THOMAS BARTRAM'S

ENCYCLOPEDIA OF HERBAL MEDICINE

ENCYCLOPEDIA
of
HERBAL MEDICINE

FIRST EDITION

Thomas Bartram

GRACE PUBLISHERS
MULBERRY COURT, STOUR ROAD, CHRISTCHURCH
DORSET BH23 1PS
TEL: (01202) 476868

Title Page: The Herball, by John Gerard (1633)

Ceres
Pomona
dedi vobis omnes herbas sementantes semen, quæ sunt
Exciderет ne tibi diuini muneris Author
Præsentem monstrat quælibet herba Deum.
THE
HERBALL
OR GENERALL
Historie of
Plantes.
Gathered by John Gerarde
of London Master in
CHIRURGERIE
Very much
Enlarged and Amended by
Thomas Johnson
Citizen and Apothecarye
of
LONDON
THEOPHRAST
DIOSCORIDES
London Printed by
Adam Islip Joice Norton
and Richard Whitakers
Anno 1633.
I. Payne sculp.

THIS ENCYCLOPEDIA is dedicated to Mr Fred Fletcher-Hyde, whose life work as a herbal consultant was complementary to the National Institute of Medical Herbalists and the British Herbal Medicine Association, which two public bodies ensured the survival of herbal medicine during the critical stages of the Medicines Bill leading to the Medicine's Act, 1968. Mr Hyde is President Emeritus of the National Institute of Medical Herbalists and of the British Herbal Medicine Association.

BRITISH LIBRARY CATALOGUING IN PUBLICATION DATA.

Thomas H. Bartram

Thomas Bartram's Encyclopedia of Herbal Medicine

ISBN 0-9515984-1-4

A practical book on phytotherapy.

The contents of this book are in no way intended to replace professional medical advice and treatment. Readers with doubts about their health and those who are pregnant are advised to consult their doctor.

Treatments in this book are intended to be used at the discretion of the reader and do not in the usual way produce side-effects, but on rare occasions an allergic response may be possible.

Phototypeset in Times by Word Perfect, The Saxon Centre, 11 Bargates, Christchurch, Dorset BH23 1PZ. Printed in Great Britain by Biddles Ltd., Guildford, Surrey.

First published by Grace Publishers, Mulberry Court, Stour Road, Christchurch, Dorset BH23 1PS, 1995.

FOREWORD

FOR over half a century I have known Mr Thomas Bartram and welcomed his unflinching advocacy of natural and herbal medicine as a Council Member and Fellow of the National Institute of Medical Herbalists. It is an honour to be invited to write a foreword for his magnum opus.

One of the compensations of increasing years is a growing maturity of judgement and a balanced objectivity. This is evident in the present work. The author is able to draw from experience in relation to established medicine and from many decades as a practitioner of herbal medicine. During his busy life Mr Bartram has read voraciously in all cognate aspects of phytotherapy. This is demonstrated in the pages of the widely acclaimed magazine "Grace" which he founded in 1960. For thirty years his gentle and kindly advice of natural and safe medication, in association with a high Christian ethic, has aided the restoration of health and hope of its readers. "Recapture the thrill of living" is the author's watchword.

This volume contains the distilled wisdom of a life spent in the cause of natural medicine: the quintessence of a herbal practitioner's experience; a book of reference and information to help the restoration and maintenance of health for all its readers. I wish it every success. Ex herbis remedia.

F. Fletcher-Hyde B.Sc. FNIMH
1st January 1995

PREFACE

IS IT NOT AMAZING, after 200 years denigration and ridicule, that herbalism is stronger than ever?

At a time of unprecedented demand for natural medicines there would appear to be a need for a comprehensive A to Z compendium of diseases and their treatment. Today, clinical effects of natural medicines are convincingly demonstrated. These were the remedies used by Pythagorus, Galen and Hippocrates. Their use today has been built upon the experience of centuries. Their data has often been confirmed at the cost of human lives – a point often overlooked by research workers. Their use extensively around the world, especially in the undeveloped countries, exceeds that of conventional medicine.

With each passing year, science proves the efficacy of the age-old craft at the back of this system of medication which today wins the confidence of peoples of the world. More consulting herbalists work in co-operation with registered medical practitioners as scientific investigation confirms empirical observation.

Herbal (phytotherapeutic) medicine is used to assist the body in its own instinctive attempts at self-healing. Non-suppressive medicines strengthen immune reserves and help overcome disease, viz: to reduce inflammation (Elderflowers), to sustain the immune system (Echinacea).

Plant medicines bring to the body a force which stimulates the energy-production system. They also de-toxify. Alteratives, diuretics, diaphoretics and antibacterials combat infection, cleanse the blood, stimulate the kidneys, empty the bowel and eliminate wastes. Each herb contains a group of valuable constituents and vital mineral material – in its natural context. A plant synthesises its own chemicals to protect itself against disease, which also proves to be effective in humans. It bridges the gap between the inorganic and the organic – the non-living and the living.

As never before, pharmaceutical laboratories are feverishly screening plants from all over the world. Success is reported by the use of a Periwinkle for leukaemia, and Wild Yam for its steroid effects. Agnus Castus increases production of progesterone and is helpful for pre-menstrual tension, infertility and hormone imbalance.

Mistletoe has been shown to produce an anti-tumour effect, as also has Wild Violet. Plants that have been used in orthodox medicine for many years include the Foxglove (digoxin), Poppy (morphine), Peruvian Bark (quinine). The medical profession took 300 years to accept quinine.

Readers may be surprised to see herbal medicines for some of the highly contagious and infectious diseases that have troubled the human race since the beginning of time. Plant medicines have always been used for cholera, diphtheria and venereal disease, though maybe not as effectively as today's orthodox medicine.

300 million people in the world are infected with STD each year. It is estimated that only 20 per cent receive the sophisticated pharmacy of the West. The remaining 80 per cent rely on native medicine.

No apology is made for inclusion of plant medicines for these and similar desperate conditions. True, they may not prove a cure, yet a wealth of medical literature testifies to their beneficient action. Sometimes they reduce severity of symptoms and may be used as supportive aids to official treatment. The anecdotal experiences of accredited physicians merit attention. Such treatments must be carried out by or in liaison with hospital specialists, oncologists, etc. A work on herbal medicine would not be complete without reference to these classic diseases of history.

If the public is to receive the best of treatment it needs the best of both worlds. Length and quality of life are more likely to be improved by a multi-disciplinary team including the herbalist.

In this book, where silicosis, pneumoconiosis, emphysema and other incurable conditions are linked with herbal medicines, no cure is implied.

Herbalism is a science in its own right. It has a rationale and modus operandi quite different from orthodox medicine. Given the opportunity, it is able to provide appropriate medication for a vast range of diseases. It offers healing properties that favourably influence chemical change, combat stress, build up resistance to infection and promote vitality.

Herbs also have an important role in improving mental and physical performance and, whether to the sportsman on the track or housewife in the kitchen, have something to offer everybody.

Self medication. The Government and health authorities of the UK and Europe express their desire that citizens take more responsibility for their own health. Also, the public's disquiet towards some aspects of modern medicine leads them to seek alternatives elsewhere. As a generation of health-conscious people approach middle age, it is less inclined to visit the doctor but to seek over-the-counter products of proven quality, safety and efficacy for minor self-limiting conditions. This has the advantage of freeing the doctor for more serious cases. Intelligent self-medication has come to stay.

Prescriptions. While specimen combinations appear for each specific disease in this book, medicines from the dispensary may be varied many times during the course of treatment. The practitioner will adapt a prescription to a patient's individual clinical picture by adding and subtracting agents according to the changing basic needs of the case. For instance, a first bottle of medicine or blend of powders may include a diuretic to clear the kidneys in preparation for the elimination of wastes and toxins unleashed by active ingredients.

The reader should never underestimate the capacity of herbal medicine to regenerate the human body, even from the brink of disaster.

Acknowledgements. I am indebted to my distinguished mentor, Edgar Gerald Jones, Mansfield, Nottinghamshire, England, to whom I owe more than I could ever repay. I am indebted also to the National Institute of Medical Herbalists, and to the British Herbal Medicine Association, both of which bodies have advanced the cause of herbal medicine. I have drawn heavily upon the British Herbal Pharmacopoeias 1983 and 1990, authentic publications of the BHMA, and have researched major works of ancient and modern herbalism including those pioneers of American Eclectic Medicine: Dr Samuel Thomson, Dr Wooster Beach, Dr

Finlay Ellingwood and their British contemporaries. All made a vital contribution in their day and generation. I have endeavoured to keep abreast of the times, incorporating the latest scientific information at the time of going to press. For the purposes of this book I am especially indebted to my friend Dr John Cosh for checking accuracy of the medical material and for his many helpful suggestions.

A wealth of useful plants awaits further investigation. Arnica, Belladonna and Gelsemium are highly regarded by European physicians. It is believed that these plants, at present out of favour, still have an important role in medicine of the future. The wise and experienced clinician will wish to know how to harness their power to meet the challenge of tomorrow's world.

Perhaps the real value of well-known alternative remedies lies in their comparative safety. Though largely unproven by elaborate clinical trials, the majority carry little risk or harm. Some have a great potential for good. The therapy is compatible with other forms of treatment.

The revival of herbal medicine is no passing cult due to sentimentality or superstition. It indicates, rather, a return to that deep devotion to nature that most of us have always possessed, and which seems in danger of being lost in the maze of modern pharmacy. It is an expression of loyalty to all that is best from the past as we move forward into the 21st century with a better understanding of disease and its treatment.

I believe the herbal profession has a distinguished and indispensible contribution to make towards the conquest of disease among peoples of the world, and that it should enjoy a place beside orthodox medicine.

Who are we to say that today's antibiotics and high-tech medicine will always be available? In a world of increasing violence, war and disaster, a breakdown in the nation's health service might happen at any time, thus curtailing production of insulin for the diabetic, steroids for the hormone-deficient, and anti-coagulants for the thrombotic. High-technology can do little without its specialised equipment. There may come a time when we shall have to reply on our own natural resources. It would be then that a knowledge of alternatives could be vital to survival.

Bournemouth 1995 — Thomas Bartram

HERBAL MEDICINES and herbs have always been with us. Up to the end of the 19th century the physician and the pharmacist shared with the herbalist a practical working knowledge of many herbal preparations and their therapeutic powers. But with the growth of scientific medicine in the 20th century medical reliance on herbal remedies has progressively diminished, although the fund of knowledge of true herbalists like Thomas Bartram continued to grow. Today, however, we hear repeatedly of threats to the natural world and its flora and fauna, alerting us to the precious heritage of herbal medicine. We realise, too, that many of our scientifically designed drugs are derived ultimately from plants; pharmaceutical research continues to draw on this source of new remedies. There is therefore a sense of urgency as we realise how much the pressures of population and of civilisation threaten the extinction of whole species of plants as well as of animals.

Public regard for herbal medicines has reawakened in the West, bringing an appreciation of the age-old herbal wisdom to be found in many other parts of the world. It is therefore of immense value to have in the publication of the Encyclopedia such a fund of information about herbs and their practical uses in everyday medical problems. It represents the fruit of many years of learning and practice by its dedicated author. All who use this Encyclopedia have good reason for gratitude to Thomas Bartram.

John Cosh MD., FRCP.
January 1995

WARNING. Recommendations are not intended to take the place of diagnosis and treatment by a medical practitioner or qualified consulting medical herbalist. All information has a record of efficacy, though treatment cannot be expected to be always successful. Any condition that persists for more than ten days should be referred to a doctor, especially if it is not in the nature of a cold or influenza. All reasonable care has been taken in the preparation of this book. The author does not imply any guarantee of cure and cannot accept responsibility for adverse effects arising from the use thereof.

IN the case of a known serious condition a doctor should be consulted.

ALL medicines should be avoided during pregnancy unless prescribed by a doctor.

UNDER-LINED HERBS. Predominant remedies are underlined. For instance, leading remedies for treatment of neuralgia are Chamomile and Valerian.

CORDIAL ACKNOWLEDGEMENTS are tendered to owners of copyright. While some of this book is from personal experience, in a work of such scope considerable research has been necessary. The author has done his best to avoid using copyright material without first asking permission. If, however, any short excerpts of this nature have been printed without formal consent, he begs the indulgence of all concerned.

ABDOMEN, INJURIES. Following accident render first-aid treatment. See: FIRST AID. Straining to lift a heavy weight or when at stool may force an intestinal loop through the muscular wall to produce a rupture. Severe cases of injury require hospitalisation; those from blows or bruising benefit from a cold compress of Comfrey root or Fenugreek seed.

Before the doctor comes: 3 drops each or any one: Tinctures Arnica, Calendula and Hypericum; hourly.

ABDOMINAL PAIN (Acute). Sudden unexplained colicky pain with distension in a healthy person justifies immediate attention by a doctor or suitably trained practitioner. Persistent tenderness, loss of appetite, weight and bowel action should be investigated. Laxatives: not taken for undiagnosed pain. Establish accurate diagnosis.

Treatment. See entries for specific disorders. Teas, powders, tinctures, liquid extracts, or essential oils – see entry of appropriate remedy.

The following are brief indications for action in the absence of a qualified practitioner. Flatulence (gas in the intestine or colon), (Peppermint). Upper right pain due to duodenal ulcer, (Goldenseal). Inflamed pancreas (Dandelion). Gall bladder, (Black root). Liver disorders (Fringe Tree bark). Lower left – diverticulitis, colitis, (Fenugreek seeds). Female organs, (Agnus Castus). Kidney disorders, (Buchu). Bladder, (Parsley Piert). Hiatus hernia (Papaya, Goldenseal). Peptic ulcer, (Irish Moss). Bilious attack (Wild Yam). Gastro-enteritis, (Meadowsweet). Constipation (Senna). Acute appendicitis, pain central, before settling in low right abdomen (Lobelia). Vomiting of blood, (American Cranesbill). Enlargement of abdominal glands is often associated with tonsillitis or glandular disease elsewhere which responds well to Poke root. As a blanket treatment for abdominal pains in general, old-time physicians used Turkey Rhubarb (with, or without Cardamom seed) to prevent griping.

Diet. No food until inflammation disperses. Slippery Elm drinks.

ABORTIFACIENT. A herb used for premature expulsion of the foetus from the womb. Illegal when used by laymen and practitioners not medically qualified. Emmenagogues may be abortifacients and should be avoided in pregnancy. Papaya fruit is used by women of Sri Lanka and India for this purpose.

ABORTION – TO PREVENT. Disruptive termination of pregnancy before twenty-eighth week. Too premature expulsion of contents of the pregnant womb may be spontaneous, habitual, or by intentional therapy. Untimely onset of uterine contractions with dilation of cervical os (mouth of the womb) dispose to abortion. Essential that services of a suitably qualified doctor or obstetrician be engaged. It would be his responsibility to ensure that the embryo (unborn baby) and the placenta (after birth) are completely expelled.

Alternatives. *Tea*: equal parts – Agnus Castus, Ladysmantle, Motherwort, Raspberry leaves, 1-2 teaspoon to each cup boiling water; infuse 5-10 minutes; 1 cup 2-3 times daily.

Tablets/capsules. Cramp bark, Helonias.

Powders. Formula. Combine Blue Cohosh 1; Helonias 2; Black Haw 3. Dose: 500mg (two 00 capsules or one-third teaspoon) thrice daily.

Practitioner. Tincture Viburnum prunifolium BHP (1983), 20ml; Tincture Chamaelirium luteum BHP (1983) 20ml; Tincture Viburnum opulus BHP (1983), 20ml; Tincture Capsicum, fort, BPC 1934, 0.05ml. Distilled water to 100ml. Sig: 5ml tds pc c Aq cal.

Black Cohosh. Liquid Extract Cimicifuja BP 1898, 1:1 in 90 per cent alcohol. Dosage: 0.3-2ml. OR: Tincture Cimicifuja, BPC 1934, 1:10 in 60 per cent alcohol. Dosage: 2-4ml.

Squaw Vine (mother's cordial) is specific for habitual abortion, beginning soon after becoming pregnant and continuing until the seventh month. Also the best remedy when abortion threatens. If attended by a physician for abortion, a hypodermic of morphine greatly assists; followed by Liquid Extract 1:1 Squaw Vine. Dosage: 2-4ml, 3 times daily.

Liquid extracts. Squaw Vine, 4 . . . Helonias, 1 . . . Black Haw bark, 1 . . . Blue Cohosh, 1. Mix. Dose: One teaspoon every 2 hours for 10 days. Thereafter: 2 teaspoons before meals, 3 times daily. Honey to sweeten, if necessary. (*Dr Finlay Ellingwood*)

Abortion, to prevent: Cramp bark, (*Dr John Christopher*)

Evening Primrose. Two 500mg capsules, at meals thrice daily.

Diet. High protein.

Vitamins. C. B6. Multivitamins. E (400iu daily).

Minerals. Calcium. Iodine. Iron. Selenium, Zinc. Magnesium deficiency is related to history of spontaneous abortion; magnesium to commence as soon as pregnant.

Enforced bed rest.

ABRASION. Superficial grazing, rubbing or tearing of the skin. Wash wound with warm water or infusion of Marigold petals, Comfrey or Marshmallow leaves. Saturate pad or surgical dressing with 10/20 drops fresh plant juice, tincture or liquid extract in equal amount of water: Aloe Vera, Chamomile, Chickweed, Comfrey, Marigold, Plantain, St John's Wort, Self-heal or other vulnerary as available. Notable products: Doubleday Comfrey Cream. Nelson's Hypercal.

ABSCESS. A collection of pus in a cavity, consisting of spent white blood cells and dead invading micro-organisms. The body's fight against localised infection may result in suppuration – the discharge of pus. An abscess may appear on any part of the body: ear, nose, throat, teeth, gums, or on the skin as a pimple, boil, stye. A 'grumbling appendix' is one form of abscess, caused by internal obstruction and irritation. Internal abscesses are usually accompanied by fever, with malaise and swollen glands under arms, groin or elsewhere. Septicaemia – a dangerous form of blood poisoning – may result where an abscess bursts and discharges purulent matter into the bloodstream.

Abscess of the rectum (anorectal, ischiorectal, perianal) can be exceedingly painful. Chiefly from E. Coli infection, it may be associated with piles, colitis, fissures or small tears in the mucosa from hard faeces. There may be throbbing pain on sitting or defecation. In all cases Echinacea should be given to sustain the immune system.

Alternatives. Abundant herb teas. Burdock leaves, Clivers, Comfrey leaves, Figwort, Gotu Kola, Ground Ivy, Horsetail, Marigold petals, Marshmallow leaves, Mullein, Plantain, Red Clover tops. 1 heaped teaspoon to each cup boiling water: drink half-1 cup thrice daily.

Mixture: Tinctures. Echinacea 30ml; Blue Flag 15ml; Bayberry 5ml; Hydrastis can 1ml; Liquorice 1ml. Dose: One 5ml teaspoon in water, honey or fruit juice thrice daily.

Tablets/capsules. Blue Flag, Echinacea, Poke root, Red Clover, Seaweed and Sarsaparilla, Garlic (or capsules): dosage as on bottle.

Powders. Formula. Echinacea 1; Marshmallow root 1; Goldenseal quarter. Dose: 500mg (one-third teaspoon, or two 00 capsules), thrice daily.

Ointments or poultices: Aloe Vera, Comfrey, Marshmallow and Slippery Elm.

Abscess of the breast. Internal mixture as above.

Abscess of the kidney. Mixture: tinctures. Equal parts: Echinacea, Bearberry, Valerian. Dose: 1-2 5ml teaspoons, thrice daily.

Topical. Ointments or poultices: Aloe Vera, Comfrey, Marshmallow and Slippery Elm.

Diet. Regular raw food days. Vitamin C (oranges, lemons, etc.). Fish oils, oily fish or other vitamin A-rich foods.

Supplements. Vitamins A, B and E.

ABSCESS ANAL. Abscess with collection of pus on one or either side of the anus. May be associated with ulcerative colitis, Crohn's disease or TB. Boil-like swelling.

Symptoms: bursting and throbbing pain, worse sitting down. Hot bath relieves.

Alternatives. *Teas:* Holy Thistle, Marigold petals, dried flowering tops. Clivers, Nettles. Wormwood. Oat husk. Thyme. 1 heaped teaspoon to each cup boiling water infused for 10-15 minutes. 1 cup 2-3 times daily.

Decoctions: Echinacea. Goldenseal. Juniper berries. Wild Indigo. 1 teaspoon to each cup water simmered gently 20 minutes. Half a cup 2-3 times daily.

Powders. Formula. Echinacea 1; Stone root half; Wild Yam half. Dose: 500mg (two 00 capsules or one-third teaspoon) thrice daily.

Liquid extracts. Echinacea 1; Goldenseal quarter; Stone root quarter; Marshmallow 1 and a half. Mix. Dose: 15-30 drops, in water, 2-3 times daily before meals.

Tincture. Tincture Myrrh BPC (1973). 15-40 drops, in water or honey, 3 times daily before meals.

Topical. Aloe Vera juice, fresh leaf or gel. Comfrey, Chickweed or Marshmallow and Slippery Elm ointment.

ABSCESS ROOT. Sweat root. *Polemonium reptans L.* Root.

Action: diaphoretic, expectorant, alterative, astringent.

Uses. Feverish conditions, bronchitis, pleurisy, coughs, tuberculosis.

Preparation. *Decoction:* 1oz to pint water, gently simmer 20 minutes. Dose: half a cup every 2 hours for febrile conditions; otherwise thrice daily.

ACACIA GUM. Gum arabic. *Acacia senegal,* Wild.

Action. Mucilaginous. Demulcent.

Uses. Emulsifying agent. Used with other herbs to soothe inflamed tissue in irritable bowel, sore throat or bronchi.

Preparation. Powder: 1-3g in honey, thrice daily.

GSL

ACEROLA. Health tree. Puerto Rican Cherry. (*Malpighia punicifolia*). Valuable source of vitamins and nutritive elements. One of the richest sources of Vitamin C.

Uses. Alcoholism, arteriosclerosis, habitual abortion, chronic infection of the cornea and eye disturbance due to diseases of the blood vessels. Rheumatic inflammatory conditions, common cold, high blood pressure, whooping cough, fatigue, stress, strokes, premature symptoms of old age.

A number of Vitamin C preparations are made from Acerola berries. Concentrated juices. Powder. Capsules, 250mg.

ACHILLES TENDON CONTRACTURE. Restriction of ankle movements due to shortening of Achilles tendon, with calf pain.

Treatment: Hot foot baths: Chamomile flowers. Paint with Liquid extract or tincture Lobelia. Gradual stretching by manipulation. Massage with Neat's foot oil.

ACHLORHYDRIA. Absence or reduction of hydrochloric acid in stomach juices. Predisposes to pernicious anaemia. Stomach acid aids absorption of proteins, iron and other minerals as well as to exterminate hostile bacteria.
To increase stomach acid: bitters, tonics, stomachics.
Alternatives. *Teas.* Balm, Calumba (cold infusion), Betony, Bogbean Centuary, Chaparral, Gentian (cold infusion). German Chamomile, Holy Thistle, Horseradish, Southernwood, Wormwood.
Tea mixture. Equal parts: Balm, Betony, German Chamomile. Mix. 1 heaped teaspoon to each cup boiling water; infuse 5-10 minutes; 1 cup 2-3 times daily.
Tablets/capsules. Ginseng, Goldenseal, Sarsaparilla, Wild Yam, Yellow Dock.
Gentian. Powder. 500mg (two 00 capsules or one-third teaspoon) before meals thrice daily.
Calumba. Powder. Prepare, same as for Gentian.
Calumba root. Tincture, EHC. Vol 1, 2-4ml thrice daily.
Cider vinegar. 2 teaspoons in glass water: 2-3 times daily.

ACID-ALKALINE BALANCE. A healthy bloodstream depends upon maintenance of an acid-alkaline balance. Blood is always slightly alkaline. Only slight variations on either side are compatible with life. When this delicate balance is disturbed by faulty elimination of acid wastes, carbon dioxide, etc., a condition appears known as acidosis, a known precursor of chronic disease. A change of diet is indicated.

To help restore the acid-alkaline balance, any one of the following teas may assist: Iceland Moss, Bladderwrack (fucus), Kelp, Irish Moss, Slippery Elm, Calamus, Meadowsweet, or Dandelion (which may be taken as Dandelion coffee).

ACID FOODS. Foods that produce acid when metabolised. Ash from these foods contains sulphur, phosphoric acid and chlorine, all essential for efficient metabolism. Breads, cereals, cheese, chicken, chocolate, cocoa, coffee, cranberries, eggs, fish, flour, fowl, grain products, lentils, meats (lean), nuts, oats, oatmeal, oysters, pasta, peanuts, peanut butter, pearl barley, plums, prunes, rhubarb, rabbit, rice (white), sugar, sweet corn, tea, veal, wholemeal bread, wheatgerm.

ACIDITY. Heartburn, with acid eructations and a sensation of distress in the stomach, chiefly associated with peptic ulcer (duodenal) or gastritis.
Symptoms: local tenderness and stomach gas. The terms *hyperacidity* and *hyperchlorhydria* refer to excessive production of hydrochloric acid in the stomach.
Alternatives. For preparation and dosage see remedy entry.
Teas: Agrimony, Balm, Black Horehound, Caraway, Catnep, Celery seeds, Centuary, Chamomile, Dandelion root coffee, Fennel, Irish Moss, Liquorice root, Meadowsweet, Parsley, Quassia, Red Sage.
Tablets/capsules. Dandelion, Papaya, Goldenseal. Dosage as on bottle.
Powders: equal parts, Slippery Elm, White Poplar, Meadowsweet. Mix. 500mg (two 00 capsules or one-third teaspoon) thrice daily and when necessary.
Tinctures. Formula: Dandelion 1; Meadowsweet 1; Nettles 1; Goldenseal quarter. Dose: 1-2 teaspoons in water thrice daily before meals.
Practitioner prescription. Dec Jam Sarsae Co conc (BPC 1949) 1 fl oz (30ml); Liquid Extract Filipendula 1 fl oz (30ml); Liquid Extract Taraxacum off. Half a fl oz (15ml); Ess Menth Pip 0.05ml. Aqua to 8oz (240ml). Sig: one dessertspoon (8ml) in warm water before meals. (*Barker*).
Diet: lacto-vegetarian. Garlic. Celery. Dried raw oats. Regular raw food days. Low fat. Powdered kelp in place of salt. Paw paw fruit. Regulate bowels.
Note. In view of the finding of gastric carcinoid tumours in rodents subjected to long-term anti-secretory agents, caution needs to be exercised over the long-term use of antacids that powerfully suppress the gastric juices.

ACID RAIN SICKNESS. Acid rain air pollution is responsible for increased hospital admissions with respiratory illness when it hangs in a haze over a polluted area. The main components of acid rain are sulphates, salts of sulphur, known to cause breathing difficulties.
Alternatives. *Teas*: Alfalfa, Angelica leaves, Boneset, Catnep, Chamomile, Coltsfoot, Comfrey leaves, Dandelion leaves, Hyssop, Lemon Balm, Lime flowers, Milk Thistle, Mullein, White Horehound, Red Clover flowers, Sage, Violet leaves, Umeboshi tea.
Tablets/capsules. Chamomile, Echinacea, Iceland Moss, Irish Moss, Liquorice, Lobelia.
Powders. Formula. Equal parts: Echinacea, Barberry bark, Elecampane root. Dose: 500mg (two 00 capsules or one-third teaspoon) thrice daily.
Formula. Tinctures. Echinacea 2; Sarsaparilla 1; Fringe Tree half; Liquorice quarter. Mix. 1-2 teaspoons thrice daily.

ACIDOPHILUS. A friendly bacteria found in the digestive system which combats the activities of invading micro-organisms associated with food poisoning and other infections. The natural balance of intestinal flora can be disturbed by diets high in animal fat, dairy produce, sugar, stress and alcohol. Lactobacillus Acidophilus assists production of B vitamins, regulates cholesterol levels, enhances the immune system and helps absorption of food. Perhaps the most popular bacteria-friendly food is yoghurt.

L.A. is available in tablets and capsules. As a vaginal douche the powder can be used for thrush. It is necessary to follow the use of antibiotics of orthodox pharmacy. Of value for candida albicans, allergies, depression and some forms of menstrual disorders.

ACIDOSIS. A general term for a number of conditions arising from an abnormal breakdown of fats with rapid consumption of carbohydrates. Diabetic, oxybutyric acids and other allied bodies appear in the urine. Diagnosis may be confirmed by a smell of acetone on the breath.
Causes. Diet too rich in fats, inability to digest fats. May be associated with diabetes, starvation wasting diseases and liverish attacks; when followed by coma, situation is serious.
Symptoms. Physical weakness, pallor, lethargy, acid stools, constant yawning, constipation, diarrhoea – in severe cases, jaundice. A liver tonic would be an ingredient of a prescription (Barberry, Balmony, Dandelion, Mulberry, Wahoo).

A reduced alkalinity of the blood allows acidosis to take over. Symptoms of diabetic coma when due to salt deficiency profoundly affects the chemistry of the blood.
Alternatives. Teas: Agrimony, Balm (lemon), Bogbean, Boldo, Centuary, Chamomile, Cleavers, Dandelion, Fumitory, Hyssop, Meadowsweet, Motherwort, Wormwood.
Tea. Formula: equal parts, Balm, Chamomile and Dandelion. 1 heaped teaspoon to each cup boiling water, infuse 10 minutes; dose – 1 cup thrice daily.
Tablets/capsules. Seaweed and Sarsaparilla, Blue Flag, Goldenseal, Wild Yam, Yellow Dock.
Potter's Acidosis tablets: Anise oil, Caraway oil, Cinnamon, Meadowsweet, Rhubarb, Medicinal Charcoal.
Formula. Equal parts: Dandelion, Blue Flag, Meadowsweet. Mix. Dose: Powders: 500mg; Liquid extracts: 30-60 drops; Tinctures: 1-2 teaspoons thrice daily.
Goldenseal tincture: 1-2ml thrice daily.
Diet. Vigorous cutback in food-fats, especially dairy products. Readily assimilable form of carbohydrate (honey), replenishing stores in the liver without working that organ too hard. Restore body chemistry. Kelp instead of salt. Powdered skimmed milk, yoghurt, plantmilk made from Soya bean. Pectin foods: raw apples help solidify the stool. Bananas, carrots, carob flour products. Vitamin B complex, B6, Folic ac., Niacin, Pantothenic acid. See: CAROB BEAN.

ACNE ROSACEA. Chronic inflammatory skin disease of middle life with redness, i.e., enlargement of the nose due to swelling of sebaceous glands. Excessive alcohol consumption said to be a cause, but is doubtful. May be accompanied by blepharitis (inflammation of the eyelids). May appear anywhere on the body due to over-function of sebaceous (grease) glands. Absence of comedones distinguishes it from acne vulgaris. Often associated with dyspepsia (Meadowsweet), or hormone disorder (Agnus Castus). *Key agent*: Barberry bark (Berberis vulgaris).
Alternatives. *Teas.* Agnus Castus, Agrimony, Clivers, Dandelion, Nettles, Red Clover, Wood Betony.
Tea. Formula. Equal parts: Agnus Castus, Dandelion, Wood Betony. 1 heaped teaspoon to each cup boiling water; infuse 15 minutes; dose – 1 cup thrice daily.
Decoction. 1 teaspoon Barberry bark to cup cold water; steep 3 hours. Strain. Dose: 1 cup morning and evening. Barberry bark is one of the few agents that yield their properties to cold infusion. Works better without application of heat.
Formula. Equal parts: Echinacea, Blue Flag, Barberry. Dose – Powders: 500mg (two 00 capsules or one-third teaspoon). Liquid extracts: One 5ml teaspoon. Tinctures: Two 5ml teaspoons. Thrice daily, before meals.
Cider vinegar. Internally and externally – success reported.
Topical. Cooling astringent creams or ointments: Chickweed, Aloe Vera, Witch Hazel, Zinc and Castor oil, Jojoba. Avocado cream, Dilute Tea Tree oil. Thyme Lotion (Blackmore).
Aromatherapy. 2 drops each: Lavender and Tea Tree oils in 2 teaspoons Almond oil: applied with cotton wool. Or Sandalwood oil.
Diet. Avoid chocolate, cow's milk, sugars and drinks that induce facial flushing. Low fat. Low carbohydrate. Raw fruit and vegetables.
Supplements. Biotin, Vitamins A, C, E. Two halibut liver oil capsules after breakfast. Vitamin B6 for menstrual acne. Betaine hydrochloride, Selenium, Zinc.
Note. Avoid foods and medicines containing iodine or bromine.

ACNE, VULGARIS. Inflammatory sebaceous skin disease with pustules, papules and cysts found frequently in adolescents at commencement of puberty when the sebaceous (grease) glands become more active. Blackheads are formed by blockage of follicles with sebum. A black pigment, melanin, concentrates on the top of the hair follicle forming a plug.

Lesions may appear on face, neck and chest. Worse in winter, better in summer. Acne vulgaris has blackheads (comedones) that distinguish it from acne rosacea. Studies show low zinc levels. The British Herbal Pharmacopoeia records Poke root singularly effective. Medicines containing iodine and bromine (Kelp) should be avoided. Dr Edward Frankel, Los Angeles, warns against use of Vaseline which, through build-up of bacteria, may cause pustular reaction.

Alternatives. *Teas.* Agrimony, Alfalfa, Burdock leaves, Chamomile, Dandelion, Figwort, Gotu Kola, Heartsease, Hibiscus, Marigold petals, Mate tea, Nettles, Redbush (rooibos), Rose Hip, Violet, Wood Betony.

Tablets/capsules. Blue Flag, Dandelion, Echinacea, Queen's Delight, Seaweed and Sarsaparilla, Poke root, Devil's Claw, Goldenseal.

Formula. Echinacea 2; Blue Flag 1; Poke root half. Dose – Powders: 500mg (two 00 capsules or one-third teaspoon). Liquid extracts: 30-60 drops. Tinctures: 1-2 teaspoons. Thrice daily before meals.

Evening Primrose oil. Success reported.

Maria Treben. Nettle tea.

French traditional. Horse radish vinegar.

Greek traditional. Marigold petal poultice.

Topical. cleanse lesions with distilled extract of Witch Hazel or fresh lemon juice. Follow with Marshmallow and Slippery Elm ointment, dilute Tea Tree oil, Evening Primrose oil, Jojoba or Aloe Vera gel. Thyme Lotion (*Blackmore's*).

Aromatherapy. Sandalwood oil. Or Lavender and Tea Tree oils.

Diet. Lacto-vegetarian. Low fat, low carbohydrate. Avoid chocolate, cow's milk, sugars and drinks that induce facial flushing. Raw fruit and vegetables.

Supplements. Vitamins A, B-complex, B6, C, E. Chromium, Selenium, Zinc.

ACONITE. Monkshood. Wolfsbane. Aconitum napellus L. *French*: Aconit napel. *German*: Wolfswurz. *Italian*: Aconito napello. *Spanish*: Caro di Venere. Part used: dried roots.

Action. Cardio-active; slows the heart via the vagus nerve. Antibacterial, antiviral, antifungal.

Uses. Used in conventional medicine for many years as a heart relaxant, to lower blood pressure and relieve capillary engorgement, but internal use now discontinued in the UK. Facial and intercostal neuralgia. Pains of rheumatism, lumbago and arthritis (liniment).

Pains of arthritis and gout: Tincture Aconite 2; Tincture Colchicum 1. 10 drops thrice daily. (*Dr Rudolf F. Weiss, "Herbal Medicine", Beaconsfield*)

Preparations. *Tincture*: Dose: 2-5 drops, thrice daily. Practitioner only. Alternative dosage sometimes used in fevers: 5 drops in 100ml water: 1 teaspoon hourly – until temperature falls or improvement is noted.

Standardised product: Aconitysat (Buerger): 5-10 drops or more.

Liniment. 1.3 parts tincture to 100 parts Witch Hazel.

Note. Widely used in its homoeopathic preparation. Pharmacy only sale.

ACOUSTIC NEUROMA. A tumour or new growth arising from the nerve of hearing – eighth auditory nerve. In middle-aged and elderly.

Symptoms: tinnitus, nerve deafness, vertigo. Herbal treatment may prove beneficial, before surgery.

Treatment alternatives. *Tea*, mixture. Equal parts: Gotu Kola, Violet leaves, Clivers. 1 heaped teaspoon to each cup boiling water: infuse 10 minutes: dose, half-1 cup thrice daily, before meals.

Powders. Formula. Equal parts: Poke root, Echinacea, Blue Flag root. Mix. Dose: 500mg (two 00 capsules or one-third teaspoon), thrice daily, before meals.

Tinctures. Equal parts: Yellow Dock, Thuja, Poke root. Mix. Dose: 1 teaspoon in water thrice daily.

Topical. 2-3 drops warm oil of Mullein injected into the meatus 3-4 times daily.

Nutrients: All vitamins. Selenium. Zinc.

Treatment by or in liaison with a general medical practitioner.

ACROCYANOSIS. Persistent blueness of hands, face, nose, ears and feet in young women due to inadequate supply of blood.

Alternatives. *Teas*: Borage, Chamomile, Gotu Kola, Motherwort, Nettles, Rosemary.

Tea formula. Equal parts, German Chamomile, Gotu Kola and Motherwort. 1 heaped teaspoon to each cup boiling water, infuse 10 minutes. Dose: 1 cup thrice daily.

Tablets/capsules. Capsicum (Cayenne), Hawthorn, Motherwort, Ginger, Prickly Ash, Ginseng, Pulsatilla, Red Clover.

Formula. Yarrow 2; Gentian 1; Prickly Ash 1; Liquorice quarter; Capsicum quarter. Mix. Dose – Powders: 500mg (two 00 capsules or one-third teaspoon); Liquid extracts: 30-60 drops; Tinctures: 1-2 teaspoons, thrice daily, before meals.

Diet. See: DIET – GENERAL.

Supplements. Vitamins: B-complex, B1, B6, B12, Folic ac., PABA, Pantothenic acid, Vitamin C (300mg daily), Vitamin E (400iu daily).

ACRODYNIA. Pink disease. The term was once confined to children of teething age who were believed to be allergic to mercury in teething, worm and dusting powders, and ointments containing mercury. The term is now increasingly used for mercury poisoning in all ages, in one of its many forms: atmospheric pollution, cereal grains, fish living in polluted waters, escape of vaporised mercury from teeth fillings, cassettes, camera mechanism, etc.

Symptoms: sweat rash, photophobia (intolerance of bright light on the iris of the eye), wasting, rapid heart beat, weakness, swollen ankles,

diminished reflexes.
Alternatives. Assist the liver in its task to eliminate poisons, and to cleanse the lymph system.
Adults: Gotu Kola, Sarsaparilla, German Chamomile: teas.
Young children: German Chamomile tea: sips, freely – as much as well tolerated.

ACROMEGALY. Increase in size of hands, feet, skull, and jaw by excessive bone growth, associated with expanding tumour of the pituitary gland. Bones become longer and the voice deepens. The change is usually gradual, the face becoming elongated and the features coarse due to thickened skin. Lips, nose and tongue enlarge. Mandible is prominent (prognathism), frontal sinuses enlarge and brows have a beetling appearance. A complexity of symptoms include: ill-fitting dentures, bite reversal, headache, enlarged fingers requiring ring to be moved from fourth to fifth finger. Shoes get tight, spine kyphotic and stiff, possible carpal syndrome, overt diabetes and visual defects.

The condition is irreversible thus no cure is possible. However, pituitary gland normalisers can assist and possibly avert decline.
Alternatives. *Tea*: Combine equal parts: Gotu Kola, Yarrow, Horsetail. 1 heaped teaspoon to each cup boiling water; infuse 15 minutes. 1 cup once or more daily.
Tablets/capsules. Bladderwrack, Borage, Kelp, Liquorice, Ginseng, Wild Yam, Damiana, Helonias.
Formula. Combine: Sarsaparilla 1; Ginseng 1; Fringe Tree half; Thuja quarter. Dose: *Powders*, quarter of a teaspoon. *Liquid extracts*: 30-60 drops. *Tinctures*: 1-2 teaspoons. In water, morning and evening.

ACTINOMYCOSIS. A suppurative disease from hard surfaces that soften and form punctured holes in the skin (multiple sinuses). Primarily a disease of cattle (hard mouth), infectious to man. Can affect lungs, abdomen, throat and mouth. Draining fistulas and 'holes' produce a pus with gram positive micro-organism (*actinomyces israeli*) which causes abscesses and hard swellings.
Differential diagnosis: tuberculosis and cancer.
Conventional treatment: antibiotics and surgical excision.
Herbal treatment: antiseptics, anti-microbials, vulneraries. In addition to basic formula, they will be given according to the organ or system involved. for skin give basic formula.
Alternatives. *Basic formula*: Combine: Echinacea 4; Goldenseal 1; Yellow Dock 2. Preparations: powders, liquid extracts, tinctures; doses taken in water or honey thrice daily.
For the lungs: add Balm of Gilead 1.
For the abdomen: add Sarsaparilla 2.
For the throat: add Red Sage 2.
For the mouth: add Myrrh quarter.
Powders. 500mg (two 00 capsules or one-third teaspoon).
Liquid Extracts: mix. Dose, 15-30 drops.
Tinctures: Dose, 30-60 drops thrice daily.
Dr Finlay Ellingwood. Echinacea liquid extract: 60 drops in water every 2 hours. Where ulcerative lesions are present: 10 drops in water applied externally.
Topical:– Lotion: 1 part oil Eucalyptus to 9 parts glycerine. shake well.
Diet: The fungus is more likely to become established where health is poor. Regular raw food days. Avoid liver-clogging eggs, ham, bacon, cream and excessive cheese.

ACTIVE PRINCIPLE. There are active and passive (in-active) constituents in all plants. An active principle is the most active constituent.

The amount of active constituent of a plant is not constant. The percentage of active constituent varies greatly. For this reason official pharmacy standardises drugs. See: WHOLE PLANT.

ACUPUNCTURE. A traditional Chinese treatment for relieving ills of the body by inserting needles into special meridians. Discovered over 5,000 years ago, it has only of recent years found tardy acceptance in Western medicine. In Russia it is taught in universities as a serious medical science.

Acupuncturists believe in lines of life force called meridians which encircle the body and are linked to all main organs. Sceptics complain that needles are inserted at points with no apparent connection with the disease. A needle stuck into the nose is intended to treat hay-fever, and a needle in the toes, migraine. Karate and Judo experts observe that such points correspond to those used by themselves.

Eastern acupuncturists believe in two channels of energy circulating the body: the Yang (positive) and the Yin (negative), and that in perfect health these two are in perfect balance. However, when one line of force dominates the other full free flow is obstructed and illness results. To release the blockage, insertion of a needle at the correct point on the meridian can often relieve pain and cure.

Chinese acupuncture was always used together with herbal medicine (Ginger, Sarsaparilla, Pennywort, etc.) and many new uses of herbs have been discovered by practitioners of the art. About 60 per cent success rate is shown where the two combined therapies are used for surgical analgesia in childbirth. Laser acupuncture may one day surpass the needle therapy in the treatment of organic problems, depression, and anxiety.
Information. British Acupuncture Association, 34 Alderney Street, London SW1V 4EU.

ACUTE. (Acute disease). A short sharp crisis of rapid onset in which the body's defences rise in protection against invasion or other menace to health. Not chronic.

ADAPTOGEN. A substance that helps the body to "adapt" to a new strain or stress by stimulating the body's own defensive mechanism. Natural substances in the form of plant medicines offer a gentle alternative to fast-acting synthetic chemical medicine in releasing the body's own source of energy to sustain the immune system.

It is when a particular stress is intense that the immune system may lack the vitality to mobilise the body's resources against a threat to its safety and well-being.

Adaptogens are concerned with the therapeutic action of the whole plant which is regarded as greater than the sum of its parts. They may affect many different kinds of cells, whereas a chemical drug has a direct action upon a particular tissue or system.

Adaptogens are powerful supportive agents against stress and its effects, initiating processes of regeneration of tissues and fluids. They release innate resources of vitality in their efforts to re-invigorate and protect.

This important group includes: Siberian and Asiatic Ginseng, Borage, Don Quai, Gotu Kola, Lapacho tea, Pollen extracts, Royal Jelly, Sarsaparilla, Shiitake Mushroom, Suma.

ADDER'S TONGUE. *Ophioglossum vulgatum L.* Leaves.
Action: emollient, anti-eczema, vulnerary (fresh leaf on wounds), anti-neoplasm (poultice of fresh leaves).
Uses. Ulcers that refuse to heal.
Ointment. 1oz fresh leaves simmered in 16oz lard until leaves are devoid of colour; strain.

ADDISON'S DISEASE. A disease causing failure of adrenal gland function, in particular deficiency of adrenal cortical hormones, mainly cortisol and aldosterone. Commonest causes are tuberculosis and auto-immune disease.
Symptoms: (acute) abdominal pain, muscle weakness, vomiting, low blood pressure due to dehydration, tiredness, mental confusion, loss of weight and appetite. Vomiting, dizzy spells. Increased dark pigmentation around genitals, nipples, palms and inside mouth. Persistent low blood pressure with occasional low blood sugar.
Crisis is treated by increased salt intake. Research project revealed a craving for liquorice sweets in twenty five per cent of patients.

Herbs with an affinity for the adrenal glands: Parsley, Sarsaparilla, Wild Yam, Borage, Liquorice, Ginseng, Chaparral. Where steroid therapy is unavoidable, supplementation with Liquorice and Ginseng is believed to sustain function of the glands. Ginseng is supportive when glands are exhausted by prolonged stress. BHP (1983) recommends: Liquorice, Dandelion leaf.
Alternatives. *Teas.* Gotu Kola, Parsley, Liquorice root, Borage, Ginseng, Balm.
Tea formula. Combine equal parts: Balm and Gotu Kola. Preparation of teas and tea mixture: 1 heaped teaspoon to each cup boiling water: infuse 5-10 minutes; 1 cup 2 to 3 times daily.
Tablets/capsules. Ginseng, Seaweed and Sarsaparilla, Wild Yam, Liquorice. Dosage as on bottle.
Formula. Combine: Gotu Kola 3; Sarsaparilla 2; Ginseng 1; Liquorice quarter. Doses. Powders: 500mg (two 00 capsules or one-third teaspoon). Liquid extracts: 30-60 drops. Tinctures: 1-2 teaspoons 2 to 3 times daily.
Formula. Alternative. Tinctures 1:5. Echinacea 20ml; Yellow Dock 10ml; Barberry 10ml; Sarsaparilla 10ml; Liquorice (liquid extract) 5ml. Dose: 1-2 teaspoons thrice daily.
Supplementation. Cod liver oil. Extra salt. B-Vitamins. Folic acid.

ADENOIDS. An overgrowth of lymphoid tissue at the junction of the throat and nose. After exposure to inflammation from colds, dust, allergy or faulty diet adenoids may become enlarged and diseased. Chiefly in children, ages 3 to 10.
Symptoms. Mouth always half open through inability to breathe freely through nose. Nose thin and shrunken. Teeth may protrude. Snoring. Possible deafness from ear infection. Where the child does not 'grow out of it' flat chestedness and spinal curvature may ensue because of inadequate oxygenation. Children gritting their teeth at night may be suspected. Children may also have enlarged tonsils. Both tonsils and adenoids are lymph glands which filter harmful bacteria and their poisons from the blood stream. Herbs can be used to facilitate their elimination from the site of infection for excretion from the body.
Alternatives. Clivers, Echinacea, Goldenseal, Marigold, Poke root, Queen's Delight, Sarsaparilla, Thuja, Wild Indigo.
Tea. Formula. Equal parts: Red Clover, Red Sage, Wild Thyme. 1 heaped teaspoon to each cup boiling water; infuse 5-15 minutes. 1 cup thrice daily.
Tablets/capsules. Echinacea, Poke root, Goldenseal. Dosage as on bottle.
Powders. Formula. Equal parts: Echinacea, Poke root, Goldenseal. 500mg (two 00 capsules or one-third teaspoon). Children 250mg or one capsule. Thrice daily.
Tinctures. Formula: Echinacea 20ml; Elderflowers 20ml; Poke root 10ml; Thuja 1ml, Tincture Capsicum 5 drops. Dose: 1-2 teaspoons. Children: 15-30 drops, in water, thrice daily.
Topical. Lotion: Liquid Extract Thuja 1; Aloe

Vera gel 2. Apply to affected area on a probe with cotton wool.
Gargle: Equal parts tinctures Myrrh and Goldenseal: 10-15 drops in glass of water, freely.
Snuff: Bayberry bark powder.
Diet. 3-day fast, followed with low fat, low salt, high fibre diet.
On retiring: 2 Garlic capsules/tablets to prevent infection.

ADHESION. May follow inflammation which causes two surfaces, normally separated, to stick together and form fibrous tissue. Peritonitis is a common cause of adhesions in the abdomen resulting in intestinal obstruction. Adhesions can occur in joint diseases, chest troubles such as pleurisy, intestinal and bowel disorders. Sometimes it is necessary for adhesions to be divided by surgery.

External. Castor oil packs.

ADJUVANT. A substance that works well with another. A remedy that enhances the effect of another. One that assists and promotes the operation of the basic ingredient of a prescription: i.e., by dilating peripheral blood vessels, Cayenne (capsicum) assists Hawthorn in its action on the heart.

ADOLESCENCE. This is the time of life when profound physical and emotional changes take place in young people, marking the beginning of puberty and proceeding throughout teenage years towards maturity. It is a time when sound nutrition should bypass many of the distressing crises which arise from heredity tendencies or an unhealthy life-style. Problems of puberty:–
Treatment. *Girls*. Delayed menarche (Raspberry leaf tea), and other menstrual disorders; hormone deficiency (laboratory tests confirm). Puberty goitre (Kelp), skin disorders: see "Acne". Listlessness, (Gentian). Loss of appetite (Chamomile). Over-activity, tearfulness, (Pulsatilla).
Boys. Constitutional weaknesses from childhood, (Sarsaparilla); puberty goitre (Kelp); Offensive foot sweat, see: DIURETICS. Aggression, over-activity, (Alfalfa). Under-developed testes (Liquorice, Sarsaparilla).

Nervousness and restlessness of many of the younger generation may arise from a number of causes, including a diet of too much sugar, coffee, caffeine stimulants (coffee, cola, strong tea) and foods deficient in nutrients and minerals. The condition can be related to the number of chemicals used in food and commercial products, pesticides and drugs.
Diet. Plenty fresh raw fruits and vegetables. Raw food days. High protein, low salt, low fat. Alfalfa tea (rich in builder minerals).
Reject: coffee, cola drinks, strong tea, alcohol, tobacco.

ADONIS. Pheasant's eye. *Adonis vernalis L.* Contains glycosides, including cymarin. *French*: Hellébore bâtard. *German*: Frühlingsadonisblume. *Spanish*: Elléboro falso. *Italian*: Ellebore bastardo.
Action. Cardiac tonic. Emmenagogue. Anthelmintic. Coronary artery dilator. Diuretic. Hypertensive.
Uses. For slowing the heart's action, increasing force of the beat, and increasing blood pressure. Dropsy. 'Heart asthma'. Palpitation. Mitral insufficiency.
Preparation. *Tincture Adonis*: 10-20 drops in water twice daily and when necessary. Pharmacy only medicine.

ADRENAL-ACTIVATOR. An agent which stimulates the adrenal glands thereby increasing secretion of cortisol and adrenal hormones. A herb with a mild cortico-steroid effect. Liquorice. Ginseng. Sarsaparilla.

ADRENAL GLANDS. Two organs situated one upon the upper end of each kidney. Each gland encloses a central part known as the medulla, and an outer cortex which exercises some control over sexual development. Addison's Disease or tumours may cause defective hormone secretion and profoundly interfere with the metabolism of salt. Stresses of modern life may exhaust the glands.

The medulla, or core of the gland, secretes adrenalin and noradrenalin, known as the 'fight or flight' hormones that move the body into top gear to meet an emergency. Mental or physical stress may cause it to swing into action; increasing the heart beat, elevating blood pressure and releasing glycogen from the liver.

The cortex secretes a hormone – aldosterone (the salt and water hormone) which regulates water retention in the body. Also, the cortex secretes cortisone which raises the level of sugar in the blood . . . insulin reduces it. Also secreted are the adrenal sex hormones that complement the gonads.

Re-vitalisers for exhausted or hypoactive adrenals: Borage, Cayenne, Ginger root, Ginseng, Gotu Kola, Hawthorn, Liquorice, Mullein, Parsley root, Sarsaparilla, Wild Yam.

ADRENALIN. A hormone secreted by the cortex of the adrenal glands. Prepares the body for 'fight or flight'. Surface blood vessels constrict, heart rate and blood pressure rises, breathing is stimulated, muscle activity increases, sweat is released, pupils contract, the mouth becomes dry and blood clots faster. One of its properties is to mobilise fatty acids from adipose tissue, thus being of value in obesity.

ADVERSE REACTIONS. Herbalists, phytotherapists, other practitioners and companies are required by the Committee on Safety of Medicines to report all adverse reactions associated with herbal products used in the treatment of disease in the UK within one month. Adverse reactions to over-the-counter alternative medicines should be reported using the yellow card scheme. (*CSM., Current Problems 1986, No 16:477.*)

ADVERTISING. References: The Medicine's Act, 1968. The Medicines Labelling and Advertising to the Public Regulations (SI 1978 No 41). The Medicines (Advertising) Regulations 1994 SI 1994 No 1932, and The Medicines (Monitoring of Advertising) Regulations 1994 SI No 1933.

In addition to the above, a Code of Practice for advertising herbal remedies has been agreed by the British Herbal Medicine Association in consultation with the Department of Health and the Scientific Committee of the BHMA. It represents an act of self-discipline within the trade and profession, acceptance and observance of which is a condition of membership of the British Herbal Medicine Association.

It is the responsibility of all placing and accepting advertisements to ensure that wording complies with statutory requirements. For any ailment or disease no claim for cure may be made.

The following extracts are few of a wide range of conditions appearing in the BHMA Code.

"The expression 'treatment' is not permitted except in respect of a 'course of treatment' by herbal medicines within the meaning of the Act.

"Advertising shall in no way induce unjustified concern that the reader is suffering from any illness, ailment or disease or that, without treatment, he may suffer more severely.

"Advertising shall not discourage the reader from seeking advice from a qualified practitioner.

"Advertising shall not invite the reader to diagnose specific medical conditions except those readily recognised by the layman and which are obvious to the sufferer. Advertising shall not use words such as: 'magic', 'Miracle', 'Mystical', 'wonder remedy', 'nature's remedy', 'breakthrough' or similar terms."

"Advertising shall not indicate medical or surgical consultation is unnecessary, or guarantee the effects of a medicine. It shall not indicate an absence of side-effects, or suggest that a product is better than or equivalent to another treatment. It shall not suggest health can be enhanced, or that health may be impaired by not taking the product. It should not be directed principally at children, or refer to recommendations by a health professional, a celebrity, etc. It shall not suggest a product is a food or cosmetic, or has a special benefit because it is 'natural'. One cannot refer to a 'licensed medicine' or approved by the Dept of Health or use similar statements."

AEROBIC ATHLETES. Taken for 30 consecutive days, runners using powdered Eleutherococcus (Siberian Ginseng) showed a 10 per cent improvement in performance. (*Arkopharma*)

AETIOLOGY. A term denoting the cause or origin of a specific disease.

AFTERBIRTH. The placenta, umbilical cord and membranes left behind but which are detached and must needs be expelled a few hours after delivery in the third stage of labour. Where retained, a strong infusion of White Horehound is indicated. Dioscorides records that Birthwort (Aristolochia longa) powder in wine "brings away the afterbirth with ease".

Tea. combine equal parts, German Chamomile, Angelica root, Pennyroyal and Basil; or as many as are available. 1-2 teaspoons to each cup boiling water; infuse 5-15 minutes; 1 cup freely.

AGAR-AGAR (*Gelidium amansii*). Gelling agent made from seaweed. Alternative to gelatine which is prepared from the bones of animals. A colloid which absorbs moisture rapidly, providing bulk and a lubricant to the intestinal tract for relief of constipation. Used for making pills, lotions and suppositories. Also known as Japanese isinglass, it is a nutrient to add weight and build up weakly constitutions. The powder is added to desserts: stewed fruits, etc. Still used as a bulk laxative for chronic constipation. GSL

AGE SPOTS. Liver spots. Pigment defects.

External: Aloe Vera juice or gel. Comfrey paste: Mix a little powder and water.

AGEING. Old age. To maintain health, prevent anaemia, ensure mobility of joints, sense of balance, reduce possibility of strokes, preserve density of the bones and ward off senility. In age, nutrients are not so well absorbed. Minerals may be provided by Mullein and Nettles (iron), Kelp (iodine), Chamomile and Horsetail (calcium), Oats (silicon), Silverweed (sulphur), Liquorice root (phosphorus), Dandelion (potassium), Carrot leaves (magnesium).

Alternatives. Garlic (anti-infective), Ginseng (anti-fatigue), Hawthorn (sustains heart), Red Clover (lymphatic cleanser), Ginkgo, (brain stimulant). Sage tea is favoured in China for longevity.

Combination. Tea. Combine equal parts: German Chamomile, Horsetail, Nettles. 1 heaped teaspoon to cup boiling water; infuse 5-15 minutes. 1 cup once or twice daily. Single teas may be made from Hawthorn blossoms or any of the above.

Belgian research has shown that the elderly are more able to resist infection by taking Selenium

supplements. They are prone to a deficiency of Selenium. See entry. Elderly subjects who complain of memory loss are unlikely to develop dementia. (*Prof Raymond Levy, London Institute of Psychiatry*).
Diet. Reduce fats, meat and sugar. High intake of fresh fruit and vegetables. Dietary fibre, muesli, oatmeal porridge. Oily fish.
Supplements. Daily. Beta carotene 5,000iu; B-complex; B12; Vitamin C to preserve blood vessels 1g; Vitamin E to sustain a robust circulation, 200iu. Selenium 100mcg.
Note. It is desirable that elderly patients should, where possible, be weaned off psychotropic drugs, as they are particularly prone to side-effects. See: DRUG DEPENDENCE.

AGNUS CASTUS. Chaste tree. *Vitex agnus castus L. Part used*: dried ripe fruits.
Contains aucubin and agnuside (iridoid glycosides), flavonoids, castin (bitter), fatty and ethereal oils.
Action: acts on the anterior pituitary gland, reducing FSH (follicle-stimulating-hormone) and increasing LSH (luteum-stimulating-hormone). Stimulates production of progesterone but reducing that of oestrogen. "Has a corpus luteum hormone effect" (*Dr Weiss 1974 322. New herbal Practitioner, March 1977*). Alternative to hormone replacement therapy (HRT).
Uses: Symptoms caused by excess FSH and low progesterone output. used as substitution therapy for primary and secondary corpus luteum deficiency. Pre-menstrual symptoms, especially nervous tension, irritability, mood-swings, depression, anxiety, crying, forgetfulness, insomnia. Amenorrhoea (by regulating sex hormones). Pain in breasts. To promote breast milk in nursing mothers; assist bust development. Acne vulgaris (to restore sex hormone balance). Water-retention (pre-menstrual) caused by oestrogen excess or progesterone deficiency. "Regular bleeding between periods decreased following temporary increase" (*Dr W. Amann, Bundesanzeiger, No 90, 15/5/1985*). Premature old age from sexual excess and masturbation. Agnus lowers sexual vitality; reduces nervous excitability. By opposing excess oestrogen it lessens the risk, however small, of endometrial carcinoma. For symptoms of the menopause and of withdrawal on giving-up The Pill.
Preparations. Extracts made from crushed roots.
Tablets: 300mg; 2 tablets after meals thrice daily.
Liquid Extract: 1:1 in 25% alcohol. Dose: 2-4ml.
Caution: Not taken in the presence of progesterone drugs.
Contra-indications and interaction with other drugs: None known.
Tincture: 10-20 drops daily morning dose during second half of menstrual cycle. GSL

AGORAPHOBIA. Fear of open spaces. Unrealistic, persistent and intense fear. Sufferer cannot leave home without feeling in need of psychological support. "Fear of a situation from which there is no immediate escape." It is not necessary to discover the original cause of such panic anxiety to cure the effect of it. Ninety per cent of agoraphobic patients are women. All have a weakened central nervous system which causes them to over-react to stress, when they can no longer control the way their balance-mechanism works; continued efforts to do so increase their stress level and produce emotional distress.

Where emotional and mental stress is caused by adrenal exhaustion the herb Pulsatilla exerts a positive influence. Other adrenal stimulants:– Sarsaparilla, Ginseng, Gotu Kola, Borage. Night cap to relax: cup of Balm tea.

As many of its symptoms are indistinguishable from caffeinism, coffee and strong tea should be avoided. Hypoglycaemia predisposes. Stop smoking. A dog makes an ideal companion for an agoraphobic, providing an impetus to get across the threshold.
Supplements: Vitamin B-complex, B1, B6, C, E. Minerals: Calcium, Magnesium, Zinc.
Aromatherapy: 6 drops Roman Chamomile oil on cotton wool for use a nosegay.

AGRANULOCYTOSIS. A condition in which there is a marked decrease or absence of polynuclear or granular white cells in the blood following prolonged septic conditions or from taking such drugs as phenothiazines, thiouracil and chloramphenicol. Other causes: radiation therapy, leukaemia, aplastic anaemia.
Symptoms: sore mouth, throat and lungs with bacterial infection.
Treatment: Should be supportive to specific medical treatment. Stop drugs that may be causative. Select from:–
Angelica, Burdock leaves, Calamus, Chamomile, Chickweed, Comfrey, Dandelion, Ginseng, Ground Ivy, Gotu Kola, Iceland Moss, Irish Moss, Liquorice root, Lime flowers, Linseed, Marshmallow leaves, Mullein leaves, Plantain, Red Clover flowers, Thuja, Violet leaves.
Tea. Combine equal parts: Red Clover, Gotu Kola, Mullein. 1 heaped teaspoon to each cup boiling water; infuse 10-15 minutes; dose, half-1 cup freely, as tolerated.
Tablets/capsules: Goldenseal, Echinacea, Iceland Moss, Ginseng. Dosage as on bottle.
Powders: Formula. Red Clover 2; Ginseng 1; Echinacea 1. Dose: 750mg (or three 00 capsules or half a teaspoon) thrice daily.
Tinctures. Combine Echinacea 2; Goldenseal 1; Fringe Tree 1. Dose: 1-2 teaspoons in water thrice daily.
Topical: Epsom's salts baths.
Diet: High protein, high fibre, low fat, low salt,

regular raw food days. Vitamins C, B-complex (especially B12), folic acid, bioflavonoids. Minerals – copper, iron, zinc.

AGRIMONY. Cocklebur, Church Steeples. *Agrimonia eupatoria*. *French*: Aigremoine. *Italian*: Agrimonia. *German*: Leberkraut. *Spanish*: Agrimonia.
Constituents: coumarins, tannins, flavonoids, phytosterol.
Action: diuretic, hepatic, astringent (mild), haemostatic, vulnerary, cholagogue, Promotes assimilation of food. Bitter tonic.
Uses: weak acid stomach, indigestion, sluggish liver and debility, gall bladder disorders, nose-bleed, sore throat, laryngitis (gargle), bed-wetting, incontinence, diarrhoea, to promote flow of gastric juices.
Local: ulceration – to cleanse and heal. Ancient remedy for suppurating sores and wounds.
Preparations. Thrice daily.
Tea: 1 teaspoon to each cup boiling water. Or, as part of *Spring Tonic combination*: equal parts, Agrimony, Raspberry leaves, Balm and Nettles. 2 teaspoons to each cup boiling water; infuse 15 minutes. Half-1 cup freely.
Liquid extract: BHP (1983). 1:1 in 25 per cent alcohol. Dose 15-45 drops (1-3ml).
Tincture: BHP (1983). 1:5 in 45 per cent alcohol. Dose 15-60 drops (1-4ml).
Tablets. Agrimony (*Blackmore's Labs*). GSL

AGUE. A term once used for an acute fever, particularly with alternating heat and shivering, i.e., malaria. See: FEVER, MALARIA, etc.

AIDS. Acquired Immune Deficiency Syndrome. Infection by HIV virus may lead to AIDS, but is believed to be not the sole cause of the disease. It strikes by ravaging the body's defence system, destroying natural immunity by invading the white blood cells and producing an excess of 'suppressant' cells. It savages the very cells that under normal circumstances would defend the body against the virus. Notifiable disease. Hospitalisation. AIDS does not kill. By lacking an effective body defence system a person usually dies from another infection such as a rare kind of pneumonia. There are long-term patients, more than ten years after infection with HIV who have not developed AIDS. There are some people on whom the virus appears to be ineffective. The HIV virus is transmitted by infected body fluids, e.g. semen, blood or by transfusion.

A number of co-factors are necessary for AIDS to develop: diet, environment, immoral lifestyle, drugs, etc also dispose to the disease which, when eliminated, suggest that AIDS needs not be fatal. However, there is no known cure. Smoking hastens onset. Causes include needle-sharing and sexual contacts. Also known as the 'Gay Plague' it can be transmitted from one member of the family to another non-sexual contact.

The virus kills off cells in the brain by inflammation, thus disposing to dementia.
Symptoms. Onset: brief fever with swollen glands. "Feeling mildly unwell". This may pass off without incident until recurrence with persistent diarrhoea, night sweats, tender swollen lymph nodes, cough and shortness of breath. There follows weight loss, oral candida. Diagnosis is confirmed by appearance of ugly skin lesions known as Kaposi's sarcoma – a malignant disease. First indication is the appearance of dark purple spots on the body followed by fungoid growths on mouth and throat.

While some cases of STDs have been effectively treated with phytotherapy, there is evidence to suggest it may be beneficial for a number of reasons. Whatever the treatment, frequent blood counts to monitor T-4 cells (an important part of the immune system) are necessary. While a phytotherapeutic regime may not cure, it is possible for patients to report feeling better emotionally and physically and to avoid some accompanying infections (candida etc).
Treatment. Without a blood test many HIV positives may remain ignorant of their condition for many years. STD clinics offer free testing and confidential counselling.

Modern phytotherapeutic treatment:–
1. Anti-virals. See entry.
2. Enhance immune function.
3. Nutrition: diet, food supplements.
4. Psychological counselling.

To strengthen body defences: Garlic, Echinacea, Lapacho, Sage, Chlorella, Reisha Mushroom, Shiitake Mushroom. Of primary importance is Liquorice: 2-4 grams daily.
Upper respiratory infection: Pleurisy root, Elecampane.
Liver breakdown: Blue Flag root, Milk Thistle, Goldenseal.
Diarrhoea: Bayberry, Mountain Grape, American Cranesbill, Slippery Elm, lactobacillus acidophilus.
Prostatitis: Saw Palmetto, Goldenrod, Echinacea.
Skin lesions: External:– Comfrey, Calendula or Aloe Vera cream.
To help prevent dementia: a common destructive symptom of the disease: agents rich in minerals – Alfalfa, Irish Moss, Ginkgo, St John's Wort, Calcium supplements.
Nervous collapse: Gotu Kola, Siberian Ginseng, Oats, Damiana.
Ear Inflammation: Echinacea. External – Mullein ear drops.
With candida: Lapacho tea. Garlic inhibits candida.
Anal fissure: Comfrey cream or Aloe Vera gel (external).
Practitioner: Formula. Liquid extract Echinacea

30ml (viral infection) . . . Liquid extract Poke root 10ml (lymphatic system) . . . Liquid extract Blue Flag root 10ml (liver stimulant) . . . Tincture Goldenseal 2ml (inflamed mucous membranes) . . . Liquid extract Guaiacum 1ml (blood enricher) . . . Decoction of Sarsaparilla to 100ml. Sig: 5ml (3i) aq cal pc.

Gargle for sore throat: 5-10 drops Liquid extract or Tincture Echinacea to glass water, as freely as desired.

Abdominal Castor oil packs: claimed to enhance immune system.

Chinese medicine: Huang Qi (astragalus root).

Urethral and vaginal irrigation: 2 drops Tea Tree oil in strong decoction Marshmallow root: 2oz to 2 pints water. Inject warm.

Diet. Vitamin C-rich foods, Lecithin, Egg Yolk, Slippery Elm gruel, Red Beet root, Artichokes. Garlic is particularly indicated as an anti-infective.

Nutrition. Vitamin A is known to increase resistance by strengthening the cell membrane; preferably taken as beta carotene 300,000iu daily as massive doses of Vitamin A can be toxic. Amino acid – Glutathione: Garlic's L-cysteine relates.

Vitamin C. "The virus is inactivated by this vitamin. Saturating cells infected with the HIV virus with the vitamin results in 99 per cent inactivation of the virus. The vitamin is an anti-viral and immune system modulator without unwanted side-effects. The ascorbate, when added to HIV cells, substantially reduced the virus's activity without harming the cells at specific concentrations. Patients taking large doses report marked improvement in their condition. Minimum daily oral dose: 10 grams." (*Linus Pauling Institute, Science and Medicine, Palo Alto, California, USA*)

Periwinkle. An anti-AIDS compound has been detected in the Madagascan Periwinkle (*Catharanthus roseus*), at the Chelsea Physic Garden.

Mulberry. The black Mulberry appears to inhibit the AIDS virus.

Hyssop. An AIDS patient improved to a point where ulcers were healed, blood infection eliminated, and Kaposi's sarcoma started to clear when her mother gave her a traditional Jamaican tea made from Hyssop, Blessed Thistle and Senna. From test-tube research doctors found that Hyssopus officinalis could be effective in treatment of HIV/AIDS. (*Medical Journal Antiviral Research, 1990, 14, 323-37*)

Circumcision. Studies have shown that uncircumcised African men were more than five to eight times more likely to contract AIDS than were circumcised men; life of the virus being short-lived in a dry environment. (*Epidemiologist Thomas Quinn, in Science Magazine*)

Study. A group of 13 HIV and AIDS patients received 200mg capsules daily of a combination of Chelidonium (Greater Celandine) 175mg; Sanguinaria (Blood root) 5mg; and Slippery Elm (Ulmus fulva) 20mg. More than half the patients enjoyed increased energy and improved immune function with reduction in both size and tenderness of lymph nodes. (*D'Adamo P. 'Chelidonium and Sanguinaria alkaloids as anti-HIV therapy. Journal of Naturopathic Medicine (USA) 3.31-34 1992*)

Bastyr College of Naturopathy, Seattle, MA, USA. During 1991 the College carried out a study which claimed that a combination of natural therapies including nutrition, supplements, herbal medicine, hydrotherapy and counselling had successfully inhibited HIV and other viral activity in all patients in controlled trials lasting a year.

Patients chosen for the trial were HIV positive, not on anti-viral drugs and showing symptoms of a compromised immune system, but without frank AIDS (generally taken to be indicated by Karposi's sarcoma and/or PCP-pneumocystitis carinii pneumonia).

Symptoms included: Lymphadenopathy in at least two sites, oral thrush, chronic diarrhoea, chronic sinusitis, leukoplakia, herpes, night sweats and fatigue.

Assessment was subjective and objective (including T-cell ratio tests). The patients did better than comparable groups in published trials using AZT.

Treatment was naturopathic and herbal. Patients receiving homoeopathy and acupuncture did not do as well as those receiving herbs.

Best results with herbs were: Liquorice (1g powder thrice daily); St John's Wort (Yerba prima tablets, 3, on two days a week only). Patients reported a great increase in the sense of well-being on St John's Wort. An equivalent dose of fresh plant tincture would be 10ml. The tincture should be of a good red colour. The College did not use Echinacea, which would stimulate the central immune system and which would therefore be contra-indicated.

Supplements given daily. Calcium ascorbate 3g+ (to bowel tolerance). Beta-carotene 300,000iu. Thymus gland extract tablets 6. Zinc 60mg (with some Copper). B-vitamins and EFAs.

To control specific symptoms: most useful herbs were: Tea Tree oil for fungal infections; Goldenseal and Gentian as bitters. Ephedra and Eyebright for sinusitis. Carob drinks for non-specific enteritis. Vitamin B12 and topical Liquorice for shingles.

Counselling and regular massage were used to maintain a positive spirit. Studies show all long term HIV positive survivors have a positive attitude and constantly work at empowering themselves.

Results showed significant improvements in symptoms suffered by HIV patients despite a slow deterioration in blood status. Methods used in the study had dramatically reduced mortality and morbidity. A conclusion was reached that AIDS may not be curable but it could be manageable. (*Reported by Christopher Hedley MNIMH, London NW1 8JD, in Greenfiles Herbal Journal*)

AIR SWALLOWING. Aerophagia. Swallowing mouthfuls of air. Usually associated with indigestion.
Treatment. Carminatives, antacids.
Teas: any one: Aniseed, Balm, Caraway seeds, Cardamom seeds, Cinnamon bark, Fennel seeds, Dill seeds, Parsley. 1 teaspoon to each cup boiling water; infuse 5-15 minutes; dose half-1 cup freely.
Ginger: powder, crystallised or tincture. *Horseradish* sauce. Few grains Cayenne pepper. *Oil Peppermint*: 1-2 drops in honey.

ALBUMINURIA. Presence of albumin in the urine which produces a white coagulate on heating. See: PROTEINURIA.

ALCOHOL. Alcohol is a chemical with definite physical and chemical properties. It may be used as the alcohol of pharmacy (ethyl alcohol, ethanol) for the making of tinctures, extracts, etc. Strength of alcohol used depends upon the phytochemistry of the plant. The weakest spirit is always chosen to serve the purpose.
Weak. 20-25 per cent. For water soluble ingredients and small amounts of volatile oils, i.e., Infusion Buchu Conc. A white wine (approximately 25 per cent) may prove adequate for most leaves, flowers and stems (i.e., Agrimony, Balm or Chamomile.
Medium Strength. 45 per cent. This is the strength, on average, used by the herbal practitioner. For tannins and small amounts of volatile oils, etc (i.e., Extract of Witch Hazel Liquid).
Moderately Strong. 60-70 per cent. Water soluble glycosides, (Tincture Digitalis, Squills, etc.).
Strong alcohols. 70-80 per cent. For alkaloids present in many plants.
Very Strong Alcohols. 90-99 per cent. For gums and resins (Myrrh), essential and volatile oils (Spirit Menth Pip., etc.).

Without alcohol, extraction of active constituents of plants would not be possible. Glycerine has not proved to be a satisfactory menstruum. For simple home-made tinctures Vodka offers a useful alternative provided it is of the strength specified.

Alcohol is not only a reliable solvent and preservative. It may be used effectively in the treatment of disease. In the form of wine it is one of the oldest drugs known to medicine. It appears in the pharmacopoeias and medical text-books of every civilised culture in the world. It may be used as an analgesic for the control of pain. It is an effective anaesthetic, vasodilator, sedative, and diuretic to stimulate kidney function. It was probably the first tranquilliser discovered. See: PRESCRIPTIONS.

Alcohol is the commonest substance to be incriminated in drug interactions. It can potentiate soporific effects in antidepressants, pain-killers and antihistamines and increase irritation of the stomach by aspirin. It can change the action of hypoglycaemic and anticoagulant remedies.

ALCOHOLS. Plant chemicals in the form of sterols and volatile oils such as pulegone in Pennyroyal.

ALCOHOL ABUSE. Three to four daily drinks for several weeks result in increased fat in liver cells. Then comes alcoholic hepatitis, inflammation of the liver tissue and destruction of cells, degenerating into an irreversible state known as cirrhosis. Complications develop such as intestinal bleeding, fluid accumulation, kidney failure and death if not arrested in time. Alcoholism is compulsive drinking leading to dependence.
Alternatives: *Teas*. Hops, Angelica, German Chamomile, or Skullcap. 1 heaped teaspoon to each cup boiling water; infuse 5-15 minutes. 1 cup 3-4 times daily.
Tablets/capsules. Cramp bark, Black Cohosh, Valerian.
Formula. Equal parts: Cramp bark and Valerian. Dose – powders: 250mg, or one 00 capsule; liquid extracts: 15-30 drops; bark tinctures: 30-60 drops; in honey or water 3-4 times daily.
Cold infusion. 1 teaspoon Oak bark cut, in cup cold water. Infuse 1 hour. Dose: sips during the day.
Tincture Cinchona, BPC (1949) , 15-30 drops, 2-3 times daily.
Tincture Myrrh BPC (1973) 5-10 drops in half glass water 2-3 times daily.
Oil of Evening Primrose improves brain function in cases of withdrawal (*Efamol Can Improve Alcohol Recovery, General Practitioner, p11, Sept 18, 1987*).
Milk Thistle. Good responses observed. Dose: 80-200mg, thrice daily.
Chinese Medicine. Kudzu vine (*Pueraria lobata*) can effectively reduce the cravings of alcohol. The flowers are used in China for alcoholic poisoning. Used for reforming alcoholics. (*Herbarium Dec 1993*)
Supplements. B-complex, A, C, E. Magnesium, Selenium, Zinc. For bone-loss of alcoholism: see: OSTEOPOROSIS.
Information. Alcoholics Anonymous, Stonebow House, Stonebow, York YO1 2NJ.

ALETRIS. True unicorn root. Star Grass. *Aletris farinosa L.* Dried rhizomes and roots.

Action. Estrogenic, due to diosgenin-derived steroid. Stomachic, anorexic, sedative, bitter tonic (fresh plant).
Uses. Relaxed conditions of the womb. Lack of vitality in teenage girls and menopausal women from blood loss or nutritional deficiency. Used in pregnancy when Raspberry leaf tea is not well tolerated. Sometimes advised for threatened miscarriage but Helonias (False Unicorn root) more effective. Loss of appetite, flatulence, dyspepsia, colic. Rheumatism (Appalachia Indians). Prolapse of the womb. Dysmenorrhoea.
Preparations. Yields very little of its properties to water.
Liquid Extract BHP (1983) 1:1 in 45 per cent alcohol; dose, 5-15 drops in water.
Powdered root: 0.3-0.6 grams.
Poultice for sore and painful breasts (*A. Vogel*).
GSL

ALFALFA. Purple medick, lucerne, Californian clover, Buffalo herb. *Medicago sativa L. German*: Luzerne. *French*: Luzerne. *Italian*: Medica. *Chinese*: Mu-su. *Part used*: leaves.
Habitat. Native to Asia but now found in temperate zones.
Constituents. Alkaloids, isoflavones, coumarins, sterols. Contains eight essential enzymes:– amylase (digests starches), coagulase (coagulates milk), invertase (converts sugar into dextrose), emulsin (acts upon sugars), peroxidase (oxidases blood), lipase (fat-splitting enzyme), pectinase (forms a vegetable jelly from pectin), protase (digests protein). Together with its rich content of vitamins and minerals, Alfalfa offers an effective aid to cover a wide range of diverse conditions.
Vitamin content: pro-Vitamin A (B-carotene), B6, C, D, E, K, P. Yields 20,000 to 40,000 units Vitamin K to every 100 grams, and is therefore a useful preventative of high blood pressure.
Minerals. Alfalfa yields 10 times more mineral value than average grains. Roots penetrate subsoil as far as 125 feet, thus enabling it to absorb vital mineral nutrients beyond the reach of other vegetation. Calcium, Magnesium, Phosphorus, Potassium.
Action. Anti-cholesterol, anti-haemorrhagic, anti-anaemia, anti-coagulant. Traditional anti-diabetic activity (South Africa).
Uses. To promote strong bones and rebuild decayed teeth. Nutrient to increase weight and vitality. Lumbago, rheumatism, dyspepsia, back ache, fistula, chronic ulcer, infections of sinus, ear, nose and throat. Affections of respiratory tract, certain forms of insulin-dependent diabetes. Rich in chlorophyll, it stimulates growth of supportive connective tissue and is useful for collagen disease – arthritis etc. Assists granulation of tissue in healing of wounds, abscesses. Relieves constipation by gently activating peristalsis of the bowels. Frequent cups of tea have a diuretic effect relieving dropsy, kidney, bladder and prostate disorders. Fattens thin people. Builds up after surgical operation. Hyperlipidaemia. Repair of radiotherapy damage.
Preparations. *Tea*: 2-3 teaspoons to each cup boiling water; infuse 5-10 minutes. Drink freely.
Diuretic tea. Herbs: Alfalfa 3, Couchgrass 2, Buchu 1, Wild Carrot 1. Mix. 1-2 teaspoons to each cup boiling water; infuse 5-10 minutes. Half-1 cup thrice daily.
Liquid extract, BHP (1983), 1:1 in 25 per cent alcohol. Dose: 5-10ml thrice daily.
Green drink. Fresh Alfalfa passed through a blender; juice drunk in wineglassful doses. Alfalfa 'sprouts' are grown from seed in a shallow tray and contain 150 per cent more protein than wheat or corn. Daily rinsed with water, they are allowed to germinate to about half inch in height when they are chopped and used in salads. See: SPROUTS.

Any one of these preparations favourably influences nutrition in cases of anorexia nervosa, neurasthenia, insomnia, feeble appetite, and to increase the flow of milk in young nursing mothers. Taken regularly, it is believed to dispose to mental and physical well-being.
Capsules (powder). 250mg: 2 capsules thrice daily during meals. (*Arkocaps*)
Tablets. 500mg. (*Meadowcroft*)
Note. Alfalfa should not be taken with Vitamin E, the action of which it vitiates.

ALGAE. A seaweed. A large group of lower plants in various forms, some of which are single-celled. Unlike fungi, they contain chlorophyll – an active healing agent. Algae has an affinity for heavy metals; mercury, lead, cadmium, etc, and is therefore useful as a detoxicating agent in the body. See: SPIRULINA.

ALIMENTARY TRACT. A long canal, the digestive tract, from the mouth to the anus, through which food passes in the process of digestion and absorption.

ALKALINE FOODS. These are foods the body breaks down into alkali. Alkaline foods are high in sodium and potassium. Almonds, apples, asparagus, bananas, dried beans, beet greens, Brussels sprouts, buttermilk, cabbage, celery, cauliflower, currants, carrots, chestnuts, coconuts, cream; all fruits except prunes, fresh plums and cranberries. Lemons, lima beans, milk, molasses, oranges, parsnips, dried peas, peaches, radishes, raisins, Soya flour, turnips, all green leafy vegetables except sweet corn. Yeast, fresh tomatoes, herb teas, lettuce, watercress.

ALKANET. Anchusa. *Alkanna tinctoria*, Tausch. Root. Astringent. Once taken internally as a tea, now externally as an ointment. Antidotes poison in those bitten by venomous snakes, (Dioscorides). Culpeper records its use for St Anthony's Fire (erysipelas).

ALKALOIDS. Alkaloids are basic organic substances, usually vegetable in origin and having an alkaline reaction. Like alkalis they combine with acids to form salts. They are natural amines, contain nitrogen and have a direct action on body tissue, chiefly of blood vessels and nerves. Some are toxic. All have a bitter taste. Most are insoluble in water but soluble in alcohol. Many herbs yield alkaloids, notably Comfrey (pyrrolizidine a.), Mistletoe, Butterbur, Blue Cohosh, Lobelia, Greater Celandine, Barberry, Boldo, Blue Cohosh, Betony, Colchicum, Ephedra, Gelsemium, Horsetail, Passion flower, Turkey corn. Some alkaloids stimulate the liver while others may be toxic.

ALLANTOIN. A substance. CHNO, found in the human body in fetal urine, etc. Formed by the oxidation of uric acid. Also found in the natural kingdom, Comfrey root and other plants. Promotes growth of epithelium over a wound as part of the final stage of healing. See: COMFREY.

ALLERGIC RHINITIS. See: HAY FEVER.

ALLERGY. Hypersensitiveness to a foreign protein which produces a violent reaction taking the form of asthma, hay fever, urticaria, eczema, migraine, catarrh, irritable bowel. Sensitivity covers a wide range of irritants including animal odours, pollens, insect bites. All kinds of food may be responsible: milk, eggs, pork, tomatoes, strawberries, coffee, tea, etc, also preservatives and artificial colourings.

Substances that cause allergic reactions are known as *allergens*. Their number are limitless. Against these, the body produces *antibodies* to fight off invaders. If we are allergic, such defence mechanisms over-react. The reaction has the effect of releasing various chemicals such as histamine which causes irritation and swelling of mucous membranes. Removal of dental amalgam fillings sometimes relieves.

Perhaps the most common allergy is hay fever. It is now known that most sufferers have a family history of the complaint. Asthma is a serious form, but with the aid of certain herbs (Lobelia, etc) sufferers may lead normal lives.

Premature babies fed on cow's milk are at risk of cow's milk allergy with increased histamine release. (*Dunn Nutrition Unit, Cambridge*)

Food allergies from shell fish and cereal grain fungi are difficult to detect. A large body of opinion favours *Garlic* (corm, tablets or capsules), being observed that Garlic eaters seldom suffer allergies. Agrimony tea.

Skin reactions may be severe. Hives, dermatitis and blisters can be the result of allergies triggered off by insect stings or animal bites, drugs, food additives, colourings, monosodium glutamate, chocolate, wines, aspirin, penicillin and other drugs. Cytotoxic tests are made to discover foods to which a person may be allergic.

Heredity predisposes, but forms vary. A 'nettle rash' father may have a 'hay fever' son. Stress is an important factor. While allergy is not a psychosomatic disturbance, there is general agreement that emotional distress – fright, fury or fatigue – can be related. An allergy can also be due to a flaw in the immune system, the body over-reacting to an allergen. Some allergies are treated with the antihistamines of orthodox pharmacy but which may induce drowsiness.

Treatment. The phytotherapist's primary agent is Ephedra.

Teas. Chamomile, Centuary, Elderflowers, Ground Ivy, Lime flowers, Nettles, Plantain, Red Sage. 1 heaped teaspoon to each cup boiling water; infuse 5-10 minutes. 1 cup 1 to 3 times daily.

Liquid Extract. Ephedra sinica BHP (1983): Dose – 1-3ml. Thrice daily.

Tincture. Ephedra sinica BHP (1983) 1:4 in 45 per cent alcohol. Dose: 6-8ml thrice daily.

A Vogel. Devil's Claw, thrice daily.

J. Christopher. Burdock, Marshmallow root, Parsley root.

Valerian. Add to prescription in cases of nervous hyperactivity.

Diet. Low salt, low fat, high fibre. Eggs and dairy products are known to cause allergies. Raw salad once daily. Add more protein, cooked and raw vegetables. Rice is not known to cause any allergic reactions.

Supplements. Daily. Vitamin A, B-complex, Vitamin C. Bromelain, Selenium, Zinc.

Note. No animals or birds in the house.

ALLOPATHY. Conventional medicine, as distinct from homoeopathy.

ALLSPICE. Pimento. Jamaican pepper. *Pimento officinalis* Lindl. Powdered fruit.

Action: stomachic, carminative, aromatic. An ingredient of 'mixed spices'. Used in condiments. Local antiseptic and anaesthetic. Source of new natural anti-oxidants. volatile oil.

Uses. Indigestion, diarrhoea, flatulence.

Preparations. *Liquid extract*: 30-60 drops. Oil Piment BPC (1949): 1-3 drops in honey. *Powder*: Half-2 grams. Dose as necessary. GSL

ALMOND OIL. Amygdala dulcis (sweet almonds). A fixed oil expressed from *Prunus amygdalus* without the aid of heat. Contains 45 per cent fixed oil and about 20 per cent protein and an enzyme, emulsin. Demulcent. Nutritive. Emulsifying agent. Used internally as a laxative, or externally as a massage oil. A nourishing skin cream is made by whisking Almond oil 2; Beeswax 1; and Aloe Vera 1; in a mixer. "Oil of Almonds makes smooth the hands and face of delicate persons, and cleanses the skin from spots and pimples" (*John Gerard*)

Oil is injected into the meatus for softening ear wax prior to removal. A good vehicle for Vitamins A, D and E in cosmetic lotions. Excellent base for ointments, together with Agar-Agar.

Sweet almonds have been used as food since ancient times, being a source of fats, iron, calcium, potassium, phosphorus, copper and zinc. Used widely in Aromatherapy. GSL

ALOE. *Aloe arborescens*. Part used: leaf.
Action. Skin protective against radiation damage from X-rays. Appears to work through anti-oxidant, free-radical scavenging effects. (*Japanese Journal of Pharmacology, Yakugaku zasshi – 1990 110(11): pp 876-84*)

ALOE VERA. *Aloe barbadensis and others*. Aloe Vera gel. Spiky cactus-like plant of the lily family. The gel is present under the outer surface of the leaf. *French*: Aloes. *Italian*: Aloe ordinario. *German*: Achter Aloe.
Action. Bactericidal against *staphylococcus aureus, streptococcus viridans* and five strains of *streptococcus mutans* – the cause of dental plaque. Antibiotic, Demulcent, Coagulant, Analgesic for mild degree pain. Antiviral.

Astringent, Vitamin B12 precursor, growth stimulator, vulnerary. Contains 18 amino acids and vitamins. Helps eliminate toxic minerals from the body. Neutralises free radicals created by toxic substances.
Uses. An important use: protection against radiation burns. Sunburn. A segment of the fresh leaf rubbed on the skin was a centuries-old sun-screen used by desert Arabs against sunburn, and who regarded the plant as a natural medicine chest. Internal: indigestion, stomach ulceration.
External. Ulceration (leg ulcer, etc.), acne, chapped skin, nappy rash. To allay the itching of dry skin conditions including shingles, eczema, poison ivy and other plant allergies, detergent dermatitis, ulcers on cornea of eye, purulent ophthalmia. Dry scalp, poor hair (shampoo), ringworm. Stretch marks of pregnancy, age lines and liver spots.
Dentistry. "In 12 years of dental practice I have not found any one item which is so versatile for the healing needs of the mouth . . . an ancient plant for modern dentistry". (*Dr B. Wolfe, "Health Consciousness", Vol 6. No 1*) Increasing use as a dental anaesthetic, and for oral infections. Uses include gel on new dentures, rinsing every 4 hours. In canal filling the gel is used as a lubricant.

Combines with Vitamin E for allergies; with Eucalyptus oil for sinus and nasal congestion; with Comfrey for healing of fractures. Combines with Jojoba oil as an invigorating body lotion. Combines with Chamomile or Henna for hair conditioner.
Preparations. Part of fresh leaf cut and thick sap-juice squeezed on affected area for sunburn, burns, injury, wounds. Pulp leaves for use as a poultice for inflamed joints, arthritis. (*East Africa*). Tablets: Combined with papaya, pineapple, apricot or acerola fruits.
Tincture: 4oz pulped leaf to 8oz Vodka. Shake bottle daily for one week. Filter. Dosage: 1 teaspoon in water, thrice daily, for internal conditions.
Aloe gel. Many preparations on the market contain pure Aloe Vera, cold-pressed to preserve its moisturising and healing properties. Most are free from artificial fragrance and colour being made without lanolin or mineral oil.
Undiluted juice. 1-2 tablespoons (20-40ml) on empty stomach. (Internal)
Pregnancy. Not used during. GSL

ALOES. Barbados aloes, Cape aloes, Socotrine aloes. Curacao, *Aloe barbadensis* Mill., *Aloe Ferox* Mill., *Aloe perryi* Baker. *German*: Aloé. *French*: Aloès. *Italian*: Aloè. *Spanish*: Aloe, Linaloe. *Chinese*: Chin-hiang. Liquid from cut leaves allowed to dry solid. Contains anthraquinone glycosides (aloin), resins.
Action: emmenagogue, abortifacient, vermifuge. Perhaps the best known laxative of history. Stimulates peristalsis. Stool softener.
Uses: chronic constipation, with a carminative to prevent griping. Said to have anti-malignant activity. An ingredient of the Natural Health Tablet.
Dose. Barbados aloes: 50mg (MD). Cape aloes: 100mg (MD). Aloin: 20mg (MD).
Tincture Aloes BPC 1949. Dose: 2-8ml. GSL

ALOPECIA. See: HAIR LOSS. HAIR CARE.

ALSTONIA BARK. Australian quinine. Fever bark. *Alstonia constricta, F.* Muell. Bark.
Action: febrifuge, anti-periodic. Used by Australian aborigines for all kinds of fevers. Contains indole alkaloids.
Other uses: high blood pressure, mild analgesic, intermittent fevers.
Preparations. Thrice daily.
Tea: 1oz to 1 pint water simmered gently 5 minutes: one wineglassful. *Liquid Extract*: 5-30 drops. *Powdered bark*: 1-3g. *Tincture*. 15-60 drops.

ALTERATIVES. "Medicines that alter the process of nutrition, restoring in some unknown way the normal functions of an organ or system

. . . re-establishing healthy nutritive processes" (*Blakiston Medical Dictionary*)

They are blood cleansers that favourably change the character of the blood and lymph to de-toxify and promote renewal of body tissue. The term has been superseded by the word 'adaptogen'. See: ADAPTOGEN. However, since the majority of professional phytotherapists still use the term 'alterative', the term 'alterative' is used through this book to describe the particular action of the group which includes:–

Alfalfa, Bladderwrack, Blue Flag root, Burdock, Chaparral, Chicory, Clivers, Dandelion, Devil's Claw, Echinacea, Garlic, Ginseng, Goldenseal, Gotu Kola, Marigold, Mountain Grape, Nettles, Poke root, Queen's Delight, Red Clover, Sarsaparilla, Thuja, Turkey Corn, Wild Indigo, Yellow Dock.

English traditional formula: equal parts, Burdock, Red Clover, Yellow Dock. Place quarter of the mixture in 2 pints water; simmer gently down to 1 pint. Dose: one-third-half cup thrice daily, before meals. Effects are to enhance elimination through skin, kidneys and bowels; to provide hormone precursors, electrolytes and minerals. The above combination may also be taken in liquid extracts, tinctures or powders.

ALTITUDE SICKNESS. Felt by those who have not adapted to the rare atmosphere of a high altitude. Ginger (crystallised).

ALUMINIUM. A soft metal readily absorbed into food, especially acid fruits. Mildly toxic. Salts of aluminium are excreted from the body with difficulty. Believed to be one of the causes of Alzheimer's disease. The element tends to dry up tissues of the body, the end result of which can be formation of fibrous tissue. There is growing concern that it is associated with hyperactivity in children. So far fish and plant life have been unable to adapt to the increase in aluminium levels in the environment. Most toxic metals are excreted by the kidneys, which organs should receive support by demulcents and diuretics where aluminium poisoning is suspected.

Toxic effects of aluminium may arise from use of baking powders, antacids, deodorants and foodstuffs. Symptoms include: memory loss, anorexia, irritative skin rash, constipation.

ALZHEIMER'S DISEASE. A progressive brain deterioration first described by the German Neurologist, Alois Alzheimer in 1906. Dementia. Not an inevitable consequence of ageing. A disease in which cells of the brain undergo change, the outer layer (cerebral cortex) leading to tangles of nerve fibres due to reduced oxygen and blood supply to the brain.

The patient lives in an unreal world in which relatives have no sense of belonging. A loving gentle wife they once knew is no longer aware of their presence. Simple tasks, such as switching on an electrical appliance are fudged. There is distressing memory loss, inability to think and learn, speech disturbance – death of the mind. Damage by free radicals implicated.

Symptoms: Confusion, restlessness, tremor. Finally: loss of control of body functions and bone loss.

A striking similarity exists between the disease and aluminium toxicity. Aluminium causes the brain to become more permeable to that metal and other nerve-toxins. (*Tulane University School of Medicine, New Orleans*). High levels of aluminium are found concentrated in the neurofibrillary tangles of the brain in Alzheimer's disease. Entry into the body is by processed foods, cookware, (pots and pans) and drugs (antacids).

"Reduction of aluminium levels from dietary and medicinal sources has led to a decline in the incidence of dementia." (*The Lancet, Nov 26, 1983*).

"Those who smoke more than one packet of cigarettes a day are 4.5 times more likely to develop Alzheimer's disease than non-smokers." (*Stuart Shalat, epidemiologist, Harvard University*).

Researchers from the University of Washington, Seattle, USA, claim to have found a link between the disease and head injuries with damage to the blood/brain barrier.

Also said to be associated with Down's syndrome, thyroid disease and immune dysfunction. Other contributory factors are believed to be exposure to mercury from dental amalgam fillings. Animal studies show Ginkgo to increase local blood flow of the brain and to improve peripheral circulation.

Alternatives. *Teas*: Alfalfa, Agrimony, Lemon Balm, Basil, Chaparral, Ginkgo, Chamomile, Coriander (crushed seeds), Ginseng, Holy Thistle, Gotu Kola, Horsetail, Rosemary, Liquorice root (shredded), Red Clover flowers, Skullcap, Ladies Slipper.

Tea. Formula. Combine, equal parts: German Chamomile, Ginkgo, Lemon Balm. 1 heaped teaspoon to cup boiling water; infuse 5-15 minutes. 1 cup freely.

Decoction. Equal parts: Black Cohosh, Blue Flag root, Hawthorn berries. 1 teaspoon in each cupful water; bring to boil and simmer 20 minutes. Dose: half-1 cup thrice daily.

Powders. Formula. Hawthorn 1; Ginkgo 1; Ginger half; Fringe Tree half. Add pinch Cayenne pepper. 500mg (two 00 capsules or one-third teaspoon) thrice daily.

Liquid extracts. Formula. Hawthorn 1; Ephedra half; Ginkgo 1. Dose: 30-60 drops, thrice daily, before meals.

Topical. Paint forehead and nape of neck with Tincture Arnica.

Diet: 2 day fluid-only fast once monthly for 6 months. Low fat, high fibre, lecithin. Lacto-vegetarian. Low salt.
Supplements. Vitamin B-complex, B6, B12, Folic acid, A, C, E, Zinc. Research has shown that elderly patients at high risk of developing dementia have lower levels of Vitamins A, E and the carotenes. Zinc and Vitamin B12 are both vital cofactors for brain enzymes.
Alzheimer's Disease linked with zinc. Zinc is believed to halt cerebral damage. Senile plaques in the brain produce amyloid, damaging the blood-brain barrier. Toxic metals then cross into the brain, displacing zinc. This then produces abnormal tissue. (*Alzheimer Disease and Associated Disorders, researchers, University of Geneva*).
Japanese study. Combination of coenzyme Q10, Vitamin B6 and iron. Showed improved mental function.
Abram Hoffer MD, PhD. Niacin 500mg tid, Vitamin C 500mg tid, Folic acid 5mg daily, Aspirin 300mg daily, Ginkgo herb 40mg daily. (*International Journal of Alternative and Complementary Medicine, Feb 1994 p11*)
Alzheimer's Disease Society. 2nd Floor, Gordon House, 10 Greencoat Piace, London SW1P 1PH, UK. Offers support to families and carers through membership. Practical help and information. Send SAE.

AMARANTH. Love-lies-bleeding. *Amaranthus hypochondriacus L.*
Part used: the flowering herb. *French*: Amarante blette. *German*: Erdamarant. *Spanish*: Amaranto. *Italian*: Amaranto. *Chinese*: Hsien.
Action: Astringent.
Uses. Internal haemorrhages (from the womb, bowel, stomach). Leucorrhoea (douche). Sore throat (gargle). Leg ulcers (decoction used as a cleanser). Irritable bowel.
Preparations. Thrice daily. Decoction: 1oz to 1 pint water gently simmered 15 minutes. Dose: wineglassful. *Liquid Extract*: 30-60 drops (2-4ml).

AMENORRHOEA. Suppression of normal menstrual flow during the time of life when it should occur. The most common cause is pregnancy but it can arise from hormonal imbalance, trauma, anaemia, fibroids, polyps, constitutional disorder or emotional problems. Though not prejudicial to health it marks a departure from normal.
Symptoms. Scanty irregular or absent periods.
Alternatives. Agnus Castus, Black Cohosh, Blue Cohosh, Chaparral, Feverfew, Helonias, Life root, Lovage, Marigold, Motherwort, Mugwort, Parsley root, Pennyroyal, Rosemary, Rue, Tansy, Thuja, Southernwood, Wormwood, Yarrow, Hedge Hyssop (*Gratiola officinalis*).
Tea: Combine: Agnus Castus, Motherwort, Yarrow. 1 heaped teaspoon to each cup boiling water; infuse 15 minutes. 1 cup thrice daily.
Formula. Combine: Helonias 2; Agnus Castus 2; Blue Cohosh 1. Doses. Powders: 500mg (two 00 capsules, or one-third teaspoon). Liquid Extracts: 30-60 drops. Tinctures: 1-2 teaspoons. In water or honey, thrice daily.
Agnus Castus. Success reported.
Due to thyroid imbalance: Kelp, Bladderwrack, Irish Moss.
Vitamins: A. B-complex. E.
Minerals: Calcium. Zinc.
Note. Patients with amenorrhoea are at risk of osteoporosis. (*Middlesex Hospital, London*)

AMINO ACIDS. Building blocks from which body protein is made. Their molecules contain nitrogen.

Some amino acid supplements are available singly, being sold by pharmacists and health stores for therapeutic or body-building purposes, including: Arginine, cysteine, cystine, glutamine, histidine, lysine, methionine, ornithine, phenylalanine, taurine, tryptophan and tyrosine.

AMMONIACUM. *Dorema ammoniacum* G. Don. Gum resin.
Action: Antispasmodic, expectorant, stimulant, diaphoretic, anti-asthmatic.
Uses: Respiratory disorders, asthma, cough, catarrh, chronic bronchitis.
Preparations: Thrice daily. *Powder*: 0.3-1g. Often an ingredient in Lobelia tablets. GSL

AMNESIA. See: MEMORY, WEAK.

AMOEBIASIS. See: DYSENTERY.

AMOEBIC LIVER ABSCESS. Usually contracted in a tropical country during foreign travel. Likely to be associated with amoebic dysentery by the organism *Entamoeba histolytica* from contaminated drinking water or decaying foods (uncooked vegetables), foods exposed to flies. Onset of the disease may not be apparent until years after original infection. It presents with tenderness over the liver. On palpation, liver area is tender and the diaphragm elevated.
Symptoms. Fever, sweating, constitutional upset.
Differential diagnosis: diverticulitis, Crohn's disease, salmonella, carcinoma, bacillary dysentery.
Alternatives:– Blue Flag, Boneset, Burdock, Chaparral, Echinacea, Elecampane, Elder flowers, Eucalyptus, Fringe Tree, Milk Thistle, Marshmallow, Queen's Delight, Thyme (garden), Wild Indigo, Wild Yam, Yarrow, Yellow Dock.
Tea. Combine: equal parts, Yarrow, Burdock leaves, Marshmallow leaves. 2 teaspoons to each cup boiling water; infuse 10-15 minutes; 1 cup freely.

Decoction. Echinacea 2; Fringe Tree bark 1; Yellow Dock root 1 2 teaspoons to 2 cups water gently simmered 20 minutes. Half a cup freely.
Formula: Combine Echinacea 2; Fringe Tree bark 1; Boneset 1; Goldenseal quarter. Dose: Liquid Extracts: 2-4ml. Tinctures: 4-8ml. Powders: 500mg (two 00 capsules, or one-third teaspoon). In water, honey, or cup of Fenugreek tea.
Cold puree. Pass Garlic corm through food blender. Eat with a spoon as much as tolerated. Blend with adjutants: carrots, raisins, apple.

AMPHOTERIC. A normaliser. A remedy that serves to harmonise the function of an organ (liver, endocrine gland) in such a way as to "improve apparently contradictory symptoms" (*Simon Mills*). A plant that acts in two different ways, having two different characters. In chemistry, an amphoteric affects both red and blue litmus, acting both as an acid and an alkali. Some plants have opposite effects, notably Lily of the Valley, according to the condition of the heart.

Thus, a plant may normalise glandular secretions, build up cell protein and enable the body to recover from exertion. This important group includes Gotu Kola, Sarsaparilla and Ginseng.

AMPUTATION. Ghost pains after surgical removal of a limb. Wash remaining limb with strong infusion of Thyme (2oz – 2 handfuls wild or garden Thyme to quart boiling water infused 15 minutes and strained). (*Maria Treben*) Comfrey Poultice. Comfrey cream or ointment.
Internal: Valerian. St John's Wort (Hypericum).

ANABOLIC AGENT. An agent which assists constructive metabolism and assimilation: Saw Palmetto, Sarsaparilla.

ANAEMIA. Blood disorder. Characterised by reduction in haemoglobin level.
Symptoms: breathlessness on exertion, fatigue, facial pallor, infection-prone, and others according to type. See appropriate entries: IRON DEFICIENCY ANAEMIA, HAEMOLYTIC ANAEMIA, APLASTIC ANAEMIA, SICKLE CELL ANAEMIA, PERNICIOUS ANAEMIA, SPORTS ANAEMIA, PREGNANCY – ANAEMIA, LEUKAEMIA.

ANAEMIA: APLASTIC. Failure of the bone marrow to produce red cells because of infection, also neutropenia and depletion of platelets in the blood through chronic disease (TB etc) elsewhere in the body, or through chemicals in food and medicine. Other causes include food preservatives, X-ray radiation, fluoride in water supply and environmental pollution. The condition is serious.

Possibility of mercurial poisoning. A 59-year-old man employed filling thermometers with mercury developed aplastic anaemia and died. His urine contained 1.01mg mercury per litre. (*D.R. Ryrie. Brit. Medical Journal, i/1970, 499. A similar report D.R. Wilson, ibid., ii/1966, 1534*)
Symptoms. Headache, dizziness, pallor of skin, loss of weight and appetite, sore or burning tongue, jaundice, bruising, nose-bleeds. A low state of the immune system exposes the subject to infection.
Treatment. Hospital supervision. Necessary to identify the causative toxic agent and eliminate it. Condition fails to respond to usual preparations of iron taken by mouth. No specific exists but supportive adaptogen herbs sustain and raise haemoglobin levels, marginally increasing red cells.

To facilitate elimination of toxic chemicals:–
Teas: Alfalfa, Red Clover, German Chamomile, Ground Ivy, Milk Thistle, Gotu Kola, Nettles, Fennel.
Tea. Formula. Equal parts: Dandelion, Nettles, Alfalfa. 1 heaped teaspoon in each cup boiling water, infuse 10-15 minutes. One cup freely.
Decoction: Gentian – 1 teaspoon in cup cold water. Steep overnight; drink on rising.
Tinctures. To stimulate bone marrow. Formula: equal parts, Echinacea, Prickly Ash bark, Horsetail. Dose: 1-2 teaspoons thrice daily, taken in water or cup of one of the above teas.
Tincture Cinnamon BP (1949). Dose: 2-4ml (30-60 drops).
Powders. Combine: Gentian 1; Yellow Dock 1; Echinacea 2; Cinnamon quarter; Cayenne quarter. Dose: 500mg (two 00 capsules or one-third teaspoon), before meals.
Liquid Extracts: Combine Echinacea 2; Black Cohosh half; Damiana 1; Ginger quarter. Dose: 1 teaspoon in cup Red Clover tea, before meals.
Diet. Dandelion coffee, high fibre, low fat, low salt, molasses, lamb's liver. Foods containing Vitamin B12.
Supplements daily. Vitamin B12. Folic acid 400mcg, Vitamin C, Floradix.

ANAEMIA: HAEMOLYTIC. A blood condition due to abnormal destruction of red blood cells in the spleen.
Causes: hereditary background with deficiency of cell enzymes or cell membrane weakness; wrongly matched blood transfusion, environmental chemicals, food additives, colourings, drugs, infections.
Symptoms. Pale face, sore tongue, headache, dizziness, palpitations, breathlessness, angina, weakness, loss of weight and appetite, jaundice (yellow skin), feverishness, vague aches and pains, enlarged spleen and pain under left ribs.
Treatment. Under hospital supervision.

Echinacea has a long reputation for regeneration of red blood cells: experience shows it beneficial for this type of anaemia. To assist

control of symptoms: Gentian, Motherwort, Mugwort, Barberry, Hops, Saw Palmetto.
Bitter herbs stimulate the stomach, liver and pancreas. By increasing the appetite they benefit digestion and are given half an hour before meals by tea or decoction: Hops, Quassia chips, Angostura, Feverfew, Bogbean.
Formula. Tea. Milk Thistle 2; Betony 1; Hops 1. Mix. 1-2 teaspoon to each cup boiling water. Infuse 5-15 minutes. 1 cup, thrice daily.
Decoction. Echinacea 1; Sarsaparilla 1; Peruvian bark half; Saw Palmetto half. Mix. 2 teaspoons to 2 cups water, simmer gently 20 minutes. Half a cup, cold, thrice daily before meals.

For weak heart add one part Hawthorn; neurasthenia (Ginkgo); swelling of ankles (Lily of the Valley); loss of hormonal balance (Ginseng).
Prognosis. Surgical removal of spleen may be necessary.
Diet. Dandelion coffee, molasses, desiccated or fresh calves' liver. Green leafy vegetables, dried beans, apricots. Shellfish, milk, eggs, Soya, meats.
Supplements. Daily. Vitamin B12 1mg; Vitamin C, 1g; Folic acid 400mcg; Floradix.

ANAEMIA: IRON DEFICIENCY. An estimated 15 per cent of the female population suffers from this form of anaemia. A deficiency of nutritional iron is responsible for oxygen starvation of the blood due to insufficient haemoglobin. Number of red cells is reduced.
Aetiology: heavy menstrual loss, feeble constitution from hereditary weakness, poor diet, hidden or known blood loss from gastric ulcer, pregnancy, bleeding piles or insufficient food minerals: iron, copper, calcium, etc, chronic liver or kidney disease, worms, anorexia nervosa, rheumatoid arthritis, tuberculosis.
Symptoms. Tiredness, dizziness, breathlessness, palpitations, pale face and mucous membranes. White of eyes may be blue. Enlarged flabby tongue often bears impression of teeth marks. Hair lifeless, fingernails brittle and ridged. There may be angina, tinnitus and general reduced efficiency.
Treatment. The object is to achieve absorption of iron to raise normal haemoglobin levels and increase red cells. Echinacea has a reputation for regeneration of red cells. Herbs used with success: Echinacea, Gentian, Motherwort, Mugwort, Barberry, Hops, Nettles, Saw Palmetto, Chaparral, Red Clover, Dandelion.

Bitter herbs stimulate absorption of vital nutrients from the stomach, toning liver and pancreas, increasing the appetite; usually given half hour before meals. See: BITTERS.
Gentian. 1 teaspoon fine-cut chips to 2 cups cold water steeped 8 hours (overnight). Dose: Half-1 cup thrice daily before meals.
Tea. Formula. Combine: Agrimony 1; Barberry bark 1; Nettles 2; White Poplar bark half. Place 1oz (30g) in 1 pint (500ml) cold water and bring to boil. Simmer 10 minutes. Drink cold: Half-1 cup thrice daily, before meals.
Powders. Formula. Echinacea 2; Gentian 1; Kelp 1; pinch Red Pepper. Dose: 500mg (two 00 capsules or one-third teaspoon) thrice daily, before meals.
Liquid extracts. Formula: Echinacea 1; Queen's Delight 1; Ginseng 1; Ginger quarter. Dose: 30-60 drops in water, thrice daily, before meals.
Infusion Gentian Co Conc BP (1949). Dose: 30-60 drops.
Diet. *Dandelion coffee*, as desired. Molasses. Desiccated liver.
Floradix. A pre-digested iron preparation. Readily assimilable by the body. Compounded by Dr Otto Greither (Salus Haus). Iron is fed onto yeast which breaks down the metal and absorbs its cells. Other tonic ingredients include extracts of nettles, carrots, spinach, fennel, Vitamin C plus supplements; Angelica root, Mallow, Horsetail, Yarrow, Juniper and Rosehips. Not chemically preserved.
Avoid chocolate, egg yolk, tea, coffee, wheat bran.
Supplements. Daily. Vitamin C (1g morning and evening). Vitamin B12, Folic acid 400mcg. Vitamin C is the most potent enhancer of iron absorption. Multivitamin containing iron.
Note. Iron absorption is decreased by antacids, tetracyclines, phosphates, phytates (phytic acid from excessive intake of wholewheat bread), and excessive calcium supplements. Lack of stomach hydrochloric acid impairs iron absorption, especially in the elderly.

ANAEMIA: PERNICIOUS. A form of anaemia following a deficiency of Vitamin B12. Usually occurs middle life, 45-60.
Symptoms. Skin of yellow tinge, failing eyesight, swollen ankles, feeble heart action, numbness of feet and legs, dyspepsia, tingling in limbs, diarrhoea, red beefy sore tongue, patches of bleeding under skin, unsteadiness and depression.
Treatment. Hospitalisation. Intramuscular injections of Vitamin B12. Herbs known to contain the vitamin – Comfrey, Iceland Moss. Segments of fresh Comfrey root and Garlic passed through a blender produce a puree – good results reported.
Alternatives:– *Teas*: Milk Thistle, Hops, Wormwood, Betony, White Horehound, Motherwort, Parsley, Nettles, Centuary.
Formula. Combine Centuary 2; Hyssop 1; White Horehound 1; Red Clover flower 1; Liquorice quarter. 1-2 teaspoons to each cup boiling water, infuse 15 minutes. 1 cup thrice daily.
Decoction. Combine Yellow Dock 1; Peruvian bark quarter; Blue Flag root quarter; Sarsaparilla 1; Bogbean half. 1 teaspoon to each cup of water, or 4oz (30 grams) to 1 pint (half litre) water.

Simmer gently 10-15 minutes in covered vessel. Dose: Half-1 cup, thrice daily.
Decoction. Combine Yellow Dock 1; Peruvian bark quarter; Blue Flag root quarter; Sarsaparilla 1; Bogbean half. 1 teaspoon to each cup of water, or 4oz (30 grams) to 1 pint (one-half litre) water. Simmer gently 10-15 minutes in covered vessel. Dose: Half-1 cup, thrice daily.
Tablets/capsules. Echinacea, Dandelion, Kelp.
Powders. Formula. Equal parts: Gentian, Balm of Gilead, Yellow Dock. Dose: 500mg (two 00 capsules or one-third teaspoon), thrice daily before meals.
Liquid Extracts. Combine, Echinacea 2; Gentian 1; Dandelion 1; Ginger quarter. Dose: 15-30 drops in water thrice daily.
Gentian decoction. 1 teaspoon dried root to each cup cold water.
Diet. Dandelion coffee. Calves' liver. Absorption of nutritious food may be poor through stomach's inability to produce sufficient acid to break down food into its elements. Indicated: 2-3 teaspoons Cider vinegar in water between meals. Contra-indicated – vegetarian diet.
Supplements. Vitamin B12, (in absence of injections). Iron – Floradix. Desiccated liver. Vitamin C 1g thrice daily at meals. Folic acid. 400mcg thrice daily.

ANAEMIA: SICKLE CELL. A form of anaemia growing into an acute social problem, affecting people of African, Asian, and Mediterranean origin. *Thalassaemias* are caused by defects of a gene that produces the globin part of haemoglobin. Such defects in the DNA can now be detected in the womb before birth. The name derives from sickle-shaped cells instead of circular red blood cells. Few sufferers survive beyond their 40th year.
Symptoms. Unhealthy pallor, listlessness, sore tongue, dizziness, vague aches and pains, rapid pulse and breathing, tinnitus, palpitation. The skull may be disproportionately large, resistance to infection feeble, chances of survival poor. This form of anaemia is linked with defective colour vision. Impaired liver function. Stunted growth, great pain. Sufferers have a higher risk of infection.
Malaria. Sufferers are less likely to die of malaria because their red cells do not support the growth of malaria parasites very well.
Carriers: Carriers of the sickle-cell gene can now be identified by a simple blood test.
Treatment. No specifics exist but supportive herbal treatment has been known to increase output of red cells and raise haemoglobin levels:– Red Clover flowers, Yellow Dock, Echinacea, Burdock, Wild Indigo, Gentian, Nettles, Birch leaves, Sage, Walnut leaves, Centaury, Gota Kola (Indian Pennywort).
Alternatives:– *Tea.* Mix equal parts: Iceland Moss, Nettles, Red Clover flowers. 2 teaspoons to each cup boiling water; infuse 15 minutes; 1 cup morning and evening.
Decoction. Mix equal parts; Echinacea, Walnut leaves, Balm of Gilead buds; 1 teaspoon to each cup water gently simmered for 20 minutes. Half-1 cup, cold, 3 times daily, before meals.
Tablets/capsules. Sarsaparilla. Ginseng. Iceland Moss. Red Clover. Echinacea. Gentian.
Powders. Formula: Echinacea 1; Fringe Tree half; Ginseng half; White Poplar bark 1. Dose: 500mg (two 00 capsules or one-third teaspoon) thrice daily before meals.
Liquid extracts. Formula. Echinacea 2; Dandelion 1; Oat Husk (*avena sativa*) 1. Mix. Dose, 1-2 teaspoons before meals, in water or one of the above teas or decoctions.
Tinctures. Same combination. Dose: 2-3 teaspoons.
Dong quai. See entry.
Pollen. Claimed to be of value.
Diet. Dandelion coffee. Molasses. Desiccated liver. Calf liver, fresh. Green leafy vegetables contain chlorophyll, iron and folic acid. Cider vinegar. Dried beans, apricots and shellfish. Dandelion leaves in salads. Milk, eggs, meats, Soya. Carrot juice to increase red cells.
Supplements. Daily. Vitamin B12. Vitamin C, 1g; Folic acid 400mcg, Floradix. Of particular value: Vitamin E 400iu. Zinc.
Note. Those at risk should submit themselves for screening. The disease cannot be cured but can be controlled largely by orthodox measures and sometimes by natural medicine.

ANAEMIA: SPORTS. A side-effect of hard training in endurance sports with low haemoglobin and haematocrit levels due to rapid depletion of iron on excessive exertion. See: IRON DEFICIENCY ANAEMIA.

ANAL FISSURE. See: FISSURE, ANAL.

ANALGESICS. PAIN-RELIEVERS. ANODYNES. Herbs taken orally for relief of mild pain. May also be applied externally. An analgesic may also be an antispasmodic, relieving cramp (Cramp bark etc.). Throughout history, Opium Poppy has always been the most effective analgesic, but must be given by a qualified medical practitioner except applied externally as a poultice. The same rule may apply to Aconite, Arnica and Belladonna.
Mild analgesics:– Black Cohosh, Black Willow, Catnep, Chamomile, Cowslip root (Bio-Strath), Cramp bark, Devil's Claw, Gelsemium, Guaiacum, Hops, Jamaican Dogwood, Ladyslipper, Lobelia, Passion flower, Rosemary, Skullcap, St John's Wort, Skunk Cabbage, Valerian, White Willow bark, Wild Lettuce, Wild Yam, Wintergreen, Yerbe Mate tea, Poke root, White Poplar.

Skullcap, Mistletoe, Valerian and Feverfew are

herbs of choice. All four are believed to have an anti-prostaglandin effect, the first three given in combination; the latter (Feverfew) appearing to work best singly.

ANALGESIC CREAM (Lane). Camphor 2 per cent; Oil of Turpentine 8 per cent; Menthol 2 per cent; Oil Eucalyptus 2.5 per cent; Methyl sal 10 per cent; Oil Mustard 0.2 per cent. To be massaged into painful joints until absorbed.

ANAPHRODISIAC. A herb that reduces excessive sexual desire. Hops, Sweet Marjoram, Camphor, Stramonium, Agnus Castus, Black Willow.

ANAPHYLACTIC SHOCK. See: SERUM SICKNESS.

ANASARCA. Collection of fluid in the tissues. General dropsy. It is not confined to isolated parts of the body such as the ankles. Due to kidney or heart disease.

ANA-SED. Each tablet contains: Hops 30mg and the aqueous extractive from 90mg Jamaica Dogwood, 180mg Passiflora, 45mg Pulsatilla, and 270mg Wild Lettuce. For pain and insomnia due to stress. (*Potter's*)

ANDROGRAPHIS. Andrographis paniculata. Ingredients: andrographolide, neoandrographolide. Widely used in Chinese medicine.
Action. Inhibits growth of Staphylococcus aureus. Antibiotic.
Uses. Urinary tract infections, boils and internal ulceration. Enteritis, shigella, colitis, osteomyelitis, pneumonia.
Courtesy. Chris Low, Member of the Register of Traditional Chinese Medicine (RTCM), scientific advisor to the Herbal Pharmaceutical Industry; The Chinese Medicine Clinic, Cambridge.

ANECDOTAL MEDICINE. A medicament, the efficacy of which has not been proved by convincing clinical investigation and double blind trials. To the scientific mind, the difference between fact and fiction depends upon satisfying the Medicines Control Agency with worthwhile evidence of efficacy before issue of a Product Licence.

ANEURYSM. A local widening (dilatation) in the wall of an artery usually the aorta or a major artery. May grow into a pulsating tumour and finally burst. Situation is important; aneurysm in chest, abdomen or head being most at risk. Where not due to excessive athletic performance, it is a sign that arteries are already diseased. Excessive athletic exercise and high living predispose.

Usually painless, it is recognised by touch as a round swelling about the size of a plum and visibly expands and contracts with each heart beat. A difference in the pulse on both sides of the body or inequality of pupils of the eyes may determine diagnosis. Tendency for blood to clot, indicating need for large doses of Vitamin E to prevent formation of a solid mass.
Symptoms: breathlessness, difficult swallowing, cough, change in tone of voice.
Treatment: Directed towards reduction of volume of blood and blood pressure. Rest in bed.
Teas: Single or in combination. Yarrow, Cactus flowers, Motherwort.
Tinctures: Lily of the Valley 1; Pulsatilla 1; Hawthorn 2. Dose: 10-30 drops in water thrice daily.
Practitioner: Tincture Selenicereus grand, 10ml . . . Tincture Crataegus Oxy., 20ml . . . Tincture Pulsatilla, 10ml . . . Tincture Scutellaria lat., 10ml. Aqua to 100ml. Dose: 5ml (3i) tds aq. cal. pc.
Diet. See: DIET – HEART AND CIRCULATION.

ANGELICA. *Angelica archangelica L. German*: Angelika. *French*: Angélique. *Italian*: Angelica. *Spanish*: Angélica. *Chinese*: Ch'ien-hu. Part used: dried root, rhizome.
Action: Smooth muscle relaxant, carminative, diuretic, antifungal, antibacterial, diaphoretic, expectorant, gentle digestive tonic, antispasmodic.
Uses. Cold conditions where increase in body heat is required. To create distaste for alcohol. Friend of the aged as a circulatory stimulant and to sustain heart, stomach and bowel. Loss of appetite, chronic dyspepsia, aerophagy.
Preparations. Thrice daily.
Decoction. Half an ounce bruised root to 1 pint water; simmer 5 minutes. Dose: Half-1 cup, thrice daily.
Liquid Extract BHP (1983) 1:1 in 25 per cent alcohol. Dose: 0.5 to 2ml.
Tincture, BHP (1983) 1:5 in 50 per cent alcohol. Dose: 0.5 to 2ml.
Powder. 250mg capsules: 2 capsules before meals. (*Arkocaps*)
Contra-indications: pregnancy, diabetes.
Cancer inhibitor. The coumarin of Angelica has an inhibitory effect on cancer. (*Planta Medica 1987, 53(6), pp 526-9*)
Note. Used in the production of Chartreuse and Benedictine. GSL

ANGELICA, CHINESE. (Angelica sinensis root). See: Dong Quai.

ANGELICA, JAPANESE. *Angelica shkiokiana*. Part used: root. Constituents include a coumarin derivative.
Action. Anti-inflammatory, adaptogen, vasodilator, anti-stress, aphrodisiac, tonic. Action

resembles Ginseng.
Uses. Diabetes. To reduce concentration of fats in the blood. Inflammation. Allergies: asthma, skin disorders.

ANGINA (Angina pectoris). A condition where the demand for oxygen by the heart exceeds supply. A syndrome, not a disease entity. Common cause is narrowing of the coronary arteries by atheroma limiting the flow of blood in the heart muscle.

Condition also caused by a spasm in the coronary circulation. 'Strangling pain in the chest', lasting 2 to 10 minutes. Aggravated by diabetes, anaemia, goitre, high blood pressure and stress.

Is it angina? Important evidence is the association of the pain with exercise and its relief by rest. Pain is similar to intermittent claudication (pain in the calf muscle). Sense of constriction in front of chest: may radiate to the jaw or left arm.

Atherosclerosis (hardening of the arteries) is caused by cholesterol deposits hindering blood flow. It is the work of the practitioner to unclog blocked arteries where possible.

Phytotherapy may increase exercise capacity, reduce the number of angina attacks, and is known to enjoy a low incidence of unwanted side-effects.
Alternatives. *Teas*. Chamomile, Hawthorn, Motherwort, Lime Flowers, Hops, Oats (avena), Orange Tree leaves.
Tablets/capsules. Cayenne, Hawthorn, Lobelia, Prickly Ash.
Powders. Formula. Equal parts: Hawthorn berries, Opuntia (Cactus flowers), Mistletoe, Motherwort. Dose: 750mg (three 00 capsules or half a teaspoon) thrice daily.
Liquid extracts: Formula: Equal parts: Cactus, Hawthorn, Prickly Ash. Dose: 1-2 teaspoons. Thrice daily.
Tinctures: Formula. Hawthorn BHP (1983) 30ml; Motherwort BHP (1983) 30ml; Prickly Ash bark BHP (1983) 20ml; Tincture Capsicum Fort BPC 1934: 0.25ml. Dose: 5ml in water thrice daily.
Practitioner. Alternatives:–
1. Tincture Aconite, BPC 1949: 2-5 drops (0.12 to 0.3ml) when necessary.
2. Liquid extract: Lobelia BHP (1983): 10-30 drops every 20 minutes when necessary.
3. Formula. Tincture Selenicereus grand (preferably fresh plant) 1oz; Tincture Ginger quarter of an ounce. Dose: 15-30 drops every 15 minutes.
4. Formula. Liquid extract: Prickly Ash bark 20ml; Liquid extract: Cactus 20ml. Mix. Dose: 5-20 drops when necessary. (*A. Barker, FNIMH*)
5. Emergency. Tincture Gelsemium BPC 1973. Dose: 5 drops (0.3ml).
Diet: See: DIET – HEART AND CIRCULATION. Vitamin E reduces the risk of angina.

ANGIO-OEDEMA. Skin eruption resembling dermatitis or urticaria. A contact allergy from plants such as poison ivy and primula, various chemicals (red-headed matches), cosmetics (make-up), nail varnish, after-shave, certain drugs and perfumes. Allergic reactions are associated with swollen eyelids, shingles, erysipelas or sinus infections. Fever sometimes present and lesions may take the form of the weals of nettle-rash. A hereditary form is rare but the condition is a frequent reaction to aspirin. Differentiate from eczema.
Alternatives. *Tea*. Formula. Equal parts: Red Clover flower, Nettles, Clivers. 2 teaspoons to each cup boiling water; infuse 10-15 minutes. 1 cup 2-3 times daily.
Tablets/capsules. Garlic. Echinacea. Blue Flag root. Poke root.
Powders. Formula. Echinacea 2; Juniper 1; Blue Flag root half. Dose: 500mg (two 00 capsules or one-third teaspoon) 2-3 times daily before meals.
Tinctures. Formula. Echinacea 2; Valerian 1; Blue Flag root half. Dose: 1-2 teaspoons in water 2-3 times daily before meals.

ANGOSTURA BARK. *Galipea officinalis* Han. *German*: Cuspabaum. *French*: Cusparie. *Italian*: Cusparia. Part used: dried bark.
Action: Aromatic, bitter, anti-periodic.
Uses. South American traditional: diarrhoea, dysentery, intermittent fevers, dropsy.
Preparations. Thrice daily. *Powdered bark* 0.3 to 1g. *Liquid extract*: 5-30 drops. *Tincture*: 10-60 drops.

ANGOSTURA. Celebrated Liqueur created by Surgeon-General Siegert, Venezuela, in 1832, and which is still popular as a powerful restorative tonic, especially after illness, anorexia, etc. Angostura bark 2oz; Chamomile flowers half an ounce; Cardamom seed 1dr; Cinnamon 1dr; Orange peel half an ounce; Raisins half a pound; Vodka or alcohol 3 pints; water 7 pints. Steep for one month, shaking daily, press and filter.

ANISEED. Anise. *Pimpinella anisum*. *German*: Anis. *French*: Anis. *Italian*: Anice. *Spanish*: Simiente de anis. *Chinese*: Huai-hsiang. *Malayan*: Jira-manis. Dried ripe fruits.
Action: Carminative, Expectorant, Antispasmodic, Oestrogenic, Anti-parasitic.
Uses: Flatulence, dry coughs, whooping cough, tracheitis, bronchitis. Externally for scabies and lice infestation.
Preparations. *Tea*. 2 crushed seeds to each cup boiling water, taken hot. *Spirit BPC (1949)*: 0.3-1.2ml in water or honey when necessary. For acidity, bad breath, infant spasms. Anise oil BP, dose: 0.05-0.2ml. GSL

ANKYLOSING SPONDYLITIS. A chronic inflammatory condition attacking joints of the

spine and sacroiliac resulting in fixation by bony ankylosis. Intercostal joints also at risk. Bamboo spine. Poker spine. Genetic factor involved. Abnormal immune response to infection. Sometimes associated with anaemia, ulcerative colitis or psoriasis. Neglected symptoms degenerate into 'an old man with a hoop'.
Symptoms. Persistent stiffness and pain in buttocks and low back. Poor chest expansion. Worse on rising and after inactivity. Rigidity develops over many years in neck and back.

The patient should be examined for bloodshot eyes. In the formative stages iritis is a classic diagnostic sign. An iritis which does not cause eyelids to be stuck down in the mornings is to be regarded with extreme caution. See: IRITIS.
Treatment. Anti-inflammatory analgesics: Guaiacum, White Willow bark, Wild Yam.
Teas. Bogbean, Celery seeds, Devil's Claw root, German Chamomile, Meadowsweet, Prickly Ash bark, White Willow bark, Wild Yam.
Tablets/capsules. Black Cohosh, Devil's Claw, Prickly Ash, Wild Yam, Bamboo gum.
Formula. White Willow 2; Celery 1; Black Cohosh half; Guaiacum quarter; Liquorice quarter. Mix. Dose: Powders – 500mg (two 00 capsules or one-third teaspoon). Liquid Extracts: 15-60 drops. Tinctures: 1-2 teaspoons. Thrice daily.
Topical. Liniment. Tincture Black Cohosh 2; Tincture Lobelia 2; Tincture Capsicum quarter; Alcohol to 20.
Cold packs: See entry.
Aromatherapy. Massage oil: 6 drops Oil Lavender in 2 teaspoons Almond oil. Jojoba, Aloe Vera, Thyme, Peanut oil.
Diet. See: GENERAL DIET. Avoid lemons and other citrus fruits.
Supplements. Daily. Pantothenic acid 10mg; Vitamin A 7500iu; Vitamin B6 25mg; Vitamin E 400iu; Zinc 25mg. Cod Liver oil: 1 dessertspoon.
General. Graduated exercises to promote good posture and free breathing. Swimming; walk-tall; sleep with board under mattress; hot baths. Gentle osteopathy to delay consolidation of vertebrae.

ANODYNES. See: ANALGESICS.

ANOREXIA. See: APPETITE, LOSS OF.

ANOREXIA NERVOSA. A neurotic and metabolic condition, mostly in young women who suppress appetite by refusing food in an effort to be thin. Such starvation may result in death.

The patient may start as a food faddist with depressive tendencies. Some gorge huge meals (bulimia) and induce vomiting later. Such women are known to be oestrogen deficient; most have a low dietary intake of calcium, resulting in reduced bone density (osteoporosis). Lack of exercise has a worsening influence, often with severe loss of weight.

It is now established that one cause is a deficiency of zinc in the diet. Individuals suffering from the condition (with its depression) may recover when given 15mg zinc daily. Starvation causes increased urinary zinc secretion, thus further reducing body levels of the mineral. Most anorectics complain of loss of sense of taste and smell which is a symptom of zinc deficiency. Loss of these two senses reduces further the desire for food.
Symptoms. Excessive thinness. Anaemia. Poor haemoglobin levels. Absence of menses. Episodic hyperactivity. Slow pulse when resting. Teeth decay, brittle bones. Heart weakness. Low blood pressure, hormonal disorders, yellowing skin, blood disorders, abnormal drowsiness and weakness. Reduced bone density may develop during the illness, the subject being prone to bone fracture for years afterwards.
Treatment. Correct anaemia with iron-bearing herbs, Vitamin B12, mineral supplements and nourishing food.

Angelica root, Barberry, Bogbean, Burdock root, Calamus, Centuary herb, Chamomile flowers, Condurango bark, Dandelion (coffee), Garden Sage, Gentian, Ginkgo, Helonias, Hops, Marshmallow root, Milk Thistle, Quassia chips, White Poplar.
Alternatives:– *Tea*. Formula. Equal parts, Centuary, Chamomile, Peppermint. 1 heaped teaspoon to each cup boiling water; infuse 5-15 minutes. Dose: 1 cup thrice daily, before meals.
Decoction. Formula. Combine Angelica root 1; Burdock root 1; Condurango bark half. 1 teaspoon to each cupful water simmered gently 20 minutes. Dose: Half-1 cup thrice daily before meals.
Powders. Formula. German Chamomile 2; Gotu Kola 1; Ginkgo 1. Dose: 500mg (two 00 capsules or one-third teaspoon) before meals thrice daily.
Tinctures. Formula. Combine: Condurango quarter; Burdock root half; White Poplar 1; Ginkgo 1; add 2-10 drops Tincture Capsicum fort. 1-2 teaspoons in water thrice daily, before meals.
Tincture: Tincture Gentian Co BP. Dose: 2-4ml (30-60 drops).
Ginger, stem. Success reported.
Milk Thistle and Turmeric: popular in general herbal practice.
Diet. High protein, low fat, low salt. Dandelion coffee. Liver. Artichokes. 2-3 bananas (for potassium) daily.
Supplements. Daily. Vitamin B-complex. Vitamin C, 1g. Vitamin E, 200iu. Zinc, 15mg. Magnesium, 250mg morning and evening.

ANOXIA. An inadequate supply of oxygen in body tissues. Ginseng. Vitamin E.

ANTACIDS. Remedies that correct effects of stomach acid and relieve indigestion: Black

Horehound, Bogbean, Barberry bark, Centuary, Dandelion, Fennel, Irish Moss, Meadowsweet. By forming a barrier between contents and lining of the stomach, demulcents may also serve as antacids.

ANTHELMINTICS. Anti-parasitics. Herbs that destroy worms (vermicides) or expel them from the body (vermifuges). Aloe, Areca nuts (tape), Assafoetida, Balmony, Betel nuts (tape), Butternut, Castor oil (thread worms), Cinnamon, Garlic, Hyssop, Kousso, Male fern (tape – now seldom used), Mugwort, Pomegranate, Pumpkin seeds, Quassia chips, Rue, Senna, Southernwood, Tansy, Thuja, Garden Thyme (hookworm), White Bryony (small doses), Wormwood.

Anthelmintics may also be given for rectal irrigation.

ANTHRAQUINONES. Anthracene purgatives form an important group including Senna, Rhubarb, Aloes, Buckthorn, Yellow Dock and Cascara. They do not act as purgatives until they reach the intestines where they are modified. They act mildly upon the colon and are useful for chronic constipation. Large doses are discouraged as the effect may be drastic on the bowel and irritative to kidneys and bladder.

ANTHRAX. Notifiable disease. Infectious disease of wild and domesticated animals, with malignant pustule and splenic fever caused by Bacillus anthracis. Its discovery in 1850 by Dr Pollander was one of the brightest events in the history of infectious disease. A disease of cattle passed on to man.

Attack is sudden. If unchecked may be fatal within three days. The germ usually enters the body through a scratch or wound penetrating the skin or internal membrane. A tiny papule may appear where skin has been injured which burns and itches angrily as inflammation spreads. The lesion fills with blood and serum which dry to form bluish scabs. Symptoms of glandular infection follow along the course of the lymphatics with enlargement of the spleen.

Symptoms. Severe chill introduces high fever, rapid breathing, vomiting stomach pains, diarrhoea and severe prostration. Heartbeat rapidly falls. Pulse is feeble. Nerve distress may end in convulsions and delirium.

While it is the belief that no cure exists apart from inoculation with antiserum, successes with plant medicines appear in medical literature. Dr W.L. Lewis, Canton, Pennsylvania, USA, records a treatment given by doctor pioneers of the 'outback' where they had to do 'everything' in emergency. "I claim," he writes, "to have discovered that Echinacea (cone flower) is a cure for anthrax if a physician has faith in it, and knows how to properly use it. I have used it on cases where its action has been a great wonder. Liquid extract: 1 teaspoonful every 4 hours throughout the day and night."

This experience is sustained by Dr Finlay Ellingwood who also achieved similar success. (*Ellingwood's Therapeutist: 8, 10, 1914, 394*)

To be treated by a general medical practitioner or hospital specialist.

ANTHROPOSOPHICAL MEDICINE. Holistic medicine based on the work of Dr Rudolf Steiner (1861-1925) an Austrian scientist who founded the Anthroposophical Society in 1913. To Steiner disease was more than a group of physical symptoms. It was a malfunction of man on one of four planes. These planes consist of (1) the physical body, which is surrounded by (2) the etheric body. (3) He also declared man to have an astral body (our inner life of emotional reactions) and (4) a consciousness of the personal ego – the "I".

Steiner equated these planes with the doctrine of the elements earth, fire, air and water as understood by the Ancient World. In health all four work together in one "harmonious integrated whole". Bad health was a sign that the balance between these states had been disrupted.

The school of thought believes that disease may be a preparation for future life towards which reincarnation is a feature. It is not possible to be an anthroposophical doctor without a fundamental relationship with the plant kingdom. It is believed that to heal the four-fold dimensions of man demands a high level spiritual awareness which is not always acquired through the usual channels of medical education. The movement has its international centre at the Goetheanum, Dornach, Switzerland. See: RUDOLF STEINER.

ANTI-ABORTIVES. Herbs that check any tendency to miscarriage. They should be prescribed by a practitioner and may include: Raspberry leaves, Cramp bark, Lobelia, etc. See: ABORTION.

ANTI-ASTHMATICS. Herbs that relieve the symptoms of asthma. According to the case the remedy may be an expectorant, antispasmodic, bronchodilator or a combination of each. A large group including:–

Belladonna, Black Haw bark, Comfrey, Ephedra, Elecampane, Euphorbia, Evening Primrose, Gelsemium, Irish Moss, Lobelia, Mullein, Senega, Storax, Stramonium, Wild Cherry bark and Wild Yam are all of practitioner use.

ANTI-BILIOUS. Herbs with an affinity for the liver and gallbladder, prescribed for inflammation of those organs and promotion of bile.

Balmony, Barberry, Betony, Bitter root, Black root, Centuary, Chamomile, Dandelion, Fringe Tree, Fumitory, Goldenseal, Holy Thistle, Hops,

Mountain Grape, Mugwort, Pomegranate bark, Vervain, Wahoo, Wild Yam, Wormwood.

ANTIBIOTICS. Herbs known to have an antibacterial or antiviral effect upon certain types of bacteria and microbes. Herbal antibiotics are not derived from micro-organisms in moulds or fungi, but from tinctures and extracts prepared from the whole plant complete with its natural context of alkaloids, enzymes, minerals, etc. Broad spectrum antibiotics may promote overgrowth of fungi in the bowel, a tendency to which is corrected by yoghurt.

Herbal, non-fungal antibiotics: Blue Flag root, Burdock, Cayenne, Chaparral, Cloves, Echinacea, Garlic, Goldenseal, Holy Thistle, Horseradish, Juniper, Lobelia, Mullein, Myrrh, Nasturtium, Poke root, Red Clover, Thyme, Wild Indigo, Wild Thyme.

ANTIBIOTICS. Bartram's shortlist for antibiotic prescribing.

Infection	*Antibiotic*
Chest infections	Wild Thyme
Tonsillitis, glands	Poke root
Cystitis	Buchu
Pyelitis	Juniper
Otitis media	Echinacea
Infective sore throats	Myrrh
Skin and soft tissue infection	Blue Flag root
Conjunctivitis	Goldenseal
Dyspepsia	Milk Thistle

ANTIBODY. A defence protein, usually a globulin. A substance prepared in the body for the purpose of withstanding infection by viruses, bacteria and other organisms. Produced by reaction of the body's immune system to an antigen. See: ANTIGENS.

ANTI-CATARRHALS. Agents that reduce the production of mucus. Angelica, Avens, Bayberry, Bistort, Blood root, Cayenne, Chamomile (German), Coltsfoot, Comfrey, Elderflowers, Elecampane, Eyebright, Fenugreek, Garlic, Ginger, Goldenseal, Gotu Kola, Ground Ivy, Hyssop, Iceland Moss, Irish Moss, Juniper, Liquorice, Marsh Cudweed, Marshmallow, Mountain Grape, Mouse Ear, Mullein, Myrrh, Parsley, Plantain, Poke root, Senega, Skunk Cabbage, White Horehound, Wild Cherry bark, Wild Indigo, Witch Hazel, Yarrow. Successful treatment of catarrh is often dependent upon efficient kidney, skin and bowel function which may require also, diuretics, alteratives and laxatives.

ANTI-CHOLINGERGICS. Remedies that inhibit release of acetylcholine as a neuro-transmitter. Given for anti-depressant therapy. May have side-effects of dry mouth, drowsiness, blurred vision. Administered by a qualified practitioner. Two chief remedies: Belladonna (*atropa*) and Henbane (*hyoscyamus*). They reduce acid secretion but are sometimes given with Comfrey and other tissue builders to promote healing. Anti-cholinergics decrease secretion of gastric juices by their control of the vagus nerve.

ANTI-COAGULANTS. Herbs that keep the blood 'flowing' by preventing clotting or clumping of the platelets. Anti-coagulants are justified after myocardial infarction, may prevent cardiac death, and are not outweighed by adverse reactions. Of value in thrombosis.

Bayberry, Cowslip root (Biostrath), Garlic, Ginseng, Lime flowers.

ANTI-CONVULSANTS. Usually refers to children with fevers. Herbs for a febrile seizure, or for prevention and reduction of epileptic fits. Usually given orally, but where this is not possible a rectal injection or a suppository (such as Valerian) may be used. Another term for 'antispasmodics'.

ANTIDEPRESSANTS. Agents that lift depression without sedation. Thymoleptics. Mood raisers. They may exert an antagonising action or specifically influence any particular organ that might be responsible i.e., Dandelion for depression caused by a congested liver; Hawthorn for circulatory stasis and Skullcap for cerebral congestion.

As indicated: Oats, Kola nuts, Balmony, Ginseng, Damiana, Lavender, Ladyslipper, Rosemary, Vervain. Yerbe Mate tea is used in Paraguay for this purpose.

For neurotic depression with obsessive and phobic states: Black Cohosh, Damiana, Kola, Betony and Oats.

No behavioural changes in children have been observed. Impressive safety record. Little effect upon the cardiovascular system.

ANTI-DIABETICS. Anti-diabetics have an ability to counter hyperglycaemia and are of value for diabetes mellitus.

1st degree. Goat's Rue, Fenugreek Seeds, Garlic, Jambul.

2nd degree. Damiana, Nettles, Pipsissewa, Olive leaves, Karela, White Horehound, Sweet Sumach, Mountain Grape, Fennel.

ANTI-DIARRHOEALS. Herbs with an ability to arrest diarrhoea or soothe an irritable bowel. According to degree, an astringent may have a similar effect. A large group including:– Avens, Bistort, Catnep, Cinnamon, Hemlock Spruce, Holy Thistle, Kola nuts, Matico, Orris root, Rhatany root.

ANTIDOTE. A substance or remedy that counteracts the action of a medicine. Used in the case of over-dosage or accidental poisoning. As discovered by early practitioners, over-dosage may be neutralised by a strong infusion of coffee, or 2 drops Tincture of Camphor in honey. Individuals of the coffee habit seldom enjoy maximum results from herbal treatment.

In China it is common practice not to drink tea or coffee on days when herbal medicine is taken. In the case of Ginseng, they not only avoid tea and coffee but eat no fish for three days.

ANTI-EMETICS. Remedies that allay a sense of nausea and prevent vomiting. Three most popular: Chamomile, Black Horehound, Meadowsweet. Others: Balm, Balmony, Barberry, Cayenne, Cinnamon, Cloves, Dill, Fennel, Fringe Tree bark, Iceland Moss, Lavender, Mountain Grape, Nutmeg, Peppermint.

A cup of Chamomile tea may sometimes alleviate the vomiting of cancer chemotherapy and radiation.

ANTI-FATIGUE HERBS. Ginseng, Gotu Kola, Saw Palmetto, Kola.

ANTIFECT. Formula: Garlic 30mg; Garlic oil 1mg; dry extract Echinacea 100=22 13.2mg. Traditional remedy for the symptomatic relief of catarrh, rhinitis and nasal congestion. (*Potters*)

ANTI-FLATULENTS. See: CARMINATIVES.

ANTI-FUNGALS. Fungicides. Herbs that destroy fungi, as in the treatment of thrush, candida, etc. Internal or external use: Aloe Vera, Tea Tree oil, Caprycin, Bitter-Sweet, Daisy, Blood root (skin), Castor oil, Common Ivy, Ground Ivy, Marigold, Eucalyptus oil, Scarlet Pimpernel, Echinacea, Life root, Myrrh, Witch Hazel, White Pond Lily, Wild Indigo, Poke root. Thuja and Garlic are perhaps the most widely used. Externally, used as dusting powders, creams, ointments.

Administration of anti-fungals should be accompanied by a sugarless diet.

ANTIGENS. Substances, usually harmful, that when entering the body stimulate the immune system to produce antibodies. Invaders may be polio virus, typhoid bacillus, or chain-like streptococcal bacteria – the usual pus-forming type found in infected wounds, or toxins they release into the blood stream.

ANTI-HAEMORRHAGICS. A group of powerful astringents clinical experience has shown to be effective in arresting mild to moderate internal bleeding.
Digestive tract: Marigold, Comfrey, Bur-Marigold, Matico, Shepherd's Purse, Holy Thistle, American Cranesbill, Goldenseal.
Anal/Rectal: Pilewort, Plantain, Matico, Rhatany root, Witch Hazel.
Mouth: Tormentil.
Nose-bleeds: Nettles.
Uterus. Shepherd's Purse, Ladies Mantle, Greater Periwinkle, Beth root, Avens, Goldenseal.
Urinary system. Bistort, Plantain, Marigold, Stone root, Horsetail, Bur-Marigold.
Lungs. Bugleweed, Elecampane, Lungwort.
Colon. Greater Burnet, Matico, Comfrey, Bistort, Wild Yam, Holy Thistle, Avens, Tormentil.
Capillary haemorrhage. Buckwheat.

ANTIHISTAMINES. Agents that arrest production of histamine and which are useful in allergic conditions.

Herbal antihistamines may lessen severity of symptoms. Not limited by sedative, anticholinergic or central nervous system side effects. Nor do they impair psychomotor skills or potentiate the effect of alcohol. Non-sedating antihistamines are available for perennial allergic rhinitis, conjunctivitis and other conditions normally responsive to antihistamines including allergic skin reactions.

Garlic has powerful antihistamine properties. It is a vaso-constrictor and thus reduces swelling of mucosa of the nose and conjunctiva of the eye. It is of special value for purulent discharge. According to the individual case it works well with Hyssop, Angelica and Peppermint. Herbal antihistamines include: Juniper, Marshmallow root, Burdock, Parsley root, Cudweed, Elder, Ephedra, Eyebright, Echinacea, Goldenseal, Peppermint, Sage, Lobelia, Chaparral. One in common use among herbalists is Marigold (calendula), directed particularly against staphylococcus.
Ayurvedic Medicine, specific: equal parts Ginger root, Black Pepper and Aniseed.

ANTI-INFECTIVES. Herbs that stimulate the body's immune system to withstand infection. Alternatives to anti-bacterial substances obtained from micro-organisms as penicillin, streptomycin etc. Those from herbs do not destroy beneficial bacteria normally present in the intestines, neither does the body get used to them.

Some essential oils are natural antibiotics. Others: Blue Flag root, Buchu, Chaparral, Butterbur, Echinacea, Feverfew, Garlic, Goldenseal, Holy Thistle, Horse Radish (Vogel), Juniper berries, Myrrh, Nasturtium, Poke root, Red Clover, Watercress (Vogel), Wild Indigo, Wild Thyme.

Vitamin C is a powerful antibiotic (1-2g daily).

ANTI-INFLAMMATORIES. A group of agents known to reduce inflammation. Action is not to suppress but to enable tissue to return to

normal on the strength of its own resources. Some members of the group are helpful for chronic conditions such as polyarthritis and rheumatism caused by a sub-acute inflammation going on quietly over a long time. Others work by blocking prostaglandin synthesis.
General. Chamomile (German, Roman), Cowslip root, Fennel, Feverfew, Heartsease, Mistletoe, Turmeric, Yellow Dock.
Specific. Bistort (bowel). Comfrey (bones). Devil's Claw (muscles). St John's Wort (nerve tissue). Lignum vitae (rheumatic joints). Poke root (lymph vessels). Eyebright (conjunctivitis: topical as an eye lotion). Horsechestnut (anus). Bogbean (liver and gall bladder).
Steroid-like action. Ginseng, Black Cohosh, Black Haw, Liquorice, Wild Yam.
Aspirin-like action. Birch, Black Willow bark, Meadowsweet, White Poplar bark, White Willow bark, Wintergreen.

Some types of inflammation may be reduced by herbs that stimulate the eliminatory organs – lungs, bowel, skin and kidneys. A timely enema may reduce a high temperature with inflammation, to expel toxins and unload an over-loaded bowel; (Dandelion root, Parsley root, Sarsaparilla).

ANTI-INFLAMMATION FORMULA. (Biostrath). Drops containing cultures combined with extracts derived from medicinal plants possessing known therapeutic properties: Arnica, Bryony, Balm, Chamomile, Horseradish, Marigold, Hypericum, Echinacea.
Indications: colic, inflammation of the alimentary tract.

ANTI-LACTEALS. Herbs that reduce milk production. Sage.

ANTI-LITHICS. Agents used for elimination or dissolution of stone or gravel. Stone root, Parsley root, Hydrangea, Pellitory of the Wall, Gravel root.

ANTI-MICROBIALS. Plant medicines that destroy or inhibit growth of disease-causing bacteria or other micro-organisms. Aniseed, Barberry, Bayberry, Bearberry, Benzoin, Blood root, Buchu, Camphor, Caraway oil, Catechu, Cayenne, Cinnamon, Clove, Cornsilk, Coriander, Echinacea, Elecampane, Eucalyptus, Fennel seed, Garlic, Gentian, Goldenseal, Guaiacum, Heather flowers (Calluna), Hemlock Spruce bark, Juniper, Kava Kava, Kino, Labrador tea, Lavender, Liquorice, Lovage root, Mandrake, Marigold, Marjoram, Meadowsweet, Mountain Grape, Myrrh, Nasturtium, Olive, Orthosiphon, Parsley root, Peppermint, Peruvian balsam, Plantain, Propolis, Rosemary, Rue, Sage, St John's Wort, Southernwood, Thuja, Thyme, Turmeric, White Pond Lily, Wild Indigo, Wood Sage, Wormwood, Yarrow.

ANTI-MYCOTICS. Remedies that arrest fungal growth on the skin or mucous membrane. See: ANTI-FUNGAL.

ANTI-NAUSEANTS. Herbs that arrest or inhibit vomiting and nausea. Black Horehound.

ANTI-NEOPLASTICS. Herbs that prevent formation or destroy tumour cells. Some reported in the literature to arrest the spread of malignancy. A neoplasm is a new growth and may be malignant or non-malignant. Bayberry (intestinal), Bryonia (lung), Clivers (Genito-urinary tract), Comfrey (general), Condurango (gastric), Dandelion (liver), Echinacea, Greater Celandine (epithelial), Mandrake (face and skin), Mistletoe, Myrrh, Plantain (throat), Poke root (breast), Queen's Delight, Red Clover (epithelial and breast), Rosebay Willowherb (gastric), Vinca rosea (leukaemia), Thuja (womb), Wild Violet (breast and womb), Yellow Dock.

ANTIOXIDANTS. Compounds that protect the body against free radical activity and lipid peroxidation. Free-radical scavengers. Low levels in the tissues reduce the span of human life. High levels enable humans to live longer. The greater the oxidation damage to the DNA, the shorter the lifespan.

Vitamins A, C and E inhibit production of free radicals. Especially effective is beta-carotene, the precursor of Vitamin A, found in carrots, spinach, yams and some green leafy vegetables. Vitamin E and Selenium work together to prevent free radical damage to cell membrane. Antioxidants act favourably on glaucoma, Parkinson's disease and rheumatoid arthritis.

This group claims to have an anti-tumour effect. Epithelial cancers may invade the respiratory and gastro-intestinal tracts, lungs, skin and cervix of the womb. The higher the level of antioxidants in the cells, the lesser the risk of epithelial cell cancer, and blindness in the aged.

Chief antioxidants: Alfalfa, Comfrey, Asparagus (fresh), Beet tops, Dandelion leaves, Ginseng, Gotu Kola, Goldenseal, Irish Moss, Parsley, Walnuts, Watercress, Wheat sprouts. Perhaps the cheapest and most effective is Garlic.
Diet. Highly coloured fruits and vegetables: oranges, red and green peppers, carrots, apricots, mangoes, liver and spinach.
Supplements. Beta carotene (Vitamin A), Vitamin C, Vitamin E, Selenium, Zinc. See: SOD, FREE RADICALS.

ANTI-PARASITICS. Another term for ANTHELMINTICS.

ANTI-PERIODICS. Remedies that prevent the return of a disease that tends to recur (malaria). Peruvian bark, Ash Tree (Fraxinus excelsior).

ANTI-PERSPIRANTS. Herbs that reduce sweating; anti-hidrotics.
Internal: White Willow bark, Red Sage.
External: Essential oils of Sage, Pine, Rosemary, Lavender. Blended with fresh lemon juice are marketed as a gentle spray without aerosol (*Weleda*). Zinc and Castor oil cream or ointment.
Bath preparations made from these oils; herbal soaps, massage oils.

ANTI-PROTOZOALS. Remedies that inhibit the action of protozoa, a class of single-celled microscopic animals. Ipecacuanha, Peruvian bark.

ANTI-PRURITICS. Agents to relieve intense itching. Chamomile, Chickweed, Clivers, Cucumber, Goldenseal, Marigold, Sarsaparilla, Peppermint, St John's Wort.

ANTI-PYRETIC. Another term for FEBRIFUGE.

ANTI-RHEUMATICS. Herbs that may relieve discomforts of rheumatism and arthritis. Bearberry, Black Cohosh, Blue Cohosh, Black Willow, Bladderwrack, Blue Flag root, Bogbean, Boneset, Burdock, Calluna (Heather flowers), Cayenne, Celery seed, Chickweed, Couchgrass, Cowslip (Biostrath), Dandelion, Devil's Claw, Guaiacum, Juniper, Lavender, Meadowsweet, Mountain Grape, Nettles, Parsley root, Poke root, Prickly Ash, Sarsaparilla, Pipsissewa, White Poplar, Wild Yam, Wintergreen, Wood Sage, Willow (Biostrath), Wormwood, Yarrow, Yellow Dock.

ANTI-SCORBUTICS. Agents that relieve or cure scurvy. Bogbean, Burdock, Chickweed, Clivers, Cubebs, Blue Flag root, Lemon juice, Sorrel, Nettles, Sarsaparilla, Yellow Parilla, Yellow Dock, Watercress.

ANTISEPTICS. Anti-infectives. Anti-microbials. Powerful plant germicides destructive to harmful bacteria, tending to prevent decay and putrefaction. This group includes the astringents and contains tannins which of themselves tend towards an antiseptic effect. Three of the most widely used are: Myrrh, Echinacea and Goldenseal which combined are a popular combination. Cinnamon is regarded as a powerful antiseptic, internally and externally, in China and the Far East; a sprinkle of the powder applied even to open wounds.
Aromatherapy oils: Borneol, Cinnamon, Eucalyptus, Juniper, Cloves, Lavender, Niaouli, Pine, Rosemary, Thyme, Ylang Ylang.
In present practice: (General) Abscess root, Black Catechu, Boldo, Barberry, Bearberry, Balm of Gilead, Buchu, Blood root, Composition powder or essence, Cudweed, Eucalyptus, Echinacea, Garlic, Goldenrod, Juniper, German Chamomile, Marigold, Myrrh, Oak bark, Peppermint, Onion, Peruvian bark, Poke root, Poplar (white), Rosemary, Sage, Sarsaparilla, Saw Palmetto, Southernwood, Thyme, Wild Indigo, Wild Thyme, White Willow bark, Wintergreen.
Eyes: Marigold, German Chamomile.
Intestines: Goldenseal, German Chamomile.
Lymph glands: Poke root, Echinacea, Garlic, Sarsaparilla, Wild Indigo.
Mucous membranes: Goldenseal, Myrrh, Echinacea, Sarsaparilla.
Genital system: Saw Palmetto, Goldenseal.
Nose: Eucalyptus (oil) injection.
Respiratory system: Balm of Gilead, Cudweed, Pine (oil of).
Skin: Myrrh, Cinnamon, Goldenseal, Sphagnum Moss, Marigold; Oils of Garlic, Thyme, Sage, Juniper, Blood root, Marigold.
Throat and mouth: Poke root, Goldenseal, Cinnamon, Sage.
Urinary system: Barberry, Bearberry, Boldo, Couch Grass, Echinacea, Juniper, Meadowsweet (mild), Onion, Wild Indigo, Yarrow.

ANTI-SCROFULOUS. An agent that tends to reduce glandular inflammation and swelling, and inhibits onset of tuberculosis of the lymphatics. See: LYMPHATICS.

ANTI-SPASMODICS. Agents for relief of muscular cramp, spasm or mild pain. To reduce spasm of smooth muscle. The key remedy is Cramp bark but all have their specific uses.
They may be general (Black Haw, Cramp bark), or those that exert their influence upon specific structures: Hyssop (lungs), Cloves (mucous membranes), Wild Thyme (bronchi), Figwort (anus).
Others in common use: Asafoetida, Balm, Betony, Black Haw (muscles generally, also womb), Black Cohosh, Blue Cohosh, Butterburr, Blood root (externally), Cayenne, German Chamomile (stomach), Dong Quai (ovaries), Eucalyptus, Hops (stomach), Ladyslipper, Liquorice, Lime Blossom, Lobelia, Mistletoe, Motherwort (heart), Nutmeg (angina), Passion Flower, Skullcap, Skunk Cabbage, Thyme, Valerian, Vervain, Wild Cherry (respiratory), Wild Carrot (kidneys and bladder), Wild Lettuce, Wild Yam. Devil's Claw (muscles).
Anti-Spasmodic Drops (Heath and Heather). Cramp, neuralgia, etc. Tincture Myrrh 6 per cent; Tincture Capsic 15 per cent; with 45 per cent ethanol extractive from Scutellaria (Skullcap) 10 per cent; Lobelia 1.25 per cent; Fennel 2.5 per

cent; American Valerian 5 per cent. Dose: 10-30 drops according to age.
John Christopher: 2oz crushed Lobelia seeds; half an ounce Lobelia herb; 1 teaspoon Cayenne; macerated in 1 pint cider 8 days. 1-2 teaspoon when necessary.
Combination: powders. Equal parts: Skullcap, Valerian, Lobelia, Black Cohosh. Myrrh quarter part. Mix. Sift. Quarter of a teaspoon in water, honey etc as necessary.
Formula. Powders. Cramp Bark 2; Skullcap 1; Cloves half; Cayenne Pepper quarter. Mix. Dose: 500mg (two 00 capsules or one-third teaspoon thrice daily. (*Indian Herbology of North America, Alma R. Hutchens*)

ANTI-STAPHYLOCOCCALS. Agents that have anti-bacterial action on most strains of staphylococcus. For treatment of pus-forming lesions, necrotic tissue and for after-surgery infections.

Angostura, Balm, Barberry, Bayberry, Bearberry, Benzoin, Bistort, Blood root, Black Cohosh, Black Currant, Buchu, Bugleweed (Lycopus virginicus and Lycopus europaeus), Butternut (Juglans cinerea), Camphor, Catechu, Cola, Cornsilk, Elecampane, Eucalyptus, Fringe Tree, Goldenseal, Guaiacum, Holy Thistle, Hops, Jaborandi, Jalap, Jambul, Juniper, Kino, Ladysmantle, Labrador tea, Lavender, Liquorice, Male fern, Mandrake, Marjoram, Meadowsweet, Mountain Grape, Myrtle (common), Oleander, Olive, Orthosiphon, Pennyroyal, Peony (common), Pine (Hemlock spruce), Pulsatilla, Rhus toxicodendron, Sage, St John's Wort, Senna, Sumach, Sumbul, Sundew, Thuja, Turmeric, Unicorn root true, Walnut (juglans regia), Wild Indigo. Propolis, a resin foraged by bees for the exclusion of draughts in the hive has proved to be an effective anti-staphylococcal.

ANTITIS. Formula: Buchu leaf 60mg; Dry extract Buchu 100=39 23.4mg. Dry extract Clivers 100=28 16.8mg; Dry extract Couchgrass 5=1 12mg; Dry extract Equisetum 5=1 12mg; Dry extract Shepherd's Purse 5=1 12mg; Dry extract Uva Ursi 5=2 80mg. A traditional remedy for the symptomatic relief of urinary or bladder discomfort. (*Potter's*)

ANTI-TUMOURS. See: ANTI-NEOPLASTICS.

ANTI-TUSSIVES. To reduce cough severity, ease expectoration and clear the lungs. Over a hundred medicinal plants are listed from which the following are a small selection: Angelica, Balm of Gilead, Coltsfoot, Comfrey, Cowslip, Elecampane, Fenugreek, Garlic, Grindeli; Hyssop, Linseed, Liquorice, Marshmallow, Irish Moss, Mousear, Mullein, Pleurisy root, Senega, Sweet Chestnut leaves, Sundew, Violet leaves, Thyme (Garden or Wild), White Horehound, Slippery Elm bark, Marsh Cudweed, .

ANTI-VIRALS. Herbs that contain Vitamin C or stimulate its metabolism in the body. Vitamin C has a broad spectrum viricidal action which is often overlooked for acute infectious diseases.

Aloe Vera, Balm, Boneset, Burdock, Echinacea, Elderflowers, Elecampane, Eucalyptus, Garlic, Goldenseal, Liquorice, Marjoram, Pulsatilla, Queen's Delight, St John's Wort, Thuja, Wild Indigo, Yarrow.

ANXIETY STATES. Acute or chronic, mild or severe.

Pathological anxiety is caused by a mood of fear, the resolution of which is usually psychological or spiritual. Apart from wise counselling it is sometimes necessary to give relaxants to reduce tension.

Causes may be fatigue, low blood pressure, emotional exhaustion, autonomic imbalance, endocrine disturbance (hyperthyroidism, premenstrual tension), stress, conflict, schizophrenia, depression.
Symptoms: dry mouth, increased sweating, fainting attacks, rapid heartbeat, shortness of breath. Prolonged consumption of strong tea, coffee and other caffeine drinks leads to a deficiency of Vitamin B1 which manifests as general anxiety, even agoraphobia.
Alternatives:– Passion Flower, German Chamomile, Lime Blossom, Skullcap, Oats, Cowslip, Damiana, Dogwood, Valerian, Wild Lettuce, Motherwort, Pulsatilla.

In cases of anxiety the heart is involved – whether physically or otherwise. A 'heart sustainer' may give the patient an unexpected 'lift' enabling him to cope.
Motherwort tea. Combine equal parts: Motherwort (heart), Balm (gentle nerve relaxant), Valerian (psycho-autonomic). 1-2 teaspoons in each cup boiling water; infuse 10-15 minutes; 1 cup 2-3 times daily.
Powders. Formula. Motherwort 2; Passion Flower 1; Valerian half. Dose: 500mg (two 00 capsules or one-third teaspoon) 2-3 times daily.
Tinctures. Combine, Oats 3; Hawthorn 1; Valerian 1. Dose: 1-2 teaspoons in water or honey thrice daily.
Anxiety before menstruation. Evening Primrose Oil capsules. OR: Liquid Extract Pulsatilla BHP (1983) 3-5 drops, thrice daily.
Anxiety with obvious heart symptoms. Hawthorn 6; Valerian 1; Cactus 1; Holly 1; Hyssop 1. (*Dr A. Vogel*)
Bach Flower remedies: Rescue remedy.
Biostrath. Kava kava of special value.
Diet. Low salt, low fat, high fibre. Avoid alcohol, coffee, sugar and refined foods. Alfalfa tea for remineralisation.

Supplements. Vitamin B-complex, Magnesium, Zinc. 2-3 bananas daily for potassium.
Supportive: Relaxation technique: yoga, etc.

AORTIC STENOSIS. An unnatural narrowing of the aortic opening of the heart or of the aortic vessel. A serious defect which may lead to chronic heart enlargement. Hardening or scarring of the valve and ultimately calcification may follow rheumatic fever, syphilis or other chronic disease and may be congenital. Incompetence of the valve may be observed in arteries that throb. More common in men.
Symptoms: pain over the breast bone, fainting, vertigo, breathlessness, headache. Where heart is resilient, compensation can minimise effects. Most popular agent among practitioners is Cactus. See entry.

Without addition of a diuretic, (Dandelion or Buchu) dropsy of legs and feet, and breathlessness tend to worsen.
Treatment. Surgical valve replacement now the treatment of choice. Improve the circulation.
Formula. Liquid extracts: Cactus 10ml; Pulsatilla 5ml; Hawthorn 20ml; Tincture Capsicum BPC 1934 0.25ml. Dose: 10-30 drops thrice daily before meals.
A. Barker FNIMH. Liquid extract Garden Thyme 15ml; Liquid extract Pulsatilla 5ml; Liquid extract Passion flower 15ml; Tincture Capsicum 0.25ml. Emuls aqua Menth Pip conc (1 in 64) 2ml . . . Aqua to 250ml. Dose: 1 dessertspoon (8ml) in water every 4 hours.
Diet. See: DIET – HEART AND CIRCULATION.

APERIENT. A mild laxative. Ispaghula seeds, Liquorice, Fenugreek, Boneset, Figs, Dandelion, Senna, Honey, Cowslip, Linseed. For stronger agents, see: LAXATIVES.

APHASIA. Loss of speech; usually from a lesion of the brain through injury, tumour, apoplexy. Ginkgo tea: 1 heaped teaspoon to each cup boiling water; infuse 5-15 minutes. 1 cup thrice daily. Also tincture, tablets or capsules.

APHONIA. Loss of voice. Treatment, as for LARYNGITIS.

APHRODISIACS. Herbs that stimulate sexual activity and libido. Aletris, Angelica, Burdock, Damiana, Ginseng, Honey, Kola, Muira-puama (Liriosma), Saw Palmetto, Pollen, Royal Jelly.
Aromatherapy: Ylang Ylang, Patchouli, Jasmine.

APHTHOUS ULCERS. See: STOMATITIS.

APOPLEXY. See: STROKE.

APPENDICITIS. Inflammation of the vermiform appendix – a small worm-like offshoot from the gut at the junction of the colon and small intestine, in the low right fossa of the abdomen. Blockage leads to stasis and infection. Pain starts from the centre of the abdomen and moves down towards the low right groin focusing on a sensitive spot known as McBurney's point (midway between the naval and the right groin). Possible history of constipation.
Symptoms. Attack may be sudden, with acute low right abdominal pain. Lost appetite. Vomiting occurs usually only once. Nausea. Temperature slightly raised (102°). Muscles rigid and boardlike. The sufferer tries to find relief by lying on his back with right leg drawn up. Rapid heartbeat.

May lapse into abscess, perforation or peritonitis. If neglected, gangrene is a possibility, therefore a modern hospital is the safest place. In any case surgical excision may be necessary to prevent a burst when pus would discharge into the surrounding cavity causing peritonitis.
Differential diagnosis. Inflammation of the right ovary, gall bladder or kidney, ileitis, diverticulitis, perforated peptic ulcer.

Skin temperature aids diagnosis. Application of Feverscan thermometer detects local skin temperature over the right iliac fossa and records at least 1°C warmer than that on the left.

An added aid to diagnosis is the facial expression which predominantly conveys an aura of malaise with an obvious upward curving of the upper lip. This is not a wince or grimace but a slower reaction, and occurs on gentle pressure over the appendix. Rectal tenderness may indicate peritonitis.

A practitioner's prescription would be raised according to the individual requirements of each case; some calling for support of nervous system (Skullcap, Lady's Slipper) or for the heart (Hawthorn, Motherwort), etc.

To be treated by or in liaison with a qualified medical practitioner.
Treatment. Acute stage – immediate hospitalisation.
Tea. Formula. For non-acute stage: equal parts – German Chamomile, Yarrow, Black Horehound. 1 heaped teaspoon to each cup boiling water; infuse 5-15 minutes. 1 cup thrice daily.
Tea: children. Agrimony.
Tablets/capsules. (non-acute stage), Goldenseal, Blue Flag root, Calamus, Cranesbill, Wild Yam. Juice: Aloe Vera.
Chinese medicine. Fenugreek seeds: 2 teaspoons to each cup water simmer 5 minutes. 1 cup thrice daily, consuming the seeds.
Powders. Formula. Echinacea 2; Myrrh half; Wild Yam half; trace of Cayenne. Dose: 750mg (three 00 capsules or half a teaspoon) thrice daily. Every 2 hours for acute cases.
Tinctures. Formula. Echinacea 2; Wild Yam half; Elderflowers 1; few drops Tincture Capsicum

(cayenne). Dose: 1-2 teaspoons in water or herb tea thrice daily or every 2 hours for acute cases.
Finlay Ellingwood MD. Equal parts, Liquid Extract Bryonia and Echinacea. Dose: 20 drops in water, hourly. For prevention of sepsis and pus formation.
Eric F.W. Powell, MNIMH. 1 teaspoon Tincture Echinacea; 10 drops Tincture Myrrh; 2 drops Tincture Capsicum; in wineglassful hot water. Each wineglass taken in sips; dose repeated hourly until pain eases; then less frequently.
Frank Roberts, MNIMH. Liquid extracts: Equal parts, Wild Yam, Echinacea, Lobelia. Mix. 30-60 drops in wineglassful water, sipped 4 times daily.
John Cooper MD, Waldron, Arkansas, USA. 20 grains Epsom's salts in hot water every 2 hours until pain ceases, then continue half that quantity. To control pain: Tincture Belladonna, 8 drops in water, when necessary.
Enema. Large enemas are not indicated. Warm strong infusion of German Chamomile proves helpful (50 flowers to 1 pint boiling water). Inject with 1 tablespoon warm olive oil.
Topical. Castor oil packs. Chamomile, Catnep, or Linseed poultices. In France, cases of acute appendicitis are treated with Tea Tree oil by abdominal massage as an alternative to surgery; good results reported.
Diet. No solid food taken as long as raised temperature persists. Herb tea and fruit-juice fast.

Remission of fever or after surgery: Slippery Elm gruel. Convalescent stage requires extra protein to make good muscle wastage and loss of weight. Low fibre.
Supplements. Daily. Beta-carotene 300,000iu. Vitamin C 2-3g. Vitamin E 400-800iu. Child: quarter of adult dose.
Acute stage: until the doctor comes. Do not eat or drink, take laxatives or painkillers. Go to bed. Hot water bottle to ease pain.

APPETITE: LOSS OF. Anorexia. Due to one of many causes including: kidney, liver or heart disorder, coeliac disease, adrenal insufficiency, glandular disorder, indigestion, hepatitis, vitamin deficiencies, pernicious anaemia, infection (influenza, colds), emotional conflict, threadworms, anxiety, stress. Refer to entry of relevant disorder. Where due to absence of menses: see AMENORRHOEA.
Alternatives: before meals, thrice daily.
Teas. Alfalfa, Agrimony, Balm, Balmony, Bogbean, Calamus, Calumba, Caraway, Centuary, Chamomile, Coriander seeds, Dandelion, <u>Fenugreek seeds</u>, Garlic, Galangal, <u>Gentian</u>, Ginger, Goldenseal, <u>Milk Thistle</u>, Horseradish, Mugwort (where linked with menstrual disorders), Peruvian bark, Quassia, Sage, Southernwood, Wormwood.
Tea mixture. Formula. Equal parts: Agrimony, Balm, Chamomile. 1 heaped teaspoon to each cup boiling water; infuse 5-15 minutes; 1 cup.
Decoction. 1 teaspoon Gentian root to each cup cold water. 1 cup.
Powders. Formula. Equal parts: Gentian, German Chamomile. Dose: 750mg (three 00 capsules or half a teaspoon).
Liquid Extract. Goldenseal BPC 1949: 5-15 drops.
Tincture Gentian BHP (1983). 15-60 drops.
Diet. Wholefood.
Supplements. Vitamin B-group. Zinc.

APPETITE – EXCESSIVE. May be due to worms, pregnancy, nervous excitability in adolescents. Unhappy anxious people tend to over-eat. With some forms of indigestion there is constant desire to eat.
To decrease appetite. Fennel, Hawthorn, Wild Lettuce, Chickweed, Comfrey.

APRICOT. *Prunus armeniaca. German*: Aprikose. *French*: Abricot. *Spanish*: Albaricoque. *Italian*: Meliaco. *Chinese*: T'ein-mei. Part used: powdered kernels.
Action: antitussive, anti-asthmatic. "Long Chinese traditional use in treating tumours." (*Kiangsu Institute of Modern Medicine, 1977, Encyclopaedia of Chinese Drugs (2 vols), Shanghai Scientific and Technical Publications, People's Republic of China.*) See: LAETRILE.

AQUAE WATERS. Aqua waters are weak and simple solutions of volatile oils in distilled water obtained either by distillation or by simple solution. Still popular as harmless carminatives in infantile colic, mild antispasmodics, etc.

A natural basis for skin lotions (Witch Hazel).
Dill water. (*Anethi*). Dill seeds 4oz; water 2 and a quarter litres. Distil down to 1 and a quarter litres. Dose: 1-3 teaspoon for children's colic.
Aniseed water. (*Anisi*). Aniseeds 4oz; distilled water 2 and a quarter litres. Distil down to 1 and a quarter litres. Antispasmodic for children's colic, teething troubles, etc. Dose: 1-3 teaspoons.
Elderflower water. (*Sambuci*). Elderflowers 8oz; distilled water 1 and a quarter litres. Distil down to one-fifth. Eye lotion.
Eyebright water. (*Euphrasia*). Eyebright herb and flowers 4oz; distilled water 2 and a quarter litres. Distil down to 1 and a quarter litres. Antihistamine eye lotion.

ARACHIS. *Arachis hypogaea L.* Peanuts, Monkey nuts, Groundnuts. Part used: nuts; oil expressed from the nuts.
Constituents. Fixed oil; Vitamins B1, B2, B3, E, bioflavonoids, tannins.
Action. Emollient.
Uses. *Internal.* Reported improvement in case of haemophilia. Promotes production of oestrogen. *External.* Massage oil, creams, lotions.

Preparations. Flour: for use by haemophiliacs. Peanut oil for cooking purposes. GSL

ARECA NUT. Betel nut. *Areca catechu L. German*: Areka palme. *French*: Noisette d'inde. *Italian*: Palma arec. *Chinese*: Ping-lang. Part used: seed. Chewing nut of the Far East.
Action: taenicide, astringent, stimulant. In absence of other remedies may be used for tapeworm. Use confined to veterinary medicine. Hardens soft gums. Treatment: for helminthiasis in dogs. To expel tape worms.
Preparations. *Areca powder*: dose, 1-4g. *Liquid Extract*; dose, 1-4ml. Thrice daily.

ARKOPHARMA. Each passing year sees encapsulated herbal powders gaining in popularity. Arkopharm Laboratories, leaders in the field, are located at Nice on the French Riviera, and offer a wide range of powders in capsules (*Arkocaps*) under the authority of a highly qualified team of pharmacists, chemists and doctors.

After the usual stringent tests of raw material on receipt from the suppliers, plants are pulverised and sieved until granulometry is down to 300 micrograms. This size particle ensures a good digestive assimilation without damaging the plant cells. Such material is then subjected to another series of quality control tests for proper potency, purity and cleanliness. This is followed by a further examination for bacteriological cleanliness before shipment. Arkopharma: Head Office: BP 28 06511 Carros (Nice) France. Marketed in the UK by Arkopharma (UK) Ltd.

ARNICA. Leopard's Bane. Wolf's Bane. *Arnica Montana L. German*: Wolferlei, Arnika. *French*: Arnica, Aronique. *Spanish*: Arnica. *Italian*: Arnica, Polmonaria di Montagna. Dried flowerheads.
Action: external use only. GSL
Uses. Bruises and contusions where skin is unbroken. Severe bruising after surgical operation. Neuralgia, sprains, rheumatic joints, aches and pains after excessive use as in sports and gardening.
Combination, in general use: 1 part Tincture Arnica to 10 parts Witch Hazel water as a lotion.
Contra-indications: broken or lacerated skin.
Preparations. Compress: handful flowerheads to 1 pint boiling water. Saturate handtowel or suitable material in mixture and apply.
Tincture. 1 handful (50g) flowerheads to 1 pint 70 per cent alcohol (say Vodka) in wide-necked bottle. Seal tight. Shake daily for 7 days. Filter. Use as a lotion or compress: 1 part tincture to 20 parts water.
Weleda Lotion. First aid remedy to prevent bruise developing.
Nelson's Arnica cream.
Ointment. Good for applying Arnica to parts of the body where tincture or lotion is unsuitable. 2oz flowers and 1oz leaves (shredded or powdered) in 16oz lard. Moisten with half its weight of distilled water. Heat together with the lard for 3-4 hours and strain. For wounds and varicose ulcers.
Wet Dressing. 2 tablespoons flowers to 2 litres boiling water. For muscular pain, stiffness and sprains.
Tincture. Alternative dosage: a weak tincture can be used with good effect, acceptable internally: 5 drops tincture to 100ml water – 1 teaspoon hourly or two-hourly according to severity of the case.

Widely used in Homoeopathic Medicine.

First used by Swiss mountaineers who chewed the leaves to help prevent sore and aching limbs.
Note. Although no longer used internally in the UK, 5-10 drop doses of the tincture are still favoured by some European and American physicians for anginal pain and other acute heart conditions; (Hawthorn for chronic).

Pharmacy only sale.

AROMATHERAPY. The external use of essential oils from seeds, resins, herbs, barks and spices for relaxant purposes.

Plant essences give plants their scent and were known to the ancient civilisations of Egypt and Greece as the 'vital force' or spirit of the plant. They were used for inhalation, rubbing on the skin or as a healthful addition to baths and footbaths. The art is complementary to phytotherapy, acupuncture and other systems of alternative medicine.

The aromatherapist uses oils individually or in blends of different oils. The natural concentrated oil is usually diluted by adding a vegetable oil before direct application to the skin. A massage oil usually comprises 6 drops essential oil to 10ml (2 teaspoons) carrier oil – Almond, Peanut or other vegetable oil.

The skin is known to be an integral part of the immune system. T-cells are scattered throughout, primarily in the epidermis or outer layer. It has been demonstrated that oils rubbed on the skin are readily absorbed and borne to distant organs in the body via the bloodstream to soothe, relax and heal. Some oils should not be used during pregnancy or lactation.

An oil may be used as a natural perfume. As a bath oil, 5-6 drops of a favourite oil may be added to bathwater. Oils freshen a room; stimulate or relax as desired when added to water on a warm radiator. Oils are never used on the skin undiluted.

The aromatherapist never uses essential oils internally. Other carrier oils may be used: Sesame seed, Sunflower seed, Apricot kernel and Wheatgerm. Usual methods of applying essential oils: massage, inhalation and baths. When adding oils to baths water should not be too hot which causes oils to evaporate.

Remedies absorbed into the body via the skin avoid metabolism by the liver as when taken by mouth.

When the therapy was used in a geriatric ward in Oxford drug expenditure on laxatives and night sedatives fell. It was reported to have given profoundly deaf patients, many of whom had multiple sensory deficits, tranquillity. The results of a randomised trial in patients on an intensive care unit showed significantly greater psychological improvement (as demonstrated with anxiety and mood rating scales) in those given aromatherapy (1 per cent Lavender and Grapeseed oil) over those massaged with Grapeseed oil only or those prescribed rest alone. (*The Lancet 1990 336 (8723) 1120*)

The governing body of the therapy in the UK is the Aromatherapy Organisations Council (AOC) which represents the majority of professional practitioners. Enquiries: AOC, 3 Latymer Close, Braybrooke, Market Harborough, Leicester LE16 8LN. Tel/Fax 01858 434242.

AROMATICS. Plants of agreeable taste and smell, chiefly due to the presence of essential oils. A healing odour stimulates the senses of taste and smell. Used to improve the taste of unpalatable medicines or to aid digestion. Angelia, Aniseed, Balm, Basil, Caraway, Catmint, Celery, Cinnamon, Cloves, Coriander, Dill, Eucalyptus, Fennel, Galangal, Hyssop, Ginger, Lavender, Lovage, Meadowsweet, Orris root, Pennyroyal, Peppermint, Rosemary.

ARRACH. Stinking arrach. *Chenopodium olidum* S. Wats. Herb.
Action. Relaxing nervine, emmenagogue, antispasmodic.
Uses. Delayed menses. Nervous excitement from menstrual disorders.
Preparations: Thrice daily.
Tea: 1 teaspoon to each cup boiling water; infuse 15 minutes. Dose: Half a cup.
Liquid Extracts: 30-60 drops in water.

ARRHYTHMIA. (Dysrhythmia). A heart beat irregularity caused by disturbance of the conducting mechanism. Arrhythmias may present as atrial fibrillation, atrial flutter, bradycardia, tachycardia or palpitation most often due to premature beats (extra systoles). See entries.

ARROWROOT. Maranta. *Maranta arundinacea L.* A white powder from the rhizomes of maranta.
Action: nutritive, demulcent.
Uses. Convalescence, weak stomach, colitis, diverticulosis. Mix 2 teaspoons with a little cold water into a smooth paste; add, slowly, half a pint boiling milk, stirring continuously. Flavour with nutmeg. Said to increase weight. The name is derived for its use for arrow wounds in tropical communities.

ARTERIOSCLEROSIS. Thickening and hardening of the arteries with loss of elasticity. While the most common cause is atherosclerosis, it is of gradual onset on old age, diabetes, kidney disorders, syphilis, lead or mercurial poisoning, and certain chronic infections. Treat as for: ATHEROSCLEROSIS.

ARTERITIS. Inflammation of an artery. Chiefly refers to temporal arteritis (giant cell) from which blindness may develop. Over 60s at risk. Associated with polymyalgia rheumatica.
Symptoms. Frontal headache – single or double-sided. Forehead tender to touch. Red line on forehead may confirm temporal arteritis. Feverishness. Erythrocyte sedimentation rate (ESR) is always high and should be frequently checked in a Haematology laboratory. Steroids may be sight-saving but should only be resorted to until effective phytomedicines are discovered.
Alternatives. *Teas*. Cactus, Feverfew, Ginkgo, Meadowsweet, Nettles, Parsley, Rutin, Skullcap.
Tea, formula. Combine equal parts: Hawthorn, Ginkgo, Valerian. 1 heaped teaspoon to each cup water gently simmered 5 minutes. Dose: Half-1 cup thrice daily.
Tablets/capsules. Bamboo gum, Ginkgo, Hawthorn, Prickly Ash, Rutavite, Wild Yam.
Practitioner. (1) Liquid extracts: Lily of the Valley 10ml; Hawthorn 15ml; Valerian 5ml. Tincture Capsicum 0.3ml (5 drops). Dose: 15-60 drops in water thrice daily.
(2) Lily of the Valley, tincture BPC 1934: dose 0.3-1.2ml.
(3) Tincture Gelsemium for severe headache.
Diet. See: DIET – HEART AND CIRCULATION. Pineapple juice.
Supplements. B-complex, Vitamin E (500-1000iu daily). Evening Primrose oil, Maxepa, Glanolin. Iodine, Magnesium, Selenium, Zinc.

ARTHRITIS – BOWEL RELATED. A form of arthritis running concurrently with a bowel disorder arising from intestinal irritation. Acute Crohn's disease or colitis may be related. Joint stiffness and inflammation subside on disappearance of the bowel condition.

Chronic bowel conditions are frequently responsible for heavy drainage of vitamins and minerals via excessive stool. Calcium may be pillaged from the bones to make up blood calcium levels which, if prolonged, may lead to rigid spine.
Treatment. Treatment of arthritis would be secondary, the primary object being to normalise the bowel. Alternatives:–
Teas or decoctions. Comfrey leaves, Calamus,

Chamomile, Avens, Agrimony, Marshmallow root, Meadowsweet, Slippery Elm bark, Wild Yam.
Tea. Formula. Equal parts: Agrimony, Balm, Chamomile. 1 heaped teaspoon to each cup boiling water; infuse 5-10 minutes; 1 cup freely.
Fenugreek seeds. Decoction. 1 cup freely.
Tablets/capsules. Calamus, Fenugreek, Goldenseal, Wild Yam.
Formula. Fenugreek 2; Wild Yam 1; Goldenseal quarter; Ginger quarter. Mix. Dose: Powders: 500mg (two 00 capsules or one-third teaspoon). Liquid extracts: 1 teaspoon. Tinctures: 2 teaspoons.
Bamboo powder. Two 320mg capsules thrice daily. (*Dr Max Rombi*)
Biostrath Willow Formula.
Diet. Slippery Elm food. Vitamin B12. Low fat. Cider vinegar.
Supportive: high enemas. Natural lifestyle. Outlook good.

ARTHRITIS, JUVENILE, CHRONIC. A group of rheumatoid conditions of unknown causation with onset before 16 years. Girls more than boys. Still's disease being the form presenting with enlargement of spleen and lymph nodes, high temperature with macular rash comes and goes. Children usually 'grow out of it' although stiffness may continue. Deformities possible. Tardy bone growth of the mandibles giving the face a birdlike look. May progress to rheumatoid arthritis (girls) or ankylosing spondylitis (boys). So strong is psychosomatic evidence that sociologists believe it to be a sequel to broken families, divorce or bereavement. Few patients appear to come from a balanced environment or happy home.
Treatment. BHP (1983) recommends: Meadowsweet, Balm of Gilead, Poke root, Bogbean, Hart's Tongue fern, Mountain Grape.
Teas: Singly or in combination (equal parts): Chamomile, Bogbean, Nettles, Yarrow. 1-2 teaspoons to each cup boiling water; infuse 5-10 minutes. 1 cup thrice daily before meals.
Tablets/capsules. Blue Flag root, Dandelion root, Poke root, Prickly Ash bark.
Formula. White Poplar bark 2; Black Cohosh half; Poke root quarter Valerian quarter; Liquorice quarter. Mix. Dose: Powders: 500mg (two 00 capsules or one-third teaspoon) (children 5-12 years: 250mg – one 00 capsule or one-sixth teaspoon). Liquid extracts: 1 teaspoon: (children 5-12: 3-10 drops). Tinctures: 2 teaspoons: (children 5-12: 5-20 drops).
Evening Primrose oil. Immune enhancer.
Topical. Hot poultice: Slippery Elm, Mullein or Lobelia.
Diet: Lacto vegetarian. Kelp. Comfrey tea. Molasses. Low fat.
General. Adequate rest, good nursing, gentle manipulation but no massage to inflamed joints. Natural lifestyle. Parental emotional support.
Oily fish. See entry.

ARTHRITIS, GONOCOCCAL. A form of arthritis arising from infection by gonorrhoea may simulate rheumatoid arthritis, affecting the joint fluid. A history of genito-urinary discharge may confirm.
Alternative formulae. *Powders.* Echinacea 2; Kava Kava 2; Prickly Ash 1; Cayenne quarter. Mix. Dose: 500mg (two 00 capsules or one-third teaspoon) thrice daily.
Tinctures. Balm of Gilead 1; Kava Kava 1; Black Cohosh half; Juniper quarter. Mix. Dose: 30-60 drops, thrice daily.
Topical. Tea Tree oil (if too strong may be diluted many times. Analgesic cream.

Treatment by or in liaison with a general medical practitioner or infectious disease specialist.

ARTHRITIS, INFECTIVE. Pyogenic. Bacterial infection may invade the body via mouth, nose or other mucous membranes. By the bloodstream it can be borne to almost any body tissues; joints of the shoulders, knees and hips. Immediate attention is necessary to avoid tissue destruction. Two virulent types are tuberculosis and gonorrhoea.

Infective arthritis may be associated with German Measles against which conventional antibiotics may be of little value. Infective organisms include: streptococcus, E. coli, staphylococcus, or others. May follow surgical operation, steroid therapy, rheumatoid arthritis or diabetes.
Symptoms. Joint hot, feverish, enlarged and painful.
Differential diagnosis: distinguish from gout and synovitis. Herbal treatment must needs be persevered with for 3 to 6 months, even longer. Good nursing is necessary. Natural life-style. Bedrest.
Treatment. For all microbial infections include Echinacea. (*Hyde*)
Teas. Nettles. Red Clover. Yarrow. 2 teaspoons to each cup boiling water; infuse 15 minutes. 1 cup 3-4 times daily.
Tablets/capsules. Devil's Claw, Alfalfa, Echinacea, Horsetail.
Alternative formulae:– *Powders.* Echinacea 2; Burdock 1; Devil's Claw 1; Guaiacum quarter. Mix. Dose: 750mg (three 00 capsules or half a teaspoon). Thrice daily.
Liquid Extracts. Echinacea 2; Juniper half; Black Cohosh half; Guaiacum quarter. Mix. Dose: 30-60 drops. Thrice daily.
Tinctures. Dandelion 2; Echinacea 2; Poke root half; Peppermint quarter. mix. Dose: 1-2 teaspoons. Thrice daily.

Above powders, liquid extracts and tinctures – effects are enhanced when each dose is taken in half-1 cup Fennel tea; otherwise, to be taken in water.

Topical. Analgesic cream. Comfrey poultice, Comfrey ointment. Tea Tree oil, Castor oil packs.
Diet. High Vitamin C foods. Dandelion coffee.

ARTHRITIS – OF INFECTIVE HEPATITIS. Inflammatory disease of a joint or joints may follow invasion of organism in infective hepatitis for which primary treatment would be directed to the liver. See: INFECTIVE HEPATITIS.
Treatment. To include liver agents: Barberry, Fringe Tree, Balmony or Milk Thistle.

ARTHRITIS – OF LEPROSY. A chronic infection of the joints associated with the disease. Treatment of the primary condition is necessary. Two historic remedies are Sarsaparilla (*Smilax*) and Gotu Kola (*Hydrocotyle asiatica*). See: HANSEN'S DISEASE.

Treatment by general medical practitioner or infectious diseases specialist.

ARTHRITIS, LUPUS. A form of arthritis associated with systemic lupus erythematosis in young girls. An auto-immune disease which may involve the heart, kidney, CNS or other systems.
Symptoms: Joint pains with feverishness, loss of weight, anaemia and red raised patches of skin on nose and face (butterfly rash). Swelling of the joints resembles rheumatoid arthritis. Chest and kidney disease possible. Personality changes with depression followed by mania and possible convulsions.
Treatment. Standard orthodox treatments: aspirin, steroids. Alternatives: Echinacea (rash), Valerian (mental confusion), Lobelia (chest pains), Parsley Piert (kidney function).
Tablets/capsules. Echinacea. Poke root. Dandelion. Valerian. Wild Yam. Prickly Ash bark.
Powders. Echinacea 2; Dandelion 1; Wild Yam half; Poke root quarter; Devil's Claw half; Fennel half. Mix. Dose: 500mg (two 00 capsules or one-third teaspoon) thrice daily. In water or cup of Fenugreek tea.
Tinctures. Dandelion 4; Valerian 1; Prickly Ash half; Poke root half; Peppermint quarter. Mix. Dose: 1 teaspoon thrice daily, in water or cup Fenugreek tea.
Tincture. Queen's Delight BHP (1983) 1:5 in 45 per cent alcohol. Dose 1-4ml (15-60 drops).
Topical. Plantain Salvo. Castor oil. Oil Cajeput or Sassafras. Comfrey or Chickweed cream.
Diet. Young girls may require diet for anaemia.
Supplementation. Daily. Vitamins A, B6, B12, C, D. Dolomite (1500mg). Calcium Pantothenate (500mg). Iron: Men (10mg), women (18mg).

ARTHRITIS – MENOPAUSAL. Joint stiffness of the menopause due to diminished output of progesterone and oestrogen. Not really a separate disease but one form in which rheumatoid arthritis may present.
Alternatives. Agnus Castus, Alfalfa, Black Cohosh, Blue Cohosh, Cramp bark, Hawthorn, Hops, Liquorice, Sage, Sarsaparilla, Wild Yam, Yarrow.
Tea. Formula. Equal parts: Alfalfa, Hops, Sage. 1 heaped teaspoon to each cup boiling water; infuse 5-10 minutes; 1 cup freely.
Chinese medicine: Sage tea.
Formula. Agnus castus 2; Black Cohosh 1; Valerian half; Juniper quarter. Mix. Dose: Powders: 500mg (two 00 capsules or one-third teaspoon). Liquid Extracts: 1 teaspoon. Tinctures: 2 teaspoons, in water, or cup of Nettle tea.
Nettle tea. Favourable results reported.
Evening Primrose oil.
Diet. Oily fish. Low fat, Low salt. High fibre.
Supplements. Vitamins A, B6, B-complex, C, E. Calcium, Magnesium, Zinc.

ARTHRITIS – FROM ATTACK OF MUMPS. While treatment would be directed towards the primary condition, Poke root should be included in any prescription.
Formula. Echinacea 1; Goldenseal half; Poke root quarter. Mix. Dose: Powders: 500mg (two 00 capsules or one-third teaspoon). Liquid extracts: 1 teaspoon. Tinctures: 2 teaspoons. Thrice daily, in water.
Poke root tablets/capsules. As recommended.

ARTHRITIS – OSTEO. Osteo-arthritis. Erosion of cartilage of a joint with pain and stiffness. "Wear and tear" arthritis of the over 50s, affecting hands, knees, spine or hips. Biochemical changes in the cartilage stimulate overgrowth of bone cells (hyperplasia) which is an effort by the body to correct the disturbance.

Common in the elderly and menopausal women. Calcium salts may be laid down in a joint believed to be due to errors of diet. Small crystals of calcium hydroxyapatite have been observed to form in cartilage and synovial fluid. (*Research group: St Bartholomew's Hospital, London*)

The aged sometimes suffer from diminished supply of hydrochloric acid in the stomach, and which is necessary for normal calcium metabolism. An effective substitute is 2 teaspoons cider vinegar in a glass of water sipped before or during meals.
Alternatives. Black Cohosh and Meadowsweet (natural sources of salicylic acid), Asafoetida (inflammation of connective tissue), Hawthorn (efficient circulation of the blood), Poke root, Bladderwrack, Guaiacum, Devil's Claw, Bogbean, White Poplar bark, Yucca leaves.
Tea. Celery seeds. 1 teaspoon to each cup boiling water. Infuse 15 minutes. Half-1 cup, 2-3 times daily, before meals. Comfrey tea.
Alternative formulae:– *Powders.* White Willow

2; Devil's Claw 1; Black Cohosh half; Guaiacum quarter. Mix. Dose: 500mg (two 00 capsules or one-third teaspoon). Thrice daily in water or Nettle tea.
Liquid extracts. White Willow 2; Devil's Claw 1; Bogbean 1; Fennel 1; Tincture Capsicum quarter. Mix. 1 teaspoon thrice daily in water or Nettle tea.
Tinctures. Bogbean 2; Meadowsweet 2; Black Cohosh 1; Guaiacum quarter; Peppermint quarter. Mix. Dose: 2 teaspoons thrice daily.
Tablets/capsules: Devil's Claw, Wild Yam, Ligvites.
Cod liver oil. Chief of the iodised oils. Can reach and nourish cartilage by the process of osmosis. Its constituents filter into cartilage, imparting increased elasticity which prevents degeneration. Known to soften-up fibrous tissue. 2 teaspoons once daily. Also helps correct uric acid metabolism.
Topical. Physiotherapy. Osteopathy. Jojoba oil packs. Capsicum Cream. Hot and cold compresses twice daily – followed by a cold compress at night, leaving on when in bed. Hot Epsom salt bath twice weekly.
Diet. Oily fish: see entry. Low fat. Low salt. High fibre. Avoid lemons and other citrus fruits. Lemon juice may remove some calculi from the body but later begins to remove calcium from the bones.
Supplementation. Pantothenic acid 10mg; Vitamin A 7500iu; Vitamin B6 25mg; Vitamin E 400iu; Zinc 25mg.
General. Warm dry climate often relieves. Surgery may be necessary. Herbs Pleurisy root, Comfrey root and Bryonia, sustain the constitution and promote tissue healing after joint replacements with ceramic substitute after the famous Charnley operation. The condition is disabling but it is possible to manage successfully, maintaining normal activities with minimum difficulty.

ARTHRITIS – PSORIATIC. A form of joint erosion possible in patients with psoriasis; fingers and toes being most susceptible. Nails may be pitted with deep ridging. Bony structures are at risk where in close contact with septic psoriasis.
Alternatives:– *Teas.* Gotu Kola, Red clover flowers, Chickweed. Singly or in combination. 1 heaped teaspoon to each cup boiling water: infuse 5-10 minutes. 1 cup thrice daily.
Decoction. Fine cut: Burdock 2; Horsetail 1; Echinacea 1; Thuja quarter. Mix. 1oz to 1 pint water gently simmered 15 minutes. Wineglassful (or half a cup) thrice daily, before meals.
Tablets/capsules. Echinacea, Poke root, Prickly Ash bark.
Powders. Formula. Sarsaparilla 1; Echinacea 1; Boneset half; Thuja quarter. Dose: 500mg (two 00 capsules or one-third teaspoon) thrice daily.
Liquid extracts. Formula. Equal parts: Echinacea, Devil's Claw, Gotu Kola. Dose: 30-60 drops thrice daily before meals.
Tinctures. Formula. Burdock 2; Echinacea 1; Boneset 1; Sarsaparilla 1; Thuja quarter. Fennel quarter. Mix. Dose: 1-2 teaspoons thrice daily.
Cod Liver oil.
Topical. Comfrey poultice, Chickweed cream, Oils of Mullein, Jojoba or Evening Primrose.
Diet. Oily fish (or fish oils). Low salt, low fat.
Supplements. Vitamins A, B-complex, C, D, E, Magnesium, Sulphur, Zinc.

ARTHRITIS – RHEUMATOID. A systemic inflammatory disease of several joints together where erosive changes occur symmetrically, and which may arise from inflammation and thickening of the synovial membrane. Cartilage becomes eroded and fibrous or even bony fusion leads to permanent fixation of a joint, or joints. Polyarthritis. An auto-immune disease.
Symptoms. Morning stiffness and pain wearing off later. Easy fatigue and decline in health. Nodules on surface of bones (elbows, wrists, fingers). Joint fluids (synovia) appear to be the object of attack for which abundant Vitamin C is preventative. Anaemia and muscle wasting call attention to inadequate nutrition, possibly from faulty food habits for which liver and intestine herbs are indicated.
Treatment. Varies in accord with individual needs. May have to be changed many times before progress is made. Whatever treatment is prescribed, agents should have a beneficial effect upon the stomach and intestines to ensure proper absorption of active ingredients. (Meadowsweet)

It is a widely held opinion that the first cause of this condition is a bacterial pathogen. An anti-inflammatory herb should be included in each combination of agents at the onset of the disease. See: ANTI-INFLAMMATORY HERBS. Guaiacum (*Lignum vitae)* and Turmeric (*Curcuma longa*) have a powerful anti-inflammatory action and have no adverse effects upon bone marrow cells or suppress the body's immune system. Breast feeding cuts RA death rate.
Of therapeutic value according to the case. Agrimony, Angelica root, Balmony, Black Cohosh (particularly in presence of low back pain and sciatica), Bogbean, Boldo, Burdock, Celery, Cramp bark, Devil's Claw, Echinacea (to cleanse and stimulate lymphatic system), Ginseng (Korean), Ginseng (Siberian), Liquorice, Meadowsweet, Poke root, Prickly Ash bark, White Poplar bark, White Willow bark, Wild Yam.
Tea. Formula. Equal parts. Alfalfa, Bogbean, Nettles. 1 heaped teaspoon to each cup boiling water; infuse 5-10 minutes, 1 cup thrice daily.
Decoction. Prickly Ash bark 1; Cramp bark 1; White Willow bark 2. Mix. 1oz to 1 pint water gently simmered 20 minutes. Dose: Half-1 cup

thrice daily.
Tablets/capsules. Black Cohosh, Celery, Cramp bark, Devil's Claw, Feverfew, Poke root, Prickly Ash, Wild Yam, Ligvites.
Alternative formulae:– *Powders.* White Willow bark 2; Devil's Claw 1; Black Cohosh half; Ginger quarter. Mix. Dose: 750mg (three 00 capsules or half a teaspoon) thrice daily.
Liquid extracts. White Willow bark 2; Wild Yam half; Liquorice half; Guaiacum quarter. Mix. Dose: 1-2 teaspoons thrice daily.
Tinctures. Cramp bark 1; Bogbean 1; Prickly Ash half; Meadowsweet 1; Fennel half. Mix. Dose: 1-3 teaspoons thrice daily.
Ligvites. (*Gerard House*)
Cod Liver oil. Contains organic iodine, an important factor in softening-up fibrous tissue, to assist metabolism of uric-acid, help formation of haemoglobin, dilate blood vessels; all related to arthritics. The oil, taken internally, can reach and nourish cartilage by the process of osmosis; its constituents filter into cartilage and impart increased elasticity.
Topical. Evening Primrose oil, Wintergreen lotion, Comfrey poultice. Hydrotherapy: hot fomentations of Hops, Chamomile or Ragwort. Cold water packs: crushed ice or packet of frozen peas in a damp towel applied daily for 10 minutes for stiffness and pain. See: MASSAGE OIL.
Aromatherapy. Massage oils, any one: Cajeput, Juniper, Pine or Rosemary. 6 drops to 2 teaspoons Almond oil.
Supportives: under-water massage, brush baths, sweat packs, Rosemary baths, exposure of joints to sunlight.
Diet. Low salt, low fat, oily fish, Mate tea, Dandelion coffee. On exacerbation of the disease cut out all dairy products.
Supplements. Daily. Evening Primrose capsules: four 500mg; Vitamin C (1-3g); Bromelain 250mg between meals; Zinc 25mg.
General. Residence in a warm climate. Yoga. Disability and deformity may be avoided by a conscientious approach to the subject.

ARTHRITIS – TUBERCULOUS. A chronic bone and joint condition due to bovine from of tuberculosis believed to be caused by drinking TB milk and cream. Mostly in children, beginning in fluids surrounding a joint before invading bone tissue. Instead of normal flesh colour a joint has a white appearance. Condition maybe secondary to disease of the lungs or glands. Pain worse at night.

Elecampane (Inula) has a direct effect on TB bacilli, controlling night sweats and localising the disease. Agents yielding salicylates (mild analgesics) Meadowsweet, White Willow, etc are of value. Echinacea increases phagocytic power of the leucocytes and may normalise percentage count of neutraphiles. To meet individual needs, it will be necessary to vary treatment many times during the course of the disease.
Alternatives. Echinacea, Elecampane, Balm of Gilead buds (Hyde), Gotu Kola, Comfrey root, Iceland Moss. Rupturewort promotes elasticity of lung tissue.
Decoction. Equal parts: Iceland Moss, Comfrey root, Elecampane root, Liquorice. Mix. 1oz to 1 pint water gently simmered 20 minutes in a covered vessel. Dose: Half a cup thrice daily.
Alternative formulae:– *Powders.* White Willow 2; Comfrey 1; Echinacea 1; Ginger quarter. Mix. Dose: 750mg (three 00 capsules or half a teaspoon) thrice daily.
Tinctures. White Willow 2; Echinacea 1; Blue Cohosh half; White Poplar half; Tincture Capsicum quarter. Mix. 1 teaspoon thrice daily before meals.
Tincture Krameria (Rhatany root), Dose: 30-60 drops in water thrice daily.
Fenugreek seed tea.
Comfrey. Potential benefit of Comfrey root outweighs risk.
Topical. Compresses: Mullein leaves, Lobelia, Comfrey root or Fenugreek. Evening Primrose oil. No massage to affected joints.
Diet. Low carbohydrate. Oily fish.
Supplements. Vitamins A, B6, B12, D, Niacin, Calcium, Iron, Phosphorus.
General. Tuberculosis is a notifiable disease for which specific medical treatment is available. Failure to comply may expose a practitioner to a charge of negligence.

ARTICHOKE. Globe artichoke. *Cynara scolymus L. French*: Artichaut. *German*: Echte Artischocke. *Italian*: Artichiocco. Leaves and blossom.
Active constituent: cynarin.
Action: cholagogue, flow of bile increase up to 60 per cent, hypo diuretic, liver restorative. Assists digestion of fats. Choleretic, hypolipaemic. Tonic. Anti-hyperlipidaemic.
Uses. Liver and gall bladder disorders. Liver damage, jaundice, nausea. Artichokes are the diabetic's potato. Hyperlipaemia – to reduce level of fats in the blood. Hypercholesterolaemia. To stimulate metabolism. Fluid retention. Detoxification. Aid to cell metabolism.
Preparations. *Tea.* 1-2 teaspoons leaves or root to each cup boiling water. Infuse 15 minutes. Half-1 cup freely.
Powder. 250mg capsules. 3 capsules, morning and evening, before meals. (*Arkocaps*)
Bio-strath artichoke formula. Artichokes eaten as a vegetable.

ASAFOETIDA. Devil's Dung. *Ferula asafoetida L. German*: Stinkasant. *French*: Ferule asafétide. *Italian*: Ferula del sagapeno. *Spanish*: Asafédita. *Chinese*: A-wei. Oleo-gum resin of the odour of fresh truffles.

Action: powerful expectorant, carminative, antispasmodic, nervine stimulant. Non-steroidal anti-inflammatory. Anticoagulant (Vitamin K antagonist). No pain-killing activity.
Uses. To expel mucous during bronchitis, asthma, whooping cough. Intestinal colic with wind. Hysteria, nervous excitability, restlessness, convulsions, autonomic imbalance, mental depression. To reduce sexual excitability. To neutralise effects of mercury, as from dental fillings. Stress situations. Research study of mixed group of 30 rheumatoid and osteoarthritic patients showed improvement was obtained in 28. (*Dr Finiefs, 1966*)
Preparations. *Tincture BHC Vol 1.* 1:5, 70 per cent ethanol. Dose: 2-4ml.
Tablets. Combination. Skullcap 45mg; Hops 45mg; Asafoetida 30mg; and the aqueous extractive from 120mg Gentian and 90mg Valerian. Special reference to shingles.
Ferula Extract (*Nelson*). GSL

ASBESTOSIS. Common affliction from prolonged exposure to asbestos, with scarring of lung tissue and obstruction of air-spaces within the lung. Not curable. Cause of malignant mesothelioma of pleura.
Symptoms. Difficult breathing, with possibility of pneumonia and bronchitis. Where the patient is a smoker the incidence of lung cancer is increased. Frequent site is the pleura, symptoms developing slowly over many years.
Treatment. Expectorants, anti-infectives. Same as for SILICOSIS.

ASCITES. An accumulation of fluid around the intestines causing swelling. Dropsy of the abdomen. Due to stagnation of the abdominal circulation. May occur as part of general dropsy by heart disease or following obstructed circulation by the liver in cirrhosis. May also be due to malignant tumour inside the abdomen especially where it obstructs the portal circulation conveying blood to the liver.

While sometimes necessary for fluid to be drawn off by a medically qualified person, certain agents assist dispersal. See: DROPSY. HEART FAILURE. NEPHRITIS.

Attention to bowels. A laxative helps relieve abdominal pressure.

ASH. White ash. European ash. *Fraxinus excelsior L. German*: Esche. *French*: Frêne. *Italian*: Frassino. *Chinese*: Ch'in-pi. *Spanish*: Fresno. Leaves. Coumarin derivatives, flavonoids.
Action: antiperiodic, diuretic, laxative.
Uses: Promotes excretion of uric acid. Intermittent fevers; one-time substitute for Quinine, (Bark). As a tea, the young leaves have a reputation for gout, rheumatism and sluggish kidney function. "To stimulate blood circulation of hands and feet" (*Russian Science Academy*).
Preparations. *Tea*: 1 heaped teaspoon, leaves, to each cup boiling water; infuse 15 minutes. Half a cup thrice daily.
Case: "A Mrs Louis, Connecticut, informed me that an Indian cured a cancer by internal and external use of the juice of White Ash that issued from the end of wood as it burned." (*Samuel Stearn*, 1741-1809, in "American Herbal".)

Poultice, for gouty and rheumatic limbs. Combines well with Devil's Claw. GSL

ASPARAGUS. *Asparagus officinalis L. French*: Asperge commune. *German*: Spargel. *Spanish*: Esparrágo. *Italian*: Asparago commune. *Chinese*: T'ien-men-tung. *Malayan*: Akar parsi. Contains steroidal glycosides, bitter glycosides, flavonoids, saponins. Root.
Action: gentle diuretic to increase flow of urine, Source of folic acid and selenium. Contains steroidal glycosides. Galactagogue, Aphrodisiac.
Uses: Cystitis. Pyelitis. Swollen ankles, oedema where of heart origin. Strong-smelling urine. Some reputation for mild diabetes. Rheumatism, neuritis. Used by the Chinese as an anti-parasitic.
Preparations. Half cup fresh root juice, thrice daily. Young shoots at meals.

ASPIRIN. Acetylsalicylic acid. Widely used drug for relief of pain and to reduce fever. Preventative against stroke, cataract, heart attack. While aspirin has been a dramatic life-saver, unwanted side-effects include stomach bleeding, nervous irritability and personality change. Should not be given to children with influenza or chicken pox. A common source of allergies and infertility.

Herbal alternatives exist but may be of limited efficacy: menstrual pain (Helonias root), muscular rheumatism (Black Cohosh), tension headaches (Ginkgo), Angina pectoris (Cramp bark), eye-strain (Eyebright), facial neuralgia (German Chamomile), swollen glands (Poke root), chest pain (Elecampane), cough (Iceland Moss), simple abdominal pain (Fenugreek).

Cures for relief of painful limbs run into hundreds. Gentle massage to release endorphins which block pain waves offers an external approach. Arthritic knees are less painful on application of Castor oil packs or one of the many preparations commended under poultices, liniments, lotions, etc.

During trials at Long Island University, USA, 189 cases of rheumatic knees and elbows were rendered painless by pollen poultices. Dissolve one tablespoon bee pollen pellets in warm water; immerse small handtowel; squeeze out excess moisture; bind over affected joint.

Cold water packs are advised by hydrotherapists for headache, stiff neck, shoulders, back and legs.

Sodium bicarbonate is the safest and most effective antidote for aspirin overdose.

Aspirin therapy almost halves the risk of venous thrombosis and pulmonary embolism in patients undergoing surgery, according to a major study. (*BMJ Jan 22 1994*)

Studies show that deaths from heart attack can be halved by prescribing half tablet daily together with a clot-dissolving remedy (Nettles, Vitamin E, etc). As an anti-coagulant aspirin is matched by Garlic.

In alternative medicine the use of aspirin is discouraged.

ASTHENIA. See: WEAKNESS.

ASTHMA. Spasmodic contraction of the bronchi following exercise, emotional tension, infection, allergens, pollens, house dust, colds.

Symptoms. Obstruction of airways with wheezing, rales or whistling sounds with a sense of constriction. Often related to eczema – 'eczema of the epithelium'. Infantile eczema treated with suppressive ointments may drive the condition 'inwards' and worsen asthma. "My son's eczema has got better, but he now has asthma" is a common observation.

Causes: hypersensitivity to domestic animals, horses and pet birds. Common salt. Red or white wine allergy. An older generation of practitioners recognised a renal-bronchial asthma encouraged by faulty kidney function. With addition of a relaxing diuretic (Dandelion, Buchu or Parsley root) to a prescription, respiratory symptoms often abate.

Broncho-dilators such as Ephedra and Wild Thyme are widely used by the practitioner. To relieve spasm: Lobelia, Pleurisy root. White Horehound, Ammoniacum, Cramp bark, Garlic, Grindelia, Hyssop.

Anti-cough agents serve to remove sticky sputum: Coltsfoot, Garden Thyme, Slippery Elm bark, Maidenhair Fern, Linseed, Bayberry bark.

For the chronic asthmatic, bacterial invasion spells distress, when Echinacea or Balm of Gilead should be added. Where an irregular pulse reveals heart involvement, add: Hawthorn or Lily of the Valley.

Lobelia is of special value for the anxious patient with spasm of the bronchi. Should be tried before resorting to powerful spray mists which frequently produce gastro-intestinal disturbance.

Alternatives. *Teas*. Coltsfoot, Comfrey, Horehound (White), Mullein, Skullcap, Marshmallow, Thyme, Valerian, Wild Cherry bark, Elecampane, Plantain. Formula: equal parts herbs Coltsfoot, Mullein, Valerian. 1-2 teaspoons to each cup boiling water; infuse 10-15 minutes; dose, 1 cup twice daily and when necessary.

Antispasmodic Drops. See entry.

Practitioner. <u>Ephedra</u>, <u>Lobelia</u>, Gelsemium, Grindelia, Euphorbia (pill-bearing spurge), Skunk Cabbage, Senega, Pulsatilla, Lily of the Valley (cardiac asthma), Thyme. Formula. Equal parts, Tincture Lobelia simp; Tincture Belladonna; Tincture Ephedra. 5-10 drops thrice daily (maintenance), 10-20 drops for spasm.

Cockayne, Ernest, FNIMH. Hyssop tea for children throughout childhood to avoid respiratory disorders.

Dr Finlay Ellingwood. Gelsemium 3.5ml; Lobelia 3.5ml. Distilled water to 120ml. One 5ml teaspoon in water every 3 hours.

Dr Alfred Vogel. Ephedra 20 per cent; Ipecac 15 per cent; Hawthorn berry 10 per cent; Blessed Thistle 5 per cent; Burnet Saxifrage 5 per cent; Garden Thyme 5 per cent; Grindelia 1 per cent. 10-15 drops in water thrice daily.

Dr Wm Thomson. 1 teaspoon Ephedra herb to cup boiling water; infuse 10-15 minutes. Half-1 cup 2-3 times daily.

Traditional. 2 teaspoons shredded Elecampane root in cup cold water; stand overnight. Next day, heat to boiling point when required. Strain. Sips, hot, with honey: 1 cup 2-3 times daily.

Potter's Asthma & Bronchitis Compound 32. 40g medicinal teabags. Ingredients: Clove BPC 4.84 per cent; Elecampane root 17.24 per cent; Horehound 26.20 per cent; Hyssop 17.24 per cent; Irish Moss 17.24 per cent; Liquorice 17.24 per cent. Dose: 1-2 teaspoons when necessary.

Chinese Medicine. Decoction or extract from the Gingko tree widely used, as also is Ephedra, Garlic, Liquorice and Bailcalensis.

Tablets/capsules. Lobelia. Iceland Moss, (*Gerard*). Euphorbia (*Blackmore*).

Powders. Formula. Lobelia 2; Hyssop 1; Elderflowers 1; Grindelia quarter; Liquorice quarter; pinch Cayenne. Dose: 750mg (three 00 capsules or half a teaspoon) 2-3 times daily.

Aromatherapy. 6 drops Rosemary oil in 2 teaspoons Almond oil for massage upper chest to relieve congestion.

Inhalation. See: INHALATIONS, FRIAR'S BALSAM.

Nebulizer. A germicidal solution is made from 5 drops oil Eucalyptus in one cup boiling water. Use in nebulizer for droplet therapy.

Ioniser – use of.

Cider Vinegar. Sips of the vinegar in water for whoop.

Supportives. Yoga. Singing. Cures have been reported of patients on taking up singing. "During singing, up to 90 per cent of the vital capacity may be used without a conscious effort to increase tidal volume." (*Dr M. Judson, New England Journal of Medicine*)

Diet. Low salt, low fat, high fibre, cod liver oil, carrots, watercress, Soya beans or flour, lecithin, sunflower seed oil, green vegetables, raw fruit, fresh fish. These foods are valuable sources of antioxidant vitamins and minerals essential for the body's defence mechanism. A diet deficient in these reduces ability of the airways to withstand the ravages of cigarette smoke and other air pollutants.

Foods that are craved are ones often causing sensitivity. Among problem foods are: milk, corn, wheat, eggs, nuts, chocolate, all dairy products, fat of meats. Check labels for tartrazine artificial colouring.

Salt intake. Linked with chest diseases. "Those who eat a lot of salt had more sensitive airways than those with low salt intake . . . excess salt tended to cause most pronounced symptoms." (*Institute of Respiratory Diseases, Oavia, Italy*)

Asthma mortality could be significantly reduced by sufferers lowering their salt consumption, an epidemiologist predicted.

Supplements. Daily. Vitamin B6 50-100mg. Vitamin C 500mg. Vitamin E 400iu. Magnesium, Zinc. Cod liver oil: 2 teaspoons.

Anti-allergic bedding. Provides a protective barrier against the house dust mite on mattresses and bedding. Droppings from the tiny pests are worse in the bedroom.

ASTRINGENTS. One of the largest groups of herbs. Herbs that contract blood vessels and certain body tissues (mucous membranes) with the effect of reducing secretion and excretion. Binders. They are used for debility, internal and external bleeding, catarrhal discharges, etc, their action due to the tannins they contain. Main astringents: Agrimony, Avens, Bayberry, Beth root, Bistort, Black Catechu, Burr-Marigold, American Cranesbill, Eyebright, Golden Rod, Great Burnet, Ground Ivy, Hemlock Spruce bark, Kola, Ladies Mantle, Meadowsweet, Mouse Ear, Mullein, Nettles, Oak bark, Periwinkle, Pilewort, Plantain, Raspberry leaves, Sage, Rosemary, Shepherd's Purse, Tormentil, Wild Cherry bark, Witch Hazel, Yarrow, White Pond Lily.

ASTROLOGY. A system of medical astrology was recorded by Culpeper in his "*Complete Physician*". Astrologers believe diseases vary according to movements of the stars and that in some unknown way plants are related to the heavenly bodies. Culpeper writes: "It is essential to find out what planet caused the disease and then by what planet the affected part of the body is governed." A remedy of a contrary nature is applied: for instance, if a disease is caused by Venus, herbs under Mars are used; if under the Sun, herbs under Saturn.

In some instances a planet cures by acting in sympathy, each planet curing its own disease; i.e. Venus and diseases of the reproductive system.

It is an ancient herbal practise for herbs to be gathered when the ruling planet is in the ascendancy. Scientific inquiry fails to support this system of medical treatment.

ATHERA. Traditional herbal remedy for symptomatic relief of minor conditions associated with the menopause. Formula: Parsley 60mg; Vervain powder 10mg; Senna leaf powder 4mg; dry extract Vervain from 90mg; dry extract Clivers from 60mg; dry extract Senna from 10mg. Tea and tablets. (*Modern Health Products*)

ATHEROMA. A degeneration of arterial walls into fatty tissue by soft waxy material which accumulates in arteries and eventually causes blockages. There is evidence that atheroma starts in childhood. Even children killed accidentally often have fatty deposits in the aorta at post-mortem.

Cause: chiefly high intake of fat meat, milk and dairy products. Atherosclerosis is the hardening process that takes place where calcium is deposited in the arteries. See: HYPERLIPIDAEMIA.

ATHEROSCLEROSIS. Atheroma is a name given to the disease where fatty and mineral deposits attach themselves to the walls of the arteries. Usually starts from a deposit of cholesterol which leaks into the inner surface of the artery causing a streak of fat to appear within the wall. As the fatty streak grows deeper tissue within the arterial wall is broken down and the mechanism for clotting blood is triggered. The result is formation of atheromatous plaque that may clog an artery, precipitate a clot (known as an embolism) and travel to a smaller artery which could become blocked. The end result of atherosclerosis is invariably arteriosclerosis in which thickening and hardening leads to loss of elasticity.

Atherosclerosis can be the forerunner of degenerative heart and kidney disease, with rise in blood pressure.

A study of Australian 'flu epidemic diseases revealed influenza as a major cause of cardiovascular disease and in particular, atherosclerosis.

Causes. Excessive smoking and alcohol, fatty foods, hereditary weakness, stress and emotional tension that release excessive adrenalin into the bloodstream. Toxic effects of environmental poisons (diesel fumes). Fevers.

Symptoms. Cold hands and feet, headache, giddiness. Diminished mental ability due to thickening of arteries in the brain. Pain on exertion, breathlessness and fatigue. Diagnosis of atheroma of main arteries: by placing stethoscope over second right intercostal space, half inch from the sternum, the second aortic sound will be pronounced.

Treatment. Surface vasodilators, Cardioactives. Anti-cholesterols.

Alternatives. *Teas*. To lower cholesterol levels and shrink hardened plaque: Alfalfa, Chamomile, Borage, Olive leaves, Mint, Nettles, Marigold,

Garlic, Lime flowers, Yarrow, Horsetail, Hawthorn, Ginkgo, Orange Tree leaves, Meadowsweet, Eucalyptus leaves, Ispaghula, Bromelain. Rutin (Buckwheat tea).
Artichoke leaves. Spanish traditional. 2 teaspoons to each cup of water; simmer 2 minutes. Drink cold: 1 cup 2-3 times daily.
Mistletoe leaves. 1-2 teaspoons to each cup cold water steeped 8 hours (overnight). Half-1 cup thrice daily.
Tablets, or capsules. Garlic, Mistletoe, Poke root, Rutin, Hawthorn, Motherwort, Ginkgo, Bamboo gum.
Liquid Extracts. Mix Hawthorn 2; Mistletoe 1; Barberry 1; Rutin 1; Poke root half. Dose: 30-60 drops thrice daily.
Tinctures. Mix: Hawthorn 2; Cactus flowers 2; Mistletoe 1; Capsicum half. Dose: 1-2 teaspoons thrice daily in water before meals.
Powders. Mix equal parts: Bamboo gum, Hawthorn, Mistletoe, Rutin, Ginger. Fill 00 capsules. Dose: 2-4 capsules, or quarter to half a teaspoon (375-750mg) thrice daily before meals.
Threatened stroke. Tincture Arnica BPC (1949): 3-5 drops in water morning and evening. Practitioner only.
Evening Primrose oil. Favourable results reported. (*Maxepa*)
Diet. Vegetarian. Low fat. Low salt. High fibre. Lecithin, polyunsaturated oils, artichokes, oily fish (see entry). Linseed on breakfast cereal. Garlic at meals, or Garlic tablets or capsules at night to reduce cholesterol.
Vitamins. A, B-complex, B6, B12, C (2g), E (400iu), daily.
Minerals. Chromium, Iodine, Potassium, Selenium, Magnesium, Manganese, Zinc.

"A man is as old as his arteries" – *Thomas Sydenham, 17th century physician.*

"A man's arteries are as old as he makes them" – *Robert Bell MD, 19th century physician.*

ATHLETE'S FOOT. Superficial infection of the skin of the feet by a fungus. Ringworm of the feet. Scaly lesions, sometimes with blisters. May be secondary infection from lymphadenitis or cellulitis – in which cases internal treatment would be indicated. Begins between the toes before spreading to plantar surface.
Differential diagnosis. Eczema, psoriasis or dermatitis from shoes.
Symptoms. Itchy redness and peeling. Sore raw areas left after removal of patches of skin. Possible invasion of other parts of the body: fingers, palms. The fungus can be picked up walking bare-feet in sport's clubs, schools or swimming baths. Worse in warm weather. Resistant to cleansing.
Treatment. *Tablets/capsules*. Echinacea, Thuja, Poke root.
Formula. Echinacea 2; Goldenseal 1; Poke root half. Mix. Dose – Powders: 500mg (two 00 capsules or one-third teaspoon). Liquid extracts: one 5ml teaspoon. Tinctures: two 5ml teaspoons. Thrice daily before meals.
Topical. Alternatives:– Thuja lotion applied on lint or suitable material (1 teaspoon Liquid extract Thuja in 1oz (30ml) distilled extract of Witch Hazel. Wild Indigo salve (1 teaspoon Wild Indigo powder in 1oz (30ml) honey – store in screw-top jar.

Aloe Vera, fresh juice or gel.

Tea Tree oil: if too strong may be diluted many times.

Comfrey cream. Castor oil. Mullein oil. Houseleek.

Black Walnut: tincture or Liquid extract. Cider vinegar. Bran bath.

Night foot-wash. With water to which has been added a few drops of tincture Thuja, Myrrh, or Tea Tree oil.

Light sprinkle of powdered Myrrh or Goldenseal in sock or shoe.

ATHLETE'S HEART. Jogger's heart. Excessive strain on the heart as in running and other sports.
Alternatives. *Teas*. Ginseng, Hawthorn, Marigold, Motherwort.
Tablets/capsules. Ginseng, Hawthorn, Motherwort.
Formula. Ginseng, Hawthorn, Mistletoe, Motherwort. Equal parts. Dose: Powders: 750mg (three 00 capsules or half a teaspoon). *Liquid extracts*: 1 teaspoon. *Tinctures*: 2 teaspoons. Thrice daily in water.
Practitioner. Tincture Arnica: 1-3 drops in honey, once or twice daily.
First-aid on the track. Ginseng. Arnica.
Diet. See DIET – HEART AND CIRCULATION.
Supplements. Vitamin E (500-1000iu daily), Chromium, Magnesium, Potassium, Selenium.

ATRIAL FIBRILLATION. Arrhythmia. Heart flutter. Disorderly uncoordinated contraction of atrial muscle wall, the ventricles responding irregularly.
Causes: thyrotoxicosis, valvular or coronary disease. Present in mitral stenosis and myocarditis. Precursor of heart failure. Carrying a bucket of coal upstairs may be sufficient to precipitate an attack.
Symptoms. Pulse irregular in time and force, breathlessness, visible pulse in neck, excessive heart beats of sudden onset or permanent, with breathlessness often from emotional excitement.
Treatment. Patient should avoid excessive physical exercise or give way to anxiety and depression.
Alternatives:– *Tea*. Equal parts: Hawthorn (berries or blossoms), Broom, Valerian. 1-2 teaspoons in each cup boiling water; infuse 5-15 minutes; dose – half-1 cup thrice daily.

Tablets/capsules. Hawthorn, Valerian, Motherwort.
Formula. Hawthorn 2; Passion flower 2; Broom 3. Mix. Dose: Powders: 750mg (three 00 capsules or half a teaspoon). Liquid extracts: 1 teaspoon. Tinctures: 2 teaspoons. In water or honey thrice daily.
Practitioner. Tincture Gelsemium (BPC 1973): 2-5 drops. Tincture Lily of the Valley: 0.5-1ml.
Undue violence. Tincture Gelsemium 1; Tincture Cactus 2. Mix. Dose: 5-10 drops. Where heart muscle is damaged, add 1 part Liquid Extract Black Cohosh.
Broom. Spartiol Drops, 20 drops thrice daily. (*Klein*)
Diet. See: DIET – HEART AND CIRCULATION.

AUSTRALIAN JOURNAL OF MEDICAL HERBALISM. Quarterly publication of the National Herbalists Association of Australia. Australian medicinal plants Government reports, case studies, books, plant abstracts. For subscription details and complimentary copy of the Journal contact: NHAA, PO Box 65, Kingsgrove NSW 2208, Australia. Tel: +61(02) 502 2938. Annual subscription (Aus) $40 (overseas applicants include $15 for air mail, otherwise sent by sea mail).

AUTISM. An abnormal condition of early childhood where the child is unable to make contact and develop relationships with people. Scanning techniques show that blood-flow in the frontal and temporal lobes is impaired. A passive child fails to become emotionally involved with other people and isolates himself. When the even tenor of his existence is disturbed he flies into a rage or retires into anxious brooding. Diagnosis is assisted by recognising young children being socially withdrawn and teenagers developing peculiar mannerisms and gait.

A child may avoid looking a person in the face, occupying himself or herself elsewhere to avoid direct contact. Obsessional motions include erratic movements of the fingers or limbs or facial twitch or grimace. Corrective efforts by parents to educate into more civilised behaviour meet with instant hostility, even hysteria. Hyperactivity may give rise to tantrums when every degree of self-control is lost. For such times, harmless non habit-forming herbal sedatives are helpful (Skullcap, Valerian, Mistletoe).

A link has been discovered between a deficiency of magnesium and autism. Magnesium is essential for the body's use of Vitamin B6. Nutritionists attribute the condition stemming from an inadequate intake of vitamins and minerals at pregnancy. Alcohol in the expectant mother is a common cause of such deficiencies. Personal requirements of autistic children will be higher than normal levels of Vitamin B complex (especially B6) C, E and Magnesium.

Such children grow up to be 'temperamental', of extreme sensibility, some with rare talents. Medicine is not required, but for crisis periods calm and poise can be restored by:–
Motherwort tea: equal parts, Motherwort, Balm and Valerian: 1-2 teaspoons to each cup boiling water; infuse 10-15 minutes; 1 cup 2-3 times daily. Honey renders it more palatable.
Alternatives:– *Teas, tablets or other preparations*: Hops, German Chamomile, Ginseng, Passion flower, Skullcap, Devil's Claw, Vervain, Mistletoe, Ginkgo.
Diet. Lacto-vegetarian. 2-3 bananas (for potassium) daily.
Supplements. Daily. Vitamin B-complex, Vitamin B6 50mg, Calcium, Magnesium, Zinc.
Aromatherapy. Inhalation of Lavender oil may act as a mood-lifter.
Note. A scientific study revealed a link with the yeast syndrome as associated with candidiasis.

AUTO IMMUNE DISEASE. An abnormal reaction of the body to groups of its own cells which the immune system attacks. In a case of anaemia, it may destroy the red blood cells. Failure of the body's tolerance mechanism.

The immune system is the body's internal defence armoury which protects from sickness and disease. White blood cells are influenced by the thymus gland and bone marrow to become "T" lymphocytes or "B" lymphocytes which absorb and destroy bacteria. There are times when these powerful defence components inflame and attack healthy tissue, giving rise to auto immune disease which may manifest as one of the numerous anaemic, rheumatic or nervous disorders, even cancer.

A watchful eye should be kept on any sub-acute, non-specific inflammation going on quietly over a long period – a certain indication of immune-inadequacy. It would appear that some unknown body intelligence operates behind the performance of the immune system; emotional and physic stresses such as divorce or job dissatisfaction can lead to a run-down of body defences. Some psychiatrists believe it to be a self-produced phenomenon due to an unresolved sense of guilt or a dislike of self. When this happens, bacterial, virus or fungus infections may invade and spread with little effective opposition. People who are happy at their home and work usually enjoy a robust immune system.

An overactive immune system may develop arthritis with painful joint inflammation, especially with a background of a fat-rich diet. A link between silicone implants and auto-immune disease is suspected.

"There is increasing evidence," writes Dr D. Addy, Consulting Pediatrician, "that fevers may enhance the defence mechanism against infection." (See: FEVER) "There is also increasing evidence of a weakening of the immune system through suppression of fevers by modern drugs. In this way, aspirin and other powerful anti-inflammatories may be responsible for feeble immune response."

White cell stimulators: Liquorice, Ginseng (Siberian), Goldenseal, Echinacea. These increase ability of white blood cells to attack bacteria and invading cells. Chinese medicine: Ginseng (men), Chinese Angelica (women).

Treatment. To strengthen body defences. Garlic, Borage, Comfrey, Agrimony, Balm, Chamomile (German), Echinacea, Horsetail, Liquorice, Lapacho, Sage, Wild Yam, Wild Indigo, Poke root, Thuja. Shiitake Mushroom. Reishi Mushroom, Chlorella..

Tea. Combine, equal parts, St John's Wort, Borage, Chamomile (German). 1 heaped teaspoon to each cup boiling water; infuse 15 minutes. 1 cup thrice daily.

Powders. Combine, Echinacea 4; Comfrey root 2; Wild Yam 1. 500mg (two 00 capsules, or one-third teaspoon) thrice daily.

Tinctures. Combine, Echinacea 4; Poke root 1; Thuja 1. 1-2 teaspoons in water thrice daily.

Tincture: Tincture Myrrh BPC 1973: 5-10 drops in water, morning and evening.

Decoctions. Horse-radish. Fenugreek seeds.

Bio-strath. Yeast-based herbal tonic. Exerts a positive influence on the immune system by rapid and marked increase in white blood cells.

Diet. Foods rich in essential fatty acids: nuts, seeds, beans, pulses, Evening Primrose oil, Cod Liver oil flavoured with mint or lemon. High protein: eggs, fish. (Low protein – acute stage). Foods rich in selenium. Yoghurt, cider vinegar, pineapple juice. Sugar has an immune suppressing effect.

Supplements. To rebuild immune system. Vitamins A, B5, B6, C, D, E. Zinc is required to produce histamine which is a vasodilator. Combination: zinc, selenium and GLA. Iron. Calcium.

Aromatherapy. Lavender oil: massage or baths.

Note. An alleged link exists between silicone implants and auto-immune disease. A new study reveals evidence that women with silicone breast implants who breast-feed their children put them at risk of developing systemic sclerosis. (*JAMA Jan 19 1994*)

AUTO-TOXAEMIA. Toxic means poisonous. Auto-toxaemia is self-poisoning of the blood and tissues from absorption of bacterial toxins formed during infection from acute or chronic inflammatory disease; or due to defective excretory organs (kidneys, bowel, etc). Raw foods produce little waste, but putrefaction of meats and other acid foods in the intestine and colon create an environment in which hostile bacteria flourish. Retrograde tissue change may be brought about by an unhealthy lifestyle and diet where an accumulation of cell wastes dispose to congestion and decomposition.

Treatment. An eliminative group of herbs include: expectorants, diuretics, lymphatics and alteratives to promote chemical breakdown and expulsion of the body's waste cell products.

Cleansing teas: Gotu Kola, Bogbean, Ginseng, Nettles, Alfalfa. Or, decoctions: Dandelion root (or Dandelion coffee), Burdock root, Yellow Dock root.

Tablets/capsules. Echinacea, Blue Flag root, Goldenseal, Ginseng, Poke root, Seaweed and Sarsaparilla, Garlic, "Natural Herb Tablet".

Powders, Liquid Extracts, Tinctures. Combine: Echinacea 2; Goldenseal 1; Myrrh quarter. Doses. Powders: Quarter of a teaspoon. Liquid extracts: 30-60 drops. Tinctures: 1-2 teaspoons. In water or honey thrice daily.

Enema: Chamomile.

Saunas and sweat-promoting exercises; epsom salts bath.

Diet. Regular raw food days. Garlic, Onions, Watercress. Low fat, low salt, high fibre. Drink distilled water. Three-day fast once monthly.

Supplements. Vitamin B-complex, Vitamin C 1g thrice daily, niacin, sulphur, zinc.

Auto-toxaemia does not refer to the toxaemia of pregnancy, known as eclampsia, for which a different group of herbs is relevant.

Removal of dental amalgam fillings is believed to assist recovery.

Note. Toxaemia may be caused by the action of toxic molecular fragments known as "free-radicals" which corrode cell membranes and kill cells. See: FREE-RADICALS.

AVENS. Herb Bennet. Colewort. *Geum urbanum L. German*: Nelkenwurz. *French*: Herb de St Benoît. *Italian*: Ambretta salvatica. *Spanish*: Gariofilea. Dried leaves and stems.

Action: anti-haemorrhagic, anti-inflammatory to the intestines and bowel. Gentle astringent, stomachic, antiseptic.

Uses. Ulcerative colitis, diarrhoea, diverticulitis, Crohn's disease. Combines well with Agrimony for these complaints.

Preparations. *Dosage*: 1-2 teaspoons herb to each cup boiling water; infuse 15 minutes. Half-1 cup 3-4 times daily. For fresh plant, double quantity of herb. *Liquid Extract* (herb or root), dose: 2-5ml. GSL

AVICENNA. 960-1037AD (*Arabic: Ibn Sina*). Famous Arabian physician. His medical system, *The Canon*, based largely on herbs, was for centuries a standard for the teaching and practice of Arabian medicine. His Advia-I-Qalbia (Precious Book of Heart Remedies) is being re-discovered and approved by Arabian medical scientists. Avicenna, himself, attached great importance to his description of 62 cardiac medicines. He was the first to note the sweet taste of the urine of diabetes.

AVOCADO. *Persea americana*, Mill. Moisturiser for the skin. Contains beta carotene precursor of vitamin A, Vitamins D, E and chlorophyll. For dry skin. Powdered seeds used by Indians for diarrhoea and dysentery. Oil or pulp softens hard skin, beautifies the complexion, stimulates hair growth, aids healing of wounds, acts as an emmenagogue and aphrodisiac.

Bactericidal against Gram-positive bacteria, especially Staphylococcus aureau (*I. Neeman et al., Appl. Microboil., 19, 470 (1970)*).

Avocados lower cholesterol levels.

AYURVEDA MEDICINE. System of sacred medicine originating from Ancient India, dating from 1000 to 3000BC. Most likely it goes back to Babylonian times. It is generally believed that Western medicine has grown out of Greek medicine which, in turn scholars claim to have come from India.

Ayur ("life") and veda ("science"), the science of life, is part of the Hindu writings – the Artharva-veda. By 500BC many of these writings, including a vast collection of 'Materia medica' gravitated to the University of Benares, to be joined 700 years later with another huge volume of medical literature which together formed the basis of the Ayurveda system. In rural India where Western medicine is absent it is still practised by 80 per cent of the population. Like the medical culture of China, that of India is among the oldest in the world. Today, its practitioners are skilled in gynaecology, obstetrics and other specialties.

It is a branch of Holistic medicine whereby body imbalances are restored by a natural regime, baths, fasting, enemas, cleansing diets and herbs. Time is given up to meditation and prayer for which many mantras exist. Those who practise it support the role of preventive medicine, insisting it is not only a system of cure but a metaphysical way of life touching body, mind and spirit. A strict daily discipline embraces yoga and special foods to maintain a sound and wholesome life. Ayurvedic medicine regards the herb Valerian as important for epilepsy.

Important Ayurvedic medicines include Borage, Liquorice, Cinnamon, Garlic, Gotu Kola and Wild Yam, renowned for their versatility. Of special importance to this system of medicine is the hypoglycaemic plant, *Gymnema sylvestre*, used since the 6th century for a condition known as "honey urine", which today grows in popularity in the West for the treatment of diabetes.

BACH, DR EDWARD 1886-1936. English Physician. Qualified in medicine at University College Hospital, before being appointed pathologist at a London hospital. He was convinced that the cause of most diseases was in the mind and devised a method of treating the patient's personality.

After years of study in a remote Norfolk village he concluded there were 38 states of mind which, if corrected led to improvement of certain physical conditions. Being 'psychic', he claimed to feel the vibrations of plants and their reactions to his body when holding them in his hand; some causing pain, nausea, nervous excitability or producing a fever. He divined the 'soul' of a number of different plants, matching each to a particular state of mind.

It was claimed that destructive moods produced body toxins which lowered vitality and natural resistance. He prepared what are now known as the Bach Remedies from the petals of wild flowers with which he overcame depression, fear and abnormal mental states. He treated the attitude of mind, illness being a cleansing process of mind and body. Thus he became the first Holistic practitioner.

He 'potentised' remedies by immersing petals in fresh spring water in the sun and preserving. Though his cures are still regarded as 'anecdotal', the remedies enjoy world-wide recognition. Dr W.T. Garton writes: "Dr Bach's remedies have the power to dispel gloom, anxiety, hate and fear, and with them go many of the physical ills which are the natural outcome of such frames of mind. The remedies are not a substitute for courageous living, but may enable us to better cope with life."

The Bach Centre, Mount Vernon, Wallingford, Oxon, England.

BACH REMEDIES. Prescribed according to mental symptoms or personality traits:

1. **Agrimony**. Those who suffer considerable inner torture which they try to dissemble behind a facade of cheerfulness.
2. **Aspen**. Apprehension and foreboding. Fears of *unknown* origin.
3. **Beech**. Critical and intolerant of others. Arrogant.
4. **Centaury**. Weakness of will; those who let themselves be exploited or imposed upon – become subservient; difficulty in saying 'no'. Human doormat.
5. **Cerato**. Those who doubt their own judgement, seeks advice of others. Often influenced and misguided.
6. **Cherry Plum**. Fear of mental collapse/desperation/loss of control and fear of causing harm. Vicious rages.
7. **Chestnut Bud**. Refusal to learn by experience; continually repeating the same mistakes.
8. **Chicory**. The over-possessive, demands respect or attention (selfishness), likes others to conform to their standards. makes martyr of oneself.
9. **Clematis**. Indifferent, inattentive, dreamy, absent-minded. Mental escapist from reality.
10. **Crab Apple**. Cleanser. Feels unclean or ashamed of ailments. Self disgust/hatred. House proud.
11. **Elm**. Temporarily overcome by inadequacy or responsibility. Normally very capable.
12. **Gentian**. Despondent. Easily discouraged and dejected.
13. **Gorse**. Extreme hopelessness – pessimist – 'Oh, what's the use?'.
14. **Heather**. People who are obsessed with their own troubles and experiences. Talkative 'bores' – poor listeners.
15. **Holly**. For those who are jealous, envious, revengeful and suspicious. For those who hate.
16. **Honeysuckle**. For those with nostalgia and who constantly dwell in the past. Homesickness.
17. **Hornbeam**. 'Monday morning' feeling but once started, task is usually fulfilled. Procrastination.
18. **Impatiens**. Impatience, irritability.
19. **Larch**. Despondency due to lack of self-confidence; expectation of failure, so fails to make the attempt. Feels inferior though has the ability.
20. **Mimulus**. Fear of *known* things. Shyness, timidity.
21. **Mustard**. Deep gloom like an overshadowing dark cloud that descends for *no known reason* which can lift just as suddenly. Melancholy.
22. **Oak**. Brave determined types. Struggles on in illness and against adversity despite setbacks. Plodders.
23. **Olive**. Exhaustion – drained of energy – everything an effort.
24. **Pine**. Feelings of guilt. Blames self for mistakes of others. Feels unworthy.
25. **Red Chestnut**. Excessive fear and over caring for others especially those held dear.
26. **Rock Rose**. Terror, extreme fear or panic.
27. **Rock Water**. For those who are hard on themselves – often overwork. Rigid minded, self denying.
28. **Scleranthus**. Uncertainty/indecision/vacillation. Fluctuating moods.
29. **Star of Bethlehem**. For all the effect of serious news, or fright following an accident, etc.
30. **Sweet Chestnut.** Anguish of those who have reached the limit of endurance – only oblivion left.
31. **Vervain**. Over-enthusiasm, over-effort; straining. Fanatical and highly-strung. Incensed by injustices.
32. **Vine**. Dominating/inflexible/ambitious/tyrannical/autocratic. Arrogant Pride. Good leaders.
33. **Walnut**. Protection remedy from powerful influences, and helps adjustment to any transition

or change, e.g. puberty, menopause, divorce, new surroundings.
34. **Water Violet**. Proud, reserved, sedate types, sometimes 'superior'. Little emotional involvement but reliable/dependable.
35. **White Chestnut**. Persistent unwanted thoughts. Pre-occupation with some worry or episode. Mental arguments.
36. **Wild Oat**. Helps determine one's intended path in life.
37. **Wild Rose**. Resignation, apathy. Drifters who accept their lot, making little effort for improvement – lacks ambition.
38. **Willow**. Resentment and bitterness with 'not fair' and 'poor me' attitude.
39. **Rescue Remedy**. A combination of Cherry Plum, Clematis, Impatiens Rock Rose, Star of Bethlehem. All purpose emergency composite for causes of trauma, anguish, bereavement, examinations, going to the dentist, etc.

BACKACHE. Back pain may arise from different causes – from prolapsed disc to a diseased vertebra requiring hospital treatment. For specific treatments reference should be made to appropriate entries: rheumatism, arthritis, fibrositis, lumbago, osteoporosis, sciatica, myalgia, 'slipped disc', etc.

Pain in upper spine and right shoulder: investigate for gallstones. Thousands suffer chronic back pain because of an enzyme defect in the blood. Such defect is the cause of an inability to clear fibrin, a protein which repairs damaged tissue.

Alternatives:– *"Whole in One" Tea*. Mix, equal parts: Hops, Valerian, Buchu, 1-2 teaspoons to each cup boiling water: infuse 15 minutes; 1 cup 2-3 times daily. Pinch Cayenne pepper enhances action.
Decoction. Mix, equal parts: Valerian, Juniper, Black Cohosh. 2 teaspoons to each cup water simmered gently 20 minutes; half cup 2-3 times daily.
Powders. To alleviate low backache accompanying fluid retention. Dandelion leaf 60. Uva Ursi 15. Couch Grass 15. Buchu 10. Dose: half a teaspoon after meals thrice daily: children over 12 years.
Tablets/capsules. Prickly Ash bark, Devil's Claw, Juniper.
Tinctures. Mix, Juniper 2; Black Cohosh 1; Guaiacum quarter. 15-60 drops 2-3 times daily.
Topical. Analgesic cream, Olbas oil, Golden Fire, Stiff Neck Salve, Epsom salts soaks. Aromatherapy: mix essential oils, Rosemary 1 drop, Juniper 1 drop, Thyme 2 drops: add to 2 teaspoons Almond oil. After massage, wrap affected area with damp hot towel.
Diet. High fibre, low salt, low fat, Dandelion coffee.
Supplements. Vitamin B-complex, Niacin, Vitamins C, E. Dolomite. Evening Primrose oil capsules. Two Garlic capsules at night. Chiropractic. Osteopathy.

BACTERIA. A vast group of single-celled microscopic organisms living in the soil, in water, or in the human body as parasites and which are responsible for much human disease. They are of three types: bacilli (rod-shaped), cocci (spherical), and spirochete (curved coils). Bacteria can only be identified with the aid of a microscope.

One school of medical thought believes bacteria to be a by-product of disease and not a direct cause of infection. Dr Pettenknofer, famous Viennese physician sought to demonstrate this when he surprised bystanders when he deliberately swallowed a glass of water containing millions of active cholera bacilli. He did not contract the disease or die as feared. Other similar demonstrations have been made to prove that before germs can harm the body, cell-soil on which they flourish must have undergone toxic degeneration. It is believed that when body resistance is low, hostile bacteria invade tissue and destroy cells. See: ANTIBACTERIALS.

BAD BREATH. Aetiology: Infection of throat, lungs, gullet, or stomach. A common cause is bad teeth and gums. The rock-like scale (plaque) on or between teeth may be due to neglected mouth hygiene. Halitosis is the anti-social disease. Where stomach and intestines are at fault, charcoal biscuits have some reputation.

Bad breath is often indicative of toxaemia or defective elimination via liver, kidneys and skin which should be the focus of treatment. Palliatives such as Papaya fruit (or tablets), Peppermint or Chlorophyll may not reach the heart of the trouble which could demand deeper-acting agents.

Liver disorders (Blue Flag root); hyperacidity (Meadowsweet); excessive smoking and alcohol (Wormwood); bad teeth and septic tonsils (Poke root); diverticulitis (Fenugreek seeds); gastro-intestinal catarrh (Senna, Agrimony, Avens); smell of acetone as of diabetes (Goat's Rue); constipation (Senna, Psyllium seed).

May be necessary for serious ear, nose and throat problems to be resolved by surgery. For blockage of respiratory channels, Olbas oil, Tea Tree oil or Garlic drops relieve congestion. Many cases have chronic gingivitis and arise from dental problems improved by 1 part Tea Tree oil to 20 parts water used as a spray. Alfalfa sprouts have a sweetening effect upon the breath. Chew Parsley or Peppermint.

Alternatives. *Teas*. Dill seeds, Fennel seeds, Sage, Nettles, Mint, Liquorice root, Alfalfa, Wormwood. Dandelion (coffee). Parsley.
Tablets/capsules. Blue Flag root, Goldenseal, Echinacea. Wild Yam. Chlorophyll. Calamus.
Powders. Mix, parts: Blue Flag root 1; Myrrh

half; Liquorice half. Dose: 250mg (one 00 capsule or one-sixth teaspoon) thrice daily before meals.
Gargle. 5 drops Tincture Myrrh to glass water, frequently.
Diet. Lacto-vegetarian. Lemon juice.
Supplements. Vitamins A, B-complex, B6, Niacin, C (500mg).

BAEL. Bengal Quince. *Aegle marmelos*, Correa. *German*: Bhelbaum. *French*: Bel Indien. *Italian*: Bella indiana. *Indian*: Bela. Dried half ripe fruits.
Action: Astringent. Contains coumarins, flavonoids, alkaloids, mucilage, nutrient.
Uses. Reputation in India as a specific for colitis, dysentery, diarrhoea. One of the sacred Hindu remedies. Said to increase fertility. Indigestion.
Preparations. *Liquid Extract*, 1 in 1. Dose: 1-2 teaspoons. Thrice daily.
Tincture. 2-4 teaspoons. Thrice daily

BALANCE – DISORDERS OF. Associated with a number of conditions including PMT, low blood pressure, etc. Treatment: same as for MENIERE'S DISEASE.

BALANITIS. Inflammation of the glans penis and prepuce.
Symptoms: soreness, itching, sometimes burning.
Aetiology: psoriasis, trichomoniasis, candida, drug reactions, sexually transmitted disease. In diabetes, balanitis is a possibility from irritation by urine. Often associated with phimosis: tightness of the foreskin. Analogous with the clitoris.
Alternatives. *Teas or Decoctions*. Blood root, Echinacea, Garlic, Goldenseal, Gravel root, Kava-Kava, Myrrh, Wild Indigo, Rosemary, Parsley root, Sarsaparilla.
Tablets/capsules. Echinacea. Sarsaparilla. Goldenseal. Chaparral.
Powders. Equal parts: Kava-Kava, Myrrh, Goldenseal. Mix. Dose: 500mg (two 00 capsules or one-third teaspoon) thrice daily.
Liquid extracts. Combine Echinacea 2; Myrrh half; Goldenseal half. Mix. 15-60 drops 3 times daily, in water.
Practitioner. Tincture Blood root, BHP (1983) 5ml . . . Tincture Gravel root BHP (1983) 20ml . . . Tincture Goldenseal BPC (1949) 5ml . . . Decoction Sarsaparilla Co Conc, BPC, to 100ml. Sig: 5ml (3i) tds Aq cal. pc. (*A. Barker*)
Topical (1) For cleansing after retraction of foreskin: one drop Tincture Myrrh to one ounce (30ml) Distilled extract of Witch Hazel. (2) Aloe Vera gel. (3) Eucalyptus oil, dilute many times.

BALDNESS. See: HAIR LOSS.

BALM. Lemon balm. Melissa officinalis L. *German*: Zitronen-melisse. *French*: Citronelle. *Spanish*: Erba cedrata. *Italian*: Cedronella. *Indian*: Badaranj. *Part used*: herb.
Action: antispasmodic, antidepressant, antihistamine, antiviral – topical application, anti-stress, antiflatulent, febrifuge, mild tranquilliser, nerve relaxant, heart-sedating effect.
Antibacterial, especially against myco-bacterium phlei and streptococcus haemolytica (*H. Wagner & L. Springkmeyer. Dtsch, Apoth., Zrg, 113, 1159 (1973)*)
Uses. Hyperthyroidism, dizziness, migraine, nervous heart or stomach, insomnia, little energy, stomach cramps, urinary infection, feverishness in children, mumps, shingles, reaction to vaccination or inoculation. Nervous excitability.
Psychiatry. To strengthen the brain in its resistance to shock and stress; low spirits, restlessness, fidgety limbs, "cold and miserable", anxiety neurosis.
Rudolf F. Weiss MD. Balm protects the cerebrum of the brain and is effective in treatment of autonomic disorders – an action similar to modern tranquillisers . . . usually combined with Peppermint. (*Herbal Medicine, Beaconsfield Publishers*)
Preparations. *Tea*: 1-2 teaspoons to each cup boiling water; infuse 5 minutes; 1 cup freely.
Liquid Extract: BHP (1983). 1:1 in 45 per cent alcohol; dose – 2-4ml.
Tincture BHP (1983) 1:5 in 45 per cent alcohol; dose 2-6ml. Thrice daily.
Powders. Two 210mg capsules thrice daily. (*Arkocaps*)
Traditional combination: Balm and Peppermint (equal parts) tea. 2 teaspoons to each cup boiling water; infuse 15 minutes; cup at bedtime for restful sleep or to improve digestion. (*Rudolf F. Weiss MD*)
Historical. John Evelyn writes: "Balm is sovereign for the brain. It strengthens the memory and powerfully chases away melancholy."
Balm Bath. 8oz dried (or 12oz fresh) herb to 10 pints (7 litres) boiling water: infuse 15 minutes: add to bathwater. For sleeplessness or nervous heart. Aromatherapy: 10-20 drops Oil Melissa (Balm) added to bath water.
Note. Combined with a pinch of Nutmeg it has a reputation for nervous headache (migraine) and neuralgia. Popular in all European pharmacopoeias. GSL

BALM OF GILEAD. Poplar buds. *Populus gileadensis*. *French*: Baumier. *German*: Mekkabalsambaum. *Spanish*: Bilsamo. *Italian*: Balsamo della Mecca. *Indian*: Gungal. Leaf buds.
Action. Mild analgesic (forerunner of aspirin), Febrifuge, Anti-inflammatory, Stimulating diuretic (resin), Antiseptic, Circulatory stimulant, Expectorant. Contains salicylates.
Uses. Laryngitis. Chronic bronchitis. Safe for children's chest troubles. Traditional: for coughs,

colds and sore throats. Buds used by North American Indians for muscular and circulatory aches and pains (*Dr A. Clapp, 1852*).
Side effects. None known.
Preparations. *Tea*. 2-3 buds to each cup boiling water; infuse 15 minutes. Half-1 cup 3-hourly, acute cases; thrice daily, chronic.
Tincture, BHC (vol 1). 1:5 45 per cent Ethanol, 4-8ml.
Balm of Gilead Cough Mixture (Potter's). Each 10ml contains Acet. Scill. BP 0.339ml; Acetic acid (5.5 per cent) extractive from Lobelia (1-12.5) 0.148ml; Ipecac Liquid extract BP 0.004ml; 30 per cent alcoholic extractive (1:1) from each of 100mg Balm of Gilead buds and 200mg Lungwort lichen in a sweetened flavoured vehicle. GSL

BALMONY. Turtlebloom *Chelone glabra L. German*: Schildblume. *French*: Galane, Chélone. *Italian*: Galana spicata.
Action: Cholagogue, Antidepressant, Antemetic, Laxative, Liver tonic.
Uses. Keynote: liver. Inflammation of gall bladder. Jaundice. Gall stones, Colic.
Preparations. Thrice daily.
Tea. 1 teaspoon to each cup boiling water; infuse 15 minutes. Half-1 cup.
Liquid Extract BHP (1983) 1:1 in 25 per cent alcohol. Dose: 2-4ml.
Tincture BHP (1983) 1:10 in 45 per cent alcohol. Dose: 1-2ml. Powdered herb: 1-2g. GSL

BAMBOO. Tabashir. *Bambousa arundinacea. German*: Bambus. *French*: Bambon. *Spanish*: Semenedia. *Italian*: Bambi. *Indian*: Bansakapura. *Arabian*: Tabashura. *Chinese*: Tan-chu. Species of bamboo. Contains 97 per cent silica.
Action: immune enhancer Aphrodisiac, tonic, pectoral. Calcium-fixer in bones.
Uses. Repair of fractured bone. Of value for osteo-arthritis, rheumatism, stiff joints, cartilage fragility as in osteoporosis, pregnancy, senile dementia, weak spine – tendency to dislocation of vertebrae. Arterio-sclerosis. Brittle hair and nails.
Preparations. *Decoction*: Quarter of a teaspoon to each cup water gently simmered 20 minutes. Dose: half a cup thrice daily.
Powder. Two 320mg capsules thrice daily (*Arkocaps*).

BAMBOO SPINE. See: ANKYLOSING SPONDYLITIS.

BANANA. Nutrient food.
Uses. Low fat, low calorie food for weight control. Rich in potassium, pectin, Vitamin B6, inositol. Part of Cape Canaveral astronaut's diet to counteract rapid heart beats in inter-space flights. Gastric ulcer: diet on bananas and cheese for one month or two. (Jamaica traditional)

BAREFOOT DOCTOR'S MANUAL. Published 1970 by the Institute of Traditional Chinese Medicine of Hunan Province, China, to supply its barefoot doctors with a basic guide in their work of serving the rural population ("... because they worked in the paddy fields like any other commune member, barefooted and with trouser legs rolled up, they were given the name 'barefoot doctors' " (*Pekin Review, 1977*)).

BARBER'S ITCH. Sycosis.
See: FOLLICULITIS.

BARBERRY BARK. *Berberis vulgaris L. French*: Vinettier. *German*: Berberize. *Italian*: Berberi. *Indian*: Zirishk. Stem bark.
Action. Liver stimulant, cholagogue, antiseptic, alterative. Tonic to spleen and pancreas, antemetic, digestive tonic. Hypotensive. Mild sedative and anticonvulsant. Uterine stimulant. Anti-haemorrhagic, Febrifuge, Anti-inflammatory, Anti-diarrhoeal, Amoebicidal, Bactericidal.
Uses. Sluggish liver, jaundice, biliousness, gastritis, gallstones, itching anus, ulcerated mouth, malaria, sandfly fever, toxaemia from drugs and environmental chemicals. Shingles, bladder disorders, leucorrhoea, renal colic. Old gouty constitutions react favourably. Cholera (animals). Leukopaenia due to chemotherapy.
Combinations. With Yarrow for malaria. With Gelsemium for pain in the coccyx (tailbone). With Fringe Tree bark for skin disorders.
Contra-indications: pregnancy, diarrhoea.
Preparations. Thrice daily.
Decoction: 1 teaspoon to each cup cold water left to steep overnight. Half-1 cup.
Liquid Extract: BHP (1983) 1:1 in 25 per cent alcohol. Dose (1-3ml).
Tincture: BHP (1983) 1:10 in 60 per cent alcohol. Dose (2-4ml).
Powdered bark, dose, 1-2g. GSL

BARKER, ARTHUR. FNIMH. Consulting Medical Herbalist. President: National Institute of Medical Herbalists. Author: The Herbal Pocket Prescriber. (*Eardley*)

BARLEY. *Hordeum distichon L.* An almost perfect food. High in fibre, calcium, iron, magnesium and potassium. High in lysine, an essential amino acid. One of the best and cheapest cholesterol blockers. A grain that should have a prominent place on the dining table. This nutritive demulcent, taken as Barley-water, is still used in kidney, intestinal and bowel disorders.

Malt extract (with, or without Cod Liver oil).
Green Barley. Juice of young Barley leaves harvested when 12 inches in height. A concentrate of vitamins, mineral nutrients, amino acids, enzymes and chlorophyll. Seven times richer in Vitamin C than oranges; five times richer in

iron than spinach; has 25 times the potassium of wheat. High in the enzyme that slows the ageing of cells – superoxide dismutase (SOD). Said to be of value for malignancy and effective against pigmentation of the skin (melanosis, and other skin diseases). (*Yoshihide Hagiwara MD, pharmacologist, Japan*)

Immune system protective. Constipation. Anaemia.

Prepare in a juicer, young Barley leaves: 1 wineglassful night and morning.

Green powder: (Green Barley essence) (*Natural Flow*)

BARTHOLIN'S CYST. Bartholin's glands are two lubricating glands at the entrance of the vagina which may be blocked by a cyst or plugged with mucous secretion.
Symptoms: Soreness and discomfort between legs, with swelling sometimes as big as a pigeon's egg. Abscesses form when drainage is impeded.
Treatment. Surgery: a permanent opening created to facilitate drainage or, in case of a cyst, its extirpation. Responses have been observed in external use of highly diluted oil of Eucalyptus.
Alternatives: internal or external use of Walnut leaves. Topical use of fresh Plantain juice. Cider vinegar.

BARTRAM, JOHN AND WILLIAM. 18th century botanists who opened up the then American wilderness in search of medicinal and ornamental plants. They blazed a trail through hostile Indian territory in early pioneering days, bringing back plants to stock the first botanical garden in America. A knowledge of healing by medicinal plants and barks enabled these simple pious Quakers to render aid to other settlers and to the Indians from whom they learnt the art of healing. It is believed their activities would have been devoted exclusively to healing had they not received a commission from King George III to explore and report on the natural history of the country. The Bartrams' talent in the practice of natural medicine impressed the Swedish explorer/botanist Peter Kalm who noted formulae in his diary.

The Bartrams' friends included Benjamin Franklin and Washington who often visited their house, resting in the garden with giant trees planted by the Bartrams. John (1699-1777) was described by Linnaeus as the "greatest contemporary natural botanist". His son, William, was also an explorer-naturalist and artist whose works are now collector's pieces.

BASIL. Sweet Basil. *Ocimum basilicum L. French*: Basilique. *German*: Basilikum. *Italian*: Bassilico. *Spanish*: Albahaca. *Indian*: Nazbo. *Chinese*: Hsiang-ts'ai. *Malayan*: Tirunitru rachchá. Part used: leaves. Contains high levels of Vitamins A and C. (*Marsh*)
Action. Antispasmodic, carminative, galactagogue, sedative (mild), stomachic, antibacterial, vermifuge, anti-depressant. Adrenal stimulant.
Uses. Nervous irritability, increase secretion of milk in nursing mothers, nausea, vomiting. Little used in present-day UK herbalism. Stomach cramp (China). Recovery after hysterectomy.

Combines well with Lemon Balm for depression.
Preparations. *Tea*. 1 teaspoon dried (2 teaspoons fresh) herb to each cup boiling water. Infuse 10 minutes. Dose: One-third-1 cup thrice daily.
Salads: addition of 2-3 fresh leaves as a nerve sustainer.
External. Basil oil protects against some types of fungus. Fresh juice – lotion for warts, stings.

No longer used in Aromatherapy, or in pregnancy.

BASTYR COLLEGE OF NATUROPATHIC MEDICINE. An institution for training and granting of the qualification, Doctor of Naturopathic Medicine, including study of two years basic medical sciences and two years clinical sciences. The philosophical approach includes personal responsibility for one's own health, natural treatment of the whole person, prevention of disease, and to awaken the patient's inherent healing powers. Of university status. Address: 144 N.E. 54th, Seattle, WA 98105, USA. See: NATUROPATHY.

BATHS. The healing and soothing action of herbs used in the bath is well-known. An infusion, usually 1oz (30g) herb (double the amount for fresh herb) is infused in 2 pints boiling water for 15 minutes. Strain and pour into bath. Use of soap destroys its effect. Alternatives are essential oils of aromatherapy: 10-15 drops to 2 pints boiling water. General tonic: Thyme. To induce sleep: Hops, Lime flowers, Lavender, Balm. To dispel body odour: Bergamot, Rosemary, Lavender.
Hyperactive children: Chamomile. Nerve stress: Valerian. Irritable rashes of eczema or psoriasis: bran (2, 3-4 handfuls).
Rheumatic joints: Mustard (2 teaspoons).
Low blood pressure: Rosemary.
Feverish conditions: Yarrow.
Any may be used for Sitz or foot bath. Crush fresh herbs with rolling pin.
Seaweed bath. Take handful freshly-gathered seaweed; tie in muslin bag (or nylon stocking); use as a sponge as a relaxing rub in bath or ablutions. Skin nutrient; sleep restorative.

BAY LEAVES. Sweet Bay. Victor's laurel. *Laurus nobilis L.* Held in high esteem as a medicine and prophylactic by the ancient Greeks. *French*: Laurier franc. *German*: Edler Lorbeerbaum. *Spanish*: Lauro. *Italian*: Lauro franco. Young stems and old leaves yield highest content of oil.

Action: antiseptic, antifungal, gastric tonic, nutritive, mild sedative. Oil has mild bactericidal and anti-fungal properties. Anti-dandruff, Carminative, Cholagogue, Vermifuge.
Uses. Weak digestion, poor appetite; hot and soothing to a 'cold' stomach. Urinary infections (decoction). Chest infections (berries). Rheumatic pains (seed oil, externally).

Reportedly used in cancer. (*J.L. Hartwell, Lloydia, 32, 247, 1969*)

Boosts insulin activity. (*American Health, 1989, Nov 8, p96*)
Preparations. Average dose: 2-4 grams. Thrice daily.
Decoction. 1oz crushed leaves to 1 pint water simmered down to three-quarters of its volume. Dose. Half a cup thrice daily.
Bay bath. Place crushed leaves in a small muslin bag and steep in hot water.
Diet: taken as a culinary herb with potatoes, salads, soups, etc. A source of oleic acid and linoleic acid.

Contact dermatitis may sometimes occur as an allergy on handling the oil.

BAYBERRY BARK. Wax Myrtle. *Myrica cerifera L.* Root bark. *German*: Wachsgagel. *French*: Cirier. *Spanish*: Arrayàn. *Italian*: Mirica cerifera. *Indian*: Kâiphala. *Malayan*: Maru tam toli.
Action. Diffusive circulatory stimulant, Deobstruent, Tonic. Astringent (local). Diaphoretic (in hot infusion). Bactericidal. Spermatocidal.
Uses. Mucous colitis, diarrhoea. Congestive catarrhal conditions of mucous membranes. Leucorrhoea, prolapse of the womb. Tuberculosis diathesis. To stimulate a sluggish circulation. Colds and fevers to promote sweating. Nasal polypi (powdered bark snuff). Bleeding from lungs, stomach and bowels. Candidiasis (douche). Leg ulcers (dusting powder). Diphtheria (local application to throat).

An essential ingredient of Dr Thomson's Composition powder. Combination: with Turkey Rhubarb, Goldenseal, Slippery Elm or Fenugreek seeds for chronic stomach/intestine disorders and irritable bowel syndrome.
Preparations. Thrice daily.
Decoction: 1 teaspoon powdered bark to each cup water; remove vessel when boiling point is reached: dose, quarter to half a cup.
Liquid extract BHP (1983). 1:1 in 45 per cent alcohol: dose, 0.6-2ml.
Powdered bark, dose 0.6-2g.
Poultices, powdered bark for ulceration.
Peerless Composition Essence (Potter's). Ingredient. GSL

BEACH, DR WOOSTER. (1794-1868) Scholar and physician. Of the eclectic school of physicians whose pharmacy was drawn from botanic medicine. In 1829 he founded the Medical Society of the United States for teaching the various branches of medical science and botanic medicine. Their methods became so popular that the American Government granted many charters for schools to teach the system.

Beach made many long visits to Britain gleaning information from the British Museum, Guy's Hospital and from consulting medical herbalists. Ex-Professor of several American universities, he organised herbal medication into a system defined in his books: *"American Practice of Medicine"*, *"Midwifery"*, and *"Family Physician"* which proved a bestseller.

BEAN HUSKS. French beans. *Phaseolus vulgaris L. French*: Haricot. *German*: Bohnen. *Spanish*: Habichuela seca. *Italian*: Fagoilo. *Indian*: Khurdya. *Chinese*: Lu-tou. *Iranian*: Bendo mash.
Constituents: phaseoline, mucilage, minerals including sulphur.
Keynote: kidneys. *Part used*: pods without beans.
Action: hypotensive, diuretic, anti-diabetic, resolvent, glycaemic – to regulate blood sugar.
Uses. Water retention. Albuminuria (proteinuria), especially of pregnancy. Oedema of cardiac origin. Premenstrual tension. Diabetes mellitus. Hyperinsulinism. To induce loss of weight. Swollen legs and ankles. Hypoglycaemia. Sometimes given in combination with Bladderwrack.
Preparations. Capt Frank Roberts Bean Cure. 40 grams of the *dried herb* soaked for 6 hours in 750ml (1 and a half pints) cold water. Boil, half an hour. Drink all over 1-2 days for water retention.
Roasted beans: nutritious coffee substitute.
French bean water (after cooking beans without salt) used traditionally in France for a soaked-lint compress for leg ulcer.
Powder. Capsules, 200mg. Dose: 8 capsules: 2 in morning, 3 at midday, 3 in the evening, at beginning of meals. (*Arkocaps*)

BEANS, BROAD (*Vivia faba*), leguminosae.

Contain natural L-dopa which penetrates the intestinal epithelial cells and is transported through the blood stream to the brain capillaries where it is converted into dopamine, of value in the nutrition of Parkinson patients.

Beans should be eaten, not when fully mature, but when young, with a thin skin and easy to digest. Ninety per cent afflicted with Parkinson's disease at an early age respond quickly. It is easily oxidised two or three days after harvest and vanishes completely as the plant stops growing and begins to dry. Patients report a marked improvement each time they eat a meal of fresh broad beans and may not require drug treatment "for many hours". The young beans are immersed in boiling water for three minutes, and may be eaten as a preventative.

BEAR GRASS. *Yucca filamentosa*. Carminative. For biliousness and temporal headache. Tea or tincture of flowers.

BEARBERRY. Arctostaphylos uva-ursi, Spreng. *French*: Busserole. *German*: Gemeine Bärrentraube. I*talian*: Uva d'orso. Dried leaves.

Contains hydroquinones, iridoids, flavonoids. *Keynote:* highly acid urine.
Action. Diuretic, urinary antiseptic, astringent, haemostatic, oxytocic.
Uses: smarting cystitis, painful micturition, urethritis, blood in the urine, urinary retention, oedema of legs or face, bed-wetting, diarrhoea, dysentery, profuse menstruation, leucorrhoea (chronic).
Combinations. With Dandelion root for dropsy. With Broom, Buchu and Clivers for inflammation of urinary tract and bladder. With Couch Grass as a urinary antiseptic.

Soothing combination for kidney relief and renal backache: Bearberry 15 per cent, Couchgrass 15 per cent, Wild Carrot 15 per cent, Buchu 10 per cent, Alfalfa 45 per cent. Tea: 1 heaped teaspoon to each cup boiling water. Infuse 10 minutes, 1 cup twice daily.
Preparations. Thrice daily.
Tea. 1 heaped teaspoon to each cup boiling water; infuse 15 minutes; Dose: half-1 cup.
Liquid extract BHC Vol 1. 1:1, in 25 per cent ethanol. Dose: 1.5-2.5ml.
Tincture BHC Vol 1. 1:5, in 25 per cent ethanol. Dose: 2-4ml.
Powder. 250mg. (One 00 capsule or one-sixth teaspoon).
Tablets. Popular combination. Powdered Dandelion root BHP (1983) 90mg; powdered Horsetail extract 3:1 10mg; powdered Uva Ursi extract 3:1 75mg. To assist urinary flow and prevent fluid retention.
Precautions. Not used in pregnancy, kidney disorders, lactation. Large doses may cause vomiting. Should not be used for more than two weeks without consulting a practitioner. GSL

BEARSFOOT, AMERICAN. *Polymnia uvedalia L*. Root
Action: Stimulant alterative, spleen tonic. Lymphatic. Anti-malarial. Analgesic (mild). Laxative.
Uses. Swollen glands. Liver congestion. Splenetic enlargement. Mastitis, to reduce benign swelling.
Preparations. Thrice daily.
Decoction: 1 teaspoon shredded root to large cup water simmered gently 5 minutes. Dose: One-third of a cup.
Liquid Extract: 30-60 drops.

Externally as a hair tonic. GSL

BECHET'S DISEASE. Ulceration of the mouth and genitals, with iritis. Hippocrates wrote of it as one of the epidemics of Ancient Greece. Prof Behcot, himself, believed it to be due to a virus. Afflicted age group: 30s-40s.
Symptoms. Vulva or penis swollen and itching. Neuritis of the eye with possible ensuing blindness. A specific disease unrelated to herpes simplex which it resembles. There is no evidence that it is venereal. Basic pathology is inflammation of the veins, arteries and capillaries (Nettles). Thrombosis is possible (Hawthorn).
Treatment. *Tea*. (1) Nettles. Or (2): place half an ounce Burdock root in 1 pint water; simmer gently 20 minutes: Add 1oz Nettles. Allow to steep for further 15 minutes. Dose: 1 cup thrice daily.
Tablets/capsules. Kelp, Echinacea, Blue Flag.
Tinctures. Combine Echinacea 2; Goldenseal three-quarters; Myrrh quarter. Dose: 1-2 teaspoons in water thrice daily.
Practitioner. Tincture Colchicum BP 1973.
Topical. Bathe with dilute cider vinegar. Cold tea. Garlic ointment. Tea Tree oil diluted many times. Houseleek.
Eyedrops. Goldenseal eyedrops.
Diet. Avoid hot peppery foods, fried foods.

Low-salt. Regular raw food days.
Supplementation. Vitamin E: 500-1000iu daily. Vitamin B-complex. Calcium and Magnesium.
Avoid: scented soap, talcum powder, wool (alternatives: cotton briefs, open gusset tights).
Information: Bechet's Syndrome Society, 3 Belgrave Street, Haxby Road, York YO3 7YY.

BEDSORES. Breakdown and ulceration of tissues from pressure on parts of the body overlying bone in those confined to bed for long periods. Poor or obstructed circulation interferes with tissue replacement and drainage, giving place to local gangrene. Weak body health disposes: anaemia, poor nutrition or absence of a fatty barrier between skin and bone. Commences with superficial redness, turning to blue and progressing to fat and muscle necrosis. Prognosis: destruction of bone and septicaemia.

Prevention is best. Wipe over possible areas with whisky or Vodka following with Oil of St John's Wort. Bed patients are encouraged to spend at least 2 or 3 hours out of bed daily. Many kinds of bed-care aids exist: inflatable rings, water beds and padded protection. Vitamin C deficiency exists in most cases.
Treatment. Herbal antibiotics: Wild Indigo, Myrrh, Milk Thistle, Goldenseal, Echinacea, Marigold. Supportives: Comfrey, Sarsaparilla, Vitamin E.
Tablets/capsules. Goldenseal, Echinacea, Sarsaparilla.
Powders. Parts: Echinacea 2; Goldenseal 1; Liquorice 1. Dose: 750mg (three 00 capsules or half a teaspoon) thrice daily.
Tinctures. Wild Indigo 1; Echinacea 2; Goldenseal quarter. 1-2 teaspoons in water

3 times daily.
Practitioner. Tincture Echinacea BHP (1983) 20ml; Tincture Goldenseal BPC (1949) 5ml; Tincture Marigold BPC (1934) 10ml. Low alcohol vodka to 100ml. Sig: 5ml (3i) tds aq. cal. AC. (*Anonymous*)
Topical. Early stages: Comfrey poultice or ointment. Marshmallow and Slippery Elm ointment; Oil St John's Wort, Rue tea. Fresh pulp of Aloe Vera. Later stages: Sunlight soap plaster. Official medicine at the turn of the century used Lassar's paste or zinc and castor oil ointment which are still effective. Distilled extract of Witch Hazel. For threatened gangrene, skin breakdown with formation of slough: (1) Zinc and Castor oil ointment (or cream) plus a little powdered Myrrh. (2) Cold poultice of Comfrey powder.

BEDSTRAW, LADIES. Cheese rennet. *Galium verum L.*
Action. Alterative, diuretic.
Uses. Kidney stone, gravel, gout.
Preparation. *Tea*: 1-2 teaspoons to each cup boiling water; infuse 15 minutes. Dose, 1 cup freely.

BED-WETTING. See: ENEURESIS.

BEECHAM'S PILLS. Ingredients: Aloes 42mg; Anise oil 200 micrograms; Capsicum oleoresin 100 micrograms (mcg); Ginger oleoresin 400mcg; Juniper oil 700mcg; light magnesium carbonate 2-5mg; Soap (hard) 9.7mg; Rosemary oil 700mcg; Ginger 20.3mcg; Coriander 4.4mg. (*Beecham Proprietaries*)

BEER. Harvester's. Ingredients: 2 gallons water, quarter of an ounce bruised root Ginger, 2 pounds Barbados sugar, 2oz Hops, 1oz Yeast.
Method: Place Hops and Ginger in a muslin bag. Immerse bag in water and boil until it sinks to bottom of the vessel. Remove bag. Add sugar. Bring to boil and simmer two minutes. Strain when warm. Spread yeast on piece of well toasted bread and float on surface of the liquor. Allow to stand 3 days. Bottle. Ready for use in 2-3 weeks.

BEER, NETTLE. Gather basket of nettles, wash and place in a pan with double their quantity of water. Simmer gently one hour. Strain. To every gallon add half an ounce ground Ginger and one pound Barbados sugar or molasses. When cool, ferment with Yeast – three-quarters of an ounce to each gallon. Allow to stand until next day before bottling. Flavour is improved by juice of a lemon.

BEETROOT. *Beta vulgaris L. French*: Bette. *German*: Baisskohl. *Spanish*: Barba bictola. *Italian*: Bictola. *Chinese*: T'ien-ts-ai.
The juice is an oxygen catalyser believed to have an anti-tumour effect. High in iron content and silicic acids, it assists regeneration of red blood cells. Hungarian research indicates anti-cancerous properties; one kilo fresh vegetable daily. Active elements are stable and unaffected by cooking. Other contents: selenium; Vitamins A, C, E, flavonoids, fibre. Side-effects – nil. Bottled juices – (*Biotta, Switzerland*) Produces red stool and urine.
Beetroot juice assists the liver to break-down stored fats and is of value for cellulite and other obese conditions.

BELAICHE, DR PAUL, Chairman, Department of Phyto-therapy, Faculty of Medicine, Bobigny, University of Paris. European authority on use of essential oils (Aromatherapy) in medicine. Commended for his work on Tea Tree oil.

BELCHING. Treatment as for FLATULENCE.

BELLADONNA. Deadly nightshade. *Atropa belladonna L. German*: Amaryllis. *French*: Belladonne d'Automne. *Spanish*: Belladonna. *Italian*: Amarilli a fiori rosei. *Indian*: Suchi.
Action. Antispasmodic, antasthmatic, anti-sweat, sedative, lactifuge.
For use by qualified practitioner only.
Uses. Spasmodic asthma; colic of intestines, gall bladder or kidney; spasm of bladder and ureters. Whooping cough, excessive perspiration (night sweats, etc), spermatorrhoea, bed-wetting (dose afternoon and at bedtime), dribbling of saliva in Parkinsonism. The common cold, hay fever, acidity – to inhibit secretion of stomach acid.
Contra-indications. Glaucoma, rapid heart, pregnancy, enlarged prostate. Side-effects – dry mouth, dilated pupils, mental disorientation. Used for a millennia in China as an anaesthetic (*Kiangsu – 1719*)
Widely used in homoeopathic medicine.
Preparations. Unless otherwise prescribed – up to thrice daily. Dried herb, 50mg in infusion.
Tincture, BHC (vol 1). 1:10, 70 per cent ethanol, 0.5ml.
Initial dose recommended per week by British Herbal Compendium, Vol 1; dried leaf, 200mg (max 1g); tincture, 2ml (max 10ml).
A weaker solution may sometimes be used with good effect: 5 drops tincture to 100ml water – 1 teaspoon hourly. (*Dr Finlay Ellingwood*)
Pharmacy only sale

BELL'S PALSY. Paralysis of the 7th (facial) nerve which controls muscles of the face. One-sided stiffness and distortion of the face which lacks expression. Inability to close eyes or whistle. Rarely painful.
Aetiology. Injury, virus infection, cold, stroke. Recovery usually spontaneous. Herpes Simp.
Alternatives. Chamomile, Wood Betony, Bryonia, Black Cohosh, Barberry, Asafoetida,

Lobelia, Rosemary, Valerian, Sage. Echinacea has been used with convincing results internally and externally.
Tea. Equal parts. Chamomile, Wood Betony. Sage. 1 heaped teaspoon to each cup boiling water; infuse 15 minutes. 1 cup 3 times daily.
Decoctions. Black Cohosh, Rosemary, Valerian, Echinacea.
Tablets/capsules. Black Cohosh. Ginseng. Echinacea. Valerian.
Powders. Formula. Rosemary 1; Echinacea 2; Valerian 1. Dose: 500mg (two 00 capsules or one-third teaspoon) thrice daily.
Tinctures. Formula. Echinacea 2; Rosemary 1; Black Cohosh 1; Pinch Tincture Capsicum. 1-2 teaspoons 3 times daily.
Evening Primrose oil. 4 x 500mg capsules daily.
Aromatherapy. 10 drops Oil Juniper to eggcup Almond oil; gentle massage affected side of face.
Diet. Lacto-vegetarian.
Vitamin E. (400iu daily).

BENZOIN. Gum Benzoin. *Styrax benzoin.* Dry. Part used: gum.
Action: astringent, carminative, expectorant, preservative, genito-urinary antiseptic, anti-fungal. Stimulates phagocytes.
Uses. Chronic bronchitis, coughs, affections of the respiratory organs (as part of Friar's balsam). Mouth ulcers, as a mouth wash: 2 drops tincture in glass of water. Infective cystitis. Tears used as incense. Tincture in dentistry for oral herpes and candida and as an anti-inflammatory after extraction.
Preparations. Tincture Benzoin BPC: 5-15 drops in water. An ingredient of Whitfield's ointment and Friar's balsam. Poultice: for suppurating ulcers and wounds.
Aromatherapy. 3-5 drops in hot water as an inhalant for colds, influenza, chills. GSL

BENZODIAZEPINE ADDICTION. See: DRUG DEPENDENCE.

BERGAMOT, RED. Bee Balm. Oswego tea. *Monardo didyma L.* Part used: herb.
Action: Antiseptic, Carminative, Expectorant.
Uses. Flatulence. Stomach cramp. Intestinal colic. Weak digestion. Nausea. Headache. Painful menstruation.
Preparation. *Tea.* 1 teaspoon to each cup boiling water; infuse 5-10 minutes. Half-1 cup as necessary. Bergamot imparts the distinctive flavour to Earl Grey tea.
Aromatherapy. Diluted oil for shingles: 6 drops to 2 teaspoons Almond oil as a soothing lotion.
BERI BERI. A disease caused by a deficiency of thiamine (Vitamin B1) by eating polished rice from which the husk (in which the vitamin is found) is discarded. Others at risk from Vitamin B1 deficiency are alcoholics, hypothyroids, pregnant women and those with a high intake of refined sugar but a low intake of fresh fruits and vegetables. Heavy coffee drinkers suffer temporary wastage.
Symptoms: weight loss, poor appetite, loss of sensation in arms and legs. Polyneuritis, muscular atrophy. Mood changes.
Of value. Slippery Elm. Dandelion. Alfalfa sprouts or tea. Psyllium husks.
Diet. Vitamin B1 is present in green vegetables, eggs, meat, nuts, yeast, natural unprocessed brown rice, cereal germ and husks, oatmeal, peas, beans, asparagus, brewer's yeast, desiccated liver.
Supplements. Vitamin B-complex. Vitamins B1 and C.

BETA BLOCKERS. The beta-blocker blocks sympathetic action at beta adrenergic receptors. Since 1964 this has transformed the orthodox practice of medicine. Its action reduces peripheral resistance and the heart rate and lowers blood pressure. Prescribed for angina, brain blood vessel disease and to reduce ischaemia. It limits the action of a neurotransmitter which stimulates the heart muscle (Propranolol).

Nearest herbal equivalents include Hawthorn, Broom and Lily of the Valley but their action is not as powerful as drugs of orthodox medicine. Cactus (Opuntia) and Magnesium are effective in mild cases; both dilate peripheral vessels, calm the nervous system, decrease heart rate and the vigour of its contractions. The traditional use of Cactus is notable for prevention of heart attacks.

BETA-CAROTENE. Precursor of Vitamin A. Increases resistance against infection. Antioxidant. Together with Vitamins C and E form a vital line of defence in protection of strands of DNA, the genetic code, from cancerous mutation. Immune booster. Increases lymphocytes and T cells, part of the defence system.
Deficiency. Sun sensitivity; exposure inducing itching, burning and swelling of the skin. Kidney, bladder, and gut infections. Severe earache in young children. Strokes, heart attacks.

It is claimed that those who eat a diet rich in beta-carotene are less likely to develop certain types of cancer.

Smokers usually have low levels of beta-carotene in the blood. Statistics suggest that people who eat a lot of beta-carotene foods are less likely to develop lung, mouth or stomach cancer. In existing cases a slow-down of the disease is possible.
Daily dose. Up to 300mg. Excess may manifest as yellow discoloration of the skin, giving appearance of sun-tan.
Sources. Mature ripe carrots of good colour. A Finland study suggests that four small carrots contain sufficient beta-carotene to satisfy the rec-

ommended daily amount of Vitamin A. Orange and dark green fruits and vegetables. Broccoli, Brussels sprouts, spinach, pumpkin, apricots, peaches, oranges, tomatoes.
Harvard Medical School study. Among 333 subjects with a history of heart disease, those who received beta-carotene supplements of 50 milligrams every other day suffered half as many heart attacks as those taking placebos. (*Dr Charles Hennekens, Harvard Medical School*)

BETH ROOT. Wake Robin. Lamb's Quarter. Birth Root. *Trillium erectum L.* Part used: rhizome.
Action. Genito-urinary anti-haemorrhagic; alterative; soothing tonic astringent. "Natural sex-hormone precursor" (*D. Hoffman*)
Uses. Used in American Indian medicine for excessive bleeding from the womb, and for easy childbirth. Bleeding from lungs, kidneys, bladder and uterine fibroids. Flooding of the menopause. Candida, leucorrhoea (decoction used as a vaginal douche).
To strengthen female constitution.
Preparations. Thrice daily.
Decoction. Half-2 grams to each cupful water simmered gently 10 minutes Dose: half-1 cup.
Liquid extract. 10-30 drops in water.
Tincture. BHP (1983) 1:5 in 40 per cent alcohol. Dose: 1-4ml in water.
Powdered root. Half-2 grams in capsules.
Poultice: for bleeding ulcers: equal parts Beth root and Slippery Elm bark powder.
Snuff: for nosebleed.
Douche (per vagina). 1oz to 2 pints water (decoction). Allow to cool; inject warm. GSL

BETONY. Wood Betony. Stachys betonica. *Betonica officinalis L. German*: Betonien. *French*: Bétoine. *Spanish*: Betónica. *Italian*: Betonica. Dried herb.
Action: Affinity for liver and nervous system. General tonic (emphasis on circulation of the brain). Bitter. Stomachic, Sedative (mild).
Uses. Headache, nervous debility, lack of energy, loss of memory, weak digestion, sciatica, chronic rheumatism, sinus congestion, temporal arteritis (temporary relief), dizziness, hiatus hernia, low back pain (to reduce). Myalgic encephalomyelitis (ME). Nightmare.
Combinations. With Valerian for anxiety states. With equal parts Agrimony and Raspberry leaves as a substitute for domestic tea. With Vervain to enhance its relaxing properties.
Caution. Avoid over-dosing in pregnancy.
Preparations. *Tea*: 1-2 teaspoons to cup boiling water; infuse 5-10 minutes. 1 cup freely.
Liquid Extract: 1 teaspoon in water.
Tincture BHP (1983) 1 in 5 in 45 per cent alcohol. Dose 30-90 drops (2-6ml). GSL

BIG TOE JOINT, INFLAMMATION. Synovitis. Treat as for gout.
Potato Poultice. 1 part potato juice to 3-4 parts hot water, applied on suitable material. Cover with protective.

BILBERRY. Huckleberry. *Vaccinum myrtillus L. French*: Petit Myrte. *German*: Echte Heidelbeere. *Italian*: Baceri mirtillo. Fresh berries, rarely leaves.
Action. Anti-inflammatory, anti-diarrhoeal, antemetic, astringent, diuretic, refrigerant, strengthens blood vessels, vein tonic. Inhibits growth of certain bacteria. Contains Vitamins A, C, P. Gather before fruit ripens.
Uses. Dropsy, gravel, violent irritable bowel, diverticulosis, nausea or vomiting, sore throat (gargle), leucorrhoea (douche), scurvy, Vitamin C deficiency. Popular in Russian Folk Medicine for gastro-enteritis and to reduce insulin intake in diabetes. Cleansing wash for old ulcers (decoction). Pharyngitis (gargle). Leukoplakia of the mouth, vagina and urethra – improvement reported. Crohn's disease. Bacillus Coli infections. By stimulating production of visual purple improves vision, especially night vision. Varicose veins. Piles. Cystitis.
Preparations. Thrice daily.
Decoction: 1oz to 1 pint water, remove vessel when boiling point is reached. Wineglass freely.
Liquid Extract, dose: 2-8ml.
Home tincture. Handful bilberries to 1 pint Vodka. Cork or cap. Shake daily for 1 week. Filter. Wineglass freely.
Formula. Combines well with Meadowsweet and Horsetail (equal parts).
Powder, capsules: 280mg. 2 capsules thrice daily between meals. (*Arkocaps*)
Diet. Cooked fresh berries are a popular dessert. Equal parts leaves of Wild Strawberry, Thyme and Bilberry substitute for domestic tea.
Fresh berries. Chew 1-3 teaspoons daily.

BILE SECRETION DEFICIENCY. Bile is a greenish-yellow alkaline substance secreted by the liver which emulsifies fat and prevents putrefaction in the intestines. An aid to pancreatic juices.
Alternatives. *To stimulate flow*, Boldo, Horsetail, Dandelion, Blue Flag root, Milk Thistle, Bogbean, Burdock. Teas, capsules, tablets, Liquid extracts, or Tinctures.
A. Vogel recommends: Barberry, Centuary, St John's Wort, Sarsaparilla.
Combination tea. Equal parts: Peppermint leaves, Milk Thistle, Dandelion root. 1 teaspoon to each cup boiling water; infuse 15 minutes, 1 cup thrice daily for limited period (1 month).
Bile in the urine. (Bilviria)
Arthur Barker: Liquid Extract Black root 1oz (30ml). Liquid Extract Cornsilk 1oz (30ml).

Essential Peppermint 30 drops (2ml). Water to 8oz (240ml). 2 teaspoons in water 3 times daily before meals.
Diet. Dandelion coffee. Artichokes.
See: CHOLAGOGUES. CHOLERETICS.

BILHARZIA. Schistosomiasis. One of the serious diseases of the tropics, caused by schistosomes, or blood flukes. Goes back into Egyptian history by 3,000 years when it was referred to as 'blood in the urine' (haematuria).

Bilharzial calcified eggs have been found in the rectum and bladder of mummified bodies. There is evidence that they received treatment with the plants Valerian and Hyoscyamus. Today, Poke root is favoured.

More than 300 million people are infected. Cure is difficult, in spite of our greater knowledge. No natural medicine has yet been discovered to kill the parasite worms except deep-acting poisons: Antimony (tartar emetic).

Causative organism pierces the skin or mucous membranes of walkers, swimmers, or farmers wading in contaminated water.

Medicinal plants are used, with varying degrees of success to discourage the flukes from invading the host and to make good their depredations.
Anti-Bilharzials – Gum arabic, Cannabis sativa (hemp), Citrullus colocynthis, Citric acid (from lemons), Cyperus esculentus, Douma thebaica, Hordeum vulgare (Barley), Phoenix dactylifera, Ricinus communis (Castor oil), Thymus capitata (Thyme), Vitis vinifera (Grapes), Pistacea terebinthus (the Mastic Tree), Morus nigra (fresh fruits, root bark and leaves of the Mulberry Tree), Ficus carica (Common Fig), Thymus vulgaris (Thyme similar to English Garden Thyme). Later in history these remedies were joined by Ginger and Ambrosia artemisia. (*Samir Yahia El-Gammal, MD, in "Medical Times", Journal for the Promotion of Eastern Medicine. Hamdard Centre, Nazimabad, Karachi, Pakistan. Vol XIX, Winter 1984*)
Ginger, powdered root and aqueous extract, prevents hatching of schistosome eggs in host. In trials with schoolchildren, bloody urine stopped and egg count in the urine dropped. (*Kucera et al., 1975; Theakston et al., 1975*)
CORIANDER SEED. Tea. Original research, Lawrence D. Hills, Henry Doubleday Research Association.
Note. Berries of a native Ethiopian plant, the endod or Soapberry (Phytolacca dodecandra) contain a potent toxin that can, in minute quantities, kill the snails carrying the schistosomes. (*New Scientist, 1989, No 1690, p21*)

To be treated by or in liaison with a general medical practitioner.

BILOUSNESS. "Liverishness". A common term used to describe sick headache, nausea and sour belching due to liver disorder. May also be associated with kidney disease, acidity, constipation or appendicitis. Most likely due to dietetic indiscretions, alcohol, fatty foods.
Alternatives:– *Tea. Mixture*. Equal parts, Black Horehound and Wood Betony. 1-2 teaspoons to each cup boiling water infused 5-15 minutes. Drink freely.
Decoction. Mixture. Parts: Fringe Tree bark 2; Parsley root 1; Dandelion root 1. One teaspoon to each cup water gently simmered 20 minutes. Half a cup 3 times daily before meals.
Tablets/capsules. Devil's Claw, Milk Thistle, Blue Flag, Wild Yam.
Powders. Formula. Equal parts: Milk Thistle and Peppermint. Dose: 750mg (three 00 capsules or half a teaspoon) thrice daily.
Tinctures. Formula. Equal parts: Wahoo and Barberry. 30-60 drops every 2 hours in water.
Barberry bark. One teaspoon shredded Barberry bark to each cup cold water allowed to infuse overnight. Half-1 cup twice daily.
Arthur Barker. Liquid Extract Black root 30ml; Liquid Extract Meadowsweet 30ml; Liquid Extract Agrimony 15ml; Emulsion Peppermint water (1 in 60) 2ml (optional). Water to 240ml (8oz). Dose: 2 teaspoons in water 3 times daily.
Prevention. Weekly dose Epsom's salts.
Milk Thistle. Acquires a reputation for the complaint.
Diet. Low fat, Dandelion coffee, artichokes. Reject alcohol and strong caffeine drinks.
See also: ACIDOSIS. LIVER.

BIOCATALYST. A herb that initiates a change in the metabolism of the body. It exercises a specific chemical action relating to vitamins, hormones, enzymes and minerals. Parsley is one of the most important. Others – Watercress, Alfalfa, Fenugreek seeds, Lettuce, Marshmallow, Carrots.

BIOFLAVONOIDS. Vitamin P factors usually found with Vitamin C. Sources: most fruits, particularly citrus, grapefruit, grapes, lemons; rutin as found in buckwheat. They are associated with maintaining the strength of capillary walls in the elderly. One of the most popular and effective sources is Ginkgo that increases oxygen and blood supply in the general circulation, particularly the brain.

BIOSTRATH A.G. Company founded by Fred Pestalozzi, Herrliberg on Lake Zurich, Switzerland. Pioneered herbal preparations in a base of *candida utilis* yeast. Yeast is fed with wild herbs plasmolysed in a fermentation process. Efficacy of products demonstrated by scientific experiment. Under special growing conditions the principles are absorbed by the yeast cells in the process of multiplication or are bound to the cell surface. They are then metabolised, i.e., undergo chemical change.

Candida utilis is a highly active wild yeast able to synthesise its own vitamins. More than 90 selected plant species from 14 countries are used in Biostrath preparations. The Company has pioneered an important advance in the preparation of herbal medicines. Results have in some instances led to completely new discoveries.

BIOSTRATH ELIXIR. Herbal yeast food supplement. Ingredients: herbal yeast plasmolysate (saccharomyces cerevisiae) 85 per cent w/w, malt extract 9 per cent w/w, honey 3 per cent w/w, orange juice 3 per cent w/w. Biostrath Drops are a similar preparation but without malt, honey and orange juice, (Vessen). Builds up resistance, promotes vitality, combats stress, examination fatigue and lack of concentration. Said to protect the body against radiation.

Live yeast Saccharomyces cerevisiae is cultivated on the herbs: Angelica, Balm, Basil, Caraway, Chamomile, Cinnamon, Elder, Fennel, Horseradish, Hyssop, Lavender, Liquorice, Parsley, Peppermint, Sage and Thyme.

BIRCH, EUROPEAN. Silver birch. *Betula alba L., B. pendula* Roth. *German*: Weissbirke. *French*: Bouleau. *Spanish*: Abidul. *Italian*: Betula. Bark and leaves.
Action: Astringent. Bitter. Anti-inflammatory. Cholagogue. Diuretic. Contains salicylates which have an aspirin-like effect. Young leaves increase the flow of urine. Popular in Scandinavia.
Uses. Rheumatism and gout (dried leaf tea). Sore mouth (gargle). Kidney and bladder complaints. Sluggish kidney function. 'Heart' oedema. Cellulitis due to retention of metabolic wastes.
Preparations. *Tea*: 1 teaspoon dried leaves to each cup boiling water; infuse 15 minutes. Strain. Wineglass thrice daily.
Methyl salicylate, a rheumatism remedy, obtained by distillation of the twigs. (*A. Vogel) Birch tar oil*. (Ointment) External use only (UK). GSL

BIRTH. North of England midwives 'birth' tea. Equal parts: Basil, Lavender and Raspberry leaves in infusion. To each cupful add few grains grated Nutmeg.

To arrest excessive bleeding: Yarrow or Nettle tea.

After the event; to restore – Alfalfa tea.

To heal the placenta: inserts of powdered Comfrey.

BIRTHWORT. *Aristolochia longa, L. Aristolochia clematis L. Aristolochia indica L.*
Part used: root. Long reputation in traditional medicine. Prescription by medical practitioner only.
Action: stimulant, emmenagogue, diaphoretic, oxytocic (hence its name – to induce childbirth delivery). Immune enhancer. Stimulates action of white blood cells.

Reduces effects of Prednisolone, Chloramphenicol and Tetracycline (*H. Wagner, "Economic & Medicinal Plant Research, vol 1, Pub: Academic Press (1985) UK*)
Uses. *Chinese medicine*: ulcers, infectious diseases.
Preparations. *Powdered root*: dose – 2-4 grams. 2-3 times daily.
Madaus: Tardolyt: a sodium salt of aristolochic acid.

BISR KHIL. The Khil plant is native to the Nile Valley. Seeds have a long traditional reputation as a kidney-stone breaker. Half an ounce seeds to 1 pint water; bring to boil and simmer for 5 minutes. All is drunk over the course of the day. Continue until positive response, allowing one week's rest after each three weeks.

BISTORT. Adderwort. *Polygonum bistorta L. German*: Matterknöterich. *French*: Bistorte. *Italian*: Bistorta. *Malayan*: Séludang. Root and rhizome.
Action: powerful astringent, anti-inflammatory, anti-catarrhal, anti-diarrhoeal, demulcent, anti-haemorrhagic.
Uses. Chiefly to arrest flow of internal bleeding. Haemorrhage from lungs, stomach or bowel. Irritable bowel, diverticulosis, incontinence of urine, uterine infection with discharge (vaginal douche), ulcerated mouth and spongy gums, nasal polypus (juice of fresh plant or decoction injected into nostrils), nosebleed (powder snuffed into nose), sore mouth (mouth wash).
Preparations. Thrice daily.
Decoction: (internal), 1 heaped teaspoon to each cup water gently simmered 20 minutes. Half cup. Decoction may also be used as a douche.
Liquid extract: 15-30 drops, in water.
Powder: half a teaspoon in water or honey.
Tincture BHP (1983) 1:5 in 25 per cent alcohol. Dose, 1-3ml (15-45 drops) in water. Gargle. Mouthwash. Ointment. GSL

BITES. Of cats, dogs, fish, domestic and other animals. Treatment as for RABIES. For weever fish sting the best treatment is hot water. For bites of insects, see INSECT BITES.

BITTER MELON. Balsam Pear. *Momardica charantia.*
Action. Alterative.
Uses. Psoriasis.
Preparations. Fresh juice: 1 to 4oz (30-120g) daily.

BITTER ORANGE. *Citrus aurantium L.* var. *Amara L.*

Leaves are antispasmodic and digestive; flowers have a tranquilliser effect; the peel is a stomachic-bitter; seeds contain linolenic acid to disperse cholesterol deposits. Essential oil (neroli) is inhaled for hysteria and fainting. Orange peel is a bitter-tonic for flatulence and depression. A tea is made from the leaves and flowers: 2 teaspoons to each cup boiling water. Used by the perfumery industry (eau de cologne). Adds a bitter-sweet flavour to 'Curacao' liquers. Stimulates appetite. Orange wine.
Aromatherapy. External use of the oil for fatigue, limited powers of endurance, recovery from prolonged illnesses and surgical operations.

BITTER ROOT. Dog's bane. *Apocynum androsaemifolium L.* Root.
Action: diaphoretic, emetic, expectorant. Heart stimulant of value in cardiac dropsy. Old-time antidote for rabies. North American Indians: for venereal disease. Traditional: jaundice, gall stone, sluggish liver conditions, migraine sick headache. Warts: an external wipe with sap of the fresh plant.
Powdered root: dose, quarter-2g.
Liquid Extract, dose: half-2ml.
Internal treatment by practitioner only.

BITTERS. Bitters are stimulants to the autonomic nervous system. They stimulate 'bitter' taste buds in the mouth that reflexly initiate secretion of a special hormone into the blood stream increasing production of stomach and pancreatic juices and impelling the liver to release bile into the duodenum. Bitters increase acid production and are given about half an hour before meals. To sweeten them is to nullify their effect.

Bitters increase the appetite, assist assimilation, and are indicated for perverted or loss of the sense of taste (zinc). They reduce fermentation in the intestines and are of value in hypoglycaemia and diabetes mellitus. Bitters are not carminatives. Some, such as Gentian, Calumba and Chamomile are also sialogogues (increasing the flow of saliva). Another effect, little understood, is an increase in white corpuscles in the peripheral circulation.

Aletris, Angostura, Avens, Balmony, Barberry, Betony, Bogbean, Boneset, Calumba, Centuary, Chicory, Condurango, Feverfew, Gentian, Goldenseal, Holy Thistle, Hops, Quassia Chips, Rue, Southernwood, White Horehound, Wormwood.

Not used in presence of gastric ulcer.

BITTERSWEET. Felonwort. *Solanum dulcamara L. German*: Bittersüss. *French*. Douce amère. *Italian*: Dulcamara. *Spanish*: Delcamara. *Indian*: Ruba barik. Twigs and root-bark.
Action: stimulating expectorant, diuretic, hepatic, anti-rheumatic, anti-fungal, alterative. Contains saponin glycoside Dulcamarin.
Uses. Chronic bronchitis. Chronic eczema with itching. Gout. Mild analgesic for rheumatism. Warts, tumours, (external).
Preparations. Thrice daily.
Decoction: half-2g twigs to each cup water simmer 10 minutes. Dose: half a cup.
Liquid extract: 2-4ml in water.
French traditional: wives boiled handful of twigs or root-bark in lard for ulcers, warts and ringworm.
Contra-indication: pregnancy and lactation.

BLACK DEATH. See: BUBONIC PLAGUE.

BLACKBERRY. *Rubus villosus, Ait.* Bramble, dewberry. *French*: Ronce. *German*: Beerstrauch. *Italian*: Rovo. Part used: leaves and root-bark.
Constituents: tannin, malic acid, pectin.
Action. Powerful astringent: root more than leaves. Anti-haemorrhage.
Uses. Diarrhoea, dysentery, infant's irritable bowel, bleeding from colon or rectum. Appendicitis (tea, freely). Enteritis (tea and enema). Sore throat (gargle). Mouth ulcers. Frequent mouth-wash claimed to fasten loose teeth. Bleeding gums (leaves chewed).

Reported isolated anti-tumour effect (*HHS Fong; J. Pharm. Sci., 61 (11), 1818, 1972*)
Combination: traditional. Equal parts dried leaves Agrimony and Blackberry; tea, 1 cup freely.

With Balm as a substitute for domestic tea.
Preparations. *Tea*. 1oz (30g) to 1 pint (500ml) boiling water, infuse 15 minutes; 1 cup freely. May be used also topically as an enema or wash for wounds.
Liquid extract. 2-4ml in water, thrice daily.
Tincture. 1-2 teaspoons thrice daily. GSL

BLACK COHOSH. Macrotys actaeae. Black Snakeroot. Actaearacemosa. *Cimicifuga racemosa Nutt. German*: Schwarzes Wanzenkraut. *French*: Cimicaire. *Chinese*: Shêng-ma-jou. Root and rhizome.
Action: relaxing nervine, sedative, spasmolytic, vaso-dilator, anti-arthritic, anti-inflammatory, anti-rheumatic, anti-cough, regulates autonomic system, emmenagogue, natural source of salicylic acid which has an aspirin-like effect. The agent works powerfully upon the female reproductive organs. Analgesic (mild).
Constituents: triterpine glycosides.
Uses. Cramps, sciatica, low back pain, facial and intercostal neuralgia, stiff neck, aches after strenuous exercise. Painful menstruation and menopausal symptoms, breast pains, threatened abortion, migraine of hormonal origin and pain in the ovaries. Tinnitus. Oestrogen-deficiency. Scarlet fever. Fatty heart.

Combines, equal parts with Bogbean for

rheumatism; with Blue Cohosh for ovaries and womb; with Elecampane for whooping cough. Psychological: of value for melancholia, hysteria and nervous depression. Peter Smith, 19th century explorer, claimed the Indians used it with success for yellow fever.
Contra-indicated in pregnancy and lactation.
Preparations. Unless otherwise prescribed, daily dose: dried rhizome and root, 40-200mg or by decoction; tincture (1:10, 60 per cent ethanol), 0.4-2ml. (*British Herbal Compendium, Vol 1*).
Antispasmodic tincture (*Potter's*)
Used in traditional Chinese medicine. GSL

BLACK CURRANT. *Ribes nigrum L. German*: Schwarze Ribsel. *French*: Bassis. *Spanish*: Grosellero. *Italian*: Grosularia nera. Garden fruit. Leaves, fruit.
Action: febrifuge (mild), astringent, diuretic, anti-rheumatic. Fruits are a rich source of Vitamin C, and have a Vitamin P effect. Anti-inflammatory for rheumatic disorders and gout. Nerve tonic. Hypotensor. Mild antispasmodic. Cooling.
Uses. As a tea in early stages of fevers until deeper-acting and more specific treatment is prescribed. Capillary fragility. High blood pressure (fruit). Sore throat (tea used as a gargle). Irritable bowel. Renal calculi, oliguria, renal colic.
Combination: equal parts: with Agrimony and German Chamomile for diverticulosis.
Preparations. *Leaves*: 1oz to 1 pint boiling water; infuse 15 minutes. One-half-1 cup freely.
Fruits: Black currant syrup, BPC.
Note. Seeds are twice as rich in gamma linolenic acid than an equivalent amount in Evening Primrose oil. Assists production of prostaglandins that control blood pressure and regulate metabolism. GSL

BLACK EYE. Bruise. Cold compress: pulped. Any one – Plantain, Houseleek, Slippery Elm, Comfrey, Rue. Juice or gel of Aloe Vera.

BLACK HAW. Sweet viburnum. *Viburnum prunifolium L.* Root bark.
Action. Uterine antispasmodic, antasthmatic, hypotensive, nervine, sedative (womb), diuretic, antidiarrhoeal. Keynote: female reproductive system.
Constituents: Coumarins, salicin.
Uses. Threatened miscarriage: give 4-6 weeks before due date of delivery. After-pains of childbirth. False labour pains. Painful menstruation. Absence of periods from general debility. Morning sickness, prolapse of the womb, flooding of the menopause. Asthma. High blood pressure. Tetanus (*Dr E. Phares, Ellingwood's Therapeutics*). Successful in the cure of two cases of cancer of the tongue (*Dr E.P. Fowler (Ellingwood Therapeutics)*)
Preparations. Thrice daily, or as prescribed.
Decoction: one teaspoon to each cup water simmered gently 10 minutes. Half-1 cup.
Liquid Extract BHP (1983) 4-8ml in water.
Powder. 2-5g by capsule or decoction.
Tincture BHP (1983) 1:5 in 70 per cent alcohol. Dose: 5-10ml. GSL

BLACK RADISH. *Raphanus sativus L.*, var nigra. Roots.
Action: cholagogue, digestive, hepatic.
Uses. Indigestion. To increase bile production in liver disorders and to increase intestinal peristalsis. Dyskinesias. Gall bladder disorders. Constipation. Dyspepsia.
Preparations. *Powder*. 230mg capsules; 3 capsules midday and evening 15 minutes before meals. (*Arkocaps*)
Freshly pressed Juice: half-1 cup daily. If too pungent mix with a little Slippery Elm powder.

BLACK ROOT. Culver's root. Leptandra. *Veronicastrum virginicum L.* Part used: root, dried rhizome. Constituents: saponins and volatile oil.
Action. Antiseptic, antispasmodic, mild liver relaxant, promotes flow of bile, a laxative that acts without griping.
Uses. Chronic indigestion associated with liver disorder BHP (1983). Chronic liver congestion, non-obstructive jaundice, inflammation of the gall bladder.
Combination: with Dandelion (2) and Black root (1) an aid to liver function in cirrhosis.
History. Used by the Menominee Indians for internal purification.
Preparations. Thrice daily.
Decoction: 1oz (30g) to 1 pint (500ml) water gently simmered 20 minutes: One-third to half a cup.
Liquid extract: 10-60 drops in water.
Tincture BHP (1983): 2.5ml-10ml.
Powder. Mix sifted powder with pinch Cayenne: 1-4g. GSL

BLACKMORE, MAURICE. Naturopath, Chiropractor. Pioneer of natural therapies in Australia of over 50 years. Founder of Australian based Blackmore Laboratories and the Maurice Blackmore Research Foundation. Manufacturers of herbal care preparations. A professional service is dedicated to the Australian Practitioner of Complementary Medicine. Address: 23 Roseberry Street, Balgowlah, Sydney, 2093 NSW, Australia.

BLACKOUTS. Transient loss of consciousness. Is it a fit or a faint?
As blood flow to the brain is reduced the person may feel light-headed, wobbly and sick. Blood pressure falls. Sight fades and consciousness is lost. Rapid breathing and 'pins and needles'. May be due to a tiny bloodclot entering the circulation of the brain, emotional shock, premenstrual pain,

a hot room, drugs that lower blood pressure. Diabetics sometimes feel faint when blood pressure is low. The heart may be responsible: with sudden drop in output, cardiac infarction with chest pains and palpitation.

An epileptic convulsion is recognisable as a fit, with possible discharge of urine and biting of the tongue. See: EPILEPSY. For a simple faint:–

Treatment. Place head between the knees to ensure an immediate flow of blood to the brain. When he 'comes-to' any of the following may be given, either in tablet, capsule or liquid form: Ginseng, Prickly Ash, Ginger, Cayenne, Peppermint, Cola, Ephedra or Composition Essence.

BLACK STOOLS. May be due to melaena or to colours left from bismuth, iron, charcoal, liquorice and certain fruits. Chocolate sandwich may sometimes induce a pseudo-melaena. Treat: as for MELAENA.

BLADDER DISORDERS. The bladder is a hollow muscular organ with a wall of smooth muscle. It stores urine received from the kidneys which is released via the urethra in an action known as micturition. Common disorders, see: ENEURESIS. FREQUENCY OF URINE. GRAVEL. HAEMATURIA. INCONTINENCE. STONE IN THE BLADDER. STRANGURY. STRICTURE. URETHRITIS. URINE – PAIN ON PASSING.

BLADDERWRACK. Black tang. *Fucus vesiculosis L. German*: Algen. *French*: Algue marine. *Italian*: Alga marina. A sea-plant which transforms inert inorganic substances from the sea into organic minerals capable of nourishing the human body. One of the richest sources of minerals (micro-nutrients) chiefly iodine, sodium, manganese, sulphur, silicon, zinc and copper.

Keynote: thyroid gland.

Action: anti-hypothyroid, anti-obesic, anti-rheumatic, blood tonic, adaptogen, stimulates the circulation of lymph. Endocrine gland stimulant. Laxative. Antibiotic. Diuretic (mild).

Uses. Thyroid disease, thyroxin deficiency, simple goitre. Obesity of low-thyroid function, myxoedema (adaptogen). Faulty nutrition, listlessness, rickets, glandular ailments, general debility; to build up old broken-down constitutions. Cases requiring increased body heat – hypothermia. Allays onset of arteriosclerosis by maintaining elasticity of walls of blood vessels. Beneficial to male and female reproductive organs, liver, gall bladder and pancreas. Militates against onset of rheumatism and arthritis. Contains Vitamin K for prevention of strokes.

Combination. Burdock root, Clivers, Ground Ivy and Bladderwrack. (*Heath and Heather*)

Preparations. Thrice daily.

Teas: half teaspoon to each cup boiling water; infuse 15 minutes. Half-1 cup.

Liquid Extract: 1:1, 25 per cent ethanol, 5-10 drops.

Tincture, BHC Vol 1. 1:5, 25 per cent ethanol, Dose: 4-10ml.

Powder: important to those who do not eat fish or sea-foods. Added to soups, salads, cottage cheese; sprinkled on muesli or on a cooked meal.

Tablets/capsules. 300mg Kelp BHP (1983) with 12mg Kelp extract. 1 tablet or capsule thrice daily after meals. Not for children under five.

Diet: Combination rich in essential nutrients: Kelp powder, Alfalfa tea, Soya bean products, Dandelion (coffee). GSL

BLEEDING. Haemorrhage. Bleeding from arteries is bright red, escaping in jerks; from the veins it is darker; steadier from the capillaries. There is an oozing of bright red blood from a cut. In an extravasation blood pours into lax tissues beneath the skin; the part becoming swollen with the appearance of a bruise.

To strengthen veins – Gentian. To enhance resistance – Echinacea. To counter failing strength – Ginseng. To promote granulation – Comfrey. To restore lacerated nerves – St John's Wort. Nettles are a well-known traditional anti-haemorrhagic.

If bleeding is serious, control with firm finger pressure. Any one of the following may be used in the form of teas, tinctures, powders, etc.

Bowels. Ladies Mantle, Avens, Horsetail, <u>Shepherd's Purse</u>, Tormentil, Raspberry leaves, Yarrow, <u>Cranesbill</u>, Bilberry.

Gums. Tea. Equal parts: Horsetail, St John's Wort. (*Maria Treben*) Or:– Paint gums with Tincture Myrrh, Blood root, Goldenseal or <u>Marigold</u>.

Post-partum. (After child-birth) Goldenseal BHP (1983); Lady's Mantle BHP (1983).

Lungs. Haemoptysis. Blood spitting. <u>Blood root</u>, Beth root, Lungwort, Mullein, Horsetail, <u>St John's Wort</u>, Cranesbill. Bur-Marigold. Sage. Mouse Ear, Bugleweed. Nettle tea is a good stand-by.

Post-menopausal bleeding: Internal: <u>Raspberry leaves</u>, Ladies Mantle, Shepherd's Purse. Plantain tea as an injection. Plugs of cotton wool saturated with Witch Hazel. To be investigated by a competent authority.

Mucous surfaces: *tongue, mouth, throat, gullet*. Marigold, Yarrow, Rue, Clematis erecta, Life root. Blood root (tincture: 10-15 drops in water). Ice to suck.

Nose. Witch Hazel. Nettles. Vinegar water: to snuff into nostrils. Apply sponge soaked in cold water to back of the neck. Or: plug nose with Witch Hazel saturated cotton wool.

Hymen. See entry.

Skin. Superficial. Buckwheat, <u>Marigold</u>, Daisy, Tormentil, Witch Hazel, Blood root (tincture),.

Stomach. Haematemesis. The vomit of blood has the appearance of coffee grounds and is a symptom of gastric ulcer. Teas: Avens, Meadowsweet, Yarrow. Bur-Marigold, Cranesbill, Mullein.
Decoctions: Cranesbill root, Beth root, Oak bark.
After Surgery. After tissue excisions, blood clotting or wound-healing disorders for safe haemostasis: Beth root, Cranesbill root, Lady's Mantle, St John's Wort.
Blood in the urine. See: HAEMATURIA.
Bleeding of menses: See: MENSTRUATION.
IUD bleeding. Bleeding from intra-uterine devices: Injection: teas – Lady's Mantle, Cranesbill, Tormentil, Marigold.

Vitamin E supplementation (*International Journal of Fertility, Vol 28. 1983*) Suggested dose: One 500iu capsule morning and evening.
Retinal haemorrhage. Buckwheat tea. Vitamin C: 1-3g daily. Evening Primrose oil.
Red cell stimulators: Yellow Dock root, Red Clover, Gentian.
White cell stimulators: Liquorice, Ginseng (Siberian) and Korean, Goldenseal, Echinacea.
Vitamins. C. D. K. P.
Minerals. Calcium, Iron, Selenium, Zinc.
Note. Any new episode of bleeding (rectal, gastric, etc) in those 45 and over should be investigated in hospital. Alteration of bowel habit, with bleeding, in young people should lead to referral to a doctor.

BLEPHARITIS. Chronic inflammation of margins of the eyes.
Aetiology. May follow children's infections, measles, seborrhoea, skin disease. Allergic reactions to cosmetics, drugs and industrial poisons.
Symptoms: irritation of eyelids, lashes glued together on rising, crust formation. Purulent conditions – Blue Flag, Echinacea. Eyelids puffy: Buchu. Treat underlying cause.
Alternatives. *Tea*. Mix: equal parts Skullcap, Vervain, Yarrow. 1 heaped teaspoon to each cup boiling water; infuse 5-15 minutes. 1 cup thrice daily.
Decoction. Mix: equal parts: Echinacea, Buchu, Burdock. 1 teaspoon to two cups water gently simmered 20 minutes. Half-1 cup thrice daily.
Tablets/capsules. Echinacea. Blue Flag root. Poke root.
Powders. Equal parts: Echinacea, Buchu, Burdock. Mix. Dose: 500mg (two 00 capsules or one-third teaspoon) thrice daily.
Tinctures. Equal parts: Echinacea, Buchu, Blue Flag. Mix. 1-2 teaspoons in water 3 times daily.
Topical. Chickweed ointment. Aloe Vera gel. Potato, cold compress.

Bathe with any of following tepid teas: Red Clover, Fennel seed, German Chamomile, Plantain, Elderflowers, Raspberry leaves, Barberry bark.

BLEPHAROSPASM. Involuntary closure of the eyelids, usually due to a painful eye condition. Combination: equal parts, Valerian, Vervain, Mistletoe. 1 heaped teaspoon to each cup boiling water; infuse 15 minutes. Dose: half-1 cup thrice daily. Or, individual herbs as tablets, powders, tinctures, etc.

Cramp Bark: Success reported.

BLOATED FEELING, in women. Abdomen feels heavy and swollen. Helonias.

BLOCKED-UP NOSE. Due to many causes from catarrh to infection. May be associated with sinus headache and nasal congestion.
Alternatives. *Teas*. Plantain leaves, Nasturtium leaves, Marigold flowers (Calendula), Thyme.
Tablets/capsules. Garlic, Goldenseal, Iceland Moss.
Tinctures. Formula. Echinacea 2; Goldenseal 1. Mix. 30-60 drops in water thrice daily.
Practitioner. Ephedra.
Topical. Decongestants. Olbas oil. Oils of Aromatherapy: Eucalyptus, Garlic, Thyme.
Supplementation. Vitamins A, C.
Bedtime: 2-3 Garlic capsules.

BLOOD CLOT. See: EMBOLISM.

BLOOD PRESSURE. The cardio-vascular vessels may be compared with a central heating system in which a volume of water is forced through a network of pipes by a pump in a closed circuit, over and over again. Our heart and circulatory system operate in the same way.

Blood pressure is recorded by two readings on a sphygmomanometer with the aid of the traditional inflatable cuff. The top pressure is known as the systolic, the bottom as the diastolic. The systolic pressure occurs when the heart contracts, the diastolic when the heart relaxes and the volume of blood is at its lowest. A practitioner interprets the pressure of blood against the wall of the brachial artery in terms of millimetres.

In a healthy young person or middle-aged adult, average systolic pressure is 120, diastolic 80. They are recorded as 120/80. A pressure of 140/90 requires investigation while one of 160/95 is high and demands treatment. Average pressure at 50 is 135/80, over 65 – 165/85. Defined hypertension is a raised pressure on three consecutive readings.

The highest pressure peak is reached in the evening after a day's work and the lowest, at night. Pressure may rise with stress when the heart responds by beating faster, or fall with physical or mental exhaustion when the heart slows down. Persistent high or low pressure is usually associated with other conditions which may require their own specific treatments: i.e. low – anaemia, high – kidney disease. See: HYPERTENSION. HYPOTENSION.

BLOOD PURIFIERS. Alteratives. The blood is a fluid from which every variety of cell and tissue derives its special form of food for the repair of constant wastage resulting from functions they perform. When the blood becomes vitiated from lack of exercise, too little oxygen, debilitating personal habits and sophisticated foodstuffs the whole body suffers. The vital fluid then needs to be cleansed of its impurities. Nature's blood purifiers are unique in the world of medicine, restoring biochemical balance and promoting healthy elimination.
Blood tonic. Decoction, tablets, tinctures or fluid extracts:– Echinacea 3; Burdock 2; Goldenseal 1.
See also: ALTERATIVES.

BLOOD ROOT. Red Indian paint. *Sanguinaria canadensis L. French*: Sanguinaire. *German*: Kanadisches Blutkraut. *Spanish*: Sanguinaria. *Italian*: Sanguinaria del Canada.
Constituents: isoquinoline alkaloids.
Action. Antiseptic, antispasmodic, cardio-active, emetic (large doses), expectorant, escharotic, antibacterial, stimulant to the womb and general circulation. Mild local anaesthetic.
Though extensively used by pharmacy in the past, is no longer used internally. Traditional among Mohawk Indians.
Uses. Internal, drop doses for asthma, croup, whooping cough, pneumonia, bleeding of the lungs as in tuberculosis, emphysema.
External. Warts, ringworm, fungoid tumour. Nasal polypi (powder injected into nostril).
Preparations. Thrice daily. Accurate dosage is not possible by infusion or decoction.
Liquid extract BHP (1983) 0.06-0.3ml.
Tincture BHP (1983) 0.3-2ml.
Ointment: tumours. GSL

BLOOD TRANSFUSION. A transmission of blood from donor to recipient subject to check for compatibility (ABO groups) and freedom from HIV, hepatitis and other viruses.
"There are as many different bloods as there are different people," wrote Dr Alonzo J. Shadman. In his practice as a physician and surgeon he claimed he never lost a case for lack of blood and never employed blood transfusion or drugs. For bloodlessness he advised normal saline to give the heart sufficient fluid-load to work on.
Normal saline solution he used was with 2 teaspoons table salt to one of sodium bicarbonate in two quarts (approximately 2 litres) water. Normal saline keeps the blood vessels "open".
Dr Shadman continues: "Where infection has occurred, expressed fresh juice from the flowering Marigold (Calendula) is mixed with sufficient alcohol to prevent fermentation. It should not be used full strength but diluted one part to ten parts water. Any left after the emergency should be thrown away." (*The Layman Speaks, April 1963, p.137-139*)
Garlic. Study showed a marked reduction in platelet aggregation over a 5-week period in a group of patients with normally increased tendency to aggregation. (*Dr F. Jung, Department of Clinical Haemostasiology and Transfusion Medicine, Saarland University*)

BLUE COHOSH. Squaw root. Papoose root. *Caulophyllum thalictroides L* Mich. Root and rhizome.
Action: anti-inflammatory, antispasmodic (womb), oxytocic, emmenagogue, anti-rheumatic. Excellent relaxing and stimulating nervine for the womb. Its principle influence is on the generative system and the sympathetic nervous system connected thereto, soothing and imparting tone to each. (*J.T. Lyle*) North American women gathered it along the trails for easy childbirth and to promote rapid recovery. Not given before pregnancy is commenced. For great exhaustion before labour with feeble results.
Uses. Early American settlers and Indians claimed its power to prevent premature labour and miscarriage, prolonged painful labours and rigidity of the os. Indicated in labour with no expulsive effort and to counter false labour pains with bearing down sensations in the abdomen. Dr Farrington (*Ellingwood's Therapeutist*) knew a single dose to arrest them after lasting several hours.
For persistent amenorrhoea and to increase menstrual flow; painful adolescent menses. Habitual abortion. Painful inflammation of the vagina, internally; and as a douche. Adolescent leucorrhoea. Acute rheumatic pains of the menopause. Combines well with Motherwort for rapid recovery after childbirth.
Preparations. Thrice daily, or as dictated for an acute condition.
Powder: by capsule or for decoction: dose, 0.3-1g.
Liquid Extract BHP (1983): 1:1 in 70 per cent alcohol; dose, 0.5-1ml.
Tincture. One to ten parts 70 per cent alcohol. Dose: 1-2ml.
Note. Chiefly used the latter half of pregnancy.

BLUE FLAG ROOT. Water flag. *Iris versicolor L.* and *I. caroliniana* Watson. *French*: Iris. *German*: Blaue Iris. *Spanish*: Mavi Susan. *Italian*: Giglio azzura. Dried rhizome, root.
Action: anti-inflammatory, astringent (liver), cholagogue, diuretic, laxative, stimulant, *anti-emetic*, blood and lymph purifier, anti-obesity. A powerful alterative for passive sluggish conditions involving the liver, gall bladder, lymphatics, veins and glandular system. Restores loss of tonicity to involuntary muscle structures.
Uses. Chronic liver conditions to increase flow of bile. Cirrhosis, psoriasis, eczema and scrofulous skin disorders, acne, shingles, anal fissure.

Combines well with Yellow Dock, Red Clover. Poke root and Queen's Delight for skin disorders BHP (1983). Soft goitre (persist for months). Migraine or sick headache of liver origin. Reported to be of value in thyroid deficiency. Jaundice (*Dr M.L. Tyler*). Uterine fibroids: combined with Goldenseal and Balmony (*Priest*). Promotes secretions of pancreas, intestines and salivary glands.
Traditional combination: With equal parts Yellow Dock and Sarsaparilla as a powerful lymph cleanser.
Henry Smith MD. "I use Blue Flag when there is any local disease involving the lymph glands. The vessels become enlarged and congested because of obstruction. Disease in these vessels is the forerunner of chronic skin disease. Blue Flag can be given in expectation of satisfactory results."
Colonel Lydius, explorer. "The Indians take the root, wash it clean, boil it a little, then crush it between a couple of stones. They spread this crushed root as a poultice over leg ulcers. At the same time, the leg is bathed with the water in which the root is boiled. I have seen great cures by the use of this remedy. (*Travels in North America, II. 606*)
Preparations. Thrice daily.
Decoction: half a teaspoon to each cup water; simmer gently 15 minutes: dose – one-third cup.
Liquid Extract, BHC Vol 1. 1:1, 45 per cent ethanol. Dose: 0.6-2ml.
Tincture, BHC Vol 1. 1:5, ethanol. Dose: 3-10ml.
Powdered root. Half-2g.

Blue Flag is an ingredient of Potter's Irisine Mixture.
Note. Tincture is best made from fresh root in early spring or autumn. GSL

BLUE FLESH. Blueness of ears, hands, feet or nose, due to slow circulation of the blood through the small vessels of the skin. See: ACROCYANOSIS.

BLURRED VISION. Refer: ALCOHOLISM, CATARACT, CONJUNCTIVITIS, DIABETES, ECLAMPSIA, GLAUCOMA, IRITIS, MIGRAINE, MULTIPLE SCLEROSIS, RETINITIS, SHOCK.

BODY ODOUR. A personal and social problem. Over-activity of the sweat glands. Offensive smell is caused by the action of bacteria on stale sweat. The purpose of antiperspirants is to reduce skin bacterial action on apocrine sweat. Almost all antiperspirants sold over the counter are made from aluminium salts which have been implicated in skin granulomas. Deodorants that bear labels describing contents as dangerous to the eyes, nose and mouth should be rejected.

Bowel and kidney function should be investigated, as body odour is not normally offensive when these organs are healthy. Zinc is a powerful deodorant – zinc and castor oil cream being a traditional combination of pharmacy. Key herbal agent is *Thuja*, but it is sometimes advisable to add to this an agent for liver and kidneys.
Alternatives. *Teas*: Sage, Pennyroyal, Thyme, Betony.
Decoctions: Sarsaparilla, Wild Yam.
Tablets/capsules. Seaweed and Sarsaparilla. Wild Yam, Thuja.
Formula: equal parts: Dandelion Root, Clivers, Thuja. Dosage – Powders: One-third teaspoon. Liquid Extracts: 30-60 drops. Tinctures: 1-2 teaspoons in water, thrice daily.
Topical. Dilute oil of Sage, or Sage tea, to underarms, hands, feet.
Diet. Lacto-vegetarian. Safflower oil.
Vitamins. B-complex.
Minerals. Zinc. Dolomite.

BOGBEAN. Buckbean. *Menyanthes trifoliata L.* *German*: Fieberklee. *French*: Trefle des marais. *Italian*: Scarfano. *Chinese*: Ming-ts'ai. Herb.
Constituents: iridoid glycosides and coumarins.
Action: *bitter*, tonic, diuretic, anti-rheumatic, anti-inflammatory, lymph-alterative.
Uses. Diseases of liver and gall bladder, stomach. Anorexia, migraine of liver origin. Gout. Rheumatism and rheumatoid arthritis; muscular rheumatism with physical weakness BHP (1983).

Combines well with Celery seed or Black Cohosh BHP (1983).
Contra-indicated: colitis, diarrhoea, dysentery.
Preparations. Thrice daily.
Tea: teaspoon in each cup of boiling water; infuse 10 minutes. Dose half-1 cup.
Liquid extract, BHC Vol 1, 1:1 in 25 per cent alcohol. Dose half-2ml.
Tincture, BHC Vol 1, 1:5 in 25 per cent alcohol. Dose 2-6ml. GSL

BOILS. Furuncles. A boil is a hard swelling arising from infection of the hair roots and sweat glands caused by staphylococcus bacteria and dead white corpuscles. It is red and inflamed, with a central point, and can occur anywhere, especially, back of the neck, under armpit, on buttocks. A pustule develops, which increases in size and tension. A poultice may be necessary to bring the boil to bursting point and to discharge its contents. Severe cases require lancing with a sharp sterile instrument. Defective personal hygiene may produce satellite lesions nearby by pus infecting other hair follicles or by burrowing under the skin (carbuncle). Where persistent, test for diabetes.

Care should be taken to trace any underlying cause which should receive primary treatment: diabetes, kidney inflammation, anaemia, etc. The 'core' or centre of the boil should be extracted, although pustular matter may disperse and erup-

tion aborted. Echinacea counters infection and hastens ripening. Goldenseal is shown to be effective for staph. aureus.
Alternatives. *Teas*. Chickweed, Clivers, Comfrey leaves, Figwort, Linseed, Marshmallow leaves, Plantain, Nettles.
Combination tea. Equal parts: Dandelion root, Nettles, Senna leaf, Burdock leaves. 1-2 teaspoons to each cup boiling water, thrice daily.
Decoctions from any of the following: one teaspoon to two cups water; gently simmer 20 minutes; strain when cold. Half-1 cup thrice daily. Blue Flag root, Burdock root, Echinacea root, Marshmallow root, Yellow Dock, Wild Indigo.
Tablets/capsules. Echinacea, Blue Flag, Queen's Delight, Poke root.
Powders. Formula: Echinacea 1; Poke root half; Goldenseal quarter. Dose: 500mg (two 00 capsules or one-third teaspoon) thrice daily.
Tinctures. Formula. Echinacea 1; Burdock 1; Yellow Dock 1; Few drops Tincture Myrrh. Mix. Dose: 1 teaspoon in water thrice daily.
Tincture Myrrh, BPC (1973). 10-20 drops in water, 3 times daily.
BHP (1983) recommends, internal – combination: Burdock, Poke root, Violet and Wild Indigo.
Topical. Self-cleansing process is promoted by hot poultices of equal parts: Marshmallow root and Slippery Elm bark (preferably in powder form). An ointment with this combination is available. In the absence of herbs, use honey on clean lint, cover with cotton wool and fix in position. Alternatives: poultices of Carrot, Cabbage, White Pond Lily, Chickweed, Comfrey, Plantain, Linseed, Fenugreek. Cover with clean linen or gauze.
Dr A. Vogel. Tincture Marigold; pulped Cabbage leaves.
Tea Tree oil. After cleansing site, use lotion: 5 drops oil in eggcup boiled water, 3-4 times daily.
Supplements. Vitamins A, C, D, E. Zinc.
Preventative: 2 Garlic capsules at night.

BOLDO. *Peumus boldus*, Molina. *French*: Boldu. *German*: Chilenischer Boldobaum. *Italian*: Boldo. Part used: leaves.
Constituents: Peumus bollidus, boldine. Grows in Central Chile where it is used against liver diseases and gall stones.
Action. Cholagogue, liver tonic, diuretic, urinary antiseptic, laxative (mild), choleretic, anti-obesity, liver-protector, anti-inflammatory, choleretic.
Uses. Inflammation of the gall bladder, gall stone, biliary colic, infective cystitis, hypothyroidism, fluid retention.
Combination. With Barberry and Fringe Tree for gall stones and hepatic disease BHP (1983).
Preparations. Thrice daily.
Tea. Quarter of a teaspoon to each cup boiling water; infuse 15 minutes. Dose: half a cup.
Liquid extract. 1-5 drops in water.
Tincture BHP (1983) 1:10 in 60 per cent alcohol. Dose: 0.5-2ml in water.
Powder. (capsules) 250mg (one 00 capsule) or one-sixth teaspoon. GSL

BONE DISORDERS. May be present at birth or due to infection (osteomyelitis, tuberculosis, etc), fractures from injury or accident, osteoporosis, Paget's disease (deformity due to mineral deficiency), tumour or sarcoma, osteomalacia, rickets due to Vitamin D deficiency. Brittle-bone disease. Arthritis. See separate entries.
Comfrey decoction. 1 heaped teaspoon to cup water gently simmered 5 minutes; strain when cold; 1 cup – to which is added 20 drops Tincture Calendula (Marigold), thrice daily. Fenugreek seeds may be used as an alternative to Comfrey.
Alternative:– *Mixture*: equal parts liquid extracts: Comfrey, Marigold, St John's Wort. One teaspoon in water or honey thrice daily.
Tablets/capsules. Fenugreek, St John's Wort.
Topical. Comfrey, Fenugreek or Horsetail poultice.
Supplements. Vitamin A, C, E. Dolomite, Zinc.
Supportive. Exposure of site to sunlight.
Comfrey. The potential benefit of Comfrey root outweighs possible risk for bone disorders.

BONESET. Feverwort. *Eupatorium perfoliatum L*. *French*: Herbe Parfaite. *German*: Durchwachsener Wasserhanf. *Spanish*: Eupatorio. *Chinese*: Tsé-lan. Herb.
Action: febrifuge, diaphoretic, bitter tonic, laxative, immune stimulant.
Keynote: children's fevers. Induces heavy sweating to reduce a raised temperature and eliminate toxins via the skin. Antispasmodic to the respiratory organs. Was official in the U.S. Pharmacopoeia for nearly a century, 1820-1916. Reported to be anti-neoplastic. (*Indian J. Chem., 13, 541 (1975)*)
Uses. Fevers, "ache-all-over" influenza. Acute pain in the bones (from which it derives its name). Fractures, to promote healing of broken bones. Used with success in malaria (*Virgil Vogel*). Dengue fever. Bronchitis.

Skin diseases accompanying children's fevers (measles, chicken pox, etc). Acquitted itself well in combating yellow fever epidemic, Philadelphia, 1793.

Combines well with Yarrow or Elderflowers or Composition for colds and feverishness in children.
Preparations. Thrice daily.
Tea. 1 heaped teaspoon to each cup boiling water; infuse 5-10 minutes; half-1 cup every 2 hours (acute). Thrice daily (chronic).
Liquid extract. 15-30 drops in water.
Tincture BHP (1983) 1:5 in 45 per cent alcohol:

dose 1-4ml.
Powder. 375mg (quarter of a teaspoon). GSL

BORAGE. *Borago officinalis L. French*: Bourrache. *German*: Boretsch. *Spanish*: Borraja. *Italian*: Borrana. Oil from seeds.
Constituents: pyrrolizidine alkaloids, choline.
Action: adrenal gland restorative, galactagogue, demulcent, emollient, diuretic, refrigerant, anti-depressive. Stimulates production of prostaglandin EI. Oil contains two important fatty acids: gamma-linolenic acid (GLA) and linoleic acid. Assists assimilation of iron.
Uses. To strengthen adrenal glands weakened by intake of steroids (cortisone, etc). Stress, mental exhaustion, depression. Helps to prevent inflammation of stomach and intestines in cases of toxicity, allergy and infection. Colitis, Gastritis, Gastric ulcer. "Borage cheers the heart and raises drooping spirits" (*Dioscorides*). Old Italian remedy to increase breast milk in nursing mothers. Chronic catarrh. Borage oil is combined with Evening Primrose oil to reduce cholesterol deposits. Leaky-gut syndrome (Borage seed oil). External use said to defer wrinkling and skin dryness of old age. Used internally under directions of a qualified practitioner.
Preparations. Thrice daily.
Tea: 1 teaspoon to each cup boiling water; infuse 15 minutes. Half-1 cup.
Home tincture: 1oz cut herb to 20oz 45 per cent alcohol (Vodka, etc) in wide-neck bottle. Macerate and shake daily for 4 days. Filter. Bottle. Dose: 1-2 teaspoons in water.
Liquid Extract: half-1 teaspoon.
Capsules: (oil) (Salus).
Fresh juice: 1 teaspoon.
Pharmacy only.

BOSWELLIA SERRATA, Roxb. Oleo-gum resin.
Action. Aromatic diuretic, laxative, demulcent, diaphoretic, astringent, expectorant, stimulant, digestive. Mild pain killer.
Uses. Urinary disorders, rheumatism.
Preparations. *Topical*. Ointments for ulcers.

BOTULISM. An uncommon disorder of the nervous system usually caused by infected canned foods. Spores C. Botulinum yields a toxin which produces symptoms: disturbance of vision, abdominal pain, diarrhoea and temporary paralysis of the breathing muscles. As the disease develops quickly and affects the central nervous system, modern hospital diagnosis and treatment are essential. However, matching antibacterials include: Echinacea, Myrrh, Wild Indigo, Goldenseal, Wild Yam. Add: Valerian for the CNS.
Alternatives. *Tablets/capsules*. Goldenseal, Echinacea, Valerian.
Tinctures. Formula. Echinacea 2; Goldenseal half; Wild Indigo half. Mix. 1-2 teaspoons in water every 2 hours.
Tincture Myrrh Co 1 part Tincture Capsicum BPC (1973) to 4 parts Tincture Myrrh BPC (1973). Dose: One-2.5ml.
Diet. 3-day fruit and vegetable juice fast.
Treatment by or in liaison with a general medical practitioner.

BOVINE SPONGIFORM ENCEPHALOPATHY (BSE) Scrapie. Notifiable disease. Fatal disease in the nervous system of cattle, unknown before 1985. Microscopic holes appear in the brain giving a spongiform appearance, but with little inflammation. Can spread from one animal to another: sheep, goats, deer, mules, mink, hamsters, mice, pigs and monkeys. Cause: not a virus. Animals itch and scrape themselves against trees or posts for relief. May spread from animals to humans, with brain infection after the character of polio.
Symptoms. (Human). Speech impairment, short-term-memory-loss, difficulty in controlling body movements. Zinc deficiency.
Treatment. Hospitalisation.
Suggested treatment for human infection, unproven.
Tinctures. Echinacea 5; Black Cohosh 3; Yarrow 2; Senna leaf 1. 2-3 teaspoons in water (or cup hot Yarrow tea) 3-4 times daily. For headache: Gelsemium.
Supplement: Zinc.
To be treated by a general medical practitioner or hospital specialist.

BOX'S INDIGESTION PILLS. Ingredients: Myrrh 18.2 per cent. Gentian 18.2 per cent. Ginger 18.2 per cent. Aloes 18.92 per cent. Capsicum 18.2 per cent. Acacia 6.3 per cent. Cajuput oil 2.7 per cent. For dyspepsia. Very popular in their day but now obsolete.

BOX'S HERBAL OINTMENT. Ingredients: Slippery Elm 10.5 per cent; Marshmallow 10.5 per cent; soft yellow paraffin to 100 per cent. General purposes. Now obsolete.

BRADYCARDIA. Slow heart rate; less than 55 beats per minute. Cause may be disease of the heart muscle or may lie in the CNS (central nervous system). May also be caused by disorder of the thyroid gland (hypothyroidism) with dropsy-like swelling of face and hands. Of recent years bradycardia has been associated with beta-blocker drugs, reserpine and digitalis alkaloids given in excess. Wrist pulse is slow. In the aged it is present as weakness and worsened by hypothermia.

In total heart block a rate of 36 or less is due to failure of conduction from atria to ventricles: requires artificial pace maker.

Modern herbalism (phytotherapy) employs: *Hawthorn berries*, Prickly Ash bark (berries preferred for circulatory disorders), *Lily of the Valley leaves*, Bugleweed (Lycopus virginicus), Broom, Heart's Ease, Holy Thistle, Cactus (Night blooming cereus), Nutmeg, Saffron, Lemon Balm, Thuja, Figwort, Ginseng. Lily of the Valley has a specific action in the heart muscle.

One of the purest and positive stimulants known for increasing the pulse rate is Cayenne Pepper. A few grains sprinkled on a meal or added to a beverage coaxes the heart to increase its output. To give the heart just that little extra support it may need, gentle cardiac stimulants can be found in the kitchen: Cloves, Ginger, Horseradish, Peppermint, Red Sage, Garden Sage.

Where a slow beat arises from a serious heart condition the underlying disorder should receive priority. In the event of an emergency the restorative, Camphor, may be given until the doctor comes:– 1-5 drops oil of Camphor in a teaspoon of honey. Even inhalation of the oil is known to increase pulse rate.

A slow pulse can be increased in pace by vagal relaxation. The pulse may be slow because of an excess of bile salts in the blood when a liver remedy (say Dandelion) would be indicated. Slow pulse of convalescence (Gentian), diabetes (Goat's Rue), glandular fever (Poke root), jaundice (Dandelion), low thyroid (Kelp), congestion in the brain (Cypripedium), nervous exhaustion (Ginseng).

Practitioner. Broom (*Spartiol Drops*), 20 drops thrice daily. (*Klein*)

Diet and supplements. See: DIET – HEART AND CIRCULATION.

BRAIN DISORDERS. Usually associated with some loss of sensation and power in another part of the body. Taste, smell, hearing, sight and movement may be affected. The following are some of the disorders that may affect the brain. *Each has a separate entry in this book.*

Abscess, Alzheimer's Disease, anoxia (oxygen starvation), coma, concussion, haemorrhage, Down's syndrome, epilepsy, tumour, hydrocephalus (water on the brain), meningitis, multiple sclerosis, stroke (rupture of blood vessel), spina bifida, syphilis (general paralysis of the insane), sleepy sickness.

Poor circulation through the brain due to hardening of the arteries: Ginkgo, Ginseng. Ginseng stimulates the hypothalmic/pituitary axis of the brain and favourably influences its relationship with the adrenal glands.

Congestion of the brain – Cowslip (Boerwicke). Irritability of brain and spine – Hops. Oats.

Inflammation of the brain (encephalitis) as in viral infection, poliomyelitis, rabies, sleepy sickness, etc: Echinacea, Passion flower, Skullcap and Lobelia. Gelsemium acts as a powerful relaxant in the hands of a practitioner: Tincture BPC (1973): dose 0.3ml.

Brain storm from hysteria, locomotor ataxia, etc – Liquid Extract Lobelia: 5ml teaspoon in water when necessary (*Dr Jentzsch, 1915, Ellingwood*) Supplement with Zinc, Vitamins C and E.

Blood clot, thrombosis: Yarrow. Neurasthenia: Oats, Basil, Hops.

Brain fag and jet-lag: Chamomile, Skullcap, Oats, Ginseng, Ginkgo.

Tumour may be present years before manifesting: Goldenseal.

Mental state: depression, anxiety, schizophrenia.

Tea. Formula. Skullcap, Gotu Kola and German Chamomile; equal parts. 1 heaped teaspoon to each cup water gently simmered 10 minutes. Strain. 1 cup thrice daily.

Unspecified tensive state. Formula. Tinctures. Hops 1; Passion flower 2; Valerian 2. Dose: 2 teaspoons thrice daily until diagnosis is concluded.

Unspecified torpor. Formula. Tinctures. Ginseng 1; Kola 1; Capsicum quarter. 2 teaspoons in water thrice daily until diagnosis is concluded.

Brain weakness in the elderly: Ginkgo. See: ALZHEIMER'S DISEASE.

Fluid on the brain: see HYDROCEPHALUS.

Abscess of the brain: see ABSCESS.

Brain restoratives. Black Haw, True Unicorn root, Galangal, Oats, Oatstraw, False Unicorn root, Kola, Hops. Vitamin B6. Magnesium.

Cerebral thrombosis. See entry.

Note. Cold water may help victims to survive: rapid loss of body heat protects the brain. (*Child Health Department, University of Wales*)

Treatment by or in liaison with general medical practitioner or hospital specialist.

BRAN. A concentrated form of food fibre (bulk). Bran can absorb nine times its own weight in water, and therefore forms easily-passed soft moist stools. In this way it regulates bowel function and may be appropriate for both constipation and diarrhoea. In the absence of Ispaghula seeds is good for irritable bowel with diverticula. High in zinc and fibre; helps reduce level of cholesterol in the blood and thus lessens risk of heart disease.

Bran wash. Fill a muslin bag with bran and immerse in boiling water for 15-30 minutes. Use as a sponge for cleansing ulcers, skin rashes, etc. Use no soap. Two or three times weekly.

Bran bath. Fill muslin bag with 1 or 2lbs (1-2 kilos) of bran. Run bath-tap. Immerse bag in bath. No soaps used. Twice weekly. Renew bran weekly. Patient remains in water 20-30 minutes.

BREAST-FEEDING. Evidence strongly demonstrates the protective effects of breast milk compared with bottle feeding, against numerous infections, especially against gastro-intestinal infections (*Hanson & Bergstrom, 1990*). Breast milk also plays a protective role against respiratory tract infections, inflammation of the middle ear and meningitis. (*Cunningham et al, 1991*)

Breast-feeding has been shown to have a protective effect against urinary tract infections in the first six months of life. (*Pisacane et al, 1992*). In other infections, such as Haemophilus influenzae Type B, breast-feeding for longer than six months has also been found to have a protective effect. (*Takala et al, 1989*)

A new study reveals evidence that women with silicone breast implants who breast-feed their children put them at risk of developing systemic sclerosis. (*JAMA Jan 19, 1994*)

BREASTS. The female breast should be examined monthly, and any dimples, lumps or change in skin texture noted. A lifestyle to avoid most breast disorders means following a wholefood diet, to the exclusion of additives, food colourings and carcinogens where possible. Drugs, artificial sweeteners, alcohol and coffee should be avoided. Consumption of caffeine (tea, coffee, etc) has been associated with cysts (fibrocystic disease, fibro-adenoma). The link is shown between tea and coffee, but not with cola and chocolate products. (*Journal of National Cancer Institute, vol 72, No. 5, p. 1015-1019, 1984*)

Exercises include the "windmill" movement, stretching the circling arms without straining. Give breasts an invigorating spray of cold water for one minute. Exchange animal fats and cholesterol for unsaturated cold-pressed oils. Daily supplementation includes: Vitamins A, C, E. Zinc, Selenium, for their anti-carcinogenic effect.

Agents known to promote healthy breasts: Red Clover flowers, Sarsaparilla, oil of Evening Primrose, Yarrow, Clivers.

Women with breast disease have high rates of sebum production, a marker of Essential Fatty Acid deficiency. (*Goolamali SK, Shuster S. Lancet 1; 428-9, 1975*) To make good such deficiency oils of safflower, corn, Soya, etc, being rich in EFAs are indicated. Animal fat should be avoided; butter and dairy products taken sparingly.

Evening Primrose oil capsules (*Efamol*) can significantly reduce breast pain, breast tenderness and formation of nodules. (*Pashby NL, Mansel RE, Preece et. al. British Surgical Research Society, July 1981*)

BREAST, ABSCESS. See: ABSCESS.

BREAST, CYST. See: FIBROCYSTIC BREAST DISEASE.

BREAST, GUITAR NIPPLE. Musician's breast.
Alternatives:– External treatment. Lotion – few drops Tincture Arnica in eggcup of water. Aloe Vera or Comfrey cream. Marshmallow and Slippery Elm ointment.

BREASTS, HARD. To soften. Creams: Calendula, Chickweed, Aloe Vera, Evening Primrose. Castor oil (cold compress).

BREASTS, MASTECTOMY. Surgical operation for removal of the breast. Follow-up treatment to promote healing with minimum scarring. Marigold, St John's Wort (Hypericum), Oil of Evening Primrose. Vitamin E. Fenugreek seeds.
Alternatives. *Tea*. Equal parts: Marigold petals, St John's Wort, Mullein. 2 teaspoons to each cup boiling water; infuse 15 minutes. 1 cup 3 or more times daily.
Tissue regeneration. Fenugreek tea.
Capsules. Oil of Evening Primrose: 2 x 250mg, 3 times daily.
Liquid Extract Blue Cohosh BHP (1983) 7-15 drops (0.5-1ml).
Topical. Oil of Evening Primrose. Comfrey dusting powder. Aloe Vera juice. Vitamin E cream.
Diet. Lacto-vegetarian.
Information. BCC, Free Help Line. UK telephone: 0500 245345.

BREASTS, MASTITIS. Inflammation of the breast. Maybe of the new born, of puberty; associated with mumps, abscess; or occurs during breastfeeding when a milk duct may become blocked and infected by bacteria – usually *Staphylococcus aureus*. Mothers should suckle the baby until the breast is completely empty. Chronic mastitis is known as fibro adenosis. Should acute mastitis get out of hand, abscess may form requiring more drastic treatment such as incision to release pus.
Symptoms. Local tenderness, feverishness, general agitation. Pain following mumps. Nipple discharge.
Alternatives. Where there is feverishness add Elderflowers (one part).
Tea. Combine equal parts: Comfrey leaves. Wild Thyme. German Chamomile. Red Clover. 1 heaped teaspoon to each cup boiling water; infuse 5-15 minutes. Drink freely.
Tablets/capsules. Poke root. Red Clover. Echinacea.
Powders. Formula: Echinacea 2; Red Clover 1; Poke root 1. Mix. Dose: 500mg (two 00 capsules or one-third teaspoon) thrice daily.
Tinctures. Formula. Echinacea 2; Marigold 1; Agnus Castus 2; Poke root 1. Dose: 1-2 teaspoons thrice daily, in water.
Poultice: (1) Fresh Plantain leaves beaten in pestle and mortar, applied cold. (2) Comfrey powder or Slippery Elm powder (or both) sprinkled on suitable material wrung out in boiling water and applied. (3) German Chamomile and Comfrey leaves. (*Arthur Hyde, MNIMH*) (4) Bring to boil, equal parts Chamomile flowers and Marshmallow leaves in milk and water.

Remove when boiling point is reached. Saturate linen or suitable material. Apply every 12 hours. (*Rev. John Wesley*) (6) Bathe with juice of Houseleek. (*Traditional, Norfolk villages*)
Evening Primrose oil: internally and externally.
Poke root. An important ingredient of prescription for acute condition.

BREASTS, MILK EXCESSIVE. To reduce.
Tea. Rosemary. 1 teaspoon to each cup boiling water; infuse 15 minutes; dose – half-1 cup thrice daily.
Tea. Sage. 2 teaspoons to each cup boiling water; infuse 15 minutes; dose – half-1 cup thrice daily.
Old hospital remedy: Epsom's salts.

BREASTS, MILK SCANTY. To promote milk production: Alfalfa, Aniseed, Borage, Caraway, Centuary, Balm, Dill, Fennel, Goat's Rue, Holy Thistle, Nettles, Burnet Saxifrage, Bitter Milkwort, Marshmallow root, Raspberry leaves, Vervain. John Parkinson (1640) recommended Agnus Castus.
Formula (1). Fenugreek seeds 2; Aniseeds 1. Mix. 2 teaspoons to each cup water gently simmered 2 minutes in a covered vessel. Dose: 1 cup 3 or more times daily. Consume seeds.
Formula (2). Equal parts: Goat's Rue, Raspberry leaves. Mix. 1 heaped teaspoon to each cup boiling water; infuse 5-10 minutes. Dose: 1 cup 3 or more times daily.
Tablets/capsules. Agnus Castus, Fenugreek, Borage.

BREASTS. NIPPLE – TO HARDEN. Bathe nipple with Vodka or gin.

BREASTS. NIPPLES, DISCHARGE. Due to a number of causes. Unlike colostrum secreted during breast-feeding after delivery. A pathological nipple discharge is non-milky, recurs from time to time, and is usually only from one nipple. It may be watery or a sticky yellow, staining being detected on bra or pyjamas. When blood-flecked it should be promptly investigated by a competent authority.

When the discharge is yellow, indicating pus, an infection is suspected which may develop into an abscess. Herbal treatment can be effective but if, after a week, the condition has not improved surgical exploration may be necessary to remove the affected duct.
Alternatives. Clivers, Goldenseal, Fenugreek, Marigold, Poke root, Queen's Delight, Wild Indigo. Taken as tea, powder, liquid extract or decoction.
Tea. Formula. Equal parts: Red Clover, Clivers, Gotu Kola. 2 teaspoons to each cup boiling water; infuse 15 minutes. Half-1 cup thrice daily.
Powders. Formula. Wild Indigo 1; Echinacea 2; Poke root 1. Dose: 500mg (two 00 capsules or one-third teaspoon) thrice daily.
Tinctures. Formula. Echinacea 2; Goldenseal 1; Poke root 1. Dose: 30-60 drops thrice daily.
Topical – for sore nipples. Wheatgerm oil, Evening Primrose oil. Lotions: Goldenseal, Marigold, distilled extract of Witch Hazel. Nipples to be washed before a child is again put to the breast. Cracked nipples: Comfrey – pulp from fresh plant, or equal parts powder and milk as a paste.
Minerals: magnesium, zinc.

BREASTS, NURSING MOTHER EXHAUSTION. Inability to cope with incessant demands of the child. Heaviness of shoulders and back. Headache, pains, possible anaemia, lack of energy, insomnia, mental depression. Usually a combination of invigorating herb teas suffices. Alcohol-based tinctures, liquid extracts, etc, are contra-indicated. Bananas, to counter potassium deficiency. Oatmeal porridge.
Alternatives. *Teas*. Oats. Raspberry leaves. Ginseng, Wood Betony, Vervain.
Gerard tea. Equal parts: Raspberry leaves, Lemon Balm leaves, Agrimony leaves. Mix. Made as ordinary tea: 2-3 teaspoons to small teapot; infuse few minutes. Drink freely.
Fenugreek tea: consume seeds as well as liquor.
Gentian root. 2 teaspoons to cup cold water left to steep overnight. Half-1 cup before meals.
Pollen..
Diet. Oatmeal porridge. Honey.
Supplements. Multivitamins, B-complex, B6, B12.

BREASTS, OVER LARGE. To reduce.
Internal:– Nettles, Agnus Castus, Poke root, Pipsissewa leaves. Teas, powders or tinctures thrice daily.
External:– Engorgement from breast-feeding – massage with Calendula cream or Almond oil.

BREAST (Female) TENDERNESS, PAIN. May be from hormonal imbalance for which Agnus Castus is almost specific.
Rosemary. 1 teaspoon leaves to cup boiling water; infuse 15 minutes. Half-1 cup 2-3 times daily.
Tea. Formula. Equal parts leaves, Agnus Castus, Rosemary, Balm. 1-2 teaspoons to each cup boiling water; infuse 15 minutes; 1 cup 2-3 times daily.
Evening Primrose oil. 10 drops (or 2 x 250ml capsules) 3 times daily.
Poke root. Internally and externally.
Yorkshire gypsy device: fix a cabbage or a rhubarb leaf beneath brassiere.
Liquid Extract Blue Cohosh BHP (1983): 0.5-1ml. Thrice daily. Alternative: Liquid Extract Rosemary BHP (1983): 2-4ml. Thrice daily.
Vitamins. All-round multivitamin and mineral supplement. Vitamin C (1g daily). Vitamin E (400iu daily).

BREASTS, UNDERDEVELOPED. To increase size and firm, native women of Costa Rica use *Saw Palmetto* berries. The traditional combination of Saw Palmetto, Kola and Damiana are available in tablet or capsule form.
Peruvian bark. Liquid Extract, BPC (1954), 0.3-1ml in water, thrice daily.
Diet. Adequate protein is essential for a healthy-looking bust.
Fenugreek seed tea. Favourable results reported.

BREASTS, WEANING. *Aloe Vera*. From time immemorial women of Northern Ethiopia have applied to their nipples raw juice of Aloe Vera to discourage the child from suckling. European tradition favours *Rosemary*, internally and externally.

BREATHING IRREGULARITIES. Accelerated inspiration, followed by slow expiration is usually not serious. May accompany fevers and certain nervous disorders for which no specific treatment is necessary. Where condition is chronic the causal factor should be investigated. Any underlying condition should be treated. For transient irregularity:–
Teas: Balm, Motherwort, Mistletoe, Lime flowers.
Tablets/capsules. Lobelia, Hawthorn, Motherwort, Valerian.

BRIGHT'S DISEASE (ACUTE). Glomerulonephritis. Recognised by slight puffiness of the eyes and a dropsical accumulation of fluid in body cavities. Blood pressure rises. Appetite disappears. Digestion is deranged, urine may be blood-stained and a variety of symptoms present as dizziness, headache, nausea. Commonly caused by post streptococcal throat infection circulating in the blood, yet it is now known that the condition may arise from exposure to common garden insecticides and toxic substances of commercial importance that alter the body's immune system and affect kidney function.

Acute toxic nephritis is possible in the convalescent stage of scarlet and other infectious fevers, even influenza. Causes are legion, including septic conditions in the ear, nose, throat, tonsils, teeth or elsewhere. Resistance to other infections will be low because of accumulation of toxins awaiting elimination. When protein escapes from the body through faulty kidneys general health suffers.

This condition should be treated by or in liaison with a qualified medical practitioner.
Treatment. Bedrest essential, with electric blanket or hot water bottle. Attention to bowels; a timely laxative also assists elimination of excessive fluid. Diuretics. Diaphoretics. Abundant drinks of bottled water or herb teas (3-5 pints daily). Alkaline drinks have a healing effect upon the kidneys. Juniper is never given for active inflammation.
Useful teas. Buchu, Cornsilk, Couchgrass, Clivers, Bearberry, Elderflowers, Marshmallow, Mullein, Marigold flowers, Wild Carrot, Yarrow.
Greece: traditional tea: equal parts, Agrimony, Bearberry, Couchgrass, Pellitory.
Powders. Equal parts: Dandelion, Cornsilk, Mullein. Dose: 750mg (three 00 capsules or half teaspoon) every 2 hours. In water or cup of Cornsilk tea.
Tinctures. Equal parts: Buchu, Elderflowers, Yarrow. Mix. Dose: 1-2 teaspoons in water or cup of Cornsilk tea, every two hours.
Topical. Hot poultices to small of the back; flannel or other suitable material saturated with an infusion of Elderflowers, Goldenrod, Horsetail or Yarrow. Herbal treatment offers a supportive role.

BRIGHT'S DISEASE (CHRONIC). Chronic glomerulonephritis. The final stage. May follow the sub-acute stage or repeated attacks of the acute stage. Kidneys small and white due to scar tissue. Amount of urine passed is considerably increased, pale and low specific gravity. Kidneys 'leak' protein in large quantities of water passed, their efficiency as filters greatly impaired. Tissues of eyelids and ankles waterlogged. Symptoms include loin pain, anaemia, loss of weight, progressive kidney damage.

A constant fear is the onset of uraemia caused by accumulation in the blood of waste by-products of protein digestion, therefore the patient should reject meat in favour of fish. Eggs and dairy products taken in strict moderation.

Where urea accumulates in the circulation 'sustaining' diuretics are indicated; these favour excretion of solids without forcing the discharge of more urine: including Shepherd's Purse, Gravel root, or Uva Ursi when an astringent diuretic is needed for a show of blood in the urine. According to the case, other agents in common practice: Dandelion root, Yarrow, Hawthorn, Marigold, Stone root, Hydrangea, Parsley Piert, Buchu, Hawthorn, Golden Rod.

The patient will feel the cold intensely and always be tired. Warm clothing and ample rest are essential. Heart symptoms require treatment with Lily of the Valley or Broom.

This condition should be treated by or in liaison with a qualified medical practitioner.
Treatment. As kidney damage would be established, treatment would be palliative; efforts being to relieve strain and obtain maximum efficiency. There may be days of total bed-rest, raw foods and quiet. Consumption of fluids may not be as abundant as formerly. Soothing herb teas promote well-being and facilitate elimination. Oil of Juniper is avoided.

Efforts should be made to promote a rapid absorption – to restore the balance between the circulation and the lymphatics. For this purpose

Mullein is effective. A few grains of Cayenne or drops of Tincture Capsicum enhances action.
Indicated. Antimicrobials, urinary antiseptics, diuretics, anti-hypertensives. For septic conditions add Echinacea.
Of Therapeutic Value. Alfalfa, Broom, Buchu, Couchgrass, Cornsilk, Dandelion, Lime flowers, Marigold, Mullein, Marshmallow, Parsley Piert, Periwinkle (major), Wild Carrot, Water Melon seed tea.
Tea. Combine equal parts: Couchgrass, Dandelion, Mullein. 2 teaspoons to each cup boiling water. Infuse 5-15 minutes. 1 cup freely.
Powders. Combine equal parts: Stone root, Hydrangea, Hawthorn. Dose: 500mg (two 00 capsules or one-third teaspoon) 3 or more times daily in water or cup Cornsilk tea. A few grains Cayenne enhances action.
Formula. Buchu 2; Mullein 2; Echinacea 1; Senna leaves half. Mix. Liquid extracts: 1 teaspoon. Tinctures: 2 teaspoons. In water or cup Cornsilk tea 3 or more times daily. 2-3 drops Tincture Capsicum to each dose enhances action.
Diffusive stimulant for the lymphatic vessels. Onion milk is an effective potassium-conserving diuretic and diaphoretic. Onions are simmered gently in milk for 2 hours and drunk when thirsty or as desired – a welcome alternative to water. May be eaten uncooked.
Diet. Salt-free, low fat, high protein. Spring water. Raw goat's milk, potassium broth. Fish oils. Avoid eggs and dairy products. No alcohol.
Supplements. Vitamins A, B-complex, C plus bioflavonoids, B6, D, E, Magnesium, Lecithin.
Herbal treatment offers a supportive role.

BRITISH HERB TEA. Equal parts: Agrimony, Great Burnet, Meadowsweet, Raspberry leaves, Wood Betony. Infuse as domestic tea, as strong and as frequently as desired.

BRITISH HERBAL COMPENDIUM 1990 provides data complementary to each monograph in the British Herbal Pharmacopoeia 1990. Sections on constituents and regulatory status, therapeutic action and indications for use. A valuable text for the practitioner, manufacturer and all involved in herbal medicine. Therapeutic Section records observations and clinical experience of senior practitioners (members of the National Institute of Medical Herbalists). Compiled by the British Herbal Medicine Association Pharmacopoeia Commission which includes scientists, university pharmacognosists, pharmacologists, botanists, consulting medical herbalists, and medical practitioners in an advisory capacity. See abbreviation BHC under preparations.

BRITISH HERBAL MEDICINE ASSOCIATION. Before the Medicine's Bill proceeded to the Statute book to become the Medicine's Act 1968, so great was the threat to the practice of herbal medicine and sale of herbal preparations, that the profession and trade were galvanised into mobilising opposition. Thus, the British Herbal Medicine Association was formed in 1964. In the ensuing struggle, important concessions were won that ensured survival.

The BHMA is recognised by the Medicines Control Agency as the official representative of the profession and the trade. Its objects are (a) to defend the right of the public to choose herbal remedies and be able to obtain them; (b) to foster research in herbal medicine and establish standards of safety which are a safeguard to the user; (c) to encourage the dissemination of knowledge about herbal remedies, and (d) do everything possible to advance the science and practice of herbal medicine, and to further recognition at all levels.

Membership is open to all interested in the future of herbal medicine, including herbal practitioners, herbal retailers, health food stores, wholesalers, importers, manufacturers, pharmacists, doctors and research workers.

The BHMA produces the British Herbal Pharmacopoeia. Its Scientific Committee is made up of senior herbal practitioners, university pharmacologists and pharmacognosists. Other publications include: BHMA Advertising Code (1978), Medicines Act Advertising guidelines (1979), the Herbal Practitioner's Guide to the Medicine's Act (*F. Fletcher Hyde*), and miscellaneous leaflets on 'Herbs and Their Uses'.

The BHMA does not train students for examination but works in close co-operation with the National Institute of Medical Herbalists, and with the European Scientific Co-operative on Phytotherapy.

Chairmen since its inception: Frank Power, 1964-1969; Fred Fletcher-Hyde, 1969-1977; Hugh Mitchell 1977-1986; James Chappelle 1986-1990; Victor Perfitt 1990-.

During the years the association has secured important advantages for its membership, particularly continuity of sale of herbal medicines in health food shops. It continues to maintain vigilance in matters British and European as they affect manufacturing, wholesaling, retailing, prescribing and dispensing.

See: BRITISH HERBAL PHARMACOPOEIA and BRITISH HERBAL COMPENDIUM.

BRITISH HERBAL MEDICINE ASSOCIATION, SCIENTIFIC COMMITTEE, 1995.
Peter R. Bradley MSc CChem FRSC (Chairman). Whitehall Laboratories.
Sheila E. Drew BPharm PhD MRPharms. Deputy Head of Technical Services, William Ransom & Son plc.
Fred Fletcher-Hyde BSc FNIMH. President Emeritus, British Herbal Medicine Association. President Emeritus, National Institute of Medical

Herbalists.
Simon Y. Mills MA FNIMH. Director, Centre for Complementary Health Studies, University of Exeter.
Hugh W. Mitchell MNIMH (Hon). President, British Herbal Medicine Association. Managing Director, Mitchfield Botanics Ltd.
Edward J. Shellard BPharm PhD DSc(Hon) (Warsaw Medical Academy) FRPharmS CChem FRSC FLS. Emeritus Professor of Pharmacognosy, University of London.
Arnold Webster CChem MRSC. Technical Director, English Grains Ltd.
Peter Wetton BSc LRSC. G.R. Lane Health Products Ltd.
Hein Zeylstra FNIMH. Principal. School of Phytotherapy, Sussex.

BRITISH HERBAL PHARMACOPOEIA. World-accepted work. New edition published: 1990, fully revised and updated. Over 80 monographs. Official publication of the British Herbal Medicine Association to set and maintain standards of herbal medicine. Does not contain Therapeutic Section and index that appear in the 1983 edition, but describes macroscopical and microscopical characteristics. Quantitative standards, methods of identification, commercial form and source and description of the powdered form. BHP 1990 vol 1 is available from BHMA Publications, PO Box 304, Bournemouth, Dorset, England BH7 6JZ (£35). Abbreviation: BHP.

BRITISH JOURNAL OF PHYTOTHERAPY. Published six-monthly by the School of Phytotherapy (Herbal Medicine), edited by Hein Zeylstra. Scientific journal for the professional. Enquiries: School of Phytotherapy, Bucksteep Manor, Bodle Street Green, near Hailsham, East Sussex BN27 4RJ, UK.

BRITISH PHARMACOPOEIA, THE. Provides authoritative standards for the quality of many substances, preparations and articles used in medicine and pharmacy, and includes the monographs of the European Pharmacopoeias. A legally enforceable document throughout the UK, most of the Commonwealth and many other countries, and is an indispensable laboratory handbook for all concerned with the quality of medicines. Published on the recommendation of the Medicines Commission pursuant to the Medicines Act 1968. Published by Her Majesty's Stationery Office, London. The most useful BPC for the herbal practitioner is the BPC 1934.

BRITTLE BONE DISEASE. Fragilitas ossium. A genetic disease where the child is unable to stand because bones of the legs would snap under slightest pressure. Legs may be broken as many as twenty times.

Alternatives. *Treatment*. Almost one third require major surgery. Herbal nutrition may build up quality of bone from within: Horsetail, Yarrow, Comfrey, Fenugreek seeds.
Powders. Formula: Comfrey root 2; Marigold 1; Horsetail 1; Mix. Dose: 750mg (three 00 capsules or half a teaspoon) thrice daily.
Tinctures. Formula: Comfrey root 2; Horsetail 1; Marigold 1. Dose: 1-2 teaspoons thrice daily.
Fenugreek tea. Consume seeds as well as liquor.
Propolis. Regeneration of bone tissue.
Comfrey. It would appear that the internal use of the root could be justified, where its benefits far outstrip its risks.
Diet and Supplements: same as for OSTEOPOROSIS.
Note: Brittle Bone Society, City Road, Dundee.

BROMELAIN. *Ananassa sativa. Ananas comosus*. Proteolytic enzyme derived from the stem of the pineapple plant.
Action. Anti-inflammatory, smooth muscle relaxant, digestant, anti-oedema. Stimulates production of prostaglandin E1-like compounds. Inhibitor of blood platelet aggregation thus preserving the normal consistency of the blood.
Uses. Cellulitis, to remove layers of fat. Has some reputation as a digestant in terminal disease. Sinusitis, weak digestion in the elderly, oedema following surgical operation, to promote post-operative healing. Used by natives of the Far East for quinsy. Part of the Bristol Cancer Diet to promote digestion of proteins.

"It is of value in modulating tumour growth, blood coagulation and inflammatory changes in the débridement of third degree burns. As an inflammatory it has been used for rheumatoid arthritis, thrombophlebitis, haematomas, oral inflammation, diabetic ulcers, rectal and perirectal inflammation, athletic injuries and general oral and plastic surgery." (*Kay van Rietschoten, British Journal of Phytotherapy, Vol 1, Nos 3/4*)
Preparations. 1-2 200mg Bromelain tablets/capsules between meals thrice daily. Patient preference: vegetarian hypoallergenic yeast-free: as an aid to digestion, 250-500mg at meals.

BROMIDROSIS. A fetid sweat caused by chemical change and the action of bacteria, usually in the armpit or on the feet. See: SWEATING, EXCESSIVE.

BRONCHIECTASIS. Damage to bronchi when ballooned beyond normal limits, usually from chronic infection. May be a legacy from lung infections, whooping cough, measles, tuberculosis, foreign body or other bronchial troubles. Predisposing factors: smoking, working with asbestos and other industrial materials. Now known that some structural changes in bronchial epithelium caused by cigarette smoking are reversible by abstinence for over two years.

A plug of tenacious mucus may be clogged in the bronchial tree and gradually sucked into the smaller bronchi, blocking them. This prevents air from passing through to replace air that has been absorbed and precipitates cough, sputum, spitting of blood. A stethoscope reveals crepitations; chronic cases may be detected by clubbing of the fingers, which sign may be missing in bronchitis and other chest infections.

Alternatives. *Treatment*. Bronchitics are most at risk and should never neglect a cold. Stimulating expectorants followed by postural drainage indicated. To control infection, plenty of Echinacea should be given. Where a localised area becomes septic a surgical lobectomy may be necessary. See: POSTURAL DRAINAGE. Cases of developed bronchiectasis can be maintained relatively well over a period of years by judicious use of herbs: Bayberry bark, Blood root, Elecampane root, Ephedra, Eucalyptus oil, Grindelia, Senega root, Mullein, Pleurisy root, Red Clover. Lobelia. Not Comfrey.

Tea. Formula. Equal parts: Yarrow, Mullein, Lungwort. 1 heaped teaspoon in each cup boiling water; infuse 5-15 minutes; 1 cup morning and evening and when necessary.

Powders. Mix: Lobelia 2; Grindelia quarter; Capsicum quarter. Dose: 500mg (two 00 capsules or one-third teaspoon) morning, evening and when necessary.

Tablets/capsules. Iceland Moss. Lobelia.

Tinctures. Formula. Ephedra 2; Echinacea 1; Elecampane root 1; Capsicum quarter. dose: 2-5ml teaspoons morning and evening and when necessary.

Practitioner. Liquid Extract Senega 1; Ephedra 1; Lungwort 2 (spitting of blood add: Blood root quarter). Dose: 2-5ml morning and evening and when necessary. In advanced cases there may be swollen ankles and kidney breakdown for which Parsley root, Buchu or Juniper may be indicated.

The sucking of a clove (or single drop of oil of Cloves in honey) has given temporary relief.

Aromatherapy. Inhalants or chest-rub – Eucalyptus, Cajeput, Hyssop, Rosemary, Sandalwood.

Diet. Wholefoods. Low fat, low salt, high fibre. Avoid all dairy foods.

Supplementation. Vitamin B-complex. Vitamin E for increased oxygenation. Vitamins A, C, D, F.

Outlook. Relief possible from regular herbal regime as dispensed by qualified practitioner. Requirements of each individual case may differ.

BRONCHITIS, ACUTE. Inflammatory condition of the bronchial tubes caused by cold and damp or by a sudden change from a heated to a cold atmosphere. Other causes: viral or bacterial infection, irritating dust and fumes, colds which 'go down to the chest'.

Symptoms: short dry cough, catarrh, wheezing, sensation of soreness in chest; temperature may be raised. Most cases run to a favourable conclusion but care is necessary with young children and the elderly. Repeated attacks may lead to a chronic condition.

Alternatives. *Teas* – Angelica, Holy Thistle, Elecampane leaves, Fenugreek seeds (decoction), Hyssop, Iceland Moss, Mouse Ear, Mullein, Nasturtium, Plantain, Wild Violet, Thyme, White Horehound, Wild Cherry bark (decoction), Lobelia, Liquorice, Boneset. With fever, add Elderflowers.

Tea. Formula. Equal parts: Wild Cherry bark, Mullein, Thyme. Mix. 1 heaped teaspoon to cup water simmered 5 minutes in closed vessel. 1 cup 2-3 times daily. A pinch of Cayenne assists action.

Irish Moss (Carragheen) – 1 teaspoon to cup water gently simmered 20 minutes. It gels into a viscous mass. Cannot be strained. Add honey and eat with a spoon, as desired.

Tablets/capsules. Iceland Moss. Lobelia. Garlic. Slippery Elm.

Prescription No 1. Morning and evening and when necessary. Thyme 2; Lungwort 2; Lobelia 1. OR

Prescription No 2. Morning and evening and when necessary. Iceland Moss 2; Wild Cherry bark 1; Thyme 2.

Doses:– Powders: one-third teaspoon (500mg) or two 00 capsules. Liquid Extracts: 30-60 drops. Tinctures: 1-2 teaspoons.

Practitioner. Alternatives:–

(1) Tincture Ipecacuanha BP (1973). Dose, 0.25-1ml.

(2) Tincture Grindelia BPC (1949). Dose, 0.6-1.2ml.

(3) Tincture Belladonna BP (1980). Dose, 0.5-2ml.

Black Forest Tea (traditional). Equal parts: White Horehound, Elderflowers and Vervain. One teaspoon to each cup boiling water; infuse 5-15 minutes; drink freely.

Topical. Chest rub: Olbas oil, Camphorated oil. Aromatherapy oils:– Angelica, Elecampane, Mullein, Cajeput, Lemon, Eucalyptus, Lavender, Mint, Onion, Pine, Thyme.

Aromatherapy inhalants: Oils of Pine, Peppermint and Hyssop. 5 drops of each to bowl of hot water. Inhale: head covered with a towel to trap steam.

Diet: Low salt, low fat, high fibre. Halibut liver oil. Wholefoods. Avoid all dairy products.

Supplements. Vitamins A, C, D, E.

BRONCHITIS, CHRONIC. The 'English Disease'. The result of repeated attacks of the acute condition. Menace to the elderly when bronchi becomes thickened and narrowed. Inelastic walls secrete a thick purulent mucus of fetid odour which plugs tubes and arrests oxygen intake. Aggravated by cold and damp, hence the need of a warm house with warm bedroom. Causes are many: smoking, industrial pollution irritants, soot, fog, etc. Breathlessness and audible breathing sounds may present an alarming spectacle.

A steady herbal regime is required including agents which may coax sluggish liver or kidneys into action (Dandelion, Barberry). Sheer physical exhaustion may require Ginseng. For purulent sputum – Boneset, Elecampane, Pleurisy root. To increase resistance – Echinacea. Where due to tuberculosis – Iceland Moss. For blood-streaked mucus – Blood root. For fever – Elderflowers, Yarrow. To conserve cardiac energies – Hawthorn, Motherwort. A profuse sweat affords relief – Elderflowers.

Alternatives. Capsicum, Ephedra, Fenugreek, Garlic, Grindelia, Holy Thistle, Iceland Moss, Lobelia, Mullein, Pleurisy Root, Wild Cherry.

Tea. Formula. Iceland Moss 2; Mullein 1; Wild Cherry bark 1. 1 heaped teaspoon to each cup water gently simmered 10 minutes. Dose: 1 cup 2-3 times daily.

Powders. Pleurisy root 2; Echinacea 1; Holy Thistle 1. Pinch Ginger. Mix. Dose: 500mg (two 00 capsules or one-third teaspoon) 2-3 times daily.

Tinctures. Formula. Iceland Moss 2; Lobelia 2; Grindelia quarter; Capsicum quarter. Dose: 1-2 teaspoons two or more times daily.

Practitioner. Liquid Extract Ephedra BHP (1983), dose 1-3ml. Or: Tincture Ephedra BHP (1983), dose 6-8ml.

Topical. Same as for acute bronchitis.

Note. In a test at Trafford General Hospital, Manchester, blowing-up balloons proved of benefit to those with chronic bronchitis. Fourteen patients were asked to inflate balloons and 14 refrained from doing so. After 8 weeks, the balloon-blowers showed considerable improvement in walking and a sense of well-being. Breathlessness was reduced. Condition of the others was either unchanged or worse.

BRONCHODILATORS. Herbs that expand the clear space within the bronchial tubes, thus opening-up airways and relieving obstruction. Effective for asthma, bronchitis, emphysema. May help cystic fibrosis, bronchiectasis and relieve cough. Ephedra, Euphorbia hirta, Lobelia, Mouse Ear, Sundew, White Horehound, White Squills, Wild Thyme.

BROOM. *Sarothamnus scoparius L. French*: Cytise. *German*: Kleestrauch. *Spanish*: Hiniesta. *Italian*: Ginestra. *Chinese*: Chin-ch'iao. Dried tops. Contains sparteine.

Action: cardio-active, diuretic, laxative, oxytocic, peripheral vasoconstrictor. Increases power of the heart, slows it down, increases urine. "Works on the conductive mechanism of the heart. Atrial and ventricular fibrillation disappear." (*Rudolf F. Weiss MD*)

Uses. 'Heart' dropsy. To reduce frequency of the heartbeat. Tendency to extrasystoles. Tachycardia. Liver conditions. Whole plant.

Reported use for tumour. (*J.L. Hartwell, Lloydia, 33, 97, 1970*)

Combination, traditional: with Agrimony and Dandelion root for dropsy.

Contra-indications: High blood pressure, pregnancy, lactation.

Preparations. Thrice daily.

Decoction: 1oz (30g) to each 1 pint (500ml) water, simmer gently 10 minutes. Dose: half-1 cup.

Liquid extract. 10-30 drops.

Tincture BHP (1983) 1:5 in 45 per cent alcohol; Dose: 0.5-2ml.

Kasbah Remedy (*Potter's*). Broom, an important constituent of.

Spartoil drops (*Klein*). GSL

BROWN SPOTS on the skin. Liver spots. Chloasma, melasma. Melanin is a dark pigment found in the skin and hair. When it is unnaturally concentrated into yellow-brown patches during pregnancy or from taking contraceptive pills it is known as chloasma. The darkness of such patches is enhanced by sunlight. Liver spots are common in the aged.

Topical. Cider vinegar. Castor oil (*E. Cayce*) Houseleek (traditional). Distilled extract of Witch Hazel. The juice or gel of Aloe Vera has reduced or removed spots after several months twice-daily applications.

BRUCELLOSIS. Undulant fever. An animal disease which may invade the human specie through contact with an infected animal (cattle, sheep, pigs, dogs or horses) or by consuming infected milk, cream or cheese. After drinking raw unpasteurised milk a hospital nurse suffered severe brucellosis; five patients quickly followed.

It is a disease of the slaughter house, veterinary surgeon, farm and meat trade worker. Young males are particularly at risk. In cows, infection may precipitate abortion of a calf but it does not affect the foetus in humans. May produce a rash on the arm of a vet handling a case.

Resembles glandular fever in the acute stage, with fever and high temperature, shivering, headache, profuse sweating, fatigue and anxiety-depression. Symptoms include enlargement of the spleen, liver, lymph glands, sore throat, possible rash, tremor and irritability. In long-standing cases a reactive arthritis may attack the joints. Often, it assumes an attack of influenza, its real nature remaining undiagnosed.

Treatment. By medical practitioner. Herbal antibiotics may be regarded as a supportive role. Antibacterials: Garden Thyme, Garlic, Elecampane, Burdock root, Pulsatilla, Echinacea,

Poke root, Myrrh, Goldenseal.
Tinctures. Formula. Blue Flag root 30ml; Poke root 15ml; Fringe Tree 30ml; Echinacea 60ml. Dose: 1-2 teaspoons in water every 2 hours (acute); 1 teaspoon thrice daily (chronic condition).

BRUISES. Contusions. Purple marks under the skin caused by capillary haemorrhage as from a blow. Spontaneous bruising may occur as a result of steroid therapy (corticosteroids, Prednisolone, etc) and haemophilia. People with a Vitamin K deficiency bruise easily.
Alternatives. *Topical.* Tincture Arnica: 5 drops in eggcup of water as a lotion. "In the absence of tincture Arnica," says Finlay Ellingwood MD, "wipe the discoloured area with Liquid extract Echinacea which stimulates an active capillary circulation and promotes recovery."

Arnica is never used on open wounds. Calendula (Marigold) is indicated.
Compress: any of the following: Arnica flowers, Chickweed, Cowslip, Hyssop, Black Bryony, Fenugreek seeds, Hemp, Agrimony, Calendula, Oak leaf, St John's Wort, Linseed, Herb Robert, Sanicle, Rue, Yarrow. Pulped Comfrey root, potato, cabbage leaf or Horsetail.
Lotions, creams, etc. Arnica, Chickweed, Comfrey, Myrrh.
Bruised bones. Comfrey, Rue. Spinal injuries: St John's Wort.
Others: ice or cold-water compresses fixed by bandages. Weleda Massage Balm.
Diet. Yoghurt: to encourage production of Vitamin K – the anti-clot vitamin.
Supplements. Vitamins: B-complex, C, E, K, bioflavonoids.

BRYONY, BLACK. Blackeye root. *Tamus communis L. French*: Bryone douce â fruits et à racine noirs. *German*: Schwarzwurzel. *Italian*: Tamarro. Root. Not used internally.

Contains steroidal spirostane glycosides.
Action: rubefacient, bruise-healer. Resolvent.
Uses. Traditional: scraped root used externally as a rub for gout, rheumatism, and painful joints; and as a cold poultice for blackeye and bruises generally. Steeped in strong wine (teaspoon to 8oz wine) for 8 days – a lotion for chilblains. Berries steeped in gin used for the same purpose.
Preparations. *Tincture*: 1 part pulp to 5 parts alcohol. Macerate 8 days, strain, for external use.
Cream: Tamus cream or ointment. (*Weleda, Nelson*)
Pulped fresh root: as a poultice for chilblains or gout.

BRYONY, WHITE. Wild vine. *Bryonia alba L. French*: Bryone blanche. *German*: Zaunrübe. *Spanish*: Brionia. *Italian*: Briona bianca. Contains cucurbitacins. Sliced dried root.
Action: diaphoretic, expectorant, powerful hydragogue, emetic, cathartic, anti-tumour, anti-rheumatic. Externally: as a rubefacient. Internal use, practitioner only.
Uses. Rheumatism worse from movement, rheumatic fever, acute arthritis. Heart disorder following rheumatic fever. For absorption of serous fluid as in pleurisy. Congested bronchi and lungs. Synovitis, malaria and zymotic diseases.
Combinations: With Black Cohosh for muscular pain. Also for tenderness of the spinal vertebre (an important indication). With Poke root for inflammation of the breast or testicles.
Preparations. Owing to difficulty of the layman to dispense accurately dosage of powder or decoction, use is best confined to liquid extract or tincture; small doses frequently repeated; large doses avoided.
Liquid Extract: 10 drops in 4oz water; dose 1 teaspoon every half hour.
Tincture: dose; 2 teaspoons every half hour (acute) cases; thrice daily (chronic).
External. Tincture used as a lotion.
Note. Not used in pregnancy, lactation or in presence of piles.

BUBOES. Painful swellings of the lymphatic glands found in cases of the bubonic plague or other highly infectious diseases as syphilis. See: BUBONIC PLAGUE.
Green's Herbal: Butter-bur.

BUBONIC PLAGUE. Though the Black Death is supposed to have passed into medical history, occasional cases are recorded which give rise to the question: "Could it really come again?"

In an atomic age the collapse of medical services provided by governments is not far removed from the bounds of possibility. Wars come and go, medical fashions change, what is regarded as scientific today, may be neglected to tomorrow's superstition. It is possible this book may be consulted long after 20th century medicine has had its day.

The preventative remedy of history is Garlic. It was given to workers on the Great Pyramid of Cheops as a known antiseptic and prophylactic against infection. A riot ensued when supplies ran out. During the Great Plague under Charles II a colony of people escaped death, living to reveal their secret – all were in the habit of eating Garlic. It was later confirmed that the plague was not found in houses in which Garlic had been consumed.

The disease is spread by fleas from the black rat by the organism: bacillus pestis. Incubation period is two to five days, followed by severe headache, shivering, dizziness, fever and rapid pulse. Before delirium, the patient may have the 'staggers' and confused speech.

Glands of the body enlarge and may suppurate.

Suppuration is a welcome sign indicating speedy elimination of pus. Haemorrhagic spots break out on the skin.

The most dangerous type is that which affects the lungs, known as 'pneumonic' and which is highly infectious; characterised by cyanosis (blueness of the face).

Occasionally there are human cases of Bubonic Plague in California and the West but today they seldom prove fatal. Public health officials point out that the incidence of the disease in China and Vietnam is lower than for centuries because of vaccine therapy. Wild animals still spread sporadic cases of the Plague.

Treatment: Health Authorities to be notified immediately and patient isolated. All bedding and personal effects to be destroyed or disinfected. Specialised nursing necessary. If hospital care is not available, the patient should receive treatment for collapse (Capsicum, Ginger or other circulatory stimulants).

In the absence of streptomycin and tetracycline, to which the organism *yersinia* is sensitive, powerful alternatives may assist: Echinacea, Wild Indigo, Poke root, Queen's Delight, Sarsaparilla, Yellow Parilla, Goldenseal, Prickly Ash.

Topical. Poultice of Slippery Elm, Marshmallow, or both combined to promote suppuration. History records pulped fresh Plantain leaves.

To be treated by general medical practitioner or Infectious Diseases consultant.

BUCHU. Bucco. Barosma betulina. *Agathosma betulina* (Berg). *French*: Buchu. *German*: Bukkostrauch. *Spanish*: Buchu. *Italian*: Diosma. Dried leaves.

Action: promotes secretion of urine. Stimulant diuretic (cold). Safe and effective anti-bacterial for urinary tract infections and recurrent inflammation of the bladder.

Keynote: urinary antiseptic.

Constituents. Volatile oil, flavonoids, tannin, mucilage, B-complex vitamins.

Uses. Cystitis, especially when caused by organism E. Coli. Pyelitis, urethritis, prostatitis, pus in the urine. Catarrh of the bladder. Fluid retention. To aid flow of urine.

Popular kidney herbs. Tea. Couchgrass 25 per cent; Buchu 15 per cent; Bearberry 15 per cent; Alfalfa 45 per cent. 1-2 teaspoons to cup boiling water.

Combinations. Teas. (1) equal parts: Buchu, Uva Ursi, Broom and Clivers; for chronic dropsy. (2) equal parts: Buchu and Juniper berries, for acute dropsy. (3) equal parts: Buchu and Marshmallow for irritable bladder.

Side effects – none known.

Preparations. Minimum heat. Should not be boiled. Covered vessel (teapot) to prevent escape of volatile oil. Thrice daily.

Tea: One teaspoon to each cup boiling water; infuse 15 minutes. Half-1 cup.

Liquid extract, BHC Vol 1. 1:1 90 per cent ethanol. Dose: 0.5-1.5ml.

Tincture, BHC Vol 1. 1:5, 60 per cent ethanol. Dose: 2-4ml.

Infusion Buchu Conc BPC 1954. 1:2.5, 25 per cent ethanol. Dose: 4-8ml.

Kasbah Remedy (Potter's). Buchu an important ingredient.

Gerard House. Formula. Pulverised Dandelion root 60mg; Pulverised Extract Buchu 3-1, 20mg; Pulverised Extract Uva Ursi 3-1, 20mg; Pulverised Extract Clivers 4-1, 4mg. Dose: 2 tablets thrice daily. GSL

BUCKWHEAT. *Fagopyrum esculentum* (Moench). *French*: Sarrasin. *German*: Buchweizen. *Spanish*: Alforfon. *Italian*: Grano saroceno. *Japanese*: Soba. Flowers and leaves.

Action: vein-restorative, hypotensive, anti-haemorrhage, vasodilator. Contains Rutin, an anti-coagulant. Source of magnesium.

Uses. Radiation damage, high blood pressure, capillary fragility, varicose veins, petechiae, retinal haemorrhage, spontaneous bruising, circulatory stasis, purple patches on skin due to capillary haemorrhages, temporal arteritis, visible pulsation of carotid artery in the neck, frostbite, chilblains.

Preparations. Green Buckwheat tea (Rutin); a caffeine-free tea. One heaped teaspoon to each cup boiling water. Half-1 cup as desired.

Formula. Tablets or capsules: Rutin 60mg; Vitamin C 20mg; Chlorophyll 20mg.

BUERGER'S DISEASE. (Thromboangiitis obliterans). An inflammatory condition of blood vessels of the legs, tobacco said to be the causative factor. Confined to men, especially Jews.

Symptoms. Intermittent claudication. Affected parts of the leg are much paler than others, the condition regressing to ulceration and possible gangrene. Inflammation of nerves, veins and arteries may lead to clot formation (thrombosis).

Treatment. Stop smoking. Vasodilator herbs.

Alternatives. Cayenne (minute doses), Bayberry, Lime flowers, Lobelia, Prickly Ash, Wahoo bark, Mistletoe, Skullcap, Cactus.

BHP (1983) recommends: Angelica root, Hawthorn berry, Wild Yam.

Decoction. Formula. Equal parts: Hawthorn, Mistletoe, Valerian. 2 teaspoons to two cups water gently simmered 10 minutes. Dose half-1 cup thrice daily, and when necessary.

Tablets/capsules. Alternatives. Prickly Ash 100mg. Hawthorn 200mg. Wild Yam 200mg. Dosage as on bottles.

Powders. Formula. Equal parts: Hawthorn, Wild Yam, Prickly Ash. Dose: 500mg (two 00 capsules or one-third teaspoon) thrice daily.

Tinctures. Formula. Equal parts: Bayberry,

Hawthorn, Prickly Ash. Dose: 1-2 teaspoons thrice daily.
Practitioner. Tincture Gelsemium BPC (1973). 0.3ml (5 drops) when necessary for relief of pain.
Diet. Low fat, low salt, high fibre.
Supplements. Daily. Vitamin E 1000-1500iu. Vitamin B-complex. Magnesium, Calcium.
Exercise. Physiotherapy exercise. From the sitting position raise legs to horizontal; rest for a few minutes. Lie down and raise legs to 45 degrees; rest for a few minutes. Reverse movements resting each time to equalise the circulation. (*Brenda Cooke FNIMH*)

BUGLE. Sicklewort. *Ajuga reptans L. German*: Lorenskraut. *French*: Bugle rampant. *Italian*: Bugula. *Part used*: herb. Contains iridoid glycosides. External use as a poultice for taking pain out of old wounds and to expedite healing.

BUGLEWEED. Water horehound. Gipsywort. *German*: Gemeiner Wolfstrapp. *French*: Lycope. *Italian*: Licopo. *Lycopus europaeus* and *Lycopus virginicus*. Properties of both plants are the same. Dried herb.
Action: "cardio-active diuretic, increasing force of myocardial contraction and reducing heart rate" BHP (1983). Palpitation, peripheral vasoconstrictor, antitussive, hypoglycaemic, sedative, anti-haemorrhagic, thyrostatic, narcotic (mild).

Mild contraceptive containing lithospermum acid which blocks gonadotropic hormones of the anterior pituitary (*Rudolf F. Weiss MD*)
Uses. To reduce rapid heart beat from over-active thyroid. Reduces high pulse rate in thyrotoxicosis with heart involvement. Raises blood sugar levels in diabetes. Internal haemorrhages, bleeding from the lungs, menorrhagia. High blood pressure.
Combinations. With Lily of the Valley (Bugleweed 2; Lily 1) for heart cases. With Elecampane (equal parts) for cough of tuberculosis. With Valerian 1 for thyrotoxicosis.
Preparations. Thrice daily.
Tea: 1 heaped teaspoon to each cup boiling water; infuse 10 minutes. Dose: half-1 cup.
Tincture BHP (1983) 1 part to 5 parts 45 per cent alcohol. Dose: 2-6ml in water. GSL

BUILDING SICKNESS SYNDROME. Work-related lethargy coming on in the afternoon may be the result of this syndrome. Air-conditioned buildings promote symptoms not encountered in naturally ventilated offices, shops, etc.
Symptoms: dry throat, eye irritation, headache, fatigue, wheezy chest and flu-like colds may be a product of modern ventilating systems. The headache may come on in the afternoon and improve on leaving work. Humidifier fever. Passive inhalation of cigarette smoke a factor.
Alternatives. *Treatment*. Ginseng, Iceland Moss, Irish Moss, German Chamomile tea.

BULIMIA. Binge-eating followed by self-induced vomiting. Disorder of young women. Frequently regarded as psychiatric in origin but has been linked with polycystic ovaries, zinc deficiency, even endorphin activity. Where nervous excitability is marked, the addition of a nerve relaxant (Skullcap, Valerian) proves of value.
Symptoms. Fatigue, digestive problems, irregular menstruation, irregular heart-beat, muscle cramps and weakness, dizziness, dehydration, dental problems, abdominal pain, low tolerance of cold, haemorrhages in the oesophagus, swollen salivary glands, breast tenderness, swollen ankles, unexplained low-potassium in the blood, frequent resort to diuretics.
Alternatives. *Teas*. Centuary, Chamomile, Hops, Fennel. 1 heaped teaspoon to each cup boiling water; infuse 15 minutes. 1 cup 2-3 times daily.
Tablets/capsules. Gentian, Chamomile, Ginkgo.
Powders. Formula. Equal parts: Burdock root, Ginkgo, Gentian. Dose: 750mg (three 00 capsules or half a teaspoon) thrice daily before meals.
Tincture. Tincture Gentian Co BP. Dose: 2-4ml.
Antidepressants. Bulimia has been effectively treated using antidepressants. See: ANTIDEPRESSANTS.
Supplementation. Vitamins B, C, E. Magnesium, Chromium, Zinc. Active exercising or jogging to stimulate beta endorphin release.
Note. One bulimic in two will recover spontaneously, even if they receive little or no treatment according to a decade-long follow-up of 50 bulimia nervosa patients. (*British Journal of Psychiatry, Jan 1994*)

BUNIONS. See: CORNS.

BURDOCK. Beggar's buttons. Lappa. *Arctium lappa L. French*: Bardane. *German*: Filzklette. *Spanish*: Bardana. *Italian*: Lappolone. Parts used: herb, root, seeds.
Constituents: fatty acids, organic acids, phenolic acids, lignans, sesquiterpenes, tannin, mucilage, inulin. Contains iron, sulphur and B-vitamins.
Action. One of the most powerful and reliable blood tonics of herbalism. Antibiotic action of the root against staphylococcus. Adaptogen, alterative, anti-fungal, hepatic, lymphatic, diaphoretic, diuretic, laxative, hypoglycaemic, orexigenic, bitter.

Anti-tumour activity reported (*Farnsworth, Kiangsu-429*)
Uses. Arthritis, gout, rheumatism, boils, styes, seborrhoea, cystitis, anaemia, anorexia nervosa. To lower blood sugar. Skin diseases – especially psoriasis, acne, eczema. To reduce cholesterol level. Measles (Chinese traditional).
Combination 1. Dandelion 2; Burdock root 1; (rheumatism).
Combination 2. Yellow Dock, Red Clover, Burdock, BHP (1983).

Inulin, present in the root. of value in diabetes (*Krantz & Carr, 1931*)
Preparations. Thrice daily. Persistence with low doses is more favourable than larger, over short periods. Some herbalists have observed more favourable results from use of the decoction.
Decoction. Half-1 teaspoon root to each cup water, simmer gently 5 minutes in a closed vessel. Half-1 cup.
Liquid Extract. BHC Vol 1 (root). 1:1, 25 per cent ethanol. Dose: 2-6ml.
Tincture. BHC Vol 1 (root). 1:5, 25 per cent ethanol. Dose: 8-12ml.
Powder. Two 250mg capsules with meals.
Topical. Compress: 2 teaspoons shredded root or powder to two cups water simmered 5 minutes and allowed to stand for 30 minutes; saturate piece of suitable material and apply.
Not used in pregnancy or lactation. GSL

BURNET, GREATER. Garden Burnet. Salad Burnet. *Sanguisorba officinalis L.* Herb.
Action: astringent tonic, anti-haemorrhagic. Mild antibacterial.
Uses. Irritable bowel, ulcerative colitis, excessive menstruation, gargle for throat infections.
Traditional: tea used as a wash for piles and anal irritation, or as a poultice for sores and wounds. Widely used in Chinese medicine.
Preparations. Thrice daily.
Tea: 2 teaspoons to each cup boiling water; infuse 5 minutes. Half-1 cup.
Liquid extract: half-1 teaspoon in water.
Tincture BHP (1983) 1:5 in 45 per cent alcohol. Dose 2-8ml. GSL

BURNET SAXIFRAGE. Lesser Burnet. *Pimpinella saxifraga L.* Dried root and herb.
Constituents: Coumarins, volatile oil, saponin.
Action. Carminative, aromatic, stimulant, expectorant.
Uses. Flatulence, Stomach upsets.
Preparation. *Tea*. 1 heaped teaspoon to each cup boiling water; infuse 5-15 minutes; 1 cup 2-3 times daily. GSL

BURNOUT. "Psychological withdrawal from work in response to excessive stress and dissatisfaction". At risk: business executives and conscientious staff who have worked too long with an over-high expenditure of adrenalin.
Symptoms: job stress, chronic overwork, scrappy meals, few holidays, snatched sex, no time for family, sleeplessness, irritability, depression, anxiety, hypochondria, tiredness. Aggravation by caffeine (coffee) and alcohol drinks.
To help prevent: lifestyle change to more normal working hours, rest periods and adequate holidays. Indicated: agents that increase energy and gently sustain the central nervous system: Ginkgo, <u>Ginseng</u>, Damiana, <u>Gotu Kola</u>. May be taken singly or in combination.
Alternatives. *Tea*. Formula. Equal parts German Chamomile and Gotu Kola. 1 heaped teaspoon herbs to each cup boiling water; infuse 5-10 minutes. Dose: 1 cup 2-3 times daily.
Formula. Gotu Kola 2, Valerian 1, Oats 2. Liquid Extracts: 1 teaspoon. Tinctures: 2 teaspoons. Powders: 500mg. Thrice daily.

BURNS & SCALDS. Scalds are caused by moist heat and burns by dry heat but their treatment is the same. There are six degrees of burns; anything beyond the first degree (skin not broken) and second degree (blisters and broken skin) should receive hospital treatment.

All burns are serious. Vulnerary herbs are available to promote healing and cell growth, including: Aloe Vera, Comfrey, Fenugreek, Marigold, Marshmallow, Slippery Elm, Chickweed, Myrrh (powder).

Even hospital authorities may find these effective, enhancing healing, reducing risk of infection, and often concluding with a minimum of scar tissue. Echinacea – to mobilise the immune system.

Exclude air from affected parts as soon as possible. Remove no clothing adhering to wound; cut round. For corrosive alkalis: bathe with cider vinegar (2-4 teaspoons to teacup water). Follow with honey: apply lint and bandage. Honey has a long traditional reputation for burns. The following are analgesic and antiseptic, keeping wounds clean and free from pus. Apply sterile dressings.
Tea for internal use: Nettles 1; Valerian 1; Comfrey leaf 2. Mix. 2 teaspoons to each cup boiling water; infuse 15 minutes. 1 cup every 2 hours. Or, cup of ordinary tea laced with 2-3 drops Life Drops.
Topical. (1) Tea Tree oil: 1 part to 20 parts Almond oil. (2) Strong Nettle tea – pain killer. (3) St John's Wort oil. (4) Aloe Vera – cut off piece of leaf and pulp; or, gel. (5) Slippery Elm – Powder mixed with little milk to form a paste. (6) Pierce Vitamin E capsule and anoint area. (7) Distilled extract of Witch Hazel. (8) Cod liver oil.
Compress. Apply piece of suitable material steeped in teas of any of the following: Chamomile, Chickweed, Comfrey, Cucumber, Elderflowers, Marigold, Plantain, St John's Wort.
Alcohol should not be taken.
Supplementation. Vitamins A, B-complex, C, D, E. Potassium. Zinc.

BURR-MARIGOLD. Water Agrimony. *Bidens tripartita L. French*: Cornuet. *German*: Sumpfzweizahn. *Italian*: Eupatoria acquatica. Dried leaves and stems.

Source of iron, phosphorus and other minerals.
Action: anti-haemorrhage, astringent, diuretic,

diaphoretic. Today used only in association with other haemostatics for internal or external bleeding.
Uses. Blood in the urine, stool. Bleeding of gastric ulcer or from the lungs. Ulcerative colitis. Heavy menstruation. Hair loss. Gout.
Preparations. Acute cases, bleeding: 2 hourly. Chronic cases, thrice daily.
Tea. One heaped teaspoon to each cup boiling water, infuse 15 minutes. Half-1 cup.
Liquid Extract. 20-60 drops in water.
Tincture BHP (1983) 1 to 5 parts 45 per cent alcohol. Dose 15-30 drops (1-2ml). GSL

BUSH TEA. See: ROOIBOSCH TEA.

BURSITIS. Tendinitis. Inflammation of a bursa – a soft-tissue elastic sac between bones that glide over one another, as in elbow and shoulder. Contains a little fluid, its purpose being to form a cushion against friction. In the knee-joint it is known as 'housemaid's knee'; over the hips as 'weaver's bottom', joints becoming red, hot and painful.

Deposits of calcium may thicken walls and form a focus of pressure, causing pain. Relief comes when the swelling disperses or bursts. In the 60-70 age group rupture of tendons is a frequent cause. Bursitis accounts for two-thirds of shoulder pains. Neglected, it may progress to 'frozen shoulder' in later life.
Teas. Celery seeds, Comfrey leaf, Nettles, Wintergreen.
Tablets/capsules. Prickly Ash, Lobelia, Wild Yam, Helonias.
Alternative formulae:– *Powders*. Turmeric 2; Prickly Ash 1; Cayenne quarter. Mix. Dose: 500mg (two 00 capsules or one-third teaspoon) thrice daily.
Liquid extracts. Equal parts: Black Cohosh, Devil's Claw, Turmeric. Mix. Dose: 30-60 drops thrice daily.
Tinctures. White Willow bark 2; Prickly Ash bark 1; Wild Yam 1; Capsicum quarter. Mix. Dose: 2 teaspoons thrice daily.
Cider vinegar. 2-3 teaspoons to glass of water 2-3 times daily.
Topical. Apply strapping plaster to arrest swelling. See: FOMENTATIONS. POTATO. BRAN OR COMFREY ROOT POULTICE.
Aromatherapy. Cajeput, Chamomile, Origans, Rosemary. 6 drops of any one oil in 2 teaspoons Almond oil for massage.
Diet. See: DIET – GENERAL.
Supplements. Vitamin A. Vitamin C (3-4g). Vitamin E (400iu). Zinc 15mg.
General. Cold packs. Compression bandages. Gentle massage under the knee where knee joint is involved. For septic bursa add Echinacea to internal medication or apply ointment. For drainage, aspiration is sometimes necessary. Protect knees with knee-pads. Turmeric acquires reputation for relief.

BUST DEVELOPER. A small bust may be due to a number of causes – chiefly hormone deficiency involving the pituitary and adrenal glands. Treatment should include stimulants for these glands.
Alternatives. *Teas*. Borage, Dill, Caraway seeds, Fennel, Goat's Rue, Holy Thistle, Agnus Castus.
Decoction. Fenugreek seeds. 2 teaspoons to each cup water gently simmered 10 minutes. Half-1 cup thrice daily. Fenugreek is a Persian remedy of antiquity for this purpose.
Tablets/capsules. Ginseng. Sarsaparilla. Evening Primrose. Agnus Castus, Liquorice.
Powders. Equal parts: Caraway seeds, Saw Palmetto berries. Dose: 750mg (three 00 capsules or half a teaspoon) thrice daily.
Tinctures. Combine Dong Quai 1; Saw Palmetto 2. Dose: one 5ml teaspoon in water thrice daily.
Topical. Cream for use at bedtime: Lanolin 1oz; Cocoa butter half an ounce; Saw Palmetto berries Tincture or Liquid Extract 30 drops (or 10 grams powder); Oil Cajeput 30 drops. Heat in a pan and pour into jar.
Diet. See: DIET – THIN PEOPLE. Improve nutrition with potassium-rich foods. Two or more bananas daily.
Supplements. Vitamins B6, C, E. Zinc.

BUTCHER'S BROOM. *Ruscus aculeatus, L.* Rhizome.
Action: diuretic, diaphoretic, laxative, deobstruent, anti-inflammatory, veinous tonic. Action similar to Wild Yam: used in synthesis of steroid hormones. Antispasmodic. Haemostatic.
Uses. Varicose veins, piles, jaundice, obstructed menstruation, sluggish circulation, oedema. To arrest haemorrhage.
Decoction: half an ounce fine-cut herb to 1 pint water simmered gently 20 minutes. Dose: half-1 cup thrice daily.
Powder, capsules: 270mg. 3 capsules twice daily during meals. (*Arkocaps*)
Endopharm capsules for piles.

BUTTERBUR. Bog rhubarb. *Petasites hybridus*. Root.
Action: Astringent, expectorant, diuretic (mild), antispasmodic, stimulant. Of limited use because of pyrrolizidine alkaloids.
Uses. Inflammation of urinary tract, gravel, skin disorders. Gall bladder disorders, bronchitis, asthma, whooping cough. Migraine of liver origin.
Preparations. 1 teaspoon crushed root steeped in each cup cold water overnight. Next day warm, not boil, and strain. Half cup thrice daily.
Petaforce. (Vogel & Webb) capsules, 25mg Butterburr extract.

Neurochol (Brenner). Combines Butterburr and Wormwood. GSL

BUTTERNUT. White Walnut. *Juglans cinerea L. French*: Noix de beurre. *German*: Butter Walnuss. *Italian*: Noce cenerino. Root bark and leaves.
Action: cholagogue, hepatic, laxative, blood tonic, anthelmintic, reputed anti-tumour.
Uses. Chronic constipation associated with liver disorder. To increase flow of bile and its release from the gall bladder. Toxic liver disorder. Skin diseases with pus. Worms in children. Piles.
Combinations. (1) equal parts, with Yellow Dock and Burdock for chronic skin disorders. (2) with Figwort 2; Butternut 1; for piles. (3) equal parts with Mugwort for worms.
Preparations. Thrice daily.
Decoction. Half a teaspoon to each cupful water gently simmer 15 minutes. Dose, half-1 cup.
Liquid Extract. 2 to 4ml in water. GSL

BYPASS OPERATION. The transplant of an artery or vein from the leg to bypass a clogged artery in the heart. Vessels may be blocked by a deposit of plaque made up of collagen, fats and cholesterol solidified by calcium and other mineral salts, and which may have been building up for 30-40 years. See: CHELATION.

London's Middlesex Hospital Intensive Care Unit has found that a 20-minute foot massage using Neroli oil significantly reduces the level of anxiety and pain experienced by post-cardiac surgery patients.

CABBAGE. For pains of rheumatism and arthritis. Cases of pain-relief are reported: iron a cabbage leaf with a hot iron and secure over the affected part. (*Welsh folklore*) Relief of breast pain, as an anti-inflammatory: pulp of the fresh leaf in gauze as an insert between breast and bra.

CACHEXIA. Severe constitutional weakness produced by wasting disease, such as cancer. Deficient nutrition.
Symptoms: loss of appetite, yellow sallow complexion, chronic constipation, low spirits. Even where the liver is not under suspicion, a liver stimulant assists metabolism (Dandelion, Chiretta, Fringe Tree). To stimulate powers of resistance and combat infection – Echinacea.
Alternatives. *Teas*. Agrimony, Black Horehound, Hops, Nettles, Gota Kola, Ginseng, Fenugreek seeds, Holy Thistle, Betony, Oats, Life root.
Formula (for weight loss). Equal parts: herbs: Agrimony, Nettles, Plantain. 1 heaped teaspoon to each cup boiling water; infuse 15 minutes. 1 cup freely.
Gentian. 1 teaspoon to 2 cups cold water steeped overnight. Half-1 cup thrice daily, before meals.
Aloe Vera. 1 teaspoon juice from leaf or gel, thrice daily.
Saw Palmetto. Marked effect on glandular tissue. Increases flesh rapidly and builds up strength.
Tablets/capsules. Saw Palmetto, Iceland Moss. Kola nuts. Damiana. Echinacea. Garlic, Ginseng, Kelp, Sarsaparilla.
Powders. (1) Equal parts: Saw Palmetto, Damiana, Kola. OR:– (2) equal parts: Oats (Avena sat) 2; Gentian 1; Dandelion 1. Dose: 750mg (three 00 capsules or half a teaspoon) thrice daily.
Tinctures. Formula. Equal parts: Ginseng, Chiretta, Kola. Dose: 1-2 teaspoons in water thrice daily before meals.
Practitioner. (1) Tincture Peruvian bark BPC (1949). 15-30 drops in water thrice daily. (2) Dec Jam Sarsae Co Conc BPC. 1 teaspoon in water before meals thrice daily.
To promote cell regeneration. Nasturtium flowers, Horse-radish, Watercress, Garden Cress. (*A. Vogel*)
Diet. High protein.
Supplementation: Superoxide dismutase. All the vitamins – multivitamin tablet or capsule. Zinc.

CACTUS. *Selenicereus grandiflorus*. Night-blooming cereus. *German*: Kaktus. *French*: Cactier. *Spanish*: Cactus. *Italian*: Cacto. Dried or fresh flowers.
Constituents: alkaloids, flavonoids.
Action: cardiac stimulant, increasing force of the heart beat. Central nervous system stimulant. Tonic to sympathetic nervous system. Increases size of the heart-beat and reduces its frequency. Not an emergency agent such as Digitalis; requires time for action. Not a depressant.
Uses. Heart weakness with low blood pressure and valvular insufficiency. Rapid pulse with loss of body strength. "Chest held in a vice". Unstable angina or coronary disease. Numbness of left arm. Relieves difficult breathing or congestion of the lungs of heart causation. As it has no known side-effects it enables heart sufferers to face the world with renewed confidence. Aneurism. Cholesterolised arteries, arteritis (temporal), heart murmur. Sexual neurasthenia, masturbation palpitation. Secondary prophylaxis following myocardial infarction.
Preparations. Thrice daily.
Tea. 2-3 flowers to each cup boiling water; infuse 15 minutes. Dose, one-third to half a cup.
Liquid Extract: 1-8 drops.
Combination: Action is enhanced by addition of Motherwort and Oatstraw (equal parts).
Tincture of Cereus, BPC 1934: dose 0.12 to 2ml (2-30 drops) in water.

CACTUS. Opuntia series, native of Mexico. Differs from Selenicereus (night-blooming cactus) of the West Indies.
Action: Astringent, haemostatic.
Uses. Irritable bowel, mucous colitis, prostatitis.
Preparations. Thrice daily.
Tea: 2-3 dried or fresh flowers to each cup boiling water; infuse 15 minutes. Dose, half-1 cup.
Liquid Extract. 5-15 drops.

CAFFEINE. Vegetable alkaloid. Found in tea, coffee, cola, cocoa, etc. Stimulant to the central nervous system. Promotes alertness for physical and mental activity and retards sleep. Recent studies show it to be a health hazard in large quantities. One cup of tea may contain 60-90mg caffeine; one cup of coffee between 60-150mg. Cola beverages may contain 40-70mg. Toxic effects include palpitation, headache, sleeplessness, irritability, anxiety and high blood pressure.
Alternatives: Ginseng, Gotu Kola, Guarana tea, German Chamomile.

Caffeine is the most widely used drug in the world. Studies show that abstinence induces a withdrawal syndrome of fatigue, headache and drowsiness within 24 hours and lasts about a week, on giving up the habit.

CAFFEINE POISONING. A Harvard study links coffee consumption with cancer of the pancreas. No association has been found between tea-drinkers and cancer. Some authorities claim coffee is not carcinogenic until roasted.

While an internal mechanism slows down the body, caffeine in tea, cola and coffee restores alertness. Caffeine acts by blocking the action of the compound, adenosine – one of the building blocks of DNA which promotes cell energy.

Caffeine interferes with natural metabolic processes. In the aged, coffee increases production of uric acid, causing irritation of the kidneys, joint and muscle pains.

Caffeinism is responsible for a wide range of disorders. Increases the heart beat, promotes excessive stomach acid and increases flow of urine. It may give rise to birth defects and should be taken with caution in pregnancy.

Symptoms. Restlessness, nervous agitation, extreme sensitiveness. Intolerance of pain, nervous palpitation, all senses acute.
To antidote. Chamomile tea.
Practitioner. Tincture Nux vom BP: 10 drops to 100ml water. Dose: 1 teaspoon thrice daily.
Inhalation: Strong spirits of Camphor.
Diet. Plenty asparagus.

CAJEPUT. Swamp tea tree. *Melaleuca leucadendron L. French*: Cajeputier. *German*: Kajeputbaum. Contains terpenoids. Oil.
Action: Antiseptic, antispasmodic, rubefacient, anthelmintic, insect repellent. Antimicrobial. Antiscorbutic. Expectorant.
Uses. Used by natives of the Molucca Islands as a lotion for painful stiff joints. Advised by physicians at the turn of the century to combat the tubercle bacillus. Infections of the bronchi. Worms in children. Toothache. Headache.
Preparation. Topically for toothache, bruises, sprains, neuralgia. Cajuput oil BPC: dose, 0.05-0.2ml.

Today it is confined to external use only as an ingredient of stimulating liniments and ointments for aching joints, fibrositis, etc. An ingredient of Olbas oil. GSL

CALAMINT. Basil Thyme. *Calaminta ascendens* Jord. *French*: Calament. *German*: Waldurze. *Spanish*: Calamento. *Italian*: Calamina. *Dutch*: Vold mynte. *Part used*: herb
Constituents: volatile oil, ketones, terpenes.
Action: expectorant, diaphoretic.
Uses: upper airways obstruction, catarrh, bronchitis, colds.
Preparation. *Tea*: 1 teaspoon to each cup boiling water; infuse 10 minutes. Dose: Half-1 cup thrice daily. GSL

CALAMUS. Sweet flag root. *Acorus calamus L.* Dried or fresh rhizome. Used since biblical times.
Action: Carminative, diaphoretic, digestant, abdominal antispasmodic, bitter, antitussive, hypotensor, anti-bacterial.
Uses. History records its use in the plague and for rabies. Much esteemed by the Dutch for stomach complaints. Loss of appetite, weight. Gastric ulcer. Root-chewing discourages smoking. Hyperacidity. Anorexia nervosa. Menominee Indians used the powder for stomach cramp. Reputation in China for rheumatoid arthritis.

Maria Treben records a case of cancer of the stomach cured by placing a level teaspoon of the crushed root into a cup of cold water. This was left to stand overnight, strained in the morning and drunk six sips a day. Must not be boiled. Dose, 1 sip before and after each meal. 1 teacupful consumed daily.

Fresh roots may be pulped in a juice extractor and taken in teaspoon doses. Appears in the British Pharmacopoeia, 1934.

Preparations according to BHP (1983). Thrice daily.
Liquid extract, 1:1 in 60 per cent alcohol. Dose: 1-3ml (15-45 drops).
Tincture, 1:5 in 60 per cent alcohol. Dose: 2-4ml.
The oil is not used, being reputed to have 'carcinogenic properties'. (*American Federal Register 9 May 1968*)
Powdered root: 1-3 grams.

CALCIUM. Mineral. Combines with protein to give structural solidarity to bones and flesh. Given with benefit for all bone problems, delayed union after injury, brittleness in the elderly, delayed dentition and weakness in rapidly growing children. Cataracts. Rickets in children; osteomalacia in adults.
Other deficiencies. Muscle cramps, spasms, tremors, nervousness, insomnia, joint pains.
Body effects. Healthy teeth and bones, blood clotting, nerve and muscle resilience.

Calcium helps reduce risk of fracture particularly in menopausal women who may increase intake to 1500mg daily. Calcium citrate malate is regarded as more effective than calcium carbonate. Calcium and Magnesium are essentials.
Sources. Dairy products, fish, sardines, salmon, watercress, hard drinking water, spinach. Dried skimmed milk may supply up to 60 per cent of the recommended daily amount.
Herbs. Chamomile, Clivers, Dandelion, Horsetail, Coltsfoot, Meadowsweet, Mistletoe, Plantain, Scarlet Pimpernel, Silverweed, Shepherd's Purse, Toadflax. Taken as teas, powders, tablets or capsules.
Herbal combination to increase intake. Comfrey 3, Horsetail 6, Kelp 1, Lobelia 1, Marshmallow root 2, Oats 4, Parsley root 1. Tea: 1 heaped teaspoon to each cup boiling water; infuse 15 minutes; 1 cup morning and evening.

Calcium tablet supplements should first be pulverised before ingestion and taken in honey, bread bolus, or other suitable vehicle. Vitamin D assists absorption – 400-800 international units daily.

CALCULI. Stone in the gall bladder, kidney or bladder. Chiefly made up of deposits of salts of chemicals, phosphates and oxalates. Agents to eliminate or dissolve are known as anti-lithics.

CALENDULA. See: MARIGOLD.

CALIFORNEAN POPPY. *Eschscholtzia californica* (Cham.) *French*: Globe du soleil. *German*: Goldmohn. *Italian*: Escolzia di California. Whole plant. Practitioner use.
Constituents: flavone glycosides.
Action: hypnotic, sedative, nerve relaxant, anodyne.
Uses. Insomnia, migraine, stressful conditions, nervous bowel, anxiety, depression, neuralgia.
Combines well with Passion Flower (equal parts) for hyperactivity and sleeplessness.
Preparations. *Tea*. 1 teaspoon to each cup boiling water; infuse 15 minutes; morning and evening.
Powder: capsule: 240mg. 2 capsules middle of afternoon; 4 capsules evening one hour after going to bed. (*Arkocaps*)

CALSALETTES. Tablets containing Aloin 62.65 per cent, starch 27.15 per cent, lactose 5.1 per cent, and stearic acid 5.1 per cent. (*Torbet Laboratories*) For constipation.

CALUMBA. Colombo. *Jateorhiza palmata*, Miers. *Indian*: Kalamb-kachri. *Iranian*: Bikle. *Arabian*: Sakel hamam. *Part used*: dried root.
Constituents: volatile oil, bitter principle, isoquinoline alkaloids, calumbin. No tannin.
Action: uterine stimulant, antifungal, bitter, tonic, orexigenic, hypotensor, carminative. Similar to Goldenseal as a gastric tonic. Anti-flatulent.
Uses: weak digestion, anorexia, menstrual disorders. Hypochlorhydria – to stimulate production of stomach acids to promote appetite. Amoebic dysentery.
Preparations. Thrice daily before meals.
Infusion: 1 teaspoon to cup *cold* water; steep overnight; dose – half-1 cup.
Infusion Calumba Conc. BP 1948. Dose, 2-4ml.
Liquid extract, BHC Vol 1. 1:1, 25 per cent ethanol. Dose: half-2ml.
Tincture Calumba BP (1948), 2-4ml.
Powder: half-2 grams.
Not used in pregnancy. GSL

CAMPHOR. *Cinnamomum camphora. French*: Laurier du Japon. *German*: Japanischer Kamferbaum. *Spanish*: Alcanfor. *Italian*: Alloro canforato. *Indian*: Kapur. *Chinese*: Chang. Gum camphor. Today its use is confined mostly to stimulating lotions for external use to increase surface heat in cold arthritic joints. Rubefacient. Chilblains, pains of rheumatism, nervous excitability and heart attack. Should not be used by epileptics.
Internal. Restricted dose: 10mg. Maximum daily dose: 30mg.
Historical. 1-2 drops on sugar 2-3 times daily, internally, to reduce troublesome sex-urge: priapism or nymphomania. Hourly, such doses were once classical treatment for cholera.
Liniment. 10 drops oil of Camphor to egg-cup Olive oil. Massage for relief of lumbago, fibrositis, neuralgia, chest and muscle pain.
Inhalant: Inhale the fumes for respiratory oppression with difficult breathing, heart failure, collapse, shock from injury, hypothermia, tobacco habit.
Camphor locket. A small square is sometimes hung in a small linen bag round the neck for prevention of infection, colds.
Camphorated oil: 1oz (30g) Flowers of Camphor to 4oz (125g) peanut oil. Dissolve in gentle heat.
Camphor lotion. Dissolve teaspoon (4-6g) Camphor flowers in 4oz Cider vinegar.
GSL as restricted dose above.
Camphor Drops. At one time a bottle brandy with a knob of Camphor at the bottom was kept in every pantry to restore vitality and warmth to those suffering from exposure to cold and damp. One drop of the mixture in honey rapidly invigorates, imparts energy, and sustains the heart. A reaction is evoked almost immediately; it is harmlessly repeated hourly. Camphor should be given alone as it antidotes many drugs and other remedies.

CANADA BALSAM. *Abies balsamea L.* No longer used internally. Used externally by American Indians for indolent ulcers, burns. Reportedly used in treating tumours. (*J.L. Hartwell, Lloydia, 33, 288 (1970)*)

CANADIAN HEMP. *Apocynum cannabinum L. French*: Apocyn. *German*: Hanfhundsgift. *Italian*: Apocino a fiori erbacei. Rhizome, root.
Action: expectorant, diuretic, diaphoretic, emetic. Contains cardiac glycosides. Action similar to strophanthus, digitalis and adonis. General medical practitioner use only.
Uses: cardiac dropsy, pleuritic effusion.
Preparations. *Liquid Extract*: 0.05 to 0.25ml.
Tincture: 0.2 to 0.5ml, in water.

CANARY FANCIER'S LUNG. Bird fancier's lung. Allergic alveolitis following antigens from pet birds: pigeons, budgerigars, canaries, chickens.
Symptoms: dry cough, difficult breathing usually at night. Loss of weight, tiredness, feverishness with rise of temperature. (*Clinical Allergy, 1984. 14,429*)
Tea. Yarrow, Elderflowers, Comfrey herb: equal parts.
Tablets/capsules. Garlic. Lobelia. Iceland Moss.
Powders. Formula. Pleurisy root 2; Hyssop 1; Iceland Moss 1. Dose: 500mg (two 00 capsules or one-third teaspoon) thrice daily.
Liquid Extracts. Formula. Pleurisy root 2; Liquorice 1; Hyssop 1. 1 teaspoon in water thrice daily, and when necessary.

CANCER. An invasive growth which gradually emerges into life and, undisciplined, eats its way into neighbouring tissues. Malignancy is the growth of abnormal cells with the ability to form a primary lesion from which cells may be blood-borne to other parts of the body (metastasis). Growth usually follows the line of the lymph vessels (Violet leaves have an affinity for lymph vessels).

Course of the disease is unpredictable, cases surviving for many years on primary or supportive herbal treatment. Suspected malignancy should be referred to modern hospital treatment immediately. Early detection is vital.

Common signs calling attention are: (1) Unusual bleeding or discharge. (2) Tired feeling all the time. (3) Thickening or lump in breast or elsewhere. (4) Sudden change in hair texture and colour. (5) Irritable cough or hoarseness. (6) Extreme mental depression. (7) Obvious change in a mole or wart. (8) Muscle weakness and cramps. (9) A sore that does not heal. (10) Change in bowel or bladder habit. (11) Sudden weakness of the eyes. (12) Difficulties in swallowing; indigestion. (13) Excess wind in stomach or bowel.

Tumour-killing effect of chemotherapy may be intensified and side-effects minimised (loss of weight, and of white blood cells) when certain neoplastic herbs are prescribed. Cytotoxic drugs inhibit the ability of Vitamin C to stimulate the body's defences. Herbs enhance the body's self-healing ability to eliminate. An inoperable cancer would appear to be good grounds for herbal medication which often relieves pain and preserves a man's dignity in his hour of extremity.

A series of medical trials in Finland revealed that terminal cases had 12 per cent lower mean serum *selenium* concentration than controls. Other similar trials point to the need for selenium supplements. Those with both low selenium and low Vitamin E levels are especially at risk.

See: GERSON CANCER THERAPY.

Exercise. High levels of fitness are associated with lower death rates. (*American study*)

Plants with a special reference to cancer include: Blue Flag, Burdock, Clivers, Condurango, Echinacea, Guaiacum, Houseleek, Poke root. There are many more referred to in medical literature.

Poke Root. John Bartram reported in the late 18th century that from his experience among the Mohawk Indians, Poke root (Phytolacca decandra) was a "cure" for cancer. (*American Indian Medicine, Virgil J. Vogel*)

Blood Root. For internal or external bleeding of cancer.

Calendula (Marigold). For the same purpose.

Mistletoe. Dr Alfred Vogel advises an extract of the plant (Loranthus europaeus) as grown on the Oak tree: dose: 10-15 drops.

Almonds. Edgar Cayce, Virginia Beach, USA, with some successes to his credit, advised eating three almonds a day to counter any tendency towards the disease.

Laetrile. From Apricot kernels that contain cyanogenic glucosides. Though competent physicians have reported positive results in some terminal cases without prior surgery or radiation, the remedy has been withdrawn from general practice because of possible toxicity.

Much needless suffering may be incurred because of out-moded resistance of doctors and governments against prescribing morphine early in cancer patients. It is estimated that 50-80 per cent of patients do not receive satisfactory pain-relief because doctors fear tolerance of the drug would increase, necessitating a higher dosage. From the beginning of time the Opium Poppy has been the most effective analgesic for the terminal condition. Morphine is a respiratory depressant and some authorities believe it should be given before the final stages in continuous doses for adequate pain control. Risks must be balanced with benefits. Dangerous in asthmatics.

Way of Life. Herbal medication of malignant disease involves the patient with his treatment. Here is something he or she can do to regain some control over their life. It can give them the satisfaction of knowing that in some way they are 'fighting back' thus influencing the quality of life and a sense of well-being.

If improvement in cancer is not possible maybe the condition can be stabilised and the patient helped to cope with the very unpleasant side-effects of chemotherapy and radiation. Thus, may be restored the body's natural balance and a possible extension of lifespan.

For this, patients and practitioners may need information and support. That is why suggestions for malignant disease are included in this book. Moreover, well-meaning friends and relatives may exert pressure on the patient 'to leave no stone unturned' in search of a cure. Thus every possible secondary treatment should be considered since any one may prove to contribute towards recovery. It is hoped that this book will invite a therapeutic alliance with members of the medical profession as well as with other practitioners.

Macmillan nurses help alleviate physical pain and the psychological distress that can accompany this illness. They are trained to help people with cancer and their families fight cancer with more than medicine.

All forms of cancer should be treated by or in liaison with a qualified medical practitioner or an oncologist.

CANCER – ANAL. Epithelioma.

Of possible value. Condor plant, Figwort, Goldenseal, Echinacea. Wm Boericke MD

advised Goldenseal. J.T. Kent MD mentions Poke root.
Powders. Formula. Echinacea 2; Figwort 1; Goldenseal half; Condurango half; Thuja quarter. Pinch Cayenne. Dose: 500mg (two 00 capsules or one-third teaspoon) thrice or more daily, as tolerated.
Tinctures. Formula. Echinacea 2; Stone root half; Condurango half; Asafoetida quarter. Few drops Tincture Capsicum. Dose: 30-60 drops thrice or more daily, as tolerated.
Topical. Comfrey ointment made from the fresh plant.
Diet. See: DIET – CANCER.

Treatment by or in liaison with a general medical practitioner.

CANCER – BLADDER. Neoplasm of bladder. One third of patients are over 70 years. Most cases today arise from exposure to injurious chemicals only partly eliminated from the body, as from food additives, analine dyes, etc. Evidence also links the disease to excessive coffee-drinking, the general consensus being that caffeine blocks the action of a compound named adenosine – one of the building blocks of DNA – involved in cellular energy. In this way it interferes with natural metabolic processes.
Symptoms: Blood in the urine with absence of pain on passing water in early stages. Then, burning frequency, especially at night. Kidneys become involved. Growths range from papilloma to tumour which may ulcerate in later stages.

The lesion is confirmed by cystoscopy (examination of the bladder by insertion of an instrument to illuminate inner surfaces and makes possible a direct view of the affected tissues). Even when the condition is healed this examination is repeatedly necessary to detect recurrence.

Two kinds: (1) papillary epithelioma (2) squamous cell epithelioma.
Tea. Formula. Equal parts: Marshmallow root, Clivers, Horsetail, Shepherd's purse. 1-2 teaspoons to each cup boiling water; infuse 10-15 minutes. 2 cups or more daily.
Decoction. Barberry bark cold infusion. 1 teaspoon to each cup cold water. Steep over night. 2 cups or more daily.
Tinctures. Formula. Horsetail 1; Clivers 2; Barberry 1. Mix. 1-2 teaspoons (5-10ml) 2 or more times daily. If inflammation is present add Meadowsweet 1.
Dr William Boericke, physician, advised Dandelion to lessen symptoms.
Diet. See: DIET – CANCER.
Supplements. Emphasis on Vitamins A and C. (*Vitamin A in epithelial tumours, 'New Scientist' (1975) 303*)

Treatment offered as a supportive to specific modern hospital techniques.

Treatment by or in liaison with a general medical practitioner.

CANCER – BONE. May be myeloma (tumour-like over-growth of bone marrow tissue, a giant cell sarcoma, a medullary tumour or secondary deposit from breast, lung, prostate cancer etc. Risk of fracture. Inflammation of the bone – Yarrow. Comfrey. See: MYELOMA, SARCOMA.

CANCER – BOWEL. See: COLORECTAL CANCER.

CANCER - BREAST. Commonest form of cancer in women. Overall mortality remains about 50 per cent at five years. Appears to run in families. Strikes hard unmarried women. Married women who have no children. Those who do not nurse their babies, or who are infertile and have no child before thirty. Eight out of ten chest lumps are benign.
Symptoms. A small lump comes to light while washing, a discharge from the nipple, change in nipple size and colour, irregular contour of the breast surface. Though tissue change is likely to be a cyst, speedy diagnosis and treatment are necessary. Some hospital physicians and surgeons are known to view favourably supportive herbal aids, and do not always think in terms of radical mastectomy. Dr Finlay Ellingwood, Chicago physician (1916) cured a case by injection of one dram Echinacea root extract twice a week into the surrounding tissues.

The condition is believed to be due to a number of causes including suppression of ovulation and oestrogen secretion in pregnant and lactating women. A high fat diet is suspected of interference with the production of oestrogen. Some women are constitutionally disposed to the condition which may be triggered by trauma or emotional shock. Increase in incidence in older women has been linked with excessive sugar consumption. "Consumption overwhelms the pancreas which has to 'push it out' to all parts of the body (when broken down by the digestive process) whether they need it or not. The vital organs are rationed according to their requirements of nutrients from the diet. What is left over has to 'go into store elsewhere'. And the breast is forced to take its share and store it. If it gets too much, for too long, it may rebel!" (*Stephen Seely, Department of Bacteriology and Virology, Manchester*)

"Women who nurse their babies less than one month are at an increased risk for breast cancer. The longer a woman breast-feeds – no matter what her age – the more the risk decreases. (*Marion Tompson, co-founder, The La Leche League, in the American Journal of Epidemiology*)

Lactation reduces the risk of pre-menopausal breast cancer. (*Newcomb P.A. et al New England*

Journal of Medicine, 330 1994)

There is currently no treatment to cure metastatic breast cancer. In spite of chemotherapy, surgery and radiotherapy survival rate has not diminished. Herbs not only have a palliative effect but, through their action on hormone function offer a positive contribution towards overcoming the condition. Their activity has been widely recorded in medical literature. Unlike cytotoxic drugs, few have been known to cause alopecia, nausea, vomiting or inflammation of the stomach.

Treatment by a general medical practitioner or oncologist.

Special investigations. Low radiation X-ray mammography to confirm diagnosis. Test for detection of oestrogen receptor protein.

Treatment. Surgery may be necessary. Some patients may opt out from strong personal conviction, choosing a rigid self-disciplined approach – the Gentle Way. Every effort is made to build up the body's natural defences (immune system).

An older generation of herbalists believed tissue change could follow a bruise on the breast, which should not be neglected but immediately painted with Tincture Arnica or Tincture Bellis perennis.

Vincristine, an alkaloid from Vinca rosea (*Catharanthus roseus*) is used by the medical profession as an anti-neoplastic and anti-mitotic agent to inhibit cell division.

Of possible therapeutic value. Blue Flag root, Burdock root, Chaparral, Clivers, Comfrey root, Echinacea, Figwort, Gotu Kola, Marshmallow root, Mistletoe, Myrrh, Prickly Ash bark, Red Clover, Thuja, Wild Violet, Yellow Dock.

Tea. Equal parts: Red Clover, Clivers, Gotu Kola, Wild Violet. 1 heaped teaspoon to each cup boiling water; infuse 5-15 minutes. 3 or more cups daily.

Decoctions. Echinacea, Blue Flag root, Queen's Delight, Yellow Dock.

Tablets/capsules. Blue Flag root, Echinacea, Poke root, Mistletoe.

Formula. Echinacea 2; Gotu Kola 1; Poke root 1; Mistletoe 1; Vinca rosea 1. Mix. Dose: Powders: 500mg (two 00 capsules or one-third teaspoon). Liquid extracts: 1 teaspoon. Tinctures: 2 teaspoons. Thrice daily and at bedtime. According to progress of the disease, increase dosage as tolerated.

Maria Treben's tea. Parts: Marigold (3), Yarrow 1; Nettles 1. Mix. 2 teaspoons to each cup boiling water. 1 cup as many times daily as tolerated.

William Boericke, M.D. recommends Houseleek. E.H. Ruddock M.D. favours Figwort.

Topical. *Treatments believed to be of therapeutic value or for use as a soothing application.*

(1) Cold poultice: Comfrey root.

(2) Poultice of fresh Marshmallow root pulped in juicer.

(3) Injection of Extract Greater Celandine (Chelidonium), locally, gained a reputation in the Eclectic school.

(4) The action of Blood root (*Sanguinaria*) is well known as a paint or injection.

(5) Ragwort poultice: 2oz Ragwort boiled in half a pint potato water for 15 minutes. See: POULTICE.

(6) Popular Russian traditional remedy: Badiaga (*Spongilla fluviatilis*), fresh water sponge gathered in the autumn; dried plant rubbed to a powder. Poultice.

(7) Maria Treben's Poultice: Carefully washed fresh Plantain leaves, pulped, and applied direct to the lesion.

(8) If lymph glands are affected, apply Plantain poultice to glands.

(9) Dr Brandini's treatment. Dr Brandini, Florence, used 4 grains Citric Acid (prepared from lemons) in 1oz (30ml) water for ulcerated cancer of the breast considered incurable. "The woman's torments were so distressing that neither she nor other patients could get any rest. Applying lint soaked in the solution, relief was instantaneous. Repeated, it was successful."

(10) Circuta leaves. Simmered till soft and mixed with Slippery Elm bark powder as a poultice morning and night.

(11) Decoction. Simmer gently Yellow Dock roots, fine cut or powdered, 1oz to 1 pint, 20 minutes. Saturate lint or suitable material and apply.

(12) Yellow Dock ointment. Half ounce Lobelia seed, half ounce Yellow Dock root powder. Baste into an ointment base. See: OINTMENT BASE.

(13) Infusion, for use as a wash. Equal parts: Horsetail, Red Clover, Raspberry leaves. 1oz to 1 pint boiling water infuse 15 minutes.

(14) Dr Christopher's Ointment. Half an ounce White Oak, half an ounce Garden Sage, half an ounce Tormentil, half an ounce Horsetail, half an ounce Lemon Balm. *Method*: Boil gently half an hour in quart water, strain. Reduce to half a pint by simmering. Add half a pound honey. Bring to boil. Skim off scum. Allow cool. Apply: twice daily on sores.

(15) Dr Finlay Ellingwood. Poke root juice. "Fresh juice from the stems, leaves and roots applied directly to diseased tissue. Exercises a selective action; induces liquefaction and promotes removal, sometimes healing the open wound and encouraging scar formation. Masses of such tissue have been known to be destroyed in a few weeks with only a scar, with no other application but the fresh juice. Produces pain at first, but is otherwise harmless."

(16) Lesion painted with Mandrake resin. (*American Podophyllum*)

(17) Dust affected parts with Comfrey powder. Mucilage from Comfrey powder or crushed root with the aid of a little milk. See: COMFREY.

(18) Dr Samuel Thomson's Cancer Plaster. "Take heads of Red Clover and fill a kettle. Boil in water for one hour. Remove and fill kettle with fresh flower heads. Boil as before in the same liquor. Strain and press heads to express all the liquor. Simmer over a low fire till of the consistency of tar. It must not burn. Spread over a piece of suitable material."
(19) Wipe affected area with cut Houseleek. (*Dr Wm Boericke*)
(20) Chinese Herbalism. Take 1-2 Liang pulverised liao-ko-wang (Wickstroemia indica), mix with cold boiled water or rice wine for local compress. Also good for mastitis.
(21) Italian women once used an old traditional remedy – Fenugreek tea.
(22) A clinical trial of Vitamin D provided encouraging results. Patients with locally advanced breast cancer were given a highly active Vitamin D analogue cream to rub on their tumours. "It was effective in one third of the tumours," said Professor Charles Coombes, clinical oncologist, Charing Cross Hospital, London.
Diet. "A diet rich in cereal products (high in dietary fibre) and green leafy vegetables (antioxidants) would appear to offer women some protection against breast cancer due to the relation between fibre and oestrogen metabolism. Meat-free diet. In a study of 75 adolescent girls, vegetarians were found to have higher levels of a hormone that women suffering from breast cancer often lack. (*Cancer Research*)
Supplements. Daily. Chromium. Selenium (600mcg). Zinc chelate (100mg morning and evening). Beta carotene. "Low levels of Selenium and Vitamins A and E are shown in breast cancer cases." (*British Journal of Cancer 49: 321-324, 1984*).

Vitamins A and D inhibit virus penetration in healthy cell walls. Multivitamin combinations should not include Vitamin B12, production of which in the body is much increased in cancerous conditions. Vitamins B-complex and C especially required.
Note. A link between sugar consumption and breast cancer has been reported by some authorities who suggest that countries at the top of the mortality table are the highest also in sugar consumption; the operative factor believed to be insulin.
Screening. Breast screening should be annual from the age of forty.
General. Mothers are encouraged to breast-feed children for the protection it offers against mammary malignancy. (*Am.J. Obstet. Gyn. 15/9/1984. 150.*)

Avoidance of stress situations by singing, playing an instrument. Adopt relaxation techniques, spiritual healing and purposeful meditation to arouse the immune system; intensive visualisation. Avoid the carcinogens: smoking, alcohol.
Information. Breast Cancer Care. Free Help Line. UK Telephone: 0500 245345.

CANCER – BRONCHIAL CARCINOMA. The most common form of cancer throughout the world. Five year survival: 10 per cent. Its association with cigarette smoking is now established beyond doubt. Other causes include such occupational poisons as asbestos, arsenic, chromium, diesel fumes, etc. The squamous cell carcinoma is the most common of the four types.

Diagnosis is confirmed by sputum test, chest X-ray, bronchoscopy or biopsy. Earliest symptoms are persistent cough, pain in the chest, hoarseness of voice and difficulty of breathing. Physical examination is likely to reveal sensitivity and swelling of lymph nodes under arms.
Symptoms. Tiredness, lack of energy, possible pains in bones and over liver area. Clubbing of finger-tips indicate congestion of the lungs. Swelling of arms, neck and face may be obvious. A haematologist may find calcium salts in the blood. The supportive action of *alteratives*, eliminatives and lymphatic agents often alleviate symptoms where the act of swallowing has not been impaired.

Broncho-dilators (Lobelia, Ephedra, etc) assist breathing. Mullein has some reputation for pain relief. To arrest bleeding from the lesion (Blood root).

According to Dr Madaus, Germany, Rupturewort is specific on lung tissue. To disperse sputum (Elecampane, Red Clover). In advanced cases there may be swollen ankles and kidney breakdown for which Parsley root, Parsley Piert or Buchu may be indicated. Cough (Sundew, Irish Moss). Soft cough with much sputum (Iceland Moss). To increase resistance (Echinacea).
Alternatives. Secondary to primary treatment. Of possible value.
Teas. Violet leaves, Mullein leaves, Yarrow leaves, Gotu Kola leaves, White Horehound leaves. Flavour with a little Liquorice if unpalatable.
Tablets/capsules. Lobelia, Iceland Moss, Echinacea, Poke root.
Formula. Equal parts: Violet, Red Clover, Garden Thyme, Yarrow, Liquorice. Dose: Powders: 750mg (three 00 capsules or half a teaspoon. Liquid Extracts: 1-2 teaspoons. Tinctures: 1-3 teaspoons. Thrice daily, and during the night if relief is sought.
Practitioner. Tinctures BHP (1983). Ephedra 4; Red Clover 4, Yellow Dock 2; Bugleweed 2; Blood root quarter; Liquorice quarter (liquid extract). Mix. Start low: 30-60 drops in water before meals and at bedtime increasing to maximum tolerance level.
Aromatherapy. Oils: Eucalyptus or Thyme on tissue to assist breathing. Inhale.

Diet. See: DIET – CANCER.

Treatment by a general medical practitioner or hospital specialist.

CANCER – CERVICAL. See: CANCER OF THE WOMB.

CANCER. CHINESE PRESCRIPTION. Decoction of:– 2 liang of each of the following fresh plants: Pai-ying (Solanum lyratum), Oldenlandia diffusa, Lobelia radicans, Scutellaria barbarta. If dried, use half quantity. Drink as tea. For severe pain add Ch'ing-mu-hsiang (Aristolochia debilis), 1 liang. Take with rice-polishing water. For haemoptysis, add 1 liang chi'hsueh-t'eng (Millettia reticulata). For severe coughing add yin-yang-huo (Epimedium sagittatum) and ai-ti-ch'a (Ardisia japonica), 3 ch'ien of each. Advised for cancer of the lungs, liver, cervix and nasopharynx.

CANCER-COLORECTAL. Arises from pre-malignant adenoma. About one in ten adenomatous polyps develop into a carcinoma. Simple excision of polyps with *in situ* carcinoma sometimes leads to complete cure.

Symptoms: bleeding, with alteration of bowel habit. Common in diverticular disease where large polyps may be undetected. Early detection by flexible sigmoidoscopy at hospital is essential to accurate diagnosis. Sudden episodes of unexplained diarrhoea and constipation.

The term refers to cancers of the ascending colon, caecum, transverse colon, hepatic flexure, descending colon, splenic flexure, sigmoid colon and rectum. The large bowel tumours are almost wholly adeno-carcinoma.

Common causes: ulcerative colitis, Crohn's disease, necrotic changes in polyps. The colon is at risk from cancer on a diet high in protein, fat and alcohol and which is low in fibre. An exception is the average diet in Finland where a high fat intake is present with a low incidence of cancer. Strong evidence advanced, includes the heavy consumption of yoghurt (acidophylus lacto bacillus) by the population.

A study of 8006 Japanese men living in Hawaii revealed the close relationship between cancer of the rectum and alcohol consumption. A family history of pernicious anaemia predisposes.

A 19-year prospective study of middle-aged men employed by a Chicago electric company reveals a strong correlation between colorectal cancer and Vitamin D and calcium deficiency. Results "support the suggestion that Vitamin D and calcium may reduce the risk of colorectal cancer". (*Lancet, 1985, Feb 9, i, 307*)

Patients with ulcerative colitis of more than 10 years standing carry the increased risk of developing colorectal cancer. There is evidence that malignancy in the bowel may be reduced by saponins.

Alternatives of possible value. Inoperable lesions may respond to: Bayberry, Goldenseal, Echinacea, Wild Yam, Stone root, Black root, Mistletoe, Clivers, Marshmallow root, Violet leaves, Chickweed, Red Clover, Thuja.

Tea. Equal parts: Red Clover, Gotu Kola, Violet leaves. 2-3 teaspoons to each cup boiling water; infuse 15 minutes. Freely, as tolerated.

Tablets/capsules. Echinacea, Goldenseal, Wild Yam.

Formula. Echinacea 2; Bayberry 1; Wild Yam 1; Stone root 1; Goldenseal half; Liquorice quarter. Mix. Dose: Powders: 500mg (two 00 capsules or one-third teaspoon). Liquid extracts: 1 teaspoon. Tinctures: 2 teaspoons. Thrice daily and at bedtime.

Mistletoe: Injections of fresh plant (Iscador). (*Dr Rudolph Steiner Institute, Switzerland*)

Violet leaves: Daily irrigations of strong infusion.

Chickweed: Bathe rectum with strong infusion. Follow with Chickweed ointment.

Chinese Herbalism. (1) Tea – Pan-chih-lien (*Scutellaria barbarta*), 2 liang. (2) Tea. Feng-wei ts'ao (Pteris multifida) 1 liang, and po-chi (water chestnut) 2 liang. (3) Concoction of suitable amount of ts'ang-erh ts'ao, for bathing affected area. (*Barefoot Doctor's Manual*)

Diagnosis. Exploration of proctosigmoidoscope to confirm.

Diet. Special emphasis on yoghurt which is conducive to bowel health; orally and by enema. A vegan uncooked raw food diet has been shown to reduce the body's production of toxins linked with colon cancer. A switch from conventional Western cooked diet to an uncooked vegan diet reduced harmful enzymes produced by gut bacteria. (*Journal of Nutrition*)

A substance has been found in fish oil believed to prevent cancer of the colon. Mackerel, herring and sardines are among fish with this ingredient.

Bowel cancer and additives. See: CROHN'S DISEASE (Note).

Preventive care. All 55-year-olds with this predisposing condition should be screened by sigmoidoscopy. Regular faecal occult blood tests advised.

Regular exercise helps prevent development of bowel cancer. (*Nottingham University researchers*)

Treatment by general medical practitioner or oncologist.

CANCER – FACIAL. In October 1967, after three previous surgically removed growths, an 85-year-old cattleman of Mesa, Arizona, refused treatment on the same fourth-recurrent growth, documented as malignant melanoma, in favour of "Chaparral tea", an old Indian remedy. Of this tea he drank 2-3 cups a day. In September 1968 he was re-examined by the Medical Centre, Utah,

USA. They found the growth had decreased from the size of a large lemon to that of a dime. No other medication was used, only the Chaparral tea. In eleven months he gained a needed 25lb with improvements in general health, as previous to Chaparral treatment he was pale, weak and lethargic. (*"Indian Herbology", Alma Hutchens. Pub: Merco, Ontaria*).

The facial lesion finally disappeared.

CANCER – KIDNEY. Cancer of the kidney may appear in the renal pelvis, the area where urine is collected, or as a hypernephroma in the kidney itself. Not common. Symptoms include blood in the urine but with little pain. Herbal anti-neoplastics may enable the body to tolerate and reduce the toxicity of chemotherapy, the following being subordinate to conventional treatment.
Formula. Corn Silk 3; Plantain (*Plantago major L*) 2; Golden Rod 1; Hydrangea 1; Valerian half. Dosage: thrice daily before meals. Liquid Extracts: 1 teaspoon. Tinctures: 2 teaspoons. Powders: two 00 capsules or one-third teaspoon. This may be used as a basic combination to be adapted to a changing clinical picture.

Treatment by a general medical practitioner or oncologist.

CANCER – LARYNX. Chiefly due to continued inflammation from faulty use of the voice, smoking, drugs or infection.
Symptoms. Cough, hoarseness, difficult swallowing. 'Always clearing the throat.' Differs from a polyp or papilloma on the vocal chords which are benign.
Of possible value:– Teas. Balm, Chamomile, Gotu Kola, Red Clover, Red Sage, Yarrow. Plantain (*Arthur Hyde MNIMH*)
Tea (mild analgesic). Mix equal parts: Balm and German Chamomile. 1 heaped teaspoon to each cup boiling water; infuse 5 minutes. 1 cup freely.
Tablets/capsules. Blue Flag root, Echinacea, Poke root.
Formula. Echinacea 2; Mullein 2; Goldenseal quarter. Mix. Dose: Powders: 750mg (three 00 capsules or half a teaspoon). Liquid extracts: 1-2 teaspoons. Tinctures: 1-3 teaspoons. Thrice daily and at bedtime.
Diet. Slippery Elm gruel.
Supplements. Vitamins A and C.

Treatment by a general medical practitioner or a hospital oncologist.

CANCER – LIVER. A primary lesion in the liver is rare. Usually invasion of carcinoma from the pancreas, gall bladder, stomach or intestines. Enlargement is rapid.
Symptoms. Jaundice. Ascites (excess fluid in the abdomen). Tenderness and enlargement of right upper abdomen; hobnail to the touch.
Alternatives: for possible relief of symptoms:–
Dandelion juice (fresh): 4 drachms (14ml) every 4 hours.
Wormwood tea freely.
Tea. Equal parts: Agrimony, Gotu Kola, Milk Thistle. Mix. 1 heaped teaspoon to each cup boiling water; infuse 5-10 minutes. 1 cup freely.
Decoction. Dandelion 2; Clivers 1; Liquorice 1; Blue Flag root half. Mix. 30g (1oz) to 500ml (1 pint) water gently simmered 20 minutes. Dose: half-1 cup 3 or more times daily.
Tablets/capsules. Blue Flag root, Goldenseal, Prickly Ash.
Formula. Dandelion 2; Milk Thistle 2; Fennel 1; Peppermint 1. Mix. Dose: Powders: 750mg (three 00 capsules or half a teaspoon). Liquid extracts: 1-2 teaspoons. Tinctures: 1-2 teaspoons. 3 or more times daily.
Biostrath artichoke formula.
Practitioner. Dandelion juice (fresh) 4oz; Wahoo bark Liquid extract 10 drops. Violet leaves Liquid extract 10.5ml. Tincture Goldenseal 10 drops. Dose: 2 teaspoons in water thrice daily. To each dose add 10 drops Liquid extract Oats (avena). (*W. Burns-Lingard MNIMH*)
Vinchristine. Success has been reported following use of the Periwinkle plant (*Vinca rosea*).
Greater Celandine has been regarded of value.
Chinese Herbalism. See: CANCER: CHINESE PRESCRIPTION. Also: Pulverised t'ien chi-huang (Hypericum japonicum) 1 liang, mixed with rock sugar, with boiled water, 3 times daily. Also of value for cirrhosis.
Epsom's salt Baths (hot): to encourage elimination of impurities through the skin.
Diet. Limit fats. Protein diet to increase bile flow.

Treatment by a general medical practitioner or hospital oncologist.

CANCER – LYMPH VESSELS. See: HODGKIN'S DISEASE.

CANCER – MOUTH AND LIPS. Epithelioma.
Causes: occupational hazards, contact with toxic metals and minerals.

A Health Department's committee found an increased risk of developing mouth cancer from "snuff-dipping", the practice of sucking tobacco from a small sachet, "tobacco teabags".
Of possible value:– *Fresh plant juices*. Houseleek, Aloe Vera.
Teas: Chickweed, Mullein, Comfrey. 1 heaped teaspoon to each cup boiling water; infuse 15 minutes; dose – 1 cup thrice daily, increasing to as much as well tolerated.
Condurango Liquid extract. 10-30 drops in water before meals.
Goldenseal Liquid extract. 3-5 drops in water before meals.
George Burford MD. Condurango and Goldenseal.
E.H. Ruddock MD 1925. "Several cases of cancer

of the lips have been cured by Goldenseal."
Topical. Wipe area with Liquid Extract Condurango, Goldenseal, Thuja, Poke root or fresh plant juices of above. Slippery Elm paste: powdered Slippery Elm in few drops milk or water.
Mouthwash. Equal parts: Liquid Extract Goldenseal, Liquid Extract Bayberry, Tincture Myrrh and Glycerine. Some may be swallowed as internal medicine. Comfrey, Mullein or Chickweed cream.
Diet. See: DIET – CANCER.

Treatment by a general medical practitioner or hospital oncologist.

CANCER – NOSE AND THROAT. Usually epithelioma with burning. Lesion may extend upwards into the base of the skull. Thickening of nasal membranes may cause deafness by compressing Eustachian tubes.

Anyone over 40 who has recurrent sore throat for more than six weeks should visit his family doctor.
Symptoms. Pain, headache, paralysis of eye muscles.
Of possible value. **Alternatives**:– *Teas.* Violet leaves, Red Clover flowers, Plantain. 1-2 teaspoons to each cup boiling water; infuse 5-15 minutes. Drink freely.
Decoction. Combination. Goldenseal 1; Poke root 1; Yellow Dock 3; Marshmallow root 3. Place half an ounce (15g) in 1 pint (500ml) water simmered gently 20 minutes. Half a cup or more, as freely as tolerated.
Formula. Echinacea 2; Goldenseal 1; Poke root half; Thuja quarter; Liquorice half. Mix. Dose: Powders: 500mg (two 00 capsules or one-third teaspoon). Liquid extracts: 1 teaspoon. Tinctures: 2 teaspoons. Three or more times daily as tolerated.
Case of Lady Margaret Marsham, Maidstone. Cured of cancer of the throat by Violet leaf tea. Boiling water was poured on fresh Violet leaves (wild, not cultivated) and allowed to stand 12 hours. Compresses were moistened and applied externally to the throat and covered with oil silk. Relief was immediate. Difficult swallowing, sense of suffocation and the visible swelling disappeared within one week, the growth on the tonsil within a fortnight.

Treatment by a general medical practitioner or hospital oncologist.
Diet. See: DIET – CANCER.

CANCER – OESOPHAGUS. Usually epithelial in character, similar to that of the lips. Mostly in males. Seldom before 45 years. Frequently in lower one-third of gullet. Dysphagia, with sense of obstruction on swallowing food. May perforate wall of trachea. Pain, worse at night, radiates from an exact spot. Eating hot food and drinking piping hot tea are heavily suspect.

At risk. Heavy smokers and alcoholics with depleted reserves of Vitamin A and zinc. These two factors play an important role in modern treatment.

Occurs in areas where the soil is low in molybdenum which causes plants to have a high level of nitrates. When such plants are stored they form nitrites which in turn form nitrosamines – which are carcinogens. Experimental rats given nitrous amines have a strong tendency to form cancer of the oesophagus. Eating pickled vegetables carries a high risk.

There are a few areas of the world where these adverse soil conditions pertain – one in Iran, another in Calvados, but the worst was in Lin Xian of the province of Honan, China. In Lin Xian, in the 1970s, it was found that villagers ate mainly persimmon and corn cakes and pickled vegetables. These, and their water, were high in nitrates. It was also their habit to eat mouldy bread which is high in amines – even nitrosamines. Their food was deficient in Vitamin C, which is likely to produce nitrous amines in the stomach.

The molybdenum problem was solved by sowing seeds with a fertiliser containing molybdenum. Piped water replaced old cistern wells and food was carefully stored. Even the chickens oesophageal cancers were cured. As a result of modern scientific investigation and treatment in which medicinal herbs made an important contribution, what was once a high gullet cancer area was resolved into one of the success stories of modern medicine.

Tannin has long been identified as a cancer-causing chemical, supported by findings of a high incidence of the disease among those who consume large quantities of tannin-containing beverages such as tea. Milk binds with tannin and is advised in tea-drinking where lemon is not taken.

Solid drugs and tablets should not be swallowed in the recumbent position without chewing a piece of banana.
Symptoms. (1) Sensation of obstruction when swallowing food. (2) Sharp pain behind breastbone. (3) "Something stuck in the gullet." (4) Stomach ache, dry throat. (5) Belching when taking food. (6) Soreness of the upper back. (*Dr Ge-ming, Lin Xian, Province of Honan, Chinese People's Republic*)
Of possible value. Alternatives:– *Tea.* Equal parts: Chaparral, Gotu Kola, Red Clover. 1 heaped teaspoon to each cup boiling water; infuse 15 minutes. Drink freely.
Powders. Combination. Goldenseal 1; Echinacea 2; Slippery Elm 3. Dose: 750mg (three 00 capsules or half a teaspoon). 3 or more times daily.
Tinctures. Combination. Goldenseal 1; Bayberry 1; Thuja 1; Condurango 1; Rosebay Willowherb 2. One teaspoon 3 or more times daily.

Chinese Herbalism. Powdered Huang yao-tzu 3 ch'ien, 3 times daily. Remedy is prepared by taking 12 liang of huang yao-tzu and steeping in 3 chin of white wine 24 hours. Then place huang yao-tzu in cold water and soak for another 7 days and 7 nights. Take out, dry and crush into powder. (*A Barefoot Doctor's Manual*)
Diet. Leafy vegetables, carrots, tomatoes and fruit help to protect against the disease.
Supplements. Especially Vitamin A, zinc and molybdenum.
Treatment by a general medical practitioner or hospital oncologist.

CANCER – OVARIES. Ovarian carcinoma. The fifth most common cause of death in women. Often together with bowel and breast cancers. Adeno-carcinoma. Prognosis poor because of delay in seeking medical advise.
Symptoms. Failing appetite, weight loss, flatulence, bowel symptoms, bladder disturbance, abdominal pain, clothes tight around the abdomen. The disease usually presents after the age of 45, users of contraceptives having a lower risk of development.
Risk of ovarian cancer has been related to women who consume too much animal fat and too little vegetable fat (*JAM Nov. 1984*). A similar risk is recorded in a report from Milan providing strong evidence of its relation to excessive coffee consumption.
Researchers at John Hopkin's University, Baltimore, USA, report success with Taxol, extracted from the bark of the Pacific Yew Tree, given intravenously to 40 women with ovarian cancer resistant to other therapies, caused a 50 per cent decrease in size of the tumours. *(New Scientist 1989, 1687, p37)*
Treatment. Should it be necessary to defer surgery or cytotoxic chemotherapy, any of the following alternatives may be taken with profit, or prescribed as secondary to primary treatment.
Tea. Equal parts: Agnus Castus, Gotu Kola, Red Clover. 1 heaped teaspoon to each cup boiling water; infuse 5-15 minutes. Drink freely.
Formula. Cramp bark 3; Liquorice 1; Thuja 1; Poke root half. Mix. Dose: Powders: 750mg (three 00 capsules or half a teaspoon). Liquid extracts: 1 teaspoon. Tinctures: 2 teaspoons. Thrice daily.
Vaginal pack. 8 parts Slippery Elm powder mixed with 1 part Thuja powder in a little water to form a paste; saturate tampon and insert.
Dr J. Christopher. For pre- and post-operative pain: Black Willow.
British Herbal Pharmacopoeia. Cramp bark for pain.
Diet. See: DIET – CANCER. Drinks of Violet leaf tea freely.
Supplements. Post-operative treatment should include Comfrey and Calcium to counter the loss of calcium on surgical removal, with possible brittle and broken bones in ageing women.
Note. When a potential lesion is found, a pelvic ultrasound scan may confirm.
Treatment by gynaecologist or oncologist.

CANCER – PANCREAS. Adeno-carcinoma. Cause: often related to chronic pancreatitis, alcoholism. Beer drinkers, more than 7 pints a week, run a three times greater risk of the disease than one in a 100 threat to the rest of the population. (*Imperial Cancer Research Report, April, 1989*) Diabetes. A study carried out at Harvard School of Public Health found strong evidence in favour of the excessive consumption of coffee. Seventh Day Adventists and Mormons, who abstain from coffee, have much lower rates than the average. Relative risk was 1-8 with up to two cups a day and 2.7 with three or more. (*New England Journal of Medicine, 1981, March 12, Vol 304, No 11, p630*)
Symptoms. Weight loss. Pain upper abdomen. Change of bowel habit. Phlebitis. Low blood sugar. Sugar in the urine. Jaundice when head of the pancreas is involved. As little benefit is said to be gained from chemotherapy or radiotherapy, and because a majority of these tumours are unresectable, there would appear to be good grounds for herbal medicine, either as primary or supportive treatment.
Of possible therapeutic value for relief of accompanying gastric and pressure symptoms only: Sarsaparilla, Liquorice, Dandelion, Peppermint, Fennel, German Chamomile.
Tea. Barberry bark. 1 teaspoon to each cup of cold water. Steep overnight. Dose: half-1 cup 3 or more times daily.
Formula. Equal parts: Barberry bark, Dandelion, Galangal. Dose: Powders: 500mg (two 00 capsules or one-third teaspoon). Liquid extracts: 1 teaspoon (5ml). Tinctures: 2 teaspoons. Thrice daily to commence: after fourteen days increase as tolerated.
Primrose oil. High doses GLA believed to improve immune system and prevent weight loss.
Macrobiotic diet. A retired English doctor had cancer of the pancreas, inoperable, the size of a cricket ball, for which conventional treatment could do nothing. Regression being almost impossible, he would die within a few months. In the meantime he was advised to try the Macrobiotic diet comprising wholefoods, compost grown vegetables, vegetable oils and natural drinks such as carrot juice and herbal teas. He and his wife, living in Italy, carefully followed the diet, drank water only from a local spring and ate vegetables organically grown on their own land. The tumour diminished in size and the doctor recovered.
Note. Cessation of cigarette smoking will result in a decreased incidence of the disease in the male

adult population. (*American Journal of Public Health 1989 79 1016*)

A substance found in fish oil has been shown experimentally to prevent cancer of the pancreas. Mackerel, herring and sardines are among fish with the ingredient.

Treatment by oncologist or general practitioner.

CANCER – PROSTATE GLAND. Adenocarcinoma. A hormone-related tumour in elderly men. Enlargement of the gland may be benign or carcinomatous. Fibrosis (hardening) may arise from inflammation. Obstruction of the outlet of the bladder through swelling of the gland (prostatism) may cause uraemia.

Symptoms. Bladder irritability; increased frequency during the night. Feeble forked stream of urine. Sometimes blood. Three quarters of such tumours are located in the posterior lobe of the prostate gland – readily accessible to the examining finger through the front wall of the rectum. Rectal examination reveals a hard rugged prostate. Cystoscopy confirms. Bone pains in the low back or pelvis reflect a stage where the tumour has already spread. Anaemia, weight loss, urgency.

All symptoms are worse by alcohol and spicy foods.

Harvard University scientists report: heavy consumption of animal fat, especially the fat in red meat appears to increase the chance that a man will develop advanced prostate cancer.

Of therapeutic value. Comfrey, Echinacea, Horsetail, Poke root, Thuja, Cornsilk, Goldenseal.

Tea. Combination. Comfrey leaves, Horsetail, Cornsilk. Equal parts. 2-3 teaspoons to each cup boiling water. Drink freely.

Formula No. 1. Echinacea 2; Comfrey 1; Poke root half; Thuja half. Mix. Dose: Powders: 500mg (two 00 capsules or one-third teaspoon). Liquid extracts: 1 teaspoon. Tinctures: 2 teaspoons. Thrice daily in water or cup of Cornsilk tea.

Formula No. 2. (Alternative) Echinacea 2; Goldenseal 1; Gotu Kola 1; Poke root half. Mix. Dose: Powders: 500mg (two 00 capsules or one-third teaspoon). Liquid extracts: 1 teaspoon. Tinctures: 2 teaspoons in water or cup of Cornsilk tea.

Bee pollen. Of value.

Garlic. Of value.

Diet. See: DIET– CANCER.

There is a very low incidence of prostate cancer in countries where Soya products are widely consumed – Soya contains a female hormone which is a protector factor.

Supplements. Morning and evening.

Vitamin A 7500iu or more. Large doses may be required. Vitamin C 1-2g. Vitamin E 200iu. Calcium 500mg. Selenium 100mcg. Zinc.

Study. Men with prostate cancer may not need to undergo radical prostatectomy (removal of the prostate gland). A 10-year follow-up study of men with early prostate cancer left untreated showed that 10 years later only 8.5 per cent of the 223 patients had died from prostate cancer. The survival rate of 86.8 per cent in the untreated group was nearly identical to a subgroup who met all the conditions for radical prostatectomy. (*Journal of American Medical Association, 22/29 April 1992*)

Commonly treated with female sex hormone or by orchidectomy.

It would appear that surgical removal of the gland offers little benefit, and possibly a disadvantage to patients wishing to leave well alone, particularly the elderly.

Treatment by a general medical practitioner or oncologist.

CANCER – PULMONARY. Cancer of the lung.

By the blood and lymph cancer may be transferred (metastasised) to the lymph nodes under the arm, liver, brain or lungs. An association has been shown between a low intake of Vitamin A and lung cancer.

Causes: occupational hazards, environmental pollution, radiation, keeping of pet birds. Cigarette smoking is a strong risk factor. Studies show that a high Vitamin A/carotene intake is protective against the disease in men. Among women, evidence of a similar protective effect has not been found. Vitamin C reduces cancer risk. The increased prevalence of smoking among women results in more female lung cancer. All smokers should drink freely carrot juice (Vitamin A).

Symptoms. Chronic irritative cough, difficult breathing, pain in the chest, recurrent spitting of blood, clubbing of fingers, weight loss.

Alternatives. Only transient benefit is obtainable, yet it may be sufficient to achieve a measure of relief from distressing symptoms. See: CANCER: GENERAL REMARKS. Mullein tea has its supporters. Bugleweed strengthens lung tissue and supports the action of the heart. Blood root is known to arrest bleeding (haemoptysis).

Tea. Equal parts: Red Clover, Gota Kola, Mullein. 2 teaspoons to each cup boiling water; infuse 5-15 minutes. 1 cup three or more times daily.

Formula No 1. Equal parts: Elecampane, Violet, Red Clover, Echinacea. Mix. Dose: Powders: 750mg (three 00 capsules or half a teaspoon). Liquid extracts: 1-2 teaspoons. Tinctures: 1-3 teaspoons. Thrice daily and, if necessary, at bedtime for relief.

Formula No 2. Tincture Blood root 10 drops; Liquid extract Dogwood 20 drops; Liquid extract Elecampane 200 drops (14ml); Liquid extract Bugleweed (*Lycopus europ*) 30 drops. Flavour with Liquorice if necessary. Dose: 1-2 teaspoons in water 3 or more times daily. (*W. Burns-Lingard MNIMH*)

Where accompanied by active inflammation, anti-inflammatories are indicated: Mistletoe, Wild Yam, etc.

Diet. A substance in fish oil has been shown to experimentally prevent cancer of the lung. Mackerel, herring and sardines are among fish with the ingredient. See: DIET – CANCER.

Chinese Herbalism. See: CANCER – CHINESE PRESCRIPTION.

Treatment by a general medical practitioner or hospital oncologist.

CANCER RECTAL – See COLORECTAL CANCER.

CANCER – SARCOMA. Cancer appearing in bone, muscle, connective tissue or cartilage. Malignant tissue which differs from carcinoma. Pain is intermittent, often relieved by exercise. The following is an example.

"I saw a man suffering from sarcomatous tumour infiltrating the body tissue of the upper jaw, extending to the nose. We recommended an operation. Dr O'Sullivan, Professor of Pathology, Trinity College, declared the growth to be a round-celled sarcoma. Of that there was no doubt. A month after excision the growth returned with increased vigour, bulging through the incision and protruding upon the face. The new tumour, almost closing the right eye, was blue, tense, firm and lobulated, but it did not break.

"Early in October the patient walked into my study. He looked better in health than I have ever seen him. The tumour had completely disappeared from the face and I could not identify any trace of it in the mouth. He said he had no pain of any kind. He has since gone home apparently well.

"He told me he had applied poultices of Comfrey root, and that the swelling had gradually disappeared. Now this was a case of which none of us had any doubt at all. Our first view was confirmed by the distinguished pathologist mentioned and by my own observation at the time of the major operation." (*Dr Wm Thompson, President, Royal College of Surgeons, Eire, in his address in Dublin*).

Vinchristine. An alkaloid of the Vinca plant.

Internal Treatment. See: CANCER – NOSE AND THROAT.

Diet. See: DIET – CANCER.

Treatment by a general medical practitioner or hospital oncologist.

CANCER – SKIN. There is strong evidence that sunlight plays a major role in the development of human skin cancers. Skin malignancy usually takes the form of Basal Cell carcinoma, squamous cell carcinoma and melanoma that may develop from pre-existing naevi.

Basal Cell Cancer. Strong sunlight on fair skins. Common on face and hands and other exposed areas. Commences as a tiny hard nodule. See – RODENT ULCER.

Squamous Cell Cancer. The role of sunlight in this type of cancer is even more positive. Other causes: photosensitisers such as pitch and PUVA photochemotherapy. Commences as a raised scaly rapidly-growing nodule.

Malignant Melanoma. Rare, but incidence rising. Four different kinds. Incidence is increased in individuals with fair or red hair who tend to burn rather than tan in the sun.

Causes may be numerous: genetic, occupational hazards or exposure to low-level radiation. Heavy freckling in youth doubles the risk. (*Western Canada Melanoma study*)

A study carried out by the New York's Memorial-Sloan Kettering Cancer Centre refers to damage to the ultra violet-blocking ozone layer by supersonic jet exhaust and aerosol propellants that can also raise the malignant melanoma rate. A University of Sydney study links fluorescent lighting with the disease.

Symptoms. Itching lesion increases in size and with growing discoloration. Colours may present as brown, black, red, blue, white, with a red inflammatory border. May progress to a dry crust, with bleeding.

Study. A study conducted by a team from Melbourne University, Anti-Cancer Council and St Vincent's Hospital, Australia, describes a summer-long experiment that showed that people who used a sun-screen lotion (in this case SPF-17) cut their chances of developing the first signs of skin cancer.

Study. Patients who receive blood transfusions are more likely to develop malignant lymphomas and non-melanomatous skin cancers. (*European Journal of Cancer (Nov 1993)*)

Eclectic physicians of the 19th century reported success from the use of American Mandrake (*podophylum peltatum*). Recent experience includes a 76 per cent cure rate achieved in 68 patients with carcinoma of the skin by treatment twice daily for 14 days with an ointment consisting of Podophyllum resin 20 per cent, and Linseed oil 20 per cent, in lanolin, followed by an antibiotic ointment. (*Martindale 27; 1977, p. 1341*) Podophyllum is an anti-mitotic and inhibits cell-division and should not be applied to normal cells.

Aloe Vera. Fresh cut leaf, or gel, to wipe over exposed surfaces.

Vitamin E oil. Applying the oil to the skin can reduce chances of acquiring skin cancer from the sun. (*University of Arizona College of Medicine*)

Red Clover. "I have seen a case of skin cancer healed by applying Red Clover blossoms. After straining a strong tea, the liquid was simmered

until it was the consistency of tar. After several applications the skin cancer was gone, and has not returned." (*May Bethel, in "Herald of Health", Dec. 1963*)
Clivers. Equal parts juice of Clivers (from juice extractor) and glycerine. Internally and externally.
Thuja. Internal: 3-5 drops Liquid Extract, morning and evening.
Topical. "Take a small quantity powdered Slippery Elm and add Liquid Extract Thuja to make a stiff paste. Apply paste to the lesion. Cover with gauze and protective covering. When dry remove pack and follow with compresses saturated with Thuja." (*Ellingwood's Therapeutist, Vol 10, No 6, p. 212*)
Echinacea and Thuja. Equal parts liquid extracts assist healthy granulation and neutralise odour.
Rue Ointment. Summer whole fresh leaves in Vaseline.
Poke Root. An old physician laid great stress on the use of concentrated juice of green leaves. Leaves are bruised, juice extracted, and concentrated by slow evaporation until the consistency of a paste, for persistent skin cancer. Care should be taken to confine to the distressed area. (*Ellingwood's Therapeutist, Vol 8, No 7, p. 275*)
Maria Treben. Horsetail poultice.
Laetrile. Some improvement claimed. 1 gram daily.
Cider vinegar. Anecdotal evidence: external use: small melanoma.
Diet. See: DIET – CANCER. Beta-carotene foods.
Treatment by skin specialist or oncologist.

CANCER – SPLEEN. Chronic enlargement with tumour. Cannot lie on the left side for pain. A common cause is the use of vaccines for which Thuja would be indicated.

Where irradiation and chemotherapy are not possible, any of the following alternatives may be taken with profit as secondary to medical treatment.
Astragalus. Popular spleen protective in Chinese medicine. Reduces toxicity of chemotherapy.
New Jersey tea. (Ceanothus americanus) has an affinity for the spleen and may sustain that organ under stress.
Chinese medicine. Ho-Shou-wu (Polygonum multiflorum).
Decoction, Red root. 1 teaspoon to each cup water simmered gently 10 minutes. Dose: half-1 cup 3-4 times daily.
Formula. Red root 2; Barberry 1; Bayberry 1. Mix. Dose: Powders: 500mg (two 00 capsules or one-third teaspoon). Liquid extracts: 1 teaspoon. Tinctures: 2 teaspoons. 3-4 times daily in water or honey.
Formula. Alternative. Tinctures. Fringe Tree 1; Goldenseal 2; Red root 3. Mix. Dose: 15-30 drops before meals and at bedtime.
Diet: See: DIET – CANCER.
Vinchristine: use in orthodox medicine reported.
Treatment by a general medical practitioner or hospital oncologist.

CANCER – SQUAMOUS CELL CARCINOMA. Given three months to live, Jason Winters, terminal cancer patient, was suffering from infiltrating squamous cell carcinoma wrapped round his carotid artery. Refusing major surgery, he travelled the world in search of native remedies. He was able to contact people who put him on the track of Wild Violet leaves, Red Clover flowers (Trifolium pratense) and leaves of the Chaparral bush (Larrea divaricata). The story of how he infused them, together with a well-known spice, is dramatically recorded in his book "Killing Cancer". After a spectacular recovery, remission has lasted for over 15 years and others have benefited from his experience.
Treatment by oncologist.

CANCER – STOMACH AND INTESTINES. Fibroma, myoma, lipoma, polyp, etc. When any of these breakdown bleeding can cause anaemia and melaena. Rarely painful. May obstruct intestinal canal causing vomiting. Periodic vomiting of over one year suspect.
Symptoms (non-specific). Loss of appetite, anaemia, weight loss; pain in abdomen, especially stomach area. Vomit appears as coffee grounds. Occult blood (tarry stools).
Causes. Alcohol, smoking cigarettes, low intake of fruits and vegetables. Foods rich in salt and nitrites including bacon, pickles, ham and dried fish. (*Cancer Researchers in Digestive Diseases and Sciences*) Long term therapy with drugs that inhibit gastric acid secretion increase risk of stomach cancer.
Of possible value. Alternatives:– *Tea*. Mixture. Equal parts: Red Clover, Gotu Kola, Yarrow. Strong infusion (2 or more teaspoons to each cup boiling water; infuse 15 minutes. As many cups daily as tolerated.
Formula. Condurango 2; Bayberry 1; Liquorice 1; Goldenseal quarter. Mix. Dose: Powders: 750mg (three 00 capsules or half a teaspoon). Liquid extracts: 1 teaspoon. Tinctures: 1-2 teaspoons. Thrice daily in water or honey.
Traditional. Rosebay Willowherb. Star of Bethlehem.
Chinese green tea. Anti-cancer effects have been found in the use of Chinese green tea extracts. Clinical trials on the therapeutic effects against early stomach cancer were promising. (*Chinese Journal Preventative Medicines 1990. 24 (2) 80-2*)
Chinese Herbalism. Combination. Oldenlandia diffusa 2 liang; Roots of Lu (Phragmites communis) 1 liang; Blackened Ginger 1 ch'ien; Pan-chih-lien (Scutellaria barbarta 5 ch'ein;

Chih-tzu (gardenia jasminoides) 3 ch'ien. One concoction/dose daily. Follow with roots of Bulrush tea.
William H. Cook, MD. "Mullein greatly relieves pain, and may be used with Wild Yam and a little Water-Pepper (*Polygonum Hydropiper*)." The addition of Water-Pepper (or Cayenne) ensures diffusive stimulation and increased arterial force.
Burns Lingard, MNIMH. Inoperable cancer of the stomach. Prescribed: Liquid Extract Violet leaves and Red Clover, each 4 drachms; Liquid Extract Cactus grand., 2 drops. Dose every 4 hours. Woman lived 30 years after treatment attaining age of 70.
Arthur Barker, FNIMH. Mullein sometimes helpful for pain.
Wm Boericke MD. American Cranesbill.
George Burford MD. Goldenseal.
Maria Treben. "After returning from a prison camp in 1947 I had stomach cancer. Three doctors told me it was incurable. From sheer necessity I turned to Nature's herbs and gathered Nettle, Yarrow, Dandelion and Plantain; the juice of which I took hourly. Already after several hours I felt better. In particular I was able to keep down a little food. This was my salvation." (*Health Through God's Pharmacy – 1981*)
Essiac: Old Ontario Cancer Remedy. Sheila Snow explored the controversy surrounding the famous cancer formula 'Essiac'. This was developed by Rene Caisse, a Canadian nurse born in Bracebridge, Ontario, in 1888. Rene noticed that an elderly patient had cured herself of breast cancer with an Indian herbal tea. She asked for the recipe and later modified it. Rene's aunt, after using the remedy for 2 years, fully recovered from an inoperable stomach cancer with liver involvement, and other terminal patients began to improve.

Rene's request to be given the opportunity to treat cancer patients in a larger way was turned down by Ottawa's Department of Health and Welfare. She eventually handed over the recipe to the Resperin Corporation in 1977, for the sum of one dollar, from whom cancer patients may obtain the mixture if their doctors submit a written request. However, records have not been kept up.

In 1988 Dr Gary Glum, a chiropractor in Los Angeles, published a book called 'Calling of an Angel': the true story of Rene Caisse. He gives the formula, which consists of 1lb of powdered Rumex acetosella (Sorrel), 1 and a half pounds cut Arctium lappa (Burdock), 4oz powdered Ulmus fulva (Slippery Elm bark), and 1oz Rheum palmatum (Turkey Rhubarb). The dosage Rene recommended was one ounce of Essiac with two ounces of hot water every other day at bedtime; on an empty stomach, 2-3 hours after supper. The treatment should be continued for 32 days, then taken every 3 days. (*Canadian Journal of Herbalism, July 1991 Vol XII, No. III*)

Diet. See: DIET – CANCER. Slippery Elm gruel.
Note. Anyone over 40 who has recurrent indigestion for more than three weeks should visit his family doctor. Persistent pain and indigestion after eating can be a sign of gastric cancer and no-one over 40 should ignore the symptoms. A patient should be referred to hospital for examination by endoscope which allows the physician to see into the stomach.
Study. Evidence to support the belief that the high incidence of gastric cancer in Japan is due to excessive intake of salt.
Note. A substance found in fish oil has been shown experimentally to prevent cancer of the stomach. Mackerel, herring and sardines are among the fish with the ingredient.

Treatment by or in liaison with hospital oncologist or general medical practitioner.

CANCER – TESTICLES. Rare, but increasing in most countries. Three main types: teratomas, seminomas and lymphomas. The latter affect older men.
Symptoms. A hard usually painless mass in the scrotum can give rise to gynaecomastia – abnormal enlargement of the male breasts.
Of possible value. **Alternatives**: – Abundant herb teas – Cornsilk, Red Clover, Violet leaves.
Decoction. Echinacea 2; Kava Kava 1; Sarsaparilla 1. Mix. Half an ounce (15g) to 1 pint (500ml) water simmered gently 20 minutes. Cup thrice daily.
Formula. Sarsaparilla 2; Kava Kava 1; Pulsatilla half; Thuja quarter. Mix. Dose: Powders: 500mg (two 00 capsules or one-third teaspoon). Liquid extracts: 1 teaspoon. Tinctures: 2 teaspoons. Thrice daily.
Vinchristine.
Diet. See: DIET – CANCER. Researchers from Cambridge University found that an extra pint of milk a day during adolescence was associated with 2 and a half times increased risk of testicular cancer. (*Journal of Epidemiology and Community Health, Oct. 1993*)

Treatment by or in liaison with a general medical practitioner.

CANCER – THROAT. See: CANCER OF THE NOSE AND THROAT.

CANCER – TO NEUTRALISE ODOUR. Dr Desmartis, in a paper to The American Academy of Sciences announced that Logwood, (*Haematoxylum campechianum*) was an antiseptic of value in cancer. This was discovered by accident. Having under his care several cancer patients presenting ulcerative sores 'emitting a nauseous odour', he composed a plaster of equal parts of Extract of Logwood and hog's lard. To his surprise, on application the fetter immediately disappeared.

CANCER – TONGUE. May be scirrhus or epithelial.
Causes. Smoking, alcohol, jagged teeth, chemical irritants, septic toxins, sprayed fruit and vegetables, poisoning by lead, arsenic and other chemicals, additives, hot foods, spicy curries and peppers, chewing tobacco.

Over 80 per cent found to be present in old syphilitic cases. Charles Ryall, surgeon, Cancer Hospital, regarded the two as comparable with that between syphilis and tabes. Dr F. Foester, Surgeon, concluded that epithelioma of the tongue as far more frequently preceded by syphilis than any other form of cancer. (*Hastings Gilford FRCS, "Tumours and Cancers"*)

The condition may arise from a gumma or patch of leucoplakia (white patches) – at one time known as smoker's tongue.
Of possible value. **Alternatives**:– Many plants have been shown to produce neoplastic activity, as observed in discovery of anti-cancer alkaloids of the Vinca plant (*Vinchristine*) and Mistletoe. Dr Wm Boericke confirms clinical efficacy of *Clivers*, promoting healthy granulations in ulcers and tumour of the tongue. Dr W.H. Cook advises a mouthwash of *Goldenseal*. For scirrhous hardening, juice of fresh *Houseleek* has a traditional reputation.
Tinctures. Equal parts Condurango and Goldenseal. 30-60 drops before meals in water; drops increased according to tolerance.
Local paint. Thuja lotion.
Case record. Dr Brandini, Florence, had a patient, 71, with inoperable cancer of the tongue. In the midst of his pain he asked for a lemon which immediately assuaged the pain. The next day gave him even greater relief. The doctor tried it on a number of similar patients with the same results, soaking lint in lemon juice.
Diet. See: DIET – CANCER.

Treatment by a general medical practitioner or hospital oncologist.

CANCER – WOMB. The second most common cancer in women. The alarming aspect of national health is the almost epidemic increase of cervical malignancy in younger women due to frequency of coitus, promiscuity, early coitus and contact with the herpes virus. All are mostly squamous cell carcinoma. Research studies have demonstrated a link between cigarette smoking and cancer of the cervix. (*Dr Don Hellberg*)
Symptoms. Low backache, bleeding after intercourse, between periods or after 'the change'. Abdominal swelling after 40 years of age. Sixty per cent of patients have no symptoms. Malodorous vaginal discharge. A positive cervical "pap" smear or cone-shaped biopsy examined by a pathologist confirms. Vaginal bleeding occurs in the later stages.

A letter in the New England Journal of Medicine suggests a strong link between increased risk of cervical cancer and cigarette smoking, nicotine being detected in the cervical fluids of cigarette smokers. This form of cancer is almost unknown in virgins living in closed communities such as those of the Church.

Conventional treatment is usually hysterectomy. Whatever treatment is adopted little ground is lost by supportive cleansing herbal teas. Mullein for pain.

Sponges loaded with powdered Goldenseal held against the cervix with a contraceptive cap can give encouraging results. Replace after three days. Vitamin A supplements are valuable to protect against the disease. The vitamin may also be applied topically in creams.

This form of cancer resists chemical treatment, but has been slowed down and halted by Periwinkle (*Vinchristine*) without damaging normal cells.

G.B. Ibotson, MD, reported disappearance of cancer of the cervix by infusions of Violet leaves by mouth and by vaginal injection. (*Lancet 1917, i, 224*)

In a study group of cervical cancer patients it was found that women with carcinoma in situ (CIS) were more likely to have a total Vitamin A intake below the pooled median (3450iu). Vitamin A supplementation is indicated together with zinc. (Bio-availability of Vitamin A is linked with zinc levels.) Vitamin A and zinc may be applied topically in creams and ointments.
Orthodox treatment: radiotherapy, chemotherapy, hysterectomy. As oestrogen can stimulate dormant cells the surgeon may wish to remove ovaries also. Whatever the decision, herbal supportive treatment may be beneficial. J.T. Kent, MD, recommends *Thuja* and *Shepherd's Purse*. Agents commonly indicated: Echinacea, Wild Indigo, Thuja, Mistletoe, Wild Yam. Herbal teas may be taken with profit. Dr Alfred Vogel advises Mistletoe from the oak (*loranthus europaeus*).
Other alternatives:– *Teas*. Red Clover, Violet, Mistletoe, Plantain, Clivers. 1-2 teaspoons to each cup boiling water. Infuse 15 minutes. 1 cup freely.
Decoctions. White Pond Lily. Thuja. Echinacea. Wild Yam. Any one.
Tablets/capsules. Echinacea. Goldenseal. Wild Yam. Thuja.
Formula No. 1. Red Clover 2; Echinacea 1; Shepherd's Purse 1; Thuja quarter. Mix. Dose: Powders: 750mg (three 00 capsules or half a teaspoon). Liquid extracts: 1-2 teaspoons. Tinctures: 1-3 teaspoons.
Formula No. 2. Equal parts: Poke root, Goldenseal, Mistletoe. Mix. Dose: Powders: 500mg (two 00 capsules or one-third teaspoon). Liquid extracts: 1 teaspoon. Tinctures: 2 teaspoons.
Diet. Women who eat large quantities of meat and fatty foods are up to four times the risk of those eating mainly fruit and vegetables.

Vaginal injection. 1. Strong infusion Red Clover to which 10-15 drops Tincture Goldenseal is added. Follow with tampon smeared with Goldenseal Salve.
2. Strong decoction Yellow Dock to which 10-15 drops Tincture Goldenseal is added. Follow with tampon smeared with Goldenseal salve.

If bleeding is severe douche with neat distilled extract of Witch Hazel.

Chinese Herbalism. See – CANCER: CHINESE PRESCRIPTION. Also: Decoction of ssu-hsieh-lu (Galium gracile) 2-4 liang.

Advice. One-yearly smear test for all women over 40.

Diet. See: DIET – CANCER.

Treatment by a general medical practitioner or hospital oncologist.

CANCRUM ORIS. Canker. Ulceration of mucous membrane of lips and mouth. Treatment as for stomatitis.

CANDIDA, OF SKIN AND NAILS. Infection by *Candida albicans*.

Internal. Goldenseal 1; Myrrh 1; Thuja half; Poke root half. Dose – Powders: 500mg (two 00 capsules or one-third teaspoon). Liquid extracts: one 5ml teaspoon. Tinctures: two 5ml teaspoons. Thrice daily before meals.

Capricin. See entry.

Topical. *Thuja lotion*: 1 teaspoon Liquid extract Thuja to 1oz (30ml) distilled extract Witch Hazel.

Aloe Vera; fresh juice or gel.

Tea Tree oil; may be diluted many times.

Comfrey cream; Castor oil, Oil of Mullen or Houseleek. Cider vinegar.

Night wash. Warm water to which is added a few drops Tincture Myrrh, Tincture Thuja or Tea Tree oil.

Diet and Supplements. Same as for CANDIDA – VAGINAL.

CANDIDA, VAGINAL. Fungus infection by *candida albicans* and other organisms including Torilopsis glabrala. Causes: oral contraceptives, broad spectrum antibiotics, iron deficiency anaemia, diabetes, steroid therapy, pregnancy, high sugar diet, alcohol. When sexually transmitted may appear together with mixed organisms which prove difficult to eliminate.

Greater incidence of the condition is found in women. By interfering with the hormone balance The Pill raises the female body to a constant state of false pregnancy. This affects the character of vaginal secretions and favours growth of fungi. Oestrogens in contraceptive pills create a tissue climate conducive to candida. Vaginal deodorants and scented soaps irritate. Because of its effect upon the Fallopian tubes it is a common cause of infertility.

Symptoms. Vulva itching, soreness, white discharge of watery to cheesy consistency. Urination painful, recurring cystitis, irritability, premenstrual and menstrual problems, anxiety, heartburn and dyspepsia.

Alternatives. *Teas*. Agnus Castus, Balm, Barberry bark, Chamomile, La Pacho (Pau d'arco), Sage, Thyme.

Tablets/capsules. Agnus Castus, Goldenseal, Pulsatilla, Poke root, Thuja, Garlic, La Pacho.

Tincture Thuja. 15-30 drops in water, once daily.

Tinctures. Combination for the average case. Echinacea 30ml; Calendula 15ml; Goldenseal 15ml; Ladysmantle 15ml. Dose: one 5ml teaspoon thrice daily. (*Brenda Cooke MNIMH, Mansfield, Notts*)

Topical. Tea Tree oil pessaries/cream. Alternative:– (1) Impregnate tampon with plain yoghurt and insert into vagina. Or: inject with spermicidal cream applicator or cardboard tampon applicator 2-3 teaspoons yoghurt into vagina 2-3 times daily. The theory is that the lacto-bacilli in the yoghurt competes with the candida and finally reduces it to normal levels.
(2) 2-3 teaspoons Distilled Extract Witch Hazel to cup of water for cooling antiseptic lotion.
(3) 1-2 drops Eucalyptus oil well-shaken in 4oz (120ml) Distilled Extract Witch Hazel. Reputed to kill colonies of candida albicans and allay irritation.
(4) Aloe Vera gel.
(5) Capricin.
(6) Cloves are anti-fungal and may be chewed.
(7) Calendula and Hydrastis pessaries.

Avoid surgical spirit antiseptics. A smear of Olive oil or yoghurt or No 3 above to allay irritation. Frequent washing, hot baths and use of soap at first soothe, but later exacerbate. Use water only. When washing, wipe from front to back to avoid spreading spores from bowel. No smoking.

Diet. Gluten-free, low fat, high fibre.

Acidophilus. A large mixed salad once daily. Cooked vegetables, seafood, Vitamin A foods. Replace salt with Celery, Garlic or Kelp powders. All meats, game and chicken to be from animals raised on steroid-free fodder. Replace alcohol with fresh fruit and vegetable juices. Eggs.

Reject: Dairy products (butter, cheese, milk). Brewer's yeast. Foods and drinks with which yeast has been associated: bread, beer, home-made wines. Dried fruit, mushrooms, monosodium glutamate, pickles and preserves, smoked fish and meats, foods known to be allergic to the patient, sugar, syrup, sweeteners, chocolate, puddings, pastry, white flour products.

Supplements. Daily. Vitamin A 7500iu, Vitamin C 200mg. Zinc.

CANDIDIASIS. Systemic candida. An infection by the yeast-like fungus *Candida albicans*.

Causes: Impaired immunity as in AIDS. High sugar diets (yeasts thrive in the presence of

sugar), alcohol, broad spectrum antibiotics, iron deficiency anaemia, diabetes, steroid therapy. A common cause frequently overlooked is the reaction between yeasts and mercury from amalgam dental fillings when methyl mercury is created in the intestine. For treatments to be effective silver fillings should be removed. A favourite breeding ground for the fungus is the low bowel.
Alternatives. *Teas*. Balm Chamomile, Gotu Kola, La Pacho (Pau d'arco), Rosemary, Thyme.
Tablets/capsules. Aloe Vera, Caprycin, *Echinacea*, Garlic, Goldenseal, Poke root, Thuja.
Candidiasis of stomach and intestines. Caprylic acid derived from coconut inhibits growth of candida in the intestines and colon without upsetting the balance of the intestinal flora.
Horseradish. Success reported: (*Rudat K.D. 1957. Journal Hyg. Epidem. Microbiol. Immol. Prague 1:123*)
Garlic. Inhibits growth of candida. (*Tynecke Z, and Gos Z*)
Formula. While a practitioner's treatment will be prescribed according to the specific requirements of the individual, the following combination may be used for the average case:–
Tinctures: Echinacea 50ml, Poke root 15ml, Vervain 15ml, Galangal 15ml, Calendula 15ml, Clivers 20ml. Mix. Dose: one 5ml teaspoon thrice daily. (*Brenda Cooke MNIMH, Mansfield, Notts*)
Diet. High fibre food essential for efficient daily clearance. Low fat, low salt, gluten-free, little milk only. 2 teaspoons Olive oil thrice daily. Reject: refined foods, yeasts (no bread), mushrooms, mouldy cheese sugar, artificial sweeteners, alcohol.
Supplements. Vitamin A, C, E, biotin, Calcium ascorbate, Zinc, Lacto-bacillus.
Chelation therapy. Anti-fungals.

CANKER. Cancrum oris. Ulceration – chiefly of the mouth and lips.
Treatment as for STOMATITIS.

CAPILLARIES. Networks of extremely fine blood vessels that allow exchange of oxygen, CO2, minerals, water, etc between the tissues and the blood. Their contents are fed by the arterioles and drained by the venules.

CAPILLARY FRAGILITY. A deficiency of Vitamins C or E allows cells to deteriorate, thus weakening capillary walls and placing them at risk of being broken, severed or mashed; with subsequent clot formation, bruising, nose-bleeds, bleeding gums or petechia (small spots due to effusion of blood under the skin).
Large amounts of Vitamins C and E may be given for this condition without toxicity.
Alternatives. *Teas*. Dried leaves. Buckwheat. Heartsease. Marigold. Yarrow, Butcher's Broom, Red Vine. One, or more in combination.
Tablets/capsules. Rutin (Buckwheat). Hawthorn. Motherwort.
Tinctures. Formula. Hawthorn 1; Marigold 1; Yarrow 2. One 5ml teaspoon thrice daily.
Dr Alfred Vogel. Yarrow 42; Horse Chestnut 30; St John's Wort 21; Arnica 7.
BHP (1983). "Fagopyrum (Buckwheat) combines well with Vitamin C in reducing capillary permeability."
Diet. Low fat. Low salt. High fibre. Bilberries.
Supplementation. Vitamin C 500mg daily. Vitamin E 400iu daily.
See also: CIRCULATION. PHLEBITIS. BRUISES, etc.

CAPRICIN. A caprylic acid formulation that facilitates absorption of calcium and magnesium. Occurs naturally in mother's milk. Antibacterial and antifungal properties. Like fish oils (EPA) this preparation, extracted from coconut, inhibits clumping of platelets and is effective against the organisms of candida, rhodotorulla, etc. Taken with a yeast-free and sugar-free diet for candida. This, and other caprylic formulations, are sometimes used as an alternative to Nystatin.

CAPSICUM. See: CAYENNE.

CAPSULES. A convenient vehicle for administration of powders, seeds, oils, balsams, Castor oil, Garlic, Rose Hip, etc, having the advantage to mask nasty tasting or smelly medicines. Ideal for regulating dosage for children. Swallowed, they soon reach the stomach where their contents are slowly released. Gelatin capsules are of animal origin but cellulose non-animal materials are available. Their use extends also to gynaecological and rectal problems, inserted into the vagina or anus.
Standard sizes range from size 5 to 000. Size 00 is most popular in European pharmacy. See: POWDERS.
To fill empty capsules, take apart the two sections, 'dab' open end into powder on a flat surface; fill to capacity and affix unfilled half-shell. Manufacturers use a special filling machine for this purpose.
Patients should remain standing for at least 90 seconds after taking capsules, and followed up with sips of water. Swallowing failure is possible when capsules are taken in the recumbent position when they may adhere to the oesophageal membrane delaying disintegration time.
Equipment suppliers: capsules and capsule-making machines – Dav-Caps, PO Box 11, Monmouth, Gwent NP5 3NX. Also: The Herbal Apothecary, 120 High Street, Syston, Leicester 1E7 8GC.

CARAWAY SEEDS. *Carum carvi L.* Dried seeds.

Action: Antimicrobial, antispasmodic, carminative, expectorant, galactagogue, emmenagogue.
Keynote: colic.
Uses. Wind and colic in children; loss of appetite; flatulent indigestion, 'summer' diarrhoea in children, colds, painful menses; to stimulate flow of breast milk. Gastric symptoms of cardiac origin.

Sometimes combined with Chamomile for digestive disorders.
Preparations. Thrice daily.
Tea: 1-2 teaspoons to each cup boiling water; infuse 10 minutes. Dose: half-1 cup.
Tincture BHP (1983) 1 part to 5 parts 45 per cent alcohol: 0.5-4ml (8-60 drops).
Powdered seeds: half-2 grams.
Oil of Caraway: 1-3 drops. GSL

CARBUNCLE. Staphylococcal infection of the skin and underlying tissue with local necrosis. Pus is discharged from more than one opening, giving the appearance of a collection of boils. See: BOILS.

CARCINOGENS. Substances that bring about a malignant change in body cells. Sources include: pollutants, asbestos, petroleum products, tobacco, Azo food dyes, nickel, X-rays, nitrites in preserved meats, the Pill and hormone replacement therapy. Direct-acting carcinogens may arise in stored food due to contamination by micro-organisms such as aflatoxin in mould-contaminated peanuts. They stimulate chemical change resulting in free-radicals. See: FREE-RADICALS.

CARCINOID SYNDROME. Flushing of the face and neck caused by an active malignant tumour in the stomach or intestines with secondary growths in the liver. Often accompanied by an explosive diarrhoea. The lesion is usually found in the ileum yet it may also appear in the bile duct, ovaries or bronchi. Other symptoms include low blood pressure, drastic reduction in weight due to loss of body fluids.
Symptoms: flushing of face and neck, diarrhoea, low blood pressure, weight loss.
Treatment: relief of symptoms only. Diarrhoea – Fenugreek seed tea. Flushing: Chamomile tea.
Vitamin and Mineral Supplementation: Because of severe drain on these food elements Multivitamins should be taken daily together with additional 1000ius Vitamin E for the disturbed circulatory system. The heart should be sustained with a preparation of the Hawthorn berry.

To be treated by or in liaison with a qualified medical practitioner.

CARDAMOM SEEDS. *Elettaria cardamomum* Maton. Dried ripe seeds. Volatile oil.
Action. Carminative, warm and soothing to digestive system. Stomachic, Orexigenic. Anti-gripe. Oil is antiseptic.
Uses. Flatulence, colic, loss of appetite.
Preparations. *Tea*. Crush seeds in a pestle and mortar. 1 teaspoon to cup of water; bring to boil; remove vessel when boiling point is reached. Infuse 10-15 minutes. Dose: half-1 cup.
Powder. Dose, 1-2 grams.
Liquid Extract. 0.3 to 2ml.
Tincture Cardamoms Co BP (1973): dose 2-4ml.
Oil – 3 drops in honey after meals promotes digestion, removes odour of garlic, onions, etc.
GSL

CARDIAC. From the Greek pertaining to the heart. Cardio-vascular pertains to the heart and blood vessels.
Cardio-actives. Herbs exercising a *direct* action on the heart due to the cardiac glycosides they contain. They increase output by sustaining the heart muscle without a demand for more oxygen. This group includes: Motherwort, Hawthorn, Broom, Lily of the Valley, Figwort, Bugleweed, Squills.

Cardiac glycosides, especially those of the Foxglove (digitalis) which is administered by a physician only, tend to accumulate in the body and may prove toxic when their elimination is retarded. The most important cardio-active used by the Consulting Herbalist is Lily of the Valley which has an action similar to Foxglove but without toxic effect. It is a reliable alternative to Foxglove for failure of the heart with retention of water in the body.
Cardio-tonics. Herbalists use other plants that do not contain cardiac glycosides but which have an *indirect* effect upon the heart. These dilate arteries and peripheral vessels, speeding the circulation, reducing high blood pressure, relieving any back-pressure on the heart caused by accumulation of blood in the lungs. There are peripheral dilators to resolve any hold-up in the circulation and others that assist a failing heart by eliminating obstruction in the bowel (laxatives), liver and kidneys (hepatics and diuretics), skin (diaphoretics and alteratives, chief of which is Figwort). The heart also may feel the benefit of a timely relaxing nervine such as Skullcap or Lime flowers. Even treatment of varicose veins indirectly assists. All of these reduce the work-load of the muscle and tend to 'normalise' function of the heart. Cardio-tonics include Ephedra, Motherwort, Rosemary, Mistletoe, Hawthorn, Lime flowers, Cayenne, Yarrow, Garlic, Balm.

Bugleweed is often overlooked as a cardiac sedative to relax capillaries and soothe arterial excitement.

CARDIAC ARREST. Dramatic failure of the heart to act as a pump to propel blood into the main vessels. The usual cause is blockage of the coronary artery by a clot, debris in the blood-

stream or valvular disease – resulting in either – asystole (total absence of contraction) or ventricular fibrillation (ineffective uncoordinated contraction).
Symptoms: disappearance of the pulse, imperceptible activity of the heart and loss of consciousness.
Treatment. Vigorous rubbing of chest wall over the heart. In many cases a sharp thump on the chest will restore function. Where ineffective, mouth to mouth resuscitation. Emergency defibrillation by electric shock to chest wall. C.Y.D. Pinch red pepper (Cayenne) in brandy: if patient incapable of swallowing, moisten gums and mouth.
Spirits of Camphor: 1-5 drops in water or honey. Use also as an inhalant.

CARDIAC DROPSY. Dropsy of heart origin is distinguished from renal dropsy by an increase in oedema as the day proceeds. In the morning there may be no swelling but by the evening legs become swollen from the ankles upwards. Fluids stagnate in the tissues from inability of the heart to perform efficiently as a pump. The condition is a symptom of heart failure with increasing breathlessness which may lead to general dropsy.
Symptoms: worse after exercise, breathlessness, headache, general weakness, feeble pulse, pale face, skin cold, swollen tissues pit on pressure.
Treatment. **Alternatives**:– *Teas*. Black Cohosh, Broom tops, Buchu, Dandelion, Hawthorn, Parsley root.
Tea. Formula. Equal parts: Broom tops, Motherwort, Yarrow. 2 teaspoons to each cup water brought to boil and simmered 5 minutes in covered vessel. 1 cup 3-4 times daily.
Tablets/capsules. Buchu, Dandelion, Hawthorn, Juniper, Motherwort.
Formula. Dandelion 2; Hawthorn 2; Stone root 1. Mix. Dose: Powders: 750mg (three 00 capsules or half a teaspoon). Liquid extracts: 1 teaspoon. Tinctures: 2 teaspoons. Thrice daily.
Practitioner. *Lily of the Valley, BPC 1934*: 5-20 drops, 2-3 times daily.
Squills, tincture: resembles Digitalis in action. Dose: 1-3 drops, as prescribed.
Tinctures. Dandelion 2; Lily of the Valley 2; Stone root 1; Cayenne (tincture) quarter. Mix. Dose: 1 to 2 teaspoons thrice daily.
Popular formula. Tincture Scilla 5.0; Tincture Crataegus 10.0; Tincture Valerian to make 30.0. 15 drops thrice daily. (*German Extemporaneous Formulae*)
Diet. High protein. See: DIET – HEART AND CIRCULATION.

CARDIODORON. Drops containing alcoholic (20 per cent) tinctures of Primula officinalis flowers (2-1) 5 per cent. Onopordon Acanthus flowers (2-1) 5 per cent, and Hyoscyamus niger herb (21-) 0.02 per cent. v/v equivalent to hyoscyamine 0.001 per cent w/v. (*Weleda*)

CARDIOGENIC SHOCK. The result of myocardial infarction. Reduction in contractility and output of the heart.
Symptoms: low blood pressure, reduced urinary output, water in the lungs, etc. See: MYOCARDITIS.

CARDIVALLIN TABLETS. Ingredients of each tablet: Capsicum 15mg. The aqueous extractive from 200mg Hawthorn berries, 125mg Mistletoe, 125mg Motherwort. The alcoholic extractive (45 per cent) from 125mg Lily of the Valley, 125mg Passion flower, 125mg Skullcap, and alcoholic extractive (60 per cent) from 425mg Cereus. To sustain the heart. (*Potter's, UK*)

This formula has been withdrawn after rendering excellent service for many years for heart weakness. No longer available to the general public as an OTC medicine. Of historic interest to the modern phytotherapist.

CARMELITE TEA. Popular in France as an "elixir of life", digestive and tonic for anaemia, poor appetite and low spirits. Formula: 3 litres spirits of wine, 500g fresh Lemon Balm leaves and flowers, 16g Angelica root, 125g Lemon Peel, 200g Coriander, 40g Nutmeg, 4g Cinnamon and 2g Cloves. Steep finely rubbed herbs and roots and powdered seeds in spirits of wine eight days in a dark place, stirring daily; decant, filter and bottle.

CARMINATIVES. Anti-flatulents. Aromatic herbs used to expel gas (wind) from the stomach and intestines. Containing volatile oils, their effect upon the digestive system is to tone mucous surfaces and increase peristaltic action. Also used with other agents to render them more palatable.

Allspice, Angelica, Aniseed, Balm, Calumba root, Caraway seed, Cardamom seed, Catmint, Cayenne, Centaury, Chamomile, Cinnamon, Cloves, Condurango, Coriander, Dill, Fennel, Galangal, Garlic, Gentian, Ginger (powder, crystallised, or tincture), Holy Thistle, Horseradish, Juniper, Kava Kava, Hyssop, Marjoram, Mugwort, Mustard, Nutmeg, Parsley, Peppermint, Sage, Southernwood, Thyme, Valerian, Wormwood.
Mixture: equal parts Aniseed, Caraway and Fennel. 1 teaspoon to each cup boiling water; infuse 15-20 minutes. 1 cup hot after meals. Crush seeds before use. (*Dr Rudolf F. Weiss*)

CAROB BEAN. St John's Bread. *Ceratonia siliqua L.* Food and medicine. Fruit is a hard woody pod containing a sweet yellow pulp that is made into a flour. Came into prominence as effective treatment for acute (summer) diarrhoea during the Spanish Civil War when it was observed that poorer children who ate the bean, also known as locust, did not contract the disease. Stools of gastro-enteritis, colitis and 'gippy tummy' are known to solidify within 48 hours. May be boiled in skimmed milk or rice water. An excellent substitute for chocolate and sugar, being taken in cocoa-like drinks. Low fat content. Does not contain tyramine, a known cause of migraine, as is found in cocoa. A favourite base for fruit or snack bars; flavoured with molasses, cherry, yoghurt, ginger. Rich source of pectin and calcium which have binding properties. Carob flour is given for diarrhoea in babies.

CARPAL TUNNEL SYNDROME (CTS). Compression of the median nerve between the transverse carpal ligament and the carpal bone. May cause damage to the sensory and motor nerves and manifest as teno-synovitis or ganglion. Affects chiefly middle-aged women.
Symptoms. Numbness or tingling in first three fingers which feel 'clumsy'. Worse at night. Muscle wasting of palm of the hand.
Diagnostic sign: the 'flick' sign – shaking or 'flicking' of the wrist when pain is worse and which is believed to mechanically untether the nerve and promote return of venous blood. (*J. Neural Neurosurgery and Psychiatry, 1984, 47, 873*)
Differential diagnosis: compression of seventh cervical spinal nerve root (osteopathic lesion) has tingling of the hands when standing or from exaggerated neck movements.
Treatment. Reduction of spasm with peripheral relaxants (antispasmodics). Also: local injection of corticosteroid or surgical division of the transverse carpal ligament.
Alternatives:– *Tea*. Equal parts. Chamomile, Hops, Valerian. 1 heaped teaspoon to each cup boiling water; infuse 15 minutes. 1 cup 2-3 times daily.
Tablets/capsules. Cramp bark. St John's Wort. Wild Yam. Lobelia. Prickly Ash. Passion flower. Black Cohosh. Hawthorn.
Powders. Formula. Cramp bark 1; Guaiacum half; Black Cohosh half; Pinch Cayenne. Dose: 500mg (two 00 capsules or one-third teaspoon) 2-3 times daily.
Bromelain. quarter to half a teaspoon between meals.
Turmeric. Quarter to half a teaspoon between meals.
Tinctures. Formula: Cramp bark 1; Lobelia half; Black Cohosh half. Few drops Tincture Capsicum. Mix. 1 teaspoon in water when necessary. To reduce blood pressure, add half part Mistletoe.
Practitioner. For pain. Tincture Gelsemium BPC 1963 5-15 drops when necessary.
Topical. Rhus tox ointment. Camphorated oil.
Lotion: Tincture Lobelia 20; Tincture Capsicum 1.
Supplements. Condition responsive to Vitamin B6 and B-complex. Some authorities conclude that CTS is a primary deficiency of Vitamin B6, dose: 50-200mg daily.
General. Yoga, to control pain. Attention to kidneys. Diuretics may be required. Cold packs or packet of peas from the refrigerator to site of pain for 15 minutes daily.

CARRAGHEEN MOSS. See: IRISH MOSS.

CARUNCLE, URETHRAL. A tender easily-bleeding bright red swelling at the urinary outlet of the vagina. About the size of a large pill. Not cancerous but painful on intercourse and on passing urine.
Treatment. Tincture Thuja, 5 drops in water morning and evening, internal. Topical application of much diluted oil of Eucalyptus over a long period has been successful. Surgical intervention usually successful.

CASCARA SAGRADA. Sacred Bark. Chittem Bark. *Rhamnus purshiana* D.C.
Constituent: to 10 per cent anthraquinone glycosides. Bark – after maturing for one year.
Action: Non-habit forming *stimulant laxative*, pancreatic stimulant, bitter tonic.
Keynote: stool softener.
Uses: habitual constipation, torpor of low bowel, congestion of liver and gall duct. To assist liver function in cirrhosis. Foul breath.

Sometimes combined with Cardamom, Coriander or Cumin as a precaution against griping. A common ingredient with Figwort, Witch Hazel or Stone root for piles.
Preparations. Once daily.
Tablets: 150mg. 1-2 when necessary.
Liquid Extract: half-1 teaspoon in water, at bedtime; honey to sweeten.
Powdered bark: 1 to 2 and a half grams.

Excessive dosage may result in dehydration with low potassium levels. GSL

CASHEW TREE FRUIT. *Anacardium occidentale L.* Active ingredient: anacardic acid – an inhibitor of prostaglandin synthetase. Kills laval mosquitoes and water snails. Dumped by natives into ponds where mosquitoes and snails breed. The apple-like fruit serves as a pesticide to control malaria, schistosomiasis and other parasitic diseases from drinking water. (*Dr Isao Kubo, University of California-Berkeley, USA*)

Leaves used by natives of West Africa for malaria.

CASTOR OIL PLANT. Palma Christi. *Ricinus communis L.* Part used: oil expressed cold drawn from the seeds without the aid of heat. Versatile

agent for skin diseases. "Biochemical precursor of prostaglandins . . . a trigger mechanism to immune system T-cells in the skin causing them to activate a local immune system reaction through the lymphatics." (*Harvey Grady, Edgar Cayce Foundation, Virginia Beach, Va., USA*)
Action: anti-allergenic, galactagogue. Canary Island nursing mothers bind leaves to the breast to increase secretion of milk. Vitality of cells is upgraded by contact with the oil. Oral contraceptive. (*V.J. Brondegaard, Plants Med. 23, 167, 1973*) A traditional purgative.
Uses. *Internal*. Rarely used, except for varied forms of allergy (penicillin, hay fever, etc): 5 drops oil in honey, 3-4 times daily. Mouth ulcers, smear with oil. Large doses avoided.
Topical. Anti-fungal, emollient, anodyne.

Application to warts, corns, bunions, skin disorders, psoriasis, eczema, nail infection, bedsores, pigmented mole, ringworm, itch, ear-infection in children (drops), leg ulcers – dab with smear for pain relief, rodent ulcers made bearable, gangrene (with tincture Myrrh drops). Oil massaged into scalp for 20 minutes daily for falling hair. Eyelids, to soothe and heal. Age spots: brown patches on face, arms or hands have been known to disappear when persevering with a smear of each – Castor oil and Bicarbonate of Soda.
Preparations. Internal use: oil – 5 to 20ml, as prescribed.
External use: Zinc and Castor oil cream, or ointment. Or, Castor oil only.
Castor oil pack, to stimulate the immune system: apply soft pad of material saturated with Castor oil; hold in position with elastic bandage for skin diseases, pains of arthritis or rheumatism; lacerated and well-sutured wounds that refuse to heal. Renew oil when pad becomes dry. Oil may be used as a vehicle for eye drops. GSL

CAT SCRATCH FEVER. A self-limiting crisis seen in children or adults. The *New England Journal of Medicine* noted that sufferers were nearly 30 times more likely to have been licked, scratched or bitten.

Kittens proved the greatest hazard, particularly those with fleas. Local inflammation with glandular swelling and fever. Organism: usually Pasteurella multocida. Often with great weakness. One of the commonest causes of swollen glands in the USA.
Treatment. Poke root to combat infection of the glandular system. Echinacea to increase powers of resistance.
Alternatives. *Tablets/capsules*. Poke root. Echinacea. Wild Yam.
Powders. Formula: Echinacea 2; Gum Myrrh half; Goldenseal half. Dose: 500mg (two 00 capsules or one-third teaspoon) every 3 hours.
Tinctures. Formula. Echinacea 2; Poke root 1; Goldenseal half. Mix. One teaspoon in water every 3 hours.

Dosage for children: see – DOSAGE.
Topical. Apply Tea Tree oil diluted. May be diluted many times.
Vitamin C. 1g morning and evening.
Calcium ascorbate powder. 1g morning and evening.

CATALEPSY. A medical curiosity occurring in some neurotic people who lose consciousness followed by muscular rigidity. Although rare, it may follow excessive stress. Suspension of heart beat, breathing. Other vital functions simulate death and are a cause for alarm. Rigidity may cause the body to assume a statue-like appearance. The subject should be carefully watched.
Treatment. Antispasmodics.

As swallowing is not possible, the gums should be rubbed with a little dilute Tincture or Liquid Extract Lobelia, Eucalyptus, Thyme, Valerian or Wild Lettuce. When swallowing is possible, a cup of Chamomile, Lime blossom or Ephedra tea assists.
Practitioner: Ephedrine, 8-60mg by mouth, thrice daily.

CATARACT. Gradual loss of sight following chemical disturbance in the lens protein of the eye resulting in degeneration and loss of transparency. Greyish white pupil which in normality is jet black. Occurs chiefly in the elderly due to injury of the lens capsule, glaucoma, the use of microwave or diet-mineral deficiency (calcium). In the ageing process there is a lack of antioxidant protection of the lens usually due to low Vitamin C, the major antioxidant in lens physiology. May also be congenital.

High blood glucose levels, diabetes, drugs, steroids, Down's syndrome, kidney failure, uraemia and chronic diarrhoea predispose. There is no pain. Vision is as if looking through a frosted glass.
Treatment. Restore lens metabolism.

"My father-in-law knew people who had been cured by steeping Wild Burdock burrs and taking a small drink 3-4 times a day" (*John Tobe, in "Cataract, Glaucoma and other Eye Disorders"*)
Cider Vinegar. 2 teaspoons to glass water, sips once or twice daily.
Chinese medicine. Hachimi jiogan to increase glutathione content of the lens.
Topical. Greater Celandine. 5-10 drops fresh juice of plant to 4oz distilled extract Witch Hazel. 10-20 drops in an eyebath half filled with warm water; use as a douche.
Cineraria maritima (Dusty Miller). 2-3 drops fresh plant juice applied to the eye with a medicine dropper. Same refers to Yucca and Chaparral. For early non-diabetic cataract.
Diet. Lacto-vegetarian. Carrot juice. Brewer's Yeast, yellow-green vegetables. Spinach as an

item of diet appears to reduce risk of cataract.
Supplementation. Vitamin C slows down the ageing process of the lens, protecting it from damage by free radicals: 1500mg daily. Vitamin B2. Vitamin E, 400iu daily. Selenium, 200mcg daily. Amino acids: cysteine, methionine, glutathione.
General. Surgical treatment is invariably successful. Cold packs and manipulation of the neck improve circulation and drainage of the head.

CATARRH. Inflammation of the mucous membrane (lining membrane) which becomes boggy and discharges excessive mucus. Aetiology: infection, allergy or toxaemia. May arise from lack of fresh air, stagnant atmosphere, irritation by dust, inflammation of the middle ear, tonsils or nasal sinuses, but chiefly from auto-toxaemia when it is a natural reaction to toxic matter – an effort to expel through the mucous membrane wastes that would otherwise leave the body via the skin, kidneys or bowel. Constipation worsens the condition.

It is often caused by a heavy intake of starches, salt, sugar, white flour products, and especially dairy products including milk. Some cases are due to poor diet, low blood calcium, vitamin and mineral deficiency. May manifest as catarrh of the nose, throat, stomach, bowels, bronchi or bladder.
Alternatives:–*Teas* made from any of the following: Angelica, Avens, Coltsfoot, Comfrey leaves, German Chamomile, Elderflowers, Eyebright, Garlic, Ginseng, Gotu Kola, Ground Ivy, Hyssop, Marshmallow leaves, Mullein, Mouse-ear, Parsley, Plantain, Marsh Cudweed, White Horehound, Yarrow.
Garlic. Good results reported.
Traditional combination. Equal parts, herbs: Angelica, Eyebright, Yarrow. 1 heaped teaspoon to each cup of boiling water.
Fenugreek seeds. 2 teaspoons to each cup water simmered 5 minutes; 1 cup thrice daily. Or grind to a powder in a blender to sprinkle on salads or cereals.
Tablets/capsules. Garlic, Iceland Moss, Lobelia, Poke root, Goldenseal (*Gerard*). Horseradish and Garlic (*Blackmore*).
Tinctures. Alternatives. (1) Goldenseal; 3-5 drops. Formulae: (2) Angelica 2; Ginger 1. (3) Lobelia 1; Goldenseal 1; Juniper 1. One teaspoon – thrice daily.
Tincture Myrrh, BPC 1973. 3-5 drops in water thrice daily.
Tea Tree oil. 2-3 drops on teaspoon honey, or in water, thrice daily.
Heath and Heather Catarrh pastilles. Squills, Menthol, Pine oil, Eucalyptus oil.
Antifect. (*Potter's*) Germicidal for blocked sinuses, etc.
Eric Powell. Liquid extracts: Angelica 1oz; Juniper 1oz; Peppermint half an ounce; Root Ginger half an ounce. 1-2 teaspoons in water thrice daily.
BHP (1983). (Bronchial) Irish Moss, Cinnamon, Liquorice.
Gargle. 3 drops Tincture Myrrh in half glass water.
Inhalation. Small handful Chamomile flowers or Eucalyptus leaves to 2 pints boiling water in washbasin. Cover head with towel and inhale 10 minutes. Or – see: FRIAR'S BALSAM.
Aromatherapy. Essential oils, diluted with 20 parts water, as injection for nasal catarrh: Eucalyptus, Thyme, Pine, Garlic, Hyssop, Tea Tree.
For catarrh of the womb and vagina: see LEUCORRHOEA.
Diet. Refer: GENERAL DIET. Commence with 3-day fast.
Supplementation. Vitamins A and D as in Cod Liver oil. Vitamins B-complex, C and E.
General. Cold sponge-down, deep-breathing exercises. Sea-bathing. Smoking promotes congestion.
Note. However inconvenient, catarrh has one useful protective role – it helps prevent bacteria and toxins reaching tissue. For instance, when present in the nasal organs it may prevent mercury vapour from teeth-amalgam reaching the brain.

CATECHU, BLACK. *Acacia catechu* Wild. dried extract from heartwood chips.
Action: antibacterial, antiseptic, haemostatic, powerful astringent to stomach and intestines.
Uses. Irritable bowel, dysentery, mucous colitis, chronic catarrh, haemorrhage, mouth ulcer, spongy and bleeding gums (mouth wash), sore throat (gargle). A wash for varicose ulcer. Nosebleed. "Indigestion in children." (*Chinese Traditional*)

Reported use in cancer (*J.L. Hartwell, Lloydia, 33, 97, 1970*)
Preparations. Thrice daily.
Powder: 0.3 to 1 gram in honey or banana mash.
Tincture BHP (1983) 1:5 in 45 per cent alcohol. Dose half-1 teaspoon (2.5-5ml) in water. GSL

CATECHU, PALE. Gambier. *Uncaria gambier* Roxb. Shoots. Leaves.
Constituents: flavonoids, tannins, indole alkaloids.
Action: *Intestinal astringent*.
Uses: similar to Black Catechu.
Preparations. Twice daily.
Powder: 0.3 to 1 gram (quarter of a teaspoon) in honey or banana mash.
Tincture Catechu BP. 1:5, with Cinnamon 1:20, in 45 per cent alcohol. Dose: 2.5 to 5ml. GSL

CATMINT. Catnep. *Nepeta cataria L.* Leaves and flowers. *German*: Katzenkraut. *French*: Cataire. *Spanish*: Nébeda. *Italian*: Cataria. *Chinese*: Chi-hsueh-ts'ao.

Action: anti-diarrhoeal, antispasmodic, emmenagogue, diaphoretic, carminative, gentle nerve relaxant for release of tension. To reduce temperature in simple fevers by inducing a free perspiration thus sweating-out toxins via the skin.
Keynote: crises of childhood.
Uses. Children: colic, restlessness, hyperactivity, convulsions, early stages of fever, hysteria with crying and violent twisting of the trunk, middle ear infection, sinuses. Colds, influenza, congestion of respiratory organs. Physical results of emotional disturbance.
Preparations. Two-hourly in acute cases, otherwise thrice daily.
Tea: (popular method) One heaped teaspoon to each cup boiling water; infuse 10 minutes. Half-1 cup. In its absence use Chamomile.
Liquid Extract: 30 drops to 1 teaspoon in water.
Enema: 2oz to 2 pints boiling water; for elimination of toxic wastes from colon.

Beloved by cats, making them frolicsome, amorous and full of fun. Not given in pregnancy.
GSL

CATUABA. Popular Brazilian folk remedy. Two species. *Juniperus brasiliens*
Keynote: aphrodisiac.
Action: brain and nerve stimulant, aphrodisiac for men and women.
Uses. Sexual weakness, male impotence, nervous debility and exhaustion.
Preparation. *Ground bark*: half-1 teaspoon to each cup boiling water; infuse 15 minutes. Half-1 cup freely.

CAVERNOUS SINUS THROMBOSIS. Thrombosis arising in the cavernous sinus of the sphenoid bone in the head.
Cause: Septicaemia or infected embolism conveyed from elsewhere – veins of the face, sinuses, head. May be a complication of meningitis.
Symptoms: headache, nausea, swelling of eyelids and forehead, pupils distended, veins of temples prominent, fever with severe constitutional disturbance.
Prognosis: usually fatal in the absence of orthodox antibiotics, but anti-staphylococcal herbs are helpful.
Tinctures. Formula. Echinacea 3; Goldenseal 2; Myrrh (Tincture) 1. 1 teaspoon in water every 2 hours (acute). Thrice daily (chronic).

Treatment by or in liaison with general medical practitioner.

CAYENNE. Red pepper. Chillies. *Capsicum minimum* Roxb. *French*: Piment capsique. *German*: Beisbeere. *Italian*: Peperone. *Indian*: Mirch. *Malayan*: Chabe-sabrong. *Chinese*: Lachiao. Bright red dried ripe pods. Powder known as Cayenne pepper.
Action: Regarded by the professional herbalist as the purest and safest stimulant known. Opens up every tissue in the body to an increased flow of blood.

Produces natural warmth, equalising the circulation in the aged. Stimulant and iron-bearer, it accelerates oxygenation of cells. Antiseptic. Antispasmodic for relief of pain. Carminative.

Prostaglandin antagonist and analgesic. (*F. Fletcher Hyde, The Herbal Practitioner (Dec. 1977)*)

Well suited to persons of feeble constitution with poor circulation, lacking in energy and fear of the slightest draft. Hypothermia. Encourages the adrenal glands to produce corticosteroids.
Uses. Poor digestion in the aged, wind, nervous depression, impotency. To increase gatrointestinal secretion and thus improve the appetite. A mere pinch (one-eighth teaspoon) of the powder may suffice.
Practitioner: Official tincture Capsicum Fort BPC (1934). 1 part to 3 parts 60 per cent alcohol. Dose 0.06-0.2ml. (1-3 drops).
Preparations. An active ingredient of Life Drops: see entry. A few grains of red pepper on food at table aids digestion and improves circulation.
Home-tincture: 1oz bruised chillies or coarse powder to half a litre 60 per cent alcohol (Vodka, etc); macerate 7 days; shake daily, decant. 2 or more teaspoons in wineglass water. 1-2 drops of the tincture enhances action of most herbal agents and may also be taken in tea or other beverages for cold hands and feet, pale lips and small feeble pulse.
Tincture Capsicum Fort. 1934: dose, 0.06-0.2ml.
External use as a rubefacient, antiseptic or counter-irritant. As a warming lotion, cream or ointment for rheumatism, neuralgia, backache, lumbago.
Cayenne salve: vegetable oil (16), Beeswax (2), Tincture Cayenne (1). Melt oil and beeswax in a stone jar in oven on low heat; add Cayenne. Stir gently few minutes to produce smooth consistency. Pour into jars.
Case Records. "I was called in haste to a lady who was dying. I found her gasping for breath with no wrist pulse and very cold. Seven specialists had treated her and were positive nothing could be done. I gave her tincture Capsicum in one drop doses, often and persistently. The specials made all kinds of fun at me. The patient became well and strong at 80 years. I suggest that if Cayenne pepper had been given in all cases where whisky had been taken for relief, many of those who are now dead would be alive today." (*C.S. Dyer, MD*)
External: "Capsicum has a peculiar action on bones of the external ear and mastoid process – abscesses round about and below the ear, and caries. It is frequently indicated in mastoid abscess. A girl seen in hospital with a constant temperature of about 100 degrees since a mastoid operation some years ago resulted in a normal

temperature ever since." (*Dr M.L. Tyler*)

Ingredient of: Peerless Composition Essence; Antispasmodic drops; Life Drops; Elderflower; Peppermint and Composition Essence. (*Potter's*) GSL

CEDAR LEAF OIL. See: THUJA OCCIDENTALIS.

CELANDINE, GREATER. Garden celandine. *Chelidonium majus L. German*: Scholkraut. *French*: Herbe aux hirondelles. *Italian*: Cheldonia maggiore. *Spanish*: Celidonia. Herb.
Constituents: alkaloids, saponins, carotene.
Action: cholagogue, bitter, antispasmodic, antifungal.

Analgesic (*Pharmaceutical Journal 8/3/1986, p.304*)

Diuretic, laxative, vesicant (fresh juice), antibacterial, antimycotic.
Constituents. Alkaloids Chelidonine, Chelerythrine and Sanguinarine. Yellow juice resembles bile.
Uses. Gall stones, inflammation of the gall bladder, jaundice with yellowness of skin, mild hepatitis, bilious headaches, aching pain in right shoulder of liver origin, skin diseases. Gonorrhoeal ophthalmia, as an eyewash 3-5 times daily. (*T.J. Lyle*)

Eye infections: traditional use – infusion as an eyewash. Warts, papillomas, condylomas and colonic polyposis.

Juice of fresh plant injected locally into cancer lesions gained a reputation in the old school. (*U.S. Dispensatory 25, 1923*)
Combination: with Barberry and Dandelion for gall bladder disease BHP (1983).
Preparations. Maximum dosage, dried herb: 2g (30 grains) thrice daily, by infusion. Daily dose not to exceed 6g.
Tea. Quarter of a teaspoon to each cup boiling water. Infuse 10 minutes; half-1 cup.
Liquid extract: 15-30 drops, thrice daily.
Tincture BHP (1983). 1 part to 10 parts 45 per cent alcohol: 2-4ml, thrice daily.
Ointment, for leg ulcer and skin diseases.
Fresh juice: warts, corns.
Side-effects, none; but large doses avoided.
Note. Herb loses its efficacy after a few months.

CELERY SEED. *Apium graveolens, L. French*: Ache. *German*: Sellerie. *Spanish*: Apio. *Italian*: Sedano. *Indian*: Chanoo Rhadodni. *Chinese*: Han-ch'in. Dried seeds.

Contains apiol, coumarins. Minerals: iron, phosphorus, potassium, sodium.
Action: alkaline reaction on the blood. Anti-rheumatic, urinary antiseptic, diuretic, anti-spasmodic, carminative, tonic digestive, galactagogue, assists elimination of uric acid. Anti-gout, anti-inflammatory, hypotensor, aphrodisiac.
Uses. Rheumatic disorders, stiffness and muscular pain, rheumatoid arthritis. Inflammation of the urinary tract, cystitis. To increase milk flow in nursing mothers. Bad breath.
Preparations. Thrice daily.
Green Drink: fresh raw celery juice prepared in a liquidiser. Blends well with carrot or apple juice. Cooling drink for a sickroom.
Decoction. Quarter to half a teaspoon bruised dry seeds to each cup water, gently simmer 10 minutes in covered vessel. Half-1 cup.
Liquid extract, BHC Vol 1. 1:1, 90 per cent ethanol. Dose: 0.5 to 2ml.
Tincture, BHC Vol 1. 1:5, 90 per cent ethanol. Dose: 2 to 8ml.
Tablets/capsules. Powdered plant 120mg; seed BHP (1983) 5mg.
Home acid tincture. 1 part bruised celery seed to 20 parts Cider vinegar. Macerate 1 month. Filter. Dose: 2-3 teaspoons in water (rheumatic aches and pains).
Essential oil: 1-2 drops in water or honey.
Diet: The vegetable is low in calories: for weight-conscious. Non-fattening.

Not taken in pregnancy. GSL

CELL PROLIFERANTS. Comfrey, Fenugreek, Calendula.

CELLULITE. Not a medical term. Puffy skin from deposition of fat. "Orange peel skin". Occurs chiefly in women as lumpy flesh on buttocks, thighs, stomach, knees and upper arm. Though not due to increased fluid in the tissues, it is sufficient to arrest the circulation. Constriction of capillaries causes toxic wastes to build up, forming nodules that lock away fat in the tissues. Hormone imbalance also suspected. Varicose veins may appear with cellulite from poorly supportive connective tissue. Usual cause: poor posture and unhealthy lifestyle.
Treatment. To activate capillary function and assist toxic elimination: Bladderwrack, Gotu Kola, Kola, Parsley tea. A diuretic may assist by eliminating excess fluid.
Gotu Kola tea: Quarter to half a teaspoon leaves to each cup boiling water; infuse 5-10 minutes. 1 cup morning and evening.
Formula. Tea. Equal parts: Alfalfa, Clivers, Fennel, Senna leaves. 1 heaped teaspoon to each cup boiling water: infuse 5-10 minutes. Half-1 cup morning and evening.
Seline. Tablets. Ingredients: Each tablet contains Lecithin 100mg; Pulverised Dandelion 100mg; Pulverised Horsetail 100mg; Pulverised extract Fucus 5:1 30mg; Vitamin C 40mg; Vitamin B6 1mg. 1 tablet thrice daily.
Aescin. Compound isolated from Horse-chestnuts to decrease capillary permeability and swelling.
Topical. Decoction of Horse-chestnuts as a lotion.

Or: infusion of Bladderwrack.
Aromatherapy and Herb essences. Combination for external use. Ingredients: Almond oil 47ml; Fennel oil 1ml; Juniper oil 1ml; Cypress essence 0.5ml; Lemon essence 0.5ml. Apply to affected areas morning and evening; small area 5 drops, large area 10 drops (*Gerard*). Gentle massage with a string glove, loofah or massage glove.
Diet. Reduce calorie intake. Raw fresh fruits and vegetable salads to account for 50 per cent of the diet. No sweet or dried fruits. Conservatively-cooked vegetables. Seafood. Iodine-rich foods. Wholegrain cereals. Protein: beans, chicken, poached eggs, fish, little lean meat: no pork, bacon or ham. Low-fat yoghurt. Cold-pressed unsaturated oils for salad dressings with lemon juice. Dandelion coffee to stimulate liver. Avoid sugar, alcohol, bananas and white flour products. Spring water.
Supportives. Stop smoking. Adopt an alternative to the contraceptive pill. To avoid fluid retention, 2-3 glasses of water daily.

CELLULITIS. Inflammation of the skin and underlying tissues by inflammation and spreading infection. Usually staphylococcal or streptococcal.
Symptoms: Hot, painful swollen skin sensitive to touch, with constitutional unrest.
Indicated: alteratives, lymphatics. Echinacea to increase resistance. See: ABSCESS. ERYSIPELAS.
Butcher's Broom combination. Butcher's Broom 100mg; Hawthorn berry 100mg; Garlic 100mg; Apple pectin 50mg; Cayenne (capsicum) 50mg; Ginger root 50mg; One capsule or tablet thrice daily.
Garlic. Good results reported.

CENTAURY. *Centaurium erythraea*, Pers. *German*: Tausendguldenkraut. *French*: Centaurée. *Spanish*: Centaura. *Italian*: Centaurea minore.
Action: tonic-hepatic, mild sedative, febrifuge, astringent (topical), bitter tonic, analgesic (mild), anti-inflammatory, antipyretic.
Uses. Weak or 'sour' stomach, heartburn, nausea, vomiting, indigestion. Liver disorders (mild). Hypertension. Kidney stone. Skin blemishes, freckles (lotion). Wound healer. Tapeworm: tea taken daily 2-3 months.
Combination. Equal parts, Centuary, Chamomile and Meadowsweet (tea). 1 heaped teaspoon to each cup boiling water: 1 cup thrice daily.
Preparations. Thrice daily.
Tea: Half teaspoon to each cup boiling water; infuse 15 minutes. Half-1 cup.
Liquid extract BHP (1983). 1:1 in 25 per cent alcohol. Dose: 2-4ml.
Tincture. 1 part Centuary herb to 20 parts Vodka; macerate 8 days. Dose: 1 wineglassful for liver and gall bladder. (*Russian traditional*) GSL

CEREBELLAR ATAXIA. Disease of the nervous system.
Symptoms: blurred speech, stumbling gait, fatigue on effort, inability to concentrate, feeling of isolation and weakness – cannot fight back.
Causes: vitamin deficiency, overwork, excess physical and mental activity. Multiple sclerosis.
Symptom relief only. *Tea*: equal parts, Mistletoe, Skullcap, Valerian. 1 heaped teaspoon to each cup water; bring to boil; simmer one minute; infuse 15 minutes. Half-1 cup thrice daily.
Ginseng. Kola. Saw Palmetto. Ginkgo. Tablets, capsules, tinctures, etc. Symptomatic relief.

CEREBRAL HAEMORRHAGE. See: STROKE.

CEREBRAL THROMBOSIS. Formation of a blood clot within vessels of the brain. May be due to atheroma or embolism causing a blockage resulting in hypoxia (oxygen deficiency).
Alternatives. *Teas*. Lime flowers, Nettles, Horsetail, Ginkgo, Oats, Mistletoe, Yarrow.
Tea. Mix equal parts: Ginkgo, Hawthorn, Yarrow. One heaped teaspoon to each cup boiling water; infuse 5-10 minutes; 1 cup thrice daily.
Tablets/capsules. Ginkgo, Hawthorn, Prickly Ash.
Diet. See: DIET – HEART AND CIRCULATION.
Supplements. Daily: Vitamin E 1000mg; B6 50mg; B12 2mcg. Selenium 200mcg; Zinc 15mg.
Strict bedrest; regulate bowels; avoid excessive physical and mental exertion.

CERVIX. Erosion of. A gynaecological problem of infection of the cervical crypts with a reddened area from the cervical os to the vaginal surface of the cervix. Cervicitis may be due to chemical irrigations and contraceptive creams or to the mechanical irritation of pessaries.
Symptoms: mucopurulent vaginal discharge, sometimes blood-stained. Backache. Urinary problems. Diagnosis confirmed by smear test, biopsy or swab culture.
Alternatives (also for cervicitis).
Teas, decoctions, powders or tinctures:– Agnus Castus, Black Cohosh, Echinacea. Myrrh. Pulsatilla.
Practitioner: Tinctures. Mix, parts: Black Cohosh 3; Gelsemium 1. Dose: 10-20 drops in water, morning and evening.
Lapacho tea (Pau d'arco tea). Soak gauze tampons with extract, insert, renew after 24 hours.
Douche: German Chamomile tea, or Lapacho tea.
Tampons: saturate with paste of equal parts Slippery Elm powder and milk. Or: saturate tampons with Aloe Vera gel or fresh juice. In event of unavailability refer to entry: SUPPOSITORY.
Diet. Lacto-vegetarian.
Vitamins. A. B-complex. C (1g daily). E (400iu

daily).
Minerals. Iron, Zinc.
Note. Women who have an abnormal cervical smear should be tested for chlamydia.

CHAMOMILE. Both Chamomiles are relaxants (mild sedatives). Both have a gentle soothing action on the fretful child, relaxing nerve tension without undue sedation and side-effects.

The difference between German (wild) and Roman:– German is stronger, acting beneficially on mucous surfaces. Roman Chamomile, is less bitter, more soothing to the lungs, and more directly hastens menstrual flow.

Externally as a compress of the pulped flowers (fresh), both kinds are used for lumbago, gouty joints, sciatica, neuralgia and local inflammation.

CHAMOMILE FLOWERS (GERMAN). Wild Chamomile. *Matricaria recutita L. German*: Hundskamille. *French*: Camomille. *Italian*: Camomilla. *Spanish*: Camomile. Part used: flowerheads. Contains chamazulene which is active against staphylococcus aureus.
Constituents: volatile oil, flavonoids, tannic acid.
Action. Anti-inflammatory, antimicrobial, antiseptic (mild), anti-peptic ulcer, anodyne (mild), antispasmodic, bitter, carminative, vulnerary. Mild nerve sedative but tonic to the alimentary canal.
Uses. Internal use. Nervous excitability, convulsions, restlessness, hyperactivity in children, insomnia, early stages of fever, measles (warm tea), travel sickness, pin and thread worms, peptic ulcer, gastro-intestinal spasm – calms down digestive system, pre-menstrual tension, hysteria from womb irritation, candida albicans, inflammation of respiratory and gastro-intestinal tracts, sore throat and mouth. Psychosomatic illness: see CHAMOMILE ROMAN. May be used in pregnancy.

External use. "Inflammation and irritation of skin and mucosa, including the oral cavity and gums, respiratory tract and anal and genital area." (EM) Conjunctivitis (cold tea). Gangrene (poultice with few drops Tincture Myrrh).
Combinations. With Valerian, Passion flower and Hops (equal parts) for nervous excitability. With Liquorice 1 and Chamomile 4 for gastric ulcer and chronic dyspepsia. Chamomile works well with Peppermint and Balm; equal parts.
Preparations. One teaspoon to each cup boiling water; infuse 5-10 minutes; one cup freely.
Powder. Quarter to half a teaspoon; tablets/ capsules.
Liquid extract BHC Vol 1. 1:1 in 45 per cent ethanol. Dose: 1-4ml (15-60 drops).
Tincture. 1 part to 5 parts 45 per cent alcohol. Dose: 5-10ml (1-2 teaspoons).
Oil of Chamomile. Prepare as for OILS – IMPREGNATED.
Essential oil (Aromatherapy). Externally for neuralgia.
Compress: See: CHAMOMILE FLOWERS. ROMAN. Rinses. Gargles.
Chamomile bath. Add strong infusion to bath water for irritable skin rash, eczema.
Chamomile enema. 1 tablespoon flowers in 2 litres (3 and a half pints) boiling water; infuse. strain and inject warm.
Side-effects: rare contact skin allergy. GSL

CHAMOMILE FLOWERS (ROMAN). Anthemis Nobilis. *Chamaemelum nobile L. German:* Romisch Kamille. *French*: Chamomille romaine. *Italian*: Camomilla odorosa. *Spanish*: Manzanilla.
Constituents: sesquiterpene lactones, flavonoids.
Action: *antispasmodic*, analgesic (mild), anti-inflammatory (simple acute), bitter, carminative, de-sensitiser (skin), tranquilliser (mild), anti-convulsant, anti-emetic, sedative (mild). One of the chief medicinal plants used by the phytotherapist.
Uses. Children's convulsions, physical stress, hyperactive children. Indigestion in excitable females. Nausea and indigestion from emotional upset. Facial neuralgia. Insomnia. Meniere's syndrome. Gastro-intestinal irritation with diarrhoea. Travel sickness (cup hot tea). Wind. Vomiting of pregnancy. Loss of appetite. Sore mouth, nasal catarrh. Infertility (sometimes successful). The oil is active against staphylococcus aureus and candida albicans. Skin disorders (steam face with hot tea). Autonomic imbalance. Hot tired feet (strong tea used as a footbath). Hair loss: strong tea, externally. Inflammation of the skin. Psychosomatic:– keynote: irritability. "Cannot bear it"; temper, everything seems intolerable, uncivil, impatient in sickness.
Preparations. As necessary. 4-6 flowerheads to each cup boiling water infuse 15 minutes; half-1 cup.
Tincture BHC Vol 1. 1:5, 45 per cent ethanol. Dose: 3-5ml.
Oil of Chamomile. Prepare as for OILS, IMPREGNATED. For cracked lips, dry hands and feet, massage or deodorant.
Essential oil (Aromatherapy): widely used as an inhalant.
Compress. Half-1oz flowers to small muslin or linen bag; immerse in half a pint boiling water; wring out and apply bag over affected area. Repeatedly moisten bag when dry.

Large doses emetic. Not used in pregnancy.
Enema. See: GERMAN CHAMOMILE.
Chamomile ointment. Nappy rash, dry skin, irritation. GSL

CHANCRE. Painless ulcer. STD. One of the early symptoms of syphilis. See: SYPHILIS.

CHAPARRAL. Creosote bush. Grease bush. *Larrea divaricata*. Leaves.

Action. Antibiotic, powerful blood cleanser, bactericidal, anti-inflammatory, alterative, respiratory and urinary antiseptic, anti-oxidant, anti-psoriasis, anti-arthritic. Contains NDGA a powerful parasiticide. Anti-tumour, anti-microbial. Strong bitter, enzyme inhibitor. All body cells feel its influence. Of low toxicity.
Uses. Regarded as a 'cure-all' by the Arizona Indians. Rheumatism, arthritis, skin disorders, bursitis, lumbago, healing of external wounds, delayed menses, indigestion, kidney disorders, piles, tetanus, itching. Early American agent for sexually transmitted diseases. History of use in skin malignancy. Chronic chest complaints (tea).
Combinations. (1) Combines well with antibiotics: Goldenseal 1; Echinacea 2; Chaparral 3. (2) Combines with Sarsaparilla (equal parts) for venereal infections and chancre. *(Dr J.M. Bigelow)*
Preparations. Best uses reported from tea or tablets.
Tea: daily bitter health beverage; half a teaspoon to each cup boiling water; infuse 15 minutes. Half-1 cup, thrice daily.
Tablets/capsules: one 150mg thrice daily.
Ointment. 1oz powdered herb to 16oz suet. Steep one hour in an oven 300-350 degrees F. Strain through sieve; pour into jar.
Note. The sale of Chaparral has been banned in the United States of America and the United Kingdom as a result of reported cases of human toxicity.

CHAPPED HANDS. Due to deficient nutrition as well as inclement weather or occupational hazard. Hands dry and painful.
Alternatives. Creams or ointments of Comfrey, Chickweed, Aloe Vera, Evening Primrose, Plantain, Avocado, Marigold, Cucumber, Vitamin E. Sunflower seed oil. Glycerine and Rosewater.
Aromatherapy. Few drops of one of the following essential oils in a heavy carrier oil (Avocado) to ensure penetration: Chamomile, Jasmine, Orange Blossom, Patchouli, Sandalwood.
Supplementation. Vitamins A, C, D, E. Zinc. 1 teaspoon Cod Liver oil in the morning.

CHARCOAL, VEGETABLE. Pulverised wood charcoal. An inert substance but with healing potential. Has power to neutralise putrid smells of cancer, diarrhoea, gangrene, and a great capacity for absorbing gases. Its latent power is brought to life by prolonged trituration (grinding finely and diluting) with sugar of milk. To counter effect of dangerous drugs.

In the absence of sterile dressings and modern hospital amenities, powdered vegetable charcoal has an ancient reputation as an astringent dressing. It absorbs bacterial toxins and is useful for chronic bowel discharge. Powdered charcoal dressings were used during World War I. Rubbed in lard, was used for purulent foul discharging wounds to neutralise smell and promote healing.

Other indications: relaxed veins, stomach tense and full of wind, constant belching. For weak and cachetic individuals where vital powers are weak.

Available in biscuits, tablets and capsules for its purifying properties and as an aid to digestion. Tablets containing a high sodium content should be avoided.

CHARCOT'S DISEASE. Neurogenic arthritis. A degenerative and destructive joint lesion due to loss of the normal protection and pain sense. It is associated with tabes dorsalis and syringomyelia. In tabes, knee is chiefly affected; in syringomyelia, the elbow. Joint swelling in late locomotor ataxia. Usually painless.
Alternatives. Cramp bark, Cayenne, Chamomile, Guaiacum, Hops, Meadowsweet, Celery, Prickly Ash, Valerian, Wild Lettuce, Wild Yam. Mistletoe (*F. Hyde*). White Willow.
Tea. Equal parts: German Chamomile, Hops, Meadowsweet. 1 heaped teaspoon to each cup boiling water; infuse 5-10 minutes; 1 cup 3 or more times daily.
Tablets/capsules. Chamomile, Mistletoe, Prickly Ash, Ligvites, Wild Yam, Valerian, Kelp.
Alternative formulae:– *Powders*. Prickly Ash 1; Valerian 1; Cramp bark half; Guaiacum quarter. Mix. Dose: 500mg (two 00 capsules or one-third teaspoon) thrice daily.
Liquid Extracts. White Willow 2; Prickly Ash 1; Celery seeds half; Liquorice quarter; Tincture Capsicum quarter. Mix. 30-60 drops thrice daily.
Tinctures. White Willow 2; Prickly Ash 1; Valerian 1; Meadowsweet 1; Tincture Capsicum quarter. Mix. 2 teaspoons thrice daily.
Topical. Comfrey poultices (*Maria Treben*). "Three oils."
Diet. Lacto-vegetarian. Dandelion coffee. Oily fish.
General. Straight knee brace for rigid support.

CHAULMOOGRA. *Hydnocarpus kurzii* (King). Brownish-yellow oil expressed from the seeds.
Action: powerful alterative, mild sedative, mild febrifuge.
Uses. Has been used for a millennia exclusively for leprosy (Hansen's disease). Of value in eczema, psoriasis and dermatitis.
Preparations. Orally, oil is taken in capsules or an emulsion: the initial doses 5-15 drops, increasing to 60 drops. Today, the oil is usually injected, weekly.

Externally, it is applied as an ointment: 10 per cent oil in 90 per cent soft paraffin. For scaly skin diseases, eczema, etc.

Specific for anal fissure.

CHELATION. From the Greek 'chele' meaning to claw or grip. Deposits of cholesterol and by-products of free radical activity may cause arteries to become brittle and block circulation. Chelation offers an internal 'house cleaning' whereby such deposits and metals are freed into the circulation for elimination from the body.

Chelation is increasingly used as an alternative to by-pass surgery for coronary disease, significantly improving the coronary circulation. Reportedly of value for improved kidney function, decreased insulin requirement for diabetes, to reduce prostate obstruction, restore near-normal breathing pattern in emphysema and to bring relief in arthritis. Specific herbs act as bonding agents to metals in blood vessel plague prior to expulsion via the kidneys and bowel.

Conventional medical chelation therapy consists of an intravenous drip of a synthetic amino acid, EDTA (ethylene diamine tetra-acetic acid) which leeches from the tissues toxic metals (lead, mercury etc) prior to elimination. Cholesterol and fats are dissolved and metabolised by the liver, and metals are excreted by the kidneys.

Supportive aid to primary treatment. Combine tinctures: Hawthorn 2; Lily of the Valley 1; Capsicum quarter. Dose: 15-60 drops in water thrice daily.

Saponin-containing herbs, by their detergent action act as binding agents to leech metals, plague etc from blood vessels and the intestinal canal.

Diet. Guar gum preparations. Low salt. Fish oils or oily fish.

Supplements. Vitamins A, C, D (Cod Liver oil), B-complex, especially Vitamin B12, biotin, PABA, chromium, selenium, zinc, methionine, superoxide dismutase, magnesium.

Information. The Arterial Disease Clinic: tel: 0942 676617.

CHELSEA PHYSIC GARDEN. Started by the Worshipful Society of Apothecaries 1673, the Chelsea Physic Garden is the second oldest herb garden in England devoted to the scientific study of plants. It provides a silent four-acre oasis in the heart of London for enjoyment by the public, but especially for research into herbs. For over 300 years the garden has supplied drugs to London doctors for relief of the sick.

Records provide one of the few sources of information about medicinal plants in cultivation during the 18th century. The famous gardener Philip Miller took over in 1722 and developed it as the finest botanic garden in the world for its amazing variety of plants. In the 18th century cotton seeds were sent from the garden to form the crop of the new colony of Georgia, America.

From Chelsea, Madagascan *Vinca rosea* was distributed and which earned a place in modern medicine (vinplastine) for the treatment of leukaemia. After many years neglect, medical botany enjoys a renaissance during which the skills of the garden's scientific staff are again in demand for the training of pharmacists and students of other disciplines. Its buildings house a valuable collection of botanical books, including John Parkinson's "Paradisus".

CHEMOTHERAPY. The treatment of cancer with chemical drugs that are conveyed to all body tissues and attack the rapidly dividing cancer cells wherever they flourish. Unfortunately they also attack normal cells as in the alimentary canal, bone marrow and elsewhere reducing white blood cells, thus exposing the patient to infection.

Symptoms include: soreness of the mouth and throat, loss of appetite, etc.

For inoperable cancer chemotherapy is often deemed first choice of treatment. To some people this therapy is an endurance test. Many wear wigs because their hair has fallen out. Nausea and vomiting are common side-effects which may have an adverse effect upon moral and physical well-being. Often there is loss of quality of life.

Severity of the vomiting may be increased by defective function of kidneys, liver and pancreas; natural treatments are aimed at strengthening these organs with a possible improvement in a patient's well-being and quality of life.

Teas. To rid the sickening taste, smell of sour brine and copper, and to dispel nausea: German Chamomile or Black Horehound. Anti-neoplasms – Vinca rosea herb or Violet leaves. 2 teaspoons to each cup boiling water; infuse 15 minutes. 1 cup freely.

Powders. Formula. Echinacea (to strengthen immune system) 2; Blue Flag root (anti-neoplasm) 1; Black Horehound (anti-emetic) 1; Ginkgo (anti-depressive) 2. Dose: 500mg (two 00 capsules or one-third teaspoon) every 3 hours with water or Violet leaf tea.

Liquid Extracts. Formula. Echinacea 2; Blue Flag root 1; Black Horehound 1; Ladyslipper 1. One 5ml teaspoon in water every 3 hours.

Vincristine. Dosage as on marked product.

External. For irritable skin rash: packs steeped in Castor oil, Aloe Vera gel or juice, or Houseleek juice.

Note. Sips of Ginger ale have been known to relieve symptoms.

CHERRY STALKS. *Prunus cerasus*. Part used: fruit stalks. *French*: Cerisier. *German*: Kinsche. *Italian*: Ciliego agerotto.

Constituents: polyphenols, potassium salts, organic acids.

Action: diuretic. Inflammation of urinary tract.

Uses: oedema, cystitis.

Preparations. *Tea*. 1-2 teaspoons dried stalks to each cup boiling water; infuse 15 minutes. Dose: 1 cup thrice daily.

Powder. Dose: 500mg (two 00 capsules or one-third teaspoon) thrice daily.

CHERVIL. Sweet Cicely. Myrrhis odorata. *Anthriscus cerefolium* 1. Hoffin. *German*: Gartenkerbel. *French*: Cerfeuil musqué. *Italian*: Felce muschiata. *Indian*: Rigi-el-Ghurab. Part used: fresh or dried leaves.
Action: expectorant, diuretic, hypotensive, digestive, tonic.
Uses. Indigestion, high blood pressure.
Preparations. *Tea*: Half-1 teaspoon to each cup boiling water; infuse 15 minutes; dose 1 cup, thrice daily.
Fresh juice: Half-1 teaspoon, or as a lotion for eczema. GSL

CHEST INJURIES. Immediate first aid treatment: Liquid extracts: Arnica, Marigold (calendula) and St John's Wort (hypericum): 10 drops each in cup water taken in wineglassful doses, and used externally. Moderate injuries will heal rapidly. If the ribs penetrate the lung complications may follow requiring hospitalisation. Comfrey root taken internally and applied as a poultice externally facilitates union of fractured bone and arrests bleeding from the lungs.

Internal use of Arnica and Comfrey root would appear to be justified in serious chest injuries.

CHEST RUB. One part volatile oil (Cajeput, Lemon, Hyssop, Niaouli, Rosemary, Eucalyptus or Sandalwood) in ten parts ointment base or peanut oil. Vick Vapour Rub. Mustard oil. See: OINTMENT BASE.

CHESTNUT, SWEET. Spanish chestnut. *Castanea sativa*, Mill. Leaves. *French*: Châtaignier. *German*: Kastanienbaum. *Italian*: Castagno. *Indian*: Ni-keri. *Russian*: Keschtan. *Dutch*: Kastangeboorn.

Constituents include tannins. Leaves and fruits.
Action: drying astringent, antirheumatic, antitussive.
Uses. Dry violent spasmodic coughs (whooping cough, croup). Copious catarrh. Diarrhoea (infants). Piles. Muscular rheumatism. Polymyalgia. Sore throat (gargle).
Formula. Chestnut 1; Celery 1; Black Cohosh quarter; and Meadowsweet 1; for polymyalgia and muscular rheumatism.
Formula. Sweet Chestnut 2; Wild Cherry bark 1; for whooping cough.
Preparations. *Tea*: 2 teaspoons shredded leaves to each cup water, bring to boil and simmer 5 minutes. Half-1 cup freely
Liquid Extract BHP (1983) 1:1 in 25 per cent alcohol. Dose 1-4ml, thrice daily.
Home tincture: 1oz shredded leaves to 20oz Vodka (40-45 per cent alcohol). Macerate 8 days. 2-4 teaspoons in water, thrice daily. GSL

CHICKEN POX. Varicella. Contagious virus disease with small red spots becoming vesicles, first on chest and back but later spreading over whole body. More children than adults.
Symptoms: Slight fever with temperature rising 39°-40° (102°-104°), sore throat, heavy nasal discharge, rashes come in crops soon to progress to milky white blisters which shrivel into scabs. Irritability. The virus may lie latent in the ganglia of sensory and somatic nerves for many years to manifest later as shingles.

Object of the therapy is to reduce the temperature and promote a healthy outcropping of the rash.
Alternatives. Ensure adequate fluid intake. Antihistamine herbs: Lobelia, Goldenseal root, Parsley root, Juniper. Mucous membranes: spots on: Goldenseal, Myrrh. Ears: spots in: Instil oil Mullein or contents of Vitamin E capsule.
Teas: Boneset, Elderflowers and Peppermint, Marigold, Chamomile.
Tea. Formula. Equal parts: Red Clover, Boneset, Yarrow.
Maria Treben's tea. Marigold 3; Nettles 1; Yarrow 1. Prepare: all teas, one heaped teaspoon to each cup boiling water; infuse 5-15 minutes. 1 cup freely.
Tinctures. Alternatives. (1) Combine, Echinacea 2; Poke root 1; Goldenseal 1. (2) Combine, Wild Indigo 2; Marigold 1; Myrrh quarter; Dose: as many drops as the age of the child, in a little water. (Adults: One 5ml teaspoon) Dose: 3-4 times daily.
Gargle and Mouthwash, where spots appear on mucous membranes: 5 drops Tincture Myrrh or Goldenseal (or combined), in warm water.
Topical. Aloe Vera. Evening Primrose oil. Oil from Vitamin E capsule. Wash with distilled extract Witch Hazel, Lavender water, or Chamomile tea.
Cayenne. Pinch Cayenne in teas, or few drops Tincture Capsicum in tinctures heightens action.
Note. For restlessness add, equal parts, Skullcap or Chamomile. For severe itching, wash with potato water or Chamomile tea.
Diet. Commence 3-day fast, with herb teas and fruit juices only. Vitamins A and C. Carrot juice.
High Temperature. If serious: tinctures – Pleurisy root 1; Lobelia 1; Catnep 2; Valerian 1. One 5ml teaspoon every 2 hours. Reduced to thrice daily when temperature abates.

Patients suffer less itching if kept cool.

CHICKWEED. *Stellaria media L. German*: Vogelmiere. *French*: Stellaire. *Spanish*: Pamplina. *Chinese*: Fran-lü. Herb.
Constituents: saponin glycosides, coumarins, flavonoids. Source of Vitamin C.
Action: alterative, demulcent, emollient, vulnerary, anti-itch, antirheumatic, mild laxative. A 'cold' (refrigerant) agent, dispelling excess body

heat. Cools, soothes and relieves irritation.
Uses. Ancient English remedy for chronic skin conditions. Boils, painful eruptions, varicose ulcers, abscess, etc. Muscular rheumatism, inflamed gouty joints (ointment or poultice). Takes the heat out of itchy skin.
Preparations. Thrice daily.
Tea: 2 teaspoons dried herb to each cup or, 1oz to 1 pint, boiling water; infuse 15 minutes. Fresh herb, double quantity; simmer 10 minutes: 1 cup.
Liquid extract BHP (1983). 1:1 in 25 per cent alcohol: dose – 1-5ml.
Tincture BHP (1983) 1:5 in 45 per cent alcohol: dose – 2-10ml.
Poultice: handful bruised Chickweed in muslin bag; use rolling pin until bag weeps juice; apply to affected area (varicose ulcer, etc). OR: 1oz dried leaves in bag; steep in boiling water; apply warm.
Chickweed Ointment. 1 part clean Chickweed to 4 parts fresh salt-free lard and 1 part vaseline. Place all in a stone jar in a hot oven. Steep 2-3 hours. Strain through a wire mesh strainer or clean cloth into another jar. When cold, ready for use.
Lotion: Use tea for cleansing.
Lotion. Take a pot or other suitable receptacle, fill with fresh Chickweed well pressed down. Pour on Sunflower seed oil to saturation point. Allow to steep for 2 weeks, strain and bottle. Apply lid or cap and use for eczema and other skin diseases. (*Christopher Hedley, MNIMH*) GSL

CHICORY. *Cichorium intybus L.* Succory. Garden vegetable. Part used: root.
Action: tonic laxative, diuretic, mild hepatic, mild sedative.
Uses. Liver congestion, jaundice. Rheumatic and gouty joints. To increase appetite. Gallstones.
Preparation. 1oz to 1 pint water gently simmered 20 minutes. Dose: half-1 cup, thrice daily. Leaves used in salads. Non-caffeine coffee substitute. GSL

CHILBLAINS. Spasm of surface blood vessels, with inflammation, due to exposure to cold. Thrombosis of vessels of the skin, with red itchy patches. Possible calcium deficiency. Vaso-dilators bring relief. Internal treatment to stimulate the circulation.
Alternatives. *Internal.* Prickly Ash, Hawthorn, Cayenne, Blue Flag, Ginger.
Tinctures. To tone the skin. Mix, equal parts: Yarrow, Blue Flag root, Prickly Ash. Few drops tincture Capsicum (Cayenne). One 5ml teaspoon in water before meals thrice daily.
Topical. Oak bark hand or foot baths: handful bark to each 1 pint (500ml) water simmered 20 minutes.
Capsicum or Black Bryony (Tamus): cream or lotion.
Friar's balsam: soak cotton wool and apply.
Traditional. Rub with raw onion. Bathe with potato water. Infusion of Wild Thyme wash (*Dr Alfred Vogel*). Cider vinegar.
Prophylactic measures: adequate footwear (socks and shoes) before winter comes.
Supplementation. 2 x 300mg Calcium lactate tablets at meals thrice daily. Vitamin E (400iu daily). Vitamin B-complex (500mg daily).

CHILDBIRTH. One of the areas in which herbal medicine proves safe and effective is childbirth. Before days of modern medicine herbalism was the only method of assistance. Although the modern hospital has taken over the management of the case, powerful plant parturients are still available for the enlightened physician.

Raspberry leaf tea (iron absorption) should be taken the last 3 months of pregnancy (1oz to 1 pint boiling water; infuse 15 minutes; all drunk at intervals during the day). Taken hot at expectation of delivery the tea favourably assists.

For last month of pregnancy to ensure easy delivery Blue Cohosh should also be taken: (Helonias or Pulsatilla in its absence).
Blue Cohosh. Strengthens muscles of the womb and pelvis. Assists labour pains and all aspects of childbirth. (An old veterinary stand-by to reduce piglet mortality.) Where labour is delayed, the os rigid, painful spasms, "all worn-out by fatigue", 10 drops Liquid Extract or 20 drops tincture in water every half hour favourably assists.
Pulsatilla. For inefficient labour, to accelerate delivery. Safe and reliable for weak and distressing pains. Thirty drops tincture or 15 drops Liquid Extract in water every 15 minutes to half hour. Even if ineffective, its action is harmless. Believed to act as well as Ergot. At time of delivery, place 20-30 drops tincture or liquid extract in 4oz water; dose – 1 teaspoon every 15 minutes as circumstances dictate. Given once daily, last month of pregnancy, 5 drops tincture or liquid extract powerfully assist women whose labour is expected to be difficult.
For sickness. Black Horehound tea.
Convulsions of childbirth: see, ECLAMPSIA.
Severe haemorrhage: Yarrow tea, as much as tolerated. OR:– Combination. Equal parts: Helonias, Black Haw, Cypripedium.
Powders: Quarter of a teaspoon.
Liquid Extracts: 30-60 drops.
Tinctures: 1-2 teaspoons in water or honey, hourly.
Sponge-down. A sponge saturated with Marigold (Calendula) tea after delivery is most comforting to the new mother.

CHILD ABUSE. In every case, bruising precedes more serious injuries. Cases detected at the bruising stage may well be saved from serious or fatal harm. Facial bruises, black eyes and ears

may be easily apparent but the inside of the mouth should always be inspected for broken or displaced teeth.
Lotion for external use: 1-2 teaspoons to cup of cold water – Tincture Arnica for bruising where skin is unbroken; Tincture Marigold (Calendula) where skin is broken and bleeding; Tincture St John's Wort (Hypericum) to allay nerve trauma. Injury through burning is a cruel form of abuse and frightening to a child: match-stick or cigarette burns may be mistaken for shingles; apply honey or Distilled Extract Witch Hazel. For great fear and effects of fright: Skullcap tea freely, internally. All first degree burns require immediate hospital treatment.

CHILDREN. Massive and long continued medication should be avoided parents acquiring some ability to distinguish between the purely miserable and the critically ill. It is easy to become alarmed at the sight of a child in the throes of a convulsion or feverishness when there may be a tendency to over-prescribe. German Chamomile tea is a splendid children's remedy. Liquid Extract and Tincture doses for children are 1 drop and 2 drops, respectively, for each year of age.

Anti-depressants should not be given for bed-wetting, drugs for sleep problems or strong laxatives for the chronically constipated. Mild herbal alternatives exist. Fresh carrot juice daily helps a child to avoid some complaints. Some herbs are not advised for children under 12, except under the care of a qualified practitioner.

Parental smoking habits are known to be responsible for crying and digestive symptoms in infants.
Sleeplessness. German Chamomile or Balm tea: children 2-10 years quarter to half a cup; over 10 years: 1 cup. Babies: 3-6 teaspoons in feeding bottle – sweeten with honey if necessary.
Night seizures, with screaming: Passion Flower tea. 1 heaped teaspoon to cup boiling water; infuse 5-15 minutes. Strain. A few teaspoons at bedtime. When a brain storm starts place pinch of salt on the tongue.
Calcium deficiency. Nettle tea. Carrot juice. Cod Liver oil with fresh orange juice.
Colic. Any tea: Dill, Catnep, Spearmint or Fennel. Few teaspoons frequently. Abdominal massage: 3 drops Chamomile oil in teaspoon olive oil.
Constipation. Prune or carrot juice. Dandelion coffee.
Cough. Oil of Thyme – few drops in water.
Crusta Lacta (milk rash). Weak teas: Plantain, Heartsease, Red Clover. Anoint with St John's Wort oil. Buttermilk, Wheatgerm.
Diarrhoea. Teas: Yarrow, Tormentil. Breast feeding during the first 4-6 months of life reduces the risk of children's diarrhoea.
Digestion, weak. Teas: Fennel, Caraway, Dill. 1 teaspoon crushed seeds to cup boiling water. Infuse 15 minutes in a covered vessel. Teaspoon doses for under 2s; half-1 cup thereafter. Also for flatulence.
Feverishness. Alarm at a baby's fever and fractiousness may attract complete medical treatment including nose drops, cough linctus, antipyretics and antibiotics, together with something to let the parents get some sleep. Avoid where possible. Mild fevers: teas – Yarrow, Marigold, Thyme, Elderflowers and Peppermint, Catmint, Carragheen Moss. Sweeten with honey. Topical: Flannels wrung out in these hot teas. Zinc can cut short the common cold. Echinacea tablets/capsules offer antiviral protection.

It is common for a child to convulse with fever. A feverish child, kept cool, is less likely to have convulsions. Remove most of child's clothes so he can lose heat through the skin. Fruit juices (Vitamin C) in abundance. Do not feed solid foods. Wash in lukewarm (not cold) water.
Eyes. Deep hollows under the eyes reveal exhaustion, for which blood and nerve tonics and iron supplements are indicated.
Growth problems. Under-developed children respond well to herbal aids: Gentian, Ginseng, Horsetail, Marigold, Oats, German Chamomile, Wood Betony, Kelp, Alfalfa. Supplementation with brewer's yeast, Calcium, Pollen and Zinc yield convincing results.
Hyperactivity. Nerve restoratives for highly-strung children: Teas: Lime flowers, Chamomile, Lemon Balm, B-vitamins. Porridge. Tablets: Passion flower, Valerian, Skullcap. Vitamins B6 and C. Powders: formula. Passion flower 2; Valerian 1; Liquorice 1. Dose: 250mg (one 00 capsule or one-sixth teaspoon) thrice daily.
Irritability and impaired school performance may be due to Tartrazine and other additives, sugar, and anticonvulsant drugs. See previous paragraph.
Infection. Infection of the upper respiratory tract may manifest as inflammation of the middle ear, nasal discharge or tonsillitis. Echinacea tablets, powder or liquid extract indicated. For specific infection such as measles, see under MEASLES, or other appropriate entry.
Skin. Reject cow's in favour of goat's milk. See appropriate entry for each skin disease (ECZEMA, etc). Care of skin after bathing: St John's Wort oil, Evening Primrose oil.

ROSEOLA. R. infantum. 'Rash of Roses' consists of small separate irregular rose-pink spots with a pale halo which appears *after* feverishness has abated. Spots that fade on pressure first appear on trunk and neck, spreading to the face and buttocks, remaining for a short duration – half to 2 days. This is the commonest cause of high fever in children under three. Causal agent: herpes virus, human, HH6. Differential diagnosis: from

German Measles where rash accompanies fever. Internally: German Chamomile tea freely. See: SKIN, above entry.
Teething. Teas: Spearmint, Roman Chamomile, Peppermint. 1 heaped teaspoon to cup boiling water; infuse 15 minutes; frequent teaspoon doses. Alternative: place one Chamomile flower in feeding bottle. Essential oils: rub gums with diluted oils: Spearmint, German Chamomile, Peppermint or Mullein.
Urinary Tract Infection, Cystitis or urethritis. *Teas*: Horsetail, Couch Grass, Golden Rod, Rosehip. Dandelion coffee. For pus in the urine: 1-5 drops Tincture Myrrh in cup of warm water: Dose: 1-2 teaspoons thrice daily. Fullness under the eyes may indicate Bright's Disease for which specialist opinion should be obtained without delay.
Diet. Wholegrain cereals, wholemeal bread, pasta, two servings fresh fruit and vegetables daily. Little lean meat, poultry, fish. Dairy products: yoghurt, cheese, milk in moderation. Fresh orange juice, raw fresh vegetable salads. Oatmeal (porridge oats) is sustaining to the nervous system.
Avoid: crisps, fizzy drinks, hamburgers, biscuits, chocolate, sugar-filled snacks, alcohol, strong tea and coffee.
Supplement. Most children may benefit from one zinc tablet weekly.
Medicine doses. See: DOSAGE.
Fish oils. As well as to help children guard against winter illnesses, Cod Liver oil supplements may help them later in life against arthritis, heart disease, psoriasis, eczema and other inflammatory disorders.
Aspirin. It is clear that a link exists between Reye's syndrome and aspirin. Aspirin is not advised for minor viral illness in children.

CHILLIE VINEGAR. Parts: Bruised Cayenne pods 1; Cider Vinegar 20. Macerate for one month and filter. A hot stimulating condiment for use at table. 5-10 drops in tea or beverage for winter's colds and chills.

CHILLIES. The pod of the Capsicum, extremely pungent and stimulant. Dried and ground to form Cayenne pepper. See: CAYENNE.

CHINESE MEDICINE. Modern Chinese medicine has rejected entirely the conception of disease due to evil spirits and treated by exorcism. Great advances in scientific knowledge in China have been made since 1949, removing much of the superstitious aspect from herbal medicine and placing it on a sound scientific basis. Advances in the field of Chinese Herbal Medicine are highlighted in an authoritative work: Chinese Clinical Medicine, by C.P. Li MD (Pub: Fogarty International Centre, Bethseda, USA).

Since the barefoot doctors (paramedics) have been grafted into the public Health Service, mass preventative campaigns with public participation of barefoot doctors have led to a reduction in the mortality of infectious disease.

Chinese doctors were using Ephedra 5000 years ago for asthma. For an equal length of time they used Quinghaosu effectively for malaria. The Chinese first recorded goose-grease as the perfect base for ointments, its penetrating power endorsed by modern scientific research.

While Western medicine appears to have a limited capacity to cure eczema, a modern Chinese treatment evolved from the ancient past is changing the lives of many who take it. The treatment was brought to London by Dr Ding-Hui Luo and she practised it with crowded surgeries in London's Chinatown.

Chinese herbalism now has an appeal to general practitioners looking for alternative and traditional therapies for various diseases where conventional treatment has proved to be ineffective.

See entry: BAREFOOT DOCTOR'S MANUAL.

Address. Hu Shilin, Institute of Chinese Materia Medica, China Academy of Traditional Chinese Medicine, Beijing, China.

CHIRETTA. Chirata. *Swertia chirata*, Buch. *German*: Driesenenzian. *French*: Swertie. *Italian*: Swertia. *Indian*: Chirata. Entire plant.
Constituents: xanthone derivatives, iridoids, alkaloids, flavones.
Action: bitter tonic, digestive, liver stimulant, febrifuge, antimalarial, anthelmintic.
Uses. Feeble digestion, lack of appetite. Wasting and cachetic conditions. Used for malaria before discovery of Peruvian bark. Liver damage and complaints. "Ascites due to liver involvement." (*Baiter, 1871, Ghani, 1913*)
Preparations. Thrice daily.
Tea: half-1 teaspoon to each cup boiling water; infuse 15 minutes; dose: Half-1 cup.
Liquid Extract BHP (1983) 1:1 in 25 per cent alcohol. Dose: 2 to 4ml.
Powder: half-2 grams. GSL

CHIROPRACTIC. A system of skeletal manipulation to restore balance and normality in cases of structural derangement. A feature is their "high velocity: low amplitude thrust." A number of herbal lotions and massage oils assist the Chiropractor to relax muscles and prepare tissues for manipulation. See: ROSEMARY AND ALMOND OIL. STIFF NECK SALVE, GOLDEN FIRE.

Chiropractors stress the importance of X-raying patients before applying manipulation. "Patients treated by chiropractors," reported the Medical Research Council in the British Medical Journal, "were not only no worse off than those treated in hospital but almost certainly fared considerably better and maintained their improvement for two years."

CHLAMYDIAL INFECTION. One of the many sexually transmitted diseases. Caused by the micro-organism *Chlamydial trachomatis*. Common among birds and animals and responsible for psittacosis, trachoma and urethritis. May be acquired by children at childbirth when it causes an eye disorder that may not be serious. Sexually acquired reactive arthritis in men may follow infection. Around 70 per cent PID cases in young women are due to the infection.
Symptoms. Irregular bleeding and moderate pain. Women can still have the infection but no symptoms. Damage to the fallopian tubes possible. Sterility may follow neglect.
Treatment. *Formula*. Echinacea 2; Goldenseal 1; Myrrh half. Mix. Dose: Powders: 250mg (one 00 capsule or one-sixth teaspoon). Liquid extracts: 15-30 drops. Tinctures: 30-60 drops. Thrice daily in water, honey or fruit juice.
Topical. Douche: 10 drops Liquid extract or Tincture Goldenseal in an ounce (30ml) Rosewater or Distilled extract Witch Hazel. If the condition persists for more than a month, add 10 drops Kava Kava.
Diet. Dandelion coffee.
On retiring at night. 2-3 Garlic tablets/capsules.
Treatment by a general medical practitioner or hospital specialist.

CHLOASMA. Increased pigmentation with light brown patches on the skin, especially in pregnancy where it appears as blotches on the face. Adrenal insufficiency. A side-effect of the contraceptive pill.
Treatment. Echinacea, Ginseng, Liquorice, Sarsaparilla, Wild Yam. (*A. Warren-Davis FNIMH*)
Tinctures. Formula. Ginseng 2; Wild Yam 1. Liquorice quarter; One 5ml teaspoon in water thrice daily.
Topical. Distilled Extract Witch Hazel. Cider vinegar.
Supplementation. Vitamin A B-complex. PABA.

CHLORELLA. An edible single-cell marine algae (a sea-moss, sea-lettuce) which contains more chlorophyll than many known foods, more Vitamin B12 than liver, producing protein 50 times more efficiently than other crops, including Soya and rice. Has the potential to solve the world's protein problems in the undeveloped countries. Contains: beta-carotene, polyunsaturated fatty acids; and 19 of the 22 amino acids, including the 8 essentials. A rich source of DNA/RNA, and of calcium iron, selenium and zinc.
Action: Liver detoxifier, hypotensive, antibiotic, metabolic stimulant. Bowel cleanser and nutrient for friendly flora. Immune sustainer. Antiviral. Anti-candida. Anti-ageing. Blood oxidant for production of red cells. Anti-cholesterol. Fat mobiliser.
Uses. High blood pressure, diabetes, hypoglycaemia, radiation sickness, high cholesterol levels, constipation, immune system insecurity, anaemia and nutrient deficiencies, bone maintenance, regeneration of tissue, asthma, the fatigue of old age. Shown to have a high binding affinity for poisonous substances in the gut and liver.
Inhibitory effect on growth of tumour cells. (*21st Japanese Bacteriology Convention, 1984*)
Reduces pain in peptic and duodenal ulcer. (*"The Treatment of Peptic Ulcer by Chlorella", by Dr Yoshio Yamagishi*)
Cases of arsenical poisoning due to contaminated Taiwan water supply were successfully detoxified. Dramatic height and weight increases in children and animals recorded. Appears to increase production of interferon, a body chemical that protects against harmful viruses. Of value for lead poisoning and heavy metal toxaemia.
Preparations. Available as tablets, capsules and health supplement granules.
Diet. Highly nutritional; yield 65 per cent protein; desirable for vegetarians and vegans. GSL

CHLOROPHYLL. Stored energy of the sun. The green colouring matter of plants. A catalyst that speeds or maintains a reaction. Promotes granulation tissue in healing of wounds and tissue building. Most herbs contain chlorophyll. Acts as an oxidant in body metabolism and enhances the effect of vitamins and minerals. To a plant, chlorophyll is what haemoglobin is to the human body.
Uses. Bad breath and offensive perspiration, gastritis, sore throat and mouth, skin conditions that refuse to heal, burns, suppurating wounds, athlete's foot. Cataract.
Preparations. Available as tablets, powders, green barley juice or essence.
Chlorophyll tablets (Potter's). Each tablet contains: 30mg Chlorophyll and 60mg Kola. (*Potter's Herbal Supplies, Wigan, England*)

CHLOROSIS. Simple iron-deficiency anaemia in teenagers; with sickly greenish grey or yellowish complexion.
Tea. Mix, equal parts: Agrimony, Lemon Balm, Raspberry leaves. 2 teaspoons to each cup boiling water; infuse 15 minutes. 1 cup freely. Honey for sweetening. Or: Burdock leaves, hot tea.
Tinctures. Formula: Black root 1oz (30ml); Echinacea 1oz (30ml); Peruvian bark half an ounce (15ml). 5ml teaspoon in water before meals thrice daily.
Cider Vinegar. 2 teaspoons to glass water,

morning and evening.
Floradix Formula Food supplement (Salus).

CHOKING. Obstruction from a fishbone – suck a lemon, which softens the bone and aids removal. Moisten gums with cider vinegar.

CHOLAGOGUES. A group of agents which increases the secretion of bile and its expulsion from the gall bladder. They are usually bitter and being slightly laxative and eliminative in character, are indicated in some liver diseases.

Aloe Vera, Artichoke, Balmony, Barberry, Belladonna, Boneset, Black root, Blue Flag, Boldo, Butternut, Chiretta, Dandelion, Fringe Tree, Fumitory, Gentian, Greater Celandine, Goldenseal, Heather flowers, Liquorice, Mountain Grape, Quassia, Wahoo, White Poplar, Wild Yam, Yellow Dock.

CHOLECYSTITIS. See: GALL BLADDER.

CHOLERA. The ancient disease cholera resurfaces from time to time. Thousands still die each year. It is an acute infectious disease caused by vibrio cholerae and is notifiable under the Public Heath (Control of Diseases) Act 1984. Human Carriers maintain infection. Incubation may be from a few hours to a number of days. See: NOTIFIABLE DISEASES.

It is spread by polluted water as in the case of the composer, Tchaikovsky, who died imprudently drinking unboiled water during a cholera epidemic, despite warnings of his friends. It is transmitted also by milk, shellfish and by the faeces of infected people.

Symptoms. Profuse rice-water diarrhoea, vomiting and shock from severe loss of body fluids. Muscle cramps, cyanosis, stupor.

Alternatives. *Powders*. Formula: Tormentil root 2; Ginger 8; Poplar bark 2; Ipecacuanha half; Gum Myrrh quarter; Cloves; Cayenne quarter; Slippery Elm 5. (*Reformed School of Medicine, W. Beach MD, USA*) No dosage recorded. Suggested hourly dose: Liquid Extract: 1 teaspoon. Tinctures: 2 teaspoons. Powders: 500mg.
Tinctures. Formula No 1. Turkey Rhubarb 3; Hops 2; Peppermint 1. Dose: 1-2 teaspoons in water hourly, as tolerated.
Tinctures. Formula No 2. Turkey Rhubarb 2; Camphor (spirits) 1; Capsicum quarter; Peppermint quarter. Dose: 1-2 teaspoons hourly, as tolerated.
Orange berries. (*Maeso lanceolata*) Tea drunk by natives before visiting cholera epidemic areas. (*Dr Isno Kufo, University of California, Berkeley*)
Barberry. Berberine alkaloid. (*Indian Journal of Medical Research, 50. 732, 1962*)
Camphor. In the Cholera epidemic of 1831, a Russian Consol-General reported 70 cases in two places, all were cured. Elsewhere, of 1270 cases only 108 died. Practitioner use: Spirits of Camphor (10 per cent Camphor in 90 per cent brandy, gin or Vodka). 0.3 to 2ml (5 to 30 drops). Effective in the early stages. Also, rub into soles of feet and use as an inhalant.
Calamint. Old European remedy.
Enema. Bring 2 pints (1 litre) water to boiling point. Allow to cool. Add 20 drops Goldenseal and 20 drops Tincture Myrrh; for soothing and healing injection.

Diet. During an outbreak of cholera: avoid unboiled or unbottled water, uncooked seafood, vegetables and fruit unless fruit can be peeled.

Strict sanitary hygiene. Wash hands frequently.
Recovery period. Replacement of body fluids: glasses of boiled water to which 2-3 teaspoons cider vinegar has been added. Make up potassium loss with 3-4 bananas daily. Calcium, Magnesium and Potassium. Multivitamins.
Alternative rehydration therapy: spring or bottled water with sugar and salt; salt to replace water in the blood, sugar to promote absorption. Glass of water to contain 1 teaspoon salt and 2 teaspoons sugar.

To be treated by a general medical practitioner or hospital specialist.

CHOLERETIC. An agent which reduces cholesterol levels by excreting cholesterol. It also causes bile to flow freely. Differs from a cholagogue in that the latter *increases* the flow of bile (Artichoke).

CHOLESTEROL. Cholesterol is a porridge-like substance found in animal fats: cream, whole milk, cheese, butter, meat, eggs, bacon, etc. There are two kinds of cholesterol in human blood serum, one of which is beneficial; the other, harmful if in excess. The beneficial, known as high density lipoprotein (HDL) is believed to keep down concentration of the harmful variety – low density lipoprotein (LDL). The desirable blood cholesterol level should be less than 5.2 mmol per litre. (*Government: "Health of the Nation"*)

Cholesterol is necessary for maintenance of brain and glandular system, the production of bile salts and certain hormones.

Excesses plug arteries with a gluey consistency. Fats may start furring up arteries from childhood, yet it may take many years for symptoms to develop. The more meat and dairy products eaten the more cholesterol is produced. 90 per cent cases of gall stones are composed of cholesterol. A link between coronary heart disease and high cholesterol levels is strong and consistent. Anger and hostility raise cholesterol level.

The first indication of narrowing of the arteries may be an attack of angina, severe chest pain occurring on exertion due to an inadequate supply of blood and oxygen to the heart muscle. No one should exceed a fat and cholesterol count of 40 per day. For those of moderate risk level, a count of below 30 is advised.

Dr Paul Durrington, consultant physician, Manchester Royal Infirmary and researcher in lipids, believes that 'reducing the amount of saturated fats in the diet and reducing weight are the most effective ways of lowering cholesterol levels'.

Treatment: same as for HYPERLIPIDAEMIA.
Diet. See: DIET – CHOLESTEROL.

CHRISTMAS ROSE. *Helleborus niger*. Part used: rhizome. *French*: Rose de Noël. *German*: Christwurz. *Italian*: Fior de Natale. *Spanish*: Eléboro negro. *Indian*: Kutki
Constituents: cardiac glycosides with Digitalis-like action. Enhances the organs of sense: mouth, nose and eyes.
Uses. Heart disorders.

An ingredient of Paracelsus's "Elixir of Life".

CHRISTOPHER, JOHN R. Well-known American herbal practitioner and writer. Books: *School of Natural Healing* (1976) – comprehensive herbal work commended to practitioners. *Childhood Diseases* (1976) Theory and practice of children's herbal medicine. Dr Christopher had many spectacular results hit the headlines, including one of his 'Walnut cures'. One of the worst cases of eczema reported in the United States Army was that of a soldier whose head was an eruptive mass. Known treatments were of no avail. Obtaining permission from the doctor concerned, he prepared his 'Walnut Tincture' by steeping Walnut shells in brandy for 3 weeks. Making a gauze cap to fit the man's head, he gave instructions for it to be kept moist with the Tincture 24 hours a day. Much to the amazement of the Army doctors concerned, the soldier was completely cured within one week.

CHROMATOGRAPHY. A laboratory technique for identification of herbs and their constituents, taking advantage of the different rates at which molecules diffuse through an absorbent column to separate them.

Herbs are composed of alkaloids, saponins, esters, oils etc. In order to trace these in sample plant material, a picture is taken by a process known as Thin-layer-chromatography (TLC) on which a silica-gel coated 'negative' makes visible a number of constituents.

To initiate this process, active constituents (alkaloids etc) are extracted and separated. Their separation is possible by dipping into a special solvent solution, after which the 'negative' is developed by spraying with a reagent that reveals the constituents in various colours. Each component of the plant has its own distinctive colour. Each herb has its own specific 'profile' which can be 'read' by the technician and checked against known control samples. Each plant can thus be accurately identified.

CHROMIUM. Trace element. Essential to human life. RDA 0.05 to 0.2mg. Key element in the glucose tolerance factor. Required by the pancreas to combat stress and to control blood sugar. The key metal in the glucose tolerance factor (GTF) known for its role in maintaining the correct balance of blood sugar. Low levels place pregnant mothers at risk.
Deficiency. Rare. Hypoglycaemia, arteriosclerosis, heart disease. Depression, irritability, sudden mood swings. A lack of Chromium may result in diabetes in young adults, and a craving for sweet foods (sugar, chocolate).
Body effects. Metabolism of sugars and fats. Blood sugar regulator. Builds up muscle. Lowers cholesterol levels. Encourages the body's insulin to perform effectively. Suppresses appetite – especially craving for sugar, chocolate etc. Sportsperson's mineral to build muscle and reduce fat.
Sources. Red meat, liver, kidney, cheese, mushrooms, wholegrain cereals, brewer's yeast, fresh fruits, nuts, honey, molasses, corn oil, raisins, grapes, beets, peppers, shellfish.

CHRONIC FATIGUE SYNDROME. See: MYALGIC ENCEPHALOMYELITIS (ME).

CHRYSANTHEMUM (GOLDEN). *Chrysanthellum americanum*. Whole plant.
Action: choleretic, hepatic, circulatory stimulant.
Uses. Circulatory disorders, varicose veins, menstrual problems, to protect against hardening of the liver in alcohol consumers. Rheumatism, gout. Heavy legs.
Preparations. *Tea*: 1 teaspoon to each cup boiling water; infuse 15 minutes. Dose: half a cup thrice daily.
Powder, capsules: 250mg. 3 capsules thrice daily before meals. (*Arkocaps*)

CIDER VINEGAR. Apple cider vinegar. Rich in potassium and other associated trace minerals. What calcium is to the bones, so is potassium to the soft tissues.
Action: detoxifier, antiseptic, anti-catarrhal, bitter, stomachic, antimicrobial.
Uses. Often successful against staphylococcal and streptococcal infection (impetigo, etc). High blood pressure, dizziness, overweight, chronic headache, chronic fatigue, chronic lack of stomach acid in old age, diarrhoea, mucous colitis, diverticulosis, Crohn's disease, nausea, vomiting, red-brick deposit in the urine. For shingles, to alleviate itching and burning: apply neat to skin, two-hourly day or night. The neat vinegar

applied, freely, for ringworm, varicose veins, and burns to remove smarting. To prevent night sweats, wipe down with neat vinegar.

Dosage is an individual matter. 1, 2 or 3 teaspoons to glass of water at each meal is helpful for destroying harmful bacteria in the digestive tract and to maintain good general health.

CIGARETTES. Herbal. Arabian. Smoking mixture containing:– Stramonium 50 per cent, Lobelia 15 per cent, Red Clover flowers 21 per cent, Aniseed 9 per cent. Traditional use: for relief of some pulmonary conditions.

CINCHONA BARK. Peruvian bark. Jesuit's bark. *Cinchona officinalis L.* Source of the alkaloid quinine used in the treatment of malaria. *German*: Chinabaum. *French*: Quinquina. *Italian*: China. Part used: stem-bark and root.
Constituents: quinoline alkaloids, (quinine is extracted from the bark) resin, tannins, glycosides.
Action: anti-protozoal, anti-cramp, anti-malarial, appetite stimulant, bitter, febrifuge, tonic.
Uses. Cinchona was named after the Countess of Cinchona, wife of the Viceroy of Peru who was cured of a malarial fever with the powdered bark. News of her recovery spread like wildfire through the high society circles of Europe which started a world demand for the bark.

Its temperature-reducing effect is felt by other fevers with shivering chill and violent shaking. Enlargement of the spleen due to abnormal destruction of blood cells. Iron-deficient anaemia. Atrial fibrillation of the heart. Alcoholism. Debility. For recovery from excessive diarrhoea, loss of blood and exhausting liver and gall bladder conditions. Persistent flatulence. Polymyalgia. Loss of appetite (with Hops).
Practitioner only use. The remedy is on the General Sales List, Schedule 2, Table A up to 50mg per dose (Rla); over 50mg per dose it is obtainable from a pharmacy only. Herbal practitioners are exempt up to 250mg per dose (750 daily).
Tincture (BPC 1949). Dose: 2 to 4ml.
Tonic Mineral Water. On open sale. A palatable way of taking quinine for malaria prevention.

CINERARIA MARITIMA. Dusty Miller. *Senecio maritimus L. German*: Aschenpflanze. *French*: Cendriette. *Spanish*: Cineraria. *Italian*: Cenerina. Originally an American plant. Now grows freely in Britain and the Continent. For affections of the anterior chamber of the eye. One or two drops of fresh sterilised juice instilled into the eye 2-3 times daily for several weeks have been known to remove cataract. Not used internally because of pyrrolizidine alkaloids.

CINNAMON BARK. *Cinnamomum zeylanicum* Blume. *German*: Zimtbaum. *French*: Cannelle. *Spanish*: Canela. *Italian*: Cannella. *Malayan*: Kayu manis. Dried inner bark, and oil distilled from bark and leaves.
Constituents: tannins, essential oil, coumarin.
Action: stimulant astringent to the stomach. Aromatic, antimicrobial, carminative, antispasmodic, anti-diarrhoea, anti-worm; a warming remedy for cold conditions. Haemostatic, anti-putrescent, antiseptic, vermifuge. "A stimulating effect on bone healing" (*Hamdard, Oct/Dec 1988, Vol XXXI No 4*) Anti-diabetic.
Uses. Weak digestion, feeble appetite, flatulence. vomiting, hyperacidity, to promote secretion of gastric juices. Irritable bowel, summer diarrhoea. Influenza and colds. Wasting and cachexia (5 drops oil in honey). Infestation: body lice (rub with oil). Chest complaints: massage chest with 3 drops oil to 2 teaspoons Almond oil. The tea is used by the Chinese to boost insulin activity.

Combines well with Chamomile for stomach upsets; with Elderflowers and Peppermint for influenza.
Preparations. Thrice daily, or as necessary.
Tea: Quarter of a teaspoon bark in cup of boiling water, hot tea, or other beverage, infuse 15 minutes.
Essence of Cinnamon: 10-20 drops in water or beverage.
Langdale's Cinnamon Essence.
Oil of Cinnamon: BP, 0.05 to 0.2ml.
Powder: half to 1 gram.
Liquid Extract BHP (1983) 1:1 in 70 per cent alcohol, dose 0.5 to 1ml. GSL

CINNAMON, CHINESE. Cassia bark *Cinnamomum cassia* Blume.
Action: antispasmodic, antidiarrhoeal, antimicrobial, anti-emetic, carminative, anti-putrescent, aromatic, febrifuge, mild analgesic.
Uses. Flatulent dyspepsia, colic, irritable bowel, diverticulosis. Influenza and colds. Leucorrhoea (5 drops oil in honey before meals). Lung affections: chest rub. Loss of weight and malaise Deficiency of stomach acid. Snakebite.
Preparations. Thrice daily, or more frequently in acute cases.
Tea: Quarter to half a teaspoon in each cup boiling water, hot tea or other beverage.
Tincture BPC (1949). Dose 30-60 drops (2-4ml).
Inhalant: Inhale steam from 20-30 drops oil or essence in 1 pint boiling water, with head covered
Chest-rub. 5 drops oil in 2 teaspoons Almond or Olive oil.

Not a front-line remedy. Much used to flavour medicines and toothpastes. Avoid in pregnancy.

Combines well with Ginger (equal parts). GSL

CIRCULATORY DISORDERS. Poor circulation may be due to a number of disorders including varicose veins, high or low blood pressure, arterio-sclerosis, thrombosis, phlebitis.

chilblains, anaemia, weak heart. A common cause is auto-toxaemia, calling for blood tonics and agents to assist elimination of wastes and poisons via the kidneys, skin and bowels.

Other causes requiring specific treatment are: thickening and narrowing of blood vessels, diabetes, Buerger's disease, Raynaud's disease (spasm of the arterioles and veins), arteritis. See appropriate entries.

As a protection against these diseases Garlic becomes increasingly popular. Control of blood fats through diet and exercise necessary.

Alternatives. Cayenne, Ginger, Hawthorn berries, Horseradish, Mustard, Prickly Ash bark, Buckwheat, Dandelion, Lime flowers, Mistletoe, Rosemary, Yarrow, Ginkgo.

Tea: Lime flowers, Hawthorn berries, Yarrow. Equal parts. Mix. Ginger, quarter part (or pinch of Red Pepper). Mix. 1-2 teaspoons to each cup water. Bring to boil. Remove vessel when boiling point is reached. Dose: 1 cup 2-3 times daily.

Tablets or capsules: Prickly Ash, Hawthorn, Mistletoe, Ginkgo.

Formula. Hawthorn 2; Yarrow 2; Prickly Ash 1; Ginger quarter. Dose: Powders: 500mg (two 00 capsules or one-third teaspoon). Liquid extracts: 1 teaspoon. Tinctures 2 teaspoons 2-3 times daily.

Practitioner. Liquid extracts: Hawthorn 2; Lily of the Valley 2; Prickly Ash 1; Tincture Capsicum (one-tenth part). Dose: 30-60 drops in water or honey, 2-3 times daily.

Diet and Supplements. See: DIET – HEART AND CIRCULATION.

CITRONELLA. *Cymbopogon winterianus*, Jowitt. Leaves.

Fragrant oil extracted from an Asian perennial grass. Rarely used internally.

Action: antirheumatic, strong insect repellent, febrifuge, diaphoretic, antispasmodic.

Uses: Muscular rheumatism.

External: Locally to repel insects and vermin.

CLARY. Clear-eye. *Salvia sclarea L. French*: Orvale. *German*: Muskatsalvee. *Spanish*: Salvia sylvestre. *Italian*: Salvia Sclarea. Part used: herb.

Action: anticonvulsive, sedative, stomachic, mucilage, antifungal, oestrogenic.

Uses. Weak stomach, indigestion, mild spasm, sleeplessness from over-excitability. A mucilage from the seeds is used as a soothing emollient for the eyes to allay inflammation or assist in removal of a foreign body. Old-time gardeners placed a single seed in the eye for removal of speck of dust. Is not advised for cases where orthodox oestrogens are prescribed. Menopause.

Preparations. Internal – Practitioner use only.

Liquid Extract. Dose, 2 to 4ml. Thrice daily, in water.

Aromatherapy. Essential oil, as an inhalant for hysteria, panic states.

To enhance relaxation of a hot bath – 5-10 drops. The oil is not used internally in the presence of uterine cancers, cysts, fibroids or endometriosis.

CLAUSTROPHOBIA. Unreasonable fear of crowded places and of being unable to escape from a confined space, with symptoms of breathlessness, tension and stress. Treatment as for anxiety. See: ANXIETY STATES.

CLEANSING HERBS. Typical formula. Senna 70 per cent; Buckthorn 5 per cent; Fennel 10 per cent; Mate 5 per cent; Elder 5 per cent; Psyllium seeds 5 per cent. Brownish green powder. Quarter of a teaspoon or more taken on retiring: children 5-10 years half this quantity, washed down with warm water. A combination of herbs, barks and seeds for the relief of occasional or non-persistent constipation.

CLINICAL ECOLOGY. Environmental medicine. Treatment of allergies by natural medicines. The science that endeavours to bridge physics and chemistry; including such disciplines as homoeopathy, acupuncture, herbalism, etc.

CLINICAL TRIAL. An investigation concerned with the administration of a medicinal product(s) on the supposition that it (they) may have a positive effect upon patients. The work is carried out under the supervision of a doctor(s) or suitably qualified staff to ascertain beneficial or harmful effects and to report.

CLIVERS. Cleavers. Goosegrass. *Galium aparine L. French*: Gratterton. *German*: Klebelabkraut. *Spanish*: Presera. *Italian*: Cappelo da tignosi.

Constituents: anthraquinone derivatives, flavonoids, iridoids, polyphonic acids.

Action. Lymphatic alterative and detoxifier, diuretic, astringent tonic, non-steroidal anti-inflammatory, anti-obesity, adaptogen, anti-neoplastic.

Uses: Enlarged lymph nodes, especially cervical neck nodes, cystic and nodular changes in the glands. Nodular goitre. John Wesley, evangelist, claimed that it dispersed some hard swellings (tea internally, poultice externally). Used in prescriptions for obesity until recent years. Even Galen wrote that it could make fat folk lean. For dry skin disorders (psoriasis, etc).

Urinary disorders: suppression, painful micturition, irritable bladder. Said to be a stone-solvent. Frequently used with Marshmallow for gravel. Dropsy (with Broom). Bed-wetting.

Cleansing drink for malignant conditions. The ancient world used it for cancer, but experiments fail to confirm.

Freckles: Clivers tea as a wash for skin.

Combination (traditional) for blood and glands: equal parts Ground Ivy, Bladderwrack and Clivers.
Combination for kidney and bladder: equal parts Uva Ursi, Buchu and Clivers: 1oz to 1 pint boiling water; infuse 15 minutes; half-1 cup thrice daily.
Combination for cystitis: equal parts Iceland Moss, Marshmallow and Clivers; prepare tea. Half-1 cup thrice daily.
Preparations. Thrice daily.
Tea. 1 teaspoon herb to each cup boiling water; infuse 5-15 minutes. Dose: half-1 cup.
Juice from fresh plant. 1-3 teaspoons. Terminal cases – half-1 wineglass or as much as tolerated.
Liquid extract, BHC Vol 1. 1:1, in 25 per cent ethanol. Dose: 2-4ml.
Tincture, BHC Vol 1. 1:5, in 25 per cent ethanol. Dose: 4-10ml.
Poultice: fresh plant crushed with aid of rolling pin. Applied cold.
Note. Eaten as a vegetable in China. GSL

CLOVES. Fragrant spice. *Eugenia caryophyllus*, Spreng. *Caryophyllus aromaticus*. *German*: Gewürznelken. *French*: Giroflier. *Spanish*: Jerofle. *Italian*: Garofano. *Indian*: Lovanga. *Arabian*: Karanaphal. *Chinese*: Ting-hsiang. *Malayan*: Karampu bunga chanke. Flower buds. Oil distilled from the buds.
Constituents: a heavy volatile oil, a camphor resin, flavonoids, sterols.
Action: Mild local anaesthetic for aching teeth. Carminative, aromatic, warming stimulant, powerful antiseptic, antineuralgic, antihistaminic, mild antispasmodic, spice.
Uses: flatulence, asthenia, diarrhoea, dyspepsia, measles, worms, hypothermia or 'cold' conditions. Asthma, bronchitis, pleurisy and lung conditions (external use, essential oil, as below).
An important ingredient of kitchen recipes.
Insect bites: oil rubbed into skin.
Gout: rub joint with oil as below.
Diabetes: to boost insulin activity. (*American Health, 1989, Nov 8, p69*)
Preparations. Cloves chewed or used in food.
External. 1-3 drops essential oil in 2 teaspoons Almond or other base oil. GSL

CLUB MOSS. Vegetable sulphur. *Lycopodium clavatum L*. Plant and spores.
At one time was popular for urinary disorders and chronic kidney disease, but no longer used internally. External use confined to irritable skin disorders as a soothing dusting powder. Once used as a vegetable snuff. Widely used in homoeopathy.

COBALT. Trace element essential to life.
RDA – none known. Has a vital relationship with Vitamin B12, a deficiency of which causes pernicious anaemia.
Deficiency. Anaemia, bowel disorders, nervousness, poor muscle tone.
Sources. Meats, liver, kidneys, eggs.

COCA LEAVES. Health Inca tea. Peruvian tea. Bolivian tea. *Erythroxylum coca*, Lam. Leaves. Leaves contain a minimal amount of cocaine.
A traditional remedy to prevent fatigue, to elevate mood, assuage hunger, increase pulse rate, stimulate the brain and nerves, and to enable great feats of endurance to be performed. Not on open sale; its use is discouraged. South Americans have been drinking coca leaf tea for hundreds of years apparently with no ill-effects and possibly some medical benefits. Natives drink 1-2 cups or more daily, as infused from decocainised leaves. Medical use: to assist withdrawal from cocaine addiction. Local anaesthetic. CD. (*Misuse of Drugs Act 1973*)

COCAINE ADDICTION. To assist withdrawal from: see COCA LEAVES.

COCCYDNIA. Pain in the 'tail bone' at the base of the spine. Cause usually ascribed to referred pain from lumbar disc tissue, neurosis or spasm of muscles of the pelvic floor. May be due to osteoporosis, old fractures, bony spurs or necrosis of blood vessels. The coccyx receives its blood supply from the median artery, damage to which contributes to avascularity of the coccyx.
Treatment. Osteopathy or plaster jacket immobilisation.
Alternatives. Ladyslipper, Barberry, Valerian, St John's Wort, Cramp bark.
Powders. Mix, equal parts: Barberry, Valerian, St John's Wort. 500mg (two 00 capsules or one-third teaspoon) thrice daily.
Tinctures. Formula. Equal parts: Hops, Valerian, St John's Wort. One 5ml teaspoon thrice daily, in water.
Practitioner. Tincture Gelsemium: 3-5 drops in water when necessary. For pain.

COCILLANA. Guapi bark. Grape bark. *Guarea rusbyi* Rusby.
Action: *expectorant* BHP (1983). Emetic.
Uses. Chronic bronchitis. Dry cough.
Preparations. Thrice daily.
Powder: dose, half- 1 gram.
Liquid Extract. BPC (1973), dose half-1ml.
Tincture, BHC, 1:10 in 60 per cent alcohol, dose 5 to 10ml.
Large doses cause vomiting and purgation. GSL

COCKROACH, The. The cockroach is a recognised source of infection, carrying more than 30 types of harmful bacteria and a dozen parasites. Infectious hepatitis and salmonella can be traced to this insect in whose body the latter may be harboured for as long as 42 days. Food can be dangerous for long periods when polluted. It will eat almost every item of human diet. When encountering exposed food it will over-indulge, then regurgitate contents of the stomach to make way for more.

The traditional repellent is Sweet Bay (*Laurus nobilis*) which is also used as external treatment for bite.

To prevent infection: Tincture Echinacea, 10-15 drops in water every 2 hours. See: SALMONELLA. INFECTIVE HEPATITIS.

Many asthma patients are allergic to presence of cockroaches.

COCOA. Cacao. *Theobroma cacao L.*

The fat is known as cocoa butter (oil of theobrom) used in the manufacture of chocolate and the beverage cocoa. Seeds contain caffeine which has a diuretic and stimulating effect. The fat is used in making ointments, pessaries, cosmetic creams and for treating wrinkles of eyes, neck or mouth.

COCONUT OIL. *French*: Cocotier. *German*: Kokospalme. *Italian*: Albero del cocco. *Indian*: Narikal. *Iranian*: Drakhte-bading. *Chinese*: Ye-taze. From the well-known fruit of the species of palm, *cocos nucifera*, the kernel of which contains 70 per cent of a fixed oil called Coconut oil or Coconut butter, used as an ingredient of emollient ointments, pessaries, suppositories, scalp creams and oils for increasing growth of hair. Caprylic acid is a natural food grade oil extracted from Coconut and is an important ingredient of the preparation "Capricin" for the control of candida albicans.

CODE OF ETHICS. The following rules are amplified in the official Code of Ethics observed by members of the National Institute of Medical Herbalists. Summarised as follows:–

Rule 1. Members shall at all times conduct themselves in an honourable manner in their relations with their patients, the public, and with other members of the Institute.

The relationship between a medical herbalist and his or her patient is that of a professional with a client. The patient puts complete trust in the practitioner's integrity and it is the duty of members not to abuse this trust in any way. Proper moral conduct must always be paramount in member's relationships with patients. Members must act with consideration concerning fees and justification for treatment.

Rule 2. No member may advertise or allow his or her name to be advertised in any way, except in the form laid down by the Council of the Institute.

Any form of commercialism in the conduct of a herbal practice is unseemly and undesirable. Particular considerations govern commencement of practice, partnerships, assistantships, door plates, signs, letter headings, broadcasts, etc.

Rule 3. Members shall comply at all times with the requirements of the Code of Practice.

Rule 4. Members shall not give formal courses of instructions in the practice of herbal medicine without the approval of the Council of the Institute.

Rule 5. It is required that members apply the Code of Practice to all their professional activities.

Rule 6. Infringement of the Ethical Code renders members liable to disciplinary action with subsequent loss of privileges and benefits of the Institute.

CODE OF PRACTICE. National Institute of Medical Herbalists.

1. It is illegal for anyone not a registered medical practitioner to attempt to procure an abortion: a member must not knowingly administer an abortifacient or known uterine muscle stimulant remedies to a pregnant patient, nor instruments for the purpose of procuring an abortion, nor assist in any illegal operation.
2. It is required that any intimate examinations on a patient of the opposite sex be conducted in the presence of a relative of the patient or a suitable assistant.
3. A member must not treat or prescribe any remedy for gonorrhoea, syphilis, or urinary affections of a venereal nature.
4. It is the duty of the practitioner to notify the District Medical Officer regarding any disease on the current list of notifiable diseases. In cases of industrial poisoning or accident the local district branch of the Health and Safety Executive should be notified.
5. A member must consider very carefully the implications of recommending a course of treatment contrary to the advice of the patient's registered medical practitioner or of not recommending referral to a registered medical practitioner in the case of serious disease or uncertain diagnosis. Members must be aware of their vulnerability in law on this issue and must ensure in such a case that all available information is given to the patient and that the patient makes the final decision without coercion.
6. A parent or supervising adult must be present at any treatment or examination of a child under the age of 16, or of a mentally-retarded patient.
7. The Data Protection Act means that any practitioner keeping patient's data on computer file must register under the terms of the Act.
8. A member must become familiar with the terms of the Medicine's Act 1968 and subsequent statutory instruments, notably the Medicines (Retail Sale or Supply of Herbal Remedies) Order 1977. Particular care should be taken to become familiar with the statutory maximum doses of those remedies listed in Schedule III of the latter order. Detailed records of prescriptions and dispensing must also be kept.

9. The Medicines Act further states that to claim exemptions from the restrictions on the supply of certain herbal remedies, the practitioner should supply said remedies from premises occupied by the practitioner and able to be closed so as to exclude the public.
10. The Medicines Act adds that to claim the said exemptions, the person supplying the remedy "sells or supplies it for administration to a particular person after being requested by or on behalf of that person and in that person's presence to use his own judgement as to the treatment required". The member should avoid treatment through telephone or postal contact, although repeat prescriptions may be supplied on this basis for a limited period.
11. Dispensing and labelling of medicines should at least comply with the terms of the Medicines Act. All medicines should be labelled to clearly indicate the correct dosage or other directions for use (especially for those remedies subject to a statutory maximum dose), and with the name and address of the practitioner and the date of dispensing.
12. A member should never claim verbally or in print to be able to cure any life-threatening or serious disease.
13. The distribution or display of letter headings, business cards or practice information should be compatible with the highest professional medical standards.

COELIAC DISEASE. See: GLUTEN-SENSITIVE DISEASE.

COFFEE. *Coffea arabica. French*: Cafier. *German*: Kaffeebaum. *Spanish*: Café. *Italian*: Albero del caffé. *Arabian*: ag. Kernels of dry seed.
Constituents: caffeine, aromatic oil, tannic acid, B vitamins.
Action. General stimulant, anti-emetic, anti-narcotic, diuretic.
Uses. A valuable agent medicinally but over-consumption may be followed by a wide range of symptoms. See: CAFFEINISM. Used for fatigue, drowsiness, headache and to reduce effects of alcohol.

Coffee stimulates the activities of all organs, increasing nervous and circulatory activity. An excess produces nervous agitation, restlessness and is the cause of many allergies. A direct heart stimulant, diuretic, it raises blood pressure hence is useful for revival in threatened heart failure or weakness.

Caffeine is present also in tea and cola drinks. Coffee is the most widely used psychotropic agent: any excess is associated with anxiety, depression and reduction of blood flow through the brain. Antagonistic to some drugs, but potentiates the action of aspirin and paracetamol. Rapidly rectifies over-dosing of many drugs. Taken with caution in pregnancy. Antidotes some poisons and neutralises therapeutic effects of many herbs. Should be avoided by those undergoing a course of herbal treatment.

Excess caffeine, as in coffee, tea, cola and chocolate, has been shown to be a factor in the development of fibrocystic breast disease in women, and breast cancer increased. (*Dr John P. Minton, in "Surgery"*)

Women who drank between 8 to 25 cups of coffee a day during pregnancy had children with an absence of fingers or parts of digits of hands and feet. A number of authorities claim a link between coffee and birth defects. Cases of pre-menstrual tension (PMT) have improved on giving up coffee.

Coffee depletes the body of B-vitamins.

COFFIN, DR ALBERT (1798-1866). Medical reformer. Fell victim of tuberculosis with severe pulmonary haemorrhages. Failing to respond to conventional medicine he accepted aid from Senecca Indians who took him into their care and treated him with simple herbal remedies, resulting in arrest of the profuse bleeding and a rapid return to normal health.

Prescribing botanic medicines for his patients from knowledge learned from his Indian friends, he met the famous medical botanist, Samuel Thomson, who taught him the elements of the craft. On his return to England lectures to his fellow doctors met with hostility. Persecution urged him to gather around him a small band of doctors and experienced laymen to study organic medicine; thus was formed the National Institute of Medical Herbalists.

Coffin left books: *"Botanic Guide to Health"* (1848) *"Lectures on Medical Botany"* (1850). He introduced Thomsonism into England thus combining British and American Herbalism.

Dr Coffin wrote: "Had we not been cured by a poor Indian woman, when all other means had failed, we should never have turned our attention to the vast resources in which nature abounds throughout the whole of her ample dominions, nor should we have dared to attempt such cures as have been performed." (*Botanic Guide to Health, by A.L. Coffin MD*)

COLA. Kola seeds. *Cola nitida. Cola acuminata. German*: Kolabaum. *French*: Café du Soudan. *Spanish*: Kola. *Italian*: Noci del sudan. *Malayan*: Kelapong. *Part used*: dried powdered seeds.
Constituents: Caffeine, theobromine, kolanin, gum, tannic acid, phenols.
Keynote: cerebro-spinal stimulant.
Action: Nerve tonic, anti-depressant, diuretic, astringent, anti-diarrhoeal. *Thymoleptic BHP (1983)*. Strengthens action of the heart by increasing its muscular power. Antidepressant. Stimu-

lates the central nervous system and strengthens the heart by increasing its muscular power.
Uses. Physical and mental exhaustion (jet-lag), brain fatigue, neurasthenia, convalescence, muscle weakness, headache, depression. Diarrhoea, dysentery. Contains caffeine which increases mental alertness, heart rate and passage of urine. Low blood pressure. Not given in presence of high blood pressure.
Traditional combinations: (1) with Damiana and Saw Palmetto for sexual weakness. (2) with Skullcap and Oatstraw for depression and nerve debility.
Burroughs and Wellcome (1900) issued a tabloid "Forced March" (Kola compound 5g) used during the South African war and continued until 1937. Today similar preparations exist for jet-travel and tired business-men.
Side-effects: over-excitability.
Preparations. Average dose: 1 to 3 grams. Thrice daily.
Decoction (powder). Half a teaspoon to each cup water gently simmered 10 minutes. Dose 1 cup. Powder/tablets: 1 to 3g.
Liquid Extract, BHC Vol 1. 1:1, 60 per cent ethanol. Dose: 0.6 to 1.2ml.
Tincture BPC (1934). 1:5 in 50 per cent alcohol. Dose: 1-4ml. GSL

COLCHICUM. Meadow saffron, Naked Ladies. *Colchicum autumnal L. German*: Herbstzeitlose. *French*: Tue-chien. *Spanish* Villorita. *Italian*: Colchico florido. Tincture made from the corm collected in early summer. Practitioner use only.
Constituents: colchicine, tannin, gallic acid, flavonoids.
Action: anti-gout, emetic, cathartic. Non-steroidal, anti-inflammatory.
Uses. Relieves inflammation and pain of acute gout but does not increase expulsion of uric acid. Used with an alkaline diuretic Used with caution, large doses producing nausea, diarrhoea and stomach irritation. Behcet's syndrome.
Preparations. *Liquid extract* of the corm, 2-5 drops every 2 hours until relief is felt: then thrice daily for one week.
Tincture Colchicum, BP 1973. dose, 0.5 to 2ml.
POM medicine.

COLDS. The common cold. A virus droplet infection of the air passages.
Symptoms: Red itching eyes, clear nasal discharge progressing to yellow and thick, slight sore throat, sneezing, mild fever, headache, blocked or running nose, malaise.

The alternative school of medicine believes a cold should not be suppressed with popular drugs of the day but allowed to run its course. That course may be dramatically reduced by use of herbs. A cold is sometimes an acute healing crisis in which Nature expels accumulated wastes and toxins. Diaphoretics promote sweating, aiding this process.
Alternatives. *Teas* may be made from any of the following: Elderflowers, Peppermint, Catmint, Bayberry, Boneset, White Horehound, Feverfew, St John's Wort.
Alternatives. Formulae:– Equal parts:– (1) Elderflowers and Peppermint. (2) Yarrow and Peppermint. (3) White Horehound and Hyssop. 1 teaspoon to each cup boiling water; infuse 5-15 minutes. 1 cup freely. A trace of Cayenne Pepper enhances potency and stimulates circulation.
Decoction. Prepared from Horseradish, Pleurisy root, Prickly Ash, Bayberry. Teaspoon, of any one, to two cups water gently simmered 20 minutes. Half-1 cup freely. Pinch of Cayenne enhances action.
Irish Moss. 1 teaspoon to 2 cups water simmered gently 20 minutes. Do not strain. Eat with a spoon with honey.
Powders. Composition. 1 teaspoon to cup of tea, or hot drink.
Powders. Formula. Bayberry bark 2; Ginger 1; Pleurisy root 1. Cayenne quarter. Sift. 500mg (two 00 capsules or one-third teaspoon) thrice daily.
Tablets/capsules. Lobelia. Iceland Moss. Vitamin C. Feverfew.
Essence of Cinnamon. Popular traditional herbal expectorant to help relieve symptoms of cold and flu.
Composition essence and Elderflowers and Peppermint. 2 teaspoons in hot water or cup of tea every 3 hours. Children less according to age.
Life Drops. See entry.
Practitioner. Colds with fever, cardiac excitability and distress out of all proportion to the infection: Tincture Gelsemium, 3-5 drops.
Laxative. A mild laxative may be advised (5-7 Senna pods, infused in cup of boiling water, or Senacot). A healthy bowel movement may cut short a cold by assisting elimination.
Aromatherapy. Few drops of any of the following antiseptic oils added to a bowl of boiling water, head covered with a towel, steam inhaled: Eucalyptus, Peppermint, Marjoram, Thyme, Niaouli. Oil of Camphor is most effective, but as it antidotes all other medicaments, should be used alone. Oil of Scots Pine (5-10 drops) used in bath. Tiger Balm. Olbas oil.
Diet. 3-day fast; no solid food, herb teas and fruit juices only. Citrus fruits (Vitamin C) in abundance. Hot lemon and honey.
Supplementation. Daily. Vitamin A (7500iu), B-complex (50mg), C (3 grams at onset: 2 grams every 3 hours thereafter).
Prophylaxis, winter months. Daily: Vitamin C (Rose Hip, Acerola, etc), Echinacea. 2 Garlic capsules at night to build-up body's resistance.

COLD – ON THE CHEST. Simple and uncomplicated. Sometimes a cold in the head will travel down to the chest with cough and difficult breathing. Tracheitis, bronchitis.
Alternatives. *Teas*. Boneset, Yarrow, Angelica. White Horehound, Hyssop.
Irish Moss. 1 teaspoon to 2 cups water gently simmered 20 minutes. Do not strain but eat with a spoon, sweetened with honey.
Tablets/capsules. Lobelia. Iceland Moss.
Foot-bath. Immerse feet in hot infusion of Chamomile or Mustard to divert blood to lower extremities.
Supplementation: Vitamin C, 2-3 grams daily.

COLD FEET. Due to poor circulation. Ginger, Cayenne Pepper condiment at meals, Essence of Cinnamon, Horseradish sauce, Mustard. Footbath: Chamomile or Mustard. Vitamins: Niacin, Pangamic acid. Honey.

COLD SORE. See: HERPES SIMPLEX.

COLI BACILLUS. Infections. Freshly-grated Horseradish root steeped in cup cold water for 2 hours. Remove root. 1 cupful freely, as tolerated. Papaya fruit.

COLIC. Spasm of the bowels, particularly the colon. Severe pain under the navel with nausea, vomiting. Patient writhes from side to side. Cause may be wind, acid bile, worms, constipation, food; aluminium, lead or other metal poisoning, strangulated hernia, appendicitis, adhesions.
Differential diagnosis: gallstones, menstrual difficulties, kidney stone.
Alternatives. Teas, any one. Roman Chamomile, Catmint, Fennel, Lovage, Caraway, Betony, Avens, Wormwood, Holy Thistle, Peppermint leaves, Aniseed, Tormentil.
Decoction, any one. Angelica root, Boldo, Calamus, Cardamom, Condurango, Coriander, Cramp bark, Ginger root, Liquorice, Wild Yam.
Tablets/capsules. Dandelion, Capsicum, Valerian, Wild Yam, Cramp bark, Blue Flag root.
Powders. Alternatives. (1) Calamus 2; Marshmallow root 1. Add pinch Cayenne. (2) Turkey Rhubarb plus pinch of Cayenne. (3) Wild Yam plus pinch of Cayenne. Dose: 500mg (one-third teaspoon or two 00 capsules) every 2 hours.
Tinctures. Formulae. Alternatives: (1) Angelica root 1; Wild Yam 1; Ginger half. Mix. (2) Dandelion 2; Wild Yam 1; few drops Tincture Capsicum. Mix. (3) Wild Yam 1; Galangal root half; Ginger half. Mix. Dose: 1 teaspoon in hot water every 2 hours.
Traditional German combination. Ginger, Gentian, Turkey Rhubarb.
Topical. Apply hot bran, oats, hops or Slippery Elm poultice, or Castor oil packs to abdomen.
Aromatherapy. Any one oil: Aniseed, Fennel, Mint, Garlic, Bergamot. Adult: 6 drops to 2 teaspoons Almond oil: child, 2 drops in 1 teaspoon Almond oil, for abdominal massage.
Enema. 1oz Catmint, Boneset or Chamomile in 2 pints boiling water. Strain, inject warm.
Diet. 3-day fast, with fruit juices and herb teas.
See: RENAL COLIC, COLIC OF PREGNANCY, CHILDREN.
Gripe water.

COLIC, INFANT. See that the infant's mouth completely latches on the nipple otherwise air-swallowing may cause colic.
Teas. Spearmint, Dill seeds or Roman Chamomile. 1 teaspoon to each cup boiling water infused until warm. Teaspoonful doses as necessary.
Aromatherapy. Gentle abdominal massage: 3 drops oil Chamomile in 1 teaspoon Almond oil. If not available, use warm Olive oil.

COLITIS. Whichever colitis, live yoghurt provides acidophilus bacteria to maintain a healthy bowel. To increase bulk and peristalsis: Ispaghula seeds or Agar-Agar (seaweed). See: ULCERATIVE COLITIS.

COLLAGEN. Collagen is the essential component of fibrous tissue. A protein in the form of fine fibrils bound together by molecular crosslinks, it is the substance that holds body tissues together, present in quantity in the skin and subcutaneous tissue, in interstitial tissue generally and in bone. It is formed by fibroblasts and is laid down by them in the process of wound repair after injury forming a scar. When weak or inadequate it stretches and tissues sag. In bone repair, with the aid of Vitamin C, collagen forms a callus in which new bone develops. In parts where circulation is poor or areas subjected to repeated trauma excess collagen may accumulate as a corn or callosity. (*John Cosh MD., FRCP*)
For deficiency states, including the "old before your time" look, and to promote repair of wounds: Bamboo gum, Carragheen Moss, Comfrey, Fenugreek, Horsetail, Marshmallow, Quince seeds, Slippery Elm, Wild Yam.
Diet. See: GENERAL DIET. Oily fish: see entry.
Supplementation. Vitamin C (1 gram thrice daily). Calcium, Zinc.

COLLAGEN DISEASES (Connective tissue diseases). Terms now largely discarded, referring to a group of rheumatic diseases of an auto-immune nature (mainly rheumatoid arthritis, systemic lupus, systemic sclerosis). Fibrous tissue and collagen are prominent in many of the lesions of these conditions, but collagen does not have a causative role.

COLLAPSE. A state of extreme prostration and weakness due to shock, haemorrhage, overwork,

surgery, or severe infective fever such as typhoid, etc.
Symptoms: cold sweat, sunken eyes, weak heart beat, reduced temperature, pallor, mental vacuity, icy coldness, low blood pressure.
Treatment. When patient is able to swallow. Recovery in quiet darkened room with electric blanket for extra warmth if cold. Herbal stimulants indicated. Life Drops, Composition powder or essence. Brandy.
Tincture Capsicum (Cayenne): Few drops in cup of tea with honey.
Tincture Camphor: 1 drop (on honey) every 15 minutes.

If patient is unable to swallow: rub gums with brandy or Tincture Camphor.
Supportive: Apply hot wet towels to anus; patient in squatting position. Sponge-down with Cider Vinegar (1) to hot water (20).

COLOSTOMY. Surgical excision to create an opening through the abdominal wall which serves as an artificial anus. Usually, part of the colon or rectum is removed because of obstruction by fibrous tissue or rectal carcinoma. It is possible by a change of bowel habits to maintain a convenient management routine. Stools are collected in a special bag over the opening in the abdominal wall. Faecal odours from the opening may be neutralised by eating charcoal biscuits or use of chlorophyll. Herbal mucilages assist stool consistency for easy evacuation: Ispaghula seeds, Carragheen Moss, Iceland Moss, Fenugreek seeds have proved of particular benefit.

For outbreak of infection: Echinacea, Goldenseal or Myrrh. Flatulence – Calamus, Dill, Chamomile flower (Roman), Cardamom seed, Fennel, Calumba, Lemon Balm.

If the stoma is large it may be difficult to fit with a bag; exoriation is caused by leakage, requiring a soothing demulcent cream or ointment: Aloe Vera, Comfrey, Marshmallow. Recurrent Crohn's disease may cause fistula or abscess formation for which combined tinctures of Echinacea (2 parts), Myrrh (1 part) and Goldenseal (1 part) are indicated: dosage, 10-20 drops thrice daily in water.
For local sepsis: Calendula cream or ointment.
For bleeding around the stoma: Witch Hazel water or Calendula lotion.
For maintenance, healthy bowel function thereafter: 2 teaspoons Fenugreek seeds in cup warm water, soak overnight; drink (together with seeds) over the course of the following day.

COLTSFOOT. Coughwort. *Tussilago farfara L.* *German*: Huflattich. *French*: Tussilage. *Spanish*: Tusilago. *Italian*: Tossalaggine. *Arabian*: Fanjiun. *Indian*: Watpan Afangium. Leaves, flowers.
Constituents: flavonoids, mucilage, pyrrolizidine alkaloids.
Action: anticatarrhal, relaxing expectorant, demulcent bitter, diuretic. Immune stimulant. Antispasmodic. Anti-inflammatory. Antitussive.
Uses. Relief of dry unproductive irritative cough, smoker's cough, whooping cough, bronchial asthma. Dr J. Cullen found a strong decoction of the leaves beneficial for tuberculosis. Dr E. Percival found it useful in hectic diarrhoea. Has been used with limited success in silicosis and pneumoconiosis. Rubbed herb once used as smoking mixture for bronchial conditions.
Combination. Dried herb: equal parts: Coltsfoot, Thyme, White Horehound. Mix. 1oz to 1 pint water gently simmered 5 minutes. Dose: half-1 cup thrice daily.
Preparations. Thrice daily.
Decoction. Half a teaspoon to each cup water gently simmered 5 minutes: dose – half-1 cup.
Liquid Extract. 1-2ml.
Tincture BHP (1983): 1:5 in 45 per cent alcohol: dose 2-8ml.
Note. Recent research advises external use only. Alternatives Thyme and Elecampane preferred for internal use. Not used in pregnancy or lactation. GSL

COMA. Deep unconsciousness in which all reflexes are absent.
Causes: reaction to drugs or alcohol, stroke, epileptic seizure, skull injury, diabetes, uraemia.
Inhalant: Eucalyptus oil.
Foot rub. Capsicum ointment or stimulating lotion.
Rub into gums: Dilute spirits of Camphor or brandy.
Supportive. Patient is usually cold. Induce warmth, but not by placing hot water bottle near the skin.

COMBINATIONS, FORMULAE. In the evolution of herbal medicine it was discovered that some remedies have affinities and assist others in therapeutic action. An older generation of herbalists learnt how to 'blend' herbs according to their properties. Although empiric, such intelligent observation over centuries has developed into lore handed down as traditional medicine.

Use of herbs in combination enhances activity of the mild ones and modifies effects of the strong. Volatile properties of one may be kept in balance by opposing alkaloids, glycosides, etc.

Present practice views with disfavour the combination of several remedies, approval being given to a maximum of no more than four plant substances.

Herbs may be combined in equal parts or in specific proportions; i.e. Elder 4, Ladies' Mantle 3 and Pulsatilla 1: represent Elder 4 parts, Ladies' Mantle 3 parts and Pulsatilla 1 part.

The object of combining medicines is (a) to

augment, correct or modify the action of a remedy, (b) to obtain a joint operation of two or more remedies, (c) to obtain a new medicine and (d) to afford a suitable form for administration.

"A combination of similar remedies will produce a more certain, speedy and considerable effect than an equivalent dose of any single one." (*Fordyce*) Some herbs used singly may be of little use, their true value lying in a correct combination. Referred to as polypharmacy where a number of remedies are used in one prescription.

COMBUDORON OINTMENT. For relief of minor burns and scalds. Anthroposophic.
Constituents: Urtica urens herba tincture (1:2) 9.5 per cent. Arnica montana planta tincture (1:2) 0.5 per cent. (*Weleda*)

COMFREY. Knitbone. *Symphytum officinale, L. French*: Grande consoude. *German*: Reinweld. *Italian*: Consolide maggiore. *Part used*: root and leaves. Considerable therapeutic versatility.
Constituents: allantoin, pyrrolizidine alkaloids (fresh young leaves and roots), mucilage, phenolic acids, steroidal saponins (root).
Action: astringent-demulcent, haemostatic, vulnerary. Rapid healer of flesh and bones by its property to accelerate mitosis (cell-division). Useful wherever a mucilaginous tissue restorative is required (repairing broken bones and lacerated flesh), especially in combination with Slippery Elm powder which prevents excess fluidity.
Uses. Ulceration anywhere along the gastro-intestinal tract; colitis, hiatus hernia.

Bleeding from stomach, throat, bowel, bladder and lungs (haemoptysis) in which it reduces blood clotting time. Once used extensively for tuberculosis (pulmonary and elsewhere). Irritating cough, 'dry' lung complaints; pleurisy. Increases expectoration. Should not be given for oedematous conditions of the lungs.

Bones – fractures: to promote formation of a callus; rickets, wasting disease. Skin – varicose ulcers and indolent irritating sores that refuse to heal. Promotes suppuration of boils and gangrene as in diabetes. Bruises. STD skin lesions, internally and externally. Blood sugar control: assists function of the pancreas. Urine: scalding. Rheumatoid arthritis: improvement reported. Malignancy: cases of complete regression of sarcoma and carcinoma recorded. Rodent ulcer, (as a paste).
Preparations: thrice daily.
Tea: dried herb, one heaped teaspoon to each cup; or, 1oz to 1 pint boiling water; infuse 15 minutes, half-1 cup for no more than 8 weeks.
Tincture (leaf). 1 part to 5 parts alcohol: dose 2.5-5ml. Maximum weekly dosage – 100ml for no more than 8 weeks.
Tincture (root). 1 part to 5 parts alcohol. Maximum weekly dosage – 80ml, for 8 weeks. (*National Institute of Medical Herbalists*)
Poultice. A mucilage is prepared from fresh root in a liquidiser or by use of a rolling pin. For sprains, bruises, severe cuts, cleaning-out old ulcers and wounds.
Compress. 3 tablespoons crushed root or powder in 1 pint (500ml) water. Bring to boil; simmer gently 10 minutes. Saturate linen or suitable material and apply. Renew 2-3 times daily as moisture dries off.
Ointment. 1 part powder, or liquid extract, to 10 parts base (cooking fat, Vaseline, etc).
Oil (external use). Ingredients: powdered Comfrey root in peanut oil and natural chlorophyll. (*Henry Doubleday Research Association*)
Notes. Contains trace element germanium, often given for cancer and arthritis. (*Dr Uta Sandra Goodman*) Helps eliminate toxic minerals. Neutralises free radicals that are created by toxic substances entering the body. Restores the body's pH balance disturbed by highly acid foods such as meat, dairy products, refined foods and alcohol.

Dr H.E. Kirschner, well-known American physician, reported being called to the bedside of a patient with a huge advanced cancer of the breast. The odour was over-powering and the condition hopeless, but he advised poultices of fresh crushed Comfrey leaves several times daily to the discharging mass. Much to the surprise of all, the vile odour disappeared. The huge sore scaled over and the swelling subsided. Within three weeks the once-malignant sore was covered with a healthy scale and the pain disappeared. Unfortunately, treatment came too late; metastases had appeared in the liver which could not be reached by the poultices.

Claims that Comfrey is a toxic plant are unsubstantiated by a mass of clinical evidence to the contrary. Attempts to equate the effects of its isolated compounds apart from the whole plant yield conflicting results. For thousands of years the plant has been used by ancient and modern civilisations for healing purposes. Risks must be balanced with benefits.

There is a growing body of opinion to support the belief that a herb which has, without ill-effects been used for centuries and capable of producing convincing results is to be recognised as safe and effective.

Experiments reveal that in sufficient doses Comfrey can cause liver disease in laboratory animals. Its risk to humans has been a matter of serious debate since the 1960s, and is still unresolved. Although the overall risk is very low, a restriction has been placed on the plant as a precautionary measure. Fresh Comfrey leaves should not be used as a vegetable which is believed to be a health risk. It is believed that no toxicity has been found in common Comfrey (*Symphytum officinale L*). No restriction has been placed on use of dried Comfrey leaves as a tea.

The debate continues.

It would appear that use of the root of Symphytum officinale may be justified in the treatment of severe bone diseases for which it has achieved a measure of success in the past, such as rickets, Paget's disease, fractured bones, tuberculosis, etc, its benefits outweighing risks. Few other medicinal plants replenish wasted bone cells with the speed of Comfrey.

GSL (external use only)

COMMINUTION. To reduce crude herbal material to particles of varying size – to small segments or to pulverise into powder by a pestle and mortar or otherwise. To crush with a rolling pin.

COMMITTEE ON SAFETY OF MEDICINES. The Committee for safety of medicines was set up in 1963 after the thalidomide disaster. It is an advisory committee which examines drugs before clinical trials, before a product licence is granted, and when passed for marketing. A product cannot be tested in the human body without the company holding a clinical trial certificate. A product licence is renewable after five years.

COMMUTER'S SYNDROME. A range of complaints blamed on the effects of commuting to and from work.
Symptoms: headaches, palpitations, skin complaints, sleeplessness, digestive disorders, chest pains and excessive perspiration. These may be due to exposure to unsatisfactory levels of bacterial and chemical pollution. Where symptoms are not due to any underlying condition, Ginseng, Gota Kola and Chaparral may usually be relied on.
Preparations: teas, tablets, liquid extracts. Professional woman's fatigue may be dispelled by German Chamomile tea.

COMPLEXION. To improve. Attention to thyroid gland. Thyroid deficiency produces a thick, coarse dry skin.
Internal: Teas: Red Clover leaves, Clivers, Chickweed.
Tablets/capsules. Blue Flag, Dandelion, Red Clover, Sarsaparilla, Echinacea, Poke root. Kelp (thyroid gland).
Topical. Preparations of Evening Primrose oil, Aloe Vera, Chickweed, Elderflowers, Marigold, Witch Hazel, Cucumber cleansing milk.
Astringent lotion. Half a cup of Witch Hazel, 1 teaspoon honey, half a teaspoon Aloe Vera gel, half a teaspoon cider vinegar. Combine.
Milk. Natural cleanser.
Bran Vinegar. Tablespoon bran in cup cider vinegar; infuse in gentle heat. To nourish the skin.
Diet. See: DIET – GENERAL.
Supplementation. Vitamins A, B-complex, C, D, E. Cider vinegar. Vitamin B6 Cod Liver oil.

COMPOSITION POWDERS. Alternatives.
1. Powders: 3oz Bayberry, 1oz Ginger, half Cinnamon, half an ounce Cloves, quarter of an ounce Cayenne. Sift. Mix. (*E.G. Jones MNIMH*)
2. 2oz Bayberry, 1oz Ginger, 1oz Pleurisy root, half an ounce Cayenne. Sift. Mix. (*Melville C. Keith MD*)
3. 2oz Poplar bark, 1oz Balmony herb, half an ounce Goldenseal, half an ounce Cinnamon, three-quarters of an ounce Cayenne. Mix. Sift. "This brought the American physiomedical doctors immortal fame." (*F.H. England MD*)

Dose: Quarter to 1 teaspoon in hot water, tea or honey. The powder may be fed into 00 capsules: 2-4 capsules swallowed or taken as above.

Composition powder is a harmless stimulant against winter's ills, influenza and for the first stages of fevers. Long traditional reputation for stomach and bowel disorders, cramp, collapse, circulatory stasis, fainting, hypothermia, to promote perspiration, to assuage moderate degree pain. In the elderly it was given to rekindle the fires of life when burning low. GSL

COMPRESSES. Fomentations. External applications to soften tissue, allay inflammation or alleviate pain. They may take the form of a piece of soft cloth or other suitable material folded double (1) wrung out in a hot herbal infusion or (2) lint or flannel wrung out in hot water to which has been added Liquid extracts or the essential oils of Aromatherapy.
Requirements. Basin, towel, kettle of water, piece of cotton wool, oilcloth, binder and safety pins.
Method: Place towel across basin; lay flannel on towel and press down. Pour on hot herbal infusion, decoction or tincture and thoroughly soak. Bring together ends of the towel and twist hands in opposite directions to squeeze out surplus fluid. Untwist towel, free the flannel, shake it out and apply direct to the skin. Smear affected skin with olive oil before application. Add a layer of cotton wool; cover with plastic or oilskin; bind in position and pin securely. Moisten compress when dry, every half hour or less.

Herbs commonly used: Chickweed, Comfrey, Elder, Linseed, Fenugreek seeds, Irish Moss, Marigold, Marshmallow, Mullein, Plantain, Slippery Elm, German Chamomile, Hounds Tongue.

CONCUSSION. Loss of brain function with unconsciousness. Cause: head injury or violent spinal jarring as when falling on the base of the spine.
Symptoms. Sudden drawing-up of knees, nausea, vomiting, pallor, shallow breathing, prostration, weak heart beat, irritability, amnesia.
Treatment. Bed rest. Protection of eyes against light. Admission to hospital in case of deep brain damage. Quietness. Tranquillisers, sedatives and

alcohol aggravate symptoms. If patient can swallow, alternatives as follows:–
Teas. St John's Wort (concussion of the spine). Skullcap (to ease headache). Ginkgo (cerebral damage).
Powders. Formula. Combine, St John's Wort 3; Skullcap 2; Oats 2; Trace of Cayenne. Dose: 750mg (three 00 capsules or half a teaspoon) two-hourly.
Tinctures. Formula as above, but with few drops Tincture Capsicum in place of Cayenne powder: 1-2 teaspoons in water hourly.
Tincture Arnica. (European practise) 2-5 drops in hot water usually sufficient to hasten recovery.
Topical. Distilled Extract Witch Hazel saturated pad over eyes and to wipe forehead.
Supplements. Vitamin B-complex. B6, C.

CONDURANGO. *Marsdenia cundurango*, Rchb. Condor plant sought by the condor eagle in the mountains of Ecuador and Peru. Dried bark.
Constituents: glycosides, essential oils.
Action: alterative, circulatory stimulant, stomach relaxant, bitter, adaptogenic, orexigenic.
Uses. Nervous indigestion, anorexia nervosa, neoplasm of stomach and intestines. Calms pain in stomach disorders following gastric ulcer and lessens vomiting (*Le Monde Medical Journal*). Condurango has found its chief use as a cancer remedy, especially those originating in epithelial structures, epitheliolma, etc. (*John Clarke MD*)
Preparations. Thrice daily.
Powder: 1-4g in honey, or milk.
Liquid Extract. Dose: 2-4ml. (30-60 drops) in water.
Tea: 1-4g to cup boiling water. Half-1 cup. GSL

CONFUSIONAL STATE. An acute distressing symptom in elderly and very young people. 'Lack of clarity in thinking.' Mild brain failure. Temporary character-change and alteration in behaviour. Absence of classical symptoms of illness. Cannot formulate answers.
Diagnosis: dementia requires six months mental impairment, whereas acute confusional states may develop in a few days. Distinguish from Alzheimer's disease.
Causes: Oxygen deficiency in the tissues (Vitamin E). Toxaemia (eliminatives). Delirium (nerve relaxants). Infections (Echinacea). Metabolism (Dandelion). Drugs (Ginseng). Hypothermia (Cayenne). Nutritional (Slippery Elm, thiamine).
Tea. Combine herbs, equal parts: Agrimony, Skullcap, Balm. 2 teaspoons to each cup boiling water; infuse 5-15 minutes. 1 cup freely.
Ginkgo: Favourable results reported.
Vitamins. B-complex. B12. Thiamine. E (1000iu daily).
Minerals. Dolomite. Zinc.

CONGESTION. Engorgement of blood vessels due to circulatory disturbance or poor venous return circulation of blood to the heart.

CONJUNCTIVITIS. Acute red eye. Inflammation of the conjunctiva. Allergic or infective. Fifty per cent cases in hay fever season are due to allergy.
Causes: environmental chemicals, drugs, feathers, animal hairs. Infections include staphylococcus, pneumococci, herpes, gonococcal (rare). Conjunctivitis never causes persistent visual disturbance.
Symptoms. Watery discharge, itching, blood vessels visibly engorged, sensation of grit, mucopus discharge may cause lids to stick together.

A casual attitude to Conjunctivitis can no longer be justified. Prolonged use of antibiotics and corticosteriods is best avoided, where possible. Eye infections of virus origin become more common. A simple douche with herb teas enables eyes to stay clear of most minor infections. If 'red eye' does not clear within 3 days refer to Eye Department of a modern hospital, especially infections from herpes (shingles).
Treatment. *External.* The following soothe and do not exacerbate herpes or cause glaucoma: Eyebright, Chamomile, Marshmallow, Mullein, Marigold, Fumitory, Rose petals, Melilot, Plantain, Elderflowers, Fennel, Rue, Raspberry leaves, Witch Hazel, Aloe Vera gel, Borage. Conjunctivitis of infants – Elderflowers, Rosewater.
Douche. 1 teaspoon any of the above herbs to cup boiling water; infuse 15 minutes. Strain. Half-fill eye-bath for tepid douche freely. Separate baths for each eye.
Internal: tablets, liquid extracts, tinctures or powders: Echinacea, Goldenseal, Myrrh, Garlic (juice, corm or capsules freely – not to children).
Dr Alfred Vogel. Apply white of an egg.
Supplements. Daily. Vitamin A 7500iu, Vitamin B2 10mg, Vitamin C 3g, Vitamin E 400iu. Zinc. Cod Liver oil.

CONNECTIVE TISSUE. Tissue that supports other tissues or organs, i.e., fibrous tissue of ligaments or cartilage covering the ends of bones in joints. To strengthen: Horsetail, Knotgrass. See: COLLAGEN.

CONSTIPATION. Failure of contents of the large bowel to be evacuated due to inactivity, chemical laxatives, ignoring body signals that the body is full, obsession with bowel movements, piles, diverticulosis with small pockets from the colon, lack of exercise, spastic condition, low-fibre foods, poor eating habits, nervous stress. Waste products stagnate, changing behaviour of intestinal flora friendly to the body and necessary for breakdown of food. Toxins formed from re-absorption may be the cause of chronic disease.

Constipation is usually due to an underlying condition which requires primary treatment: i.e. anaemia.

The habit of taking purgatives lessens ability of the bowel to do its work. Gentler-acting remedies are advised: Isphagula (Psyllium seeds, light). In prescriptions, it is good practice to include a remedy for the liver (Barberry, Wahoo) and the digestive system (Dandelion, Liquorice). For constipation of pregnancy – see PREGNANCY.

Alternatives. *Senna*. 1-2 teaspoons leaves or 5-7 pods to cup cold water left to stand overnight.

Combined tea. Equal parts: Senna leaves, Chamomile flowers, Fennel seeds. 1-2 teaspoons to each cup boiling water; infuse 15 minutes. 1 cup, evening.

Psyllium seeds (Ispaghula, pale) 1, 2, 3 or more teaspoons aided down with sips of water, morning or evening.

Decoctions. Any of the following: Black root, Blue Flag, Buckthorn, Cascara sag, Dandelion root, Turkey Rhubarb, Wahoo, Yellow Dock.

Tablets/capsules. Dandelion. Calamus. Blue Flag. Seaweed and Sarsaparilla. Turkey Rhubarb. Damiana. Senokot.

"Natural Herb Tablet": Holy Thistle 60mg; Aloes BP 50mg; Fennel powder BPC 15mg; Myrrh powder BPC 15mg; Extract Skullcap 10mg; Powdered Valerian BPC 30mg; Powdered Lime flowers BPC 1949 30mg. Two or more tablets as necessary. Variations of this formula are on sale throughout Europe and the UK.

Powders. Combinations. Alternatives. (1) Turkey Rhubarb, with trace Cayenne. Use powder, or rubbed Rhubarb root with aid of kitchen grater. (2) Equal parts: Barberry, Liquorice, Senna pods. (3) Turkey Rhubarb 6; Slippery Elm 1; Liquorice 1. (4) Senna 70; Buckthorn 5 Fennel 10; Mate 5; Elder 5; Psyllium (pale) 5. Dose: 500-750mg (2-3 00 capsules or one-third-half a teaspoon) once or twice daily, as necessary.

Tinctures. Formulae: (1) Turkey Rhubarb, with trace of Capsicum. (2) Dandelion 2; Cascara sag, 2; Barberry 2; Liquorice 1; Tincture Ginger half. Half-2 teaspoons in hot water, evening.

Standard sales. A large number of preparations are on sale including Potter's "Lion Cleansing Herbs", Monastery herbs, Priory herbs. Fybogel Orange to increase bulk in colon. Regulan, for high fibre regimen.

Enema or gravity douche: half an ounce Chamomile flowers to 2 pints boiling water allowed to cool. Inject warm; repeat twice weekly until normal function is established.

Diet. Milk-free diet often curative. Teaspoon powdered Agar Agar with meals once or twice daily. Prunes soaked overnight. Yoghurt. Crude black molasses. Increase fibre-foods. Dandelion coffee.

Hay Diet. Impressive results reported.

Supplementation. Cod Liver oil.

Vitamins: A. B-complex, Thiamine, Niacin, C. P (bioflavonoids).

Minerals: Calcium. Potassium. Zinc.

CONTACT LENS FATIGUE. Irritation, soreness, friction, inflammation. "People who use extended-wear soft contact lenses are more likely to develop serious microbial keratitis infection than users of other lenses." (*Research team, Moorfields Eye Hospital, London*) Risk of keratitis was seen to increase when soft lenses were worn for more than six days.

Alternatives:– *Douche*. Simple teas: Fennel or German Chamomile; half a teaspoon dried herb or teabag to cup boiling water. Infuse 15 minutes. Half-fill eye-bath and use as douche, tepid. OR: quarter of a teaspoon distilled extract Witch Hazel in eye-bath; half-fill with water. Natural lubricant for contact lens is Evening Primrose oil (contents of a capsule). See: EYES, INFECTION.

Supplements. Daily. Vitamin A 7500iu, Vitamin B2 10mg, Vitamin C 400mg, Vitamin E 400iu, Beta carotene. Zinc 15mg.

CONTRA-INDICATED. Not indicated. Against medical advice. A remedy which is contra-indicated is unsuitable for use.

CONTUSIONS. See: BRUISES.

CONVALESCENCE. During the period of recovery from the passing of an illness to normal health the individual may still be weak, requiring adequate rest and rehabilitation. Restorative herbs include:

Alternatives. *Teas*. Alfalfa, Oats, Ginseng, St John's Wort, Vervain, Yarrow.

Carragheen Moss. See entry.

Decoctions. Angelica root, Echinacea, Fenugreek seed, Fringe Tree bark.

Gentian root. 1 heaped teaspoon to each cup cold water steeped overnight. Half-1 cup thrice daily. Popular German tonic.

Tablets or capsules: Damiana, Ginseng, Echinacea, St John's Wort. Siberian Ginseng.

Angustura: see entry.

Powders. Formula: Siberian Ginseng 2; Gentian 1. Pinch Cayenne. Dose: 500mg (two 00 capsules or one-third teaspoon) thrice daily.

Dr Charles Millspaugh. "Bark of the root of Fringe Tree as a tonic after a long and exhaustive illness is one of great merit." (Tincture 1:5 in 45 per cent alcohol BHP (1983); dose 2-3ml thrice daily)

Diet. See: DIET – GENERAL. Avoid alcohol, smoking, coffee and other caffeine drinks. Slippery Elm gruel.

CONVULSIONS. Seizure, fit. Muscular spasms with alternate contraction and relaxation of muscles arising from brain disturbance. Epilepsy.

Occurs when serum calcium, serum magnesium, or blood sugar is low. Feverish conditions are responsible for most convulsions in children. This is where herbal anti-febrile agents are helpful: Chamomile, Peppermint, Catnep, etc. Many parents unwittingly help to provoke a febrile convulsion.

Treatment would depend on diagnosis which may be one of a number of conditions: alcoholism, toxic drugs, meningitis, epilepsy, diabetic coma, dentition, expanding brain tumour, excessive crying or coughing – as in whooping cough, bowel irritation, emotional upset.

Symptoms. Aura, crying out, heavy breathing, loss of consciousness, rigidity, incontinence of urine and faeces.

Treatment. Cause the body to lose heat. For insulin coma give glucose, honey, or something sweet. Remove tight clothing. If the case is a child, lay on its side; sponge with cold water. If available, insert Valerian or other relaxant herb suppository. Catnep tea enema brings relief (*Dr J. Christopherson*).

Teas. Any one: German Chamomile, Hops, Lobelia, Motherwort, Passion flower, Skullcap, Wood Betony.

Decoctions. Any one: Cramp bark, Black Cohosh, Blue Cohosh, Skunk Cabbage, Valerian, Lady's Slipper.

Tinctures. Any one: Cramp bark, Black Cohosh, Blue Cohosh, Lobelia, Valerian, Wild Yam, Lady's Slipper. OR: Formula – Equal parts: Black Cohosh, Blue Cohosh, Valerian. Dose: 1 teaspoon in hot water, every half hour.

Camphor, Tincture or spirits of: 2-5 drops in honey or bread bolus offers a rapid emergency measure for adults. Inhalant also.

Peppermint, Oil. 1-2 drops in honey or milk.

Practitioner. Tincture Gelsemium BPC 1983. Dose: 0.3ml in water.

Supplements, for prevention: Calcium lactate 300mg 6 daily. Magnesium. Vitamin B6.

COPAIBA. Balsam copaiva. *Copaifera langsdorffi*, Desf. Oleoresin obtained by cutting deeply into trunk of the Copaiva tree.

Constituents: volatile oil, terpenic acids, resins.

Action. Antiseptic (urinary), carminative, alterative, diuretic, stimulant, cathartic.

Uses. Chronic inflammation of the genito-urinary tract, mild STD attacks, for its antiseptic effect. Chronic catarrh of the bladder, vagina and of the respiratory organs. Pruritus of anus and genitals. Irritable bladder of old women. Leucorrhoea.

Preparations. Because of its disagreeable taste it is usually given in capsules. Oil of Copaib: dose, 5 drops, thrice daily. Combined with alkali diuretics.

Lotion: oil of Copaiva 1 part, Glycerine 10 parts.

COPPER. Important nutrient. Required for conversion of iron into haemoglobin. See: HAEMOGLOBIN. Tyrosinase is organic copper and as such is the missing link between anaemia and iron. Copper has long been known as a preventative and treatment for anaemia. Its levels increase steadily during pregnancy. A lack of the metal turns the hair white and predisposes to schizophrenia. If allowed to accumulate in the body its effect may be toxic. High levels are mostly found in high blood pressure, smokers and those with heart failure.

While deficiencies are not common, it increases red blood cell count, maintains bone health and strength, and assists enzyme function.

Copper is "pro-oxidant", promoting formation of free radicals (highly unstable molecules capable of damaging walls of arteries when in excess). Potential narrowing of arteries may occur when high levels of copper are present with a high LDL cholesterol and low Selenium. RDA 0.05 to 0.2mg.

Sources. Calves liver, kidney, shellfish (especially oysters), brewer's yeast, chocolate, Brazil nuts.

CORIANDER. *Coriandrum sativum, L. German*: Koriander. *French*: Coriandre. *Spanish*: Cilantro. *Italian*: Coriandro. *Russian*: Coriandro. The Persians grew Coriander as a mild antiseptic and spice over 3000 years ago. It added fragrance to the Hanging Gardens of Babylon. Contains volatile oil, coumarins, phenolic acids, sterols, etc.

Action: stimulant, carminative. The aromatic herb contains a volatile oil, warming to the stomach and dispelling wind. Aromatherapists discover its use as an anti-rheumatic.

Uses. Well-known Chinese remedy for measles. Schistosomiasis. Hypoglycaemic and of value in diabetes. Aerophagy (air-swallowing). Gastro-enteritis.

Preparations. The tea serves as a gripe water for infant's colic. Half-1 teaspoon bruised seeds to each cup boiling water: cover with saucer to prevent escape of volatile oil. Drink before meals or as necessary for flatulence.

Powder: Half-1 gram, thrice daily.

Liquid Extract: Half-2ml in water thrice daily.

Aromatherapy. For rheumatic muscles and joints, lotion: 1 part oil of Coriander to 10 parts Almond oil. GSL

CORN SILK. Stigmata maidis. *Zea mays, L. German*: Turkisches Korn. *French*: Maïs. *Arabian*: Durah shami. *Iranian*: Khôshahe-makki. *Chinese*: Yu-kao-liang. *Malayan*: Jagung. Dried silky flower threads of maize. Constituents include: rutin, flavonoids.

Constituents: allantoin, saponins, Vitamin C and K.

Keynote: kidneys and bladder.

Action: antilithic, mild stimulant, *soothing urinary demulcent, diuretic*.
Uses. Kidney and bladder disorders. Cystitis, uncontrollable bladder, retention, pus in the urine, bed-wetting, prostate gland enlargement, irritation of the urinary tract by phosphatic and uric acids, urethritis, expulsion of gravel. Gonorrhoea, in combination with powerful alteratives: Yellow Dock, Burdock, Queen's Delight.

Heart failure with oedema and scanty urine; used with success. (*William Boericke MD*) Chronic malaria – in strong infusion the shucks have been used with success. (*Dr E.C. Lowe*) Nephritis (with equal parts Marshmallow) for temporary relief. Its value is increased by adding to it (equal parts) Dandelion root and Shepherd's Purse herb. (*J.H. Greer MD*) Of special value for bed-wetting: with Agrimony herb (equal parts). Diabetes. (*Chinese medicine*)
Preparations. It is a consensus of professional opinion that the infusion (tea) is the best form. 3-4 teaspoons to each cup boiling water; infuse 15 minutes; drink freely.
Liquid Extract: 1-2 teaspoons, in water.
Tincture: 1-3 teaspoons, in water. GSL

CORNS, BUNIONS. A bunion (hallux valgus) is a bony prominence on the inner side of the foot at the base of the big toe due to injury, flat feet, arthritis or narrow shoes. A corn (clavus) is an area of thickening and hardening of the skin, worse from friction or pressure on the toes.

Relieve pressure on the tender area by use of thick felt rings.
Alternatives. *Internal* (to reduce inflammation). Prickly Ash, Lignum Vitae (Guaiacum). Celery seed tea for elimination of uric acid.
Topical. Lobelia, Comfrey or St John's Wort fomentation. Zinc and Castor oil ointment or cream. Comfrey cream. Bind a slice of lemon over bunion or corn at night. Wipe surface with a cut raw onion or garlic 2-3 times daily. Wipe with expressed orange-coloured juice of the fractured stem of Greater Celandine.

Paint with Liquid Extract Lobelia. (*Ernest Cockayne FNIMH*)

For corns, soak feet in hot soapy water; scrape away the corn and when dry cover with a plaster. Successful results reported with Houseleek steeped in Cider vinegar. Hundreds of corn-cures exist.
Old Yorkshire tradition: 2 teaspoons Epsom salts to a bowl of hot water for a foot-soak; finish off with a Castor oil wipe.
Greek traditional: Rub corn or bunion with lemon juice and leave on lemon rind overnight. Onion juice.
Preventative: Anoint feet with Plantain oil believed to be effective. Cider vinegar as a lotion.
Aromatherapy. Massage feet after soaking: Lavender, Geranium.

CORNEAL ULCER. See: EYES, INFECTION.

CORONARY HEART DISEASE. The cause of: coronary occlusion, coronary blockage, coronary thrombosis. A heart attack occurs when a coronary artery becomes blocked by swellings composed, among other things, of cholesterol. Such swellings may obstruct the flow of blood leading to a blood clot (thrombus). Cholesterol is a major cause of CHD.

Coronary thrombosis is more common in the West because of its preference for animal fats; whereas in the East fats usually take the form of vegetable oils – corn, sunflower seed, sesame, etc. Fatty deposits (atheroma) form in the wall of the coronary artery, obstructing blood-flow. Vessels narrowed by atheroma and by contact with calcium and other salts become hard and brittle (arterio-sclerosis) and are easily blocked. Robbed of oxygen and nutrients heart muscle dies and is replaced by inelastic fibrous (scar) tissue which robs the heart of its maximum performance.

Severe pain and collapse follow a blockage. Where only a small branch of the coronary arterial tree is affected recovery is possible. Cause of the pain is lack of oxygen (Vitamin E). Incidence is highest among women over 40 who smoke excessively and who take The Pill.

The first warning sign is breathlessness and anginal pain behind the breastbone which radiates to arms and neck. Sensation as if the chest is held in a vice. First-line agent to improve flow of blood – Cactus.

For cholesterol control target the liver. Coffee is a minor risk factor.

Measuring hair calcium levels is said to predict those at risk of coronary heart disease. Low hair concentrations may be linked with poor calcium metabolism, high aortic calcium build-up and the formation of plagues. (*Dr Allan MacPherson, nutritionist, Scottish Agricultural College, Ayr, Scotland*)

Evidence has been advanced that a diagonal ear lobe crease may be a predictor for coronary heart disease. (*American Journal of Cardiology, Dec. 1992*)

Tooth decay is linked to an increased risk of coronary heart disease and mortality, particularly in young men. (*Dr Frank De Stefano, Marshfield Medical Research Foundation, Wisconsin, USA*)
Treatment. Urgency. Send for doctor or suitably qualified practitioner. Absolute bedrest for 3 weeks followed by 3 months convalescence. Thereafter: adapt lifestyle to slower tempo and avoid undue exertion. Stop smoking. Adequate exercise. Watch weight.
Cardiotonics: Motherwort, Hawthorn, Mistletoe, Rosemary. Ephedra, Lily of the Valley, Broom.
Cardiac vasodilators relax tension on the vessels by increasing capacity of the arteries to carry more blood. Others contain complex glycosides

that stimulate or relax the heart at its work. Garlic is strongly recommended as a preventative of CHD.

Hawthorn, vasodilator and anti-hypertensive, is reputed to dissolve deposits in thickened and sclerotic arteries BHP (1983). It is believed to regulate the balance of lipids (body fats) one of which is cholesterol.

Serenity tea. Equal parts: Motherwort, Lemon Balm, Hawthorn leaves or flowers. 1 heaped teaspoon to each cup boiling water; infuse 5-15 minutes; 1 cup freely.

Decoction. Combine equal parts: Broom, Lily of the Valley, Hawthorn. 1-2 teaspoons to each cup water gently simmered 20 minutes. Half-1 cup freely.

Tablets/capsules. Hawthorn, Motherwort, Cactus, Mistletoe, Garlic.

Practitioner. Formula. Hawthorn 20ml; Lily of the Valley 10ml; Pulsatilla 5ml; Stone root 5ml; Barberry 5ml. Tincture Capsicum 1ml. Dose: Powders: 500mg (two 00 capsules or one-third teaspoon). Liquid extracts: 1 teaspoon. Tinctures: 2 teaspoons. Thrice daily in water or honey.

Prevention: Vitamin E – 400iu daily.

Diet. See: DIET – HEART AND CIRCULATION.

Supplements. Daily. Vitamin C, 2g. Vitamin E possesses anti-clotting properties, 400iu. Broad spectrum multivitamin and mineral including chromium, magnesium selenium, zinc, copper.

Acute condition. Strict bed-rest; regulate bowels; avoid excessive physical and mental exertion. Meditation and relaxation techniques dramatically reduce coronary risk.

CORTICOSTEROIDS. Chemical substances produced naturally in the body by the adrenal glands (the corticosteroids) which affect carbohydrate, fat and protein metabolism, adjust salt and water requirements, and increase the body's resistance against stress. Synthetically prepared, they are used to fight inflammation and to spare the body's defence system excessive activity, especially when it over-reacts. A number of diseases respond dramatically to steroids, such as temporal arteritis and rheumatism. Shrinkage of the adrenal glands may be caused by stress or steroid drugs.

As serious side-effects are possible herbal alternatives may be sought which, though not producing spectacular results, can usually be relied upon to evoke a favourable response. Steroid side-effects include: retention of sodium which may raise blood pressure, Cushing's syndrome (moon-face), reduction of body immunity against bacterial infection, bleeding of the intestines, weight gain, weakness of muscles, prominent blood vessels on the eyelids, anger, aggression.

Aloe Vera gel has received some support as an anti-inflammatory (JAM). To sustain the adrenal glands – Ginseng, Liquorice, Sarsaparilla, Black Cohosh, Borage, Thuja. Wild Yam, long known to herbalists, contains diosgenin of the dioscorea family used in the synthesis of progesterone. Other plant steroids include constituents of Soya, Agave and Bittersweet (*solanum dulcamara*). Butcher's Broom contains the same steroid content as found in Wild Yam. (*Lapin and Saunie – French*)

CORTISONE. One of the corticosteroid hormones produced by the outer layer (cortex) of the adrenal glands. Corticosteroid drugs are synthetic derivatives that have similar properties as those produced in the body. They are used in pharmacy for allergies, Addison's disease, rheumatism and inflammatory conditions. Prolonged over-use is known to weaken response of the body's immune system to invasion of bacteria and infection.

Alternatives of limited efficacy: see entry – CORTICOSTEROIDS. These are known to produce increased output of adrenal hormones by their cortisone-like effect.

CORYDALIS. Stagger-weed. Root. *Corydalis cava*.

Action. Powerful alterative and antiseptic. Nervine.

Uses. Has a long traditional reputation for ulcerations, chancre, sore throat of syphilis and the chronic nerve dystrophy that follows. An analogue of Goldenseal. Parkinsonism. (*Wm A.R. Thomson MD*)

Said to work well with Poke root.

Combined with Skullcap for epilepsy.

Preparation. *Tincture*: from the bulbous root when plant is in flower. 10 drops in water thrice daily.

Once used in herbal pharmacy. Of historic interest only.

CORYZA. See: COLDS.

COSMETIC HERBS. Today it is possible to blend age-old beauty lore with modern scientific pharmacy. Wide ranges of products are based on totally natural ingredients such as Rosemary, Avocado, Chamomile, Lime flowers, Aloe Vera and Jojoba in the form of make-up, skin-care, hair-care and toiletry preparations.

COT DEATH. See: SIDS.

COTTON ROOT. *Gossypium herbaceum L. German*: Baumwollenbaum. *French*: Cotonnier en arbre. *Italian*: Cotone arbusto. *Arabian* Kuttun. *Indian*: Karpas. *Iranian*: Pambah. Dried root bark. Cotton fibre leaves.

Constituents: mucilage, flavonoids, fixed oil, resin, tannin.

Action: abortifacient. Parturient. Traditional

male contraceptive (unproven). Oxytocic, (fresh gathered).
Uses. For procuring abortion. Claimed to contract the womb after the action of Ergot, but safer. Alabama Indian squaws made a tea of the freshly-gathered roots to ease pains of childbirth. For absent or painful menstruation. Pain in ovaries. Morning sickness. Reduces sperm count and sexual urge in the male.
Reference. Rats were made temporarily infertile without change of mating behaviour, without reducing the male hormone (testosterone) and without heart abnormalities. (*Dr Yun-feng-Ren, People's Republic of China*)

Not used in pregnancy. Hypokalaemia may follow overdose.
Preparations. *Liquid Extract, BPC (1934)*. Dose, 2-4ml.
Tincture BPC (1934). Dose 30-60 drops. GSL

COUCH GRASS. Twitch Triticum repens. *Agropyron repens* (Beauvais). *German*: Quecke. *French*: Chiendent. *Spanish*: Grama. *Italian*: Caprinella. Dried or fresh rhizome.
Constituents: volatile oil, Vitamin A.
Keynote: bladder and kidneys. This is the grass to which a dog is said to go instinctively when sick, hence its name – dog grass.
Action: Soothing demulcent diuretic for simple inflammation of the urinary tract. Uric acid solvent. Laxative. Urinary antiseptic. Nutritive, emollient. Anti-cholesterol.
Uses. Cystitis, nephritis, urethritis, painful and incontinent urination, liver disorder, renal colic, kidney stone, gravel, gout, rheumatism, back-ache. Reduction of blood cholesterol. Chronic skin disorders.

Combines with Hydrangea (equal parts) for prostatitis.

Herbal tea for kidneys and bladder: Couchgrass 15 per cent; Buchu 15 per cent; Wild Carrot 15 per cent; Bearsfoot 15 per cent; Alfalfa 45 per cent. 2 teaspoons to each cup water, gently simmer 5 minutes. Half-2 cups thrice daily.
Preparations. Thrice daily.
Decoction. 2-3 teaspoons to each cup water, gently simmer 5 minutes. 1-2 cups.
Liquid Extract BHP (1983) 1:1 in 25 per cent alcohol. Dose: 4-8ml.
Tincture BHP (1983) 1:5 in 40 per cent alcohol. Dose: 5-15ml (1-3 teaspoons)
Powder. 250mg in capsules; 3 capsules thrice daily. (*Arkocaps*)
Kasbah remedy. Alpine herb teabags.
Antitis tablets (*Potter's*) GSL

COUGH. A protective reflex for the expulsion of an obstruction or irritant from lower respiratory organs. Causes are legion, smoking being most common. A cough is often secondary to an underlying condition which should receive prompt attention, (bronchitis, pleurisy, croup, etc).

The modern herbalist does not use suppressives but favours expectorants or 'eliminatives' to soothe irritated surfaces and expel excess mucus. If a dry unproductive irritating cough persists despite treatment, a qualified practitioner should be consulted.

Addition of a nervine (Skullcap, Wild Lettuce, etc) acts as a relaxant. May be a particular help for nervous cough. Add Hawthorn or Motherwort to sustain the heart where necessary.
Alternatives. *Teas*. Any one: Aniseed, Caraway, Blessed Thistle, Coltsfoot, Comfrey leaves, Ground Ivy, Hyssop, Liquorice (shredded root), Marshmallow, Mouse Ear, Mullein, Plantain, Soapwort, Iceland Moss, Wild Violet, Thyme, White Horehound, Lungwort. Formulae: (1) Equal parts; Coltsfoot, White Horehound, Liquorice. (2) Equal parts; Hyssop, White Horehound, Valerian. (3) Equal parts; Mullein, Lemon Balm, Valerian.
Decoctions. Any one: Balm of Gilead buds, Elecampane root, Fenugreek seeds, Grindelia, Marshmallow root, Pleurisy root, Wild Lettuce, Wild Cherry bark. Valerian (nervous cough). Formula: Equal parts: Elecampane root, Marshmallow root, Wild Cherry bark. 1 heaped teaspoon to 2 cups water gently simmered 20 minutes. Half-1 cup freely.
Tablets/capsules. Lobelia, Iceland Moss, Garlic.
Powders. Formula: equal parts, Lobelia, Liquorice root, Elecampane. Dose: 750mg (three 00 capsules or half a teaspoon) 2-3 times daily.
Liquid Extracts. (1) Formula: Lobelia 2; Sundew 3; Red Clover 3; Ginseng 6. 30-60 drops in hot water, every 2 hours. (*George Slack*) (2) Formula Elderflowers 1; Boneset 1; Hyssop 2; Liquorice half. 1 teaspoon in cup hot water, every 2 hours.
Tinctures. Formula. Elecampane 2; Black Cohosh 2; Lobelia 1; Few drops Tincture Capsicum. Dose: 30-60 drops in hot water every 2 hours.
BHP (1983) recommends: Elecampane, Hops, Mullein, Wild Cherry bark, Wild Lettuce.
Potter's. Balm of Gilead Cough Mixture.
Onion juice and honey.
Topical. Rub back and chest with Olbas oil, or warm Camphorated oil. Bran or Slippery Elm poultices to chest.
Aromatherapy. Chamomile and Thyme, 5 drops each in cup boiling water, with towel over the head, as an inhalant.
Preventative. 2 Garlic capsules or tablets at night. Honey. German Chamomile tea.

See: WHOOPING COUGH. CROUP.

COUGH SYRUP. Onion juice and honey. Slices of raw onion steeped overnight in 1lb honey jar, quarter full, with screw cap. Taken by teaspoonful for obstructive airways disease, wheezing, etc.

COUGHING OF BLOOD. See: BLEEDING (haemoptysis).

COUMARINS. Powerful anti-coagulant plant chemicals (Di-coumarol). Used to prevent blood clotting. Adverse effects: nettlerash, hair loss, bleeding from the gums. Used in orthodox medicine for the manufacture of Warfarin against thrombosis. Aspirin enhances their action. Should not be used in pregnancy or when breast-feeding. Coumarins include: Tonka seed or Tonquin bean, Melilot, Ash, Bael, Black Haw, Rupturewort.

COUNCIL FOR COMPLEMENTARY AND ALTERNATIVE MEDICINE. A General Medical Council style organisation with a single Register, common ethics and disciplinary procedures for its members. To promote high standards of education, qualification and treatment; to preserve the patient's freedom of choice.

Founder groups: The National Institute of Medical Herbalists, College of Osteopaths, British Naturopathic and Osteopathic Association, The British Chiropractic Association, The Society of Homoeopaths, The British Acupuncture Association, The Traditional Acupuncture Society and the Register of Traditional Chinese Medicine.

Objects: to provide vital unified representation to contest adverse legislation; to promote the interests of those seeking alternative treatments; to maintain standards of competent primary health care; to protect the practice of alternative medicine if Common Law is encroached upon. The Council prefers to work in harmony with the orthodox profession in which sense it is complementary. Council's first chairman: Simon Mills, FNIMH. Address: 10 Belgrave Square, London SW1X BPH.

COUNTER IRRITANT. An agent which produces vaso-dilation of peripheral blood vessels by stimulating nerve-endings of the skin to generate irritation intended to relieve deep-seated pain. Arnica, Balm of Gilead, Black Mustard, Bryony (white), Cajuput (oil of), Camphor, Canada Balsam, Cayenne, Eucalyptus, Nutmeg (oil of), Sassafras, Thuja.

COURVOISER'S LAW. With a history of gall stones walls of the gall bladder become fibrotic. Fibrosis robs the walls of their elasticity. The bladder will therefore be unable to expand to permit passage of the stone. Jaundice results. Thus if jaundice exists in the presence of a distended gall-bladder, the diagnosis cannot be gall stones. It is more likely to be caused by pressure from another organ; for instance, tumour at the head of the pancreas.

COW PARSLEY, HIMALAYAN. *Heracleum brunonis* benth, (umbellifera). Contains coumarins. Related to Angelica.
Action. Photosensitiser, antifungal, tuberculostatic. (*Journal of Natural Products 1987, 50(5), pp997-8*)
Uses. Leucoderma. Vitiligo. Reputed fading of coloured areas of skin.

COW'S MILK ALLERGY (CMA). An estimated 8 per cent of infants suffer from cow's milk intolerance.
Symptoms. Irritable bowel, respiratory troubles (asthma), skin disorders (eczema) and behavioural problems. Symptoms disappear when dairy products are discontinued but re-appear when they re-enter the diet.
Treatment and prevention. Garlic, for reduction of symptoms. A switch from cow's to goat's milk proves effective. Cases are on record of goat's milk checking irritable bowel and the spread of eczema.

COWSLIP. Peagle. Primula officinalis L. *Primula veris L. German*: Petersblume. *French*: Primerolle. *Spanish*: Vellorita. *Italian*: Primavera. Dried flowers (tea). Root (decoction).
Constituents: flavonoids, saponin glycosides, phenolic glycosides.
Keynote: hyperactivity.
Action: Analgesic, anti-inflammatory, anti-rheumatic, antipyretic, antispasmodic, hypnotic, sedative, vasodilator. Platelet anticoagulant. (*Biostrath*) Mild diuretic and laxative. Antitussive, expectorant.
Uses. Temporal arteritis, varicose veins, intermittent claudication, parasthesia (pins and needles), lumbago, sciatica, rheumatism . . . decoction. Restlessness in children, nervous headache, anxiety, sleeplessness, whooping cough, chronic bronchitis . . . tea.
Preparations. Early evening for sleeplessness, otherwise thrice daily.
Tea. 2 teaspoons dried flowers to each cup boiling water; infuse 10 minutes. Half-1 cup.
Decoction. Half-1 teaspoon (half-2g) dried root to each cup water simmered gently 10 minutes. Dose: Half a cup.
Liquid extract BHP (1983) 1:1 in 25 per cent alcohol: dose 1-2ml. GSL

COXSACKIE INFECTION. Named after a city in New York State where it was first isolated from a family of viruses that can cause a number of serious inflammatory disorders, including Bernholm disease and meningitis. While cases require hospital attention, herbal antivirals may be used in the absence of specific treatment: Echinacea, Wild Indigo, Myrrh, Goldenseal.
Tinctures. Formula. Echinacea 3; Goldenseal 1; Myrrh quarter. One teaspoon in water every 2 hours (acute) thrice daily (chronic).

CRABS. Pediculosis pubis. Pubic hair lice. STD. Contracted during intercourse, infested blankets, toilet seats.
Symptoms. Nightly itching of pubic hair due to toxin excreted by this vampire-like louse.
Treatment. Remove nits or eggs with fine tooth comb.
Topical. Tea Tree oil, neat or diluted. Camphor, tincture or liniment. Garlic, oil or lotion. Use any one, not washing off for at least 24 hours.

CRAMP. Sustained contraction of a muscle. Charley Horse.
Causes: oxygen starvation, lactic acid build-up. A common cause is depletion of salt from excessive sweating. Night cramps may be due to impaired blood supply or mineral deficiency: Calcium, Iron, Magnesium. Spasm takes many forms: writer's, swimmer's, pianist's, harpist's, trumpeter's, hornplayer's or emotional stress due to tightening of the facial muscles (German Chamomile). Athlete's cramp from mechanical stress may be relieved by Cramp Bark as well as manipulation. Repetitive strain injury (RSI).

Cramp of the heart muscle is known as angina (Cramp Bark, Motherwort). Where due to spasm of blood vessels from atherosclerosis it may take the form of intermittent claudication (Prickly Ash bark, Cramp bark, Nettles, Vitamin E). For cramp in the back (Cramp bark, Ligvites); stomach (Fennel, Cardamoms, Turkey Rhubarb); womb (Squaw vine, Wild Yam, Cramp bark); kidney and bladder (Horsetail); muscles (Devil's Claw).
Alternatives. *Teas*. Mild cases. Any one: German Chamomile, Lime flowers, Holy Thistle, Motherwort, Silverweed, Skullcap, St John's Wort, Betony.

Combination: equal parts, Skullcap, German Chamomile, Motherwort. 1 heaped teaspoon to each cup boiling water; infuse 5-10 minutes. 1 cup thrice daily or as necessary.
Decoction. More severe cases. Any one: Cramp bark, Valerian, Peruvian bark, Wild Yam, Prickly Ash bark.
Tablets/capsules. Black Cohosh, Cramp bark, Prickly Ash bark, Devil's Claw, Wild Yam, Ligvites.
Combination. Equal parts, Butterburr and Cramp bark. Dose: powders 500mg (two 00 capsules or one-third teaspoon thrice daily); Liquid extracts: one 5ml teaspoon. Tinctures: 1-2 teaspoons. Thrice daily or as necessary.
John William Fyfe MD. "After 20 years broken sleep from leg cramps a patient found relief with 15 drops Liquid Extract Black Haw, thrice daily for 3-4 days." This was used successfully in his practice for over 30 years.
Aromatherapy. Massage oil. 3 drops Marjoram, 3 drops Basil, in 2 teaspoons Almond or other vegetable oil. Or: Cypress oil, Mustard bath for feet.
Diet. See food sources of Calcium, Iron and Magnesium.
Supplements. Daily. B-complex 100mg; B6 100mg; Dolomite tablets (1000mg); Vitamin E (400iu); Vitamin C (2g); Calcium ascorbate (800mg); Magnesium 300mg (450mg, pregnancy). Zinc (25mg).

For cramp of pregnancy – see PREGNANCY.

CRAMP, ANAL. Spasmodic pain in the anal muscles, mostly suffered by sports-persons after running. Pain may last 10 minutes before dispersing as a deep dull ache. Worse by constipation. Check for anal fissure, which is a small tear in the skin. Readily disperses after taking a pinch of Cayenne or Ginger in honey. Those subject, should open their bowels before a run or at onset of pain.
Powders. Formula. Cramp bark 2; Stone root 1; Cayenne quarter. Dose: 500mg (two 00 capsules or one-third teaspoon in hot water) once or more daily.
Tinctures. Formula. Cramp bark 2; Stone root 1; Horseradish quarter. Dose: one 5ml teaspoon in hot water as necessary.
Tinctures. Alternative Formula. Equal parts: Tincture Peruvian bark and Stone root. Dose: one to two 5ml teaspoons in hot water as necessary.
Supplements. Magnesium, Calcium.

CRAMP BARK. Guelder rose. Snowball tree. *Viburnum opulus L. German*: Schling. *French*: Obier. *Spanish*: Rosa da qúeldres. *Italian*: Viburno loppo. Dried bark.
Constituents: coumarins, hydroquinones.
Keynote: cramp.
Action: antispasmodic, astringent, nerve and muscle relaxant, sedative.
Uses. Muscular cramp, spasmodic pains in abdomen, womb, ovaries, back, stomach, intestines, bladder. Convulsions in children. Epididymitis. Painful menstruation, flooding menses of the menopause. Polymyalgia. Nervous irritability. Heart cramp (angina), intermittent claudication, arteritis, palpitation. Earache. Acute bronchitis, asthma. Muscular rheumatism. Bedwetting.
Preparations. Thrice daily.
Tablets. Two 200mg tablets before meals.
Decoction. 1-2 teaspoons to each cup water: simmer 15 minutes: dose, half-1 cup.
Powder. 2-5g.
Liquid extract. Half-2 teaspoons in water.
Tincture BHP (1983) 1 part bark to 5 parts 70 per cent alcohol. Dose: 5-10ml in water. GSL

CRANBERRIES. (English) *Vaccinium oxycoccos*. (American) *Macrocarpa oxycoccos*.
Action: Antiscorbutic.
Uses. Urinary tract infections. Unpleasant odour of urine. Believed to be of value for diabetes mel-

litis. Suppresses symptoms of bacterial infection. Prevention of Vitamin C deficiency states. Hay fever. Food and chemical allergies.

Preparations. *Cranberry Juice Capsules*. Ingredients: Oil (vegetable Soya) 243mg; Cranberry Juice Concentrate 12.1-140mg (equal to 1680mg of fresh cranberries); Gelatine 118mg; Vitamin C (ascorbic acid) 100mg; Glycerine 71mg; Beeswax 14mg; Lecithin 13mg; Vitamin E (d'Alpha-Tocopheral) 2iu. 2 capsules daily. (*Power Health*)

Fresh juice. "For mild urinary infections – drinking 15fl oz cranberry juice daily prevented bacteria clinging to the urinary tract." (*Dr Anthony Sobota, Professor of Microbiology, Youngstown University, Ohio, USA*)

CRANESBILL, AMERICAN. Storksbill. Wild Geranium. *Geranium maculatum L*. Herb. Dried Root.

Constituents: Tannic and gallic acid.

Action: Haemostatic, astringent, anti-inflammatory, vulnerary, styptic tonic, antiseptic. A vaso-compressor to increase the vital potency of living matter of the ganglionic neurones. Anti-diarrhoea. For over-relaxed conditions.

Uses. Urinary system: frequency, incontinence in the young and aged, bed-wetting, blood in the urine. An ingredient of Captain Frank Roberts' prescription for ulceration of stomach, duodenum and intestines. Ulceration of mouth and throat (tea used as a mouth wash and gargle). Irritable bowel. Summer diarrhoea of children.

Combines with Beth root (equal parts) as a vaginal douche for leucorrhoea or flooding of the menopause; with tincture Myrrh for cholera and infective enteritis.

Dr Wm Winder reported in the 1840s how the Indians of Great Manitoulin Island held it in high favour as a healing styptic antiseptic, "the powdered root being placed on the mouth of the bleeding vessel . . . Internally, they considered it efficacious for bleeding from the lungs". (*Virgil J. Vogel, University of Oklahoma Press, USA*)

Preparations. Thrice daily.

Tea. Half-2 teaspoons dried herb to each cup boiling water; infuse 15 minutes. Half-1 cup.

Decoction. Half-1 teaspoon dried root to each cup water simmered gently 20 minutes. Half a cup.

Tablets BHP 270mg. (*Gerard House*)

Liquid extract: 15-30 drops.

Tincture BHP (1983). 1 part root to 5 parts 45 per cent alcohol. Dose: 2-4ml (30-60 drops).

Powdered root, as a snuff for excessive catarrh and to arrest bleeding from the nose.

Vaginal douche. 1oz root to 2 pints water simmered 20 minutes. Strain and inject. GSL

CRAWLEY ROOT. Dragon's claw. *Corallorhiza odontorhiza*, Nutt. Rhizome.

Keynote: fevers (early stages).

Action: febrifuge, diaphoretic, relaxant.

Uses. Once used widely in North American medicine for fevers, the rational being to induce a heavy sweat to reduce a high body temperature and relieve arterial excitement. Pleurisy. Typhoid fever.

Preparations. *Tea*. Not given in this form, losing its strength on application of heat.

Tablets/capsules. 200mg. Two, every two hours, acute cases.

Tincture. 30-60 drops.

CREAM. A cream is an emulsion, either oil in water or water in oil. Usually soothing and nourishing, mixing readily with secretions of the skin.

Example: ingredients: olive oil, beeswax, lanolin, herb.

Method: Infuse half an ounce herb (Chickweed, Elderflowers, Comfrey, etc) in half a pint boiling water for 20 minutes, strain. Place 1oz olive oil in a double saucepan or basin, standing in a vessel of hot water (not boiling). Add: half an ounce beeswax and half an ounce lanolin. In a separate vessel warm 3 tablespoons infusion and dissolve into it half a teaspoon borax. When beeswax and lanolin are well melted in the olive oil, reduce heat and stir in the infusion. Continue stirring until warm, adding a few drops of perfume if desired. When it begins to thicken pour into pots and keep in a refrigerator. When opened should be used within a few weeks. Purpose of borax is to prevent formation of mould.

CROHN'S DISEASE. Chronic inflammation and ulceration of the gut, especially the terminal ileum from changes in the gut blood vessels. Commences with ulceration which deepens, becomes fibrotic and leads to stricture. Defective immune system. Resistance low. May be associated with eye conditions and Vitamin B12 deficiency.

Symptoms: malaise, bloody alternating diarrhoea and constipation; right side colicky abdominal pain worse after meals; flatulence, loss of weight and appetite. Intestinal obstruction can usually be palpated.

Blood count. A blood count high in whites indicates an abscess – a serious condition which may require surgical repair during which segments of the gut may have to be removed. Malignant change rare.

Differential diagnosis. Ulcerative colitis, appendicitis, appendix abscess, irritable bowel syndrome.

Cracks or ulcers at corners of the mouth may be a good marker of Crohn's Disease.

Treatment. Select one of the following. Herbal treatment offers a safe alternative to steroids by inducing remission in acute exacerbation. Good responses have been observed from the anti-bacterials Wild Yam and Goldenseal. Fenugreek seeds are of special value. Comfrey (tissue regen-

eration). Irish Moss.
Teas: Chamomile, Comfrey leaves, Hops, Marshmallow leaves, Meadowsweet, Shepherd's Purse (*Dr A. Vogel*), Lobelia. Silverweed and Cranesbill are excellent for internal bleeding; Poke root for intestinal ulceration.
Decoction. Fenugreek seeds: 2 teaspoons to large cup water simmered gently 10 minutes. 1 cup freely. The seeds also should be consumed.
Tablets/capsules. Wild Yam, Fenugreek, Ginger, Goldenseal, Lobelia, Slippery Elm.
Powders. Formula. Wild Yam 2; Meadowsweet 2; Goldenseal 1. Dose: 500mg (two 00 capsules or one-third teaspoon) thrice daily.
Liquid Extracts. (1) Formula. Wild Yam 1, Echinacea 2. 30-60 drops in water thrice daily. Or, (2) Formula: Turkey Rhubarb 2, Goldenseal 1, Caraway half. 20-30 drops in water thrice daily.
Tinctures. Formula. Bayberry 2, Goldenseal 1, Cardamoms 1. Dose: One to two 5ml teaspoons thrice daily.
Ispaghula seeds. 2-4 teaspoons thrice daily.
Tea Tree oil Suppositories. Insertion at night.
Diet. Bland, little fibre, Slippery Elm gruel. Irish Moss preparations. Increase fluid intake. Reject: broccoli, tomatoes, lima, Soya, Brussels sprouts, pinto beans, cocoa, chocolate, cow's milk, peas, onions, turnips, radishes. Accept fish oils.
Addenbrookes Hospital, Cambridge. Reject foods containing wheat and all dairy produce.
Supplements. Vitamins A, B12, C, Calcium, Iron, Magnesium, Potassium, Zinc.
Study. In a study carried out by UK researchers (1993) food allergies were found to be the most common cause of the disease. Results suggested that dietary changes may be as effective as corticosteroids in easing symptoms. The most common allergens were corn, wheat, milk, yeast, egg, potato, rye, tea, coffee, apples, mushrooms, oats, chocolate. An elemental diet with a formula of nutrients (E028, produced by Hospital Supplies, Liverpool) was used in trials. (*The Lancet, 6.11.1993*)
Notes. Crohn's Disease is associated with Erythema nodosum, more frequently recognised in childhood. A frequent cause is cow's milk intolerance. Smoking adds to the risk of Crohn's disease.

In susceptible people, the food additives titanium dioxide and aluminosilicates may evoke a latent inflammatory response resulting in Crohn's disease, ulcerative colitis or bowel cancer. These chemicals may be found in the intestinal lymphoid aggregations in gut mucosa. (*Jonathan Powell, Gastro-intestinal Laboratory, St Thomas's Hospital, London*) (Titanium dioxide rarely occurs naturally but is added to confectionery, drinking water and anti-caking agents.)

CROUP. Laryngo-tracheo-bronchitis. Acute bacterial or viral inflammation of the respiratory tract. Spread by airborne infection.
Symptoms: difficult breathing. Breathing-in is noisy, spasmodic and prolonged. Effusion of a plastic-like material which coagulates to form a false membrane. Fretfulness. Symptoms of a 'cold' disappear but towards evening skin becomes hot, pulse rises, and a sense of anxiety takes over.

Laryngeal muscles are held in spasm, calling for antispasmodics. If the course of the disease has not been arrested on the third or fourth day a crisis is at hand and modern hospital treatment necessary. The condition is always worse at night. Treatment varies with each individual case. Stimulating diaphoretics induce gentle sweating, de-toxicate, and relieve tension on respiration.

Lobelia is unsurpassed as a croupal remedy and may be given alone either by infusion (tea) liquid extract or acid tincture. Given as a powder it works too slowly in a condition where speed saves lives.

While copious drinks of Catnep (Catmint) tea help, stronger medicines are indicated. Where resistance runs low, add Echinacea. Should any of these induce vomiting, it would be regarded as a favourable sign after which a measure of relief is felt.

Alternatives. *Liquid extracts*. Formula. Pleurisy root 2; Lobelia 1; Ginger half. Dose: one 5ml teaspoon in hot water every 2 hours. Infants: 10-30 drops.
Tinctures. Formula: Pleurisy root 2; Blue Cohosh 1; Lobelia 1. One to two 5ml teaspoons in hot water every 2 hours. Infants 10-20 drops.
Practitioner. Formula: 2 drops Tincture Belladonna BP 1980, 4 drops Tincture Ipecuanha BP 1973. Water to 2oz. One 5ml teaspoon in water every 15 minutes for 2 or 3 doses to enable child to sleep until morning; then once every hour or two for 3 days. Not to press medicines on children feeling comfortable.
Inhalant. Friar's Balsam. Steam kettle on hand. Or:–
Aromatherapy. Inhale. Drops. Thyme 1; Eucalyptus 2; Hyssop 1. In bowl of boiling water at the bedside at night or when necessary.
Drowsiness requires diffusive stimulants: Tinctures: Echinacea 2; Ginger quarter; Pleurisy root 1. One to two 5ml teaspoons in hot water every 2 hours; infants 5-20 drops according to age.
Collapse. When confronted with an ashen face, depression and collapse, powerful stimulants are necessary: tinctures – Formula. Prickly Ash bark 3; Blue Cohosh 2; Ginger 1. One 5ml teaspoon in hot water every 10 minutes; (infants 5-20 drops).
Topical. Relaxing oil. Ingredients: 3oz olive oil; half an ounce Liquid Extract or tincture Lobelia; Tincture Capsicum (Cayenne) 20 drops. Shake vigorously. Rub freely on throat, winding round a strip of suitable material wrung out in hot water.

Cover with protective bandage or plastic film. Renew hot flannel every 10-15 minutes until paroxysms subside.
Poultice. Dissolve coffeespoon Cayenne powder or chillies in cup cider vinegar. Simmer gently 10 minutes. Strain. Saturate a piece of suitable material and wind round throat to relieve congested blood vessels.
Diet. No dairy foods which increase phlegm. No solid meals. Herb teas, vegetable and fruit juices only.

Steam kettle on hand, or Friar's Balsam inhalation. See: FRIAR'S BALSAM. Regulate bowels. The condition is worsened in a dry hot atmosphere; reduce central heating to ensure adequate ventilation. Many a serious stridor and cough have been relieved by running some hot water into a bath or basin and sitting the child in a home-made Turkish bath.

Treatment by or in liaison with a general medical practitioner.

CUBEBS. Tailed pepper. *Piper cubeba L.*
Constituents: lignans, gum resins, volatile oil.
Action: powerfully stimulates genito-urinary mucous surfaces and for this purpose was used by the Old School extensively for gonorrhoea and other STDs. As an expectorant was once used for chronic cough and bronchitis (lozenges).
Preparations. Thrice daily.
Liquid Extract BPC (1934) 1 in 1. Dose: 2-4ml.
Tincture Cubebs BPC 1949; dose, 2-4ml.
Powder: dose, 2-4g. GSL

CUCUMBER. *Cucumis sativus*.
Action: cooling astringent, diuretic anodyne, sedative, alterative (mild), action similar to Hydrangea, reducing specific gravity of urine.

Its properties are destroyed by heat.
Uses. Irritation of the urinary tract, sharp pain in loins, and rheumatic pains in shoulders. (*Scudder*) Relieves spasm of low back pain after changing turbid discharge to a free easy flow of urine. (*J. Henry Finch MD, Savannah, Ga, USA*) Inability to urinate. Cystitis. Burns (external). Eyestrain: slice of cucumber over each eye when resting.

Tapeworms. "Take 60g (2oz) ground seeds and mix with honey. Take fasting and followed after 2 hours by a cathartic." (*David Hoffmann MNIMH*)
Preparation. Cucumber passed through a liquidiser yields a clear pea-green fluid. Dose: 2-4 teaspoons, neat or with water, every 3 hours. Cucumber and Yoghurt face pack to rid skin of impurities and discourage wrinkles: blend equal parts fresh cucumber and yoghurt in a liquidiser and apply.

CUDWEED, MARSH. *Gnaphalium uliginosum L. German*: Ruhrkraut. *French*: Immortelle. *Italian*: Canapicchie. *Part used*: herb.
Action: Astringent, antitussive, antiseptic, anti-catarrhal, anti-inflammatory.
Uses. Quinsy, sore throat, tonsillitis, pharyngitis (tea used as a gargle every 2 hours). Inflammation of the parotid gland (mumps). Bleeding from respiratory mucous surfaces. Whooping cough, croup. Lice infestation (wash hair with tea). High blood pressure. (*Russia*)
Preparations. Thrice daily.
Tea. 1 heaped teaspoon to each cup boiling water; infuse 15 minutes, half cup freely, acute cases; thrice daily, chronic. Addition of 2 drops Tincture Myrrh enhances action.
Powder: dose, 2-4g.
Liquid Extract: half-1 teaspoon in water.
Tincture BHP (1983) 1 part to 5 parts 45 per cent alcohol. Dose: 1-4ml (15-60 drops).

CULPEPER, NICHOLAS (1616-1654). Astrologer-physician. In 1649 he issued his "Physical Directory" which attracted the fury of the College of Physicians. Followed by *"The Complete Herbal"*, (1653) Family Dispensary and Natural System of Healing, which became the herbal best-seller – even today. He practised in Spitalfields, beloved by the poor of the East End. Revolutionary in medicine and politics, was wounded in the chest whilst serving as a Roundhead in the Civil War. See: ASTROLOGY.

CUMIN. *Cuminum cyminum L.* Old Egyptian spice. Dried ripe fruits.
Constituents: amino acids, flavonoids, volatile oil.
Action: carminative, antispasmodic, stimulant, aphrodisiac, diuretic, emmenagogue.
Uses: Traditional Indian remedy for indigestion, which is one reason why it appears in many recipes for curry.
Powder: a sprinkle (1-2g). Disagreeable taste when taken alone. Masked by honey.

Not taken during pregnancy. GSL

CURRY POWDER. Madras Special. Parts: Coriander 13; Black Pepper 5; Cayenne 1; Cumin 6; Fenugreek 6; Turmeric 6. Mix. Grind. Sift. Store in airtight jar. A rich source of copper.

CUSHING'S SYNDROME. A glandular disorder occurring mostly in females, aged 30 to 50.
Causes: a tumour on the adrenal glands or excessive medication with large doses of corticosteroid drugs to make up for adrenal insufficiency. There is diminished resistance to infection. (*Echinacea*)
Symptoms. Fat plethoric 'moon' face. Limbs thin, trunk obese. Skin easily bruises (Arnica). Fatigue, weakness, pink streaks on skin. Cessation of menstruation. Loss of sex drive in men. High blood pressure and sugar in the urine are common. Bone softening leads to pain. Acne (Agnus Castus). Excess body hair. Personality change.
Treatment. Adrenal stimulants may obviate

surgery or irradiation to the adrenal glands: they include Ginseng, Liquorice, Sarsaparilla, Holy Thistle (Hyde), Samphire (Hyde).
Men. Tinctures. Formula. Ginseng 3; Sarsaparilla 2; Liquorice 1. One to two teaspoons in water thrice daily.
Women. Tinctures. Formula. Agnus Castus 2; Helonias 2; Pulsatilla 1. One to two teaspoons in water thrice daily.

Good responses have been observed from Pulsatilla and Black Cohosh.

CUTS. A cut is a minor injury which permits the escape of blood and may thus lead to infection. Cuts should never be neglected because of possible invasion by the tetanus organism ubiquitous in the soil and airborne dust.
Treatment. If the wound is a small puncture, wash with soap and water and dry. Wipe with distilled extract of Witch Hazel, or with a solution made from 1 teaspoon Tincture St John's Wort (Hypericum) or 1 teaspoon Tincture Marigold (Calendula) to a cup of water. Cover with clean dry dressing.

Many natural healing ointments are available: Comfrey, St John's Wort, Marigold, Chickweed, Slippery Elm, Foxglove leaves. In days of the Civil War Comfrey leaves were used as bandages and washed Sphagnum Moss as cotton wool. Leaves or gel of Aloe Vera plant enhance healing and reduce scarring. Bruised leaves of Cranesbill, Bistort, Hyssop.

Literally hundreds of natural substances promote healing and prevent infection, including: Goldenseal, Myrrh, Echinacea, Cinnamon, Pot Marjoram, Chamomile, Fenugreek, Self-heal, Woundwort, etc. The Menominee Indians used the powdered root of Skunk Cabbage for injuries and wounds that refused to heal. (*John Bartram, 1699-1777*)

To minimise scar formation after healing: wipe with castor oil or contents of a Vitamin E capsule.

Honey is a popular domestic application for cuts and grazes "to draw out the dirt".

Products: Nelson's Hypercal, Doubleday Comfrey Cream.

CYPRESS. *Cupressus sempervirens*. *German*: Zypresse. *French*: Cyprès. *Spanish*: Ciprés. *Chinese*: Pien-po. Part used: essential oil – external use only.
Action: vaso-constrictor, vein-tonic, antiseptic, aromatic, antispasmodic, sedative, diuretic.
Uses: varicose veins, oedema, piles, menopausal cramps, leg-cramp, intermittent claudication. Incontinence and frequency of urine.
Preparation. *Tincture*: 1 part cone shavings to 5 parts 60 per cent alcohol; macerate 14 days, strain. Dose: 5-30 drops in water thrice daily before meals. Traditional remedy: no longer taken internally.
Aromatherapy: 10 drops in 2 teaspoons Almond oil for massage lower abdomen or limbs according to condition.

CYPRIPEDIUM. See: LADY'S SLIPPER.

CYST. An abnormal sac-like swelling covered by a supporting membrane containing fluid of different consistencies which cannot escape into the general circulation.
Breast. Harmless breast tumours and cysts are common in women over 40. They may form a lump, be with or without pain. Sometimes there is a light blood-stained discharge from the nipple (Poke root).
Ovary. See OVARIES.
Dermoid. May be made up of hair and skin (Greater Celandine).
Hydatid. Caused by parasitic infection (Thuja).
Sebaceous. Caused by blockage of a gland of the skin by a plug of fat (Marigold ointment).

A spot, often on the upper back, may irritate and itch and be diagnosed as a lipoma. Before resorting to surgery, external application of any one of the following may prove helpful: Castor oil, Liquid Extract Thuja, Blood root.
Cervical. Chaparral tea douche.
Dr John R. Christopher recommends: Poultice of Walnut leaves or bark. Chaparral, externally. Apple cider vinegar.

CYSTIC FIBROSIS. A genetic condition in children in which a defective gene is responsible for altered body chemistry, with excess secretion from the mucous glands. Thick mucus in the lungs may cause breathing distress; in the liver it may block ducts and inhibit function. Liver, pancreatic and salivary glands may be involved. Selenium and Vitamin E levels low (supplementation advised).
Symptoms. Respiratory difficulties and irritating cough. Thick sputum changes colour with infection. Sweat is high in salt. Evil-smelling stool. Treatment by or in liaison with general medical practitioner only.

Until recent years the condition was fatal by death from pneumonia. Carriers may be symptomless. Survival is largely in the hands of physiotherapists and osteopaths who give postural drainage.
Differential diagnosis. Infant's asthma, bronchitis, coeliac disease.

Having regards to missing enzymes (digestive and others) a hard look at food proves rewarding. Individuals may lack the necessary enzymes to break down wheat; one reason why wheat products should be avoided. Production of mucous is reduced considerably by the gluten diet in which oats, wheat, rye and barley are avoided. See: GLUTEN-SENSITIVE DISEASE.

To avoid infection, herbal antibiotics: Wild

Yam, Echinacea, Wild Indigo, Goldenseal, Myrrh.
Alternatives. To stimulate production of pancreatic enzymes, and peristalsis. Daily physiotherapy to prevent retention of viscid secretions.
Supportive treatment. To liquefy mucus.
Teas: Hyssop, White Horehound, Gotu Kola. Fenugreek seed. Alfalfa.
Tablets/capsules. Lobelia. Iceland Moss. Goldenseal. Echinacea. Wild Yam.
Powders. Formula: equal parts: Elecampane, White Horehound, Dandelion; pinch Cayenne. Dose: 500mg (two 00 capsules or one-third teaspoon) thrice daily.
Tinctures. Formula: equal parts: Elecampane, Lobelia, Dandelion. Few drops Tincture Capsicum. One to two 5ml teaspoons in water 3-4 times daily.
Friar's Balsam. Inhalation helps to thin mucus from the bronchi.
Supplementation. In addition to Selenium and Vitamin E: Vitamins A, B-complex, C, D. Pancreatic enzymes. High calorie intake.

CYSTINURIA. The presence of cystin in the urine, sometimes during pregnancy. Hereditary. A weakness of metabolism associated with increased urinary excretion of cystine – an amino acid – which leads to the formation of kidney stone. Its presence increases the risk of urinary tract infection, obstruction and the possibility of renal failure. Cases will require specialist hospital treatment, being necessary to screen urine at 3 to 6 months of pregnancy.

Plenty of fluids are indicated. Where these are supplied by herb teas a double purpose is served; these advised being of proven value for pregnancy and parturition.
Tea. Equal parts: Raspberry leaves, Cornsilk. 2 teaspoons to each cup boiling water; infuse 5-15 minutes. 1 cup 3-4 times daily.

CYSTITIS. Inflammation of the bladder, usually acute. Scalding pain on passage of water. Rapid onset. Patient feels off-colour. Pain in centre low abdomen worse when urine is passed. Frequent passing of small amounts, or mere sensation of 'wanting to go' Most cases resolve themselves without need for deep-acting agents. The exciting cause may be a chill.

Bacteria invades where there has been continued irritation, such as that of 'sand' or 'gravel' in the urine. Bacillus coli resides in the rectum but may invade the bladder. Urine is often turbid and evil-smelling. By travelling down the ureters, kidney infection may be conveyed to the lining of the bladder.

A common cause is dietetic indiscretion such as too much spicy food (curries, peppers), vinegar, coffee, alcohol, tea – too much and too strong, cola and other stimulants. Too much meat concentrates the urine, as do other high purine foods. Eighty per cent of women have at least one experience of cystitis during their lifetime. Other common causes: vaginal deodorants, freshener tissues, pants washed in biological washing powders, tampons, bubble-bath liquids, sexual aids such as spermicidal creams. The Pill.

Plenty of fluid should be drunk, either in the form of herbal teas (Alfalfa, etc) or bottled waters rather than coffee or tea. These dilute the irritating effect of uric acid in the urine.
Treatment. Bed-rest, abundant herb teas, non-caffeine drinks or plain water. Barley water.
Alternatives. Agrimony, Bearberry, Buchu (urinary antiseptic), Cornsilk (soothing to mucous surfaces), Couchgrass, Elderflowers, Juniper (not with inflammation), Lime flowers, Parsley, Parsley Piert, Pellitory, Plantain, Wild Carrot, Marshmallow (burning), Mullein, Rupturewort, Yarrow.
Tea: formula No 1. Equal parts: Cornsilk, Elderflowers, Marshmallow. Mix. 1-2 teaspoons to each cup boiling water; infuse 5-10 minutes; 1 cup freely.
Tea: formula No 2. Equal parts: Bearberry, Buchu, Couchgrass. Mix. 1 heaped teaspoon to each cup boiling water; infuse 5-10 minutes; 1 cup freely.
Barberry bark. 1 teaspoon to each cup *cold* water; steep overnight. 1 cup freely, next day.
Maria Treben's tea. Equal parts: Horsetail, Ladysmantle, Shepherd's Purse, Yarrow. 2 teaspoons to each cup boiling water. Infuse 15 minutes: 2-3 cups daily.
Tablets/capsules. Buchu, Dandelion, Echinacea, Goldenseal, Potter's "Antitis".
Formula. Marshmallow root 2; Echinacea 2; Goldenseal 1. Mix. Dose: Powders: 500mg (two 00 capsules or one-third teaspoon). Liquid extracts: 1 teaspoon. Tinctures: 2 teaspoons. 2-3 times daily.
E.G. Jones MNIMH. Tinctures, equal parts: Kava Kava, Saw Palmetto, Sweet Sumach. 20-30 drops in water thrice daily. Consistent results reported.
Practitioner. Where much pus is present in the urine, inject: 5 drops Tincture Myrrh to each cup warm water, per catheter.
External. Fomentations to low centre abdomen (including genital area). Two towels are required: one squeezed out in hot water and placed in position for 5 minutes. Replace with one squeezed out in cold water; apply for 1 minute. Repeat applications for half an hour daily. Hot hip baths twice weekly.
Aromatherapy. 5 drops each: Cajeput and Juniper in bathwater.
Diet. Fresh and conservatively-cooked vegetables, adequate protein (vegetable), polyunsaturated oils. Organic foods with an absence of additives and tartrazine colourings, potassium

broth, watermelon, carrots and carrot juice, baked potatoes, whole grains, parsnips, Garlic. Yoghurt, pumpkin seeds; Slippery Elm gruel at almost every meal. Herb teas. Avoid hot spices, condiments, coffee, tea and cola drinks.
Supplements. Vitamins A, B, C, E, bioflavonoids, beta carotene, dolomite, propolis, zinc.

CYTOSTATIC. A herb which tends to slow-down mitosis (division and multiplication of cells) that can be of value as a supportive aid in malignancy.

Goldenseal, Mistletoe, Red Clover, Violet leaves. See also: ANTI-NEOPLASTIC.

DAISY. Woundwort. Bruisewort. *Bellis perennis L. German:* Wildes Massliebchen. *French*: Marguerite. *Spanish*: Margarita. *Italian*: Bellide. Keynote: conditions arising from bruises. Fresh or dried flowerheads.
Constituents: ammoniacal salts, saponin, tannic acid, inulin.
Action: vulnerary. Acts upon muscle fibres of blood vessels. "A princely remedy for the aches and pains of old gardeners." (*Dr C. Burnett*) Discutient.
Relations: Arnica, Calendula, St John's Wort, Witch Hazel.
Uses: Tumours resulting from a blow. Injuries, sprains, bruises, excessive tiredness.
Preparation. *Infusion*. Half a cup fresh or dried flowerheads to two cups water. Bring to boil; remove vessel when boiling point is reached; strain when cold. Use externally as a lotion or with suitable material as a compress. Internal: 2 teaspoons thrice daily.
Note. A glycosidase inhibitor has been found in the leaves of the common daisy which is very similar to castanospernine and other HIV drugs. It is believed this may prevent the spread of the HIV virus.

DAMIANA. Curzon. *Turnera diffusa* Willd. Leaves and stems.
Constituents: flavonoids, volatile oil, arbutin.
Action: aphrodisiac, antidepressant, diuretic, stomachic, thymoleptic BHP (1983), stimulating tonic to the central nervous system and reproductive organs.
Uses. To enhance sexual performance, especially in the male. Impotence, frigidity, sterility, prostatitis, physical weakness and nervous exhaustion. Depression, anxiety states.
Combines well with Skullcap and Oats for senile dementia and feeble constitution. Traditional combination: (equal parts), Damiana, Saw Palmetto and Kola.
Preparations. Thrice daily.
Tea. 1 teaspoon to each cup boiling water; infuse 15 minutes. Half-1 cup.
Liquid extract. Half-1 teaspoon.
Tincture. 1-2 teaspoons, in water.
Tablets/capsules. One 300mg capsule or capsules after meals thrice daily. GSL

DAMP HAY DISEASE. Farmer's lung. A disease contracted from working in mouldy hay. A wet summer means much moist hay, ideal breeding ground for micro-organisms.
Symptoms: inflammation of the lung and high temperature with dry cough.
Tea: Equal parts; Elderflowers (to reduce temperature). Comfrey leaves (cough), Thyme (antibiotic), Peppermint (to assist breathing). 2 teaspoons to each cup boiling water; infuse 5-15 minutes. 1 cup freely.
Alternative: Combine *Tinctures*: Pleurisy root 2; Lobelia 1; Ginger half. One or two 5ml teaspoons in water 3-4 times daily.

DANDELION. *Taraxacum officinalis* Wiggers. Parts used: dried root and herb. *French*: Pissenlit. *German*: Kuhblume. *Spanish*: diente de léon. *Italian*: Dente de Lion.
Constituents: carotenoids, sesquiterpene lactones.
Action: powerful diuretic, bitter tonic, pancreatic regulator, galactagogue, cholagogue, anti-rheumatic, pancreatic and bile duct stimulant, stimulant to the portal circulation, laxative (mild), urinary antiseptic, anti-eczema, detoxicant, choleretic. Contains Vitamins A, B and C. Rich in nutrient minerals. Promotes elimination of plasma cholesterol.
Uses. Liver disorders, inflammation of the gall bladder, to counter tendency to form gallstones; mild jaundice, to clear a yellowish complexion and brighten the eyes; to stimulate flow of bile. Not given in presence of blocked bile duct. Indigestion, lack of appetite, sweating in the anal cleft, muscular rheumatism, hypoglycaemia, anorexia nervosa, cachexia and other wasting diseases. Congestive heart failure: should be prescribed for every case of oedema of heart origin. Warts: express milky sap and wipe wart frequently. Has a reputation for splenic and pancreatic disorders as an ingredient of diabetic and anaemia prescriptions. A decoction of the root has been taken with success for infective hepatitis. An older generation of gardeners chewed the root for bladder disorders. Combine: with Alfalfa and Kelp for nutrient minerals; with Yarrow and Lime flowers (equal parts) for high blood pressure. Promotes loss of weight during dieting.
Preparations. Thrice daily.
Tea (leaf). 3-4 teaspoons to each cup or, 2oz to 1 pint boiling water; infuse 15 minutes. Half-1 cup freely.
Decoction, root. 1 teaspoon to each cup boiling water gently simmer 15 minutes. Half-1 cup freely.
Liquid Extract. Dose: half-2 teaspoons.
Tincture, BHC Vol 1. 1 part to 5 parts 25 per cent ethanol. Dose: 5-10ml (1-2 teaspoons).
Juice of fresh root (by liquidiser or blender) 1-4 teaspoons
Tablets/capsules. Popular combination. Powdered Dandelion BHP (1983) 90mg; powdered Horsetail extract 3:1 10mg; powdered Uva Ursi extract 3:1 75mg. To assist urinary flow and prevent fluid retention. Waterlex tablets. (*Gerard House*)
Dandelion coffee, roots roasted and ground. Freely.
Diet. Leaves used in salads or cooked as spinach. In all preparations a pinch of Ginger renders it more diffusive.
Note: The elderly need gentle control of blood

pressure with a minimum of side-effects, without loss of potassium and magnesium, for which the root (dandelion coffee) is an alternative to synthetic drugs. GSL

DANDRUFF. Scurf. Flakes of desquamated cells shed by the scalp.
Topical. Clary sage, Burdock root, Eucalyptus, Lavender, Nettles, Rosemary, Sage, Southernwood, Thyme, Peppermint. Internally as teas, tinctures etc, or externally as lotions.
Hair conditioner: live yoghurt, rub into scalp after washing and rinsing. Leave 15 minutes, again rinse with warm water. Finally rinse with 1 part cider vinegar to 10 parts warm water.
Shampoos: Rosemary, Sage Thyme.
Dressing. 25ml Castor oil in 100ml Vodka. Shake well and rub gently into scalp.
Aromatherapy. Jojoba, Evening Primrose, Borage. 10 drops any one oil to 1 pint (500ml) warm water as a rinse.
Diet. See: DIET, SKIN DISORDERS.
Supplements. Vitamins B6, C. Minerals: Selenium, Zinc. Essential fatty acids.

DEAD NETTLE. *Lamium album L.* Part used: herb.
Constituents: flavone glycosides, mucilage, tannin.
Action: anti-catarrhal.
Uses. Nasal catarrh, leucorrhoea. Anaemia.
Preparations. *Tea*. As a medicament or daily 'health' tea. 1-2 teaspoons to each cup boiling water; infuse 10-15 minutes. 1 cup as desired.
Vaginal douche: 2oz dried (or handful fresh herb) to 2 pints boiling water; infuse, and inject warm. May also be used as a lotion for skin disorders.

DEAFNESS. See: HEARING LOSS.

DEATH. "Death is often, at the start, in a particular organ, i.e. local. If the part can be saved in time life may be preserved. At the approach of death the value of a particular organ strikes one forcibly. There may be no need for constitutional medication. The one suffering part may be the whole case. In many chronic cases certain organs claim and must have special attention." (*Dr J. Compton Burnet*)

Most important of such organs are the heart, which can be sustained by a few grains of Cayenne; the brain (Ginkgo, Skullcap, Kola); stomach (Peppermint); liver (Dandelion); spleen (New Jersey tea). See: LIFE DROPS.

When all desire for food has ceased, sips of honey-water or Balm tea sweetened with honey offer a comforting and sustaining support.

DEATH CAP, or other poisoning by fungi. Fungus contains toxic amanitines.
Symptoms: vomiting, nausea, abdominal pain. Leads to rapid liver degeneration.
Tinctures. Formula. Echinacea 3; Goldenseal 1; Myrrh 1. Dose: 30-60 drops every 2 hours.
Practitioner. Stomach irrigation. 50mg ampoules of Silymarin (Madaus) injected by a physician.

DEBILITY. See: WEAKNESS.

DECOCTION. A preparation obtained by bringing to the boil and simmering dense herbal materials; barks, roots and woody parts of a plant to extract active constituents. Being watery in character it lasts for a day or two only.

A decoction is usually made in the ratio of 30g (1oz) of the cut or crushed crude material simmered in 750ml water until the volume is reduced by one quarter. It is then cooled, strained and taken in divided doses throughout the day. Bring to boil in a stainless steel, glass, earthenware, ceramic, non-aluminium, non-plastic saucepan or other suitable vessel. Decoctions should be made in a covered vessel to prevent escape of volatile components into the atmosphere. Store in a thermos flask. Standard dose: half-1 teacup thrice daily.

DECONGESTANT. (Bronchi and lungs). Combine, parts: Mullein herb 2; Lobelia 1; Wild Cherry bark 2; Liquorice 1; Ginger half. Take as decoction, powders, liquid extracts or tinctures.

DEFECATION. Another term for a bowel movement to expel wastes from the body. Also applies to a colostomy where faeces are voided through an artificial opening.

DEHYDRATION. Loss of natural body fluids when diarrhoea strikes. Loss of water through bowel overaction. Untreated dehydration may result in circulatory collapse in the young and elderly. See: DIARRHOEA.

Re-hydration, after heavy fluid loss: glass water containing 1 teaspoon salt and 2 teaspoons sugar.

Check elderly patient's armpits for moisture – a useful way to rule out dehydration.

DELHI BELLY. Treatment same as for irritable bowel or diarrhoea.

DELIRIUM TREMENS. D.T.s Occurs when heavy drinkers are deprived of alcohol, or from mental shock. Hallucinations, during which he talks to himself. Imagines he is chased by horrible creatures: reptiles, birds, insects. Violent tremors, sleeplessness, irritability and fever require careful nursing in a darkened room. A small amount of alcohol may be necessary to ensure sleep. Overdoses of coffee can have a similar effect.
Alternatives. *Teas*. Hops, Passion flower. Motherwort (with heart symptoms). Oats.

Tablets/capsules. Motherwort, Passion flower. Mistletoe.
Powders. Formula. Passion flower 2; Hops (lupulin) 1; Jamaica Dogwood 1. Dose: 750mg (three 00 capsules or half a teaspoon) every 2 hours.
Tinctures. Formula. Equal parts: Passion flower; Hops; Oats. Dose: one to three 5ml teaspoons in water, every 2 hours.
Practitioner. Tincture Stramonium, Dr Fyfe, Eclectic Medical Review, advises: "With mania present in acute inflammation. Furious, noisy, raving: one drop Tincture Stramonium every two hours."
Tincture Cinchona (Peruvian bark) BPC (1949). 2-4ml 2-3 times daily. 2-3 drops Tincture Capsicum enhances its action.
German traditional. Arnica. Suggest: Tincture Arnica, 2-5 drops in water 2-3 times daily.

DEMENTIA (Atherosclerotic). Arteriosclerotic disease. Due to atheromatic change in blood vessels of the brain. Infarcts.
Symptoms. High cholesterol levels, pathological laughing and crying, depression, delusion.
Alternatives. Evening Primrose, Oats, Alfalfa, Garlic. German Chamomile, Gotu Kola, Ginkgo, Ginseng. Hawthorn, Rutin.
Powders. Formula: Hawthorn 3; Ginkgo 2; Lily of the Valley 1. Dose: 500mg (two 00 capsules or one-third teaspoon) thrice daily.
Liquid Extracts. Formula as for powders. Dose: one 5ml teaspoon thrice daily.
Tinctures. Formula as above. Dose: two 5ml teaspoons thrice daily.
Guar gum. Lowers serum fat levels, body weight and blood pressure.
Aromatherapy: massage and inhalation: Rosemary.
Arnica. Lotion: 1 part Tincture Arnica to 20 parts distilled extract Witch Hazel. Wipe over forehead and hair-line 1-3 times daily.
Diet. Egg-yolk, Lecithin, Oatmeal porridge.
Supplements. Vitamins A, B-complex, B12, C and E. Choline, Folic acid, Magnesium, Manganese, Zinc.

DEMENTIA, (Senile). Progressive loss of brain cells, atrophy; caused by stress and a number of diseases: Huntingdon's Chorea, Alzheimer's Disease, Pick's Disease, syphilis, trauma, and by certain sedative, anxiolytic, diuretic and hypotensive drugs.
Symptoms. Disorientation, failure of memory for recent events, failure to comprehend, unable to form elemental judgements, confusion, ataxia (lack of coordination of muscles), emotional instability with outbursts, forgetful.
Alternatives. Remedies known to sustain the brain. Nervines and alteratives believed to leach from the body deposits of toxic minerals: aluminium, sulphur, mercury, etc. Gotu Kola, Ginseng, Ginkgo, Vitamin E conserve oxygen. Pulsatilla – success reported for mental outbursts. Vasodilator of value. Ginkgo favourably reported.
Teas. Basil, Ginseng, Gotu Kola, German Chamomile, Horsetail, Yarrow.
Tea. Formula. Equal parts, Ginkgo, German Chamomile, Yarrow. 1 heaped teaspoon to each cup boiling water; infuse 5-15 minutes; 1 cup thrice daily.
Tablets/capsules. Prickly Ash, Ginseng, Ginkgo, Kelp, Pulsatilla.
Powders, Liquid Extracts, Tinctures. Combine: Gotu Kola 3; Vervain 2; Rosemary 1. Doses. *Powders*: 500mg; two 00 capsules or one-third teaspoon. *Liquid Extracts*: 1 teaspoon. *Tinctures*: 2 teaspoons. In water, honey or fruit juice thrice daily.
Incontinence. A frequent problem for which American Cranesbill is indicated.
Aromatherapy. Inhalation: Feverfew, Thyme.
Contra-indicated: Black Cohosh.
Diet. Low salt. Low fat. High fibre. Egg yolk. Lecithin.
Supplements. Folic acid, Vitamins B-complex, B12, C and E. Selenium, to conserve oxygen. Magnesium, Manganese, Zinc.
General. Home help. Meals on Wheels. Service from local Psychogeriatric unit.

DEMULCENT. Anti-irritant. A herb rich in mucilage that is soothing, bland, offering protection to inflamed or irritable mucous surfaces. Herbalist's alternative to glycerine. A demulcent is almost always used together with anti-lithics for stone to protect surrounding mucosa (i.e. Parsley Piert).

Agar Agar, Aloe Vera, Arrowroot, Chickweed, Coltsfoot, Cornsilk, Fenugreek seeds, Iceland Moss, Irish Moss, Ispaghula seeds, Linseed, Liquorice root, Marshmallow root, Meadowsweet, Mullein, Oatmeal, Plantain, Slippery Elm bark, Tragacanth gum, White Pond Lily.

DEMYELINATING DISEASES. Disorders that destroy myelin, a fatty substance which forms a sheath round nerve fibres and appears in the central nervous system. A typical example is multiple sclerosis.

Essential fatty acids have an important role in the function of the nervous system, being closely related to the fatty (myelin) sheath and cell membranes. Disturbance in their metabolism may result in nerve disorder. Thus, vegetable oils of Soya, corn, safflower and sunflower should replace animal fats and dairy products.
Symptoms. Numb, prickling, tickling sensation on the skin, paralysis, incoordination, physical weakness and visual complaints.
Treatment. Indeterminate diagnosis.
Tablets/capsules. Prickly Ash, Black Cohosh,

Ginseng, Ginkgo.
Powders, Liquid Extracts, Tinctures. Formula. Equal parts: Black Cohosh, Prickly Ash, Ginseng. Doses. Powders: two 00 capsules or one-third teaspoon, (500mg). Liquid Extracts: 1 teaspoon. Tinctures: 2 teaspoons. In water, honey or fruit juice.
Evening Primrose oil capsules or tablets: two 500mg thrice daily.
Aromatherapy. Rosemary spinal rub: 6 drops Oil Rosemary in 2 teaspoons Almond oil.
Diet. High protein, low fat, oily fish or 2 teaspoons Cod Liver oil daily. Gluten-free diet. Cholesterol-free – avoid milk, meat fat and dairy products. Avoid coffee and other caffeine stimulants. Dandelion coffee.
Supplements. B-complex, B3, B6, B12, C, E. Dolomite, Manganese, Zinc

DENGUE. Breakbone fever. An acute tropical disease caused by the mosquito *Aedes aegypti*. Rarely fatal, lasting 3-4 days.
Symptoms: intensely irritable measles-like rash which responds to Chickweed ointment. Fever, vomiting, painful muscles, headache. A number of relapses may occur before recovery. Each attack is followed by depression and physical weakness.
Treatment. Guaiacum can usually be relied upon to reduce the fever. Abundant herb teas indicated: Yarrow, Elderflowers, Boneset, Chamomile, Golden Rod, Wild Thyme.
Formula. Powders, Liquid Extracts, Tinctures. Combine Yarrow 3; Fringe Tree 1; Guaiacum quarter. Doses. Powders: 500mg (two 00 capsules or one-third teaspoon). Liquid Extracts: 1 teaspoon. Tinctures: 2 teaspoons. Thrice daily.

DENTAL PROBLEMS. See: TEETH DECAY, TEETH EXTRACTION, ALOE VERA.

DEOBSTRUENT. That which clears obstruction by dilating natural passages of the body. Usually of the intestines (Ispaghula seeds) or colon (Buckbean).

DEODORANTS. Herbs, including essential oils, that resolve fetid smells of the breath or body – as from discharging ulcer, cancer, etc.

Bad breath may often be overcome by gentle stimulation of liver and kidneys by the teas, Agrimony, Parsley, Balm. Chlorophyll tablets. Charcoal tablets. Lemons. Nettle beer.
External use: Essential oils of Peppermint, Eucalyptus, Lavender, Wintergreen, Bergamot, Thymol. Zinc and Castor oil cream. Cider vinegar (neat or dilute). Raw lemon juice. See: ANTI-PERSPIRANTS.

DEPRESSION. A persistent change of mood deeper than superficial sadness. Of symptoms, headache is the commonest presenting complaint (Feverfew, Skullcap). Release from symptoms may be obtained from teas, powders or liquid extracts of the following.
Liver causation: Dandelion (Coffee), Wild Yam, Goldenseal.
In the elderly: Skullcap, Sage.
With restlessness: Lemon balm, Californian Poppy.
With palpitations: Hawthorn, Motherwort.
From abuse of coffee: German Chamomile.
Unable to relax: Passion Flower.
Epileptic: Mistletoe. Vervain.
Parkinsonian: St John's Wort, broad beans.
To correct hormone imbalance: Helonias, Raspberry leaves.
Pre-menstrual tension: Evening Primrose, St John's Wort, Rosemary.
With painful menstruation: Black Cohosh.
Associated with glaucoma: Rutin tea.
The hidden alcoholic: Ginseng.
Pregnant depressive: Raspberry leaves.
Obese depressive: Cider vinegar.
Enuresis schoolchild: Liquorice.
With swollen prostate gland: Pulsatilla.
In heart cases, and to counter side effects of beta blockers: Hawthorn, Lily of the Valley.
Drug-induced: St John's Wort, Californian Poppy, Ginseng.
General anti-depressives: Lemon balm, Celery, Chamomile, Borage, Ginkgo, Damiana, Kola, Mistletoe, Mugwort, Oats, Rosemary, Skullcap, Southernwood, Valerian, Vervain, Wormwood, St John's Wort, Peppermint.
BHP (1983) combination: Kola nuts, Skullcap, Oats, Damiana.
Evening Primrose: 4 x 500mg capsules daily.
Temporary depression from physical and mental exhaustion: Life Drops (see entry). Pinch of Cayenne in cup of tea.
Old men. Low cholesterol levels are linked to depression among older men.
Practitioner: Persistent depression from shock: Tincture Arnica, 2-5 drops in water, thrice daily. (Practice among German physicians.)
Aromatherapy. Inhalant: any one oil: Rose, Tangerine, Geranium.
Diet. Low caffeine. Oats: good for depression (oatmeal porridge, oatcakes, etc). Spinach for iron and calcium.
Supplementation. Vitamins: B-complex, B6, B12, C. Thiamine, Niacin. Minerals: Dolomite, Iron, Chromium, Iodine, Zinc.
Note. Depression may trigger mechanisms that introduce chronic disease by lowering immune response, hence need for conscientious patient compliance.

DEPRESSION – POST-NATAL. Extreme anguish after birth of a child. Mental illness: "sinking into gloom". Baby blues. Bursting into tears; every small problem seems magnified; ago-

raphobic tendency.
Etiology. Some mothers have a genetic predisposition to the condition. Death of a close relative, stressful pregnancy, redundancy, moving house, or sheer physical and mental exhaustion.
Treatment. Conventional medicine advises strong anti-depressants. Alternatives, until "hormones settle down": Agnus Castus, Helonias, Milk Thistle. Raspberry leaf tea (tablets/capsules/liquid extracts/tinctures). Special attention to the thyroid gland.
Diet. See: GENERAL DIET.
Supplements. Vitamins: B group, E. Minerals: Calcium, Iodine, Magnesium, Zinc. Tyrosine.
Supportives: Astute GP, helpful health visitor, thoughtful husband.

DEPURATIVE. Blood purifier. Another term for an alterative.

DERMATITIS, CONTACT. Redness and possible blistering caused by a sensitive substance such as chromium, nickel, other metals, rubber, paints, cosmetic materials, plants (primula), house dust mites, aerosols, deodorants, photocopying, dyes in clothing, etc. A patch test establishes diagnosis. A suspected irritant is applied to the skin and after two days its reaction is noted. If inflammation is present the test is positive. Symptoms may include vesicles with weeping, scaling, and presence of dropsy.

In a study of 612 patients attending the Royal Hallamshire Hospital, Sheffield, more than half of the women who had ears pierced reported skin reactions to metallic jewellery, while a third had sensitivity to nickel. (*British Journal of Dermatology, Jan 1992*)
Treatment. Remove article or cause of irritation. Garlic is claimed to be successful, either in diet or by capsule when the condition is caused by histamines. Other agents: Betony, Burdock leaves, Chickweed, Dandelion, Figwort, Gotu Kola, Plantain, Red Clover.
Internal. Burdock tea. Clivers tea.
Tablets/capsules. Garlic, Devil's Claw, Blue Flag.
Topical. Avoid use of Calamine, if possible. Creams or salves: Aloe Vera, Comfrey, Evening Primrose, Witch Hazel, Jojoba. All are alternatives to corticosteroids.

Tamus (Black Bryony) tincture.

Distilled extract of Witch Hazel.

DERMATITIS, EXFOLIATIVE. Erythroderma. Redness and thickening of the skin which later peels off in layers (desquamation). Follows some chronic skin disorders: leukaemia, Hodgkin's disease or fungoid invasion. May involve the whole of the body.
Alternatives. *Teas*. Betony, Burdock leaves, Bogbean, Chickweed, Clivers, Dandelion, Gotu Kola, Ground Ivy, Figwort, Red Clover, Violet, Yarrow.
Cold tea. Barberry bark: one heaped teaspoon to each teacup cold water; stand overnight, drink 1 cup morning and evening next day (most effective).
Tablets/capsules. Blue Flag root, Burdock, Devil's Claw, Echinacea, Garlic, Poke root, Queen's Delight, Red Clover, Seaweed and Sarsaparilla.
Formula. Equal parts: Dandelion, Echinacea, Yellow Dock root. Dose – Powders: 500mg (two 00 capsules or one-third teaspoon). Liquid extracts: one 5ml teaspoon. Tinctures: two 5ml teaspoons. Thrice daily before meals.
Topical. Alternatives to corticosteroids. Tamus tincture or salve – see Black Bryony. Aloe Vera, Witch Hazel, Comfrey, Evening Primrose, Jojoba, Thuja. Bran bath.
Diet. See: DIET – SKIN DISEASES.

DERMATITIS, HERPETIFORMIS. Red inflammation of the skin with blisters. Not eczema. Common cause: gluten, as present in cereals barley, oats, rye, wheat.
Alternatives. *Teas*. Betony, Burdock, Elderflowers, German Chamomile, Hops, Gotu Kola, Mullein, Plantain, Red Clover, Valerian.
Tea formula. Equal parts, Mullein, Red Clover, Valerian. Mix. 1 heaped teaspoon to each cup boiling water; infuse 15 minutes; 1 cup thrice daily.
Tablets/capsules. Blue Flag, Dandelion, Devil's Claw, Echinacea, Poke root, Red Clover, Seaweed and Sarsaparilla, Valerian.
Powders. Formula. Equal parts: Burdock root, Dandelion root, Valerian root. Two 00 capsules or one-third teaspoon thrice daily, (500mg).
Liquid extracts or tinctures. Formula. Chickweed 10ml; Poke root 5ml; Meadowsweet 10ml; Valerian 10ml. Dose: liquid extracts, one 5ml teaspoon; tinctures, two 5ml teaspoons. Thrice daily in water.
Topical. Apply dilute Tea Tree oil 3-4 times daily. Witch Hazel, Aloe Vera, Vitamin E cream, Evening Primrose oil, or Marshmallow and Slippery Elm ointment. Bran bath.
Diet. Gluten-free.

DERMATITIS, LIGHT. Photo dermatitis. Reddening and blistering of the skin on exposure to sunlight. See: SUNBURN.

DERMATITIS, PSEUDOMONAS. Itchy rash contracted in swimming pools, sports clubs or public baths caused by *pseudomonas aeruginosa*. Runs a self-limiting course from 7-14 days. Garlic and Echinacea specific.

DERMATITIS, SEBORRHOEIC. See: SEBORRHOEA.

DERMATOGRAPHIA. A form of nettle rash (hives). Rubbing a sensitive surface produces raised rough patches. 'Skin writing.' Treat as for NETTLE RASH.

DERMATOMYOSITIS. Degeneration of muscles with inflammation and swelling of the skin (oedema), sometimes associated with malignancy. Remedies indicated: Poke root, Thuja, Mistletoe, Melilot, Guaiacum, Cramp bark. (*Hyde*)

DETERGENT. A herb of strong cleaning properties such as Soapwort for use on the skin. Balmony, Southernwood, Marigold, Chickweed, Goldenseal, Daisy.

DETOXIFIERS. Plant medicines that aid removal of a poison or poisonous effect, reducing toxic properties of certain substances by inducing chemical changes in the offending substance and assisting its excretion from the body. For instance: Sarsaparilla is said to aid the elimination of mercury salts, and the plant Chorella the toxic effects of radiation.

For internal cleansing. Urinary tract – Dandelion, Burdock. Liver – Dandelion, Milk Thistle. Mucous membrane – Goldenseal. Blood – Burdock, Red Clover, Yellow Dock. Intestinal tract – Slippery Elm, Fenugreek, Meadowsweet. Womb – Raspberry leaves. Lymphatic system – Figwort, Poke root. Lungs – Mullein, Angelica root. Skin – Yellow Dock, Chamomile.

DEVIL'S CLAW. *Harpagophytum procumbens* D.C. Rhizome. Native of the Kalahari Desert.
Keynote: rheumatism. A versatile remedy.
Constituents: flavonoids, iridoid glycosides.
Action: anti-inflammatory, antirheumatic, analgesic (mild), liver tonic, cholagogue, diuretic, sedative, detoxicant, stomachic, lymphatic, stimulant, cortisone-like action.
Uses. Inflammatory arthritic stiff joints. Gout. Lumbago, sciatica, polymyalgia, neuralgia, liver congestion. Gall bladder disorders. Itching skin conditions. Piles. Inflammatory conditions of the veins. Avoid in pregnancy. Not given in presence of gastric or duodenal ulcer.
Preparations. Thrice daily.
Tablets: dosage as on bottle.
Alternative: a tea is made by dissolving tablets in a cup of boiling water.
Decoction. Quarter to half a teaspoon in each cup water gently simmered 15 minutes. Dose: half a cup.
Liquid Extract, BHC Vol 1. (1:1, 25 per cent ethanol). Dose: 1-2ml.
Powder. 250mg capsules; maintenance dose, 2 capsules thrice daily with meals. Or applied to open wounds for healing. GSL

DIABETES, MELLITUS. Sugar diabetes. Chronic disorder of fat, protein and carbohydrate metabolism. A decrease of insulin by the pancreas gives rise to high level blood sugar (glucose) which is eliminated in the urine by the kidneys. With low insulin production the body cannot convert food into energy. In Britain over 30,000 new cases are diagnosed each year. One in five people go blind because of diabetes. The genetic factor is important; it may run in families due to defect in the immune system. Women who have German measles during the first three months of pregnancy can have a child who develops diabetes during adolescence.
Etiology. The more severe form, in younger patients, needs insulin treatment, without which ketosis and diabetic coma are possible. The milder form in older patients can be managed with diet and hypoglycaemic agents. Now considered due to auto-immune attack on Islet of Langerhams cells in pancreas which secrete insulin. "The Pill" often raises blood sugar. Lack of trace minerals (chromium and zinc). Zinc is a component of insulin and Chromium produces enzymes to stimulate metabolism of sugars. Diabetes can cause heart attack, stroke, hardening of arteries, blindness. It is the leading cause of kidney failure and gangrene.
Symptoms. Great thirst. Urine of high specific gravity. Weakness, emaciation, skin ulcers, loss of tactile sensation in the fingertips (Vitamin B6). In men there may be inflammation of the glans penis and in women, itching of the vulvae. Boils are common. In spite of large appetite there may by severe weight loss. Magnesium deficiency.

Diabetics are subject to glaucoma and detachment of the retina. There is a high incidence of cataract of the eye. While surgery may be necessary, effective supportive herbal treatment can do much. Regular visits to the Hospital Specialist help detect in time future eye, kidney and circulation damage.

High fibre, low fat, high carbohydrate. To help control blood sugar a diabetic must avoid sweets. Exercise lowers blood sugar.

Agents used with some success: Alfalfa, Damiana leaves, Fenugreek seeds, Aloe Vera juice, Dandelion, Fringe Tree, Guar gum, Garlic (anti-diabetic action shown by Dr Madaus, West Germany, 1967), Bilberry berries, Goat's Rue (dried aerial parts reduce blood sugar BHP (1983), Olive leaves, onions, Nettles, Pipsissewa, White Horehound, Sweet Sumach, Jambul seeds rapidly reduce sugar in the urine. Karela. Gurmar, (*Gymnema sylvestre*) leaves are chewed in India to reduce sugar in the urine (mild cases). Balsam pear. Bitter melon (*Momordica charastia*).

Hypoglycaemic herbs can be effective where the pancreas still functions. Type 1 diabetes, suffered by children whose insulin-producing cells have been destroyed and who produce no insulin at all will always require administered insulin. Maturity-onset diabetes (Type 11) occurs in middle life, insulin-production being insufficient. This form is usually associated with obesity for which herbs are helpful.

Diabetics are specially prone to infections; a course of Echinacea at the onset of winter is beneficial. Coronary artery disease is common in diabetics (especially women) who may develop atherosclerosis at an early age. High blood pressure places undue strain upon kidneys which may excrete too much protein (Yarrow, Lime flowers, Hawthorn). Lack of sensation in the feet exposes the subject to unconscious bruising and injury from which septic ulceration may arise (Chamomile foot baths).

Alternatives. Liver herbs work positively on the pancreas. Diabetic cases should receive treatment for the liver also, Dandelion and Fringe Tree being a reliable combination. Dr John Fearn, California (*Ellingwood*) used Fringe Tree for all his cases of sugar in the urine: 10 drops, Liquid Extract, 4-5 times daily.

Tea. Equal parts: Peppermint leaves, Dandelion leaves, Goat's Rue leaves. 1-2 teaspoons to each cup boiling water infuse 5-15 minutes. Cup 2-3 times daily.

Teas from any one of the following: Bilberry berries or leaves, Nettles, White Horehound, Alfalfa, Olive leaves.

Decoction. Fenugreek seeds. 2 teaspoons to each large cup water simmered gently 5 minutes. One cup daily, consuming the seeds.

Powders. Equal parts: Sweet Sumach, Jambul seeds, Dandelion. Dose: 750mg (three 00 capsules or half a teaspoon) thrice daily.

Tinctures. Formula. Equal parts: Jambul, Fringe Tree, Goat's Rue. Dose: 1 teaspoon thrice daily and at bedtime.

Tablets. Dr Alfred Vogel: tablet containing: Bilberry, Kidney Bean, Tormentil, English Walnut leaves, Alfalfa leaves, Cuckoo flowers.

Karela (*Momordica Charantia*) Hypoglycaemic action gave good results in clinical trials. Daily dose: 50/60ml fresh juice.

Evening Primrose. See entry.

Guar Gum. 5g unit dose sachets (*Guarina*) containing dispersible granules. This gum has shown beneficial effects for insulin-dependants.

Hypoglycaemics (second degree). Allspice, Bugleweed, Burdock, Ginseng, Lily of the Valley, Wormwood, Nettles.

Diabetic gangrene. Tinctures: equal parts, Echinacea, Thuja. Internally and externally. Internal dose: 30-60 drops.

Diabetic neuralgia. Cayenne pepper (Capsicum). Frequently successful.

American traditional. It is claimed that 500mg Bayleaf, Cinnamon, Cloves and Turmeric halve the need for insulin in diabetics.

Diet. Dietary treatment has changed over the past few years. Patients are now advised by the British Diabetic Association to eat food rich in complex carbohydrates (starches) and high in fibre as in wholemeal bread, oats and wholegrain breakfast cereals, wholewheat pasta, brown rice, beans and lentils, vegetables and fruit. Fat intake should be carefully watched (lean meat); skimmed milk, polyunsaturated or low-fat cheeses and salad dressings. Certain foods are known to encourage the pancreas to produce more insulin: banana, barley, cabbage, lettuce, oats, olive, papaya, turnip, sweet potato.

Coffee intake should be limited to prevent hypoglycaemic symptoms.

Barley. A study has shown that the use of barley flour as a substitute for wheat in bread helps to control diabetes, in Iraq. (*Naismith D, et al, 'Therapeutic Value of Barley in Management of Diabetes': Annals Nutr Metab, 35, 61-64 1991*)

Supplementation. Vitamins A, B-complex, C, D, E, F. Vitamin B6. Brewer's yeast. Minerals: Chromium 50mcg; Manganese 15mg; Magnesium 300mg; Zinc 25mg; to normalise glucose metabolism.

Note. Over 400 traditional plant medicines have been documented for diabetes, but few have been evaluated for efficacy. In the undeveloped countries they are chiefly used for non-insulin dependent diabetes. (*Diabetes Care, 1989, Sept 12, p553*)

Insulin dependents. Whether adults or children, insulin dependents should under no circumstances discontinue insulin injections.

Treatment by or in liaison with general medical practitioner.

Information. British Diabetic Association, 10 Queen Anne Street, London W1M 0BD, UK. Send SAE.

DIAGNOSIS. The specific disease or other condition defined after investigation has taken into consideration all the facts, evidence and information bearing on the case.

The practice of medicine, orthodox or alternative, is beset by many variables. Care should be taken not to assume that the obvious clinical findings are the cause of the symptoms; but to look deeper. The danger comes when a patient or practitioner is persuaded to ignore dangerous symptoms. If the malaise associated with a progressive disease like cancer is not properly investigated, then when it is eventually recognised in its later stages it may be more difficult to treat.

Accurate diagnosis is the touchstone of correct treatment. The modern herbalist will employ basic medical techniques as supported by examinations of the blood, urine and other body fluids carried out by the pathological, haematological or other specialist ancillary service in a modern hospital.

Immediate reduction of symptoms often indicates an absence of deep-seated disease. (*Dr J.T Kent*) It is sometimes necessary to remove a small sample of tissue (biopsy) for further tests. It is good when disease moves from the inside to the outside (skin).

When in doubt, alternative practitioners should not hesitate to seek a second opinion, preferably from a competent independent medical practitioner. The safety of a second brain engaged on the problem reduces the risk of incorrect treatment.

DIAPHORETICS. Herbs that induce increased perspiration. Diaphoresis is regarded as a process of internal cleansing. Toxic wastes are eliminated via the pores of the skin thus assisting kidney function. Widely used in feverish conditions to reduce a high temperature and to equalise the circulation. Of this large group, commonly used are: Balm (relaxing), Bayberry (mild), Boneset, Catnep (relaxing), Cayenne, Elderflowers, Ephedra, Galangal, Garlic, Ginger, Golden Rod, Hemlock Spruce, Holy Thistle, Lime flowers, Hyssop, Marigold, Peppermint, Pleurisy root, Prickly Ash bark, Queen's Delight, Rosemary, Senega, Thyme, Vervain, Yarrow.

For a more profuse abundant sweating *Sudorifics* are employed: Red Sage, Boneset, Ginger, Angelica root, Virginia Snakeroot, Cayenne, Crawley root.

DIARRHOEA. The world's biggest killer of children. Inflammation of the bowel by production of too much mucous secretion.

Causes: faulty absorption of fats, bacterial or viral infection, nervous bowel, anxiety or psychosomatic disturbance, malfunction of the thyroid gland, etc.

Looseness of the bowels may sometimes occur as an acute cleansing eliminative effort by Nature to expel wastes and impurities. Dehydration can be serious in children. For presence of mucous or blood in the stool refer to DIFFERENTIAL DIAGNOSIS.

Differential diagnosis. Crohn's disease, Gastroenteritis, Diverticulosis, Ulcerative colitis, Dysentery, Salmonella.

Travel diarrhoea: 'blight of holiday and business trips abroad' due to E. Coli. Acute, usually non-persistent self-limiting condition. Ginger, crystallised or powder in capsules or tablets is known to reduce the incidence in high risk areas.

Imported bloody diarrhoeas – salmonella, shigella or amoebic infections should receive special investigation by a competent authority, a consultant in infectious diseases. First-aid until the practitioner comes: 2-5 drops oil of Peppermint in water.

Children's diarrhoea. Re-hydration after severe loss of fluids – glass of water containing 1 teaspoon salt and 2 teaspoons sugar.

Over 13,000 children die from this preventable disease every day, many in the developing countries. This simple combination of sugar and salt prevents dehydration, the most common cause of death from acute diarrhoea, and has helped save tens of thousands of lives.

Alternatives. Rest. Avoid caffeine and alcohol drinks. Plenty of astringent herb teas to reduce the associated hyperperistalsis. Children – half-dose.

Teas. Any one of the following: Agrimony, Avens, Burmarigold, Black Walnut leaves, Burnet (greater or garden), Ground Ivy, Ladysmantle, Hops (nervous bowel), Plantain, Peppermint, Periwinkle (vinca major), Meadowsweet, Silverweed, Shepherd's Purse, Tormentil. Sage. Formulae: (1) equal parts; Raspberry leaves, Agrimony, Avens. Or (2) equal parts; Raspberry leaves, Plantain, Silverweed. 2 teaspoons to each cup boiling water; infuse 5-15 minutes. Half-1 cup freely. For nerve exhaustion: add a sprinkle of Valerian.

Seeds. Coriander, Caraway or Fenugreek. Half a teaspoon to each cup water, brought to boil; vessel removed as soon as boiling point is reached. Half-1 cup freely.

Decoctions. Any one of the following: Bayberry, Cranesbill (American), Rhatany root, Sweet Chestnut leaves, Oak bark, Wild Yam, Iceland Moss.

Powders. Any one: Calamus, Bayberry, Oak bark, Cinnamon, Black Catechu, Wild Yam. Add pinch of Ginger.

Tinctures. (1) Combine Bayberry 2; Ginger 1. Or (2) Combine Bayberry 1; Raspberry leaves 2. One to two 5ml teaspoons thrice daily after meals.

Tincture, or spirits of Camphor: 5-10 drops in water every 3-4 hours for severe depletion of body fluids. Adults only.

Aloe Vera. Scientific papers confirm efficacy.

Dr Finlay Ellingwood. Castor oil: 5 drops every 2 hours.

Bilberry juice. Half-1 cup freely.

Goldenseal. Antibacterial. 5-10 drops, tincture, 3-4 times daily. Adults only.

Diet. Avoid cow's milk. 3-day fast on fruit juices and herb teas alone, followed by gruel made from Slippery Elm, Oatmeal or Arrowroot. Yoghurt. Bilberry fruit. Carob bean products: chocolate or other preparations. Ensure adequate fluid intake.

Supplementation. Vitamins A, B12, C, D. Minerals: Calcium, Iron, Magnesium, Potassium, Zinc.

Preventative. 2 drops oil of Peppermint morning and evening.

DIET – CANCER. GENERAL DIET use as a base.

Life is our most precious gift. But at some point that gift might be at risk. It is at such time that food and drink may contribute to our sense of well-being.

Rapidly accumulating evidence links cancer to a growing public awareness of the role of diet. Also, involvement of supplements in cancer prevention are a fruitful area of research.

Vital food enzymes are not destroyed in

cooking when a large proportion of food is eaten raw. All food should be free from additives.

A high fat intake is a risk factor in cancer of the ovary, womb and prostate gland. It also affects the bowel flora, changing bile acid metabolism and the concentration of carcinogenic bile acid metabolites. Obesity significantly increases risk of cancer.

Epidemiological studies in man show that people with low Vitamin A levels are more susceptible to lung cancer. Cancer risk is increased by low levels of Vitamin A, particularly Beta Carotene, Vitamin E and Selenium.

Antioxidants control the activity of free-radicals that destroy body cells, and source foods containing them are therefore of value in cancer prevention. Most cancers generate a high degree of toxicity and this is where antioxidants, particularly Vitamin C are indicated. A deficiency of Vitamin C has been associated with cancer of the oesophagus, stomach, lungs and breast. This vitamin is known to increase life expectancy in terminally ill patients and is a mild analgesic for pain. Vitamin B6 may be of value for nausea.

Vitamins and minerals of value: Vitamins A, B6, C, E, Calcium, Chromium, Magnesium, Molybdenum, Selenium, Zinc.

Stimulants should be avoided: cocoa, alcohol, sugar, coffee (including decaffeinated). Tea should not be too strong as it inhibits absorption of iron. Choice should be over a wide range of foods, to eat less fat and more wholegrain cereals and raw fresh fruit and vegetables.

DIET – CHOLESTEROL. To lower cholesterol. Avoid all animal fats and dairy products, bacon, ham, lobster, shell fish, milk (use skimmed), rich sauces, gravies, the use of cream, eggs, offal, ice cream, cheese (cottage cheese accepted), cream puffs, fried foods, crab, salami, pork, beef steak, veal, baked custard, mayonnaise made with eggs, milk chocolate, fried fish and chips. Alcohol, refined sugars.
Accept: white fish, lean meat, chicken, skimmed milk, Tofu products, nuts except cashew and coconut, bread, breakfast cereals, cottage cheese, plenty of fruits and fruit juices, raw green vegetables and salad materials. For cooking – polyunsaturated oils such as sunflower, corn or Soya. No more than 3 eggs per week. 2-3 fatty fish meals each week to prevent clumping of platelets. Artichokes. Dandelion coffee.

DIET – GENERAL. It is sometimes not possible to achieve worthwhile results from herbal medicine without due regard to the quality and type of food that enters the body. Suggested foods are those which experience has shown to assist recovery and conserve body energies that might otherwise be diverted towards elimination of metabolic wastes.

"A good and proper diet in disease is worth a hundred medicines and no amount of medication can do good to a patient who does not observe a strict regimen of diet." (*Charaka Samhita 300AD*)

A healthy diet helps maintain the immune system, builds up reserves and hastens recovery from illness.

A good general diet includes foods low in fat, salt and high in fibre. All white sugar and white sugar products (chocolates, sweets, etc) should be replaced with natural sugars (honey, dates, figs, molasses, raisins etc). It should contain plenty of raw fresh fruit and vegetables; best prepared in a juice-press.

Vegetables should be conservatively cooked in very little water with little salt in a covered vessel. At least one mixed raw vegetable salad should be taken daily. Bread can be replaced by jacket potato, Soya-bean flour products or ripe bananas. Puddings, pastry and suety meals should be avoided.

Lean meat should be restricted to two or three parts a week with liberal inclusion of oily fish. Tofu, a Soya bean product, is an excellent alternative to meat. Three or four eggs, only, should be taken weekly.

Dairy produce (milk, butter, cream) contain cholesterol which thickens the blood, blocks arteries and increases resistance against the heart and major blood vessels, and should be taken sparingly.
Accept: Garlic, Onions, Lecithin, Muesli or Oatmeal porridge for breakfast or at other times during the day, yoghurt, honey.
Reject: fried foods, biscuits, confectionery.
Salt: replace with powdered Garlic, Celery or Kelp.
Alcohol: replace with fresh fruit or raw vegetable juices. Coffee is a risk factor raising cholesterol concentration; Dandelion coffee, Rutin or any one of many herbal teas available offer alternatives.

Avoid over-eating and meals when tired. Foods should be well masticated without liquid drinks; dry-feed. Plenty of liquid drinks, water etc should be taken between meals.
Supplements: Vitamin C 200mg, Vitamin E 200iu, morning and evening. Evening Primrose oil. Efamol produce a combined Evening Primrose and Fish oil capsule.

Dietary fibre can prevent certain colonic diseases. Treatment of disease by diet is preferred to drugs because it has the advantage of being free from side-effects.

DIET – GLUTEN-FREE. Some people cannot absorb the protein gluten present in wheat, barley, rye and oats, and hundreds of foods made from them. Nutritional deficiencies may result in coeliac disease, schizophrenia, allergies and irritable bowel syndrome.

Foods containing gluten include: many breakfast cereals, shredded wheat wheat germ flakes, white and wholemeal bread, cakes, puddings, biscuits, porridge, rye and wheat crispbreads, crumbled fish and meat, semolina, baked beans, macaroni, baby foods, soups in packets and tins, chocolate, cocoa, spaghetti, muesli, custard, sausages, batter, beer, instant coffee, bedtime drinks and all kinds of pasta.

Natural gluten-free foods include maize, peas, millet, Soya, lima beans, rice. Brown rice is the basic cereal food: cornflakes, puffed rice, rice cereals. Millet flakes, sago, tapioca. These may be prepared in skimmed milk. Gluten-free flours and bread. The potato comes into its own in the gluten-free kitchen, especially for thickening soups and casseroles.

One school of medical thought associates certain nerve dyscrasies with nutritional deficiencies, the gluten-free diet being advised for cases of multiple sclerosis, myasthenia gravis, poliomyelitis, syringomyelia, motor neurone disease.

Book. Gluten-Free cooking Recipes for Coeliacs and Others, by Rita Greer.

DIET. THE HAY DIET. Diet plays an important role in modern herbal medicine. A faulty diet may ruin the effect of the best of medicine. In some instances it may seriously hinder recovery. The Hay Diet works well with herbal medicine and comprises three principles.

1. Starches and sugars are not eaten with protein and acid fruit. Acid fruits should be eaten with protein meals.
2. Sugars, proteins, fats and starches are eaten only in small quantities. Vegetables, salads and fruits should form 80 per cent of the diet – all these are necessary to maintain the alkaline reserve.
3. All refined sugars and starches are avoided.

Example: potatoes or bread are not eaten with meat or fish. Sugar or honey are not used on acid fruits. Sugar and honey are only compatible with starch fruits such as bananas. There are, however, certain foods that are compatible with all meals: mushrooms, oils, butter, cream, raisins, nuts, milk, egg yolks (the white is one of the most acid foods known).

Dr Hay advised against eating refined or processed foods – white sugar, white flour, etc, and against eating one kind of meal within four hours of a meal of the same kind.

Book: "*Food Combining for Health*", by Doris Grant and Jean Joice. (*Thorsons*)

The Hay Diet has proved beneficial for Crohn's disease, Colitis, Indigestion, Migraine, Raynaud's disease, Irritable Bowel Syndrome, Heart disease, Allergies and certain other disturbances.

DIET. HEART AND CIRCULATION. It is now widely accepted that changes in diet and lifestyle can dramatically reduce the risk of heart disease. Use DIET – GENERAL as a base.

Unsaturated fatty acids, as in vegetable oils, should replace animal fats (saturated fatty acids) that increase deposits of cholesterol on the inner coat of arteries and encourage hardening. Vegetable oils contain lecithin – a homogeniser which thins and separates the cholesterol, sweeping it along through the bloodstream and preventing deposits to form on walls of the arteries.

A study on the European population has shown a strong link between oily fish consumption and a reduced risk of heart disease. Populations that eat a lot of fish, such as Greenland Eskimos (about 400g a day) and Japanese fishermen (about 200g a day) have low rates of heart disease.

Another study, by the Leiden University of the Netherlands, has found that men who ate more than 30g of fish per day were less than half as likely to die from coronary heart disease as those who ate no fish. A diet high in fish lowers plasma cholesterol, triglyceride and very low density lipoprotein levels and is of value in the treatment of hyperlipidaemia (abnormally high concentration of fats in the blood).

Indicated: Magnesium-containing foods, lecithin, Evening Primrose oil for gamma linoleic acid which is converted into prostaglandin E1 in the body and helps reduce high blood pressure and prevents platelet clumping. Coffee carries a risk factor and should be taken sparingly – alternatives: herbal teas Rutin, Lime flowers and others as available in bulk or tea-bags. Green grapes.

Supplements, daily: Vitamin C 1g; Vitamin E 400iu; Magnesium 300mg – 450mg for pregnant women and nursing mothers. Iodine. Chromium, Selenium. Garlic tablets/capsules – 2-3 at night.

Flora margarine is high in essential polyunsaturated fats – made from sunflower seed oil.

Hay diet: good results reported.

DIET, HIGH FIBRE. A diet high in rich carbohydrate foods with sufficient protein to promote efficient elimination and supply vital trace elements in the form of minerals. Such foods produce moist bulky stools easy to pass and reduce blood cholesterol. It reduces LDLs and increases HDLs.

Fibre-deficient foods lead to poor elimination of body wastes and constipation, disposing the colon to a toxic state. This induces depression, a coated tongue and tiredness during the day. Such foods bring about a change in the balance of bowel bacterial flora, and form gas which may cause pouches of diverticulitis to develop. One of its less obvious effects is to enhance the risk of tooth and gum disease. Soon calcium is expelled by the urine and the intake of magnesium reduced, thus favouring the development of stone.

All plant material; leaves, stalks, seeds etc contain fibre. High-fibre foods include: whole grains, wholemeal bread, wholemeal flour (100 per cent extraction rate), crispbreads, biscuits (digestive, bran, oatmeal or coconut), raw green salad materials, potatoes boiled in their jackets, breakfast cereals (porridge, muesli, All-Bran, Shredded Wheat), brown rice, bran (2 teaspoons thrice daily; increase if necessary), fresh or dried fruit once or twice daily.

DIET, LOW PROTEIN. Reduce intake of foods, taking small helpings: meat, eggs, poultry, fish, milk, cheese, dried peas and beans, pulses, nuts, bread, pasta, wheat flour.
Accept: rice, cornflour, honey, salad vegetables, all fruits, preserves.

DIET, LOW SALT. Salt is present in most foods. Spices, herbs and peppers (Black or Cayenne) may be used for flavouring. No salt should be used in cooking or added at table. Salty foods such as the following should be avoided:
Reject: canned foods (except fruit), packet mixes, all bought cooked meats – sausages, bacon, ham. Cakes containing baking soda, chocolate, toffee, treacle, bought biscuits, kippers and other smoked fish, yeast extracts, chutneys, sauces, excessively salted cheeses, butter and margarine.
Accept: rice, pasta, cereals, home-made cottage cheese, eggs (3 per week), all meats, chicken, poultry, whitefish, shellfish, herring, salmon, unsalted bread, butter, margarine, vegetable oils, restricted milk and cream, all vegetables and fruits, fruit juices, brown sugar, wines.

Excess salt leads to retention of fluid in body tissues and adds to work the heart will perform.

DIET – MACROBIOTIC. A plant-based diet with small amounts of poultry, fish or meat for non-vegetarians. A return to the traditional diet of local natural foods as found in some primitive communities and which is believed to increase immunity against degenerative diseases of the civilised world.

The average macrobiotic diet is made up approximately of the proportions: whole grains 45 per cent; vegetables 25 per cent; beans, legumes and seeds 10 per cent; nuts 5 per cent; fruit 5 per cent; seaweeds 5 per cent; poultry 2.5 per cent; fish 2.5 per cent.

Whole grains: wheat, barley, rye, oats, brown rice, buckwheat, millet, corn. Vegetables: green leaves and roots – grown organically. Beans, legumes and seeds: all beans, aduki, lentils, chickpeas. Seeds: sesame, sunflower, etc. Seaweeds: hiziki, wakama, dulse, Carragheen moss, kelp. Very low sugar. Moderate fats and oils.

DIET. SKIN DISORDERS. Low fat, low salt, high fibre. Dairy-free (no milk, cream, cheese, eggs). Soya milk is more suitable for children and adults than cow's milk and provides protein, calories, calcium and vitamins. Polyunsaturates: oils of safflower, corn, Soya, sunflower seed, etc which are rich in essential fatty acids, low levels of which are frequently found in the blood of those with chronic skin disorders. Evening Primrose oil is a rich source of EFAs. Gluten-free diet has proved successful in some cases.
Accept. Goat's milk, yoghurt, eggs – twice weekly. The high potassium and low salt content of bananas help reduce itching. Lecithin. Oily fish. Purslane is a non-fish source of EPA and suitable for the vegetarian approach. Cottage cheese. Pumpkin seeds as a source of zinc. Dandelion coffee. Artichoke: such as Schoenenberger plant juice. Salad dressing: emulsify 1 teaspoon Cider vinegar to each 2 teaspoons safflower seed oil.
Reject: Fried and greasy foods, pastries, chocolates, sweets, ice cream, spicy foods, seasoning, sausage meats, white flour products, white sugar products, alcoholic drinks, meat from the pig (ham, pork, bacon), peppers, horseradish, condiments. Powdered kelp in place of salt, powdered garlic or celery.

Foods known to contain artificial colours and preservatives. All soft drinks, except those made at home from fresh fruits or raw vegetables; coffee, strong tea, oranges, Cola drinks, chocolate, milk, cream, cheese, whey.
Supplement. Beta carotene.
Study. A flare-up can be caused by nuts, jams, fruits, artificially coloured or flavoured foods. (*British Journal of Dermatology, 110, 457, (1984)*)

DIET, SLIMMING. Diet should be based on 1200 calories a day, eating habits being changed to a simple regime. Low-fat, high carbohydrate and fibre.

Eat plenty of fresh fruit and raw vegetables for vitamins and minerals as well as for fibre. As a substitute for mayonnaise use low-fat plain yoghurt. Vegetable fats should replace animal fats: instead of butter – margarine from Sunflower or Safflower oils.
Carbohydrates. At liberty: porridge, muesli, wholemeal bread and wholegrain products, pasta, potatoes, beans, peas, brown rice. These are high in fibre and low in fat. Processed foods should be avoided and those with natural goodness preferred, except for All-Bran which is rich in iron.
Protein. Meat should be taken in small quantities only – turkey, poultry, steamed fish, replace red with grilled lean white meats. Chicken is the most versatile, least expensive and most nutritious of meats. Cottage cheese is low in calories. Food should not be fried but grilled, roasted or baked.
Fluids. Juices, or drinks made with skimmed milk, herb teas. Dandelion coffee. In place of alcohol – carrot, tomato and other fresh vegetable juices.
Reject. Fried foods, white and brown sugar prod-

ucts, honey, sweets, confectionery, jams, biscuits, chocolates, canned fruits, thick soups. Frankfurters, beefburgers, hamburgers, everything from the pig: bacon, ham, pork, lard. Avoid between-meal snacks but chew a carrot or piece of other raw vegetable or fresh fruit.

There is increasing support for a well-balanced vegetarian diet for weight reduction as it contains no animal fats. Protein is preferred from such foods as beans, pulses, nuts eggs; and calcium from cottage cheese and milk. The Hay Diet also has been found to be frequently effective.

DIET, THIN PEOPLE. Often more difficult to 'put on' than to 'take off' weight. Eat plenty of carbohydrates: bread and wholemeal products. Butter, margarine and other fats, meats, eggs, cream and cheese. In order to metabolise these effectively, without kidney or liver congestion, large quantities of fresh fruits and vegetables and juices should be eaten. Increase daily Vitamin B-complex intake. See: THIN PEOPLE.

DIET, VEGAN. A vegan is a strict vegetarian who does not eat meat, fish, eggs, milk and dairy products generally, He, or she, eats no animal products at all. By selecting a number of products from the plant kingdom they claim their diet is adequate.

As the Vegan diet is deficient in Vitamin B12 which may lead to anaemia, supplements are available. Some Vegan products have this vitamin added.

Their rule is to combine legumes with other cereals, seeds or nuts at the same meal. The combination is claimed to be equal to one animal based.

DIGESTIVES. Digestants. Agents that stimulate the processes of digestion: Meadowsweet, Peppermint, Gentian, Cardamom, Fennel, Chamomile, etc.

DIGITALIS. See: FOXGLOVE.

DIGOXIN INTOXICATION. Digoxin poisoning is possible from over-prescription of the drug, a crystalline glycoside, a powerful heart tonic for cardiac weakness. Doses may have been given over a long period during which toxicity builds up and manifests as nausea and vomiting, slow heart rate, faulty vision where objects appear green. Effective herbal alternatives to digoxin exist, reducing the current high mortality rate. Patient might die if not treated quickly.

Treatment: Once a patient is established on any of the digitalis (Foxglove) drugs it is very difficult to discontinue. Smaller doses are advised in the process of weaning to Lily of the Valley (*Convallaria majalis*) which has a digitalis-like effect by reversing heart rhythm disorders.

Dosage: dried leaves 60-200mg or by infusion. Liquid Extract, 0.6 to 2ml. Tincture, 0.5 to 1ml. Thrice daily.

Treatment by general medical practitioner or qualified phytotherapist.

DILL. *Anethum graveolens L. German*: Dill. *French*: Aneth. *Spanish*: Encido. *Italian*: Aneto odoroso. *Malayan*: adas. Dried or fresh seeds. *Keynote*: wind.
Constituents: flavonoids, volatile oil, coumarins, Zanthone derivatives.
Action: aromatic carminative, stomachic, antispasmodic.
Uses. Flatulence, infant's colic, bad breath. To increase breast milk in nursing mothers. Aerophagy (air-swallowing).
Preparations. *Tea*. Half-1 teaspoon bruised seeds in each cup of boiling water; infuse 10 minutes. Dose: 2, 3 or more teaspoons (babies): half a cup (older children): half-1 cup (adults).
Dill water: distilled extract: 30-60 drops in water.
Woodward's Gripe Water. Dill (concentrated 3.6 per cent) is an important ingredient. GSL

DIOSCORIDES. Greek physician (1st century AD) who accompanied the Roman armies as physician through many countries. He left the first illustrated comprehensive book on medicinal substances and their uses (*De Materia Medica*) which was a major work on pharmacology for over a thousand years. He embraced the work of Hippocrates from whose scrolls he borrowed 150 descriptions of plants for inclusion in his own work of well over 600. Many of these are still in use today, and easily recognisable from the primitive illustrations. The Herbal was 1870 years old before it was translated into English by John Goodyer, in 1933. At Mt Athos, Greece, MSS of Dioscorides can be found in the libraries. A 12th century copy at the Lavra monastery pictures girls gathering violets.

DIPHTHERIA. An acute infectious disease caused by Gram positive *Corynebacterium diphtheria* by droplet infection. Incubation: 2-4 days. Isolation.
Symptoms: low grade fever, malaise, sore throat, massive swelling of cervical lymph glands, thick white exudate from tonsils, false membrane forms from soft palate to larynx with brassy cough and difficult breathing leading to cyanosis and coma. Toxaemia, prostration, thin rapid pulse. Throat swabs taken for laboratory examination. See: NOTIFIABLE DISEASES.
Treatment. Bedrest. Encourage sweating.

Recommendations are for those parts of the world where medical help is not readily available and may save lives. Alternatives:–

1. Combine: Tincture Echinacea 3; Tincture

Goldenseal 2; Tincture Myrrh 1. Dose: 30-60 drops in water, two-hourly.
2. Combine equal parts: Tincture Lobelia; Tincture Echinacea. Dose: 30-60 drops in water, two-hourly.
3. Combine Tincture Poke root 2; Tincture Echinacea 3. Dose: 30-60 drops in water, two hourly.
4. *G.L.B. Rounseville, MD, Ill., USA*. I have treated diphtheria since 1883. I have treated diphtheria until I am sure the number of cases treated run into four digits. I have never given a hypodermic of antitoxin on my own initiative, nor have I ever lost a case early enough to inhibit conditions. I have depended upon *Echinacea* not only prophylactic but also as an antiseptic . . . In the line of medication the remedies are: *Aconite*, *Belladonna*, *Poke root* and *Cactus grand*, according to indications. But remember, if you are to have success, Echinacea must be given internally, externally and eternally! Do not fear any case of diphtheria with properly selected remedies as the symptoms occur. Echinacea will also be your stimulant, diaphoretic, diuretic, sialogogue, cathartic and antipyretic. (*Ellingwood's Physiomedicalist, Vol 13, No 6, June, 1919, 202*)
5. *Alexander M. Stern MD, Palatka, Florida, USA*. Combine: tinctures Echinacea 1oz, Belladonna 10 drops, Aconite 10 drops. Water to 4oz. 1 teaspoon 2-hourly.
6. *F.H. Williams, MD, Bristol, Conn., USA*. I took a case which had been given up to die with tracheal diphtheritic croup. I gave him old-fashioned *Lobelia* (2) seed and *Capsicum* (1) internally and externally and secured expulsion of a perfect cast of the trachea without a tracheotomy.
7. *Gargle, and frequent drink*. To loosen false membrane. Raw lemon juice 1, water 2. Pineapple juice. Teas: Red Sage, fresh Poke root.
Cold packs – saturated with Echinacea (Tincture, Liquid Extract or decoction) to throat.
Note: Capsicum and Lobelia open up the surface blood flow of the body thus releasing congestion on the inner mucous membranes.
Diet. Complete lemon-juice and herb tea fast with no solid foods as long as crisis lasts.

To be treated by a general medical practitioner or hospital specialist.

DISCUTIENT. See: ANTI-NEOPLASTIC.

DISEASE – Definition of: "I find diseases are crises of purification, of toxic elimination. Symptoms are the natural defences of the body. All diseases are but one. Their cause is also but one. They manifest themselves by means of different symptoms according to the location in which they appear." (*Hippocrates – 460BC*)

"Herbal medicines offer a technique for catalysing the patient's own in-built bio-regulatory mechanisms to effect a cure of his diseased condition." (*Mervyn Werbach, Third-Line Medicine, Modern Treatment for Persistent Symptoms*)

DISINFECTANTS. Herbs that act on bacteria of communicable diseases and help prevent spread of infection. Camphor, Eucalyptus, Thyme, Terebene, Pennyroyal, Pine. Tinctures or essential oils.

DISLOCATIONS. Luxations. Displacement of a structure, usually bone, as in an osteopathic lesion. May occur spontaneously as a result of weak ligaments or from injury, posture. Common in the shoulder. Many dislocations of the spine and skeleton are resolved by osteopathy.
Alternatives. To strengthen ligaments: Comfrey (topical). Wild Yam, Irish Moss, Slippery Elm bark, Horsetail, Fenugreek seeds. St John's Wort, Ginseng.
Supplementation. Calcium and Zinc, Vitamin C (1 gram thrice daily).

DISMUTASE ENZYMES (SOD). A dismutase enzyme is a biologically active enzyme complex present in most human cells and capable of converting tissue-damaging oxygen free radicals (highly reactive cellular toxins) into less harmful chemical substances that can be excreted from the body through the usual eliminatory channels.

Evidence shows that a number of chronic diseases including MS, diabetes, arthritis, even cancer, are the result of free radical damage. SOD is derived from a natural wheat sprout extract from specially cultured wheat that is hypoallergenic. It stimulates and supports the immune system, neutralises toxins, and minimises tissue damage in wasting diseases and organ transplantation. Protecting oxygen levels in body cells, it allays the ageing process and alleviates circulatory disorders.

DIURETICS. Agents that increase the flow of urine from the kidneys and so excrete excess fluid from the body. As well as elimination of fluid, diuretics cause potassium to be expelled. To restore the chemical balance, potassium is often prescribed. The advantage of some herbal diuretics is their ability to make good the loss without the use of synthetics, i.e., Dandelion root contains an abundance of potassium (three times as much as some). Liquorice reduces the action of a diuretic by causing fluid and salt retention.

Demulcent diuretics (Marshmallow root, Corn Silk, Couch Grass) protect the delicate parenchyma of the kidneys against irritation by gravel, stone or inflammation. All detoxifying prescriptions, as given for such chronic diseases as rheumatism, arthritis, etc, would include a diuretic to ensure complete excretion of by-products and metabolism.

Diuretics are prescribed for high blood pressure, water retention, inflammation of kidneys or bladder and oedema. They are usually combined with 'heart' remedies (Hawthorn, Lily of the Valley, Broom, etc) for dropsy of cardiac origin. Best taken cold on an empty stomach.

The possibility of diuretic abuse should be borne in mind when women and sportsmen seek to lose weight by such means. The following is a selection from over 300 herbs known as diuretics.

Agrimony, Bearberry, Bilberry leaves, Blue Flag root, Bogbean, Boldo, Boneset, Broom, Buchu, Bugleweed (cardio-active diuretic to increase force of the heart beat), Burdock, Celery seed, Clivers, Corn Silk, Couchgrass, Dandelion, Devil's Claw, Elder, Fennel seed, Gravel root, Heather flowers, Juniper berries, Kava Kava, Kola, Life root, Lignum Vitae, Lily of the Valley, Lime flowers, Marshmallow, Mullein, Pai Shu, Parsley Piert, Pellitory, Pumpkin seed, Sarsaparilla, Saw Palmetto, Sea Holly, Stone root, Vervain, Wild Carrot, Yarrow, Yerba Mate tea, Garden Nasturtium.

See: POTASSIUM. DANDELION.

DIVERTICULOSIS. Weakness of the colonic wall due to "Western" diet responsible for dry, hardened and less bulky stools. Characterised by pouchings or "blow-outs" of the mucosa (diverticula) which when inflamed and under pressure (as from straining at stool) lead to a condition known as diverticulitis.

Two types: (1) multiple pockets with no pain. (2) hypertrophy of muscles of the colon with chronic spasmodic pain. Also an occupational hazard of saxophone players.

Symptoms. Continuous cramp-like pain in the left abdomen (iliac fossa), distension, flatulence, incomplete emptying of rectum. Colon is tender to touch and mass may be palpated. Constipation and left-sided pain are the hallmarks. Complications include abscess, faecal peritonitis from burst pouch.

Differential diagnosis. On rectal examination, ulcerative colitis has fever, abdominal pain, and bloody diarrhoea.

Alternatives. *Tea*. Equal parts, herbs: Agrimony (to stimulate a healthy flow of bile). Avens (to check excessive secretion by toning-up of bowel tissue). Hops (an alvine nervine for strengthening the walls). Liquorice (to support the immune system). Red Clover (anti-neoplastic to discourage malignancy).

For local sepsis. Suggested by high white cell count. Echinacea, Wild Indigo or Goldenseal. Where general toxaemia co-exists: Myrrh. For the chronic case with a silent abdomen, Fenugreek seeds relieve in most cases.

Fenugreek Seeds. 1 heaped teaspoon to each cup water gently simmered 10 minutes. Dose: 1 cup 2-3 times daily, seeds consumed as well as the liquor.

For constipation. Ispaghula seeds, (psyllium) in the form of Isogel, Normacol, Regulan or other brand. To increase bulk, soften and render stools easier to pass.

For abdominal discomfort. Peppermint oil: 1-2 drops in honey or milk.

Tinctures. Formula. Wild Yam 2; Marshmallow 1; Elderflowers (to reduce inflammation) 1; Ginger quarter. Dose: one teaspoon before meals thrice daily; every two hours acute cases.

Aloe Vera. Good responses observed.

Diet. The Hay Diet. Fluid intake important. For acute *inflammatory* cases food should be bland. Little muesli without bran. Bran makes an irritable bowel worse, fibre husk increasing irritability. Oatmeal porridge oats with mashed banana, molasses and honey. Arrowroot, Slippery Elm drinks. Fruit juices, grapes (no seeds), papaya fruit.

Avoid: ham, bacon, fried foods, pickles, caffeine drinks and alcohol. In chronic, *non-inflammatory* cases, bran relieves, producing soft easy-passing stool. On passing of the acute inflammatory stage the patient should gradually take into the diet fibre-rich foods with sufficient protein. See: DIET: HIGH-FIBRE.

Supplementation. Vitamin B-complex, Vitamin C, folic acid, Bromelain enzymes. Bioflora, Lactoflora.

Surgical operative measures may be necessary.

DIZZINESS. Giddiness. Light-headedness, temporary unsteadiness. Not to be confused with vertigo which is a spinning sensation.

Alternatives. A simple herb tea may disperse. Any one: Skullcap, Ginkgo, Wood Betony, Gotu Kola, Hops, Chamomile, Lemon Balm, Lime Blossom, Motherwort, Peppermint, Betony, Catnep, Spearmint.

For persistent dizziness: treat as for VERTIGO.

DNA. Deoxyribonucleic acid. The substance that makes up the genetic blueprint of every living cell. Molecules that store information that affects the life of a man or woman: hair texture, height, colour of eyes or skin, etc all of which are determined in advance and recorded in the body's DNA. Chemical decision-maker that decides all the characteristics of a child on coming into the world. DNA finger-printing is a unique method of identifying a person by DNA present in his body fluids or cells. A criminal may be convicted by leaving behind a tell-tale bit of skin, hair, etc.

Human nuclei have 46 chromosomes, each consisting of long, thin strands of DNA. The strands are so long because all required information contained in 3 to 4 million genes is stored in sequence in the DNA. In human bone it can survive for a millennium. A most important discovery has been the location of the gene for Huntington's chorea on chromosome 4 made public in *"Nature", 18.3.93*. Discoveries have also revealed genes relative to cystic fibrosis and sickle-cell anaemia.

DOCTRINE OF SIGNATURES. It was believed by some ancient civilisations that the Creator has placed his seal on plants to indicate their medicinal use. Nicholas Culpeper was an outstanding advocate. The seeds of Skullcap (headache) resemble tiny skulls; Lungwort has white spotted leaves relative to the tubercula lung; Garlic, with its hollow stalk, relates to the windpipe; White Willow growing in damp places was believed good for rheumatic disorders (it was from the bark of this tree that aspirin was first isolated). Examples are numerous. It is a curiosity that many liver remedies have yellow flowers, those for the nerves (blue), for the spleen (orange), for the bones (white). Serpentaria (Rauwolfia) resembles a snake and is an old traditional remedy for snake-bite.

Herbalism confirms the Doctrine of Signatures but is not based on it.

DODOENS, REMBERT. 1517-1585. Dutch physician. Born at Malines. Practised Leyden, Holland. Physician to the Emperor. His famous Herball, *Cruydtboeck*, (1578) translated by Lytes Cary became one of the standard works in England, classifying plants not alphabetically but according to their medical properties. To Dodoens every hillside was a pharmacy.

DOG BITE. Treatment as for RABIES.

DOG ROSE. Wild briar. Rose hip tree. *Rosa canina L. French*: Eglantine. *German*: Weisse Rose. *Italian*: Rosa Bianca. *Spanish*: Rosa blanca. Ripe fruits.
Constituents: flavonoids, tannins, vitamins, carotenoids.
Natural source of Vitamin C.
Action. Antidiarrhoeal, anti-stress.
Uses. Rose hip capsules or tablets are taken as a prophylactic against colds and infections.
Teabags offer a popular daily 'health' tea as an alternative to caffeine drinks. See: VITAMIN C.
GSL

DOGS. As a general rule herbs may be used for the relief of disease in dogs and pets generally, dosage depending upon the animal. Dosage for dogs, according to size of the animal, is approximately one-third that of an adult human dose.

All dog worming programmes should include Garlic, tablets or capsules for *Toxocara canis*, the common dog roundworm.
Alternatives: Wormseed powder in capsules. Pomegranate seeds. Quassia chips: 2 teaspoons steeped in cup Cider Vinegar; strain and add two teaspoons of the liquor to drinking water.

Epileptic seizures. Add one teaspoon Brewer's yeast and quarter of a teaspoon powdered Skullcap or Vervain to feed, once or twice daily.
General health maintenance: Garlic capsules, 1-2 daily.

DOLOMITE. Source of minerals for maintenance of nervous and muscle tissue. From deep-mined limestone. A supplement of magnesium and calcium for dietary deficiency. The two minerals work together to maintain normal growth of bone, healthy teeth, efficient heart function and sound collagen structures. Women have a special need of both.
Typical combination. Magnesium carbonate 200mg; Calcium carbonate 240mg.
Uses. Mineral deficiencies, osteoporosis, to maintain healthy teeth.
Note. Not used by the elderly or those with digestive weakness.
Dolomite supplements should first be pulverised before ingestion, taken in honey, a bread bolus or other suitable vehicle.

DONG QUAI. *Angelica sinensis*, Oliv. Chinese angelica. Dried root. Keynote: conditions arising from disordered female reproductive system.
Action: antispasmodic, analgesic (mild), blood purifier, circulatory stimulant, hormone regulator, nutritive.
Uses. Covers a wide range of female disorders: amenorrhoea, dysmenorrhoea, menopause. Cramps. Hypothermia. Infertility. Sleeplessness, nerve debility, high blood pressure. Toxic shock syndrome. Asthma. Hay fever. Osteoporosis. Anaemia; particularly in Asian women. To heighten resistance against disease. Avoid in pregnancy.
Preparations. Thrice daily.
Dried root. One heaped teaspoon in cup water gently simmered 20 minutes, dose: half a cup.
Liquid Extract (1:1) half-2ml (quarter to half a teaspoon).
Tincture (1:5) 4-6ml (1-1 and a half teaspoons).
Powder (4:1) quarter to half a gram.
Note. Referred to in the East as "female Ginseng". Most popular "female" herb in the Far East.

DOSAGE. The best time to take herbal medicine is half hour before meals. Acute conditions: doses should be taken a few days until cessation of symptoms or on practitioner's instruction. Chronic cases: treatment may continue for weeks but with the break of a week after each period of 6 weeks.

Dosage may vary from herb to herb but today's standard doses are as follows unless stated otherwise. Dried herbs may be swallowed with water (Psyllium seeds) or drunk as a tea or decoction. Dosage is usually thrice daily for chronic conditions and every 2 hours for acute cases.

Refer to appropriate entries for dosage of teas (infusions), decoctions, powders, liquid extracts, tinctures.
Children. 5 to 12 years. One quarter to half adult dose except where otherwise stated. Medical opinion is that after 12 years a child is regarded as an adult. For babies and children, teas and decoctions have much to commend them. Alcohol-based preparations should be avoided where possible.
Babies. 1 to 5 years. 1 to 5 teaspoons tea or decoction. Should a baby fail to take extract internally, a strong tea or decoction may be prepared and used as a footbath or poured into the bath water. This would need to be ten times as strong as for an internal dose. In this way medicaments may indirectly enter the circulation by absorption through a baby's soft receptive tissue. Other liquid medicines: one drop for each year of age to 5 years; two drops thereafter to 12 years.
Measurement. 1 millilitre = 15 drops. 1 teaspoon = 5ml (5 millilitres or 75 drops liquid medicine). For liquid medicines always use a medicine glass graduated in millilitres, or a standard dropper. Take liquid extracts or tinctures in water (25ml) or honey.

DOUCHE. A term used to describe lavage of certain parts of the body, for washing wounds and ulcers, for eye douches with aid of an eye-bath, but especially for cleansing or applying medication to the vagina. Douches with herbal teas (or decoctions) are given for their antiseptic and anti-bacterial properties being used to irrigate the vagina in cases of infections or to soothe inflammation. They are best performed sitting on the toilet, the douche or enema can about two feet above the thighs. Fluid is retained for 5-10 minutes. Not advised in pregnancy. Once or twice daily for one week.

A strong tea is prepared from one of a number of agents according to indications.
Infections: Blue Flag root, Yellow Dock root, Echinacea, Marshmallow root, Sarsaparilla.
Leucorrhoea: Motherwort, Plantain, Bayberry, Black Cohosh.
Endometritis: Raspberry leaves.
Candida: injection of neat yoghurt or, half cup cider vinegar to 2 pints warm water.
Acute discomfort, itching, inflammation: equal parts Chamomile, Marshmallow, Ladies Mantle. 1oz to 2 pints boiling water; infuse, inject warm.

Alternative to herbs: use liquid extracts, 2-4 teaspoons to two pints water.
Thuja douche: Thuja, Liquid Extract half an ounce; Ginger Tincture 10 drops; Glycerine 1oz. Hot water to 1 pint. Candida, leucorrhoea, Polypi.

DOWN'S SYNDROME. Mongolism. Trisomy 21. Not a disease but a defect in mental and physical development. In the normal human being there are 46 chromosomes; in Down's there are 47 – one extra No 21 chromosome. The syndrome increases with the age of the mother after the age of 35. Over the age of 40 the chances of a mother having such a child are 1-2 per cent. Children with the defect have low levels of zinc.

Cases of Down's have followed use of nonoxynol-9 (vaginal contraceptive device) such as the polyurethane sponge. The sponge, when left *in situ* for a long time, may cause Down's to follow.

Certain physical characteristics are present. The most important feature is impaired mental development. Almost all are coeliacs.
Symptoms. Low IQ, short fingers, small flat head, flattened nose, low-set ears. May be subject to umbilical hernia, and heart disease. No treatment can cure, but certain herb teas rich in minerals (Alfalfa, Red Clover) together with Kelp (either in tablet or powder form) may help children, with possible improvements in IQ. Vitamin supplements – A, D, Thiamine, Riboflavin, B6, B12, C and E improve a child's physical and mental health – as do also the minerals: Magnesium, Calcium, Zinc, Manganese, Copper, Iron and Iodine.

Children with Down's syndrome run an increased risk of coeliac disease, due to disturbed immunity. A substantial evidence is held in America that links a low level of Selenium in the mother. Unnecessary X-rays should be avoided. Ensure fitness before conception by gentle exercise and nutrients: Folic Acid, Selenium and Zinc.

Children with the condition are noted for their happy disposition and warmth of feeling towards others.

DREAMS. Everybody dreams, but bad dreams may be due to stress, liver congestion, indigestion, circulatory troubles and other causes. A nightcap of German Chamomile tea settles the stomach and alimentary canal, Lime flower tea reduces nerve tension, Motherwort tea equalises the circulation to ensure a restful night's sleep. For sexual problems: Agnus Castus.

Dreams, frightening; wakes in a sweat.
Teas: Alfalfa, Balm. Of far-fetched embarrassing situations: nervous tension on waking with or without urinary incontinence – Liquid Extract Kava Kava. 15-60 drops in water at bedtime.

DROPSY: CARDIAC. Oedema (excess fluid in the tissues) may be due to poor circulation from impaired heart action. The condition is worse at the end of the day.
Treatment. Agents in frequent use: Broom, Lily of the Valley, Hawthorn (blossoms or berries), Motherwort.
Tea. Combine equal parts: Dandelion root, Motherwort, Yarrow. 2 teaspoons to each cup boiling water; infuse 5-15 minutes; 1 cup thrice daily.

Powders. Equal parts: Dandelion root, Juniper berries, Hawthorn berries. Mix. Dose: 500mg (two 00 capsules or one-third teaspoon).
Practitioner. Lily of the Valley. Dose as BHP (1983): Liquid Extract: 1:1 in 25 per cent alcohol, 0.6-2ml. Tincture: 1:5 in 40 per cent alcohol, 0.5-1ml. Thrice daily.
Dropsy in children: cucumber juice extracted from vegetable with aid of a juicer. As many cupfuls as well-tolerated. If vomiting is induced, it should be regarded as favourable.
Diet. Lacto-vegetarian, salt-free, bottled or spring water, honey.

DROPSY, RENAL. Oedema. Hydrops. Not a disease but a condition. An abnormal accumulation of fluid in a body cavity or beneath the skin. Due to weakened walls of capillaries caused by circulating toxins obstructing the flow of blood or lymph. Gross oedema of nephrotic syndrome associated with low plasma protein level and high proteinuria.

Renal dropsy is worse in the early morning, with loose tissues under the eyes.
Treatment. When fluid rapidly collects it may have to be aspirated (drawn off) but before this stage is reached herbal diuretics and cardiac tonics have much to offer. In acute conditions, sweat glands should be stimulated by suitable diaphoretics to assist elimination of excess fluid through the skin. Attention to the bowels is important; a timely copious bowel action greatly assisting elimination. A well-known diuretic for dropsy is *Juniper*, 3 to 5 drops taken in honey 2 or 3 times daily.
Alternatives. *Teas*. (Simple infusions): Agrimony, Bearberry, Boldo, Boneset, Borage, Buchu, Celery seed, Clivers, Corn Silk, Dandelion leaves, Parsley leaves, Elderflowers, Bogbean, Heartsease, Lime flowers, Parsley Piert, Pellitory, Plantain, Sea Holly, Wild Carrot, Yarrow.
Decoctions. Broom tops, Lovage, Burdock root, Couchgrass, Dandelion root, Juniper berries, Blue Flag root.
Bean Cure (*Phaseolus vulgaris*). 1 tablespoon kidney (haricot) bean pods, sliced, in cup water simmered gently for 5 minutes. 1 cup morning and mid-day.
Sassafras root. An old Swedish colonist of the late 18th century related how his mother cured many cases of dropsy with a decoction of Sassafras root. (*American Indian Medicine. Virgil Vogel, p.363*) Of historic interest only, this root is no longer used in herbal practice.
Tablets/capsules. Buchu. Dandelion. Juniper. Celery. Garlic. Blue Flag.
Powders. Equal parts: Buchu, Dandelion root, Stone root, Senna leaf. Mix. Dose: 500-750mg (2 x 3 x 00 capsules or one-third to half a teaspoon) thrice daily.
Liquid Extracts. Equal parts: Buchu, Clivers, Blue Flag. Mix. 30-60 drops, thrice daily.
Practitioner. Alternatives with a record of efficacy. Tinctures.
Formula 1. Burdock, 20ml; Buchu, 20ml; Bearberry, 20ml; Aqua to 100ml. Dose: 5ml 3 times daily in water.
Formula 2. Juniper, 10ml; Buchu, 20ml; Broom, 10ml; Dandelion, 10ml. Aqua to 100ml. Dose: 5ml, 3 times daily, in water.
Topical. Poultice over kidney area: quarter of an ounce Irish Moss gently simmered in half a pint water to a jellied mass and applied on linen or suitable material to the small of the back. Repeat 2 or 3 times with fresh hot poultices.
Diet. High protein, low salt. Fresh conservatively-cooked vegetables, polyunsaturated oils. Bottled or spring water.
Supplementation. Vitamin A, B-complex, B1, B6, C, E, Potassium.
General. Elevation of affected limbs above level of abdomen.

This condition should be treated by or in liaison with a qualified medical practitioner.

DROSERA. *Drosera rotundifolia L.* See: SUNDEW.

DROWNING. Prompt action is necessary for survival. Water-logged lungs arrest the pulmonary circulation. Blood coagulates in the pulmonary veins. A strong stimulant is essential; one of the best is brandy. Others:– Life Drops. Composition Essence or powder. If the act of swallowing is not possible, swab out mouth with the above, diluted.
Treatment: Quarter of a teaspoon powdered or tincture Myrrh in water; spray or pour into throat. Massage back with Capsicum ointment or Lotion. Warm blankets.

DRUG DEPENDENCE. One third of those taking tranquillisers become addicted. One of the problems of psychological dependence is the discomfort of withdrawal symptoms.
Symptoms. Tremors, restlessness, nausea and sleep disturbance. The greater potency of the drug, the higher the rebound anxiety. Many drugs create stress, weaken resistance to disease, tax the heart and raise blood sugar levels.

Drugs like Cortisone cause bone loss by imperfect absorption of calcium. Taken in the form of milk and dairy products, calcium is not always absorbed. Herbs to make good calcium loss are: Horsetail, Chickweed, Slippery Elm, Spinach, Alfalfa.

Agents to calm nerves and promote withdrawal may augment a doctor's prescription for reduction of drug dosage, until the latter may be discontinued. Skullcap and Valerian offer a good base for a prescription adjusted to meet individual requirements.

Alternatives. *Teas*: German Chamomile, Gotu Kola, Hops, Lime flowers, Hyssop, Alfalfa, Passion flower, Valerian, Mistletoe, Oats, Lavender, Vervain, Motherwort. 1 heaped teaspoon to each cup boiling water; infuse 5-15 minutes; half-1 cup thrice daily.

Decoctions: Valerian, Devil's Claw, Siberian Ginseng, Lady's Slipper. Jamaica Dogwood, Black Cohosh.

Tablets/capsules. Motherwort, Dogwood, Valerian, Skullcap, Passion flower, Mistletoe, Liquorice.

Powders. Formulae. Alternatives. (1) Combine equal parts Valerian, Skullcap, Mistletoe. Or, (2) Combine Valerian 1; Skullcap 2; Asafoetida quarter. Dose: 500mg (two 00 capsules or one-third teaspoon) thrice daily. Formula No 2 is very effective but offensive to taste and smell.

Practitioner. Tincture Nucis vom. once or twice daily, as advised.

Aloe Vera gel (or juice). Russians tested this plant on rabbits given heavy drug doses and expected to die. Their survival revealed the protective property of this plant: dose, 1 tablespoon morning and evening.

Aromatherapy. Sniff Ylang Ylang oil. Lavender oil massage for its relaxing and stress-reducing properties.

Diet. Avoid high blood sugar levels by rejecting alcohol, white flour products, chocolate, sugar, sweets and high cholesterol foods.

Supplements. Daily. Multivitamins, Vitamin B-complex, B6, Vitamin C 2g, Minerals: Magnesium, Manganese, Iron, Zinc. Change of lifestyle. Stop smoking. Yoga.

Notes. "Do not withdraw: insulin, anticoagulants, epileptic drugs, steroids, thyroxin and hormone replacement therapy (the endocrine glands may no longer be active). Long-term tranquillisers e.g., Largactil or any medicament which has been used for a long period. Patients on these drugs are on a finely-tuned medication the balance of which may be easily disturbed." (*Simon Mills, FNIMH*)

Counselling and relaxation therapy.

The Committee on Safety of Medicines specifically warns against the abrupt cessation of the Benzodiazepines and similar tranquillisers because of the considerable risk of convulsions.

DRUG ERUPTIONS. Reactions on the skin due to drug allergy. Symptoms may manifest as urticaria or exanthemata. Aspirin may produce urticaria. Mercury, arsenic, gold, mepacrine and others manifest in their own distinctive rash or vesicles.

Treatment: same as for NETTLE RASH.

DRUMSTICK FINGERS. Thickening or widening of the fingertips caused by tumour or other permanent congestion, heart or lung trouble. See: HEART DISEASE, TUBERCULOSIS, CHRONIC LUNG COMPLAINTS.

DRUNKENNESS. See: ALCOHOLISM. Also: WORMWOOD TEA.

DRYING HERBS. Herbs should be harvested from unsprayed dust-free zones and spread out on racks or suitable fittings. Smaller batches may be hung in bunches. Rotting may set in if fresh herbs are left compressed in bags, baskets, etc. Never wash herbs before drying or place one above another. Turn or agitate daily. They should be dried in a well-ventilated room in the absence of excessive heat, sunlight or bright lights which may destroy the volatile oils of aromatic herbs. They should not be cut until thoroughly dried.

Only roots should be washed soon after lifting, and cut before drying into hardness. In a few cases drying of roots may be assisted by added heat.

DUMPING SYNDROME. A common complication of gastric surgery. Due to rapid passage of starches into the small intestine causing a decrease in the volume of circulating blood (early dumping). May be caused also by rapid rise in blood sugar followed by a rapid fall – a rebound hypoglycaemia (late dumping).

Symptoms: appearing after meals – palpitation, sweating with sense of weakness, nausea, abdominal pain and sometimes collapse.

Preventative day-starter: Chamomile tea.

Alternatives. Anti-cholinergics.

Teas: Betony, Black Horehound, Chamomile. Fenugreek seeds. Guar gum, or pectin added to orange juice slows down gastric emptying and ameliorates symptoms. Slippery Elm gruel.

External cold packs to upper abdomen.

Diet: fibre foods are important as they delay the transit of carbohydrates into the intestines. No solid food at bedtime.

Supplementation: Vitamin B-complex, chromium.

Note: Guar gum is resistant to stomach acid and digestive enzymes. It passes unchanged to the colon where it is degraded.

DUODENAL ULCER. See: PEPTIC ULCER/DUODENAL.

DUPUYTREN'S CONTRACTURE. The Thatcher Finger. Fibrosis of the palm of the hand leading to deformity. Inability to straighten the ring and little finger due to fixed flexion. A tightened sinew. High serum fat levels are present, the disease affecting men from the age of 20 and women after the menopause.

"It is believed that oxidation of the lipids by free radicals (which are also present in high numbers in patients who have Dupuytren's contracture) produces toxins which kill fibroblast cells in the palmar fascia. The surrounding tissue overreacts

by producing many more fibroblasts, a bit like callous formation after a wound. The rapid increase in fibrous tissue leads to the contracture. This explains why the contracture is so common among patients with diabetes, epilepsy and alcoholism – serum lipid levels are raised in all these groups . . . However, the disorder occurs only if the patient has a genetic predisposition to the disease." (*Mr Paul Sanderson, Orthopaedic Surgeon, Wrightington Hospital, Wigan, in the Journal of Bone and Joint Surgery, Nov. 1992*)
Treatment. Directed towards prevention. Same as for HYPERLIPIDAEMIA.

DWARF BEAN. See: FRENCH BEAN.

DWARF ELDER. Danewort. Ground Elder. *Sambucus ebulus L. French*: Petit sureau. *German*: Attichwurzel. *Spanish*: Sauro enano. *Italian*: Ebbio. Part used: leaves.
Action: expectorant, diaphoretic, diuretic, purgative.
Uses. Dropsy, kidney and bladder torpor, rheumatism.

Combine, equal parts Dwarf Elder, Greater Plantain and Parsley Piert for gravel.

Combine, equal parts Dwarf Elder, Wild Carrot, Broom and Motherwort for oedema of heart origin. Combine, equal parts Dwarf Elder and Celery seeds for polymyalgia and rheumatism. (*W.T. Hewitt, FNIMH*)
Preparations. Thrice daily.
Tea. 2 teaspoons leaves to each cup boiling water; infuse 10 minutes. Half-1 cup.
Tincture. 1 part in 5 parts 45 per cent alcohol. Macerate 8 days. Decant. 5-10ml (1-2 teaspoons).

DYSENTERY, AMOEBIC. Amoebiasis. Ulcerative colitis of the large bowel chiefly with *entamoeba histolytica* from infected food, water, or by 'carriers'. Penetration through colon walls may lead to increased peristalsis. Period of infection – one to six months. Travelling upwards via the portal vein.
Symptoms: may invade the liver causing abscess. Colic, changed bowel habits. Where severe – fever, bloody stools and pain in iliac fossa.

Treatment by or in liaison with general medical practitioner.

Attention to water supply. Water should be boiled for five minutes to destroy cysts. Avoid fruits and salad materials from unhygienic sources and exposure to flies.
Alternatives. Agrimony, Balm, Bayberry, Bistort, Blue Flag, Burdock, Calamus, <u>Catechu (black)</u>, <u>Cranesbill</u>, <u>Echinacea</u>, Fenugreek, Garlic, Goldenseal, Holy Thistle, Ipecacuanha, Ladies Mantle, Marshmallow, Mullein, Nettles, Pulsatilla, Raspberry leaves, Red Clover, Shepherd's Purse, Slippery Elm, Spurge (hirta), Tormentil root, Thyme (garden), <u>Wild Yam</u>, Witch Hazel, Yarrow.
Tea. Equal parts: Holy Thistle, Marshmallow, Thyme. 2 teaspoons to each cup boiling water; infuse 5-15 minutes; 1 cup thrice daily or every 2 hours acute cases.
Decoction. Combine, Wild Yam 1; Marshmallow root 1; Echinacea 2. One heaped teaspoon to two cups water. Simmer gently 20 minutes. Half-1 cup thrice daily: every 2 hours acute cases.
Formula. Equal parts: Bayberry, Burdock, Echinacea, Peppermint. Dose: Liquid extract: one 5ml teaspoon. Tinctures: one to two 5ml teaspoons. Powders: 750mg (three 00 capsules or half teaspoon) in water, honey or fruit juice, thrice daily: every 2 hours for acute cases.
Practitioner. (1) Tincture Ipecacuanha (BP 1973). Dose: 0.25-1ml as prescribed.
(2) Formula. Liquid Extract Echinacea 15ml; Liquid Extract Monsonia ovata 4ml; Liquid Extract Marigold 4ml; Tincture Goldenseal 2ml; Oil Cinnamon 1ml. Distilled water to 240ml (8oz). Dose: 1 dessertspoon (8ml) every 3 hours. (*A. Barker*)
Preventative: two Garlic capsules at night.
Note. Fenugreek tea: frequent cupfuls. Good results reported.
Drink plenty of fluids: milk, oatmeal porridge, vegetable juices.

DYSENTERY, BACILLARY. Severe watery diarrhoea caused by a microscopic single-celled organism of the genus *shigella* which may enter through the mouth, pass the stomach barrier and multiply in the lower intestine and bowel. Diarrhoea gives way to scanty slimy stools mixed with blood and shreds of mucous membrane due to abscesses on the villi. The classical bowel trouble of the armies of history. See: NOTIFIABLE DISEASES.
Symptoms. Fever, cramping abdominal pain, weight loss, serious fluid loss, appetite disappears.
Treatment. Herbal antibiotics. These include carminatives to allay griping and deal with the infection. Powerful astringents should not be given as they delay elimination of bacteria. Teas may be taken internally as supportive to primary treatment, and can also offer a soothing enema.

A daily gruel of Slippery Elm bark forms a soothing coating on the bowel and helps to carry off the bacillus in the stool. Cases require good nursing, warmth, and condition of the heart monitored.

Relief has been reported by the use of purgative doses of castor oil combined with Lobelia and Valerian (to relieve pain). Prescriptions would include an analgesic. Always beneficial is a daily wash-out of the bowel with a strong infusion of Boneset, Chaparral, Ladies Mantle or carrot juice.

Dr Melville Keith, physician, recommended

Raspberry leaf tea in frequent drinks.
Alternatives. Agrimony Balm, Bistort, Calamus, Catnep, Cranesbill, Echinacea, Fenugreek, Goldenseal, Ladies Slipper, Nettles, Raspberry leaves, Red Clover, Sage, Shepherd's Purse, Smartweed, Wild Indigo, Wild Yam, Yarrow.
Tea. Formula. Equal parts: Yarrow, Shepherd's Purse, Fenugreek seeds. 2 teaspoons to each cup water; bring to boil; simmer for 5 minutes; allow to cool; 1 cup every two hours.
Decoction. Formula. Equal parts, Fenugreek seeds, Cranesbill, Echinacea, Valerian. One heaped teaspoon to 2 cups water. Simmer gently 20 minutes; cool; 1 cup every two hours.
Formula. Echinacea 2; Cranesbill 1; Valerian 1; Peppermint half. Dose – Liquid Extracts: One 5ml teaspoon. Tinctures: two 5ml teaspoons. Powders: 750mg (three 00 capsules or half a teaspoon). In water, honey or Fenugreek tea thrice daily. Acute cases: every 2 hours.
Clove of Garlic crushed in honey.
Enema. Any teas from above agents injected. Carrot juice as an enemata.
Practitioner. (1) Ipecacuanha BP (1973). Dose 0.25-1ml.
(2) Alternative. Combined tinctures – Aconite 10 drops; Ipecacuanha 20 drops, Wild Indigo 20 drops. Distilled water to 4oz. Dose: one teaspoon hourly. (*Dr Finlay Ellingwood*).
History. Dr Wooster Beach, New York Medical Society, writes: "500 Oneida Indians went down with dysentery in one season. All recovered by the use of Blackberry root while their white neighbours fell before the disease."
Traditional. 2 teaspoons dried Blackberry root to each 2 teacups water gently simmered 20 minutes. Dose: half-1 cup every 2 hours.
Diet. No solid foods. Plenty of fluids – oatmeal porridge, boiled rice, semolina, pasta, Slippery Elm.

Treatment by or in liaison with general medical practitioner.

DYSLEXIA. A term to describe impaired learning ability, reading and writing disorders. A surprising inability found in a person inconsistent with his/her intelligence. Not a sign of low intelligence. Affects about 10 per cent ten-year-olds who tend to have higher levels of toxic metals (copper, cadmium, lead, etc) in the blood. Zinc-deficiency parents can contribute. See: AUTO-TOXAEMIA.

DYSMENORRHOEA. Painful menstruation – two types – (1) primary or spasmodic (2) secondary – secondary to pelvic disease. Herbal treatment is the same for both types.

The womb goes into spasm with pains as in labour; teenager screams aloud. Causes may be glandular inadequacy, prolapse of the womb, inflammation and congestion of the lining, scars on the cervix, psychological disorders. The most likely cause is hormonal imbalance. Where due to a chill, a hot bath and herbal teas (Agnus Castus, Pennyroyal, or Raspberry leaves) are indicated. Where accompanied by emotional excitability, the addition of Skullcap or Motherwort is beneficial.

Cause of the pain is mostly a high concentration of prostaglandins – chemical hormone-like substances that have an astringent effect upon walls of the womb thus arresting blood supply. Herbal vaso-dilators or relaxants have an anti-prostaglandin effect.
Treatment. The first concern of the practitioner is to administer a uterine vaso-dilator to increase the capacity of the blood vessels to transport blood. This effect can be obtained by employing antispasmodics, and nerve relaxants. Those having a specific effect upon the womb are: Agnus Castus, Black Cohosh, Black Haw, Blue Cohosh, Butterbur, Caraway, Cramp bark, Helonias, Jamaica Dogwood, Goldenseal, Lovage, Motherwort, Mugwort, Peppermint, Pulsatilla, St John's Wort, Skullcap, Squaw Vine, Valerian, Wild Thyme, Wild Yam.
Teas. Lovage, Motherwort, Mugwort, Peppermint, Skullcap, Chamomile, Wild Thyme, Agnus Castus, Raspberry leaves. Add a pinch of Ginger.
Decoctions. Black Cohosh, Black Haw, Blue Cohosh, Butterbur, Cramp bark, False Unicorn root, Jamaica Dogwood, Squaw Vine, Valerian, Wild Yam. A pinch of Ginger enhances action.
Formula. Skullcap 2; Black Cohosh 1; Cramp bark 1. Dosage. Powders: 500mg or one-third teaspoon. Liquid extracts: half-1 teaspoon. Tinctures: 1-2 teaspoons. In honey, water or fruit juice thrice daily, before meals.

In the absence of the above, the following are also reliable: Black Haw, Helonias, Squaw Vine. Jamaica Dogwood combines well with Black Haw.
Antispasmodic drops.
Supplements. B-complex, B6, Calcium, Magnesium.
Supportives: Heat to the feet. Hot water bottle and electric blanket. Bedrest helps relax pelvic tissues.

DYSPAREUNIA. Difficult sexual intercourse felt by a woman. See: VAGINISMUS.

DYSPEPSIA. Acute: non-recurring indigestion may be caused by isolated episodes of overeating, excessive alcohol, rapid eating and irregular eating habits. Chronic indigestion may indicate some serious disorder such as gastric ulcer, duodenal ulcer, gall bladder disorder or hiatus hernia: see appropriate entry. Symptoms vary according to each disturbance, but for simple indigestion are usually confined to abdominal discomfort, nausea and gastric reflux.

Of Value. Agrimony, Balm, Balmony, Boldo, Calamus, Caraway, Cardamom, Catnep, Cayenne, Centuary, Cinnamon, Condurango (tumour), Dandelion, Dill, Fennel, Galangal, Gentian, Ginger, Hops (nervous stomach), Peppermint, Quassia, Thyme, Wild Yam, Wormwood, German Chamomile.

Herbal mucilages protect walls of the digestive tract from erosion by strong acid secretions: Slippery Elm, Marshmallow root, Iceland Moss, Irish Moss. One of these may be combined with any of the above, as appropriate to the individual case. A simple combination is Meadowsweet and Marshmallow root (equal parts).

Alternatives. *Teas*. (1) Formula. Equal parts: Agrimony, Chamomile, Dandelion. (2) Formula. Meadowsweet 2; Balm 2; Hops 1. Prepare: 1-2 teaspoons to each cup boiling water, infuse 5-10 minutes. Half-1 cup freely.

Decoction. Gentian root (shredded): 1 teaspoon to each cup cold water, steep overnight. Half-1 cup on rising. For weak digestion.

Acid insufficiency (especially in the elderly): 2 teaspoons Cider Vinegar in glass water; drink freely.

Tablets/capsules. Dandelion, Goldenseal, Papaya, Slippery Elm, Chamomile, Meadowsweet.

Powders. Formula. Dandelion 2; Gentian 1; Ginger quarter. Dose: 750mg (three 00 capsules or half a teaspoon) thrice daily.

Liquid extracts. Combine equal parts: Chamomile, Meadowsweet, Marshmallow. One to two 5ml teaspoons thrice daily.

Tincture. Tincture Cardamom Compound BP (1973) Dose: 15-60 drops (2-4ml) in water thrice daily.

Aloe Vera. Juice from crushed leaves (1-2 tablespoons).

Papaya. To assist protein digestion: leaf tea, fresh juice, or papain in tablet form.

David Hoffman. "For all kinds of infants indigestion, Balm herb acts like a charm. Two teaspoons of the herb, finely cut, is placed in a teacup, filling with boiling water. When cool, give hourly, one or two teaspoons to the very young and half to one cup to the over-sevens."

Dr A. Vogel. To strengthen stomach, increase appetite, and stimulate bile flow: Cola nut 16 per cent, Peruvian bark 16 per cent, Frankincense 4.5 per cent, Myrrh 4.5 per cent, Sweet Myrtle 16 per cent, Yellow Gentian 10 per cent, Bitter Orange 16 per cent. Dose: 10-15 drops.

Banana Cure. The banana is a traditional treatment for gastric ulcer in India. Research has shown how three quarters of a treatment group on powdered banana had complete or partial relief of pain. The banana could be a useful early therapy before beginning more expensive forms of treatment. (*All India Institute, Delhi*)

Diet. The Hay diet. Slippery Elm gruel. Honey.

Supplements. Vitamins B-complex, B1, B6, Folic acid, Niacin.

Note: German Chamomile is the most widely used for simple dyspepsia; Roman Chamomile being important as an anti-inflammatory where dyspepsia is accompanied by feverish conditions.

EAR DROPS. Used for a number of purposes from softening wax to arresting a discharge. Alternatives:
1. Oil Cajeput 4 per cent; Oil Rosemary 4 per cent; Oil of Almond (or Mullein) to 100 per cent. For infection.
2. 30 drops Goldenseal; 30 drops Tincture Myrrh; half an ounce Almond oil. For pus-discharging infection. Otorrhoea.
3. Practitioner: Effective stock ear drops: Oil Cajeput 2 per cent; Oil Tea-Tree 2 per cent; Menthol 2 per cent; Oil of Almond (or Mullein) to 100 per cent.
4. Garlic capsule. Pierce tip and squeeze contents into the ear for staphylococcus aureus.
5. Vitamin E capsule. For tinnitus.
Wash hands; lie or sit down; tilt head to bring ear uppermost; pull ear backwards; insert 3-4 drops. Remain in same position for 2 minutes.

EAR DRUMS, PERFORATED. Sliced Garlic treatment. Peel corm, leaving transparent epithelial-layer attached. Cut slice and shape it to cover the perforation; push it against the eardrum so that its cut surface hugs the perforation. Pack the external auditory meatus with an alcohol-moistened plug of cotton wool. Water must not enter the ear and forceful nose-blowing avoided. Replace Garlic slice once or twice a week until healing is complete. If middle ear becomes inflamed with excessive exudate, stop treatment and give an anti-inflammatory (*such as Echinacea, author*). Any exudation usually stops when treatment is discontinued. (*Chinese Medical Journal, May 1977*)

EARS. Middle ear inflammation. See: OTITIS MEDIA. External ear inflammation. See: OTITIS EXTERNA. Glue ear. See: OTITIS MEDIA, SECRETORY FORM.

EARACHE. Severe throbbing pain inside the ear, usually due to pressure from a blocked Eustachian tube or a respiratory infection. The condition may be treated by herbal antibiotics, antihistamines or nasal decongestants. Simple earache may resolve itself without inflammation from the inside and pus formation. Where pai persists more than 24 hours a practitioner's opinion should be sought.
Before the practitioner comes: instil into the ear: few drops Onion or Garlic juice, Houseleek, Aloe Vera or Plantain juice; oils of Mullein, St John's Wort or Almond. Moistened Chamomile flower sachet; apply to ear to ease pain.
Feverfew. A traditional way to relieve was to hold the ear over hot steaming Feverfew tea.
Supportive: A number of strong yawns while pinching the nostrils and blowing the nose vigorously may free obstruction and normalise pressure on both sides of the drum. Hot foot baths divert blood from the head and reduce pain.

EAR DISCHARGE – OTORRHOEA. May be due to a perforated eardrum or to inflammation of the external ear (otitis externa). Whatever cause, antibacterials and alteratives would be required. See: OTITIS EXTERNA. OTITIS MEDIA.

EARS. WAX. A little wax is normal. When it collects and thickens removal by syringe is necessary. To soften in preparation for the syringe: instil 3-4 drops Castor, Mullein, Garlic or Almond oil into the ear and insert small plug cotton wool. If not available: use Peanut oil.

EAU de COLOGNE. Sydney Gold Medal. Mix, parts: oils of Bergamot (1), Citronella (2), Neroli (1), Rosemary (1), Alcohol (say vodka) 20 parts. Dissolve. For perfumery, or to neutralise sick-room effluvia of the terminally ill.

EBERS PAPYRUS. The first medical records of Ancient Egypt containing 876 substances, most of them herbal including Castor oil, Valerian, Dill, Senna leaves; and goat fat as a base for ointments. The papyrus, written about 1500 BC contains prescriptions and formulae covering wide range. Medicines still in use today: Myrrh, Wormwood, Peppermint, Anise, Fennel, Lotus flowers, Linseed, Juniper berries, Gentian, etc.

ECHINACEA. Cone flower, Black Sampson. *Echinacea pallida*, Nutt. *Echinacea angustifolia* (DC) Heller. *Brauneria pallida*, Nutt. *Echinacea purpurea*. *Part used*: rhizome and whole of the plant.
Constituents: Echinacosides (in Echinacea angustifolia), alkaloids, polysaccharides, flavonoids, essential oil.
Action. Antimicrobial, antiseptic, anti-inflammatory, tonic, detoxicant, parasiticide, antibiotic (non-toxic), vasodilator, lymphatic. Does not act directly upon a virus but exerts an antiviral effect by stimulating an immune response. Raises white blood cell count and increases the body's inherent powers of resistance. Has power to stimulate 'killer' cells that resist foreign bacteria. T-cell activator. Vulnerary.
Uses. Boils, acne, abscesses, sore throat: streptococcal and staphylococcal infections generally. Ulcers of tongue, mouth, gums, tonsils, throat (mouth wash and gargle). Duodenal and gastric ulcer. Systemic candida. Putrefaction and fermentation in the alimentary tract. Skin disorders: eczema. Infection of the fallopian tubes.Ill-effects of vaccination. A cleansing wash and lotion for STDs and varicose ulcers. Vaginal candidiasis.
Tonsillitis and infective sore throat: "In all cases do not forget the value of Echinacea. I rely on it to restore a poisoned system." (*I.F. Barnes MD,*

Beverley, Mass, USA)

Appendicitis. "Seven cases of fully diagnosed appendicitis were completely cured by 5 drops liquid extract Echinacea, in water, every 1-3 hours." (*Henry Reny MD, Biddeford, Maine, USA*)

Gangrene. "Echinacea retards and prevents gangrene." (*Finlay Ellingwood MD*)

Shingles. Genital herpes. Echinacea purpurea. Self-medication by "T.S., London" for neuralgic pains caused by the virus 'moving down the nerves' preceding appearance of a herpetic lesion. "Each time an attack has been aborted – pains subsiding within six or so hours."

Phytokold capsules. Arkopharma.

Listeria. Complete protection against. (*Dr H. Wagner, Munich University*)

Preparations. Thrice daily.

Decoction. 1g dried root or rhizome to each cup water simmered 15 minutes. Dose: 1 cup.

Powder. 250mg (one 00 capsule or one-sixth teaspoon).

Liquid extract: 3-15 drops in water.

Alcoholic and aqueous extract from 360mg root. 1 tablet.

Tincture, BHC Vol 1. (1:5, 45 per cent ethanol). Dose: 2-5ml.

Formula. Tincture Echinacea 2; Tincture Goldenseal 1. Dose – 15-30 drops in water every 2 hours (acute) thrice daily (chronic).

Echinacea and Garlic tablets/capsules. Echinacea 60mg; Garlic 20mg; powders to BHP (1983) standard. Versatile combination for minor infections: colds and influenza. (*Gerard House*)

Historical. "Many years ago American Indians observed that by tantalising the rattlesnake it would in its wrath bite itself. The creature was seen to become immediately restless and sought to retreat. On following the snake it was observed that it went straight to a certain shrub and there became a veritable 'sucker'. When it finished sucking the plant it would seek a hole in which to hide, but not to die. It would recover. This led to the discovery of the plant, Echinacea. It was from the medicine-men of the Mohawk and Cherokee Indians we obtained our first knowledge of this remarkable herbal remedy." (*J.H. Henley MD, Enid, Oklahoma, USA*)

Often positive results may not follow because too small a dose is given. For desperate conditions, Dr L.W. Hendershott, Mill Shoals, Illinois, USA, advised frequent 1 dram (4ml) doses. (*Ellingwood, Vol 10, No 4*)

Echinacea has an 'interferon' effect by enhancing body resistance to infection. (*Wagner and Proksch*) GSL, *schedule 1*

ECLAMPSIA. Pre-eclampsia. Toxaemia of last 3 months of pregnancy. Due to a number of causes, one of which is calcium deficiency. Calcium controls muscular spasms that are a feature of the condition. Eclampsia is due, in part, to a traffic jam of blood through the placenta causing a compensatory rise in blood pressure. Black women run 12 times the risk of developing pre-eclampsia during their first pregnancy as non-black women. (*American researchers*)

Women who use barrier contraceptives are more than twice as likely to develop pre-eclampsia in pregnancy than those using non-barrier methods. (*North Carolina Memorial Hospital*)

Symptoms. Headache, dizziness, nausea, upper abdominal pain, twitching of face and limbs, albumin in the urine. Extreme cases: high blood pressure, rigidity, congestive heart failure.

Treatment. Hospitalisation. To be treated by qualified obstetrician.

Formula. Cramp bark 2; Motherwort 1; Black Cohosh 1. Dose: Powders: 750mg (three 00 capsules or half a teaspoon). Liquid extracts: one to two 5ml teaspoons. Tinctures: 1-3 teaspoons. Hourly, or more frequently as tolerated; in water or honey. Magnesium sulphate for fits.

Suppression of urine. Dilation of kidney arterioles to increase flow of blood and to re-start kidney function.

Bearberry (Uva Ursi) tea. 1-2 teaspoon to each cup boiling water; infuse 15 minutes; 1 cup freely.

Bearberry Liquid extract. 2-4ml hourly, or as tolerated, in water or honey.

White Willow. Conventional treatment places high-risk women on low-dose aspirin therapy. As White Willow is a source of natural aspirin, it would appear to offer some benefit. White Willow reduces platelet aggregation, and encourages placental blood flow. Aspirin of pharmacy cuts the risk of pregnancy-induced high blood pressure by two-thirds.

Diet. Pre-eclampsia: oily fish or fish oil supplements. (*Journal of Obstetrics and Gynaecology 1990, 97 (12) 1077-79*)

Supplements. Calcium. Magnesium.

Note. A serious condition which can be fatal but which can be prevented by regular antenatal examinations by a qualified obstetrician.

ECLECTIC MEDICINE. The eclectics were a group of North American physicians who selected from various systems of medicine such principles as they judged to be rational. Their materia medica was based almost entirely on herbal medicine. Part of their knowledge was acquired from the native Indian population and they enjoyed an extraordinary degree of success in the treatment of some of the deeper disturbances of the human race. However, their work was eclipsed by the advance of science and the medical revolution with its brilliant discoveries that have long since been adopted by the orthodox profession. Impressive results were reported in their professional magazine, *Ellingwood's*

Therapeutist, which continued in publication from the turn of the century until 1920. The recorded experiences of those early pioneers awaken renewed interest today.

ECZEMA. The most common skin disease; recognised by minute blisters (vesicles) which fill with colourless fluid and burst leaving the skin cracked, scaly and weepy with possible bleeding. Successful treatment depends upon recognising the type and distribution. Partly a metabolic imbalance.

Atopic eczema. Allergic eczema. May run in families together with hay fever, asthma or inflamed nasal membrane. May appear anywhere but prefers elbows, knees (flexures), ankles or face. Often seen in infants. May return again and again throughout adult life. Scratching exacerbates.

As regards babies, some paediatricians believe breast-feeding to be protective. A stronger case follows investigation into pollutants from the atmosphere or as additives in food. Industrial chemicals find their way into breast milk that may not be easily excreted but stored in fat.

Cow's milk is particularly suspect because of exposure of the animal to herbicides and pesticides. For this reason, goat's milk has met with some success in treatment of this condition, as has Soya milk. Now known that food plays an important part in effective treatment. Chief allergy-stimulators: dairy produce, eggs, cow's milk. Each individual case must identify those foods that are responsible.

Seborrhoeic eczema leads to scaling of the scalp and redness of the ears, eyebrows, side of the nose and possibly armpits and groin.

Stasis eczema (or varicose eczema) may arise from varicose vein problems, usually limited to the lower third of the leg.

Discoid eczema has coin-shaped patches preferring extensor surfaces of arms and legs.

Contact eczema may be caused by washing-up detergents, etc. See: CONTACT DERMATITIS.

While emotional or psychic disturbance may worsen, eczema is seldom a psychosomatic disorder arising from stressful situations. Contact with water may worsen. Hairdressers and those allergic to dyes may require patch tests.

Eczema patients, especially atopic, have a metabolic deficiency of linoleic acid (a dietary fatty acid) to y-linolenic acid, which is found in Evening Primrose oil. Eczema may develop in bottle-fed babies due to absence of GLA (gamma-linolenic acid) in commercial powdered milk. GLA is present in Evening Primrose.

A cross-over trial in 99 patients (adults and children) by Bristol (England) dermatologists found Evening Primrose oil (Efamol capsules) produced an overall 43 per cent improvement in eczema severity: doses – 4 to 6 capsules twice daily (adults); 2 capsules twice daily (children). Lower doses were not effective.

Alternatives. Barberry, Bladderwrack, Blood root, Blue Flag root, Bogbean, Burdock, Clivers, Devil's Claw, Echinacea, Figwort, Fringe Tree, Fumitory, Garlic, Guaiacum, Goldenseal, Mountain Grape, Gotu Kola, Nettles, Plantain, Poke root, Queen's Delight, Red Clover, Sarsaparilla, Sassafras, Wild Indigo, Heartsease, Yellow Dock.

Tea. Combine herbs: equal parts: Gotu Kola, Clivers, Red Clover. 1-2 teaspoons to each cup boiling water; infuse 5-10 minutes; 1 cup thrice daily, before meals (Dry eczema).

Formula: equal parts, Burdock root, Yellow Dock root, Valerian root. Dose. Liquid Extracts, 1 teaspoon. Tinctures, 1-2 teaspoons. Powders, two 00 capsules or one-third teaspoon. Thrice daily, before meals.

Practitioner: specific medication.

Dry eczema. Equal parts, tinctures: Yarrow, Dandelion, Calendula, Echinacea.

Weeping eczema. Combine tinctures: Barberry 1; Clivers 2; Echinacea 2.

Seborrhoeic eczema. Combine tinctures: Blue Flag root 1; Meadowsweet 2; Boneset 1.

Discoid eczema. Combine tinctures: Yellow Dock 2; Mountain Grape 1; Echinacea 1.

Varicose eczema. Combine tinctures: Echinacea 2; Calendula (Marigold) 1; Hawthorn 1.

Dosage for the above: One to two 5ml teaspoons in water thrice daily before meals.

Skin Care. May reduce necessity for steroid creams. It is best to avoid: lanolin and Coconut oil compounds that may contain coal tar. Wash in soft water (rain water) or water not containing chemical softeners.

Indicated: soothing softening herbal lotions, ointments or creams: Marshmallow, Chickweed, Comfrey, Witch Hazel, Aloe Vera gel, Jojoba oil, Evening Primrose oil. For seborrhoeic eczema: Bran Bath or Bran Wash, twice weekly, soapless, followed by Rosemary shampoo. Vitamin E lotion or cream.

Note. A study carried out at the University of Manchester, England, found that children with eczema had significantly low levels of serum zinc than control-cases. (*British Journal of Dermatology, 1984, 111, 597*)

Evening Primrose oil. For Omega 6 fatty acids.

Diet. Gluten-free. Oily fish: see entry. Avoid cow's milk, wheat products.

Supplements. Daily. Vitamins: A (7500iu). C (500mg). E (400iu). Bioflavonoids (500mg). Zinc (15mg). Betaine hydrochloride.

Note. The disorder may be due to a deficiency of essential fatty acids (EFAs) brought about by a deficiency of zinc which is necessary for EFA metabolism.

Chinese herbs. A study has shown herbal treatment to be far superior to placebo in clinical trials. British children with (dry) atopic eczema responded favourably to treatment which included the following herbs known as Formula PSE101.

Ledebouriella sesloides, Potentilla chinesis, Anebia clematidis, Rehmannia glutinosa, Peonia lactiflora, Lophatherum gracile, Dictamnus dasycarpus, Tribulus terrestris, Glycyrrhiza uralensis, Schizonepta tenuifolia. Non-toxicity confirms their safety. (*Sheeham M et al. "A controlled trial of traditional Chinese medicinal plants in widespread non-exudative atopic dermatitis", British Journal of Dermatology, 126: 179-184 1992*)

When 10 Chinese herbs were analysed by a team at the Great Ormond Street Hospital, London, it was revealed that no single active ingredient or herb was responsible for success. "It was a combination of all 10 herbs that gave the medicine its healing properties." This is an example of the synergistic effect of combined plant remedies and supports the herbalist's belief in use of the whole plant.

EJACULATION, PREMATURE. Emission of semen before sexual partner is prepared for orgasm. Agnus Castus, Vervain, Cramp bark, Mistletoe, Valerian.

ELDER. Black Elder. *Sambucus nigra L.* Flowers, bark, berries. *German*: Holunder. *French*: Sureau. *Spanish*: Sauco. *Italian*: Sambreo.
Constituents: flavonoids, oil, tannins.

Berries contain Vitamin C and iron. Elderblossom works well with Peppermint or Yarrow, as a tea.

Action: anti-inflammatory, laxative (especially berries and bark), anticatarrhal, relaxing diaphoretic, hydragogue (inner bark), cathartic (inner bark). Elderblossom is an emollient skin care product. Emetic (inner bark). Diuretic (urinary antiseptic). An ancient household remedy for promoting flow of urine (cold infusion). Expectorant (hot infusion).

Uses: the common cold, influenza, winter's chills, early stages of fevers with dry skin and raised body temperature. Nasal catarrh, sinusitis. Tonsillitis, inflammation of mouth, throat and trachea (mouth wash and gargle). Night sweats (cold infusion). Chilblains (local).

"The inner bark of Elder has been used with success in epilepsy by taking suckers or branches 1-2 years old. The grey outer bark is scraped off and 2oz of it steeped in 5oz boiling water for 48 hours. Strain. Give a wineglassful every 15 minutes when a fit is threatening. Have the patient fast. Resume every 6 to 8 days." (*Dr F. Brown (1875)*)

Croup (combined with Coltsfoot – equal parts). Eyestrain, conjunctivitis, twitching: cotton wool pads soaked in cold Elder tea applied to the closed lids, patient lying down.

Preparations. *Tea* (flowers) 2 teaspoons (2-4g) in each cup boiling water; infuse 5 minutes. Half-1 cup two-hourly for acute conditions. Cold tea is laxative and sedative. Hot tea excites and stimulates. Cold tea soothes and heals chapped hands and useful for sunbathing.
Distilled Elderflower water: for inflamed eyes.
Liquid Extract. 1 teaspoon in water, thrice daily.
Home tincture (traditional). Chippings of inner green bark macerated in white wine for 8 days, strain; for dropsy and constipation.
Ointment. 3 parts fresh Elder leaves. Heat with 6 parts Vaseline until leaves are crisp; strain and store. (*David Hoffmann*)
Elderberry wine: traditional.
Powder: dose, 3-5g.
Veterinary. "If sheep or farm animals with foot-rot have access to the bark and young leaves, they soon cure themselves." (*Dr John Clarke, Dictionary of Materia Medica*) GSL

ELDERFLOWERS. Peppermint and Composition Essence. Active ingredients: Each 10ml contains: Liquid extract Pleurisy root (1:1, 35 per cent alcohol) 0.15ml. Liquid extract Elecampane (1:1, 21 per cent alcohol) 0.15ml. Liquid extract Horehound (1:1, 20 per cent alcohol) 0.15ml. Liquid extract Skunk Cabbage (1:1, 21 per cent alcohol) 0.15ml. Tincture Lobelia (1:12.5, 5.8 per cent Acetic Acid) 0.225ml, in a syrup base. Chills and feverish colds. (*Potter's, UK*)

ELECAMPANE. Scabwort. *Inula helenium L.* Root and rhizome. *German*: Alant. *French*: Inule. *Italian*: Enula elemie. *Arabian*: Ussul-ur-rasun. *Indian*: Phatmer. *Iranian*: Pil-gush. *Keynote*: lung disorders. Grows freely in Russia where it is cultivated and the fresh root preserved in strong vodka for chest and stomach complaints.
Constituents: sesquiterpene lactones, inulin, resin.

Action: antispasmodic, alterative, stimulating *expectorant*, diaphoretic, antiseptic, stomachic, anticatarrhal.

"Performs a double action (1) as a bacteriostatic in chronic bronchitis and (2) its biochemical action in alleviating rheumatism." (*Hamdard Foundation, Pakistan*).

Helenin inhibits growth of tubercle bacillus (*Ellingwood, 12.4. Apr 18. 126*)

Uses: Has a long record for old coughs, especially of tuberculosis. Haemoptysis, whooping cough, croup. Advanced chest diseases to facilitate removal of mucous. Silicosis, pneumoconiosis, emphysema. Chronic catarrh. Night sweats. Leucorrhoea. To strengthen a feeble digestion. Stitches in the side (spleen). Hyperventilation.

Combines well with Yarrow and Marshmallow. *Popular combination*. Decoction: mix equal parts; Yarrow, Marshmallow root and Elecampane root. 1oz (30g) in 1 pint (500ml) water simmered 20 minutes. Dose: half-1 cup, 2-3 times daily. In the absence of any one ingredient, substitute Wild Cherry bark.

Preparations. Thrice daily.

Powder: quarter to half a teaspoon.

Decoction, root. Quarter to half a teaspoon to each cup of water; simmer gently 10 minutes in a covered vessel. Dose: 1 cup

Liquid extract BHC Vol 1. (1:1, in 25 per cent ethanol). Dose: 1-2ml.

Not used in pregnancy and lactation.

Note. Difficult to maintain chemical stability of the root which may explain why best results have followed pulping or decoction of the fresh root. Dosage of pulp: 2-4 teaspoons. GSL, *schedule 1*

ELEPHANTIASIS. Swelling of feet, arms, legs, genitals, breasts, commencing with scaly skin rash and progressing to gross swelling of the flesh. Mostly tropical. Infestation of lymph glands by worm *Wuchereria bancrofti* from a mosquito. Draining of fluid from the tissues via the lymph system is obstructed. Chronic oedema of limbs and scrotum.

Alternatives. Secondary to conventional treatment.

Teas. Clivers, Fenugreek (decoction), Yarrow. Oriental traditional remedy: Gotu Kola.

Formula. Combine Poke root 1; Echinacea 2; Dandelion 3. Doses. Powders: 750mg (three 00 capsules or half a teaspoon). Liquid Extracts: 1 teaspoon. Tinctures: 2 teaspoons. Thrice daily. Longstanding-cases: add 1 part Thuja.

ELEUTHEROCOCCUS. *Eleutherococcus senticosus*. See: GINSENG – SIBERIAN.

ELIMINATIVE. A herb to disperse and promote excretion from the body accumulated poisonous substances, metabolites, that may have been ingested as additives in food, inhaled as part of the environment, or acquired as morbid products of inflammation left behind after some acute disease, such as influenza.

Some eliminatives have a biochemical action on cell wastes and toxins, breaking them down preparatory to voiding from the body. Others stimulate organs of elimination to speed them on their journey: liver, kidneys, skin, bowel. This group will therefore include diuretics, hepatics, lymphatics, expectorants, diaphoretics or laxatives according to indications of the case.

ELIXIR. A sweetened alcoholic extract for internal use. To active ingredients, flavours, sorbitol or syrup may be added to mask unpleasant taste or make the medicament more acceptable. The use of elixirs is discouraged by the modern herbalist who seeks to avoid sugar in favour of honey. Example: Weleda's Cough Expectorant Elixir. An elixir serves as a vehicle for Wormwood, Rhubarb, Senna, etc.

ELLINGWOOD, Dr FINLAY. Distinguished Chicago physician with a practice based on herbal medicine. Of the school of American physiomedicalists including John K. Scudder, M.D., Wooster Beach, MD. Editor: *Ellingwood's Therapeutist* published beginning of this century and still consulted by progressive herbalists. Books: *Ellingwood's New American Materia Medica, Therapeutics and Pharmacognosy. Ellingwood's Practice of Medicine*. Commended.

This pioneer and frontiersman was one of the first of the eclectic physicians to discover the remarkable versatility of Echinacea root.

EMBOLISM. A situation in which a blood clot is lodged in an artery and obstructs blood flow. Anticoagulants are indicated. If of septic origin, microbials such as Echinacea would be added to combination.

Alternatives. *Formula*. Equal parts: Motherwort to open up blood vessels, Hawthorn to increase force of heart-beat, Broom to reduce risk of oedema.

Tea. 1 heaped teaspoon to each cup of water gently simmered 5 minutes. 1 cup freely.

Powders. Dose: 750mg (three 00 capsules or half a teaspoon). Liquid extracts: 1 teaspoon. Tinctures: 2 teaspoons. In water or honey 3-4 times daily.

Diet. See entry: DIET – HEART AND CIRCULATION.

EMETIC. A herb to induce vomiting. Given to expel poisons. Physiomedical doctors of the 1880s employed emetics at the onset of a feverish condition, setting much store on emptying and cleansing the stomach, relaxing the skin, regulating the bowels, claiming that a fever could often be aborted or cut short in its early stages.

While emetic therapy is no longer popular, it has a tradition of use for dropsy, dysentery, jaundice, bilious attacks and acidity – even swollen testicles!

Important agents: Balm, Boneset, Catmint, Elderflowers, Elecampane (mild), Holy Thistle (mild), Poke root, Senega, Squill, Queen's Delight, Grape bark (Guarea). Mustard: 1 tablespoon to 8oz warm water. Simple emetic: 1 teaspoon Lobelia herb to cup boiling water.

To restore stomach-tone after use of emetics give bitters: Centuary, Gentian, Angostura, Chamomile, Bogbean, Poplar bark, White Horehound, Vermuth.

EMETIC TREATMENT. As practised by members of the Thomsonian medical fraternity.

An emetic treatment may be administered with good effect when the body is powerless to throw off toxic matter in a healing crisis (acute disease). Uneliminated by-products of carbohydrate and protein metabolism may obstruct the abdominal

circulation and congest the tissues. A few days fast followed by emesis has resolved many an acute gastro-intestinal problem.
Requirements: towel, large bowl, strainer, and a bowl of cold water in which a container may be cooled should infusions be too hot.

Before emesis the bowels should be evacuated. A full bowel inhibits the emetic effect and absorbs fluid.

Prepare three one-pint infusions, in separate vessels; cover to prevent escape of essential oils. Infuse 15 minutes.
1. *Catnep*. 1oz to 1 pint boiling water.
2. *Bayberry* (or Composition). 1 heaped teaspoon, powder, to 1 pint boiling water.
3. *Lobelia*. Half an ounce to 1 pint boiling water.
Proceed: (a) Drink a cup of Catnep tea (b) follow with a cup of Bayberry (or Composition) tea (c) drink a second cup of Catnep (d) drink a second cup of Bayberry (or Composition). Four cups will be taken at this point, all of which will stimulate mucous surfaces. (e) Follow with a cup of Lobelia tea (a relaxant). (f) Repeat the procedure. Vomiting usually occurs before 8 cups. Repeat the sequence as long as can be borne. About half the intake will be returned. Vomit will be found to be exceedingly viscous and ropy and a healthy sense of well-being can follow its exit from the body. After vomiting three times, or as much as tolerated, discontinue treatment and rest.

EMMENAGOGUES. Plant substitutes for hormones that stimulate the pituitary gland to produce more gonadotropic hormones. Herbs that initiate and promote the menstrual flow. Most are uterine tonics and stimulants to restore normal function of the female reproductive system. Not used in pregnancy, except when a practitioner has good cause to do so in the first few weeks. They include: Agnus Castus, Angelica, Basil, Barberry, Autumn Crocus, Blood root, Beth root, Black Cohosh, Black Haw, Blue Cohosh, Caraway, Celery seeds, Chamomile, Coltsfoot, Cramp bark, Cinnamon, False Unicorn root, Fenugreek, Feverfew, Gentian, Ginger, Goldenseal, Greater Celandine, Holy Thistle, Juniper berries, Lime flowers, Lovage, Marigold, Marjoram, Motherwort, Mugwort, Myrrh, Parsley root, Pennyroyal, Peppermint, Poke root, Pulsatilla, Raspberry leaves, Red Sage, Rosemary, Rue, Senna, Shepherd's Purse, Southernwood, Squaw Vine, St John's Wort, Tansy, Thuja, Thyme, True Unicorn root, Valerian, Vervain, Wormwood, Yarrow.
Combination. Equal parts: Mugwort, Senna, Chamomile. 2 teaspoons to each cup boiling water; infuse 15 minutes. 1 cup morning and midday.
Papaya fruit. Contraceptive used to halt pregnancy. Papain, an enzyme in the tropical fruit, attacks progesterone, the hormone essential to pregnancy.

EMOLLIENT. A herb, usually mucilaginous, which has a protective and soothing action upon the surface of the body. A demulcent has a similar action but on internal surfaces (mucous membranes), Almond oil, Balm of Gilead, Borage, Chickweed, Comfrey, Elecampane, Fenugreek seeds, Iceland Moss, Irish Moss, Linseed oil, Lungwort, Marshmallow, Mullein, Oatmeal, Peanut oil, Plantain, Sesame Seed oil, Soya oil, Slippery Elm bark, Wheatgerm oil. Used in creams, lotions and poultices.

EMOTIONAL ILLNESS. A number of different mental and emotional conditions may arise. Some are hereditary, others acquired through anxiety and a sense of insecurity. A sound constitution and strong nervous system are a bulwark against disintegration of the personality. For this purpose nerve restoratives and anxiolytics are indicated.
Alternatives. *Teas*: German Chamomile, Oats, Skullcap, Valerian, Gotu Kola.
Tablets. Devil's Claw, Ginseng, Pulsatilla, Mistletoe, Motherwort, Valerian.
Gotu Kola: used extensively in traditional Indian medicine for mental ailments.
Diet. Protein, Salt-free. Lacto-vegetarian.
Vitamins. B-complex, B1; B6; B12; Niacin, Folic Acid. C, E, F.
Minerals. Dolomite. Zinc.

EMPHYSEMA. In normal breathing the lungs spring back into their usual shape after expansion by the act of breathing-in. In emphysema, elasticity has lost its spring so the lungs become permanently expanded. Differs from chronic bronchitis by destroying walls of the air sacs. The chest is barrel-shaped through hyperinflation. Trumpeter's lung; glass-blower's disease, smoker's disease. Stethoscope reveals 'distant' heart sounds of right heart failure, for which Hawthorn is indicated. Breathlessness on exertion. The victim cannot dispel the sensation of puffed-up lungs.

Through a lack of oxygen other muscles weaken. Rate of breathing may increase from 14-30 times per minute. Always 'clearing the throat'. Overweight worsens.
Alternatives. Lobelia, Wild Thyme, Coltsfoot. Ephedra (practitioner only).
To loosen and thin tough mucus: Iceland Moss, Garlic, Coltsfoot, Gum ammoniac, Fenugreek seeds, Liquorice, Khella.
Decoction. Equal parts: Valerian, Liquorice root. 1-2 teaspoons to each cup boiling water; simmer 15 minutes. Dose: 1 cup once or twice daily and at bedtime.
Tablets/capsules. Lobelia, Iceland Moss, Garlic.
Formula. Equal parts: Elecampane, Iceland Moss, Wild Thyme. Dose: Powders: 750mg (three 00 capsules or half a teaspoon). Liquid

extracts: 1-2 teaspoons. Tinctures: 1-3 teaspoons. In water, honey or banana mash, thrice daily, and during the night if necessary

Practitioner. Alternatives.

Formula (1). Liquid extracts: Ephedra 2; Elecampane 1; Lobelia 1. Dose – 500mg (two 00 capsules or one-third teaspoon). Liquid extracts: 1-2 teaspoons. Tinctures: 1-3 teaspoons in water etc as above.

Formula (2). Liquid extracts: Ephedra 2; Liquorice 1. Dosage same as Formula 1. The action of both formulae is improved when taken in cup of Fenugreek decoction.

Hyssop Wine. Good responses observed. 1oz herb macerated in 1 pint white wine or Vodka for 3-4 weeks; shake daily.

A. Barker FNIMH. Liquid extract Mouse Ear 60 drops; Liquid extract Pleurisy root 30 drops; Tincture Goldenseal 30 drops; Tincture Myrrh 20 drops; Tincture Ginger 20 drops. Pure bottled or distilled water to 8oz (240ml). Dose: 2 teaspoons every 3 hours.

Diet. Low salt. High fibre. Avoid all dairy products.

Supplements. Daily. Vitamin A 7500iu. Vitamin E 400iu. Folic acid 1mg. Vitamin C 200mg. Iodine, iron.

Deep-breathing exercises. 2 Garlic tablets/capsules at night. For acute respiratory infections that irritate emphysema add Echinacea.

EMPYEMA. Accumulation of pus in a cavity, especially bacterial infection of the lung or in pleural space.

Treatment. May be necessary for practitioner to draw away pus through a tube. Treat underlying cause. Herbal antibiotics.

Liquid Extracts. Formula. Echinacea 2; Goldenseal 1; Thuja half. Dose: 30-60 drops.

Tinctures: same formula, double dose. In water thrice daily.

Australian practice. Tea Tree oil: 2-5 drops in honey or other vehicle, thrice daily. If too strong may be diluted many times.

Treatment by or in liaison with registered medical practitioner.

EMULSION. A medication in which an oil is suspended in water with the addition of an emulsifier: Quillaia bark (Soap bark), Lecithin, Acacia or other gum. A convenient way of applying oils to the skin, aiding penetration. Drying and cooling. Usually one part oil to ten parts water.

ENCEPHALITIS. Inflammation of the brain. A notifiable disease. See: BRAIN DISORDERS.

ENDOCARDITIS. Two types – simple and ulcerative. Inflammation of the membrane lining of the heart with the appearance of small fibrin accumulations on the valves. These may form during a specific fever – rheumatic, scarlet, etc, due to bacterial infection. In Bacterial Endocarditis, fragments of tissue may be shed from the main seat of infection and borne to other parts of the body, promoting inflammation or ischaemia elsewhere.

Affects more women than men, ages 20 to 40 years. Most cases have a history of rheumatic fever as a child. Thickening of the valves renders them less efficient in regulating the flow of blood through the heart thus allowing leakage by improper closure. Increased effort is required from the heart muscle to pump blood through the narrowed valves giving rise to fatigue and possible heart failure.

Prolapsus of the mitral valve is now recognised as predisposing to bacterial endocarditis. It is concluded that herbal antibiotic prophylaxis is justified in heart patients undergoing dental extraction, or other surgery where there is exposure to infection.

Symptoms: Breathlessness on exertion. Swelling of legs and ankles, palpitations, fainting, blue tinge to the skin and a permanent pink flush over the cheek bones. Clubbing of fingers. Enlarged spleen. Stethoscope reveals valvular regurgitation. The most common organism remains *streptococcus viridans*, by mouth. It may reach the heart by teeth extraction, scaling and intensive cleaning which may draw blood, posing a risk by bacteria.

Treatment. Acute conditions should be under the authority of a heart specialist in an Intensive Care Unit. Absolute bedrest to relieve stress on the heart's valves. For acute infection: Penicillin (or other essential antibiotics). Alternatives, of limited efficacy: Echinacea, Myrrh, Wild Indigo, Nasturtium, Holy Thistle.

Avoid: excitement, chills, colds, fatigue and anything requiring extra cardiac effort. Convalescence will be long (weeks to months) during which resumption to normal activity should be gradual.

Aconite. With full bounding pulse and restless fever. Five drops Tincture Aconite to half a glass (100ml) water. 2 teaspoons hourly until temperature falls.

To sustain heart. Tincture Convallaria (Lily of the Valley), 5-15 drops, thrice daily.

To stimulate secretion of urine. Tincture Bearberry, 1-2 teaspoons, thrice daily.

Rheumatic conditions. Tincture Colchicum, 10-15 drops, thrice daily.

Various conventional treatments of the past can still be used with good effect: Tincture Strophanthus, 5 to 15 drops. Liquid Extract Black Cohosh, 15 to 30 drops. Spirits of Camphor, 5 to 10 drops. Bugleweed (American), 10 to 30 drops. To increase body strength: Echinacea. To sustain heart muscle: Hawthorn. Endocarditis with severe headache: Black Cohosh.

Teas: single or in combination (equal parts) – Nettles, Motherwort, Red Clover flowers, Lime flowers. 2 teaspoons to each cup boiling water; infuse 15 minutes. 1 cup 2-3 times daily.
Decoction: equal parts: Hawthorn berries, Echinacea root, Lily of the Valley leaves. Mix. 2 teaspoons to each 2 cups water in a non-aluminium vessel, gently simmer 10 minutes. Dose: 1 cup 2-3 times daily.
Formula. Echinacea 20; Cactus 10; Hawthorn 10; Goldenseal 2. Mix. Dose: Powders: 750mg (three 00 capsules or half a teaspoon). Liquid extracts: 1-2 teaspoons. Tinctures: 1-3 teaspoons. Thrice daily.
Diet. See entry: DIET – HEART AND CIRCULATION. Pineapple juice.
Treatment by or in liaison with general medical practitioner or cardiologist.

ENDOCRINE GLANDS. Ductless glands that secrete chemicals (hormones) direct into the blood stream to be borne to other parts of the body. Chiefly: pituitary gland, thyroid gland, parathyroid gland, adrenal glands. The gonads are also endocrines, producing sex hormones. Similarly, the pancreas secretes insulin which is discharged directly into the blood. Certain herbs act specifically on these glands as normalisers (adaptogens): Ginseng, Gotu Kola, Echinacea, Liquorice, Wild Yam, etc.

ENDOMETRIOSIS. The presence of tissue normally found on the walls of the womb in an abnormal site, i.e. endometrial tissue implants may appear in the pelvic cavity where they multiply causing obstruction or retrograde tissue change. Scars and adhesions may form between womb and bowel. An ovary may be affected by a tissue thread passing through a Fallopian tube as an aftermath of menstruation. The condition may disappear at pregnancy or menopause. Such fibrous adhesions prevent proper conception and fertility.
Symptoms. Sharp stabbing pains are worse by intercourse. Pain radiates down the back; worse two weeks before menstruation. Incidence has increased since introduction of the vaginal tampon. Enlarged 'boggy' uterus. Menstrual irregularity and pain. Diagnosis confirmed by laparoscopy.
Treatment. Official treatment is by Danol hormone therapy which induces a state of artificial pregnancy. Shrinkage and remission of symptoms follow as long as medication is continued. Where the condition has not regressed too far, a number of phyto-pharmaceuticals may bring a measure of relief. These are believed to reduce levels of gonadotrophins and ovarian steroids and abolish cyclical hormonal changes. They are best administered by a qualified herbal practitioner: (MNIMH). Prescriptions vary according to the requirements of each individual case and are modified to meet changed symptoms and progress.
Formula.

Tr Zingiber fort BP (1973)	5
Tr Xanthoxylum 1:5 BHP (1983)	20
L.E. Glycyrrhiza BP (1973)	10
Tr Phytolacca 1:10 BPC (1923)	5
Tr Chamaelirium 1:5 BHP (1983)	50

Aq ad 250ml
Sig 5-10ml (3i) tds aq cal pc.
For pain episodes: pelvic antispasmodics – say Anemone: 10-20 drops (tincture) prn. Extra Ginger, pelvic stimulant, may be taken once or twice daily between meals. Chamomile tea: 1-2 cups daily to maintain endocrine balance.
Formula. Mrs Janet Hicks, FNIMH. Blue Flag root 30ml; Burdock root 20ml; Hawthorn berries 20ml; Pulsatilla herb 40ml; Vervain 50ml; Dandelion root 30ml; Ginger 10ml. Dose: 5ml in water, thrice daily. (*Medical Herbalist, Alresford, Nr Winchester, UK*)
Formula. Mrs Brenda Cooke, FNIMH. Helonias, Wild Yam, Vervain, Black Haw, Parsley Piert, Marigold, Butternut, aa 15. Goldenseal 10, Ginger 2.5. 5 mls tds., pc. (*Medical Herbalist, Mansfield, Notts, UK*)
Topical. Castor oil packs to low abdomen, twice weekly.
Note. Vigorous exercise appears to reduce the risk of women developing the condition.
Danazol drug rash. Echinacea. Chickweed cream.

ENDOMETRITIS. Inflammation of the endometrium (lining of the womb).
Causes: curettage, abortion, sepsis, bacterial or viral infection (tuberculosis, etc), STD diseases (gonorrhoea, etc). Commonly follows miscarriage or abortion.
Symptoms: low backache, unpleasant purulent vaginal discharge, fever, painful periods.
Treatment. Bedrest. Herbal antibiotics, anti-infectives. To reduce pus formation and strengthen body resistance – Echinacea. To check bleeding between periods – Raspberry, Beth root. To repair mucous membrane – Goldenseal. Constitutional remedy: Thuja, see entry. With hormonal disturbance – Agnus Castus.
Tea. Formula: equal parts, Raspberry leaves, Yarrow, Agnus Castus.
Beth root. See entry.
Helonias. Long history of use by north American Indians. See entry.
A. Barker, FNIMH. Prescription. Tincture Goldenseal 30 drops, Liquid Extract Clivers 60 drops, Liquid Extract Cornsilk 1 fl oz, Liquid Extract Damiana 60 drops. Liquid Extract Marshmallow 1 fl oz. Water to 8oz. Dose: 2 teaspoons every 4 hours.
Topical. Douches: Thuja, Echinacea, Goldenseal. or Myrrh. Raspberry leaf tea.

ENDORPHINS. Body chemicals synthesised by the brain and which play a part in regulation of mood as well as affecting the brain's perception of pain. Endorphins have been shown to fall in menopausal women causing depression, mood swings, lack of interest in sex and lower pain thresholds.

Agnus Castus and Helonias are believed to encourage production of endorphins thus improving a sense of well-being in menopausal women.

ENEMA. A rectal infusion chiefly water given as an aid to evacuation of the bowel or, injected slowly can be an aid to dehydration. An enema may also be of great value in the treatment of some diseases. Injection of fluid (herb teas, etc) through a tube into the rectum, via the anus, to relieve constipation or convey medication or nutriment. A herbal tea may be given as a stimulating nervine (to rouse from severe prostration as in apoplexy, meningitis); relaxant (when the body is feverish and tense); or to re-activate after collapse and shock. Usual enemata: 2 pints herb tea.

Bayberry bark, Burdock root, Catnep, Lobelia, Fenugreek seeds, Raspberry leaves, Chickweed, Tormentil, Lime flowers, Mullein.

Evacuant Children. Catnep tea, with 2 teaspoons honey. Adults. Catnep, Raspberry leaves.

Stimulating nervine: Skullcap, Oatmeal, Oats, Bayberry bark.

Relaxant: Lobelia, Lime flowers, Mullein.

To re-activate after collapse: Teaspoon Composition powder, Ginger; or 20 drops tincture Myrrh.

To soothe pain of diverticulosis: Fenugreek seeds, Marshmallow root, Oatmeal.

Alternatives to coffee for cancer: Raspberry leaves, Red Clover flowers, Burdock root, Yellow Dock.

For bowel infections: typhoid (Boneset and Skullcap – equal parts): dysentery (raspberry leaves 10, Myrrh 1): diverticulitis (German Chamomile 8, Goldenseal 1). Impacted faeces: Chamomile tea with teaspoon Olive Oil.

When the stomach rejects a medicine an alternative route is by enema into the bowel.

Olive Oil enema: 5oz Olive Oil in 20oz boiled water.

Myrrh enema: 20 drops Tincture Myrrh in 20oz boiled water for bowel infections.

Slippery Elm enema: half a teaspoon Slippery Elm powder in 20 boiled water.

Raspberry leaf enema: 1oz Raspberry leaves in 1 pint (20oz) boiling water; infuse until warm, strain and inject for irritable bowel and other conditions.

Enemas should not be given to children.

ENEMA, COFFEE. Injection of a strong infusion of coffee into the rectum is given in some cases of terminal disease to cleanse the bowel, and for sedative effect to assuage the pain of malignancy. When cancer cells are released into the bloodstream they are borne to the liver where they are broken down and expelled from the body via the eliminative organs. Such organs may be congested by by-products of disease. Coffee enemas are used for their detoxifying effect.

3 heaped tablespoons of ground coffee (not Instant) to 2 pints (1 litre) water. Bring to boil. Simmer 20 minutes. Strain when warm. Inject one or more pints according to tolerance. "Coffee retention enemas may be given at frequent intervals where well-tolerated, with no side effects." (*Mayo Clinic*) (*JAMA 245, 591, 1981*)

ENERGY – LACK OF. *Teas*: Agrimony, Betony, Gotu Kola, Ginseng.

Decoction: Gentian.

Tablets: traditional combination – Kola, Saw Palmetto, Damiana. Ginseng.

Powders: equal parts Ginseng and Kola. Half a teaspoon.

Liquid Extracts: equal parts, Damiana, Saw Palmetto, Wild Yam. 30-60 drops in water thrice daily.

Diet: porridge oats. Bee Pollen. Cayenne. Life Drops.

ENGLAND Dr F.H. Physician and Professor of Materia Medica, College of Medicine and Surgery, Chicago. Pioneer in the introduction of American Herbalism into Britain at the turn of the 20th century.

ENTERITIS. See: GASTRO-ENTERITIS.

ENURESIS. Bed-wetting. Unconscious persistent discharge of urine in bed by children over three years. Possible hereditary tendency. Some cases psychological in origin: lack of security, marital disharmony, etc. Adenoids or worms sometimes responsible. Occurs mostly in boys where foreskin is too tight. Circumcism may be necessary. Parents should not scold but reserve extra affection and attention to patient.

Treatment. No drinks at night. Empty bladder at bedtime. Wake child 2 hours later to again empty bladder. During the day all caffeine drinks should be avoided: coffee, tea, Cola, etc.

Alternatives. *Day-time drinks*. Teas from any one:– American Cranesbill, Agrimony, Heartsease, Corn Silk, Liquorice root, Marshmallow root, Mullein, Raspberry leaves, Vervain, Shepherd's Purse, Ladies Mantle, Uva Ursi. Formula. Bearberry 1; Cornsilk half; Skullcap 1. 1-2 teaspoons to each cup boiling water; infuse 15 minutes; half-1 cup hour before bedtime.

Tablets/capsules. Cranesbill (American). Passion flower. Valerian.

Formula. Equal parts: Ephedra, Valerian,

Cranesbill (American). *Dose*. Powders quarter of a teaspoon. Liquid Extract 1 teaspoon. Tinctures 1-2 teaspoons. In water or honey, early evening and at bedtime.
Eclectic School, America. (1) Horsetail 1; Cramp bark half. (2) Mullein 2; Cramp bark half. (3) Oil Thyme, 3 drops night and morning. (4) Oil Mullein (traditional, but still effective) 5 drops.
Thuja. "I have never failed to cure eneuresis in children and young people 3-15 years by giving 2-15 drops Liquid Extract Thuja in a tablespoon of water before each meal and at bedtime. (*J.M. Stephenson MD*)
Practitioner. Dec Jam Sarsae Co Conc BPC (1949), 1 fl oz. Liquid Extract Rhus Aromatica (Sweet Sumach) half a fluid ounce. Liquid Extract Passiflora 60 drops. Syrup Althaea 2 fl oz. Aqua to 8oz. Dose: 2 teaspoons in water thrice daily; last dose at bedtime. (*Arthur Barker*)
Tinctures. Formula. Equal parts: Agrimony, Corn Silk, Horsetail. Dose: 15-60 drops in water thrice daily.
Tincture Arnica: 1-2 drops in water at bedtime; not under 5 years.
Tincture Sweet Sumach. 10-15 drops in water thrice daily.
Diet: piece of cheese or peanut butter at bedtime helps level off the blood sugar level during sleep – important for normal brain function. Citrus fruits and chocolate aggravate. Cow's milk suspect.

ENZYMES. An enzyme is a substance produced in the body, acting as a catalyst to trigger chemical change in another. Complex substances are thereby broken down into simple compounds to facilitate assimilation and absorption, as in the digestive juices.

EOSINOPHILIC MYALGIA SYNDROME (EMS). An increase in the number of eosinophils in the blood. May occur in a number of allergies, infections, and is sometimes responsible for leukaemia. Among other causes, food supplement tryptophan has been linked. See entry.
Symptoms. Stiffness and severe muscle pain.
Treatment. *Formula*. Echinacea 2; Burdock 1; Yarrow 1; Poke root quarter. Dose: Liquid Extracts: 1-2 teaspoons. Tinctures: 2-3 teaspoons. Powders: 750mg (three 00 capsules or half a teaspoon). Thrice daily.

EPHEDRA. *Ephedra sinica* stapf., *Ephedra equisentina* Bunge and *Ephedra gerardiana* Wall (including *Ephedra nebrodensis* Tineo). Twigs. *German*: Meerträubchen. *French*: Ephèdre. *Italian*: Uva di mare. *Iranian*: Huma. *Japanese*: Ma oh. *Indian*: Butshur. *Chinese*: Ma Huang.
Constituents: Alkaloids – ephedrine, pseudoephedrine.
Action: brain, heart and circulatory stimulant, antasthmatic, bronchodilator, anti-allergic, vasodilator, hypertensive, diaphoretic. Dilates vessels of the heart causing a rise in blood pressure. Cough sedative. Febrifuge, antispasmodic. The essential oil has antibacterial and antiviral properties.
Uses. Practitioner's first choice for asthma. Bronchitis, breathlessness, whooping cough. Used for such chest conditions for over a millennia in Chinese medicine.
Allergies: hay fever, irritative skin rashes. Low blood pressure. Hypothermia. Bed-wetting. Myasthenia gravis BHP (1983). Chinese Barefoot doctors inject the tea into nostrils for hay fever.
Usually given with expectorants: Liquorice, Lobelia, Senega, Sundew. "Combines well with Lobelia and Skunk Cabbage for bronchitis; and with Horsetail for frequency of urine." (*Fletcher Hyde*)
Contra-indications: hypertension, coronary thrombosis, thyrotoxicosis, glaucoma. Not given with anti-depressants (MAO inhibitors).
Preparations. Thrice daily. Average dose: 15-60mg.
Tea. Quarter to half a teaspoon herb to cup water simmered gently 5 minutes. Half a cup.
Liquid extract. BHP (1983) 1:1 in 45 per cent alcohol. Dose: 15-45 drops (1-3ml).
Tincture BHP (1983) 1 part to 4 parts 45 per cent alcohol. Dose: 6-8ml.
Ephedrine. Maximum dose: 30mg. Maximum daily dose 60mg.
Store in airtight container out of the light.
Pharmacy only medicine. Practitioners only.

EPIDIDYMITIS. The epididymus is the tube which receives the ducts of the testicle; in acute bacterial infection it becomes swollen and painful. The cause may be invasion from an infected bladder or urethra.
Symptoms: difficulty in passing urine, painful scrotum.
Indicated: antibacterials. Pulsatilla (*American Dispensary*)
Alternatives. *Teas*. Cornsilk, Marshmallow leaves.
Decoction. Marshmallow root.
Tablets/capsules. Pulsatilla, Saw Palmetto. Echinacea. Goldenseal.
Powders. Formula. Equal parts, Saw Palmetto, Pulsatilla, Black Willow, pinch of Cayenne. Dose: 500mg (two 00 capsules or one-third teaspoon) 3-4 times daily.
Liquid Extracts. Alternatives. (1) Formula: equal parts: Black Willow, Echinacea, Pulsatilla. Dose: 30-60 drops. (2) Echinacea 2; Saw Palmetto 2; Thuja 1. Dose: 30-60 drops. 3-4 times daily.
Topical. Scrotal ice packs. Cold Dogwood poultice.

EPILEPSY. An epileptic fit is a temporary spasmodic disturbance in the brain of sudden onset caused by a spurious discharge of electrical energy by brain cells. Can be sparked off by an excess of zinc. Loss of consciousness signalled by an aura and a fall to the ground with a cry. Breathing is noisy, eyes upturned.

General causes: hereditary, severe head injury (even before birth), chronic disease, stroke, tumour, hardening of the arteries, drugs, lack of oxygen. An attack may be triggered by the flickering of a television or computer screen. Screen-addicted children may develop photosensitive epilepsy, suffering fits while using electronic games.

Three forms: major (grand mal); temporal lobe; and minor (petit mal). In petit mal the period of unconsciousness consists of brief absences lasting less than 15 seconds.

Treatment. Orthodox medical: Carbamazepine, phenytoin and many other drugs.

Alternatives. BHP (1983) recommends: Grand mal: Passion flower, Skullcap, Verbena. Petit mal: Hyssop. Standard central nervous system relaxants are Hops, Lobelia, Passion flower, Vervain, Valerian, Skullcap. Wm Boericke used Mugwort. Peony leaf tea had a long traditional use. In nearly all epileptics there is functional heart disturbance (Hawthorn Lily of the Valley, Motherwort). Mistletoe can help in the struggle to control seizures and improve the quality of life.

Two important remedies are Skullcap and Passion flower. Both work quickly without risk of respiratory arrest. If dose by mouth is not possible insert gelatin capsules containing powders, per rectum, child or adult lying prone. This method is particularly suitable for feverish convulsions or Grand mal. Repeat after 5 minutes if patient continues in convulsion. Where neither of these powders are available, Chamomile, Valerian or Mistletoe may be used.

"The remedy I have relied on most," writes C.I. Reid, MD (*Ellingwood's Journal*) "is Passion flower. Use this alone or in combination with Gelsemium – more often alone. I cannot say I obtain an absolutely curative effect, but the spasms disappear and do not return while the remedy is continued. It has none of the unpleasant effects of other medicines. I give the liquid extract in doses from 25-30 drops, 3-4 times daily, for continued use. It may be given more frequently for convulsions."

Alfred Dawes, MNIMH. Green tincture of Mistletoe, 3-5 drops. Or, combine equal parts: Liquid Extract Skullcap, Valerian and Black Horehound.

Finlay Ellingwood MD combines White Bryony, Prickly Ash, Skullcap and St John's Wort.

Samuel Thomson MD. Lobelia 2; Cayenne 1; (antispasmodic drops) given at the premonitary stage. 1-2 teaspoons.

Edgar Cayce. Passion flower tea. Hot Castor oil packs.

Excess acidity and intestinal toxaemia. There is considerable opinion that these trigger an attack. Combination: Liquid Extracts – Skullcap 15ml; Mistletoe 10ml; Meadowsweet 10ml; Elderflowers 10ml. Two 5ml teaspoons in water thrice daily.

West African Black Pepper. (Piper guineense) is used by traditional Nigerian healers to good effect.

Associated with imperfect menstruation. Liquid Extracts, single or in combination: Black Cohosh, Life root, Lobelia. Dose: 5-15 drops thrice daily.

Associated with mental weakness. Liquid Extract Oats (avena sativa). 2-3 teaspoons in water thrice daily.

Aromatherapy. (Complex partial seizures) Massage with essential oils found to be beneficial. (*The Lancet, 1990, 336 (8723) 1120*)

Diet. Salt-free lacto-vegetarian. Oatmeal porridge. A cleansing 8-day grape juice fast has its advocates.

Vitamin E. In 24 epileptic children refractory to anti-epileptic drugs (AEDs) with generalised tonic-clonic and other types of seizures, addition of Vitamin E 400iu daily to existing AEDs was accompanied by a significant reduction in 10 of 12 cases. (*Epilepsy 1989; 30(1): 84-89*)

Supportives: osteopathic or chiropractic adjustments.

Note. A number of Italian physicians linked a salt-rich diet with epileptic fits. Number and violence diminished when discontinued and did not recur for weeks. Dr W.P. Best found that, in children, circumcism made a valuable contribution.

Drug-dependency. Herbal medication may offer a supportive role to primary medical treatment. Under no circumstances should sufferers discontinue basic orthodox treatments except upon the advice of a physician.

Information. British Epilepsy Association, 40 Hanover Square, Leeds LS3 1BE, UK. Send SAE.

To be treated by or in liaison with a qualified medical practitioner.

EPITHELIOMA. See: CANCER.

EPSOM SALT BATH. Half fill bath with water, temperature about 98°F. Add two handfuls crude (cattle) Epsom salts. Bath stay 20-30 minutes, topping up with hot water as necessary. Massage affected parts under water. Follow with tepid sponge-down and bed with no exposure to cold.

To increase elimination through the skin. As it has a drying effect should not be taken by those with irritative skin disorders. Follow with moisturising lotion next morning. Also not taken in the presence of high blood pressure.

EQUISITUM. See HORSETAIL.

ERGOT of rye. Secale. *Claviceps purpurea*, Tulasne.
Constituents: indole alkaloids, tyramine, acetylcholine.
Action: abortifacient, parturient, haemostatic, hypertensive, uterine stimulant, oxytocic.
Uses. Obstetrics.
Difficult childbirth. Applied to excite uterine contractions in the third stage of labour.
Preparations. *Liquid Extract*. BPC 1954, dose, 0.6 to 1.2ml.
Registered medical practitioner only. POM

ERYTHEMA NODOSUM. Appearance of red oval nodules on the skin, later passing from red to brown. Onset sudden. Infection is usually streptococcal for which Myrrh and Goldenseal are specific. Non-infective. Lesions are preceded by sore throat. Stony-hard nodules break down to discharge pus.
Symptoms: lesions mostly on shins and forearms; fatigue, aching joints and muscles, sometimes fever. Much physical activity stimulates out-cropping.
Treatment. Bedrest where necessary. Treat underlying cause which may be ulcerative colitis, tuberculosis, toxicity from The Pill, drug reactions.
Alternatives:– *Tea*. Red Clover, Gotu Kola, Clivers. Combine. 1 heaped teaspoon to each cup boiling water; infuse 5-10 minutes; half-1 cup thrice daily.
Tablets/capsules. Blue Flag root, Devil's Claw, Poke root, Seaweed and Sarsaparilla, Wild Yam.
Formula. Burdock 1; Dandelion 2; Sarsaparilla 1. Dose – Powders: 500mg (two 00 capsules or one-third teaspoon). Liquid Extracts: 1 teaspoon. Tinctures: 2 teaspoons. Thrice daily in water.
Diet. See: DIET – SKIN DISEASES.
Note. Erythema nodosum associated with Crohn's disease, more frequently recognised in childhood.

EROTOMANIA. See: SATYRIASIS. NYMPHOMANIA.

ERUPTION. A lesion on the skin, red and raised above the surface. See appropriate skin disease.

ERUCTATION. See: REFLUX.

ERYSIPELAS. St Anthony's Fire. An acute contagious disease caused by Group A Beta Haemolytic *Streptococcus erysipelatis*, or *pyogenes*. Onset with chilliness followed by rigor, thirst, feverishness, drowsiness. Burning, irritating skin lesions which ulcerate with great pain. Symptoms include nervous prostration, delirium from pain, fast and full pulse, swollen eyes and turgid face.
Treatment. Bedrest. Alteratives, analgesics, sedatives. Spreads via the lymphatic system (Poke root, Clivers). Sustain heart (Hawthorn or Lily of the Valley); kidneys (Buchu or Juniper); as appropriate. Yarrow – to reduce temperature. Echinacea to strengthen immune system.
Tea: Formula: Yarrow 1; Raspberry leaves 1; Red Clover 1; Clivers 1; Liquorice root half. 2 teaspoons to each cup boiling water; infuse 5-15 minutes. Half-1 cup every 2 hours, or as tolerated. If ingredients not available: substitute Elderflowers, Boneset, or Balm.
Alternatives. *Tablets/capsules*. Echinacea, Lobelia.
Powders. Formula: Sarsaparilla 2; Poke root 1; Liquorice 1. Dose: 500mg (two 00 capsules or one-third teaspoon) every 2 hours or as tolerated.
Tinctures. Alternatives: (1) Echinacea 2; Fringe Tree 1. (2) Sarsaparilla 2; Queen's Delight 1. (3) Clivers 2; Echinacea 2. 1-2 teaspoons in water every 2 hours, or as long as tolerated.
Topical. Ointments or creams: Marigold, Comfrey, Evening Primrose, Echinacea, Logwood, Aloe Vera gel.
Traditional: Equal parts Houseleek and dairy cream.
Early Florida settlers: Powdered Slippery Elm as a dusting powder or with a little milk to form a paste.
Maria Treben. Application of crushed leaves of cabbage, Coltsfoot, Houseleek and Speedwell all have their successes in reducing pain and facilitating healing.
Cleansing wash: warm infusion of Yarrow or Marshmallow.
Diet. Lacto-vegetarian. Abundant Vitamin C in lemon and other fruit juices.
Supplements. Vitamin A, B-complex, C, D.
To be treated by or in liaison with a general medical practitioner.

ERYTHEMA MULTIFORM. An acute skin reaction to a virus, possibly streptococcal or herpes simplex. Often associated with infection of the mucous membranes. May manifest as a reaction to barbiturates and other drugs.
Symptoms: low blood pressure, skin lesions, toxaemia, collapse.
Treatment. Same as for ERYTHEMA NODOSUM.
Local antipruritics to relieve irritation.

ERYTHRAEMIA. See: POLYCYTHAEMIA VERA.

ESCHAROTIC. A herb with a caustic action on the skin, i.e. the milky juice of Sun Spurge (Euphorbia) has a corrosive effect upon warts and hard schirrhous lesions. Once used on small malignant spots to dry-up and enhance formation of a crust or scab that in the course of time might detach itself. Blood root.

ESCOP. European Scientific Cooperative for Phytotherapy. Established June 1989 by representatives of six European associations for phytotherapy. To advance the scientific status of phytomedicines (herbs) and to assist with harmonisation of their regulatory status at the European level. Represents about 1500 active members (physicians, pharmacists and scientists), many tens of thousands of prescribers and practitioners and many millions of consumers. This represents about 30 per cent of the entire pharmaceutical market.

Aims and objects. To develop a coordinated scientific framework to assess phytopharmaceuticals. To promote acceptance of phytopharmaceuticals, especially within the therapy of general medical practitioners. To support and initiate clinical and experimental research in phytotherapy. To improve and extend the international accumulation of scientific and practical knowledge.

National associations represented.

Federal Republic of Germany: Gesellschaft für Phytotherapie e.V.

The Netherlands: Nederlandse Vereniging voor Fytotherapie.

Belgium: Société Belge de Phytothérapie, Belgische Vereniging voor Phytotherapie.

France: Institut Francais de Phytothérapie.

United Kingdom: British Herbal Medicine Association.

Switzerland: Schweizerische Medizinische Gesellschaft für Phytotherapie.

The Scientific Committee, with two delegates from each member country, has embarked on a programme of compiling proposals for European monographs on the medicinal uses of plant drugs. This task is expected to take about ten years to complete.

In preparing monographs the Committee assesses information from published scientific literature together with national viewpoints as expressed by delegates or included in the results of national reviews. Leading researchers on specific plant drugs are invited to relevant meetings and their contributions substantially assist the Committee's work. Draft monographs prepared by the Scientific Committee are circulated for appraisal and comment to an independent Board of Supervising Editors, which includes eminent academic experts in the field of phytotherapy.

The monographs are offered to regulatory authorities as a means of harmonising the medicinal uses of plant medicines within the EC and in a wider European context. Phytotherapy (Herbalism) makes an important contribution to European medicine.

ESSENTIAL FATTY ACIDS (EFA). A group of unsaturated fatty acids essential for growth and body function. EFA activity requires three polyunsaturated fatty acids (linolenic, linoleic and arachidonic). The most essential are linoleic and arachidonic which are closely involved in metabolism, transport of fats, and maintenance of cell membranes. While linolenic and arachidonic acids can be synthesised in the body, linoleic cannot.

EFA deficiency may be caused by alcohol, particularly Omega-6. Deficiencies may be responsible for a wide range of symptoms from foul-smelling perspiration to psoriasis, pre-menstrual tension and colic. EFAs are precursors of prostaglandin formation.

EFAs are present in oily fish and reduce the adhesion of platelets and the risk of heart disease. They reduce blood cholesterol and increase HDLs.

Common sources: cold pressed seeds, pulses, nuts and nut oils. Evening Primrose oil (15-20 drops daily). The best known source is Cod Liver oil (1-8 teaspoons daily); (children 1 teaspoon daily to strengthen immune system against infection); bottled oil preferred before capsules. To increase palatability pour oil into honey jar half filled with orange or other fruit juice, shake well and drink from the jar.

Margarines, salad dressings, cooking and other refined vegetable oils inhibit complete absorption of EFAs and should be avoided. EFAs require the presence of adequate supply of Vitamins A, B, C, D, E and minerals Calcium, Iron, Magnesium and Selenium.

ESSENTIAL OILS. Volatile oils. Out of 250,000 flowering plants only 2,000 yield essential oils. Soluble in alcohol, colourless. Contained in plants, they are responsible for taste, aroma and medicinal action. Organic properties give the flower its scent. May be anti-bacterial, antispasmodic, sedative, expectorant, antiseptic, anti-inflammatory. The smell of a flower roughly conveys the potency of its oil. An example is menthol in the mint family.

Oils used in Phytotherapy: Almond, English Chamomile, Aniseed, Bergamot, Black Pepper, Buchu, Camphor, Cedarwood, Cloves, Coriander, Cypress, Eucalyptus, Geranium, Juniper, Lavender (French), Lavender (English), Lavender (Spanish), Lemon, Marjoram, Orange (sweet), Patchouli, Peppermint, Pine (Scots), Rosemary, Sage, Sandalwood, Thyme, Spearmint, St John's Wort, Turpentine, Ylang Ylang.

Most oils are obtained by steam distillation. Being highly concentrated, internal use is by a few drops, diluted. About 30-40 are used medicinally; each having its own specific healing properties. Some are convenient as inhalants; a few drops on a tissue for relief of catarrh, colds, etc. Fragrant burners and electronic diffusers are available for vapour-inhalation. Bring to boil 2 pints water; allow to stand 3-4 minutes; sprinkle on the surface 5-10 drops Eucalyptus oil and with towel over head, inhale steam, 5-10 minutes.

Examples: (a) equal parts dilute oils of Thyme and Hypericum (acute middle ear inflammation) 3-4 drops injected into ear 2-3 times daily. (b) 10 drops oil Marjoram in bath water for cramp. Eucalyptus is a useful antibacterial; Cinnamon (anti-inflammatory), Juniper (urinary antiseptic), Orange blossom (anti-depressant), Lavender (sedative).

Essential oils should never be used neat, except as prescribed by a suitably qualified practitioner. While aromatherapists do not prescribe internally, Dr Paul Belaiche, one of France's leading experts on essential oils, advises oral medication at a maximum daily dosage of 12 drops according to the oil. He advises drops on the tongue, on activated charcoal, in capsule form using a suitable excipient or vegetable oil, or mixed with a little honey. Anal injection has proved successful, (8-10 drops in 10ml vegetable oil) or suppositories made from 200-300mg (8-10 drops) essential oil to 2 grams of base per suppository. Oils should never be allowed to touch the eyes.

Capsules of Garlic oil may be inserted into the rectum for worms or prostate disorder. OR: 10 drops oil mixed with 10ml vegetable oil and injected with the aid of a pipette. Dilute oil of Thyme is used as a massage-rub for chest infections. Oil of Cloves is not only an antiseptic but an analgesic to assuage moderate dental pain. Volatile oils reflexly stimulate the medulla through the olfactory nerve, thus promoting appetite and flow of saliva. All stimulate production of white blood cells and thereby support the immune system.

Oils not used: Basil, Bitter Almonds, Boldo, Calamus, Horseradish, Mugwort, Mustard, Pennyroyal, Rue, Sassafras, Savin, Tansy, Thuja, Wormseed.

Oils not used in pregnancy: Bay, Buchu, Chamomile, Clary Sage, Cinnamon, Clove, Fennel, Hyssop, Juniper, Marjoram, Myrrh, Peppermint, Rose, Rosemary, Sage, Thyme. All other oils – half the normal amount.

Tea: 2-3 drops, selected oil, on teabag makes 3 cups tea.

Inhalant: 10 drops on tissue, or same amount in hot water to inhale steam.

Bath water: add: 10-15 drops.

Compress: 10-15 drops in half a cup (75ml) milk or water. Soak suitable material and apply.

Massage: 6 drops in two teaspoons 'carrier' vegetable oil (Almond, Peanut, Olive, etc).

Fragrant oils replace hospital smell.

Essential oil suppliers: Butterbur and Sage, 101 Highgrove Street, Reading RG1 5EJ. Also: Shirley Price Aromatherapy, Wesley House, Stockwell Road, Hinckley, Leics LE10 1RD.

ESSIAC TEA. See: CANCER – STOMACH AND INTESTINES.

ETIOLOGY. The cause of a specific disease.

EUCALYPTUS. Blue gum tree. *Eucalyptus globulus*, Labill. Oil distilled from the fresh leaves. *Keynote*: general antiseptic. *French*: eucalyptus. *German*: blauer gommibaum. *Italian*: eucalypto.

Constituents: flavonoids, volatile oil.

Action: acts powerfully upon mucous membrane; antibiotic, anti-viral, anti-fungal, antispasmodic, stimulant restorative. Said to have the power of destroying miasma in fever-stricken areas, arresting the spread of pestilential fever. Widely used by the aborigines of Australia. Hypoglycaemic.

Uses. Early stage of fever, colds, asthma, nasal catarrh, sinusitis, sore throat and respiratory disorders generally as an inhalant or internal medicine. Senile bronchitis as a chest rub. For lung conditions, may be inhaled or used in pastilles. Once used for diphtheria and relief of tubercula cough. Diabetes mellitis. Congestive headache, pyrrhoea and bleeding gums.

In Arabian medicine a few drops of the oil in wine dispelled offensive odours as from growths and infected wounds. The leaves have been smoked for relief of asthma.

Chinese Barefoot medicine: a cleansing douche made from 15-30 drops in 2 pints warm water for sexual transmitted disease. Reduction of caruncle at vaginal opening.

Preparations. Thrice daily before meals or, in acute cases, as necessary. 2-5 drops of the oil in honey.

Decoction: 3-4 leaves to each cup water gently simmered 10 minutes in a covered vessel. Dose: half-1 cup.

Spray or vaporiser: 5-10 drops of oil in 1oz Olive oil.

Chest rub: 3-5 drops oil in 2 teaspoons Almond or Olive oil.

Antiseptic wash: a strong decoction made from a handful of leaves to 1 pint water simmered 20 minutes offers a healing cleansing wash for leg ulcers, discharging wounds; and as an enema for worms and amoebic dysentery.

Powder: capsules, powdered leaves, 250mg: 2 capsules between meals thrice daily.

Note. Not given with Goldenseal with which it is antagonistic.

EUONYMUS. See: WAHOO.

EUPHORBIA. Asthma weed. Pill-bearing spurge. *Euphorbia hirta, L. Euphorbia pilulifera*. Dried herb.

Constituents: terpenoids, flavonoids, gallic acid.

Action. Antasthmatic, antispasmodic, anticatarrh, expectorant.

Uses. Asthma, laryngitis, chronic nasal and bronchial catarrh. An ingredient of an external application used by the Cardiff Cancer Curers (Rees-Evans family) of the early 20th century. Its use for tumours recorded (*J.L. Hartwell, Lloydia, 32, 153, 1969*)

Preparations. Thrice daily.

Tea. Quarter to half a teaspoon to each cup boiling water; infuse 10 minutes; dose quarter of a cup sweetened with honey.

Liquid extract. Dose – 1-5 drops in water.

Tincture BPC 1923. 1:5 in 60 per cent alcohol: dose – 0.6 to 2ml. GSL

EUROPEAN JOURNAL OF HERBAL MEDICINE. Published three times a year by The National Institute of Medical Herbalists, 9 Palace Gate, Exeter, Devon, England EX1 1JA. Material of high quality on all subjects relevant to the practice of herbal medicine, creating a forum for sharing information and opinion about developments in the field, including scientific, professional and political issues of importance to the medical herbalist.

EUROPEAN PHARMACOPOEIA, legal status of. Under the 1964 Convention on the Elaboration of a European Pharmacopoeia the standards of the European Pharmacopoeia are required to take precedence over the standards of the national pharmacopoeias of the contracting parties, thus ensuring a common standard. In the United Kingdom this has been achieved by means of section 65(7) of the Medicines Act 1968. In addition to the United Kingdom the countries party to the Convention are Austria, Belgium, Cyprus, Denmark, Finland, France, German Federal Republic, Greece, Iceland, Ireland, Italy, Luxembourg, The Netherlands, Norway, Spain, Sweden, Switzerland and Portugal. (*Mail 54, June 1988*)

EVANS, WILLIAM C. (B.Pharm., B.Sc., Ph.D., F.R. Pharm. S) Formerly Reader in Phytochemistry, Department of Pharmacy, University of Nottingham. Research interests: secondary metabolites of the Solanaceae and Erythroxylaceae. Principal author of Trease and Evans' Pharmacognosy. Visiting lecturer, School of Phytotherapy (*Herbal Medicine*).

EVENING PRIMROSE. *Oenothera biennis L. German*: Echte Nachtkerze. *French*: Onagre. *Italian*: Stella di sera. *Keynote*: Prostaglandin precursor. Unrefined oil is expressed from the seeds that yield gamma linolenic acid and an essential fatty acid. Whole plant is edible.

Action. Anticoagulant, nutritive, demulcent, anti-eczema. Reduces blood clotting time, which is of value for thrombosis. A precursor of Prostaglandin E1 which inhibits abnormal cell proliferation and reduces blood pressure. Reduces serum cholesterol levels. Externally: to protect moisture balance of the skin.

Uses. Stops platelet-clumping. Dilates coronary arteries and removes obstructions. Intermittent claudication. Raynaud's disease. Said to slow down the progress of multiple sclerosis. Pre-menstrual tension and breast pain. Said to arrest rheumatoid arthritis in moderate cases. Prevention of liver damage. Dry scaly skin disorders; eczema, acne (with zinc). Soft brittle finger nails. Abnormal tear production. Hyperactive children. Mental depression. Diabetic retinitis. To allay the ageing process. Alleviates hangovers. Alcohol habit. Pruritus. Combined with Vitamin E which acts as a protective antioxidant. Trials have shown that the oil has significantly improved sensory function: muscle weakness, arm tendon reflex and numbness – which signs may be reversed in diabetes.

Preparations. *"Efamol" 500*: comprising 500mg Evening Primrose oil; 10mg natural Vitamin E. 4-6 capsules daily depending on requirement, for 6-8 weeks.

To maintain EFA and GLA levels. "Efamol" 250: comprising 250mg Evening Primrose oil; 200mg Safflower oil; 50mg Linseed oil; 10mg Vitamin E. 3-4 capsules daily, regularly.

Vitamins B6 and C; and minerals Magnesium and Zinc assist its action. Features in a wide range of cosmetic products as a moisturiser.

Poultice: leaves and flowers for abscesses, boils, etc.

Not given in epilepsy. GSL

EXAMINATIONS JITTERS. Excessive nervousness. Overwhelmed by cumulative effects of prolonged worry, chronic fatigue, feeling of unwellness, loss of appetite, stomach upsets, poor concentration. To relax nerves, aid digestion and healthful sleep:

Alternatives: tablets, capsules, tinctures, extracts etc. Alfalfa, Primrose flowers, Ginseng, Vervain, Skullcap, Valerian, Passiflora, Ginkgo, Siberian Ginseng, Hops.

Powders, Liquid Extracts, Tinctures. Formula. Equal parts: Skullcap, Valerian, Mistletoe. Doses. Powders: 500mg (two 00 capsules or one-third teaspoon). Liquid Extracts: 1 teaspoon. Tinctures: 2 teaspoons. In water thrice daily.

On retiring. Cup Passion flower tea. (1-2 teaspoons to cup boiling water)

EXCIPIENT. A substance which is not an active part of a preparation, but is combined with active ingredients to achieve a suitable dose or for the purposes of colouring, preservation, etc. Usually believed to be inert and non-toxic.

EXFOLIATIVE DISEASE. See: DERMATITIS.

EXHAUSTION. Extreme fatigue. May follow stress conditions or limited powers of endurance, surgical operations, exposure or prolonged illnesses. Physical Exhaustion, (Ginseng). Nervous Exhaustion, (Hops). Mental Exhaustion, (Capsicum, Peppermint, Life Drops). Heart Exhaustion, (Hawthorn). Jet fatigue (Passion flower).
Alternatives. *Teas*. Gotu Kola, Ginseng, Sage, Oat husks, Wood Betony, Hyssop, Agrimony, Wormwood, Angustura, Hops, Chamomile, Hibiscus flower, Hawthorn blossoms.
Gentian. 1 teaspoon to each cup cold water; allow to steep overnight. Half-1 cup before meals.
Tablets or capsules. Iceland Moss, Alfalfa, Gentian, Siberian Ginseng, Damiana, Pollen.
Life Drops. See entry.
Tinctures. Equal parts: Siberian Ginseng and Hawthorn – one 5ml teaspoon in water thrice daily.
Aromatherapy. Oil Rosemary massage. 6 drops in 2 teaspoons Almond oil or other vegetable oil.
Diet. Oats (porridge, etc). Emphasis on protein. Bee pollen. Honey.
Nutrients. Vitamins A, Vitamin B12, B-complex, Folic acid, C, D. Chromium, Molasses (iron), Manganese, Zinc. Kelp for minerals. Biostrath.
Note. ME (Myalgic encephalomyelitis) is the end result of nervous exhaustion. Specific treatment on the heart, with adequate sleep and rest have proved of benefit.

EXOPHTHALMUS. Abnormal protrusion of the eyeballs. May be a symptom of hyperthryroid states. A rare cause is a tumour at back of the eye. Abnormal exposure of the white of the eye, with double vision.
Treatment. The underlying condition should be treated – overactive thyroid. Many cases arise from infection.

"Internal remedies should be carefully selected, because each case is different," writes Margaret Wilkenloh, MD, Chicago (*Ellingwood*). "The best remedies to my mind are Echinacea, Pulsatilla, Skullcap and Hawthorn." These are available as herbs, tablets, powders, liquid extracts or tinctures.
Specimen combination: Liquid extracts: Echinacea 2; Pulsatilla half; Skullcap 1; Hawthorn 1. Mix. One to two 5ml teaspoons in water thrice daily.

EXOSTOSIS. Bony out-cropping from the surface of a bone. May appear in those with gouty tendencies as small unsightly lumps on knuckles, toes or upper edges of lobes of the ears. Not painful, except on pressure. Existing nodules cannot be reduced but future ones may be prevented by herbs known to facilitate elimination of excess uric acid from the body: Guaiacum, Sarsaparilla, Celery seed, Dandelion root. Turkey Rhubarb.
Teas: Celery seed, Meadowsweet, Yarrow. Yerba Mate.
Tincture Rhei Co BP (1948). 30-60 drops in water thrice daily.
Burdock and Sarsaparilla health drink.
Liquid Extract: Guaiacum: 5-10 drops in water thrice daily.
Diet. Low protein (especially fish and shellfish). Dandelion coffee. Vegetable juices. Reject alcohol, coffee, strong tea.

EXPECTORANTS. Herbs that increase bronchial mucous secretion by promoting liquefaction of sticky mucus and its expulsion from the body. Their secondary action is that of a vasoconstrictor which, in the case of a stuffy nose, relieves by reducing blood supply to the inflamed lining of the nasal passage. They improve the outlook for respiratory troubles.

Aniseed, Ammoniacum gum, Asafoetida, Balm of Gilead, Blood root, Boneset, Chickweed, Coltsfoot, Comfrey, Elderflowers, Elecampane, Eucalyptus, Fenugreek seeds, Garlic, Goldenseal, Grindelia, Heartsease, Holy Thistle, Hyssop, Iceland Moss, Irish Moss, Life root, Liquorice, Lobelia, Lungwort, Marshmallow, Mouse Ear, Mullein, Maidenhair Fern, Myrrh, Parsley root, Pleurisy root, Queen's Delight, Red Clover, Senega, Skunk Cabbage, Slippery Elm, Squill, Thuja, Thyme, White Horehound, Wild Cherry, Wild Violet, Yerba Santa.

EXPLODING HEAD SYNROME (EHS). Explosive bomb-like sensation – 'like a thunderclap' – coming from the back of the head. Not a morning-after-the-night-before feeling or pain in the head, but an unexplained loud noise occurring during sleep. Sufferers are mostly women, middle-aged or elderly, with no other symptoms and usually in good health.

Described as "seems as if my head was bursting, with a flash of light". Reaction is one of fear and violent heart beat. Attacks unrelated to alcohol or excitement of the previous evening. No circulatory changes in the brain or cerebrospinal fluid are known to cause such a symptom.
Treatment. Cup of one of the following teas at bedtime: Buckwheat, Yarrow, Hawthorn flowers, Skullcap, Oats. Morning and evening: one 500mg Evening Primrose capsule; one 400iu Vitamin E capsule.
Diet: low-salt. Cholesterol-rich foods should be kept to a minimum.

EXTRACT. The Exeter Traditional Medicines, Pharmacology and Chemistry Project. An expert data-base system that integrates on a cumulative basis annotated information about the chemistry, pharmacology and therapeutics of medicinal plants and their constituents from a range of sources. The conventional phytochemical literature, often exhaustively searched and assessed, is augmented by evidence from the areas of clinical pharmacology and ethnopharmacology, and the personal and recorded experience of practicing phytotherapists and herbalists. The material is entered into a knowledge base which is programmed to provide intelligent integration and weighting of the data. Director: Simon Y. Mills MA FNIMH, Centre of Complementary Health Studies, University of Exeter Devon EX4 4PU.

EYEBRIGHT. Bright-eye. Birds-eye. *Euphrasia officinalis. German:* Augentrost. *French*: Casselunettes. *Dutch*: Oogentroost. *Spanish*: Eufrasia. *Arabian*: Adhil. Herb: whole of the plant gathered while in bloom. *Keynote*: mucous membrane.
Constituents: tannin-mannite, iridoid glycosides, volatile oil.
Action: anti-inflammatory (eye lotion), antihistamine, anti-catarrhal, astringent.
Uses. Has special reference to eyes, nose and sinuses. Conjunctivitis, red eye, stye (lotion), poor visual acuity due to eyestrain or diabetes, eyes itch and sting. For purulent ophthalmia: (tea: Eyebright 1; Goldenseal quarter). Corneal opacity. Blepharitis (local bathing). Watery catarrh, hay fever, chronic sneezing, inflamed nasal mucosa (douche). Relaxed tonsils and sore throat (gargle).

Practitioners have advised Eyebright lotion during measles to prevent eye troubles. Many causes of eye trouble in later life date from measles in childhood. The presence of a prominent red rim around the eye of an adult, especially if eyelids are missing, may be due to childhood measles when Eyebright lotion might have proved helpful.

The tea is said to strengthen a weak memory and improve circulation of the brain. Was used by Dioscorides for eye infections when accompanying the Roman legions through many countries.
Preparations. Thrice daily. Average internal dose: 1-4g.
Tea. 1 teaspoon to each cup boiling water; infuse 10 minutes. Dose (internal) half-1 cup. External, in an eyebath as a douche.
Liquid Extract. Half-1 teaspoon in water.
Tincture BHP (1983). 1 part to 5 parts 45 per cent alcohol. Dose: 2-6ml. Capsules also available.
Eyebright water, (lotion). Unsuccessful as a compress or poultice, Chamomile flowers being more effective.
Douche. Half fill an eyebath with Eyebright water or warm tea. GSL

EYE DROPS. Alternatives.
1. Liquid Extract Witch Hazel 60 drops; Liquid Extract Goldenseal 20 drops; 4oz pure spring water, or distilled water. Mix. For conjunctivitis. Instil 3-5 drops, 3-4 times daily.
2. Tincture Goldenseal 5 drops; Liquid Extract Eyebright 30 drops; Rosewater (or pure spring water) 3oz. Mix. (*A. Barker FNIMH*) Apply, as above. For eye infections.
3. Teas made from any of the following: Raspberry leaves, Eyebright, Clary Sage, Chamomile, Mullein, Plantain, Elderflowers. Prepare: 1 teaspoon to each cup boiling water, infuse 15 minutes. Strain. Half fill eyebath for tepid douche, freely. For tired strained eyes.
4. Soothing eye-drops for inflammation: 1-2 drops Castor oil. Administering eye drops can be an awkward procedure. To overcome problems of direction and dose an eye-drop dispenser has been developed by Dispomed Ltd, 114 Northgate Street, Chester, UK. The device, Opticare, is on prescription in the UK.

EYES. See entries:– CONJUNCTIVITIS, CONTACT LENS FATIGUE, GLAUCOMA, IRITIS, PALMING, RETINITIS, RETINITIS PIGMENTOSA, RETINOPATHY, SCLERITIS AND EPISCLERITIS, XEROPHTHALMIA (dryness of the eyes).

EYES – FOREIGN BODY. From coal dust, insects, pollen, etc.
Symptoms: blinking, watering, acute discomfort. Sensation of grit in the eye does not always imply foreign body, but symptoms of conjunctivitis or keratitis. Automatic blinking is sometimes enough to clear offending object.
Treatment. External. Evert lid and remove. Swab out with dilute Witch Hazel on cotton wool. Inject one drop Castor oil, (also good for scratched cornea), Aloe Vera gel or juice. Fenugreek seed puree. Juice of Houseleek and dairy cream.
Difficult case. Removal of particles of iron or dust, apply mucilage of Slippery Elm powder to eye – patient lying on his back, a second person injecting it into corner of eye, the patient moving eye in opposite direction. Safe and healing. Clean eye and bathe with warm milk.

Referral to consultant ophthalmologist.

EYES – INFECTION. Whatever the infection, dendritic ulcer, corneal ulcer, herpes simplex or stye, treatment should be internal as well as external.

A study carried out at Moorfields Eye Hospital, London, has shown that those who use extended-wear soft contact lenses are more likely to develop microbial keratitis than users of other lenses.
Treatment. *Internal*: Powders, Tinctures or Liquid Extracts. Combine Echinacea 2; Blue Flag 1; Goldenseal 1. Doses: Powders: 500mg (one-third teaspoon or two 00 capsules). Liquid Extracts 30-60 drops.
Tinctures: 1-2 teaspoons. In water, or honey.
Comfrey. To promote epithelial regeneration.

Potential benefit far outweighs possible risk.
Evening Primrose capsules.
Topical. Alternatives. (1) Goldenseal Eye Lotion: 1 part Goldenseal root macerated in 40 parts distilled extract of Witch Hazel 2-3 days. Strain. 5-10 drops in eyebath half filled with warm water; douche. Wipe eyelids. (2) Aloe Vera juice or gel. (3) Moisten Chamomile teabag with warm water and fix over eye for styes, etc. (4) Bathe with Periwinkle minor tea: 2 teaspoons to cup boiling water allowed to cool and strain. (5) Elderflower water. The above to relieve pain, redness and gritty sensation. (6) Evening Primrose lotion. (7) Raw carrot compress to ripen stye. Nasturtium seed compress.
Supplements. Daily. Vitamin A 7500iu, Vitamin B2 10mg, Vitamin C 3g, Vitamin E 400iu, Zinc 15mg.
Referral to consultant ophthalmologist.

EYE INJURIES. From blows, burns, chemicals or haemorrhage. Hospital treatment may be required. Petechial haemorrhage (Witch Hazel douche). For infection, add Echinacea. For shock, German Chamomile tea.
Topical. Alternatives. Flashburns from welding etc – fresh juice Aloe Vera gave instant relief and speeded recovery. (*New England Journal of Medicine, Vol 311, 6, p.413*) Houseleek juice. Wounds that refuse to heal: cotton wool pad saturated with Castor oil overnight. Chamomile compress. Bathe with teas of Plantain, Horsetail, Chickweed, Blessed Thistle, Self-Heal, Comfrey especially commended to encourage epithelial healing.
Diet. Bilberries, rich in flavonoids which are anti-inflammatory and healing. As desired.
Supplements. Daily. Vitamin A 7500iu, Vitamin B-complex, Vitamin C 3g, Vitamin E 1000iu, Beta-carotene. Selenium 300mcg, Zinc 15mg.
Referral to a consultant ophthalmologist.

EYES. MACULAR DEGENERATION. Zinc and selenium, supported by doses of Vitamin E and amino acid taurine produced dramatic results in some cases; effect said to be due to antioxidant activity mopping up free radicals associated with degenerative diseases (*Journal of Nutritional Medicine*)
A preliminary therapeutic trial in patients with ageing macular degeneration or diabetic retinopathy showed that supplementation with Beta-carotene, Vitamin C, Vitamin E and Selenium halted the progression of degenerative changes and in some cases even brought some improvement. (*Age and Ageing 1991, 20(1) 60-9*). Bilberries.
Referral to a consultant ophthalmologist.

EYES. NIGHT BLINDNESS. Inability to see at night or in imperfect light due to a deficiency of visual purple (rhodopsin) in the rods at the back of the eye due to low level Vitamin A. Night myopia usually affects people during twilight. "One in five people are not fit to drive at night." May occur in glaucoma and other eye disorders. Other causes: old age, free radical damage.
Alfalfa tea freely.
Of value: Kelp, Irish Moss, Iceland Moss.
Diet. Vitamin A foods, carrots, bilberries, Cod Liver oil.
Supplements. Vitamin A, Beta-carotene. C (2g), E (400iu). B-complex, B2, Niacin, Zinc.

EYES – PAIN. A number of causes including reflex pain from inflammation of the middle ear or decayed teeth. Eyeball tender to touch.
Alternatives. Plantain, Ginkgo. Teas, tablets, etc.
Topical. Cold compress: Witch Hazel.
Supplements. Daily. Vitamins C (500mg); E (400iu). Beta-carotene.
Palming.

EYES – POUCHES UNDER. Due to a number of causes including kidney disturbance.
Tea. Equal parts: Clivers, Wild Carrot, Yarrow. Mix. 1 heaped teaspoon to each cup boiling water; infuse 15 minutes. Half-1 cup 2-3 times daily.
Topical. Soak cotton wool pads with Witch Hazel Distilled Extract and place over the closed eyelids for ten minutes, once or more daily.

EYES. RETINAL HAEMORRHAGE. See: BLEEDING.

EYES. SHADOWS UNDER. Due to nervous excitability (Valerian), physical exhaustion (Ginseng), pre-menstrual tension (Agnus Castus), spinal weakness (Ladyslipper), liver disorder (Blue Flag), dyspepsia (Meadowsweet), weakness of immune system (Echinacea).
Diet. Low salt, low fat. High fibre. Dandelion coffee.
Supplements. Evening Primrose, one 500mg capsule morning and evening. Vitamin B-complex. Brewer's yeast, 2 teaspoons. Zinc, 15mg.

EYES – SIGHT DETERIORATION. Presbyopia. General deterioration of the eye, usually from long-sightedness. A natural ageing process. Nutritional deficiency is a common cause, promoted by smoking, alcohol and denatured foods. If the eyes are treated nutritionally good sight lasts much longer. Strong emotions such as anger, and infections such as colds may weaken.
Services of a qualified optician should be sought after limits of the Bate's Method of eyesight training have been reached.
Alternatives. *Tablets/capsules.* Ginseng. Gotu Kola.

Powders. Mix. Parts: Gentian 2; Dandelion 1; pinch Cayenne. Dose: 500mg, (two 00 capsules or one-third teaspoon) thrice daily. (To build-up good general health)
Cider Vinegar. 2 teaspoons to tumbler water; sips during the day.
Topical. Teas. Any one: Eyebright, Fennel, German Chamomile, Plantain, Rue. 1 teaspoon to each cup boiling water; infuse 15 minutes, strain, half fill eyebath and use as a douche.
Diet. Low salt. High fibre. Bilberries.
Supplements. Daily. Vitamin A, 7500iu. Beta-carotene. B-complex. Vitamin C, 100mg. Vitamin E, 100iu. Zinc.
Supportive. Palming. Bate's exercises.

EYES – SORE. Persistent sensitivity. Bruised feeling in eyes. 1 teaspoon Rue herb to each cup boiling water; infuse 15 minutes. Strain. Half fill eyebath with warm infusion; douche. Evening Primrose capsules: 1 x 500mg, twice daily.
Fennel eye compress. Steep teabag in cold water and apply.
Chickweed Lotion. Take a handful of Chickweed, wash well, crush with a rolling pin, infuse in two cups boiling water until cool. Use as a compress or in an eye bath two or more times daily.
Supplements. Daily. Vitamin A 7500iu. Vitamin B2 10mg. Vitamin C 1g. Vitamin E 400iu. Zinc.
Palming. Bilberries.
If persistent, consult eye specialist.

EYES – TIRED. Non-persistent overstrain and ache. Internal: 2 teaspoons Cider Vinegar to glass cold water: half-1 glass freely. Bilberries.
Topical. Soak cotton wool pads with Distilled Extract Witch Hazel and apply to eyelids for 5-10 minutes.
Potato. Apply slices of raw potato, or potato poultice.
Teabag. Moisten Chamomile or Fennel teabag with cold water and apply.
Cucumber, fresh. Apply slices to closed eyes.
Supplements. Vitamin A 7500iu. Vitamin B2 10mg. Vitamin E 100iu. Vitamin C 1g. Zinc 15mg.
Bates Method eye exercises. Palming.

EYES – VISUAL DISORDERS. May be due to strain, ageing, hereditary. Poor sight may be related to poor food.
Symptoms. Sensitivity to light, near or far sight deficient, squint.
Treatment. Attention to general condition, circulation and nervous system. Ginseng, Garlic, Kelp, Bilberries, Cider vinegar.
Diet. See: DIET — GENERAL.
Supplementation. Vitamins A, B-complex, B2 (10mg daily), C (500mg daily), D, E (100iu daily). Zinc.
General: Refer to a qualified optician. Palming.

EYES – WATERY. Lacrimal disorder of secretion. See: HAY FEVER.

EYEBROWS. Disappearance of: as in thyroid deficiency, or in the use of certain cosmetics, eyebrow pencils, acne, etc. Emphasis should be on wholefood diet with adequate minerals and supplements, especially Alfalfa tea which enriches hair growth. Anoint brows with Jojoba oil.

FABRY'S DISEASE. Rare. Chiefly due to passage of a gene from a parent to an offspring, preventing production of an enzyme giving rise to symptoms including a pin-prick blood vessel rash, loss of weight, allergies, but the person is reasonably fit.
Symptomatic relief. Rutin, Hawthorn, Echinacea. Vitamin E: 200iu daily.

FACIAL PAIN. Many causes, including neuralgia, frontal sinusitis, eye troubles (pain of glaucoma being referred to the temples), dental problems, shingles, psychogenic, migraine; pain referred from lungs or heart. See appropriate entries for each of these complaints.
Maria Treben's Facial Pack: of any of the following – Thyme, Mullein, Chamomile or Yarrow. Fill small muslin bag and steep in boiling water. Ring out. Apply as hot as possible.
Internal: Chamomile tea.

FAINTING. Cardiac or vasomotor syncope. A temporary arrest of flow of blood through the brain leading to loss of consciousness. (a) Due to slowing of the heart beat by temporary emotional experience, pain, low blood pressure, blood loss, fluid loss, drug effects. (b) Heart-shock, heart-block or sudden distress.

In the elderly fainting can be associated with adverse drug reactions.
Symptoms. Dilated pupils, pallor, sweating, yawning.
Treatment. Towards recovery: cup of Chamomile tea. Life Drops in tea. Elevation of legs to restore circulation.
Topical. Whiff of Camphor or oil of Rosemary to the nose. Smelling salts. Sponge-down with Cider Vinegar (1) and water (20). Wipe face with Witch Hazel, distilled extract.
General. Remove tight clothing about the neck. Dash water in face. Recovery in 'heart-cases' should be followed by investigation in a cardiac care unit.

FALLOPIAN TUBES. Two small tubes rising from either side of the womb, connecting with the womb cavity, one from each ovary. After ovulation the egg (ovum) passes along a Fallopian tube on its way to the womb. From the womb sperm swim up the Fallopian tube to engage the egg. Inflammation may cause scarring of the lining of the tube, with blockage, and lessen chances of conception. See: SALPINGITIS.

FARMER'S LUNG. Allergic alveolitis. An occupational lung disease due to inhaling dust and mouldy grain, hay or other mouldy vegetable produce. Usually affects farm workers and those exposed to its wide range of allergens.
Symptoms: Influenza-like fever, breathlessness, cough.
Prognosis: Chronic lung damage and progressive disability.
Indicated: antifungals, antibiotics.
Alternatives. *Teas.* Marigold, Ground Ivy, Scarlet Pimpernel, Yarrow. 1 heaped teaspoon to each cup boiling water; infuse 5-15 minutes; 1 cup freely.
Tablets/capsules. Garlic, Echinacea, Goldenseal, Thuja.
Powders. Combine, parts, Echinacea 3; Goldenseal 1; Thuja 1. Dose: 500mg, (two 00 capsules or one-third teaspoon) thrice daily.
Decoction. Irish Moss, to promote expectoration and eliminate debris.
Tinctures. Alternatives. (1) Echinacea 2; Lobelia 1; Liquorice 1. (2) Equal parts: Wild Indigo, Thuja and Pleurisy root. (3) Echinacea 2; Marigold 1; Thuja half; Liquorice half. Dosage: two 5ml teaspoons in water thrice daily. Acute cases: every 2 hours.
Topical. Inhalation of Eucalyptus or Tea Tree oils.
Diet. See: DIET – GENERAL. Yoghurt in place of milk.
Note. Bronchodilators of little value. Those at risk should have an X-ray at regular intervals.

FASTING. 3-day fast. To eliminate accumulated wastes; to mobilise body energies for internal cleansing. To lose weight or excess fluids, strengthen the immune system, free nervous energy blocks and to eliminate toxins.

FAT HEN. Lamb's quarter. White Goosefoot. Pigweed. *Chenopodium album L.* Close relation of Good King Henry, *Chenopodium bonus-henricus. Keynote*: nutritive.

Plant with a long root system capable of penetrating deeply into mineral-rich sub-soil to attract trace elements not reached by shallower rooted plants. Source plant for minerals: calcium, iron, manganese, etc. Chickens thrive on it. Comes into its own in times of famine when it will sustain life as a cooked vegetable.

FATHER PIERRE'S MONASTERY HERBS. Contain Frangula 2.5 per cent, Senna leaves 65.25 per cent, Ispaghula 6.75 per cent, Meadowsweet 5.125 per cent, Mate leaves 13.5 per cent, Nettles 6.75 per cent. Non-persistent constipation.

FEBRIFUGE. Anti-fever. Anti-pyretic. Herbs used for reduction of an abnormally high body temperature. Alternatives to aspirin, antibiotics and salicylates. Agents such as Elderflowers, Pleurisy root and Yarrow lower temperature by dilating blood vessels of the skin thus allowing heat to escape. Some febrifuges are also diaphoretic which promote sweating and elimination of cell wastes – a further aid to temperature reduction. Given at the commencement of a fever, a febrifuge may effectively abort high temperature and severity of attack. Febrifuges are usually anti-stressors, sleep-inducing and mild analgesics.

Angelica, Avens, Balm, Boneset, Borage, Catmint, Cayenne, Elderflowers, Eucalyptus, Holy Thistle, Hyssop, Lobelia, Marigold, Pennyroyal, Peppermint, Peruvian bark, Pleurisy root, Prickly Ash, Raspberry leaves, Sage, Thyme, White Willow bark, Wild Indigo, Yarrow.

"It is wonderful what an enema does to bring down a child's temperature." (*Dr Han Suyin*)

FEET – HOT, SWEATY, SMELLY. Excessive foot-sweat directs our attention to constitutional weakness, kidney malfunction or to general toxic condition. For fungoid infections: see under FUNGUS. Kidney remedies (diuretics) often reduce foot sweat (Juniper, Buchu, Golden Rod, Horsetail, Parsley root or leaves, Plantain, Thuja). Teas, decoctions, etc.
Constitutional treatment (oral): Liquid Extract Thuja: 5-10 drops morning and evening.
Topical. Foot baths: with teas from Chamomile, Sage, Rosemary, Juniper, or Southernwood. Half an ounce dried or fresh herb in 2 pints boiling water; infuse until warm. Weleda Foot Balm.
Diet. Dandelion coffee. Raw food days. Avoid eggs. Increase protein.
Vitamins. B-complex. B6. B12. E.
Minerals. Dolomite. Zinc.
General. Ban rubber shoes (plimsolls) which prevent adequate ventilation.
See: SWEATING, ABNORMAL.

FEET – PAIN IN. (*Metatarsalgia*)
Causes: foot-strain, deformity, osteoporosis, high heels throwing the body out of its normal posture, tight shoes.

Feet are often painful because one or more of the bones are out of alignment and which may be adjusted by simple osteopathy. The process can be assisted by foot-baths of Chamomile flowers, Arnica flowers, or Comfrey to relax muscles and tendons.
Alternatives. Alfalfa, Chaparral, Ligvites, Prickly Ash.
Topical. Aromatherapy. (Sensitive feet) Oils of Pine, Eucalyptus or Thyme – 6 drops, any one, to 2 teaspoons Almond oil. Warm. Massage into foot and wrap round with damp hot towel.
General. Acupuncture. Shoes should be bought in the afternoon, particularly if feet swell during the day. Shoes that fit well in the morning may have become too tight by tea-time.

FELON. See: WHITLOW.

FEMALE RESTORATIVE. Female corrective. A medicine which restores healthy menstrual function by correcting hormone imbalance. Herbs: Agnus Castus, Cramp bark, Motherwort, Oats (endosperm), Raspberry leaves, True Unicorn root (aletris), Wild Yam.
Tea: Agnus Castus, Motherwort, Oats or Raspberry leaves.
Tablets. Agnus Castus, Cramp bark, Motherwort, Raspberry leaves, Wild Yam.
Formula. Agnus Castus 2; Cramp bark 1; Motherwort 1. Dosage: powders: quarter of a teaspoon. Liquid Extracts: 1 teaspoon. Tinctures: 2 teaspoons. In water or honey thrice daily.

FENNEL. *Foeniculum vulgare*, Mill. *German*: Fenchel. *French*: Fenouil. *Spanish*: Hinojo. *Italian*: Finocchio. *Chinese*: Shih-lo. Seeds, roots and leaves. Seeds contain an important essential oil (anethol).
Constituents: coumarins, volatile oil, flavonoids (rutin), sterols.
Action: a gentle warming agent for delicate stomachs; carminative, aromatic, antispasmodic (children), digestive, orexigenic, rubefacient, diuretic (soothing), galactagogue, stimulant (mild), anti-inflammatory in polyarthritis, anticoagulant (Vitamin K antagonist). Antimicrobial. Expectorant. Oestrogen-effect – Aberdeen University.
Uses. To disperse windy colic in infants; griping; to arouse appetite, sweeten a sour stomach, soothe an irritable bowel. To increase milk in nursing mothers. Obesity (traditional tea). Wrinkle smoother (tea). Old Chinese remedy for cholera. Externally, an eyewash for red-eye and blepharitis.
Preparations. As necessary.
Tea. Fresh or dried leaves: 3-4 teaspoons to teapot; add boiling water. Dose: adult; half-1 cup; infants, 2-3 teaspoons.
Tea. Crushed seeds: quarter to half a teaspoon to each cup boiling water; infuse 15 minutes. Quarter to half a cup (infants, 2-3 teaspoons).
Liquid Extract BHP (1983) 1:1 in 70 per cent alcohol. Dose: 0.8 to 2ml.
Fennel water (distilled). 5-15 drops.
Powder. 300mg capsules; 2 capsules before meals thrice daily.
Lotion. Half a teaspoon crushed seeds in cold water. Infuse 1 hour. Half fill eyebath and use as a douche.
Diet. Young shoots and root as a cooked vegetable. Seeds sprinkled on salads.
Note. Fennel seeds were discovered among personal chattels of Egyptian rulers salvaged from among the tombs.
Side-effects: slight return of periods in menopausal women. GSL

FENUGREEK. *Trigonella foenum-graecum L. German*: Griechisches Bockshorn. *French*: Fenugrec. *Italian*: Fieno greco. *Indian*: Methi.

Arabian: Halbah. *Iranian*: Shembalita. *Malayan*: Halba. Seeds. Properties similar to Irish Moss.
Constituents: flavonoids, volatile oil, saponins, alkaloids.
Action: leaves a soothing protective coating over irritated surfaces (internal demulcent, external emollient); nutrient, anti-inflammatory, galactagogue, hypoglycaemic. A natural lubricant for the colon. Oxytocic. Febrifuge. "A stimulating effect on bone healing." (*Hamdard Medicus, Oct/Dec 1988, Vol XXXI No 4*)
Uses. Soothing and healing to mucosa of stomach, intestines. Gastric and duodenal ulcer. Diverticulosis, dysentery, colitis, diarrhoea, irritable bowel, fistula, Crohn's disease. Weak digestion, poor appetite and general debility. Convalescence. Reduces level of blood sugar; transient effects in diabetes. For thin people anxious to put on weight. Cancer of the bowel, as a soothing mild analgesic. Sore gums, mouth ulcers, chronic cough, bronchitis. Has been used for kidney complaints in China as early as 1057 AD. Protection against thrombosis, embolism and angina. To increase milk in nursing mothers. Hiatus hernia, impotence.
Arabian medicine: "for alluring roundness of the female breast."
Topical. Decoction used as a poultice for boils, abscesses, wounds.
Preparations. Freely.
Decoction. 1-2 teaspoons crushed seeds to each cup water gently simmered 15 minutes. Dose: half-1 cup; seeds should be eaten. More efficacious than alcoholic preparations.
Popular combination. (Tablets, powders) Fenugreek 275mg; Rhubarb root 6mg; Slippery Elm 9mg; Bayberry 6mg; Goldenseal 3mg.
Poultice. Powder or crushed seeds – see POULTICE.
Diet. Sprouts. Seeds readily germinate on a moistened surface to provide rich source of natural vitamins, lecithin and iron for addition to green salads. GSL

FEVER. Fever is a reaction of the immune system to (1) defend the body against attack from viral or bacterial infection, (2) trauma, or (3) to decompose morbid matter into simpler compounds suitable for elimination. It is also the result of toxins released by infective agents. It may be a healing crisis. Dr Samuel Thomson writes: "Fever should not be suppressed with drugs. The body's increased heat is a sign that the body is engaged in an extraordinary effort to cleanse itself of a disease influence. We are to support it, but see that temperature does not get out of hand."

"There is an increasing amount of evidence," writes Dr D. Addy, Consulting Paediatrician, "that fevers may enhance the defence mechanism against infection. There is little evidence that fever itself is harmful except in 3 per cent of children who are prone to develop febrile convulsions."

When a fever is identified (scarlet fever, measles, etc) specific treatment with agents of proven efficacy are required. See appropriate entries. For unidentified fever, before the doctor comes, diaphoretics (Yarrow, etc) may be given to induce sweating to relieve tension on lungs and other internal organs. Also, diuretics (Yarrow, etc) stimulate elimination of wastes through the kidneys. Two herbs, Elderflowers and Peppermint, given at the chill stage have probably saved lives of tens of thousands from fever. A timely laxative to clean out stomach and bowels may favourably reduce temperature.

Perseverance with strong Nettle tea may also assist the work of the awaited practitioner. Excellent for simple fevers is the formula: Liquid Extracts: Elderflowers 1oz; Peppermint quarter of an ounce; Cinnamon quarter of an ounce; Skullcap 1oz. One 5ml teaspoon in hot water every 2 hours until fever abates – patient in bed. Sponge down body with vinegar and water. Patient should not leave bed until temperature falls. Abundant Vitamin C drinks, fresh lemon, orange juice.

A fever may be accompanied by: flushed face, rapid breathing, headache, hot skin, shivering, thirst and sweating.

Discharges are often a necessary part of the cure. Once toxins are eliminated by skin, kidneys, bowel or by respiration, symptoms abate and a feeling of well-being appears. It is often a turning point towards recovery: the body is trying to throw off toxins and poisons. A fever is an effort of the system to fight back.

FEVERFEW. Nosebleed. Midsummer daisy. *Tanacetum parthenium L.* Schultz Bip., (dark green leaf). Healing properties of *Chrysanthemum parthenium* (gold leaf) are less conclusive. *Part used*: leaves. *Keynote*: migraine. Extracts of Feverfew inhibit prostaglandin biosynthesis.
Constituents: sesquiterpene lactones, volatile oil, parthenolides.
Action: Anti-migraine, anti-rheumatic, febrifuge, bitter, carminative, tranquilliser, diuretic, antispasmodic, laxative, vermifuge. Anti-thrombotic (inhibits deposition of platelets). Vasodilator. Anti-inflammatory.
Uses: Protection against clot formation. Meniere's disease, vertigo; painful, absent or irregular menstruation, threatened miscarriage, psoriasis. Inflammatory rheumatism, arthritis. After 12 years with osteo-arthritis of the hands, a patient ate 3 leaves a day and was soon able to turn most taps without a tapeze.

Migraine preventative. Dr John Hill (*Hill's Family Herbal, 1808*) recommended it for violent

headache and as an antidote for mercurial poisoning. In psychosomatic medicine for depression or hysteria due to menstrual disorders. Especially effective for migraine relieved by hot packs.
Preparations. The herb is said to be less effective when subjected to heat, hence its popular use as the fresh leaf, powder, tincture or essence prepared 'cold'.
Fresh leaves. 1 or 2 large or 3 or 4 small, every day until positive results achieved. If too acrid, may be eaten with bread in a sandwich or in mashed banana. 125mg of the leaf provides 0.2 per cent parthenolides which a Canadian authority regards as a minimum dose.
Tablets. One 125ml tablet or capsule is equivalent to 2 leaves daily.
Tincture. The tincture best captures its therapeutic properties where laid down within 2 hours of harvesting. To prepare: 1 part pulp Feverfew leaves (fresh) to 5 parts 45 per cent alcohol. Macerate 7 days. Filter. Dose: 5-20 drops every 2 hours for acute conditions; thrice daily, chronic.
Liquid Extract. Dose: 3-15 drops.
Poultice. Crushed leaves for aching muscles and joints.
Suppositories. For piles.
Allergic effects (rare). Mouth ulcer, sore tongue, skin rash.

Not used in pregnancy or by women on the contraceptive pill.
Note. Extracts and products should be kept out of a bright light and stored below room temperature. Roots and stalks are of no value. (*Dr S. Heptinstall, Nottingham University Medical School*) GSL

FEVER POWDER No. 10. Equal parts: Lobelia herb, Pleurisy root, Crawley root, Catmint (Catnip), Sage. In powder form. Dose: One heaped teaspoon in cup; fill with boiling water; steep half an hour. 3-5 tablespoons every half hour while fever is on. Dose: small child, quarter of a teaspoon; child, half a teaspoon. For most kinds of fever it is a safe and efficient febrifuge. Never allow fever powder to be boiled. (*Dr Melville Keith*)

Widely used by the Eclectic School during second half of the 19th century.

FIBRE. It has been discovered that various cultures round the world, e.g. the Hunza Colony near Pakistan, the 7th-Day Adventists and others who eat high fibre foods have fewer cases of diabetes, heart disease, arthritis and other degenerative diseases. Natives of Hunza may live to great ages and have few dental problems, emotional illness and never require a laxative. Today, foods may be over-processed.

Other diseases recognised to be characteristic of modern western civilisation and claimed to be causally related to diet are: appendicitis, coronary heart disease, hiatus hernia, diverticulosis, piles and other anal disorders, obesity, gall stones, hypertension, deep vein thrombosis and varicose veins.

Low fibre intake results in slow transit of food and exposes potential carcinogens a longer period of time in contact with the alimentary canal. A high fibre diet tends to absorb a variety of environmental pollutants and eliminate them from the body.

Foods rich in fibre: wholemeal bread, grains, cereals, brown rice, beans, peas, boiled cabbage, sweetcorn, banana, prunes (stewed), dried apricots. One of the highest is All Bran, which has the highest proportion of dietary fibre among breakfast cereals with no preserves, artificial colouring or flavouring. Contains one-third fewer calories than most breakfast cereals and because of its glycaemic effect is useful in diabetic diet.

FIBRINOLYTICS. Agents that prevent deposition of fibrin in veins. Fibrin deposits may block nutrients and oxygen, which state is a precursor of venous ulceration. Nettles.

FIBROCYSTIC BREAST DISEASE (FBD). Most lumps are harmless, including cysts (adenosis) and benign tumours. Not forerunners of cancer. Largely due to hormone imbalance. Fluid may be aspirated from a cyst. Thickened patches of fibrous tissue are freely movable and occur chiefly during years of menstruation depending upon the presence of oestrogen. An accurate diagnosis is necessary by a competent authority. Excessive sugar consumption suspected.

Prominent cyst formations have been reduced, even eliminated by Poke root, internally and externally, though surgery is sometimes indicated. Diuretics influence the kidneys to expel more body fluids and are sometimes helpful to reduce size. Cold water packs may be applied to the affected area two or more times daily, as practical.
Alternatives. *Tea*. Formula. Equal parts: Ground Ivy, Clivers, Horsetail. One heaped teaspoon to each cup boiling water; infuse 15 minutes. 1 cup morning and evening.
Poke root. Tablets, powders. Tincture. 5-10 drops in water 3 times daily.
Evening Primrose oil. Two 500mg capsules, 3 times daily. Trials carried out by departments of Surgery at the University of Wales and the University of Dundee found Evening Primrose oil effective and safe.
Poultice. Poke root. Horsetail.
Diet. As salt favours retention of fluid in cystic tissue it should be restricted.
Supplements. Daily. Beta carotene; B-complex; B6, Vitamin C 1g; Zinc. Vitamin E contra-indicated.

Treatment by or in liaison with a general medical practitioner.

FIBROIDS. Myoma of the womb. Non-malignant, non-painful growth of smooth muscle tissue enlarging into a mass on the wall of the womb. Accounts for most hysterectomies. Women may have them without knowing. Responsible for heavy menstruation and clots. Surgical removal is known as myomectomy.

Fibroids depend on oestrogen for their growth. High levels, as in The Pill, are believed to increase their size. Low levels cause shrinkage. Size: anything from a marble to a turnip, producing a sense of fullness. After the menopause when oestrogen declines they may shrink and finally disappear. When enlarged, they cause frequency of urine and constipation, sometimes resultant anaemia. A common cause of infertility. Not all are removed by surgery. Women with fibroids should not take steroids.

Alternatives. Anti-mitotics – Damiana, Motherwort, Helonias, Goldenseal, Life root, Prickly Ash, White Pond Lily, Thuja, Violet leaves (wild), Blue or Black Cohosh.

To arrest bleeding: add Shepherd's Purse or Beth root.

For pain: Cramp bark. Goldenseal has a mixed success record and can constipate.

Tea. Formula. Equal parts: Corn Silk, Shepherd's Purse, Violet. 2 teaspoons to each cup boiling water; infuse 15 minutes; dose, one cup thrice daily.

Decoction. Formula. Equal parts: Violet leaves, Clivers, Yellow Dock. 1 teaspoon to each cup of water simmered 20 minutes. Half-1 cup thrice daily.

Tinctures. Alternatives:

(1) Combine Cornsilk 3; White Pond Lily 2; Goldenseal quarter. Dose: 15-30 drops in water thrice daily. (*Edgar G. Jones, MNIMH*)

(2) Yellow Parilla, 60 drops; Yarrow 1oz; White Pond Lily 60 drops; Tincture Goldenseal 60 drops. Water (preferably distilled) to 8oz. Dose: 2 teaspoons in water after meals. (*Arthur Barker, FNIMH*)

Powders. Formula. Blue Cohosh 1; Poke root 1; Goldenseal half. Dose: 500mg (two 00 capsules or one-third teaspoon) thrice daily.

A.W. & L.R. Priest. Combination: Goldenseal, Balmony, Galangal. (Oral and local suppository)

Douche. 1 litre boiled water. Allow to cool. Add 30-40 drops Liquid Extract Goldenseal, Bayberry or Thuja.

Castor oil packs over affected area. Three thicknesses cotton wool or suitable material soaked in Castor oil. Cover with an electric heating pad. Apply 3-4 nights a week for 6 months. Disappearance of fibroid reported. *ARE Journal, Vol 19, May 84, p.127*

Note. Correction of anaemia, if present. Simple iron deficiency – Nettle tea. Floradix. Special care during pregnancy.

FIBROSITIS. Muscular rheumatism. Painful, sore and aching muscles due to over-exertion, septic foci (bad teeth, grumbling appendix, infected sinuses etc), or an over-growth of fibrous tissue due to inflammatory change in muscles. Also due to injury or faulty food combinations.

Alternatives. Bladderwrack, Bogbean, Cayenne, Dandelion, Black Cohosh (especially after violent exercise), Ginger, Horseradish, Sweet Chestnut, St John's Wort, Rosemary.

Tea. Celery seed.

Tablets/capsules. Black Cohosh, Celery, White Willow, Devil's Claw, Ligvites, Wild Yam.

Alternative formulae:– *Powders*. Formula. White Willow 2; Cramp bark half; Guaiacum quarter; Liquorice quarter. Mix. 500mg (two 00 capsules or one-third teaspoon) thrice daily.

Liquid Extracts. Formula. Rosemary 1; St John's Wort 1; Black Cohosh half; Valerian half. Mix. Dose: 30-60 drops thrice daily.

Tinctures. Formula. Dandelion 2; Celery 1; Bogbean 1. Fennel half. Dose: 1-2 teaspoons thrice daily.

Topical. Aromatherapy. 2 drops each, Origan (Wild Marjoram), Scots Pine, Rosemary, to 2 teaspoons vegetable oil (Almond, etc). Massage. Capsicum liniment.

Poultice. Leaves of Lobelia, Ragwort or Wintergreen.

Analgesic cream. Hot Epsom Salts bath, once weekly.

Diet. Lacto-vegetarian. Oily fish. Dandelion coffee.

Supplements. Daily. Vitamin B6 (50mg), C (500mg), Calcium Pantothenate (500mg), Dolomite.

FIGWORT. Throatwort. *Scrophularia nodosa L. German*: Knötige. *French*: Schofulaire des bois. *Spanish*: Scrophularia nudoso. *Italian*: Scrofularia maggiore.

Constituents: flavonoids, iridoids, phenolic acids.

Action: relaxing alterative, anodyne (mild – as applied to piles), diuretic (mild), laxative, anti-inflammatory, vulnerary, lymphatic, cardiac stimulant.

Uses. Skin eruptions that exude matter: scrofulous eczema, psoriasis, pemphigus. Severe itching. Swollen glands. Piles: hard, swollen and painful. Appendicitis. Lumps in the breast (traditional). It is called scrofula plant because of its reputation for discharging abscesses, boils, infected wounds, etc.

Combines well with Yellow Dock. Figwort 2; Yellow Dock 1.

Preparations. Thrice daily.

Tea. 1 heaped teaspoon to each cup boiling water; infuse 15 minutes; dose – half-1 cup.

Powder. 500mg (two 00 capsules or one-third teaspoon).

Liquid extract. Dose: 1-2ml.

Tincture BHP (1983) 1:10 in 45 per cent alcohol; dose – 2-4ml.
Note. Contra-indicated in tachycardia (rapid heart beat). GSL

FILAREE. Storkbill. "Clocks". Pinkets. Plant common in the Western United States, especially California. Used by early settlers to fatten herds of cattle. A galactogogue increasing the supply of milk in animals and humans in child rearing. Fresh plant used in spring as a substitute for Alfalfa when the latter is scarce. Dogs, domestic and farmyard animals, especially racehorses savour it. A green tea may be prepared from the fresh plant. Used in salads.

FINGERNAILS, SPLITTING. Most usual cause is nutrition. High in minerals, Alfalfa tea is known to toughen soft or splitting nails. Liquid Extract Echinacea: 10-20 drops in water, thrice daily. Paint nails with Tincture Myrrh.
Supplementation: zinc.

FIRST AID AND MEDICINE CHEST. Various aspects of first aid are described under the following: ABRASIONS, BLEEDING, CUTS, SHOCK, EYES, FAINTING, FRACTURES, INJURIES, POISONING, WOUNDS, WITCH HAZEL.

Avoid overstocking; some herbs lose their potency on the shelf in time, especially if exposed. Do not keep on a high shelf out of the way. Experts suggest a large box with a lid to protect its contents, kept in a cool dry place away from foods and other household items. Store mixtures containing Camphor separately elsewhere. Camphor is well-known as a strong antidote to medicinal substances. Keep all home-made ointments in a refrigerator. However harmless, keep all remedies out of reach of children. Be sure that all tablet containers have child-resistant tops.

Keep a separate box, with duplicates, permanently in the car. Check periodically. Replace all tablets when crumbled, medicines with changed colour or consistency. Always carry a large plastic bottle of water in the car for cleansing dirty wounds and to form a vehicle to Witch Hazel and other remedies. Label all containers clearly.
Health care items: Adhesive bandages of all sizes, sterile gauze, absorbant cotton wool, adhesive tape, elastic bandage, stitch scissors, forceps (boiled before use), clinical thermometer, assorted safety pins, eye-bath for use as a douche for eye troubles, medicine glass for correct dosage.
Herbal and other items: Comfrey or Chickweed ointment (or cream) for sprains and bruises. Marshmallow and Slippery Elm (drawing) ointment for boils, abscesses, etc. Calendula (Marigold) ointment or lotion for bleeding wounds where the skin is broken. An alternative is Calendula tincture (30 drops) to cupful of boiled water allowed to cool; use externally, as a mouth rinse after dental extractions, and sipped for shock. Arnica tincture: for bathing bruises and swellings where the skin is unbroken (30 drops in a cup of boiled water allowed to cool). Honey for burns and scalds. Lobelia tablets for irritating cough and respiratory distress. Powdered Ginger for adding to hot water for indigestion, vomiting, etc. Tincture Myrrh, 5-10 drops in a glass of water for sore throats, tonsillitis, mouth ulcers and externally, for cleansing infected or dirty wounds. Tincture Capsicum (3-10 drops) in a cup of tea for shock, or in eggcup Olive oil for use as a liniment for pains of rheumatism. Cider vinegar (or bicarbonate of Soda) for insect bites. Oil Citronella, insect repellent. Vitamin E capsules for burns; pierce capsule and wipe contents over burnt area. Friar's balsam to inhale for congestion of nose and throat. Oil of Cloves for toothache. Olbas oil for general purposes. Castor oil to assist removal of foreign bodies from the eye. Slippery Elm powder as a gruel for looseness of bowels. Potter's Composition Essence for weakness or collapse. Antispasmodic drops for pain.

Distilled extract of Witch Hazel deserves special mention for bleeding wounds, sunburn, animal bites, stings, or swabbed over the forehead to freshen and revive during an exhausting journey. See: WITCH HAZEL.

Stings of nettles or other plants are usually rendered painless by a dock leaf. Oils of Tea Tree, Jojoba and Evening Primrose are also excellent for first aid to allay infection. For punctured wounds, as a shoemaker piercing his thumb with an awl or injury from brass tacks, or for shooting pains radiating from the seat of injury, tincture or oil of St John's Wort (Hypericum) is the remedy.

FISH OILS. It is now accepted that oily fish is good for the heart, arthritis, skin disorders and some cases of chronic headache.

In Greenland, where much oily fish is eaten, heart disease is scarcely known. Each year over 200,000 people in Britain alone die of heart disease. Western affluence-diseases from a diet of excess saturated fat (from meat, butter, etc) may be reduced by modest amounts of oily fish.

A daily intake of 800 milligrams of essential fatty acids as contained in herring, mackerel, cod, etc., can play a decisive role in cardiac treatments. Such fish may be eaten twice weekly. On days when not taken, supplement with pure fish oil or fish oil capsules. As little as 1oz (30 grams) of mackerel, herring or other similar fish is sufficient.

When eating oily fish only twice a week a teaspoon of pure fish oil or dessertspoon cod liver oil daily is sufficient.

Labels of fish oils should be carefully studied for their DHA and EPA content in milligrams.

Add together to a total 800 milligrams – average daily dose.

Fish oils can lower the level of triglycerides and reduce 'stickiness' of the blood – its tendency to clot and possibly block coronary vessels. As fish oil Vitamin A contains 10,000iu of Retinol, it should not be taken for extended periods without the advice of a practitioner.

FISHERMAN'S FRIEND THROAT AND CHEST LOZENGES. Contain Eucalyptus oil 0.153 per cent, Cubeb oil 0.305 per cent, Tincture Capsicum 0.02 per cent, Liquorice extract 7.317 per cent, Menthol 0.9 per cent. Specially formulated for Fleetwood Deep Sea fishermen working in Icelandic frost and fog conditions to relieve bronchial congestion, and ease breathing. (*Lofthouse*)

FISSURE, ANAL. A small split or ulcer on the skin or mucous membrane at the entrance of the anus. Motions are passed with much pain. The anus is tightly contracted because of muscle spasm. Pain at the anal verge on straining at stool; possible stain of bright red blood on toilet paper. Torn tag of epithelium. May be associated with piles, Crohn's disease or colitis. Appearance resembles crack at corner of the mouth.

Alternatives. Sometimes has to be resolved by surgical operation.

Tea. Formula. Equal parts: Chamomile, Comfrey herb, Figwort. 2 teaspoons to each cup boiling water. Infuse 15 minutes. 1 cup thrice daily.

Decoction. Equal parts. Bistort root. Cranesbill root. Frangula bark. 1 teaspoon to each cup water simmered gently 20 minutes. Half-1 cup thrice daily.

Powders. Formula. Bistort root 1; Slippery Elm 2; Fenugreek 1. Pinch red pepper. Mix. Dose: 750mg (three 00 capsules, or half a teaspoon) thrice daily.

Liquid extracts. Formula. Bistort root 2; Marshmallow root 1; Frangula bark 1. Dose: 30-60 drops thrice daily, before meals.

Tincture. Tincture Bistort BHP (1983) (1:5 in 45 per cent alcohol). Dose: 30-60 drops, thrice daily.

Topical. Comfrey or Calendula cream: smear on anal dilator or suppository to relieve spasm and heal. Vitamin E cream. Insert 1-4 Garlic capsules into rectum at night.

Practitioner ointment. Figwort 10; Belladonna 1. Ointment base to make 100 parts.

Diet. Low residue. Dandelion coffee.

Supplements. Plenty of Vitamin C. (Oranges, citrus fruits)

Attention to bowels: Psyllium seeds.

FISTULA, ANAL. An unnatural drainage tract from an abscess on the anus or in the rectum leading to the skin surface. May have one or more openings.

Causes: persistent anal or rectal abscesses from ulcerative colitis, TB, granuloma, carcinoma or a breakdown of internal piles.

Symptoms. Itching anus, discharge of pus from a point near the anus.

Echinacea may arrest pus formation but not heal; which would require assistance of Comfrey root and Marigold (Calendula) where healing is possible.

Alternatives. Poke root, Ground Ivy, Horsetail, Marigold, St John's Wort, Yarrow, Yellow Toadflax. <u>Comfrey leaves or tincture</u>. <u>Echinacea</u>.

Tea. Mix: Equal parts: Comfrey leaves, Horsetail, Yarrow. One heaped teaspoon to each cup boiling water, infuse 15 minutes. 1 cup thrice daily before meals.

Decoction. Equal parts: Fenugreek seeds; Stone root. One teaspoon to each cup water simmered gently 20 minutes. Dose: half cup thrice daily.

Fenugreek seeds. One heaped teaspoon seeds to each cup water simmered gently 15 minutes. Half cup morning and evening: consume seeds.

Formula. Butternut 1; Poke root 1; Stone root half. Dose: powders – 500mg (two 00 capsules or one-third teaspoon). Liquid Extract: 30-60 drops in water. Tinctures: 1-2 teaspoons in water, thrice daily.

Topical. After emptying bowel insert one 400iu Vitamin E capsule. Inject mucilage of fresh Comfrey root. Distilled extract of Witch Hazel lotion to anus. Horsetail poultice.

Poke root. Used with success. (*Edgar G. Jones MNIMH*)

Important to treat associated disease.

Diet. Bland. Slippery Elm powder in soups etc. Little fibre. Avoid peppers and spicy foods.

FLATULENCE. Gas in the stomach or intestines. A common cause is feeble secretion of stomach acid and a fall in folic acid levels.

Anti-Flatulence herbs are known as carminatives. See entry.

Powdered Cinnamon: quarter to half teaspoon in water or milk.

Seeds: Aniseed, Caraway, Celery, Coriander, Cumin, Fennel, Mustard. 1 level teaspoon to cup boiling water; infuse 10-15 minutes. Sip.

Oils: Peppermint, Thyme, Aniseed. 1-3 drops in milk.

Herb teas: Balm, Catmint, Centuary, Chamomile, Holy Thistle, Hyssop, Marjoram (not in pregnancy), Parsley. 1-2 teaspoons to each cup boiling water: infuse 5-15 minutes. Dose: half-1 cup freely.

Tinctures. Gentian, Cardamoms, Cayenne, Galangal, Ginger, Juniper, Valerian.

Life Drops. Charcoal biscuits (not for children under 5).

FLAVONOIDS. Flavones. Natural chemicals

that prevent the deposit of fatty material in blood vessels. A group of coloured (yellow) aromatic plant constituents with a spicy taste and smell, chiefly due to the presence of benzene. Efficient absorption of Vitamin C is dependent upon them. Their action is chiefly diuretic, antispasmodic and antiseptic. Some strengthen fragile capillaries and tone relaxed blood vessels, as in veinous disorders. They lower blood pressure.
Notable examples: Buckwheat, Coltsfoot, Citrus fruits, Hawthorn, Euphorbia, Figs, Heartsease, Pellitory of the Wall, Rutin, Skullcap, Lime flowers, Elderflowers, Shepherd's Purse, Silver Birch, Wild Carrot, Yerba Santa and members of the labiatae family. All are immune enhancers and useful for chronic conditions where prolonged treatment produces no known toxicity. Of value in heart medicines.

Flavonoids are also pigments usually responsible for the colour of flowers and fruits and protect the plant against stress. A diet rich in raw fruit and vegetables provides adequate flavonoids.
Zutphen Elderly Study. Revealed that tea, onions and apples provided the majority of flavonoids in the overall diet. The mortality rate from coronary heart disease and myocardial infarction was lower in those with a high flavonoid intake. (*Hertog MGL, National Institute of Public Health, Holland, et al The Lancet, 1993. Oct 23, 1007-11*)

Among red wines, Italian Chianti has the most flavonoids, with 20mg per litre, fostering healthy changes in the blood. All flavonoids are antioxidants and platelet inhibitors. Antioxidants stop oxygen from binding with LDL, a type of cholesterol. The oxygen-LDL pair clings to blood vessel walls, impeding blood flow. Flavonoids seem to suppress the stickiness. Platelet inhibitors prevent blood clots.

A diet rich in flavonoids would appear to prevent heart disease.

FLEABANE. Canada fleabane. *Erigeron canadensis L. German*: Grosses Flohkraut. *French*: Pulicaire. *Italian*: Psillo. *Part used*: herb, seeds.
Constituents: flavonoids, oil, tannins, gallic acid.
Action: haemostatic, astringent, antirheumatic, vulnerary, diuretic.
Uses. Extravasation of blood, black eye, bruises; bleeding from gullet, lungs, kidneys or bowel, piles. Kidney disorders. Diarrhoea, Bronchitis, Sore throat. Canadian Indians' wound herb. Insect repellent.
Preparations. Thrice daily.
Tea. 1 teaspoon to each cup boiling water; infuse 15 minutes; dose – half cup.
Liquid extract. 5ml in water.
Tincture – fresh plant when in bloom. 1 part to 5 parts 60 per cent alcohol. Dose – 5-10ml in water.
Oil. Dose – 2 drops in honey.

FLEAS. See: LICE.

FLESH-EATING DISEASE. Necrotising fasciitis, in which flesh and muscle are destroyed at a rate of inches an hour. Can spring from a range of streptococcal bacteria of which there are over 80 sub-types.

It seems that this common bacteria, in some unknown way, receives a booster by taking on viral DNA. Lungs, liver and stomach may be attacked, while red blood cells are disrupted and their haemoglobin released. Among other conditions caused by streptococcus is the bright red rash of scarlet fever, sinusitis, meningitis and rheumatic fever. Flesh-eater disease may take just twenty hours to kill a man ("galloping gangrene").
Symptoms. High temperature – body hot, hands and feet freezing cold. 'Strep' sore throat (pharyngitis). Bright red skin rash. Pains in arms and legs as if straining a muscle.
Treatment. The disease is resistant to penicillin. Frequent hot lemon drinks well-laced with honey.
Tinctures. Echinacea 2; Goldenseal 1; Myrrh half. Dose: 10-20 drops in dessertspoon water or honey, hourly, acute cases.

Treatment by or in liaison with medical practitioner or infectious diseases specialist.

FLETCHER-HYDE, Frederick. Distinguished herbal authority. President Emeritus both of the National Institute of Medical Herbalists and of the British Herbal Medicine Association. Degree in Chemistry and a first class honours degree in the special examination in Botany granted in 1932 at London University. Founder of the Education Fund and the School of Herbal Medicine. Former member of the Commitee on Review of Medicines and other government bodies. He gave herbal medicine a place on the Statute Book (Medicines Act 1968) after 400 years. For 16 years, chairman of the British Herbal Pharmacopoeia Committee. Entered the National Institute of Medical Herbalists (then NAMH) in 1931, and directed the Research and Analytical Department for 50 years.

Hyde organised the fight for the survival of herbal medicine endangered by the Medicines Bill and was able to modify some clauses that would have put an end to herbal medicine under the Medicines Act, 1968. The BHP is indebted to his expertise and clinical experience. As a consultant and teacher he inspired many students and practitioners. A Doctorate of Botanic Medicine was conferred on him by the School of Botanic Medicine, London.

FLOODING (Menses). See: MENORRHAGIA.

FLOATERS, Black. Usually clumps of red cells

which invade the vitreous humour from the retinal vessels. "Spots before the eyes". See: LIVER.

FLORADIX. A biological food supplement providing organic iron, extracts of carefully selected herbs, fruits, vitamins, specially cultured yeast and ocean kelp. In addition, contains extracts of wheat germ and rose hips. For women (including expectant and nursing mothers), men, growing children and persons whose diet is lacking in natural iron and vitamins.

Important components of Floradix preparations are herbal extracts of various medicinal plants. Those rich in iron include: Stinging Nettle, Couch grass roots and algae Macrocystis pyrifera and Spinach. Extracts to aid digestion and metabolism (as well as strengthen the system) include: Hawthorn for heart function; Fennel, Angelica root and Wormwood for digestion; and Juniper berries to aid metabolism. See: SALUS-HAUS.

FLUID EXTRACTS. Another term for liquid extracts, chiefly used in America and among a modern generation of herbal practitioners. Largely solutions of alcohol and water, strength 1:1. Prepared from crude material or solid extract, the alcohol content differing with each product. See: LIQUID EXTRACTS.

FLUID RETENTION SYNDROME (FRS). Accumulation of fluid beneath the skin; frequent sites – fingers, abdomen, breast, ankles.
Symptoms. Headache, frequency of urine, palpitation, possible irritable bowel syndrome. "My feet are killing me", "I can't get my wedding ring off" are typical complaints by women with FRS. Sometimes a complication of diabetes, or follows abuse of laxatives or diuretic drugs. A part of the premenstrual syndrome.
Alternatives. *Teas*. Any of the following: Buchu, Dandelion, Hawthorn, Motherwort, Yarrow. One or more cups daily, cold.
Tablets. Popular combination. Powdered Dandelion root BHP (1983) 90mg; powdered Horsetail extract 3:1 10mg; powdered Uva Ursi extract 3:1 75mg. (*Gerard House*)
Formula. Equal parts: Hawthorn, Dandelion, Broom. Dose: Powders: 750mg (three 00 capsules or half a teaspoon). Liquid extracts: 1 teaspoon. Tinctures: 1-2 teaspoons. Thrice daily.
Practitioner. Tincture Lily of the Valley (Convallaria) BHP (1983) (1:5 in 40 per cent alcohol). Dose 8-15 drops (0.5-1ml). Thrice daily.
Aromatherapy. 6 drops Lavender oil on wet handkerchief: use as a compress for relief of ankles during a journey.
Traditional Gypsy Medicine. The sufferer is exposed to the rising smoke of smouldering Juniper berries which exudes volatile oils and has a gentle diuretic effect.
Diet. Salt-free. High protein. Dandelion coffee.
Supplements. Vitamin B-complex, Potassium, Copper.

FLUKES. Trematoda. Parasitic flatworms: (*Fasciola hepatica*) occurs mostly in sheep and in the freshwater snail. Larval forms of the latter encyst on water plants, commonly Watercress. On invasion into the human body, settles in the liver and bile duct.
Liquid Extract Butternut. 1:1 in 25 per cent alcohol BHP (1983), dose: 2-6ml, thrice daily.
Butternut. Powder, with few grains Cayenne. 750mg (three 00 capsules or half a teaspoon) thrice daily.
Wormwood tea. 1-2 teaspoons to cup cold water steeped overnight. Consume on rising.
Molasses. Half a teaspoon Wormseed powder in a little molasses, night and morning, for 3 days, followed by laxative. For desperate cases.
Dandelion and Burdock, traditional drink. Freely.
Diet. Strong Dandelion coffee.

FLUORINE. Trace element. Imparts 'tone' to walls of blood vessels and muscles.
Deficiency. A diet deficient in Fluorine induces relaxed conditions: varicose veins, weak ligaments. Bone-wasting diseases – osteoporosis, dental decay.
Body effects. Maintains vascular, bone and dental health.
Sources. Meat, fish (where bones are consumed) sardines, salmon. Plants: Garlic, Watercress.
Note. Excess causes: fluorosis – mottling of teeth, arthritic joints and increased density of the bones. Controversial government policy promotes addition of Sodium flouride to water to achieve a minimum of one part per million.

FOLLICULITIS. Sycosis. Barber's itch. Inflammation of the hair follicles commencing as scattered pimples progressing to pustules on the scalp or beard.
Cause: mostly staphylococcal or streptococcal.
Key agent: Thuja.
Alternatives. Blue Flag root, Burdock root, Clivers, Garlic, Poke root, Red Clover flower, Yellow Dock root, Echinacea root. Devil's Claw, Guaiacum resin, Sarsaparilla.
Decoction. Burdock and Sarsaparilla; equal parts. Mix. 1oz to 1 pint water gently simmered 20 minutes. Half-1 cup thrice daily.
Powders. Combine equal parts, Echinacea and Garlic. 500mg or one-third teaspoon in water or honey, thrice daily.
Practitioner. Tinctures: Guaiacum BPC (1949) 0.5ml; Rheum Palmatum BPC (1934) 5ml; Thuja 0.5ml; Trifolium pratense BHP (1983) 5ml; Arctium lappa BHP (1983) 5ml; Rumex Crispus BHP (1983) 5ml. Aqua et 100ml. Sig: 5ml (3i) tds

Aq. cal. pc.
Topical. 10 drops Tea Tree oil in eggcup Almond, Safflower or Sunflower oil. Evening Primrose oil. Aloe Vera gel.
Diet. See: DIET – SKIN DISEASES.
Vitamins. A. B-complex, B2, B6, D, F, Biotin, Niacin, Zinc.
Note. There is a form which is part of the constitutional disease resulting from gonorrhoea which presents with dry soft spongy cauliflower warts. See: GONORRHOEA.

FOMENTATIONS. Compresses consisting of a cloth or other suitable absorbant material immersed in a herbal tea and wrung out. Almost any herb may be used for this purpose. Before application the skin is smeared with Olive oil to avoid burning. May be hot or cold. Heat relaxes, cold tones. Wrung-out material is held in position by a plastic cloth or other suitable protective covering. Fomentations have many uses: they convey heat and medication to arthritic joints and to cold extremities in old age (Ginger, Prickly Ash). May be given for abscesses (Slippery Elm); tennis elbow (Comfrey); abdominal inflammation (Castor oil); Neuralgia (German Chamomile): Marshmallow or Blue Flag stimulate activity of the lymphatic system for swollen glands; and disperse local congestion of the circulation. They relax surface nerve-endings, dilate blood vessels, alleviate pain.

FOOD POISONING. A notifiable disease under the Public Health (Control of Diseases) Act 1984.
Symptoms: vomiting, diarrhoea and abdominal pain. Diseases include Salmonella, Botulism (rare), typhoid and paratyphoid. Ptomaine is now an obsolete term for bacterial decomposition.
Treatment: *First aid*: Capsicum, Ginger, Cinnamon. Cider vinegar in water, sip slowly every few minutes until specific treatment is available. Spices are powerful germicides. See: SALMONELLA, LISTERIA, SHIGELA, etc.
Re-hydration, after heavy loss of fluids: glass of water containing 1 teaspoon salt and 2 teaspoons sugar.
Preventative: 2-3 Garlic tablets/capsules at night.
To be treated by or in liaison with a qualified medical practitioner.

FOOT POWDER. For foot-sweat and general discomfort. Mix into 1oz (30g) cornflour a few drops of any of the following oils, according to personal choice: Lavender, Geranium, Eucalyptus, Lemon, Pine.

FORBIDDEN TREATMENT. No remedies may be offered for treatment of sexually transmitted diseases, diabetes, tuberculosis, cancer, epilepsy, fits, locomotor ataxia, Bright's disease, any kidney disease, cataract, paralysis, glaucoma. No claims must be made by letter, telephone or otherwise that a vendor or practitioner can 'cure' or favourably affect the course of any of such conditions. A practitioner has the right to exercise his own judgement should, in the course of his duties, he diagnose one of these conditions except for sexually transmitted diseases for which specialised treatment is given at approved official veneral diseases centres.

FORCED MARCH TABLET. Active principles of Kola nut, Coca leaves (caffeine and cocaine). Chiefly used in war. To allay thirst, hunger and sustain strength under mental and physical strain. Instruction to physicians: "Cola is a stimulant, tonic and restorative, decreasing the sensation of fatigue in prolonged muscular exertion or mental effort."
Dose: One dissolved on the tongue daily. (*Burroughs Wellcome during World War I*)

FO-TI-TIENG. *Tea*: fine-cut herbs: Hydrocotyle 10 per cent; Meadowsweet 10 per cent; powdered Kola 80 per cent.
Capsules: each contains Hydrocotyle 60mg; Meadowsweet 60mg; Kola 480mg.

FOXGLOVE. *Digitalis purpurea L. French*: Doigts de la Vierge. *German*: Fingerhut. *Spanish*: Dedalera. *Dutch*: Vingerhoed. *Italian*: Guancelli. *Chinese*: Mao-ti-huany. Dried leaves.*Keynote*: heart. The most important cardiovascular agent in modern medicine. Digitalis lanata is superior to the purpurea.
Constituents: Cardenolides, saponins, flavonoids, anthraquinones.
Action: Digitalis stimulates the vagus nerve thus slowing the heart rate. Prolongs diastole which increases the heart's filling-time and improves coronary circulation. Effects of digitalis are cumulative. The herbalist uses an alternative: Lily of the Valley for the failing heart.
Preparation. *Tincture B.P.* Each millilitre possesses one unit of activity and is equivalent to 0.1 gramme of the International Standard digitalis powder. Prepared from the leaf in 70 per cent alcohol by a pharmacist. Dose: 0.3ml to 1ml (5-15 drops). Used only under medical supervision.
Digoxin toxicity occurs at levels above 2.6m mol/litre. Schedule 1 P. (POM) (UK)

FRACTURES. Open or closed. In open fractures the skin is pierced; closed, the skin is not broken. As the incidence of neck-of-the-femur fractures associated with osteoporosis increases, with delayed healing in the elderly infirm, herbal mitotics have much to offer. Taken internally with Calcium supplements all kinds of fractures, including hip replacements, are assisted.
Treatment. Acute: give no food or drink in case anaesthetics are needed later. Do not bandage

over open fractures. To promote collagen and callous formation: Horsetail, Mouse Ear, Fenugreek, Alfalfa, Marshmallow root, Mullein, Parsley, Comfrey leaves or tincture.
Decoction. Welsh traditional. Equal parts, Comfrey and Horsetail. 1 heaped teaspoon to each cup water gently simmered 20 minutes: half-cup thrice daily.
Dr J. Christopher USA. Equal parts, Mullein, Comfrey, Oak bark, Lobelia, Skullcap, Walnut, Marshmallow root, Wormwood, Gravel root.
Guaiacum. Liquid extract. 5-10 drops in water thrice daily.
Cinnamon. Healing effect on fractures.
Fracture with nerve laceration. St John's Wort.
Topical. Comfrey paste or poultice.
Diet. High protein.
Supplements. Vitamins A, C, D, E. Calcium citrate malate (more effective than the carbonate), Dolomite, Magnesium, Zinc.

FRANGULA BARK. Buckthorn bark. *Frangula alnus*, Mill. *Rhamnus frangula L.* Dried bark, after two years. Fresh bark causes griping. Contains anthraquinone glycosides.
Action: bitter, diuretic, cholagogue, stimulating laxative.
Uses. Chronic spastic constipation. Torpid liver.
Preparations. *Decoction*: half-1 teaspoon to each cup water simmered 10 minutes: half-1 cup.
Liquid extract: 1-2 teaspoons in water once or twice daily.
Powder. Capsules (200mg). 2 capsules before meals.
Hoxsey Cancer Cure (1950s): Ingredient of.
Contra-indications. "Inflammatory colon diseases (e.g. ulcerative colitis, Crohn's disease, ileus, appendicitis, abdominal pain of unknown origin." (*European monograph, ESCOP*)
Side-effects. If used correctly side-effects will be minimal.
Not recommended during pregnancy, lactation or for children. GSL *Schedule 1*

FRANKINCENSE. Olibanum. *Boswellia thurifera.*
A milk-like sap from the trunk of the tree hardens into resinous tears. The chlorophyll of the ancient world, with power to neutralise offensive odours. Used as incense in religious ceremonies. Modern use chiefly external.
Action: mild expectorant, carminative, diuretic, urinary antiseptic, stimulant.
Uses: bronchitis and congested nasal passages (inhalant). Leprosy (China). Avicenna (10th century physician) advised it for ulceration and tumours. Used in embalming of bodies, and as a preservative in pharmacy.
Preparations. In the ancient world it was steeped in strong wine for use in drop doses for the pestilence and as an antiseptic wash for infections. Modern use: throat pastilles.
Inhalant. 1 teaspoon, tincture, is added to a bowl of boiling water and the steam inhaled.

FRECKLES. Cold infusion of Clivers tea 2-3 times daily and used as a wash on affected parts. Handful fresh Clivers simmered gently in 1 pint water for 10 minutes. Rub affected parts with lemon juice or paste of bitter almonds and milk.
Greek traditional: Lime flower tea (wash).

FREE RADICALS. Both vegetable and animal tissues produce free radicals as a normal metabolic byproduct. They are found in many areas of human activity.
A radical is a group of atoms which can combine in the same way as single atoms to make a molecule. Free means uncombined. A free radical is a state in which a radical can exist before it combines – an incomplete molecule containing oxygen which has an uneven electrical charge. High energy oxygen atoms are known to form atheroma.
As well as being substances that take part in a process of metabolism, free radicals can be found in industrial fumes and cigarette smoke. They are oxidants and have an anti-bacterial effect. But their activity is not confined to bacteria alone. When produced in large amounts as in inflammation and infection, they may have a damaging effect upon the lining of blood vessels and other tissues. An excess is produced in ischaemic heart disease. They have been shown to be involved in jet lag, Alzheimer's disease, rheumatoid arthritis, thrombosis, heart failure, cancer, irradiation sickness and a weak immune system. Damaging to the DNA, they are probably the greatest single cause of ill health. They hasten the ageing process. Vitamins A, C, E, being antioxidants and the mineral Selenium stimulate certain enzyme systems to limit damage done by these destructive elements.
Losing weight is believed to generate free radicals – a metabolic side-effect of dieting. See: ANTIOXIDANTS.

FREEDOM OF INDIVIDUAL TO CHOOSE THERAPY. The British Government supports freedom of the individual to make an informed choice of the type of therapy he or she wishes to use and has affirmed its policy not to restrict the sale of herbal medicines.
A doctor with knowledge of herbal medicine may prescribe them should he consider them a necessary part of treatment.

FREQUENCY OF URINE. Bladder instability. Urine is usually passed 4 to 6 times daily; anything in excess of this is known as 'frequency'. In the elderly it may be due to weak bladder muscles and sphincter, or to unrecognised overflow due to prostatic obstruction.

Causes may also be psychological: worry, excitement, emotional crises such as school exams. Where the trouble is persistent attention should be focussed on the bladder (cystitis), inflammation of the kidneys, even the presence of stone.

Simple frequency may arise from cold weather, nervous excitement, or early pregnancy. Other predisposing factors are: diabetes mellitis, enlarged prostate gland, stone in the kidney or bladder.

Alternatives. *Teas*. American Cranesbill, Agrimony, Cornsilk, Horsetail, Passion flower, Plantain, Skullcap, Uva Ursi, Huang Qi (Chinese). Saw Palmetto (prostate gland).

Tablets/capsules. Cranesbill (American), Gentian, Liquorice.

Powders. Equal parts: Cranesbill, Horsetail, Liquorice. Mix. Dose: 500mg (two 00 capsules or one-third teaspoon). Thrice daily.

Tinctures. Equal parts: Cramp bark and Horsetail. Dose: 30-60 drops, thrice daily.

Practitioner. Tinctures. Alternatives:–

Formula 1. Ephedra 30ml; Geranium 20ml; Rhus aromatica 20ml; Thuja 1ml. Aqua to 100ml. Sig: 5ml (3i) tds aq cal pc.

Formula 2. Equal parts: Ephedra and Horsetail. 15-60 drops thrice daily; last dose bedtime.

A. Barker FNIMH. Dec Jam Sarsae Co Conc BPC 1 fl oz (30ml) . . . Liquid extract Rhus 240 minims (16ml) . . . Liquid extract Passiflora 60 minims (4ml) . . . Syr Althaea 2 fl oz (60ml) . . . Aqua to 8oz (240ml). Dose: 2 teaspoons thrice daily; last dose bedtime.

Tincture Arnica. German traditional. 1 drop in honey at bedtime.

Pelvic exercises. Alternate hot and cold Sitz baths. Swimming, Cycling.

Address. Incontinence Advisory Service, Disabled Living Foundation, 380-384 Harrow Road, London W9 2HU.

FRIAR'S BALSAM. Tincture Benzoin Co (BPC).

Action. Expectorant for chronic bronchitis, asthma and other respiratory disorders.

Use. An inhalant. One 5ml teaspoon of the balsam to 500ml boiling water; patient inhales the vapour with a towel over the head.

Still used as an alternative to pressurised devices that may evoke a diminished response by over-use. Children may develop an unhealthy dependence upon a nebuliser resulting in bronchitis, the area of aerosol mists being an area of controversy. Friar's balsam may still be used with effect.

Formula: macerate Benzoin 10 per cent, prepared Storax 7.5 per cent, Tolu balsam 2.5 per cent and Aloes 2 per cent with alcohol 90 per cent. GSL

FRIGIDITY. Absence of sexual desire. Inability to reach orgasm, usually in women.

Causes: Sexually transmitted diseases, tension, stress, absence of menses, dry vaginal entrance, fibroids, cystic ovaries, Vitamin E deficiency. Vegetarians have lower levels of oestrogen.

Alternatives. Endocrine balancers: Helonias, Life root, Wild Yam, Damiana, Saw Palmetto, Ginseng, Motherwort.

Tea. Combination: equal parts, Motherwort, Oats, Gotu Kola. 2 teaspoons to each cup boiling water; infuse 15 minutes. Half-1 cup daily.

South American traditional: Saw Palmetto, Kola and Damiana. Available as tablets and other preparations.

Far East traditional: Ginseng.

Agnus Castus. Deficient secretion of luteal hormone.

Diet. Oats (porridge, etc). High fibre.

Vitamins. E (400iu daily). B-complex.

Minerals. Zinc.

FRINGE TREE. Old man's beard. Snowdrop tree. *Chionanthus virginicus L. German*: Schneeflockenbaum. *French*: Chionanthe. *Italian*: Chionanto. Root bark. *Keynote*: liver.

Constituents: saponin glycoside, chionanthin.

Action: liver stimulant, cholagogue, laxative, diuretic, alterative. Tonic action on spleen and pancreas.

Uses. Liver disorders, inflammation of the gall bladder and duodenum; gall stones. Jaundice, to liquefy bile and assist its elimination from the blood. Excess sugar in the urine; of value in diabetes. Suited to liverish temperaments, malaria liver, constipation, high blood pressure due to congestion of the portal circulation.

In the presence of yellow or greenish discolouration of the skin, eyes; highly coloured urine, clay-coloured stools and pain on the right side of the body: Fringe Tree is indicated.

Weil's disease: with Echinacea BHP (1983).

Combines well with Barberry and Wild Yam (equal parts).

Preparations. Thrice daily.

Tea. 1 teaspoon to each cup water, simmer 1 minute, infuse 15 minutes: dose – half cup.

Liquid extract BHP (1983) 1:1 in 25 per cent alcohol. Dose – 1-3ml.

Tincture BHP (1983) 1:5 in 45 per cent alcohol. Dose – 2-3ml.

Powder: dose – 2-4g. GSL

FROZEN SHOULDER. Treatment, same as for osteo-arthritis.

FROSTBITE. May attack those who face cold exposure as an occupational hazard, or who wear inadequate clothing in severe weather. Frost-nip of cheeks and chin. Dermis is frozen. May lead to Raynaud's Disease, or long-term vein disease.

Dullness of sensation.
Treatment: frozen limbs should not be rubbed or manipulated, but thawed out in luke-warm water, a hand still remaining in the glove or foot in the boot. Vasodilators to equalise the circulation.
Teas. Boneset, Chamomile, Elderflowers, Feverfew, Hyssop, Lime flowers, Peppermint, Sage, Gotu Kola, Yarrow. Buckwheat.
Echinacea: tablets, liquid extract, tinctures.

Never give alcohol or use hot water bottles. Paint with Friar's balsam followed by smoothing-in a little Olive oil. Abundant Vitamin C drinks. Life Drops in tea. Ginger, Capsicum. Horseradish.
Old Norwegian remedy: cold mashed onion poultice.
Supplements. Hourly: Vitamin C 1g; Vitamin E 500iu.

FUMIGANT. A herb, usually a gum which, when burnt, releases mixed gases into the atmosphere to cleanse against air-borne infection. An aerial disinfectant such as Myrrh, Frankincense, Incense.

FUMITORY. Earth smoke. *Fumaria officinalis L. German*: Erdrauch. *French*: Fiel de terre. *Spanish*: Fumaria. *Italian*: FUmosterno. *Arabian*: Shahteraj. *Indian*: Pitapapra. *Chinese*: Tszü-hua-ti-ting. *Iranian*: Shahturuz. Dried aerial parts.
Keynote: eczema.
Constituents: fumaric acid, isoquinoline alkaloids.
Action: alterative, diuretic (mild), antispasmodic (mild), laxative. Popular as a spring blood tonic. Hepatic stimulant, anthelmintic, anti-inflammatory, choleretic, cholagogue.
Uses. Eczema, dry skin diseases. Migraine of liver origin, torpid liver, gall stone colic, constipation.
Preparations. Thrice daily.
Tea. 1-2 teaspoons to each cup boiling water; infuse 10 minutes. dose: half-1 cup. Tea used also as an eyewash for conjunctivitis.
Liquid Extract: 30-60 drops in water, before meals.
Tincture 1:5 in 25 per cent alcohol. Dose, 1-4ml.
Powder, capsules: 160mg. 6-8 capsules daily in two doses before meals. (*Arkocaps*) GSL

FUNGICIDES. See: ANTI-FUNGALS.

FUNGUS INFECTION. Treatment – same as for Athlete's Foot. Wipe with contents of a Vitamin E capsule. Tea Tree oil, Thuja, Marigold. See: ANTI-FUNGALS.

FUNGUS POISONING. Even the harmless mushroom may produce allergy from its alkaloid muscarine. Every year there are hundreds of deaths. Symptoms include vomiting, abdominal pain and diarrhoea, followed by jaundice.
Treatment. Abundant herb teas, singly or in combination: Agrimony, Balm, Raspberry leaves. Charcoal tablets bind the toxins. Holy (or Blessed) Thistle tea is traditional. For practitioner use Belladonna has a reputation. Hospitalisation may be necessary for wash-out.

FURUNCULOSIS – FOLLICULITIS. A furuncle is another name for a boil caused by staphylococcal infection. Folliculitis is bacterial infection of a hair follicle. A carbunkle: a cluster of boils with more than one opening and deeply pus-forming. See: BOILS.

GALACTAGOGUE. A herb to increase flow of breast milk in nursing mothers. Agnus Castus, (*John Parkinson, 1640*) Aniseed, Basil, Caraway, Centuary, Cumin, Fennel, Goat's Rue, Holy Thistle, Nettles, Raspberry, Vervain.

GALACTORRHOEA. Abnormal breast secretion. See: BREAST.

GALANGAL. Colic root. Chinese Ginger. *Alpinia officinarum*, Hance. Dried rhizome.
Keynote: colic.
Constituents: galangol, oil.
Action: carminative, stomachic, stimulant, diaphoretic, anti-neoplastic. "Antifungal against various candida species." (*Planta Medica 1988, 54(2), pp 117-20*)
Uses: flatulent indigestion, chronic nausea and vomiting, seasickness. Ulceration of gums and skin. Benign tumour.
Preparations. Average dose: 1-2g. Thrice daily.
Decoction. Half a teaspoon to each cup water gently simmered 20 minutes. Dose: quarter to half cup morning and evening.
Liquid Extract BHP (1983) 1:1 in 25 per cent alcohol. Dose, 1-2ml.
Tincture BHP (1983) 1:5 in 45 per cent alcohol. Dose, 2-4ml.
Powder (internal use) 1-2 grams. Also as snuff.
GSL

GALBANUM. *Ferula gummosa*, Boiss. Gum-resin. Similar in action to Asafoetida. Rarely used in modern herbalism.
Constituents: volatile oil, gum, resin acids.
Action: antimicrobial against staphylococcus aureus; expectorant, carminative, antispasmodic.
Uses. Chronic infections of mucous surfaces. Lotion for infected wounds. An ingredient of the biblical incense of Exodus 30, 34.
Preparations. *Liquid Extract*: 5-10 drops, thrice daily, in water.
Powder: dose, 1-2g (root).
Ointment for wounds that refuse to heal.

GALEN. 130-200 AD. Greek physician and philosopher. Born in what is now known as Turkey, (129-199 AD). Prolific writer on medical subjects, gathering recorded knowledge up to his time and confirming it on such a foundation of truth that his works were studied up to the 17th century. He gained such a reputation in Rome that he received, but declined, an offer of the post to Physician to the Emperor. He attended Marcus Aurelius and his son, heir to the throne. He was an accurate observer, especially of muscles and bones, and demonstrated that arteries carry blood and not air.

In his diagnosis he laid great stress on the pulse, which is observed today. He believed in 'critical days' when men and women are more accident-prone and gave diminished performance due, he believed, to the moon.

Galenist physicians who followed him did not deviate from his ancient formulae, for better or worse, largely of herbs of the whole plant given in tincture or extract form. Apothecaries and chemists departed from the tradition when they isolated what they believed to be the active principles of the plant – often in a form of extreme concentration and small bulk.

GALL BLADDER, INFLAMMATION. Cholecystitis. Acute or chronic. One of the commonest acute abdominal emergencies. An impressive rise in incidence in the young female population has been linked with the use of oral contraceptives. Other causes: heavy consumption of animal fats, sugars.
Symptoms. Severe upper abdominal pain, often radiating to the shoulder and right midback. Constancy of the pain contrasts with the repeated brief attacks of gall-stone (biliary) colic. Sweating, shallow erratic breathing, tenderness upper right abdomen, distension, flatulence, nausea, intolerance of fatty foods.

In cases of suspected cholecystitis, bitter herbs help liquefy bile and prevent consolidation.
Prevention: Blue Flag, or Wild Yam, 2 tablets at night.
For infection: Echinacea.
Alternatives. BHP (1983) selection: Barberry, Mountain Grape, Balmony, Fringe Tree, Wild Yam, Wahoo, Chiretta, Dandelion, Black root; according to individual case. Milk Thistle.
Teas. Agrimony, Milk Thistle, Fumitory, Black Horehound, Wormwood. 1 heaped teaspoon to each cup boiling water, infuse 15 minutes. Half-1 cup freely.
Cold tea. One teaspoon Barberry bark to each cup cold water. Steep overnight. Half-1 cup freely.
Tablets/capsules. Blue Flag. Echinacea, Wild Yam, Milk Thistle.
Powders. Equal parts: Echinacea, Wild Yam, Milk Thistle. Dose: 500mg (two 00 capsules, or one-third teaspoon) thrice daily.
Tinctures. Equal parts: Wild Yam, Blue Flag, Milk Thistle. 1 teaspoon thrice daily in water.
Topical. Castor oil pack over painful area.
Diet. Low fat. Avoid dairy products.
Supplementation. Vitamins A, B-complex, C. Bromelain, Zinc.
Note. See entry: COURVOISER'S LAW.

GALL-STONES. Any obstruction to the free flow of bile causes stagnation within the gall-bladder. Deposits of bile pigments form (bile sand). Under chemical change, these small masses become encrusted with cholesterol and converted into gall-stones. Common in overweight middle-aged women, "fair, fat and forty". Fifteen per cent of the world's population are affected. Pain may be mistaken for heart disorder.

Stones are of two main types: cholesterol and bile pigment. Cholesterol stones are composed of about 70 per cent cholesterol. Bile pigment stones are brittle and hard and brown or black. Stones cause gall duct obstruction, inflammation of the gall bladder and biliary colic.

Biliary colic can be one of the most excruciatingly painful conditions known.

Symptoms: extreme tenderness in upper right abdomen, dyspepsia, flatulence, vomiting, sweating, thirst, constipation. Prolonged obstruction leads to jaundice. Pain should be evaluated by a competent authority: doctor or hospital. Large stones will require surgery.

Alternatives. Combinations should include a remedy for increasing the flow of bile (cholagogue); to disperse wind (carminative); and for painful spasm.

BHP (1983) – Barberry, Greater Celandine, Balmony, Wahoo, Boldo, Chiretta, Dandelion.

Indicated: Cholagogues, Bitters to meet reduced secretion of bile. To prevent infection – Echinacea. Preventative measure for those with tendency to form stone – 2 Blue Flag root tablets/capsules, or half a teaspoon Glauber salts in morning tea, or 420mg Silymarin (Milk Thistle), daily.

Teas. Boldo, Black Horehound, Horsetail, Parsley Piert, Milk Thistle, Strawberry leaves, Wood Betony. Dr Hooper's case: "An Indian Army officer suffered much from gall-stones and was advised to take Dandelion tea every day. Soon the symptoms left him and he remained free from them for over 20 years." (*John Clarke, MD*)

Decoction. 1oz each: Milk Thistle, Centuary, Dandelion root, in 3 pints water. Bring to boil. Simmer down to 2 pints. Strain. One cup 3 times daily an hour before meals.

Tablets/capsules. Cramp bark (acute spasm). Wild Yam (spasmolytic and bile liquifier).

Powders. Equal parts: Cramp bark, Wahoo, Dandelion. Dose: 750mg (three 00 capsules or half a teaspoon) every 2 hours for acute cases.

Study. Silymarin 420mg daily on patients with a history of gall-stones. Results showed reduced biliary cholesterol concentrations and considerably reduced bile saturation index. (*Nassuato, G. et al, Journal of Hepatology 1991, 12*)

Captain Frank Roberts. Advises Olive oil and Lemon treatment (see below) followed by his prescription: Liquid Extract Fringe Tree 1oz (30ml); Liquid Extract Wahoo 1oz; Liquid Extract Kava-Kava 1oz; Liquid Extract Black root 1oz; Honey 2oz. Dose: teaspoon after meals – minimum 3 meals daily – in wineglass tepid water.

Liquid Extract Barberry: 20-60 drops in water every 2 hours.

Finlay Ellingwood MD. Liquid Extract Fringe Tree bark 10ml; Liquid Extract Greater Celandine 10ml; Tincture Gelsemium 5ml. Dose: 10 drops in water half hourly for acute cases.

Alfred Vogel. Suggests Madder root, Clivers and Knotgrass have solvent properties.

Juices believed to have solvent properties: Celery, Parsley, Beet, Carrot, Radish, Lemon, Watercress, Tomato.

Olive oil and Lemon treatment. Set aside a day for the operation. Take breakfast. No meals for the rest of the day. About 6pm commence by drinking 1 or 2 ounces of the oil. Follow with half-1 cup fresh Lemon juice direct from the fruit in a little warm water. Dilute no more than necessary. Alternate drinks of Olive oil and Lemon juice throughout the evening until one pint or more Olive oil, and juice of 8-9 Lemons been consumed. Drink at intervals of 10 minutes to half an hour. Following 3 days pass stools into a chamber and wash well in search for stones and 'bile sand'.

Practitioner. For spasm on passing stone: Tincture Belladonna: 20 drops in 100ml water: 1 teaspoon hourly.

Compresses: hot wet. Castor oil packs, or hot water packs over painful area.

Enema. Strong Catmint tea – 2 pints.

Diet. Commence with 3 day juice-fast: no solid food. Turmeric used at table as a condiment. Avoid cheese, sugar. Vegetarian diet. Studies show those who eat meat are twice as likely to develop stone. Less saturated fat and more fibre. Vegetable margarine instead of butter. Dandelion coffee or juices in place of caffeine beverages. High vegetable protein; high carbohydrate; high fibre. Oats. Artichokes, honey, molasses, unrefined cereals. Vegetable oil in cooking.

Supplements. Daily. Vitamin C, 2-3g. Vitamin E, 500iu. Choline 1g.

Note. Subjects with a sensitive skin who enjoyed sunbathing are at a raised risk of having gall-stones. (*Journal of Epidemiology and Community Health*)

Gall-stones may form if weight is lost rapidly when on a low calorie diet.

GAMMA LINOLENIC ACID (GLA). A polyunsaturated fatty acid; an essential ingredient in the body's production of prostaglandins. Present naturally in mother's milk. The body produces GLA from linoleic acid present in food as an essential fatty acid (EFA). Vital to growth, cell structure and cardiac health.

Sources: Evening Primrose oil; Sunflower seed oil, Borage and Blackcurrant. Preparations from the fermentation of rotten carrots. Helps lower blood pressure and prevent cholesterol build-up in the blood.

GANGLION (plural: ganglia). Harmless cystic swelling of the sheath of a tendon, chiefly on the wrist. Deposits of calcium may thicken walls and form a focus of pressure causing pain. May also appear on the ankle. Relief comes when the

swelling disperses or bursts.
Treatment. Topical Castor oil packs or Rue lotion are said to be effective. Internal treatment of no value. A ganglion may be dispersed by sudden pressure by the thumbs or by a smart blow with a book.

GANGRENE. Decay or death of tissue from inadequate blood supply. Two kinds, dry and moist: in the dry the flesh withers, in the moist there is putrefaction.
Causes are many: blood-clotting, burns, frostbite, boils, Raynaud's Disease, injuries, ulcerated bed-sores. Diabetics and arteriosclerotics are most at risk, where even minor injuries to fingers or toes may result in necrosis.
Symptoms: wounds swollen and painful with oozing of brown exudate of sickly odour. Fever, low blood pressure, sweating and bronze discoloration around lesion.
To be treated by or in liaison with a general medical practitioner.
Treatment. Hospitalisation. Thuja and Echinacea make a powerful combination for senile or diabetic gangrene. Externally, also, they break down the odour, stimulate tissue to renewed activity and promote healthy granulation. Echinacea strengthens the body's powers of resistance. Treatment may also have to be aimed at releasing spasm of the peripheral blood vessels.
Alternatives. *Tinctures*. (1) Combine, Echinacea 4; Thuja 1. (2) Combine, Echinacea 3; Goldenseal quarter; Myrrh quarter. (3) Combine, Sarsaparilla 2; Wild Indigo 1; Lobelia 1. Dose: 1-2 teaspoons in water every 3 hours. (4) Thuja, (singly): 5 drops in water every 3 hours.
Abundant herb teas to support: Lime flowers, Nettles, Marshmallow root.
Topical. Powdered Myrrh wrapped over affected area for 24 hours. Renew for same period. Repeat as necessary. When condition clears leave undisturbed for few days. OR: Lint soaked with tincture Myrrh applied to affected area; replenish when dry. OR: Aloe Vera pulp or gel. OR: Tea Tree oil, neat. May be diluted many times. (*Dr Paul Belaiche, Paris*) For diabetic gangrene.
Diet. 3-day fruit juice fast, followed by diet as for heart and circulatory disorders.
General. Regulate bowels.

GARLIC. *Allium sativum L. German*: Knoblauch. *French*: Ail. *Italian*: Aglio. *Arabic*: Som. *Indian*: Lashuna. *Chinese*: Swan. *Iranian*: Sir. *Malayan:* Bawang puteh. Bulb. Contains allicin, amino acids; iodine, selenium, sulphur and other minerals. Pliny, of ancient Rome, advised Garlic for more than 60 different health problems. A valued medicament to the civilisations of China, Egypt, Chaldea and Greece.
Constituents: volatile oils, B group vitamins, minerals.
Action: antibiotic, bacteriostatic, anti-parasitic, anti-viral, anti-carcinogen, antispasmodic, antiseptic, fungicide, anti-thrombic, cholagogue, diaphoretic, hypoglycaemia, hypotensor, expectorant, anthelmintic. A wide range of anti-infection activity reported. Hypolipidaemic. Non-sedating antihistamine. Anticoagulant – reduces blood platelet clumping, raises HDL. Lowers total cholesterol after a fatty meal in normal subjects. As a vasodilator tends to reduce blood pressure. Bacteria do not become resistant to it. (*Dr Stephen Fulder*) Detoxifier.
Uses. Prevents build-up of cholesterol in the blood. Lowers a too high blood pressure and raises one too low. Beneficial in thrombosis and arteriosclerosis.
"Helps clear fat accumulating in blood vessels, reducing the tendency to heart disease: also can drastically reduce the level of sugar in the blood, which could help diabetics." (*Lancet i 607, 1979*)
Bronchitis (loosening phlegm), asthma, cough, whooping cough and as a preventative of influenza and colds. Sinusitis; catarrh of the stomach, throat and nose. Catarrhal discharge from the eyes returning every night; catarrhal deafness. Intestinal worms. To stimulate bile for digestion of fats. Mucous colitis, allergies including hay fever, ear infections, paroxysmal sneezing, candida and some other fungus infections, vaginal trichomoniasis.
"Anti-tumour activity reported." (*Y. Kimura and K. Yamamoto, Gann, 55, 325 (1964); Chem. Abstra, 63, 1089d 919650*)
The therapeutically active ingredients of Garlic are the smelly ones. Deodorised Garlic has not the efficacy of the odoriferous. (*Dr Stephen Fulder, JAM Feb. 1986*) Chewed Parsley may mask the odour of Garlic on the breath.
Preparations. *Fresh clove*: eaten at meals.
Fresh juice: half-1 teaspoon in honey or water.
Capsules: one before meals or three at night to prevent infection.
Powder: 300mg capsules; 5-10 capsules twice daily during meals.
Tincture BHP (1983): 1:5 in 45 per cent alcohol. Dose, 2-4ml in water.
Compress: mashed clove or oil on suitable material.
Ear or nasal drops: pierce Garlic capsule and squeeze oil into ear or nose for infection.
Notes. Source of the important trace element, Germanium. Combines well with Echinacea.
GSL

GASTRIC REFLUX. See: REFLUX.

GASTRIC ULCER. See: PEPTIC ULCER.

GASTRITIS. Acute or chronic inflammation of the stomach mucosa.
Causes: acidity, vitamin or mineral deficiencies,

nervous disorders, excess smoking, alcohol, drugs, bad teeth, infected tonsils, stress. May follow acute infective diseases: dysentery, sepsis, typhoid.
Symptoms. Nausea, vomiting, impaired appetite, pain.
Alternatives. BHP (1983) recommends: Calamus, Cinnamon, Fenugreek seeds, Goldenseal, Ground Ivy, Iceland Moss, Carragheen Moss, Liquorice, Marshmallow, Mountain Grape, Rose Hips, Slippery Elm, Sundew, Thyme (garden).
Teas. Fenugreek seeds, 2 teaspoons to each cup of water simmered gently 15 minutes. 1 cup freely. German Chamomile. Meadowsweet.
Traditional – Provence, France. Equal parts, Balm, Fennel, Peppermint. 1 heaped teaspoon to each cup boiling water: 1 cup freely.
Decoction. Combine: equal parts; Marshmallow root, Meadowsweet; 2 teaspoons to each cup of water simmered gently 10 minutes. 1 cup freely. Pinch of Cinnamon improves.
Carragheen Moss. 2 teaspoons to each cup water simmered 20 minutes. Do not strain. Eat from a spoon with honey.
Tablets/capsules. Goldenseal, Calamus, Fenugreek. Iceland Moss. Slippery Elm.
Powders. Combine: Carragheen Moss 2; Goldenseal 1. Dose: 750mg (three 00 capsules or half a teaspoon) thrice daily.
Captain Frank Roberts: equal parts – Tinctures: Agrimony, Oats, Comfrey and Goldenseal. 40 drops in half a cup warm water 3-4 times daily, after meals.
Dr Alfred Vogel recommends: Combination – Centuary, Bitter Orange, Myrrh, Frankincense, Silverweed, Yellow Gentian.
Rudolf F. Weiss MD. Equal parts: Fennel seed, Peppermint leaves and Calamus root. 1 teaspoon to cup boiling water; infuse 10 minutes. Drink warm, in sips, 2-3 times daily.
Aloe Vera juice or gel.
Tinctures. Combine equal parts Goldenseal, Myrrh. 5-10 drops in water before meals thrice daily.
For gastric weakness or old age and to promote acid production: Cider vinegar: 2 teaspoons to glass of water, freely.
Diet. Slippery Elm powder drinks. Papaya fruit.
Supplementation. B-complex, especially B6 and B12. Folic acid, Evening Primrose for linoleic acid. Dessicated liver, brewer's yeast and molasses for iron. Vegetable charcoal biscuits.

GASTROENTERITIS. Disorders of the stomach and intestines. A non-specific term for a number of infections caused by viruses, bacteria and protozoa. May be caused by domestic pets, dogs, birds, poultry, farm animals, milk, drugs, environmental poisons.
Symptoms. Onset sudden, with abdominal pain, nausea, vomiting, wind, malaise, shock, loose stool.
Alternatives. Commence 3-day fast. Agrimony, German Chamomile, Milk Thistle, Ladies Mantle, Marshmallow root, Slippery Elm.
Tea. Combine, equal parts: Agrimony, Gotu Kola, Meadowsweet. 1 teaspoon to each cup boiling water; infuse 10-15 minutes. Half-1 cup thrice daily, or more frequently as tolerated.
Decoction. Fenugreek seeds. 2 teaspoons to each cup water gently simmered 15 minutes. 1 cup freely.
Formula. German Chamomile 2; Marshmallow root 1; Goldenseal half; Liquorice quarter. Dose: Powders – 750mg (three 00 capsules or half a teaspoon). Liquid Extracts: 1-2 teaspoons. Tinctures: 1-3 teaspoons. Thrice daily.
Aloe Vera, gel or juice. (*Linus Pauling Institute of Science and Medicine*)
Enemata. 15 drops Tincture Myrrh in 2 pints (1 litre) warm water.
Diet. Commence 3-day fast. Slippery Elm gruel. Bilberries.

GASTRO-OESOPHAGEAL REFLUX DISEASE. See: REFLUX.

GELSEMIUM. Yellow Jasmine. *Gelsemium sempervirens L. German*: Gelber Jasmine. *French*: Gelsémie luisante. *Spanish*: Gelsomina. *Italian*: Gelsomino della Carolina. *Chinese*: Hu-wan-ch'iang. Dried root and rhizome.
Constituents: alkaloids, coumarins, tannins, iridoids.
Action: powerful relaxant to the central nervous system, vasodilator, analgesic; to calm down physical violence in hysteria and reduce a dangerously high pulse rate. Antispasmodic, hypotensive (transient). Tranquilliser. Combines well with Hawthorn for cardiac arrhythmias. No evidence of dependence in clinical use.
Uses. Pressive nervous headache (constrictive migraine). Facial neuralgia, cramp, intermittent claudication, pain in womb and ovaries, temporal arteritis. Pain in tail bone at base of the spine (coccydynia). Spasm of the osteopathic lesion. Great restlessness, convulsions, contracted pupils and circulatory excitement.

Avoid in heart disease and low blood pressure.
Practitioner use. Tincture Gelsemium, 2-5 drops, 2-3 times daily. Pharmacy only sales.

A weaker tincture may frequently be used with good effect: 5 drops to 100ml water – 1 teaspoon hourly. (*Dr Finlay Ellingwood*)

GENITO-URINARY. Pertaining to the organs of fluid excretion or reproduction. Genito-Urinary astringent – Horsetail. Genito-Urinary tonics – Beth root, Saw Palmetto, Damiana. Genito-Urinary relaxant – Black Willow.

GENTIAN. *Gentiana lutea L. German*: Gelberenzian. *French*: Gentiane jaune. *Italian*: Genziana gialla. *Arabian*: Jintiyania. *Indian*: Pakhanbhed. *Iranian*: Gintiyana. Dried rhizomes and roots.
Constituents: Xanthones, iridoids, alkaloids, phenolic acids, pectin, gum, no tannin.
Action: well-known traditional European bitter (all bitters are liver and pancreatic stimulants). Haemopoietic action speeds production of red blood cells. (Should not be given for overproduction of red blood cells as in polycythaemia.) Emmenagogue, sialagogue, antispasmodic, anti-inflammatory, anthelmintic. King of tonics. Digestant, increases gastric juices by 25 per cent, without altering pH. Appetite stimulant.
Uses. Alkalosis, feeble digestion in the elderly from gastric acid deficiency. Thin people anxious to put on weight. Jaundice – promotes flow of bile. Nausea, vomiting, travel sickness (with or without Ginger), bitter taste in mouth, diarrhoea with yellow stool, malaria (as a substitute for Quinine), post-influenzal or ME depression and lack of appetite, severe physical exhaustion (Ginseng). To antidote some types food-poisoning (salmonella, shigella, etc).
Preparations. Thrice daily. Average dose half-2g. Before meals.
Decoction: half-1 teaspoon to cup *cold* water; steep overnight. Dose: half a cup.
Tincture: 1 part powdered root to 5 parts Vodka; macerate 8 days. Dose: 1-2 teaspoons.
Tablets: formula. Skullcap 45mg; Hops 45mg; Asafoetida 30mg, and the aqueous extractive from 120mg Gentian and 90mg Valerian. Two tablets thrice daily for nervous exhaustion and stress disorders.
Anorexia nervosa, specific combination: equal parts – Gentian and Valerian roots. One heaped teaspoon to each cup cold water; steep overnight. Dose – half a cup the following day, morning and evening.
Contra-indications: pregnancy, hyperacidity. Gastric ulcer.
Note. An ingredient of anti-smoking preparations. Well-known in Chinese medicine. GSL

GERARD, JOHN. 1545-1611. Elizabethan physician. Born at Nantwich, Cheshire. Writer of the famous herbal: *"Anatomie of Plants"* (1597) in which is revealed considerable scientific insight into the medicinal character of plants. Herbalist to James I. Shakespeare must have visited his garden in Holborn, subsidised by the King. Also a surgeon, becoming a Master of Chirurgy. He was one of the first to discover the 'companionship of plants', referring to the affinities and antipathies in the plant kingdom.

First to grow potatoes in England. His garden at Holborn, London, and now Fetter Lane, was then a village.

GERARD HOUSE. Founded by Thomas Bartram, 1958, with formulae used with success in his busy practice as Consulting Medical Herbalist, Bournemouth, England. Objects: to spread knowledge of herbal medicine and to provide a reliable service of safe alternatives to drugs. Foundation named after John Gerard in the belief that the science of the herbalist makes an important contribution towards national health.

GERMAN MEASLES. Rubella. An infectious virus disease spread by droplet transmission. Incubation: between 2-3 weeks. A notifiable disease.
Symptoms. Mild fever, temperature rising to 101°F (38°C), headache, drowsiness, runny nose, sore throat, swelling of glands side of neck and behind ears; itchy rash of small pink spots spreads from face downwards to whole of the body, lasting 3 days.
Complication: inflammation of the brain (rare).

If patient is pregnant professional care is necessary as congenital defects, stillbirth or abortion may follow in early pregnancy. There is evidence of a link between the virus and juvenile joint disease and arthritis later in life.
Treatment. Bedrest. Plenty of fluids (herb teas, fruit juices). Should not be suppressed by drugs.
Alternatives:– *Teas*. Any one. Balm, Chamomile flowers, Elderflowers and Peppermint, Hyssop, Wild Thyme, Marigold. Sage, Peppermint. Combination: equal parts, Marigold flowers, Elderflowers, Yarrow. Prepare: 2 teaspoons to each cup boiling water; infuse 15 minutes. Half-1 cup freely.
Tablets/capsules. Echinacea.
Tinctures. Echinacea: 5-30 drops in water every 2 hours. OR: Combine, equal parts Echinacea and Wild Indigo with few drops Tincture Capsicum; 5-30 drops every 2 hours.
Absence of urine: add 1 part Pleurisy root.
For swollen glands: add 1 part Clivers.
For nervousness: add 1 part Skullcap.
For sore throat: Cinnamon.
Diet. Commence 3-day fast with no solid food. Abundant Vitamin C drinks, fruit juices, etc.

To be treated by or in liaison with a qualified medical practitioner.

GERMANDER. *Teucrium chamaedrys L.* Herb, in flower.
Constituents: iridoid glycosides, tannins, volatile oil.
Action: anti-diarrhoea, anti-inflammatory, anti-rheumatism, antimicrobial, antiseptic (mild), stomach bitter, diaphoretic, brain tonic, antispasmodic. Has been associated with cases of liver disease and is not now used internally.
Uses. Summer diarrhoea in children, irritable bowel, acute dyspepsia, lack of appetite, chronic bronchitis, skin disorders, pyorrhoea and inflam-

mation of the gums (tea used as a mouth wash). To induce weight loss in slimming diets. Travel sickness, cellulitis, flatulence. Gout.
Preparations. Average dose: 2-4g. Thrice daily.
Tea. 1 teaspoon to each cup boiling water; infuse 15 minutes. Dose half a cup.
Liquid extract. Half-1 teaspoon in water.
Powder, capsules: 250mg. Dose: 2 capsules between meals.
Note. Given to facilitate weight loss it has been known to be hepatotoxic. Of historic interest only.

GERMANIUM. Rare white metal. Symbol: Ge. Atomic No 32. Plays an important role in all biochemical life. Found in traces in soil and Lourdes water. Present in certain foods and helps eliminate toxic metals from the body. Neutralises free radicals. Restores the body's pH balance disturbed by highly 'acid' foods: meat, dairy products, refined foods and alcohol. Immune enhancer, mild analgesic and energy modulator.

The metal is claimed to have a beneficial effect on asthma, high blood pressure, Raynaud's disease, heart and circulatory disorders. Believed to be a challenge to cancer cells and metastasis.
Source plants: Aloe Vera, Comfrey (*Symphytum pereginum*), Chlorella, Bandai udo (*Aralia cordata*) and Bandai Moss; Pearl Barley.

Ginseng becomes defenceless against viruses and bacteria where there exists a deficiency of Germanium in the soil. (*Dr Kazuhike Asai, Tokyo, Japan*)

Garlic is rich in this trace element. (*Dr Uta Sandra Goodman*)

GERSON CANCER THERAPY is described in *A Cancer Therapy; Results of Fifty Cases*, Gerson, Max; 3rd edition, 1977, Pub: The Gerson Institute Bonita, CA 92002, USA.

Basically, the therapy consists of a vegetarian diet with meals of vegetables, fruits and whole grains, fresh or freshly prepared. Drinking water is replaced by hourly, fresh, raw juices of vegetables and fruits. Refined, altered, denatured or enhanced foodstuffs are forbidden. The diet is sodium, chloride, fat and protein restricted. Supplemental potassium, iodine, thyroid and crude liver extract comprise the medical armamentarium. A repeatable choleretic, enemas of a solution of boiled coffee, is administered to lower serum toxin levels. Coffee is a potent enhancer of the carcinogen detoxifying enzyme system, glutathione S-translerase (*Wattenburg*). The Gerson cancer therapy reduces accumulated tissue sodium and chloride, promoting diuresis. *Gerson Therapy Center: Hospital de Baja California, at La Gloria, Mexico*
Diet. Lunch and dinner contain ample cooked food, mainly to act as a 'blotter' to the daily intake of 5.25 pints fresh raw fruit juices that are the backbone of the therapy. Ingredients of the juices include 4lbs raw organic carrots a day, with no harm to the liver. (*JAM, May 1991, p5. Beata Bishop on her recovery from metastasised malignant melanoma*)

The Gerson therapy is based on the 'holistic' philosophy which states that cancer represents a clinical manifestation of an underlying toxic condition. Such condition should receive primary treatment that is lifestyle orientated. The theme is: detoxification through internal cleansing. The diet and supplements are re-inforced by 'positive thinking' and supported by meditation and emotional balance.

GIANT CELL ARTERITIS. See: ARTERITIS.

GIARDIASIS. A disease of the duodenum and small intestine caused by the protozoan, *Giardia lamblia*. Acquired from contaminated drinking water. Common in children. Sometimes associated with ME (chronic fatigue syndrome).
Symptoms. Explosive diarrhoea, flatulence, abdominal pain, pale fatty stools.
Treatment. Cup Fenugreek tea into which has been added 5-10 drops Tincture Goldenseal. 1 cup thrice daily.

GIDDINESS. See: VERTIGO.

GIGANTISM. Abnormal height resulting from excessive growth hormone secretion by the pituitary gland in the adolescent. See: PITUITARY GLAND.

GINGER. Jamaican Ginger. *Zingiber officinale*, Roscoe. *German*: Ingwer. *French*: Gingembre. *Spanish*: Gengibre. *Italian*: Zenzero. *Arabian*: Zengabil. *Indian*: Alenadu. *Malayan*: Alia. *Chinese*: Kan-kiang. *Iranian*: Zinjabile. Dried rhizome. *Keynote*: diffusive stimulant.
Constituents: phenolic compounds, gingerols, mucilage, volatile oil.
Action: anti-inflammatory, carminative, antispasmodic, expectorant, vasodilator, anti-cholesterol. Circulatory stimulant not as sharp as Cayenne. Anti-emetic. Diaphoretic. Traditional ingredient in prescriptions to ensure absorption through the stomach to all parts of the body.
Uses. Travel sickness, flatulent colic, irritable bowel and diarrhoea where no inflammation exists; colds and influenza – to promote perspiration and thus reduce body temperature. Cold hands and feet, hypothermia: a pinch of the powder in a beverage sends blood to the surface. Uncomplicated stomach and intestinal problems; appetite loss; hiccups; to promote secretion of gastric juices in the elderly and in achlorhydria. Brain fatigue (with Kola nuts, equal parts). Atherosclerosis and coronary artery disease (diet). Suppressed menstruation from cold. Improves sex life. Loss of appetite. Jet lag,

general weakness. Nausea and vomiting. Morning sickness of pregnancy. Sickness of chemotherapy and after surgical operation. Traditionally eaten with raw fish which effectively destroys *anisakis larvae* and some other parasites.

Preparations. *Tea*. Quarter to half a teaspoon to each cup of boiling water or domestic tea, freely.

Tablets/capsules. Powdered Ginger, quarter to 1g thrice daily.

Weak tincture BP (1973) Dose: one and a half to 3ml.

Strong tincture: 3 to 10 drops in water.

Liniments, for external use.

Contra-indicated in kidney disease. Best taken with food. GSL

GINGIVITIS. Inflammation of the gums. Chiefly caused by build-up of plaque or bacterial invasion from the teeth.

Etiology. Poor dental hygiene, diabetes, pregnancy, leukaemia, Vitamin C deficiency, drugs, debilitating diseases. The condition has spread rapidly due to oral sex. Untreated, teeth may loosen and fall out.

Symptoms. Bleeding gums, pain, swelling, possible ulceration (Trench mouth). Breath reminiscent of stale cabbage.

Alternatives. Formula. Equal parts tinctures Goldenseal and Myrrh: dose – 5-10 drops in water thrice daily.

Tablets/Capsules. Echinacea – dosage as on bottle; plus Blue Flag root on retiring.

Old Dorset, combination of herbs. Equal parts: Marjoram, Chamomile, Garden Sage. Mix. 1 heaped teaspoon to each cup boiling water. Infuse 15 minutes in a covered vessel. Dose – half-1 cup freely. Used also as a mouth wash.

Topical. Mouth washes: Avens, Bayberry, Black Catechu, Echinacea, Goldenseal, Ladies Mantle, Myrrh, Poke root, Rhatany root, Sage, Silverweed, Tormentil, Wild Indigo.

Tea Tree oil, mouth wash. 1 drop to each cup of warm water. May be diluted many times yet still be effective.

Bilberry tea. Special reference to this condition. Good results reported.

Aloe Vera. Brush gums with fresh juice, or gel, to firm-up loose teeth.

Diet. Avoid sugar, refined foods, dairy products and hot spicy foods. Low-salt.

Supplements. Daily. Vitamin C 1-2g, Vitamin Q10 60mg, Vitamin E 200iu, Selenium 50mcg, Zinc 15mg.

GINKGO. Maidenhair tree. *Ginkgo biloba*. Sole survivor of its own genus. Seeds, leaves. *Keynotes*: brain and lungs.

Constituents: terpenes, tannins, lignans, flavonoids, and gingkolide B which is a platelet activating factor (PAF).

Action: nutritive, tuberculostatic. A compound (BN 52021) from the tree antagonises bronchospasm and tends to resolve breathing difficulties. Circulatory stimulant. Increases brain blood flow, Peripheral vasodilator, Energy enhancer. (*JAM, Vol 6, No 2*)

Uses. Respiratory complaints, especially asthma. Inhibits platelet clumping: of value in coronary artery disease. Tinnitus. Intermittent claudication. Raynaud's disease. Thrombosis. Cold hands and feet. Spontaneous bruising. Early stages of Alzheimer's disease. Cerebral insufficiency in old age. Varicose veins. Some antitumor activity against sarcoma in mice recorded. Piles. Temporal arteritis. Cramp in the calves – walking-distance increased. Tired brain, impaired memory. Coronary artery disease. Hearing loss, depression, vertigo, headache. To increase resistance to adverse environmental factors. Chronic fatigue syndrome (ME). Subclinical neurosis. Headache. Depression. Impaired mental ability. Hangover.

Preparations. Thrice daily. Large doses may be required.

Tea (leaves). 1 heaped teaspoon to each cup of water gently simmered 5 minutes. Dose: half-1 cup.

Tablets/capsules. 250mg. Maintenance dose: one tablet or capsule increasing to two in acute cases.

Chinese Medicine. "Seeds moisten the lungs, stop coughing, and strengthen the body."

"I have seen a reduction in severity and frequency of asthma attacks and a marked reduction in use of brocho-dilating drugs by the use of Ginkgo." (*Brown D., Phytotherapy Review and Commentary, Townsend Letter to Doctors, October 1990 pp648-9*)

German medicine. No drug interactions and very low levels of side-effects. Important remedy to the German Health Service at a cost of 286 million DM in 1989. (*Kleijnen J. & Knipschild P. The Lancet 1992, 340, Nov 7*)

GSL

GINSENG. American. Five-fingers. *Panax quinquefolium L.* Dried root. *Keynote*: stress with stomach symptoms.

Action: adaptogen, digestive relaxant, hypoglycaemic, aphrodisiac, old-age re-vitaliser.

Uses. Irritable or nervous stomach caused by pressure of work and other stresses. Lack of appetite. Low blood pressure. Sustains nerves and immune system in physical exhaustion and infection.

Preparations. Average dose: half-4 grams dried root. Thrice daily.

Powder: made palatable in honey. GSL

GINSENG. King plant. *Panax schinseng*, Nees. *Panax ginseng*. *German*: Gensang. *French*: Panax. *Italian*: Ginseng. *Chinese*: Huang shen. C.A. Meyer. Roots. More suited to men than

women. Used as a medicine in the Far East for over 4,000 years. Source of natural steroids (oestrogens), raising natural immunity. All Ginsengs enhance the natural resistance and recuperative power of the body. Produces opposite effects; i.e. it is both sedative and stimulant; in some it raises, in others it lowers blood pressure. Raises some cholesterol factors while reducing the overall amount in the blood. Hypoglycaemic. Aphrodisiac. Heart tonic. Old age re-vitaliser. Adaptogen. Used by the People's Republic of China for a wide range of disorders. Source of the element Germanium.
Constituents: gum, resin, starch, saponin glycosides, volatile oil.
Uses. Physical weakness, neurasthenia, recovery after surgery. Promotes physical and intellectual efficiency. A mood-raiser. Induces a feeling of well being and stability. Depression, sexual debility, sleeplessness. The sportsman's remedy, improving running ability and endurance. Retards build-up of lactic acid which normally occurs during hard exercise and causes fatigue. Increases resistance to excess cold or heat exposure and to a working environment with a noisy background. Lessens side-effects of insulin in diabetes. To help the body adapt to a changed environment (jet lag). Enhances mental performance in students. Promotes biosynthesis of DNA and RNA.
Preparations. Miscellaneous products available. Single morning dose.
Decoction. Half-1 teaspoon to each cup water gently simmered 10 minutes, or added to a cup of domestic tea.
Powder. Half-1g daily.
Contra-indications: hyperactivity in children, pregnancy, high blood pressure, menopause. Not taken continuously but for periods from 1 week to 1 month. Should not be taken with coffee. GSL

GINSENG. Siberian. *Eleutherococcus senticosus*, Maxim. *Part used*: root. Believed to be stronger and more stimulating than Panax Ginseng.
Action. Anti-stress, antiviral, adaptogen, aphrodisiac, vasodilator, hypoglycaemic, tonic, adrenal hormone stimulant, anti-toxic activity in chemotherapy. Beneficial for boosting the body's natural defence system, to resist viruses, free-radical toxins and even radiation. Increases immune resistance.
Uses. Conditions related to stress. Improves capacity for mental and physical exertion, to re-vitalise a run-down constitution, shingles, myalgic encephalomyelitis (ME), atherosclerosis in heart and arterial conditions, increases cerebral circulation in the elderly, non-caffeine invigorator, depression from overwork, jet-lag, children – classroom stress, recovery from surgical operation, radiation injury, immune stimulant in cancer therapy. To increase fertility. Enables patient to tolerate higher doses of radiation. Counters nuclear reactor leakage. Inhibits HIV-1 replication in cells acutely or chronically infected.
Preparations. Miscellaneous products available.
Tea. Quarter of a teaspoon powdered root to each cup boiling water. OR: dissolve 1-2 capsules in cup of boiling water, once daily.
Tablets/capsules. 150mg, one thrice daily.
General uses and contra-indications: see GINSENG (PANAX). GSL

GIPSYWORT. *Lycopus europaeus*. The European equivalent of the American plant *Lycopus virginicus* (Bugleweed). See: BUGLEWEED.

GLADLAX TABLETS. Active Constituents: Aloes (Cape) BP 50.00mg. Pulverised Fennel (BHMA Master File 006/2) BHP (1983) 15.00mg. Pulverised Valerian BP 30.00mg. Pulverised Holy Thistle BHP (1983) (BHMA Master File 51/1) 60.00mg. A traditional herbal remedy for the relief of occasional or non-persistent constipation. Not for pregnancy or nursing mothers. (*Gerard House*)

GLAND BALANCER. There are times when the endocrine orchestra fails to strike its normal note; when energies of life flow slowly and body tone is low. Such is when stimulation of the thyroid, pancreas, and adrenals by natural precursors of their hormones is helpful. The following has a hormone-effect and proves useful for general weakness, change of life, persistent fatigue, sterility, puberty and adolescence, frigidity, metabolic disorders:
Formula. Ginseng 2; Liquorice 1; Sarsaparilla 1; Ginger half; Kelp half. Dose – powders: half a teaspoon; tinctures 1-3 teaspoons; liquid extracts: 1-2 teaspoons; in water or honey thrice daily.

GLANDULAR FEVER. Mononucleosis. An *infectious* viral disease caused by a herpes virus (Epstein Barr). Spread by saliva, nasal secretion as in kissing. Most commonly young adults, 15-25. Incubation 10-15 days.
Symptoms. Mild fever, sore throat, headache, tiredness, malaise, swelling of glands under arm and in neck. These progress to high fever with painful lymph nodes. Puffiness of upper eyelids.
Treatment. Bedrest, when febrile.
Alternatives:– Echinacea, Eucalyptus, Garlic, Mountain Grape, Myrrh, Poke root, Wild Indigo, Wormwood, Elecampane, Blue Flag root.
Tea. Yarrow or Elder – early stages of fever in children.
Decoction: Formula. Equal parts, Echinacea, Blue Flag root. Half an ounce to 1 pint water gently simmered 20 minutes. Half-1 cup every 3 hours, with pinch of Cayenne. Children: 5-

12 years three-quarters dose.
Formula. Echinacea 2; Blue Flag 1; Goldenseal half; pinch Cayenne. Dose: Powders: 500mg (two 00 capsules or one-third teaspoon). Liquid Extracts: 1 teaspoon. Tinctures: 1-2 teaspoons. Thrice daily. Children 5-12 years – as many drops as years of age.
Convalescence. Give a general tonic. See: TONICS.
Garlic. 2 capsules at night.
Diet. Commence with 3-day fast with herb teas (Marigold petals, Red Clover or Yarrow) and fruit juices, followed by vegetarian, salt-free diet. Vitamin C, 1g morning and evening. Vitamin B-complex.
Supplements. Daily. B-complex. Vitamin C 3g.
To be treated by or in liaison with a qualified medical practitioner.

GLANDS – SWOLLEN. Lymphadenitis. *Non-infectious*. Can be localised, e.g. armpit only, due to lymphatic drainage of a local inflammation or generalised due to systemic infection (AIDS) or some malignant conditions.
Symptoms. Swelling of glands of armpit, neck and groin.
Alternatives. *Tea*: combine equal parts: Clivers, Red Clover, Gotu Kola. 2 teaspoons to each cup boiling water; infuse 15 minutes. Dose: half-1 cup thrice daily.
Decoction. Formula. Equal parts, Yellow Dock, Plantain, Clivers, Liquorice root. 1oz to 1 pint water gently simmered 20 minutes. Half a cup thrice daily.
Powders. Formula. Bayberry 1; Echinacea 2; Poke root half; a trace of Cayenne. Dose: 500mg (two 00 capsules or one-third teaspoon) thrice daily.
Tinctures. Combine equal parts: Poke root and Echinacea. One 5ml teaspoon in water thrice daily.
Poke root. A leading remedy for the condition.
Agnus Castus. Swollen glands in young girls.
Dr Finlay Ellingwood: Liquid Extracts: equal parts, Blue Flag root and Poke root. 30-60 drops in water thrice daily.
Diet. See: DIET – GENERAL. See: LYMPHATICS.

GLAUBER SALTS. One pinch Glauber salts in an early morning cup of tea, every day, was once taken as a preventative for gout.

GLAUCOMA. Expressionless eye with pin-point pupil (pupil constriction). The iris is compressed against the cornea thus arresting fluid circulation and raising intra-ocular pressure. Medical emergency. Two kinds: acute (closed angle) and chronic.
Acute. Eye is brick red and brick hard. Agonisingly painful, vision much reduced, pupil dilated and oval, the cornea steamy and the iris greenish, sees rainbow rings around lights, misty vision, pain in head and eyes, colours appear dull, can read for only short periods, unable to walk confidently downstairs, damage to retina and optic nerve from build-up of fluid.
Etiology: Damage from past inflammations, high blood pressure, steroids, stress, diet deficiencies, injury. Develops more in far-sighted people.
Ocular emergency requiring immediate hospital specialist treatment. If admission to hospital is delayed Pilocarpine may save the day: 1 drop of 1 per cent solution to each eye to constrict the pupil and open the drainage angle. This lasts 4-5 hours. Apply 1 drop 4 times every 24 hours. In the absence of Pilocarpine, a practitioner may prescribe Tincture Gelsemium BPC 1963, 5 drops in water not more than thrice daily.
A history of eyelids that are stuck down in the mornings reveals blockage from inflammatory exudate, tension rises and may precipitate glaucoma.
Chronic (gradual and long-continued). Usually in the elderly. Sometimes genetic. Chronic rise in painless intra-ocular pressure arrests blood supply to the optic discs thus disrupting bundles of retinal nerve fibres. 'Deeply cupped discs'. Condition usually unsuspected. A sight destroyer.
Symptoms: bumping into objects and people. As above.
Treatment. Surgical drainage incision through the iris relieves tension. The object is to contract the pupil and focussing (ciliary) muscle which promotes the escape of watery fluid from the eye. Agents which contract the pupil are Pilocarpine, Adrenalin. Promotion of the body's own supply of Adrenalin is mildly assisted by Ginseng. All cases should receive Echinacea to enhance resistance. Herbal medicine often stabilises the condition, with remedies such as Pulsatilla.
Alternatives:– *Maintenance anti-inflammatory*. *Tea*: fresh or dried herbs. Equal parts: Nettles, Marigold petals, Horsetail. Mix. 2 teaspoons to each cup boiling water; infuse 15 minutes. Dose: half-1 cup thrice daily.
Traditional. It was common practice in the South of France to douche the eye with dilute lemon juice, doubtless because Vitamin C has an osmotic effect, drawing away fluid.
Rutin (Buckwheat). 20mg thrice daily. Tablets, powder, etc.
Canasol. A non-hallucinogenic alkaloid of the marijuana plant (cannabis) has been used with success.
Blood Tonics. See entry. Healthy blood contributes to healthy eyes and common blood tonics have been responsible for some cures in the early stages.
Bilberries. Mr Eric Wright suffered from glaucoma for many years. At 74 he was nearly blind, walked with a white stick, and couldn't read or

write. Improvement was impressive after taking Bilberry extract. His specialist agreed that his sight was at its best in three years since surgery to reduce intra-ocular pressure.
Diet. Begin 3-day fast, followed by 3 days on fruit and vegetable juices. Wholefoods thereafter. Increase protein intake. Repeat fast every 3 months. Fresh Bilberries as desired. Dr Rolf Ulrich links coffee with glaucoma. (*Clinical Physiology*)
Supplements. Daily. Vitamin A 7500iu, Vitamin B1 15mg, Vitamin B2 10mg, Vitamin B6 10mg, Vitamin C 3g, Vitamin E 500mg, Zinc.
Notes. Stress automatically raises intra-ocular pressure for which relaxation techniques are indicated. Tobacco worsens by causing constriction of blood vessels supplying the optic nerve. Abstain alcohol. Glaucoma becomes more prevalent in an ageing population. Patients with a strong history and with high blood pressure and diabetes should be screened.

To be treated by a general medical practitioner or hospital specialist.

GLENTONA HERBAL BLOOD PURIFIER. Popular blood tonic of the 1930s, 1940s and 1950s. Ingredients: Liquid Extract Liquorice 5 per cent, Infusion Gentian Co Conc 10 per cent, Infusion Senna Conc 5 per cent. And 25 per cent alcoholic extractive from Burdock 5 per cent, Red Clover 5 per cent, Queen's root 2.5 per cent, Yellow Dock root 1.25 per cent, Poke root 2.5 per cent, Sarsaparilla 2.5 per cent. (*Carter Bros*)

GLOBUS HYSTERICUS. Sensation of a 'lump in the throat' causing a choking under stress of emotion. Related to hysteria with spasm of the pharynx.
Indicated: German Chamomile, St John's Wort, Balm, Valerian or Lobelia. In the form of tincture, tea, liquid extract or tablets.

GLOSSITIS. Inflammation of the tongue, with burning sensation. Geographical tongue. Often associated with inflammation of the mouth (stomatitis) and gums (gingivitis). Tongue may be ulcerated, with difficulty in swallowing.
Etiology: mouth breathing, dental faults, hot spicy foods, alcohol, smoking, anaemia, drug induced, septic teeth.
Symptoms: pain and swelling.

Chronic gastritis may reflect in a persistent form requiring treatment specific to the stomach. The underlying condition should be treated.
Alternatives. Change of lifestyle, food habits, etc.
Teas. Sage, Tormentilla, Balm of Gilead, Bedstraw. Drink freely and use as a mouth wash.
Decoction. 2 teaspoons Fenugreek seeds to each cup water gently simmered 15 minutes. 1 cup freely and as mouth wash.
Juices, gels: Aloe Vera, Houseleek. Houseleek has a mild anaesthetic effect and has been used for schirrhus induration.
Tinctures. Combine Sarsaparilla 4; Goldenseal 1. One to two 5ml teaspoons in water 3-4 times daily.
Mouth Wash. 5-10 drops Tincture Myrrh in glass water; freely.
Diet. Slippery Elm drinks. Dandelion coffee.
Vitamins. B-complex. A. C.
Minerals. Zinc.

GLOTTIS – SPASM OF. May be caused by a reflux from the stomach. Cramp bark.
Formula. Liquid Extracts: Goldenseal 1 drachm, Gelsemium 1 drachm, Stone root 2 drachms, Burdock 4 drachms. Water to 4oz. Dose: 1 teaspoon after meals, thrice daily. (*W.W. Fraser, MD*). Practitioner use.

GLUE EAR. See: OTITIS MEDIA.

GLUTEN-SENSITIVE DISEASE. Adult coeliac disease, coeliac sprue, non-tropical sprue, idiopathic steatorrhoea. Allergy to gluten which disturbs the small intestine by preventing the body from absorbing food nutrients. A child's condition may worsen when put on solid cereals containing wheat, barley, rye or oats. "Allergic to pasta" disease. A change in the mucous membrane of the intestines with enzyme deficiency.
Symptoms: diarrhoea, abdominal swelling and pain, irritability, inability to gain weight, neuritis, ulcers on tongue and mouth, low blood pressure, debility, lactase-deficiency. Breast-feeding stops coeliac disease.
Alternatives. *Tea*. Mix, equal parts: Raspberry leaves, Agrimony, Lemon Balm. 2 teaspoons to each cup boiling water; infuse 15 minutes. 1 cup freely.
Tablets/capsules. Goldenseal, Slippery Elm. Calamus. Fenugreek seeds, Papaya. Wild Yam.
Powders, Liquid Extracts, Tinctures. Formula. Equal parts: Sarsaparilla, Wild Yam, Stone root. Dose. Powders: 500mg (two 00 capsules or one-third teaspoon). Liquid Extracts: 30-60 drops. Tinctures: 1-2 teaspoons. In water, banana mash or honey, thrice daily.
Papaya (papain) digests wheat gluten and assists recovery. Half-1g with meals.
Aloe Vera juice. Promotes improved bowel motility, increases stool specific gravity, and reduces indication of protein putrefaction, flatulence and bloating after meals. (*J. Bland PhD. JAM June 1985, p.11*)
Topical. Warm hip baths of Lemon Balm, Chamomile, etc. (*Alfred Vogel*)
Diet. Gluten-free. Rice. Unpasteurised yoghurt. Buttermilk. Sweet acidophilus milk. Raw carrot juice. Bananas mashed with a little Slippery Elm or dried milk powder, carob bean powder and Soya milk.

Supplementation. Vitamins A, B-complex, B6, B12, Folic acid, C, D, E, K (Alfalfa tea). Calcium, Iron and Magnesium orotates.

GLYCOSIDES. Including cardiac glycosides. Discovered by Dr Withering (1785) who was the first physician to prescribe Foxglove for heart disorders. Glycosides are water-soluble constituents of a plant which when heated with dilute acid, or in the presence of an enzyme are resolved into two or more substances, one of which is sugar. Thus, the root of Horseradish contains the glycoside sinigrin which is decomposed in the presence of water by the ferment myrosin. Cardiac glycosides occur in Lily of the Valley (used as an alternative to Foxglove), Bitter root and Strophanthus. An important group of glycosides (flavonoid glycosides) are found in the labiatae family – a family well-represented among medicinal plants.

GOAT DISEASE. The disease (caseous lymphadenitis) attacks the lymphatic system and may spread to sheep and humans. Breaks out sporadically in goats imported from abroad. Those in close contact with infected animals are at risk.
Symptoms: loss of weight, wasting illness, skin abscesses.
Treatment. *Tea*: Aniseed 1; Senna leaf 1; Nettles 2. 2 teaspoons to each cup boiling water; infuse 10-15 minutes in covered vessel. 1 cup thrice daily. Add to each dose: 30 drops Tincture Echinacea.

GOAT'S RUE. French Lilac. *Galega officinalis L.* Dried leaves and stems.
Constituents: flavonoids, saponins, galegine.
Action: anti-diabetic, hypoglycaemic, diuretic, diaphoretic, galactagogue.
Uses. Diabetes mellitis; to reduce sugar in the urine. Insulin must be continued until improvement is clinically confirmed. Increases secretion of milk in women and animals. For women anxious to increase size of the breast (daily tea). Combines well with Agnus Castus for the latter.
Combines well with Fenugreek seeds for increase in milk and breast development.
Preparations. Thrice daily.
Tea. 1 teaspoon to each cup boiling water; infuse 15 minutes. Half-1 cup.
Liquid extract BHP (1983) 1:1 in 25 per cent alcohol. Dose, 15-30 drops (1-2ml).
Tincture BHP (1983) 1 part to 10 parts 45 per cent alcohol: dose, 30-60 drops (2-4ml).
Note. An alternative to rennet in cheese-making.

GOITRE. See: THYROID GLAND.

GOLDEN FIRE. Salve for rheumatic joints, stiff muscles, lumbago, backache and to prepare the spine or skeleton for manipulation as in osteopathy.
Ingredients: Cayenne pods 2oz (or Tincture Capsicum 60 drops); Camphor flowers quarter of an ounce; Peppermint oil 20 drops; Cajuput oil 50 drops; Eucalyptus oil 20 drops; Beeswax 2oz. Sunflower seed oil 16oz.
Method: Gently heat Sunflower seed oil. If Cayenne pods are used: add pods, steep for one and a half hours. Stir. Strain. Over gentle heat add wax stirring gently until dissolved. Add other ingredients (including Tincture Capsicum if used), stirring well. Pour into jars while fluid.

GOLDENROD. *Solidago virgaurea L. German*: Goldrute. *French*: Verge d'or. *Italian*: Verge d'oro. Dried or fresh leaves and flowers.
Constituents: phenolic glycosides, saponins, rutin.
Action: anticatarrhal, anti-inflammatory, antiseptic to mucous membranes, diuretic, diaphoretic.
Uses. Weak stomach, nausea, vomiting, hiccups, persistent catarrh of nose and throat. Thrush and sore throat (gargle). Irritable bowel in children. Bronchitis, with purulent phlegm. Blood in the urine. Tonsilitis, with pus. Reduces mass in kidney stone and gravel (anecdotal). Prostatis. Kidney and bladder conditions where urine is dark, scanty and reddish brown.
Dr Gallavardin cured her husband of kidney trouble after he was compelled to use a catheter for over a year, by giving him tea made from the dried leaves and flowers, morning and evening.
Preparations. Standard dose: half-2 grams. Thrice daily.
Tea. Half-1 teaspoon to each cup boiling water; infuse 15 minutes. Dose: 1 cup.
Liquid Extract. Dose, half-2ml.
Tincture BHP (1983) 1:5 in 45 per cent alcohol. Dose: 0.5 to 1ml.
Compress (cold), for wounds and ulcers. GSL

GOLDENSEAL. Yellow root. Eye Balm. *Hydrastis canadensis L.* Dried rhizome and roots. One of phytotherapy's most effective agents. Versatile, with a wide sphere of influence.
Constituents: berberine, hydrastine, canadine, resin.
Action: alterative, choleretic, antiseptic, anti-inflammatory, anti-microbial, bacteriostatic against staphyococcus. (*Complementary Medical Research Vol 2, No 2, p. 139*) Bitter, diuretic, haemostatic, laxative, oxytocic, powerful stomach and liver tonic, detoxifier. Increases blood supply to the spleen.
Uses. Mucous membranes generally. Ulceration of mouth, throat, intestines. Heartburn, chronic dyspepsia, gastric and duodenal ulcer, diverticulosis, ulcerative colitis, liver damage. To assist function of old age. Drying to mucous surfaces and therefore indicated in all forms of catarrh (respiratory, vaginal etc). Proteinuria. Painful,

excessive menstruation and bleeding from the womb for which the addition of Beth root (equal parts) enhances action. Itching of anus and genitals. Ear infections: internal and topical medication. Prostatitis. Bleeding gums. Tinnitus. Has a long history for use in sexually transmitted diseases. Once used to stimulate contractions of the womb to hasten delivery.

Preparations. Standard dose: half-1 gram. Thrice daily.

Decoction. Quarter to half a teaspoon dried rhizome to each cup water simmered gently in a covered vessel 20 minutes. Dose: half a cup.

Liquid Extract, BHC Vol 1. 1:1 in 60 per cent ethanol; 0.3-1ml, (5-15 drops).

Tincture, BHC Vol 1. 1:10, 60 per cent ethanol; 2-4ml, (15-60 drops).

Formula. Popular. All BHP (1983) standard powders:– Marshmallow root 100mg; Goldenseal 10mg; Cranesbill 30mg; Dandelion root 60mg. Traditional for the relief of indigestion, heartburn, flatulence, nausea and gastric irritation.

Powder. Dose: half-1g.

Lotion. Equal parts, Tincture Goldenseal and glycerine. For painting mouth, throat and lesions elsewhere.

Goldenseal solution. 250mg powder shaken in 3oz Rosewater or Witch Hazel: filter. 5-10 drops in eyebath half-filled with water; douche 3 or more times daily.

Goldenseal ointment. 1 teaspoon (5ml) tincture in 1oz Vaseline; dissolve in gentle heat.

Mouth Wash. 5-10 drops tincture in glass water.

Vaginal douche or enema. 10 drops tincture to 2 pints boiled water; inject warm.

Notes. Liquid extract may be used instead of tincture, in which case half quantity is used. Not given in pregnancy, lactation or high blood pressure Not given with Eucalyptus to which it is antagonistic. GSL, schedule 1

"GONE ALL TO PIECES" SYNDROME. Nervous disarray and weakness from severe emotional or physical shock.

Tablet: 45mg each, Skullcap, Lupulin, Hydrocotyle; and the aqueous extractive from: 90mg Gentian, 75mg Jamaica Dogwood.

GONNE. Mild pain-relieving balm for rheumatism, muscular aches and pains. Menthol BP 5 per cent; Camphor BP 2 per cent; Oil of Cajeput BPC '79 2.5 per cent; Oil of Eucalyptus Ph.Eur. 2.5 per cent; Oil of Turpentine BP 8 per cent; Methyl Sal Ph.Eur. 10 per cent. (*G.R. Lane*)

GONORRHOEA. A venereal infection that may be acute or chronic. Affects the mucous membrane of the urethra in the male or the vagina in the female. Almost always the result of sexual contact. One million cases are reported in the United States annually and perhaps as many as two million go unreported. Causative organism: *Neisseria Gonorrhoeae*.

In the initial attack in the male bacteria produces inflammation, with pus, which spreads to the prostate gland and other organs. In women there may be a painful abscess at the opening of the vagina, with characteristic yellowish discharge. It is particularly destructive to the lining of the womb, Fallopian tubes and ovaries, producing sterility or miscarriage. *A notifiable disease*.

Symptoms occur from two to eight days with scalding pain on passing water; urgency, frequency, and irritation of the urethra. A profuse discharge sets in and the urine contains visible yellowish threads of pus as the bladder is affected. Inflammation is followed by fibrosis producing urethral stricture; narrowing of the canal makes the passing of water difficult in men and swelling of the prostate gland may result in acute retention of water. Glands in the groin may enlarge, suppurate. Abscess formation in various parts of the body. Infection of the eyes and pharynx possible through transferred infection.

If severe, valves of the heart may be affected (endocarditis). The chronic form is accompanied by rheumatic pains in the joints, especially knee, ankle and wrist. Untreated patients may remain anonymous carriers months before detection.

Alternatives. It was observed that on South Sea Islands where Kava Kava (*piper methysticum*) is a popular native remedy, gonorrhoea was rare. It was claimed that, used by the native doctors, it was capable of curing the disease in visiting sailors. Once given in combination with Black Cohosh and Marshmallow root.

Tincture Thuja. 5-10 drops thrice daily.

Sandalwood oil. 5-10 drops thrice daily.

Formula. Hydrangea 10; Black Cohosh 5; Gelsemium 1. If headache follows, reduce dose. Dose: 20 drops in water 2-hourly. If discharge does not lessen within 3 days give external douche: 10 drops Goldenseal in an ounce of Witch Hazel distilled extract, or rosewater to bladder and urethra. If a thin discharge prevails on the fifth day, add to each dose 5 drops Liquid Extract or 10 drops tincture Kava Kava. (*Dr G.A. West, Ellingwood's Physiomedicalist*)

"I used Echinacea for gonorrhoea, both internally and by injection" writes Dr A.G. Smith, Washington, claiming success in recent and chronic cases.

Early Australian settlers used: Tea Tree oil internally (drop doses) and as a douche: 3-5 drops in half a pint boiled milk allowed to cool.

Powders. Formula. Kava Kava 2; Hydrangea 1; Cinnamon half. Dose: 500mg (two 00 capsules or one-third teaspoon) thrice daily.

Elderflower tea. If fever is present give abundant Elderflower tea. OR: 5-15 drops tincture Aconite

BP. 2-3 times daily.
Diseases due to suppressed gonorrhoea (arthritis, etc): Liquid Extract Thuja, 5 drops thrice daily.
Eye infections from gonorrhoea, Great Celandine. (*Priest*)
For genital lesions, Tincture Myrrh and Goldenseal lotion: (20 drops each) to 1oz Evening Primrose oil. Thoroughly mix by shaking before external use.
Diet: Avoid alcohol, condiments and hot spicy foods, curries, etc which worsen the irritation.
Exercise: Avoid all violent exercise.
To be treated by STD specialist only.

GOTU KOLA. Hydrocotyle asiatica, Indian Pennywort, European Water-marvel. *Centella asiatica L. French*: Hydrocotyle. *German*: Wassernabel. *Italian*: Idrocotile. *Indian*: Brahami. *Chinese*: Chi-hsueh-ts'ao.
Constituents. flavonoids, terpenoids, volatile oil.
Action. Adaptogen, alterative de-toxifier, bitter, diuretic, digestant, powerful blood tonic, central nervous system relaxant, laxative, emmenagogue, Ginseng-like effect, antibiotic (ointment and dusting powder).
Uses. Mentioned in most Eastern religions and medical systems. Has a reputation for longevity. Under the name Fo-ti-tieng it was prescribed and taken by Professor Li-Ching-Yun, Chinese herbalist who died 1933 at the reputed age of 256. (*Guinness Book of Records*) The herb is active in Ayurvedic Medicine, having a long history for leprosy and tumour. Prominent as a mild analgesic to alleviate pains of the female generative organs, for mental illness. Some success has been reported for cancer of the cervix. In Chinese medicine it covers a wide range including infertility, insomnia, crumbling nails, impaired vision, chronic sinusitis, sexual debility and some venereal diseases (juice of the fresh leaves).
It is a medicine of some versatility. In the West it has been used for recovery from surgical operation, drug withdrawal. Addison's disease (copper-coloured complexion), rheumatism. For skin disorders: discharging ulcers, acne, pemphigus and lupus (where not ulcerative). It is said to heal without a scar. Of value for tiredness, depression, loss of memory, and to improve the nervous system generally in Parkinson's disease.
Recent research reports improved memory and the overcoming of stress, fatigue and mental confusion.
Preparations. Average dose: half-1g. Thrice daily.
Tea. Quarter to half a teaspoon to each cup boiling water; infuse 10 minutes; dose – 1 cup.
Liquid extract: 1:1. Dose – 2-4ml (half-1 teaspoon).
Bengal tincture. 1 part coarsely powdered dried plant in 5 parts by weight of strong alcohol. Macerate 8 days in well-corked bottle in a dark place; shake daily; strain; filter. Dose – 1-2 teaspoons in water.
Use for not more than 6 weeks without a break.
Not used in pregnancy or epilepsy. GSL

GOUT. Acute gouty arthritis. A disturbance of protein metabolism in which production of uric acid is increased, resulting in deposits of uric acid crystals around joints, especially fingers and toes. Uric acid is a breakdown product of nucleic acid and found in all living tissue. Excess amounts are usually excreted in the urine but any hold-up may cause crystals to be formed. Untreated, it affects the arterial system. Male preponderance 20-1.
Etiology. May be hereditary. Excess alcohol, meat or starchy foods without adequate fresh vegetables and fruit. Alcohol increases synthesis of urates and inhibits secretion. High beer intake. There is a link between gout and the good life.
Symptoms. Joints hot, painful, inflamed, shiny and swollen. Temperature rises in acute cases. Urine strong-smelling, but little passed. Urate deposits (tophi) present a ready diagnostic sign on elbows or lobes of ears. Swollen big toe common. Joints normal between attacks.
Autumn Crocus (Colchicum) is the oldest and still one of the most effective plant medicines for relief and appears to act by inhibiting prostaglandin activity.
The symptoms of pseudo-gout are similar, focus of pain mostly in the knee. Instead of uric acid, pyrophosphoric acid crystals are laid down and calcium salts deposited in cartilages. For this, Colchicum is of little value, though reportedly good results follow use of White Willow.
Influenza vaccination injections may trigger acute gout in some patients.
Alternatives. Autumn Crocus (Colchicum), Black Cohosh, Boldo, Burdock root, Celery seeds, Gravel root, Guaiacum, Meadowsweet, Sarsaparilla, Valerian, White Willow, Wild Lettuce, Yarrow, Devil's Claw.
Alternatives for acute conditions:– *Tea*. Equal parts: Boldo, Celery seeds, Meadowsweet. Mix. 1-2 teaspoons to each cup boiling water; infuse 15 minutes. 1 cup every 2 hours.
Decoction. Black Cohosh 1; Gravel root 1; White Willow 2. Mix. 1-2 teaspoons in 2 cupfuls water gently simmered 20 minutes. Half a cup every 2 hours.
Tablets/capsules. Boldo, Black Cohosh, Celery, Garlic, White Willow, Devil's Claw, Prickly Ash. Colchicine USP, one 0.5mg tablet every 2 hours.
Powders. Formula. Black Cohosh 1; White Willow 3. Guaiacum quarter. Dose: 500mg (two 00 capsules or one-third teaspoon) every 2 hours.
Tinctures. Formula. White Willow 2; Celery 1; Black Cohosh quarter; Guaiacum quarter; Liquorice quarter. Dose: 1-2 teaspoons every 2 hours in water.
Cider vinegar. Traditional. (*Vermont, USA*)
Colchicum. Extract Colchici Liquid, dose: 2-

5 drops. Tincture Colchici; 5-15 drops. In water as prescribed by a practitioner.
Topical. Cider vinegar as a lotion. Warm potato poultice for pain. Lotion: 1 part Oil of Sassafras to 20 parts Safflower seed oil. Slippery Elm poultice: mix well 2-3 teaspoons powdered Slippery Elm into 1 pint (500ml) equal parts Cider vinegar and water. Epsom salts bath. Comfrey ointment. Chamomile soaks.
Aromatherapy. Wipe affected parts with any one diluted oil: Sage, Burdock, Bryony, Rosemary, St John's Wort.
Diet. Low protein, fat, salt. Nettle tea. Plenty of water. No tea, coffee or alcohol. *Reject*: purine foods – organ meats, kidney, liver, brain, sweetbread, red meat, meat extracts. *Accept*: bananas for potassium – 3 daily, and oily fish. For gout, a vegetarian diet has much to commend it.
Supplements. Daily. Bromelain 200mg. Folic acid 30mg. Vitamin C 3g. Vitamin E 200iu. Iron – Floradix. Magnesium.
General. Reduce acidity. Gout is a rewarding condition for the phytotherapist. Rest affected parts. Good responses with Guaiacum. For kidney involvement add Wild Carrot. For prevention, an older generation of physicians advised quarter to half a teaspoon Glauber Salts in breakfast tea, or cup of Nettle tea. Cradle affected joint against pressure from shoes or bedclothes.

GRANULOMA. Same treatment as for TUMOUR. Of the skin – Aloe Vera, Chickweed, Comfrey.

GRAPES. *Vitis vinifera L.*
Dr Joanna Brandt knew that grapes may sometimes check malignancy. Facing up squarely to the reality of cancer, she resolved not to take any medicines to check its course or alleviate the pain . . . neither would she submit to the surgeon's knife.
For nine years she had been desperately seeking something to destroy the growth effectively, to eliminate virulent cancer toxins and rebuild new tissue.
At the conclusion of a seven-day fast she developed a craving for grapes. From the first mouthful she felt their purifying influence and a lift physically and mentally. She was miraculously cured.
As in other cases, improvement was attended by the senses becoming abnormally acute, dim eyes became bright, faded hair took on a new gloss, a lifeless voice became vibrant, the complexion cleared; teeth, loose and suppurating in their sockets became fixed and healthy.
In "The Grape Cure", she records: "While the system is drained of its poisons, external wounds are kept open with frequent applications of Grape poultices and compresses . . . No scabs or crusts are formed as long as the lesions are kept moist . . . From glistening bones outwards, the process of reconstruction goes on. Healthy, rosy granulations of new flesh appear and cavities are filled in."
The body is prepared for the regime by fasting for 2-3 days, drinking plenty of pure cold water and by taking a two-pint enema of lukewarm water daily.
After the fast, she advises – "Drink one or two glasses of cold water on rising. Half hour later, have a meal of grapes, discard seeds, chew skins thoroughly, swallowing a few for medicine and fibre. Have a grape meal every two hours from 8am to 8pm (7 meals daily). Continue two weeks – even for one month. Begin with 1, 2 or 3 ounces per meal, increasing gradually to half pound. The maximum should not exceed 4 pounds. Patients taking large quantities should allow 3 hours for digestion and not take all skins."
After years of suffering, Dr Brandt discovered a cure which worked in her particular case and which she was able to repeat in a number of others.

GRAPE SEED OIL. High in polyunsaturates. Contains nearly 75 per cent linoleic acid. Made from crushed seeds of white grapes. Contains more polyunsaturated fats than corn or sunflower oil. Used chiefly in cooking for coronary patients.

GRAVEL ROOT. *Eupatorium purpureum, L.*
Keynote: stone. Rhizome and root.
Constituents: Eupatorin, resin, volatile oil, flavonoids.
Action: antilithic, antirheumatic, soothing diuretic, astringent.
Uses. Stone in the kidney, gravel, stricture, urethritis, painful urination, prostatitis, lumbago of kidney origin, rheumatism, gout. Some success in diabetes. For stone: combines well with Parsley Piert, Pellitory and Hydrangea BHP (1983).
Preparations. Average dose: 2-4 grams. Thrice daily.
Decoction. 1 teaspoon to each cup water gently simmered 20 minutes. Dose: half cup.
Liquid extract. 2-4ml.
Tincture BHP (1983) 1:5 in 40 per cent alcohol. Dose: 1-2ml (15-30 drops).

GRAVE'S DISEASE. Hyperactive thyroid gland. See: THYROID.

GRAVEL. A sediment in the urine composed of mineral salts or small masses of uric acid. Grains of urinary calculus may be made up of successive layers of material. Gravel is said to be *vesical* when lodged in the bladder and *renal* when in the pelvis of the kidney. As its name suggests, gravel is much smaller than stone.
Causes: drinking water with a high degree of hardness. When rhubarb, gooseberries, chocolate or spinach are eaten calcium oxalate is formed

between the water and oxalic acid in these foods.
Treatment. A pelvic nervine is sometimes added to formula.
Alternatives. *Teas*. Cornsilk, Couchgrass, Cranesbill (American), Clivers, Hollyhock, Marshmallow leaves, Parsley, Parsley Piert, Pellitory-of-the-wall, Sea Holly, Wild Carrot.
Tablets/capsules. Parsley Piert.
Powders. Hydrangea 2; Gravel root 1; Valerian half. Mix. Dose: 500mg (two 00 capsules or one-third teaspoon) thrice daily.
Decoction. Clivers 4; Gravel root 1; Valerian half. Mix. Half ounce to 1 pint water simmered gently 20 minutes. Strain. Dose: half-1 cup thrice daily.
Formula. Pellitory 2; Hydrangea 1; Stone root half; Valerian quarter. Mix. Dose: Liquid extracts: 1 teaspoon. Tinctures: 2 teaspoons. Thrice daily.
Practitioner. Tincture Hydrangea 20ml; Gravel root 10ml; Ephedra 20ml; Stone root 10ml; Sig: 5ml in cup of Marshmallow tea. Thrice daily and when necessary. Tincture Belladonna for sudden pain.
Diet. Dandelion coffee. Slippery Elm beverage or gruel. No dairy products, calcium of which disposes to gravel formation. No tap water, only bottled low-calcium waters. Vitamins A, B6, C and E. Magnesium is credited with dissolving gravel.

GREASY SKIN. Blue Flag, Goldenseal, Queen's Delight, Garlic.

GREEN HEALTH CUP. Feed into an electric juicer leaves of any one kind of leaf (Mint, Alfalfa, etc). For Green Multicup juice any number of different leaves: Alfalfa, Chard, Dandelion, Carrots, Parsley, Beet Greens, Filaree, Spinach, Celery, Mint, Kale. Discard stems.

Green drinks are important sources of chlorophyll, vitamins and minerals and are regarded as preventive medicine.

GREEN TEA. *Camellia thea*. *Part used*: first two leaves and the buds of spray. Domestic tea which has not been processed into black tea. China tea.
Action: anti-fat, diuretic.
Uses. Obesity, swollen ankles, oedema.
Preparations. *Tea*: prepare as domestic tea.
Powder. 500mg or two 250mg capsules thrice daily at meals.
Note. Anti-cancer effects have been observed in Chinese green tea extract. Clinical trials on therapeutic effects against early stomach cancer were promising. *(Chin.J. Prev. Med. 1990, 24 (2) 80-2)*

GRIEF. One of life's most stressful experiences is associated with bereavement following the death of a partner and which may give rise to the "I am out of control" syndrome.

Evidence exists that bereavement is related to a suppression of white cell function. As long as one year may elapse before a normal blood pattern is regained. *(Dr Stephen Schleifer, Mount Sinai School of Medicine, New York City)*
To help restore lymphocyte count and relieve depression/anxiety: Combine equal parts Red Clover (blood): Valerian (nerves) and Motherwort (heart).
Tea: 1-2 teaspoons to each cup boiling water; infuse 15 minutes; half-1 cup 2-3 times daily.
Alternative. *Tea*: equal parts Motherwort, Balm and Chamomile. 2 teaspoons to each cup boiling water; infuse 5-15 minutes. 1 cup as desired.
Liquid Extracts: 20-60 drops in water, 2-3 times daily.
Pulsatilla. *(Nalda Gosling, FNIMH, Herbal Practitioner: Apr 79, p.11)*
Note. Grief is known to make changes in hormone production and invariably centres on the reproductive system manifesting as a uterine or prostate disturbance.

GRINDELIA. Gumweed. Tarweed. *Grindelia camporum*, Greene. Flowering tops. *Keynote*: asthma.
Constituents: flavonoids, diterpenes, fat, wax, resins.
Action: antispasmodic, expectorant, hypotensive, sedative, diuretic, reduces the heart rate. Antidote to rhus poisoning, internally and externally.
Uses. Bronchial asthma where associated with rapid heart action. Emphysema, whooping cough, catarrh – nose and throat. Poison Ivy dermatitis – as a topical wash by decoction. Once used by the Western Indians, USA, for venereal disease.
Tincture BHP (1983) 1:10 in 60 per cent alcohol. Dose: half-1ml.

Large doses irritate kidneys. GSL

GRIPING PAIN. Acute pain in the abdominal cavity. Non-recurring.
Tea. Combine equal parts: Avens, Catmint, Thyme. 2 teaspoons to each cup boiling water; infuse 5 minutes. Half-1 cup freely.
Alternative: quarter of a teaspoon powdered Ginger, or Cinnamon in honey.
Enema: Catmint, Chamomile or Balm.

See: COLIC.

Persistent griping should be investigated.

GROMWELL. Lithospermum officinale. Borage family. *Part used*: seeds and leaves.
Action: anti-gonadotropic. Mild contraceptive.
Uses. Sometimes used as an alternative to The Pill.

GROUND IVY. Glechoma hederacea. *Nepeta hederacea L. German*: Gundermann. *French*: Lierre terrestre. *Spanish*: Hiedra terrestre. *Italian*: Edera terrestre. Dried herb. *Keynote*: catarrh.
Constituents: flavonoids, oil, sesquiterpenes, a bitter principle.

Action: Anti-catarrhal, expectorant, diuretic, an important astringent for stomach, intestines and colon. Diaphoretic, anti-scorbutic, tonic, anti-inflammatory.
Uses. Catarrh: chronic bronchial, nasal; catarrhal deafness, tinnitus (buzzing in the ears). Sinusitis. Kidney disease (supportive to primary treatment). Dyspepsia. Piles.
Reported to have been used with success for cancer of the bladder.
Combinations. Combines well with Agrimony (equal parts) for irritable bowel. Combines with Goldenseal 1; (Ground Ivy 4) for cystitis.
Preparations. Average dose: 2-4 grams. Thrice daily.
Tea: 1-2 teaspoons to each cup boiling water; infuse 15 minutes. Half-1 cup.
Home tincture: 1oz dried or fresh herb to 5oz 25 per cent alcohol (Vodka, etc). Macerate 8 days; shake daily. Strain. Dose: 1-2 teaspoons in water.
Liquid Extract: 2-4ml. GSL, schedule 1

GROWING PAINS. A vague term for pains in children. Generally rheumatic in character and not related to rapid growth. Usually a hot bath and warm bedrest suffices, but if the heart is affected a child should receive treatment for rheumatic fever. Bad teeth and enlarged tonsils may be an underlying cause requiring priority treatment. Alfalfa Tea. Treat for RHEUMATISM.

GUAIACUM. Lignum vitae tree of the West Indies. *Guaiacum officinalis L. German*: Guajakbaum. *French*: Bois de gaïac. *Spanish*: Guayaco. *Italian*: Guaiaco. *Parts used*: heart wood and gum resin. *Keynote*: rheumatism.
Constituents: terpenoids, lignans, resin acids.
Action: anti-rheumatic, anti-inflammatory, adaptogen, diuretic, powerful blood cleanser, anti-psoriasis, anti-tuberculin, diaphoretic, acts on fibrous tissue.
Uses. Inflammatory rheumatism: takes the heat out of any rheumatic or arthritic flare-up. Rheumatoid arthritis, gouty nodes on fingers, knees, etc. Osteo-arthritis. Mercurial poisoning is ever present in the modern world: Guaiacum is a natural antidote for this metal for the many conditions it causes including rheumatism. Shrunken tendons of hands (Dupuytrens contracture). Overpowering body odour. Psoriasis, eczema, boils, abscesses. In the 16th and 17th centuries it had a reputation for syphilis.
Combines well with Sarsaparilla for the above: (Guaiacum 1; Sarsaparilla 2 parts).
Preparations. Thrice daily.
Decoction: quarter of a teaspoon wood chips or sawdust to each cup water simmered gently 20 minutes. Dose: quarter to half a cup.
Liquid Extract: 1-2ml.
Tincture, BPC 1934: 1:5 in 90 per cent alcohol, dose 1-4ml. GSL, schedule 1

GUAR GUM. From the Indian bean *Chyamopsis tetragonobulus*. A normaliser of carbohydrate intolerance. Previously used as an emulsifier and thickener in foods like yoghurt and ice-cream. When combined with water forms a sticky gel. Slows rate of entry of sugar into the blood, improving insulin sensitivity. Anti-hyperglycaemic and hypocholesterolaemic.
Guar has an effect upon sugar metabolism, blood fat levels, body weight and blood pressure. (*Dr J. Tuomilehto, University of Turku, Finland*)
A study at Hammersmith Hospital, London, showed Guar efficacious in reducing blood sugar levels. Its cholesterol-lowering action is of benefit in diabetics.
Guar induces weight loss in obese subjects; reduces risk of kidney stone. Granules of the gum may be taken with water or sprinkled direct on food – fluid being taken at the meal to ensure swelling of the granules.
By slowing the rate of sugar absorption, it reduces the post-prandial peak in blood sugar level, making possible a reduction of insulin.
Contra-indications: obstruction of the intestines and diseases of the gullet.
Guarina or Guarem, sachets: 5g unit dose sprinkled over food. Adults: one sachet daily, increasing if necessary to a maximum of 3 sachets. A preparation Glucotard is taken as dry minitablets, washed down in portions with a glass of water.
Alternative: Powdered Guar gum – 15 grams daily.
Note. Effectiveness for weight loss unproven. Guar gum may cause throat obstruction in rare cases and should be prescribed by a medical practitioner only.
See: DIABETES. HYPERLIPIDAEMIA. CHOLESTEROL.

GUARANA. Brazilian cocoa. *Paullinia cupana. French*: Quarane. *Italian*: Quarana. *Spanish*: Quarana. Legendary sacred fruit of the Amazon Indians. Seeds, roasted and ground to a fine powder. Popular stimulant drink throughout South America. Dietary supplement. *Keynote*: revitaliser.
Constituents: theobromine, theophyllin, caffeine (7 per cent), saponins, tannins, choline.
Action: anti-stress agent, tonic, nutrient, nerve relaxant, astringent, adaptogen, diuretic. Sustains the immune system. Aphrodisiac. Gentle stimulant for adrenals. Revitaliser. Antidepressant.
Uses. Sportsman's strength and stay. Increases stamina, adapts the body to stresses of modern living. Jet-lag, nervous depression, diarrhoea. Recovery from illness, hang-over symptoms. To adapt circadian rhythm after long-distance travel. To sustain the brain during prolonged mental effort. Stress-related headaches.
Preparations. *Capsules* contain 500mg sun-dried powder. Two capsules on rising. Tablets

(350mg) two thrice daily. The *powder* may be mixed with Cassava flour and water to make a paste which stirred into water provides a strengthening beverage. A popular Brazilian drink: half-1 teaspoon powder to glass lemonade. (*Rio Trading Co. Ltd., Brighton*)

GUAREA. See: COCILLANA.

GUGULON. *Commiphora mukul*. Resin. Myrrh-like exudate.
Action: anti-inflammatory, anti-rheumatic, anti-cholesterol.
Uses. Internally: rheumatism, gout. Regulate cholesterol levels. Lumbago. Osteoarthritis.
Preparations. *Tincture*: 1-5 drops in water, thrice daily.
Powder: two 300mg capsules thrice daily. (*Arkocaps*)

GUILLAIN-BARRE SYNDROME (GBS). Named after the French neurologist. A type of polyneuritis, causing sensory loss and muscle weakness. May follow minor viral infections. Recovery usually spontaneous, but death may result if paralysis affects the respiratory system. Antibodies produced during an infection may attack the myelin sheath of the nerves which weakens muscle control.
Symptoms: muscle weakness. A hand may drop objects. Legs too weak for walking. Asks himself: "Will I ever walk again?" Pain is similar to banging a 'funnybone' – but never lets up.
Treatment. Good nursing and family support. Agents that recoat the nerves. A warm bath helps relieve pains.
Alternatives:– *Tea*: mix equal parts: Skullcap, Oats, Catmint. 1 heaped teaspoon to each cup boiling water; infuse 5 minutes. Dose: half-1 cup, freely.
Tablets, tinctures or extracts: Cramp bark, Valerian, Mistletoe. Ginseng.
Vitamins. B1, B2, B6, B12, B-complex. Pantothenic acid.
Minerals. Magnesium. Dolomite. Zinc.

GULLET, STRICTURE OF. See: OESOPHAGEAL STRICTURE.

GUMS. Painful from ill-fitting dentures or injury caused by new dentures, with soft sensitive gums. Same treatment as for GUMS, RECEDING. Leave out artificial teeth at night to allow gums to "breathe". Sage tea as a mouth rinse – success reported. Coenzyme Vitamin Q10: 60mg daily.

GUMS, RECEDING. Neglected professional dental attention may result in deposits of plaque or tartar on the teeth, responsible for gum recession and loose teeth. Gums become soft and sensitive. Usually associated with refined sugar intake, carbonated beverages, the aftermath of infections, etc. Recession may be caused by incorrect brushing of the teeth.
To harden gums: 5-10 drops Tincture Myrrh in tumbler of water as a mouth rinse, freely. To inhibit plaque: chew sticks of Marshmallow root, Liquorice root, or Orris root. Saliva from such chewing inhibits lactic acid; reduces adherence of *Saliva mutans*.
Mouth wash. Leaves of Comfrey, Sage or Walnut. 2 teaspoons to each cup boiling water; infuse 15 minutes.
Marie Treben's Mouth Rinse. Equal parts, Ladies Mantle, Oak bark, Sage, Knotgrass. Mix. 2 teaspoons to cup boiling water; infuse 15 minutes. Strain off.
Bloodroot makes a mouth wash for reducing plaque and blocks enzymes that destroy collagen in gum tissue. (*American Herbal Association*)
Cider Vinegar. 2 teaspoons in glass of water. Sips throughout the day.
Diet. Alfalfa tea. Sugar-free, salt-free diet. Reject foods known to contain additives.
Supplementation. Vitamin C (1 gram daily). Calcium. Dolomite.

GUNSHOT WOUNDS. To prevent suppuration and pyaemia – Marigold.
Internally: Marigold petal tea freely.
Externally: Marigold (Calendula) ointment, cream or fomentation with petals. During the Coup d'etat in Paris in 1849, a Dr Jahr saved many limbs with Marigold. Echinacea to allay infection. See entry: WOUNDS.

GYNAECOMASTIA. Excessive enlargement of the breasts in male or female. In the male it is sometimes associated with atrophy of the testicles. Subjects usually enjoy excellent physical health.
Causes: failure of the liver to detoxicate oestrogens in the blood, pituitary tumour, drug therapy, Cimetidine (an ulcer-healing drug).
Alternatives. Rosemary, Sarsaparilla, Agnus Castus, Dandelion, Red Clover.
Tea. Combine, equal parts: Gotu Kola, Red Clover, Dandelion. 1-2 teaspoons to each cup boiling water; infuse 15 minutes. 1 cup thrice daily.

HAEMATINICS. Agents used to increase haemoglobin in the blood. May be advised for iron-deficiency anaemia. Burdock, Devil's Claw, Nettles, Red Clover, Yellow Dock.

HAEMATOMA. A blood clot forming in tissue following operation or injury.
Internal. Garlic capsules – two every two hours.
Topical. Horsetail poultice. See entry.
Supplements. Vitamins C, E.

HAEMATURIA. Blood in the urine. From the bladder – bright red. From the kidneys – smoky dark brown but not in clots. May not be long-lasting, clearing up without incident. Some food dyes and confectionery dye the urine red.
Symptoms. Where due to kidney: pain in the back on same side as affected kidney. May indicate tumour. Professional help should be sought. The main symptom of nephritis. Should not be confused with blood of the menstrual flow.
Alternatives. BHP (1983) recommends: Bur-Marigold, Horsetail, Sea Holly, Common Plantain, Beth root. HAMDAD recommends Grape seeds.
Cinnamon oil. Long traditional reputation in Malaysia for blood in the urine – 5-10 drops oil (or half a teaspoon powder) to control until medical attention is available or other measures adopted.
Formula. Sea Holly 3; Bur-Marigold 2; Beth root 1. Mix. *Dose*. Powders quarter of a teaspoon (375mg). Liquid Extracts 30-60 drops. Tinctures 1-2 teaspoons. In water thrice daily. Acute cases: every 2 hours.
Dr Finlay Ellingwood. Formula. Liquid Extracts: Black Cohosh 20ml; Hydrangea 10ml; Chimiphila 5ml; Gelsemium 0.5ml. Mix. 20-40 drops in water every 2 hours, acute cases.
John Wesley (evangelist). Copious draughts of Yarrow Tea.
Note. Small stone or gravel are a common cause of blood in the urine. Rhubarb favours formation of stone, being able to induce oxaluria. Where drinking water has a high degree of hardness and rhubarb is eaten, calcium oxalate stones may be formed between the action of the water and the oxalic acid in the rhubarb.
Treatment by or in liaison with a general medical practitioner or hospital specialist.

HAEMOLYTIC. A herb that lyses red blood cells by causing them to rupture. Soapwort.

HAEMOLYTIC DISEASE OF INFANTS. Severe disease of the newly born and infants with jaundice and anaemia. Occurs when a Rhesus negative mother gives birth to a Rhesus positive child. There may be degeneration of nerve cells of the brain through circulating bile. Followed by water-logging of tissues lining lungs, abdomen or heart (hydrops).
Treatment. Purpose of medication is to stimulate flow of bile and support the liver.
Arthur Hyde, MNIMH recommends a selection from the following according to individual case: Balmony, Barberry, Dandelion, Goldenseal, Hops, Ladyslipper, Mistletoe, Passion flower, Stone root.
Tinctures. Formula. Marigold 2; Barberry 2; Ginkgo 1. Dose: 2 drops in feed, or in water, thrice daily. Infants 3-5 years: 10 drops.
To be treated by or in liaison with a qualified medical practitioner.

HAEMOLYTIC-URAEMIA SYNDROME (HUS). An uncommon cause of kidney failure in children. The association of three processes: reduced platelets, haemolytic anaemia and kidney failure. Foodborne infection is spread by micro-organisms (E. coli, etc) with an affinity for the alimentary canal. The central nervous system is involved.
Onset: diarrhoea with streaks of blood, vomiting, breathlessness, feverishness, dizziness, jaundice and enlargement of the spleen.
Other causes may be mismatched food transfusion, environmental chemicals, nitrite food preservatives and analgesic drugs.
Alternatives. *Tea*. Combine herbs: Red Clover (to increase platelets) 3; Yarrow (kidneys) 2; Hops (cerebrospinal supportive) 1. 1-2 teaspoons to each cup boiling water; infuse 15 minutes. Half-1 cup freely.
Formula: Combine, Tinctures. Red Clover 2; Fringe Tree 1; Hops half. Dose: one 5ml teaspoon. Babies: 2 drops in feed; infants 3-5 years 10 drops in water and honey thrice daily.
Supplementation. Vitamin B-complex. C.
To be treated by or in liaison with a qualified medical practitioner.

HAEMOPHILIA. A sex-linked hereditary bleeding disease associated with a deficiency of Factor VIII in the blood. Closely related to Christmas disease which has a deficiency of Factor IX. Transmitted by mothers with the recessive gene. Disease exclusive to males, blood failing to clot, resulting in bleeding from minor injury, such as tooth extraction. Possible blood in the urine (haematuria). No cure. A course of Goldenseal (liquid extract) 3-5 drops for 1 week, at bedtime, every 3 months, is said to be of value.
Alternatives. **Treatment**. To increase tone in blood vessels (Gentian). To promote healing and toughen vessels (Horsetail). Blood in the urine (Shepherd's Purse). Tendency of mucous surfaces to bleed (Goldenseal). Bleeding from the lungs (Elecampane); from the alimentary tract, bowel (American Cranesbill); from the throat (Sage). From the nose: inject equal parts Cider vinegar and water.

To strengthen vascular system. Tea. Equal parts: Horsetail, Nettles, Mullein. 1-2 teaspoons to each cup boiling water; infuse 15 minutes. One cup once or twice daily.
Topical. For bleeding of skin: Witch Hazel (distilled extract). Marigold tincture, cream, etc.
Diet. High calcium and phosphorus diet. Low salt. An article in a scientific journal describes how one sufferer arrested attacks with handful of unsalted peanuts.
Supplementation. Niacin, Vitamin C, Calcium, Zinc.
See: HAEMOSTATICS.
Treatment by a general medical practitioner or hospital specialist.

HAEMOPTYSIS. The coughing up of blood, or sputum mixed with blood from the lungs. See: BLEEDING, FROM THE LUNGS.

HAEMORRHAGE. See: BLEEDING.

HAEMORRHOIDS. Varicose veins around the anus and low bowel due to poor local circulation. First degree haemorrhoids, remain inside the rectum, but may bleed. Second degree haemorrhoids, bleed and protrude beyond the anus but return after defecation. Third degree haemorrhoids, remain outside the anus and have to be pushed back manually. Blood is bright red.
Causes: constipation, sluggish liver, grumbling appendix, pregnancy, etc. Underlying cause must be treated. Pilewort and Stone root are key remedies.
Alternatives. Teas from any of the following: Butcher's Broom, Balmony, Bilberry, Beth root, Bistort, Comfrey, Cranesbill, Figwort, <u>Ground Ivy</u>, <u>Horsechestnut</u>, Ladies Mantle, Nettles, Oak bark, <u>Pilewort</u>, Plantain, Silverweed, Stone root, Tormentil, Wild Yam, Witch Hazel, St John's Wort.
Alternative formulae. *Tea.* (1) Equal parts, Yarrow, Witch Hazel leaves, German Chamomile. (2) Equal parts, Yarrow, Pilewort, Mullein. (3) Equal parts, Plantain, Figwort, Pilewort. 1-2 teaspoons to each cup boiling water; infuse 15 minutes. Half-1 cup thrice daily before meals.
Tablets/capsules. Pilewort. Cranesbill. Wild Yam. Blue Flag root.
Powders. Formula. Equal parts, Pilewort 1; Figwort 1; Stone root half. Dose: 500mg (two 00 capsules or one-third teaspoon) thrice daily.
Tinctures. Formula. Butternut 1; Figwort 1; Cascara quarter. One 5ml teaspoon in water thrice daily. Alternative: Combine Hawthorn 2; Stone root 1. Dose: 30-60 drops in water thrice daily.
Enema. Strong infusion of Raspberry leaves: 2oz to 2 pints boiling water. Steep 20 minutes, strain. Improves with addition of 5 drops Tincture Myrrh.
Suppositories. 1 part Liquid Extract Witch Hazel or German Chamomile to 5 parts Cocoa butter.
Ointments: Pilewort, Chickweed, Figwort, Aloe Vera, Horse Chestnut, Houseleek.
Psyllium seeds (light) (Ispaghula) increases bulk of the stools making them softer and easier to pass.
To alleviate itching and assist healing: insert into the anus fresh peeled Aloe Vera or Houseleek. Alternatives: make a paste of quarter of a teaspoon of any of the following powders with few drops of milk: Comfrey, Pilewort, Stone root and apply externally, holding in position with a binder.
Vitamin E capsules. Piles that had resisted all other forms of treatment rapidly cleared. Insert one capsule into rectum night and morning.
Diet: Low salt, low fat, high fibre.
Supplements. Vitamins A, B-complex, B6, C, and E. Calcium. Zinc.
Supportives. Sitz bath. Sponge anus with cold water.

HAEMOSTATICS. Agents that arrest bleeding. <u>Bayberry</u>, Blackberry, Cayenne, Cinnamon, <u>Cranesbill (American)</u>, Ephedra, Goldenseal, Herb Robert, Horsetail, <u>Marigold</u>, Mullein, <u>Oak bark</u>, St John's Wort, Turmeric, Uva Ursi, Witch Hazel, Yellow Dock, Tormentil, <u>Rhatany root</u>, Cinquefoil, Comfrey. This group is made up chiefly of astringents and coagulants. All serious cases of bleeding should be referred to a qualified practitioner.

HAHNEMANN, Dr SAMUEL (1755-1843). Born: Meissen, Germany. Discovered a science of healing which he called Homoeopathy, based on the immutable law of *similia similibus curentur* (like cures like). It brings to the treatment of human and animal sickness a universal law, which in the field of medicine ranks with Newton's Law of Gravity in physics.
Far in advance of his time in preventive medicine, he denounced the hazardous treatments of his day thus arousing the animosity of his contemporaries. His major work, "The Organon" is the homoeopathist's bible to this day. "Cinchona bark was to Hahnemann what the falling apple was to Newton and the swinging lamp to Galileo." See: HOMOEOPATHY.

HAIR ANALYSIS. Hair is believed to be a "time capsule" of a person's metabolic activity. Believed to be a useful means of acquiring information regarding the concentration of mineral nutrients and toxins. Alone, it does not provide sufficient evidence for purposes of diagnosis, but helpful in building a picture of the nutritional state of the patient.

HAIR CARE. Hair, like nails and skin, is a protein material built up on amino acids. It is rich in minerals, especially sulphur. A sebaceous gland at the base of the hair follicle secretes sebum, an oily substance, which acts as a lubricant. When vital minerals and vitamins are lacking in the blood the quality of fibre and sebum deteriorates resulting in lustreless hair and change of texture. Healthy hair depends upon good personal hygiene, brushing, and washing with gentle-acting materials instead of harsh detergent shampoos which remove natural oils from the scalp and spoils its condition.

An adequate daily intake of essential fatty acids is assured by the golden oils (Sunflower, Corn, etc) which can be well supported by Evening Primrose oil capsules.
Internal: Bamboo gum. Nettle tea, Alfalfa, Horsetail, Soya.
Topical. Shampoo. Soapwort or Yucca. Chop 2 tablespoons (dry) or 1 tablespoon (fresh) leaves or root. Place in cup of warm water. Stir until a froth is produced. Decant and massage liquor into scalp.

Aloe Vera gel is noted for its moisturising effect and to provide nutrients. It may be used as a shampoo, hair set and conditioner. Jojoba oil has been used for centuries by the Mexican Indians for a healthy scalp; today, it is combined with Evening Primrose and Vitamin E with good effect. Olive oil stimulates strong growth.

One of several herbs may be used as a rinse, including Nettles, Rosemary, Southernwood, Fennel, Chamomile, Yellow Dock and Quassia. Hair should be washed not more than once weekly with warm water and simple vegetable soap; rinse four times with warm rinse, finishing off with cold. Brunettes should add a little vinegar; blondes, lemon juice. Selenium once had a reputation as a hair conditioner; recent research confirms. Selenium shampoos are available.
Supplements: Vitamins B (complex), B6, Choline, C and E. Copper, Zinc, Selenium, Vitamin B12 (50mg thrice daily).
Aromatherapy. 2 drops each: Sage, Nettles, Thyme; to 2 teaspoons Gin or Vodka, and massage into the scalp daily.

HAIR – DRY. Internally, and externally where lotions, creams etc are available. Burdock root, Comfrey, Elderflowers, Geranium, Marshmallow, Nettles, Parsley, Sage.
Itchy scalp. Catmint leaves and flowers, Chamomile, Comfrey.

HAIR FALLING. To arrest *recent* fall-out where baldness has not been established. See: HAIR LOSS for internal treatments.
Topical. Massage scalp with creams or lotions of Jojoba, Aloe Vera, or wash with strong teas made from Burdock, Sage, Elder leaves, Walnut leaves or Nettles. Apple Cider vinegar.
Aromatherapy. 2 drops each: Sage, Nettles, Thyme to two teaspoons Gin, Vodka or strong spirit. Massage into scalp daily.

Supplements. Biotin, a growth factor, seems to slow down hair loss and is a substitute for oestrogen in a penetrating cream applied to the scalp. Inositol 300mg; Zinc 15mg, daily.

HAIR – GREYING. Rinse hair with strong decoction of Rosemary, Red Sage or Oak bark: believed to temporarily allay greying of the hair.
Supplements: PABA, Vitamin B-complex, Kelp, Selenium, Zinc.

HAIR LOSS. Alopecia. Baldness. Shedding of the hair in patches leaving glossy bald areas. It is normal to lose about one hundred hairs a day, but severe stress such as unemployment, divorce or death in a family may considerably increase hair loss. Losses of long-standing are seldom recovered.
Causes: hormone deficiency (Agnus Castus) in females, where it may be associated with failing thyroid or ovarian function. In such cases, other agents include: Helonias, Motherwort, Black Haw bark. Other causes may be pregnancy, the menopause, or simply discontinuing The Pill. Certain skin diseases predispose: ringworm (Thuja), eczema (Yellow Dock), from thyroid disorder (Kelp, Blue Flag root).

Exposure to some cosmetics, excessive sunlight, strong chemicals and treatment of cancer with cytotoxic drugs may interfere with nutrition of the hair follicles. To ensure a healthy scalp a correct mineral balance is essential calling for supplementation of the diet with vitamins, selenium, zinc and silica. Yellow Dock is believed to counter toxicity of chemicals; Pleurisy root opens the pores to promote sweat and action of surface capillaries.

Baldness sometimes happens suddenly; eyelashes or beard may be affected. Though emotional stress and a run-down condition is a frequent cause, most cases are not permanent, returning to normal with adequate treatment.

Baldness of the eyebrows alerts us to a lowered function of the thyroid gland, being an early outward sign of myxoedema. A pony-tail hair style or the wearing of a crash helmet may cause what is known as traction alopecia. Heavy coffee drinkers invariably lose hair lustre.

Soviet Research favours silica-rich plants internally and as a lotion: Horsetail, Burdock, Nettles, Bamboo gum.

Growth of hair is assisted by improving surface circulation of the scalp which is beneficial for conveying nutrients to the hair roots and facilitating drainage. Herbal vasodilators stimulate hair follicle nutrition and encourage growth: Cayenne, Pleurisy root, Black Cohosh and Prickly Ash, taken internally. A convenient way of taking Cayenne is the use of a pepper-shaker at table.
Topical. Hair rinse. 2-3 times weekly. Infusion: equal parts Yarrow, Sage and Rosemary. 1oz (30g) to 1 pint (500ml) water. Simmer gently five

minutes. Allow to cool. Strain before use.

Cider vinegar – minimal success reported.

Day lotion. Liquid Extract Jaborandi half an ounce; Tincture Cantharides half an ounce; Oil Jojoba to 4oz. Shake well before use.

Oily lotion. Equal parts Olive and Eucalyptus oils.

Bay Rhum Lotion. Oil of Bay 50 drops; Olive oil half an ounce; Rum (Jamaica or other) to 4oz. Shake well before use.

Oil Rosemary: rub into hair roots.

Russian Traditional. Castor oil half an ounce; Almond oil 1oz; Oil Geranium 15 drops; Vodka to 6oz. Rub into hair roots.

Aromatherapy. To 1oz Castor oil and 1oz Olive oil add,10 drops each – Oils Neroli, Lavender and Rosemary.

Gentian plant extract. Japanese scalp massage with extract from roots to thicken thinning hair. Some success reported.

Supplements. B-vitamins, Kelp, Silicea Biochemic salt. Zinc. Low levels of iron and zinc can cause the condition.

Note. Studies show that male occipital baldness confers a risk of heart disease, being associated with a higher total cholesterol and diastolic blood pressure than men with a full head of hair. Frontal baldness has not been found to be associated with increased risk of coronary heart disease and myocardial infarct. "It seems prudent for bald men to be specially vigorous in controlling risk factors for such conditions." (*S.M. Lesko, Journal of the American Medical Association, Feb 24, 1993, 269: 998-1003*)

HAIR – OILY. To condition. Calendula, Clary, all kinds of mints, Horsetail, Lavender, Lemon Balm, Rosemary, Southernwood. Internal and external.

HAIR – SURPLUS. See: HIRSUTISM.

HAKIMS. A group of herbal therapists, usually Indian or Muslim, who practise the Ayurvedic system of medicine. See: AYURVEDIC.

HALFA SUDANI. Sudanese grass. Hamareb. Traditional reputation in Egypt and the Sudan for breaking-up gravel and stone. Due to high salt content in soil and water, gravel is a common native affliction.

Tea: whole plant: 1oz to 1 pint water simmered 5 minutes. 1 cup freely until all is taken during the day. Continue until positive results ensue.

HALITOSIS. See: BAD BREATH.

HALLUCINOGENS. Herbs that enhance the special senses, increasing sensibility and perception. Psycho-active plants. More than 90 hallucinogenic plants are known besides Cannabis sativa – none of which are used in the practice of herbalism.

HALLUX RIGIDUS. Stiffness of the great toe due to injury by stubbing the toe, or to arthritic change.

Formula. Prickly Ash bark 1; Celery 1; Bogbean 1; Guaiacum quarter. Dose: in a cup of Dandelion coffee. Powders: 500mg (two 00 capsules or one-third teaspoon). Liquid extracts: half-1 teaspoon. Tinctures: 1-2 teaspoons. Thrice daily.

Bamboo gum.

Topical. Castor oil pack. Hot poultice of Lobelia and Comfrey. Gentle manipulation to induce a wider range of movement. Chamomile foot baths.

HAMDARD NATIONAL FOUNDATION, PAKISTAN. Greco-Arabian and Ayurvedic Medicine. Islamic Research and scholarship. Research into natural medicines on the Indian Continent and Far East; traditional medicines of Pakistan. President: Hakim Mohammed Said, distinguished physician, researcher and publisher.

Publications include: *Hamdard Pharmacopoeia of Eastern Medicine; Greco-Arabian Concepts of Cardio-vascular Disease; Avicenna's Tract of Cardiac Drugs and Essays on Arab Cardiotherapy.* Scientific journal: *Hamdard Medicus* – informative articles by world authorities. Hamdard Foundation, Nazimabad, Karachi-18, Pakistan.

HAND. TIGHTENING OF SINEWS. See: DUPUYPTREN'S CONTRACTURE.

HAND CREAM. *Dry skin*: Avocado or Elderblossom cream.

Oily skin: Witch Hazel cream, cleansing milk or skin freshener.

To maintain healthy skin: Cucumber cleansing cream, or milk; Marigold cream.

Formula: Almond oil 2; Apricot kernel oil 1; Beeswax 1. Dissolve in a pan in gentle heat; pour into pots. To soothe chapped hands, wind burn, and for general kitchen use.

HANGOVER. After-effects of excessive alcohol consumption.

Symptoms. Dry mouth, thirst, increased output of urine, fatigue, irritability. Alcohol increases REM (rapid eye movement) during sleep. Brain cell excitability is followed by depression.

Potassium loss may be severe, as also loss of Vitamins B, B6 and C. Bananas are rich in potassium.

Alternatives. *Tea.* 1-2 cups Chamomile tea. Ginger. Gin-and-tonic with juice of lemon, plus teaspoon honey.

Morning-after tea. Meadowsweet (antacid) 1; Centuary (bitter) 1; Black Horehound (anti-emetic) 1; Gentian (tonic) quarter; Ginger (stomach settler) quarter. Mix. 2 teaspoons to

each cup boiling water; infuse 10 minutes. Drink freely.
Diet. Honey for energy. Slippery Elm gruel. Avoid coffee.
Supplements. B-complex, C, E. Essential fatty acids. Potassium, Magnesium, Selenium, Zinc.
Note. Alcohol is a strong diuretic which drains the body and brain cells of vital fluids. Alcohol also contains congeners, the chemical by-products of fermentation which have a poisonous effect upon the body. The most important treatment is water – long drinks to rehydrate the body and brain. Water also helps the kidneys and liver to wash out the poisons.

HANSEN'S DISEASE. Leprosy. Progressive infection by *Mycobacterium leprae*. Two forms: (1) tuberculoid; infection of the nerve endings and membranes of the nose, with loss of feeling and pale patches on the body. (2) Lepromatous; with inflamed thickened painful red skin exacerbated by ulceration, fever, neuritis and orchitis. Distorted lips and loss of nasal bone as infection progresses.
Symptoms: numbness, nerves may swell like iron rods. Infected nerves kill all sensation. In endemic areas, pins and needles in hands may call attention to it. A disease of nerves rather than skin. NOTIFIABLE DISEASE.

Many laymen and practitioners will never have seen a case. In the absence of modern medicine some good can be achieved by traditional remedies. Ancient Hindu and Chinese records refer to the use of Gotu Kola (internally and externally). Dr C.D. de Granpré (1888) refers. (*Martindale 27; p.441*)

Oil of Chaulmoogra was used up to one hundred years ago before introduction of modern drugs. It fell into dis-use until discovered by a Director of Health in the Philippine Islands during World War I when he used it successfully in combination with camphor. In South America, where the disease is still active, Sarsaparilla has a long traditional reputation. Walnut oil is used as a dressing, in China. An anti-staphylococcal fraction has been isolated from the seeds of *Psoralea corylifolia* for use in leprosy. (*Indian Journal of Pharmacy 26: 141, 1964*)
Tea. Gotu Kola. Half a teaspoon to each cup boiling water; infuse 15 minutes. Drink freely. Stronger infusions may be used externally to cleanse ulceration.
Decoction. Combine: Sarsaparilla 1; Gotu Kola 1; Echinacea 2. Half an ounce to 1 pint water gently simmered 20 minutes. Dose: Half a cup 3 times daily.
Formula. Echinacea 2; Sarsaparilla 1; Gotu Kola 2. Dose. Powders 500mg. Liquid Extracts 3-5ml. Tinctures 5-10ml. Thrice daily.
Note. Antibody-positive cases of AIDS are vulnerable to leprosy, both diseases being caused by a similar bacterium.

To be treated by infectious diseases specialist.

HANTAAN VIRUS. Haemorrhagic fever with kidney syndrome (HFRS). Has been known for years by the Chinese and other nations of antiquity. Over 3,000 cases recorded during the Korean War (1951-1952), the disease taking its name from the River Hantaan, South Korea.
Cause: a virus spread by field mice, rats and other rodents. Incubation period: 2-3 weeks.
Symptoms: fever, headache, backache, severe nervous prostration, low blood pressure, red patches on skin, failure of kidneys, high protein levels in urine. Small red or purple spots indicate bleeding beneath the skin.
Treatment. *Traditional*. Ayurvedic:– Gotu Kola, Juniper. Dr Mattiolus regards Juniper as a preventative of the pestilence.

To be treated by or in liaison with a qualified medical practitioner.

HARPAGOPHYTUM. See: DEVIL'S CLAW.

HART'S TONGUE. Fern. *Phyllitis scolopendrium L. Scolopendrium vulgare L.* Dried leaves.
Keynotes: liver and spleen.
Constituents: flavonoids, tannins, mucilage.
Action: spleen and liver astringent, pectoral, laxative, diuretic.
Uses. Disorders of liver and spleen BHP (1983). Gravel.

Combines well with Fringe Tree BHP (1983).
Preparations. Average dose 2-4g. Thrice daily.
Tea. 1 heaped teaspoon to each cup of boiling water; infuse 15 minutes; dose half-1 cup.
Liquid extract. Half-1 teaspoon in water.
Tincture BHP (1983) 1:5 in 45 per cent alcohol; dose 2-6ml. GSL

HARVESTING OF HERBS. Older generations of herbalists attached great importance to the time of collection. The most auspicious hour may vary from herb to herb and is recorded in the old herbals. The kind of weather, with presence or absence of sunlight, are now known to affect the potency of a plant. Much herb lore of history has been vindicated by today's scientific research, with the discovery that the quality of active ingredients depends upon such variables as season, location, and the time of day when gathered. Different parts of herbs are gathered at different times.

Herbs should be collected in dry weather after the dew has lifted. Where not possible to cull by hand, a sharp knife or scythe should be used. In general, aerial parts should be gathered before flowering. Rhizomes and roots are gathered in the autumn when the leaves decline for maximum therapeutic action. Wash and clean roots, and ensure they do not touch when drying. Flowers are picked just before breaking into full bloom.

Barks and twigs are collected in the spring when the sap is rising.

Spread out fresh material to dry in a thin layer, without delay. Use trays, wire racks, even lengths of string netting. Packed into bundles without circulation of air encourages bruising, fermentation and mould that destroy medicinal properties.

Almost any shed can be adapted as a drying shed, provided there is adequate ventilation. Artificial heat may be required for complete drying. Leaves should not be dried to the point where they powder when rubbed between the palms. Most herbs and roots lose about four-fifths of their weight on drying. When the hand is plunged into a bag of well-dried herbs they should feel warm and crisp to the touch. Roots are dried to the point of brittleness, breaking easily.

Present-day growers achieve high standards of drying. Since passage of the Medicine's Act, 1968, the quality of herbs on sale has been good. Dried herbs should be stored away from direct sunlight, or they will lose their colour and efficacy.

HASHIMOTO'S DISEASE. Hashimoto's thyroiditis. Inflammation of the Thyroid gland with increase of fibrous tissue and intrusion of excess white blood cells. Forerunner of myxoedema. It is an auto-immune disorder resulting in thyroid damage. Middle-aged women prone. Painless swelling.
Alternatives. *Treatment*. Echinacea is the key remedy.
Others indicated: Red Clover flower, Blue Flag root, Horsetail, Poke root, Bladderwrack. May be taken singly, as available.
Tea: Combine Bladderwrack 2; Echinacea 2; Horsetail 1. 1-2 teaspoons to each cup boiling water; infuse 15 minutes. Half-1 cup thrice daily.
Tinctures. Combine: Bladderwrack 2; Echinacea 2; Horsetail 1. Dose: one to two 5ml teaspoons in water thrice daily.
Diet. Iodised salt. Avoid cabbage which contains a factor which depresses the thyroid gland.
Supplementation. Vitamin A. B-complex. Kelp.

HAWTHORN. White thorn. *Crataegus oxyacanthoides* Thuill. Or *C. monogyna Jacq. French*: Aubépine. *German*: Hagedorn. *Spanish*: Espina blanca. *Italian*: Marruca bianca. *Parts used*: Dried flowers, leaves, fruits. *Keynote*: heart.
Constituents. Flavonoids, phenolic acids, tannins, amines.
Action. Positive heart restorative. Coronary vasodilator BHP (1983), antispasmodic, antihypertensive, adaptogen, diuretic, sedative to nervous system, cholesterol and mineral solvent. Action lacks the toxic effects of digitalis. Useful where digitalis is not tolerated.
Uses. To increase blood flow through the heart. Strengthens heart muscle without increasing the beat or raising blood pressure. Enhances exercise duration. Myocarditis with failing compensation. Improves circulation in coronary arteries. Arteriosclerosis, atheroma, thrombosis, rapid heart beat, paroxysmal tachycardia BHP (1983), fatty degeneration; angina, enlargement of the heart from over-work, over-exercise or mental tension, alcoholic heart, Buerger's disease, intermittent claudication, risk of infarction, dizziness (long term), mild to moderate hypertension, insomnia. Used by sportsmen to sustain the heart under maximum effort.
Preparations. Thrice daily.
Tea. Leaves and flowers. 1-2 teaspoons to each cup boiling water; infuse 5-10 minutes. Dose: 1 cup. Traditional for insomnia or for the heart under stress.
Decoction. Fruits. 1-2 heaped teaspoons haws to each cup water; simmer gently 2 minutes. Dose: half-1 cup.
Tablets/capsules. Two 200-250mg.
Liquid extract. 8-15 drops in water.
Tincture. 1:5 in 45 per cent alcohol, dose: 15-30 drops (1-2ml).
Popular combinations:–
With Mistletoe and Valerian (equal parts) as a sedative for nervous heart.
With Lily of the Valley 1; Hawthorn berries 2; for cardiac oedema.
With Lime flowers, Mistletoe and Valerian (equal parts) for high blood pressure.
With Horseradish or Cayenne, as a safe circulatory stimulant.

Gradual onset of action. Low incidence of side-effects. No absolute contra-indications.
Note. Dr D. Greene, Ennis, County Clare, Eire, attained an international reputation for treatment of heart disease keeping the remedy a secret. Upon his death his daughter revealed it as a tincture of red-ripe Hawthorn berries. Pharmacy only

HAY FEVER. An allergic condition with hypersensitivity of eyes, nose, throat and sometimes the skin due to grass and flower pollens in May and June. These and similar allergens cause the body to produce an excess of histamine which manifests as catarrh and nasal congestion. Hay fever may simulate allergy to cow's milk (in children), additives and colourings in foods and sweets.
Symptoms: sneezy runny itchy nose and eyes, nose-block and sensitive palate. The upset may be mild or very disabling.
Alternatives. *Teas*. Cudweed, Elder, Ephedra, Eyebright, Ground Ivy, Nettles, Plantain, Peppermint, Sage.
Formula. Equal parts, Eyebright, Ephedra, White Horehound. 2 teaspoons to each cup boiling water; infuse 15 minutes. Dose: half-1 cup freely.
Tablets/capsules. Iceland Moss, Garlic, Lobelia, St John's Wort.
Powders. Formula. Equal parts: Eyebright, Ephedra, Plantain. Dose: 500mg (two 00 capsules

or one-third teaspoon) thrice daily.
Tinctures. Alternatives. (1) Formula. Eyebright 3; Echinacea 2; Bayberry bark 1. (2) Formula. St John's Wort 2; Uva Ursi 2; Bayberry bark 1. Dose: one 5ml teaspoon thrice daily. Infants: one drop each year of age.
Practitioner. Alternatives. (1) Equal parts: Ephedra (anti-allergic) and Nettles (anti-histamine). (2) Tinctures: Ephedra 2ml; Yarrow 5ml; Elder 5ml; Capsicum 0.5ml. Doses: 15-30 drops thrice daily in water.
Topical. Eyes should be treated separately. Bayberry bark powder for use as a snuff. Compresses of Chamomile for inflamed itchy eyes. Witch Hazel eye douch. Olbas oil on a handkerchief as an inhalant. Potter's Anti-fect. Nasal douche: 1-2 drops Blood root in water. Dr Bourgeois, French Allergist, recommends Halibut liver oil nasal spray, frequently.
Diet. Avoid dairy products, caffeine drinks and alcohol entirely during the hay fever season. Low fat yoghurt contains an antihistamine. Abundant grated carrot for Vitamin A. Green tea. Raw vegetable salad once daily.
Supplementation. Vitamins A, B-complex, C (1 gram daily), E. Propolis, Pollen, Honeycomb as chewing gum, Magnesium, Zinc.
Preventative. 2 Garlic capsules, with high oil content, at night for 1-2 months before season begins.
Purulent cases. 5-10 drops Tincture Myrrh in water, thrice daily.

HE SHOU WU. Polygonum multiflorum. Chinese remedy. *Part used*: tuber.
Action. Antibacterial, antispasmodic, laxative, tonic, blood tonic, diuretic.
Uses. Menopause. Mild kidney disturbance. Greying of hair early in life.
Preparations. Thrice daily.
Tea. 2-4g root to each cup water gently simmered 5 minutes (decoction). Dose: half-1 cup.
Tincture. Dose: 1 teaspoon.
Caution. Not used in presence of irritable bowel syndrome.

HEADACHE, COMMON. Usually due to muscular tension. Where persistent the underlying cause should be treated. Causes are many and varied including fevers, infected sinus cavities, kidney disorders, dental problems, thrombosis, neuralgias, nasal congestion, arteritis, pressure within the eyes, spread of pain from bones, etc.

See separate entry for migraine.
As indicated: relaxants, antispasmodics, hepatics (liver agents), laxatives. BHP (1983) recommends: Betony, Hops, St John's Wort, Yerba Mate, Catmint, Passion flower, Jamaican Dogwood, Pulsatilla, Rosemary. A diuretic may release excess body fluid and surprisingly relieve headache as in pre-menstrual tension.
Frontal headache: Agnus Castus.
From eyestrain: Rue, Witch Hazel.
After heavy physical work: Ginseng.
Neuralgia of the skull: Gelsemium.
Low blood pressure: Gentian.
High blood pressure: Lime flowers.
Depressive conditions: Cola.
Pain, back of the head: Oats, Ladyslipper.
Pre-menstrual: Cramp bark, Agnus Castus.
Excess mental exertion: Rosemary.
Following anger: Sumbul.
In children: see CHILDREN'S COMPLAINTS.
Pain, top of head: Pulsatilla, Cactus.
Throbbing headache: Chamomile.
Sick headache: Blue Flag.
Tension headache: Skullcap, Betony, Passion flower.
Cluster headache, associated with shingles: Vervain, Skullcap.
Menstrual headache: see entry: MENSTRUAL HEADACHE.
Alternatives. *Tea*. Combine equal parts: Skullcap, Betony, Chamomile. 1-2 teaspoons to each cup boiling water; infuse 15 minutes. Half-1 cup when necessary.
Decoction. Combine equal parts: Valerian, Blue Flag, Barberry bark. 1 teaspoon to each cup water gently simmered 20 minutes. Half-1 cup when necessary.
Tablets/capsules. Blue Flag, Valerian, Chamomile, Passion flower.
Powders. Formula. Equal parts: Skullcap, Rosemary, Valerian. 500mg (two 00 capsules or one-third teaspoon) when necessary.
Tinctures. Combine equal parts: Mistletoe, Valerian, Skullcap. One to two teaspoons in water every 3 hours as necessary.
Tincture Rosemary. 15-30 drops in water as necessary.
Practitioner. Tincture Gelsemium 5 drops to 100ml water (half cup) – 1 teaspoon hourly.
Traditional combination: Skullcap, Valerian, Mistletoe.
Topical. Hot footbaths. Cold compress to head.
Aromatherapy. Anoint forehead with few drops: Lavender, Chamomile, Rosemary, Mint, Balm, or Tiger Balm essential oils.
Diet. Low fat. Low salt. Avoid meats preserved in sodium nitrite (bacon, ham, red meats, etc).
Supplementation. Vitamins A, B-complex, B6 (50mg), B12, C (up to 1 gram), E (up to 1000iu). Magnesium, Zinc.

HEALING HERBS. Herbs with outstanding ability to promote granulation and healing of flesh as in injury, ulceration and breakdown of tissue. There are many, chief of which are: Comfrey, Fenugreek, Iceland Moss, Marigold, Witch Hazel.

HEALTH STORES (WHOLESALE) LTD. Registered as a Friendly Society (1932) under the Industrial and Provident Societies Act. The buying society of the independent health food trader. Owned and managed entirely by retailer members and concerned with food standards. Stringent rules govern membership and conduct of business. Members are the only shareholders, who are required to hold 20 withdrawable shares of £5 each.

Financial advantages to members include earning profit-sharing discounts: suppliers are relieved of the burden of collecting separate accounts and benefit from having their products approved by the retailers own organisation. Its meetings are a focal point for reporting on up-to-date research and protecting the public interest.
Address: Queen's Road, Nottingham NG2 3AS.

HEARING LOSS. Otosclerosis: a common cause of deafness in healthy adults. Gradual progressive hearing loss with troublesome tinnitus. The stapes may be fixed and the cochlea damaged. Bones may become spongy and demineralised. While deafness is a matter for the professional specialist, herbal treatment may prove useful. Examine ear for wax.
Internal. Elderflower and Peppermint tea (catarrhal). Ginkgo tea.
Tablets/capsules. Ginkgo. Improvement reported in moderate loss.
Topical. Garlic oil. Injection of 3-4 drops at night.
Wax in the ear. Mixture: 30 drops oil Eucalyptus, 1 drop Tincture Capsicum (or 3 of Ginger), 1oz (30ml) Olive oil. Inject 4-5 drops, warm.
Black Cohosh Drops. It is claimed that John Christopher (USA) improved many cases of moderate hearing loss with topical use of 5-10 drops Liquid Extract in 1oz oil of Mullein (or Olive oil).
Pulsatilla Drops. Tincture Pulsatilla and glycerol 50/50. 2-3 drops injected at bedtime. Assists auditory nerve function. (*Arthur Hyde*)
Nerve deafness due to fibroma of the 8th cranial nerve, or after surgery – oral: Mistletoe tea for temporary relief.

HEART. See: ANEURISM, ANGINA, AORTIC STENOSIS, ARTERITIS, ATHEROSCLEROSIS, ATHLETE'S HEART, ATRIAL FIBRILLATION, BRADYCARDIA, CARDIAC ARREST, CORONARY HEART DISEASE, ENDOCARDITIS, MITRAL STENOSIS, MYOCARDITIS, PALPITATION, PERICARDITIS, SMOKER'S HEART, TACHYCARDIA, THROMBOSIS.
For all heart disorders. Weight reduction, stop smoking. Reduction of excessive physical exertion. Correction of aggravating factors such as anaemia and dietetic tendency to eat too much animal fat. Specific herbal treatment may be taken with profit before surgery (coronary bypass grafts). Cardiac herbs reduce oxygen consumption by the heart muscle (myocardium) by having a beta-blocker-like effect, lowering the heart rate particularly during exercise and reducing systolic blood pressure, thus decreasing the demand for oxygen.

HEART. OVER-STRAINED. See: ATHLETE'S HEART.

HEART BLOCK. A disorder that occurs in the transmission of impulses between the atria (upper chambers) and ventricles (lower chambers) of the heart. A blocking of the normal route of electrical conduction through the ventricles not responding to initiation of the beat by the atria. Beats are missed with possible blackouts.
Causes: myocardial infarction, atherosclerosis, coronary thrombosis or other heart disorder.
Symptoms: slow feeble heart beats down to 36 beats per minute with fainting and collapse, breathlessness, Stoke Adams syndrome.
Treatment. Intensive care. Until the doctor comes: 1-5 drops Oil of Camphor in honey on the tongue or taken in a liquid if patient is able to drink. Freely inhale the oil. On recovery: Motherwort tea, freely. OR, Formula of tinctures: Lily of the Valley 2; Cactus 1; Motherwort 2. Mix. Dose – 30-60 drops in water thrice daily. A fitted pace-maker may be necessary.
Spartiol. 20 drops thrice daily. (*Klein*)

HEARTBURN. A burning sensation in the gullet, as felt behind the breastbone, caused by a laxity of the oesophago-gastric sphincter, with acid rising from the stomach. May be due to bending, tight clothing, hiatus hernia, acid dyspepsia or gastritis. Bitter acid taste in the mouth.
Alternatives. Most antacids relieve heartburn and gastric reflux in conditions such as acid dyspepsia, gastritis and hiatus hernia. Teas selected from Barberry, Black Horehound, Centuary, (*Dr A. Vogel*) Dandelion, Chamomile tea. (*Charles Wesley*) Marshmallow, Meadowsweet.
To give mucosal protection: Irish Moss, Iceland Moss, Slippery Elm. St John's Wort. (*Dr A. Vogel*)
Powders. Alternatives. (1) Meadowsweet 2; Galangal 1. (2) Equal parts: Dandelion root, Fennel. Doses: 500mg (two 00 capsules or one-third teaspoon) thrice daily.
Tinctures. Alternatives. (1) Dandelion 1; Meadowsweet 2; Liquorice root half. (2) Meadowsweet 2; Black Horehound 1. Liquorice half. Dose: One 5ml teaspoon in water thrice daily before meals.
Tablets/capsules. Sarsaparilla, St John's Wort. Meadowsweet. Iceland Moss. Slippery Elm.
Aloe Vera juice. 1-2 tablespoons juice from crushed leaves.
Nervous stomach. German Chamomile tea.
From alcohol and tobacco habit. Liquid Extract

Stone root: 15-60 drops, (or Tincture BPC (1934) 30-120 drops) in water thrice daily.

For heartburn of pregnancy – see PREGNANCY.

Diet. Dandelion coffee. See: THE HAY DIET.

Avoid bending and stooping, eat small regular meals. Avoid hot spicy foods.

Avoid wearing tight clothing, cut out smoking. If suffering is at night, prop up head end of mattress by 4-6".

HEART DISEASE – CONGENITAL. Heart disease arising from abnormal development. Some cases are hereditary, others due to drugs taken during pregnancy. Many owe their origin to illnesses of the mother such as German measles. Structural abnormalities of the heart take different forms but whatever the case, when under abnormal pressure and stress, all may derive some small benefit from the sustaining properties of Hawthorn berry and other phytomedicines.

Alternatives. To sustain.

Teas. Lime flowers, Motherwort, Buckwheat, Hawthorn.

Tablets/capsules. Hawthorn, Mistletoe, Motherwort.

Formula. Hawthorn 2; Lily of the Valley 1; Selenicereus grandiflorus 1. Powders: 500mg (two 00 capsules or one-third teaspoon). Liquid extracts: 1 teaspoon. Tinctures: 2 teaspoons. In water morning and evening.

HEART – DEGENERATION, IN THE ELDERLY. May take the form of degeneration of healthy cardiac tissue replaced by broken fatty patches. As cardiac muscle wastes fibrous tissue takes its place.

While cure is not possible, atheroma may be arrested by a cup of herbal tea: Hawthorn blossoms, Motherwort, Horsetail: single or in combination. 1-2 teaspoons to each cup boiling water; infuse 5-15 minutes; 1-2 cups daily.

Formula. Hawthorn 2; Ginkgo 2; Horsetail 1; Ginger quarter. Dose. Powders: 500mg (two 00 capsules or one-third teaspoon). Liquid extracts: 1 teaspoon. Tinctures: 2 teaspoons. Twice daily: morning and evening in water or honey.

Diet. See: DIET – HEART AND CIRCULATION. Few grains of Cayenne pepper as seasoning on food once daily.

Stop smoking.

HEART – ENLARGEMENT. A heart may dilate (enlarge) to compensate for valvular disease. One of two types: (1) Swelling (dilation) of the cavities with thickening of the walls, (hypertrophy of the heart muscle). (2) Dilation of cavities with thinning of the walls.

(1) Arises from the exertions of professional athletes. Extra strain enlarges the heart and calls for compensation. Other causes: high blood pressure and diseased valves.

(2) From anaemia, thyroid disorder, or extra strain demanded by fever. Thin walls always lead to heart weakness, robbing the organ of its maximum power.

Treatment. When compensation is delayed cardiac supportives include Bugleweed (American) to increase force of contractions of the heart and reduce the rate BHP (1983).

Right ventricular enlargement – Stone root.

Left ventricular enlargement – Lily of the Valley.

Both remedies have the advantage of being diuretics, thus aiding elimination of excess fluids.

Diet. See: DIET – HEART AND CIRCULATION.

HEART – EXTRA BEATS. Extra-systoles. An occasional beat or beats may arise prematurely from an abnormal focus in atrium or ventricle. Such is a common occurrence and is little cause for alarm. Simple arrythmia may be the outraged protest of a heart under the influence of alcohol, heavy meals, too much tea or coffee, smoking or excitement. If persistent, examination by a trained practitioner should be sought. For uncomplicated transient extra-systole:–

Alternatives. *Teas*: Balm, Motherwort, Hawthorn flowers or leaves.

Tablets: Hawthorn, Motherwort, Mistletoe, Valerian.

Tincture Lily of the Valley: 8-15 drops when necessary.

Broom: Spartiol drops. (*Klein*) 20 drops thrice daily.

Broom decoction. 1oz to 1 pint water gently simmered 10 minutes. 1 cup morning and evening.

HEART – FATTY DEGENERATION. A deposit and infiltration of fat on the heart in the obese and heavy consumers of alcohol. Distinct from true degeneration in which there is no destruction of tissue.

Symptoms. Breathlessness and palpitation on slight exertion. Anginal pain: see ANGINA. Mental dullness. May follow enlargement of the heart and acute infections such as influenza.

Alternatives. *Teas*. Alfalfa, Clivers, Yarrow, Motherwort.

Tablets/capsules. Poke root, Kelp, Motherwort.

Formula. Equal parts: Bladderwrack, Motherwort, Aniseed, Dandelion. Dose. Powders: 500mg (two 00 capsules or one-third teaspoon). Liquid extracts: 1 teaspoon. Tinctures: 2 teaspoons in water thrice daily.

Black Cohosh. Introduced into the medical world in 1831 when members of the North American Eclectic School of physicians effectively treated cases of fatty heart.

Diet. Vegetarian protein foods, high-fibre, whole grains, seed sprouts, lecithin, soya products, low-fat yoghurt, plenty of raw fruit and vegetables,

unrefined carbohydrates. Oily fish: see entry. Dandelion coffee. *Reject*: alcohol, coffee, salt, sugar, fried foods, all dairy products except yoghurt.
Supplements. Daily. Broad-spectrum multivitamin including Vitamins A, B-complex, B3, B6, C (with bioflavonoids), E, Selenium.

HEART – FIBROUS DEGENERATION. Distinct from fatty degeneration Due to thickening of walls by atheroma. Heart muscle (myocardium) fibres waste away due to lack of nourishment and are replaced by fibrous tissue. The condition usually runs with kidney weakness. Incurable. Partial relief of symptoms – treatment as for arteriosclerosis.

Every cardiac prescription for this condition should include a gentle diuretic to assist kidney function. The kidneys should be borne in mind, the most appropriate diuretic being Dandelion which would also make good any potassium loss.

HEART – LEFT VENTRICULAR FAILURE (LVF). Failure of the left ventricle to receive blood from the pulmonary circulation and to maintain efficient output of incoming blood to the arterial system. Failure to do so leads to congestion of blood in the lungs followed by fluid retention. If uncorrected, leads to kidney disturbance, low blood pressure, cyanosis (blueness of the skin). Onset may be tragically sudden. Failure of the left ventricle may occur in cases of pericarditis, disease of the aortic valve, nephritis or high blood pressure.

Left ventricular failure is often of sudden onset, urgent, and may manifest as "cardiac asthma".
Causes: blood clot, anaemia, thyroid disorder, coronary disease, congenital effects, drug therapy (beta blockers, etc), and to fevers that make heavy demands on the left ventricle.
Symptoms: breathlessness, wheezing, sweating, unproductive cough, faintness, bleeding from the lungs, palpitation. Cardiac asthma at night: feels he needs air; better upright than lying flat. Exertion soon tires. Sensation as if heart would stop. Blueness of lips and ears from hold-up in circulation of the blood through the lungs. Frequent chest colds. Awakes gasping for breath. Always tired. Cold hands and feet. Symptoms abate as compensation takes place. 'Cream and roses' complexion. The failure of left ventricle soon drags into failure of the right ventricle.

Right ventricular failure leads to congestive heart failure, with raised venous pressure in neck veins and body generally, causing oedema, ascites and liver engorgement.
Treatment. Agents to strengthen, support, and eliminate excess fluids from the body. BHP (1983) advises four main remedies: Hawthorn, Motherwort, Broom and Lily of the Valley. The latter works in a digitaloid manner, strengthening the heart, contracting the vessels, and lessening congestion in the lungs.
Tinctures. Hawthorn 2; Stone root 1. Lily of the Valley 1. Dose: 15-45 drops thrice daily.
Broom tea. 2 teaspoons flowers, or 2-3 teaspoons tops and flowers, in cup water brought to boil and simmered one minute. 1 cup freely.

To remove fluid retention in the lungs, diuretics are indicated; chief among which is Dandelion root because of its high potassium content to prevent hypokalaemia. Dandelion coffee. As urinary excretion increases, patient improves.
Vitamin E. Not to be taken in left ventricular disorders.
Diet. See entry: DIET – HEART AND CIRCULATION.
UK Research. Researchers found that left ventricular failure was reduced by a quarter when patients were given magnesium intravenously for the first 24 hours after admission to the coronary care unit. They conclude that it should be given before any other heart therapy is commenced, and that patients should receive regular infusions if no other drug treatment is used. (*The Lancet, 2.4.1994*). This supports the use of magnesium sulphate (Epsom's salts) by a past generation of herbal practitioners for the condition.

HEART – NERVOUS. Condition with no specific organic lesion present, but one in which palpitation or cardiac distress may be precipitated by nervous or emotional stimuli.
Alternatives. *Neuralgia of the Heart*: Lobelia.
Palpitation with sense of suffocation: Pulsatilla.
From physical exhaustion: Ginseng.
With rapid heart beat: Lily of the Valley, Gelsemium.
Tea. Equal parts, Valerian, Motherwort, Lime flowers. Mix. 1-2 teaspoons to each cup boiling water allowed to cool. Drink cold 1 teacup 2 or 3 times daily.
Decoction. Equal parts, Valerian, Hawthorn, Mistletoe. Mix. 1 heaped teaspoon to each cup water simmered gently for 20 minutes. 1 teacup 2 or 3 times daily.
Tablets/capsules. Hawthorn, Mistletoe, Motherwort. Valerian. Passion flower. Lobelia.
Formula. Equal parts: Hawthorn, Lily of the Valley, Mistletoe. Dose: Powders: 500mg (two 00 capsules or one-third teaspoon). Liquid extracts: 1 teaspoon. Tinctures 2 teaspoons. Thrice daily.
Practitioner. Formula. Tincture Hawthorn 2; Tincture Gelsemium 1. Dose: 15-30 drops 2-3 times daily.
Alternative formula. Tincture Valerian 2; Strophanthus 1. Dose: 15-30 drops thrice daily.
Diet. Oats (oatmeal porridge), low fat, low salt, high fibre. See also: DIET – HEART AND CIRCULATION.

HEART, RAPID BEAT. See: TACHYCARDIA.

HEART. RHEUMATIC HEART. Hearts can be damaged by rheumatic fever but they yearly become less, due to the advance of medical science, better nutrition and living conditions. Damage to the valves may not come to light until years later. Mostly a legacy from rheumatic fever in early childhood.
Alternatives. Regular treatment may not be necessary except for periods of unusual tension, exposure and stress.
Teas: Nettles, Borage, Mate, Figwort, Gotu Kola, Motherwort.
Decoctions: Blach Cohosh, Cramp bark, Hawthorn, Lily of the Valley, White Willow, Sarsaparilla. Any one.
Formula. Combine Black Cohosh root half; White Willow bark 2; Gotu Kola 1; Hawthorn berries 1. 1oz to 1 pint water; bring to boil; simmer gently 15 minutes; strain when cold. Dose: half-1 cup thrice daily, and when necessary.
Ligvites. Guaiacum resin BHP (1983) 40mg; Black Cohosh BHP (1983) 35mg; White Willow bark BHP (1983) 100mg; Extract Sarsaparilla 4:1 25mg; Extract Poplar bark 7:1 17mg. (*Gerard House*)
Powders. Combine, Hawthorn 1; Cactus 2; Black Cohosh half; White Willow bark 1; with pinch Cayenne. 750mg (three 00 capsules or half a teaspoon) 2-3 times daily.
White Bryony. Liquid Extract: 15-60 drops, thrice daily. Good results reported.
Colchicum, Tincture. Indicated in presence of gout: Dose: 0.5-2ml in water. (Practitioner use only)
Vitamin E. Should not be taken in rheumatic heart disorders.
Diet. See: DIET – HEART AND CIRCULATION.

HEART – RIGHT VENTRICULAR FAILURE (RVF). Failure of the right ventricle to hold its own with the return flow of blood and to re-direct it through the lungs where it is re-oxygenated before entering the left ventricle for completing the circulatory cycle. Usually secondary to failure of the left ventricle. May be caused by valvular disease, especially narrowing of the orifice of the mitral valve.

Mitral disease leads to heart failure either by a narrowing of the orifice (stenosis) or a regurgitation blocks the passage of blood from the left atrium (auricle) to the left ventricle. The left atrium enlarges (hypertrophies) in an effort to counter the impediment. Real compensation – increased thrust of the blood – is provided by the right ventricle. In order to overcome a mitral impediment the right ventricle has to enlarge.

Sooner or later the right ventricle cannot enlarge any further and general heart failure sets in. Though caused primarily by a lesion of the mitral valve, it may be secondary to left ventricular failure (LVF), thyroid disorder (thyrotoxicosis), pericarditis, congenital heart disease, or any disease which weakens ventricular muscle.

Venous congestion and back pressure of RVF leads to congestion and accumulation of fluid in the lungs, cough and spitting of blood, painful swelling of the liver, nausea, loss of appetite and severe wasting.

Where the right ventricle fails to move the blood forward as it arrives from the systemic circulation, generalised dropsy sets in. Congestion of the kidneys leads to reduced urinary excretion and presence of albumin in the urine.

The picture is well known to the cardiac practitioner: blueness of the skin, congestion of the brain circulation with sleeplessness and delirium. Soon the tension of water-logged tissues results in pain and extreme anxiety. Feet are swollen and ankles pit on pressure; chest cavities fill with fluid and the abdomen swells (ascites).
Alternatives. Cardio-tonics would be given to strengthen the ventricle and diuretics to correct fluid retention: Lily of the Valley, Hawthorn, Motherwort, Broom. BHP (1983).
Due to rheumatic fever: Hawthorn.
High Blood Pressure: Mistletoe.
Effort Syndrome: Motherwort.
Tinctures. Combine, Lily of the Valley 2; Hawthorn 2; Motherwort 3. Dose: 1 teaspoon thrice daily after meals.
Diet. Low salt, low fat, high fibre. Restricted fluids, vegetarian protein foods, yoghurt. See also: DIET – HEART AND CIRCULATION.
Supplements. Potassium (bananas), Vitamin B6.
General. Stop smoking. Correction of overweight. Complete bed-rest with legs raised above level of the abdomen and patient propped-up to relieve difficult breathing.

HEART. SIMPLE HEART WEAKNESS. General debility of the heart in the absence of structural defect or serious disorder. A feeble heart may sometimes be well served by nervines alone: Skullcap, Chamomile, Betony, Valerian, especially if accompanied by a sinking feeling.
Alternatives. *Tea*. Combine equal parts: Motherwort, Valerian, Borage. 1-2 teaspoons to each cup boiling water; infuse 10 minutes. 1 cup once or twice daily.
Decoction. Combine equal parts: Hawthorn berries, Valerian. 1-2 teaspoons to each cup water simmered gently 10 minutes. 1 cup once or twice daily.
Tablets/capsules. Hawthorn, Motherwort, Cayenne, Valerian, Skullcap.
Alternative formulae. *Tinctures*.
(1) Cactus 15ml; Hawthorn 15ml; Capsicum 1ml. Dose: one teaspoon in water thrice daily.
(2) Hawthorn 15ml; Valerian 15ml; Ginseng 10ml. Dose: one teaspoon in water thrice daily.

(3) Saw Palmetto 20ml; Damiana 10ml; Hawthorn 20ml; Capsicum 1ml. Dose: 1-2 teaspoons in water thrice daily.
Practitioner. Tincture Arnica 1-2 drops in water morning and evening for 7 days.
Diet. Foods rich in Vitamins B, B6, C, E. See also: DIET – HEART AND CIRCULATION.

HEARTSEASE. Wild Pansy. *Viola tricolor L. French*: Pensee. *German*: Dreifarbiges Veilchen. *Spanish*: Pensamiento. *Italian*: Pensiero. Leaves and flowers. *Keynotes*: skin and mucous membranes.
Constituents: mucilage, gum, saponin, flavonoids.
Action: anti-inflammatory, antirheumatic, expectorant, diuretic. Alterative. Depurative. Laxative. Rich in zinc. Anti-allergic. Anti-acne.
Uses. Chronic skin disorders with purulent sticky discharge. Moist eczema, milk crust, ringworm. Some success reported by Dr Schlegel, Moscow, for sexually transmitted diseases generally, with ulceration. A daily tea made from the herb is still taken in Russia by those with a tendency to tuberculosis, scrofula.
Capillary fragility BHP (1983). To prevent capillary haemorrhage when under corticosteroid therapy. Rheumatism. Acute bronchitis, whooping cough and respiratory distress in children.

Action is enhanced with Mouse Ear (equal parts) for whooping cough; and with Red Clover (equal parts) for skin disorders.
Preparations. Average dose: 2-4 grams. Thrice daily. Chiefly used as a tea made from the dried or fresh herb: 2 teaspoons to each cup boiling water; infuse 15 minutes. 1 cup.
Liquid Extract BHP (1983). 2-4ml.
Tablets/capsules. Two 250mg. GSL

HEAT EXHAUSTION. Collapse of the circulation from exposure to excessive heat. Possible in the presence of diarrhoea, vomiting or excessive sweating (dehydration) or alcohol consumption.
Symptoms: heavy sweating, failure of surface circulation, low blood pressure, weakness, cramps, rapid heartbeat, face is pale, cool and moist. Collapse. Recovery after treatment is rapid.
Alternatives. Cayenne pepper, or Tincture Capsicum, to promote peripheral circulation and sustain the heart. Prickly Ash bark restores vascular tone and stimulates capillary circulation. Bayberry offers a diffusive stimulant to promote blood flow, and Cayenne to increase arterial force.
Decoction. Combine equal parts Prickly Ash and Bayberry. 1 teaspoon to each cup water gently simmered 20 minutes. Half a cup (to which 3 drops Tincture Capsicum, or few grains red pepper is added). Dose: every 2 hours.
Tablets/capsules. Prickly Ash. Bayberry. Motherwort. Cayenne.
Tinctures. Formula. Prickly Ash 2; Horseradish 1; Bayberry 1. 15-30 drops in water every 2 hours.
Traditional. Horseradish juice or grated root, in honey.
Life Drops.

HEAT RASH. See: PRICKLY HEAT.

HEATH AND HEATHER, LTD. From small beginnings this unique herbal enterprise grew into a national concern. Founded: 1920 by James Ryder, St Albans, Herts. On his death in 1937 the company passed to Mrs Joan Ryder. Vendors of fine herbal preparations and publishers of a number of booklets including: *Gateway to Health* and *Famous Book of Herbs*. Following the company's 'take-over' from Booker Health Foods in 1987, it passed to The London Herb and Spice Co. Ltd., who maintain it as a brand leader in the health food trade.

Herbal combinations include: *Rheumatic Pain tablets No 100*: formula:– Guaiacum resin BPC '49 50.0mg; Capsicum oleoresin BPC 0.6mg; the solid extracts of: Rhubarb (alc 60 per cent 1-4) BPC '54 15mg; Uva Ursi (Aq 4:10) BPC '34 12.0mg; Bogbean (Aq 1:4) 30.0mg; Celery seed (Aq 1:4) BPC '49 30.0mg.
Indigestion and Flatulence tablets No 80: formula:– Capsicin BPC '23 0.25mgm; dried aqueous extract of Skullcap (3-10) BPC '34 3mgm; Valerian BPC 14mgm; Fennel seed BPC 14mgm; Myrrh BPC 19mgm; Papain BPC '54 1mgm; Peppermint oil BP 0.0006ml.

HEATHER FLOWERS. Ling. *Calluna vulgaris L. French*: Brande. *German*: Heidekraut. *Spanish*: Breyo. *Italian*: Brendolo. *Russian*: Weresk. *Swedish*: Liung. *Part used*: flowers. *Keynote*: urine.
Action: urinary antiseptic, diuretic, anti-rheumatic.
Uses. Cystitis, urethritis, gravel in the bladder, gout, muscular rheumatism.
Preparations. Average dose: 1-2 grams. Thrice daily.
Tea: half-1 teaspoon to each cup boiling water; infuse 15 minutes.
Liquid Extract BHP (1983) 1:1 in 25 per cent alcohol. Dose: 15-30 drops (1-2ml).

HEATHERCLEAN. (*Heath and Heather*) Senna leaves 75 per cent, Fennel 15 per cent, Frangula 5 per cent, Mate 2.5 per cent, Elder leaves 2.5 per cent. Non-persistent constipation.

HEATSTROKE. Sunstroke. Should not be confused with heat exhaustion.
Symptoms: skin hot, dry and flushed. High temperature and high humidity dispose. Sweating mechanism disorganised. Delirium, headache, shock, dizziness, possible coma, nausea, profuse sweating followed by absence of sweat causing skin to become hot and dry; rapid rise in body

temperature, muscle twitching, tachycardia, dehydration.

Treatment. Hospital emergency. Reduce temperature by immersion of victim in bath of cold water. Wrap in a cold wet sheet. Lobelia, to equalise the circulation. Feverfew to regulate sweating mechanism. Yarrow to reduce temperature. Give singly or in combination as available.

Alternatives. *Tea*. Lobelia 1; Feverfew 2; Yarrow 2. Mix. 2 teaspoons to each cup boiling water; infuse 15 minutes. Half-1 cup freely. Vomiting to be regarded as favourable.

Tinctures. Combine: Lobelia 1; Pleurisy root 2; Valerian 1. Dose: 1-2 teaspoons in water every 2 hours.

Decoction. Irish Moss; drink freely.

Practitioner. Tincture Gelsemium BPC (1973). Dose: 0.3ml (5 drops).

Alternate hot and cold compress to back of neck and forehead. Hot Chamomile footbath.

Diet. Irish Moss products. High salt. Abundant drinks of spring water.

Supplements. Kelp tablets, 2 thrice daily. Vitamin C (1g after meals thrice daily). Vitamin E (one 500iu capsule morning and evening).

Vitamin C for skin protection. Increasing Vitamin C after exposure to the sun should help protect against the sun's ultra violet rays, as skin Vitamin C levels were shown to be severely depleted after exposure. (*British Journal of Dermatology 127, 247-253*)

HEAVY ACHING LEGS. See: OEDEMA, CRAMPS, VARICOSE VEINS.

HEAVY METAL TOXICITY. Pollution of the blood and tissues by environmental poisons and traces of chemicals is a source of chronic disease. The most common toxic metals are lead, aluminium, cadmium, mercury and arsenic in that order. Copper is also toxic but is essential in small amounts.

Lead disrupts neurotransmitters in the brain and disposes to nervous excitability, aggression and hyperactivity. Aluminium is associated with senile dementia and Alzheimer's disease, accumulating in the brain. Cadmium induces changes in behaviour with reduced mental ability. Mercury is present in the amalgam used in dental surgery as part-filling for teeth. Arsenical poisoning may occur in food contamination or paints.

An internal chelating or cleansing of tissues of the lungs, urinary system, blood and lymph may be assisted by a combination of relative expectorants, diuretics, hepatics and adaptogens among which are: Barberry, Blue Flag root, Chaparral, Burdock, Echinacea, Red Clover, Yellow Dock. To bind with metals and assist their passage through the intestinal canal to the outside of the body: Irish Moss, Iceland Moss or Slippery Elm. Garlic.

The Medicines Control Agency of the Ministry of Health (UK) has given consideration to the content of heavy metal impurities and rules that a limit of 75 micrograms of total heavy metals shall be the acceptable maximum daily intake.

Licence-holders are required to carry out tests on all incoming material. Some seaweeds may be heavily polluted with mercury, arsenic and radioactive particles as a result of micro-biological contamination. The MCA requires Bladderwrack and other seaweeds to contain minimum levels.

HELONIAS. False Unicorn root. Blazing Star root. *Chamaelirium luteum* LA Gray. *Parts used*: roots, rhizome. *Keynote*: female reproductive system.

Constituents: helonin, saponins, chamaelirin.

Action. Powerful uterine tonic. Emmenagogue. Adaptogen. (*Simon Mills*) Precursor of oestrogen. Anthelmintic, diuretic, emetic.

Uses. Weakness of female reproductive organs. Absent or painful periods. Endometriosis, leucorrhoea, morning sickness, female sterility, inflammation of the Fallopian tubes, vaginitis, pruritus. Symptoms of the menopause: hot flushes, heavy bloated feeling, headache, depression, and to maintain normal fluid balance. Ovarian neuralgia. Spermatorrhoea in the male. Threatened abortion: miscarriage.

Preparations. Thrice daily. Average dose: 1-2g.

Combines well with Beth root. (*F. Fletcher Hyde*)

Tea. Does not yield its properties to simple infusion.

Decoction. Half-1 teaspoon to each cup water gently simmered 20 minutes. Dose: half-1 cup.

Liquid extract BHC Vol 1. 1:1 in 45 per cent ethanol. Dose: 1-2ml.

Tincture BHC Vol 1. 1:5 in 45 per cent alcohol. Dose: 2-5ml.

Powder. Equal parts Helonias and Beth root: 500mg (two 00 capsules or one-third teaspoon).

Popular combination. Tablets/capsules. Powdered Helonias BHP (1983) 120mg; powdered Parsley BHP (1983) 60mg; powdered Black Cohosh BHP (1983) 30mg; powdered extract Raspberry leaves 3:1 – 16.70mg. (*Gerard House*)

Note. Large doses may cause vomiting.

GSL, schedule 2

HEMIPLEGIA. Paralysis on one side of the body. Spastic weakness and increased muscle tone and tendon reflexes on affected side.

Causes: brain tumour or ruptured blood vessel, haemorrhage, thrombosis.

While total hemiplegia cannot be cured, the CNS may be supported by:–

Tinctures. Combine: Oats (stimulant nutrient) 3; Hops (central nervous system restorative) 1; Black Cohosh 1; Damiana (tonic nervine) half; few drops Tincture Capsicum. Dose: 1-2 teaspoons thrice daily in water. For unstable bladder add 1 part Ephedra, Cramp bark or Bearberry. Teas for unstable bladder: see INCONTINENCE.

Elderly patients with diabetes are prone to the development of hypoglycaemia. This may be responsible for temporary weakness. Hemiplegics should be investigated for tendency to hypo-glycaemia as improvement in neurological symptoms may follow treatment for that condition. See: HYPOGLYCAEMIA.

HEMLOCK. *Conium maculatum L. French*: Ciguë. *German*: Schierling. *Spanish*: Cicuta. *Italian*: Cleuta. *Indian*: Kirdâman. *Iranian*: Bikhi-i-Tafti. *Arabian*: Banj-e-rumi. *Parts used*: leaves, fruit.
Constituents: alkaloids, volatile oil.

Poisonous, taken internally but has been used with success as a poultice or ointment topically for malignant glands. Continued use has had a shrinking effect reducing the gland from stony hardness. Schedule 1. Poultice for use by a medical practitioner only. Other external uses: itching anus, piles. Pharmacy only medicine

HEMP AGRIMONY. Water Hemp. *Eupatorium cannabinum, L.* Herb. *German*: Hanfwasserdost. *French*: Chanvre d'Eau. *Italian*: Canapa salvatica. *Chinese*: Tse-lan. *Indian*: Allepa.
Constituents: flavonoids, pyrrolizidine alkaloids, sesquiterpene lactones, volatile oil.
Action: anti-tumoral, diuretic, cathartic. Echinacea-effect to enhance immune system.
Uses. Blood impurities. Tumour. Internal use discouraged except by a general medical practitioner.
Preparations. *Tea*: 1 teaspoon to each cup boiling water: infuse 15 minutes. Dose: half a cup, thrice daily.
Liquid Extract: 30-60 drops in water.
Externally as a poultice.

HENBANE. See: HYOSCYAMUS.

HENNA. *Lawsonia alba*, Lamk. Leaves. Regarded as a valuable medicine by the ancient world.
Constituents: naphthaquinones, flavonoids, coumarins.
Action: astringent, anti-fertility, anti-fungal, antibacterial, antispasmodic, anti-haemorrhagic. Oxytocic.
Uses. Tea used by the Chinese for simple headache. Smallpox, jaundice, leprosy (*Ancient Arabian*). Salmonella, brucellosis, staphylococcus aureus, streptococcus. Splenic enlargement.
Preparations. *Tea*: no longer taken internally, but used as a skin lotion.

Externally as a natural hair dye and conditioner. Rinses, dyes, shampoos, etc. Overuse turns the hair red.

HENRY VIII, King, Herbalist's Charter. From the Book of Statutes, 1215-1572. "At all times from henceforth it shall be lawful to every person being the King's subject, having knowledge and experience of the nature of Herbs, Roots and Waters, or of the operation of the same, by speculation or practice within any part of the realm of England, or in any other of the King's dominions, to practise, use and minister in and to any outward sore, uncome, wound, apostemations, outward swelling or disease, any herb or herbs, ointments, baths, pultes and amplaisters, according to their cunning, experience and knowledge in any of the diseases, sores and maladies before-said, and all other like to the same, or drinks for the Stone and Strangury, or Agues, without suit, vexation, trouble, penalty, or loss of their goods."

Since 1542 there have been many attempts to expunge this law from the Statute Book. A formidable attack was launched by the Pharmacy and Medicines Bill, 1941, which was fought so vigorously by a Mr Montgomery and Mrs Hilda Leyel that herbalists won the concession to continue the right to practise.

HEPATIC. A herb that assists the liver in its function and promotes the flow of bile. Hepatoprotective.

Agrimony, Balm, Balmony, Barberry, Black root, Blue Flag, Boldo, Bogbean, Centuary, Clivers, Dandelion, Fringe Tree, Fumitory, Gentian, Goldenseal, Greater Celandine, Hyssop, Mountain Grape, Prickly Ash, Wahoo, Wild Indigo, Wild Yam, Wormwood, Yellow Dock, Stone root, Black Radish. Milk Thistle.

HEPATITIS. See: LIVER.

HERB PILLOW. To promote sleep. Fill linen bag with herbs: Hops, Chamomile, Bergamot, Basil, etc. Stitch together ends. Expose to heat before use.

HERB ROBERT. *Geranium robertianum. German*: Germe robert. *French*: Herbe à Robert. *Spanish*: Geranio. *Italian*: Geranio Robertia. Leaves. *Keynote*: bleeding.
Action: haemostatic, astringent, anti-diarrhoeic, styptic, anti-diabetic.
Uses. Bleeding throughout the gastro-intestinal tract. Bleeding from nose, mouth, throat.
Irritable bowel. As a cleansing wash for discharging ulcers.
Preparations. *Tea*: 1oz to 1 pint boiling water; infuse 15 minutes. Half-1 cup freely.
Poultice: rheumatism.

HERB SOCIETY, THE. Founded as the Society of Herbalists in 1927 by Hilda Leyel who carried on a consulting service together with retailing herbs and preparations under the name of

"Culpeper".

Practical medical herbalism in Britain received an impetus under the work of Mrs Leyel until the 1968 Medicine's Act which made this alternative therapy available to all. In 1974 the Society became a registered educational charity and its name changed to The Herb Society. The brand name "Culpeper" was franchised to a private company which continues to trade as the "Culpeper" retail chain of shops.

Today, The Herb Society promotes interest in and knowledge of all aspects of herbs, as well as herbal medicine. Information is available from: The Secretary, The Herb Society, PO Box 599, London SW11 4RW.

HERB TEA. Old English. Combine equal parts: Agrimony, Balm, Dandelion, Peppermint and Raspberry leaves. Alternative to caffeine drinks. Pick-me-up of piquant natural flavour.

HERB TEAS. Day-to-day drinks available in filterbags: Blackberry leaf, Chamomile, Dandelion, Devil's Claw, Fennel, Hawthorn, Horsetail, Lemon Balm, Lime flowers (Linden), Marshmallow, Mate, Mistletoe, Nettles, Orange Blossom, Peppermint, Rosehip, Sage, St John's Wort, Thyme, Yarrow, Vervain.

HERBAL MEDICINE. "There is a large body of opinion to support the belief that a herb that has, without ill-effects, been used for centuries and capable of producing convincing results, is to be regarded as safe and effective." (*BHMA*) Claims for efficacy are based on traditional use and inclusion in herbals and pharmacopoeias over many years. Their prescription may be prefixed by: "For symptomatic relief of . . ." or "An aid in the treatment of . . ."

To establish efficacy of treatment for a named specific disease by herbs, the DHSS requires scientific data presented to the Regulatory authorities for consideration and approval.

A product is not considered a herbal remedy if its active principle(s) have been isolated and concentrated, as in the case of digitalis from the Foxglove. (*MAL 2. Guidance notes*)

A herbal product is one in which all active ingredients are of herbal origin. Products that contain both herbal and non-vegetable substances are not considered herbal remedies: i.e. Yellow Dock combined with Potassium Iodide.

The British Government supports freedom of the individual to make an informed choice of the type of therapy he or she wishes to use and has affirmed its policy not to restrict the general availability of herbal remedies. Provided products are safe and are not promoted by exaggerated claims, the future of herbal products is not at risk. A doctor with knowledge and experience of herbal medicine may prescribe them if he considers that they are a necessary part of treatment for his patient.

Herbalism is aimed at gently activating the body's defence mechanisms so as to enable it to heal itself. There is a strong emphasis on preventative treatment. In the main, herbal remedies are used to relieve symptoms of self-limiting conditions. They are usually regarded as safe, effective, well-tolerated and with no toxicity from normal use. Some herbal medicines are not advised for children under 12 years except as advised by a manufacturer on a label or under the supervision of a qualified practitioner.

World Health Organisation Guidelines

The assessment of Herbal Medicines are regarded as:–

Finished, labelled medicinal products that contain as active ingredients aerial or underground parts of plants, or other plant material, or combinations thereof, whether in the crude state or as plant preparations. Plant material includes juices, gums, fatty oils, essential oils, and any other substances of this nature. Herbal medicines may contain excipients in addition to the active ingredients. Medicines containing plant material combined with chemically defined active substances, including chemically defined, isolated constituents of plants, are not considered to be herbal medicines.

Exceptionally, in some countries herbal medicines may also contain, by tradition, natural organic or inorganic active ingredients which are not of plant origin.

The past decade has seen a significant increase in the use of herbal medicines. As a result of WHO's promotion of traditional medicine, countries have been seeking the assistance of WHO in identifying safe and effective herbal medicines for use in national health care systems. In 1989, one of the many resolutions adopted by the World Health Assembly in support of national traditional medicine programmes drew attention to herbal medicines as being of great importance to the health of individuals and communities (WHA 42.43). There was also an earlier resolution (WHA 22.54) on pharmaceutical production in developing countries; this called on the Director-General to provide assistance to the health authorities of Member States to ensure that the drugs used are those most appropriate to local circumstances, that they are rationally used, and that the requirements for their use are assessed as accurately as possible. Moreover, the Declaration of Alma-Ata in 1978 provided for *inter alia*, the accommodation of proven traditional remedies in national drug policies and regulatory measures. In developed countries, the resurgence of interest in herbal medicines has been due to the preference of many consumers for products of natural origin. In addition, manufactured herbal medicines from their countries of origin often follow in the wake of migrants from countries where traditional medicines play an important role.

In both developed and developing countries, consumers and health care providers need to be supplied with up-to-date and authoritative information on the beneficial properties, and possible harmful effects, of all herbal medicines.

The Fourth International Conference of Drug Regulatory Authorities, held in Tokyo in 1986, organised a workshop on the regulation of herbal medicines moving in international commerce. Another workshop on the same subject was held as part of the Fifth International Conference of Drug Regulatory Authorities held in Paris in 1989. Both workshops confined their considerations to the commercial exploitation of traditional medicines through over-the-counter labelled products. The Paris meeting concluded that the World Health Organisation should consider preparing model guidelines containing basic elements of legislation designed to assist those countries who might wish to develop appropriate legislation and registration.

The objective of these guidelines, therefore, is to define basic criteria for the evaluation of quality, safety, and efficacy of herbal medicines and *thereby to assist national regulatory authorities, scientific organisations, and manufacturers to undertake an assessment of the documentation/submission/dossiers in respect of such products*. As a general rule in this assessment, traditional experience means that long-term use as well as the medical, historical and ethnological background of those products shall be taken into account. Depending on the history of the country the definition of long-term use may vary but would be at least several decades. Therefore the assessment shall take into account a description in the medical/pharmaceutical literature or similar sources, or a documentation of knowledge on the application of a herbal medicine without a clearly defined time limitation. Marketing authorisations for similar products should be taken into account. (*Report of Consultation; draft Guidelines for the Assessment of Herbal Medicines. World Health Organisation (WHO) Munich, Germany, June 1991*)

HERBAL PRACTITIONER. WHAT THE LAW REQUIRES. The consulting herbalist is covered by Part III of *The Supply of Herbal Remedies Order, 1977*, which lists remedies that may be used in his surgery on his patients. He enjoys special exemptions under the Medicines Act (Sections 12 (1) and 56 (2)). Conditions laid down for practitioners include:

(a) The practitioner must supply remedies from premises (apart from a shop) in private practice 'so as to exclude the public'. He is not permitted to exceed the maximum permitted dose for certain remedies, or to prescribe POM medicines.

(b) The practitioner must exercise his judgement in the presence of the patient, in person, before prescribing treatment for that person alone.

(c) For internal treatment, remedies are subject to a maximum dose restriction. All labels on internal medicines must show clearly the date, correct dosage or daily dosage, and other instructions for use. Medicines should not be within the reach of children.

(d) He may not supply any remedies appearing in Schedule 1. Neither shall he supply any on Schedule 2 (which may not be supplied on demand by retail).

He may supply all remedies included in the General Sales List (Order 2129).

(e) He must observe requirements of Schedule III as regards remedies for internal and external use.

(f) He must notify the Enforcement Authority that he intends to supply from a fixed address (not a shop) remedies listed in Schedule III.

(g) Proper clinical records should be kept, together with records of remedies he uses under Schedule III. The latter shall be available for inspection at any time by the Enforcement Authority.

The practitioner usually makes his own tinctures from ethanol for which registration with the Customs and Excise office is required. Duty is paid, but which may later be reclaimed. Accurate records of its consumption must be kept for official inspection.

Under the Medicines Act 1968 it is unlawful to manufacture or assemble (dispense) medicinal products without an appropriate licence or exemption. The Act provides that any person committing such an offence shall be liable to prosecution.

Herbal treatments differ from person to person. A prescription will be 'tailored' according to the clinical needs of the individual, taking into account race as well as age. Physical examination may be necessary to obtain an accurate diagnosis. The herbalist (phytotherapist) will be concerned not only in relieving symptoms but with treating the whole person.

If a person is receiving treatment from a member of the medical profession and who is also taking herbal medicine, he/she should discuss the matter with the doctor, he being responsible for the clinical management of the case.

The practitioner can provide incapacity certificates for illness continuing in excess of four days for those who are employed. It is usual for Form CCAM 1 5/87 to be used as issued on the authority of the Council for Complementary and Alternative medicine.

General practitioners operating under the UK National Health Service may use any alternative or complementary therapy they choose to treat their patients, cost refunded by the NHS. They may either administer herbal or other treatment themselves or, if not trained in medical herbalism can call upon the services of a qualified herbalist. The herbal practitioner must accept that the GP remains in charge of the patient's clinical management.

See: MEDICINES ACT 1968, LABELLING OF HERBAL PRODUCTS, LICENSING OF HERBAL REMEDIES – EXEMPTIONS FROM.

HERBALENE (Lusty's). Formula: Senna leaf BP 64 per cent; Fennel BPC 16 per cent; Buckthorn BPC 1934 4 per cent; Maté 8 per cent; Elder leaves 8 per cent. Laxative. Relief of non-persistent constipation.

HERBS, SOURCE OF. Today's practice: only first grade organically grown herbs (European, British, American, etc) without the aid of pesticides or herbicides are the general rule, but standards vary in different countries. Some herbs are freshly picked and processed on the same day, and it is modern practice to cultivate in a remote location to avoid wind-blown chemical contamination.

Herbs are soft-stemmed plants that die back in winter. No artificial additives; no cruelty to animals; and no damage to the environment is the ideal in the preparation of herbal remedies.

All herbs are subject to natural variations such as weather, climate and constituents of the soil. In herbal pharmacy products are standardised as carefully as possible under strict laboratory conditions.

HERNIA. Rupture. Swelling caused by an organ pushed out of its usual position into neighbouring tissues. Abdominal hernias may be inguinal, femoral or umbilical. An external hernia is when a part of the intestine protrudes through a weak spot in the abdominal wall. Vomiting, with pain over the affected area, indicates strangulation which calls for emergency hospital treatment. Hernias may be worse on coughing or straining at stool. For internal hernia, see: HIATUS HERNIA.

Treatment. Most abdominal hernias can be pushed back manually. Where this is not possible it is known as irreducible. Umbilical hernias in children usually disappear by the fourth year.

Alternatives. *Teas*. Fenugreek, Aloe Vera, Rupturewort. 1 teaspoon fresh or dried herb to each cup boiling water. Strain when cold. 1 cup thrice daily.

Lobelia. (*Priest*) Liquid Extract. 2-10 drops in water thrice daily.

Thuja (infants). Liquid Extract. 1-2 drops in water thrice daily.

Yarrow. (*Wm Boericke MD*)

Marshmallow root decoction. Traditional European.

Topical. Massage affected area with hot Castor oil (rotary motion), first to left, then to right. 2-3 tablespoons being absorbed by the body. Improvement may lead to athletic support in place of truss. (*Wm A. McGarey MD*)

Compress Comfrey root: pulp of fresh root. (*Fletcher Hyde*).

Witch Hazel packs, left in position day and night.

Strangulated hernia. Put patient to bed, lying on his back, with head low, feet raised above level of body. Rub affected part with No 6 Thomson's Compound, followed by Chickweed ointment. Give Thomson's 3rd Preparation (Antispasmodic tincture); teaspoon doses in a cup of hot water every 20 minutes. After massage with the ointment for half an hour tissues relax and with gentle manual pressure the protrusion may be restored. (*Sarah A. Webb MD*)

HERPES, GENITAL. Venereal disease. Caused by *Herpes simplex virus, type 2*, (HSV2) which infects the skin and mucosa of the genital organs and anus. The strain is more virulent than HSV1 which attacks face and lips. Contagious. STD. Blisters appear 4-7 days after coitus. May be transmitted by mother to baby at delivery. The condition is often misdiagnosed as thrush. To dispel doubts, refer to urological department of nearest hospital. Evidence exists between genital herpes and cancer of the cervix. Clinical diagnosis should be confirmed by virus culture. Attacks are recurrent and self-infective.

Symptoms: redness, soreness, itching followed by blisters on the penis or vulva. Blisters ulcerate before crusting over. Lesions on anus of homosexual men.

Treatment by general medical practitioner or hospital specialist.

Alternatives. Sarsaparilla, Echinacea, Chaparral and St John's Wort often give dramatic relief to itching rash. See entry: ECHINACEA.

Tea. Formula. Equal parts: Clivers, Gotu Kola, Valerian. One heaped teaspoon to each cup boiling water; infuse 5-10 minutes. Dose: 1 cup thrice daily.

Decoction. Combine: Echinacea 2; Valerian 1; Jamaican Dogwood 1. One heaped teaspoon to each cup water gently simmered 20 minutes. Half-1 cup thrice daily.

Tablets/capsules. Poke root. Valerian. Passion flower. St John's Wort. Echinacea. Chaparral. Pulsatilla. Red Clover.

Powders. Formula. Echinacea 2; Valerian 1; Jamaica Dogwood 1. Dose: 500mg (two 00 capsules or one-third teaspoon) thrice daily.

Tinctures. Formula. Echinacea 2; Sarsaparilla 1; Thuja quarter; Liquorice quarter. Dose: 1-2 teaspoons thrice daily.

Topical. Apply any of the following 3, 4 or more times daily. Pulp or gel of Aloe Vera, Houseleek, Echinacea lotion. Garlic – apply slice of fresh corm as an antihistamine. Yoghurt compresses

(improved by pinch of Goldenseal powder). Zinc and Castor oil (impressive record). Apply direct or on tampons.
Diet. Porridge oats, or muesli oats.
Supplementation: same as for Shingles.
Prevention. Women should be advised to submit for an annual cytosmear.
Information. Herpes Association, 41 North Road, London N7 9DP, UK. Send SAE.

HERPES SIMPLEX. Fever sore. Caused by *Herpes simplex, type 1*, (HSV1). Infects face, mouth and eyes. Maybe transmitted by kissing. Cold sores around mouth which ulcerate and form a scab. Recurrent, painful. May be a devastating disease when attacking the brain (herpes simplex encephalitis). Infection may come en route via mouth, lips or elsewhere in the body. Cold sores around the eyes should receive medical attention.
Alternatives. Balm tea. Melissa officinalis is active against the herpes simplex virus and clinical trials yield excellent results. (*European Journal of Herbal Medicine, Vol 1, No 1*)
Russian traditional. Handful of pulped Wild Garlic leaves (Ramsons) macerated in Vodka to saturation point; 7 days. 1-2 teaspoons in water thrice daily.
Oil of Cloves (3-5 drops). Anti-viral activity against herpes simplex.
Other anti-virals. Garlic, Echinacea, Aloe Vera, Eucalyptus, Yarrow, Elderflowers, Burdock, Wild Indigo. St John's Wort.
Tea. Formula. Equal parts, Yarrow, Balm, Gotu Kola. 1-2 teaspoons to each cup boiling water; infuse 15 minutes. Half-1 cup thrice daily, before meals.
Powders. Combine: Echinacea 2; Goldenseal quarter, Myrrh quarter. 500mg (two 00 capsules or one-third teaspoon) thrice daily.
Tinctures. (1) Combine: Echinacea 2; Chamomile 1; Liquorice half. Or (2) Combine: Peruvian bark half; Meadowsweet 1; Chamomile half. Dose: 1-2 teaspoons in water thrice daily.
Thuja. 70 per cent ethanolic extract of Thuja occ., inhibits herpes simplex (HSV) in vitro. (*Institute of Pharmaceutical Biology, Munich; C. Gerhäuser, et al*)
Topical. Houseleek juice. Wipe with sliced Garlic corm. Oils of Cade, Cajeput, Sesame, Aloe Vera, dilute oil Eucalyptus.
Diet. Wholefoods, high fibre, low fat. Plenty fresh raw fruit and vegetables, yoghurt.
Supplementation. Same as for Shingles.
Self-Care. Towels, face cloths and other personal linen should not be shared.

HERPES ZOSTER. Shingles. An acute inflammatory virus infection of one or more posterior root ganglion of the spine, or of the trigeminal nerve. Caused by a DNA virus (varicella zoster). May be due to re-activation of the chicken-pox virus which lies latent in the ganglia of sensory and somatic nerves and present in the body from childhood infection. Severe in the elderly. Should be distinguished from herpes simplex. Shingles cannot be re-activated by close proximity of a case, but may be caught by direct contact with a burst blister.
Symptoms: Two-to-four-day fever precedes a red rash which develops into clear blisters. Blisters dry up to form scabs that drop off leaving scars. Lesions and pain follow the path of the infected nerve. Pain described as intense, burning, itching: may persist for months as post-herpetic neuralgia. When virus affects the fifth cranial nerve vision will be impaired. In the elderly it may reveal some underlying malignancy. Patients having chemotherapy or radiotherapy are at risk.
Alternatives. Specific anti-viral therapy. Remedies in general use: Asafoetida, Jamaica Dogwood, Marigold, Mistletoe, Nettles, Passion flower, Poke root, Queen's Delight, Valerian, Wild Lettuce, Wild Yam. St John's Wort plays a role in reducing the long-lasting neuralgia. Echinacea imparts strength to endure the ordeal. The addition of a stomachic remedy (Gentian) to a prescription may prove beneficial. Mild short-term analgesics include: Oats, Valerian, Asafoetida, Passion flower, Wild Lettuce, Hops.
Tea. Formula. Equal parts: Oats, Nettles, St John's Wort.
Decoction. Formula. Echinacea root 2; Valerian half; St John's Wort 1.
Tablets. Formula. Hops BHP (1983) 45mg; Passion flower BHP (1983) 100mg; Extract Valerian 5:1 20mg. (*Gerard 99*)
Powders. Combine: Echinacea 2; Jamaican Dogwood 1; Gentian root 1. 500mg (two 00 capsules or one-third teaspoon) thrice daily.
Tinctures. Alternatives. (1) Formula. Equal parts Goldenseal and Lupulin (Hops). Or, (2) Formula. Queen's Delight 1; Valerian quarter; Goldenseal quarter; Asafoetida quarter. Dose: 1 teaspoon in water thrice daily.
Practitioner. Tincture Gelsemium: 5 drops (0.3ml) in water, as indicated, for pain.
Formula. Liquid Extract Hops, half an ounce; Liquid Extract Echinacea, 1oz; Tincture Goldenseal, 30 drops; Tincture Rhubarb BP, 1oz. Essence of Peppermint 20 drops. Water to 8oz. Dose: 2 teaspoons in water after meals. (*Arthur Barker, FNIMH*)
Topical. Aloe Vera. Houseleek – fresh juice or pulp. Evening Primrose oil. Wash with decoction of seaweed (Bladderwrack, Kelp): follow with Zinc and Castor oil cream or ointment. Slippery Elm made into a paste (powder mixed with few teaspoons of milk): apply after cleaning with Olive oil. Castor oil compress. Dilute Tea Tree oil. Ice-cube – 10 minutes on, 5 minutes off.
Russian study. Liquorice powder ointment.

Diet: Oatmeal porridge. Muesli with oats. Yoghurt. Wholefoods.
Supplementation. One high potency multivitamin daily. Anti-herpes amino acid L-lysine; one 500mg tablet, twice daily. Vitamin B12, 10mg daily. Upon relief, reduce L-lysine to one daily. (*Dr L. Mervyn*)
Minerals: Calcium, Selenium, Zinc.
Self-Care. Resist temptation to touch sores. No sharing of face cloths, towels, etc.
Note. The chicken-pox virus is believed to lie dormant in nerve cells around the spine for many years, after people catch the childhood infection. Virgorous massage of the spine may trigger an attack by activating the dormant virus.
Information. Herpes Association, 41 North Road, London N7 9DP, UK. Send SAE.

HIATUS HERNIA. The gullet (oesophagus) passes through an opening in the diaphragm which separates the chest from the abdomen. A hiatus hernia results when part of the upper stomach bulges through the opening. May be congenital or acquired. There is a relationship between air-swallowing and hiatus hernia.
Symptoms: distension, regurgitation, belching, pain, heart-burn worse lying down or when stooping, food may 'stick in the gullet', worse when straining at stool.
Alternatives. *Teas.* Wood Betony. (*Dr John Clarke*) To prevent reflux: Hops, Black Horehound, Meadowsweet. Day-starter: Chamomile tea.
Tablets. Slippery Elm. Chew 3-5 tablets when necessary. Vegetable Charcoal; Papaya: 2 before meals.
Fennel. Quarter of a teaspoon crushed seeds in cup boiling water.
Goldenseal, Liquid Extract. 5 drops in water, thrice daily.
Slippery Elm gruel.
Externally. Cold water packs to upper abdomen.
Diet. Cup fresh Carrot juice before each meal. Potato water. Avoid rich fatty foods. No solid foods at bedtime.
Supplementation. Vitamin B-complex (high formula). 1 Dolomite tablet at meals. Vitamin E 400iu daily to oxygenate the blood.

Reduction of weight favourably affects a sliding hiatus hernia. Relief from sleeping on left side is supported. Practice yawning. Relaxation techniques.

HICCUPS. Repeated involuntary contraction of the diaphragm.
Causes: eating too fast, carbonated drinks, stomach irritation (hot peppers, vinegars, alcohol). Where persistent, there may be constriction of the lower gullet by early neoplasm caused by drinking piping-hot tea when X-ray and specialist advice should be sought.
Alternatives. *Teas.* Celery seed. Spearmint. Mustard seed. Fennel seed, Dill seed, Coriander seed, Peppermint. Caraway seed.
Decoction. Blue Cohosh. Black Cohosh. Calamus. Valerian.
Tablets/capsules. Capsicum (Cayenne), Papaya, Peppermint, Cinnamon, Celery seed, Liquorice, Ginger.
Old English traditional. 1-2 teaspoons Onion juice every few minutes.
Cinnamon, oil of. 3 drops on sugar. (*John Wesley*)
Blue Cohosh, or Black Cohosh. 10 drops Tincture in little water, hourly.
Cloves, oil of. 1-2 drops in teaspoon honey.
Wild Yam. Liquid Extract. 15-30 drops in water, every 10 minutes.
Capsicum (Cayenne). Tincture, 3-5 drops in water, hourly.
Cramp Bark. (Muscle relaxant).
Slippery Elm gruel.
Supportives: deep breathing; holding the breath as long as possible. Hot foot bath. Stick a finger in each ear for 20 seconds.

HINDOO FLOWER ATTAR. Perfume or sick-room disinfectant. Mix, parts: Sandalwood oil 50 drops; Eugenol 20 drops; Bergamot 10 drops; Jasmine 20 drops. Use as a spray on handkerchief, or place an electric light bulb in fluid causing slow evaporation of 20-40 drops in a little water.

HIP REPLACEMENT OPERATION. Athroplasty. Success rate: high. Commonest indication: osteo-arthritis of hip. A lesser risk of sepsis occurs in first operation than in subsequent ones. Infection is suspected when acetabular loosening is present in conjunction with femoral loosening. Echinacea is the key remedy for combatting infection and for enhancing the patient's resistance. Comfrey root promotes healing of bone tissue. St John's Wort gives partial relief in post-operative pain. Horsetail is a source of readily absorbable iron and calcium. For slow healing, a liver agent (Fringe Tree) may be indicated.
Alternatives. *Teas.* Comfrey leaves, Calendula, St John's Wort, Gotu Kola, Plantain.
Tablets/capsules. St John's Wort.
Formula. Comfrey root 2; St John's Wort 1; Echinacea 2; trace of Cayenne (Capsicum). Dose – Powders: 750mg (three 00 capsules or half a teaspoon). Liquid Extracts: 1-2 teaspoons. Tinctures: 1-3 teaspoons. Effect is enhanced when doses are taken in cup of Comfrey herb tea.
Other agents to promote renewal of tissue. Slippery Elm bark, Fenugreek seeds, Wild Yam, Carragheen Moss.
Discomfort from a scar. Aloe Vera gel, Calendula, Comfrey or Chickweed cream or ointment. See: CASTOR OIL PACK.
Diet. High protein, oily fish or fish oils.

Supplements. Vitamin C: 3-6g daily. Calcium ascorbate, Zinc. Magnesium. Cod Liver oil for Vitamins A and D; 2 teaspoons daily.
Note. Where titanium alloy implants are used for this operation serum levels of the metal are likely to show up higher than normal. Raised serum titanium has been linked with lung cancer, osteoporosis, and platelet suppression. A New Zealand study has found deaths from cancer were significantly higher in patients having had a metal hip replacement. See: CHELATION.
Comfrey. Potential benefit far outweighs possible risk.

HIPPOCRATES. Greek physician. 460-circa 377 BC. The first to lead medical thinking from superstition to science. He related the working of the human body to the action of healing substances. The father of medicine, who practised on the Isle of Cos chosen because of its ecologically-pure atmosphere. He used as his healing agents all the natural edible vegetables and fruits, seeds, beans, peas and herbs as a means of restoring health.

He said: "Ill health is a disharmony between man and his environment" and "Let medicine be your food, and food your medicine". The long list of herbs used in his practice are still popular among herbalists today. He taught that diseases were disturbances in the balance of the four humours. For centuries he was regarded as a model for doctors and it is claimed he 'gave medicine a soul'.

HIPPOCRATES – OATH OF. "I Swear . . . To my master in the healing art I shall pay the same respect as to my parents, and I shall share my life with him and pay all my debts to him. I shall regard his sons as my brothers and I shall teach them the healing art if they desire to learn it, without fee or contract. I shall hand-on precepts, lectures and all other learning to my sons, to my master's sons and to those pupils who are duly apprenticed and sworn, and to no others.

I will use my power to help the sick to the best of my ability and judgement. I will abstain from harming or wronging any man.

I will not give a fatal draught to anyone, even if it is demanded of me, nor will I suggest the giving of the draught. I will give no woman the means of procuring an abortion.

I will be chaste and holy in my life and actions. I will not cut, even for the stone, but I will leave all cutting to the practitioners of the craft.

Whenever I enter a house, I shall help the sick, and never shall I do any harm or injury. I will not indulge in sexual union with the bodies of women or men, whether free or slaves.

Whatever I see or hear, either in my profession or in private, I shall never divulge. All secrets shall be safe with me. If therefore I observe this Oath, may prosperity come to me and may I earn good repute among men through all the ages. If I break the Oath, may I receive the punishment given to all transgressors."

HIRSUTISM. Presence of hair in areas where it is not usually found and excessive growth. Due to excess of the male hormone, testosterone in the blood. More common in women. Women smokers face threat of hirsutism. Ovarian cyst is often a forerunner of hirsutism, as also is hormone imbalance.
Alternatives. Agnus Castus, (tea, tablets or tincture). Evening Primrose oil capsules: 500mg thrice daily.

Red Clover tea. (*Walter Thompson, MNIMH*)

Vitamin E capsules: 400iu thrice daily. Vitamin A-rich foods. Zinc supplement.

HIV. Human immunodeficiency virus. The virus responsible for AIDS. Destroys the body's natural defences against disease, exposing it to fatal infections and cancer (Kaposi's sarcoma). WHO estimates that by the year 2000, thirty million children may be infected.

A number of plant medicines inhibit HIV-1 replication including, Turmeric, Siberian Ginseng and Garlic.

HIVES. See: NETTLERASH.

HODGKIN'S DISEASE. (Lymphadenoma. Lymphogranulomatosis). Chronic enlargement of the lymph nodes often together with that of the liver, spleen and bone marrow. Affects more males than females, 30-40 years. High white blood cell count. Cancer of the lymph vessels. Follows a typical clinical course with anaemia until necrosis supervenes. The disease is suspected by a combination of enlargement of lymph nodes (especially the neck), severe itching and unexplained fever. Symptoms vary according to part of the body affected.
Symptoms. Hard rubbery glands are general, chiefly detected under the arm and groin. Enlarged nodes may compress nearby structures to produce nerve pains. Weight loss. Accumulation of fluid in lungs and abdomen. Obstruction of bile duct leads to jaundice. Patient may be prone to shingles. High fever heralds approaching fatality. Blood count, bone marrow aspiration and node biopsy confirm. Tubercula glands may simulate Hodgkin's disease.

Some success reported by the use of the Periwinkle plant. (*vinca rosea – Vinchristine*) Wm Boericke, M.D. refers to Figwort as a powerful agent in Hodgkin's disease.
Alternatives. Although there is no known cure, emphasis on the cortex of the adrenal gland may reduce skin irritation and pain in the later stages (Gotu Kola, Liquorice, Sarsaparilla). To arrest

wasting and constitutional weakness: Echinacea. Anti-pruritics, alteratives and lymphatics are indicated.
Tea. Formula. Equal parts, Nettles, Gotu Kola, Red Clover. 1 heaped teaspoon to each cup boiling water; infuse 15 minutes. 1 cup 3 or more times daily.
Decoction. Formula. Equal parts – Yellow Dock, Queen's Delight, Echinacea. 1 teaspoon to each cup water gently simmered 20 minutes. Half-1 cup 3 or more times daily.
Tablets/capsules. Poke root. Blue Flag root. Echinacea. Mistletoe.
Powders. Formula. Echinacea 2; Poke root 1; Bladderwrack 1. Dose: 500mg (two 00 capsules or one-third teaspoon) 3 or more times daily.
Tinctures. Mixture. Parts: Echinacea 2; Goldenseal quarter; Thuja quarter; Poke root half; Periwinkle 1. Dose: 1-2 teaspoons, 3 or more times daily. Where active inflammation is present – add Wild Yam 1.
External. Castor oil packs to abdomen.

Treatment by a general medical practitioner or hospital specialist.

HOLISTIC MEDICINE. A school of thought which regards disease as a manifestation of an inner disturbance of the vital force, and not merely abnormality of certain groups of nerves, muscles, veins, or even the mind itself. Article 43 of Dr Samuel Hahnemann's *Organon of the Healing Art* describes it:

"No organ, no tissue, no cell, no molecule is independent of the activities of the others but the life of each one of these elements is merged into the life of the whole. The unit of human life cannot be the organ, the tissue, the cell, the molecule, the atom, but the whole organism, the whole man."

Holistic medicine relates disease to a patient's personality, posture, diet, emotional life, and lifestyle. Treatment will be related to body, mind and spirit. It encourages a positive psychological response to the disease from which a patient suffers. For instance, its gentle approach to cancer embraces stress control, meditation, forms of visualisation and other life-enhancing skills.

Diet may be vegetarian, even vegan.

HOLLYHOCK. *Althaea rosea L. Part used*: flowers contain mucilage. Action similar to Marshmallow.

HOLY THISTLE. Blessed thistle. Carbenia benedicta *Cnicus benedictus L. German*: Benediktendistel. *French*: Chardon bénit. *Spanish*: Cardo santo. *Italian*: Cardo beneditto. Herb.
Constituents: sesquiterpene lactones, mucilage, lignans, oil.
Action: Febrifuge, anti-haemorrhage, antibiotic, bacteriostatic, bitter, splenic tonic, expectorant, galactagogue, diaphoretic, emmenagogue, carminative. Externally as an antiseptic. Anti-diarrhoeal. Anti-flatulent.
Uses. Dyspepsia, loss of appetite, gastro-enteritis, liver and gall-bladder disorders. To increase a mother's milk after pregnancy. Migraine, painful menstruation, sluggish circulation.
Combination, with Agrimony (equal parts) for anorexia nervosa.

Used in the production of Benedictine.

Externally, as a cleaning wash for discharging ulcers.

Preparations. Thrice daily.
Tea. Dried flowerheads 1 teaspoon in each cup boiling water; infuse 15 minutes. Dose: 1 cup.
Liquid extract. 1-3ml (15-45 drops).
Tincture, BHC Vol 1. 1:5, in 25 per cent ethanol. Dose: 3-6ml.
Poultice. Flowerheads.
Diet. Flowerheads cooked as artichokes.

Large doses emetic. Avoid in pregnancy or hyperacidity. GSL, schedule 1

HOMOEOPATHY. A medical doctrine teaching that drugs capable of producing disease symptoms in a healthy person can, in infinitesimal doses, cure the same group of symptoms met in a particular disease.

Hippocrates was aware of the universal law *similia similibus curentur* (like cures like). He taught that some diseases were cured by similars, and others by contraries. *Stahl* (1738) was also aware of this law of healing: "diseases will yield to and be cured by remedies that produce a similar affection". But it was Samuel Hahnemann (1755-1843) who proved to the world this doctrine held the key to the selection of specifically acting medicines. His early experiments with nux vomica, arnica, ignatia and veratrum showed how the medicine which cured produced a similar condition in healthy people.

While no one has yet discovered the 'modus operandi' of the science, it has grown up largely through empiric experience, especially during certain historical epidemics in different parts of the world. For example, in 1836 cholera raged through most of the cities of Austria. Orthodox medicine could do little. Out of desperation, the Government commissioned the aid of homoeopathy. A crude hospital was hastily prepared and patients admitted. Results convinced the most hardened sceptics. Physician-in-charge, Dr Fleischman, lost only 33 per cent, whereas other treatments showed a death rate of over 70 per cent.

It is said that reduction of inflammatory fevers by homoeopathic Aconite, Gelsemium, Baptisia and Belladonna played no small part in reducing the practice of blood-letting in the early 19th century.

Since Hahneman, homoeopathy has been the object of intense professional bitterness by its opponents but since the 1963 Medicines Act (UK) provision has been made for homoeopathic treatment on the "National Health Service". Conversion of medical opinion has been gradual and today many registered medical practitioners also use the therapy.

"It is the general theory that the process of dilution and succussion (a vigorous shaking by the hand or by a machine) "potentises" a remedy.

"*To prepare*. A remedy is first prepared in solution as a "mother tincture". In the decimal system of dilution a small quantity is then diluted ten times by the addition of nine parts by volume of diluent – either alcohol or water and then shaken vigorously by hand or machine (succussion). A small quantity of this is then diluted to one tenth and successed a second time; this process is repeated again and again, producing solutions identified as 3x, 6x, 30x according to the number of times diluted. It may even be continued a thousand times (1 M). The resulting solutions are adsorbed on to an inert tablet or granules, usually of lactose, and in this form it is claimed that they remain therapeutically active indefinitely.

"For higher dilutions the centesimal system is used, when each dilution is by 1 in 100. The resulting solutions or tablets are referred to as 3C, 6C, 12C etc according to the number of times diluted.

"When dealing with a remedy which is insoluble, e.g. Carbo Veg, the first three dilutions and succussions are done in powder form, i.e. to "3x" beyond which the remedy is sufficiently soluble for further dilutions to proceed in liquid form.

"In homoeopathy a remedy may in some cases be given in a dilution so great that no single molecule of the original substance remains. The concept of "memory laden" water implies that the effect lies in a pattern impressed on the water molecules and that this is carried over from one dilution to the next." (*John Cosh MD., FRCP*)

Homoeopathic medicines can stand most tests for safety, since it is widely held that they are completely safe and non-addictive, with no side-effects.

HOMOEOSTASIS. An assumption that the body has within itself the resources and materials to restore normal function when disordered by disease. Some herbs, including Ginseng, Echinacea and Capsicum are known to trigger a response and mobilise body defence. This group contains adaptogens, alteratives, etc.

HONEY. Beverage and medicine. Whilst not a herb, honey is processed by bees from the nectar of flowers and has an ethereal quality that enhances its healing properties. A source of vitamins and minerals.

Action. Many bacteria cannot live in the presence of honey since honey draws from them the moisture essential to their existence. It is a potent inhibitor of the growth of bacteria: salmonella, shigella and E. coli. Taken internally and externally, hastens granulation and arrests necrotic tissue. A natural bacteriostatic and bactericide.

Of an alkaline action, honey assists digestion, decreasing acidity. It has been used with success for burns, frostbite, colic, dry cough, inflammations, involuntary twitching of eyes and mouth; to keep a singer's throat in condition. Some cases of tuberculosis have found it a life-preserver.

A cooling analgesic: dressings smeared with honey and left on after pain has subsided to prevent swelling – for cuts, scratches, fistula, boils, felon, animal bites; stings of mosquitoes, wasps, bees, fleas, etc. May be applied to any kind of wound: dip gauze strips in pure honey and bind infected area; leave 24 hours.

Insomnia: 2 teaspoons to glass of hot milk at bedtime.

Arterio-sclerosis: with pollen, is said to arrest thickening of the arteries.

2, 3 or more teaspoons daily to prevent colds and influenza.

2 teaspoons in water or tea for renewed vitality when tired.

Rheumatism and arthritis: 2 teaspoons honey and 2 teaspoons Cider vinegar in water 2-3 times daily.

"The taking of honey each day is advised in order to keep the lymph flowing at its normal tempo and thus avoid degenerative disease which shortens life. The real value of honey is to maintain a normal flow of the tissue fluid called lymph. When this flow-rate slows down, then calcium and iron are precipitated as sediment. When the lymph flow is stagnant, then harmful micro-organisms invade the body and sickness appears." (*D.C. Jarvis MD*)

Where sweetening is required to ensure patient compliance, honey is better than sugar. Its virtues deteriorate in open sunlight. Should not be heated above 40°C.

HONEY AND ALMOND CREAM. Make up sufficient for single application: Teaspoon honey, into which has been mixed with a spatula or spoon – 10 drops Almond oil and 10 drops Witch Hazel water.

HOOKWORM. Ancylostomiasis. Infestation of the small intestine with tiny worms (*Ancylostoma duodenale*). Common in children from hot, damp earth in which larvae thrives. Worms enter feet via the skin and are borne to lungs and intestine. Prolonged infestation leads to anaemia and retarded development in children.

In the 1860s Thymol was the important medicine, but was later superceded by Chenopodium (oil of American Wormseed) as an anthelmintic for expulsion of hookworms.

Should be supervised by a practitioner.

Patient to receive a light meal at night followed next morning by the oil in a capsule: 6-8 years, 6 drops; 9-10 years, 8 drops; 11-16 years, 10-12 drops; over 16 years, 12-16 drops. Dose is repeated two hours later. Two hours afterwards, give Senna purgative. No food should be taken until after bowel movement. Repeat procedure after one week. Less drastic treatments are available, but for the intractible stubborn hookworm desperate measures are sometimes called for.

HOPS. *Humulus lupulus L. German*: Hopfen. *French*: Houblon. *Spanish*: Hombrecillo. *Italian*: Luppolo. *Chinese*: Lei-mei-ts'ao. *Russian*: Chmel. Dried flowers (strobiles). *Keynote*: nervous tension. Chiefly used in combination with other remedies.
Constituents: oestrogens, volatile oil, resin.
Action: sedative, sustaining nervine, hypnotic, mild analgesic, spasmolytic on smooth muscle, bitter, tonic, astringent, antimicrobial (externally), liver and gall bladder relaxant, anaphrodisiac, diuretic.
Uses. Nervous anxiety, hysteria, nervous diarrhoea, nervous stomach, Crohn's disease, intestinal cramps, nervous bladder, insomnia, neuralgia, excessive sexual excitability. Loss of appetite, menopause, restless legs.
Chinese medicine – tuberculosis of the lungs.

"Of value in cancer." (*J.L. Hartwell, Lloydia, 33, 97, 1970*)
Combination. Combines well with Passion flower and Valerian.
Preparations. Average dose: half-1 gram. Thrice daily.
Tea. 1 teaspoon to each cup boiling water; infuse 15 minutes. Dose: half cup.
Liquid Extract: 0.5-1ml.
Tincture BHC Vol 1. One part to 5 parts 60 per cent ethanol. Dose: 1-2ml.
Popular tablet/capsule: powdered Hops BHP (1983) 45mg; powdered Passiflora BHP (1983) 100mg; powdered Extract Valerian 5:1 20mg. For minor stresses and strains, irritability and nervous headaches. For over-activity of children over 12 years. (*Gerard House*)
Diet: young shoots cooked as Asparagus.
Hop pillow: for healthful sleep.
Fresh Hops require careful handling on drying to prevent loss of pollen. May cause an allergic dermatitis in those susceptible.
Contra-indication: depression.
Powder. 250mg. One 00 capsule or one-sixth teaspoon. GSL, schedule 1

HOREHOUND, BLACK. *Ballota nigra L. German*: Schwarze Bulte. *French*: Marrube noir. *Spanish*: Hoarhound. *Italian*: Marrobio nero. Dried herb. Important agent used by the modern herbalist. *Keynote*: vomiting.
Constituents: iridoids, diterpenoids.
Action: anti-emetic, gastric relaxant, antispasmodic.
Uses. Nausea, vomiting (especially vomiting of pregnancy), nervous indigestion, hypoglycaemia, persistent diarrhoea. Vomiting stimulated by motion, as in travel sickness. Mad-dog bite. (*Dioscorides*) Low spirits.

Combines well with Raspberry leaves for vomiting of pregnancy: with Chamomile for gastritis.
Preparations. Thrice daily, as necessary.
Tea. One teaspoon to each cup boiling water; infuse 5-10 minutes. Half-1 cup freely.
Liquid Extract BHP (1983). 1:1 in 25 per cent alcohol. (1-3ml) in water.
Tincture BHP (1983). 1 in 10 parts 45 per cent alcohol. Dose: 1-2ml.

HOREHOUND, WHITE. *Marrubium vulgare L. German*: Maurerandorn. *French*: Marrube blanc. *Spanish*: Marrubio. *Italian*: Marrobio bianco. *Dutch*: Gemeene malrove. Flowering tops and leaves. *Keynote*: chest.
Constituents: Marrubiin, volatile oil, tannins, alkaloids, diterpene alcohols.
Action: stimulating expectorant, mild antispasmodic, sedative, amphoteric, vulnerary, diuretic, stomach and liver bitter tonic.
Uses. Chronic bronchitis, whooping cough, hard cough with little phlegm, common cold, loss of voice, snake bite, dog bite. Chronic gall bladder disease, fevers, malaria, hepatitis, "Yellowness of the eyes".
Combinations. Teas. (1) with Coltsfoot and Hyssop (equal parts) for hard cough. (2) with Lobelia and Iceland Moss for chronic chest complaints.
Preparations. Thrice daily.
Tea. 1 teaspoon to each cup boiling water; infuse 15 minutes. Dose: half-1 cup.
Liquid extract BHC Vol 1. 1:1, 20 per cent ethanol. Dose: 1-2ml.
Tincture BHC Vol 1. 1:5, 25 per cent ethanol. Dose: 3-6ml.
Horehound ale: wholesome beverage.
Horehound, Hyssop and Honey Mixture. Traditional English syrup.
Note: Horehound, Horseradish, Coriander, Lettuce and Nettles are the five bitter herbs eaten by the Jews at their Passover feast according to the Old Testament. GSL

HOREHOUND AND ANISEED Cough Mixture. Active ingredients: Each 10ml contains Liquid Extract Pleurisy root (1:1, 35 per cent alcohol) 0.15ml. Liquid Extract Elecampane (1:1, 21 per cent alcohol) 0.15ml. Liquid Extract Horehound (1:1, 20 per cent alcohol) 0.15ml. Liquid Extract Skunk Cabbage (1:1, 21 per cent alcohol) 0.15ml. Tincture Lobelia (1:12.5, 5.8 acetic acid) 0.225ml, in a syrup base.

Adults and elderly: two 5ml teaspoons thrice daily.
Children over 5: one 5ml teaspoon thrice daily.

Expectorant and demulcent to soothe irritable cough. (*Potter's, UK*)

HORMONAL HERBS. To promote production of hormones of the male and female sex organs (androgens and oestrogens), hormones of the adrenal cortex, pituitary, thyroid and other glands. Agnus Castus, Beth root, Black Cohosh, Blue Cohosh, Damiana, Helonias, Hydrangea, Kelp (Fucus v.), Liquorice, Oats, Sarsaparilla, Saw Palmetto, Squaw Vine.

HORMONE REPLACEMENT THERAPY (HRT). Within a few years medical scientists have introduced into the domestic scene a steroid which has changed the whole course of female history. HRT has solved some basic medical problems by making good the loss of oestrogen in a woman's body when menstruation is finished and her body learns to adjust.

A lack of oestrogen induces hot flushes, night sweats, thinning of the bones (osteoporosis) with possible fractures, and a wide range of physical and emotional disorders.

HRT also prevents the increased frequency of coronary disease which may follow the menopause. With oestrogen only, HRT appears to increase the incidence of cancer of the uterine body. Use of oestrogen and progestogen avoids this.

HRT is available as a tablet, transdermal patch, implant or topical cream. Most women notice temporary improvement in their appearance and hot flushes as long as treatment is continued. HRT is not prescribed by the herbal practitioner. Soya and Hops are a mild alternative.

Side-effects of such treatment include blood pressure rise, weight gain and periods probably continue with a monthly bleed. Elderly women taking HRT for osteoporosis may develop bleeding problems, the risk of blood clot and gall bladder diseases.

Helonias has proved a useful alternative, effective in eliminating excess fluids, reducing hot flushes, and relieving that bloated feeling, thus helping the older woman to live a normal life.

Damiana. 1 heaped teaspoon leaves to each cup boiling water; infuse 5-10 minutes; strain. 1 cup 2-3 times daily for 3-6 weeks.

Sarsaparilla. 1oz (30g) root in 1 pint (500ml) water; simmer gently 20 minutes; strain. 1 cup 2-3 times daily for 3-6 weeks.

Supplementation. Daily. Vitamin E, 400iu. Vitamin B-complex (high potency). Evening Primrose oil capsules, 500mg morning and evening. Dolomite, for Calcium and Magnesium, 2 tablets morning and evening.

Note. An extensive study of breast cancer risks with HRT revealed a positive link between the risk of cancer and length of use. Risk of the disease increased with all types of women using HRT with every year of use. Pre-menstrual women were more than twice at risk. It would appear that oestrogens cannot be taken without risk. (*Centre for Disease Control, Atlanta, USA*)

See: OESTROGENS.

HORMONES. Chemical substances manufactured by the endocrine glands and secreted directly into the bloodstream. As the heart pumps blood through the body they are borne to cells remote from their point of origin where they have a specific effect. Hormones are to physiology what radium is to chemistry.

HORSE CHESTNUT. *Aesculus hippocastanum L. German*: Gemeine Rosskastanie. *French*: Aescule. *Spanish*: Castano de Indias. *Italian*: Eschilo. *Part used*: horse-chestnuts and bark. Contains aescin (saponin).

Constituents: hippocaesculin and other saponins.

Action: anti-inflammatory, vasodilator, astringent, tones and protects blood vessels, anti-oedema. Vitamin P action. As regards the veinous system, properties are similar to rutin. Stimulates production of prostaglandin F-alpha which contracts veins.

Uses. Bleeding piles and uterine bleeding, varicose veins, phlebitis. Tea is taken internally or used externally as a soothing and astringent wash to cleanse leg ulcers and suppurating wounds. Heavy legs. Swollen ankles. Chilblains. Night cramp: 20 drops of Tincture at bedtime. Thrombo-phlebitis. Bruises (ointment or gel). Slipped disc: to assist dispersal of extruded nucleus pulposus (ointment or gel).

Preparations. Average dose: 1-2 grams. Thrice daily.

Tea: half a teaspoon powdered dried Chestnut to each cup boiling water; infuse 15 minutes. Dose: quarter to half cup; sweeten with honey if necessary.

Home tincture: 1 part powder (or scrapings) to 10 parts 45 per cent alcohol (vodka or strong wine); macerate 8 days; filter. Dose: 1 teaspoon in water.

Liquid extract (bark): 15-30 drops.

Combination: with Cowslip root for varicose veins. (*Biostrath*)

Reparil. Over-the-counter-product. Contains Aescin, oedema-inhibiting principle of Horse-Chestnut. For local oedema of all types: traumatic oedema, oedema following fractures, cerebral oedema due to head injuries, thrombotic oedema, lymph stasis, venous stasis, varicose oedema. (*Dr Madaus & Co., Cologne, W. Germany*)

Powder, capsules: 200mg. 3 capsules twice daily. (*Arkocaps*) GSL

HORSE RADISH. Cochlearia armoracia L. *Armoracia rusticana*, Gaertn. *Part used*: root. *Constituents*: asparagine, B vitamins, Vitamin C, sinigrin and other glucosinolates, resin.
Action: efficient alternative to Cayenne pepper, Diuretic, urinary antispetic, diaphoretic, carminative; liver, spleen and pancreatic stimulant. Bacteriostatic action on Gram-negative bacilli. (*Rudat K.D. (1957) Journal Hyg. Epidem. Microbiol. Immunol. Prague 1 213*)

To raise vital force in the elderly. Antibiotic. Circulatory stimulant with warming effect. Digestive aid. Anti-thyroid.
Uses. Feeble circulation, hypothermia, hyperthyroidism, frostbite, chilblains, absence of stomach acid in the elderly, dropsy following fevers, proteinuria (albuminuria), to arrest vaginal discharge. Hoarseness (1 teaspoon juice in honey). Rheumatic joints (poultice). Common cold, influenza and early stages of fever: cup of Horse Radish tea every 2-3 hours. Combine with Juniper berries (equal parts) for dropsy and kidney stone. Purulent wounds: cold decoction used as a lotion.
Preparations. Average dose: 1-2 grams; thrice daily.
Tea: 1 teaspoon grated fresh root in each cup boiling water; infuse 20 minutes. Half-1 cup in sips, freely.
Horse Radish vinegar. 1oz scraped fresh root to 1 pint cider vinegar. 1-2 teaspoons in water for catarrh, sinusitis, poor circulation or as a male tonic.

Steeping slices of the fresh root in cider produces a copious discharge of urine in dropsy.
Tablets, Blackmore's Labs: Horse Radish powder 350mg; Dolomite 140mg; Gum Acacia 20mg; Magnesium stearate 10mg.
Diet: Mayonnaise: whip double cream until stiff and fold in fresh grated root, flaked almonds, lemon juice and seasoning, with a little Paprika.
Note: One of the five bitter herbs eaten by the Jews during the Passover Festival.

HORSETAIL. Shave grass. Pewterwort. Nature's hoover. *Equisetum arvense L. German*: Ackerschachtelhalm. *French*: Equisette. *Spanish*: Belcho. *Italian*: rasperella. *Chinese*: Wên-ching. Dried stems. *Keynote*: genito-urinary system. A natural source of silicic acid, ashes containing 70 per cent silica soluble in water and alcohol.
Constituents: flavonoids, alkaloids, sterols, silicic acid.
Action: haemostatic for bleeding of genito-urinary organs, styptic, a soothing non-irritating diuretic. Increases coagulability of the blood. Remineraliser. Anti-atheroma. Antirheumatic. Astringent. Immune enhancer. White blood cell stimulator.
Uses. Blood in the urine, prostatitis, bed-wetting, dropsy, chronic bladder infections, incontinence in the aged, catarrh of the urinary organs, gravel, urethritis of sexual transmission with bleeding, stricture, severe pain in the bladder unrelieved by passing water, constant desire to pass water without relief. Carcinoma of the womb: cure reported. Foetid discharges of STD. Arteriosclerosis.

Silica, as in Horsetail, preserves elasticity of connective tissue; controls absorption of calcium and is a necessary ingredient of nails, hair, teeth and the skeleton. Its cleansing properties rapidly remove urates, uric acid and cellulites from the system. Hastens repair of tissue after lung damage of tuberculosis or other diseases.
Combinations. (1) With Shepherd's Purse for blood in the urine. (2) With Pulsatilla to inhibit growth of uterine fibroid. (3) With Buchu for cystitis. (4) With Oats and Goldenseal for renal exhaustion. "Combines well with Hydrangea for non-malignant prostatitis." (*F. Fletcher Hyde*) Arteriosclerosis. (*Dr Max Rombi*)
Preparations. Horsetail has a heavy mineral content (silica, selenium and zinc) therefore treatment is best staggered so as to avoid kidney strain – one month, followed by one week's break. Average dose: 1 to 4 grams; thrice daily.
Tea: half-1 teaspoon to cup water; bring to boil; simmer 5 minutes; infuse 30 minutes. Dose: half-1 cup, cold.
Liquid extract BHC Vol 1. 1:1 in 25 per cent ethanol. Dose: 1-4ml (15-60 drops).
Home tincture: 1 part herb to 5 parts 25 per cent alcohol (gin, Vodka, etc). Steep 14 days, shake daily. Dose: 2-5ml (30-75 drops) in water.
Poultice: "Place double handful herb in a sieve and place over a pot of boiling water (double boiler, etc). The soft hot herbs are placed between a piece of linen and applied to ulcer, adenoma, cyst or tumour." (*Maria Treben*)
Bath. 9oz leaves: bring to boil in 1 gallon water. Simmer 5 minutes; strain. Add to bath water.
Enema: 1 pint weak tea for infants with kidney disorders. GSL

HOSPICE. A hospital for accommodation and treatment of the terminally ill. Emphasis is not only upon appropriate physical treatment but upon the mind and psyche by generating a positive attitude to their illness. The patient is treated with compassion and accorded the special care to enable them to complete their days with dignity. Gradually, hospices are adopting some of the rational aspects of natural therapy in which is seen the increasing role of essential oils as used in Aromatherapy.

Information of the Hospice Movement is obtainable from The Hospice Information Service, St Christopher's Hospice, 51-59 Lawrie Park Road, London SE26 6DZ, on receipt of a large self-addressed envelope stamped for 200g.

HOT FLUSHES. Hot flashes (*American*). Flushing and sweating experienced by menopausal women. Waves of redness and intense heat sweep upwards from the neck to face at any time of the day or night. A similar condition (non-hormonal) may happen to men after eating curries or hot spicy foods, or who suffer from diabetes or certain skin complaints. (See: INDIGESTION, DIABETES, etc).

Alternatives. Agnus Castus, Ho-Shou-Wu, Black Cohosh, Damiana, Goldenseal, Lime flowers, Lobelia, Mistletoe, Rue, Sarsaparilla, Shepherd's Purse, Wild Yam, Chamomile tea. Teas, tablets, liquid extracts, powders, tinctures.

Official treatment may include oestrogenic preparations (HRT) with risks of blood clotting and thrombosis.

Non-hormonal relief: combination.

Tea, equal parts, Lime flowers, Motherwort, Wild Carrot. 2 teaspoons to each cup boiling water; infuse 5-15 minutes. 1 cup freely.

Liquid extracts. Formula. Black Cohosh half; Mistletoe 1; Agnus Castus 1. Dosage: 1 teaspoon thrice daily in water.

Tinctures: same formula, double dose.

Evening Primrose (capsules).

Wessex traditional. Hawthorn flowers and leaves 4; Hops 1. 2 teaspoons to each cup boiling water; infuse 5-10 minutes; 1 cup freely.

Diet. Lacto-vegetarian.

Supplement. Vitamin E, 400iu morning and evening.

HOUNDSTONGUE. Dogstongue. *Cynoglossum officinale L.* Herb.

Constituents: pyrrolizidine alkaloids, allantoin, resin.

Action: sedative, anodyne, demulcent, astringent.

Uses. Traditional: mad dog bites (rabies). Tea taken internally; poultice externally. Catarrh, diarrhoea, dysentery, wound healing, irritating cough, external ulcers. Piles (poultice).

Preparations. Thrice daily.

Tea: 1oz to 1 pint water, simmer gently 10 minutes; infuse 5-10 minutes. Dose: half a cup. Drink freely for dog-bite fevers. Tea used also as a lotion.

Tincture: 1 part herb to 5 parts 45 per cent alcohol; macerate 8 days; filter. Dose: 1-2 teaspoons in water.

Because of its P-alkaloids no longer used in general practice.

HOUSELEEK. Bullock's eye. *Sempervivum tectorum L. German*: Hauswurz. *French*: Joubarbe. *Spanish*: Siempreviva. *Italian*: Sempervivo dei tette. *Chinese*: Ching-t'un. Plant thrives on roof tiles. Fresh leaves.

Constituents: malic acid, lime salts, tannin, mucilage.

Action: anti-inflammatory, astringent, analgesic (mild), refrigerant.

Uses. Long European reputation for scirrhous induration of the tongue, burning skin rashes, urticaria, nettle stings, and chronic mouth ulcers. Galen advised juice of fresh leaves to dispel pain of shingles and erysipelas. Dioscorides mentions its use for weak and inflamed eyes (eye-drops). Injected into the ear for relief of earache. Wiped over the forehead, juice from the fresh leaf may relieve migraine and chronic headache. Has been used with success for cancer of the breast, tongue and cervix.

Preparations. Has a better record of success from use of the fresh leaf than by alcohol.

German traditional: mix juice with equal volume of fresh cream.

Poultice: bruised fresh leaves for inflamed skin, shingles, etc.

Much neglected agent.

HOUSEMAID'S KNEE. See: BURSITIS.

HOXSEY, Harry M. M.D. Cancer specialist. Great Grandson of John Hoxsey, American physician, who in 1840 observed one of his horses with cancer cure itself by foraging for certain herbs. Noticing the herbs (Alfalfa, Red Clover, etc) he gathered them and fed them to other animals with the disease with conspicuous success.

The Hoxsey Cancer Clinic was founded in Dallas, which became a mecca for the herbal treatment of that disease. However, he received such persecution from the American Medical Association that he was persuaded to sign a contract transferring to them his herbal formulae, medicines and ointments, and to abandon his practice. This he did in good faith but the opposition continued. Worn out by long prison sentences for practising medicine without a licence, he died a broken man.

Though it is still illegal to offer the Hoxsey treatment in the United States, his main formula is still used by individuals left to their own resources.

Formula. Liquid Medicine: Red Clover, Burdock root, Queen's Delight root, Barberry root, Liquorice, Poke root, Cascara sagrada, Potassium iodide, Prickly Ash bark, Buckthorn powder.

Pills: Red Clover, Queen's Delight root, Poke root, Buckthorn, Pepsin.

A popular version revised by Paul Bergner, American Medical Herbalist reads: Liquorice 4 parts; Red Clover 4 parts; Burdock 2 parts; Queen's Delight 2 parts; Mountain Grape 2 parts; Poke root 2 parts; Prickly Ash bark 1 part; Frangula bark 1 part. (*P. Bergner, 'Botanic Medicine: Alterative Medicine'. Townsend Letter for Doctors, Nov. 1988, No 64, p487-8*)

HUANG QI. *Astragalus membranaceus*. Chinese anti-viral, anti-bacterial. Immune system

enhancer. 2,000-year old herb drunk as tea in China.
Action. Anti-infective against Coxsackie virus. Immune stimulant. Antiviral.
Uses. Myalgic encephalomyelitis (ME). Upper respiratory infection. For increased white blood cell count, improved sleep habits and to stimulate appetite in patients receiving chemotherapy and radiation. (*American Health 1989 8th Oct. –100*) To increase production of interferon. Gastric ulcer therapy. Influenza. The common cold. To combat Coxsackie B myocarditis. Of value for incontinence and frequency of urine. Inhibits HIV-1 replication in cells acutely or chronically infected.
Preparation. *Decoction*. Dried root: 2 teaspoons to each cup of water simmered gently 20 minutes. Half-1 cup thrice daily.

HUNTINGDON'S CHOREA. Degenerative disease of the cortex and basal ganglia of the brain with mental retardation, jerky movements of face and limbs. Onset: 30-45 years. Hereditary.
Differential diagnosis: arterio-sclerosis, Sydenham's chorea.
Action. Emotional instability ranging from apathy to irritability. Complicated by menstrual problems (Motherwort, Helonias, Black Cohosh). Regresses into dementia. No cure possible, but anti-convulsants may reduce contortions and restlessness. Institutional care may be necessary. Scientists claim the gene that causes Huntingdon's disease has been identified.
Alternatives. *Of Therapeutic Value*. Betony, Black Cohosh, Chamomile (German), Cramp bark, Helonias, Ladyslipper, Motherwort, Oats, Passion flower, Sarsaparilla, Skullcap, Valerian, Feverfew.
Tablets/capsules. Motherwort, Passion flower, Skullcap, Valerian.
Formula. Combine: equal parts, Black Cohosh, Mistletoe, Helonias. Dose: Powders: 500mg (two 00 capsules or one-third teaspoon). Liquid extract: 1 teaspoon. Tinctures: 2 teaspoons. Thrice daily in water or honey.
Traditional, UK. Combine equal parts, Skullcap, Valerian, Mistletoe. 1oz (30g) to 1 pint (500ml) water; bring to boil; remove vessel when boiling point is reached. Dose: half-1 cup thrice daily.
Diet. Lacto-vegetarian. Yoghurt. Low salt. Oatmeal porridge, Muesli, regular raw food days.
Supplements. Vitamin B-complex, Vitamin B6, Kelp, Calcium, Magnesium, Zinc.
Note. It would appear the Ginkgo would be an object of scientific study for the complaint.
Treatment by or in liaison with general medical practitioner only.

HYDATID DISEASE. An infection caused by a tapeworm *Echinococcus granulosis*, which infests cattle, foxes, sheep and especially dogs from which it finds its way into humans by contaminated food. Eggs pass through the wall of the gut to develop in body tissue as a hydatid cyst. Many years may pass before symptoms reveal its presence. Surgical operation is the only effective cure although certain vermifuges, taken from time to time, create in the intestine an inhospitable environment for the parasite: Wormwood, Malefern, Fennel, Pumpkin seeds; given in capsule or powder form. Such worms deplete reserves of Vitamin B12 and may cause megaloblastic anaemia.
Supplementation. Vitamin B12.

HYDRAGOGUE. A herbal cathartic that causes watery evacuation and drastic purgation. White Bryony, American Mandrake. (Practitioner use only)

HYDRANGEA. Seven Barks. *Hydrangea arborescens L.* Dried root. *Keynotes*: gravel, prostatitis.
Constituents: gum, resin, flavonoids, ferrous salts, phosphoric acids. Contains no tannins.
Action: antilithic, diuretic, sialagogue.
Uses. Used by the Cherokee Indians for gravel in the urine. Survived to be an important medicine in the modern herbalist's dispensary. "As many as 120 calculi have been known to come from one person under its use." (*Mrs M. Grieve*) Prostatitis (important agent). Incontinence, catarrh of the bladder, uric acid diathesis, blood in the urine, diabetes (supportive to primary treatment).
Combines well with Barberry bark (equal parts) for prostatitis; with Gravel root (equal parts) for gravel.
Preparations. Average dose: 2-4 grams. Thrice daily.
Decoction. 1 teaspoon to each cup water; simmer gently 20 minutes. Dose: half a cup. Often taken as a preventative by those prone to form stone.
Liquid Extract. Quarter-1 teaspoon in water.
Tincture BHP (1983). 1:5 in 45 per cent alcohol. Dose: 2-10ml in water. GSL

HYDROCELE. Excessive collection of fluid in the scrotum, the protective covering of the testicles. In infants the condition usually disappears on its own and requires no treatment. In adults, onset is mostly in middle life when it may be withdrawn by needle and syringe. One cause is inflammation of the testicle or of the epididymus.
Treatment. Aspiration or surgery. Pulsatilla is a key remedy. Ellingwood recommends Thuja. Poke root.
Pulsatilla: tablets, tincture. Liquid Extract: thrice daily.
Thuja. Tea, liquid extract or tincture. See entry.
Poke root. Tablets, Decoction, liquid extract or tincture. See entry.
Supportives: cold hip bath. Attention to bowels; a laxative may relieve pressure.

HYDROCEPHALUS. An accumulation of cerebrospinal fluid between the membranes of the brain or when fluid collects in the ventricles resulting in brain damage. Head abnormally large.
Causes. Injury, tumour, blood clot, meningitis, or congenital malformation obstructing the aqueduct.
Symptoms. Headache on the crown of the head, enlarged pupils, double vision, eyes squint and appear abnormally small, convulsions, slow onset of fever, high blood pressure, delirium, flushed cheeks, patient shuns the light.
Treatment. As a supportive aid to conventional treatment by hospital specialist or general medical practitioner.
Formula. Yarrow 2; Lily of the Valley 2; Ginkgo 1. Dose: Powders – 750mg (three 00 capsules or half a teaspoon). Liquid extracts – 1 teaspoon. Tinctures – 1-2 teaspoons every 2 hours for acute cases, otherwise thrice daily.
Ivy. Dr John Clarke, homoeopathic physician, reports the case of a colleague, Dr L. Cooper, who cured a case with one single dose of 1 drop mother-tincture of Ivy (Hedera helix). "Clear fluid (cerebrospinal rhinorrhoea) dripped from his nostrils for three weeks; 20-30 handkerchiefs being used a day." Evidence of efficacy of the traditional reputation of 1-2 drops Ivy juice for the condition is lacking.
Diet. 3-5 day fast on fruit juice only. Yarrow tea. No solid food until fever abates; then Slippery Elm and Complan.
Note. Pregnant mothers are advised by the Medical Research Council to take folic acid – part of the Vitamin B-group – to help protect against neural tube defects; severe birth defects of spina bifida and hydrocephalus. See: FOLIC ACID.

HYDROCHLORIC ACID. Deficiency of. See: ACHLORHYDRIA.

HYDROCOTYLE. See: GOTU KOLA.

HYDRONEPHROSIS. One or two-sided swelling of the pelvis of the kidney due to back-pressure from an obstruction (stone, enlarged prostate gland or tumour).
Symptoms. Swelling and pain in the loins.
Treatment. Temporary relief only. Until doctor arrives.
American Cranesbill. Valerian.
Hydronephrosis from prostatitis. Treat Prostate gland.
Hydronephrosis from stone in the kidney. Colic indicates stone. Treat stone.
Hydronephrosis from tumour. See Tumour of the Kidney.
Hydronephrosis with infection. Echinacea and Goldenseal.

HYDROPHOBIA. See: RABIES.

HYDROQUINONES. Artificial alkaloids. Cramp bark, Uva-Ursi.

HYDROTHERAPY. The use of water in the treatment of disease. Improves function of the entire circulatory and nervous system. It may take the form of a poultice, douche, pack, sauna, fomentation, shower, immersion or colonic irrigation. Use goes back to Hippocrates and the Ancient World. In Europe, it was re-discovered by Father Sebastion Kneipp (1821-97). Water may be used as steam cold or hot packs . . . even ice! Cold water has the effect of drawing away blood from the seat of inflammation. It opens pores, dissipates heat and causes the body to sweat out impurities. Alternation of hot and cold water by a Sitz bath tones and soothes pelvic structures.
Herbs used in Hydrotherapy: Chamomile, Rosemary, Clary-sage, Bergamot, Thyme or Lavender. Peppermint, Red Clover flors.
Foot Freshener. Soak feet in hot water for 3 minutes. Follow, by plunging them into cold water for 1 minute. Repeat 15-30 minutes. Finish-off with cold.

HYDROTHERAPY, COLON. Irrigation of the low bowel.

When elimination of body wastes is held up by a chronically-overloaded bowel general health may suffer. A constipated colon, with accumulations of hard faeces, obstructs peristalsis and loses its ability to evacuate effectively. Toxaemia follows, with gross interference of digestion of food.

As contents putrefy, toxins are re-absorbed, poisoning the blood. Such self-induced disease may lie at the root of sluggish liver function, skin disease, blood pressure, and aches in muscles similating rheumatism.

To clean out a clogged colon, injection of a herbal tea into the rectum not only proves effective but brings about a healthful purgation and release from tension. 2-3oz herb is brought to the boil in 1 gallon water, simmered for one minute, and allowed to cool. The tea is strained when warm and injected.
Enema herbs include: Soapwort, Chamomile, Marshmallow, Catmint, Raspberry leaves, Chickweed.
Alternative: 20-30 drops Tincture Myrrh added to boiled water allowed to cool.

HYDROTHORAX. A collection of fluid in the pleural cavities.

HYMENAL BLEEDING. The maidenhead, thin band of membrane at the entrance of the vagina (the hymen) may be ruptured at first intercourse followed by bleeding. Bleeding may occur

from time to time thereafter.
Alternatives. Seldom necessary. Prolonged pressure with the finger against the source of the bleeding usually suffices. Insert tampon saturated with Witch Hazel water. Marigold or Yarrow tea.
Internal. Two Cranesbill tablets every 15 minutes. Raspberry leaf or Ladies Mantle tea.
Topical. Douche – Raspberry leaf infusion.

HYOSCYAMUS. Henbane. *Hyoscyamus niger, L. German*: Schwarzes Bilsenkraut. *French*: Jusquiame noire. *Spanish*: Beteno. *Iranian*: Sickran. *Arabian*: Bazrul-banj. *Italian*: Jusquiame nero. *Indian*: Khurasani ajvayan. *Chinese*: Lang-tang. Leaves and flowering tops.
Constituents: The leaves contain hyoscine, hyoscamine, scopolamine, choline, mucilage.
Action: Powerful brain relaxant, antispasmodic on smooth muscle, sedative. Inhibits release of acetylcholine as a neuro-transmitter (action similar to Belladonna). Analgesic, narcotic.
Uses. Rabies, delirium tremens, delirium of fevers, cystitis, travel sickness, bronchitis, asthma, renal colic, whooping cough. See: TRANSDERMAL PATCHES.
Preparations. *Poultice*. Leaves once used for painful rheumatism.
Pharmacy only. Herbal practitioners are exempted up to 300mg daily (100mg per dose).

HYPERACIDITY. See: ACIDITY.

HYPERACTIVITY. Hyperkinesis. Physically over-active. "Like a human jet engine at top velocity." Excessive motor-nerve activity.
Causes: considerable evidence implicates side-effects of sugar, caffeine, mercurials and other mineral salts that find their way into the body in food additives, dental fillings, etc. Other related factors: exposure to television radiation, fluorescent lighting, environmental toxins, stress, genetic. Studies show a lack of zinc to be a factor.
Symptoms. Always thirsty yet urine is highly concentrated, revealing a deficiency of essential fatty acids (for which Evening Primrose is indicated). Impulsive disposition, nasal congestion, pallor, dark circles under eyes. Insomnia. Difficulty concentrating, clumsiness, low tolerance to failure.
Alternatives. Since an individual's chemistry is unique, it may be necessary to experiment with one or two agents before concentrating on ones more effective.
To normalise motor activity: Passion flower, St John's Wort, Xia ku cao (*Chinese*).
Tea. Formula. Equal parts: Passion flower, Skullcap, Valerian. Mix. 1-2 teaspoons to each cup water brought to boil and simmered one minute. Infuse 15 minutes. Dose: half-1 cup thrice daily.
Powders, liquid extracts, tinctures. Formula: Valerian 1; Hops (Lupulin) 1; Wild Lettuce 2. Dose: Powders, 500mg (two 00 capsules or one-third teaspoon). Liquid Extracts, 30-60 drops. Tinctures, 1-2 teaspoons, thrice daily.
Evening Primrose oil capsules. One 500mg capsule morning and evening.
Diet. Wholefoods, raw-food days, reformed dietary pattern.
Aromatherapy. Oil of Lavender.
Supplementation. Daily: Vitamin B-complex; Vitamin C 500mg; Vitamin B6 50mg; Vitamin E 500iu; Niacin; Magnesium, Zinc.

HYPERCALCAEMIA. Presence of abnormally high concentration of calcium in the blood. In infants, may follow too much Vitamin D in dried milk, with mental consequences. Also found in malignancy with bone metastases and parathyroid tumour.
Symptoms: Vomiting, loss of appetite, large volume of urine, constipation, intense thirst, extreme exhaustion, debilitating sweats. Regarded as a medical emergency for which phosphates, oral and rectal may be given.
Treatment. Plant medicines to lower calcium levels. Nettle tea.

HYPERCHLORHYDRIA. Secretion of too much hydrochloric acid in the stomach which prepares the mucosa for gastric ulcer. Treatment as for gastric ulcer.

HYPERCHOLESTEROLAEMIA. A high blood-cholesterol level over 300mg per 100ml that disposes to atheroma – a degenerative arterial disease with high blood pressure and coronary thrombosis. Treatment same as for Hyperlipidaemia.

HYPEREMESIS. Persistent vomiting.
Of gastric flu: See, INFLUENZA.
Of intestinal obstruction: Wild Yam. Black Horehound.
Of pregnancy: (Hyperemesis Gravidarum). A serious form of morning sickness causing dehydration with rapid loss of fluids; should receive hospital treatment.
Treatment: herbal sedatives and antinauseant remedies. See: MORNING SICKNESS.

HYPERGALACTIA. See: BREAST MILK.

HYPERGLYCAEMIA. See: DIABETES. To reduce sugar in blood – Guar gum.

HYPERHIDROSIS. Excessive sweating. See: PERSPIRATION.

HYPERICUM. St John's Wort. *Hypericum perforatum L. German*: Tupfelharthen. *French*: Mille pertuis. *Spanish*: Hierba de San Juan.

Italian: Perforata. *Iranian*: Dadi. *Arabian*: Hynfarikun. *Chinese*: Chin-ssŭ-t'sao. Leaves and flowers. *Keynote*: pain.
Constituents: flavonoids, hypericins, essential oil.
Action: alterative, astringent, antiviral, relaxing nervine, anti-depressant, sedative, anti-inflammatory, cardio-tonic. Analgesic (external).
Topical. Antiseptic, analgesic (mild). To promote coronary flow and strengthen the heart.
Uses. Neuralgia (facial and intercostal), sciatica, concussion of the spine, post-operative pain and neuralgia, physical shock. Pain in coccyx, polymyalgia with tingling of fingers or feet, to reduce pain of dental extractions. Injuries to flesh rich in nerves – finger tips or sole of feet. Shooting, stitching pains. Punctured wounds: bites of dogs (rabies), cats, rats where pain shoots *up* the arm from the wound. Painful piles. Chorea. Tetanus. Temporary relief reported in Parkinsonism. Has been used with some success in relieving cramps of terminal disease. Anxiety, stress, depression. Menopausal nervousness. Menstrual cramps.

Researchers have shown that the herb possesses radioprotective properties. (*Biol. Nauki. 1992 (4) 709*)
Preparations. Average dose: 2-4 grams, or equivalent in fluid form. Thrice daily.
Tea: 1 heaped teaspoon to each cup of boiling water; infuse 15 minutes. Half a cup.
Liquid Extract: 15-60 drops in water.
Tincture BHP (1983). 1:10 in 45 per cent alcohol. Dose: 2-4ml.
Flowers: steeped in Olive oil offer a good dressing for burns, sores and stubborn ulcers.
Oil of St John's Wort, (topical).
Compress, or wet pack for wounds or rheumatism: tea rinse.
Keynote: depression GSL

HYPERLIPIDAEMIA. Presence in the blood of excess lipids (fatty substances) including cholesterol, often a forerunner of arterial disease, coronary thrombosis, strokes. Related to diabetes and heart disease. There is an inherited form giving rise to family history of coronary disease at an early age.
Causes. Diet of too much animal fat, smoking, overweight, little exercise.
Symptoms. Same as those for ischaemic heart disease, acute pancreatitis, indigestion, abdominal pain.
Alternatives. Hawthorn berries, Lime flowers, Goat's Rue. Garlic – raw bulb with salads or 2-3 capsules at night. Herb Purslane (*Portulaca oleracae*): rich in EFA's (essential fatty acids) in general, and EPA in particular.
Garlic powder significantly reduces serum cholesterol and triglyceride levels in hyperlipidaemia. (*German Association of General Practitioners, Study Group on Phytotherapy*)
Guar gum. Lowers serum fat levels, body weight and blood pressure: see entry. Add Hawthorn for angina; Goat's Rue for diabetes; Ispaghula seeds (Regulan) for intestinal and bowel health and to reduce blood-fats.
Fenugreek seeds. Lowers blood cholesterol levels in healthy people and in diabetics. Contain galacto-mannan which aids fat digestion.
Diet. Low fat. High-complex carbohydrate diet. Sugar and refined starches raise but Oats and Bran lower cholesterol levels. High levels reduced by oleic acid (Olive oil). French research workers claim three apples a day can lower plasma and liver cholesterol levels by as much as 30 per cent. The effect is believed to be due to vegetable fibre, especially pectin. Those who stopped eating their three apples after the trial showed a return to higher levels. Replace unsaturated with vegetable polyunsaturated fats. Two or three fatty fish meals weekly to prevent clumping of platelets. Linseed, Grape juice, Artichokes. See entry – OILY FISH.
Supplement: Nicotinic acid.
Stop smoking. Limit intake of alcohol.

HYPERPARATHYROIDISM. Disorder of the parathyroid gland with excessive secretion of parathormone. Leads to high level of calcium in the blood and a leeching of calcium from the bones.
Symptoms: thirst, voiding of large quantities of urine, lack of appetite, physical weakness, constipation, nausea, high blood pressure. An association with pancreatitis and peptic ulcer.

Most common cause is a tumour on one of the glands or swelling of all four. Bone fragility leads to fractures and deformity.
Alternatives. *Formula*. Equal parts: Gotu Kola, Red Clover, Goat's Rue, Bladderwrack.
Tea: 1 heaped teaspoon to each cup boiling water; infuse 15 minutes; dose, 1 cup.
Liquid Extracts: one to two 5ml teaspoons in water.
Tinctures: one to three 5ml teaspoons in water.
Powders: 500mg (two 00 capsules or one-third teaspoon). Thrice daily.

HYPERSENSITIVITY. A reaction of the body to stimuli as a result of allergy. Hyperaesthesia. May manifest as asthma, colitis, hay fever, etc.
Treatment: Garlic, to eat corm at table, or two Garlic capsules morning and evening.
Practitioner: Ephedra. Decoction or liquid extract. See: EPHEDRA.

HYPERTENSION. High blood pressure. The World Health Organisation defines high blood pressure (arterial hypertension) as that with a persistent sphygomanometer reading of 160/90, and over. Average blood pressure is 120/80 for men but lower in women. The diastolic pressure (lower figure) represents pressure to which the arterial walls are subject and is the more important figure.

Main causes of a raised pressure include increase in blood thickness, kidney disorder or loss of elasticity in the arteries by hardening or calcification.

Well defined physical problems account for 10 per cent of high blood pressure cases. By the age of 60, a third of the peoples of the West are hypertensive. Other causes: genetic pre-disposition, endocrine disorders such as hyperactive thyroid and adrenal glands, lead and other chemical poisoning, brain tumour, heart disorder, anxiety, stress and emotional instability.

Other causes may be food allergies. By taking one's pulse after eating a certain food one can see if the food raises the pulse. If so, that food should be avoided. Most cases of high blood pressure are related to lifestyle – how people think, act and care for themselves. When a person is under constant stress blood pressure goes up. It temporarily increases on drinking the stimulants: alcohol, strong tea, coffee, cola and caffeine drinks generally.

Symptoms. Morning headache (back of the head), possible palpitation, visual disturbances, dizziness, angina-like pains, inability to concentrate, nose-bleeds, ringing in the ears, fatigue, breathlessness (left ventricular failure).

Dr Wm Castelli, Director of the Framlingham Heart Study in Massachusetts, U.S.A., records: "The greatest risk is for coronary heart disease (CHD). Hypertensives have more than double the risk of people with normal blood pressure and seven times the risk of strokes."

In countries where salt intake is restricted, a rise in blood pressure with age is not seen.

Simple hypotensive herbs may achieve effective control without the side-effects of sleep disturbance, adverse metabolic effects, lethargy and impaired peripheral circulation.

Essential hypertension is where high blood pressure is not associated with any disease elsewhere; it accounts for 90 per cent cases. Most of the remainder have kidney disease except for a few other abnormalities.

Alternatives. Balm, Black Haw, Black Cohosh (blood pressure of the menopause), Cactus, Cramp bark, Chamomile (German), Garlic, Buckwheat, Lily of the Valley, Balm, Mistletoe, Motherwort, Passion flower, Nettles, Lime flowers, Wood Betony, Yarrow, Rosemary, Hawthorn flowers, Olive leaves, Dandelion. Where there is nerve excitability: Valerian.

Tea No 1. Equal parts: Hawthorn leaves and flowers, Mistletoe, Lime flowers. Mix. 2 teaspoons to each cup boiling water; infuse 5-10 minutes. 1 cup 2-3 times daily. Alternative:–

Tea No 2. Equal parts: Nettles, Lime flowers, Yarrow, Passion flower. Mix. 2 teaspoons to each cup boiling water; infuse 5-10 minutes. 1 cup 2-3 times daily.

Nettles. Nettle tea is capable of removing cholesterol deposits ("fur") from artery walls, increasing their elasticity. Like so many herbs they are rich in chlorophyll. The tea may be made as strong as desired.

Mistletoe. 2-3 teaspoons cut herb (fresh or dried) to cup cold water. Allow to infuse overnight (at least 8 hours). 1 cup morning and evening.

Garlic. Juice from one Garlic corm expressed through a juicer taken morning and evening. Garlic dilates blood vessels. Alternative: 2-3 Garlic capsules at night.

Blood pressure of pregnancy: See – PREGNANCY.

Tablets/capsules: Cramp bark, Mistletoe, Motherwort, Rutin, Garlic.

Powders. Formula. Buckwheat (rutin) 1; Motherwort 1; Mistletoe half; Valerian quarter. Dose: 500mg (two 00 capsules or one-third teaspoon) thrice daily.

Liquid extracts, tinctures. Formula. Equal parts: Cactus, Mistletoe, Valerian. Dose: liquid extracts, one 5ml teaspoon; tinctures, two 5ml teaspoons; thrice daily.

Practitioner Formula. Tinctures: equal parts: Lily of the Valley, Mistletoe, Valerian. Dose: 30-60 drops thrice daily.

Where high blood pressure is due to faulty kidney function diuretics such as Dandelion or Bearberry will be added according to individual requirements. Dandelion root is one of the most widely-used potassium-conserving agents for increasing flow of urine, as well as being a mild beta-blocker to reduce myocardial infarction. Broom (*Sarothamnus scoparius*) (diuretic) is not used in cases of high blood pressure. It is good practice to assess kidney function in all new cases of hypertension for renal artery stenosis.

Evidence from two major studies confirms that diuretics rather than beta-blockers should be the treatment of choice for most elderly hypertensives. The addition of a diuretic (Yarrow, etc) to prescriptions for the elderly is commended.

Prevention. Chances of developing high blood pressure are said to be reduced by a daily dose of Cod Liver oil. Results from studies at the University of Munich, Germany, show that when an ounce of Cod Liver oil was added to the typical Western diet, better pressure readings and lower cholesterol levels followed. When the flavour renders it objectionable to the palate, taste may be masked by stirring briskly into fruit juice.

General. Stop smoking. Watch weight. Moderate exercise. Avoidance of stress by relaxation, yoga, music, etc. These relieve constriction of peripheral blood vessels. Curb temper

Diet. Avoid processed and fast foods high in fat and salt, and empty calories. Cheese and meat sparingly. Eat plenty of natural foods. Positively reject coffee, strong tea and alcohol. "There is a significant drop in plasma cortisol with a fall in blood pressure after stopping alcohol." (*Dr J.F. Potter, University of Birmingham, England*) It is well-documented that a vegetarian diet is associated with a lower blood pressure.

Salt. The association of salt with blood pressure is larger than generally appreciated and increases with age and initial blood pressure. Even a small reduction in salt (3g) may reduce a systolic and diastolic pressure by 5mmHg and 2.5mmHg respectively. All processed foods containing salt should be avoided.

Supplementation. Inositol, zinc, Vitamin C, Vitamin B6. (*Dr C. Pfeiffer*) Vitamin E to improve circulation. Check with practitioner pressure level before starting 200iu increasing to 400iu daily. Magnesium: 300mg daily. Choline.

See: BLOOD PRESSURE.

HYPERTENSIVE. Hypertensor. An agent that increases blood pressure.

Broom, Ephedra, Gentian, Shepherd's Purse.

HYPERVENTILATION (HV). Breathing at an abnormally rapid rate while resting. Diverse causes range from psychiatric disorders, asthma or unsuspected lung disease, hyperthyroidism, habit disorders, heart disease, hiatus hernia, phobia. May precipitate tetany. Air-swallowing (aerophagia) may occur when a person both eats and talks when at food.

For serious cases requiring medication: Lobelia, Gelsemium. A cup of Lime flower tea may reduce the breathing rate.

Elecampane decoction: good results reported.

Supportive: instruct patient to swallow when exhaling. Magnesium supplementation.

HYPNOTICS. Herbs that relieve anxiety and induce normal sleep without unpleasant after-effects. No association with hypnotism. Aniseed, Cowslip, Hops, Fennel seeds, Jamaican Dogwood, Ladyslipper, Mistletoe, Passion flower, Skullcap, Wild Lettuce Valerian.

HYPO-ALLERGENIC. Some excipients used in the manufacture of tablets may have an allergenic effect. They may include additives, colourings, yeast, iodine, etc to which an increasing number of people are allergic. Present-day tablet-makers move away from these chemical binders and fillers, using natural alternatives such as vegetable oils, calcium phosphate, acacia gum and alginic acid from seaweeds. The term also refers to products, including herbal preparations made without sugar, starch, salt, wheat, yeast or artificial preservatives: suitable for vegetarians.

HYPOCALCAEMIA. Lower than normal level of calcium in the blood. Due to (a) Vitamin D deficiency, (b) underactivity of parathyroid glands. Muscular spasms may follow from tetany or seizure. Babies fed on cow's milk may be at risk.

Symptoms: breathlessness, vomiting, spasm, convulsions. The calcium balance is governed by hormones from the parathyroid gland. Absorption of the mineral depends upon dietary calcium and Vitamin D. (See: CALCIUM, VITAMIN D)

Abnormality may be shown by decrease of serum calcium levels in the blood, or by increase in size and density of bones and other tissues.

Causes: tumour, hardened arteries, bone-wasting diseases, chronic kidney disease.

Alternatives. Horsetail tea. Comfrey root powder: 2-4g, 1 to 3 times daily. Comfrey: potential benefit outweighs possible risk.

Diet. Cod Liver oil. Fish oils generally. Fresh Carrot juice.

Supplementation. Vitamins A, C, D (up to 20,000 units daily). Calcium, Magnesium, Beta Carotene, Dolomite, Phosphorus.

See: CALCIUM DISORDERS: RICKETS: OSTEOPOROSIS: OSTEOMALACIA.

HYPOCHLORHYDRIA. See: ACHLORHYDRIA.

HYPOCHONDRIASIS. An obsession in which a person is too pre-occupied with personal health and may believe he has imaginary diseases. Usually associated with anxiety, and perfectionist attitudes. May develop into a number of serious disorders, including anorexia nervosa.

Symptoms. Varied, arising from the alimentary canal, heart, genital organs (fear of venereal disease), etc.

Alternatives. Treat underlying anxiety or depression. Valerian. *BHP (1983)* Skullcap, Squaw Vine. (*Priest*)

See: DEPRESSION. ANXIETY.

HYPOGLYCAEMIA. Low blood sugar. Hyperinsulinism. "The 20th Century Epidemic." Low blood sugar levels brought about by over-stimulation of insulin production by the pancreas.

From food we eat, sugar (glucose) is converted into glycogen which is stored in the liver and muscles. To ensure its removal from the blood-stream to storage areas a balancing mechanism causes the pancreas to produce insulin for this purpose. Exhaustion of the pancreas may follow too frequent release of insulin for reducing high levels of sugar. All symptoms are temporarily relieved by eating sweet foods, chocolate, etc, or by drinking stimulating beverages: tea, coffee, cola, alcohol, etc.

Convincing evidence shows how large amounts of refined and concentrated sugars overwork the pancreas, causing wide swings in blood sugar levels. This is the reverse of diabetes which occurs from a lack of insulin.

Another factor is over-stimulation of the

adrenal glands that produce adrenalin which has the power to release stored sugars. When adrenalin is discharged too frequently into the bloodstream the conversion of glycogen to glucose is impaired. This leads to a craving for sweet foods and stimulating beverages.

Symptoms are numerous and often confuse the doctor: constant hunger, tightness in the chest, dizziness, headaches, twitching of limbs, digestive disorders, fatigue, weakness in legs, irritability, migraine, nervous tension, nervous mannerisms, insomnia, memory lapses, phobia – sense of panic, cold sweats. Cold hands and feet, visual disturbances, vague aches and pains and depression.

Life becomes a succession of erratic rises and falls of the blood sugar. Symptoms are worse when the person is passing through a 'low' period. All this is reflected upon the sympathetic nervous system and affects the emotional life. A special blood test is carried out to assess the situation; the Glucose Tolerance Test.

Alternatives. *To raise low blood sugar levels*: Avens, Balmony, Bayberry, Calamus, Centuary, Chamomile (German), Dandelion root, Echinacea, Feverfew, Gentian (Yellow), Ginger, Ginseng, Goldenseal, Holy Thistle, Hops, Horehound (White), Liquorice, Quassia, Southernwood, Betony.

Teas. Chamomile (German), Ginseng, Avens, Centuary, Hops, Betony.

Decoctions. Yellow Gentian (cold infusion), Calamus (cold infusion), Dandelion root (hot infusion), Angustura bark (hot infusion).

Tablets/capsules. Calamus, Dandelion, Ginseng, Goldenseal, Echinacea, Liquorice, Kelp.

Powders. Formula. Balmony 2; Bayberry 2; White Poplar 1; Ginger 1. Dose: 500mg (two 00 capsules or one-third teaspoon) thrice daily, before meals.

Liquid Extracts. Formula. Goldenseal 10ml; Dandelion root 20ml; Holy Thistle 20ml; Cayenne 1ml. 30-60 drops thrice daily in water before meals.

Tinctures. Same formula, double dose.

Angostura wine. Wineglassful daily.

Diet: Herb teas, juices and mineral water instead of tea, coffee and other drinks containing caffeine. Honey. Wholefoods. Adequate protein intake. Small meals throughout the day. Avoid: alcohol, sugary snacks, white flour and white sugar products.

Supplementation. Daily. B-complex, B6 50mg, E 200iu, C 1g, Chromium 125mcg, Calcium Pantothenate 500mg, Kelp, Lecithin, Zinc.

Notes: Brewer's yeast tablets contain chromium which assists sugar metabolism. Smoking causes both glucagon and insulin to be released thus aggravating the condition. Diabetics should carry in their pocket some form of sugar against emergency.

HYPOGLYCAEMIC. A herb with ability to lower blood-sugar levels. Of value in diabetes mellitis.

Bean pods, Bladderwrack, Goat's Rue, Jambul, Nettles, Onion, Fenugreek seeds, Olive leaves, Periwinkle (Vinca rosea), Sweet Sumach.

Eucalyptus. (*R. Benigni et col Planti Medicinali, 1962, vol 1, 562*)

Reduction of blood sugar by Garlic has been reported.

HYPOKALAEMIA. Presence of abnormally low levels of potassium in the blood. May occur, with dehydration, in the elderly or in diabetics. A common cause is the prolonged use of the thiazides and loop diuretic drugs that leech potassium from the body. In severe degree may cause muscle weakness or paralysis. May also be caused by excessive fluid loss due to chronic diarrhoea.

Symptoms: Always tired. Lethargy. Irregular heart-beats from heart-muscle irritability. Possible cardiac arrest. Breathlessness.

Alternatives. *Teas*. Plantain, Chamomile, Mullein, Coltsfoot. Mistletoe. Nettles, Gotu Kola, or Yarrow.

Decoction. Irish Moss, Agar-Agar, Kelp, Dandelion root.

Powders. Formula. Dandelion, Hawthorn, Liquorice. Equal parts. Dose: 500mg (two 00 capsules or one-third teaspoon) thrice daily.

Tinctures. Formula. Equal parts: Hawthorn, Dandelion, Liquorice. Dose: 1-2 teaspoons, thrice daily.

Diet. Bananas: (fruit with highest potassium). Dates, Raisins. Oily fish. Figs. Prunes, Carrot leaves, Cider vinegar (impressive record), Black Molasses.

HYPOPARATHYROIDISM. Disorder of the parathyroid gland with diminished secretion of parathormone. Part of the gland may be removed in excision of part of the thyroid, or from injury.

Symptoms: Low levels of calcium in the blood (hypocalcaemia). See entry. One diagnostic sign is a twitching or spasm of the muscles (tetany).

Alternatives. *Teas*. Horsetail, Nettles, Plantain, Oats, Comfrey leaves, Silverweed, Scarlet Pimpernel. Skullcap, Bay.

Tablets/capsules. Iceland Moss, Irish Moss, Skullcap, Kelp.

Powders. Formula. Equal parts: Fenugreek, Horsetail, with pinch of Ginger. Dose: 750mg (three 00 capsules or half a teaspoon) thrice daily.

Liquid Extracts. Formula. Equal parts: German Chamomile, Ginkgo, Horsetail. Dose: 1 teaspoon thrice daily.

Tinctures. As Liquid Extract formula; double dose.

HYPOPITUITARISM. Diminished function of the pituitary gland with insufficient production of

hormones. Children fail to develop and may be small. Tumour accounts for many cases. May occur from pituitary damage due to severe major haemorrhage (Sheehan's syndrome).
Symptoms. Fatigue, weight loss, sense of weakness, low blood pressure, visual problems, headaches. Adults – hair loss. Women – absence of menstruation; unable to provide milk after pregnancy. Feeble sex drive. Few specifics exist, yet any of the following provides a basic stimulation for the whole endocrine system.
Alternatives. Sarsaparilla, Walnut, Prickly Ash, Ginseng, Wild Yam, Ginkgo, Gotu Kola.

The action of these herbs upon the endocrine system appears to be one of 'normalising' – decreasing over-activity and boosting under-activity. They are regarded as harmonisers, and may be required for months – even years.
Tablets/capsules. Sarsaparilla, Ginseng, Prickly Ash, Kelp, Ginkgo, Wild Yam.
Powders. Formula. Ginseng 2; Kelp 1; Ginkgo 2. Dose: 500mg (two 00 capsules or one-third teaspoon) thrice daily.
Liquid Extracts. Formula as powders. Dose: one 5ml teaspoon thrice daily.
Tinctures. Double dose.
Teas. Alfalfa, Holy Thistle, Wormwood, Bogbean, Ginkgo.

HYPOTENSION. Insufficient pressure to propel contents of the circulatory vessels throughout the body. Persistent low blood pressure is usually the result of blood loss following accident, infection, anaemic disorders or shock from heart attack. Blood pressure is naturally low during sleep.
Causes: failure of the adrenal glands, tuberculosis, neurasthenia, psychological shock, constitutional debility. Blood pressure is consistently below 110mmHg. Myocardial infarction. Fainting attack.
Symptoms. Dizziness, headache, fatigue, fainting, ringing in the ears, feels low, panicky, unable to concentrate, neurotic impulses, anxiety.
Alternatives. Underlying cause must be treated. Rest, tonics, good food, sunshine. When due to shock, hospital treatment may be necessary. Tonics and adrenal stimulants assist in raising pressure. Rosemary of special value. Hypotensives and anti-depressant should not be given.
In general use. Broom BHP (1983), Cactus (*Dr A. Vogel*), Camphor (circulatory stimulant), Cayenne (*Dr S. Thomson*), Echinacea, Ephedra, Garlic, Gentian, Ginseng BHP (1983), Goldenseal, Peppermint, Hawthorn (*D. Hoffmann*), Hyssop (*Dr A. Vogel*), Kola, Nettles, Prickly Ash bark, Lily of the Valley, Rosemary, Betony. Bladderwrack, Bogbean (*A. Thompson*), Wormwood, Hyssop. Fenugreek tea of special value.
Tonic Tea. Mix equal parts: Betony, Rosemary, Alfalfa, Peppermint. 1-2 teaspoons to each cup boiling water; infuse 15 minutes. 1 cup 2-3 times daily.
Rosemary leaves. 1 teaspoon to cup boiling water, infuse 15 minutes. Drink cold: half-1 cup morning and evening.
Tablets/capsules. Ginseng, Prickly Ash, Garlic, Hawthorn, Damiana, Kola, Ginkgo.
Powders. Formula. Rosemary 2; Kola 1; Ginger quarter. Dose: 500mg (two 00 capsules or one-third teaspoon) thrice daily.
Liquid Extract. Kola nuts BPC (1934). Dose: 10-20 drops thrice daily.
Tincture. Kola nuts BPC (1934). Dose: 15-60 drops thrice daily.
Practitioner. Tincture Ephedra 1:4 in 45 per cent alcohol BHP (1983). Dose: 6-8ml morning and evening.
Alternative Formula. *Tinctures*. Cactus 2; Rosemary 1; Ephedra 2; Ginger quarter. Dose: 1-2 teaspoons, thrice daily.
Dr A. Vogel. Formula. Hawthorn 6; Valerian 1; Cactus 1; E. Holly (Ilex Aqui) 1; Hyssop 1.
Aromatherapy. Essential oils of Olive, Lemon, Milk-Thistle, Rosemary, for external application. Oil of Camphor (circulatory stimulant) as an inhalant.
Diet. Potassium-rich foods, citrus fruits, bananas, potatoes, nuts, oatmeal porridge. Cayenne at table as a condiment. Brewer's yeast to produce albumin which forms 60 per cent of protein in plasma of the blood. Avoid eggs.
Supplements. Kelp, Garlic, Multivitamin, Zinc.
Note. People with low blood pressure tend to live longer than others.

See: BLOOD PRESSURE.

HYPOTENSIVE. Hypotensor. A herb used to reduce blood pressure. Ganglionic blocking agent. There is no clear demarcation between normal and abnormal blood pressure. It varies widely in any individual under different circumstances such as cold, emotion and food. Arterial pressure rises with age. It is now shown that 'resting pressure' decides risks of complications, or a fall in life expectancy. Insurance companies have ruled the limits of normal blood pressure as 140mmHg systolic, and 90mmHg diastolic pressure, approximately. Hypotensive drugs may be responsible for cardiac risks of potassium loss. The herbal clinician discovers that herbs used for high blood pressure usually conserve potassium and that heart failure due to potassium loss is reduced, with no known side-effects.

Black Haw, Buckwheat, Chervil, Garlic, Gelsemium, Hawthorn, Lime flower, Mistletoe, Valerian, Yarrow.

HYPOTHERMIA. Injury by exposure to damp and cold. Small babies and emaciated elderly people may not generate sufficient heat in wintry

weather.
Causes: fatigue, poor physical condition, inadequate nutrition.
Symptoms: death-like cold on surface of abdomen and under armpits, arrested pulse, slow breathing, partial loss of consciousness, blue puffy skin, stumbling, hallucinations, function of vital organs slows down.

A Glasgow survey shows cases are usually due to "the person dying of something else, drinks or drugs, or low thyroid function". Cold induces platelet agglutination which is a hazard for sufferers of thrombosis and heart disease. Even short exposures in the elderly with atheroma (*see definition*) are a hazard.
Preventative: Garlic.
To thin down thick blood: Nettle tea. Lemons.
Treatment. Circulatory stimulants. Under no circumstances should sedatives, antidepressants or tranquillisers be given. More than a few drops of alcohol increases heat loss and worsens the condition.
Alternatives. *Life Drops*: 5-10 drops in cup of tea.
Cayenne pepper on food. Composition powder or essence.
Camphor drops rapidly dispel the shivering reaction. All these open surface blood vessels and promote a vigorous circulation.
Teas: Chamomile, Balm, Yarrow.
Diet. Hot meals, hot drinks, adequate protein as well as carbohydrates. No alcohol. Oats warms the blood. Oatmeal porridge is indicated for people habitually cold. One teaspoon honey thrice daily in tea or other hot drink.

Wear a hat; nightcap at night. Electric blanket. Sleep in well-heated room. Wear thick wool underclothing. Serious cases admitted to Intensive Care Unit.

HYSSOP. *Hyssopus officinalis L. German*: Ysop. *French*: Hyssope officinale. *Spanish*: Hisopo. *Iranian*: Ush-naz-daoud. *Indian*: Juphá. *Arabian*: Zupho. Herb. *Keynote*: lungs.
Constituents: volatile oil, flavonoids, terpenoids, Mucilage, Resin.
Action: to induce heavy sweating in fevers, hypertensive to increase blood pressure, expectorant, emmenagogue, mild analgesic, diuretic. Antispasmodic. (*Mills*) External antiseptic.

Antiviral action against herpes simplex virus reported. (*E.C. Herrmann, Jr., & L.S. Kucera, Proc. Soc. Exp. Biol. Med., 124, 874, 1967*)
Uses. Bronchitis, colds, chills, catarrh, sore throat. Has been used in hysteria, anxiety states and petil mal BHP (1983). Respiratory disorders of nervous background in children.
Externally: eczema, bruises.
Combinations: with Betony (tea: equal parts) for tendency to epileptic episodes.
Preparations. Average dose: 2-4 grams. Thrice daily.
Tea: 1 heaped teaspoon to each cup boiling water: infuse 15 minutes. Half-1 cup freely in acute conditions; childrens' fevers.
Liquid Extract: 30-60 drops, in water.
Tincture BHP (1983) 1:5 in 45 per cent alcohol; dose 2-4ml.
Essential oil. 1-2 drops in water or honey after meals (digestive). 5-6 drops in 2 teaspoons Almond oil (chest rub for congested bronchi). 1-2 drops in honey between meals for worms in children.

HYSTERECTOMY. Surgical removal of the womb. In a total hysterectomy both cervix and ovaries are removed. It may be performed for ovarian cyst, prolapse, persistent heavy bleeding, fibroids and other disorders. After removal, conception is not possible and menstruation comes to an end.

The nervous as well as the endocrine system may take time to adjust. For instance, there will be no internal sources of oestrogen that may have to be provided by supplementation. General health needs must be built-up with adequate rest and wholefoods rich in minerals and vitamins. Herbs to assist recovery and mildly assuage pain.
Alternatives. *Tea*. Combination. Equal parts: Alfalfa, Agrimony and Raspberry leaves. 1-2 heaped teaspoons to each cup boiling water; infuse 5-15 minutes. 1 cup freely.
Tablets/capsules. Ginseng, Kelp, Black Cohosh.
Powders, liquid extracts or tinctures. Combination. Chamomile 1; Black Cohosh 1; Marigold 2; Sarsaparilla 2. Powders: one-third teaspoon. Liquid Extracts: 1 teaspoon. Tinctures: 2 teaspoons. In water or honey thrice daily.
Topical. Castor oil packs to low abdomen.
Diet. Oily fish – mackerel, herring, salmon. Slippery Elm, Irish Moss.
Supplements. Daily. Vitamin C 1g; Vitamin E 400iu; B-complex. Magnesium 200-400mg. Dolomite, Zinc 2 each morning and evening.

HYSTERIA. A mild form of neurosis which cannot be defined as mental illness. Often related to an individual's personality and which may manifest as physical illness. Children may demand attention and display exaggerated behaviour. Sometimes a person may have 'hysterics', usually in the presence of others. Unresolved sexual tension may predispose (Agnus Castus).
Symptoms. May be many and varied; acute outbreaks of temper tantrums (Valerian); episodes of self-pity, paranoia; apparent paralysis; preparing for examinations. Subjects may be in constant need of reassurance. May be associated with loss of speech, muscle weakness, migraine, backache, 'pain-in-the-neck'. Painful menses (Raspberry leaves, Motherwort).
Alternatives. General practice: Asafoetida,

Betony, Cowslip, Hyssop, Lime flowers, Passion flower, Pulsatilla, Rosemary, Skullcap, Valerian, Vervain BHP (1983). Blue Cohosh, Oats, Ladies Slipper, Mistletoe. (*Priest*)
Combination: Blue Cohosh, Squaw Vine, Wild Yam. (*Priest*)
Tea: Mix, equal parts: Betony. Skullcap, Lime flowers. 1-2 teaspoons to each cup boiling water; infuse 15 minutes. 1 cup freely.
Traditional. Equal parts, Skullcap, Valerian and Mistletoe. Mix. 1-2 teaspoons to each cup water. Bring to boil; remove vessel when boiling point is reached. Half-1 cup thrice daily.
Formula. Black Cohosh 2; Liquorice 1; Asafoetida quarter. Doses: Powders: 375mg (quarter of a teaspoon). Liquid Extracts: 15-30 drops. Tinctures: 30-60 drops. In water or honey, thrice daily.
Antispasmodic Drops.
Serious cases: Lobelia tea enema.
Practitioner: Liquid Extract Gelsemium, 1-3 drops, in water, when necessary.
Local. Hot foot bath. Cold water to head. Loosen tight clothing. Divert blood from the brain. Electric blanket.

IATROGENIC DISEASE. A most likely reaction to occur from a complication arising from therapeutic endeavour. A red angry irritant skin reaction which later scales off. May be due to drugs (antihistamines, aspirin, and chemical medicine). Special offenders are binders, artificial colourings and other ingredients added to medicines for cosmetic or preservation purposes. Urticaria and toxic erythema are common.

BCG innoculation may produce tuberculous ulceration; deep X-ray therapy a characteristic rash; steroids a redness of the face, thinning of the skin and easy bruising.

Sufferers from psoriasis and other chronic skin disorders experience a worsening of the condition with possible pus formation. "The Pill" has been responsible for erythema nodosum (red patches and nodules) as well as vaginal candidiasis. Some drugs cause shingles. Skin looks as if it is scalded. Internally, the mucous membranes may be seriously eroded.

As the liver is responsible for breaking down foreign substances in the body, most prescriptions contain at least one liver remedy. One for the lymphatic system is also advised. Effective antidote to drug intoxication: *Nux vomica*, which is given by a practitioner.

By their specific action on liver, spleen and glandular system certain plant medicines stimulate those vital organs to eliminate drug poisons. They include alteratives: Yellow Dock, Echinacea, Blue Flag. Carefully combined herbal medicine can offer something constructive before it is too late.

Alternatives. *Teas*. Alfalfa, Nettles, Figwort, Violet leaves, Betony, Mullein. 1-2 teaspoons to each cup of boiling water; infuse 10-15 minutes; dose, 1 cup thrice daily.

Tablets/capsules. As available: Echinacea, Blue Flag root, Dandelion, Devil's Claw, Red Clover, Seaweed and Sarsaparilla, Burdock, Queen's Delight, Garlic.

Formula. Goldenseal quarter; Poke root half; Echinacea 2. Doses. Powders: one-third teaspoon. Liquid extracts 30-60 drops. Tinctures: 1-2 teaspoons. In water or honey thrice daily; 2-hourly for acute cases.

Topical. Evening Primrose oil, Aloe Vera gel or fresh juice, Jojoba. Ointments: Chickweed, Comfrey or Marshmallow. Use of lanolin-based ointments is discouraged.

Diet. *Accept*: whole grains, meat, organ meats, molasses, wheatgerm, dessicated liver, green leafy vegetables, legumes, citrus fruits, broccoli, green peppers, cold-pressed vegetable oils, sweet potato.

Reject: red meat, ham, pork, bacon, white sugar, alcohol, nuts.

Supplements. Vitamin A, B-complex, B2, B6, B12, Folic acid, C, D, E (500iu).

ICELAND MOSS. *Cetraria islandica, L. German*: Torfmoos. *French*: Sphaigne. *Spanish*: Hiusgo. *Italian*: Stagno. *Indian*: Lahana. Dried lichen. *Keynote*: cough.

Constituents: cetrarin, lichen acids, terpenes, lichenin.

Action: demulcent, expectorant, antitussive, nutrient, antemetic. Helps arrest permanent respiratory damage in wasting diseases. Highly active in chest infections. Bitter tonic. Mucilage.

Uses. Loss of weight in terminal or wasting diseases with exhaustion and vomiting. To improve digestion. Vomiting – to arrest. Catarrh of nose, throat and chest. To break-up tough mucus in respiratory organs. Chronic bronchitis, cough. Blocked sinuses.

Combinations: with Goldenseal for wasting diseases: with Lobelia for chronic respiratory disorders.

Preparations. Average dose: 1-2 grams. Thrice daily.

Decoction. 1 teaspoon to each cup water, gently simmer 20 minutes. Dose: half-1 cup.

Tincture BHP (1983). 1 part to 5 parts 40 per cent alcohol. Dose: 1-1.5ml.

Tablets/capsules. Popular formula: Iceland Moss BHP (1983) 250mg; Liquorice BP 30mg; Lobelia BP 20mg.

ILEOSTOMY. An artificial opening through the abdominal wall by which the ileum is brought to the surface, and through which the intestinal contents may be discharged instead of passing through the colon.

Treatment: same as for colostomy.

Information. Ileostomy Association, PO Box 23, Mansfield, Notts NG18 4TT, UK. Send SAE.

IMMUNE SYSTEM. See: AUTO-IMMUNE DISEASE.

IMPETIGO. Skin disease with pus-filled itching lesions from bacterial infection. Primarily in children, particularly the under-nourished. Causative organisms: *staphylococcus* or *beta haemolytic streptococcus*. Vesicles burst and crust over. Gold-crusted lesions appear mainly on the face, hands and knees. Sometimes severe kidney infection may follow streptococcus invasion. Most common source of infection is the nose for which Garlic or Goldenseal are appropriate. May progress to boils or cellulitis.

Alternatives. Blue Flag root (commended), Buchu, Chaparral, Clivers, Echinacea (profuse suppuration), Garlic, Goldenseal, Holy Thistle, Juniper, Marigold (Calendula), Myrrh, Poke root, Red Clover, Thyme (Wild), Wild Indigo, Wormwood, Yellow Dock (weeping).

Teas. Burdock leaves, Chaparral leaves, Clivers, Dandelion leaves, Figwort, Red Clover.

Tablets/capsules. Blue Flag root, Dandelion root,

Echinacea root, Devil's Claw, Poke root, Seaweed and Sarsaparilla, Garlic.
Formula. Echinacea 2; Garlic 2; Goldenseal 1. Dose – Powders: 500mg (two 00 capsules or one-third teaspoon). Liquid Extracts: 1 teaspoon. Tinctures: 2 teaspoons.
Topical. Remove crusts with liquid paraffin or strong infusion of Soapwort.
Cream: Comfrey, Marshmallow and Slippery Elm, Aloe Vera or Evening Primrose.
Tea Tree oil: 3 drops to each teaspoonful water; wipe over area with aid of cotton wool.
Tea Tree oil and Castor oil: equal parts; use as a 'wipe-over'.
Diet. See: DIET, SKIN DISORDERS.
Supplements. Vitamin A (7,500iu); Vitamin C (500mg); Vitamin E (400iu). Zinc (15mg). Daily.
On retiring at night: 2-3 tablets/capsules, Garlic.

IMPOTENCE. Absence of sexual power. Lack of sexual performance in the male whereby erection cannot be maintained to complete a satisfactory orgasm between two people. Or failure to ejaculate. Impotence puts a marriage under serious strain. Marriage Guidance Council: "About a third of sex problems we deal with concern impotence." Pre-disposing factors: stress, marital problems, diabetes, drugs. Some cases are due to piles, fissures and other diseases of the rectum. First relieve the rectum and the impotence should look after itself. Smoking.
Alternatives. With the use of Ginseng and other plant extracts it is possible for sexual desire not to diminish with age, even in the eighties. Some have children in their seventies. Reduce alcohol to a minimum. Drunk males are poor performers.
Aphrodisiacs: Damiana, Siberian Ginseng, Saw Palmetto, Muira-pauama. Sarsaparilla stimulates secretion of the male hormone – testosterone. Helonias (*Ellingwood*). Agnus Castus. (*Whitehouse*)
Tablets or capsules: Sarsaparilla, Agnus Castus, Ginseng, Ginger.
Formula. Equal parts: Saw Palmetto, Kola, Damiana, Powders: 500mg (two 00 capsules or one-third teaspoon). Liquid Extracts: 1 teaspoon. Tinctures: 2 teaspoons. In water or honey, thrice daily.
Evening Primrose: two 500mg capsules morning and evening.
Australian Herbalism. Ginseng (panax), Withania Somnifera, Siberian Ginseng (Eleutherococus senticosus), Wu Wei Zi (Schisandra chinensis), Liquorice (Glycyrrhiza glabra), Di huang (Rehmannia glutinosa), Saw palmetto (Serenoa serrulata), Damiana (Turnera diffusa). (*David McLeod, Australian Journal of Medical Herbalism 1993, Vol 5 (2) 41-4*)
Diet. See: DIET – GENERAL.
Supplementation. Zinc, 30mg daily. Vitamin E 500iu daily. Bee pollen.
Counselling. Impotents Anonymous.

INCAPACITY CERTIFICATE. Certificates of incapacity for work issued by the National Institute of Medical Herbalists are acceptable by the Department of Social Security. The official form should bear the patient's name and diagnosis. Wording: I CERTIFY that I have examined you on the undermentioned date and that in my opinion you were incapable of work at the time of that examination by reason of . . . In my opinion you will be fit to resume work today/tomorrow or on . . . day. The date to be indicated must not be more than 3 days after the date of examination This is followed by the practitioner's signature, address, date of examination, date of signing, and other relevant remarks.

INCENSE. The formula for incense used by the *old Jewish Church* at the time of Moses is given in Exodus 30: 34-36. "Take unto thee three spices – stacte, onycha (powdered shellfish shell) and galbanum . . . with pure frankincense . . . equal parts. Thou shalt make it a perfume, a confection after the art of the apothecary, tempered together, pure and holy. And thou shall grind some of it small and place it before the testimony of the tabernacle of the congregation."
Incense of the Anglican Church. Parts: Olibanum 4; Thus 4; Benzoin 4; Tolu 41; Storax 2. Mix powders.

INCONTINENCE. Bladder instability. Sudden expulsion of a few drops (or more) of urine from the bladder from nervous or emotional strain, coughing, sneezing or lifting heavy weights. Where not due to defects of supporting muscles, may be the action of a psychogenic bladder. Trigger factors vary from acute stress to pressure from the womb or other local organ. The term also applies to inability of the bowel to hold back evacuation. Other causes may be injury, degenerative disease of the spinal cord and gynaecological problems.

Herbal urinary astringents help tighten up a sphincter muscle which has lost tone.
Treatment. Alternatives:– *Tea*: Bearberry, Cranesbill (American), Horsetail.
Tablets/capsules. Cranesbill (American).
Formula. Cranesbill (American) 2; Horsetail 2; Liquorice half. Dose – Powders: 750mg (three 00 capsules or half a teaspoon). Liquid Extracts: 1 teaspoon. Tinctures: 1-2 teaspoons. In water or honey thrice daily.
Practitioner. Tinctures: Ephedra 20ml; Cramp bark 20ml; Passion flower 10ml. Mix. Aqua to 100ml. Sig: 5ml (3i) tds aq cal pc.
Urinary problems, old men: Tincture Thuja, 5 drops in water thrice daily.
Sitz bath: alternating hot and cold water. See:

SITZ-BATH.
Smoking. Researchers at the Medical College, Virginia, USA, estimate that 29 per cent of cases of incontinence can be attributed to smoking after examining results of their case-control study of 606 women with an average age of 46.

INDIAN PENNYWORT. See: GOTU KOLA.

INDIGESTION. See: DYSPEPSIA.

INFECTION. Invasion of the body by pathogens such as bacteria, viruses, fungi, protozoa and other harmful organisms that can be communicated to another person. Transmission of disease may be by direct contact, by airborne droplets, contaminated food, through animals, and a number of causes. Effective treatment of a particular condition under consideration depends upon accurate diagnosis. Where this is not known, or where the patient is awaiting arrival of a qualified practitioner, a general anti-infectious formulation such as the following may prove helpful.
Essential oils: Eucalyptus (smithii) 25ml; Tea Tree 3ml; Thyme (T. vulgaris) 2ml. Mix. Dose: 10-20 drops, applied externally four times an hour, for four hours, each time on different areas of the body; then twice an hour for four hours. (*Daniel Pénoël, British Journal of Phytotherapy, Vol 2, No 4 1991/1992*)
Oral administration: Echinacea.

Treatment of infectious disease should be supervised by physicians and practitioners whose training prepares them to recognise serious illness and to integrate herbal and supplementary interventions safely into the treatment plan.

INFERTILITY. Failure of two people to bring about a pregnancy after one year of normal sexual intercourse. Where the cause is known accurate and effective treatment is possible. For instance, where it is likely to be caused by candida, focus on that condition with anti-fungals.
Causes (female). Absence of menses, dry vaginal entrance, tension, stress, tiredness, deformed or retroverted womb, cervical polyps, inflammation of the cervix or ovaries, fibroids, cystic ovaries, diabetes, drugs, steroids, psychogenic factors. Women who use intra-uterine devices may become infertile from tubal infection. The Pill affects fertility. Vitamin E deficiency. Professor Richard Morisset (World Health Organisation) asserts STD's account for more than 50 per cent infertility in women. Alcohol is a factor.
Causes (male). Inadequate seman, testicular or prostate infection, orchitis (from past mumps), kidney failure, chronic lung disease from smoking, thyroid deficiency, liver and other infections, calcium or Vitamin E deficiency. Low sperm count is found in regular drinkers of alcohol. 30 per cent cases of infertility are found to be due to the male.

"Women who drink more than one cup of coffee a day may find it harder to become pregnant." (*American study reported in The Guardian, 28.12.88*)

"Vegetarian women have lower levels of oestrogen. The amount of fibre women eat is believed to affect oestrogen levels in their blood." (*Dr Elwyn Hughes, University of Wales Institute of Science and Technology*)

"Drinking more than four cups of coffee a day and smoking more than 20 cigarettes could be a dangerous combination for male fertility." (*Research study, North Carolina, USA*)

Women whose mothers smoked when they were pregnant are only 50 per cent as fertile as women who were not exposed (when in the uterus) to a mother's tobacco smoke. (*C. Weinberg, "Reduced Fecundity in Women with Prenatal exposure to cigarette smoking." American Journal of Epidemiology 1989; 129 p1072*)

Margarine has been implicated in low sperm counts.
Alternatives. Endocrine balancers.
Female. Tea. Equal parts: herbs – Motherwort, Agnus Castus and Oats. Mix. 2 teaspoons to each cup boiling water; infuse 15 minutes. Dose, 1 cup 2-3 times daily.
Tablets: Agnus Castus, dosage as on bottle.
Liquid Extracts: equal parts Agnus Castus and Helonias: 1 teaspoon in water 2-3 times daily.
Maria Treben: 25 drops fresh Mistletoe juice in water, on empty stomach, night and morning.
External: Castor oil abdominal packs twice weekly.
Male. Ginseng, Gotu Kola, or the traditional combination of Damiana, Saw Palmetto and Kola. Tablets, liquid extracts, powders or tinctures. Tinctures (practitioner): Capsicum Fort BPC 5ml; Saw Palmetto (1:5) 10ml; Damiana (1:5) 50ml; Prickly Ash (1:5) 10ml. Aqua to 100ml. 1 teaspoon in water, thrice daily. (*Arthur Hyde FNIMH*)

An orange a day helps keep sperm OK. (*Important role of Vitamin C – New Scientist 1992 NO.1812 p20*)
Fasting. Mrs A. Rylin, Sweden, had been trying to conceive for 2 years. Conventional medicine proved ineffective until both she and her husband decided to fast for ten days. Within a month she conceived. Other successes reported.
Diet. (For both partners) Vitamin A foods. Wholefoods, oatmeal products (breakfast oats, etc). Regular raw food days. No alcohol. The key mineral for infertility is zinc, a deficiency of which may be made up with bran which is not only high in zinc but in soluble fibre. Not to eat any green peas, which are mildly contraceptive.
Supplements. Daily. Vitamin C (1 gram). Vitamin E (500iu). One B-complex tablet, including B6. The calcium ion is the key regulator of human sperm function – Calcium Lactate 300mg (2 tablets thrice daily at meals). Zinc – 2 tablets or capsules

at night. Folic acid, 400mcg. Dolomite. Iron.
Notes. Consider Vitamin B12 and Iron deficiency when evaluating anaemia in infertile couples.

20 per cent of men suffer infertility and produce high levels of superoxide radicals in their semen. Vitamin E, an antioxidant, is believed to mop up their superoxide radicals.
Observe sign of zinc deficiency: white flecks on nails.

INFLAMMATION. "A healing crisis (rise in temperature, etc) is an acute reaction resulting from the ascendance of Nature's healing forces over disease conditions. Its tendency is towards recovery. It is therefore in conformity with Nature's constructive principle." (*Catechism of Natural Medicine*).

It can be a reaction of tissue to infection, injury, surgery, radiation, chemicals, heat or cold, cancer or auto-immune disease.

Every medical student has to commit to memory four classical symptoms: heat, redness, pain and swelling.

As inflammation is a natural process, its progress should not be hindered by too much interference. Invading micro-organisms are destroyed by antibodies and white blood cells. During the encounter white cells may also be destroyed and expelled from the body in the form of pus. They are assisted in their action by an Anti-inflammatory. Most anti-inflammatories are also antiseptics. An external injury should be washed and treated with one.

Selection of remedies varies according to area and degree of inflammation. When occurring in the colon, it was known as 'colicon' by Celsus, Roman physician, in the 1st century. His prescription is as apt today:– Aniseed, Parsley, Pepper, few drops Castor oil and a pinch of powdered Myrrh.

Treatment for inflammation would be appropriate to the disease or condition, i.e. inflammation of the inner lining of the heart requires specific treatment as appears in entry for ENDOCARDITIS. For simple external inflammation, a tea of Chickweed, Comfrey or Marshmallow root may be indicated. See: ANTI-INFLAMMATORIES.

Treatment by or in liaison with a general medical practitioner.

INFLUENZA. La grippe. An acute contagious viral infection. There are three distinct antigenic types, A, B and C. Droplet infection. Incubation period 48 hours.
Symptoms: chill, shivering, headache, sore throat, weakness, tiredness, dry cough, aching muscles and joints, body temperature rise, fever. Virus tends to change, producing new strains.

Influenza lowers the body's resistance to infection. For stomach influenza, see: GASTRO-ENTERITIS. Effects of influenza may last for years.
Treatment. (Historical) One of the most virulent strains of history was during the outbreak after World War I. The American Eclectic School of physicians treated successfully with: 5 drops Liquid Extract Lobelia, 5 drops Liquid Extract Gelsemium, and 10 drops Liquid Extract Bryonia. Distilled water to 4oz. 1 teaspoon 4-5 times daily.

Bedrest. Drink plenty of fluids (herb teas, fruit juices). Hot bath at bedtime.
Alternatives. *Teas*. Elderflowers and Peppermint, Yarrow, Boneset, Pleurisy root.
Tablets/capsules. Lobelia, Cinnamon.
Potter's Peerless Composition Essence.
Powders. Cinnamon, with pinch of Cayenne. Dose: 500mg (two 00 capsules or one-third teaspoon) every 2 hours.
Formula. Lobelia 2; Pleurisy root 1; Peppermint quarter; Valerian half. Dose: Liquid Extracts: one 5ml teaspoon. Tinctures: two 5ml teaspoons. Acute cases: every 2 hours in hot water. On remission of temperature: thrice daily.
Nurse Ethel Wells, FNIMH. Half an ounce each: Elderflowers, Yarrow, White Horehound, Peppermint, Boneset. Infuse 2 tablespoons in 1 pint boiling water in a clean teapot. Drink teacupful at bedtime and the remainder, cold, in teacupful doses the following day.
Inhalant. Aromatherapy: 5 drops each, Niaouli, Pine and Eucalyptus oils in bowl of hot water; inhale steam with head covered. See also: FRIAR'S BALSAM. 4 drops Peppermint oil in bath.
Diet. 3-day fast, where possible, with herb teas and fruit juices.
Supplements. Daily. Vitamin A 7,500iu. Vitamin C 3g.

INFURNO. (*Carter's*) Embrocation for stiff joints, aching muscles and rheumatic tendency. Capsicin 1.25 per cent; Eucalyptus oil 4.25 per cent; Rectified oil of Camphor 4.25 per cent; Menthol 0.8 per cent; Methyl salicylate 17 per cent.

INFURNO MASSAGE CREAM. Contains Methyl sal 12.4 per cent, Capsicin 0.86 per cent, Menthol 0.5 per cent, Eucalyptus oil 2.4 per cent, rectified Camphor oil 2.4 per cent. Rheumatic aches and pains.

INFUSED OILS. Extraction of active ingredients of a plant by maceration in oil for external use for massage or ointments, creams, etc. See: OILS, IMPREGNATED.

INFUSION. A herbal tea or tisane. See: TEAS.

IN-GROWING TOENAIL. Nail grows into surrounding soft tissue causing inflammation and

possible infection, usually of the big toe.
Causes: tight shoes, inadequate footcare, cutting nails, etc. Cut nails straight across and not in a curve.
Topical. After thorough cleaning with soap and hot water, dab affected area with tincture Myrrh or tincture Goldenseal. Thin-down whole of the nail with a nail file after which affected border of nail can be easily cut. Fasten slice of Lemon on nail at night to soften. Bathe nail with strong sea-salt solution. Nelson's Hypercal Cream.

INHALATIONS. Herbs containing essential oils are sometimes used as inhalations. 1oz (30g) herb is infused in 2 pints (one and a quarter litres) boiling water for 15 minutes, strained, and the steam inhaled with the aid of a towel above the head. Soothing to irritable and sensitive mucous surfaces. Anti-microbial effects on colds, whooping cough, croup, laryngitis, coryza, asthma and early stages of fevers. To relieve spasm of bronchioles: Lobelia, Stramonium, Eucalyptus, Aloe Vera.
Important inhalants: Eucalyptus, Thyme, Hyssop, Rosemary, Lavender, Chamomile, Mint, Tea Tree. Aromatherapy offers oils of the above herbs: 6-12 drops floated on the surface of 2 pints boiling water after being allowed to stand 3 minutes. See: FRIAR'S BALSAM. TEA TREE.
Alternative method. In place of a basin use an aluminium hot water bottle into which boiling water is poured. Add few drops Friar's Balsam, Olbas, or essential oil. Insert a large funnel into which the mouth and nose are placed to breathe the vapour. Stop up any free space in the neck of the bottle with a tissue.
Camphorated oil. 4 teaspoons to litre boiling water. Inhale steam with aid of a towel over head.
Inhalant Salve for nasal congestion and frontal sinusitis. Oil Pine 1ml; Oil Eucalyptus 2ml; Oil Peppermint 2ml; Vaseline to 30 grams. Melt the Vaseline. Add oils. Stir until cold. For direct use or inhaled from boiling water. (*F. Fletcher Hyde, FNIMH*)
Note. Inhalation: also through a tissue, steam or air-diffuser. Odours act upon the sense of smell and influence mucous secretion of the respiratory organs.

INSECT BITES. Reaction to any insect bite is due to either venom released or allergic response.
Symptoms: redness, pain, itching, swelling. Remove sting where possible.
Alternatives. External.
Tinctures: Arnica, Acid tincture of Lobelia, Echinacea, Marigold, Myrrh, St John's Wort.
Fresh plants. Crush and apply: Comfrey, Garlic, Houseleek, Marigold, Onion, Plantain.
St John's Wort: specific – horsefly.
Witch Hazel Lotion.
Cider Vinegar: wasp bites.
Bee and ant bites: in absence of any of the above: bicarbonate of soda.
Aromatherapy. Any one oil – Eucalyptus, Clove, Lavender.
For shock: with faintness and pallor: few grains Cayenne pepper in honey or cup of tea.
Supplements. Vitamin A and B-complex.

INSECT REPELLENTS. *Oils*: Lavender, Pennyroyal, Cloves, Thyme. Apply to exposed areas. Avoid contact with mucous membranes.
Popular Indian: 2-3 drops oil Citronella on handkerchief and dabbed behind ears, on neck, hair, etc. Garlic repels all insects and beetles. Cedarwood essential oil kills houseflies, mosquitoes and cockroaches in concentrations of less than 1 per cent. (*Central Institute for Medicinal Plants, Lucknow*)

INSECTICIDE. A herb destructive to insects.
Tinctures: Arnica, St John's Wort, Myrrh or Marigold.
Oils: Clove, Eucalyptus or Pennyroyal.
Mucilage from: Comfrey, Plantain, Houseleek.
Cider vinegar. Pyrethrum. Derris.

INSOMNIA. Inability to sleep. During sleep the central nervous system is at rest. One-third of every day should be spent in this form of recovery.
Causes: these are many and varied, including low blood glucose levels, excessive tea, coffee, Cola or other stimulants, cold, heat, cough, anxiety, depression. Sleep tends to decline with age, and is a cause of restless leg syndrome.
Alternatives. *Transient insomnia*: Roman Chamomile, Betony, Cowslip flowers, Hops, Balm, Passion flower, Skullcap, Vervain, Valerian. Ginseng. Lime flowers.
Chronic insomnia: Jamaica Dogwood, Ladyslipper, Valerian. Wild Lettuce, Mistletoe, Californian Poppy.
Tea. Any one of the above. Teas, medicines, etc may be sweetened with honey.
Maria Treben tea. Combine parts: Cowslip flowers 10; Lavender 5; St John's Wort 2; Hops 3; Valerian 1. 1 heaped teaspoon to cup boiling water; infuse 3 minutes. Sip, warm, before sleep.
Dr A. Vogel. (*Dormeason*) sleeping drops; parts: Balm 40; Oats 38; Passion flower 10; Hops 9; Valerian 2; Hop grains (lupulin) 1. Dose: 10-15 drops.
Insomnia from wind. Tea: Equal parts, Lime flowers, Passion flower, Spearmint. 1 heaped teaspoon to each cup boiling water: infuse 15 minutes. Half-1 cup freely.
Tablets. Motherwort formula. Pulverised Passiflora BHP (1983) 90mg, Pulverised Extract Motherwort 4:1 50mg, Pulverised Extract Lime flowers 3:1 67mg. (*Gerard House*)
Lobelia: 2 tablets at bedtime.
Tinctures. Formula. Equal parts: Passion flower,

Valerian, Jamaica Dogwood. 1 teaspoon in warm water at bedtime, and again for restlessness during the night. OR:– Skullcap. 1:1 in 25 per cent alcohol. 15-60 drops in water at bedtime.
Tincture. 1oz Passion flower herb steeped in 1 pint white wine 14 days. Shake daily. Filter. Dose: 1 wineglassful when necessary. On failure to sleep, repeat after half hour of dose.
Aromatherapy. Hot bath to which 10 drops oil of Lavender is added.
Insomnia from pain: Jamaica Dogwood.
Insomnia from nervous excitability: Chamomile, Vervain, Valerian.
Practitioner: desperate cases: equal parts Tinctures Gelsemium and Valerian. 10 drops hour before retiring.
Diet. Breakfast porridge oats. Avoid caffeine-containing drinks: tea, coffee, cola, cocoa and heavy meals in the evening. Honey drink at bedtime: 2 teaspoons honey in hot milk.
Supplementation: Vitamins, B-complex, B6, B12, Niacin, C, D. Calcium.
Complementary: Hot bath.
Notes. No caffeine drinks at bedtime. Deep-breathing exercises. Ensure bedroom is not too hot or cold. Keep regular hours for sleeping periods. A quiet room and a warm bed. If after one week sleep is still absent, a practitioner should be consulted.

INSTITUTE OF HEALTH FOOD RETAILING. Professional body to ensure status of those whose career is in the health food industry. Encourages training, research and education in health food retailing, health and nutrition, and furthers these objects with meetings and seminars. Holders of the NAHS Diploma of Health Food Retailing may apply for membership. On acceptance they are awarded a certificate with authority to use the designatory letters M Inst HFR.
Address: Byron House, College Street, Nottingham NG1 5AQ.

INTERFERON. An enhancer of the immune system produced by T-lymphocyte cells that destroy cells of viruses and cancer. Echinacea is found to have an interferon effect. Other agents to promote interferon: Boneset, Liquorice and Goldenseal.

INTERMITTENT CLAUDICATION. Lameness or spasmodic pain in the legs when walking a certain distance due to deficient blood supply to the muscles. Associated with artery disorders, muscular weakness. The diseased artery cannot carry enough blood to supply the oxygen needs of the muscles.
Treatment. Circulatory stimulants. Vaso-dilators.
Alternatives. BHP (1983) – Prickly Ash bark, Cramp bark, Black Cohosh, Angelica root, Hawthorn, Wild Yam. Prophylactic – Garlic.
Decoction. Mix, equal parts: Black Cohosh, Prickly Ash bark, Hawthorn berries. One teaspoon to each cup of water simmered gently 20 minutes. Half-1 cup thrice daily.
Formula. Hawthorn 2; Black Cohosh 1; Prickly Ash 1. Dose: Powders: 500mg (two 00 capsules or one-third teaspoon). Liquid Extracts: one 5ml teaspoon. Tinctures: two 5ml teaspoons. Thrice daily in water or honey.
Tablets/capsules. Prickly Ash. Hawthorn. Black Cohosh. Garlic, 2 at night. Cramp bark. Ginkgo.
Life Drops. 3-10 drops in cup of tea to relieve spasm.
Ginkgo biloba. "Walking distance is definitely increased." (*Rudolf F. Weiss MD. Herbal Medicine, Beaconsfield Publishers*)
Garlic. 80 patients with symptomatic state II occlusive disease (claudication), randomised, to take either Garlic powder 800mg a day in tablet form (equivalent to Kwai) or placebo for 12 weeks. A significantly greater improvement in walking distance, apparent after just 4 weeks, occurred in the Garlic-treated group compared with the placebo group. (*Professor H. Kiesewetter, Department of Clinical Haemostasiology, University of Saarland, Germany*)
Diet. Lacto-vegetarian.
Supplements. Vitamin E, 400iu morning and evening.
General. Venesection sometimes necessary. No smoking or alcohol. See: BUERGER'S DISEASE, RAYNAUD'S DISEASE, ARTERIOSCLEROSIS, PHLEBITIS, THROMBOSIS.

INTERTRIGO. An irritative 'hot and humid' skin eruption which occurs when two opposing moist surfaces touch and interferes with evaporation of sweat; i.e. under the breasts or between the thighs.
Indicated. Anti-bacterials, anti-inflammatories, antifungals.
Alternatives. *Teas.* Clivers, Dandelion leaves, Figwort, Marigold, Meadowsweet, Red Clover.
Tea: formula. Equal parts: Meadowsweet, Mullein, Red Clover. 1 heaped teaspoon to each cup boiling water; infuse 15 minutes; 1 cup thrice daily.
Tablets/capsules. Blue Flag, Dandelion, Devil's Claw, Echinacea, Poke root, Seaweed and Sarsaparilla.
Powders. Equal parts: Echinacea and Garlic. 500mg (two 00 capsules or one-third teaspoon), thrice daily.
Liquid Extracts. Formula. Echinacea 2; Clivers 1; Blue Flag 1. Dose: 30-60 drops. Thrice daily.
Tinctures. Formula. Echinacea 2; Goldenseal 1; Myrrh 0.5. Dose: 1 teaspoon. Thrice daily.
Topical. Anti-moisturisers. Distilled extract of Witch Hazel.
Diet. Gluten-free.
Supplements. Daily. Vitamins A, C, D, E. Selenium 200mcg. Zinc 15mg.

INTESTINAL OBSTRUCTION. Any blockage or hindrance arresting the flow of contents of the intestines. May be mechanical (adhesions, hernias, tumours, etc) or paralytic.
Symptoms: distension, dehydration, atony, vomiting, constipation.
Alternatives. Wild Yam. Calamus. Papaya.
Condition may have to be resolved by surgery.
Simple obstruction: large doses (4-8 teaspoons) Isphaghula seeds. Lime flower tea. See: COLITIS.

IODINE. Trace element. RDA 0.14 to 0.15mg.
Deficiency. Goitre, low metabolism, fatigue, sleepiness.
Body effects. Promotes thyroid hormones.
Sources. Seafood, meat, fruit and vegetables.
Herbs: Bladderwrack, Dulse, Garlic, Kelp, Iceland Moss, Irish Moss.
Iodine status check. Paint a small (about 2") patch of tincture of Iodine on the inside of the thigh before going to bed. Allow to dry. It should be yellowish-orange. Next morning check results:–
1. Colour completely gone: significant shortage of iodine.
2. Colour barely detectable: shortage of iodine.
3. Colour slightly faded: adequate iodine.
4. Colour almost as strong: adequate iodine.
5. Colour turns red: indicates chemical sensitivities helped by Selenium supplementation.
6. Colour turns black: associated with food sensitivities.
7. Colour stays for several days: indicates iodine excess.
(*Dr Robert Erdmann, PhD., 'Balance your Metabolism with Iodine', in "Here's Health", Nov 1991*)

IPECACUANHA ROOT. *Cephaelis ipecacuanha* (Brot.) A. Rich. *German*: Brachwurzel. *French*: Ipecacuanha. *Spanish*: Ipecacuanha. *Italian*: Ipecaquana. Rhizome and root. Practitioner use only. Contains alkaloid and saponin emetine, glycosides, tannins.
Action: expectorant, diaphoretic, antiprotozal BHP (1983), emetic (large doses). Acts upon the pneumogastric nerve. Antispasmodic. Stimulant to mucous membranes.
Uses: to liquefy bronchial phlegm and promote expectoration. Sore throat, whooping cough, stubborn cough. Amoebic dysentery. Expulsion of mucus from the chest. Alternative to a stomach pump to induce vomiting.
Combinations: with Lobelia for respiratory disorders. With Tincture Myrrh for bowel infection, orally or by enema.
Preparations. Average dose, rhizome and roots: 25-100mg. Thrice daily. Dose more accurately controlled by use of liquid extract or tincture rather than infusion or decoction.
Liquid extract BP 1973: dose 0.025 to 0.1ml. Emetic dose – 0.5 to 2ml.
Tincture BP (1973). Dose 0.25 to 1ml. Emetic dose 5 to 20ml.
Cough mixtures: an ingredient of. (*Potter's Balm of Gilead*) etc.
Contra-indications: shock, heart disease.
GSL, schedule 1

IRISH MOSS. Carrageen. *Chondrus crispus L.* Seaweed. Whole plant (thallus).
Constituents: trace minerals, polysaccharides. Source of minerals, iodine, iron, bromine.
Action. Antitussive, nutrient, demulcent, pectoral, antibacterial. Detoxicant. Anticoagulant, hypotensive. Lowers blood cholesterol levels.
Uses. Bronchitis and respiratory disorders generally. Pulmonary tuberculosis. Dry cough. To cleanse mucous membranes. Thin people desiring to put on weight. Wasting diseases, cachexia. Inflammation of the alimentary canal. Irritable stomach, gastric and duodenal ulcer, recovery from surgical operation. To protect lining of stomach from acidity. Inflammation of kidneys or bladder.
External. A base for ointments, cosmetic creams, etc.
Preparations. Thrice daily, or as necessary.
Decoction. Dried seaweed, 5 to 10 grams to each large cup water gently simmered 20 minutes. Cannot be strained. Half a cup eaten with spoon. Honey enhances action.
Diet. Use of the powder to thicken soups, jellies, aspic and for inclusion in recipes requiring a thickener. A fingerful (powder) in early morning tea for chest protection in winter. GSL

IRITIS. Inflammation of the iris.
Causes: juvenile polyarthritis, ankylosing spondylitis, sexually transmitted diseases, tuberculosis, injury, etc.
Symptoms. Eyeballs stuck down in the mornings from exudate, contraction of the pupil, pain, photophobia, discoloration of the iris. If exudate is with pus: Echinacea, Goldenseal, Poke root. Salmon-coloured zone around the cornea. Pupil fails to respond to light.
There is a type of eye inflammation associated with arthritic change in the body and which should not be mistaken for conjunctivitis but can be damaging to the eyeball. The iritis of early poker-spine is not local but internal and responds only to anti-arthritic and anti-inflammatory agents such as Guaiacum.
Alternatives. Dilation of pupil by a mydriatic administered by a medical practitioner. Alternatives (internal):–
Black Cohosh: Dose: Liquid Extract: 5-15 drops. Tincture: 10-30 drops. Every two hours, acute cases, otherwise thrice daily.

Pulsatilla. Dose: Liquid Extract: 5-10 drops. Tincture: 10-20 drops. Acute cases: every two hours, otherwise thrice daily.
Formula. Tinctures, Eyebright and Goldenseal, equal parts. Dose: 10-20 drops in water or cup of German Chamomile tea.
Topical. Elderflower tea or lotion eye douche, morning and evening. Aloe Vera, gel or pulp from fresh plant leaves.
Supplements. Vitamins A, C, D, E. Zinc.

IRON. Mineral. Essential for production of haemoglobin (see entry). Haemoglobin absorbs oxygen from the lungs from which it is borne throughout the body by the red blood cells. Iron is a component of enzymes that play a vital role in oxidation of food and release of energy. As the metal is not produced in the body it has to be obtained from external sources. Iron is also conserved by the body following breakdown of old red blood corpuscles. RDA 10mg (men), 12mg (women), 13mg (pregnant women), 15mg (nursing mothers).
Deficiency. Iron-deficiency anaemia is the most common deficiency disease in the world. Children require adequate level for cell growth and healthy development. Senior citizens may have inability to absorb. Sportspeople carefully watch their iron levels.

Studies reveal that iron absorption is reduced by coffee consumption. A single cup of coffee can effect a reduction of 30 per cent when consumed at the same time iron or iron containing foods are taken. (*American Journal of Clinical Medicine, 1983*)
Sources. Red meat, liver, kidney, almonds, dried fruits (especially figs), All Bran, spinach, watercress.
Herbs. All seaweeds. Burdock, Devil's Claw, Couch Grass root, Meadowsweet, Mullein, Rest Harrow, Nettles, Toadflax, Wild Strawberry leaves, Yellow Dock, Gotu Kola, Parsley, Silverweed.
Floradix Herbal Iron Extract: absorbable iron in a yeast extract dietary supplement. Contents include Nettles, Fennel, Angelica root, Horsetail, Spinach, Yarrow, etc.

IRRITABLE BOWEL SYNDROME (IBS). Previously known as "mucous colitis", "spastic colon". Believed to be associated with psychomatic rather than allergic phenomena. Food is said to be responsible for one-third cases. X-ray fails to reveal evidence; prostaglandins implicated. Females more susceptible than men. Cow's milk and antigens in beef can precipitate.
Symptoms. Spastic colon: colon held in spasm. The two main symptoms are abdominal pain and altered bowel habit. Pain relieved on going to stool or on passing wind. Diarrhoea with watery stools on rising may alternate with constipation. Sensation that the bowel is incompletely emptied. Flatulence. Passing of mucus between stools. The chronic condition may cause anaemia, weight loss and rectal blood calling for treatment of the underlying condition.
Indicated: astringents, demulcents, antispasmodics.
Treatment. If possible, start with 3-day fast.
Alternatives. *Teas*. (1) Combine equal parts; Agrimony (astringent), Hops (colon analgesic), Ephedra (anti-sensitive). (2) Combine equal parts; Meadowsweet (astringent) and German Chamomile (nervine and anti-inflammatory). Dose: 1 heaped teaspoon to each cup boiling water; infuse 15 minutes. 1 cup freely, as tolerated.
Bilberry tea. 2 tablespoons fresh or dried Bilberries in 1 pint water simmered 10 minutes. Half-1 cup freely.
Note. Old European: Chamomile and Caraway seed tea. 1 cup morning and evening.
Decoction. Formula. Tormentil root 2; Bistort root 2; Valerian root 1. Dose: 2 teaspoons to each cup water simmered 20 minutes. Half-1 cup 3-4 times daily.
Tablets/capsules. Calamus. Cramp bark. Goldenseal. Slippery Elm, Cranesbill.
Formula. Cranesbill 2; Caraway 2; Valerian half. Dose: Powders: 750mg or half a teaspoon). Liquid Extracts: 1-2 teaspoons. Tinctures: 2-4 teaspoons. Thrice daily.
Practitioner. RX tea: equal parts herbs Peppermint, Balm and German Chamomile. Infuse 1-2 teaspoons in cup boiling water and add 3 drops Tincture Belladonna.
Formula. *Tinctures*. Black Catechu 2; Cranesbill 1; Hops quarter. Dose: 1-2 teaspoons in water or honey, thrice daily.
Psyllium seeds (Ispaghula). 2-5 teaspoons taken with sips of water, or as Normacol, Isogel, etc. For pain in bowel, Valerian.
Fenugreek seeds. 2 teaspoons to cup water simmered 10 minutes. Half-1 cup freely. Consume seeds.
Cinnamon, tincture or essence: 30-60 drops in water 3-4 times daily.
Menstrual related irritable bowel. Evening Primrose.
Irritable Bowel Syndrome, with neurosis. Treat thyroid gland (Bugleweed, Kelp, etc).
With severe nerve stress: add CNS (central nervous system) relaxant (Hops, Ladies Slipper, Roman Chamomile)
Oil of Peppermint. A simple alternative. 3-5 drops in teaspoon honey, or in enteric-coated capsule containing 0.2ml standardised Peppermint oil B.P., (*Ph.Eur.*)
Intestinal antispasmodics: Valerian, Chamomile, Balm, Rosemary.
Diet. "People with IBS should stop drinking coffee as it can induce a desire to defecate." (*Hallamshire Hospital Research Team*)

Dandelion coffee. Fenugreek tea. Carrot juice.

Bananas mashed into a puree with Slippery Elm powder. Yoghurt. Gluten-free diet.
Supplements. Calcium lactate tablets: 2 x 300mg thrice daily at meals. Floradix. Lactobacillus acidophilus to counteract toxic bacteria. Vitamin C (2-4g). Zinc. Linusit.
Note. Serious depression may underlay the condition. Anti-depressants sometimes relieve symptoms dramatically.
Chronic cases. Referral to Gastrology Outpatient Department.

ISCADOR. A specific developed from Mistletoe for cancer, pre-cancerous conditions, AIDS, ME (post viral fatigue syndrome) and immune system disorders. Mistletoe (Viscum album) grows on a number of trees, the one most preferred for medical purposes being that from the pine tree.

Iscador is based on the philosophy of anthroposophy founded by Dr Rudolph Steiner and requires a special process of manufacture based on time of gathering and aspect of the moon.

ISPAGHULA SEEDS (Pale). Spogel seeds. Psyllium seeds. Ispaghula husk BP. *Plantago ovata*. Dried ripe seeds. *Keynote*: constipation and bowel irritation.
Constituents: mucilage, triterpenes, alkaloids.
Action: gentle bulk *laxative* without irritation; *antidiarrhoeal*, demulcent, bacteriostatic. Increases stool output while decreasing transit time in healthy people. Anti-inflammatory.
Uses. Chronic constipation, particularly in the elderly. Irritable bowel syndrome, mucous colitis. Amoebic dysentery. (*Indian traditional*) To assist management of diverticular disease. To reduce incidence of bowel complaints. An alternative to constant use of purgatives that decrease sensitivity of alimentary mucous membranes. Useful in pregnancy. Hyperlipaemia. Lowers cholesterol level by eliminating excess bile salts. To assist slimming regime in obesity.
Preparations. Average dose: 3-5 grams (2 grams, children).
Seeds: 1-2 teaspoons once or twice daily, helped down with sips of water. (May be soaked overnight in warm water.) In the intestines seeds swell into a gelatinous mass many times their normal size thus 'lubricating' contents of the bowel for easy defecation. Isogel.
"Regulan" Ispaghula husk BP. Sachets containing 3-6 grams. Average dose: 1 sachet thrice daily.
Psyllium seed husks, plus pectin, Vitamin C and Guar gum to cleanse the colon while leaving behind important nutrients. Aids detoxification and absorption of iron. Regulates blood sugar levels and nutrient absorption. (*JAM. Nov 86, p.23*)
Poultice. With Slippery Elm for boils, abscesses, etc. GSL

ITCHING. Pruritus. Itching is a symptom of many conditions the underlying cause of which should receive treatment. Generalised itching may direct attention to the liver: cirrhosis, jaundice or hepatotoxic drugs. Other causes: chronic kidney failure, glandular disorders, blood disorders (worse by hot bath), hyper- and hypo-thyroidism, malignancy or carcinoid syndrome (due to release of histamine), anabolic steroids, oral contraceptives, the third trimester of pregnancy (Raspberry leaves). Diabetes is usually credited with general itching but this is rare; its itching being chiefly in the anus and vulva for which Helonias is helpful.
Alternatives. All types of irritation, including itching of anus and vulva.
Teas. Chaparral, Chickweed, Figwort, Dandelion, Boneset, Marigold, Nettles, Red Clover.
Tea formula. Equal parts: Figwort, Meadowsweet, Juniper berries. 1 heaped teaspoon to each cup boiling water; infuse 15 minutes; 1 cup thrice daily.
Tea (cold). Barberry bark: one heaped teaspoon to each cup cold water steeped overnight. Dose: 1 cup thrice during the following day.
Tablets/capsules. Blue Flag, Dandelion, Echinacea, Devil's Claw, Poke root, Seaweed and Sarsaparilla, Wild Yam.
Formula. Echinacea 2; Dandelion 2; Poke root half. Dose – Powders: 500mg (two 00 capsules or one-third teaspoon). Liquid Extracts: one 5ml teaspoon. Tinctures: two 5ml teaspoons).
Practitioner. Tinctures BHP (1983). Barberry (Berberis vulgaris) 2; Kava Kava 1; Figwort 1. Dose: 1-2 teaspoons in water thrice daily for severe anal or vulval attack.
Topical. Wipe affected area with: (a) Witch Hazel water. (b) Witch Hazel water plus 2-3 drops Tincture Goldenseal (severe, anus or vulva). (c) Cider vinegar. (d) Jojoba oil. (e) Aloe Vera (anus and vulva). (f) Well diluted essential oils of Aromatherapy: Lavender, Aniseed. (g) 2-3 drops Australian Tea Tree oil to 100ml water. (h) Zinc and Castor oil cream. (i) Bathe with strong infusion Tansy (anus).
Evening Primrose oil capsules. Contain gamolenic acid which has a significant effect on relieving itching by its antihistamine action.
Diet. Gluten-free.
Vitamins. A. B-complex. B3. B6. B12. D. F.
Minerals. Zinc.
Note. Constantine Hering MD, physician, sums up the law of cure: "The direction of disease is inwards and upwards. The direction of cure is downwards and outwards. Symptoms that move deeper into the body and from the surface towards the head are considered dangerous. Any skin eruption, or itching, or nervous symptoms moving from the head towards the feet would be regarded as favourable.

"Itch is an effort of the central nervous system

to move a deeper disturbance towards the skin where the irritation may be distressing but where it is least damaging."

Perhaps the most common cause of chronic itching in the 1990s is candida.

IVY. English Ivy. *Hedera helix L. German*: Efeu. *French*: Lierre. *Spanish*: Diedra o Yedra. *Italian*: Edera. Leaves, berries. Contains the saponins, hederine and emetine. Practitioner use.
Action: cathartic, diaphoretic, stimulant, anti-spasmodic, expectorant, febrifuge, anthelmintic, amoebicidal.
Uses: whooping cough, to liquefy bronchial phlegm. Berries macerated in vinegar to make an acid tincture used in the London plague. Hydrocephalus (single drop doses of fresh plant juice) traditional.
Preparations. Locally, Ivy leaf poultice for swollen glands and chronic leg ulcer.
Ivy Leaf Corn Cure.

JAMAICA DOGWOOD. Fish poison bark. *Piscidia Erythrina L. German*: Kornelbaum. *French*: Cornouiller. *Spanish*: Corniro. *Italian*: Corniola. *Part used*: root bark.
Constituents: piscidin, calcium oxalate, isoflavones, organic acids.
Action: sedative, antispasmodic, nerve relaxant, mild analgesic, hypnotic, antitussive, anti-inflammatory.
Synergy: action resembles Wild Yam, Black Haw, Pulsatilla, Bryonia, Black Cohosh and Gelsemium regarding nerve symptoms.
Uses. Infantile hyperactivity, brain excitability, nervous instability, neuralgia, insomnia from excess coffee or mental activity, toothache, spasm of the womb, migraine.

Combines well with Valerian and Hops for over-excitability and sleeplessness.
Preparations. Thrice daily.
Dried root bark. 2-4g or in decoction.
Liquid extract BPC 1934. (1:1 60 per cent alcohol). Dose: 2-8ml.
Tincture. 1 part to 5 parts alcohol (45 per cent). Dose: 5-15ml.
Tablets/capsules. The remedy is frequently combined with Valerian, Skullcap, Black Cohosh and Cayenne for nerve weakness and tension.

Not given in pregnancy or weak heart. GSL

JAMBUL. Eugenia jambolana. *Syzygium cumini L. German*: Jambosenbaum. *French*: Jambosier. *Italian*: Mela rosa. *Indian*: Jamuna. Seeds. *Keynote*: anti-diabetic.
Constituents: jambosine (alkaloid), phenols.
Action: astringent diuretic, carminative, reputed hypoglycaemic (not specific).
Uses. Diabetes. (*India – traditional*) To reduce sugar in the urine. Colic, with severe griping pain.
Preparations. 0.3 to 2 grams. Thrice daily.
Decoction: half-1 teaspoon to each cup water gently simmered 5 minutes. Dose: one-third to half a cup.
Liquid Extract BHP (1983) 1:1 in 25 per cent alochol; dose 2-4ml in water.
Tincture: from powdered fruit stones: 1 part to 5 parts alcohol. Macerate 8 days; shaking daily. Dose: 30-60 drops.
Powdered seeds: 0.3 to 2 grams. GSL

JASMINE. *Jasminum officinale. Jasminum grandiflorum L. German*: Echter jasmin. *French*: Jasmin cummum. *Italian*: Gelsomino. *Indian*: Chambelli. *Chinese*: So-hsing. *Malayan*: Pŭkan.
Constituents: jasminine (alkaloid), salicylic acid, resin.
Action: nerve relaxant, aphrodisiac, astringent, bitter, mild anaesthetic.
Uses. Sexual debility, hepatitis, pains of cirrhosis of the liver.
Preparation. *Tea*: half-1 teaspoon flowers to each cup boiling water; infuse 10 minutes; dose, half a cup, thrice daily.

JAUNDICE. Increased level of bile pigment in blood and tissue due to obstruction to bile ducts, e.g. in liver (hepatitis) or in the main duct (stone). Also due to excess production of pigment, e.g. in haemolytic anaemia. Underlying cause should be treated; gall stones, pressure from the pancreas, etc.
Symptoms: yellow tinge of the skin and whites of eyes, urine is dark greenish brown, tongue furred, pulse slow, appetite poor, indigestion, nausea, vomiting, very offensive stools which are pale because of lack of bile, bitter taste in mouth, itching of skin.

Bitter herbs keep the bile fluid and flowing.
For itching: Aloe Vera. See ITCHING.

The following recommendations regarding diet, supplementation, etc, refer to the general condition. For herbal treatment refer to specific type of jaundice.
Diet. Commence with 3-day fruit juice fast. Raw carrot juice. Followed by low-fat diet. High protein, high carbohydrate. Dandelion coffee.
Supplementation. Vitamins: B-complex, B6, B12, C (1 gram every 3 hours for acute conditions), D, E (1000iu daily). Dolomite.
George Stevens. Some cases may require a relaxing nervine (Vervain, Lobelia) as spasm of the gall duct may be responsible.
External. If pain on right side is severe, apply hot fomentation of Hops (1 handful to half a pint boiling water) which tends to relax the biliary duct, expediting expulsion of obstruction or stone.
John Wesley. Found relief from a tea of equal parts, Nettles and Burdock leaves.

JAUNDICE, CATARRHAL. Now usually termed VIRAL HEPATITIS. Swelling of liver cells obstructs drainage. Plugged mucus in the bile duct; often caused by gluten foods. Aftermath of chills and colds or from excess milky or starchy foods. Congestion may be dispersed by speeding elimination of waste products of metabolism via the bowel (Blue Flag), the kidneys (Dandelion), and the skin (Devil's Claw). Anti-catarrhals with special reference to the liver: Gotu Kola, Plantain, Goldenseal, Mountain Grape, Barberry.
Alternatives. *Teas*. Agrimony, Boldo, Balmony, Dandelion, Plantain, Gotu Kola.
Cold infusion. 2 teaspoons Barberry bark to each cup cold water; steep overnight. Half-1 cup every 3 hours.
Tablets/capsules. Goldenseal, Dandelion, Blue Flag, Devil's Claw.
Formula. Equal parts: Dandelion, Devil's Claw, Barberry. Dose – Powders: 500mg (two 00 capsules or one-third teaspoon). Liquid Extracts: one 5ml teaspoon. Tinctures: two 5ml teaspoons. Every 3 hours.

JAUNDICE, HAEMOLYTIC. Caused by disease toxins that kill off red blood cells, or auto-immune disease.
Treatment: emphasis is on new red cell production. Dosage would be according to individual tolerance.
Alternatives. *Tea*. Mix equal parts: Agrimony, Clivers, Red Clover flowers. 2 teaspoons to each cup boiling water; infuse 5-15 minutes; one cup every 3 hours.
Decoction. Equal parts: Fringe Tree, Gentian, Milk Thistle. 2 teaspoons to each cup water gently simmered 20 minutes. Half-1 cup every 3 hours, or as much as tolerated.
Tablets/capsules. Red Clover, Ginseng.
Formula. Equal parts: Fringe Tree, Yellow Dock root, Dandelion. Dose – Powders: 500mg (two 00 capsules or one-third teaspoon). Liquid Extracts: one 5ml teaspoon. Tinctures: two 5ml teaspoons. Every 3 hours in water or honey.

JAUNDICE, INFECTIVE. Caused by toxins produced by infections: influenza, malaria, etc.
Indicated: anti-bacterials, anti-microbials that activate the body's immune system to inhibit growth of bacteria and germs. The following have special reference to the liver.
Alternatives. *Teas*. From any of the following: Holy Thistle, Thyme.
Tablets/capsules. Echinacea. Goldenseal. Blue Flag.
Formula. Echinacea 2; Milk Thistle 1; Blue Flag root 1. Dose – Powders: 500mg (two 00 capsules or one-third teaspoon). Liquid Extracts: one 5ml teaspoon. Tinctures: two 5ml teaspoons. Every 3 hours.
Tincture Myrrh BPC (1973) 20-30 drops in water every 3 hours.
See: NOTIFIABLE DISEASES.

JAUNDICE, OBSTRUCTIVE. May be due to hold-up in flow of bile from the liver down the bile duct. Bile enters the blood and is borne round the body by the circulation. Obstruction may be due to a gall stone lodged in the gall duct, or to a swelling of the liver or pancreas.
Symptoms: skin has a yellow tinge especially whites of the eyes. Motions become clay-coloured due to absence of bile in the intestines. Bitter herbs keep the bile fluid and flowing.
Alternatives. *Teas*. Agrimony, Bogbean, Clivers, Hyssop. Mix. One heaped teaspoon to each cup boiling water; infuse 15 minutes. 1 cup freely.
Decoction. 2 teaspoons shredded Gentian root to each cup cold water. Allow to stand overnight. Half cup every two hours.
Tablets/capsules. Dandelion, Goldenseal, Prickly Ash.
Formula. Milk Thistle 2; Blue Flag root 1; Valerian half. Dose – Powders: 500mg (two 00 capsules or one-third teaspoon). Liquid Extracts: one 5ml teaspoon. Tinctures: two 5ml teaspoons. Every 3 hours.
Frank Roberts MNIMH. Liquid extracts: Celandine (greater), Butternut, Fringe Tree, Dandelion; 2 drachms (8ml) of each. Purified or spring water to 12oz. Dose: tablespoon every 2 hours.

JAVA TEA. *Orthosiphon stamineus*. Indian Bean Tree. *Part used*: leaves.
Constituents: Flavones, glycosides.
Uses. Kidney disorders. (*Traditional*)
Preparation. *Tea*. 1-2 teaspoons leaves to each cup water gently simmered 15 minutes. 1 cup 2-3 times daily.

JELLY FISH STING. Antihistamines indicated: (*topical*). Plant juices: pulp of leaves of any one – Plantain, Aloe Vera, Houseleek, Garlic, Marigold, Comfrey. Oil Eucalyptus. Witch Hazel water. Neat Cider vinegar.
Internal: Echinacea. Acid tincture of Lobelia (10-20 drops). Wounds may be severe enough to require surgical exploration, herbal antibiotic therapy or tetanus prophylaxis. Pain control is essential (Black Willow, Black Cohosh) as pain may be intense and patient restless from respiratory and cardiac distress. Wash with strong spirit (methylated, whiskey, etc).

JET LAG. A conflict is created when natural body rhythms do not synchronise with real time. Sufferers feel wide awake at night and cannot sleep during the day. Treatment is focussed on the pineal gland – the biological clock.
Symptoms: lethargy, disorientation, clinical depression and tiredness associated with long-haul flights.
Treatment. Herbs for pushing forward (or back) the internal clock so that biological time accords with chronological time: Ginseng, Garlic, Gotu Kola, Kola, Capsicum. These may be supported by a good multivitamin capsule. Ginseng is a melatonin stimulant. Treat transient hypothyroidism.
Topical. Inhalant: aromatherapy oil – Rosemary.
Diet. Day before 'take-off' should be a 'feast' day, but the day of departure should be a 'fast' day. Coffee, tea and other caffeine-containing beverages should be taken only in the evenings of 'fast' days when going east, and in the mornings going west. Circadian disturbance is more easily adjusted on 'fast' days. This regime assists the production of melatonin, a natural hormone of the pineal gland which manipulates the body's response to the light/dark cycle. Avoid alcohol.
Supplements. Daily. Vitamin B6 10mg; Vitamin C 2g; Vitamin E 400iu. Magnesium, Selenium, Zinc.
Note. On day of departure change watch to the time at your destination. During the flight eat only if it is daytime there. Take plenty of fluids. On

arrival the body clock is already adjusted to local time – go to bed.

JOJOBA. Peanut of the desert. *Simmondsia chinensis. Part used*: nut-bean. An animal fat (wax) substitute. Contains myristic acid. Once an important medicinal fruit among Southern Arizona Indians.
Action: anti-oxidant, emollient, digestant, anti-inflammatory, detergent, anti-foaming agent, vulnerary for cuts and injuries, appetite-depressant, helps restore pH balance, tuberculostatic. The oil is not readily broken-down by the digestive juices, thus it more directly benefits the intestines.
Uses. Used by the native population for indigestion from a 'cold' stomach, for wounds that refuse to heal, and by the squaws for painless delivery. Internally, said to inhibit the spread of tuberculosis.
External: Mexican men still apply the oil to their eye-brows and hair for growth while their women use it to dress their braids and tresses. To the scalp the oil removes excess sebum, moistens dry skin and expels dandruff. Used for minor skin disorders, acne, sunburn, minor burns, chapped skin, nappy-rash, soft fingernails and facial blemishes.
Preparations. Nuts – eaten freely by Mexicans, their children and farm animals. Roasted to make coffee. Meal left over after oil extraction contains no less than 17 amino acids. With its 35 per cent protein Jojoba is a valuable nutrient. Oil is obtained from Mexican beans by cold pressing to ensure that properties provided by nature are not destroyed by chemical processing. It has now replaced some animal oils, especially whale oil (spermaceti) as a base for ointments, creams, bath oils, suntan lotions, and other cosmetic preparations. So successful it is as a substitute for whale oil that the sperm whale now has a new lease of life. It is both non-toxic and non-allergenic. May substitute Olive oil in salads.

JUICES. As expressed from fresh plants and used within 2-3 days or preserved with equal parts alcohol or glycerine. Use of home juicer suffices. Plantain, Horseradish, Marigold petals, Marshmallow leaves or root.

JUNIPER BERRIES. *Juniperus communis L. German*: Wacholder. *French*: Genièvre. *Spanish*: Junipero. *Italian*: Ginepro. *Chinese*: Kuli. *Iranian*: Abhala. *Arabian*: Habul hurer. *Indian*: Hanbera. Dried ripe berries. *Keynotes*: kidney and bladder.
Constituents: volatile oil, resin, grape sugar, diterpene acids, tannins, Vitamin C.
Action: urinary antiseptic, stimulating diuretic, digestive tonic, emmenagogue, parasiticide (externally), carminative, sudorific. The action of gin as a diuretic is due to oil expressed from the berries. Anti-diabetic (unconfirmed).
Uses. Cystitis, renal suppression (scanty micturition), catarrh of the bladder, proteinuria (albuminuria). Digestive weakness caused by poor secretion of gastric juices, flatulence. Aching muscles due to excess lactic acid. Amenorrhoea.
External. Aromatherapy for gout: lotion for joints. As an ingredient of massage oils for rheumatism and arthritis. Cirrhosis of the liver: upper abdominal massage.
Combination: Parsley Piert enhances action in bladder disorders. Combines well with Wild Carrot and Hydrangea for stone.
Preparations. Thrice daily, or as prescribed.
Tea: half-1 teaspoon crushed berries to each cup boiling water; infuse 30 minutes. Half-1 cup.
Tablets/capsules. 250mg. 1-2.
Tincture BHP (1983): 1 part to 5 parts 45 per cent alcohol. 1-2ml.
Basis of Martini and gin (gin and tonic).
Oil: 5-6 drops in honey after meals.
Aromatherapy. 3-6 drops in two teaspoons Almond oil or other base oil, for massage.
Precaution. Not used internally without a break for every two weeks.
Contra-indicated: pregnancy, Bright's disease.
GSL

KALMS. Formula. Each tablet contains: Hops 45mg; Extract Valeriana officinalis 33.75mg; Extract Gentiana lutea 4:1 22.50mg. To relieve periods of worry and irritability. Two tablets thrice daily after meals. Non-habit-forming, with no known side-effects. Not suitable for children, pregnancy or lactation. (*Lane's UK*)

KAPOSI'S SARCOMA. Vascular tumour. Begins with small reddish-purple plaques and skin nodules on the legs and feet. May remain benign for many years. Usually associated with AIDS, but the classical form may also be seen in renal transplant and elderly male patients receiving cortisone preparations. The tumours may appear anywhere in the body, especially around eyes and nose, giving a bruised appearance.

Diagnosis is difficult to the inexperienced practitioner. Referral to a dermatologist for skin biopsy. Homosexuals are at risk from semen ejaculated into a foreign environment. The blood abnormality extends to the lymph system for which Lymphatics such as Echinacea, Saw Palmetto and Poke root are indicated. See: AIDS.

Treatment by a general medical practitioner or hospital specialist.

KARELA. Balsam pear. Bitter gourd. *Momordica charantia*. Traditional Asian remedy for diabetes. *Part used*: vegetable juice.
Uses. Improves diabetic condition without extra pancreatic activity to secrete more insulin.
Diet: Karela sometimes appears in Eastern pickles and curries. Eaten as a vegetable it assists the body in utilising glucose and is helpful for diabetics not on insulin.

KAS-BAH. (*Potter's*) A herbal remedy for backache and urinary disorders. Winged Lion. Formula: Buchu BPC 1963 6.25 per cent; Broom 18.75 per cent; Clivers 12.5 per cent; Equisetum (Horsetail) 18.75 per cent; Senna leaf BP 6.25 per cent; Couch Grass 12.5 per cent; Liquorice BP 12.5 per cent; Uva Ursi 12.5 per cent. Well-known for over one hundred years as a demulcent diuretic and urinary antiseptic. 1 tablespoon infused in 1 pint boiling water in a covered vessel (teapot), to be drunk throughout the day. (*Potter's Herbal Supplies, Wigan, England*)

KAVA KAVA. Ava Pepper. *Piper methysticum*, Forster. *German*: Kawa pfeffer. *French*: Kawa. *Spanish*: Kava kava. *Italian*: Pepe kava. *Parts used*: rhizome and root.
Constituents: Pipermethysticine (alkaloid), Pyrone derivative.
Action: antimicrobial with special reference to STDs with mucopurulent discharge, including gonorrhoea. Also effective against Bacillus Coli. Antiseptic stimulant, mild analgesic for painful spasm, antispasmodic, nerve relaxant, diuretic, stimulant, tonic.
Uses. Genito-urinary infections, orchitis, vaginitis, urethritis, candida, violent itching, ichthyosis, metritis, inflammation of the Fallopian tubes, incontinence in the aged with bladder weakness, infection of kidney, bladder and prostate gland, conditions arising from excess of uric acid, joint pains of rheumatism following STD infection, bed-wetting. A powerful soporific for chronic insomnia, ensuring dreamless sleep with no known ill-effects on rising.
Combinations: with Sarsaparilla for STDs. With Black Cohosh for rheumatism following STDs.
Preparations. Average dose: 2-4g. Thrice daily.
Decoction. 1oz to 1 pint (30g to 500ml) water, simmer in gentle heat down to three-quarters volume. Dose: half-1 cup.
Liquid Extract. Half-1 teaspoon in water.
Powder: 2-4g.
Lotion. 1oz powdered root to 8oz glycerine, macerate 8 days, shake daily. External: for pruritus and most forms of intolerable itching. Add 10 drops Oil Eucalyptus for chronic cases. GSL

KELOID. A dense smooth overgrowth of connective tissue, or scar formation. May follow injury, especially burns, surgery, acne, smallpox.
Treatment. *Internal*: St John's Wort. Vitamin E (400iu daily).
Topical: Castor oil. Oil from Vitamin E capsule.
Juice: Aloe Vera or Houseleek.

KHELLA. *Amni visnaga*. Known to early Egyptian medicine.
Action. Antispasmodic to respiratory and cardiovascular system. Alternative to use of steroids in children.

"A potent coronary vasodilator. Has been employed in the treatment of angina pectoris and bronchial asthma; a decoction is made for whooping cough." (*Hakim Mohammed Said: Hamdard Foundation, Pakistan*)
Uses. Has a long reputation in Arabian medicine for asthma. On record for the treatment of diseases of the coronary vessels, gall bladder, kidney, bladder. To relieve painful spasm of stone in kidney or bladder. Myocardial infarction. Allergies.

Vitiligo, psoriasis. (*Abdel-Fattah et al 1982/1983*)

Seeds yield sodium cromoglycate, a preparation which is inhaled from a nebuliser or aerosol.

KIDNEY DISORDERS. The kidneys are responsible for the excretion of many waste products, chiefly urea from the blood. They maintain the correct balance of salts and water. Any of the individual kidney disorders may interfere with these important functions. See: ABSCESS (kidney). BRIGHT'S DISEASE. CARDIAC DROPS. RENAL FLUID RETENTION.

GRAVEL. HYDRONEPHROSIS. NEPHROSIS. PROTEINURIA. PYELITIS. RENAL COLIC. RETENTION OF URINE. STONE IN THE KIDNEY. SUPPRESSION OF URINE. URAEMIA.

KNEIPP, FATHER SEBASTIAN. 1821-1897. Herbalist and hydrotherapist who re-discovered the healing properties of a number of simple plants for the treatment of major diseases of the day (gout, arthritis, etc) when 19th century German pharmacy was beginning to extract and use concentrated alkaloids, glycosides (Foxglove) of plants. He insisted on use of the *whole* plant. Clinical experience of this tireless investigator led to the belief that Horsetail (*Equisetum*) arrests the growth of tumours, and where conditions are favourable may dissolve them. See: WHOLE PLANT.

KNOTGRASS. "Hundred jointed." *Polygonum aviculare L. German*: Vogelknöterich. *French*: Centinode. *Spanish*: Centinodia. *Indian*: Kuwar. *Arabian*: Anjuhar. *Chinese*: Liao. *Part used*: herb.
Constituents: gallic and tannic acids, silicic acid, polyphenolic acids, mucilage.
Action: astringent, haemostatic.
Uses. Bleeding from bowel, lungs, nose, throat, stomach. Bleeding piles, excessive menstruation. Children's summer diarrhoea, mucous colitis.
Preparations: *Decoction*: 1-2 teaspoons leaves, roots, stalks, to each large cup water gently simmered 15 minutes. Dose: one-third to half a cup thrice daily.
Tincture: 1 part to 5 parts 45 per cent alcohol; macerate 8 days, shake daily, filter. Dose: 1 teaspoon thrice daily.

KOLA NUTS. See: COLA.

KRAMERIA ROOT. Rhatany root. *Krameria triandra*. Dried root.
Action: anti-tubercle, haemostatic, powerful astringent, anti-microbial.
Uses. Basis of treatment for tuberculosis with Umckaloabo in the 1920s. See: UMCKALOABO. Spongy bleeding gums, bleeding piles, nasal polyps (powder used as snuff), haemoptysis, incontinence of urine.
Preparations. Average dose, half-2g. Thrice daily.
Decoction. Half-1 teaspoon to each large cup water gently simmered 20 minutes. Dose: one-third to half a cup.
Tincture Krameria BPC (1949). Dose 30-60 drops (2-4ml).
Liquid extract BPC 1923. Dose: 2-4ml.

KWASHIORKOR. A disease of poor nutrition following a diet lacking adequate protein. Children 1-5 years vulnerable when fed too much starch, sugar and milk. Growth is retarded, hair scanty and skin unhealthy.
Symptoms. Feeble appetite, irritable bowel, oedema, nervous irritability.
Alternatives. *Teas*. Alfalfa, Nettles, Oats, Betony, Red Clover. Irish Moss.
Tablets/capsules. Echinacea, Kelp, Slippery Elm, Seaweed and Sarsaparilla.
Formula. Echinacea 2; Gentian 1; Ginger 1. Dose – Powders: 500mg (two 00 capsules or one-third teaspoon). Liquid Extracts: one 5ml teaspoon. Tinctures: two 5ml teaspoons. Thrice daily before meals.
Diet. High protein. Sugar-free. Salt-free. Slippery Elm gruel.
Supplementation. All vitamins. Intramuscular injections of B12. Chromium, Copper, Iron, Magnesium, Selenium.

L-DOPA. An amino acid present in some foods and plants. Prepared synthetically in the laboratory when used as the basic medication for Parkinson's disease. Has enabled millions of elderly sufferers to lead a useful and less painful life with reduced muscle tension. On entering the brain the substance is known as dopamine.

In old age the concentration of L-dopa in the brain decreases. This substance is available in very high concentrations in the plant Vivia faba (broad bean). Highest concentration is found in type WH 305. Research has shown that regular eating of these golden beans can prolong life expectancy, slow down the ageing process and possibly allow a reduced dosage in medication.

LABELLING OF HERBAL PRODUCTS. The law requires labels to carry a full description of all ingredients. No label should bear the name of a specific disease or promote treatment for any serious disease or condition requiring consultation with a registered medical practitioner. Labels must not contravene The Medicines (Labelling and Advertising to the Public), SI 41, Regulations, 1978.

Misleading claims and the use of such words as "organic", "wholesome", "natural" or "biological" cannot be accepted on product labels. The Licensing Authority treats herbal manufacturers no differently than manufacturers of allopathic products for serious conditions.

The Advertising Standards Authority does not allow quotation of any medicinal claims, except where a Product Licence (PL) has been authorised by the Licensing Authority.

All labels must include: Name of product (as on Product Licence), description of pharmaceutical form (tablet, mixture etc), Product Licence No., Batch No., quantity of each active ingredient *in each unit dose* in metric terms; dose and directions for use; quantity in container (in metric terms); "Keep out of reach of children" or similar warning; Name and address of Product Licence Holder; expiry date (if applicable); and any other special warnings. Also to appear: excipients, method/route of administration, special storage instructions, and precautions for disposal, if any.

Where licences are granted, the following words should appear on the label of a product: "A herbal product traditionally used for the symptomatic relief of . . .". "If symptoms persist see your doctor." "Not to be used in pregnancy" (where applicable). "If you think you have . . . consult a registered medical practitioner before taking this product." "If you are already receiving medical treatment, tell your doctor that you are taking this product." These warnings are especially necessary should symptoms persist and be the start of something more serious than a self-limiting condition.

Herbal preparations should be labelled with the additives and colourings they contain, if any. This helps practitioners avoid prescribing medicines containing them to certain patients on whom they may have an adverse reaction.

Labels of medicinal products shall comply with the Medicines (Labelling) Regulations 1976 (SI 1976 No. 1726) as amended by the Medicines (Labelling) Amendment Regulations 1977 (SI 1977 No. 996), the Medicines (Labelling) Amendment Regulations 1981 (SI 1981 No. 1791) and the Medicines (Labelling) Amendment Regulations 1985 (SI 1985 No. 1558).

Leaflets issued with proprietory medicinal products shall comply with the requirements of the Medicines (Leaflets) Regulations 1977 (SI 1977 No. 1055).

See also: ADVERTISING: CODE OF PRACTICE. BRITISH HERBAL MEDICINE ASSOCIATION.

LABELLING OF HERBAL PRODUCTS BY A PRACTITIONER. Labelling regulations require every dispensed product, i.e. a container of medicine, lotion, tablets, ointment, etc, to be labelled with the following particulars:–

1. Name of the patient.
2. Name and address of the herbal practitioner.
3. Directions for use of the remedy.
4. Liquid preparations for local or topical use to be clearly marked: *For external use only*.

Statutory Instruments: Medicine (Labelling) Regulations 1976 No. 1726. Medicines (Labelling) Regulations 1977 No. 996.

LABOUR. If the mother has avoided over-eating heavy rich foods, an excess of meat, alcohol, domestic tea and coffee; and if she has drunk Raspberry leaf tea with Squaw Vine drops for the last three months, her delivery is likely to be easy and without incident. When labour commences let cupfuls of warm Raspberry leaf tea with a little Composition, Red Pepper or Ginger, be taken every 20 minutes. If contractions are strong, the stimulants Composition, Red Pepper and Ginger may not be needed.

Oxytocic herbs for sustaining vigorous contractions are effective and may be used when necessary. Chief among them is Goldenseal (which is never used during pregnancy); dose, Liquid Extract 5 drops in water, or honey, every 20 minutes. A number of Indian tribes including the Potawatomis, held Blue Cohosh in high esteem, as an effective parturient. Dose: same as for Goldenseal.

False labour pains: Black Cohosh, Blue Cohosh, Black Horehound, Cramp bark, Motherwort, Helonias, Valerian, Wild Lettuce, Wild Yam.

Premature labour pains: Black Horehound, Blue Cohosh, Motherwort, Black Haw bark BHP (1983).

Prolonged labour: to relax os. Feverfew, Lobelia, Ladyslipper, Blue Cohosh.

Practitioner use: Tincture Gelsemium 5 drops.
Labour contractions alarmingly inefficient: Black Cohosh, Blue Cohosh.
Post partum haemorrhage. To be given before completion of delivery: Marigold, Witch Hazel, Bayberry, Goldenseal. Dr T.J. Lyle strongly advises Beth root.

LABRADOR TEA. St James tea. Wild Rosemary. (*Ledum Latifolium*, Jacq.) (*Ledum Greenlandicum*). *German*: Sumpfporst. *French*: Romarin sauvage. *Italian*: Ledone. *Part used*: leaves. Grows in wild damp northern places where only goats eat it and where the Swedes still drink it for gout.
Action: tonic, pectoral, diaphoretic. Expectorant.
Uses. Dyspepsia, cough, dysentery, violent itching, chest infections. Cold shivery conditions with chattering teeth. Inflamed or malignant sore throat – to cleanse and sweeten bad breath. Antidotes the effects of alcohol. Gout.
External: gnat bites and punctured wounds, (*Dr Teste*) bee-sting, needle-pricks leading to whitlow, body lice, (strong decoction).

Ledum palustre (Marsh tea, Wild Rosemary, Porsch), is more powerful than Ledum latifolium – for practitioner use only.
Preparation. Average dose: 1-4g.
Tea. Quarter to half a teaspoon to cup water, gently simmer 15 minutes. Dose: half-1 cup.

LACTOSE. A disaccharide; concentration in cow's milk about 4g/100ml. In normal digestion the enzyme lactase breaks it down into glucose and galactose. A milk-sugar constituent of tablets, capsules or other preparations and which is used as a base for a medicinal substance or formulation. It is obtained exclusively from milk solids, not fats.
Example: Propolis in lactose. Propolis powder 5 per cent; Lactose powder 95 per cent; presented in a gelatin capsule.

LACTOSE INTOLERANCE. Similar to Irritable Bowel Syndrome. Lactose is a carbohydrate found in milk, and requires lactase (an enzyme) to break it down into galactose and glucose before absorption is possible. Some people are not able to produce enough lactase to digest lactose in milk. When this happens, it is left to bacteria in the colon to do the breaking-down. Lactose cannot readily be absorbed in the colon; it attracts water and precipitates diarrhoea.

A substitute for the lactase enzyme is commercially available, "Lactaid". See: DIARRHOEA.

LADY'S MANTLE. Lion's foot. *Alchemilla vulgaris L.* Dried herb (oral), root (topical). *Keynote*: bleeding.
Constituents: tannins.
Action: powerful styptic and astringent because of its high tannin content. Haemostatic. Alterative. Drying and binding. Menstrual regulator.
Uses. Excessive menstruation. Non-menstrual bleeding of the womb between periods. Children's summer diarrhoea, colitis with bleeding. Gastric and duodenal ulcer. Children's convulsions. (*Swedish traditional*)

Not used in pregnancy.
Combinations. (1) with Avens for gastritis and mucous colitis. (2) with Agnus Castus for menstrual disorders.
Preparations. Average dose: 2-4g. Thrice daily.
Tea: 1-2 teaspoons to each cup boiling water; infuse 15 minutes. One cup.
Liquid extract BHP (1983) 1:1 in 25 per cent alcohol. Dose: 2-4ml.
Powdered root. Dose, 2-4g.
Vaginal douche: 2oz to 2 pints (60g to 1 litre) boiling water. Infuse 30 minutes. Inject warm for leucorrhoea, candida, inflammation; or as a lotion for pruritus.
Decoction (roots) offer a powerful deterrant to passive bleeding. GSL

LADY'S SLIPPER. Nerve root. American Valerian. *Cypripedium pubescens*, Willd. *German*: Frauenschuh. *French*: Sabot de Vénus. *Spanish*: Zucco. *Italian*: Calceolo. Dried root and rhizome. Time-honoured North American Indian remedy. *Keynote*: central nervous system.
Constituents: tannin, resin.
Action: nerve relaxant, autonomic regulator, mild pain-killer, thymoleptic. A fine brain and spinal remedy and should be at the hand of every spinal manipulator. Antidote to caffeine poisoning.
Uses. Nervous excitability, insomnia, irritability, neuralgia, muscle twitching, anxiety states, schizophrenia, pressive headache, nerve tension, epilepsy, pre-menstrual tension, spermatorrhoea, post-influenzal depression, weepiness.

"Yellow Lady's Slipper was held in big esteem by the Indians as a sedative and an antispasmodic, acting like Valerian in alleviating nervous symptoms . . . said to have proved itself in hysteria and chorea." (*Virgil Vogel*)
Combinations. (1) with Oats and Skullcap for anxiety states and (2) with Hops for insomnia with depression BHP (1983).
Preparations. Average dose: 2-4g. Thrice daily.
Tea. Half-1 teaspoon to each cupful water; bring to boil; simmer 2-3 minutes in covered vessel; infuse 15 minutes. Half-1 cup.
Liquid Extract BHP (1983) 1:1 in 45 per cent alcohol. Dose: 2-4ml.
Powder. Dose, 2-4g. GSL

LAETRILE. Amygdalin. From apricot or peach kernels. Dramatic claims of cures of malignancy reported in 1950. In spite of extensive anecdotal efficacy, performance has not lived up to early promise. Powdered kernels are usually taken with additional vitamins and pancreatic enzymes. Purpose of the enzymes is to break down the muco-protein capsule which enables the cyanide in the remedy to penetrate the wall of the cancer cell and destroy its contents. Dr Ernest Krebs claimed the body's own immune response broke down the cyanide content to produce a substance with an ability to destroy cancer cells. Apple pips are also said to be a good source of this property. POM

LAMB'S QUARTERS. Known as Beth root in America and Fat Hen in the UK. Refer to entries.

LANE G.R. Health Products Ltd, Gloucester. Lanes traces its origins to the early 1920s when Gilbert Lane, a talented and far-sighted scientist, interested in agriculture, botany and the importance of a sensible diet for sound health, began the study of the curative properties of plants. By so-doing he created a range of herbal preparations that today are distributed throughout the world.
Products include: Quiet Life, Lecigram, Glanolin, Kalms and Olbas oil.

LANOLIN. Derived from sheep's wool and has a fatty content. Skin emollient as part of an ointment base including herbs or essential oils. Holds water well and is used in cosmetics. No animal is harmed, it being derived from the wool and not the body. See: OINTMENTS.

LAPACHO TREE. *Tabebuia avellanedae*. Ipe Roxo, Pau d'arco. LaPacho herb tea. Taheebo. 1,000 year-old Inca cancer-cure. Used for centuries by the Callawaya Tribe. Still used in Bolivia, Paraguay, Brazil and the Argentine. Laprachol occurs in heartwood of some trees of the genera Tecoma and Tabebuia (N.O. Bignonaiceae). Aids immune system health. Anti-tumour. Anti-microbial. Analgesic. Anodyne. Diuretic. Antidotal. Fungicidal. Anti-fever. Anti-candida. Anti-cancer. Anti-inflammatory, analgesic, anti-haemorrhagic. Anti-leukaemic. Indian plant C.D. shows reducible activity in Walker 255 Carcinosarcoma system in rats. Exhibits significant antitumour activity with relatively little effect on body weight. Anti-cancer experiments in human patients confirm experiments made in animals bearing malignant neoplasies. Low toxicity. Adenocarcinoma (liver, breast and prostate) and epidermoid carcinoma of womb and floor of the mouth: temporary reductions of lesions and decrease of pain. (*Manoel Antonio Schmidt*)
Folk history: cancer remedy (anti-mitotic action), diarrhoea, boils, leprosy, chlorosis, dysentery, eneuresis, fever, pharyngitis, snakebite, syphilis, wounds. (*J.A. Duke*) Large doses produce nausea and anti-coagulant tendency. Strongly commended by Professor Emeritus, Walter Accorsi, University of Sao Paulo (USP) for its therapeutic value.
Oral candidiasis: good results reported.
Decoction. 15-20g bark to 500ml (1 pint) water, gently simmered 20 minutes. 1 cup thrice daily.
Tincture. 1 part to 5 parts 60 per cent alcohol; macerate 8 days; filter. Dose: 30-60 drops thrice daily. For acute cases, dose may be doubled.
Lapacho works best taken orally.
Teabags, capsules: Rio Trading Company, Brighton, England.

LARCH RESIN OINTMENT. For tired or strained eyes.
Constituents: 100g contains: Ananarsa fruct. 5g; Larch Resin 2g in a base containing Lanolin and yellow soft paraffin. (*Weleda*)

LARYNGITIS, ACUTE. Inflammation of the vocal cords. May be associated with the common cold, influenza, and other viral or bacterial infections.
Causes: smoking, mis-use of the voice in talking or singing (Ginseng).
Symptoms: voice husky or absent (aphonia). Talking causes pain. Self-limiting.
Treatment. Stop talking for 2 days. Care is necessary: neglect or ineffective treatment may rouse infection and invade the windpipe and bronchi resulting in croup.
Differential: croup is alerted by high fever and characteristic cough, requiring hospital treatment.
Alternatives. *Teas*: Red Sage. Garden Sage. Thyme, wild or garden.
Effective combination: equal parts, Sage and Raspberry leaves. Used also as a gargle.
Tablets/capsules. Poke root. Lobelia. Iceland Moss.
Cinnamon. Tincture, essence or oil of: 3-5 drops in teaspoon honey.
Horseradish. 1oz freshly scraped root to steep in cold water for two hours. Add 2 teaspoons runny honey. Dose: 2-3 teaspoons every two hours.
Topical. Equal parts water/cider vinegar cold pack round throat. Renew when dry.
Traditional: "Rub soles of the feet with Garlic and lard well-beaten together, overnight. Hoarseness gone in the morning." (*John Wesley*) Friar's balsam.
Aromatherapy. Steam inhalations. Oils: Bergamot, Eucalyptus, Niaouli, Geranium, Lavender, Sandalwood.
Diet. Three-day fruit fast.
Supplements. Daily. Vitamin A (7500iu). Vitamin C (1 gram thrice daily). Beta carotene 200,000iu. Zinc 25mg.

LARYNGITIS, CHRONIC. The main symptom is hoarseness or loss of voice from malfunction of the vocal cords by disease, stroke, stress, or nerve disorder. Pain on speaking. "Raw throat."

Constitutional disturbance: fever, malaise.

Many causes, including: drugs, drinking spirits. Gross mis-use of voice (singing or talking) may produce nodules (warts) on the cords. The smoker has inflammatory changes. Nerve paralysis in the elderly. Carcinoma of the larynx. Voice changes during menstruation are associated with hormonal changes (Agnus Castus). Professional singers, members of choirs benefit from Irish Moss, Iceland Moss, Slippery Elm or Poke root.

Alternatives. Cayenne, Caraway seed, Balm of Gilead, Lungwort, Queen's Delight, Thyme, Wild Indigo, Marsh Cudweed, Mullein, Marshmallow.

For most infections: Equal parts, Tinctures Goldenseal and Myrrh: 3-5 drops in water 3-4 times daily; use also as a spray or gargle.

Tea. Formula. Equal parts: Mullein, Marshmallow root, Liquorice. 2 teaspoons to each cup water brought to boil; vessel removed on boiling. Drink freely.

Practitioner. Combine equal parts: Senega, Ipecacuanha and Squills (all BP). 5-10 drops thrice daily in water. Also gargle.

Poke root. Reliable standby. Decoction, tablets/capsules. Tincture: dose, 5-10 drops thrice daily in water or honey.

Topical. Aromatherapy. Steam inhalations. Oils: Bergamot, Eucalyptus, Niaouli, Geranium, Lavender, Sandalwood. Any one.

Diet. Slippery Elm gruel. Salt-free. Avoid fried foods.

Supplements. Daily. Vitamin A (7500iu). Vitamin C (1 gram thrice daily).

To prevent voice damage. The voice should not be strained by talking too much, shouting or singing – especially with a cold. Try not to cough or keep clearing the throat but instead, swallow firmly. Do not whisper – it will strain the voice.

A common cause of laryngitis is growth of a nodule, cyst or polyp on the vocal cords. They are visible on use of an endoscope. There are two vocal cords which, in speech, come together and vibrate like a reed in a musical instrument. In formation of a nodule they cannot meet, air escapes and the voice becomes hoarse. Relaxation technique.

Where the condition lasts for more than 4 weeks an ENT specialist should be consulted.

LASSA FEVER. First reported at Lassa, Nigeria. A disease of arenavirus borne by rodents or infected people. A viral fever with haemorrhage. Incubation period 3-31 days. See: NOTIFIABLE DISEASES.

Symptoms: High fever, headache, sore throat, sleepiness, loss of appetite, severe pain in muscles, abnormal decrease in white blood cells, slow pulse.

High mortality rate, (50 per cent) especially in pregnant women. Each case is a matter for an infectious disease consultant.

Treatment. Isolation. Bedrest.

Alternatives. *Teas*. Gotu Kola, Chaparral, Red Clover, Yarrow.

Formula. Equal parts: Mullein, Yarrow, Thyme. One heaped teaspoon to cup water slowly brought to boil; vessel removed on boiling. Infuse 15 minutes. 1 cup freely.

Tablets/capsules. Red Clover.

Formula. Yarrow 2; Guaiacum quarter; Gotu Kola 1; Liquorice quarter. Dose – Powders: 500mg (two 00 capsules or one-third teaspoon). Liquid Extracts: 30-60 drops. Tinctures: 60-120 drops (4-8ml). Every 3 hours.

Diet. 3-day fast on fruit juices and abundant herb teas.

To be treated by or in liaison with a qualified medical practitioner.

LASSITUDE. See: WEAKNESS.

LAVENDER. *Lavendula vera. Lavendula angustifolia*. Flowers.

Constituents: flavonoids, coumarins, triterpenes, volatile oil.

Action: inhalant, antidepressive, antispasmodic, cephalic, pleasant antiseptic, carminative, rubefacient (oil), sedative, anticonvulsant. Antimicrobial. (*B.N. Uzdennikov, Nauch, Tr. Tyumen. Sel-Khoz. Inst., No 7, 116 1970*)

Uses. Nervous headache, neuralgia, rheumatism, depression, sluggish circulation, chilblains, insomnia, for transient reduction in high blood pressure; windy colic, physical and mental exhaustion, neurasthenia, sense of panic and fainting (1-3 drops in honey). Toothache, sprains, sinusitis, bladder infection. To relieve stress; calm and relax. Migraine (hot).

Combines well with Lime flowers (Lavender 1; Lime flowers 3) for transient high blood pressure.

Preparations. Dried flowers, dose: half-2 grams. Thrice daily.

Tea. 1 teaspoon to each cup boiling water: infuse 15 minutes. Dose: one-third to half cup.

Home liniment. Place handful (approximately 50g) flowers in 1 pint (500ml) 60 per cent alcohol (vodka, etc). Macerate 8 days in cool shady place; shake daily. Filter. Massage into affected area.

Tincture BHP (1983). 1 part to 5 parts 60 per cent alcohol. Dose: 2-4ml.

Tablets/capsules. 500mg (two 00 capsules or one-third teaspoon).

Aromatherapy: oil used for a wide range of conditions.

Lavender oil, Used externally for neuralgia, rheumatism, aching muscles or to smear over forehead for migraine.

Lavender bath. 1oz (30g) fresh flowers and tips to 1 pint (500ml) water. Bring to boil. Remove vessel when boiling point is reached. Strain. Add to bath water. Tonic effect. GSL

LAXATIVE. For non-persistent constipation.

An aperient for stool-softening purposes, milder than a cathartic. Sometimes given with a carminative to prevent griping.

Agar-agar, Balmony, Barberry, Black root, Blue Flag root, Bogbean, Boneset, Buckthorn, Burdock, Clivers, Dandelion, Figs, Frangula bark, Fenugreek, Fringe Tree bark, Lignum Vitae, Liquorice root (mild), Ispaghula seeds, Mountain Grape, Rhubarb root, Senna pods, Wahoo, Yellow Dock. If constipation persists or worsens a practitioner should be consulted.

Tea: Formula:– Dandelion root, crushed or shredded, 1; Senna leaves 2; Peppermint 3. Mix. 2 teaspoons to each cup boiling water, infuse 15 minutes. Cup 1-3 times daily.

Tablet: Active constituents: Aloes (Cape) BP 50mg; Pulverised Fennel BHP (1983) 15mg; Pulverised Valerian BP 30mg; Pulverised Holy Thistle BHP (1983) 60mg. A traditional herbal remedy for the relief of occasional or non-persistent constipation. (*Gladlax – Gerard House*)

Long term use of laxatives should be avoided.

LEAD POISONING. Lead colic. Toxic hazards of lead may arise from the use of lead pipes in plumbing, petrol, paints in decoration, drinking water, ingestion by children by painted toys, and many other environmental causes. As lead is slowly excreted by the body, its symptoms differ according to tissue in which it accumulates: brain, nerves, intestines, muscles, teeth, gums, liver, pancreas and bones.

Symptoms: pain, constipation, nausea, 'always tired', vertigo, headache, irritability, breathlessness, burning in throat, cramps, convulsions.

Alternatives. Stomach wash-out (acute cases). Chelating herbs assist in removal of lead from tissues: Comfrey, Slippery Elm, Quince seeds, Marshmallow root, Aloe Vera, Houseleek.

Teas. Catmint, St John's Wort, Chorella, Chickweed, German Chamomile.

Decoctions. Irish Moss, Iceland Moss, Fenugreek seeds, Dandelion root, Echinacea root, Yellow Dock.

Tablets/capsules. Echinacea. Poke root. Dandelion. Comfrey. Slippery Elm. Iceland Moss.

Formula. Fringe Tree 1; Ginkgo 1; German Chamomile 1; Goldenseal quarter. Dose – Powders: 500mg (two 00 capsules or one-third teaspoon). Liquid Extracts: one 5ml teaspoon. Tinctures: two 5ml teaspoons. Thrice daily.

Diet. Lacto vegetarian. Low salt. 2/3 fatty meals weekly. Guar gum preparations

Supplementation. Vitamins: A, B-complex, B12, C, D. Minerals: Iodum (Kelp), Chromium, Selenium, Magnesium, Zinc.

Note. Cholesterol and fats are metabolised by the liver while metals are excreted by the kidneys. Potential benefits of Comfrey for this condition outweigh possible risk.

LECITHIN. A stabiliser and emulsifier from Soya beans, corn, peanuts and egg-yolk. Cholesterol-reducer. Used to reduce the thickness of fats. Consists of a wide complex of fats, essential fatty acids, the B-vitamins choline, inositol and the mineral phosphorus. Required in the body for cell-membrane protection and replacement. Lecithin helps burn up fats and inhibits cholesterol deposits by keeping them in movement round the body. A sufficiency is necessary to obtain the maximum effect of fat-soluble vitamins A, E, carotene and D.

A useful supplement for hardening of the arteries, angina; as a preventative of strokes, heart attacks, skin troubles, gall stones (chiefly made of cholesterol), congested liver, anxiety, depression and Alzheimer's disease.

Lecithin belongs to a group of chemicals known as phospholipids, components of the body's cell membranes.

Dosage: one to two tablespoons daily.

LEG ULCER. See: VARICOSE ULCER.

LEGIONNAIRE'S DISEASE. Non-contagious acute infection affecting the mucous membrane of the lungs. A form of pneumonia, caused by the organism *Legionella pneumophilla*.

Onset: 2-10 days.

Sources of infection: water-cooling and air-conditioning plants, Aerosols.

Usually attacks those with existing lung weakness. Those with low natural resistance and smokers are most at risk. Epidemic or single cases. Diagnosis confirmed by Haematological laboratory.

Symptoms. High body temperature (above 39°C). Rigor. Shivering. Diarrhoea. Dry cough. Bleeding from stomach and intestines. Mental confusion. Chest pains, shortness of breath, occasional diarrhoea.

Differential diagnosis. Glandular fever. Other forms of pneumonia.

Indicated: anti-microbials and expectorants.

Treatment. *Formula*. Pleurisy root 2; Echinacea root 2; Grindelia quarter. Dose – Powders: 500mg (two 00 capsules or one-third teaspoon). Liquid extracts: one 5ml teaspoon. Tinctures: two 5ml teaspoons. Every 3 hours. Take together with:–

Fenugreek tea. 2 heaped teaspoons seeds to each cup water simmered gently 10 minutes. Drink freely 1 cup. Seeds should be swallowed.

Enema. Strong Yarrow tea enema to control bowel bleeding.

LEGS. Locking at the knee (Prickly Ash bark). Legs aching from no known cause (Hawthorn, Motherwort). Legs, pins and needles (Cramp bark). Legs swollen, due to heart weakness or kidney disorder (Broom). Ankles, 'giving way' sensation (Cramp bark).

LEISHMANIASIS. Dum-dum fever. Kala-Azar. Delhi-boil. Oriental sore; a tropical infectious disease caused by protozoan parasites (usually caused by sandflies) manifesting as influenza with (1) internal visceral disturbance, or (2) skin eruptions with ulcerated nose and throat. Often a disease of Mediterranean infants. The case should be seen by a tropical diseases specialist. Until he arrives: decoction Barberry (Berberis vul); half an ounce to 1 pint warm water; steep 20 minutes. 1 cup or more every 2 hours.
Alternatives. *Powders*. Formula. Echinacea 2; Blue Flag 1; Senna leaf 1. Dose: 500mg (two 00 capsules or one-third teaspoon), every 3 hours.
Liquid Extracts. Formula. Echinacea 2; Burdock 1; Senna leaf 1. Dose: 30-60 drops in water or honey every 3 hours.
Tinctures. Formula. Echinacea 2; Myrrh 1; Goldenseal 1. Dose: one 5ml teaspoon every 3 hours.
Topical. Cleanse skin with washes or lotions of Aloe Vera, Comfrey, Marshmallow, Plantain, Witch Hazel, etc. Treat bite immediately. Do not walk in the bush at dusk. Always take insect repellent and antiseptic cream.

LEMON. *Citrus limonum*. Refreshing and fragrant essential oil.
Constituents: flavonoids, coumarins, mucilage, Vitamin C, calcium oxalate.
Action: prevention and treatment of scurvy, anti-infective, anti-inflammatory, anti-fat, antihistamine.

Contains citric acid which is an anti-bacterial capable of destroying some viruses and bacteria.
Uses. Coughs, colds, influenza and onset of fevers generally. Traditionally a whole lemon was roasted or baked in a moderate oven for half an hour and as much juice drunk as tolerated. Sore throat (gargle). Diphtheria: impressive cures reported. Persist until false membrane is detached: Neat lemon juice gargle hourly, swallowing 1-2 teaspoons. If too strong, may be diluted. Often overlooked for hiccoughs. Dropsy: lemon fast. 3-4 days on lemon juice alone: no solid food, tea, stimulants, etc. Biliousness, sick headache: juice of a lemon morning and evening; sweeten with honey if necessary. Malaria: half a teacup juice in water every 2-3 hours. Rheumatism: juice of half lemon before meals and at bedtime; may be diluted. For rheumatism, anecdotal success has been reported by combining equal parts lemon juice and molasses: tablespoon thrice daily before meals. Cellulitis. A lemon mask helps to fade spots.
External: erysipelas, corns, lesions of scurvy. "For a felon (whitlow) cut off end of a lemon; insert finger and bind securely. In the morning remove exudation of matter." (*Chinese Barefoot doctor*)
Preparations. *Tincture Limonis P (1948)* (dose, 2-4ml) is sometimes available but recorded successes have been chiefly due to use of the juice. Oil Lemon BP. Used also in Aromatherapy.
Note. When drinking lemon juice care should be taken to see juice does not come in direct contact with the teeth, the enamel of which it erodes. The juice may remove some calculi from the body, but after having cleared the bloodstream it leeches calcium from the teeth and bones. It is a known cause of arthritis, inducing dryness and subsequent erosion of cartilage of the joints.

LEPROSY. See: HANSEN'S DISEASE.

LEPTOSPIROSIS. Weil's disease. An infection from cattle (pigs, dogs, rats, etc) caused by spirochete bacteria. It may live in a cow's kidneys, humans being infected by direct contact or soil affected by the animal's urine. Rivers may be infected by animals urinating. Those usually affected are veterinary surgeons, cowmen, milkers. Frequently diagnosed in freshwater sports enthusiasts and after children have visited farms.
Symptoms: May resemble influenza, with which it is often mis-diagnosed. Other symptoms are those of liver and kidney damage. Loss of weight. A devastating headache confirms.
Alternatives. Cases respond to herbal antimicrobials, key remedies being Echinacea, Fringe Tree and Buchu.
Abundant herb teas: Yarrow, Couchgrass, Dandelion, Ho-Shou-wu, Gotu Kola, Brigham tea, Horsetail, Betony, Apricot leaves, Red Clover, Chaparral.
Formula. Echinacea 2; Fringe Tree 1; Buchu half. Dose – Powders: 750mg (three 00 capsules or half a teaspoon). Liquid Extracts: 1-2 teaspoons. Tinctures: 2-3 teaspoons. In water or honey. Acute cases: every 3 hours; chronic cases: thrice daily.
Notifiable disease. Treatment by general medical practitioner or hospital specialist only. Potentially fatal disease.

LEUCORRHOEA. Whites. A whitish or yellowish discharge from the vagina due to inflammation of the mucus membrane. Infection of the womb is a common cause, either by trichomonas or sexually transmitted disease. Often a symptom of general debility and toxic state.
Alternatives. General use: Aletris, Avens, Bayberry, Beth root, Bistort, Black Catechu, Cranesbill, Echinacea, Goldenseal, Helonias, Life root, Marigold, Mountain Grape, Myrrh, Nasturtium, Yarrow, Oak bark, Periwinkle (greater), White Pond Lily, Wild Indigo, Horsetail, Deadnettle, Ladies Mantle, Raspberry leaves.
Internal. Tea. Combination. Equal Parts: Ladies Mantle, Raspberry leaves. 2 teaspoons to each cup boiling water; infuse 15 minutes. 1 cup freely.
Tablets/capsules. Raspberry leaves, Helonias, Cranesbill, Echinacea. Goldenseal.

Formula. Echinacea 2; Goldenseal 1; Myrrh half. Doses – Liquid Extracts: one 5ml teaspoon. Tinctures: one to two 5ml teaspoons. Powders: 500mg (two 00 capsules or one-third teaspoon). Thrice daily.
BHP (1983) combination: Helonias and Beth root.
Vaginal douche. 1oz Raspberry leaves to 1 pint boiling water. Allow to cool. Add: 5-10 drops Tincture Goldenseal. Inject warm. Alternative: 1oz Marigold flowers (or herb) to 1 pint boiling water. Allow to cool. Add: 5-10 drops Tincture Myrrh. Tampon may be immersed and inserted into the vagina, after douching.

LEUKAEMIA. Greek word 'white blood'. (Leukosis) Acute myeloid and lymphoblastic. Cancer of the white blood cells of two main types; myeloid, involving the polymorph type and lymphatic involving lymphocytes. Each type may take acute or chronic form, the acute being more serious. The disease is not an infection.
Causes: exposure to chemicals, X-rays or radioactive material. Genetic factors are believed to predispose. The condition may be acute or chronic and may follow chemotherapy.

Remissions are known to have been induced by a preparation from the Periwinkle plant (*Vinca rosea*) now re-classified as Catharanthus roseus.

"Smokers suffer a significantly increased risk of developing acute myelocytic leukaemia." (*"Cancer": 1987 vol 60, pp141-144*)
Acute Leukaemia. Rapid onset with fatality within weeks or months. Fever. Proliferation of white cells in the bone marrow which are released and blood-borne to the liver, spleen and lymphatics. There may be bleeding from kidneys, mouth, bowel and beneath the skin. (Shepherd's Purse, Yarrow) The acute form is known also as acute lymphoblastic or acute myeloblastic leukaemia. May be mis-diagnosed as tuberculosis.
Chronic Leukaemia. Gradual onset. Breathlessness from enlargement of the spleen. Swelling of glands under arms, in neck and groin. Loss of weight, appetite, strength, facial colour and body heat. Anaemia, spontaneous bleeding and a variety of skin conditions. Diarrhoea. Low grade fever.

No cure is known, but encouraging results in orthodox medicine promise the disease may be controlled, after the manner of diabetes by insulin. Successful results in such control are reported by Dr Hartwell, National Cancer Institute, Maryland, USA, with an alkaloid related to Autumn Primrose (*Colchicum officinale*). Vinchristine, a preparation from Periwinkle is now well-established in routine treatment. Red Clover, also, is cytotoxic to many mammalian cells. Vitamin C (present in many herbs and fruits) inhibits growth of non-lymphoblastic leukaemia cells. Good responses have been observed by Dr Ferenczi, Hungary, by the use of raw beet root juice.

Also treated with success by Dr Hartland (above) has been lymphocytic leukaemia in children which he treated with a preparation from Periwinkle.

Choice of agents depends largely upon the clinical experience of the practitioner and ease of administration. Addition of a nerve restorative (Oats, Kola, Black Cohosh or Helonias) may improve sense of well-being. To support the heart and circulatory system with cardiotonics (Hawthorn, Motherwort, Lily of the Valley) suggests sound therapy.

Herbal treatment may favourably influence haemoglobin levels and possibly arrest proliferation of leukaemic cells and reduce size of the spleen. It would be directed towards the (a) lymphatic system (Poke root), (b) spleen (Tamarinds), (c) bone marrow (Yellow Dock), and (d) liver (Blue Flag root).

An older generation of herbalists prescribed Blue Flag root, Yellow Dock, Poke root, Thuja and Echinacea, adding other agents according to indications of the particular case.
Tea. Formula. Equal parts: Red Clover, Gotu Kola, Plantain. 1-2 teaspoons to each cup boiling water; infuse 10-15 minutes. 1 cup thrice daily.
New Jersey tea (ceanothus). 1 teaspoon to each cup boiling water. Half-1 cup thrice daily.
Periwinkle tea (Vinca rosea). 2 teaspoons to each cup boiling water; infuse 15 minutes. 1 cup thrice daily.
Decoction. Formula. Equal parts: Echinacea, Yellow Dock, Blue Flag root. 1 teaspoon to each cup water gently simmered 20 minutes. 1 cup before meals thrice daily.
Formula. Red Clover 2; Yellow Dock 1; Dandelion root 1; Thuja quarter; Poke root quarter; Ginger quarter. Dose: Liquid Extract: 1 teaspoon. Tinctures: 1-2 teaspoons. Powders: 500mg (two 00 capsules or one-third teaspoon). Thrice daily.
Vinchristine. Dosage as prescribed. In combination with other medicines.
Wheatgrass. Juice of fresh Wheatgrass grown as sprouts and passed through a juicer. Rich in minerals. One or more glasses daily.
Beetroot juice. Rich in minerals. Contains traces of rare rabidium and caesium, believed to contribute to anti-malignancy effect. (*Studies by Dr A. Ferenczi, Nobel Prize-winner, published 1961*)
Diet: Dandelion coffee.
Supplements. B-complex, B12, Folic acid, Vitamin C 2g morning and evening, Calcium ascorbate 2g morning and evening. Copper, Iron, Selenium, Zinc.
Childhood Leukaemia. Research has linked the disease with fluorescent lighting. "Fluorescent tubes emit blue light (400mm wavelength). Light penetrates the skin and produces free radicals. Free radicals damage a child's DNA. Damaged

DNA causes leukaemia to develop. The type and intensity of lighting in maternity wards should be changed. This could be prevented by fitting cheap plastic filters to fluorescent lights in maternity wards." (*Peter Cox, in "Here's Health", on the work of Dr Shmuel Ben-Sasson, The Hubert Humphrey Centre of Experimental Medicine and Cancer Research, Jerusalem*)

Treatment by hospital specialist.

LEUKODERMA. Pale patches on skin due to loss of pigmentation. May follow a skin disease or from handling chemicals. Vitiligo is a modified form of the disease. There is no known cure, although Dr Wm Burton (*Ellingwood*) found Butternut useful. Seeds of *Psoralea corylifolia* appear to be indicated. (*Indian Journal of Pharmacy 26:141.1964*)

See entry: HIMALAYAN COW PARSLEY.

LEUKOPLAKIA. A disorder of the skin similar to vitiligo but appearing on mucous membrane (internal skin) of the body – on vulva, penis, mouth or on the tongue. May be followed by ulceration and hard infiltration or cancer.

Causes: smoking, alcohol, friction of dentures, habitual diet of hot curries and spices; genetic.

Topical. No known cure. Goldenseal and Myrrh have their advocates. Fresh juice of Houseleek and Aloe Vera are old traditional remedies. Blueberries. (*Ellingwood*)

It is known that Vitamin A protects against oral cancer, from which it is believed that it might have an effect upon leukoplakia which is common among tobacco chewers in India and the Philippines.

LICE. Infestation. Head louse (*pediculosis capitas*). Body louse (*pediculosis corporis*). Pubic louse (*pediculosis pubis* – crabs). Fleas. Lice are among man's earliest companions and bearers of disease. The head louse lays small grey eggs (nits) which adhere to the hair shafts. Body lice may be responsible for Trench fever and typhus. Their appearance may be accompanied by swelling of the occipital lymph glands for which alteratives such as Burdock, Yellow Dock and Echinacea should be given.

Herbs are least effective where personal hygiene is poor. A wholesome lifestyle is the best preventative. Liberal quantities of Garlic in the diet are said to confer immunity. See also: NEEM.

Treatment. External. Vigorously scrub with soap before applying Tea Tree oil. May be diluted many times. A good response has been observed when wiping with cider vinegar. Some practitioners use 1 part Oil Rosemary to 2 parts Peanut oil rubbed into affected parts.

Dr Finlay Ellingwood. Wrap the head at night with suitable material dipped in oil of Turpentine.

Aromatherapy. Essential oils: Sassafras, Quassia, Aniseed.

Tansy herb. Strong decoction.

Traditional, Russian. Saturate the hair with Vodka or strong spirit and allow to evaporate.

General – Use of 'nit' comb. Scrub toilet seats. Change bedding frequently. Tell children not to wear another's clothes. Thorough daily combing with one or two drops of any of the above oils on the comb.

LICENSING OF HERBAL REMEDIES. See: PRODUCT LICENCE.

LICENCING OF HERBAL REMEDIES – EXEMPTIONS FROM. There are remedies that may be manufactured or assembled by any person carrying on a business or practice provided he or she is occupier of the premises which are closed to exclude the general public. The person (i.e. practitioner) supplies or sells the remedy to a particular person (i.e. patient) having been requested by or on behalf of that person and in that person's presence to use his/her own judgement as to treatment.

Anyone may administer a herbal product to a human being, except by injection. Under Section 12 of the Medicines Act 1968, any remedy may be sold or supplied which only specifies the plant and the process. The remedy shall be called by no other name. This applies to the process producing the remedy consisting only of drying, crushing and comminuting. It must be sold without any written recommendation for use.

Those who have a manufacturer's licence, or who notify the Enforcement Authority (the Secretary of State and the Pharmaceutical Society) can sell dried, crushed or comminuted herbs which have also been subjected to certain other limited processes (tablet-making, etc) but not those herbs contained in the Schedule to the Medicines (Retail Sale or Supply of Herbal Remedies) Order 1977 (SI 1977 No.2130).

This Schedule has three parts.

Part 1 contains substances that may only be sold by retail at registered pharmacies under the supervision of a pharmacist.

Part 2 refers to remedies that can be sold only in a registered pharmacy. There is, however, an important exception, as follows.

Part 3 contains a list of considered toxic herbs. A practitioner can prescribe all remedies that a shopkeeper can sell. He may also prescribe and sell remedies on Part 3 of the Schedule which a shopkeeper cannot. Such supply must be in premises closed to the public and subject to a clear and accurate indication of maximum dosage and strength. These remedies are as follows:–

Common name	*Maximum dose and Maximum daily dose*	*Percentage. Concentration for External use*
*Aconite		1.3 per cent
Adonis vernalis	100mg (md) 300mg (mdd)	
Belladonna herb	50mg (md) 150mg (mdd)	
Belladonna root	30mg (md) 90mg (mdd)	
Celandine	2g (md) 6g (mdd)	
Cinchona bark	250mg (md) 750mg (mdd)	
Colchicum corm	100mg (md) 300mg (mdd)	
*Conium leaf		7 per cent
*Conium fruits		7 per cent
Ephedra	600mg (md) 1800mg (mdd)	
Gelsemium	25mg (md) 75mg (mdd)	
Hyoscyamus	100mg (md) 300mg (mdd)	
*Jaborandi		5 per cent
Lily of the Valley	150mg (md) 450mg (mdd)	
Lobelia	200mg (md) 600mg (mdd)	
*Poison Oak (Rhus tox)		10 per cent
*Quebracho	50mg (md) 150mg (mdd)	
*Ragwort		10 per cent
Stramonium	50mg (md) 150mg (mdd)	

*Modern herbal practice no longer uses internally: Aconite, Conium, Jaborandi, Poison Oak, Quebracho and Ragwort.

LICHEN PLANUS. An inflammatory skin eruption with small shiny pimples starting from the wrists and spreading towards the trunk. Associated with lesions on mucous surfaces – vulva, penis, mouth. Cause is unknown but sometimes related to tuberculosis or drug poisoning. Usually over front of wrists, trunk and shins.
Symptoms: Severe itching. Thickened skin with shiny red patches which later become brown and scaly. Distinguish from psoriasis. Nails ridged and split.
Alternatives. Relief from itching by use of anti-histamines: Garlic, Goldenseal, Ephedra, Lobelia.
Teas. Nettles, Boneset, Chickweed, Heartsease, Yucca.
Decoctions. (1) Combine: equal parts: Burdock, Sarsaparilla, Passion flower. OR (2) Combine: equal parts: Echinacea, Blue Flag root, Sarsaparilla. Half an ounce (14g) to 1 pint (500ml) water gently simmered 20 minutes. Dose: half-1 cup thrice daily.
Cold infusion. One heaped teaspoon Barberry (*Berberis Vul*) to cup cold water. Steep overnight. Half-1 cup thrice daily.
Powders, Liquid Extracts or Tinctures. Equal parts: Wild Yam, Blue Flag root, Fringe Tree bark. Powders: 500mg. Liquid Extracts: 30-60 drops in water. Tinctures: 1-2 teaspoons in water. Thrice daily before meals.
Mouth ulcers: Rinse mouth with Goldenseal and Myrrh drops, in water.
Topical. Ointment or pulp from any one: Aloe Vera, Comfrey, Chickweed, Houseleek, Marshmallow.
Vaginal lesion. Aloe Vera pulp or gel.
Diet. Avoid citrus fruits and milk.
Vitamins. A. B-complex, B12, C. E. F. PABA.
Minerals. Dolomite. Zinc. Cod Liver oil: one dessertspoon daily.

LICORICE ROOT. See: LIQUORICE ROOT.

LIFE DROPS. A combination of tinctures devised to stimulate a healthy reaction from the major organs of the body. For promoting body warmth in winter; mobilising resources to fight off colds, chills, or threatening infection. When the fires of life burn low, a few drops in a cup of tea has power to revive and rouse the vital force.
Ingredients: Tincture Capsicum fort 70 per cent, (general stimulant). Ess Menth Pip 20 per cent (stomach and intestines). Tincture Elder flowers 5 per cent (to promote vigorous peripheral circulation). Tincture Cola vera 2 per cent (to activate brain cells). Tincture Hawthorn (or Cactus grand) 3 per cent (to sustain the heart).
Formula: Edgar G. Jones MNIMH

LIFE FORCE, THE. The spirit of the body concerned with life and survival. An extension of the spirit of the Creator in the human body. The intelligence and power behind the immune system.

A weak immune system, with little ability to withstand infection or injury, may be genetic in origin. May be acquired by faulty diet, chemicalised food and medicine, antibiotics, vaccines, and steroid drugs that exhaust the glandular system.

The Life Force can be sustained by a diet of wholefoods, organically grown vegetables and an absence of chemicals in medicine, food and environment. It is safe-guarded by a relaxed life-style which predisposes to a balanced personality capable of meeting the stresses of modern living with equanimity and self-possession. Only the spirit can restore. It is the work of the practitioner to aid in its work.

LIFE ROOT. Squaw weed. *Senecio aureus L.* Dried herb. *Keynote*: menopause.
Constituents: sesquiterpenes, pyrrolizidine alkaloids.
Action: Tonic for relaxed womb, emmenagogue, astringent, mild expectorant.
Uses. Hot flushes of the menopause with nervous instability. Absent, painful or profuse menstruation. Ovarian pain. Stone, gravel. Diarrhoea. Bleeding from mucous surfaces. Prostatitis.
Combinations: with Motherwort for suppressed menses. With Oats for menopause.
Preparations. Average dose: 1-4 grams. Thrice daily.

Tea: half-2 teaspoons to cup boiling water; infuse 15 minutes. Dose: half-1 cup.
Liquid Extract. Half-1 teaspoon, in water.
Powder: 1-4 grams.
Not now used internally.

LIGNUM VITAE. Quaiacum officinale.

LIGVITES. Tablets: formulated in accordance with traditional and modern scientific phytotherapy to provide an over-the-counter (OTC) product for the symptomatic relief of rheumatic aches and pains as in lumbago, fibrositis, backache, stiffness of joints and other systemic connective tissue disorders. Formula: Guaiacum resin BHP (1983) (anti-inflammatory) 40mg. Black Cohosh BHP (1983) (soothing and sedative) 35mg. White Willow bark BHP (1983) (analgesic, anti-inflammatory) 100mg. Extract Sarsaparilla 4:1 (antiseptic) 25mg. Extract Poplar bark 7:1 (to reduce pain) 17mg. Product Licence No 1661/5016R. (*Gerard House*)

LILY OF THE VALLEY. May Lily. *Convallaria majalis L. German*: Lilienkonvallen. *French*: Muguet. *Spanish*: Lirio de los valles. *Italian*: Mughetto. *Keynote*: heart. *Part used*: dried leaves. The herbalist's "digitalis". Practitioner use only. In official use in Russia for heart conditions where it is used in place of digitalis, but at a low dosage. Similar action on the heart as digitalis. (*Martindale 27th edn., p.489*) Specific action on heart muscle alone.
Constituents: cardioactive glycosides, flavonoid glycosides.
Action: increases force of the heart, regularises the beat for distension of the ventricles. Restores an irritable heart. Increases size and strength of the pulse; slows down a rapid feeble pulse; restores regular deep breathing. Is a secondary diuretic which eliminates fluid retained in the tissues (oedema), leaving no depression or depletion of potassium. Cardiac stimulant. Mild gastric tonic.
Uses. Left ventricular failure, mitral insufficiency, sense that "the chest is held in a vice". Congestive heart failure, endocarditis, cardiac dropsy with swollen ankles, cardiac asthma, renal hypertension. Effective in painful and silent ischaemic episodes. Bradycardia.
Combines well with Motherwort and Selenicereus grandiflorus for heart disease BHP (1983). With Echinacea and Poke root for endocarditis. Never combine with Gotu Kola. (*Dr John Heinerman, Texas, USA*)
Preparations. Maximum dose: 150mg dried leaf. Thrice daily.
Tea: 1 teaspoon shredded leaves to each cup water gently simmered 10 minutes. One-third of a cup.
Liquid Extract BPC 1934: dose: 0.3-0.6ml (5 to 10 drops).
Tincture BHP (1983): 1:5 in 40 per cent alcohol; dose – 0.5 to 1ml (8 to 15 drops).
Juice. Fresh leaves passed through a juicer. 3-5 drops thrice daily.
Contra-indicated in high blood pressure.
Sale: Pharmacy Only.

LIME FLOWERS. *Tilia platyphyllos* Scop. *Tilia cordata* Mill. *German*: Lindenbaum. *French*: Tilleul. *Spanish*: Tilo. *Italian*: Tiglio.
Part used: dried flowers.
Constituents: volatile oil, mucilage, tannins, phenolic acids, flavonoids.
Action: antispasmodic, diaphoretic, diuretic, sedative, hypotensive, anticoagulant, anxielytic, immune enhancer. One of the few herbs with very low tannin content. Tannins present in ordinary tea inhibit true protein digestibility thus favouring Lime, or Linden tree flowers for efficient digestion.
Uses. Headache from high blood pressure. Hardening of the arteries. Nervous excitability, hysteria, insomnia. Once had a reputation for reducing severity of epileptic attacks. Teabag or loose-leaf infusion is a substitute for caffeine drinks in coronary heart disease and arterial complaints (temporal arteritis). To aid digestion. Muscular weakness of the eyes.
For relief of early stages of influenza, colds, and fevers of childhood (Lime blossom tea drunk hot and freely). Combines well with Lemon Balm to reduce nerve tension.
Preparations. Average dose: 2-4g dried flowers or equivalent. Thrice daily.
Tea: 1 teaspoon to each cup or, 1oz to 1 pint boiling water; infuse 10 minutes; dose, 1 cup. Teabags available.
Liquid Extract: 1:1, in 25 per cent alcohol. Dose 2-4ml in water.
Home tincture: 1 part to 5 parts white wine (25 per cent) alcohol. Macerate 8 days, shake daily. Decant. 4-8 teaspoons.
An ingredient of blood pressure mixtures. GSL

LINCTUS. A thick syrupy anti-cough medicine. An electuary containing at least one expectorant or demulcent.
1. Tincture Ipecac 5 drops; Tincture Aniseed 5 drops; Syrup Squills 60 drops; Syrup Tolu 20 drops. Mix. Dose: 5-15 drops in teaspoon honey.
2. Tincture Camphor 20 drops; Oxmel of Squills 20 drops; Syrup Tolu 20 drops. Mix. Dose: 5-15 drops in teaspoon honey.
Of historic interest only.

LINIMENTS. May be made from any herb: 4oz herb to 1 pint alcohol (gin, vodka, etc) or cider vinegar. Add 20 drops Tincture Capsicum. Essential oils – Eucalyptus, Wintergreen, Tea Tree oil, etc, may be added for penetration and antisepsis. Sometimes soapy in character. For

external use by rubbing but not for internal use.
See also: MASSAGE OILS.

LINOLEIC, and linolenic acids. Essential fats known as Vitamin F and which are necessary for the maintenance and repair of the membrane that encloses a cell.
Important sources: Grape, Sunflower, Evening Primrose, Black Currant and Sesame oils. Fatty acids are prone to attack by free radicals.
See: FREE RADICALS.

LINSEED. Flaxseed. *Linum usitatissimum L. German*: Flachs. *French*: Lin. *Italian*: Lino usuale. *Chinese*: Hu-ma-esze. *Indian*: Tesi-mosina. *Arabian*: Bazen. *Part used*: oil from the seeds (Linseed oil), seeds.
Constituents: oil, mucilage, protein.
Action: demulcent, emollient, anti-cough, nutrient body-builder, antispasmodic (stomach and bowel). Source of polyunsaturated fatty acids, mucins and minerals. Expectorant. Bulk laxative and bowel lubricant. Rich in linoleic acid for breaking down cholesterol deposits, and to produce specific types of prostaglandins. Linseed is around six times richer in Omega-3 (the polyunsaturate present in fish oil) than most fish.
Uses. Its healing mucilage is beneficial for inflammation of the digestive and respiratory tracts, and of the gall duct. To soothe irritable mucous membranes. Spasmodic cough, bronchial asthma, bronchitis. To reduce the risk of atherosclerosis and thrombosis. Heart disease. Persistent constipation.
Preparations. Average dose: 3-6 grams or equivalent. Thrice daily.
Tea: 2-3 teaspoons to cupful boiling water; infuse 15 minutes. Drink without filtering, with honey for sweetening if necessary. One-third-1 cup.
Cold tea for stomach disorders: Half a teaspoon crushed Linseed to cup water soaked overnight. Drink next morning. Heat if desired.
Tincture: 1-2 teaspoons in water.
Poultice: Crushed seeds. Half fill small muslin bag with seeds; immerse in boiling water until swollen seeds fill the bag; apply to abscesses, boils, or to relieve chest pain.
Linseed oil. An ingredient of liniments for burns and scalds.
Linusit: organically cultivated golden Linseed.
Diet: 3 tablespoons crushed Flaxseed daily ensures adequate supply of Omega-3 fatty acids, sprinkled on breakfast cereal, or as an ingredient of muesli. Also increase fluid intake.
Capsules. Emulsified Linseed oil. 1,000mg organic cold-pressed Linseed oil: 1-5 daily. (*Bio-Care*)

LION CLEANSING HERBS. Elder leaf 8 per cent, Fennel 18 per cent, Frangula 8 per cent, Ispaghula 8 per cent, Mate 8 per cent, Senna leaf 50 per cent. Non-persistent constipation. (*Potter's*)

LIPODERMATOSCLEROSIS. Post phlebitis. An important fore-runner to leg ulceration without resolution of which an ulcer may reappear indefinitely. A condition due to pressure on the vascular system which causes deposition of excess fibrin in the capillaries and veins which arrests the circulation of oxygen and nutrients to the skin.
Symptoms. Those of a prelude to ulceration: eczema, pigmentation, pain.
Treatment. Aim should be (1) to reduce internal pressure on the veins and (2) to resolve deposition of fibrin.
Alternatives. *Teas*: Alfalfa, Nettles, <u>Plantain</u>. Brigham tea, <u>Clivers</u>, Bladderwrack.
Capsules: Evening Primrose oil (4 x 500mg) daily.
Tablets/capsules. Fucus (*Bladderwrack*). Motherwort. Chlorophyll, Rutin.
Formula. Equal parts: Dandelion and Burdock: add pinch or few drops Cayenne. Powders: half a teaspoon. Liquid Extracts: 2 teaspoons. Tinctures: 2-3 teaspoons. In water, thrice daily before meals.
Topical. Graduated elastic stocking compression reduces tension on veins and prevents further deposition of fibrin. Juice, gels, or oils:– Aloe Vera, Houseleek, Evening Primrose, Comfrey, Chickweed, Zinc and Castor oil.

LIPOMA. A benign tumour of fat, more unsightly that harmful. May be multiple. Rounded, with well-defined border. May grow large, giving rise to symptoms by pressure and interference with function.
Dr Compton Burnett regarded Thuja as the remedy for fatty tissues which he believed to be sycotic by nature.
Alternatives. *Liquid Extract Thuja*: 5 drops in water, 3 times daily.
Formula: Liquid Extracts: American Bearsfoot half an ounce, Bayberry 1oz, Barberry 60 drops, Syrup Marshmallow 2oz, water to 8oz. Dose: two teaspoons after meals. (*Arthur Barker, FNIMH*)
Topical. Wipe area with Liquid Extract Thuja 2-3 times daily. Surgical excision usually successful.

LIPOPROTEIN. A protein found in the blood lymph and plasma which combines with fats such as cholesterol. It is important for transport of fats in the lymph vessels and blood stream.
High density lipoproteins (HDLs) are blood-fats known to delay deposits of cholesterol on blood vessels, while low density lipoproteins (LDLs) have the opposite effect.
See: HYPERLIPIDAEMIA. HYPERCHOLESTEROLAEMIA. CHOLESTEROL.

LIPS. Cold sores, sensitive, cracked, blistered. Not to be confused with herpes simplex.
Causes: lowered resistance, menstrual disorders,

constitutional weakness, shock, Vitamin C deficiency, food allergies.
Alternatives. *Teas*: Singly, or in equal parts combination: Red Clover. Gotu Kola, Plantain.
Decoctions: Echinacea, Burdock root, Yellow Dock root, Poke root.
Tablets/capsules. Echinacea. Poke root. Slippery Elm.
Tinctures. Formula. Equal parts: Echinacea, Red Clover, Gotu Kola. Dose: 1-2 teaspoons thrice daily in water or honey.
Topical. Aloe Vera gel or fresh pulp. Houseleek juice. Chickweed ointment. Jojoba oil. Comfrey (moist). Witch Hazel (dry).
Aromatherapy. 3-5 drops of any one of the following oils in a heavy carrier oil (Avocado) to ensure penetration: Chamomile, Jasmine, Orange Blossom, Patchouli, Sandalwood.
Diet. See: DIET – SKIN DISORDERS.
Supplements. Vitamin A, B-complex, C (3-6g daily). Vitamin E (400iu morning and evening). Calcium, Biochemic silicea, Zinc.

LIQUFRUTA. Cough medicine with European mass market. Made with honey and lemon. Each 5ml contains: active ingredients: Ipecacuanha liquid extract BP 13.9mg. Liquid Glucose USP 5.08g. Menthol BP 1.32mg. Honey 0.33g. Lemon juice 1.1ml. Liqufruta Ltd, London E4 8QA.

LIQUID EXTRACT (L.E.). Fluid Extract (F.E.). The most concentrated form in which a herbal medicine can be prepared. Stronger than a tincture. Almost all liquid extracts contain alcohol. Made by a number of methods including cold percolation, evaporation by heat, or under pressure. A popular commercial form of administering herbs as a medicine. Usually taken in water.
Strength: "One part by volume of liquid is equal to 1 part by weight of herb." Thus, one ounce of fluid is equal to one ounce of crude material. For instance, 1oz Stone root liquid extract would have the same therapeutic potency as 1oz Stone root.

In the making of liquid extracts there is often a loss of valuable volatile constituents which is believed to reduce efficacy of a plant. For this reason tinctures are becoming popular among practitioners. Dosage of L.E.s may vary from 5 to 60 drops according to the plant. For instance, the maximum dosage of Goldenseal is 15, Black Cohosh 30, and Yarrow 60 drops. A general average would appear to be 15-60 drops, though a practitioner would be more specific. The bottle should be shaken vigorously before use to remix any natural sediment.

One millilitre = 15 drops. One teaspoonful = 5ml (5 millilitres) or 75 drops liquid medicine. For liquid medicines, always use medicine glass graduated in millilitres, or standard dropper.

LIQUORICE ROOT. The universal herb. Sweet root. *Glycyrrhiza glabra L.* Shredded or powdered dried root. Long history for strength and long life in Chinese medicine. Sweet of the Pharoahs of Ancient Egypt. Carried by armies of Alexander to allay thirst and as a medicine.
Constituents: volatile oil, coumarins, chalcones, triterpenes, flavonoids.
Action: demulcent expectorant, glycogen-conservor, anti-inflammatory, mild laxative. Adrenal restorative (has glycosides remarkably similar to body steroids). ACTH-like activity on adrenal cortex (*Simon Mills*). Female hormone properties (*Science Digest*). Regulates salt and water metabolism (*Medicina, Moscow, 1965*). Anti-stress. Anti-ulcer. Antiviral. Increases gastric juices up to 25 per cent, without altering pH. Aldosterone-like effect. Liver protective. Anti-depressive.
Uses. Adrenal insufficiency – sodium-retention properties suitable for Addison's disease. Hypoglycaemia. Peptic ulcer – reduces gastric juice secretion. Inflamed stomach. Mouth ulcer. Duodenal ulcer. Respiratory infections: dry cough, hoarseness, bronchitis, lung troubles, catarrh. Tuberculosis (*Chinese traditional*). In the absence of more effective remedies of value in food poisoning. To prevent urinary tract infections.
Combinations: with Iceland Moss for wasting and cachexia to nourish and increase weight; with Lobelia for asthma and bronchitis: with Raspberry leaves for the menopause; with Comfrey for dental caries.

"Liquorice is recorded as a cancer remedy in many countries." (*J.L. Hartwell, Lloydia, 33, 97. 1970*)
Preparations. Average dose: 1-5 grams. Thrice daily before meals.
Decoction: half-1 teaspoon to each cup water, simmer 15 minutes. Half-1 cup.
Liquid Extract: 1:1. Dose: 2-5ml.
Sticks: for chewing.
Powdered root: 750mg (three 00 capsules or half a teaspoon).
Diet: Pontefract cakes – use in kitchen for adrenal failure; because of their sodium-retaining properties may be taken as sweets without added sugar. Low salt when taken.
Contra-indicated: In pregnancy, cirrhosis (liver) and in the presence of digitalis.
Note. If over-consumed may result in low potassium levels, high blood pressure and falls in renin and aldosterone. Where taken for a long period, increase intake of potassium-rich foods. May cause fluid retention of face and ankles which could be tolerated while primary disorder is being healed. GSL

LISTERIA. Listeriosis. A form of food poisoning by the bacterium *listeria monocytogenes* which from the soil enters the human food chain on unwashed vegetables, infected milk through

udder infection or faecal matter or the carcasses of slaughtered animals. A common route is unpasteurised milk in soft cheeses. The organism can survive a long time in extreme conditions of heat or cold – even microwave cooking.
At risk: pregnant females, babies, the elderly and immuno-suppressed groups. Notifiable disease.

There may be few gastrointestinal signs but it may lead to endocarditis and CNS disturbance: encephalitis and meningitis. When faced with a previously healthy person with acute diarrhoea and vomiting, food poisoning should be suspected.

Treatment. Dosage: thrice daily (chronic conditions); 2-hourly (acute conditions).
Formula. Equal parts: Wild Yam, Goldenseal, Valerian. Dose: Liquid Extracts: 30-60 drops in water. Powders: 500mg (two 00 capsules or one-third teaspoon). Tinctures: two 5ml teaspoons. Tablets: one tablet of each taken together.
Diet. Slippery Elm gruel. No tea, alcohol or caffeine drinks. Lemon balm tea freely. Listeria is inhibited by unsaturated fatty acids.
Prevention. 2 Garlic tablets/capsules at night.

Treatment by or in liaison with a general medical practitioner.

LITHAGOGUE. Herb with the ability to dissolve or expel stone, gravel (renal calculi). Bearberry, Buchu, Corn Silk, Couchgrass, Golden Rod, Gravel root, Horse Radish, Hydrangea, Nettles, Pellitory of the Wall, Parsley Piert, Sea Holly, Stone root, Violet leaves, Wild Carrot.

LITTLE LIVER PILLS. For bilious headache, inactive liver, constipation.
Ingredients: Aloin gr. 1/10. Ipom resin gr. 1/10. Capsic gr. 1/50. Podoph. resin. gr. 1/10. Jalapin gr. 1/10. Olearesin. Ginger. gr. 1/70.
Dose: One or two pills at bedtime or after dinner.

Historical interest only.

LIVER. The largest gland in the body. Situated on the right side under the dome of the diaphragm. At times, it may hold as much as a quarter of the body's blood supply. Blood from the spleen, stomach and intestines passes to the liver via the portal vein from which it issues much changed. The liver works in close association with the pancreas, bitter remedies being beneficial to both. It detoxicates offending bacteria and drugs which may enter through the intestines.

One vast laboratory, the liver secretes bile, cholesterol and lecithin; breaks down old red cells; and its anti-anaemic factor (Vitamin B12) is necessary by the bone marrow for production of red blood cells for protection against pernicious anaemia. It aids the digestion of fats, and ensures the storage of carbohydrates in the form of glycogen, together with Vitamins D and K.

A faint yellow tinge of the skin and eyeballs may be the first indication of liver disturbance. The liver has great powers of recovery, herbal agents powerfully influencing regeneration of cells.

In all liver disorders the liver is less taxed on a low-fat or fat-free diet. Most effective remedies are Dandelion and Burdock. Treatment will depend upon the particular disturbance. Dandelion relieves portal vein congestion.
Simple test to spot liver disease: check that stools are the right colour and that the urine does not stain.

LIVER – ABSCESS. May follow inflammation of the liver from a number of causes, the most common being a manifestation of amoebic dysentery. Through blood infection it may appear on the surface of the liver or other organs.
Symptoms: pain under the right lower rib which may be referred to the right shoulder or under shoulder blades.
Treatment. Official treatment is aspiration or opening-up the abscess followed by drainage. Whether or not this is necessary, alternative antibacterials such as Myrrh, Goldenseal, Echinacea and Blue Flag may be used with good effect.
Alternatives. *Teas*: Milk Thistle. Grape leaves. 1 heaped teaspoon to each cup of water, thrice daily.
Decoctions: Echinacea, Blue Flag, Goldenseal, Parsley root. One heaped teaspoon to each cup water gently simmered 20 minutes. Half a cup thrice daily.
Tablets/capsules: Blue Flag, Echinacea. Goldenseal. Wild Yam. Devil's Claw.
Tinctures. Formula. Fringe Tree 3; Meadowsweet 2; Goldenseal 1. One to two 5ml teaspoons, thrice daily.
Practitioner. Ipecacuanha contains emetine which is specific for liver abscess; at the same time it is effective as an anti-amoebic-dysentery agent. Where dysentery is treated with Ipecacuanha liver abscess is rare. Tincture Ipecacuanha BP (1973). Dose: 0.25-1ml.
Diet. Fat-free. Dandelion coffee. Vitamins B6, C and K. Lecithin.

Treatment by or in liaison with a general medical practitioner.

LIVER – ACUTE INFECTIOUS HEPATITIS. Inflammation of the liver from virus infection. As the commonest form of liver disorder, it is often without jaundice or marked liver symptoms apart from general malaise and abdominal discomfort. 'Gippy tummy', 'chill on the liver'. For feverishness, add a diaphoretic.
Treatment. Bitter herbs keep the bile fluid and flowing.
Alternatives. *Teas*. Agrimony, Lemon Balm, Boldo, Bogbean, Centuary, Dandelion, Hyssop, Motherwort, Wormwood, Yarrow.

Maria Treben. Equal parts: Bedstraw, Agrimony, Woodruff. 2 teaspoons to cup boiling water.
Cold tea: 2 teaspoons Barberry bark to each cup cold water. Infuse overnight. Half-1 cup freely.
Tablets/capsules: Blue Flag. Dandelion. Wild Yam. Liquorice.
Formula. Equal parts: Turkey Rhubarb, Dandelion, Meadowsweet. Dose: Liquid Extracts: 1-2 teaspoons. Tinctures: 2-3 teaspoons. Powders: 500mg (two 00 capsules or one-third teaspoon). 3-4 times daily.
Alfred Vogel. Dandelion, Devil's Claw, Artichoke.
Antonius Musa, physician to Emperor Augustus Caesar records: "Wood Betony preserves the liver and bodies of men from infectious diseases".
Preventative: Garlic. (*Old Chinese*)
Milk Thistle: good responses observed.
General. Bedrest until motions are normal. Enema with any one of above herb teas.
Diet. Fat-free. Fasting period from 1-3 days on fruit juices and herb teas only. Artichokes. Dandelion coffee. Lecithin.

See: COCKROACH, The.

Treatment by or in liaison with a general medical practitioner.

LIVER – HEPATITIS, CHRONIC. Term referring to hepatitis where the condition is the result of acute attacks of more than six months duration.
Causes: alcohol excess, drugs (Paracetamol prescribed for those who cannot tolerate aspirin), autoimmune disease, toxaemia, environmental poisons. Clinically latent forms are common from carbon monoxide poisoning. May lead to cirrhosis.
Symptoms. Jaundice, nausea and vomiting, inertia.
Treatment. Bile must be kept moving.
Alternatives:– *Decoction*. Formula. Milk Thistle 2; Yellow Dock 1; Boldo 1. 1 heaped teaspoon to each cup water gently simmered 20 minutes. Half-1 cup thrice daily.
Formula. Barberry bark 1; German Chamomile 2. Dose: Liquid Extracts: 2 teaspoons. Tinctures: 2-3 teaspoons. Powders: 750mg (three capsules or half a teaspoon) thrice daily.
Tablets/capsules. Blue Flag root. Goldenseal.
Astragalus. Popular liver tonic in Chinese medicine. A liver protective in chemotherapy.
Diet. Fat-free. Dandelion coffee. Artichokes. Lecithin.
Supplements. B-vitamins, B12, Zinc.

Treatment by or in liaison with a general medical practitioner.

LIVER – HEPATITIS A. The most common cause of inflammation of the liver from a virus known as Hepatitis A. May be caught by eating shellfish contaminated by sewage or polluted water. Distinct from alcohol and drugs. The virus is ingested in the mouth, grown in the intestines and passes out of the body on defecation.
Treatment. Same as for acute infectious hepatitis.

LIVER – HEPATITIS B. Regarded as more serious than Hepatitis A. A main symptom is a flu-like illness followed by jaundice. Transmitted sexually, blood transfusion or by infected blood as from contaminated needles used by drug abusers. It is the first human virus to be identified with cancer in man. High mortality rate.
Symptoms: nausea and vomiting, fever, dark urine, loss of appetite, skin irritation, yellow discoloration of the skin and whites of eyes, weakness and fatigue.
Treatment. Internal. Silymarin (active principle of Milk Thistle) has been used with good responses. (*R.L. Devault & W. Rosenbrook, (1973), Antibiotic Journal, 26;532*)
Wormwood tea. 1-2 teaspoons herb to each cup boiling water in a covered vessel. Infuse 10-15 minutes: 1 cup thrice daily.
Formula. Equal parts: Balmony, Valerian, Wild Yam. Dose: Liquid Extracts: 1-2 teaspoons. Tinctures: 1-3 teaspoons. Powders: 750mg (three 00 capsules or half a teaspoon) thrice daily.
Astragalus. Popular liver protective used in Chinese medicine.
Phyllanthus amarus. Clinical trials on 78 carriers of the virus revealed that this plant effectively eliminated the virus from the body in 59 per cent of cases. Treatment consisted of 200mg dried powdered herb (whole plant minus the roots) in capsules, thrice daily for 30 days). (*Thyagarajan, S.P., et al "Effect of Phyllanthus amarus on Chronic Carriers of Hepatitis B Virus." The Lancet, Oct.1988 2:764-766*)
External. Castor oil packs for two months.

Treatment by or in liaison with a general medical practitioner.

LIVER – HEPATITIS C. Paul Bergner describes 4 cases of patients with chronic hepatitis C successfully treated. All were given Milk Thistle, and prescribed an alternative tea: equal parts, Burdock, Dandelion, Barberry, Liquorice, Cinnamon and Fennel. Chologogue action is important in chronic liver disease. Not used in acute inflammation. All patients felt better within 2 weeks, and had liver function tests at 3-monthly intervals, showing a gradual decline in elevated values until normal or almost so. All patients became symptom-free. (*Medical Herbalism, Vol 6, No 4*)

LIVER – ACUTE YELLOW ATROPHY. Necrosis. Fatal disease in which the substance of the liver is destroyed. Incidence is rare since the public has been alerted to the dangers of certain chemical toxins, fumes from synthetic glues, solvents, and poisonous fungi.
Symptoms: jaundice, delirium and convulsions.

As it is the work of the liver to neutralise incoming poisons it may suffer unfair wear and tear, alcohol and caffeine being common offenders.
Treatment for relief of symptoms only: same as for abscess of the liver.

Treatment by or in liaison with a general medical practitioner.

LIVER – AMOEBIC HEPATITIS. Patients with amoebic dysentery may develop liver complications, usually by blood borne infection via the portal system. Small lesions coalesce to form abscesses capable of destroying liver cells.
Treatment: as for LIVER ABSCESS.

LIVER – CIRRHOSIS. A disease of the liver with hardened and fibrotic patches. Scar tissue obstructs the flow of blood through the liver, back pressure causing damage. As they wear out liver cells are not renewed.
Causes: damage from gall-stones, aftermath of infections, drugs; the commonest is alcohol. Usually made up of three factors: toxaemia (self-poisoning), poor nutrition, infective bacteria or virus.
Symptoms. Loss of appetite, dyspepsia, low grade fever, nosebleeds, lethargy, spidery blood vessels on face, muscular weakness, jaundice, loss of sex urge, redness of palms of hands, unable to lie on left side. Mechanical pressure may cause dropsy and ascites. Alcohol-induced cirrhosis correlates with low phospholipid levels.
Treatment. Bitter herbs are a daily necessity to keep the bile fluid and flowing. Among other agents, peripheral vaso-dilators are indicated. Regulate bowels.
Teas. Balmony, Milk Thistle, Boldo, Bogbean. Dandelion coffee. Barberry tea (cold water).
Tablets/capsules. Calamus, Blue Flag, Wild Yam.
Formula. Wahoo 2; Wild Yam 1; Blue Flag root 1. Dose: Liquid Extracts: one 5ml teaspoon. Tinctures: two 5ml teaspoons. Powders: 500mg (two 00 capsules or one-third teaspoon). Thrice daily.
Milk Thistle (Silybum marianum). Based on its silymarin contents: 70-210mg, thrice daily.
Practitioner. For pain. Tincture Gelsemium: 5-10 drops in water when necessary.
Enema. Constipation may be severe for which warm water injection should be medicated with few drops Tincture Myrrh.
Diet. High protein, high starch, low fat. Reject alcohol. Accept: Dandelion coffee, artichokes, raw onion juice, turmeric as a table spice.
Lecithin. Soy-derived lecithin to antidote alcohol-induced cirrhosis. (*Study: Bronx Veterans Affairs Medical Center & Mount Sinai Hospital School of Medicine, New York City*)
Supplements. B-complex, B12, C (1g), K, Magnesium, Zinc.

Treatment by or in liaison with a general medical practitioner or gastro-enterologist.

LIVER – CONGESTION. Non-inflammatory simple passive congestion is usually secondary to congestive heart failure, injury, or other disorders.
Symptoms: headache, vomiting of bile, depression, furred tongue, poor appetite, lethargy, sometimes diarrhoea. Upper right abdomen tender to touch due to enlargement, pale complexion.
BHP (1983) recommends: Fringe Tree, Wahoo, Goldenseal, Blue Flag, Butternut bark, Boldo, Black root.
Treatment. Treat the underlying cause, i.e. heart or chest troubles. Bitter herbs.
Alternatives:– *Teas*. Balmony, Bogbean, Centuary. 1 heaped teaspoon to each cup boiling water infused 15 minutes. Half-1 cup 3 or more times daily.
Decoction. Dandelion and Burdock roots. Mix. One teaspoon to large cup water simmered gently 20 minutes. Cup 2-3 times daily.
Tablets/capsules. Blue Flag, Goldenseal, Wild Yam.
Formula. Dandelion 2; Wahoo 1; Meadowsweet 1; Cinnamon 1. Dose: Liquid Extracts: 1-2 teaspoons. Tinctures: 1-3 teaspoons. Powders: 750mg (three 00 capsules or half a teaspoon) thrice daily.
Alfred Vogel recommends: Barberry bark, Centuary, Boldo, St John's Wort, St Mary's Thistle, Sarsaparilla.
Epsom salt baths (hot) to promote elimination of impurities through the skin.
Diet. Fat-free. Dandelion coffee. Artichokes. Lecithin.

LIVER ENLARGEMENT. From a number of causes ranging from persistent infections to chemical poisoning.
Formula. Fringe Tree bark 2ml; Black root 7ml; Echinacea 4ml; Distilled water to 4oz (120ml). Dose: teaspoon every two hours. (*W.H. Black MD, Tecumseh, Oklahoma, USA*)
Hypertrophy. Equal parts: tinctures Goldenseal and Fringe Tree. 15-60 drops in water before meals and at bedtime.
Diet. Low fat. Artichokes, Dandelion coffee, lecithin.
Supplements. Vitamin B6.

LIVER – FATTY. Destruction of normal liver cells and their replacement by fat.
Causes: obesity; environmental chemicals, toxins from fevers (influenza, etc).
Alternatives. *Teas*. Boldo, Clivers, Motherwort, Chaparral. One heaped teaspoon to each cup boiling water infused 15 minutes. 1 cup freely.
Tablets/capsules. Seaweed and Sarsaparilla.
Formula. Fringe Tree 2; Clivers 1; Bladderwrack (fucus) 1. Dose: Liquid Extracts: 1 teaspoon. *Tinctures*: 1-2 teaspoons. Powders: 750mg (three 00 capsules or half a teaspoon) thrice daily.

Cider Vinegar. 2-3 teaspoons to glass water. Drink freely.
Evening Primrose oil. 4 x 500mg capsules daily.
Diet. Fat-free. Dandelion coffee. Artichokes.
Supplementation. Vitamin B6. C. K. Zinc. Kelp.

LIVER – INJURIES. As bleeding cannot be ruled out, no time should be lost seeking hospital treatment. An immediate surgical repair may be necessary. However, there are ways in which healing can be speeded and body defences sustained. The following promote healing: Fringe Tree being most relevant. To prevent infection it should be combined with Echinacea (anti-microbial).
Alternatives. *Teas*. Comfrey, Horsetail, Marigold, St John's Wort, Plantain.
Decoction. Equal parts: Fringe Tree bark; Echinacea root. 1 heaped teaspoon to each large cup water simmered gently 20 minutes. Half-1 cup or as much as tolerated, every 2 hours.
Tinctures. Equal parts: Milk Thistle, Echinacea root. 20-60 drops in water every 2 hours.
Castor oil packs. Applied over liver area.

LIVER SPOTS. See: AGE SPOTS.

LOBELIA. Indian tobacco. Puke weed. *Lobelia inflata L. German*: Indianischer tabak. *French*: Tabac indien. *Italian*: Lobelia. *Part used*: dried herb collected when part of capsule is inflated.
Constituents: lobeline, resin, wax, gum, lignin, fixed oil.
Action: antasthmatic, antispasmodic, mild sedative and gentle relaxant. Expectorant, diaphoretic, anti-cough. Broncho-dilator containing the alkaloid lobeline. Claimed to destroy pneumococcus. Amphoteric. Emetic. Smoking deterrent (tablets). *Respiratory stimulant*.
Uses. Broad spectrum therapy: chest, throat, sinuses, middle ear, urinary tract, chronic bronchitis. An effective means of controlling difficult breathing without risk of serious side-effects: croup, whooping cough, pleurisy, etc. For deteriorating asthma where there has been a declining response to routine broncho-dilator treatment. Well tolerated by those allergic to penicillin and for side-effects arising from that therapy. Tetanus (*Dr H. Hart, Chi Med Journal*). Irritability and hypersensitivity. Nicotine addiction.
External. Use of tincture or liquid extract for gouty joints, big toe, etc.
Ear troubles in children: Inject 2 drops Oil Lobelia.
Preparations. Thrice daily.
Dried herb, 50 to 200mg in infusion (BHC Vol 1).
Liquid Extract: 0.2 to 0.6ml (3 to 10 drops).
Tincture Lobelia acid: 1 part to 10 parts cider vinegar; macerate 8 days; decant. Dose: 5 to 10ml (1-2 teaspoons).
Simple Tincture Lobelia BPC (1949), 1:8 in 60 per cent alcohol. Dose, 0.6 to 2ml.
Tablets/capsules. Lobelia compound. Powdered Lobelia BP 60mg; Powdered Gum Ammoniacum BPC 30mg; Powdered extract Squill 2:1, 30mg. Respiratory stimulant for blocked sinuses, catarrh and coughs.
Contra-indicated: feeble pulse or nerve response, pregnancy, shock, paralysis. Large doses induce vomiting. GSL

LOBELIA. Dr Thomson's 3rd Preparation. Equal parts, powders, Lobelia (herb or seed), Cayenne pepper, Lady's Slipper root. Add to 20 parts tincture Myrrh. Mix and shake well. Always shake before use. Dose: 30-160 drops, in hot water.

LOCKJAW. See: TETANUS.

LOCOMOTOR ATAXIA. Loss of co-ordination of the muscles from terminal syphilis. See: TABES DORSALIS.

LOGWOOD. Peachwood. *Haematoxylon campechianum L. German*: Campechebaum. *French*: Campèche. *Italian*: Campeggio. *Part used*: Heart wood chips or raspings.
Constituents: Haematoxylin, volatile oil, resin, tannin.
Action: astringent.
Uses: diarrhoea, dysentery, summer diarrhoea. Bleeding from the lungs, womb or bowels. Nasal polypi (douche).
Preparation. Half an ounce to 1 pint water simmered down to three-quarters volume. Dose: one-third to half a cup; children 2-4 teaspoons; thrice daily.
Liquid extract Logwood BPC (1934), dose, 2-8ml.

LOTIONS. Liquid preparations applied externally for protection or medication of the skin or mucous membranes. May be made with alcohol, (Tincture Calendula); water (Witch Hazel water); or glycerine (Goldenseal and glycerine). Preparations containing oil are generally known as liniments. Lotions may be made from flowers, herbs, etc, with the aid of glycerine.
Marigold Lotion. Flowerheads are passed through a juicer. Combine equal parts juice and glycerine. Hand lotion for children's sensitive skin with tendency to chafe and smart.

LOTUS. The sacred lotus of the East. *Nelumbo nucifera*, Gaertn. *Nelumbrium nelumbo L. German*: Lotusblume. *French*: Lotus du Nile. *Arabian*: Nilufar. *Indian*: Komol. *Malayan*: Telipok. *Chinese*: Ho Lein-hua. *Iranian*: Nilofer. *Parts used*: flowers, seeds, roots.
Constituents: an alkaloid similar to nupharine, tannin, resins.
Action: astringent, haemostatic to arrest bleeding,

tranquilliser, anaphrodisiac, antispermatorrhoeic.
Uses: In his *Supplement to the Pharmacopoeias* (1818), S.F. Gray writes: "Root astringent . . . as also the liquor that runs out of the footstalk when cut, used in looseness and vomiting, also diuretic and cooling; seeds nutritive."

Young rhizomes and seeds yield Chinese Arrowroot, a starch made into a porridge for diarrhoea and dysentery. Has a reputation to reduce excessive sexual activity, and was taken by priests of Buddha to assist their practice of relaxation.

LOVAGE. *Levisticum officinalis*, Koch. *German*: Agyptischer Kümmel. *French*: Ammi. *Italian*: Sisone. *Arabian*: Amus. *Indian*: Ajwain. *Malayan*: Homama Azamoda. *Iranian*: Zhinyan.
Parts used: root, rhizome.
Constituents: coumarins, butyric acid, volatile oil.
Action: antibiotic (mild), diaphoretic, expectorant, anti-catarrhal, emmenagogue, carminative, diuretic (mild), sedative, antispasmodic.
Uses: flatulent dyspepsia, anorexia, rheumatism, gout, absent or painful menses, mild feverishness in children, renal dropsy (mild), cystitis.
Locally: as a gargle for tonsillitis mouth wash for mouth ulcers BHP (1983).
Combinations. With Agrimony for indigestion. With Buchu for renal dropsy. With Raspberry leaves for menstrual disorders. Usually combined with other diuretics.
Preparations. Average dose: half-2g. Thrice daily.
Decoction. Half-1 teaspoon to each cup water gently simmered 15 minutes. Dose: one-third-1 cup.
Liquid Extract: 5-30 drops in water.

Oil used in aromatherapy and perfumes. GSL

LOZENGE. A compressed tablet for sucking in the mouth for inflammatory conditions of throat, mouth and chest. Usually has a base of sugar, a demulcent (Comfrey, Marshmallow root, Slippery Elm, Tolu, or Balm of Gilead), together with a binder, such as gum acacia or gum tragacanth. Recipe for simple lozenge: half an ounce (15g) powdered herb; half an ounce sugar; powdered gum 1 teaspoon (3g). Pure spring water – a sufficiency. Mix into a paste, thin-out the mass and press out lozenges with small gauge mould and dry.

LUMBAGO. Low back pain is responsible for loss of millions of working hours. Acute or chronic persistent pain in the sacroiliac, lumbar or lumbo-sacral areas.
Causes: referred pain from a disordered abdominal organ, displacement of pelvis, lumbosacral spine, slipped disc and lumbar spondylosis. See: LUMBAR INTERVERTEBRAL DISC PROLAPSE.

Paget's disease or lumbago not associated with sciatica (radiating pain down the back of the leg via the sciatic nerve).
Symptoms. Local tenderness, reduced range of movement, muscle spasm. Usually better by rest; worse by movement.
Differential diagnosis: exclude other pelvic disorders such as structural bony displacements, infection from other organs, carcinoma of the womb or prostate gland. Pain in the small of the back may indicate kidney disease or stone. See: KIDNEY DISEASE, GYNAECOLOGICAL PROBLEMS.
Frequent causes: varicosities of the womb and pelvis. These are identical to varicose veins elsewhere, venous circulation being congested. Pressure on a vein from the ovaries may manifest as lumbago – treatment is the same as for varicose veins.

Root cause of the pain should be traced where possible. As most cases of backache defy accurate diagnosis the following general treatments are recommended. For more specific treatments, reference should be made to the various subdivisions of rheumatic disorders. See: RHEUMATIC AND ARTHRITIC DISORDERS, ANKYLOSING SPONDYLITIS, etc.
Alternatives. Barberry (commended by Dr Finlay Ellingwood), Black Cohosh, Bogbean, Buchu, Burdock, Celery, Devil's Claw, Horsetail, St John's Wort (tenderness of spine to the touch), White Willow, Wild Yam (muscle spasm).
Celery tea. Barberry tea. See entries.
Decoction. Formula. White Willow 3; Wild Yam 2; Juniper half; Valerian half. Prepare: 3 heaped 5ml teaspoons to 1 pint (500ml) water; simmer gently 15-20 minutes. Dose: 1 wineglassful (100ml or 3fl oz) thrice daily.
Tablets/capsules. Black Cohosh, Celery, Devil's Claw, Wild Yam, Ligvites.
Formula. Devil's Claw 2; Black Cohosh 1; Valerian 1; Juniper half. Mix. Dose: Powders: 500mg (two 00 capsules or one-third teaspoon). Liquid extracts: 1 teaspoon. Tinctures: 2 teaspoons. Action is enhanced where dose is taken in cup Dandelion coffee, otherwise a little water.
Practitioner. Tincture Black Cohosh 4; Tincture Arnica 1. Mix. Dose: 10-20 drops, thrice daily. Black Cohosh and Arnica are two of the most positive synergists known to scientific herbalism. Both are specific for striped muscle tissue. Common disorders of the voluntary muscles quickly respond. (*James A. Cannon MD, Pickens, SC, USA*)
Practitioner: alternative. Tincture Gelsemium. 10 drops to 100ml water; dose, 1 teaspoon every 2 hours.
Topical. Castor oil pack at night. Warm fomentations of Lobelia and Hops. Warm potato poultice. Cayenne salve. Camphorated, Jojoba or Evening Primrose oil. Lotion: equal parts tinctures:

Lobelia, Ragwort and St John's Wort; mix: 10-20 drops on cotton wool or suitable material and applied to affected area. Arnica lotion. Wintergreen.
Chiropractic technique. Ice and low back pain. Patient lies on his stomach with two pillows under abdomen, the low back in an arched position. Apply ice-bag or packet of peas from the freezer on top of lumbar area; pillow on top to hold ice firm. Patient not to lie or sit on ice-pack.
Diet. Oily fish.
Supplements. Daily. Vitamin B-complex, Vitamin C (500mg); Vitamin D 500iu; Vitamin E (400iu). Dolomite. Niacin.
Supportives. Bedrest in acute stage. Diathermy. Spinal support. Relaxation techniques to reduce muscle tension.

LUNG WEAKNESS. There is no reason why lung weakness of childhood should not, in later life, resolve into vigorous respiration. However, some cases present a life-long hazard, arresting full development and reducing the body's ability to defend itself. To strengthen alveolar tissue, allay infection and enhance respiratory function a good pectoral may ensure against future disorders of lungs, trachea, bronchi and bronchioles.
Tablets/capsules. Iceland Moss.
Decoction. Irish Moss.
Tea. Combine equal parts, Comfrey, White Horehound, Liquorice. 1 heaped teaspoon to each cup water simmered gently 1 minute. Dose: half-1 cup morning and evening. Pinch Cayenne improves.

Potential benefits of Comfrey for this condition outweigh risk.

LUNGWORT. *Pulmonaria officinalis L. Lobaria pulmonaria L.* Lichen. Leaves bear a resemblance to the human lung – see: DOCTRINE OF SIGNATURES. So-named because of its traditional use for tuberculosis. *Keynote*: upper respiratory organs.
Constituents: palmitic acid, linoleic acid, tannins, ergosterol, saponin.
Action: expectorant, demulcent astringent, haemostatic, orexigenic, antibiotic (mild).
Uses: asthma, laryngitis, sore throat, children's dry cough, whooping cough, haemoptysis, nasal catarrh, bronchitis.
External: open wounds – to avoid infection.
Combinations. With Coltsfoot and White Horehound for TB cough. With Ephedra for difficult breathing.
Preparations. Average dose: 2-4g. Thrice daily.
Tea: 1 teaspoon to each cup boiling water; infuse 15 minutes; dose: one-third-1 cup. Or may be boiled in milk.
Liquid Extract BHP (1983): 1:1 in 25 per cent alcohol. Dose: 2-4ml.
Balm of Gilead Cough Mixture . GSL

LUPUS ERYTHEMATOSUS. Auto-immune disease – antibody to DNA. Non-tubercula. Two kinds: (1) discoid lupus erythematosus (DLE) and (2) systemic lupus erythematosus (SLE). DLE occurs mostly in middle-aged women, but SLE in young women. Activity may be followed by period of remission. The condition may evolve into rheumatic disease.
Symptoms (SLE): Loss of appetite, fever. Weight loss, weakness. Thickened scaly red patches on face (butterfly rash). May invade scalp and cause loss of hair. Sunlight worsens. Anaemia. Joint pains. Enlarged spleen. Heart disorders. Kidney weakness, with protein in the urine. Symptoms worse on exposure to sunlight. Low white blood cell count. Many patients may also present with Raynaud's phenomenon while some women with silicone breast implants may develop lupus.
Treatment. Anti-virals. Alteratives. Anti-inflammatories, anticoagulants.
Alternatives. *Teas*: Lime flowers, Gotu Kola, Ginkgo, Aloe Vera, Boneset.
Decoctions: Burdock. Queen's Delight. Helonias.
Tablets/capsules. Echinacea. Blue Flag root. Wild Yam. Ginkgo.
Formula. Dandelion 1; Black Haw 1; Wild Yam half; Poke root half. Dose: Liquid Extracts: one 5ml teaspoon. Tinctures: two 5ml teaspoons. Powders: 500mg (two 00 capsules or one-third teaspoon). Thrice daily.
Topical. Sunlight barrier creams: Aloe Vera, Comfrey. Horsetail poultice. Garlic ointment. Castor oil packs.
Diet. See: DIET – SKIN DISORDERS.
Supplements. Calcium pantothenate, Vitamin A, Vitamin E, Selenium.
Note. The disorder is frequently misdiagnosed as rheumatoid arthritis, multiple sclerosis or ME. Lupus antibodies have been linked with premature heart disease in women and transient strokes.

LUPUS VULGARIS. Tubercula skin disease, with small apple-jelly yellow nodules progressing to ulceration. Distribution: face, neck and mucous surfaces of mouth and nose. Non-itching. Skin thickens and discolours. Nose may be eroded and deformed.
Treatment. Because of plastic surgery deformities are now seldom seen, yet herbalism may still have a case in the absence of conventional drugs.
Teas. Elecampane. Gotu Kola.
Red Clover compound.
Arthur Barker. Liquid Extract Echinacea 1oz; Liquid Extract Queen's Delight half an ounce; Tincture Goldenseal 30 drops. Syr Senna 2oz. Distilled, or pure spring water to 8oz. Dose: 1 dessertspoon after meals.
Topical. Marshmallow and Slippery Elm poultices or ointment. Oil of Mullein. Aloe Vera. Castor oil packs.

LYME DISEASE. An acute infection following bite of tick from deer, forest ponies or other animals. A spirochaete – *Borrelia burdorfer* is responsible.

Symptoms. Headache, disorientation, confused speech, sensitive to light, partial paralysis of face. Practitioners who see patients with Bell's palsy should consider Lyme disease as a possible cause.

Treatment: anti-infective therapy. Internal:–

Formula. Equal parts: Echinacea, Lobelia. Dose: Liquid Extracts: 1 teaspoon. Tinctures: 2 teaspoons. Powders: 500mg (two 00 capsules or one-third teaspoon), 3-4 times daily.

Topical. Disinfect bite sting with alcohol (methylated spirit, whiskey, etc). With tweezers or fingers (protected with rubber gloves or tissue) grasp the tick and pull upwards. Take care not to squeeze or puncture the body of the tick; dispose by flushing down the toilet. After removal, again wipe skin with alcohol; wash hands; apply antiseptic lotion or cream: Echinacea, Aloe Vera, Witch Hazel, Garlic, Eucalyptus etc.

LYMPHADENITIS. LYMPHADENOMA. See: LYMPHATIC SYSTEM.

LYMPHATICS. A group of herbs that expend their influence upon the lymphatic system, stimulating the circulation of lymph and tending to disperse glandular swellings.

Agnus Castus, Bladderwrack, Blue Flag root, Burdock, Celandine (Greater), Clivers, Echinacea, Fenugreek, Figwort, Fringe Tree, Marigold, Pipsissewa, Poke root, Queen's Delight, Red Clover, Sarsaparilla, Saw Palmetto, Thuja, Violet (Wild), Wild Indigo, Yellow Parilla.

LYMPH GLANDS. Traps in the lymphatic system that collect byproducts of body infection and which support the immune system in its role as body protector.

LYMPHATIC SYSTEM. Lymph is the same fluid which oozes from a cut when bleeding stops. It surrounds every living cell. Lymph conveys to the blood the final products of digestion of food. It also receives from the blood waste products of metabolism. This is a two-way traffic.

Lymph fluid, loaded with waste, excess protein, etc, is sucked into the lymph tubes to be filtered by the spleen and the lymph nodes. The tubes are filled with countless one-way valves referred to collectively as the lymphatic pump, which propels the flow of lymph forwards. Lymph ultimately is collected in the main thoracic duct rising upwards in front of the spine to enter the bloodstream at the base of the neck.

A number of disorders may arise when the fluid becomes over-burdened by toxaemia, poor drainage and enlarged nodes (glands). Such uneliminated wastes form cellulite – unwanted tissue formation and swelling. Thus, the soil may be prepared for various chronic illnesses from glandular disorders to arthritis. If the lymph is circulating freely it is almost impossible to become sick.

This system is capable of ingesting foreign particles and building up an immunity against future infection. Some herbal Lymphatics are also antimicrobials, natural alternatives to conventional antibiotics.

Treatment. Clivers is particularly relative to glandular swellings of neck and axillae.

For active inflammation: Echinacea, Goldenseal, Ginseng (Panax).

Alternatives. *Teas*: Clivers, Red Clover, Agnus Castus herb, Bladderwrack, Violet leaves, Marigold petals.

Decoctions: Blue Flag, Echinacea, Fenugreek seeds, Saw Palmetto.

Tablets/capsules. Agnus Castus, Echinacea, Bladderwrack, Red Clover, Thuja, Poke root, Fenugreek.

Formula No 1. Echinacea 2; Clivers 1; Burdock 1; Poke root half. Dose: Liquid Extracts: one 5ml teaspoon. Tinctures: two 5ml teaspoons. Powders: 500mg (two 00 capsules or one-third teaspoon). Thrice daily.

Formula No 2. Equal parts: Blue Flag root, Poke root, Senna. Dose: as above.

Topical. Poultices: Slippery Elm, Fenugreek seeds, Marshmallow. Horsechestnut (Aesculus) ointment.

LYMPHOEDEMA. A swelling caused by congestion of lymph in the tissues from obstruction of the lymphatic circulation due to inflammation, injury or tumour. See: LYMPHATIC SYSTEM.

Booklet: "Lymphoedema", How the patient can alleviate symptoms. Beaconsfield Publishers Ltd, 20 Chiltern Hills Road, Beaconsfield, Bucks.

LYMPHOGRANULOMA VENEREUM (LGV). **Treatment**: same as for Gonorrhoea.

LYMPHOMA. Malignant tumour of the lymphatic system. A rare disorder. May be nodular or diffuse. The onset is encouraged by suppression of the immune system by steroids, especially in organ transplant recipients. Not the same as Hodgkin's disease. Enlargement of lymph nodes in neck, under arm and groin. Nodes become hot, red, hardened with intense stabbing pains. (Agnus Castus, Echinacea)

Conventional treatment includes surgical extirpation, chemotherapy, radiotherapy and anti-viral drugs. Herbalism has something to offer, especially when immuno-suppression regimes are discontinued. Blood tonics and Lymphatics may stimulate recovery of a depleted immune system and include Echinacea, Goldenseal, Myrrh. Treat as for Hodgkin's disease.

A type of lymphoma, known as Burkett's, is

usually confined to African children, believed to be of viral causation. See: ANTIVIRALS. Has been effectively treated with Vinchristine, from the plant *Vinca rosea*.

Treatment by or in liaison with a general medical practitioner.

LYMPHOSARCOMA. A malignant tumour appearing on lymph tissue, with enlargement of the glands, liver and spleen. Treat as for Hodgkin's disease.

MACE. *Myristica fragrans*, Houtt. *Part used*: outside shell of nutmeg seeds. Contains myristicin.
Action: carminative.
Uses: flatulent dyspepsia.
Preparation. *Powder*. Half-1 gram in honey or banana, thrice daily.

MACERATION. Partial extraction of the active constituents of a plant by the action of a solvent, usually alcohol. The process takes a few days, usually seven, in a closed vessel at room temperature and frequently shaken. The liquor is strained off, the marc (spent herbs) pressed out and the expressed liquor added. The whole is filtered and sediments removed. All herbs can be macerated, fresh or dry, for the making of tinctures. Glycerine is sometimes used as a solvent.

MAD-COW DISEASE, HUMAN. Creutzfeldt-Jakob disease. See: BOVINE SPONGIFORM ENCEPHALOPATHY.

MADAUS, DR & Co. West Germany. The firm was founded in Bonn in 1919 by the brothers Dr Gerhard Madaus, Friedemund Madaus and Hans Madaus, as a result of a personal family experience. As a child one of the brothers was seriously ill and his recovery was greatly aided by treatment with medicinal plants and herbs. Impressed by this experience the eldest brother studied medicine. After the First World War the three brothers began the manufacture of medicaments on a small scale.

In 1936 the first Biological Institute was established, in which the effects of constituents were examined. Intensive research work induced Dr Gerhard Madaus to publish, in 1938, a three volume work entitled "Manual of Biological Medicine" which, even today, still enjoys a high reputation in the professional world.

The House of Madaus has its own research departments in pharmacology, pathology, botany and immunisation biology.

Their preparation of Convallaria (Lily of the Valley) in natural compound form has outstandingly proved itself in heart failure. Work on Horse Chestnut, Echinacea and Agnus Castus has advanced herbal pharmacy worldwide.

MADDER. *Rubia tinctorum, L.*

Of historic interest only, as a cholagogue, emmenagogue and diuretic. No longer used in medicine. Used in the dyeing industry as Turkey Red.

MAGNESIUM. Important mineral. Magnesium limestone (dolomite rock). Essential for use of Vitamins B1 and B6, a deficiency of which affects the nervous system. Vasodilator. Platelet inhibitor.
Deficiency. May lead to disorders of arteries or kidneys; brittle bones, pre-menstrual tension, heart disease, muscle cramps, hypoglycaemia, insomnia, palpitation, tremor of hands or lower limbs; anorexia, anxiety, depression, tiredness, dizziness, confusion. Studies reveal that two-thirds of patients with peripheral vascular disease are magnesium-deficient. Absorption is blocked by the contraceptive pill, a high milk or high fat intake. Chronic fatigue syndrome.

Heart attack. "An imbalance in the Magnesium/Calcium ratio may contribute to myocardial infarction." *(Dr H.J. Holtmeier, University of Freiburg, Germany)*
Body effects. Co-ordination of nerves and muscles. Healthy teeth and bones. This metal activates more enzymes in the body than any other mineral. Heart patients on Digoxin have less palpitation when magnesium level is normal.
Sources. Most foods. Meat, milk, eggs, seafood, nuts (peanuts etc), brown rice, wheatbran, cocoa, Soya beans and flour, almonds, walnuts, maize, oats.
Fruits: apples, avocado, bananas, black grapes, seeds.
Herbs: Bladderwrack, Black Willow bark, Broom, Carrot leaves, Devil's Bit, Dulse, Dandelion, Gotu Kola, Kale, Kelp, Meadowsweet, Mistletoe, Mullein, Okra, Parsley, Peppermint, Primrose flowers, Rest Harrow, Silverweed, Skunk Cabbage, Toadflax, Walnut leaves, Watercress, Wintergreen. Teas made from any of this list can be effective for low-grade magnesium deficiency.

RDA 300mg: 450mg (pregnant women and nursing mothers).

MAIDENHAIR FERN. Venus hair. *Adiantum capillus-veneris*. *German*: Venushaar. *French*: Adianthe. *Italian*: Adianto. *Iranian*: Hansa padi. *Indian*: Mubarakha. *Arabian*: Shuir-el-jin. *Parts used*: the fern and rhizomes.
Constituents: terpenoids, flavonoid glycosides.
Action: demulcent expectorant, pectoral stimulant, anti-tussive, mucilaginous, galactagogue, anti-dandruff.
Uses: detoxicant for alcoholism; coughs, sore throat, bronchitis.
Preparations. Average dose, half-2 grams. Thrice daily.
Tea. quarter-1 teaspoon to each cup boiling water; infuse 15 minutes. Half a cup.
Liquid Extract BHP (1983) 1:1 in 25 per cent alcohol. Dose, half-2ml.
Powder: half-2 grams. GSL

MAIDENHAIR TREE. See: GINKGO TREE.

MALABSORPTION SYNDROME. Arising from poor assimilation of nutrients, minerals, fat

soluble vitamins by the intestines. Patient not getting maximum nourishment from food.
Multiple causes: diseases of the gut; strictures, fistulas, Crohn's disease, obstructions, parasites, infections, drugs, X-rays, endocrine disease, gastric surgery. A common cause is gluten sensitivity due to ingestion of gluten foods (wheat, oats, rye, barley).
Symptoms: Wasting of muscles, weight loss, flatulence, loss of appetite, distension, fat in the faeces, large pale frothy stools, vitamin and mineral deficiencies.
Alternatives. *Teas*: Alfalfa, Agrimony, Gotu Kola, Meadowsweet, Red Clover, Oats.
Decoctions: Irish Moss, Dandelion root, Fenugreek seeds, Bayberry bark. Calamus or Gentian, in cold infusion.
Formula. Dandelion 1; Echinacea 2; Saw Palmetto 1; few grains Cayenne or drops Tincture Capsicum. Dose: Liquid Extracts: 1 teaspoon. Tinctures: 1-2 teaspoons. Powders: 500mg (two 00 capsules or one-third teaspoon). Thrice daily.
Irish Moss, strengthening. Echinacea to sustain natural powers of resistance.
Diet. Gluten-free. Soya products. Avoid dairy products. Slippery Elm gruel.
Vitamins: B-complex, B1, B6, B12, Folic acid, PABA, C, E.
Minerals: Calcium, Iron, Copper, Zinc.

MALARIA. Notifiable disease. The world's No 1 public health enemy. Affects 108 nations. Still kills millions of people each year. Probably has claimed more lives than all the wars of history. In the 1960s was believed to have been eradicated but has made a dramatic reappearance due to the malaria-carrying mosquito's resistance to insecticides. Few modern drugs have proved a match for malaria; quinine drugs of proven reliability still used. Quinine (Peruvian bark) has a history of safety and efficacy.
The disease is transmitted by the anopheles protozoa. Old cases present with fever, jaundice, diarrhoea and confusion.
Symptoms: incubation 2-5 weeks. Onset sudden, with shivering and high fever (104°F), headache, vomiting. Symptoms recur every 2-3 days. Blood sample examination confirms.
Treatment. Drugs once useful in the fight against malaria are losing their effectiveness. Drug resistance becomes a major problem; in which case the remedies of antiquity have something to offer.
Alternatives. Yarrow was once regarded as the Englishman's Quinine. Nettle tea (*Dr Compton Burnett*). Prickly Ash (*Ellingwood*). Barberry, Chiretta, Peruvian bark BHP (1983). Mountain Grape (Berberis aquifolium) (*Ellingwood*). Wild Indigo, cases of extreme prostration (*Dr Wm Boericke*).
Sweet Wormwood. The Chinese Qing Hao (Artemisia annua) proved beneficial for millennia before Quinine arrived on the scene. Its re-discovery by Professor Nelson is declared 'very effective'.
Formula. Liquid Extracts: Boneset 1; Yarrow 1; Barberry half; Valerian half. Few drops Tincture Capsicum. Dose: 1-2 teaspoons every 2 hours.
Malaria was rife in parts of America, especially Arkansus. During the Civil War it was difficult to obtain Quinine and various alternatives were tried. Where symptoms of chills and intermittent fever presented, Gelsemium gained considerable reputation as a substitute, also as a preventative. A favourite prescription was three drops tincture in a little brandy every 2-3 hours before the chill, and repeated every hour.
Dr M.H. Grannell, Sinaloa, Mexico. "I do not doubt that I treat more malaria than any other five physicians in the United States. My sole remedy, unless other indications present themselves, is Gelsemium. I give the following with never-failing results: 30 drops Tincture Gelsemium in 4oz water. Dose: 1 teaspoon hourly." (*Ellingwood, June 1920*)
Thomas Nuttall, botanist. In 1819, when on tour in Arkansus, relieved a malarial attack with decoction of Boneset.
David Hoffman, MNIMH. 1 teaspoon Peruvian bark in each cup boiling water; infuse 30 minutes. Thrice daily.
Diet. 3-day fast.
Treatment by or in liaison with a general medical practitioner.

MALE FERN. *Dryopteris filix-mas, L. German*: Wurm-Schildfarn. *French*: Fougère mâle. *Spanish*: Polypodio. *Italian*: Felche maschia. Frond bases and buds of the rhizome, collected in the autumn.
Constituents: filicin, triterpenes, resins, volatile oil.
Action: taenifuge, vermifuge, deobstruent.
Uses: tapeworms (*Traditional*). Treatment is taken fasting under medical supervision. Dr C. Hering advised an ounce of the grated root, gathered fresh, to be taken in the morning, the tapeworm usually making a speedy exit by the afternoon. Present-day dosage is much less: quarter to half an ounce taken over a longer period and mixed with a demulcent (i.e. Slippery Elm).
Dioscorides was aware of its power to induce abortion and infertility. Reported use by Chinese for tumours.
Preparations. Extract Filicis, BP. Dose: 3-6ml.
Powder: dose, 1-10 grams. Male Fern capsules BP (1958).
Note: Today seldom used. Of historical interest.

MALIGNANT. That which has a tendency to become worse. A tumour that destroys tissue in which it originates and tends to spread to another site. See: CANCER.

MALLOW, Common. High mallow. *Malva sylvestris, L. Parts used*: flowers, herb.
Constituents: mucilage, malvin, flavonal glycosides.
Action: mucilaginous, antitussive, emollient, children's laxative. Phagocyte stimulant, immune enhancer, antibacterial, laxative.
Uses: Respiratory ailments and the common cold. Coughs and irritation of the bronchi. Inflammation of mouth or throat Being a demulcent, the peeled root was once used by infants for teething troubles. Chinese eat leaves boiled as spinach.
Preparations. Thrice daily.
Tea: 1 teaspoon to cup boiling water; infuse 15 minutes. Half-1 cup.
Tincture: 1 part to 5 parts 45 per cent alcohol; macerate 8 days, shaking daily, filter. 30-60 drops in water.
Powder: capsules, 190mg. 2 capsules 4 times daily between meals. (*Arkocaps*)

MALNUTRITION. See: MALABSORPTION.

MANAGER'S STRESS. All in charge of other people are subject to a wide range of environmental stress, working conditions, conflict with superiors. Some are more predisposed to stress than others.
Alternatives. Ginseng, Valerian. Skullcap, Oats, Gotu Kola.
Tea. Skullcap 1; Oats 2; Valerian half. Mix. 1 teaspoon to each cup boiling water. 1 cup as desired.
Life Drops. Few drops in tea.
Lime flower tea, at night.
Ginkgo. For brain fatigue.
Diet. Avoid strong tea, coffee, alcohol.

MANDRAKE, AMERICAN. May apple. *Podophyllum peltatum L.* Dried root or rhizome. For practitioner use only.
Constituents: flavonoids, lignans, gums, resin.
Action: slow-acting purgative, hepatic, hydragogue, cholagogue, alterative, emetic, "vegetable mercury". Internal use has been superceded by less violent purgatives. Continues in use as an anti-neoplastic.
Uses: "a cure-rate of 76 per cent was achieved in 68 patients with carcinoma by treatment, twice daily for 14 days with an ointment consisting of Podophyllum resin 20 per cent, and Linseed oil 20 per cent in lanolin, followed by antibiotic treatment . . . In 14 patients treated with Podophyllotoxin 5 per cent in a Linseed oil/lanolin base, the cure rate was 80 per cent. There was no evidence of systemic toxicity." (*F.R. Bettley, Br.J. Derm. 1971. 84,74*)

One-time treatment as a paint for soft venereal and other warts.
Preparations. *Liquid Extract*: 0.3ml in water, twice daily.
Tincture Podophyllum BPC 1934: dose, 0.3 to 4ml.
Powder. Dusting powder for malignant ulceration.
Paint of Podophyllin Compound, BPC. Contains 14.6 per cent of Podophyllum resin in compound Benzoin tincture. For external use. POM

MANGANESE. Trace element. RDA 2.5mg.
Deficiency. Bone diseases.
Body effects. Bone health.
Sources. Tea. Wholegrains, oatmeal, avocados, nuts, seeds, pulses, bananas, beans, beets, kale, lettuce, oatmeal, peas, prunes, brown rice, spinach, calves liver.
Note. Excess may cause injury to the brain.

MANGO LEAVES. *Part used*: leaves. Contains Mangiferin.
Action: anti-viral.
Uses. Herpes simplex virus (HSV-1).

MANNA. "Bread of Heaven" *Tamarix mannifera*, ehr. Believed to be the food of the Old-Testament Israelites during their 40 years wanderings through the wilderness. "Even to this day a "manna" falls like dew or hoar frost and lands like beads on grass, stones and twigs. It is sweet like honey and sticks to the teeth. A secretion exuded from the tamarisk trees and bushes when pierced by a certain kind of plant-louse or small insect which lives off the tree indigenous to Sinai. They exude a kind of resinous exudation the shape and size of a coriander seed. When it falls to the ground it is white in colour but later becomes a yellowish browny. When left a long time it solidifies, tastes like honey, and is an exportable commodity. Carefully preserved it is the perfect 'iron ration' keeping indefinitely as discovered by the Arabs since biblical times." (*Dr Werner Keller, "The Bible as History", Pub: Hodder and Stoughton*)

MANUFACTURING. Criteria for manufacture of herbal preparations are efficacy, safety and purity. To ensure Government requirement, manufacturers test all incoming crude material by first placing it in quarantine, an area specially set aside for quality control. Material is inspected against standard samples by sight, taste, touch and microscopic analysis. Samples are taken for chemical reaction in a laboratory equipped for this purpose.

Herbal preparations are required to meet the same high pharmaceutical standards as conventional medicine.

Today's exacting standards ensure an absence of sugar, yeast, gluten, milk derivatives, cornstarch, wheat, artificial colours, flavours, and preservatives.

The Department of Health expects manufacturers to standardise active constituents where possible and to ensure purity by eliminating from crude material pesticide residues, aflatoxins and heavy metal contaminants. Chromotography, in one of its forms (thin-layer, gas or high-pressure liquid) are used to assess purity, potency, accurate identity and contamination by lead, cadmium, etc. A Geiger-counter reveals the presence or absence of radio-activity. Each plant has its own signature or 'fingerprint' showing density and other important characteristics.

Failure to meet Government requirements empowers a purchaser to return the whole consignment to the supplier. Thus, a high standard of manufacturing practice is maintained.

See: *Medicines Act leaflet 39, Revised Guidelines DHSS Nov 1985*

MARASMUS. Same treatment as for MALABSORPTION.

MARBURG DISEASE. A severe infection by virus encephalitis, originating in Africa. A notifiable disease. Rapidly fatal, requiring immediate hospitalisation. The powerful anti-viral, Echinacea, should prove of value together with recommendations as for meningitis for limited relief of symptoms.

MARFAN'S SYNDROME. A collagen disease in infants (hereditary) with lax joints permitting easy dislocation and strain.
Features: long fingers and arm span, high palate, kyphosis, etc.
Symptoms. Backache, pain in joints, dislocations.
Alternatives. Alfalfa, Fenugreek, Irish Moss, Kelp, Horsetail, Marshmallow, Bamboo gum.
Teas. Alfalfa, Comfrey leaves, Horsetail, Plantain, Silverweed. Any one: 1 heaped teaspoon to each cup boiling water; infuse 10-15 minutes. 1 cup thrice daily.
Decoction. Fenugreek seeds 2; Horsetail 1; Bladderwrack 1; Liquorice half. Prepare: 3 heaped teaspoons to 1 pint (500ml) water gently simmered 10 to 20 minutes. 1 wineglass thrice daily.
Fenugreek seeds decoction.
Diet. High protein, oily fish.
Supplements. Calcium, Dolomite, Zinc.

MARIGOLD. Pot marigold. *Calendula officinalis L. German*: Ringelblume. *French*: Souci des Jardins. *Spanish*: Calendula. *Italian*: Calendola. Dried florets. One of the most versatile and important herbal medicines. This is the same Calendula as used by the homoeopaths but the method of preparation and therapy is different. Contains high levels of nitrogen, phosphoric acid and Vitamin A.
Keynote: injuries. Not the same plant as French Marigold (*Tagetes patula*).
Constituents: volatile oil, flavonoids, triterpenes.
Action: immune stimulant, anti-protazoal, anti-inflammatory, anti-fungal, anti-spasmodic, anti-haemorrhage, anti-histamine, anti-bacterial effect particularly against staphylococcus and streptococcus, anti-emetic, anti-cancer, antiseptic, styptic, haemostatic, diaphoretic, anthelmintic, oestrogenic activity (extract from fresh flowers), menstrual regulator.
Uses. *Internal*. A remedy which should follow all surgical operations. Enlarged and inflamed lymphatic glands, gastric and duodenal ulcer, jaundice, gall bladder inflammation, absent or painful menstruation, balanitis, rectum – inflammation of, gum disease, nose-bleeds, sebaceous cysts, measles (cup of tea drunk freely), pneumonia – a cooling drink which is anti-inflammatory. Vaginal thrush.
Uses. *External*. Rapid epithelisation process in damaged skin tissue, especially alcoholic extract; rapid wound adhesion and granulation without suppuration. (*Weleda*)

Wounds where the skin has been broken: laceration with bleeding (Arnica for unbroken skin). Sores, leg ulcers, abscess etc. Sore nipples in nursing mothers, varicose veins, nosebleeds, grazed knees in schoolchildren. Bee, wasp and other insect stings. Chilblains, fistula, inflamed nails, whitlow, dry chapped skin and lips, wind burn, air pollution.
Dentistry: Tooth extractions: rinse mouth with infusion of the florets or much-diluted tincture – 5-10 drops in water.
Malignancy: strong tea, 1-2oz to 1 pint boiling water; use as a wash to cleanse exudations.
STD purulent discharge: inject douche of strong infusion as above.
Wm M. Gregory MD, Berea, Ohio, USA. "I have never seen one drop of pus develop in any wound, however dirty."
Preparations. For internal or external use. Average dose, 1-4 grams, or equivalent. Thrice daily.
Tea: dried petals/florets. 1-2 teaspoons to each cup boiling water; infuse 15 minutes. Drink freely.
Home tincture. 1 handful petals/florets (approximately 50g) to 1 pint (500ml) 70 per cent alcohol (Vodka); stand 14 days in a warm place, shake daily. Filter. Dose: 5-20 drops in water.
Poultice. Handful petals/florets to 1 pint boiling water; infuse 15 minutes. Apply on suitable material to injuries where skin is broken; replenish when dry.
Herbalist's Friend. 1 part Tincture Calendula to 4 parts Witch Hazel, for phlebitis and painful varicose veins.
Weleda. Calendula lotion locally, or as a mouth wash and gargle. GSL

MARJORAM. Sweet marjoram. *Origanum vulgare. Origanum majorana L. German*: Diptam. *French*: Amaraque. *Spanish*: Mejorana. *Iranian*: Mirzan gush. *Italian*: Amaraco. *Indian*: Kame phatusa. Herb.

Constituents: miscellaneous acids, flavonoids, volatile oil.
Action: Gastro-intestinal stimulant, anaphrodisiac, expectorant, emmenagogue, rubifacient. Mild antiseptic because of its thymol content, diuretic, carminative, diaphoretic, antispasmodic (mild), antiviral, anti-stress.
Uses: aid to digestion, coughs, colds, influenza, antiseptic mouth wash and gargle, tension headache, masturbation in the young, to promote menstrual flow suppressed by cold.
Preparations. Thrice daily.
Tea: 1-2 teaspoons to each cup boiling water; infuse 15 minutes. Half-1 cup.
Aromatherapy: 4 to 6 drops Oil of Marjoram added to 2 teaspoons Almond oil as a rub for muscular pains, neuritis, sprains and rheumatic aches.
Widely used in cooking. Avoid in pregnancy. Marjoram is related to Oregano but is sweeter and milder.

MARSHMALLOW. Schloss tea. Guimauve tea. *Althaea officinalis L. German*: Malve. *French*: Guimauve. *Spanish*: Malvavisco. *Italian*: Malvavisce. *Iranian and Indian*: Gul-Khairu. *Chinese*: K'uei. Dried peeled root. *Keynote*: anti-mortification.
Constituents: mucilage, flavonoids, tannins, scopoletin.
Action. Soothing demulcent, emollient, nutrient, alterative, antilithic, antitussive, vulnerary, diuretic. Old European remedy of over 2,000 years.
Uses: Inflammation of the alimentary canal, kidneys, bladder. Ulceration of stomach and duodenum, hiatus hernia, catarrh of respiratory organs and stomach, dry cough open wounds – to cleanse and heal, cystitis, diarrhoea, septic conditions of moderate severity. Plant supplies an abundance of mucilage for protection of mucous membranes of the mouth, nose and urinary tract in the presence of stone. A poultice or ointment is applied topically to boils, abscesses, ulcers and old wounds to draw effete matter to the surface before expulsion from the body.
Combinations. With Comfrey and Cranesbill (American) for peptic ulceration. With White Horehound, Liquorice and Coltsfoot for pulmonary disease.
Preparations. Average dose, 2-5 grams dried root. Thrice daily. For best results plant should not be boiled.
Cold decoction. Half-1 teaspoon shredded root or powder to each cup cold water; stand overnight. Dose, half-1 cup. Also used externally as a douche for inflamed eyes.
Liquid Extract BHP (1983). 1:1 in 25 per cent alcohol. Dose, 2-5ml.
Tincture. 1 part root to 5 parts alcohol (25 per cent). Dose: 5-15ml.
Traditional 'Drawing' ointment: Marshmallow and Slippery Elm.
Ointment (home): 5 per cent powdered root in an ointment base. See: OINTMENTS.
Poultice. Bring powdered root to the boil in milk; add a little Slippery Elm, apply. GSL

MARTINDALE, THE EXTRA PHARMACOPOEIA. The world's most comprehensive source of drug information in a single volume. Provides an accurate and concise summary of the properties, actions, and uses of plant and other medicines in clinical use. All information evaluated by expert editorial staff of the Pharmaceutical Society of Great Britain.

MASSAGE. For relief of cramp, back and skeletal pain, constipation, insomnia or lift a mood. To stimulate the lymph circulation.
Massage oils. (1) Oil Eucalyptus 13 per cent; Oil Scots pine 9 per cent; Camphor 3 per cent; Sunflower oil 75 per cent. (*Dr Alfred Vogel*)
(2) Tincture Capsicum; essential oils of Camphor. Thyme, Cajeput, Terebinth, in a base of Sunflower seed oil. (*David Williams*)
(3) *Rheumatism*. 1 drop Oil Juniper; 2 drops Oil Rosemary; 1 drop Oil Sassafras. Two teaspoons Almond oil. Massage affected muscles and joints and cover with a moist hot towel 2-3 times daily.
(4) *Backache*. 30 drops Oil Rosemary; 20 drops Oil Peppermint; 10 drops Oil Eucalyptus; 10 drops Oil Mustard: 20 drops Oil Juniper; 50 drops Tincture Cayenne (Capsicum). Mix. Shake briskly; store in a cool place. Heat and apply warm. The old Golden Fire oil.
(5) *Aromatherapy*. It is usual practice to combine 6 drops essential oil to 10ml (2 teaspoons) Almond or other vegetable oil. Anti-inflammatory and pain-easing combination: Lavender, Thyme, Hypericum and Yarrow.
(6) *European traditional*. Oil Camphor 7; Oil Cloves 2; Oil Wintergreen 3; Oil Eucalyptus 3; Oil Origanum 3. Mix. General purposes: pain, stiffness, backache, sciatica, lumbago.
(7) Olbas oil.
(8) Weleda Massage oil (Arnica, Lavender and Rosemary).
Tonic. Gently thump the centre of the chest seven times with the closed fist to stimulate the thymus gland, activate the immune system and help loosen congestion in the lungs.
Note. Massage also has a beneficial effect upon the mind. The sense of touch helps release physical and emotional tensions and has a place in mental health and well-being.
Lymphatic massage. A specific form of massage concentrated on the lymph glands to stimulate their activity and assist expulsion of toxins from the body.
Massage should never be carried out on patients with thrombosis and blood-clotting problems, varicose veins or inflammation of the veins.

MASTECTOMY. See: BREAST.

MASTERWORT. *Peucedanum ostruthium (L.) Koch. Imperatoria ostruthium L. German*: Meisterwurz. *French*: Benzoin Francais. *Italian*: Imperatoria. *Part used*: rhizome.
Constituents: flavonoids, furocoumarins, oil.
Action: antispasmodic, carminative, gastric stimulant, aromatic, expectorant, bitter, diaphoretic.
Uses. Indigestion and flatulence, loss of appetite, asthma, bronchial catarrh, menstrual pain, migraine relief.
Preparations. Thrice daily.
Tea. 1oz to 1 pint boiling water; infuse 15 minutes. Dose, half-1 cup, thrice daily.
Liquid Extract: 1-2 teaspoons in water. GSL

MASTITIS. See: BREAST.

MASTODYNIA. Pain in the breast.
Tea: equal parts, Agnus Castus and Balm. 2 teaspoons to each cup boiling water; infuse 15 minutes; 1 cup 2-3 times daily or when necessary.
Liquid Extract. Blue Cohosh BHP (1983) 1:1 in 70 per cent alcohol; dose 7-15 drops.

MASTOIDITIS. An infection of the mastoid bone behind the ear, with possible destruction of bone. Usually due to extension of infection (streptococcal, etc) from the middle ear (otitis media) when that condition is wrongfully or neglectfully treated.
Symptoms: Mastoid bone behind the ear is tender to touch. Feverishness, red flush over mastoid area, deafness with throbbing earache, malaise, heavy discharge from the ear through perforated eardrum.
Diagnostic sign: pinna (external ear) is displaced.
Treatment. *Indicated*: anti-microbials, anti-bacterials, alteratives with nervines as supportives.
Yarrow tea.
Decoction. Combine: Echinacea 3; Wild Indigo 2; Poke root 1. 1 teaspoon to each cup water gently simmered 20 minutes. Half-1 cup every 2 hours with pinch of Cayenne.
Formula. Echinacea 2; Wild Indigo 1; Pulsatilla 1; few grains of Cayenne or Tincture Capsicum drops. Dose: Liquid Extracts: 30-60 drops (2-4ml). Tinctures: 4-8ml. Powders: 500mg (two 00 capsules or one-third teaspoon). Every 2 hours according to age. Children under 5 years – one-quarter dosage; under 12 years – half dosage.
Vitamin C. Copious fluids: fruit juices. Yarrow tea.
Topical. Goldenseal Ear Drops. Oil of Mullein, Sage or Lavender. Gentle massage with Tea Tree oil or Rosemary oil around the mastoid bone and in front of the ear 3/4 times daily.

Treatment by or in liaison with a general medical practitioner.

MASTURBATION. Stimulation of a person's own genitals to induce orgasm. Treatment also for NOCTURNAL EMISSION.
Alternatives. Anaphrodisiacs. Agnus Castus (female specific). Black Willow, Lady's Slipper, Oatstraw, Thuja, Sweet Marjoram (*Dr Wm Boericke*).
Tea: Combine equal parts: Agnus Castus, Valerian, Oats. 1 heaped teaspoon to each cup boiling water; infuse 15 minutes. Thrice daily.
Decoction: Combine Black Willow 2; Valerian 1. 1 teaspoon to cup water simmered gently 20 minutes. Half cup thrice daily.
Tablets/capsules. Agnus Castus, Passiflora, Valerian, Thuja.
Formula. Black Willow 2; Agnus Castus 1; Valerian half. Dose: Liquid Extracts: 1-2 teaspoons. Tinctures: 2-3 teaspoons. Powders: 750mg (three 00 capsules or half a teaspoon). Once or twice daily.
To arrest mental and physical deterioration: Wood Betony, Black Cohosh root, Hops, Cayenne, Skullcap, Lady's Slipper.
Vitamins. B-complex. B6. B12. Folic acid.
Minerals. Calcium. Magnesium. Phosphorus.

MATE TEA. Yerba mate. Paraguay tea. Jesuit's Brazil tea. *Ilex paraguariensis*, Hook. *Keynote*: Reviver. Dried leaves.

National drink of Paraguay and Brazil. Less astringent and contains less tannin than ordinary tea. Contains caffeine, but regarded as a good substitute for ordinary tea.
Action: stimulant to the brain and nervous system. Anti-rheumatic, diuretic. General tonic, mild antispasmodic, assists elimination of uric acid.
Uses. Physical exhaustion from stress. Rheumatism, gout. Nervous headache (*Fletcher Hyde*).
Preparations. Average dose, 1-4 grams. Thrice daily.
Tea: 1-2 teaspoons to each cup boiling water; infuse 10 minutes. Freely.
Liquid Extract (seldom used): 1 teaspoon in water, as necessary. GSL

MATERIA MEDICA. The science which deals with the source, origin, distribution, composition, preparation and action of medicinal plants used in herbalism. Although the modern herbalist no longer forages his own herbs from fields and hedgerows, a knowledge of materia medica is important.

"Crudes" are mostly imported from abroad, cut fine, and sold by skilled suppliers or druggists to herb shops for sale in their native state or for compounding into preparations by practitioners.

The art of preparing medicines is known as pharmacy; that of herbal medicine is often referred to as biopharmacy or "green pharmacy".

There are certain disadvantages of buying crude material from other than specialist sources; the risk of stale or otherwise inactive material is one.

An accredited manufacturer will compound materials according to a fixed formula published in an official pharmacopoeia. A practitioner writes his prescription which he compounds himself or gives it to an assistant who acts as a dispenser. This art of dispensing evolves as Herbal Pharmacy.

The traditional herbalist will endeavour to relieve a condition by giving a remedy which produces an opposite effect. For instance, a loose condition of the bowels, as in colitis, would be reversed by astringents; a 'tight' colon, as in some forms of constipation, would be relaxed by laxatives. They thus work to a system of cure known as *contraria contraribus curantur*.

Rational herbalism has evolved from a knowledge of the behaviour of disease patterns and an understanding of remedies used to combat them. Periwinkle (*Vinca*), for instance, kills off white blood cells over-produced in leukaemia without harming the body. Treatment of leukaemia with Vinca in the form of Vinplastine or other derivatives is therefore rational.

It is well-known that alkalies inhibit secretion of gastric juice. Hyper-acidity (over-secretion of acid) is the common cause of many forms of indigestion. A herbal pharmacopoeia describes effective plants with a positive alkaline action. Herbal alkalies are therefore rationally indicated.

Plant medicines obtain their objective by chemical means. During its life, a plant will take up from the soil various minerals from which it synthesises alkaloids, glycosides, saponins, etc, that are the real activators. Their strength depends upon the quality of soil on which they are grown.

MATICO. *Piper angustifolium*, R & P. Soldier's herb. *German*: Soldatenkraut. *French*: Herbe du soldat. *Italian*: Erba di soldato. *Part used*: leaves.
Constituents: resins, tannins, camphor oil.
Action: stimulant, astringent, anti-haemorrhage, urinary antiseptic, styptic, diuretic.
Uses: Copious mucous discharge, diarrhoea, piles, leucorrhoea. Bleeding from lungs, bowel or bladder.
Externally: styptic for healing wounds.
Preparations. Thrice daily.
Tea: 2-3 teaspoons to each cup boiling water; infuse 15 minutes; dose, half-1 cup.
Liquid Extract: 1-2 teaspoons in water.
Powder: dose, 2-8g.
Tincture BPC 1923: dose: 4-8ml.

MAYTENUS. Medicinal plant which produces maytansine, a substance with anti-cancer properties. "It is a well-known Japanese remedy," says Dr Rene Haller. "You grind up the stem, mix it with vaseline. Applied to skin cancers it is effective."

M.E. Myalgic encephalomyelitis. Chronic Fatigue Syndrome. See: MYALGIC ENCEPHALOMYELITIS.

MEADOWSWEET. Spireae ulmaria. *Filipendula ulmaria L. German*: Mädesüss. *French*: Ulmaire. *Spanish*: Ulmaria. *Italian*: Ulmaria. Leaves and stems. Contains salicin. The herbalist's bicarbonate of soda. Contains salicylic acid which has an aspirin (anti-thrombotic) effect on blood vessels.
Constituents: flavonoids, oil, phenolic glycosides.
Action: *antacid*, anti-rheumatic, stomachic, astringent, antiseptic (internal), diaphoretic, diuretic, hepatic, anti-ulcer, anti-inflammatory, mild urinary analgesic, anti-coagulant.

"A calming influence in an overactive digestive system." (*Simon Mills*)

Uses: effective symptomatic relief of indigestion and other upper gastro-intestinal conditions associated with flatulence and hyperacidity. Gastric ulcer, gastric reflux, liver disorder, summer diarrhoea in children, cystitis, rheumatism, foul breath. Red sandy deposits in the urine with an oily film on the surface. Arthrosis, chronic rheumatism, oedema, urinary stone, cellulitis.

Combines well with Goldenseal and Marshmallow for gastric ulcer. Balanced combination of antacids with anti-flatulent: Meadowsweet, Parsley and Black Horehound (equal parts as a tea).

Preparations. Average dose 2-6 grams dried herb or in infusion. Reduced dose for children and the elderly.
Tea: 1-2 teaspoons to each cup boiling water; infuse 15 minutes. Half-1 cup.
Liquid Extract BHC Vol 1. 1:1 in 25 per cent ethanol. Dose: 2-6ml.
Tincture BHC Vol 1: 1:5 in 25 per cent ethanol. Dose: 2 to 4ml.
Powder, capsules: 250mg. 2 capsules thrice daily before meals. (*Arkocaps*)

MEASLES. An acute contagious notifiable disease with catarrh of upper respiratory passages and watery eyes, characterised by papular eruption. Incubation: 1-2 weeks. Usually affects children. Common spring and autumn. Fever may reach 40°C (104°F), with coughing and sore throat. About two days before the rash, white spots (Koplik's spots) may appear in mouth, but which fade when rash disappears.
Rash: blotchy and orange-red. Commencing behind the ears, it rapidly invades the whole body.
Complications: inflammation of the middle ear, brain, and eyes.
Prophylactic: Pulsatilla.

A Danish study confirms that suppression of measles with drugs and vaccines can contribute to dermatitis, arthritis and cancer later in life.

Treatment by or in liaison with a general

medical practitioner.
Alternatives. Marigold petal tea popular: 2-6 teaspoons to 1 pint boiling water. Make in vacuum flask. Consume 1-2 flaskfuls daily.
Other teas. Lime flowers, Chamomile, Elderflowers and Peppermint, Vervain. Formula (France): equal parts, German Chamomile, Catmint, Thyme. 2 teaspoons to each cup boiling water; infuse 15 minutes. 1 cup freely. Children: 2-5 teaspoons each year to 5 years; quarter to half cup to 10 years.
Jethro Kloss. 1 teaspoon Pleurisy root; quarter of a teaspoon powdered Ginger. Steep in 1 pint boiling water. For hyperactive child, add 1 teaspoon Skullcap. Infuse 20 minutes. Dose: half-1 cup freely. Children: 2-5 teaspoons each year to 5 years; quarter to half cup to 10 years.
Traditional. First give laxative to clear stomach and bowels. Then, bruise Houseleek, adding equal weight of honey. Dessertspoon every 2 hours. Cup of Balm tea assists reduction of temperature.
Topical. Wash with warm Elderflowers or Chamomile tea. Aloe Vera juice.
Aromatherapy. To inhale or for bath: Lavender essential oil.
Enema. Constipation. Injection of warm Chamomile tea.
Eyes. Impairment of sight possible. For inflamed eyes and lids bathe with warm Elderflowers or Chamomile tea.
Note. There is always debility and chilliness followed by a throwing out of the skin morbific materials. Diaphoretic drinks are important so that no undue stress is placed on the kidneys. These include teas of Yarrow, Lemon Balm, Lime flowers, Hyssop, Ginger, Elderflowers and Peppermint.
Tincture. Echinacea. Adults: 1 teaspoon. Child: 1 drop each year to 5; thereafter 2 drops each year to 12 years.
Diet. 3-day fast, if possible. No solid food. Abundant Vitamin C drinks, fruit juices. All cases should receive Vitamin A supplements, halibut liver oil. Foods rich in beta-carotene (carrots).

MEDICAL ACCIDENTS. Legal guidance sought by the sufferer when making claims against a doctor or health authority is available from: Action for Victims of Medical Accidents (AVMA), Bank Chambers, 1 London Road, Forest Hill, London SE23 3TP.

MEDICINE. Definition:– "A substance or combination of substances presented for treating or preventing disease; or with a view to making a medical diagnosis or to restoring, correcting or modifying physiological functions." (*Directive EC 65/65*)

Take medicines as instructed by the practitioner. Never take the contents of unlabelled bottles or cartons. Never share prescribed medicines with other people. Never transfer medicines from one container to another. Keep all medicines out of the reach of children.

MEDICINE'S ACT, 1968. An enabling Act allowing subsequent definitive statutory instruments to be issued at the discretion of the Medicines Control Agency. The Act controls all aspects of the sale of medicines in the United Kingdom; with no exceptions.

Medicines fall into three categories: POM (Prescription Only Medicines), P (Pharmacy Only), and OTC (Over The Counter). POM and P medicines must be prescribed by a registered medical practitioner and dispensed by a pharmacist. P medicines can be sold only by a registered pharmacist. Health stores are concerned with the OTC products, the sale of which is governed by S.I. Medicines General Sales List, Order 1980, No 1922.

All medicines and substances used as medicine bearing a medicinal claim on label or advertising material must be licenced. Without a licence it is not lawful for any person, in his business, to manufacture, sell, supply, export, or import into the United Kingdom any medicinal products unless some exemption is provided in the Act or subsequent regulations. The prefix ML, followed by the Manufacturer's number must appear on the label together with the product licence number prefixed by the capitals PL. For example, if any person other than a pharmacist sells a medicinal product which claims to relieve indigestion or headache, but the label of which bears no licence number, that shopkeeper (and the manufacturer) will be breaking the law.

All foods are exempt from licencing provided no claims are made of medicinal benefits.

A special licence (manufacturer's) is required by any person who manufactures or assembles a medicinal product. (*Section 8*) He must hold a Product Licence for every product he manufactures unless some special exemption is provided by the Act. He may of course act to the order of the product licence holder. (*Section 23*)

"*Manufacture*" means any process carried on in the course of making a product but does not include dissolving or dispersing the product in, or diluting or mixing it with some other substance used as a vehicle for the purpose of administering it. It includes the mixture of two or more medicinal products.

"*Assembly*" means enclosing a medicinal product in a container which is labelled before the product is sold or supplied, or, where the product is already enclosed in a container in which it is supplied, labelling the container before the product is sold or supplied in it. (*Section 132*)

From the practitioner's point of view, herbal medicines are exempt from the Act and no licence is required.

The consulting herbalist in private practice who compounds his own preparations from medicinal substances may apply to the Medicines Control Agency, 1 Nine Elms Lane, London SW8 5NQ for a manufacturer's licence to authorise mixture and assembly, for administration to their patients after he has been requested in their presence to use his own judgement as to treatment required. Products thus sold, will be without any written recommendation and not advertised in any way.

The "assembly" aspect of his licence refers to his ability to buy in bulk, repackage and label. Where he uses prepackaged products and does not open the packet, or relabel, a licence is not required. He will not be able to use terms, "Stomach mixture", "Nerve mixture", etc, implying cure of a specific condition.

It is necessary for the practitioner to have a personal consultation with his patient before making his prescription. Subsequent treatment may be supplied by a third person or by post at the discretion of the practitioner.

A licence is required where one or more non-herbal ingredients (such as potassium iodide, sodium citrate, etc) are included. Dispensing non-herbal remedies constitutes "manufacture" for which a licence is required. (*MAL 24 (3)*)

The main thing the licensing authority looks for before granting a licence is evidence of safety. The manufacturers' premises must be licenced. A wholesaler or distributor, also, must have a licence.

Where a product is covered by a Product Licence certain medicinal claims may be made. Where claims are made, the Act requires a warning to appear on the label worded: "If you think you have the disease to which this product refers, consult a registered medical practitioner before taking this product. If you are already receiving medical treatment, tell your doctor you are also taking this product." (*SI 41,s.5*)

Labels of all medicines, tablets, etc, must carry the words: "Keep out of the reach of children".

Under the Act it is illegal for medicines to be offered for sale for cancer, diabetes, epilepsy, glaucoma, kidney disease, locomotor ataxy, paralysis, sexually transmitted diseases and tuberculosis; these diseases to be treated by a registered medical practitioner only.

Definition of a herbal remedy. A "herbal remedy" is a medicinal product consisting of a substance produced by subjecting a plant or plants to drying, crushing or any other process, or of a mixture whose sole ingredients are two or more substances so produced, or of a mixture whose sole ingredients are one or more substances so produced and water or some other inert substances. (*Section 132*)

No licence is required for the sale, supply, manufacture or assembly of any such herbal remedy in the course of a business in which the person carrying on the business sells or supplies the remedy for administration to a particular person after being requested by or on behalf of that person, and in that person's presence, to use his own judgement as to the treatment required. The person carrying on the business must be the occupier of the premises where the manufacture or assembly takes place and must be able to close them so as to exclude the public. (*Section 12 (1)*)

No licence is required for the sale, supply, manufacture or assembly of those herbal remedies where the process to which the plant or plants are subjected consists only of drying, crushing or comminuting and the remedy is sold or supplied under a designation which only specifies the plant or plants and the process and does not apply any other name to the remedy; and without any written recommendation (whether by means of a labelled container or package or a leaflet or in any other way) as to the use of the remedy. (*Section 12 (2)*) This exemption does not apply to imported products. Except where a herbal product is supplied for a medicinal use, legally it is not even a medicinal product.

The 1968 Act has been a great step forward in the history of herbal medicine, The British Herbal Medicine Association and the National Institute of Medical Herbalists fought and won many special concessions. In years following the Act standards rose sharply. Practitioners enjoy a measure of recognition, with power to manufacture and dispense their own medicines and issue official certificates for incapacitation for work.

See: BRITISH HERBAL MEDICINE ASSOCIATION. NATIONAL INSTITUTE OF MEDICAL HERBALISTS.

MEDITATION. Essential oils are used in prayer, zen, yoga or meditation to induce rest and reflection. Bergamot, Balm (Melissa), Sage, Lavender, Orange Blossom. Any one used as an inhalant or to anoint the forehead with a smear.

MEDITERRANEAN FEVER. An intermittent fever related to brucellosis. Colchicum. (*Martindale 27th Ed. p.370*)

See: BRUCELLOSIS.

MEIER, Beat. Privatdocent ETH, Dr sc nat Pharmacist. Head of R & D Dept at Zeller AG, Herbal Medicines, Romanshorn, Switzerland. Medical plant researcher at ETH, Department of Pharmacy, Zurich. Developed modern strategies for analysis of herbal medicines, especially in the field of HPLC. University teacher in pharmacognosy and phytochemistry. C/O Zeller AG, Ch-8590 Romanshorn, Switzerland.

MELAENA. Presence of blood in the faeces from bleeding in stomach or upper intestines due to ulceration, infection, aspirin or other drugs.

Symptom: black or tarry stools.
Alternatives. *Teas*: Nettles, Shepherd's Purse. American Cranesbill. Meadowsweet.
Decoctions: Beth root. Marshmallow root.
Formula. Cranesbill root 2; Echinacea 1; Goldenseal quarter. Dose: Liquid Extracts: 1 teaspoon. Tinctures: 2 teaspoons. Powders: 500mg (two 00 capsules or one-third teaspoon). In honey or water, thrice daily before meals.
Diet. 3-day fast.
Vitamins. C. K.
Minerals. Calcium. Iron. Zinc.

MELANOMA. See: CANCER – SKIN.

MELILOT. Sweet Clover. *Melilotus officinalis*, Willd. *German*: Steinklee. *French*: Couronne royale. *Spanish and Italian*: Meliloto. *Arabian*: Aklil-ul Malika. *Indian*: Iklil-ul-mulk. *Chinese*: Hsün-ts'ao. Dried flowering plant. *Keynote*: thrombosis.
Constituents: coumarin derivatives, flavonoids, tannin, dicoumarol (anticoagulant).
Practitioner use.
Action: aromatic, antispasmodic, anti-inflammatory, diuretic, expectorant, antibiotic (seeds). Contains Coumarin, an anticoagulant and antithrombotic. Sedative. Mild analgesic (leaves and flowers). Antiflatulent. Styptic, to arrest haemorrhage.
Uses: thrombosis, facial or intercostal neuralgia (compress), conjunctivitis (infusion as an eye douche), rheumatic aches and pains, wounds, externally, for the healing of, (compress). Swelling of lymph glands. Flatulent colic. Phlebitis, heavy legs, varicose veins, menopausal disorders, insomnia, nervousness.
Combines with Milk Thistle or Goldenseal.
Preparations. *Tea*: 1-2 teaspoons to each cup boiling water; infuse 15 minutes. Dose: half-1 cup, thrice daily. (Cold as an eye douche)
Powder. 375mg (quarter of a teaspoon).
Tincture. Dose: 3-5ml thrice daily.
Fomentation. Aches and pains.
Externally: herb pillow.
Contra-indications. Emetic in large doses. Should not be used without supplementation with Vitamin K. Not used in presence of Warfarin.

MEMORY, WEAK. Amnesia – from slightly impaired to complete loss. Forgetfulness associated with ageing, depression, alcoholism, low thyroid function, Alzheimer's disease.
Alternatives: to improve concentration.
Teas, Liquid extracts, tinctures or powders: Ginseng, Gotu Kola, Hawthorn (berries or blossoms), Holy Thistle, Horsetail, Kola nuts, Periwinkle (minor), <u>Rosemary</u>, Skullcap, Vervain, <u>Ginkgo</u>.
Ginkgo: impressive results reported.
Practitioner. Ephedra.
Supplements. B-complex, B6, B12, E. Phosphorus, Zinc.

MENARCHE. A girl's first menstrual period. Hormones from the pituitary gland stimulate the ovaries to produce oestrogen, the female sex hormone which initiates body changes towards maturity. There follows enlargement of the breasts and the appearance of pubic hair. Signs include listlessness, irritability, bloated feeling and emotional disturbances.

Where the menarche is delayed, Raspberry leaf tea or Chamomile tea may be all required. Other agents in general use: Mugwort, Pennyroyal, Ginseng, Kelp, Peppermint, Marjoram, Sage, Squaw Vine, Blue Cohosh.
Where long delayed. Formula. Motherwort 2; Helonias 2; add few grains powder or drops of tincture Ginger. Dose: Liquid Extracts: 1-4ml; Tinctures: 4-8ml; Powders: 500mg (two 00 capsules or one-third teaspoon) thrice daily in water or honey.
Diet. High fibre, low fat, low sugar.
Vitamins. B-complex, B6, C, E, F.
Minerals. Calcium, Iodine, Iron, Zinc.
Supportive. A mother's friendly advice helps allay anxiety in this dramatic change in a girl's life.

MENIERE'S DISEASE. Inner ear disorder. Constriction of cerebral blood vessels (vasospasm) increases pressure of fluids in the balancing mechanism. Ages 40-60; more in men.
Etiology. Obscure; though cases may be traced to auto-toxaemia, Vitamin B deficiency, menstruation, malaria drugs (chloroquine).
Symptoms: dizziness, nausea, vomiting, tinnitus, sound distortions, heavy sweating, loss of hearing; usually in one ear only. Early diagnosis essential for effective treatment. This may mean reference to a department of otolaryngology or otoneurology.
Treatment. Antispasmodics. Nervines. Sometimes a timely diuretic reduces severity – Uva Ursi, Dandelion root, Wild Carrot.
Alternatives. Current European practice: <u>Betony</u>, German Chamomile, <u>Passion flower</u>, Hawthorn, Hops, Feverfew, White Willow.
Tea. Combine, equal parts: Valerian, Wild Carrot, Agrimony. 2 teaspoons to each cup boiling water; infuse 15 minutes. Half-1 cup every 2 hours during attack; thrice daily thereafter.
Decoction. Mistletoe: 2 teaspoons to each cup cold water steeped overnight. Bring to boil. Allow to cool. Half-1 cup, as above.
Tablets/capsules. Feverfew, Mistletoe, Prickly Ash.
Formula. Ginkgo 2; Dandelion 1; Black Cohosh 1. Dose: Liquid Extracts: 1 teaspoon. Tinctures: 2 teaspoons. Powders: 500mg (two 00 capsules or one-third teaspoon). Thrice daily.

Feverfew tincture. See: FEVERFEW.
Dr J. Christopher: inject into ears, at night, few drops oil of Garlic (or contents of Garlic capsule).
Cider vinegar. 2 teaspoons to glass water: as desired.
Aromatherapy. Inhalants: Eucalyptus or Rosemary oils.
Diet: gluten-free, low salt; good responses observed. High fibre. Avoid dairy products and chocolate.
Vitamins: B-complex, B1; B2; B6; E; F. Brewer's yeast, Niacin.
Minerals: Calcium. Magnesium. Phosphorus. Dolomite.

MENINGITIS. Cerebrospinal fever. Inflammation of the pia mater and arachnoid covering of the brain and spinal cord. A notifiable disease. Hospitalisation. Diagnosis is difficult without a lumbar puncture. Caused by a wide range of virus, bacteria, protozoa and fungi. Three most common bacterial causes in England and Wales are N. Meningotidis, H. influenzae and streptococcus-like infection with sore throat; then fever, vomiting, headache and mental confusion; half-open eyes when asleep, delirium, sensitive to light, possibly drifting into coma. Sometimes onset is gradual over 2-3 weeks. Treatment by hospital specialist.

Poor housing and passive smoking suspected. Its association with non-germ meningitis, and inflammatory drugs is well recognised. Also caused by injury or concussion.

Commence by cleansing bowel with Chamomile enema.
Cerebrospinal relaxants indicated: Passion flower (cerebral), Black Cohosh (meningeal), Ladyslipper (spinal meningeal). (*A.W. & L.R. Priest*)

If patient is cold, give Cayenne pepper in honey to promote brisk circulation.
Aconite and Gelsemium. "For irritation of the meninges of the brain and spinal cord *Aconite* is indispensible. Combined with Gelsemium for restlessness it is an exceptional remedy. Tincture Aconite (5-15 drops) with Gelsemium (3-10 drops) hourly. Also used in combination with other agents as may be dictated by the course of the disease. (*W.W. Martin MD., Kirksville, Mo., USA*)
Crawley root. Decoction: 1 teaspoon to half a pint water, simmer 20 minutes. Dose: 1 teaspoon or more 3-4 times daily for children over 6 months. A powerful diaphoretic and sedative. (*Dr Baker, Adrian, Michigan, USA*)
Lobelia and Echinacea. Equal parts, Liquid Extract 30 drops in water every 3 hours. (*Dr Finlay Ellingwood*)
Lobelia, alone. Hypodermic injections of Lobelia in five cases of epidemic spinal meningitis, with complete recovery in every case. Dose: 10 drops hourly until symptoms abate, then twice daily. (*Dr A.E. Collyer, Ellingwood Therapeutist*)
Ecclectic School. Echinacea commended.
Before the Doctor comes. As onset is rapid, often less than 5 hours, an anti-inflammatory is justified. Teas or decoctions from any of the following: Catmint (Catnep), Prickly Ash berries, Pleurisy root, Boneset, Wild Cherry bark, Bugleweed (Virginian), Ladyslipper. When temperature abates and patient feels better: Chamomile tea or cold Gentian decoction with pinch Cayenne.
Hydrotherapy. Hot baths make patient feel worse. Sponge down with cold water.
Protective throat spray: equal parts, Tincture Myrrh and Tincture Goldenseal.
Protective gargle: 10-20 drops Tincture Myrrh and Goldenseal to glass of water.
Garlic. Dr Yan Cai, Department of Neurology, Ren Ji Hospital (affiliated to Shanghai Second Medical University), China, referred to the extensive use of Garlic in Chinese folk medicine and his hospital's experience with Garlic products – diallyl trisulphide in particular – to treat viral infections including crypotococcal meningitis for which disease results were impressive.

Garlic appears to be a reliable preventative.
Diet. Fast as long as temperature is elevated; with fruit juices, red beet juice, carrot juice or herb teas.
Note. GPs and other practitioners may help stop meningitis claiming lives by giving massive doses of Echinacea before they are admitted to hospital.
Note. The infection is often difficult to diagnose. At the end of each year (November and December) when the peak in cases approaches, every feverish patient with headache should be suspected, especially where accompanied by stiff neck.

The above entry is of historic interest only; more effective orthodox treatment being available.

MENOPAUSE. Conclusion of menstruation at the end of reproductive life – between the years 45-50 – and lasting about 4 years. Ovulation fails, hormonal activity wanes. Intervals between periods longer. Periods may stop gradually or suddenly and become scantier.
Symptoms. Not all present at once. Hot flushes, weight gain, depression, urinary frequency, headaches, backache, painful breasts, vaginal discomfort, cannot sleep or concentrate and gets irritable. Cries easily. Poor sexual response.

The hot sweats must not be misdiagnosed. They may be due to an over-worked thyroid gland which requires Kelp, Bugleweed. Palpitations may be due to tachycardia – see: CARDIO-VASCULAR AGENTS: Hawthorn, Lily of the Valley, Motherwort, etc. Tiredness often points to anaemia – see: ANAEMIA.

Oestrogen deficiency predisposes to osteoporosis (weakening and softening of the bones), height loss. Increased flow, or spotting, after an interval of 6 months should be investigated. Excessive blood loss may be due to fibroids.
Alternatives. Herbs to enable women to adjust naturally to the menopause are many and varied. In general use: Agnus Castus (ovarian hormone precurser), Black Haw (Uterine relaxant), Broom (gentle diuretic and heart restorative), Clivers, Goldenseal, Helonias (ovarian hormone precurser), Lady's Mantle, Life root, Lime flowers, Marjoram, Motherwort, Nettles, Oats (nutrient), Parsley tea, Pennyroyal, Raspberry leaves, Skullcap (tension), St John's Wort (anxiety), Valerian (nervous excitability).
For menopausal flooding, see: MENORRHAGIA.
Hot flushes: see entry.
With circulatory disorders, add Rosemary.
Alternative formulae. *Teas*. (1) Motherwort and Raspberry leaves. (2) Lady's Mantle, Lime flowers, Yarrow. (3) Raspberry leaves, Broom, Clivers. Place 1 heaped teaspoon in each cup boiling water; infuse 15 minutes; 1 cup thrice daily. (4) Sage tea. (*Chinese traditional*)
Vitamin E. Hot flushes and circulatory distress.
Evening Primrose oil capsules.
Formula. Agnus Castus 2; Black Haw 1; Valerian half. Dose: Liquid Extracts: 1 teaspoon. Tinctures: 2 teaspoons. Powders: 500mg (two 00 capsules or one-third teaspoon). Thrice daily.
Diet. Infrequency of hot flushes and other menopausal symptoms in Japanese women are believed to be related to their Soya-rich diet, Soya containing isoflavonoids which are similar to human oestrogen. Avoid coffee. Reduce tea, Cola drinks, Alcohol.
Vitamins. The condition makes heavy demands upon the vitamin reserves. C, 1g morning and evening. E, 500iu morning and evening. B-complex, B6.
Minerals. Calcium helps reduce risk of fracture, particularly in menopausal women who may increase their intake to 800mg daily – calcium citrate malate being more effective than the carbonate. Dried milk powder contains high percentage of Calcium.

MENORRHAGIA. Abnormally heavy menstrual bleeding; more than normal flow and lasting longer.
Causes: iron deficiency, shock, thyroid gland disturbance, ovarian insufficiency, prolapse, polypi, fibroids, congestion of the womb, or failure of the blood to coagulate – for which coagulants and Vitamin K are indicated. Hormone imbalance. Use of intra uterine devices (IUD).
Symptoms: legs and hands cold, pale face, alternate heats and chills, loss of appetite, nervous exhaustion, pain in the back and loins.
General use. Uterine astringents.
Alternatives. Bayberry bark, Beth root, Black Haw, Blue Cohosh, Broom, Cranesbill (American), Goldenseal, Lady's Mantle, Life root, Periwinkle (greater), Raspberry leaves, Rhatany root, Shepherd's Purse, Yarrow. For reduction of menstrual flow without arrest.
Raspberry leaves. A gentle astringent tea for mild cases.
Agnus Castus. Heavy bleeding between periods.
Formula. Tea. Equal parts: Lady's Mantle, Raspberry leaves, Shepherd's Purse. 2 teaspoons to each cup boiling water; infuse 15 minutes. 1 cup freely.
Formula. Powders. Black Haw 3; Bayberry bark 3; Cinnamon 1. Dose: 750mg (three 00 capsules or half a teaspoon) 3-4 times daily.
For the severe case. Formula. Bur-marigold 2; Lady's Mantle 2; Beth root 1. Dose: Liquid Extracts: 1-2 teaspoons; Tinctures: 2-3 teaspoons; every 2 hours.
Prophylactic: Mistletoe, taken at least 14 days before period. For prolonged heavy loss, refer patient to a gynaecologist.
Diet. Vitamin K foods. Iron foods. Prunes. Kelp. Irish Moss.
Supplements. Daily. Vitamin A, 7,500iu, Vitamin C, 1g. Vitamin E, 200iu. Vitamin K, 5mcg. Bioflavonoids. Calcium. Iodine. Iron – Floradix.
Sitz bath. Has a toning effect upon the pelvic organs, arresting high blood loss. See: SITZ BATH.

MENSES: suppression of.
See: AMENORRHOEA.

MENSTRUAL CRAMP. Cramp in the womb. See: DYSMENORRHOEA.

MENSTRUAL HEADACHE. Menstrual migraine. Headache with lowering mood, muddled thinking, sluggish dopey feeling preceded by visual or sensory aura, dizziness, pain around eyes, persistent tiredness. These suggest underlying hypothalamic disturbance – a nerve-cause which, together with progesterone deficiency may trigger menstrual migraine.
Treatment. Uterine restoratives, nerve relaxants.
Formula. Tea. Equal parts: Raspberry leaves; Skullcap; Agnus Castus. 1 heaped teaspoon to each cup boiling water; infuse 5-15 minutes; drink freely.
Alternative formula. Agnus Castus 2; Black Cohosh 1. Dose: Liquid Extracts: 1-2 teaspoons. Tinctures: 2-3 teaspoons. Powders: 750mg (three 00 capsules or half a teaspoon). Thrice daily.
Feverfew: good results reported.
Evening Primrose oil capsules. 500mg thrice daily.
Sleep. One in two patients find relief in 'sleeping it off' any time of the day or night. Hot bath. Passion flower tea or tablets.

Diet. High fibre, low fat, low salt. Hot soup. A cooked meal but not with rich fatty or spicy foods. Oatmeal porridge.
Supplements. Vitamin B6. 50mg daily. Magnesium, Zinc.
Preventative: Raspberry leaf tea 3 days before periods.

MENSTRUATION. Periodic shedding of the lining of the womb during the reproductive years as a result of hormonal change. This natural body function is regulated by a delicate balance between hormones produced by the pituitary gland and the ovaries. The pituitary produces the follicle stimulating hormone (FSH), and the luteinizing hormone (LH) which stimulates the ovary to produce oestrogen and progesterone respectively.

The ovaries secrete oestrogen and progesterone. Oestrogen thickens the lining of the womb while the LH produces progesterone which prepares the lining of the womb for the fertilised egg. When fertilisation leading to pregnancy does not take place, the womb lining is shed in the process of menstruation and the cycle is repeated. This is a sign of adult womanhood.

Monthly periods begin about 12 years and continue for about 30 years, interrupted only by pregnancy, lactation or a uterine disorder. Disorders of menstruation include:
(1) Its absence or scanty periods (amenorrhoea).
(2) Painful, with cramps (dysmenorrhoea).
(3) Heavy blood loss (menorrhagia).
(4) Cessation of periods (menopause).
(5) Irregular.
(6) Pre-menstrual tension (PMT).
(7) Dysfunction because of fibroids, vaginal or cervical infection, or pressure from adjacent pelvic organs.
(8) Young girls beginning to menstruate (menarche).
(9) Bleeding from the womb when it is not due (metrorrhagia).

See appropriate entries.

Even in healthy menstruation a loss of blood means a loss of iron; therefore the diet should not be deficient in iron (and iodine) and Vitamin C which assists iron absorption.

MENSTRUATION, PROLONGED. May be caused by a decline in hormone levels.
Indicated: Agnus Castus, Black Cohosh.
See: MENORRHAGIA.

MERCURY POISONING. The toxic effect of mercury has been known since days of the medieval alchemists. Charles II presented all the symptoms we now recognise as mercurial poisoning, presumably the result of medication received over many years. Its symptoms simulate multiple sclerosis, when chronic. They are: constant fatigue, pins and needles in the limbs, resting tremor, nausea, dizziness, ataxia, pains in the bones and joints, drooling (excessive salivation), blue line along the gums. In children they may include all kinds of vague aches and pains, chorea, hyperthyroidism and facial neuralgia. Weakness, walking difficulties, metallic taste in the mouth, thirst, mental deterioration. It is now known to cause a number of serious nerve dystrophies.

Mercury has an affinity for the central nervous system. Soon it concentrates in the kidney causing tubular damage. A common cause is the mercurial content (50 per cent) in the amalgam fillings in teeth which, under certain conditions, release a vapour. Fortunately, its use in dentistry is being superceded by an alternative composite filling.

A common cause of poisoning was demonstrated in 1972 when 6,000 people became seriously ill (600 died) from eating bread made from grain treated with a fungicide containing methylmercury. For every fungus in grain there is a mercuric compound to destroy it. The seed of all cereal grain is thus treated to protect its power of germination.

Those who are hypersensitive to the metal should as far as possible avoid button cells used in tape recorders, cassette players, watch and camera mechanisms. As the mercury cells corrode, the metal enters the environment and an unknown fraction is converted by micro organisms to alkylmercury compounds which seep into ground waters and eventually are borne to the sea. When cells are incinerated, the mercury volatilises and enters the atmosphere. (*Pharmaceutical Journal, July 28/1984*)

Mercury poisoning from inhalation of mercury fumes goes directly to the brain and pituitary gland. Autopsies carried out on dentists reveal high concentrations of mercury in the pituitary gland. (*The Lancet, 5-27-89,1207 (letter)*)

Treatment. For years the common antidote was sulphur, and maybe not without reason. When brought into contact sulphur and mercury form an insoluble compound enabling the mercury to be more easily eliminated from the body. Sulphur can be provided by eggs or Garlic.

Old-time backwoods physicians of the North American Medical School used Asafoetida, Guaiacum and Echinacea. German pharmacists once used Bugleweed and Yellow Dock. Dr J. Clarke, USA physician recommends Sarsaparilla to facilitate breakdown and expulsion from the body.

Reconstructed formula. Echinacea 2; Sarsaparilla 1; Guaiacum quarter; Asafoetida quarter; Liquorice quarter. Dose: Liquid Extracts: 1 teaspoon. Tinctures: 2 teaspoons. Powders: 500mg (two 00 capsules or one-third teaspoon). Thrice daily.

Chelation therapy.
Formula. Tinctures. Skullcap 2-15 drops; Pleurisy root 20-45 drops; Horehound 5-40 drops. Mercurial salivation. Thrice daily. (*Indian Herbology of North America, by Alma Hutchens*)
Dental fillings: replace amalgam with safe alternative – ceramic, etc. Evidence of a link between tooth fillings containing mercury and ME has caused the use of dental amalgam to be banned in Sweden.

METABOLISM. Concerns chemical changes and physical processes whereby (1) energy is created for the body's vital activities and (2) old cells are replaced by new ones. Metabolism is dependent upon a chemical interaction promoted by enzymes. A wide range of illness may follow metabolic disturbance, from debility to hyperactivity. Requires attention to the liver, digestive organs, and endocrine glands.
To stimulate: Boldo, Barberry, Dandelion, Devil's Claw, Artichoke, Knotgrass, Garlic, Gentian, Bee pollen, Ginseng, Kelp, Oats, Peppermint, Prickly Ash, Wild Yam.
Tea: combine equal parts: Agrimony, Dandelion root, Betony. 1 heaped teaspoon to each cup boiling water; infuse 15 minutes. Thrice daily.
Formula. Dandelion 1; Devil's Claw half; Ginseng half; Liquorice 1. Powders: quarter of a teaspoon. Liquid extracts: 30-60 drops. Tinctures: 1-2 teaspoons. In water, honey or suitable vehicle, thrice daily.
Diet. See: DIET – GENERAL. Watercress.
Vitamins: B-complex, B6, B12. Folic acid. C. D.
Minerals: Iron, Manganese, Zinc.

METEORISM. A collection of gas in the epigastrium, distending the intestines. Fermentation with full bloated stomach. Often a symptom of arteriosclerosis of the mesenteric blood vessels.
See: FLATULENCE.

METRORRHAGIA. Bleeding from the womb between periods. May indicate fibroid, polyp, abortion, cervical erosion, tuberculosis, syphilis or other disease of the womb. Refer to appropriate entry.
Keynote: Agnus Castus.
Others in general use: Beth root, American Cranesbill, Lady's Mantle, Black Haw.
Dr Alfred Vogel's combination: Goldenseal, Shepherd's Purse and Yarrow.
Teas: Agnus Castus, Lady's Mantle, Shepherd's Purse, Yarrow. 1 heaped teaspoon to each cup boiling water; infuse 15 minutes. 1 cup 3-4 times daily.
Formula. Agnus Castus 2; Beth root 1; American Cranesbill 1. Dose: Liquid Extracts: 1 teaspoon. Tinctures: 2 teaspoons. Powders: 500mg (two 00 capsules or one-third teaspoon). 3-4 times daily.
Diet. Foods rich in iron, calcium, potassium.

MICTURITION. Discharge of urine from the body.

MIGRAINE. Recurring headache commencing with constriction of blood vessels of the brain, followed by expansion which allows engorgement of vessels. Single or double-sided. With nausea, vomiting, speech difficulties, visual disturbances, emotional stress, tension.

"Half of all migraine patients suffer from anxiety, and one in five experiences depression," according to a study carried out at Manchester University. (*Dr Jennifer Devlen*)
Causes: many and varied. Alcohol, excess coffee and caffeine stimulants, gluten food allergies, dairy products, chocolate, citrus fruits. Related to carbohydrate metabolism. May be associated with menstruation or emotional disturbance, nervous or physical fatigue; liver, stomach or kidney disturbance, or The Pill.
Symptoms: temporary blindness, or sight may be only half the visual field. Flashing lights, throbbing headache, loud noises worsen, nausea, vomiting, depression.
Treatment. In the initial (constrictive) stage any of the following simple teas may resolve: German Chamomile, Betony, Skullcap, Wild Thyme, Valerian.

Where the condition has progressed to vasodilation (engorgement of cerebral blood vessels) give any of the following alternatives. Whilst the requirements of each individual case is observed, inclusion of a remedy for stomach and liver may enhance efficacy. Sometimes a timely diuretic to reduce volume of the blood aborts an attack.
Associated with menstrual disorders: Agnus Castus, Evening Primrose oil.
Tea: Formula. (1) Equal parts: Betony, Valerian, Dandelion root. (2) Alfalfa 1; Valerian half; Hops quarter. One heaped teaspoon to each cup boiling water; infuse 15 minutes. Half-1 cup 2-3 times daily.
Formula. Skullcap 2; Mistletoe 1; Hops half. Dose: Liquid Extracts: 1-2 teaspoons. Tinctures: 1-3 teaspoons. Powders: 750mg (three 00 capsules or half a teaspoon) 2-3 times daily.
Valerian. German traditional.
Feverfew. 2-3 fresh leaves on bread. Tincture (or essence) 5-10 drops.
Practitioner: Tincture Gelsemium, BPC (1963) 5 drops.
Diet: Fruit juice fast. Oily fish. Hay diet. Salt-free.
Vitamins. A. B-complex, B6, B12, C (up to 1000mg). E, Niacin.
Minerals. Manganese, Calcium, Magnesium, Zinc.
Rose-tinted glasses. Ophthalmology Department, Birmingham University.
Information. British Migraine Association, 178A High Road, West Byfleet, Surrey KT14 7ED. Send SAE.

MILIARIA. Sweat rash. See: PRICKLY HEAT.

MILK. To promote flow after childbirth: Agnus Castus, (*John Parkinson 1640*) Aniseed, Borage, Caraway seeds, Cumin seeds, Centuary, Dill seeds, Fennel, Fenugreek seeds, Goat's Rue, Holy Thistle, Nettles, Raspberry leaves, Vervain.
Vitamins. A. B-complex, C. E.
Minerals. Calcium, Iron, Zinc.

MILK LEG. See: VENOUS THROMBOSIS.

MILK FEVER. The flow of milk does not naturally commence until the third day after delivery when a slight feverishness with chill may be experienced. With filling of the breast and suckling by the child relief is felt. The condition is not usually in need of medication but where difficult, as it can be to anorexics and those in feeble health, a cup of Chamomile tea suffices. Combine with Skullcap for those of nervous disposition.

MILK THISTLE. Marian thistle. *Silybum marianum L.* Gaertn. *German*: Mariendistel. *French*: Chardon Marie. *Spanish*: Carod de Maria. *Italian*: Cardo di Maria. *Parts used*: seeds, leaves. One of the best liver remedies.
Constituents: silymarin and other flavo-lignans.
Action: bitter tonic, cholagogue for promoting flow of bile up to 60 per cent in liver disorders, choleretic, antidepressant. Antioxidant to inhibit action of free radicals. Stimulates synthesis of protein. Liver protector, producing new cells in place of the old. Detoxifier. Antiviral. Gall bladder protective.
Uses: to assist digestion of fats, hypertensive, stitch-in-the-side, toxaemia from drug addiction, to correct pale stools, cirrhosis. Of value as supportive treatment for hepatitis B. Lowers blood fats. Varicose ulcer (powdered seed locally). Inflammation of gall bladder and duct. Food allergy. Damage caused by alcoholism and environmental poisons. Fatty liver. To raise bilirubin levels. Pre-menstrual tension. Mushroom poisoning. Candida. To assist liver function in chronic degenerative disease. To increase flow of milk in nursing mothers.
Preparations. Dose: 80 to 200mg, thrice daily. With a history of gall stones: 420mg daily as a protective.
Tea: quarter to half a teaspoon to each cup boiling water; infuse 15 minutes. Dose: quarter to half a cup thrice daily.
Tincture: 10-30 drops in water. An ingredient of Biostrath.
Liver-gall Formula No 6 Biostrath. An ingredient of.
Extract. Capsules 100mg. Milk Thistle Extract, Lactose, Magnesium stearate, Silica. 1-3 capsules daily. (*Reevecrest, Healthcare*)
Legalon tablets. Contain 35mg Silymarin: 2-4 tablets after meals for 4-6 weeks; thereafter 1 tablet thrice daily. (*R.F. Weiss MD*)
German Pharmacopoeia. Rademacher's Milk Thistle: 20 drops thrice daily in water or cup of Peppermint tea.
German Medical Research. Noted that Milk Thistle protected the liver from carbon tetrachloride poisoning.
Note. As an antioxidant is more powerful than Vitamin E.
Chronic alcoholism. Silymarin increases SOD activity of both red and white blood cells. (*Journal of Hepatology, 12 pp290-5, 1991*)

MILLS, Simon, MA FNIMH. Joint Director of the Centre for Complementary Health Studies, University of Exeter (England). President, National Institute of Medical Herbalists (1983-1988) and (1990-1991). Member of the Therapeutics Revision Committee, The British Herbal Pharmacopoeia. UK representative to ESCOP. Mr Mills is in private practice as a herbal consultant in Exeter, England.

MINERAL NUTRIENTS. Dietary minerals. See entries: CALCIUM, CHROMIUM, COBALT, COPPER, DOLOMITE, FLUORINE, IODINE, IRON, MAGNESIUM, MANGANESE, MOLYBDENUM, PHOSPHORUS, POTASSIUM, SELENIUM, SODIUM, SULPHUR, ZINC.

MISCARRIAGE. Termination of a pregnancy before the embryo or foetus can live apart from its mother. An abortion refers to an induced termination. Spontaneous termination is usually referred to as a miscarriage. See: ABORTION.
Lupus erythematosis – accounts for a significant number of unexplained miscarriages. Some lupus sufferers may have ten or more miscarriages (*Swedish study*). In lupus there is a sluggish blood supply – microscopic blood vessels between baby and the mother may silt up, the nutrient supply cut off and the baby dies. Agents with blood-thinning properties (anti-coagulants) can keep blood flowing smoothly to the baby. Some women with severe lupus symptoms may require the stronger anti-coagulants of general medicine (heparin).
Pregnancy. Should be carefully monitored with one-month scans to make sure the baby is alive. All women who miscarry should be tested to see if they are carrying lupus antibodies, and have a lupus test after their first miscarriage.
Influenza. Epidemiologists found that women whose pregnancies were more likely to have had flu-like illness during pregnancy can miscarry. Evidence of a link between influenzal infection during pregnancy and miscarriage or stillbirth has been uncovered. Such infection during pregnancy may also cause schizophrenia in offspring.

Information. Miscarriage Association, C/O Clayton Hospital, Northgate, Wakefield, West Yorks WF1 3JS, UK. Send SAE.

MISO. Rich vegetable source of Vitamin B12, protein, fats, carbohydrates and minerals. After the atom bomb was dropped in Japan during World War II it was discovered that those who included Miso in the diet did not suffer from radiation trauma.

MISTLETOE. *Viscum album L. German*: Mistel. *French*: Gui blanc. *Spanish*: Liga. *Russian*: Olma. *Indian*: Banda. *Italian*: Visco quercino. *Arabian*: Kishmish-j-kawaliyan. *Chinese*: San-shang-chi-shêng. Leaves and terminal twigs. Practitioner use only.
Constituents: alkaloids, glycoproteins, polypeptides, flavonoids.
Action: tranquilliser, vasodilator – reducing blood pressure after an initial rise. Cardiac depressant. Used as an alternative to beta-blocking drugs when they produce sore eyes and skin rash. Stimulates the vagus nerve which slows the pulse. Contains acetylcholine. Diuretic. Immune enhancer. Anti-inflammatory.
Uses. Arterial hypertension, insomnia, temporal arteritis, nervous excitability, hyperactivity, limb-twitching, epilepsy, (petit mal), chorea, tinnitus, rabies (*Dr Laville*). Benzodiazepine addiction – to assist withdrawal. Arteriosclerosis (with Horsetail). Headache, dizziness, fatigue.
Cancer: some success reported in isolated cases. Juice of the berries has been applied to external cancers since the time of the Druids. Present-day pharmacy: Iscador (*Weleda*), Viscotoxin. Pliny the Elder (AD 23-79) and Hippocrates record its use in epilepsy and for tumours. The berries may be prescribed by a medical practitioner only (UK). As an immune enhancer it is used as an adjunct to surgery and radiotherapy for patients for whom cytotoxic drugs are inappropriate because of adverse side-effects. Lymphocytes divide more readily by production of interferon.
Combinations: (1) with Skullcap and Valerian for nervous disorders (2) with Motherwort and Hawthorn for myocarditis (3) with Blue Cohosh for menstrual irregularity (4) with Hawthorn and Lime flowers for benign hypertension. Never combine with Gotu Kola. (*Dr John Heinerman*)
Preparations. Average dose: 2-6g, or equivalent. Thrice daily.
Tea: 1 heaped teaspoon to each cup cold water steeped 2 hours. Dose: half-1 cup.
Green Tincture. 4oz bruised freshly-gathered leaves in spring to 1 pint 45 per cent alcohol (Vodka, strong wine, etc). Macerate 8 days, shaking daily. Filter and bottle. Dose: 3-5 drops: (every 2 hours if an epileptic attack is suspected).
Powder, capsules: 300mg. 2 capsules thrice daily before meals. (*Arkocaps*)
Plenosol. (*Madaus*)
Liquid Extract (1:1): 8-10 drops.
Sale: pharmacy only.

MITCHELL, Hugh, MNIMH (Hon.), F.Inst.H.F.R., Past Manager, Crude Drugs Division, Potter & Clarke, London. Later, joint Managing Director, Brome & Schimmer Ltd. Chairman, Mitchfield Botanics Ltd. President, British Herbal Medicine Association. Past Chairman, British Herbal Pharmacopoeia. Chairman, Board of Governors, School of Phytotherapy. Founder member of ESCOP and member of the Executive and General Council.

MITOGENICS. Cell proliferants. Comfrey, Marigold.

MITRAL DISEASE. A serious defect of the mitral valve of the heart. Two kinds: (1) a permanently deformed narrowed valve (mitral stenosis), or (2) a dilated, over-stretched or distorted valve through enlargement of the left ventricle. In this case imperfect closure causes back pressure which produces chest symptoms. Incompetence leads to enlargement of the heart. Often a legacy from rheumatic fever in children. Sooner or later the liver congests with possible jaundice. Presence of albumin in the urine follows kidney involvement.
Treatment. See: HEART – LEFT VENTRICULAR FAILURE.

MOLES. Flat or raised, a mole is a coloured spot on the skin. It contains a dark pigment, melanin, and may be covered with hair. While easy to remove by plastic surgery, advice should be sought before excision. Under the influence of friction a mole may become malignant. Studies show that moles carry an elevated risk of malignant melanoma. When a mole changes in character, a qualified practitioner should be consulted. By herbal means they are never completely eradicated.
Traditional. Rub with raw Garlic bulb. Apply juice of Dandelion, Milkweed, Greater Celandine, or Jojoba oil over a long period.
Linda Clark. Moles have been known to disappear on wiping with Castor oil.
Internally: Liquid Extract, Thuja. 3-5 drops in water, once daily, for 1 month, repeated again after 3 months.
Vitamin E.
Minerals. Silicon, Sulphur.

MOLYBDENUM. Trace element. RDA 0.15 to 0.5mg.
Deficiency. Sexual impotence in aged men. Decayed teeth, allergy, palpitation.

Believed to be linked with cancer of the gullet in China where soil is deficient in this element.

Body effects. Male sexual libido, dental health, iron metabolism, function of some enzymes.
Sources. Most foods. Liver, oats, buckwheat, barley, wholegrains, lima beans, sunflower seeds, pulses, Soya beans and flour.
Note. High levels of uric acid (a cause of gout and gravel) have been linked with a high content of the element in some native soils – especially in Armenia.

MONILIASIS. Thrush. Now known as candida. Infection caused by the organism *Candida albicans*, a yeast fungus. Invades parts of the body that are warm and moist.
Symptoms: white patches on background of red skin, beneath the breasts, in the groin or vagina. In babies appears as nappy rash. Internally, it may invade the urinary tract, intestines or lungs.
See: CANDIDA.

MONONUCLEOSIS. See: GLANDULAR FEVER.

MONOSODIUM GLUTAMATE SYNDROME. Pains in arms, neck, shoulders and spine from excessive consumption of monosodium glutamate which increases the body's salt levels.
Tea. Mix, equal parts: Agrimony, Centuary, Meadowsweet.
Decoction. Mix, equal parts: Dandelion root, Echinacea root.
Tablets/capsules. Blue Flag. Devil's Claw. Wild Yam.
Formula (1). Turkey Rhubarb, with pinch of Cayenne or drops of Tincture Capsicum. Dose: Liquid Extracts: 1 teaspoon. Tinctures: 2 teaspoons. Powders: 500mg (two 00 capsules or one-third teaspoon). Thrice daily.
Formula (2). Dandelion 2; Meadowsweet 1; Goldenseal quarter. Dose: as above.

MORNING SICKNESS. See: PREGNANCY.

MOTH REPELLENT. Sew into small linen bags any of the following: Cinnamon, Sandalwood chips, Camphor, Cloves. Add: sprinkle of Cedarwood for greater potency.

MOTHER SEIGEL'S SYRUP. See: SHAKERS, The.

MOTHERWORT. *Leonurus cardiaca L.* *German*: Herzgespann. *French*: Agripaume. *Spanish*: Agripalma. *Italian*: Cardiaca. *Chinese*: T'ui. *Part used*: herb.
Constituents: flavonoids, iridoids including rutin, diterpenes.
Action: *antispasmodic*, laxative, diaphoretic, emmenagogue, vaso-constrictor. (*Simon Mills*) Nerve and heart sedative. Hypotensive. Action similar to Valerian. (*Dr Rudolf F. Weiss*) Cardiotonic.
Uses: angina on effort, simple uncomplicated heart conditions to enhance exercise duration; tachycardia from hyperactive thyroid, hypertension, absent or painful menstruation (hence its name), menopausal flushes, schizophrenic tendency, pre-menstrual tension.
"Drink Motherwort tea and live to be a source of continuous astonishment and frustration to waiting heirs." (*Old saying*)
Not given in pregnancy.
Combines well with Vervain (equal parts) for relaxing nervine.
Practitioner combinations: *Menstrual disorders*, equal parts: Black Cohosh, Cramp bark, Motherwort.
Heart disorders: Motherwort 1; Hawthorn 1; Lily of the Valley half.
Benzodiazepine addiction to assist withdrawal: equal parts, Motherwort, Skullcap and Valerian. Infusions, extracts or tinctures.
Preparations. Thrice daily.
Tea: 1-2 teaspoons to each cup boiling water; infuse 15 minutes. Half-1 cup.
Tea combination: equal parts, Motherwort, Balm and Lime flowers. 2 teaspoons to cup boiling water: infuse 15 minutes, 1 cup thrice daily. Angina and heart symptoms – to ameliorate.
Liquid Extract: 1:1, 25 per cent alcohol. Dose: 2-4ml (30-60 drops).
Tincture: 1:5, 25 per cent alcohol. Dose: 5-10ml (1-2 teaspoons).
Powders. 2 to 4g.
Tablets/capsules. Popular combination. Powdered extract Motherwort 4:1 – 50mg. Powdered Passion flower BHP (1983) – 90mg. Powdered extract Lime flowers 3:1 – 67mg. For a calming and sedating effect in stressful situations and insomnia. (*Gerard House*)
Note. Motherwort needs to be taken for weeks.
GSL

MOTION SICKNESS. Nausea and vomiting caused by lack of air and restricted vision upsetting the balance of the inner ear.
Cup of Chamomile, Balm, or Meadowsweet tea. Liquorice helpful, but most popular is Ginger taken in the form of Ginger wine, or powdered root (quarter to half a teaspoon). Chrystalised Ginger from sweetshop is one of the safest and cheapest: 2-3 pieces sucked or chewed half hour before journey and at intervals thereafter.
Avoid tobacco which reduces oxygen count.
Potter's Ginger root capsules.
Peppermint. Before travelling, glass water with 2 drops.
Aromatherapy. Inhalant. 2-3 drops Peppermint oil on tissue.
Diet. No alcohol or fatty foods. Accept Papaya fruit, Lemons or Lemon juice, Honey,

Acidophilus.
Supplements. Alternatives to the above. Seven days before journey: B-complex, magnesium 200mg, calcium 400mg.

MOTOR NEURONE DISEASE (MND). Degeneration of nerve cells of the brain and spinal cord with reduced muscle activity. Disability comes without warning. Muscle wasting and weakness commences with hands and feet, rising upwards. It is believed that exposure to the polio virus in childhood increases the likelihood of developing MND. Bulbar palsy is one of the group with difficulties in talking and swallowing.
Symptoms. Slurred speech, muscle wastage, shortness of breath, difficult swallowing. The intellect is not affected. Bladder and bowel control are retained.
Treatment. There is no specific treatment. Black Cohosh gives added power to feeble nerve impulses. The husks of oats, Avena sativa, offers a strengthening nutrient containing tocopherol and protein for the debility. Ginkgo and Kola nuts are cerebral stimulants. Damiana (Curzon) has a tonic effect upon the central nervous system.
Tablet: Damiana, Kola, Saw Palmetto.
Tinctures. Combine – Ginkgo 3; Avena sativa 2; Damiana 1; Black Cohosh half. Dose: 2-4ml (30-60 drops), in water.
Evening Primrose oil: of value in rehabilitation of the patient.
Note. Treatment should be supervised by a neurologist whose training prepares him/her to recognise serious illness and to integrate herbal treatment safely into the treatment plan.
Diet. Gluten-free. Low animal fats, high unsaturated fats, low sugars: give preference to honey. Avoid beer, sweetened bottled fruit juices.
Supplements. To make good possible vitamin and mineral deficiencies; directed towards regeneration of wasted nerve cells. Multivitamin capsule/tablet containing the B group, but the Vitamin B12 (10mcg thrice daily) should be taken separately. Magnesium relieves chronic nervous fatigue. Zinc contributes to motor neurone health. Amino acids, including L-leucine to restore the glutamate dehydrogenase (GDH) to slow down degeneration.
Cases have been known to evolve from physical injury or trauma, such as falling downstairs, in which case the use of the homoeopathic remedy *Arnica* might be indicated.
Aluminium. Aluminium is suspect in playing an etiological role in the onset of MND. As a precautionary measure aluminium anti-perspirants, antacids and cooking vessels are best avoided.
Supportives. Deep-breathing exercises. A range of communication aids are available under the National Health Service, England.
Information. Motor Neurone Disease Association, PO Box 246, Northampton NN1 2PR, UK.

MOUNTAIN GRAPE. Oregon grape. *Berberis aquifolium*, Pursh. *French*: Berberis. *Spanish*: Berberis. *Italian*: Berberi. *Parts used*: root, rhizome.
Constituents: isoquinoline alkaloids (berberine, hydrastine, etc).
Action: cholagogue, hepatic, alterative, anti-diarrhoeal.
Uses: similar to those of Barberry (*Barberry vulgaris*). Dyspepsia. Blood impurities. Skin diseases: especially eczema, psoriasis.
Preparations. Thrice daily.
Decoction. Quarter to half a teaspoon to each cup water simmered 20 minutes. Dose: half a cup.
Liquid extract: 10-30 drops in water.
Powder: 1-2g.

MOUSE-EAR. Mouse-ear hawkweed. *Hieracium pilosella L.* Dried herb. *Keynote*: cough.
Constituents: flavonoids, coumarin.
Action: antitussive, anticatarrhal, expectorant, diuretic, sialogogue, antispasmodic, astringent, antibiotic (fresh plant only). A drying agent for profuse mucous discharge.
Uses: whooping cough, cough productive of much mucus. Profuse catarrh, haemoptysis (blood in the sputum), brucellosis (Malta fever), colitis. Bruised fresh plant used by Spanish shepherds for injuries in the field. Nosebleeds. Liver disorders.
BHP (1983) combination: Mouse-ear, White Horehound, Mullein and Coltsfoot (whooping cough).
Preparations. Average dose: 2-4 grams, or equivalent; thrice daily (5-6 times daily, acute cases). Works best as a tea or in combination of teas rather than in alcohol.
Tea: 1-2 teaspoons to each cup boiling water; infuse 15 minutes; dose, half-1 cup.
Liquid Extract: 30-60 drops, in water.
Home tincture: 1 part to 5 parts 45 per cent alcohol (Vodka, gin, etc). Macerate 8 days, shake daily. Filter. Dose: 1-3 teaspoons in water.
Powder. 500mg (two 00 capsules or one-third teaspoon). GSL

MOUTH INFECTIONS. See: STOMATITIS, CANCRUM ORIS, CANKER, ULCERATION.

MOUTHWASH. The protective influence of a mouth rinse or gargle are well-known. Not only the patient, but those in close proximity may find a mouth wash limits the virulence of infection by seasonal fevers, measles, etc two or more times daily. 3 drops of any one tincture: Myrrh, Cinnamon, Goldenseal, Marigold, Blood root, Thyme, Peppermint, Echinacea. OR: 5 drops fresh juice of Marigold petals, Horseradish or Marshmallow after passing fresh plant through a juicer – in warm water.

MUCILAGE. A herb containing an abundance of sticky, viscous sap of value for inflamed surfaces, often with healing properties. Bistort, Comfrey, Fenugreek, Iceland Moss, Irish Moss, Ispaghula, Linseed, Marshmallow, Quince seed, Slippery Elm, White Pond Lily.
See: DEMULCENT, EMOLLIENT.

MUCOLYTICS. Agents that disperse or dissolve mucus. Of use for such conditions as glue ear or abdominal complications associated with cystic fibrosis in children. Quillaia bark, Lungwort.
See also: EXPECTORANTS.

MUGWORT. Wild Wormwood, Felon herb. *Artemisia vulgaris L. German*: Mugwurz. *French*: Herbe de St Jean. *Spanish*: Artemisia. *Arabian*: Afsantin-e-hindi. *Iranian*: Artemassaya. *Indian*: Duna murwa. *Chinese*: Ai-hao-ai. *Part used*: leaves.
Constituents: vulgarin, flavonoids, coumarin derivatives, oil.
Action. Menstrual regulator, nervine, diuretic, choleretic, stomachic, diaphoretic, orexigenic, bitter, anti-diabetic. Has an affinity for the womb, stomach and nerves. Re-mineraliser.
Uses: menstrual obstruction, pain or delay. Menopause. To temporarily allay the tremor of Parkinsons; reduce excitability of epileptics before an attack, convulsions in children; early stages of colds, influenza and other fevers. To stimulate the appetite in anorexia nervosa. Pin worms, sleep-walking, abdominal cramp. Malaria. (*China*)
Combination: with Helonias, Pennyroyal and Southernwood for menstrual irregularity BHP (1983).
Preparations. Average dose, half-2 grams, or equivalent, thrice daily.
Tea: half an ounce to 1 pint boiling water; infuse 15 minutes. Half-1 cup thrice daily.
Liquid Extract BHP (1983). 1:1 in 25 per cent alcohol. Dose: half to 2ml in water.
Powder, capsules: 250mg. 3 capsules at meals, morning and evening. (*Arkocaps*)
Contra-indications: pregnancy, lactation, large doses. GSL

MUIRA-PUAMA. *Liriosma ovata*, Miers. Root.
Keynote: impotence.
Action: aphrodisiac.
Uses: impotence, infertility, neurasthenia.
Preparations. Average dose, half-2 grams, thrice daily.
Decoction: half-1 teaspoon to each cup water gently simmered 20 minutes; dose one-third-1 cup.
Liquid Extract BHP (1983): 1:1 in 60 per cent alcohol. Dose, half-2ml. GSL

MULLEIN. Candlewort. Aaron's rod. *Verbascum thapsus L. German*: Wollkraut. *French*: Bouillon blanc. *Spanish*: Gordolobo. *Italian*: Candela regia. *Iranian*: Busir. *Arabian*: Makizahraj. *Parts used*: leaves and flowers.
Constituents: rutin, hesperidin, saponin, volatile oil.
Action: a soothing relaxant for irritable respiratory conditions; pectoral demulcent, anti-tussive, mild sedative, diuretic, vulnerary, mild antispasmodic.
Uses: asthma, deep hollow cough, emphysema, tracheitis, hay fever, wet pleurisy, bronchitis, bed-wetting (1-2 drops oil thrice daily).
Topical: for earache and temporary deafness, inject 1-3 drops oil to relieve irritation and promote sleep. The oil is used as an emollient for wounds, ulcers, piles, pain in the rectum, itching anus, and to soften hard dry schirrhous tumours. A bruised fresh leaf over the anus was once a gardener's pile relief.
Quinlan Cure. Dr Quinlan initiated what became an Irish traditional treatment for tuberculosis. He obtained best results with green leaves of Mullein. Hot-house cultivation makes it possible for leaves to be available throughout the year. Irish peasantry prepared it by boiling one handful in 2 pints fresh milk, strained, and sweetened with honey. The whole quantity was drunk once or more times daily, as tolerated. Soothes the lungs, increases weight and restores vitality.
Preparations. Average dose, leaves: 4-8 grams. (Flowers: 1-2 grams.) Thrice daily.
Tea: 2-3 teaspoons to cup, or 2oz to 1 pint boiling water; infuse 15 minutes; half-1 cup. Best results have followed the tea, instead of alcohol.
Liquid Extract: 1-2 teaspoons in water.
Tincture is made from the fresh plant at the time of flowering: 1 part to 5 parts 45 per cent alcohol, macerated 8 days; dose, 2-3 teaspoons in water.
Oil of Mullein: gently heat 1 pint Olive, Sunflower, Safflower or Almond oil in a non-aluminium vessel. Add fresh flowers to saturation point. Continue in gentle heat until all colour fades from the flowers. Press out, bottle. As an injection for ear troubles, a chestrub for respiratory disorders, healer for ulcers, and for general purposes.

MULTIPLE SCLEROSIS. Or disseminated sclerosis. A brain and spinal cord disorder with damage to nerve sheaths. Nerve fibres are protected by a sheath known as myelin. Like an electrical flex, it insulates nerve structures. When damaged in different places, demyelination shows in the form of 'plaques' which interfere with transmission of nerve impulses and tissue nutrients. Symptoms depend upon the particular nerves affected. Not all cases present a consistent symptom picture but generally include: pins and needles in arms or legs, muscle cramps, weakness of legs, walking difficulties, "always tired", urinary bladder problems, blurring of vision, clumsy movements, vertigo.

As described by the French physician, Charcot, over 100 years ago, it is not infectious. Symptom-free periods may extend for months, even years, though relapses may be triggered by emotional crises, physical injury, the contraceptive pill, influenza and other infections.

While the cause is unknown, some studies have revealed a link between the disorder and the distemper virus in dogs. Others have linked the disease with mercury toxicity from amalgam dental fillings shown to generate electromotive forces which propel ionised mercury particles into the body from teeth. A further link is persistent infective sinusitis.

MS is high in families that eat excessive meat fat, butter and dairy products but with too little vegetable fat (corn, Soya, sunflower oil, etc). Linoleic acid levels in the blood of MS patients are abnormally low, especially during relapse. (*Schwartz JH, Bennett B. Int Arch Allergy Appl Immunol 45; 899-904, 1973*) Evening Primrose oil is claimed to make up the deficiency. Ethnic peoples with a diet wholly of fish (Eskimos) seldom develop this disease.

While cure is not possible, herbal medicine may in some cases arrest deterioration. Treatment of severe nerve conditions should be supervised by neurologists and practitioners whose training prepares them to recognise serious illness and to integrate herbal and supplementary intervention safely into the treatment plan.

Nerve sheaths require calcium; herbs to increase its levels: Oats, Lobelia, Horsetail.

Evening Primrose oil makes good a deficiency of linoleic acid (Vitamin F) for efficient function of the brain.

Alternatives:– *Tablets/capsules*. Black Cohosh, Cramp bark, Prickly Ash, Skullcap, Ginseng.

Formula. Ginkgo 2; Prickly Ash 1; Black Cohosh; Ginger quarter. Dose: Liquid Extracts: one 5ml teaspoon. Tinctures: two 5ml teaspoons. Powders: 500mg (two 00 capsules or one-third teaspoon). Thrice daily.

Formula, for pain. Lobelia 1; Ladyslipper 1; Ginger quarter. Dose: Liquid Extracts: 30-60 drops. Tinctures: one 5ml teaspoon. Powders: 250-500mg.

Rue tea. Traditional remedy for MS.

Evening Primrose: 4 x 500mg capsules, daily.

Aromatherapy. Spinal massage. 10 drops oils of Rosemary and Lavender in egg-cup Almond oil (or other vegetable oil).

Purslane herb. A rich source of non-fish EPA – suitable for a vegetarian approach.

Diet. A diet rich in essential fatty acids appears to arrest deterioration. (*MS Unit, Central Middlesex Hospital, London*)

High protein, low fat with oily fish. Lecithin. Sugar-free. Gluten-free (see Gluten diet). Cholesterol-free (avoid milk and dairy products). Grape juice. Dandelion coffee. One tablespoon Cod Liver oil daily. Red beet. Vegetable oils (safflower, sunflower, etc). Avoid coffee and caffeine stimulants.

Vitamins. Dismutase enzymes (see entry). B-complex, B3, B6. Vitamin C, 500-1000mg. Vitamin E, 200iu. Daily. Some authorities advise maximum dosage of Vitamin B12.

Minerals. Dolomite. Manganese. Zinc.

Information. Multiple Sclerosis Society, 25 Effie Road, London SW6 1EE, UK. Send SAE.

MULTIVITAMIN FORMULA. Alternative to vitamin and mineral supplements. The following are rich in vitamins and minerals, and may be taken singly or in combination:– Alfalfa, Horsetail, Iceland Moss, Irish Moss, Kelp, Nettles, Oats, Parsley root, Spirulina.

MUMPS. Parotitis. Inflammation of the salivary glands with painful swelling in front of the ears, caused by a virus. Common, children. In adults, mumps may include inflammation of the testicles in men which may lead to sterility; or of the ovaries in women; or of the pancreas in both sexes. A notifiable disease.

Symptoms: fever, malaise, headache, one or two days before sudden rise in temperature to about 40°C (104°F).

Treatment. Maintain adequate fluid intake.

Tea. Formula. Angelica 2; Centuary 1; Marigold 1. 2 teaspoons to each cup boiling water; infuse 15 minutes. Add pinch Cayenne. Quarter-1 cup every 2 hours, according to age. Where recovery is tardy, add 3-4 drops Spearmint oil.

With nervousness: add 1 part skullcap.

With swollen testicles or ovarian involvement: Agnus Castus.

Absence of urine: Yarrow.

Alternative formula:– Echinacea 2; Poke root 1; Yarrow 2. Dose: Liquid Extracts: one 5ml teaspoon. Tinctures: two 5ml teaspoons. Powders: 500mg (two 00 capsules or one-third teaspoon). Children: 1 drop for each year to age of 5; 2 drops thereafter to age of 10. Thrice daily.

Tablets/capsules. Poke root. Echinacea.

Malecite Indians: Cramp bark. Echinacea. Decoction.

European traditional. Balm tea, internally, half-1 cup freely. Externally to bathe face and genitals.

Tinctures: Formula. Equal parts: Pulsatilla, Ginkgo, Vinca major. Adults: 1-2 teaspoons in water thrice daily. Children: 1 drop for each year to 5 years; thereafter 2 drops each year to 12.

Metastasis. Equal parts, Liquid Extracts. Pulsatilla (testes and mammae); Skullcap (Brain); Vinca major (pancreas). Dosage as Liquid Extract.

Gargle. 5-10 drops Tincture Myrrh in glass of water freely.

Hot compress. St John's Wort oil to neck or face

(*Dr A. Vogel*).
Poultice to reduce swelling: fresh Mullein leaves.
Vitamins. A. B-complex, C. D. E.
Minerals. Calcium. Iodum. Zinc. Dolomite.
To be treated by or in liaison with a qualified medical practitioner.

MUSCAE VOLTANTES. Moving specks, threads or black spots before the eyes. Floating debris in the vitreous humour of the eye and which are visible as 'floating spots'.
Treatment: directed towards stomach, liver and alimentary canal.
Teas: Centuary, Holy Thistle, Meadowsweet, Wormwood, Balmony, Agrimony, Chiretta.
Formula. Tea: equal parts, Agrimony, Meadowsweet, Dandelion root. 1 heaped teaspoon to each cup boiling water; infuse 15 minutes. 1 cup thrice daily.
Decoction. 1 teaspoon Barberry bark steeped overnight in large cup cold water. One-third cup before meals, thrice daily.
Formula. Equal parts: Meadowsweet, Fringe Tree, Echinacea. Dose: Liquid Extracts: 1 teaspoon. Tinctures: 1-2 teaspoons. Powders: 500mg (two 00 capsules or one-third teaspoon). Thrice daily.
Diet. See: DIET – GENERAL DIET.

MUSCULAR DYSTROPHY. Slow progressive muscle wasting and weakness in childhood, developing usually before the fifth year. Peroneal muscular atrophy. Few survive after adolescence. "Waddling" gait, frequent falls, deformity. Another type: facio-scapular-humeral develops in early adult life. No cure possible.
Associated with a deficiency of taurine, (an amino acid) and Vitamin E.
Treatment. No specific therapy. Surgery sometimes able to correct. Herbs to support the constitution. Herbs contain vital complexes of minerals which may arrest progress of the disease.
Teas: Plantain, Alfalfa, Fenugreek seeds.
Tablets/capsules. Alfalfa, Kelp, Irish Moss, Saw Palmetto, Damiana.
For pain. See: ANTISPASMODIC DROPS. Wild Lettuce.
Evening Primrose. 4 x 500mg capsules, daily.
Diet. Bananas for potassium. Oats: oatmeal porridge.
Vitamins. A. B6. B12. C. E. Pantothenic acid.
Minerals. Dolomite, Potassium. Zinc.
Aromatherapy. Massage spine Three drops each – Rosemary and Lavender in 2 teaspoons Almond oil.
Treatment by or in liaison with a general medical practitioner.

MUSCLES. General aches, pain and soreness. Non-specific.
Alternatives. *Internal*. Prickly Ash bark, Plantain, Mullein, Yarrow, White Willow, Black Cohosh, Guaiacum, Feverfew.
Tablets/capsules. Prickly Ash bark, Black Cohosh, Guaiacum.
Formula. White Willow 2; Black Cohosh 1; Guaiacum quarter; few grains Cayenne or drops Tincture Capsicum. Dose: Liquid Extracts: 1 teaspoon. Tinctures: 2 teaspoons. Powders: 500mg (two 00 capsules or one-third teaspoon). Thrice daily.
Topical. Castor oil packs. Massage oils. Gold Fire ointment, Epsom salt baths.
Supplements. Niacin, B-complex, B6, Kelp, Dolomite, Calcium, Zinc.
See: RHEUMATIC and other relative disorders for specific treatments.

MUSHROOM POISONING. Poisoning by toxic fungi. Symptoms relative to each particular specie. Should treatment induce vomiting, this should be regarded as favourable.
Swiss traditional. Fresh Mistletoe berry swallowed whole.
Fresh lemon juice, 1-2 tablespoons.
Teas: Black Horehound, Dandelion, German Chamomile, Wormwood, Basil.
Tablets/capsules. Goldenseal. Mistletoe, Papaya, Slippery Elm, Wild Yam.
Formula. Equal parts: German Chamomile, Black Horehound. Dose: Liquid Extracts: 1-2 teaspoons. Tinctures: 2-3 teaspoons. Powders: 750mg (three 00 capsules or half a teaspoon). Thrice daily.
French traditional. Chamomile tea.
English traditional. Grated nutmeg; few grains.

MUSICIAN'S CRAMP. Overuse syndrome. Occupational tenosynovitis. Pain in hands, limbs, shoulders, neck.
Treatment. Radical rest, avoiding turning door handles, taps, writing, housework.
Teas, decoctions: St John's Wort, Ginseng, Valerian, Alfalfa, Oats.
Tablets/capsules. Cramp bark. Valerian. St John's Wort, Ginseng, Black Cohosh.
Formula. Cramp bark 1; Ginseng 1; Ginger half. Dose: Liquid Extracts: 1 teaspoon. Tinctures: 2 teaspoons. Powders: half a teaspoon. Thrice daily.
Topical. Arnica cream or lotion.
Supplements. Vitamins B6, C, E. Calcium, Dolomite, Magnesium.

MUSTARD, COMMON. White or black mustard. *Brassica alba L., Brassica nigra L. German*: (white) Echter senf, (black) Senfkohl. *French*: (white) Moutarde blanche, (black) Moutarde noire. *Spanish*: Mostaza (black and white). *Italian*: Mostardo. *Arabian*: Khardal. *Indian*: Raigis. *Malayan*: Savi sasavi. *Iranian*: Sipandan. Seeds.

Constituents: sinigrin (black), sinalbin (white), mucilage, sinapine.
Action: diaphoretic, diuretic, emetic, rubefacient, stimulant. As a counter-irritant it induces inflammation causing dilation of blood vessels, thus increasing flow of blood to a specific area, externally.
Uses. *Internal*. As a tea for colds, influenza and early stage of fevers for profuse sweat to reduce a raised temperature. Hypothermia (quarter of a teaspoon powder in honey, banana mash or tea) to stimulate body heat. Today, rarely used internally.
Emetic: 1 tablespoon powder or seeds in pint tepid water.
Uses. *External*. As a poultice for painful chests to promote increased circulation for the relief of bronchitis, pleurisy, intercostal neuralgia. Chilblains. Cold, painful joints of old age.
Foot-bath: 1 tablespoon in muslin bag to 2 pints boiling water. Cool, stir well.
Preparations. As necessary. Quarter of a teaspoon powder to each cup boiling water (honey increases palatability).
Powder: sprinkle in boots or shoes for fisherman's cold feet.
Oil: for cold arthritic joints: 1 part Mustard powder or seeds gently simmered in 20oz vegetable oil half hour. Strain. Bottle.

GSL external use only
Internal use – practitioner only

MYALGIA. Pain in a muscle.
Treatment: same as for NEURALGIA.

MYALGIC ENCEPHALOMYELITIS (ME). Chronic fatigue syndrome (CFS). Iceland disease. Post Viral Fatigue. A chronic neuromuscular illness with psychological disturbance ranging from depression to severe behavioural abnormality. Follows persistent infection by enteroviruses with viral material in the muscles. May follow influenza and so-called 'burn-out'. While virus enters the body through the intestines, it tends to invade the central nervous system and depress the immune system. Occurs chiefly in women and young energetic executives pursuing vigorous activity when a feverish condition is latent.

Exercise worsens symptoms by reduced muscle tissue oxygen. (*Swedish study*)

The function of the immune system is to arrest the action of viruses and bacteria, but when it ceases to act the body intelligence cannot tell the difference between a normal reaction and an alien one. It begins to attack its own weapons of defence – the antibodies.
Symptoms. Exercise-induced muscle fatigue and weakness after walking or other activity. Movements are slow. Headache, dizziness, chest pain, difficult breathing, sore throat, swollen glands, stomach unrest. Mental weariness. "Cannot fight back". Wants to sleep all the time. Difficulty in finding the right words, to remember things, to concentrate on problems and has to force the brain to work. He or she looks basically healthy but is unhappy and may awake crying in response to the pressures of life.
Treatment. Lymphatics, hepatics, nervines, oral anti-fungals (anti-candida).
Alternatives. Clivers, Galangal, Gentian, Ginkgo, Ginseng, Goldenseal, Milk Thistle, Liquorice root, Garlic, Astragalus radix, Poke root, Shitake Mushroom, Wild Indigo, Wormwood.
To enhance immune response: Echinacea.
Of value: Ginseng (anti-depressant), Evening Primrose (GLA), Vitamin E (antioxidant).
Formula: Tea: equal parts Gotu Kola, Ginkgo, Caraway. One teaspoon to each cup boiling water; infuse 15 minutes; 1 cup thrice daily.
Formula. Echinacea 2; Astragalus 1; Ginseng 1. Dose: Liquid Extracts: 1 teaspoon. Tinctures: 2 teaspoons. Powders: 500mg (two 00 capsules or one-third teaspoon). Thrice daily.
Diet. Low salt and fat, high fibre. Wholegrains, sprouting seeds, fresh fruit and vegetables, fish oils. Avoid sugar, yeast and dairy products.
Supplements: daily. Beta carotene, Vitamin B12, Vitamin C, Magnesium asparate 1g, Potassium 1g, Zinc.
Contra-indications: tranquillisers that decrease physical and mental activity.
Evening Primrose. Clinical trials (*Efamol*) prove to help treat symptoms, especially when in combination with fish oils.
Supportive: cranial osteopathy. Aromatherapy massage. Complete rest, with long sleep periods.
Information. MEA, Stanhope House, High Street, Stanford-le-Hope, Essex SS17 0HA, UK. Send SAE.

MYASTHENIA GRAVIS (MG). Autoimmune disorder. Nerve weakness due to defective nerve impulse transmission. Rare. Neuro-muscular disease with spells of extreme weakness. Sight, voice and breathing are most at risk. Often misdiagnosed as neurosis. Muscles fail to respond to directions from the brain. May be associated with a tumour of the thymus, removal of which is curative.
Symptoms: weakened eye muscles producing drooping eyelids (ptosis). Double vision (diplopia). Weakness of neck muscles served by the cranial nerves. Thymus gland abnormality. Difficult swallowing, chewing, slurred speech, fatigue, 'simply cannot hold her head up'.

Lid-lag test and Tensilon tests establish diagnosis.

Treatment should give support to the thymus gland.
Alternatives. To improve nerve transmission: but not cure. Ephedra tea BHP (1983). 1 teaspoon to each cup boiling water; infuse 15 minutes, thrice

daily.
Formula. Oats 2; Ginseng 1; Sarsaparilla 1; pinch Cayenne or drops Tincture Capsicum. Dose: Liquid Extracts: 1 teaspoon. Tinctures: 2 teaspoons. Powders: 500mg (two 00 capsules or one-third teaspoon). Thrice daily.
Practitioner: Ephedrine.
Diet: Gluten-free.

MYELOMA. Bone marrow tumour. Neoplastic, with presence of high globulin levels in the blood. Bone marrow becomes impregnated with plasma cells. Lesions appear in pelvis and dorsal spine, skull and rib cage.
Symptoms: weight loss, back pain, anaemia, impaired kidney function. Usual symptoms of anaemia: weakness, fatigue, pallor, drowsiness, indigestion.
Differential diagnosis. Important. Early X-ray confirms. Patient may be treated for back pain long before true condition is revealed.
Special investigations: for anaemia, plasma cells in the bone marrow. Check ESR (erythrocyte sedimentation rate), kidney function and for excess calcium in the blood.
Treatment. Chemotherapy; radiotherapy. Anti-tumour agents with a tendency to reduce side-effects: Echinacea, Poke root. Comfrey: potential benefit outweighs possible risk. Thuja.
Tea. Combine, equal parts, Red Clover, Gotu Kola, Clivers, Plantain. 1 heaped teaspoon to each cup boiling water; infuse 15 minutes. 1 cup 3 or more times daily.
Decoction. Combine: Echinacea 2; Comfrey root 1; Poke root half. 1 heaped teaspoon to each cup water simmered gently 20 minutes. Half-1 cup 3 or more times daily.
Tablets/capsules: Echinacea, Comfrey, Poke root.
Liquid Extracts: Echinacea 2; Comfrey 1; Poke root half; few drops Tincture Capsicum. Dose: 1 teaspoon, thrice daily.
Tinctures: Echinacea 2; Yellow Dock 1; Horsetail 1; Tincture Capsicum quarter. Dose: 2 teaspoons, thrice daily.
Powders: Echinacea 2; Comfrey 1; Yellow Dock 1; pinch Cayenne. Dose: 500mg (two 00 capsules or one-third teaspoon), thrice daily.
Dr William Boericke. Poke root often assuages pain in bone cancers and tumours.
Supplements. Vitamins B12, C D, E, Selenium.

At the discretion of the physician, any of the above alternatives may be used secondary to hospital treatment.

Treatment by a general medical practitioner or hospital specialist.

MYOCARDIAL INFARCTION (MI). Disease of the heart in which a segment of left ventricular muscle dies as a result of blockage of a coronary artery. Obstructed blood supply may lead to thrombosis and heart failure. Chief symptom is severe pain in the chest, arms and possibly throat (angina).
Alternative Treatment:– *Tea*. Combine equal parts Hawthorn flowers and leaves, Lime flowers, Motherwort. 1-2 teaspoons in each cup of boiling water; infuse 10-15 minutes. 1 cup thrice daily.
Alfalfa tea: anti-cholesterol.
Liquid Extracts. Motherwort 1; Hawthorn 2; Valerian 3. Dose: 30-60 drops thrice daily.
Tinctures: dose, 60-120 drops.
Tincture Lily of the Vally BHP (1983). 1:5 in 40 per cent alcohol; dose: 0.5-1ml, thrice daily.
Diet. See: DIET – HEART AND CIRCULATION.
Supplements. Daily. Vitamin A 7500iu; Vitamin B6 50mg; Vitamin C 200mg; Vitamin E 400iu; Magnesium 300mg; Selenium 200mcg; Zinc 15mg.

MYOCARDITIS. Inflammation of the heart muscle due to (a) infective bacteria – virus influenza, streptococcus, etc, or (b) toxins they produce. May follow scarlet or enteric fever.
Alternative Treatment:– Rest. Stress-free lifestyle. Stop smoking. Few hot drinks but fruit juices and herb teas.
To strengthen the heart: Hawthorn.
To counter infection: Echinacea.
Rheumatic myocarditis: Meadowsweet.
BHP (1983) combination: Hawthorn, Cactus, Lime flowers, Mistletoe, Skullcap.
Tea. Combine equal parts: Mistletoe, Lime flowers, Broom. 1-2 teaspoons to each cup water. Bring to boil and simmer 1 minute. 1 cup thrice daily.
Tablets/capsules. Hawthorn. Mistletoe. Broom.
Tinctures. 20ml Hawthorn, 5ml Marigold (Calendula), 20ml Cactus grand., 10ml Echinacea. Mix. Dose: one teaspoon thrice daily.
Liquid Extracts. (*Arthur Barker*) Combine: Hawthorn 15ml; Cactus 15ml; Hops 4ml. Dose: 15-30 drops thrice daily.
Spartiol Extract. (*Klein*)
Anti-coagulants: indicated after an attack. (*Practitioner*)
Spirits of Camphor. To reduce blood pressure and strengthen heart muscle. To regulate the pulse in chronic myocarditis with wild palpitation. One to five drops in honey, as necessary. (*Dr Finlay Ellingwood*)
Oil of Camphor. Alternative. 1-2 drops in honey when necessary.
Diet. See: DIET – HEART AND CIRCULATION.
Supplements. Daily. Vitamins A 7500iu; B-complex; C 1g; E 1000iu.

MYRRH. Balsamodendron myrrh. *Commiphora molmol*, Engl. *German*: Echter Myrrhenbaum. *French*: Arbre à myrrhe. *Spanish*: Arbol de Mirra. *Italian*: Albero del mirra. *Indian*: Bal. *Arabian*: Mukala. Gum resin. *Keynote*: purification.
Constituents: Myrrhol (volatile oil).

A leuco-cytogenic agent – increases number of white cells in the blood. "From the days of Moses to the time of Christ and since then to the 20th century, Myrrh has proven over and over again to be one of the finest antibacterial and antiviral agents placed on earth." (*John Heinerman, in Science of Herbal Medicine*)
Action: bacteriostatic against staphylococcus aureus and other gram-positive bacteria. Perhaps the most widely used herbal antiseptic. Bitter, astringent, anti-inflammatory, carminative, vulnerary, antifungal, expectorant, diaphoretic, deodorant, emmenagogue, anti-thrush.
Uses. The whole body feels its influence. Internal and external ulceration; especially of mouth, throat, pharynx, spongy gums, pyrrhoea, etc (mouth wash and gargle). Candida – 5-10 drops emulsified in yoghurt. Suppurating wounds that refuse to heal, boils, abscesses. Fungal infections. Myrrh is effective in lowering blood fats and therefore useful for reducing deposits of cholesterol and triglycerides in coronary heart disease.
Powerful antiseptic combination: equal parts powders or tinctures: Echinacea, Goldenseal and Myrrh.
Capsicum and Myrrh. Capsicum enhances its action. The two are synergistic and capillary stimulants. Both may be used with impressive effect for chronic conditions along the alimentary canal.
Preparations. Thrice daily.
Tincture Myrrh BPC 1973: 1:5, 90 per cent alcohol. Dose: 5 to 15 drops.
Thomson's Tincture of Myrrh Co (as once used by members of the National Institute of Medical Herbalists). 1 part Tincture Capsicum BPC to 4 parts Tincture Myrrh. Dose: 1 to 2 and a half ml.
Powders: Fill number 00 capsules. 1 capsule thrice daily. May be used as a dusting powder on wounds.
Enema. Add 20-30 drops Tincture Myrrh to 2 pints boiling water; allow to cool, inject warm.
Contra-indications: pregnancy. GSL

MYXOEDEMA. Deficiency of thyroid hormones in the circulation. Hypothyroidism, under-active thyroid, with possible secondary increase in TSH (thyroid stimulating hormone). Many causes, chief of which is the gradual destruction of the gland by inflammation (chronic thyroiditis). As hormones produced by the gland determine the body's metabolic rate, the condition is responsible for a slowing-up of the individual in body and in mind. When occurring in infancy is known as cretinism.
Symptoms. The patient does not feel particularly unwell, but on examination is found to present a dry, scaly, thickened, puffy skin. Only a few signs may be detected: brittle lack-lustre hair, gross facial features, fatigue, slow pulse, slowness of expression and movement, aches and pains in joints, malar flush, deafness, anaemia, constipation, slurred speech, profuse menses. Later the voice assumes a deep masculine quality. The patient may be subject to carpel tunnel syndrome, and almost always complains of being icy cold. 90 per cent of cases are auto-immune.
Treatment. Official medication is the administration of Thyroxin, an iodine-containing hormone. Sometimes a herbal combination is given to supplement its action. On progress of the condition no permanent cure is possible but it is believed that certain herbs may arrest deterioration.
Alternatives: Carragheen Moss, Iceland Moss, Parsley herb, Kelp, Sarsaparilla, Ginseng, Ginkgo.
Simple tea. For energy and vitality. Combine equal parts: breakfast Oats, Alfalfa herb, Gotu Kola herb. 1 teaspoon to each cup boiling water; infuse 5-10 minutes. One cup morning and evening.
Formula. Equal parts: Ginseng, Kelp, Ginkgo. Add a few grains Cayenne Pepper or drops of Tincture Capsicum. Dose: Liquid Extracts, 1 teaspoon; Tinctures, 2 teaspoons; Powders, 500mg (one-third teaspoon). Morning and evening.
Note. Snoring may be a feature of myxoedema.
Diet. The following have an adverse effect upon the thyroid gland and should be eaten in small amounts: Cabbage, Kale, Cauliflower, Spinach, Brussels Sprouts, Soya beans, Turnips and Beans.
Supplements. Vitamins A, C, D, E, PABA, Calcium, Iodine, Selenium, Zinc. Selenium is an essential component of an enzyme required by the gland. A deficiency of this mineral can be responsible for an under-active thyroid.

NABOTHIAN CYST. A cyst on the cervix of the womb. Ducts of the glands may be plugged with mucus and manifest as white pimples of the size of grape shot and which cause little harm. Often the result of irritation from contraceptives.
Treatment: usually by cauterisation.
See: CYST, CERVICAL.

NAIL BITING. Chewed nails and cuticles wound the skin on one of its most exposed areas. Chronic nail-biting has been known to cause osteomyelitis of finger bones due to staphylococcus aureus from direct spread through macerated tissue. After ablutions, paint nails with Tincture of Myrrh, daily.

NAILS. Nail loss. Paronychia. Clubbing. Brittle nails. Deformity (koilonychia). Spoon-shaped, as from iron-deficiency anaemia. A wide range of diseases affect the nails which, themselves, provide useful clues to underlying constitutional disturbance. Brittle and malformed nails are usually due to mineral deficiency. Ridging and grooving show altered nutrition and damage to the nail bed. Psoriasis nails are pitted.

Infections include candidiasis (monilia), ringworm, staphylococcal or streptococcal bacteria. Biting of fingernails reveals anxiety. Colour change and atrophy of nails may be caused by antibiotics, antimalarials, betablockers, gold and arsenic medicines, steroids, "The Pill"; requiring Eliminatives, liver, kidney and possibly Lymphatic agents.

For in-growing toenail – see entry.
Alternatives. General, internal. For antifungals, see: WHITLOW. Mineral-rich herbs for nutrition.
Teas: Alfalfa, Carragheen, Horsetail, Gotu Kola, Red Clover, Oats (for silicon salts), Plantain, Silverweed, Clivers, Dandelion.
Decoctions: Yellow Dock, Burdock, Sarsaparilla, Queen's Delight.
Tablets or capsules: Alfalfa. Kelp. Bamboo gum.
Formula. Horsetail 2; Gotu Kola 1; Thuja quarter. Dose: Liquid extracts: 1 teaspoon. Tinctures: 2 teaspoons. Powders: 500mg (two 00 capsules or one-third teaspoon). Thrice daily.
Cider Vinegar. See entry. Efficacy recorded.
Topical. Alternatives:– Apply to the nail:
(1) Liquid Extract or Tincture Thuja. (*Ellingwood*)
(2) Blood root. (*J.T. Kent MD*)
(3) Evening Primrose oil.
(4) Contents of a Vitamin E capsule.
(5) Tincture Myrrh.
Diet. Nails are almost wholly protein. High protein. Onions, Garlic, Soya products, Carrot juice, Cod Liver oil, Kelp.
Vitamins. A. B-complex. B6. B12. Folic acid.
Minerals. Calcium. Dolomite. Copper. Iron. Silica. Stannum, Zinc.

NAPIER'S OF EDINBURGH. Britain's oldest herbal establishment. Founded by Duncan Scott Napier, 1860, 17, Bristo Place. While run in the light of modern pharmacy it is still complete with its mahogany fittings, antique tincture bottles and bygones of the Victorian herbalist.

In those early days almost all herbs were collected locally and extracts made on the premises for the queues of patients which formed outside until ten o'clock at night. Today crude material comes from abroad for manufacture into their many preparations: Lobelia syrup, Compound Barberry bark, Composition Essence, Skullcap Herb Compound, Heart Tonic, etc. Ginseng, a supposed modern discovery, has been handled by Napier's for over a century.

NAPPY RASH. An inflammatory skin disorder around the anus and genitals caused by urine reacting with faecal bacteria to produce ammonia. By nature it is a chemical 'burn' and is aggravated by monilia, a wet nappy, or detergents used to wash the nappy.
Causes: nappies sealed in plastic pants for hours on end. Eggs.
Seborrhoea is a common type.
Treatment. After soiling, the nappy area should be washed in warm water and powdered with cornflour (cornstarch); this may be used as a substitute for talcum powder for reducing friction. Nappy rash is rare in Greece where it is a mother's habit to clean a baby's soiled bottom with a stream of warm water from a mixer tap, holding the infant over the left arm in the washbasin, and washing with the right hand.
Topical. Emollient herbal creams: Comfrey, Marshmallow, Chickweed, Slippery Elm, Aloe Vera, Marigold (Calendula). Evening Primrose oil. Zinc and Castor oil ointment. A paste made from Slippery Elm and teaspoon Vitamin E oil. Fresh juice of Plantain or Comfrey.
Tea Tree oil: 10 drops in glass warm water. Saturate handkerchief or sterile dressing and apply.
Diet. Slippery Elm gruel. Avoid eggs.

NARCOTIC. A medicine that diminishes sensibility to pain. See: ANALGESICS.
Deep-acting narcotics are not used in phytotherapy.

NARCOLEPSY. Overpowering desire to sleep at any time of the day and in any situation. Psychiatrists believe it to be an escape mechanism, a form of hysteria. Seems to run in families. Official definition favours a neurologic brain disorder rather than a psychogenic disorder which has its origin in the mind. May be mis-diagnosed and treated as schizophrenic with antipsychotic drugs.
Symptoms. Tired and apathetic. Muscle weak-

ness. May hear voices and have terrifying hallucinations. Causes may be emotional, autotoxaemic, psychic disturbance or spirit possession.
Treatment. Central nervous system stimulants, antidepressants.
Alternatives. Ginkgo, Siberian Ginseng, Camphor, Horseradish, Prickly Ash bark, Gotu Kola, Kola.
Yerbe mate tea.
Tablets/capsules. Prickly Ash, Thuja, Ginseng, Gotu Kola.
Formula. Ginkgo 2; Prickly Ash 1; Ginseng 1. Doses – Powders: 500mg (two 00 capsules or one-third teaspoon). Liquid Extracts: 1 teaspoon. Tinctures: 2 teaspoons. In water or honey, thrice daily.
Practitioner. Ephedra – 1 teaspoon to each cup boiling water; half-1 cup at bedtime. Ephedrine.
Note. Researchers have discovered a "biologic marker for the disease – an antigen called HLA.DR2 found in almost 100 per cent of narcoleptic patients". The antigen appears in only 25 per cent of the general population. This unusual finding may also be evidence that the immune system is somehow involved in the onset of narcolepsy. (*American Family Physician, July 1988*)

NASAL DECONGESTANT. Lobelia, Poke root, Ephedra.

NASTURTIUM (Garden). *Tropaeolum majus*. *German*: Kapuziner-kresse. *French*: Capucine grande. *Spanish*: Nasturcia. *Italian*: Asturzia. Aerial parts used.
Constituents: mineral salts including iodine, iron, phosphates and a sulpho-nigrogenous oil.
Action: antibiotic, antitussive, diuretic, expectorant.
Uses: lung emphysema (fresh juice drunk in milk). Bronchitis, colds, influenza, dry cough. Cystitis, bladder disease. Alopecia – fresh juice rubbed into the scalp is said to stimulate hair growth. Wounds (external use).
Preparations. Thrice daily.
Tea: 2-3 bruised fresh leaves to cup boiling water. Infuse 15 minutes. Dose: one-third-1 cup.
Tincture: 1 part fresh leaves and flowers to 5 parts 45 per cent alcohol (Vodka, gin, etc). Macerate 8 days; shake daily. Filter. Bottle. Dose: 1-3 teaspoons in water.
Tromacaps. (*Dr Madaus, West Germany*) Antibiotic resistant pneumonia; monilial infections of the genito-urinary tract; acute pyelitis. Adults and children over 8 years: on the first day 2 capsules thrice daily; thereafter 1 capsule thrice daily.
Diet. Its pungent flavour adds a zestful stimulant to a salad. Eaten for general health and especially for skin infections.

NATIONAL ASSOCIATION OF HEALTH STORES (NAHS). Founded 1931. Objects:
(a) To promote and protect the interests of Health Foods Stores among members.
(b) To set standards in retailing of health foods and herbs.
(c) To encourage production, marketing and sales of products derived from purely natural and vegetable sources.
(d) To provide qualifications by certificate and diploma courses for those engaged in the industry.

The Association provides advice on aspects of health food and herb retailing and is able to help its members with professional advice and merchandising. NAHS Diploma of Health Food Retailing qualifies for membership of the Institute of Health Food Retailing.
Address: Bastow House, Queens Road, Nottingham NG2 3AS.

NATIONAL HERBALIST ASSOCIATION OF AUSTRALIA. Professional association of qualified consulting medical herbalists. Founded 1920. Membership is by examination. Members required to adhere to a strict Code of Ethics. Quarterly publication: see – AUSTRALIAN JOURNAL OF MEDICAL HERBALISM.
Address: NHAA – PO Box 65, Kingsgrove, NSW 2208, Australia. Tel: +61(02) 502 2938.

NATIONAL INSTITUTE OF MEDICAL HERBALISTS. Est. 1864. The oldest and only body of professional medical herbalists, now known as phytotherapists, in Europe. Membership by examination after completion of course of training. A stipulated period of clinical practice must be completed before the final examination is taken.

Members are directly involved with patient-care, carrying full responsibility for their recommendations, prescribing medication suitable to the individual biological requirements of each patient. Their role includes patient-counselling, health education and research.

Official recognition of the Institute, indicating its growing importance in the field of medicine came with the historic Grant of Arms by Her Majesty's College of Heralds. Members regard this as evidence that the Royal Charter of King Henry VIII still stands and that there is no monopoly in healing the sick. See: HENRY VIII, HERBALISTS' CHARTER.

The Institute played a major role in winning vital concessions for the survival of the herbalist in the passage through Parliament of the Medicine's Bill. See: MEDICINE'S ACT, 1968.

In connection with the NIMH degree courses in herbal medicine are available at a London University, and Exeter University.

The Institute provides professional indemnity cover for its members, and is engaged in a series of clinical trials to evaluate traditional remedies.

All members are required to adhere to a strict professional Code of Ethics and are entitled to carry after their names the letters of qualification: MNIMH or FNIMH.

Members have a key role in preventative medicine and health promotion in their contribution to improvement of the nation's health.
Address: 56 Longbrook Street, Exeter EX4 6AH, from which a list of members is obtainable.

NATRACALM. For symptomatic relief of nervous tension and stress. Active ingredient: aqueous alcoholic extractive from 500mg Passion flower (*Passiflora incarnata*). One tablet thrice daily; and at bedtime if required. *English Grains Ltd*

NATUROPATHY. A distinct system of healing – a philosophy, science art and practice which seeks to promote health by stimulating the body's inherent power to regain harmony and balance. It regards as self-evident laws:
(1) only nature heals, providing it is given the opportunity to do so;
(2) let food be your medicine and medicine your food;
(3) disease is an expression of purification; and
(4) all disease is one.

The philosophy of Naturopathy is based upon two basic principles. The first principle is that the body possesses the power to heal itself through its internal vitality and intelligence. All the practitioner does is to create the most favourable conditions to stimulate and enhance this healing power of nature.

In 1964 a Naturopathic Commission drafted a definition of Nature Cure and defined the therapies of dietetics, fasting, structural adjustments, hydrotherapy, natural hygiene and psychotherapy to be of primary importance.

Naturopathy enlists the aid of water, light, air, diet and manipulation. Mechanical factors to be rectified are spinal mal-alignments and muscular tensions due to occupational or postural causes.
Address: British College of Naturopathy and Osteopathy, 6 Netherhall Gardens, London NW3 5RR. Tel 071-435-8728.

See also: BASTYR COLLEGE OF NATUROPATHIC MEDICINE.

NAUSEA. Sensation of sickness with tendency to vomit.
Common causes: stomach upset from food indiscretion, emotional episode. May precede active vomiting in sick headache, migraine or liver disease.
For simple nausea: a cup of German Chamomile, Peppermint, Ginger, Black Horehound or Balm tea, or suck segment of crystalised Ginger, or Liquorice.
For nausea of pregnancy: see: MORNING SICKNESS.
Entry: VOMITING also refers.

If nausea persists for a number of days a practitioner should be consulted.

NEBULISER. A dispenser designed to convert a remedy solution into a mist of droplets to effectively convey medication to the respiratory organs. Essential oils suitable for this purpose: Peppermint, Eucalyptus, "Olbas". For asthma, bronchitis, sinusitis, hay fever.

Nebulisers should carry a warning against misuse. Failure to respond should not be a signal to increase dosage, but an indication that asthma or the complaint is deteriorating.

NEEM. East Indian Neem tree (*Azadirachta indica*) with a long history as a teeth cleaner in Southern Asia. Common ingredient of toothpowders and toothpastes in India and Pakistan. Popular in folk-medicine as an alterative for skin diseases and as an anti-inflammatory for fevers and infections. Antifungal. Cattle feed. Said to bring added 'heart' to impoverished soil. Antimalarial. Simulates some steroids in its action. Insect-repellent properties.
India, traditional. Swollen glands, diseases of the gums, jaundice, intestinal parasites. Snakebite, to delay blood-clotting. The fruits are used for urinary disorders and piles. The seed-oil is used as a contraceptive.
Topical. Decoction used as a skin wash for lice and scabies: 1oz of the rasped bark to 1 pint water simmered 20 minutes.

NEOKLENZ. Contains Senna leaf 40 per cent, Frangula bark 22.5 per cent, Psyllium seeds 27.5 per cent, Fennel 10 per cent. For non-persistent constipation.

NEOPLASM. New growth. Tumour. Usually regarded as cancerous. See: CANCER. ANTI-NEOPLASMS.

NEPHRITIS. See: BRIGHT'S DISEASE.

NEPHROSIS. Degeneration of the kidney, with high discharge of albumin in the urine. Anaemia, dropsy and protein loss.
Causes: recurrent attacks of nephritis, bacterial toxins, environmental poisons, mineral drugs (mercury etc).
Treatment. Specific hospital treatment essential, (dialysis etc). Simple phytomedicines may bring a measure of relief as supportives to conventional medicine.
Teas. Barley water, Buchu, Clivers, Cornsilk, Couchgrass, Goldenrod, Parsley, Plantain, Wild Carrot.
Decoctions. Broom tops, Dandelion root, Marshmallow root, Hydrangea root, Parsley root.

Powders. Alfalfa 45; Bearberry 15; Buchu 10; Couchgrass 15; Wild Carrot 15. Dose: 500-750mg (2-3 00 capsules or one-third to half a teaspoon) thrice or more daily.
Tinctures. Echinacea 2 (to enhance powers of resistance). Parsley root 2; Ginseng 1; Ginger quarter. Dose: 1-2 teaspoons in water thrice or more daily.
Restharrow herb. For weak kidneys and bladder. (*R.F. Weiss MD. Book: Herbal Medicine, Beaconsfield Publishers*)
Diet. High protein, salt-free, herb teas. Spring water in abundance.
Supplements. Vitamin A, B-complex, B2, C, E. Calcium, Iron, Magnesium.
Supportives. Hot abdominal packs. Castor oil packs. Sweat packs. Induce sweating with aid of diaphoretics.

Subsequent treatment by or in liaison with a qualified medical practitioner.

NERVE RELAXANT. See: SEDATIVE.

NERVE RESTORATIVES. All degenerative changes in the nervous system arise from breakdown of cell integrity through causes including stress, disease or faulty nutrition. J.M. Thurston classifies the restorative effect of herbs as:
Stomach and intestines: Wild Cherry bark, Black Haw.
Heart: Lily of the Valley, Cactus.
Liver: Wild Yam.
Eye: Blue Cohosh, Poke root.
Brain: Oats, Black Cohosh.
Spine: Damiana, Oats, Kola, Unicorn root (Aletris). Hops.
Womb: False Unicorn root (Helonias).
General Restoratives: St John's Wort, Vervain.

NERVE STIMULANTS. Often necessary to bring added vitality to the body or one of its parts. Often combined with circulatory stimulants to help support the nervous system in the presence of nerve weakness and paralysis.
Ephedra, Ginseng, Siberian Ginseng, Oats, Damiana, Kola, Gotu Kola, Thuja, Vervain.

NERVE TONICS. To invigorate and restore. Regarded as nutrients for strengthening nerve fibres and their protective sheaths. Help resolve effects of stress and replace mineral deficiencies in nerve tissue. They bring a new vigour in place of enervation and debility.
Betony, Damiana, Oats, St John's Wort, Skullcap, Vervain.
Combination. Tea: Equal parts, Skullcap, Betony, Vervain. 1 heaped teaspoon to each cup boiling water; infuse 15 minutes. Half-1 cup freely.

NERVOUS BOWEL SYNDROME. Frequent urging to stool due to nervous irritability or emotional distress.
Indicated: astringents, nerve relaxants.
Teas. Hops, Vervain, Chamomile, Cranesbill.
Tablets/capsules. Chamomile, Calamus, Wild Yam, Fenugreek.
Formula. Bayberry 2; Wild Yam 1; Valerian half. Dose: Liquid extracts: 1-2 teaspoons. Tinctures: 2-3 teaspoons. Powders: 750mg (three 00 capsules or half a teaspoon). Thrice daily.
Tincture. Black Catechu BHP (1983). 1:5 in 45 per cent alcohol. Dose 2.5 to 5ml in water, thrice daily.
Fenulin. (*Gerard House*)
Diet. Slippery Elm gruel.
Supplements. Vitamins A, B6, C, Calcium, Dolomite.

NERVOUS DEBILITY. Nerve weakness; loss of strength and power.
To strengthen nerves and generate vitality: Ginseng, Bee pollen, Oats, Ginkgo, Saw Palmetto, Damiana.
Tea. Formula. Equal parts: Betony, Balm, Skullcap. One heaped teaspoon to each cup boiling water; infuse 5-15 minutes. 1 cup thrice daily.
Gentian. One teaspoon fine-cut root in cup cold water; infuse overnight. Strain; drink cold following morning.
Tablets/capsules: Damiana, Skullcap, Lady's Slipper, Ginseng, Ginkgo.
Formula. Equal parts: Gentian, Oats. Gotu Kola. Dose: Liquid Extracts: 2 teaspoons. Tinctures: 3 teaspoons. Powders: 750mg (three 00 capsules or half a teaspoon). Thrice daily.
After surgical operation: St John's Wort. Hawthorn.

NERVOUS EXHAUSTION. See: EXHAUSTION.

NERVOUS STOMACH. Stomach hypersensitivity, with absence of acidity or organic disturbance.

Calamus, Cinnamon, Burnett Saxifrage, Lovage, Fumitory, Rosemary, Wormwood, Oats, Skullcap. German Chamomile tea.

NERVE TENSION. Nervous excitability, irritability, prone to over-reaction by anger or other destructive emotion.
Teas. Cowslip flowers, St John's Wort flowers, Passion flower, Valerian, Hops, Lime flowers, Balm, Motherwort, Woodruff, Skullcap, Oats.
Formula, tea: equal parts, Balm, Motherwort, Passion flower. 1 heaped teaspoon to each cup boiling water; infuse 5-10 minutes. 1 cup thrice daily.
Tablets. Valerian. Pulsatilla. Natracalm. (*English Grains*) 500mg Passion flower tablets: 1 tablet thrice daily.

See: SEDATIVES.

NERVOUS SHOCK. Non-medical term for nervous collapse. "All gone to pieces" syndrome following a period of abnormal stress or shock. Nervous breakdown. Psychiatric illness. Post-traumatic stress disorder.
Alternatives. Betony, Black Cohosh, Hops, Lady's Slipper, Mistletoe, Oats, Skullcap, Valerian.
Tea. Formula. Equal parts: Skullcap, Mistletoe, Valerian. 1 heaped teaspoon to each cup water gently simmered 10 minutes. Dose: half-1 cup thrice daily.
Formula. Equal parts: Hops, Rosemary, Valerian. Dose: Liquid Extracts: 1 teaspoon. Tinctures: 2 teaspoons. Powders: 500mg (two 00 capsules or one-third teaspoon). Thrice daily.
Supplements. B-complex, B12, B6, E. Magnesium, Dolomite. Calcium.

NERVOUSNESS IN YOUNG WOMEN. With menstrual problems, menopausal women, ovarian pain, or weak nerves after childbrith.
Tea. Combine equal parts: Raspberry leaves, Skullcap, Motherwort. 1 heaped teaspoon to each cup boiling water; infuse 15 minutes. 1 cup freely.
Formula. Equal parts: Black Cohosh, Helonias, Valerian. Dose: Liquid Extracts: half a teaspoon. Tinctures: 1 teaspoon. Powders: 250mg thrice daily.
Supplements. B-complex. Vitamin C to aid iron absorption.

NETTLERASH. Hives. A rash resembling the sting of a nettle. Itchy red or red-white patches appear chiefly on face and trunk. A transient eruption or watery swelling may appear by release of histamine due to allergy. May be a reaction to environmental irritants from plants, insect stings, chemicals or certain foods as after eating strawberries, lobster. Numerous allergens include food additives, acid fruits, pork, bacon, ham, eggs.
Alternatives. Oral anti-histamines include: Burdock, Goldenseal, Juniper berries, Marshmallow, Lobelia, Myrrh, Echinacea, Nettles, Parsley root.
Teas. Betony, Boneset, Celery seed, Chamomile, Chickweed, Elderflowers, Hops, Meadowsweet, Motherwort, Red Clover, Sarsaparilla, Skullcap, Yarrow.
Tea, formula. Equal parts: Meadowsweet, Nettles, Red Clover. 1 heaped teaspoon to each cup boiling water; infuse 15 minutes; 1 cup thrice daily.
Decoction (cold). One teaspoon Barberry bark to each cup cold water steeped overnight. Half-1 cup thrice the following day.
Tablets/capsules. Blue Flag. Echinacea.
Formula. Echinacea 2; Blue Flag 1; Valerian 1. Dose – Powders: 500mg (two 00 capsules or one-third teaspoon). Liquid extracts: 1 teaspoon. Tinctures: 2 teaspoons. Thrice daily.
Practitioner's prescription. Tinctures: Echinacea ang. 20ml; Ephedra sinica, 20ml; Urtica dioica, 10ml. Aqua et 100ml. Sig: 5ml (3i) tds Aq cal. pc.
Alternative:– Liquid extract Echinacea ang. 1 fl oz (30ml). Liquid extract Urtica dioica. 1 fl oz. Liquid extract Humulus lupulus. Half fl oz (15ml). Syrup Senna. 2 fl oz (60ml). Aqua et 8 fl oz (240ml). Sig: 8ml (3i) tds aq cal. pc. (*Arthur Barker, FNIMH*)
Topical. Wash with infusion of Chickweed, Elderflowers, Mullein, Chamomile or Eucalyptus leaves.
Oil of Evening Primrose. Aloe Vera gel.
Creams: Vitamin E, Chickweed, Elderflowers, Comfrey, Plantain.
Diet. See: DIET – SKIN DISEASES.
Supplements. Daily. Vitamin A (7500iu). Vitamin C (2g).

NETTLES. *Urtica dioica L. German*: Grosse Brandnetel. *French*: Grande ortie. *Spanish*: Ortiga. *Italian*: Grande ortica. *Part used*: dried herb.
Constituents: Chlorophyll (high), vitamins including Vitamin C, serotonin, histamine, acetyl-choline, minerals including iron, calcium, silica.
Action: blood tonic, hypoglycaemic, antiseptic, tonic-astringent (external), diuretic, haemostatic (external), expectorant, vasodilator, hypotensive, galactagogue, splenic, circulatory stimulant, amphoteric (can increase or reduce flow of breast milk, making its own adjustment). Strengthens natural resistance. Re-mineraliser, antirheumatic. Eliminates uric acid from the body. Anti-haemorrhagic. Mild diuretic.
Uses: iron-deficiency anaemia, gout (acute painful joints – partial amelioration). First stage of fevers (repeat frequently), malaria. Uvula – inflammation of. Foul-smelling sores. To stimulate kidneys. Detoxifies the blood. Pregnancy (Nettle and Raspberry leaf tea for iron and calcium). To withstand onset of uraemia in kidney disease; chronic skin disease, melaena with blood in stool, splenic disorders, high blood sugar in diabetes, burns (first degree), feeble digestion due to low level HCL; bleeding of stomach, bowels, lung and womb. Has power to eliminate urates; expulsion of gravel. On taking Nettle tea for high blood pressure passage of gravel is possible and should be regarded as a favourable sign. For women desiring an ample bust. Lobster and other shell-fish allergy, strawberry allergy. Nettle rash. Hair – fall out – tea used as a rinse.
"No plant is more useful in domestic medicine." (*Hilda Leyel*)
Frequent drinks of Nettle tea often allay itching of Hodgkin's disease.
Preparations. Thrice daily.
Tea: 1oz herb to 1 pint boiling water; infuse 15 minutes. 1 cup.

Liquid Extract: 3-4ml in water.
Tincture BHP (1983): 1 part to 5 parts 45 per cent alcohol. Dose, 2-6ml in water.
Powder: 210mg capsules, 6-8 capsules daily. (*Arkocaps*)
Floradix Herbal Iron Extract contains Nettles. (*Salus-Haus*)
Nettle shampoo and hair lotion.
Diet. Nettles cooked and eaten as spinach. Fresh juice: 1-2 teaspoons. GSL

NEURALGIA, FACIAL. Trigeminal Neuralgia. Severe lancing pain along one or more branches of the fifth cranial nerve.
Causes include: dental problems, ill-fitting dentures, laughing, yawning, bad teeth.
Symptoms: nervous exhaustion, contracted pupils, flushed face.
Alternatives. Black Cohosh, Cactus, Celery seed, Bogbean, Chamomile, Lady's Slipper, Ginseng, Hops, Jamaica Dogwood, White Willow, Wild Lettuce, Skullcap, St John's Wort, Valerian.
Tea. Combine equal parts: Chamomile, Hops, Skullcap. 1 heaped teaspoon to each cup boiling water; infuse 5-10 minutes. 1 cup freely.
Decoction. Combine: Rosemary 2; Ladyslipper 1; Jamaica Dogwood 1. 1 heaped teaspoon to each cup water gently simmered 20 minutes. Half-1 cup every 2-3 hours.
Tablets. Passion flower. Ginseng. St John's Wort, White Willow.
Formula. Equal parts: Jamaica Dogwood, Wild Lettuce, Valerian. Dose: Liquid extracts: 1 teaspoon. Tinctures: 2 teaspoons. Powders: 500mg (two 00 capsules or one-third teaspoon). Thrice daily.
Cayenne pepper (Capsicum). Frequently successful.
Practitioner. Tincture Gelsemium BPC (1973). Dose: 0.3ml (5 drops).
Topical. Poultice: Chamomile, Hops, Linseed or Bran. Acute cases (cold), chronic cases (hot). Grated or bruised Horseradish root. Evening Primrose oil. Hot cider vinegar. Tincture Arnica or Hypericum.
Aromatherapy. 2 drops each: Juniper, Lavender, Chamomile to 2 teaspoons vegetable oil. Light massage.
Diet, and supplements. Same as for general neuralgia. Australian researchers found that hot curries and spices actually trigger the trigeminal nerve causing a burning sensation.

NEURALGIA, GENERAL. Pain along a nerve, i.e. pain in the shoulders from pressure on a spinal nerve serving the neck.
Alternatives. Black Cohosh, Cactus, Chamomile, Lady's Slipper, Ginseng, Hops, Jamaica Dogwood, White Willow, Wild Lettuce, Valerian.
Chamomile tea (mild analgesic).
Tablets/capsules. Any of the above.
Formula. Ginseng 4; Black Cohosh 2; Skullcap 2; Mistletoe 1; Motherwort 1. Dose: Liquid Extracts: 1 teaspoon. Tinctures: 2 teaspoons. Powders: 500mg (two 00 capsules or one-third teaspoon). Thrice daily. Children: see: DOSAGE.
Cayenne pepper (Capsicum) sometimes successful.
Topical. Poultice: Chamomile, Hops, Linseed or Bran. Acute cases (cold), chronic cases (hot). Grated or bruised Horseradish root. Evening Primrose oil. Hot Cider vinegar, Tincture Arnica or Hypericum.
Aromatherapy. 2 drops each: Juniper, Lavender, Chamomile to 2 teaspoons vegetable oil. Light massage.
Diet. High protein. Calcium-rich foods.
Supplements. Vitamin B-complex, B6, B12, Niacin, Magnesium, Dolomite, Zinc.
See: FACIAL and INTERCOSTAL NEURALGIA; DYSMENORRHOEA (neuralgia of the womb). ANTISPASMODICS.

NEURALGIA, INTERCOSTAL. Pain along a sensory nerve serving the chest, without loss of sensation and power of movement. Differs from neuritis in which nerves are inflamed.
Causes: all kinds of infective diseases. Rheumatism, bad teeth, bony spinal lesions, gall stone, liver disorder, thickening of pleura, fractured ribs, shingles – see: SHINGLES. In simple cases a cup of Chamomile tea may suffice. Persistent cases require one of the following alternatives.
Alternatives. *Decoction*. Combine equal parts: Black Cohosh, Jamaica Dogwood (or White Willow), Pleurisy root. 1 heaped teaspoon to each cup water gently simmered 20 minutes. Half-1 cup thrice daily.
Formula. Cramp bark 2; Black Cohosh 1; Valerian 1. Pinch of Cayenne or few drops Tincture Capsicum. Dose: Liquid Extracts: 1 teaspoon. Tinctures: 2 teaspoons. Powders: 500mg (two 00 capsules or one-third teaspoon). Thrice daily.
Neuralgia associated with bronchi and lung: Formula: Cramp bark 2; Pleurisy root 2; Liquorice half. Dose: as above.
Practitioner. Tincture Gelsemium BPC (1973). 0.3ml (5 drops) in water as necessary.
Dr Finlay Ellingwood. Tincture Pleurisy root (Asclepias). 20 drops, every 2 hours.
Topical. Poultice: Chamomile, Hops, Linseed or Bran. Acute cases (cold), chronic cases (hot). Grated or bruised Horseradish root. Evening Primrose oil. Hot Cider vinegar. Tincture Arnica or Hypericum.
Aromatherapy. 2 drops each: Juniper, Lavender, Chamomile, to 2 teaspoons vegetable oil. Massage.
Diet, vitamins, minerals. Same as for general neuralgia. Cold water packs.

NEURASTHENIA. A vague term now superceded by 'debility' and 'depression'. The condition usually responds well.
Symptoms: loss of appetite, weight, energy and sleep. Often follows the toxaemia of faulty nutrition and metabolism. Sexual abuse, mental or physical shock. Feeble mental health. May herald the onset of chronic illness. Blood pressure may be low (Hawthorn, Broom, Kola). Treatment should be directed towards building up the consitution by a healthy lifestyle and wholesome mental habits.
Alternatives. *Teas*. Betony, Hops, Oats, Skullcap, Passion flower (undue restlessness), Lime flowers (easily stimulated). Gentian or Mistletoe: 1-2 teaspoons to cup *cold* water allowed to steep overnight; half cup morning and evening the following day.
Decoction: combine: Oats 2; Skullcap 1; Peruvian bark half; Hops half. 1oz to 1 pint water; bring to boil; simmer 2 minutes. Drink cold, 1 cup before meals, thrice daily.
Tablets/capsules. Combination (Kola, Damiana, Saw Palmetto). Gentian. Ginseng. Ginkgo.
Powders. Combine: Kola 2; Peruvian bark 1; Fringe Tree half; Liquorice half. Dose: 300mg thrice daily.
Liquid Extracts. Combine Valerian 1; Hops 1; Wild Yam half; Oats 2. Dose: 1 teaspoon thrice daily.
Tinctures. Combine: Peruvian bark 2; Valerian 1; Pulsatilla half; Fringe Tree half. Dose: 1-2 teaspoons thrice daily.
Diet. Oatmeal porridge. Cider vinegar. High protein.
Vitamins. B-complex, B6, B12. C, E.
Minerals. Dolomite. Iron complex. Zinc.
Note. Some authorities believe neurasthenia and chronic fatigue syndrome are the same.

NEURITIS. Inflammation or deterioration of a nerve, usually peripheral. Peripheral neuritis. When more than one nerve is involved it is known as polyneuritis which may occur in various parts of the body.
Causes: injuries, bone fractures, alcoholism, viral infection, Vitamin B12 deficiency, diabetes. Nerves become inflamed when poisons are taken into the body in the form of lead, mercury, arsenic and other heavy metals. Gout, leukaemia, and infectious diseases generally, may leave a legacy of polyneuritis. The neuritis of beri-beri is due to lack of Vitamin B1 (thiamine). Neuritis of the optic nerve – Gelsemium.
Symptoms. Swelling, redness and pain in affected area. When squeezed, muscles are tender. Knee-jerks and other reflexes may be lost. 'Pins and needles'.
Treatment. Appropriate to all types. To enhance growth of new nerve fibres as well as to assuage pain.
Alternatives. Catnep (inflammation), Chamomile, Cramp bark, Gelsemium, Ginseng, Fringe Tree bark, Ladyslipper, Hops, Oats, Valerian, Wild Yam.
Tea. Combine equal parts: Catnep, Skullcap, Chamomile. 1 heaped teaspoon to each cup boiling water; infuse 15 minutes. 1 cup freely.
Decoction. Combine equal parts: Cramp bark, Valerian. One heaped teaspoon to each cup water gently simmered 10-20 minutes. Half-1 cup thrice daily.
Tablets/capsules. Chamomile, Cramp bark, Ginseng, Skullcap, Valerian.
Powders. Combine, Cramp bark 1; Liquorice half; Valerian half; Wild Yam half. Dose: 500mg thrice daily.
Liquid Extracts. Combine: Chamomile 1oz; Hops half an ounce; Skullcap 60 drops; Cramp bark 1oz; water to 8oz. Dose: 2 teaspoons in water after meals. (*A. Barker*)
Tinctures. Formula: Cramp bark 3; Chamomile 2; Hops 2; Peppermint 1. Dose: 2 teaspoons thrice daily.
Practitioner. Tincture Gelsemium BPC (1973). Dose: 0.3ml (5 drops).
Topical. Oil of St John's Wort. Cloves, Cajeput, Chamomile.
Poultices. Chamomile, Yarrow.
Vitamins. B1, B2, B6, B12, B-complex. Pantothenic acid.
Minerals. Magnesium. Dolomite. Manganese.

NEUROBLASTOMA. A malignant tumour on a nerve ganglia. Exceedingly painful.
Treatment: to sustain the nervous system and help reduce pain. By medical practitioner. Hospitalisation. Sedatives. Antispasmodics. Anti-neoplastics.
Passion flower, Black Cohosh, Lobelia, Asafoetida, Mistletoe.
Formula. Periwinkle (Madagascar) 2; Black Cohosh 1; Passion flower 1. Liquid Extracts: 1-2 teaspoons. Tinctures: 2-3 teaspoons. Powders: 750mg. Three or more times daily.
Vinchristine. Response to vinca alkaloids.

NEW JERSEY TEA. Red root. Wild snowball. *Ceanothus americana L. German*: Säckelblume. *French*: Céanothe. *Italian*: Ceanoto. Leaves. Leaves were used as a substitute for tea during the American War of Independence. *Keynote*: spleen.
Action: alterative, febrifuge, astringent, stimulating tonic, expectorant.
Uses. Enlargement of the spleen from infection or toxic self-poisoning. Deep-seated pain in the left hypochondrium. Cannot lie down for pain on left side.
"It is a curious fact that many dropsical patients can be cured by spleen remedies." (*Dr Rademacher, 1879*)
Combines well with Fringe Tree bark.

Preparations. Thrice daily.
Tea. 1 teaspoon to each cup boiling water. Dose: quarter to half a cup.
Liquid extract. 5-30 drops.
Injection for gonorrhoea, leucorrhoea or chronic vaginal discharge: 2oz herb to 2 pints water; bring to boil, simmer for 1 minute; strain when warm. Inject. Use confined to practitioner.

NIGHT BLOOMING CEREUS. See: CACTUS.

NIGHTMARE. A frightening dream. Night terrors in children.
Causes: excessive mental activity during the day, a heavy meal late in the evening, indigestion, obstruction of free blood return from the brain.
Teas: Alfalfa. English Herb Tea.
Dioscorides, and Pliny, both record: Paeony root. Prepare: 1 part powdered Paeony root mixed with 4 parts honey. 1-2 teaspoons to cup boiling water at bedtime.
France: traditional – Marjoram tea.
Dr Wooster Beach, USA. Cup Skullcap tea with honey and pinch of Cayenne on retiring.
Aromatherapy. Bedtime inhalation or anointing of forehead: oil of Frankincense.
Nightly footbath. Practice relaxation at night before falling asleep.

NINE RUBBING OILS (*Potter's*). For rheumatism, fibrositis, painful joints and muscles. Oil for external use.
Ingredients: Amber oil 4 per cent; Clove oil BP 1 per cent; Eucalyptus oil BP 4 per cent; Linseed oil 10 per cent; Methyl sal BP 4 per cent; Volatile Mustard oil 0.03 per cent; Turpentine oil BP 12.3 per cent; Thyme oil 2 per cent; Peppermint oil BP 2.1 per cent; Arachis oil BP to 100.

NIPPLES, Cracked. See: BREASTS.

NOISES IN HEAD (ears). See: TINNITUS.

NORMACOL. For relief of non-persistent constipation. Combines the bulking agent Sterculia, with the natural stimulant Frangula. Useful in pregnancy and for management of colostomies and ileostomies. For 'high residue diet' management of diverticular disease of the colon and other conditions requiring a high fibre regime. For the initiation and maintenance of bowel action after rectal and anal surgery.
Preparation: Oral administration. Brown coated granules containing Sterculia BP 62 per cent and Frangula BPC (1949) 8 per cent. Dosage: adults: 1-2 heaped 5ml spoonfuls, once or twice daily, after meals. Children (6-12 years) half above amount.
Overdosage or where not adequately washed-down with fluid may lead to intestinal obstruction.
Contra-indication: intestinal obstruction.

NOSEBLEED. Epistaxis. Often Nature's way of relieving high blood pressure.
Causes: high blood pressure, accident, anticoagulant drugs, infection, blood disorder. As many as fifty-four causes. Usually innocent, from ruptured small vessel on anterior part of the nasal septum. May be spontaneous in the elderly, in which case blood vessels may be strengthened by Nettle tea.
Teas. Marigold flowers, Ephedra, Nettles, Melilot, Yarrow, Shepherd's Purse, Ladies Mantle, Tormentil.
Decoction. Burdock root.
Tablets/capsules. Cranesbill. Goldenseal.
Powders. Alternatives. (1) Cinnamon. (2) Bayberry. (3) Cranesbill. Half a teaspoon in milk or honey.
External. Instil juice of Houseleek into nostril. Soak cotton wool in Witch Hazel and plug nostril. Pound fresh Nettles to a pulp in pestal and mortar and instil the juice or pulp. Beth root powder. Artichoke. Soak cotton wool in Cider vinegar and plug nostril. Other astringents, as available. See: ASTRINGENTS. Cold compresses to back of neck.

NOSE DROPS DRILL. To have effect upon the nasal mucosa, drops for congestion of the upper respiratory tract should be correctly instilled otherwise they may arrive in the stomach. The patient should lie on his back with his head hanging over the edge of the bed. Drops, blood heat, should be instilled into the nostrils and the patient remain in the same position for two minutes. Drops should be used in this way for no more than three days. Ephedrine BPC, Garlic, Lobelia, Menthol, etc.
Effective oil: Tea Tree oil (1 part) to 20 parts Almond, Olive or Corn oil.
Alternative. Adopt Mecca position. Kneel down, place head on ground and tuck under. The spray will reach the maximum surface of action in the nasal cavity.

NOTIFIABLE DISEASES. Notifiable diseases under the Public Health (Control of Disease Act, 1984) are:–
Acute encephalitis, acute meningitis, acute poliomyelitis, anthrax, cholera, diphtheria, dysentery (amoebic and bacillary), food poisoning, infective jaundice, leprosy, leptospirosis, lassa fever, mumps, malaria, marburg disease, measles, German measles, ophthalmia neonatorum, paratyphoid fever, plague, rabies, relapsing fever, scarlet fever, smallpox, tetanus, tuberculosis, typhoid fever, typhus, viral haemorrhagic fever, whooping cough and yellow fever.
Six communicable diseases are internationally notifiable to the World Health Organisation:
yellow fever, plague, cholera, smallpox, louse-borne relapsing fever, louse-borne typhus.

Notification has to be made to local and central Government authorities. Certain occupational diseases and all cases of cancer must be registered and notified.

It is required that the above diseases and certain others receive modern medical therapy in a hospital or treatment under the supervision of a qualified physician. Failure to conform may expose a practitioner, registered or unregistered, to a charge of negligence.

NSAIDS. Non-steroidal inflammatory drugs. Pain-killers for muscular rheumatism and other painful disorders, (aspirin). NSAIDS work by blocking prostaglandin synthesis; usually therapeutically for inflamed joints. Reactions may follow their use, sometimes creating gastrointestinal problems and liver, kidney and skin disorders. Bleeding and internal ulcer may sometimes follow, the elderly specially at risk.
Alternatives: anti-inflammatories, analgesics.
To assist withdrawal – Devil's Claw (inflamed joints), Meadowsweet (stomach), Blue Flag (liver and skin).
Formula. Devil's Claw 2; Black Willow 2; Wild Yam 1; Valerian 1. Mix. Dose – Powders: quarter to half a teaspoon; Liquid Extracts: 1 teaspoon; Tinctures: 2-3 teaspoons; in water or honey thrice daily.

Patients on NSAID drugs should not take salt substitutes containing potassium. A quarter of patients on long-term NSAIDS suffer oesophagitis. Lesions may be caused in the gullet by 'pill oesophagitis' where delayed passage into the stomach of pills and tablets damages the oesophageal mucosal membrane.

NUMBNESS. Local parasthesia. Pins and needles. Mild weakness of a limb. Most cases are due to prolonged pressure; a neuralgia as when falling asleep with legs crossed, or from wearing tight jeans. Where persistent, may be due to nerve damage, carpal tunnel syndrome, cervical rib or other conditions from pressure Osteopathy may resolve.
Simple temporary numbness: Tea: equal parts, Nettles, Skullcap, St John's Wort. Singly, or in combination. 1 heaped teaspoon to each cup boiling water; infuse 15 minutes. 1 cup when necessary.
Persistent, but of no known cause: Liquid Extract Asafoetida: 1-3 drops in honey thrice daily.
Practitioner. Tincture Gelsemium BPC (1973). Dose: 0.3ml (5 drops).

NUTRIENT. A non-irritating, easily-digested agent which provides body nourishment and stimulates metabolic processes.

Alfalfa, Arabic gum, Arrow root, Carob flour, Fenugreek seed, Iceland Moss, Irish Moss, Okra pods, Sago root, Slippery Elm, Oats, Barley.

NUTMEG. *Myristica fragrans*, Houtt. *German*: Muskatnussbaum. *French*: Miscadier. *Spanish*: Nuez Moscado. *Italian*: Noce moscato. *Arabian*: Jour-ut-tib. *Indian*: Jaephal. *Iranian*: Jowz bôyah. *Chinese*: Jou-tou-kou. *Part used*: dried kernels. *Constituents*: volatile oil.
Action: prostaglandin inhibitor, anti-diarrhoeal, anti-inflammatory, antispasmodic, sedative, diaphoretic, brain stimulant, carminative, aromatic (oil), digestive stimulant.
Uses: children's diarrhoea, dysentery, colic, nausea, vomiting, to promote acid content of gastric juice. Claimed to dissolve gall-stones. Nervous stomach, throbbing headache caused by stress, palpitation. Relief of muscle tension back of neck.

"To comfort head and nerves." (*Dr Joseph Mill*)
Preparations. Average dose, 0.3-1 gram or equivalent. Thrice daily, after meals. Grains obtained by rubbing a Nutmeg over a metal kitchen grater; may be taken in a beverage, honey, mashed banana, etc.
Powder: Fill No 3 gelatin capsules; 1 capsule or 50mg.
Oil: an alternative for internal conditions. 1-2 drops daily.
Massage oil for rheumatic pains and to stimulate circulation: Nutmeg oil (1), Olive oil or Almond oil (10).
Home tincture: one freshly grated Nutmeg to macerate in half pint 60 per cent alcohol (Vodka, gin, etc) 7 days. Decant. Dose: 5-10 drops.

Avoid large doses. GSL

NUTRITION ASSOCIATION, The. To assist people to find a nutritionist in their area. Concerned with all aspects of diet – proteins, carbohydrates, fats, fibre, vitamins, minerals and other trace components of food. Factors which may affect a person's nutritional status such as dietary imbalances, food allergies, food processing, additives, drug therapy, metabolic and digestive disorders, personal life-style, stress, exercise and environmental factors. Maintains a directory of practising nutritionists. Promotes educational courses, encourages research.
Address: 24, Harcourt House, 19, Cavendish Square, London W1M 0AB.

NU ZHEN ZI. *Ligustrum lucidum. Part used*: berries.
Action. Diuretic, immune-stimulant, tonic. Kidney regulator.
Uses. Mild kidney disorders, menopause, irritability, hyperactivity. Recovery after hysterectomy.

NYMPHOMANIA. Insatiable desire for sex in women.
Indicated: Agnus Castus, Hops, Black Willow, Ladyslipper, (*Albert Priest*) Sweet Marjoram.

Traditional: White Pond Lily (emblem of purity).
Chinese Barefoot medicine – Sage tea.
Teas. Agnus Castus, Hops, Sweet Marjoram.
Decoction. Black Willow bark.
Tablets/capsules. Agnus Castus, Black Willow.
Formula. Equal parts: Black Willow, Agnus Castus, Wild Lettuce. Dose: Liquid extracts: 2 teaspoons. Tinctures: 2-3 teaspoons. Powders: 750mg (three 00 capsules or half a teaspoon). Thrice daily.
Oregano (origanum vulgare). Spanish traditional. 5-20 drops tincture or 1 drop oil in honey between meals, thrice daily.
Home-tincture: handful Oregano steeped in bottle of white wine.

OAK. English oak. *Quercus robur L.* Dried inner bark. *German*: Stieleiche. *French*: Bouvre. *Italian*: Rovere.
Constituents: tannins, quercin, pectin, resin.
Action: astringent, styptic, antiseptic, anti-inflammatory, haemostatic.
Uses. Alcoholism, diarrhoea, dysentery, colitis. To cleanse external ulcers and suppurating wounds. Mouth ulcers, spongy gums, sore throat, tonsillitis, (gargle and mouth-wash). Non-infectious vaginal discharge, leucorrhoea, (douche). Chilblains (decoction as a lotion). Piles (decoction as an enema).
Preparations. Average dose, half-2 grams, or equivalent. Thrice daily.
Decoction. Half an ounce to 1 pint water gently simmered 20 minutes. Dose, one-third to half a cup (internally).
Liquid extract BHP (1983). 1:1 in 25 per cent alcohol; dose, 1-2ml.
Tincture of acorns. Dehusk and pulverise acorns. 1 part to 5 parts 45 per cent alcohol (vodka etc). Macerate 8 days, shake daily. Filter. Dose, 15-30 drops. External: 1 part to 20 parts boiled water.
Powder, inner bark or acorns, for dusting foul-smelling ulcers and septic wounds.
Oak Bath. 6-8oz bark to 10 litres (7 pints) water simmered 20 minutes. Add to bath water.
Oak Compress. Soak a piece of lint in decoction and fix firmly for acute eye troubles. GSL

OATMEAL BATH. For irritated, itching skin as in eczema or shingles. Tie one pound uncooked oatmeal in a piece of gauze and run-on the hot bath tap. When softened, use as a sponge during the bath.

OATS. Oatstraw. *Avena sativa L.* Husks of oats. *German*: Evenhafer. *French*: Avoine. *Spanish*: Avena. *Italian*: Biada.
Constituents: glycosyl flavones, proteins, Vitamin E, oil, proteins.
Action: nerve restorative, antidepressant, tranquilliser, brain tonic. Cardiac tonic BHP (1983). Nutrient with selective action on brain and nerve cells. Source of minerals. Thymoleptic. Improves performance of athletes and stamina.

"Oats have the highest content of iron, zinc and manganese of all grain species." (*Dr A. Vogel*)
Uses. Benzodiazepine, Valium or other drug addiction – with Valerian and Skullcap to assist withdrawal. Alcoholism. Nerve and physical weakness with depression and anxiety. Debility following illness; recovery from surgical operation. Neurasthenia. Tension and irritability through overwork. Headache with pain at back of the neck; sleeplessness, shingles, hyperactivity in children. Nerve tremor in the aged not caused by Parkinson's or other nerve degenerative diseases. May be taken with benefit for general well-being in chronic nerve dyscrasies but with limited improvement in basic condition. Sometimes proves of benefit for schizophrenic tendency. Sexual weakness with night losses and impotence. Combines well with Saw Palmetto for spermatorrhoea. Combines with Valerian and Wood Betony for nerve weakness, to minimise attacks of petit mal, chorea and other convulsive states. Does not combine well with Passion flower or Cypripedium.
Contra-indicated in cases sensitive to gluten.
Preparations. Average dose, 1-2 grams or equivalent. Thrice daily. An older generation of herbalists prepared their tinctures and extracts from the green flowering unripe wild Oats as the effective constituent is unstable. Taken hot, effects are more immediate.
Tea: oatstraw: 1-2 teaspoons to each cup boiling water; infuse 15 minutes. Drink freely.
Tincture BHP (1983) 1 part to 5 parts 45 per cent alcohol. Macerate and shake daily for 8 days; dose, 1-5ml.
Extracts, groats and oatmeal products are all beneficial but are not of the same efficacy as the fresh green plant.
Oatstraw bath: 2-3 handfuls oatstraw. Simmer in 2-3 litres water for 5 minutes; strain; add to bathwater.
Liquid Extract: dose: 1-2ml in water.
Traditional combination: equal parts – Oats, Passion flower, Hops and Valerian.
Diet. Porridge, but not to be eaten by the gluten intolerant.
Side-effects: none known. GSL

OBESITY. Excessively overweight due mainly to fat which is carried under the skin and around internal organs.
Main cause: over-eating.

Some people may be 'slow burners' requiring metabolic stimulants. Almost all types profit by eating less. Low thyroid and adrenal disorders lead to slowing down and overweight. Excess starchy foods, particularly those containing sugar are converted into fat. Fruit, vegetables, meat and fish do not cause obesity. Select from the following alternatives.
Treatment. Increase metabolic rate and decrease body lipid content. Combine a laxative, diuretic and carminative.
Tea. Equal parts, Juniper, Senna leaves, Aniseed. 2 teaspoons to each cup boiling water; infuse 5-15 minutes. 1 cup morning and midday.
Phytomedicines in common use:–
Aniseed, Chickweed, <u>Clivers</u>, <u>Bladderwrack</u> (fatty degeneration of the heart), Fennel, Gotu Kola, Mate, Violet, Parsley, Garlic (Spanish traditional – 1 corm or 4 capsules daily), Black Cohosh (obesity of the menopause), <u>Motherwort</u>, Kelp (rich in iodine).
Any one – add Lady's Mantle where associated with menstrual problems.

Tablets/capsules. Any of the above. Poke root.
Formula. Bladderwrack 2; Clivers 1; Hawthorn 1; Frangula bark half. Pinch Cayenne or few drops Tincture Capsicum. Dose: Liquid extracts: 1-2 teaspoons. Tinctures: 2-3 teaspoons. Powders: 750mg (three 00 capsules or half a teaspoon). Morning and midday.
Cider vinegar. Claimed to reduce weight.
Evening Primrose oil. Brings about a rise in plasma glycerol in the blood; an indicator that body fat is being mobilised. Dose: 4 x 500mg capsules daily.
Diet. 3-day fruit juice fast. Follow with lacto-vegetarian meals. Avoid frying pan. Reduce dietary fat. Jerusalem artichokes.
Supplements. Dolomite, Iron, Sulphur, Zinc.
Supportive. Weight-watchers exercises.

OEDEMA. Accumulation of fluid beneath the skin or in a body cavity. See FLUID RETENTION SYNDROME.

OESOPHAGEAL SPASM. Constriction of the gullet and throat. Sense of rising pressure from chest to jaw that can simulate early heart attack.
Causes: emotional tension, hiatus hernia, food allergy and the damaging potential of hot drinks.
Alternatives. Acute case: Cramp bark. German Chamomile tea, freely. Phytomedicines for chronic condition or as preventatives: Passion flower, Skullcap, Wild Yam, Lobelia, Mistletoe, Valerian.
Formula. Cramp bark 2; Chamomile 1; Peppermint 1. Dose – Liquid extracts: 1-2 teaspoons. Tinctures: 2-3 teaspoons. Powders: 750mg (three 00 capsules or half a teaspoon) 3 or more times daily.
Milk. Drink whole glass cold milk, with or without 1 drop oil Peppermint, immediately on onset of pain. May relieve spasms in seconds.

OESOPHAGEAL STRICTURE. An abnormal narrowing of the (lower) gullet.
Causes: injury, scarring by chemical medicines, drugs swallowed with insufficient water, antacids for heartburn, piping-hot tea. It is important to exclude oesophageal cancer.

Those with 'gullet-reflex' such as the elderly, are at risk. A relationship exists between toothlessness and this condition. Eating of soft fibreless foods does not expand the tube down which food passes.
Alternatives. Horsetail, Irish Moss. Echinacea. Marshmallow. Goldenseal. Sarsaparilla. Calendula (Marigold), Chamomile.
Tea. Formula – equal parts, Horsetail, Chamomile, Marshmallow. 1 heaped teaspoon to each cup boiling water; infuse 5-15 minutes. 1 cup thrice daily.
Tablets/capsules. Echinacea, Goldenseal, Sarsaparilla, Chamomile.
Formula. Irish Moss 1; Comfrey 1; Calendula half; Goldenseal quarter. Dose – Liquid extracts: 1-2 teaspoons. Tinctures: 2-3 teaspoons. Powders: 750mg (three 00 capsules or half a teaspoon) in water before meals.
Diet. High fibre. Raw carrots with prolonged mastication. Hot drinks are potentially damaging.

OESOPHAGITIS. Inflammation of the lower oesophagus (gullet).
Causes: reflux of acid from the stomach due to incompetence of sphincter muscle. This muscle can be weakened by drugs, coffee, smoking, alcohol, piping-hot drinks or the presence of hiatus hernia.
Treatment: same as for HEARTBURN.

OESTROGENS. Phytoestrogens. Oestrogens are steroid sex hormones secreted mainly by the ovary, and in smaller amounts by the adrenals, testes and placenta. They control sexual development and regulate the menstrual cycle. In puberty they are responsible for pubic hair and secondary female sex characteristics.

Some herbs, having a similar effect, are known as *oestrogenics*, and which are given usually during days 1 to 14 of the menstrual cycle for oestrogen-deficiency disorders: night sweats, hot flushes, urinary and menopausal problems.

This group should not be given to patients taking oestrogens of orthodox pharmacy, or in the presence of growths on the female organs: fibroids, endometriosis, cancer, cysts. It has an important role in the metabolism of amino acids, vitamins and minerals.

More than 300 plants are known to possess oestrogenic activity including wholewheat and soya products.
Important oestrogenics: Aniseed, Beth root, Black Cohosh, Elder, Don quai, Evening Primrose, Fennel, Helonias (False Unicorn root), Hops, Liquorice, Sage, Sarsaparilla, True Unicorn root (Aletris). Any one, or more in combination, may be used for symptoms of the menopause or oestrogen deficiency.

The closer we enhance ovarian and uterine function to give true hormone replacement, the more effective is the science of phytotherapy.

See: OSTEOPOROSIS.

OILS, IMPREGNATED. Properties of herbs may be extracted into an oil base, such as Olive or other vegetable oil in the proportion of 250g dried or 750g fresh herb to 1 pint (500ml) oil.

Bruise herbs with a rolling pin (double quantity for fresh herb). Add oil. Simmer in low heat until herbs change colour – about 1 hour. Strain into bottles.
Alternative. Place crushed herb, preferably flowers, in the oil in a wide-mouthed bottle or jar. Cover. Shake daily. After 3 days, strain off and

replenish with fresh material Repeat the process 3 or 4 times until the oil is saturated with essence of the flowers (or herb). Strain and bottle. Method suitable for Lavender, Rosemary, Bergamot, Rose petals, Mullein and Chamomile.

Sunflower oil is used in general practice, although Olive or other vegetable oil proves satisfactory.

OINTMENT BASES. Ointments are semi-solid preparations of a plant remedy in a non-aqueous base to protect, nourish or convey medication to the skin. They are made from a base. A herbal powder or fine-cut material is usually added to the base which will vary according to the substance used. Vaseline is popular as a base, yet many combinations are serviceable from which the following are a small selection. Ointments should not be made in plastic or aluminium vessels.

Perhaps the simplest base is lard or butter, as used by Maria Treben. 2 handfuls (4oz or 120g) finely chopped herbs are digested in 500g lard or butter. Heat gently one hour. Stand overnight. Should be sufficiently fluid next morning to filter through muslin or a wire-mesh strainer. Pour into jars. Very effective but its life is not more than a few weeks.

(a) Vaseline base. Dissolve vaseline. Place 1oz (handful) fresh herb (say . . . Chickweed) or tablespoon dried herb (or 2 teaspoons powder) in 7oz (100g) vaseline melted in low heat. Simmer gently 15 minutes, stirring all the time. Strain through a wire-mesh strainer while hot and pour into air-tight containers.

(b) Vaseline base. To incorporate essential oils; i.e. Oil of Eucalyptus 2ml; Oil of Pine 1ml; Oil of Peppermint 2ml; vaseline to 30 gram. Melt the vaseline. Add oils. Stir until cold. Makes a useful inhalant ointment applied directly to the frontal sinus areas, or inhaled from boiling water. (*Fred Fletcher Hyde*)

(c) Mixed base, suitable for holding liquid extracts, tinctures. Ingredients: parts, Almond oil 12; Liquid Extract (say . . . Comfrey) 5; powdered gum Acacia 3; water (preferably distilled) to 100. *Method*: Rub together a small equal amount of well-sieved Acacia powder and water to form a paste – best performed in a pestle and mortar. Add the Almond oil. Mix. Add liquid extract, tincture or oil slowly until a good consistency is reached. Slowly add remaining water and stir. Store in air-tight glass jars.

(d) *Olive and Beeswax base* Ingredients: 2oz beeswax; 16oz Olive oil.
Method: cut beeswax into slices and dissolve in the Olive oil on a low heat. Stir until all beeswax is dissolved. Place in a stone jar or pyrex vessel 12oz aerial parts of fresh herb material (Marigold, Plantain, Chickweed etc) or 4oz hard woody parts, roots or barks (Comfrey, Marshmallow, etc). Pour on the Olive oil and beeswax. Place in a warm oven for 3 hours; give an occasional stir. While still hot, strain through a wire-mesh strainer into pots. Store in a refrigerator. Where powders are used, the proportion is 2oz for every 16oz Olive oil.

(e) *Coconut oil base*. Dissolve 7 parts Coconut oil. Add 5 parts powdered herbs and 6 parts beeswax. Simmer gently 1 and a half hours. Strain through warm wire mesh strainer or muslin. Filter if necessary. Pour into jars.

(f) *Pile ointment*. Prepare, vaseline base. Add, Liquid Extract Pilewort 5 per cent, Liquid Extract Witch Hazel 5 per cent; Tincture Benzoin 5 per cent; Menthol 2 and a half per cent.

(g) *Pain Reliever*. Prepare, vaseline base. Add Menthol 2 per cent; Eucalyptus 2 per cent; Camphor 2 per cent; Oil of Mustard 0.2 per cent.

(h) *Russian traditional*. It is still common in country practice to simmer popular herbs (Marigold, Arnica, St John's Wort) in butter, as above.

Preservatives. Length of life of above ointments is increased by addition of Benzoic acid, Nipagen, etc. Benzoinated lard was once a popular base used in pharmacy. Ointments containing volatile oils should be kept in porcelain or glass pots in preference to synthetic containers. All ointments should be stored out of the light and in a cool place.

Marshmallow and Slippery Elm ointment has a long traditional reputation as a general purposes ointment.

OLBAS OIL. European household remedy over many years. A blend of plant oils originated in Switzerland. Stomachic, bactericidal and antiseptic. Has a wide sphere of therapeutic influence, used externally for relief of the pain of rheumatism, lumbago, etc; internally as a medicament for flatulence and minor stomach disorders. Inhaled, to clear nasal congestion caused by colds, bronchial catarrh, influenza and sinusitis.
Ingredients: Cajuput oil 18.5 per cent, Clove oil 10 per cent; Eucalyptus oil 35.45 per cent, Juniper berry oil 2.7 per cent, Menthol 10 per cent, Peppermint oil 25.45 per cent, Wintergreen oil 3.7 per cent. (*Lane's, UK*)

OLBAS PASTILLES. Oil Eucalyptus 1.16 per cent, Oil Peppermint 1.12 per cent, Menthol 0.1 per cent, Oil Juniper berry 0.067 per cent, Oil Wintergreen 0.047 per cent, and Oil Clove 0.0025 per cent. Respiratory obstruction and cough. (*Lane's, UK*)

OLD AGE. See: AGEING.

OLEANDER. *Nerium oleander L. French*: Laurier rose. *German*: Lorbeerrosen. *Italian*: Lauro roseo. *Spanish*: Adelfa baladre. *Arabian*: Sumul-himar. *Indian*: Karabi.

Constituents: neriodorin, neriodorein, essential oil.
Action: has a digitalis-like effect. Cardioactive. Diuretic. Seldom used in modern herbalism.

OLIBANUM. Frankincense. *Boswellia carteri*, Birdw. Gum.

Since ancient times is still used in China, India, other Far Eastern countries and the Catholic Church as incense. With it, Egyptians embalmed their dead.
Action: used internally in drop doses of the tincture as an antimicrobial, antiseptic, diuretic and tonic.
Uses. Historic remedy for venereal disease, open sores, suppurating wounds, tumour and cancer. Not confirmed by present-day research.
Preparation. *Tincture*: 1 part gum to 20 parts 90 per cent alcohol; macerate 8 days; shake daily, filter, bottle. Dose: 1-5 drops in water thrice daily. Or use as a lotion for suppurating external lesions; may be diluted many times.

OLIVE. Olive oil. Sweet oil. Lucca oil. *Olea europaea, L. German*: Olbaum. *French*: Olivier. *Spanish and Italian*: Olivo.
Constituents: palmitic, stearic and linoleic acid glycerides.
Action: demulcent, emollient, laxative, nutrient.
Uses, internal. While positive properties for the healing of wounds are present in a decoction of the leaves, it is for its oil that the tree is universally known. Taken for constipation and lead colic. Pin worms in children: 1 teaspoon daily for one month. Orally, the oil forms a barrier on the surface of the stomach thus arresting secretion of gastric juice. For this purpose it has been used with success for gastric and duodenal ulcer. Cases are on record of daily drinking a dessertspoonful of the oil to prevent heart disease and arteriosclerosis, and to alleviate muscular pain.

Olive oil is beneficial for increasing high-density lipoprotein (HDL) and to decrease low density lipoprotein (LDL) which can have a detrimental effect upon the blood when in excess.
Uses, external. In some Levantine counries it is still the belief that rubbing the body with the oil prevents rheumatism, gout and kindred conditions. It is a common ingredient in liniments and lotions for aches and pains of the muscles.

The oil should be expressed by the 'cold press' method to preserve its active constituents. Cases are on record where the swallowing of a single black Olive stone (pit) has relieved serious low back pain within hours.
Aromatherapy. Used as a base oil in the absence of Almond oil. GSL

OLIVE LEAVES. *Olea europea L.* Other names: see OLIVE.
Action: hypoglycaemic, hypotensive, diuretic, antispasmodic (mild), astringent diuretic, febrifuge, vulnerary, vasodilator, cholagogue.
Uses. To dilate coronary arteries and improve circulation of blood through the heart. Moderately high blood pressure. Infection of the urinary tract. Nephritis. To lower blood sugar – diabetes. To facilitate passage of gall-stones.
Preparations. Thrice daily.
Tea. 20-30g in 500ml (1 pint) boiling water; infuse 20 minutes. Dose: half-1 cup.
Decoction. 50-60g in 500ml water, gently simmer 10 minutes; stand 20 minutes. Dose:quarter to half a cup.
Powder, capsules: 210mg, 2 capsules. (*Arkocaps*)

OLIVE OIL AND LEMON TREATMENT. See: GALL-STONES.

ONION. *Allium cepa*. The domestic onion. Held in high esteem by Galen and Hippocrates. *Part used*: bulb.
Constituents: flavonoids, volatile oil, allicin, vitamins, sterols, phenolic acids.
Action: hypoglycaemic, antibiotic, anticoagulant, expectorant, hypotensive, antibacterial, antisclerotic, anti-inflammatory, diuretic. Shares some of the properties of Garlic. Mild bacterical (fresh juice). Promotes bile flow, reduces blood sugar, stimulates the heart, coronary flow and systolic pressure.
Uses. Oedema, mild dropsy, high blood pressure. Inclusion in daily diet for those at risk from heart attack or stroke through low HDLs (high-density lipoprotein) levels.

"An Onion a day keeps arteriosclerosis at bay." (*Dr Victor Gurewich, Professor of Medicine, Tuft's University, Boston, USA*)

Onions clear arteries of fat which impedes blood flow. Of value for sour belching, cystitis, chilblains, insect bites, freckles. Two or three drops juice into the auditory meatus for earache and partial deafness. Burns and scalds (bruised raw Onion). Claimed that juice rubbed into the scalp arrests falling hair.

"I have observed that families using Onions freely as an article of diet have escaped epidemic diseases, although their neighbours might be having scarlet fever, etc. I believe Onions are reliable prophylactics. I have prevented the spread of contagious disease in the same household by their timely use." (*Dr L. Covert*)

The traditional roasted Onion is still used as a poultice for softening hard tumours and pains of acute gout.
Preparations. *Decoction*. Water in which Onions are boiled is a powerful diuretic and may also be used for above disorders.
Home tincture. Macerate Onions for 8 days in Holland's gin, shake daily; strain, bottle. 2-3 teaspoons in water, thrice daily for oedema, dropsy or gravel.

Note. A research team at the National Cancer Institute, China, has shown that the Onion family (Chives, Onions, Leeks and Garlic) can significantly reduce the risk of stomach cancer.

OOPHORITIS. Inflammation of an ovary. See: OVARIES.

OPIUM ADDICTION. Oatgrass (Avena sativa) has a long Indian tradition for opium addiction.

OPIUM POPPY. *Papaver somniferum L.* Prescription by a medical practitioner only. Contains morphine alkaloids and codeine. Analgesic, narcotic.

Although medication with opiates is addictive and its abuse ranges from dependence to death, use of crushed poppyheads as a topical poultice for crippling pain, as in terminal disease of chest or abdomen, is worthy of consideration. In an age before modern drugs and anaesthetics this was one of the few solaces available. Even today, there are a few situations for which this deep-acting pain-killer is indicated as, for instance, wounds healed but not without pain.

In spite of the plethora of modern drugs to combat the pain of terminal illness, few are as effective as the greatest anodyne of all time which led the eminent Sydenham to say ". . . if it were expunged from the pharmacopoeia, I would give up the practise of medicine".

ORAL ADMINISTRATION. Giving a remedy by mouth. Such a route leads to its passage through the mucous membrane lining the intestines and from there into the bloodstream.

ORANGE. Sweet orange. Bitter orange. Seville orange. *Citrus aurantium var sinensis, Citrus aurantium var amara L. German*: Orangebaum. *French*: Oranger. *Spanish*: Azahar. *Italian*: Arancio. *Chinese*: Chu. *Parts used*: fruit, juice, oil.
Constituents: the peel contains hesperidin, isohesperidin and other flavonoids, volatile oil, coumarins, Vitamin C (juice), pectin.
Action: aromatic, digestive, carminative, anti-inflammatory, antifungal, antibacterial.
Preparation. *Tincture Orange BP*, fresh fruits, Orange wine BP.

ORANGE BERRIES. *Maeso Lanceolata*. Native remedy for cholera. Potent antibiotic effect in gram-negative bacteria in laboratory animals.
Active principle: "maesanin" (*Dr Isno Kubo, University of California-Berkeley*)

Recommended by the Bwana-mganga medicine-men as a tea to be drunk one week before visiting Lake Victoria, an area where cholera is endemic.

ORCHITIS. Inflammation of the testicles.
Causes: injury, mumps, or infection from other parts of the body, as from epididymitis.
Symptoms: testicles enlarged and painful; fever. Nausea. Sensation of weight.
Treatment. Analgesics, anti-inflammatories.
Teas: Clivers, Fumitory, Burdock root (decoction). Freely.
Tablets/capsules. Poke root. Echinacea. Prickly Ash. Pulsatilla. (*Pulsatilla useful: American Dispensary*)
Formula. Equal parts: Pulsatilla, Lobelia, Poke root. Dose – Liquid extracts: 30-60 drops. Tinctures: 60-120 drops. Powders: 375mg (quarter of a teaspoon). Thrice daily.
A. Barker, FNIMH. Dec Jam Sarsae Co Conc BPC 1oz. Liquid Extract Wild Carrot 1oz. Liquid Extract Corn Silk half an ounce. Mist Senna Co BP 2oz. Water to 8oz. Dose: 2 teaspoons in water thrice daily after meals.
External. Slippery Elm or Black Bryony poultice. Camphorated oil. Ice pack.

OREXIGENIC. A herb which increases or stimulates the appetite.

Balmony, Boldo, Burdock (leaves and root), Calumba, Cardamom, Chiretta, Cinnamon, Condurango, Fennel, Fenugreek, Gentian, Holy Thistle, Hops, Lungwort, Mugwort, Peruvian bark, Quassia, Wormwood.

OROTATES. Orotic acid aids absorption of minerals by cells, and ensures against loss of these important nutrients through the action of free-radicals or infection. Orotic acid is found in Wild Yam and some root vegetables, sweet potatoes and whey from milk. It assists excretion of uric acid and stimulates phagocytic activity of the white cells.
Common orotates:–
Chromium: 1mg, providing 50mcg elemental Chromium per tablet.
Calcium: 500mg, providing 50mg elemental Calcium per tablet.
Copper: 7mg, providing 1mg elemental Copper per tablet.

ORRIS ROOT. Wild purple flag. *Iris florentina L. Iris germanica L.* Dried rhizome gathered in the autumn. *Part used*: rhizome.
Constituents: isoflavones, triterpenes, essential oil.
Action: demulcent, expectorant, anti-diarrhoeal. The fresh root is laxative and diuretic; stimulates elimination of excess fluid.
Uses. Irritable bowel, summer diarrhoea in children. To loosen phlegm in stubborn cases of respiratory congestion. Sore throat. Coughs.
Preparation. Rhizomes are ground into a flour for internal use; quarter-1 gram in cup of boiling water: infuse 15 minutes. Dose: half a cup thrice

daily. Powder is used as a tooth powder or natural face powder. Small segment sucked by a child in place of a dummy.
Contra-indication: large doses are purgative and cause vomiting. Hypersensitive individuals may react with urticaria on handling.
GSL, external use only

ORTHOSIPHON. *Orthosiphon staminus, Benth.*
Action. Diuretic, antiseptic, cholagogue.
Uses. Oedema: swollen ankles.

OSGOOD SCHLATTER DISEASE. Degenerative changes in the growth centres of bones in children due to calcium or other mineral deficiency. Herbs rich in calcium, iron, and magnesium are indicated. (Horsetail, Chamomile, Plantain, Silverweed, Nettles, Mullein, etc)

Selenium 50mcg and Vitamin E 400iu are recommended by Jonathan Wright MD, for decreasing the pain of disease, decreasing over 3 months. (*Health Update USA, June 1990*)

OSTEO-ARTHRITIS. See: ARTHRITIS, OSTEO.

OSTEOMALACIA. Bone-softening due to lack or poor absorption of Vitamin D in the diet. Occurs in the elderly and immigrants with dark skins and of indoor habits. In children it is similar to rickets, producing bow legs, kyphosis or compressed spinal vertebrae. Almost unknown in sunny lands.
Symptoms. Bone pains in back, hips, legs and ribs. Children learn to walk late. Teeth badly formed. Thinning and softening of the skull.

Comfrey root promotes bone cell growth. Marigold (Calendula) encourages granulation. Horsetail assists calcium metabolism. Cayenne is a positive circulatory stimulant.
For bone bruised by injury: Rue.
Alternatives. *Tea*. Combine: Oats 3; Comfrey leaves 2; Horsetail 1; Marigold petals 1. One heaped teaspoon to each cup boiling water; infuse 5-15 minutes. 1 cup freely.
Fenugreek tea. See entry.
Tablets/capsules. Bamboo gum, Black Cohosh, Echinacea, Kelp, Prickly Ash.
Formula 1. Powders. Bamboo gum 3; Fenugreek 2; Calendula 2; Echinacea 2; Liquorice 1. Cayenne quarter. Mix. Dose: 750mg (three 00 capsules or half a teaspoon) thrice daily.
Formula 2. Burdock root 1; Horsetail 1; Calendula half. Mix. Liquid extracts: 1 teaspoon. Tinctures: 1-2 teaspoons. Doses enhanced when taken in cup of Fenugreek tea. Thrice daily.
Comfrey root. Use of this root would appear to be of value, its potential benefit outweighing possible risk.
Diet. Oily fish. Natural spring water. Low salt. Irish Moss and Slippery Elm for minerals.
Reject: soft drinks, alcohol, heavy meat meals.
Supplements. Vitamin B12 (50mcg); Vitamin C (500mg); Vitamin D; Vitamin E (400iu), Magnesium, Zinc.
Supportives: sunbathing, stop smoking.

OSTEOMYELITIS. An acute infective inflammation of the bone marrow by pyogenic bacteria – most commonly, Staphylococcus aureus. May take the form of a fistula (abnormal passage between the bone and the skin surface) which becomes a vent for elimination of blood and watery pus.

Infection is usually blood-born from dental abscess, tonsils, boil, or old wounds. Prompt modern hospital treatment is necessary to avoid thrombosis or necrosis of bone. Herbal medication can play a substantial supportive role. Differential diagnosis should exclude Infective Arthritis, Cellulitis, Rheumatic Fever, Leukaemia.
Symptoms. Affected bone painful and hot. Throbbing. Fever. Dehydration. Raised E.S.R. Severe general illness.
Treatment. Should enhance resistance as well as combat infection. Comfrey and Echinacea are principle remedies. Infected bone areas are not well supplied with blood, so oral antibiotics may not reach them; this is where topical herbal treatments can assist. Anti-bacterial drinks are available in the absence of conventional antibiotics.
To promote cell proliferation and callous formation: Comfrey root, Marigold, St John's Wort, Arnica. (*Madaus*)
To stimulate connective tissue: Thuja.
Comfrey root. Potential benefit outweighs possible risk.
Teas. Nettles. Plantain. Silverweed, Yarrow. Boneset. Marigold petals. St John's Wort. Comfrey leaves. Singly or in combination. Abundant drinks during the day.
Formula. Echinacea 2; Comfrey 1; Myrrh half; Thuja quarter. Dose – Liquid extracts: 2 teaspoons. Tinctures: 2-3 teaspoons. Powders: 750mg (three 00 capsules or half a teaspoon). Three or more times daily in water or honey.
Madaus: Tardolyt. Birthwort: a sodium salt of aristolochic acid.
Maria Treben: Yarrow and Fenugreek tea. Half cup Yarrow tea 4 times daily. To two of such cups, add half a teaspoon ground Fenugreek seeds.
Dr Finlay Ellingwood: Liquid Extract Echinacea 20-30 drops in water four times daily. And: Liquid Extract Lobelia 20-30 drops in water twice daily. Calcium Lactate tablets.
Topical. Comfrey root poultices to facilitate removal of pus, and to heal.
Diet. No solids. Fruit and milk diet for 5 days, followed by lacto-vegetarian diet. Herb teas as

above. Plenty of water to combat dehydration.
Supplements. Daily. Vitamin B12 (50mcg), C (3g), D (500iu), E (1000iu). Calcium (1000-1500mg) taken as calcium lactate, Zinc.
General. Regulate bowels. Surgical treatment in a modern hospital necessary for removal of dead bone (sequestrum) and for adequate nursing facilities.

Treatment by a general medical practitioner or hospital specialist.

OSTEOPATHY. A system of skeletal manipulation to restore balance and normality where there is structural derangement. A number of herbal lotions and massage oils assist the osteopath to relax muscles and prepare tissues for manipulation.

See: ROSEMARY AND ALMOND OIL. STIFF NECK SALVE. GOLDEN FIRE.

OSTEOPOROSIS. "Brittle bones". The Silent Epidemic. Weakness and softness of the bones due to wastage of minerals, chiefly calcium. Crippling, painful, deforming. 'Bone-thinning' leads to hundreds of thousands of crush and spontaneous fractures every year. Vertebra of the spine may collapse with loss of height and stooping. Sufferers show body levels of zinc about 25 per cent lower than normal. May run in families.

Affects women more than men by 10:1 especially after menopause, whether this is natural or due to destruction or removal of ovaries in early adult life.

By means of a calcium-rich diet after 35 years it is a preventable disease. Like so many degenerative diseases a common cause is widespread consumptions of refined, processed, chemicalised foods. It is possible that dental caries is in reality osteoporosis.

In men, alcohol is the chief cause. It wreaks its greatest havoc in women 10-15 years after the menopause. Increased calcium will not restore tissue already lost by wasting. Emphasis is therefore on prevention. It is estimated that a quarter of women over 50 in the West suffer bone loss after the menopause when reduced oestrogen speeds loss of calcium with possible bone damage to wrist, spine and especially hip. The chances of such fractures in women reaching seventy are one in two.

Vitamin D deficiency predisposes, as also does over-prescription of thyroxine for hypothyroid cases.

Fat-free diets can break bones.

In menopausal women, increased bone loss is associated with disorders of the ovaries, which organs should receive treatment. Specially at risk are anorexic women with absence of periods. Secondary causes: hyperthyroidism, long-term use of steroids, liver disease, drugs (Tamoxifen, Antacids).

Common fractures are those of hips, spine and wrist. Wrist bone mineral content and grip strength are related. Squeezing a tennis ball hard three times each morning and evening reduces risk of fractures of the wrist.

Drinking of Lemon juice contributes to brittle bones. The habit of daily drinking of the juice causes enamel of teeth to crumble and the removal of calcium from the bones.

Cod Liver oil (chief of the iodised oils) reaches and nourishes cartilage, imparting increased elasticity which prevents degeneration.
Coffee. Two or more cups of coffee a day significantly reduces bone mineral density in women, but drinking milk each day can counter it.
Alternatives. Alfalfa, Black Cohosh, Chamomile, Clivers, Fennel, Dong quai, Fenugreek, Liquorice, Meadowsweet, Mullein, Pimpernel, Helonias, Plantain, Rest Harrow, Shepherd's Purse, Silverweed, Toadflax, Unicorn root. Nettle tea.
Tea. Equal parts. Alfalfa, Comfrey leaves, Nettles. Mix. 2 teaspoons to each cup boiling water; infuse 5-15 minutes; 1 cup thrice daily.
Decoction. Equal parts: Comfrey root, Irish Moss (for minerals), Horsetail. Mix. 3 heaped teaspoons to 1 pint (500ml) water gently simmered 20 minutes. Dose: 1 cup thrice daily.
Tablets/capsules. Bamboo gum, Helonias, Iceland Moss, Irish Moss for minerals, Kelp, Prickly Ash.
Formula. Horsetail 2; Alfalfa 2; Helonias 1. Mix. Powders: 500mg (two 00 capsules or one-third teaspoon). Liquid extracts: 1 teaspoon. Tinctures: 2 teaspoons. Action is enhanced by taking in a cup of Fenugreek tea.
Comfrey decoction. 1 heaped teaspoon to cup water gently simmered 5 minutes. Strain when cold. Dose: 1 cup, to which is added 10 drops Tincture Helonias, morning and evening. Fenugreek seeds may be used as an alternative to Comfrey root. Comfrey and Fenugreek are osteoprotectives. For this condition the potential benefit of Comfrey outweighs possible risk.
Propolis. Regeneration of bone tissue.
Dr John Christopher. Mix powders: Horsetail 6, de-husked Oats 3; Comfrey root 4; Lobelia 4. Dose: quarter to half a teaspoon 2-3 times daily.
Diet. Fresh raw fruit and green vegetables. Consumption of raw bran (which contains calcium-binding phytic acid) and wholemeal bread should be suspended until recovery is advanced. Natural spring water. Fish and fish oils. Reject high salt intake which aggravates bone loss and places the skeleton at risk by creating increasing loss of calcium and phosphorus through the kidneys. Avoid soft drinks, alcohol. Heavy meat meals inhibit calcium metabolism. Incidence of the disease is lower in vegetarians. High protein.
Supplements. Daily. Vitamin A, Vitamin B12

(50mcg); Vitamin C (500mg); Vitamin D, Vitamin E, Folic acid 200mcg; Vitamin B6 (50mg); Calcium citrate 1g; Magnesium citrate 500mg. Boron and Vitamin D. Zinc 15mg.
Calcium helps reduce risk of fracture particularly in menopausal women who may increase their daily intake to 800mg – Calcium citrate malate being more effective than the carbonate. Dried skimmed milk can supply up to 60 per cent of the recommended daily amount of Calcium.

Stop smoking.
Information. National Osteoporosis Society, PO Box 10, Radstock, Bath BA3 3YB, UK. Send SAE.

OSWEGO TEA. See: BERGAMOT, RED.

OTITIS EXTERNA. Swimmer's ear. Inflammation of the *outer* ear.
Causes: fungal or bacterial infections acquired when swimming, scratching with dirty fingernails, diabetes mellitus, eczema or excessive sweating.
Symptoms: earache, itching, discharge, moderate deafness.
Alternative Treatment:– *Tea.* Combine equal parts: Nettles, Clivers, Red Clover. 1-2 teaspoons to each cup boiling water; infuse 5-15 minutes. 1 cup thrice daily.
Tablets/capsules. Echinacea. Blue Flag. Garlic. Poke root. Red Clover. Devil's Claw. Thuja.
Powders. Combine parts: Echinacea 2; Blue Flag 1; Thuja quarter; Liquorice quarter. Dose: 500mg (two 00 capsules or one-third teaspoon) thrice daily.
Tinctures. Combine parts: Echinacea 2; Devil's Claw 1; Goldenseal quarter; Liquorice quarter. Dose: 1-2 teaspoons, thrice daily.
Evening Primrose. 4 x 500mg capsules daily.
Cider Vinegar: 2-3 teaspoons in glass water, 2-3 times daily.
Topical. Dry conditions: Jojoba oil, Mullein oil. Evening Primrose oil.
Moist suppurative conditions: Goldenseal Drops (see entry).
Simple inflammation without discharge: warm drops Houseleek juice. Pack external ear with saturated cotton wool.
Diet and supplements: same as for otitis media.

OTITIS MEDIA. Inflammation of the middle ear. Usually spreads from the nose or throat via the Eustachian tube. Tonsillitis, sinusitis or 'adenoids' predispose. A frequent complication of measles, influenza or other children's infections. Sometimes due to allergy.
Symptoms. Effusion of fluid into the middle ear with increasing deafness, discharge, tinnitus. Infant shakes head. Perforation in chronic cases. Inspection with the aid of an auriscope reveals bulging of the ear-drum. Feverishness.
Treatment. Antibiotics (herbal or others) do not remove pain therefore a relaxing nervine should be included in a prescription – German Chamomile, Vervain, etc.
Before the doctor comes. Any of the following teas: Boneset, Feverfew, Holy Thistle, Thyme. One heaped teaspoon to each cup boiling water; infuse 15 minutes; one cup thrice daily.
Formula. Practitioner. Echinacea 2; Thyme 1; Hops half; Liquorice quarter. Dose – Powders: 500mg (two 00 capsules or one-third teaspoon). Liquid Extracts: 1 teaspoon. Tinctures: 1-2 teaspoons. Acute: every 2 hours. Chronic: thrice daily.
Topical. Dry-mop purulent discharge before applying external agents. Inject warm 2-3 drops any one oil: Mullein, St John's Wort, Garlic, Lavender or Evening Primrose.

Once every 8-10 days syringe with equal parts warm water and Cider Vinegar. Repeat cycle until condition is relieved.
Diet. Salt-free. Low-starch. Milk-free. Abundance of fruits and raw green salad vegetables. Freshly squeezed fruit juices. Bottled water. No caffeine drinks: coffee, tea or cola.
Supplements. Vitamins A, B-complex, B2, B12, C, E, K, Iron, Zinc. Evening Primrose capsules.
Notes. Where pressure builds up against the drum, incision by a general medical practitioner may be necessary to facilitate discharge of pus. Grossly enlarged tonsils and adenoids may have to be surgically removed in chronic cases where treatment over a reasonable period proves ineffective. A bathing cap is sometimes more acceptable than earplugs.
Breast-feeding. Significantly protects babies from episodes of otitis media. Commenting on a study published in the Obstetrical and Gynaecological Survey, Dr Mark Reynolds, author of a breast-feeding policy by the Mid-Kent Care Trust said: "Breast milk is known to reduce respiratory infection – a precursor of otitis media."
Hopi ear candles.

OTITIS MEDIA – GLUE EAR. *Secretory form.* A common form of inflammation of the *middle* ear in children and which may be responsible for conduction deafness.
Causes: chronic catarrh with obstruction of the Eustachian tubes of dietetic origin. Starchy foods should be severely restricted. The ear is clogged with a sticky fluid usually caused by enlarged adenoids blocking the ventilation duct which connects the cavity with the back of the throat.

Conventional treatment consists of insertion of 'grommets' – tiny flanged plastic tubes about one millimetre long – which are inserted into the eardrum, thus ensuring a free flow of air into the cavity. Fluid usually disappears and hearing returns to normal.
Treatment. Underlying cause treated – adenoids,

tonsils, etc. Sinus wash-out with Soapwort, Elderflowers, Mullein or Marshmallow tea. Internal treatment with anti-catarrhals to disperse.
Alternatives:– *German Chamomile tea.* (*Traditional German*).
Teas. Boneset, Cayenne, Coltsfoot, Elderflowers, Eyebright, Hyssop, Marshmallow leaves, Mullein, Mint, Yarrow.
Powders. Combine: Echinacea 2; Goldenseal quarter; Myrrh quarter; Liquorice half. Dose: 500mg (two 00 capsules or one-third teaspoon), thrice daily.
Tinctures. Combine: Echinacea 2; Yarrow 1; Plantain 1. Drops: Tincture Capsicum. Dose: 1-2 teaspoons thrice daily.
Topical. Castor oil drops, with cotton wool ear plugs, Oils of Garlic or Mullein. If not available, use Almond oil. Hopi Indian Ear Candles for mild suction and to impart a perceptible pressure regulation of sinuses and aural fluids.
Diet. Gluten-free diet certain. No confectionery, chocolate, etc. Salt-free. Low-starch. Milk-free. Abundance of fruits and raw green salad materials.
Supplements. Vitamins A, B-complex, C. E.

OVARIES. Two female reproductive organs situated below the Fallopian tubes, one on each side of the womb, comparable to testes in the male. An egg cell or ova develops inside the ovary and when mature bursts through the surface into the abdominal cavity where it is attracted into a Fallopian tube and conveyed to the womb. If fertilised, the egg attaches to the lining of the womb and develops into a foetus. Otherwise it is expelled from the womb during menstruation. In addition to producing eggs, ovaries secrete hormones essential to body function. Ovarian disorders include:–
1. Inflammation (oophoritis – usually with salpingitis).
Causes: mumps, tuberculosis, gonorrhoea or, if following childbirth or abortion, sepsis. Inflammatory adhesions may cause ovary and tube to mat together and ulcerate.
Symptoms: feverishness, pelvic pain, abdominal swelling.
Treatment. Decoction, powders, liquid extracts or tinctures.
Formula. Echinacea 2; Helonias 1; Cramp bark 1; Liquorice quarter. Dosage. Decoction: half-1 cup. Powders: one-third teaspoon. Liquid extracts: 1 teaspoon. Tinctures: 2 teaspoons. Thrice daily in water/honey.
External. Castor oil pack to abdomen.
2. Cysts. Single or multiple hollow growths containing fluids may grow large, obstruct abdominal circulation, interfere with digestion and cause shortness of breath. They are caused by excessive stimulus from the pituitary gland. A fluid-filled sac on the ovary grows in preparation for egg release but fails to rupture. The follicle continues to grow, accumulating fluid and a cyst results.
Liquid Extract Thuja: 5-10 drops, thrice daily. Of value.
Notes. Bulimia Nervosa (eating disorder) has been linked with polycystic ovary disease. (*St George's Hospital Medical School, London*)

The presence of acne is a valuable clue to ovarian disorder: a treatment for acne reacts favourably on ovaries.
3. Tumour (non-malignant). May avoid detection. Usually revealed by laparoscopy or X-ray. When a tumour or cyst twists on an ovary's ligament severe abdominal pain is followed by vomiting and shock.
Treatment. Secondary to surgery. Decoction, powders, liquid extracts, or tinctures. Combination. Cramp bark 2; Poke root 1; Thuja half. Dosage. Decoction: half-1 cup. Powders: 500mg (one-third teaspoon). Liquid extracts: 1 teaspoon. Tinctures: 1-2 teaspoons in water/honey thrice daily.
Following surgical removal of ovaries: Pulsatilla.
Pre- and post-operative pain: Cramp bark BHP (1983). Black Willow. (*Dr J. Christopher*)
Supplements: calcium, magnesium.
Note. Increased bone loss is associated with ovarian disturbances in premenopausal women. (*Canadian Study* in "New England Journal of Medicine") See: OSTEOPOROSIS.

Polycystic ovaries have an important association with heart attacks in elderly women. (*Professor Howard Jacobs, Middlesex School of Medicine*)

OVER-THE-COUNTER PRODUCTS. Herbal products are chiefly used to relieve symptoms of self-limiting conditions. Such products are either P (pharmacy only) or GSL (General Sales List). The Medicines (Labelling and Advertising to the Public) Regulations 1978 (SI 1978 No 41) state the range of conditions on schedule 2, parts I-IV. Dried herbs on sale under their plant or botanical name over the counter are exempt, provided no medicinal claims are made.

OXALIC ACID. *Plants containing*:– Cranberry, Beetroot leaves, Gooseberries, Rhubarb, Swiss Chard, Spinach.

To be avoided in gall bladder disorders, as stone-promoting.

OXALURIA. Excessive urea and increased specific gravity in the urine. Key remedy – Senna.

OXIDATION. A chemical reaction essential to life. By removal of hydrogen atoms biological oxidation is effected. A reaction in which a molecule or atom loses electrons, and provides energy for vital cell maintenance.

OXYMEL. A combination of honey (5 parts) and Vinegar (1 part) used to mask the unpleasant taste of certain herbs (Squills, Asafoetida, etc). Medicaments are added and the whole simmered gently until the consistency of treacle. Dose, according to medicament. Internally, or as a mouthwash and gargle.

OXYTOCIC. A herb which hastens the process of childbirth by initiating contraction of the uterine muscle.

Angelica, Bearberry, Beth root, Black Cohosh, Blue Cohosh, Castor oil, Goldenseal, Juniper berries, Raspberry leaves, Rue, Squaw Vine, Wild Ginger.

OZENA. Nasal disorder with offensive discharge.
Powders, liquid extracts, tinctures. Combine, Sarsaparilla 2; Burdock 1; Goldenseal quarter. Powders: quarter of a teaspoon. Liquid extracts: 1 teaspoon. Tinctures: 1-2 teaspoons. In water, honey, etc thrice daily.

OZONE RADIATION. Harmful ultraviolet radiation from depletion of the ozone layer may affect general health and cause skin cancers, cataracts and immune deficiency. The protection offered by antioxidant nutrients can play a part in reducing the incidence of lens cataract. Until scientific medicine discovers effective treatment it would appear that Vitamins A, E, and Evening Primrose oil have a role to play in protection of the eyes and skin. Horsetail, rich in silica, is believed to delay progression of cataract when taken internally.
Topical. Creams to prevent burning: Vitamin E, Evening Primrose, Houseleek, Aloe Vera. Honey. Most creams contain Vitamin E which acts as a filter and moisturiser.
Diet. Foods rich in beta-carotene, Vitamins C and E.
Supplements. Vitamins A and E.
Note. Use of sunglasses and sun screens on sunny days to avoid burning. Wearing of a hat.

PACHO TEA. Inca cancer cure. See: LAPACHO TREE.

PAEONY. *Paeonia lactiflora*, Paeonia suffruticosa. *German*: Paeonie. *French*: Pivoine. *Italian*: Peonia. *Iranian*: Fawania Aod-el-Salib. *Indian*: Ud salap. *Chinese*: Bai shae Yae. *Parts used*: root and root bark.
Constituents. Alkaloids, benzoic acid, asparagin, volatile oil.
Action: antispasmodic, sedative, diuretic, emmenagogue. CNS relaxant, antibacterial, hypotensive, anti-inflammatory, analgesic, liver protector, stimulant to circulatory vessels.
Uses. Old English traditional: epilepsy, chorea. Painful spasm induced by gall or renal stone, whooping cough, children's convulsions, anal fissure, piles, ulceration of the perineum or coccyx (suppositories, or bathing with strong infusion).
Preparations. *Strong infusion*: 2oz bruised leaves to 1 pint boiling water infuse 15 minutes. External use only.
Tincture of the fresh root gathered in spring. 2oz bruised root in 1 pint 45 per cent alcohol. Macerate 8 days, shake daily; filter. Bottle in stoppered amber-coloured bottle. Dose, 10-20 drops thrice daily for the above conditions or when epileptic attack is suspected.
Contra-indications: large doses toxic.
For use by medical practitioner only.

PAGET'S DISEASE. (*Sir James Paget, 1814-99*) Osteitis deformans. Chronic inflammation of bone at focal points (Pagetic sites), often widespread. Chronic. Progressive softening followed by thickening with distortion. Renewal of new bone outstrips absorption of old bone. Enlargement of the skull ('Big head') and of the long bones. Broadened pelvis, distorted spine (kyphosis) from flattened vertebra. Male predominence. Over 40 years. Spontaneous fractures possible. Paget's disease and diabetes may be associated in the same family.

Some authorities believe cause is vitamin and mineral deficiency – those which promote bone health being calcium and magnesium (dolomite). Supplementation helps cases but evidence confirms that some pet-owners are at risk – a virus from cats and dogs possibly responsible. The prime candidate is one exposed to canine distemper. Dogs are involved twice as much as cats. The virus is closely related to the measles virus in humans.
Symptoms. Limbs deformed, hot during inflammatory stage. Headaches. Dull aching pain in bones. Deafness from temporal bone involvement. Loss of bone rigidity. Bowing of legs.

Surgical procedures may be necessary. Appears to be a case for immunisation of dogs against distemper.
Alternatives. Black Cohosh, Boneset, Cramp bark, Bladderwrack, German Chamomile, Devil's Claw, Helonias, Oat husks, Prickly Ash, Sage, Wild Yam.
Tea. Oats (mineral nutrient for wasting diseases) 2; Boneset (anti-inflammatory) 1; Valerian (mild analgesic) 1; Liquorice quarter. Mix. 1 heaped teaspoon to each cup boiling water; infuse 15 minutes. 1 cup thrice daily.
Decoction. Cramp bark 1; White Willow 2. Mix. 4 heaped teaspoons to 1 pint (500ml) water gently simmered 20 minutes. Dose: half-1 cup thrice daily.
Tablets/capsules. Cramp bark, Devil's Claw, Echinacea, Helonias, Prickly Ash, Wild Yam.
Formula. Devil's Claw 1; Black Cohosh 1; Valerian 1; Liquorice quarter. Dose: Powders: 500mg (two 00 capsules or one-third teaspoon). Liquid extracts: 1 teaspoon. Tinctures: 2 teaspoons. Action enhanced when taken in cup of Fenugreek tea. Thrice daily. Every 2 hours acute cases.
Practitioner's analgesic. Tincture Gelsemium: 10 drops in 100ml water. Dose: 1 teaspoon every 2 hours (inflammatory stage).
Topical. Comfrey root poultice.
Diet. High protein, low salt, low fat. Oily fish.
Supplements. Daily. Vitamin C (500mg); Vitamin D (1000mg); Calcium citrate (1 gram); Dolomite (1 gram); Beta-Carotene (7500iu). Kelp.

PAGET'S DISEASE OF THE NIPPLE. Cancer of the mammary ducts (rare). Nipple: encrusted, red, inflamed. See: CANCER OF THE BREAST.

PAIN. Agonising physical distress caused by sensory nerve irritation. Nature's warning that something is wrong. Where persistent, investigation by a qualified person is essential. For mild pain natural non-suppressive herbs are available. The following are helpful until the doctor comes.
In the chest. When in the gullet it can closely resemble pain in the heart and can be mistaken for angina. Gullet pain, worse by acid and hot drinks, is always a background pain and fails to resolve after exercise. See: OESOPHAGEAL SPASM.
Aching muscles. Bio-strath Willow Formula.
In the hips. Ligvites. (*Gerard House*)
Ovarian. See: OVARIES.
Fibrositis, polymyalgia. Low degree pain in muscles. Any one:– Black Cohosh, Devil's Claw, Wild Lettuce, Wild Yam, Wintergreen, Lavender, Parsley, Fenugreek seeds, Meadowsweet, German Chamomile.
In the chest. (Lungs) Balm of Gilead. (Heart) Motherwort.
Breast. Evening Primrose oil.
Spine. St John's Wort.
Aching teeth. Oil of Cloves.
Lumbago, sciatica, backache. Bio-Strath Willow

formula.
Gout, rheumatism, osteo-arthritis. Poultice or compress – Comfrey, Plantain leaves, Olbas oil, Weleda Massage oil.
The acute abdomen. Carminative herbs for flatulent colic.
Pain in bowels. (Internal) Wild Yam, Cinnamon, Ginger, Caraway. (External) Cold-pack with Castor oil, Chamomile poultice.
Sprains, bruises. 5 drops Oil of Camphor to egg-cup Olive oil, rub-in relief.
Facial stabbing pains. Plantain, Chamomile, Rosemary, or Wintergreen (external) compress, lotion, tincture.
Womb. Raspberry leaf/Motherwort tea (equal parts), internal.
Head. Feverfew, Skullcap, Passion flower.
Nerve pains. Valerian. Jamaica Dogwood.

See: ANALGESICS, ANTISPASMODICS, NEURALGIA, PLEURODYNIA, etc.
Aromatherapy. Combine, equal parts Oils of Clove, Sassafras and Camphor. Add 10 drops to egg-cup Olive oil: use as a rub for aching muscles and stiff joints.

Drugs suppress pain without necessarily removing the underlying cause. The natural response to pain is to tighten, but if the patient lets go and relaxes into it, then he finds he can better control it.

PAIN-RELIEVERS. See: ANALGESICS.

PALMA CHRISTI. See: CASTOR OIL.

PALMING. To strengthen the eyes and overcome fatigue. Sit in a comfortable chair. Free the mind of apprehensions. Loosen up. Relax completely. Close the eyes and cover with palms of the hands; leave the nose free. Without undue pressure exclude the light, gazing into the darkness. Support the arms and 'palm' for 20 or more minutes. To rub the hands with Aloe Vera is said to heighten its effect.

Palming was initiated by Dr William Bates who, suffering from physical exhaustion and eye strain cupped his eyes in his palms to relax the tension. A few minutes later he felt refreshed and his eyes no longer ached. From this experience he devised the Bates Method to strengthen the eyes.

PALPITATION. An awareness of the heartbeat. Increase in the normal rate of sudden onset or lasting a few hours, with or without vertigo or fainting. Temporary acceleration may be common, often entirely innocent. Where the beat reaches 100 to 140 per minute it is likely to be due to sinus tachycardia, but higher rates, 180 plus, of sudden onset and offset are due to paroxysmal tachycardia from an abnormal focus of rhythm in atrium or ventricle.

May be caused by anxiety, exercise, smoking, alcohol, caffeine, anaemia, thyroid disorder, a specific fever or presence of a 'coronary'. Extrasystoles may be felt as a thumping in the chest. May also be caused by excessive digitalis therapy.
Treatment. Where due to shock (Passion flower), overstrain (Ginseng), flatulence (Chamomile), sense of oppression in the chest (Hawthorn), suffocation (Aconite), worse lying on the left side (Cactus), highly sensitive women (Pulsatilla), mental depression (Cactus), congestion of the lungs (Lobelia).
Tea. Combine equal parts – Motherwort and Passion flower. 1-2 teaspoons to each cup boiling water; infuse 15 minutes; 1 cup as necessary.
Tablets/capsules. Chamomile, Hawthorn, Lobelia, Mistletoe, Motherwort, Pulsatilla, Passion flower (Passiflora), Valerian.
Formula. Equal parts: Lily of the Valley, Passion flower. Dose: Powders: 500mg (two 00 capsules or one-third teaspoon). Liquid extracts: 1 teaspoon. Tinctures: 2 teaspoons. Thrice daily in water or honey.
Practitioner. Tincture Aconite, BPC 1949. Dose: 0.12 to 0.3ml (2 to 5 drops). OR:– Spartiol (Broom) 20 drops thrice daily. (*Klein*).
Diet. See: DIET – HEART AND CIRCULATION.
Vitamin E. One 400iu capsule (or tablet) daily.
Minerals. Magnesium 300mg daily.

PANCREATANT. An agent to influence activity of the pancreas.

Barberry, Goat's Rue, Mountain Grape, Karela, Fringe Tree.

All bitters have a toning effect on the pancreas.

PANCREATITIS. Acute or chronic disease of the pancreas, usually by spread of infection from the gall bladder, or due to temporary blockage of the gall duct by stone. Alcoholism is common. Haemorrhage and extravasation of pancreatic juice results in profound general shock, gangrene and suppuration.
Symptoms. Upper abdominal pain, fever, nausea, backache, low blood pressure, high white cell count.
Treatment: anti-inflammatories, herbal antibiotics for bacterial infection. Allspice, Bearberry, Elecampane, Goldenseal, Liquorice root, Mullein, Nettles, Wahoo. Others as follows:–
Teas: Haronga Tree, Chamomile, Mullein, Uva Ursi, Burdock leaves, Marigold petals, Liquorice. Cup every 3 hours.
Decoctions: Sarsaparilla (hot). Barberry (cold). See: DECOCTION.
Tablets/capsules. Blue Flag root, Chamomile, Sarsaparilla, Kelp.
Formula. Echinacea 2; Blue Flag root 1; Liquorice root 1. Dose – Liquid extracts: 1 teaspoon. Tinctures: 2 teaspoons. Powders: 500mg (two 00 capsules or one-third teaspoon); every 3 hours for acute cases, otherwise thrice daily.

Goldenseal, tincture: 10 drops once daily maintenance prophylactic dose.
External. Poultice over upper abdomen: Mullein, Chamomile or Castor oil.
Diet. Abundant citrus fruits.
Supplements. Vitamin C, methionine and selenium to mop up free radicals. Without the supplements toxins strike the pancreas, leading to severe pain. In this way they can be used as an alternative to pain-killers. (*Researchers, Manchester Royal Infirmary*)
Vitamin C. Lack of Vitamin C may trigger acute pancreatitis in susceptible patients. (*Mr Patrick Scott, Manchester Royal Infirmary*)

PAPAIN. See: PAPAYA.

PAPAYA. Paw paw fruit. Melon tree. *Carica papaya L. German*: Papayabaum. *French and Italian:* Papago. *Indian*: Popoyiah. *Arabian*: Anabahe-hindi. *Iranian*: Anobahe-hindi. *Malayan*: Bate. *Chinese*: Mukua-wan-shou-kuo.
Part used: juice of the unripe tropical fruit that contains papain, a non-animal enzyme which assists digestion of protein. Acts best with an alkali such as Meadowsweet. Has a similar action to pepsin, an enzyme secreted with the gastric juices of the stomach. Digests wheat gluten, thus assisting recovery from coeliac disease. High in beta-carotene (A).
Uses: acidity, flatulence, incomplete digestion of meats. Patient preference vegetarian hypo-allergenic yeast-free, freeze-dried Papaya. For slimming diet.
Tablets/capsules. Popular combination. Papain BPC 1954 60mg; powdered Charcoal BP 100mg; powdered Slippery Elm BHP (1983) 60mg; powdered Goldenseal BHP (1983) 10mg. Digestive disorders.
External. Juice of the fresh plant used for wounds that refuse to heal. William Scharf, 31, became desperately ill after a kidney transplant. Strong antibiotics failed to heal the infected wound. The surgeon of the Transplant Department of Guy's Hospital laid strips of fresh paw-paw fruit across the wound. After one week's treatment Mr Scharf was cured.
Diet. Paw-paw fruit or juice, raw, at meals.
Note. The fruit has a contraceptive effect in its ability to halt pregnancy by attacking progesterone, the hormone essential to pregnancy. (*Researchers: Sussex University*)
The large green fruit is widely used as a contraceptive in India and Sri Lanka. If a woman wants to become pregnant, she simply avoids eating them.

PAPILLOMA. An epithelial tumour in which cells cover ridges of stroma including warts, polypi, skin horns, condylomata, spongy swellings.
Causes: hereditary, or following vaccination.
Internal. Thuja. 5-10 drops liquid extract, or 10 drops tincture, thrice daily.
Topical. Paint with liquid extract Thuja, or Blood root. Horsetail poultice. (*Maria Treben*) Rub with cut Lemon or Houseleek; juice from the stalk of a Dandelion or Greater Celandine.

PARACELSUS. 1490-1541. Theophrastus Bombastus Hohenheim. Physician and alchemist. Owed his early education to his father, a physician. Learned the practice of medicine from many sources but lost faith in the orthodox profession of his day. Supported the Doctrine of Signatures, which is really a doctrine of analogies that suggest every herb reveals by its shape, colour and scent the disease it can cure. See: DOCTRINE OF SIGNATURES. The first to introduce into pharmacy the minerals antimony, mercury and sulphur, now known to be inimical to health and which have led the practice of medicine further away from the pure Hippocratic concept. He taught that diseases were specific entities and should be cured by specific remedies.

PARACETAMOL TOXICITY. For symptoms of overdosing or withdrawal from Paracetamol when discontinued, nervines are sometimes of value.
To break dependency: White Willow bark, Guaiacum, Oats, Passion flower.
Overdosing may cause liver damage for which Fringe Tree bark is indicated.
Nutrients: Vitamins B-complex, C. Zinc.

PARALYSIS. Loss of ability to move a limb or the whole body. Flaccid paralysis (with wasting of muscle) is due to lesion of a spinal or peripheral nerve. Spastic paralysis is due to "stroke" in the brain.
Diagnosis: wasting follows damage to a surface nerve. In damage of the spinal cord there will be no wasting but loss of use of muscles.
Treatment. Depends upon the cause. Though cure is impossible, some herbs tend to prevent stiffening, and ameliorate symptoms. Others may assist function as in paralysis ileus (paralysis of muscles of the intestinal walls) where Ispaghula seeds provide bulk and promote peristalsis. To strengthen the nervous system: Oats. Circulatory stimulants and nerve restoratives are indicated. Nettle tea is helpful. Limbs have regained temporary sensation on being beaten with the herb; others have lost rheumatism. Virginia Snake root had its reputation among early American Eclectics.
For a mild or temporary condition:– *Teas*: Nettles. Yerbe Mate.
Other alternatives:– *Tablets/capsules*. Prickly Ash. Black Cohosh.
Formula. Equal parts: Gentian, Ginger, Ginkgo.

Dose – Liquid extracts: 1-2 teaspoons. Tinctures: 1-3 teaspoons. Powders: 750mg (three 00 capsules or half a teaspoon). Thrice daily.
Cystitis: to relieve: Bearberry or Cranesbill tea.
Practitioner. Tincture Nux vomica: 10 drops in 100ml water. Dose: one teaspoon every two hours (temporary).
Thomson School. 1 teaspoon Cayenne pepper mixed with 2 teaspoons Lobelia herb or seeds. Half a teaspoon to each cup boiling water; infuse 15 minutes. Half a cup 2-3 times daily with honey.
Diet. Lacto-vegetarian.
Supplements: B-complex, B6, B12, E. Calcium, Magnesium, Zinc.

For other paralytic conditions see: MOTOR NEURONE DISEASE, MULTIPLE SCLEROSIS, MYASTHENIA GRAVIS, POLYMYELITIS, STROKE, SYRINGOMYELIA.

Treatment of severe nerve conditions should be supervised by neurologists and practitioners whose training prepares them to recognise serious illness and to integrate herbal and supplementary intervention safely into the treatment plan.

PARANOIA. A psychotic state often found with alcoholism, dementia and depression. Obsessional suspicion and aggression. Morbid jealousy. Such symptoms are often of physical causation and will not improve until the condition is remedied. Consider low thyroid function (Kelp), drug dependency (Valerian), auto-toxaemia (Echinacea).

Even as too low body fluids may kindle emotions of anger and irritability, so too much water has a depressing effect, bringing about an emotional state simulating paranoia. Administration of a timely diuretic (Parsley or Juniper berry tea) is sometimes known to raise the spirits.
Pulsatilla. (*N. Gosling FNIMH, Herbal Practitioner, Apr 1979, p.11*)

PARAPLEGIA. Paralysis of the legs due to injury or disease of the spinal cord, usually accompanied by loss of bladder control.
Treatment. Condition incurable yet circulatory stimulants and nerve restoratives may improve general well-being. Accompanying bladder condition may be relieved by Bearberry tea.

See: PARALYSIS.

PARASITICIDES. Herbs that destroy animal or vegetable parasites in the alimentary canal, on the head or skin.

Aniseed, Benzoic acid as in Storax and the balsams of Tolu and Peru. Chaparral, Cinnamon oil, Garlic, Poke root, Rosemary, Rue, Thymol (oil of Thyme), Sassafras oil. (*Topical use only*)
Quassia chips (cold infusion for head lice, fleas, scabies.

PARATHYROID GLANDS. Glands that control the level of calcium in the blood. The four glands appear, two on each side, implanted in the thyroid gland in the front of the neck.

Disorders are (1) hypoparathyroidism and (2) hyperparathyroidism. See entries.

PARATYPHOID. A form of enteric fever caused by bacteria of the Salmonella group. A notifiable disease. Treatment the same as for TYPHOID FEVER.

PARKINSON, JOHN. 1567-1650. Apothecary to two kings; first James I. When Charles I came to the throne he was named Botanicus Regis Primarius. Books: *Paradise in Sole Paradisus Terristris* (1629). It was a pun on his name: Park-in-suns Earthly Paradise, and referred to as a 'speaking garden'. *Theatre of Plants* (1640). Describes 3,800 plants. A herbal in every sense of the word; most comprehensive in the English language.

PARKINSON'S DISEASE (PD). Paralysis agitans. First described by James Parkinson, 1817. His description is as apt today as when it appeared in his book "Essay on the Shaking Palsy". He wrote: "It is characterised by involuntary tremulous motion, with lessened muscular power in parts not in action and even when supported. There is a tendency to bend the trunk forward and to pass from a walking to a running pace. The senses and intellect are uninjured."

Added to the above are:– muscular rigidity, loss of reflexes, drooling – escape of saliva from the mouth. Muscles of the face are stiff giving a fixed expression, the back presents a bowed posture. The skin is excessively greasy and the patient is unable to express emotional feelings. Loss of blinking. Pin-rolling movement of thumb and forefinger.
Causes: degeneration of groups of nerve cells deep within the brain which causes a lack of neurotransmitting chemical, dopamine. Chemicals such as sulphur used by agriculture, drugs and the food industry are suspected. Researchers have found an increase in the disease in patients born during influenza pandemics.
Treatment. While cure is not possible, a patient may be better able to combat the condition with the help of agents that strengthen the brain and nervous system.
Tea. Equal parts: Valerian, Passion flower, Mistletoe. 1 heaped teaspoon to each cup water; bring to boil; simmer 1 minute; dose: half-1 cup 2-3 times daily.
Gotu Kola tea. (CNS stimulant).
Tablets/capsules. Black Cohosh, Cramp bark, Ginseng, Prickly Ash, Valerian.
Formula. Ginkgo 2; Black Cohosh 1; Motherwort 2; Ginger 1. Mix. Dose. Powders: 500mg (two 00 capsules or one-third teaspoon). Liquid

extracts: 1 teaspoon. Tinctures: 1-3 teaspoons in water or honey.
Fava Bean Tea.
Case report. Two patients unresponsive to Levodopa treatment reported improvement following meals of fresh broad beans. (*Vicia faba*) The beans contain levodopa in large amounts. (*Parkinson Disease Update Vol 8, No 66, p186, Medical Publications, PO Box 24622-H, Philadelphia, USA*) See also: BROAD BEANS. L-DOPA.
Nacuna Pruriens. Appropriate. Essential active constituent: L-dopa. (*Medicinal plants and Traditional Medicine in Africa, by Abayomi Sofowora, Pub: John Wiley*)
Practitioner. To reduce tremor: Tincture Hyoscyamus BP. To reduce spasm: Tincture Belladonna BP. To arrest drooling: Tincture Stramonium BP.
Diet. It is known that people who work in manganese factories in Chile may develop Parkinson's disease after the age of 30. Progress of the disease is arrested on leaving the factory. Two items of diet highest in manganese are wheat and liver which should be avoided, carbohydrates in place of wheat taking the form of rice and potatoes.
Supplements. Daily: B-complex, B2, B6, niacin. C 200mg to reduce side-effects of Levodopa. Vitamin E 400iu to possibly reduce rigidity, tremors and loss of balance.

Treatment of severe nerve conditions should be supervised by neurologists and practitioners whose training prepares them to recognise serious illness and to integrate herbal and supplementary intervention safely into the treatment plan.
Antioxidants. Evidence has been advanced showing how nutritional antioxidants, high doses of Vitamin C and E, can retard onset of the disease, delaying the use of Levodopa for an average of 2 and a half years. (*Fahn S., High Dose Alpha-tocopherol and ascorbate in Early Parkinson's Disease – Annals of Neurology, 32-S pp128-132 1992*)
For support and advice: The Parkinson's Disease Society, 22 Upper Woburn Place, London WC1H 0RA, UK. Send SAE.

PARONYCHIA. See: NAILS

PAROTITIS. See: MUMPS.

PARSLEY. *Petroselinum crispum,* Hill. *German*: Petersilie. *French*: Persil. *Spanish*: Perejil. *Italian*: Prezzemolo. *Indian*: Bilati. Dried root, seeds and leaves. Seeds contain apiol. Source of precursor of carotene, Vitamins C, E, bioflavonoids, iron and folic acid.

Also contains apiole and myristicin (volatile oils) coumarins and flavonoids.
Action: anti-microbial, antispasmodic, anti-rheumatic, emmenagogue, laxative, mild brain tonic, diuretic, carminative, expectorant, gastric tonic, uterine tonic. A warming remedy for cold conditions, wasting, cachexia; avoided in fevers. Mild activator of adrenals and thyroid gland. Galen, Greek physician, advised it for disorders of womb and bladder.
Uses. Retention of excess fluid in the tissues, dropsy, bladder disorders, painful urination for those who pass water only after long intervals. Absent or painful menses. Windy colic. Inflammation of the prostate gland. PMT and menopausal hot flushes. To dispel fatigue. Mashed and unheated, leaves were once applied to the breasts of nursing mothers to arrest the flow of milk. Rich in minerals, calcium, potassium and silica; is said to strengthen hair, nails and skin. Eliminates smell of onions on the breath. Liver disorders, inflammation of gall bladder. To relieve cramps.
Preparations. Thrice daily. More widely used as a tea (infusion) from leaves of the fresh or dried plant. 1 heaped teaspoon to each cup water gently simmered 5 minutes in a covered vessel. Dose: 1 cup.
Liquid Extract: (root or seeds). 1 teaspoon in water.
Tincture: (root or seeds). 2 teaspoons in water.
Juice from fresh plant: 1-2 teaspoons as extracted in a juicer.
Diet. Fresh leaves used in cooking. Eaten raw in salads in Russia.
Contra-indication: pregnancy, inflammation of the kidneys.

PARSLEY PIERT. Parsley breakstone. *Aphanes arvensis L. Alchemilla arvensis L. German*: Feldsinau. *French*: Alchemille des champs. *Italian*: Spacca pietra. Dried herb. *Keynote*: kidney stone. The practising herbalist's choice for gravel, kidney and bladder stones where not too large.
Action: anti-lithic, soothing diuretic, demulcent.
Uses: kidney and bladder complaints, painful urination, oedema of kidney or liver origin BHP (1983).

Spoken of highly by Gerard, 17th century herbalist.
Preparations. Average dose 2-4g. Thrice daily.
Tea: 1-2 teaspoons to cup boiling water; infuse 15 minutes. Dose: half-1 cup.
Liquid Extract: 30-60 drops.
Tincture BHP (1983): 1:5 in 45 per cent alcohol; dose 2-10ml. GSL

PARTURIENT. A herb which clinical experience has shown to be of benefit in pregnancy and delivery, reducing time and uneasiness of labour. Motherwort, Raspberry leaves, Squaw Vine, etc. See: CHILDBIRTH.

PASSION FLOWER. Maypop. *Passiflora incarnata L. German*: Wilde Passionsblume. *French*: Passiflore sauvage. *Spanish*: Passionaria. *Italian*: Granadiglia incarnata. Dried leaves and flowers. *Keynote*: general relaxant.
Constituents: alkaloids, flavonoids, rutin, saponarin.
Action: hypnotic, vasodilator, antispasmodic, mild sedative and analgesic without leaving depression. Hypotensor. Tranquilliser. CNS relaxant. Strengthens the heart muscle.
Uses. Sleeplessness due to mental restlessness. Nervous excitability, over-active brain, hyperactive children, hysteria, alcoholism, twitching of limbs, neuralgia, constrictive headache. Temporary relief of tremor in the elderly. Benzodiazepine and Valium addiction, to assist withdrawal. Rapid heart beat. Pain of shingles (partial relief). Anxiety neurosis (with Hawthorn – equal parts).
Combination: with Oats, Hops and Valerian for drug addiction.
Preparations. Three or four times daily.
Tea: quarter to half a teaspoon to each cup boiling water; infuse 15 minutes. Dose, half a cup morning and evening for above or at night for sleeplessness.
Liquid Extract: half-2ml in water.
Tincture BHC Vol 1: 1 part to 8 parts 25 per cent ethanol. Dose: 2-4ml.
"*Natracalm*". Aqueous alcoholic extractive from 500mg Passion flower. (*English Grains*)
Powder, capsules: three 230mg capsules morning and evening. (*Arkocaps*)
Low doses in pregnancy. GSL

PASSOVER HERBS. The five bitter herbs directed to be eaten at the Jewish Feast of the Passover are Horehound, Lettuce, Nettles, Hyssop, Coriander.

PATIENT, The. There is a strong body of opinion among the medical profession that a patient should not cease conventional treatment without the doctor's knowledge. He will also require knowledge that they are taking phytotherapy (herbal medicine).

PATIENT'S ASSOCIATION. Advice on self-help groups and other services which may be able to assist patients and carers. Advice to patients and carers on patient's rights.
Publications: Patient Voice (quarterly).
Address: 18 Victoria Park Square, Bethnal Green, London E2 9PF. Tel: 081 981 5676.

PAW PAW. See: PAPAYA.

PEACH TREE. *Amygdalus persica L. Prunus persica*, Stokes. *German*: Pfirsich. *French*: Pécher. *Italian*: Pesco. *Chinese*: Too.
Constituents: oleic acid glycerides.
Action: mild tranquilliser, expectorant, soothing diuretic.
Uses, internal. Morning sickness, leaf tea. (*Wm Boericke, MD*) Hard dry cough, whooping cough, bronchitis.
Preparations. *Tea*: half an ounce bark, or 1oz dried leaves in 1 pint boiling water; infuse 15 minutes. Dose: quarter to half a cup, as necessary.
Peach oil. Rich in triglycerides (compound fats), the oil is used as an emollient in the cosmetic industry for creams to prevent moisture-loss and to render the skin soft and smooth. GSL

PEANUT POISONING. Shelled peanuts may, with age, develop a mould called aflatoxin which attacks vital organs such as the kidneys and liver and can cause cancer if large quantities are eaten over a long period of time.
Teas: German Chamomile. Gotu Kola. Chaparral. 1-2 teaspoons to each cup boiling water; infuse 15 minutes. Half-1 cup thrice daily.
Aloe Vera gel (or fresh juice). 2-3 teaspoons.
Formula. Equal parts: Echinacea, Dandelion, Chamomile. Dose – Liquid Extracts: 2 teaspoons. Tinctures: 3 teaspoons. Powders: 750mg (three 00 capsules or half a teaspoon). Thrice daily.

PECTORAL. Pertaining to the chest and lungs. See: EXPECTORANTS.

PEDICULOSIS. See: LICE.

PELLAGRA. A deficiency disease caused by a shortage of nicotinic acid (niacin), one of the Vitamin B complex. Common in populations whose diets are mainly of Corn. Also from alcoholism.
Symptoms. Diarrhoea, weight-loss, appetite-loss, red tongue, 'always tired', depression, anxiety, sore mouth, skin is brown, scaly and itchy.
Treatment. Pellagra responds well to Thuja, in tincture or liquid extract; 30 drops in 4oz water. 1 teaspoon every 2 hours. OR:–
Practitioner. Combine: Tinctures. Barberry 1; Echinacea 1; Liquorice half; Thuja quarter. Dose: 1-2 teaspoons thrice daily.
Topical. Thuja lotion or ointment.
Diet: High protein.
Vitamins. B-complex, niacin, B12. Folic acid.

PELLITORY OF THE WALL. *Parietaria diffusa*, Mert and Koch. *German*: Glaskraut. *French*: Perce-muraille. *Italian*: Parietaria. *Dutch*: Glaskruid. *Polish*: Noc i Dzien. *Spanish*: Canarroya. Herb. Rich in sulphur, calcium, potassium and other trace minerals; flavonoids. *Keynote*: stone.
Action: demulcent diuretic, laxative, stone-solvent.

Uses. Stone in the kidney, gravel, pyelitis, suppression or painful passage of urine, dropsy, cystitis.
Old English traditional: equal parts, Pellitory, Wild Carrot and Parsley Piert (stone).
Combines well with Buchu for urinary tract infection.
Preparation. Fresh herb yields best results. Taken freely.
Tea: 1-2 teaspoons to each cup boiling water; infuse 15 minutes. Half-1 cup.
Liquid Extract: half-1 teaspoon in water.
Home tincture. 1 part fresh herb in 5 parts Holland's gin; macerate 8 days, shake daily. Decant. 1-2 teaspoons in water.
Compress: pulped clean fresh plant applied to ulcers and wounds that refuse to heal.
Contra-indications: hayfever. GSL

PEMPHIGUS. A general term for a number of skin diseases erupting as large bullae (fluid-filled blisters), which on bursting itch and burn.
Treatment: same as for Impetigo.

PENIS – INFLAMMATION. Inflammation of the glans penis and prepuce. See: BALANITIS.

PENNYROYAL. *Mentha pulegium L. German*: Poleiminze. *French*: Menthe pouliot. *Spanish*: Poleo. *Italian*: Puleggio. Fresh or dried flowering plant. First used by physicians of the ancient world.
Constituents: pulegone oil, menthol, limonene, bitter principle, tannins.
Action: carminative, diaphoretic, emmenagogue, stimulant, antispasmodic. External: insect repellent, antiseptic. A hot remedy for cold conditions.
Uses. Menstruation arrested by cold or chill, windy indigestion, nausea and vomiting, abdominal spasm (womb, stomach and intestines). Constrictive headache. To ward off midges and gnats. The common cold. To encourage a 'sweat-out' in feverish conditions.
Combinations. With Mugwort and Motherwort for painful menstruation. With Elderflowers for children's feverish conditions.
Preparations. Average dose, 1-4g. Thrice daily.
Tea: half-2 teaspoons to each cup boiling water; infuse 15 minutes, dose one-third to half a cup.
Liquid Extract: 15-60 drops, in water.
Aromatherapy: as an inhalant for nervous headaches, in drop doses.
Contra-indications: pregnancy and nursing mothers, kidney disorders. GSL

PENNYWORT. *Umbilicus rupestris*. Navelwort. The stem goes down from the centre ("navel") of the round leaf.
Action: demulcent, anodyne.
"I have found Pennywort to be a specific in earache . . . fresh leaves are pressed to extract the juice . . . rapid and complete easing of severe pain . . . safe with young children . . . not advised where there is damage to the drum." (*David Hoffmann, The Holistic Herbal, Thorsons*)

PEPPERMINT. *Mentha piperita L. German*: Pfeffer minze. *French*: Menthe poivre. *Spanish*: Menta. *Italian*: Menta prima. *Parts used*: oil distilled from fresh flowering tops; herb.
Constituents: essential oil, flavonoids, azulines, carotenes.
Action: digestive, carminative, antispasmodic, diaphoretic, anti-emetic, mild sedative, emmenagogue, peripheral vasodilator. Source of potassium and magnesium, enzyme activators. External: insect repellent, antiseptic.
Uses. Dioscorides wrote that a spray of Peppermint worn on his cloak raised his depressed spirits. Crohn's and diverticula disease. Refreshingly effective in simple indigestion. Travel sickness, flatulence, colic, nausea and vomiting, poor appetite, catarrh, ulcerative colitis, infant's convulsions. Of value in gall bladder disease.
Preparations. *Teabags or simple infusion*: 1-2 teaspoons dried herb to each cup boiling water; infuse 5-10 minutes; drink freely.
Oil of Peppermint: 1-2 drops in water, honey or banana mash.
Life Drops: an active ingredient of.
Obbekjaer's Peppermint products. Danish firm that supplies most of Europe's demands. Sugar-free, fibre-free tablets (suitable for diabetics). Capsules containing the oil in a base of Sunflower seed oil for slow release in the intestines.
Tincture. 1 part to 5 parts 45 per cent alcohol. Dose: 2-4ml.
Concentrated Peppermint oil. Dissolve 1 part Peppermint oil in 30 parts 90 per cent alcohol. Add, gradually, with repeated shaking, 50 parts distilled water (purified water). 5-20 drops freely.
Powdered herb: 2-4 grams.
Massage oil. 5-6 drops in 2 teaspoons Almond or Olive oil for cramps, spasms, muscular pains, low backache, sport's injuries, stiffness of shoulders and joints.
Inhalation: oil vapour for headache, fainting, shock, difficult breathing, colds, mental exhaustion. Widely used in aromatherapy.
Contra-indications: pregnancy, anxiety neurosis and nervous excitability. GSL

PEPSIN. A ferment secreted by the stomach to break down protein by converting it into albumose and peptones. Often used in medicine for feeble digestion. It is obtained from the stomach of pigs, calves and sheep.
Plant alternatives: Calamus, Meadowsweet, Paw Paw.

PEPTIC ULCER/GASTRIC. Loss of gastric lining; confined in space.

Etiology: reduced mucosal resistance to the eroding effect of acid and pepsin, chronic gastritis, diet, drugs, smoking, alcohol, piping hot tea.
Symptoms: weight loss, vomiting, poor appetite, acid vomiting. Epigastric pain relieved by food and alkalis.
Differential diagnosis: liver, gall bladder, pancreas and other disorders.
Treatment. Gastric diet, antacids, alcohol restriction, sustain nerves, stop smoking.
BHP (1983) recommends: Calamus, Comfrey root and leaf, Liquorice, Marigold, Marshmallow root, Slippery Elm.
German Chamomile tea. Freely.
Slippery Elm gruel. Freely.
Tea. Combine equal parts: Agrimony, Meadowsweet, Comfrey leaf. 1-2 teaspoons to each cup boiling water; infuse 5-15 minutes. 1 cup before meals 3 or more times daily.
Tablets/capsules: Cranesbill, Dandelion, Liquorice, Goldenseal, Wild Yam.
Formula. Irish Moss 2; Meadowsweet 1; Liquorice 1; Goldenseal quarter. Dose – Liquid extracts: 1-2 teaspoons. Tinctures: 1-3 teaspoons. Powders: 750mg (three 00 capsules or half a teaspoon) before meals 3 or more times daily.
Tinctures. Echinacea 2; Goldenseal 1; Liquorice half. 1 teaspoon in cup of German Chamomile tea before meals 3 or more times daily.
Maria Treben. Combine Comfrey root 1; Marigold half; Knotgrass half. 2 teaspoons in cup cold water to steep overnight. Next day bring to boil. Dose: 1 cup, warm, thrice daily.
Aloe Vera. One ounce juice every 2 hours. Success reported.
Diet. Small frequent meals. Low fibre. Low protein. Dandelion coffee. Taken at bedtime, a gruel made from Slippery Elm powder will inhibit stomach acid production during the night when mucosal damage may occur. Late night food stops ulcers healing. Well-chew all foods, avoid spices and never eat when upset, angry or anxious. Avoid eating more than three meals a day and never drink with meals.
Supplements. Vitamin A, B-complex, B2, B12, Folic acid, C, E, K, Iron complex. Bromelain.
Comfrey. Potential benefit outweighs possible risk.

PEPTIC ULCER/DUODENAL. Ulceration of the duodenal mucous membrane. Acid and pepsin secretion are not the only factors involved.
Causes: emotional, stress, smoking, alcohol, diet, environment, certain drugs such as aspirin and other pain-killers, tranquillisers, piping-hot foods.
Symptoms: irregular painful episodes. Gnawing epigastric pain relieved by alkalis and food. Poor appetite, acid vomiting, weight loss. An acid attack at night is a most important sign.
Differential diagnosis: diseases of gall bladder, pancreas, liver and other stomach disorders.
Treatment. Stop smoking, alcohol restriction, gastric diet, herbal antacids. Release emotional stress. Sustain nerves.
BHP (1983) recommends: Marshmallow root, Marigold, American Cranesbill (herb or root), Liquorice, Comfrey leaves, Slippery Elm root.
Tea. Combine equal parts: Comfrey leaves, Yarrow, Meadowsweet. 1-2 teaspoons to each cup boiling water; infuse 5-15 minutes. 1 cup freely.
Other drinks: spring water, Carrot juice, vegetable juices, potato water (made by boiling 3-4 large potatoes in water 20 minutes).
Tablets/capsules. Goldenseal, Dandelion, Cranesbill, Wild Yam, Echinacea.
Formula. Comfrey root 2; Echinacea 1; American Cranesbill half; Goldenseal quarter. Dose – Liquid extracts: 1-2 teaspoons. Tinctures: 1-3 teaspoons. Powders: 750mg (three 00 capsules or half a teaspoon) before meals 3 or more times daily.
Comfrey. Potential benefit outweighs possible risk.
Frank Roberts, MNIMH. Liquid Extracts: Goldenseal, Poke root, Echinacea, American Cranesbill, Marshmallow root – 3 and a half ounces each. Mix, store in amber bottle or out of the light. This is the entire treatment lasting 3-4 months continuous medication. Dose: 15-30 drops in water between meals (2 hours after breakfast, lunch and evening meal).
Aloe Vera. Successful results reported.
To sustain nerves: Lime flowers, Skullcap, Chamomile, Valerian.
Liquid Extract, German Chamomile BHP (1983). Dose: 1-4ml (15-60 drops), thrice daily.
Raw white cabbage juice. Prepare in a juicer, adding a little water. 1 cup between meals for a limited period (4-6 weeks).
Liquorice. Complete or partial healing. For best results chew thoroughly and swallow on an empty stomach while standing.
Slippery Elm food. Taken at bedtime, a gruel made from the powder will inhibit stomach acid production during the night when mucosal damage may occur. Protects against alcohol.
Diet. Low fibre, protein and fats. Lacto-vegetarian. Avoid hot peppery spicy foods, salt. Accept: mashed bananas and Slippery Elm; skim milk powder, soya bean milk, Plantmilk. Late night foods arrest healing. Chew well all foods. Never eat when upset, angry or anxious. Avoid spices and eat no more than three meals daily. No drink should be taken at meals.
Supplements. Vitamin A, B-complex, B2, B12, Folic acid, C, E, K, Iron complex, Bromelain.
Note. Cigarette smoking is main risk factor with recurrence.

PERCOLATION. A process for the extraction of soluble constituents of a plant by the descent of a solvent (alcohol, ethanol, glycerine, etc). Plant material is first moistened and then evenly packed into a tall slightly conical vessel having an outlet at the lower end. The outlet is closed and the percolating liquid, or *menstruum*, is poured onto the material and allowed to steep for a certain length of time. On opening the outlet, the percolate falls in drops into a suitable collecting vessel. The spent material is known as the *marc* which is discarded. Many tinctures and liquid extracts are prepared by percolation.

PERFITT, Victor D. MNIMH (Hon), F.Inst.NFR. Founder member of ESCOP (European Scientific Cooperative on Phytotherapy). UK Member of ESCOP Council. Chairman, British Herbal Medicine Association, 1994-. Member of the Scientific Committee, BHMA. Managing Director, Gerard House.

PERFUMES. Essential oils are frequently used to provide a fragrant natural perfume: Bergamot, Lavender, Patchouli, Rose.

PERICARDITIS. Inflammation or disease of the pericardium – a double membranous sac surrounding the heart and which enables that organ to function without friction.
Etiology: gout, myxoedema (thyroid disorder), congestive heart failure, injury, radiation, inflammation of the kidneys, rheumatic and other eruptive fevers, sepsis, tuberculosis.

May be dry, due to deposits of fibrin between two opposing surfaces (adherent pericarditis) revealed as a friction scraping sound when investigated by stethoscope. Or sac may fill with an effusion of fibrinous exudate (serous pericarditis) when it becomes distended. If accumulation is excessive it may constrict the heart, with serious consequences.
Symptoms: pain, centre of chest; sweating; fever with small rapid pulse, difficult breathing, restlessness, breathlessness, anxiety and hacking cough.

Although specific modern hospital treatment is necessary, much useful supportive work can be offered by herbal medicine.
Treatment. Seek underlying cause. Heart should be well-sustained by Hawthorn, Lily of the Valley, and infection treated with antibiotics (Poke root, Echinacea). Echinacea increases powers of resistance; Pleurisy root reduces inflammation of serous membranes and promotes absorption of effusion.
Dry Pericarditis. Alternatives:– *Tea*: equal parts: Yarrow, Mullein, Motherwort. Mix. 1oz (30g) placed in a previously warmed vessel and covered with 1 pint (500ml) boiling water. Allow to stand 15 minutes. Drink freely.
Decoction. Formula. Hawthorn 2; Echinacea 2; Pleurisy root 1; Goldenseal quarter. Place 1oz (30g) in 1 pint (500ml) water; simmer gently until volume is reduced by a quarter. Dose: half-1 cup thrice daily. Every 2 hours acute cases.
Tinctures. Formula. As above. Dose: 1-2 teaspoons in water thrice daily. Every 2 hours acute cases.
Effusive Pericarditis. Alternatives:– *Decoction*. Formula. Broom 3; Lily of the Valley 2; Echinacea 2. Mix. 1oz (30g) in 1 pint (500ml) water. Simmer gently 10-15 minutes. Dose: half-1 cup thrice daily; every 2 hours acute cases.
Formula. Broom 3; Echinacea 2; Lily of the Valley 1. Mix. Dose: Powders: 500mg (two 00 capsules or one-third teaspoon). Liquid extracts: 1 teaspoon. Tinctures: 2 teaspoons. Every 2 hours (acute).
Spartiol extract, (Klein). A preparation of Broom.
Practitioner. Stitching pain in left chest: Tincture Spigelia – 1-2 drops every 2 hours. Effusive pericarditis with rheumatic heart disease – Tincture Bryonia 5-15 drops thrice daily; every 2 hours acute cases.
Diet. 3-day fast with spring water and above fluids followed by low salt, low fat, high fibre, lacto-vegetarian proteins. Abundant citrus fruits for Vitamin C – oranges, lemons, Pineapple juice.
Supplements. Daily. Vitamin A 7500iu; Vitamin C 3g; Vitamin E 1000-1500iu.
General. Absolute bedrest. Tapping of pericardial cavity by medical specialist may be necessary to aspirate fluid which in some cases may be as much as a litre. Regulate bowels.

PERINEAL TEARS. Tears in the perineum – the area between the anus and the lower edge of the pubis at the front of the pelvis. In the female it includes the opening into the vagina. Tears may occur during childbirth, and are usually easily and rapidly healed, though some may require stitches. Where healing is prolonged the following may prove of value.
Tinctures. Equal parts: Pilewort, Butternut, Figwort. Mix. Dose: 1-2 teaspoons thrice daily. Comfrey tea freely.
Topical: Comfrey cream or ointment.

PERIODS, MENSTRUAL (heavy). See: MENORRHAGIA.

PERIOSTITIS. Inflammation of the membrane covering bones (periosteum). The acute condition is often caused by fracture; the chronic, by infection such as tuberculosis, osteomyelitis or nearby ulceration.
Teas. Comfrey leaf, Yarrow. Freely.
Formula. Comfrey root 2; Echinacea 1; Marigold 1; Thuja quarter. Dose: Powders: quarter to half a teaspoon. Liquid extracts: 1 teaspoon. Tinctures: 2 teaspoons in water, honey, etc, thrice daily and at bedtime.
Comfrey root. Potential benefit outweighs possible risk.
Compress: 10 drops *Tea Tree oil* to 4oz boiled

water. Soak suitable material in the solution and apply warm. Replace when dry. If too strong, may be diluted many times. Comfrey ointment. Aloe Vera gel or fresh juice.

PERIPHERAL. Refers to the outermost parts of the body, i.e. skin, surface of the body, etc. Peripheral vasodilators are agents which dilate surface blood vessels thus encouraging general circulation. See: VASO-DILATORS.

PERISTALSIS. A worm-like muscular activity of the oesophagus, stomach and intestines to propel their contents onwards. Any obstruction may result in intense contractions causing colic and spasmodic pain.
Peristalsis, to promote: Butternut. English Rhubarb, Mountain Grape. Most popular remedy: Senna pods. Sometimes peristalsis is assisted by an increase in bulk of contents passing through the intestines, in which case Ispaghula seeds are used.
Peristalsis, to reduce: see COLIC, etc.

PERITONITIS. Inflammation of the peritoneum, a membrane lining the abdominal cavity and enveloping the liver, spleen and intestines.
Causes: infection from a perforated appendix, peptic ulcer, diverticulitis, etc. TB infection is possible.
Symptoms. Severe abdominal pain with fever, vomiting and restlessness.
Treatment. Hospitalisation as an emergency. Stomach emptied through a naso-gastric tube. If this is not possible – fasting, with abundant herb teas for 3 or more days.
Herb teas; as available: Marshmallow, Lime flowers, Mullein, Balm, Yarrow, Brigham tea. Catmint.
Basic treatment (to be adapted to individual case).
Alternatives:– (1) *Liquid Extract*. Echinacea, 20-30 drops doses, hourly. Especially helpful for septic condition. (*Finlay Ellingwood*)
(2) *Decoction*. Combine Pleurisy root 1; Lobelia 1; Ginger quarter. 1oz to 1 pint water; bring to boil; simmer 5 minutes. Half a cup with or without honey, taken hot every 2 hours. In absence of Pleurisy root – Wild Yam.
External. Castor oil pack. Soak small handtowel in cold water; wring out and smear with Castor oil; apply over abdomen. Renew when dry. OR:– Poultice: Lobelia 1; Marshmallow root 3.

Treatment by or in liaison with a general medical practitioner.

PERIWINKLE. Madagascar periwinkle. *Catharanthus Roseus*. Leaves. Used by herbalists in South Africa, England, Australia and the West Indies for diabetes.
Action: hypoglycaemic, cytostatic. Anti-neoplastic that slows down growth of cells by suppression of immune response. Vinblastine and Vinchristine, as prepared from the plant, may prolong remission of leukaemia to more than five years. Both these chemotherapeutic agents are toxic to the nervous system where given by injection intravenously or intrathecaly. Should be given by mouth only.
Uses. Vinblastine is used for breast cancer and Hodgkin's disease. The herb was once added to anti-cancer agents Marshmallow, Poke root and Goldenseal for cancer of the glandular system and inoperable malignancies of the breast, brain, testicles and bronchi. Of value for acute leukaemia in children. Simple herbal infusion can be supportive of treatment by the oncologist.
Preparations. Average dose, 2-4g. Thrice daily, or more according to practitioner recommendation.
Decoction. 1oz to 1 pint water simmered 5 minutes. Dose, half-1 cup.
Tincture: 1 part to 5 parts 45 per cent alcohol; macerate 8 days, shake daily. Filter. Dose, 1-2 teaspoons.

Vinblastine and Vinchristine are usually prescribed by a physician.

Should not be given in the presence of bacterial infection, ulcerated skin, cachexia or pregnancy.

PERIWINKLE, GREATER. *Vinca major L. German*: Sinngrün. *French*: Violette de Sorcier. *Spanish*: Pervinca. *Italian*: Mortine. *Part used*: herb.
Constituents: tannins, indole alkaloids including reserpinine.
Action: astringent tonic, anti-haemorrhagic.
Uses. Excessive menstrual flow. Bed-wetting.
Preparations. Average dose, 2-4g; thrice daily.
Tea: 1oz to 1 pint boiling water; infuse 15 minutes. Dose, half-1 cup. Also used as a douche for leucorrhoea.
Liquid Extract BHP (1983). 1:1 in 25 per cent alcohol. Dose, 2-4ml.

PERIWINKLE, LESSER. *Vinca minor. French*: Violette de Sorcier. *Geman*: Sinngrün. *Italian and Spanish*: Pervinca. Has to be taken many weeks for maximum efficacy. *Parts used*: leaves and root. Contains alkaloid vincamine.
Action. Astringent. Circulatory stimulant: improves blood flow through the brain. Leaves are stomachic and bitter.
Uses. Gastric catarrh, chronic dyspepsia, belching and flatulence. The root is hypotensive, being used in parts of Africa for high blood pressure. (*Medicinal Plants and Traditional Medicine in Africa, by Abayomi Sofowora: Pub: John Wiley*)

Headache, dizziness, impaired memory, tinnitus (ringing in the ears), Meniere's syndrome, hearing loss and behaviour disorders with restlessness.
Recommended: taken as tea.

Preparations. Average dose: 2-4g. Thrice daily.
Tea. 1oz dried herb to 1 pint boiling water: infuse 15 minutes, dose half-1 cup.
Tincture. 1 part root to 5 parts material in 45 per cent alcohol. Macerate 8 days; shake daily, filter. Dose: 1-2 teaspoons in water.
Bioforce. Immergrün Drops.
Contra-indication: brain tumour.

PERTUSSIS. See: WHOOPING COUGH.

PERUVIAN BARK. See: CINCHONA.

PESSARIES. A pessary is a device to convey medicinal preparations to walls of the vagina. Similar to suppositories but shaped for insertion into the vagina. Wash hands before insertion. See: SUPPOSITORIES. Pessary moulds are obtainable from: The Herbal Apothecary, 120 High Street, Syston, Leicester 1E7 8GC.

PETECHIA. A small red spot in the skin due to effusion of blood. Indicates capillary fragility. Vitamin C deficiency.
Treatment. Buckwheat tea. Nettle tea.
Vitamin: C (1 gram daily).
Topical. Calendula (Marigold) lotion or cream. Witch Hazel water.

PETIT MAL. See: EPILEPSY.

PFAFFA. Brazilian ginseng. Suma. Paratudo. *Pfaffia paniculata*. Fam: aramanthaceae. Roots. Rich source of vitamins and mineral nutrients. Contains Germanium. *Keynote*: hormone imbalance.
Action: nerve and glandular restorative, anti-tumour, anti-melanoma. Adaptogen – to achieve more perfect endocrine balance.
Uses. To strengthen immune system against the progress of malignancy. Restorative after illness. Infertility. Menopausal and menstrual symptoms. To minimise side-effects of "The Pill" (anecdotal). Not given in pregnancy. To restore acid-alkali balance, thus facilitating blood-flow to cells and neutralising toxins. Osteomyelitis, high blood uric acid, PMT, high blood cholesterol.
Preparations. *Powdered root*. Half-1 teaspoon to each cup boiling water; infuse 15 minutes. Dose: half-1 cup thrice daily. (1 cup drunk freely by native population of Brazil).
Capsules. Powdered root, 500mg. 2 capsules on rising. (*Rio Trading Company, Brighton*)

PHARMACOGNOSY. The science of description of plants. Applies chiefly to the whole plant either cut, powdered or in liquid extract, standards for which are laid down in the British Pharmacopoeia (BP) and the British Herbal Pharmacopoeia (BHP). Such standards specify ash content levels, macroscopical definition, microscopic examination, presence of foreign matter, chemical tests to confirm that certain constituents are present and the degree of their concentration as determined by gas and thin layer chromatography.

PHARMACOLOGY. A science concerned with the action of medicinal substances on man. It is dependent upon the sciences of chemistry, physiology and pathology. The mode by which a medicinal plant and its practical application in the treatment of disease produces an action will be determined by principles governing these three sciences.

The art of applying remedies to disease is known as therapeutics. Herbal therapeutics deal with the synergistic action between a number of complex chemical constituents present in a plant. The skilful use of remedies upon the sick is possible only after the student has acquired some knowledge of pharmacology. Any practitioner of medicine, herbal or conventional, must have a knowledge of the changes induced in body tissue by the remedies he uses.

The object of pharmacology is the relief of human suffering and preservation of life. It is always advancing as an experimental science. New discoveries bring to light with greater accuracy the presence and action of vital plant constituents, with the result that new remedies of proven efficacy gradually replace some of the older ones shown to be of limited value, some even toxic in character.

PHARMACOPOEIA. An official publication containing information on the preparation, action, dosages and legal requirements of strength and quality of medicinal substances. Each country has its own. The British Pharmaceutical Codex (1934) contains the largest number of active herbal medicines among modern pharmacopoeias. A European Pharmacopoeia will control the use of drugs and medicinal substances in EC countries. See: BRITISH HERBAL PHARMACOPOEIA.

PHARYNGITIS. Acute inflammation of the pharynx. Sore throat.
Causes: usually by virus. Associated with adenoid swelling, glandular fever, tonsillitis and other infections.
In common practice. Agnus Castus (with lymphatic swelling), Poke root (with swollen lymph nodes), Boneset (with catarrh), Myrrh (streptococcal infection), Echinacea (to sustain immune system), Peruvian bark (febrifuge), Sage (antispasmodic), Wild Indigo (antimicrobial).
Tea: Chamomile or Sage tea. 1 heaped teaspoon to each cup boiling water; infuse 5-15 minutes. Half-1 cup freely.
Tablets/capsules. Agnus Castus, Poke root,

Myrrh, Echinacea, Devil's Claw.
Formula. Sage 2; Peruvian bark 1; Echinacea 1. Dose – Liquid extracts: 1 teaspoon. Tinctures: 1-2 teaspoons. Powders: 500mg (two 00 capsules or one-third teaspoon) 3 or more times daily.
Gargle. 5 drops Tincture Myrrh or Goldenseal in glass water, freely. Cider vinegar. Sage or Chamomile tea.
External. Cold pack to neck.
Diet. 3-day fast, with fruit juices and abundant Vitamin C.
Supplements. Riboflavin. Zinc.

PHILLIPSON, Dr J.D. MSc PhD MPS. Professor of Pharmacognosy, University of London. Scientific papers on herbal medicine.

PHLEBITIS. Inflammation of a vein; commonly of the leg. See: VENOUS THROMBOSIS.

PHOBIAS, NEUROSES, PSYCHOSES. A deviation of mental health from normal. Where not due to an underlying anxiety, they may follow mineral or hormone deficiency. Nervine relaxants and restoratives create an environment in which the body is better able to recover. Vitamins and minerals play an important part in health of both mind and body. Vitamins B and C and the mineral phosphorus increase the metabolic rate of the brain.
Teas: German Chamomile, Skullcap, Ginseng, Damiana, Oats, Vervain, Valerian.
Combination: equal parts: Skullcap, Valerian, Mistletoe. 1 heaped teaspoon to each cup water simmered gently one minute. Dose: half-1 cup thrice daily.
Tablets/capsules: Ginseng, Devil's Claw, Valerian. Pulsatilla. Mistletoe, Motherwort.
Diet. Protein. Salt-free. Lacto-vegetarian.
Supplements. B-complex, B1; B6; B12; Niacin, Folic acid. C, E, F, Dolomite, Zinc.

PHOSPHORUS. Non-metallic element. RDA 800mg. 1200mg for pregnant women and nursing mothers.
Deficiency. Affects every tissue in the body, particularly muscles, nerves, brain, teeth and spinal cord. A frequent cause of aches and pains. Nervous disorders, physical weakness, loss of appetite, bone pains, respiratory disorders.
Body effects. Strong healthy bones and teeth. Resilient musculature.
Sources. Most foods. Meat, dairy products, seeds, fish, peas, beans, brewer's yeast, Soya beans and flour, cola.
Herbs: Caraway seed, Chickweed, Liquorice root, Marigold flowers, Meadowsweet.

PHOTOCOPIER SYNDROME. When photocopiers are used at work, day in and day out, emission of ozone and carbon monoxide gases from dry copies (ammonia from wet copies) prove a hazard to health. Good ventilation is essential. No one should work full time in the same room all the time.
Symptoms. Sore wheezy chest, nasal irritation, skin sensitisation, dry eyes.
Treatment. Incoming poisons are neutralised by the liver, which organ easily sustains damage if toxicity is beyond its capacity. Elimination would be through lungs, bowel, skin or kidneys, which organs may become exhausted by their efforts to eliminate the noxious invader. The following sustains those organs and the liver:
German Chamomile. Dandelion. Sarsaparilla. Ginseng, Blue Flag root. Take as teas, decoctions, powders, liquid extracts or tinctures.
Garlic. 2-3 Garlic capsules at night.
Diet. Regular raw food days. See: DIET – GENERAL.
Supplements. A, B-complex, C, E.

PHTHISIS. See: TUBERCULOSIS.

PHYSICAL FITNESS. To maintain good health: daily:
Tea. Combine equal parts: Alfalfa, Agrimony, Balm.
Alternative: English Herb tea. As desired.
At breakfast: tablets or capsules; 2 of each: Ginseng, Halibut Liver oil, Dolomite.
On retiring at night: 2 Garlic capsules high in Garlic oil.
Diet. Low-fat. Low-salt. High fibre. Replace cow's milk with Soya milk. Abundant raw fresh fruit and vegetables. Avoid: condiments, frying-pan foods, white sugar and white flour products, coffee, cola and caffeine stimulants. Prefer spring water.

PHYSIOMEDICALISM. A movement founded by Dr Samuel Thomson towards the end of the 18th century to reform the practice of medicine in America. It was based chiefly on herbal medicine as used by the Indians. Many of the early pioneers became competent herbalists on their travels westward. The rationale of their system was to gently stimulate the body's own defence mechanism and enable it to heal itself from its inner resources. In this activity it was assisted by other complementary therapies such as naturopathy and hydrotherapy.

Dr Albert Coffin, English physician, went to America where he was successfully treated for tuberculosis by a practitioner of the movement. He returned to England with enthusiasm for the system but he was met with indifference by his orthodox colleagues. Thereafter, he turned his attention to the herbal fraternity and worked for the recognition of herbal medicine.

PHYTOMEDICINES. "Plant medicines.

Medicinal products containing as active ingredients only plants, parts of plants or plant materials, or combinations thereof, whether in the crude or processed state."

The above ESCOP definition is followed by their Addendum:

1. The ESCOP definition is in accordance with the principles outlined in the glossary to 'Quality of Herbal Remedies' in 'The Rules governing medicinal products in the European Community, Volume III, Guidelines on the quality, safety and efficacy of medicinal products for human use', ISBN 92-825-9619.
2. Plant materials include juices, gums, fatty oils, essential oils, and any other substances of this nature.
3. Chemically defined isolated constituents are not considered as phytomedicines.
4. Phytomedicines may contain excipients in addition to the active ingredients.
5. It is understood that medicines may contain plant materials and/or plant drug preparations combined with chemically defined substances but these are not considered to by phytomedicines by ESCOP.

PHYTO PHARMACEUTICALS. Phyto Products Ltd are a specialist manufacturer of herbal tinctures produced by the original process of cold maceration in accordance with the British Pharmacopoeia and the British Pharamaceutical Codex. Tinctures specifically derived from organically grown materials are prepared from raw botanicals that have been grown under controlled conditions. Tinctures, creams and plant juices. Phyto Products Ltd, 3 Kings Mill Way, Hermitage Lane, Mansfield, Notts NG18 5ER.

PHYTOTHERAPY. Name given to traditional medicine which goes back to biblical times. It has a longer history than modern pharmacy with its chemicals and synthetics. Efficacy is being established through a millennia of trial and error as its crude beginnings evolve into a therapy which is no longer empirical but founded on scientific proof. Phytotherapy is the modern natural pharmacy taking over herbalism of the ages. All over the world clinical studies establish new standards and criteria for efficacy, safety and purity.

Properties and active ingredients which were once unknown are now accurately documented together with vitamins and minerals. It is the prescription of these in preparations of the 'whole' plant, as opposed to isolates, that this new version of an old craft offers its greatest benefits. Efficacy of the whole plant is greater than the sum of its isolated parts and, if rightly used, has no side-effects.

PHYTOTHERAPY, SCHOOL OF. Training establishment of candidates preparing for membership of the National Institute of Medical Herbalists or other professional body. Courses offered:–

1. *The Four Year Full Time Course* consists of theoretical and practical training. After successfully passing the final examination, students obtain a Diploma in Phytotherapy and a certificate. They may then apply for membership of the N.I.M.H.
2. *The Four Year Tutorial Course*. A self-study course mainly by correspondence, apart from one week's practical training at the School each year. Students receive the same clinical training as the Full Time School and after passing examinations receive a School Diploma.
3. *The One-Year Course* for those interested in the basics of herbal medicine – health food shop managers, herb growers, housewives, laymen, etc.
4. *A Specially Structured Course* for General Practitioners of orthodox medicine and Osteopaths who have already received training in medical science and with substantial experience in the treatment of patients.

Faculty of Materia Medica. Study and observation of medicinal plants in the School's Herb Garden, including cultivation and preparation. Identification and authentication of fresh, dried and powdered material. Herbarium. Phytotherapy and pharmacological properties of medicinal plants. Indications and therapeutic uses. Pharmacy, dispensing.

Faculty of Medicine. Theory of pathology, medicine, specialities – immunology, gynaecology, geriatrics, psychology. Clinical examination, differential diagnosis, case-taking etc.

Facilities. Plots for students to grow their own herbs in the Herb Garden, commercial herb growing. Microbiology Laboratory for medical microbiology, histology, pharmacognosy. Laboratory for preparation of medicines – plasters, suppositories, lotions, emulsions, tinctures etc. Thin Layer Chromatography Laboratory for analytical plant research. Library.

Publication: Journal of Phytotherapy – articles, research.

Principal: Hein H. Zeylstra, Analytical chemist.

Address: Bucksteep Manor, Bodle Street Green, Hailsham BN27 4RJ. Tel: 0323 833812/4.

PID. Pelvic inflammatory disease. Refers to a group of miscellaneous infections of the female reproductive system. Recurrent conditions include endometritis (womb), oophoritis (ovaries), pelvic cellulitis, and salpingitis (Fallopian tubes – the most common site of infection). Around 70 per cent PID cases in young women are due to chlamydia infection, followed by gonorrhoea and some anaerobic organisms. Women can still have chlamydia but no symptoms. Usually there is irregular bleeding and moderate pain. Damage to the Fallopian tubes is possible. Sterility may follow neglect.

Women are at greatest risk of pelvic inflammation in the 20 days after having an intra-uterine contraceptive device (IUCD) fitted. But after this time, risk of the disease stays low for up to eight years. (*World Health Organisation study*)
Treatment. Orthodox treatment – antibiotics, surgery.
Phytotherapy: *tinctures, liquid extracts, powders*. Combine: Echinacea 3; Marshmallow root 2; Goldenseal 1; Cramp bark 1; Ginger 1. Tinctures: dose, 1-2 teaspoons. Liquid extracts: 1 teaspoon. Powders: one-third teaspoon. In water or honey, thrice daily. For pain-relief – Cramp bark tablets or capsules. Above for the general condition. More specific, see: ENDOMETRITIS, OOPHORITIS, SALPINGITIS, CHLAMYDIA.
Give attention to bowel to counter toxicity – Fenugreek seeds, Ispaghula seeds, etc. Consider Candida albicans which is usually present. For feverishness – Yarrow tea (diaphoretic) 2-3 times daily. For excessive pain – Pulsatilla.
Diet. Dandelion coffee to assist elimination of toxins. A sprinkle of Cayenne pepper on meals stimulates pelvic circulation. Important: avoid coffee, chocolate, cola drinks.
Note. Women who smoke risk both PID and infertility. (*American Journal of Obstetrics and Gynaecology*)
Supportives. To enhance immune system: relaxation, meditation, positive thinking.
At bedtime – 2 Garlic tablets/capsules.

PIERRE, FATHER. See: FATHER PIERRE'S MONASTERY HERBS.

PILES. See: HAEMORRHOIDS.

PILEWORT. Lesser Celandine. *Ranunculus ficaria L. German*: Scharbocks-hahnenfuss. *French*: Ficaire. *Spanish*: Celidonia. *Italian*: Scrofularia minore. *Part used*: herb.
Constituents: anemonin, tannins, saponins.
Action: anal astringent and demulcent.
Uses. Specific for non-bleeding piles. Itching anus. To soothe inflamed anal membranes.
Preparations. Average dose, 2-5 grams. Thrice daily.
Tea: 1 heaped teaspoon to each cup boiling water: infuse 15 minutes. Dose: quarter to 1 cup.
Liquid Extract: half-1 teaspoon (2 and a half-5ml) in water.
Ointment (home). 1 part whole fresh plant while in bloom to 3 parts benzoinated lard; macerate in gentle heat 24 hours. GSL

PILL, The. A hormone preparation to prevent pregnancy. Blocks the gonadotropic hormones of the anterior pituitary gland and inhibits ovulation.
Side-effect symptoms include: headache, depression, brown discoloration of face, "Spotting" – slight blood loss from the womb. Weight increase, mild nausea, breast tenderness, muscle fatigue, hair loss, impairment of fertility, aggravation of diabetes. Risk of thrombosis in over 35s. See also: HORMONE HERBS.
For side-effects: Black Cohosh: Dose: *Liquid extract*, 15-60 drops. *Tincture*, 1 teaspoon. In water thrice daily.
Mineral. Zinc: continued use of The Pill may give rise to deficiency. Dose: 15-30mg daily.
Notes. Women taking The Pill are advised to discontinue it for a month before major surgery, there being a higher risk of a blood clot following operation in women taking oestrogens.
Researchers of the Southern California University found in a study .of more than 580 women that those who had oral contraceptives doubled their risk of adeno-carcinoma of the cervix.

PILLS. Constituent powders are mixed in a mortar and kneaded into a firm mass with a suitable excipient and binder. The mass is passed through a pill machine to the desired form and size. They are coated or uncoated and intended to dissolve in the stomach. Pills have almost entirely been replaced by tablets which permit greater accuracy of strength and content. Examples: Lignum Vitae, Buchu, Cayenne.
Patients should remain standing for at least 90 seconds after taking pills and follow with a drink of water. Swallowing failure is possible when in the recumbent position when the pill may adhere to the oesophageal membrane, delaying disintegration time.

PIMPERNEL, SCARLET. Shepherd's Weatherglass. *Anagallis arvensis L* (red flowers). *German*: Roterbauchheil. *French*: Mouron rouge. *Spanish*: Centonchio rosso. *Italian*: Anagallo. *Arabian*: Marijaneh. *Iranian*: Jonk mari. *Indian*: Jam ghani. Whole plant used.
Constituents: cucurbitacins, glycosides, saponins.
Action: cholagogue, vulnerary, antitussive, diuretic, hepatic.
Uses. To stimulate flow of bile, nose-bleed, snake bite, cataract, liver congestion.
"Measles and other eruptive fevers." (*John Hill, 1772*)
"Hydrophobia (*rabies*), epilepsy and maniac depression." (*Gray, 1818*)
The Greeks said it induced euphoria, their name for it being "loud laughter".
Preparations. Thrice daily. Practitioner use only.
Tea: half a teaspoon dried herb to each cup boiling water; infuse 10 minutes: sips hourly for oedema and water retention.
Liquid Extract: 30-60 drops, in water.
Powder: 1-4g.
Poultice: for bite of mad dog, other animal or snake bite. GSL

PIMPLE. A spot. A small papule or pustule usually appearing on the face. Treatment as for ACNE.

PINE BUDS. *Pinus sylvestris L. German*: Gemeine Kiefer. *French*: Pin Silvestre. *Italian*: Pino salvatico. *Parts used*: needles, shoots, resin.
Action. Antiseptic, antiviral, expectorant, antipruritic, alterative.
Uses. Traditional remedy for pulmonary tuberculosis and upper respiratory disorders.
External: ointment for skin disorders and hair loss.
Preparations. *Tincture*: 1 part to 20 parts 90 per cent alcohol; macerate 14 days, strain. Dose: 5-10 drops in water thrice daily.
Cough mixtures: ingredient of.
Powder, capsules: (200mg). 6 to 8 capsules daily between meals. (*Arkocaps*) Or in a stable base, powder is used as an ointment for eczema.

PINEAL GLAND. A small gland behind the third ventricle of the brain: the 'third eye'. It secretes a hormone, melatonin that regulates little known body cycles such as the 'biological clock'. Light sensitive, melatonin production is high when daylight is poor. It acts on the brain, deeply influencing behaviour and mood. Jet-lag may be due to disrupted melatonin production.

Disorders manifest as sleeplessness and disorientation.
Formula. Horsetail 1; Gotu Kola 1; Guaiacum quarter. Dose: powders 500mg. Liquid Extracts: 30-60 drops. Tinctures: 1-2 teaspoons. In water, or honey, thrice daily.
Also relative to pineal disorders. Ginseng, Kelp, Safflower, Wild Indigo.
Supplements: Pantothenic acid. B6. B17. C. D. E. Iodine. Zinc.

PINEAPPLE (Juice). *Ananassa sativa. Ananas comosus.*
Action. Anti-inflammatory.
Uses. Gargle with fresh juice for sore throat.
Topical. A slice of the inner peel is placed over a corn, held in position by a skin adhesive and left on at night. In the morning the foot is soaked in hot water and debris scraped away; 2-3 applications may be necessary.

PINK DISEASE. See: ACRODYNIA.

PINKROOT. Carolina pink. *Spigelia marilandica L. German*: Indianisches Wurmkraut. *French*: Spigelie anthelminthique. *Spanish*: Spigelie. *Italian*: Spigelia. Root. Practitioner use only.
Constituents: spigeline, tannin, oil.
Action: anthelmintic, mild analgesic. Cardioactive.
Uses. "One of the most powerful medicines we have for worms, especially the common round worms; the powdered root being more efficacious." (*Dr Benjamin Rush*)

Usually followed by an evening dose of Senna. Of value in valvular disorders and enlargement of the heart.
Preparations. *Powdered root*. 1-2 grams, twice daily in water.
Tincture. 1 part root to 5 parts 60 per cent alcohol, macerated 8 days, shake daily; filter. Dose, 5-15 drops in water; morning and evening.

"PINS AND NEEDLES". Parasthesia. Tingling sensation of the skin.
Causes: external pressure on a nerve as when sitting cross-legged; may be related to a mild constitutional disorder such as iron-deficient anaemia which requires primary treatment.
For simple "pins and needles": tablets or cup of tea: German Chamomile, Skullcap, Devil's Claw, or Ginseng.

Vitamin B6.

PINUS BARK. Hemlock Spruce, Pinus canadensis. *Tsuga canadensis*, Carr. Dried bark.
Constituents: tannins, resin, oil.
Action: astringent tonic, antimicrobial, diaphoretic. Antiseptic (external).
Uses. *Oral*: diverticulosis, colitis, diarrhoea, cystitis.
Topical: douche: leucorrhoea, prolapse of the womb, candida. Mouthwash and gargle: sore throat, inflammation of the mouth or gums.

An ingredient of Composition powder.
Preparations. Average dose, 1-2 grams; thrice daily.
Decoction: half an ounce dried bark or powder to 1 pint water gently simmered 20 minutes. Dose, half a cup.
Decoction for use as a douche or enema: 2oz bruised bark to 2 pints water gently simmered 20 minutes. Strain. Inject warm.
Liquid Extract: BPC (1934), dose: 1-4ml. Diluted 1 in 10 parts of water, the liquid extract was once used as an injection for irrigation in cases of gonorrhoea and leucorrhoea. GSL

PIPSISSEWA. Prince's Pine. Ground Holly. *Chimaphila umbellata*, Nutt. *Part used*: leaves.
Keynote: urinary system.
Constituents: flavonoids, methyl salicylate, quinones, triterpenes.
Action: antiscorbutic, alterative, tonic, urinary antiseptic. Contains salicylic acid which has a mild pain-killing effect. Official in the United States Pharmacopoeia 1820-1916 as an astringent-tonic and diuretic. Diaphoretic, diuretic.
Uses. Dropsy following measles and other children's fevers. Of value in kidney disorders generally; stone, gravel. Clears scanty urine of high colour and ropy with catarrhal discharge. Ulcers, sores (tea as a lotion).

"It is reputed that North American Indians used hot infusions of the leaves to induce profuse perspiration in the treatment of typhus . . . that the Ojibwas used it as a stomachic tea . . . and that the Menominees considered it valuable for female ailments." (*Virgil J. Vogel*)
Preparations. Average dose, 1-3g. Thrice daily.
Tea. 1-2 teaspoons to cup boiling water; infuse 10 minutes. Half-1 cup.
Liquid Extract: 2.5 to 5ml in water. GSL

PITUITARY GLAND. Hypophysis. The 'master-gland' conducting performance of the whole endocrine orchestra. Size of a cherry, lying in a basin-like bony depression near the hypothalamus with which it works in close association.

The gland has two parts: the frontal lobe (anterior) and rear lobe (posterior). The anterior secretes hormones to stimulate other endocrine glands to produce their own specific hormones. The anterior lobe produces (a) TSH (thyroid-stimulating-hormone) to which Bugleweed relates; (b) ACTH which stimulates the adrenal gland cortex to produce corticosteroids; (c) FSH (follicle-stimulating-hormone) and LH (luteal-stimulating-hormone) for ovaries and testes; (d) GH (growth hormone) essential for normal growth in childhood years, and (e) prolactin, to assist milk production.

The rear part of the gland is a storage chamber for two hormones: vasopressin (anti-diuretic) and oxytocin (the pregnant womb contractor).

Malfunction of the gland lies at the root of many baffling diseases – mental and physical. For inexplicable conditions defying diagnosis, treatment should include an agent to sustain the pituitary gland and the endocrine system generally. It may reap unexpected rewards. Malfunction may be due to tumour, emotional shock, etc.

When there is an excessive secretion of HGH (human growth hormone) as by tumour, a condition known as acromegaly develops. See: ACROMEGALY.
Ginseng is known to act upon the gland, influencing relationship between adrenals and the brain.
Agnus Castus exerts an influence which ultimately affects the ovaries and testes.
Walnut (black or golden) and *Wild Yam* influence the anterior lobe while *Prickly Ash* relates to the posterior lobe.
Formula. Equal parts: Gotu Kola, Hawthorn, Prickly Ash, Agnus Castus. Dose: powders: 500mg (two 00 capsules or one-third teaspoon). Liquid extracts: 1 teaspoon. Tinctures: 1-2 teaspoons. Thrice daily.
Also relative to pituitary disorders: Gotu Kola, Iceland Moss, Irish Moss, Kelp, Parsley, Prickly Ash, Safflower, Sarsaparilla.

PITYRIASIS ROSEA. A skin disease with fine scaling over a small area, forming an itchy rash on the trunk, seldom on the face and lasting only a few weeks. Mostly affects the young and elderly as spring or autumn epidemics.
Symptoms: large scaling pimple on the trunk (herald patch). Lesions are redder and more scaly on the outer rim. 'Christmas-tree' arrangement along ribs.

Food allergy is a common cause, chief antigens being eggs and milk. Tartrazine colouring also implicated.
Alternatives. *Internally*. Echinacea, Blue Flag, Burdock, Clivers, Fumitory. Seaweed and Sarsaparilla.
Topical. Ointments, oils, creams: Comfrey, Aloe Vera (gel), Evening Primrose oil, Chickweed, Slippery Elm, Witch Hazel, Tincture Lobelia.
Aromatherapy: 6 drops Oil Myrrh in 2 teaspoons Almond oil.
Diet: Gluten-free. Oily fish: see entry. Avoid citrus fruits. Standard diet at the Great Ormond Street Hospital, London, excludes eggs, milk, chicken, beef, colours and preservatives.
Vitamins. A. B12. C. E. F.
Minerals. Dolomite. Sulphur as in Garlic.

PLACEBO. A harmless therapeutically-inactive herb or substance given to lead the patient to believe he is obtaining rational treatment. Any practitioner may, on occasion, need to break the sequence of therapeutic effect, but the patient will still expect continuous medication, if only to satisfy the "something must be done syndrome". Power of the mind may produce physiological change associated with healing – a placebo effect.

May be used in psychological medicine to determine cases of malingering. In investigating remedy-efficacy, introduction of the double-blind trial eliminates any possible placebo effect.

A sugar pill or bottle of coloured water.

PLAGUE, The. See: BUBONIC PLAGUE.

PLANTAIN. Waybread. Common Plantain. Rat's tail. *Plantago major L. German*: Wegerich. *French*: Plantain. *Spanish*: Plâtano. *Italian*: Piantaggine. *Chinese*: Ch'ê-ch'ien. *Part used*: leaves.
Constituents: flavonoids, tannin, iridoids.

One of the most versatile of herbal medicines. Seeds, roots, leaves. Rich source of minerals: potassium, magnesium, phosphorus. All body tissues feel its beneficient influence.
Action: anti-histamine, anti-bacterial, anti-allergy, blood tonic, lymphatic, anti-haemorrhagic, diuretic, expectorant, demulcent, astringent, antacid (tea).
External: as an emollient, vulnerary. Action of Ribwort Plantain (Plantago lanceolata) is similar, but Plantago major is preferred.
Uses. Chronic blood disorders. A neuralgic remedy of the first order. Non-poisonous liquid

extract or tincture is painted over painful areas of shingles, etc.

Diabetes (tea). Intermittent fever. Kidney and bladder disorders. Bed-wetting (tea: 2 or more cups daily, as necessary). Irritable bowel, dysentery, bleeding piles, diverticulosis (enema). Ulcers, internal and external: internal – bleeding gastric ulcer, blood in the stool: external – lesions not healed by Comfrey. Bleeding malignant ulcers: infusion to cleanse before dressing with Plantain salve.

Excess menstrual loss, hyperacidity, bronchitis. Bruises. Chronic discharging skin eruptions: erysipelas, scalds, burns, wounds that refuse to heal. Cystitis with blood. Blood in the urine. Thrush or purulent discharge (strong tea as a vaginal douche). Skin disorders: eczema, acne.

Bleeding gums, toothache. Mouth wash with tea or fresh juice. (*Herbal of Dodoens*) The tea makes a cooling drink where fevers have gone on long. Syphilis and STD: traditional in China. Old Chinese remedy for bites of snakes, animals, and insects.

Combination: Prickly Ash 1; Plantain 3; for Meniere's disease.

Preparations. Average dose, 2-4g. Thrice daily.

Tea. 1oz dried (2oz fresh) herb to 1 pint boiling water; infuse 15 minutes. Dose, half-1 cup. External: also used as a cleansing wash.

Powder, capsules: 200mg. 2 capsules thrice daily. (*Arkocaps*)

Liquid Extract: half-1 teaspoon in water. Children, 10-15 drops.

Home tincture: 1 part fresh plant pulp to 5 parts 25 per cent alcohol (Vodka, gin, etc). Macerate 8 days; shaking daily. Filter. Dose, 1-2 teaspoons in water.

Compress. Bruised fresh leaves applied to assuage pain, irritation and itching.

Juice of fresh plant. Shred leaves; pass through a juicer. 1-2 teaspoons juice in honey or other vehicle. Also for cuts, scratches, minor wounds, bites of animals and insects.

Enema. 2oz leaves infused in 2 pints boiling water for half an hour. Stir, strain, inject warm.

Salve. Take parts: fresh Plantain leaves 12; Vegetable oil (Peanut, Safflower or Olive) 16; beeswax 2.

Method: melt beeswax in the oil by gentle heat in a suitable vessel: earthernware, pyrex etc (not aluminium or metal). Add bruised or shredded Plantain leaves and place in a warm oven for 3 hours. Strain off when hot into pots. For healing purposes. GSL

PLASTERS. For external use. Leaves, roots or other components are bruised and placed between two pieces of cloth, muslin, etc, and applied to the affected area.

Examples: Mustard, Linseed, Marshmallow root, Comfrey root, Marigold petals, Plantain. Creams, ointments or tinctures of such plants offer an alternative, the area covered with clingfilm.

PLEURISY. Dry. Inflammation of the pleura without accumulation of fluid. The pain of dry pleurisy is stabbing, cutting or tearing, stitch-like in the side preventing sleep. Distribution, usually under arm or beneath breasts. Worse on respiration. Movement on affected side limited. Contour of chest little altered. Palpation reveals vocal fremitis (friction sounds present). Percussion: some resonance. Stethoscope reveals pleural "rub".

Treatment. Hot bath and bedrest. Extra warmth if patient complains of chilling. Abundant drinks of Yarrow tea.

Formula. Equal parts: Mullein, Yarrow, Pleurisy root. Dose: Liquid Extracts: 1 teaspoon. Tinctures: 2 teaspoons. Powders: 500mg (two 00 capsules or one-third teaspoon). Every 2 hours (acute); thrice daily (chronic) in water or honey.

Albert Orbell FNIMH. Simple acute. Tea: equal parts Elderflowers (to reduce temperature), Thyme (antibiotic), Peppermint (to relieve breathing), Coltsfoot (cough). One heaped teaspoon to each cup boiling water; infuse 10 minutes. Half-1 cup every 2 hours, or as tolerated.

External. Sponge-down with vinegar and water. Hot packs made by immersing suitable material (flannel etc) in one of the following teas: Mullein, Linseed, Comfrey root. Apply to chest. Renew when cold. OR:– hot Camphorated oil rub.

Diet. 3-day fast with plenty of fluids: Yarrow tea, fruit juices, spring water.

Note. To prevent an attack in those prone to respiratory weakness: 2-3 Garlic capsules at night.

Treatment by or in liaison with a general medical practitioner.

PLEURISY, WITH EFFUSION. Accumulation of fluid in a pleural cavity. Expectoration may be absent or slight.

Symptoms. Sensation of malaise, pain in chest worse on breathing, coughing and exertion. Difficult breathing. Swelling of eyelids, thirst, dry cough followed by thin mucus. Swelling of ankles and legs in evening. Palpitation, anxiety, dry skin. Worse lying down.

Inspection: side of chest visibly enlarged; heart displaced towards the opposite side. Palpitation: vocal fremitis almost always absent. Percussion: flat-sounding note with sufferer's increased sense of resistance. Stethoscope reveals: diminished or absent breath sounds.

Treatment. Hot bath and bedrest. Assist drainage.

Teas. Boneset, Buchu, Cowslip, Dandelion, Elderflowers, Elecampane, Yarrow.

Tea. Formula. Equal parts: Boneset, Elderflowers, Peppermint. 1 heaped teaspoon to

each cup boiling water; infuse 5-10 minutes; 1 cup freely.
Powders. Dandelion root 2; Elecampane 1; Squills half; Ginger quarter. Mix. Dose: 750mg (three 00 capsules or half a teaspoon) every 2 hours (acute); thrice daily (chronic).
Practitioner. Tinctures: Pleurisy root 10ml; Elecampane 20ml; Lily of the Valley 10ml; Yarrow 20ml. Capsicum fort 5 drops (0.3ml). Aqua to 100ml. Dose: 1 teaspoon (5ml) in water or cup Elderflower tea every 2 hours (acute); thrice daily (chronic).
External treatment. Same as for dry pleurisy.

Attention to bowel. Laxative may relieve intra-thorax pressure.

Treatment by or in liaison with a general medical practitioner.

PLEURISY ROOT. Butterfly weed. *Asclepias tuberosa L. Part used*: root.
Constituents: flavonoids, cardenolides, amino acids.
Action: febrifuge, antispasmodic, amphoteric, expectorant, diaphoretic, carminative. Stimulates function of mucous and serous surfaces. Stimulant to the autonomic system. Equalises the circulation by opening up surface capillaries and promoting free blood flow.
Uses. Pleurisy. Painful respiration, especially at the base of the lung. Pericarditis. Pneumonia, pneumonitis, bronchitis, dry cough, irritation of the larynx, hoarseness. Influenza, the common cold, catarrh. To slow down a rapid pulse. Peritonitis.

"The Natchez Indians believed this plant to be the best agent for pneumonia. They boiled the roots and took a cupful at a time. If one was sick with a hot dry fever," wrote Dr John Swanton, "drank this and wrapped himself up well in bed he would soon perspire freely." (*Virgil J. Vogel*)
Preparations. Average dose, 1-4 grams, or equivalent. Thrice daily. Every 2 hours for acute cases.
Tea. Half-2 teaspoons to cup boiling water; infuse 15 minutes. Dose, half-1 cup.
Liquid Extract. 1-4ml in water.
Tincture BHP (1983). 1:10 in 45 per cent alcohol. Dose, 1-5ml. GSL

PLEURODYNIA. A sharp pain in the chest which may be misdiagnosed as pleurisy. Pain is often muscular in character, many cases being resolved by osteopathy.
Treatment: same as for FIBROSITIS.

PLEURODYNIA, epidemic. Devil's Grip. Bornholm disease. An infectious disease (*Coxsackie*) in children in late summer and autumn, with pain in the diaphragm.
Symptoms: fever, chest muscle tenderness, nausea, malaise, headache.
Treatment. *Formula*. Pleurisy root 2; Ginger 1; Cramp bark 1. Dose – Liquid extracts: 1 teaspoon. Tinctures: 2 teaspoons. Powders: 500mg (two 00 capsules or one-third teaspoon). Thrice daily and when necessary.
German Chamomile tea.
External. Compress: 10 drops Tea Tree oil to 4oz boiled water. Soak suitable material in the solution and apply warm. Replace when dry. If too strong may be diluted many times. Comfrey cream or ointment. Aloe Vera gel or fresh juice.
Diet. 3-day fast.

PLINY THE ELDER. 23-79 AD. Roman naturalist who pursued the good life by taking a daily cold bath followed by a frugal meal of raw foods and a siesta between long spells of writing. An attendant read to him while in the bath and when receiving his daily massage or 'anointing' with essential oil of plants. Asthma contributed to his dramatic death. Eager to witness the great eruption of Vesuvius in 79 he strayed too near and was overcome by the stifling fumes. In his *Natural History* he records the beneficial herbs of his time. Famous for curing soldier's army of scurvy with Bistort (*Polygonum bistorta*).

PNEUMOCONIOSIS. Occupational lung disease from inhalation of dust particles. Three main types:
(1) Simple pneumoconiosis, from inert dust which may be painless (iron, carbon).
(2) Irritant dusts which cause scarring and erosion (silica, asbestos).
(3) Organic dusts which cause allergies (fungi, pollen).
Symptoms: cough, bronchitis, breathlessness, finger-clubbing, progressive lung deterioration.
Treatment: same as for SILICOSIS.

PNEUMONIA. Inflammation of the lungs. Different types ranging from acute lobar of bacterial origin to suppuration pneumonia with formation of abscesses in the lungs. It may appear also as a serious complication of another disease, i.e. typhoid fever.

The three stages of pneumonia are *engorgement*, the lung congested with blood; *red hepatisation* where air spaces are filled with coagulated fluid; and *grey hepatisation* in which pus cells give the lung a grey colour.

The condition usually starts with general malaise, cold sores around the mouth (Vitamin C deficiency), shivering, high temperature sometimes approaching 104 degrees with chest pain. A child may be convulsed.

When the pulse is erratic and not in proportion to the breathing rate, the second stage commences. The patient feels hot, coughs up a little rusty-coloured sputum, and has great anxiety. If the condition is widespread the face will be livid blue (cyanosis), with temperature high even during the day.

On the seventh or eighth day the patient may face a crisis: temperature drops suddenly, sweating increases. Temperature drops slowly by lysis to normal in a few days. Where delirium, breathlessness and cyanosis continue without improvement the situation is regarded as grave.

With the coming of Penicillin mortality rate from the disease has fallen dramatically. Antibiotics are likely to hold the stage for many years. However, should they no longer become available through national emergency or war, certain plant materials (at one time mainline treatment) are still available.

Today, it would appear that herbal medicines for pneumonia have been superseded by more effective orthodox medicines; however, they may still be given as a positive supportive aid to the physician's primary treatment. They are of special value to communities beyond the reach of modern medicine.

All cases of pneumonia should be treated by or in liaison with a qualified medical practitioner.

Treatment. Where the patient presents with different symptoms, treatment will differ. Each treatment will be tailored to the biological needs of the individual. The American School of Physiomedicalists were practising physicians who had plenty of experience in this desperate condition and left their testimonies to a group of agents which have passed into medical history but which, used with knowledge and keen clinical observation can, even today, give a convincing performance of their therapeutic efficacy. Medicines used were liquid extracts or tinctures.

Aconite. A reliable standby where skin is hot and dry, throat sore and burning, pulse small and frequent. 5 drops tincture to 100mls (3 and a half fluid ounces) water. Dose: 1 teaspoon hourly. Should there be stomach irritation: add 1 drop Tincture Ipecacuanha. Testimony of a member: "I've always used Aconite for my pneumonia cases. I only lost three cases in all my 40 years practice, and these took a form of typhoid."

Green Hellebore (veratrum viride). High temperature, dry tongue with red streak down middle, full bounding pulse, wasted condition. Add 10 drops tincture to 100mls (half glassful water). Dose: 1 teaspoon hourly until temperature falls.

Gelsemium. Pulse strong and full. Pupils contracted to pin-point indicating severe nervous agitation. Face flushed high scarlet. This agent relieves nerve irritation and pressure on the brain, forcing blood from the arteries into the veins, thus equalising the circulation. 10 drops Gelsemium tincture to 100mls water. Dose: 1 teaspoon hourly.

Belladonna. Indicated where pupils are large, occupying almost the whole of the iris; patient drowsy approaching coma, face pale. Capillaries engorged; blood trapped in the veins. Belladonna is the opposite of Gelsemium, and promotes oxygenation of the blood. 5 drops tincture to 100mls water. Dose: 1 teaspoon, hourly, or more frequently as urgency demands.

Formula. Equal parts: Elecampane root, Echinacea, Iceland Moss.

Tea.1 heaped teaspoon of the mixture to each cup water gently simmered 10-15 minutes. Dose: as much as well tolerated every 1-2 hours.

Liquid extracts: half-1 teaspoon; tinctures: 1-2 teaspoons; in water.

Diet. No dairy products. First few days: fruit juices and herb teas only.

Where the heart is weak, it needs to be strengthened by Tincture Cactus (Opuntia) or Tincture Crataegus oxyacanthoides: five drops in water when necessary.

Where possible the patient should be bathed with warm water and bed attire changed when sweating has been profuse. Long drinks of home-made lemon and other fruit juices should be available and massive supplementation of Vitamin C given with benefit.

To allay pains and laboured breathing rub the chest with hot Camphorated oil and follow with hot packs (towels wrung out in hot water) as hot as can be borne and replaced when dry. This practice has largely been superseded by dry packs impregnated with essential oils: Niaouli, Rosemary, Hyssop, Cajeput, Eucalyptus, etc.

In the early stages of any fever, an older generation of doctors gave an aperient to flush the bowel of morbid matter. This internal cleansing may effect some reduction of a high temperature. Throughout the whole course of treatment careful attention must be given to bowels and kidneys for speedy elimination of wastes.

It is also possible to disperse a certain amount of heat and internal tension by use of herbs that stimulate activity of the skin. Diaphoretics (Yarrow, Boneset, Elderflowers, etc) promote sweating. To revive after collapse – Cayenne.

Most of the aforegoing remedies calm the delirium. Where the chest is painful, Linseed or Comfrey poultices may relieve. Fresh air is important but draughts should be avoided. Blueness of the face indicates a lack of oxygen in the circulation. It may be necessary for oxygen to be administered by a catheter or oxygen tent.

At all times the heart should be carefully monitored. While herbal cardiac remedies are available, desperate conditions demand desperate cures. The time-honoured stimulant, brandy, has much to commend it in such a situation – up to two ounces a day.

While temperature is above normal little solid food should be given, emphasis being on fresh ripe fruits. When appetite returns, a little fish and minced chicken are allowed.

No one would deny use of the best that science

has to offer. However, in the absence of the amenities of modern pharmacy and hospital facilities, a hard-pressed practitioner may be glad of an alternative line of defence for a last ditch stand against this critical condition.

PNEUMOTHORAX. The presence of air within a pleural cavity. May occur from abnormality of the lung, chronic bronchitis, emphysema, asthma, tuberculosis, fibrotic conditions, carcinoma, trauma (when it is often associated with haemorrhage) or ascent in an aeroplane. Apical cysts or bullae on the lung may burst resulting in air leaking into the pleural cavity. A poor blood supply to the apex of the lung predisposes.

Pneumothorax leads to a fall in arterial oxygenation for which Vitamin E is indicated.

Symptoms: acute chest pain (pleuritic in nature), radiating towards the shoulder and neck. Pain rarely central and does not radiate down the arm. Breathlessness, dry tickling cough.

Treatment. Same as for Pleurisy, with emphasis on Vitamin E (1,000iu) and Vitamin C (1g) daily.

POISONING. INTERNAL. Certain substances when taken into the body may have a harmful effect on tissue. They may be swallowed chemicals or inhaled noxious fumes. Internal poisons irritate the stomach and bowels causing pain, vomiting and purgation. Some corrosives burn. Others excite or depress the nervous system causing painful spasm or paralysis.

Treatment. Summon emergency hospital service. Until the practitioner comes give drinks of Chamomile tea, Irish Moss or Slippery Elm decoctions.

Practitioner. Tincture Nux vomica. 5 drops to half glass water (3 and a half fluid ounces). Dose: 1 teaspoon hourly.

POISONING. OF THE SKIN. Certain plant poisons may be absorbed through the skin, setting up intense irritation, i.e. Nettles, poison oak and poison ivy.

Symptoms include rash with blisters and intense itching, face swollen, eyes closed. Many pesticides and herbicides have the same effect, for which the following are appropriate.

Internal: Echinacea, Valerian, Black Cohosh, Kava Kava.

Topical. Cold poultices: Slippery Elm powder. Comfrey, Marshmallow, Mugwort, Witch Hazel, Plantain, Elecampane, Spinach or any green vegetable leaves crushed with a rolling pin and applied.

Dr F. Ellingwood: "Liquid Extract Echinacea applied to the skin relieves."

Aloe Vera. Good responses observed.

POKE ROOT. Pigeon berry. *Phytolacca americana L. Phytolacca decandra L. German*: Gewöhnlicheker mesbeere. *French:* Herbe de la Laque. *Italian*: Fitolacca. Wide range of versatility. Leaves, root, berries. Ashes said to contain caustic potash which may account for its powerful action.

Constituents: lectins, tannin, triterpenoid saponins, resin, gum.

Action: lymphatic alterative, anti-neoplastic, fungicide, parasiticide, anti-rheumatic, anti-inflammatory. Dr Tyler Kent referred to it as the vegetable 'mercury'. Its action on the blood is slow but powerful.

Uses. Swollen glands and lymph nodes, mumps, tonsillitis, sore throat. Inflammation of prostate gland, ovaries, testicles. Chronic irritative skin disorders: ringworm, eczema, psoriasis, pityriasis, acne, scrofula, lupus; itching of genitals and anus. Ulceration (internal and external). Polymyalgia, rheumatism, arthritis. Breasts: mastitis, mammary abscess, fissured nipples, fibrotic nodules and hard lumps that have been diagnosed benign. Chronic fatigue syndrome (ME).

Obesity: eliminates excessive fat in fatty degeneration. Birds that feed on its berries lose most of their fat. To arrest erosion of periosteum in bone. Itching piles. Diverticulosis, ulcerative colitis (enema). Once traditional for syphilis and STDs. Sore throat (mild to diphtheria), chronic follicular pharyngitis; early physicians gave the fresh juice for spasmodic and membranous croup; mercurial poisoning from dental amalgam in teeth fillings. Lipoma (persistent internal and external treatment). Dr W.A. Dewey, Ann Arbour, Michigan, USA, saw an epithelium of the lip cured.

Some forms of cancer spread via the lymphatics for which Poke root has an inhibitory effect. Dr Johann Schöpf advised a tincture for carcinoma. John Bartram, explorer and medical botanist (1799-), after 50 years among North American Indians was convinced the root offered a cure or relief of symptoms for some forms of cancer.

Combines well with Echinacea and Myrrh for glandular disorders. Combines with Thuja (equal parts) for epithelioma and malignant ulcer.

Preparations. Average dose: not more than 8ml per week.

Pulp of fresh root or leaves: 1-2 teaspoons.

Tablets/capsules. Poke root 150mg: 2 tablets. Children 5-12 years: half tablet morning and evening.

Decoction. 60-300mg powder to each cup water simmered gently 5 minutes; dose, half-1 cup. Does not yield all its properties to water.

Liquid Extract: 2-5 drops in water. 2-hourly for acute cases.

Tincture, from fresh root gathered in winter. 1 part to 10 parts 45 per cent alcohol; macerate 8 days; shake daily, filter. Dose: 3-10 drops.

Poultice or compress. Apply pulp of fresh leaves or root with suitable dressing.

Ointment. Powder, 10 per cent; suitable base to

100 per cent. See: OINTMENT BASE.
Contra-indication: large doses cause vomiting.
Note. Berries contain a property which kills off snails carrying schistosomiasis (bilharzia) parasite. (*New Scientist 1989 No 1690 p21*)

POLIOMYELITIS. Highly contagious disease. Infantile paralysis. Caused by one of three polioviruses. Incubation: 7-14 days. Transmission by human contact. Has been known to spread through domestic pets. Enters the body by the stomach and intestines. See: NOTIFIABLE DISEASES.
Symptoms. Onset, flu-like fever, headache, vomiting, general malaise. Then come aching limbs, stiff neck and increasing violence of the headache. May be mistaken for meningitis. Irritability, drowsiness. At this point the patient may recover without incident, while another may develop paralysis. Invasion of the throat and respiratory organs may be fatal. The disease should be treated by or in liaison with a qualified medical practitioner.
Treatment. Hospitalisation, with good nursing facilities. Gentle splinting. Abundant fluids to prevent dehydration. Until the doctor comes: singly or in combination, Elderflowers, Skullcap, Yarrow. 2 teaspoons to each cup boiling water; infuse 5-15 minutes; drink freely. The addition of 3-5 drops Tincture Capsicum (or antispasmodic drops) increases efficacy.
Sister Kenny treatment. Hot packs and internal diaphoretics (as above) to induce sweating.
Dr Finlay Ellingwood. Relied on Echinacea, only; large doses, 4-8 grams Liquid Extract.
Alternative:– *Tinctures*: Cramp bark 1; Echinacea 2; Yarrow 1. Few drops Tincture Capsicum. 1 teaspoon in water, every 2 hours.
Practitioner. Where headache is severe, add: 1-2 drops Tincture Gelsemium to each dose.
External. Sponge down body with warm water and vinegar.
Fomentations of Hops, Chamomile or Ragwort over affected area.
Enemas: where necessary; Boneset, Catnep or Chamomile.
Diet. No solid food until temperature is back to normal, then Gluten-free.

POLLEN. The male sex cell of plants. Gathered by bees from flowers, preferably from unsprayed land. Revitalising concentrated cell nutrient with pH value of 6. A curative and strength-imparting natural product. Taken by athletes for added strength and greater performance. Contains vitamins, proteins, fat, sugar, carbohydrate, growth hormones, co-enzymes, and 21 of the known 23 amino acids. Contains both DNA and RNA that improve the memory and psychological health.
Uses. Chronic prostatis, colitis, diverticulosis, constipation, tiredness, loss of appetite, lowered resistance to illness, premature ageing, depression, poor nutrition. Covers a wide range of allergies. Stress conditions.
Kalorinska Institute, Stockholm: Annual Congress of Physicians reports impressive results for encephalitis, hepatitis, bronchitis and some forms of sclerosis.
Preparations. *Tablets*. Bee-collected pollen; 500mg tablets. 2-3 tablets once daily on an empty stomach, ideally on rising.
Pollen cream. Smooth textured to promote growth of healthy skin tissue.
Home salve. Add pollen powder to sufficient honey to form a paste. General purposes healing, and cosmetic.

POLLUTION, ENVIRONMENTAL. Diseases arising from: see – TOXAEMIA.

POLYARTERITIS NODOSA. A disease of unknown causation in which areas of inflammation appear on the walls of arteries, leading to formation of degenerative nodules, giving the skin a mottled tinge.
Symptoms. Fever, abdominal pain, nervous irritation, skin ulcers and unexplained blood pressure or blood in the urine. A collagen disorder, allied to rheumatoid arthritis, affecting the lining of arteries instead of the joints. A hazard is thrombosis. Hospital laboratory test, including erythrocyte sedimentation rate, confirms. Causes may be bacterial or drug-induced.
Alternatives. Hawthorn, Meadowsweet, Mistletoe, Wintergreen, Guaiacum. Chickweed, Prickly Ash. (*Hyde*)
Decoction. Mixture. Equal parts: Hawthorn berries, Mistletoe, Prickly Ash bark. 1-2 teaspoons to each cup water simmered gently 20 minutes. Half-1 cup 3 times daily.
Herb tea combination. Equal parts: Gotu Kola, Yarrow, Skullcap. 1-2 teaspoons to each cup boiling water. Half-1 cup thrice daily.
Tablets/capsules. Dandelion. Prickly Ash. Mistletoe. Hawthorn. Rutin. Kelp.
Formula. Prickly Ash 2; Fringe Tree 1; Hawthorn 1; Rutin 1. Dose – Liquid extracts: 1 teaspoon. Tinctures: 2 teaspoons. Powders: 500mg (two 00 capsules or one-third teaspoon). Thrice daily.
External. Wipe over area with Distilled extract Witch Hazel.
Diet. Vegetarian, salt-free. Regular raw food days. Abundant fresh Vitamin C drinks: orange, lemon, etc.
Supplements. Vitamins A, C, E. Zinc.

POLYCYTHAEMIA. A rare disease of the bone marrow which produces a surfeit of red blood cells, increasing blood haemoglobin as high as 110-160 per cent. "Too much blood in the body". There will be a corresponding decrease in the volume of plasma. Condition is the opposite of anaemia. Viscosity of the blood is increased and the spleen enlarged due to hyperplasia. May be associated with high blood pressure which exerts extra pressure on the heart with possible heart failure and cerebral accident.

Polycythaemia vera, a variation of the disease, is accompanied by an increase in platelets, and white blood cells also – sometimes reaching 24,000 per cubic millimetre.

Symptoms. Sense of fullness in the head, vertigo, lassitude, convulsions, tinnitus, fragility of blood vessels, breathlessness, nose bleeds, bleeding gums. Possible internal bleeding identified by black stools. Dyspepsia, facial cyanosis, plethora, jaundice, respiratory distress, oedema of the legs. Spleen is palpable in 75 per cent cases.

Alternatives. Cannot be cured, but phlebotomy (removal of blood regularly from the veins) prolongs life. Radioactive phosphorus is used to suppress proliferation of red cells. Few known alternatives exist. The condition is worsened by diuretics, yet a hepatic such as *Fringe Tree* may assist function of the liver which sooner or later becomes enlarged.

Cider vinegar. Believed to normalise red blood cell count: 2 teaspoons in glass water 2-3 times daily.

Nettle tea. Cider vinegar and Nettle tea may be taken intercurrently, not together.

Rutin. To maintain integrity of blood vessels.

Hawthorn. Where condition is accompanied by a failing heart.

Cayenne. (Capsicum) increases red cells and is contra-indicated.

Mistletoe. Constricts blood vessels and stimulates heart beat and is contra-indicated.

Yarrow. Bone marrow disease.

Formula. Yarrow 3; Lime flowers 3; Rutin 1; Fringe Tree 2. Dosage – Powders: 750mg (three 00 capsules or half a teaspoon). Liquid Extract: 1-2 teaspoons. Tinctures: 1-3 teaspoons. Thrice daily. Every 2 hours acute cases.

Lemon. An earlier generation of herbalists believed lemons to have the property of reducing the volume of the blood.

Lime flowers. Hypotensive, anti-cholesterol, anti-coagulant.

Garlic. Has been used in past treatments.

Diet. Gluten-free foods. Salt, which concentrates the blood, should be rejected. Abundant citrus fruits (mild anticoagulants). Low fat, high fibre.

Supplements. Vitamins A, C, E.

POLYMYALGIA RHEUMATICA. A rheumatic disease of rapid onset in the over-fifties and elderly – chiefly women. Auto-immune disease. Raised blood sedimentation rate: ESR over 50mm/hr. May accompany inflammation of an artery or arteries (arteritis), particularly manifesting in temporal vessels of forehead. Occasionally, involvement of the retinal artery leads to sudden blindness – of the brain, to stroke.

Diagnosis. Among other signs, an absence of pulse in temporal artery. Condition is regarded as a manifestation of giant cell arteritis. Cause unknown.

Symptoms. Painful morning stiffness of shoulders and buttocks with local tenderness. Seldom occurs in joints. Headache, associated with scalp tenderness; weight loss, fever, wasting, impairment of vision.

Alternatives. Oral corticosteroid hormone drugs may be necessary, yet many cases respond favourably to phytotherapy.

Tea. Hawthorn, to support weak circulation 2; Yarrow for inflammatory rheumatism 1; Meadowsweet, natural source of salicylic acid 1; White Willow (analgesic) 2. Mix. 1 heaped teaspoon to each cup boiling water; infuse 15 minutes; 1 cup thrice daily.

Fenugreek tea.

Tincture Black Cohosh. Dose: 2-4ml. Favourable results reported.

Formula. Prickly Ash bark 2; Hawthorn 2; Dong Quai 1; Liquorice 1. Mix. Dose: Powders: 500mg (two 00 capsules or one-third teaspoon). Liquid extracts: 30-60 drops. Tinctures: 1-2 teaspoons. Thrice daily. In water or cup Fenugreek tea.

Topical. Distilled extract of Witch Hazel over temple area for headache.

Aromatherapy, pain relief: any one oil, Chamomile, Eucalyptus, Rosemary, Wintergreen. 6 drops in 2 teaspoons Almond oil.

Analgesic cream.

Diet. Abundance of raw fresh fruit and vegetables. Vitamin C drinks: citrus fruits. Oily fish.

Supplements. Daily. Vitamin B3 (100mg); Vitamin C (500mg); Calcium pantothenate (500mg). Kelp. Magnesium for mild pain relief and to increase levels of red blood magnesium. Zinc.

POLYNEURITIS. Inflammation of a group of nerves. See: NEURITIS.

POLYP. A small benign growth with a stalk on a mucous membrane. May appear anywhere on the body, usually in the nose, ear, womb or rectum. Commonest site is the nose.

Treatment. Numerous cases are recorded of successful use of Garlic internally, and by inserting powder, oil, or sliver of fresh corm into the nostril or meatus of the ear, whichever is affected.

Powdered Blood root or Thuja used as a snuff twice daily. Other agents: powders: Bayberry bark, Black Walnut, Myrrh, Goldenseal, Catthyme. 1-3 drops Tincture Thuja (internally) assists.

POLYPHARMACY. The use of more than one herb in a prescription is known as polypharmacy. By mixing a number of compatible plant medicines, a disease may be combatted from more than one angle.

Some herbs assist the action of others. Their influence becomes more than the sum of the individual remedies. Jason Winters enjoyed a spectacular cancer cure after experimenting with three different herbs separately. In desperation he mixed all three together and the result was a 'life-saver'. "Each single herb did not work," he writes, "but *together* they brought about a miracle."

Each combination of herbs would be carefully compounded of those known to be compatible; thus, they increase their synergistic effect. Moreover, an ingredient of a prescription exerts its influence upon a particular part of the body. For instance, in treatment of a case of acne, elimination of blood toxins may call for a blood cleanser, skin depurative, and lymphatic gland stimulant. Thus, a prescription may include Red Clover (blood), Agrimony (liver and skin depurative) and Figwort (lymphatic stimulant).

Modern practice is towards a minimum number of ingredients in a formula. However, it is claimed by some that multipharmacy is of value, as in Maria Treben's combination for leukaemia:–
20g Speedwell, 25g Bedstraw, 25g Yarrow, 20g Wormwood, 30g Elder shoots, 30g Calendula, 30g Greater Celandine, 30g Nettles, 15g St John's Wort, 15g Dandelion root, 25g Goat's Beard. 1 heaped teaspoon of the Mixture to 1 cup of boiling water. "During the day at least 2 litres are sipped."

POLYPODY ROOT. *Polypodium vulgare L. German*: Engelsüss. *French*: Polypode commun. *Spanish*: Polipodio. *Italian*: Polipodio. *Arabian*: Kather-el-riyl. *Indian*: Kalabchva. *Chinese*: Kou-chi. Root.
Constituents: essential oil, tannin, saponin glycosides.
Action: expectorant, alterative, laxative, anti-stress, cholagogue, stomachic tonic.
Uses. Stubborn cough, bronchitis, loss of voice, weak digestion, catarrh, to promote flow of bile.
Preparations. Thrice daily.
Decoction. Half a teaspoon (root) to each cup water simmered 15 minutes; dose, half a cup.
Powder. Half a teaspoon to each cup boiling water sweetened with honey; dose, half a cup.
Liquid Extract. Dose, 1-4ml (15-60 drops) in water.

POLYVALENT. A versatile plant medicine with the reputation of a 'cure-all'. A herb said to relieve a number of unrelated symptoms.

Chamomile, Garlic, Ginseng, Peppermint.

POM. Prescription only medicine obtainable from a registered pharmacy only and may not be sold by a retailer.

POMEGRANATE. *Punica granatum L. German*: Granatbaum. *French*: Grenadier. *Spanish*: Granada. *Italian*: Granato. *Iranian*: Ruman. *Arabian*: Kilkul. *Indian*: Dalim. *Malayan*: Dalima. Root bark; fruit rind.
Constituents: alkaloids, ellagitannins.
Action: taenifuge, vermifuge, bitter, aphrodisiac, demulcent (seeds).
Uses. Round and pin worms. Tape worms – patient fasting one or two days before taking teacupful doses of the decoction. Irritable bowel, dysentery. Cystitis (fruit eaten). Leucorrhoea (decoction used as a douche). Sore throat (gargle).
Preparation. Except for tape worm, used in small frequent doses; large doses nauseate. Decoction (bark or fruit rind): 2oz to 2 pints water simmered down to 1 pint; dose, winglassful thrice daily. Follow with a strong laxative: i.e. Cascara.

POMPHOLYX. Form of eczema with itching blisters on hands (cheiro-pompholyx) or feet (podo-pompholyx). Small vesicles like sago grains first appear, which fill with clear fluid before bursting. On the hand, may be caused by the allergen nickel.

See: ALLERGIC CONTACT DERMATITIS. ECZEMA.

PORPHYRIA. Excessive secretion of porphyrins in the liver and blood, usually as a result of a congenital disorder. Porphyrins are required for formation of haemoglobin. There are two types: (1) red blood cell and (2) liver.
Symptoms: (1) red teeth, pink urine, blisters worse in sunlight. (2) Abdominal pain, swelling and vomiting. Discoloured urine.
Treatment. Children must avoid sunlight. Adults should avoid drugs. No herbal cure.
Believed to be of value:– *Tea*. Combine, equal parts: Nettles, Lime flowers, Yarrow. 1 heaped teaspoon to each cup boiling water; infuse 5-15 minutes; 1 cup morning and evening.
Formula. Equal parts: Shepherd's Purse, Mistletoe, Buckwheat (rutin). Dose – Liquid extracts: 1 teaspoon. Tinctures: 2 teaspoons. Powders: 500mg (two 00 capsules or one-third teaspoon). Thrice daily.
Tablets/capsules. Rutin, Mistletoe.
Diet. Lacto-vegetarian.
Supplements. Vitamins C, E. Magnesium.

POSTGRADUATE DEGREE IN COMPLEMENTARY HEALTH STUDIES. Exeter University. The aim of the BPhil course is to generate a cadre of advanced professionals who are able to relate their therapeutic skills to the wider historical, cultural and social contexts in which they work. Many graduates from the course are expected to become the future leaders of their professions, not just as therapists but as educators

and initiators of reform in health-care delivery within the United Kingdom and the European Community. The degree may be taken over either one year full-time or two years part-time.
Subjects covered include: research skills, comparative medical traditions, environmental and dietary factors in health; law, social policy, social care; the therapeutic relationship, case studies, teaching and learning, dissertation (a significant project to demonstrate the student's ability to design and execute a responsible academic study). Enquiries to The Centre for Complementary Health Studies, University of Exeter, Streatham Court, Rennes Drive, Exeter, Devon EX4 4PU, UK. Tel: (0392) 433828.

POSTURAL DRAINAGE. A form of gravitational drainage to assist removal of phlegm in bronchitis, bronchiectasis and other congestive respiratory disorders. Patient lies crosswise with legs on the bed but with the upper half of the body bent, face downwards, off the bed. Forearms on the floor act as a support, while the position is held for about ten minutes. The patient may need some physical assistance to prevent falling. At this body angle expectoration is much easier than in the upright position. The patient is advised to cough-up mucus into a bowl or on to waste material – tissue etc. Perform 2-3 times daily.

POT POURRI. Recipe. Thoroughly dry flowers, with no moisture whatsoever which would form mould.
Best flowers: Roses (Damask), Moss Roses, old Cabbage Roses. Lavender, Clove Carnations, Woodruff, Rosemary, Violets, Sweet Verbena; any sweet-smelling flowers.
Leaves: Sweet Bay, Sweet Briar, Balm, Lemon, Thyme, Mint. Rind of Lemon, Tangerine, Oranges; cut.
Mix: 1lb kitchen salt, half a pound Bay salt, half an ounce storax, 6 drachms Orris root, grated Nutmeg, half a teaspoon ground Cloves, half a teaspoon all-spice, 1oz Oil of Bergamot. Grind to powder the Bay salt, kitchen salt, etc, and mix in all the dry ingredients. Add the Oil of Bergamot. Re-mix. Take a jar and place a layer at the bottom. Add a layer of the dried flowers. Alternate the layers of special mixture with layers of dried flowers. Close jar. (*Old Scotch recipe*)

POTASSIUM. Metallic element whose atoms when ionised carry an electrical charge. Essential for body function. Found within, while sodium appears outside body cells. A loss of potassium is followed by a loss of cell fluid causing a shrinkage of the cell. Illness may bring about an excess of this element (hyperkalaemia) or a deficit (hypokalaemia) leading to heart, nerve and muscle disorders. Hyperkalaemia is chiefly caused by kidney disease; hypokalaemia by excessive fluid loss.

An excess of the adrenal hormone aldosterone may cause fluid retention by displacing potassium which is excreted through the urine and leads to hypokalaemia.
Deficiency. Low blood pressure, abdominal distension, loss of appetite, muscular weakness, 'pins and needles'. There is mounting evidence that a low level of potassium in the blood is associated with heart problems. Abnormal heartbeats are more common in people with low potassium levels. Sudden deaths from heart disease have a high incidence in those in need of this mineral.
Body effects. Potassium works with Magnesium to open the coronary arteries and other blood vessels. When associated with Calcium it closes and constricts vessels. A deficiency causes irregular heart beat and breathing. Regulates the body's acid/alkali balance.
Sources. Meat, milk, cream, wholegrain cereals, potatoes, green vegetables, fresh fruit, Cider vinegar.
Herbs: Alfalfa, Chamomile, Carrot leaves, Dandelion root, Kelp, Nettles, Plantain leaves.
Diet. The best article of food for the mineral is the banana which quickly increases dietary potassium. To replace loss of potassium, three bananas daily suffice. This is recommended for all heart patients on conventional diuretics. Apricots, Orange juice and citrus fruits of value.
Notes. Absorption of the element is reduced by certain prescription drugs used in arthritis and high blood pressure. A common cause of potassium loss is the use of diuretics – drugs that promote secretion of urine. The phytotherapist has the benefit of such potassium-sparing diuretics as Uva Ursi and Dandelion. Most important of the group is Dandelion, itself rich in potassium.

RDA 1875 to 5625mg.

POTATO. *Solanum tuberosum L. German*: Kartoffel. *French*: Pomme de terre. *Italian*: Putata. *Dutch*: Ardappel. *Iranian*: Seb-zamini. Tubers. Source of valuable minerals and salts. Raw pulp or juice: not water in which potatoes are boiled.
Action: mild anodyne (external use). Antispasmodic.
Uses, external. Cut potato (or pulp) applied direct to piles, ulcers, gouty joints, itching skin rash, inflammation of big toe joint, bruises, synovitis, water-on-the-knee (or shoulder), lumbago, rheumatic muscles and joints.
Uses, internal. Potassium deficiency. To relieve pain of gastric or duodenal ulcer and intestinal colic.
Preparations. Thrice daily, or more frequently for acute cases.
Juice from fresh uncooked potatoes; dose, 2-3 teaspoons.

Liquid extract: 2 parts fresh juice to 1 part glycerine; dose, 3-4 teaspoons.
Poultice: grated fresh potato.

POTTER'S. "In 1812 when Napoleon was on the retreat from Moscow a young man called Henry Potter founded the first herb supply company in the UK. He would never have imagined that he had just laid the foundations of what was to become one of the UK's largest herbal medicine manufacturers. He prospered, retiring a wealthy man in 1846 when the business was taken over by his nephew Henry Potter II."

"But it was Henry Potter III who really built the business." By the time of his death in 1928 the company had maintained its position as leading supplier. Other members of the family carried on the business until 1952 when it was reorganised to become Potter's Herbal Supplies Ltd, Wigan, Lancs. While their Lion Cleansing herbs, Kasbah Remedy and Motherhood tea have been household words for over a hundred years, Potter's are equally well-known by the public and herbal practitioners for their liquid compound mixtures, fluid extracts, tinctures, tablets, galenicals, ointments and crude herbs.

POTT'S DISEASE. Tuberculosis of the spine. Erosion of a vertebra by TB osteitis (inflammation of the bone) which results in kyphosis (hunchback). Severe pain may accompany spinal cord compression. A notifiable disease.
Treatment. Bedrest. Tuberculostatics, chief of which are Elecampane, Comfrey, Echinacea, Iceland Moss.
Decoction. Combine: Elecampane 2; Comfrey 1; Iceland Moss 1. 1oz (30g) to 1 pint (500ml) water gently simmered 20 minutes. Half-1 cup thrice daily.
Powders, liquid extracts or tinctures. Combination and proportions, same as above. Powders: quarter to half a teaspoon. Liquid Extracts: 1 teaspoon. Tinctures: 2 teaspoons. In water or honey, thrice daily.
External. Removal of pus or bone. Comfrey poultices.
Diet. Lacto-vegetarian. Slippery Elm gruel. Alfalfa tea.
Vitamins. Daily. A. B6. B12. C (1g). E (400iu), D.
Minerals. Calcium, Iron, Phosphorus, Magnesium, Zinc.

POTTER'S ASTHMA CIGARETTES.
Constituents: active principles of Stramonium leaves equivalent to 0.15 per cent w/w of alkaloids calculated as hyoscyamine. (*Potter's*)

Preparation now obsolete; of historic interest only.

POTTER'S CATARRH PASTILLES. A relief for catarrh, colds, coughs and hay fever.
Formula: Sylvestris Pine oil 0.41 per cent; Pumilio Pine oil BPC 0.41 per cent; Eucalyptus oil BPC 0.02 per cent; Creosote BPC (1959) 0.20 per cent; Menthol BP 0.83 per cent; Thymol BP 0.02 per cent; Aqueous extractive from Marshmallow BPC (1949) 0.50 per cent; Basis to 100 per cent.

POTTER'S MENTHOL AND EUCALYPTUS PASTILLES. For coughs and catarrh associated with colds.
Formula: Menthol BP 0.8 per cent w/w; Eucalyptus oil BP 0.6 per cent w/w. Basis to 100 per cent.

POULTICES. Poultices are packs of powders, dried or fresh herbs, enclosed in a muslin bag or within the folds of a piece of flannel or linen (man's handkerchief) and soaked in boiling water. Mix with a little honey or vegetable oil, equal parts, into a paste. Where there is fear of infection a few drops Tincture Myrrh may be added. Poultices are best applied on sterile lint.
Common poultices: Comfrey (fractures, ulcers). Linseed (chest infections, chronic cough, bronchitis). Bran (sciatica, neuritis, synovitis). Chamomile, Hops: singly or combined (painful neuralgia, muscle pains). Potato, cold, fresh (bruises, sprains). Slippery Elm bark (ulceration).
Traditional combinations. Equal parts. Marshmallow and Slippery Elm (to 'draw' pus from boils, abscesses). Slippery Elm and Lobelia (ulcers, wounds, swellings). (*Dr Melville Keith*) Slippery Elm and Chickweed (inflammation).
Fresh plants may be broken down to pulp with a rolling pin or in a kitchen blender. Hard resins require pestle and mortar. St John's Wort, Marigold, Arnica and others require a supporting matrix: mix into a little cornflour, flour or Slippery Elm powder. The latter makes one of the most useful poultices in the whole range of medicine. See: COMPRESSES for preparation.

Poultices should be renewed every 2-3 hours.

POWDERS. One great advantage of the use of herbal powders is the absence of a binder or filler, as in tablets. Some people find alcohol objectionable but may tolerate powders. Powders are a convenient form of taking bitter herbs.

Loose powders may be taken in water, honey, milk, yoghurt, mashed banana or other vehicle: encapsulated or as a fraction of a teaspoon dose. A more accurately measured dose is possible by capsule or tablet.

The most widely used capsule in European phytotherapy is 00 with a capacity to hold 200-250mg powdered herb. Number of capsules per dose varies according to density of the agent. Standard dose of 00 capsule: 2-3 capsules, 2-3 times daily.

One teaspoon equals 1.5 grams (1,500 milligrams); half teaspoon – 750mg; quarter teaspoon – 375mg; one-third teaspoon – 500mg; one-sixth teaspoon – 250mg.

PRECURSOR. Precursor means forerunner. A substance that can be used in the production of another substance by the body, such as beta-carotene – a precursor of Vitamin A.

An example is Agnus Castus which, when taken combines with other substances in the body to produce the female group of hormones. Where the appropriate stimulus is provided, the body can synthesise its own enzymes and biological molecular compounds. In short, in some unknown way a precursor encourages the endocrine glandular system to produce its own hormones.

PREGNANCY. Albuminaria (proteinuria) of. Cornsilk tea, freely.

Antenatal Care. Should begin before pregnancy. This important event in the life of a woman will repay all the effort and study caring parents can give it. High on the list of priorities is the relief of fear and anxiety, and a mental and spiritual bonding between mother and baby even before it is born. A loving concern does much to ensure healthy function of the glands.

Treatment during pregnancy is discouraged, except when by or in liaison with a registered medical practitioner. There is, however, one exception – Raspberry leaves taken the last four months for its traditional use as a parturient.

Calcium, iron and other minerals necessary for the formation of bones, blood and soft tissues are present in herbs in a form easily assimilated. Additional iron and calcium is essential to prevent anaemia and to meet the need for an increase in blood volume by one-fifth of the body's normal level. The iron supplement, Floradix, is commended.

Herbs rich in iron are: Nettles, Chickweed, Dandelion leaves, porridge Oats. Horsetail, Centuary, Yellow Dock.

Calcium-rich herbs are: Watercress, Sesame seeds, Comfrey, Horsetail, Nettles.

Smoking increases the risk of post partum haemorrhage. X-rays retard growth while alcohol encourages miscarriage. Diazepam and other drugs may threaten life. No Weight-Watching unless toxaemia develops. Loud music causes distress to a developing foetus. In a study of pregnant mice exposure to 80 decibels of sound resulted in congenital defects in offspring. Alcohol may put a baby at risk.

The golden rule is not to take any medicaments unless absolutely necessary.

A group of herbs known as 'womb stimulants' would *not* be used in pregnancy. While not harmful in the usual way, their action may be too vigorous at a time when every effort is made to encourage relaxation and serenity. They include: Basil, Blood root, Barberry, Autumn Crocus, Cinnamon, Celandine (greater), Goldenseal, Cotton root, Thuja, Mistletoe, Thyme, Myrrh, Juniper, Male Fern, Pennyroyal, Poke root, Rue, Sage, Southernwood, Tansy, Wormwood. Marjoram, Parsley, Celery seed, Coltsfoot.

Hot baths. The pregnant woman should not spend more than 10 minutes lying in a bath if the water temperature is 40°C or higher. There is some evidence that temperature above 38.9°C can harm an unborn child.

Gestation. Taken for the last three months, few remedies have more to offer than Raspberry leaves, rich in minerals. It should be remembered that both domestic tea and coffee inhibit absorption of iron. Lime flower tea or Chamomile tea are helpful for nervous subjects and may keep blood pressure within normal limits. Whichever teas are taken, all are improved by the addition of 5 drops Liquid Extract Black Haw, once daily, to prevent miscarriage. Apart from these, no herbal medicine should be given during the first six months of pregnancy, except as prescribed by a practitioner.

The EPA of oily fish or fish oil supplements assist development of the foetal brain. They prolong gestation and increase birth weight.

Aspirin and pain-killers should be avoided. Of women whose babies had heart defects, one in three took analgesic drugs during pregnancy.

Last 3 months of pregnancy. 5 drops Liquid Extract Helonias or Squaw Vine should be added to Raspberry leaf tea once daily to prepare the circulation, nervous system and womb for childbirth. Daily, last term of pregnancy, the abdomen should be gently massaged with Almond or Olive oil.

In the absence of Helonias and Squaw Vine, use Cramp bark or True Unicorn root (Aletris).

Diet. Adequate protein. Low salt. Regular raw food days. See Iron-rich foods (dried Apricots are specially rich in iron). Vitamin and mineral supplements daily: folic acid, Vitamin B6, B-group vitamins together with magnesium, zinc, manganese, chromium, dolomite. (*Dr Pfeiffer*)

Iron supplements are of mixed value as they interfere with the uptake of zinc. In pregnancy, there is a high need for zinc, required for the rapid multiplication of cells. Zinc deficiency is linked with low birth weight and painful labour and is suspected of a relation to spinal bifida. (*Dr Nigel Meadows, Bart's Hospital, London*)

Spina bifida may arise from a deficiency of folic acid in the diet. Folic acid foods should prove preventative. Supplements are given under the supervision of a practitioner.

Avoid: unpasteurised cow's milk and all sheep and goat's milk, unless boiled, and all yoghurts and cheeses made from them. Avoid undercooked poultry, shell-fish, raw eggs. Cook egg whites and yolks until solid. Avoid raw meat and liver. Liver contains high levels of Vitamin A (retinol) which can cause abnormalities. Cod Liver oil is also

high in retinol. For Vitamin A oily fish (makerel) should be taken. Jacket potato skins (especially green) contain the toxin Solanine, link with spina bifida, and should be avoided. An excess of alcohol can cause defects. Moderate drinking is the equivalent of a glass of wine a day. Vitamin A supplements are to be avoided in pregnancy.
Backache. As the unborn baby grows the spine stretches and its curve increases. Such a pull may cause backache frequently relieved by gentle manipulation. Where persistent, a practitioner may prescribe Ladyslipper, Black Cohosh or Cramp bark.
Blood Pressure. High blood pressure may lead to placental fluid retention, with oedema.
Indicated: Hawthorn, Lime flowers, Buckwheat, Passion flower.
Diet: oily fish or fish oil supplements.
Supplements. Calcium supplements should not be given to women who are pregnant, except in the form of Nettle tea, etc.
Breasts excessively enlarged. *To reduce*: Wild Strawberry leaves, tea. 2 teaspoons to each cup boiling water. Half-1 cup, 2-3 times daily. Footbaths of Lavender or Yarrow.
Breasts, painful. *External*: Evening Primrose oil, Calendula (Marigold) cream, Comfrey cream. Old gypsy device is to insert beneath the brassiere leaf of cabbage or rhubarb. Fresh Poke root juice.
Internal: Evening Primrose oil supplements.
Mastitis: Local warm poultice of German Chamomile flowers and Comfrey leaves; or tinctures of either plants – 10 drops to each cup warm water as a lotion.
Anaemia, of pregnancy. The body of the normal woman contains up to 4 grams of iron. An additional gram is needed in pregnancy and dietary intake should be about 600mg. In pregnancy, the haemoglobin level must be over 11. Anything below this is regarded as a matter of concern. As chemical iron leads to zinc deficiency, iron should be provided only in foods, herbal teas containing iron: Horsetail, Nettles, Yellow Dock, Centuary. Floradix.

When a supplement of 60mg elemental iron was combined with 2.4 retinol (Vitamin A) and given to anaemic pregnant women for eight weeks, the resulting normalisation rate (97 per cent) was shown to far exceed simple iron (68 per cent) or simple Vitamin A (16 per cent). (*Randomised, double-masked, placebo controlled field trial, West Java, Indonesia – The Lancet, Nov 27 1993 pp1312-1313*)
Constipation. Care should be taken in selection of suitable laxative out of more than the 100 herbs used for this purpose. With still much to commend them are Senna pods, 5-10 pods in cup of boiling water allowed to stand overnight. Pinch of Ginger may be added in morning when all is drunk on rising or before breakfast. Senokot. Psyllium seeds (light) offer a harmless non-chemical laxative which is also nutrient, increasing bulk of stools for easy elimination. 2 teaspoons to each cup boiling water. 1 cup 2-3 times daily. Linseeds. 1 teaspoon to each cup boiling water: 1 cup 1-2 times daily. Figs, prunes, etc.
Cracked nipples. Often due to Vitamin C deficiency. Wash nipple and apply creams, ointments or lotions of Calendula (Marigold), Comfrey, Chickweed, Marshmallow and Slippery Elm. Cucumber moisturiser. Honey and Rosewater. Fresh juice of Poke root, Comfrey root, or lukewarm compresses: Marshmallow, Lemon Balm, Coltsfoot or Ladies Mantle. Evening Primrose oil (also internally).
Cramp, mild. (Not eclampsia, which may occur at the end of pregnancy or delivery.)
German Chamomile tea.
Practitioner. Formula. Squaw Vine 1; Cramp bark 1; Ginger half. Dose – Liquid extracts: 2-4ml. Tinctures: 3-6ml. Powders: 500mg (two 00 capsules or one-third teaspoon). As necessary.
Eclampsia. See entry.
Emotional Stress. Irritability, depression, irrational fears.
Teas: Lime flowers, Chamomile, Lemon Balm, Hops.

Passion flower is a soothing relaxant to the nervous system. Valerian tablets or tincture.
Aromatherapy. 3 drops Oil of Clary to 1 teaspoon Almond oil, dabs on forehead, behind ears, and on handkerchief for inhaling.
Heartburn, of pregnancy. Teas: Chamomile, Meadowsweet, Slippery Elm powder as a gruel, Dandelion, Marshmallow, Liquorice.
Formula. Herbs, mix. Dandelion 1; Meadowsweet 1; German Chamomile half; Liquorice root shredded quarter. Pinch Ginger. 1-2 teaspoons to each cup boiling water; infuse 15 minutes. 1 cup when necessary.
Labour. See: LABOUR.
Lactation, of pregnancy. To promote production of milk in the nursing mother: Goat's Rue, Centuary, Vervain, Nettles, Fennel, Holy Thistle, Milkwort, Fenugreek seeds, Aniseed, Caraway seeds.
Formula. (1) Seeds. Parts: Caraway 1; Fenugreek 2; Aniseed 1. Mix. Crush 2 teaspoons seeds to each cup boiling water; cover and infuse 15 minutes. Stir well. 1 cup 2-3 times daily.
(2) Herbs. Parts: Goat's Rue 2; Nettles 1; Holy Thistle 1. Mix. 2 teaspoons to each cup boiling water. Infuse 15 minutes. 1 cup 2 or 3 times daily.
(3) Agnus Castus.
To arrest supply of milk: Red Sage, Garden Sage, Rosemary flowers or leaves; any one. One heaped teaspoon to each cup boiling water. Infuse 15 minutes. Half-1 cup 2 or 3 times daily.
Miscarriage. See: ABORTION.
Morning Sickness. Usual in pregnancy but not limited to the morning. Worse around tenth and fourteenth weeks. Popular agents: Raspberry

leaves, Chamomile flowers. Both are also good for weak and nervous stomach. Where sickness is severe leading to dehydration consider thyroid imbalance.

Teas. Catnep, Chamomile, Black Horehound, Raspberry leaves. 1 heaped teaspoon, any one, to each cup boiling water, infuse 5-10 minutes. Half-1 cup 2-3 times daily.

Ginger, powder. 250mg (one-sixth teaspoon) morning and evening.

Black Haw, tincture: 1-2 teaspoons in water thrice daily.

Diana, Princess of Wales. Discovered Royal Jelly, product of bees, successful.

Mother's milk. Natural childbirth, mother feeding her baby, has much to commend it. "Mother's milk is therapeutic for certain infections transmitted from mother to baby including *Giardia lamblia* and other protozoa. These and other infections are killed by low concentrations of normal human milk." *(Dr Frances Gillin and Dr David Reiner, San Diego; and Chi-Sun Wang, Oklahoma, USA in "Science" Vol 221 No 4617)*

A breast-feeding baby can tell when its mother has had beer or spirits – and may react by taking less milk. Even small amounts of alcohol affect the smell of breast milk.

Nervous restlessness of pregnancy.

Teas. Lime flowers, Valerian, German Chamomile, Passion flower, Hops, Raspberry leaves.

Swollen ankles, of pregnancy. Oedema due to fluid retention. Cornsilk. 1oz to1 pint water simmered gently down to half a pint. Drink: half-1 cup, 3 times daily.

Toxaemia of late pregnancy. See: ECLAMPSIA.

Toxoplasmosis. See entry.

Varicose Veins. *Causes*: fluid retention, high progesterone levels, tight underwear or jeans.

Tea: Shepherd's Purse.

Liquid Extract: Helonias.

External. Tincture Marigold (Calendula) 20/30 drops in a little water. Strong decoction Oak bark. Distilled Extract Witch Hazel.

Viral infections. See appropriate entry: MEASLES, HERPES, etc.

Note. Medication during pregnancy is best administered by a qualified practitioner.

PRE-MENSTRUAL SYNDROME (PMS). For 20 days of a month, a woman may be perfectly happy and well-balanced. For the next week or ten days her whole outlook can be changed. From a capable, able-to-cope woman she suddenly finds herself at the mercy of a bewildering diversity of symptoms leaving her depressed and irritable. This phenomenon is due largely to a hormonal imbalance resulting in high levels of oestrogen and low levels of progesterone. Sometimes the condition is complicated by fluid retention, for which diuretics are indicated (Dandelion).

Symptoms. Acne, anxiety, backache, bloating, breast tenderness, craving for sweets, crying, depression, dizzy spells, puffiness, fainting, fatigue, headache, insomnia, irritability, increased appetite, inefficiency, mood swings, weight gain, confusion, heart pounding, cramp. A tendency towards hypoglycaemia. To avoid PMS a woman requires more progesterone.

Treatment. Many alternatives are shown below in case of non-availability of some agents.

Keynote: Agnus Castus (hormone precursor).

PMS with cramp: Cramp bark.

With high blood pressure: Lime flowers.

With extreme nervous excitability: Skullcap or Valerian.

With puffiness of hands and feet due to fluid retention: Dandelion or Parsley.

Diuretics are best taken the last week of the menstrual cycle.

Evening Primrose oil, usually in capsules. ". . . depends upon severity of symptoms.For bad cases: 3,000-4,000mg daily for 3 months, reducing to 2,000-3,000mg for a further 2 months, and finally, as low a dose as the patient discovers will keep her symptom-free. This is usually 1,500-2,000mg daily during the pre-menstrual phase of the cycle. Commence treatment day or two before symptoms are expected to start; continue until day after menstrual bleeding commences." *(Dr Caroline Shreeve, "The Curse that can be Cured." Thorsons)*

Chamomile tea. 1-2 cups for temporary relief.

Simple tea. Combine, equal parts: Agnus Castus, Yarrow, Valerian. 1 heaped teaspoon to each cup boiling water; infuse 15 minutes. Half-1 cup freely.

Tablets/capsules. Agnus Castus, Helonias, Valerian, Liquorice.

Powders, liquid extracts, tinctures. Combination. Equal parts: Black Haw, Passion flower, Valerian. Dosage. Powders: quarter of a teaspoon. Liquid extracts: 1 teaspoon. Tinctures: 2 teaspoons. In water/honey, thrice daily.

Practitioner. Tr Valerian simplex, 10ml; Tr Cypripedium 10ml; Tr Scutellaria BHP (1983), 5ml; Tr Viburnum opulus BHP (1983), 10ml; Tr Humulus lupulus BHP (1983), 5ml. Tr Pulsatilla BHP (1983), 2ml. Distilled water to 100ml. Dose: 5ml in medicine glass water, thrice daily, after meals.

PMS formula. Evening Primrose oil, Vitamin B6 and Agnus Castus.

Aromatherapy. Drops of Oil Geranium on tissue as a palliative.

Vitamin E. An effective low-risk treatment for reduction of certain PMS symptoms, particularly tenderness of the breasts.

Diet. Reject chocolate, sugar, salt, tea, coffee, alcohol, dairy, wheaten products, processed foods and fat. Accept: fresh green vegetable salads, oats, rye, barley, millet, beans, nuts, seeds, cold-

pressed Sunflower or Safflower oil for cooking and margarine. Skimmed milk. Fresh fish. Oatmeal porridge (oats are an anti-depressant). Extra calcium (yoghurt, wholemeal bread). Hay diet: good results reported.
Supplements. B-complex, B6 (30-50mg daily), C (1-3g daily), E (500iu daily), Iodine, Iron, Magnesium, Zinc. Bromelain.

Stop smoking. Do not expose the body to abnormal stress or excessive exercise

PRESCRIPTION. Prescriptions may be dispensed by a practitioner in his dispensary and take the form of liquids, tablets, capsules, etc. The traditional 'bottle of medicine' in which a number of extracts have been compounded still proves popular, making for greater accuracy of dosage and concentration. However, the Licensing Authority does not view with favour packed products or medicines containing a large number of ingredients, other than excipients. This applies especially to products on sale through business channels for which they require to know to which ingredients therapeutic claims refer.

Ingredients in a prescription are usually built up rationally by the practitioner according to the individual needs of the patient. Some remedies work well together. Others are antagonistic. It is the skill of the practitioner to mix compatible herbs to ensure they make the maximum impact. He will treat his patients according to the laws of physiology. For instance, for acne rosacea he may select Barberry bark for the liver, Senna for the bowel, Poke root for the lymphatic system, and Red Clover flowers for the blood; all to work in harmony.

People objecting to an alcohol content in liquid medicines may release it by pouring their doses into *hot* water; the spirit content vaporises, passing off into the atmosphere leaving elements of the plants for drinking when cold.

PREVENTATIVE MEDICINE. Simple herb teas may serve as well as sophisticated preparations such as liquid extracts, tinctures, etc. Lime flower tea tends to prevent hardening of the arteries while Milk Thistle is a powerful liver protective and pancreatic sustainer. Garlic is a well-known preventative.

PRIAPISM. Persistent erection of the penis with pain. May be congestion of veins associated with sickle-cell anaemia, stone in the bladder, urethritis, prostatitis or enlarged pelvic veins with thrombosis.
Alternatives. *Teas*: Catnep, Hops, Passion flower, Black Willow, Sage Agnus Castus, Betony, Mistletoe.
Formula: tea. Equal parts: Betony, Hops, Passion flower. 1-2 teaspoons to each cup boiling water; infuse 5-15 minutes; 1 cup 2-3 times daily.
Tablets/capsules. Mistletoe, Valerian, Agnus Castus.
Formula. Black Willow 2; Mistletoe 1; Valerian half. Liquid extracts: 1 teaspoon. Tinctures: 2 teaspoons. Powders: 500mg (two 00 capsules or one-third teaspoon). Dose: 2-3 times daily.
Alternative formula. Wild Lettuce 2; Skullcap 1; Hops (Lupulin) quarter. Liquid extracts: 1 teaspoon. Tinctures: 2 teaspoons. Powders: 500mg (two 00 capsules or one-third teaspoon). Dose: 2-3 times daily.
External. Cold packs to base of spine.
Diet. Lacto-vegetarian. Salt-free.
Vitamins. B-complex, B12.
Minerals. Magnesium. Phosphorus.

PRICKLY ASH BARK. Toothache bark *Zanthoxylum clavaherculis L. German*: Zahnwehgelbholz. *French*: Clavalier. *Italian*: Clava erculea. Bark. Much esteemed by American Indian communities in the pioneer days.
Constituents: coumarins in Zanthoxylum americanum; alkaloids in both species; herculin in Zanthoxylum clava-herculis; tannin, oil.
Action: alterative, bitter, antispasmodic, carminative, tonic, diaphoretic, positive diffusive stimulant to arterial and capillary circulation. Anti-malarial (*Ellingwood*). Ingredient of the Hoxsey cancer cure (1950s).
Uses. Cramp. Cramp-like pain in leg on walking. Muscular rheumatism, arthritic tendency, Raynaud's disease, temporal arteritis, toothache (chewed), pain in the coccyx. Improves circulation of blood through the brain, and is therefore of value in chronic fatigue syndrome.
Combination: *American traditional*: half an ounce each – Prickly Ash bark, Bogbean herb and Guaiacum shavings. Boil in 1 and a half pints water down to 1 pint; add 3 Cayenne pods. Dose, wineglassful, thrice daily.
Preparations. Thrice daily.
Decoction: quarter to half a teaspoon to each cupful water simmered 20 minutes; dose, half-1 cup.
Liquid extract BHC Vol 1. 1:1, 45 per cent ethanol. Dose: 1-2ml.
Tincture BHC Vol 1. 1:5, 45 per cent ethanol. Dose: 2-5ml. GSL

PRICKLY ASH BERRIES. *Zanthoxylum clavaherculis L.* Dried fruits.
Action: similar to the bark, but with greater emphasis on the circulatory system (intermittent claudication, etc).
Preparations. Average dose, 0.5 to 5g thrice daily.
Liquid Extract BHP (1983): 1:1 in 45 per cent alcohol; dose, 0.5 to 5ml in water. GSL

PRICKLY HEAT. Milaria. Acute inflammation

of the skin with red rash, usually commencing on the trunk. Chiefly associated with residence in hot, wet climates of high humidity. Profuse sweating causes water-logging of the skin, the sweat ducts becoming plugged by keratin debris. Ducts swell to form itchy blisters that rupture. Itching leads to scratching and possible invasion by staphylococci.

Treatment. Antihistamines – anti-itch measures.
Teas. Chamomile, Ephedra.
Tea combination. Ephedra 2; Burdock leaves 1; Gotu Kola 1. 1 heaped teaspoon to each cup boiling water; infuse 10 minutes, strain. 1 cup taken cold freely.
Formula. Ephedra 2; Chamomile 2; Burdock root 1. Liquid Extracts: 1-2 teaspoons. Tinctures: 2-3 teaspoons. Powders: 750mg (three 00 capsules or half a teaspoon) thrice daily.
Vitamin C. Ascorbic acid. Cured by half-1 gram daily. (*T.C. Hindson (1968) Ascorbic Acid and Prickly Heat, The Lancet*)
Topical. Emolient creams: Aloe Vera, Calendula, Evening Primrose oil, Chickweed, Houseleek.
Diet. Avoid anything that may cause sweating – hot drinks, curries, peppery spices and all hot foods. Vegetarian diet commended. Reduce salt intake. Drink plenty spring water.
Supplements. Sodium, Potassium, Zinc.

Frequent cold showers. After bathing rub the body with a slice of lemon.

PRIMARY BILIARY CIRRHOSIS (PBC). Chronic liver disease in which the bile ducts are destroyed. Cause unknown. No known cure. An auto-immune condition. Damage to bile ducts by the action of free-radicals. Ducts coalesce, obstructing the flow of bile and causing break-down of liver tissue into scars.
Symptoms. Indigestion, nausea, jaundice (yellow eyes and skin), tan-like darkening of the skin, dry eyes, dry mouth, always tired, pale stools, dark urine. A most important diagnostic symptom is the extreme skin irritation.
Treatment. *Liver specific*. Milk Thistle (*Silybum marianum*).
Fluid retention. Buchu.
Itching. Aloe Vera (external). Blue Flag root (internal).
Bone wastage. Fenugreek tea. Calcium supplements. Vitamin D.
Dry eyes. Evening Primrose (internal). Castor oil eye drops.
Bleeding. Vitamin K. Calendula.
Headache. Feverfew.
Diet. Low fat, low salt, high fibre. Turmeric as table spice. High protein, high starch. Dandelion coffee. No alcohol.

Treatment by a general medical practitioner or gastro-enterologist.

PRIMROSE. *Primula vulgaris*, Huds. *German*: Primel. *French*: Primevère. *Spanish*: Primula. *Italian*: Primavera. *Part used*: herb, root.
Constituents: phenolic glycosides, flavonoids, saponins.
Action: antispasmodic, anthelmintic, astringent, anti-inflammatory, emetic.
Uses. Plant is seldom used today. Once used for muscular rheumatism, gout, pain in the back.
Preparations. *Tincture*, fresh plant: 10oz to 1 pint 45 per cent alcohol; macerate 8 days, filter. Dose, 1-10 drops twice daily. (*Professor E. Scudder*)
Ointment. 1oz herb to 10 parts of suitable base. See: OINTMENT BASE. For healing ulcers and wounds.
Poultice. Herb.

PRIORY CLEANSING HERBS. *Ingredients*: Senna leaf powder BP 70 per cent w/w. Buckthorn powder (Frangula) BP 10 per cent w/w. Fennel powder BHP (1983) 10 per cent w/w. Psyllium seeds pale BPC 1963 10 per cent w/w. Herbal powder for relief of non-persistent constipation.

PROCTALGIA. Neuralgic pain deep in the rectum; may be unidentifiable, occurring at night. The coccyx should be examined and palpated to exclude coccydynia.
Causes: many and diverse including constipation, osteopathic spinal lesion, etc.
Treatment. A little food or drink sometimes relieves. Pressure with finger on area between anus and genitals (perineum). Warm baths. Massage of levator muscle by finger in rectum.
Anal relaxants: Black Cohosh, Cramp bark, Lobelia, Peppermint.
Teas. Betony, German Chamomile, Hops, Peppermint, Vervain.
Fenugreek seeds. 2 heaped teaspoons to each cup water gently simmered ten minutes. 1 cup 1-3 times daily; consuming the seeds.
Tablets/capsules. Black Cohosh, Cramp bark, Lobelia, Peppermint.
Formula. Cramp bark 1; Peppermint 2; Fennel 2. Liquid extracts: 1 teaspoon. Tinctures: 2 teaspoons. Powders: 500mg (two 00 capsules or one-third teaspoon). Thrice daily.
Alternative Formula. Equal parts: Marigold, Figwort, Peppermint. Liquid extracts: 1-2 teaspoons. Tinctures: 1-3 teaspoons. Powders: 750mg (three 00 capsules or half a teaspoon). Thrice daily.
Practitioner. For severe pain. 5 drops Tincture Belladonna to 100ml water. 1 teaspoon hourly.
Diet. Lacto-vegetarian. Salt-free. Slippery Elm gruel.

PROCTITIS. Inflammation of the anus and rectum with pain and frequent desire to pass stool, sometimes with blood and mucus. Underlying cause should receive treatment.

Treatment. *Tea.* Combine equal parts: Avens, Chamomile, Senna leaves. 2 teaspoons to each cup boiling water; infuse 5-15 minutes. 1 cup 2-3 times daily.

Tablet. Pilewort compound: Pulverised extract Pilewort 5:1, 12mg. Pulverised Senna leaf BP, 30mg. Pulverised extract Cranesbill 3:1, 80mg. Pulverised extract Cascara BP, 54mg. (*Gerard House*)

Formula. Equal parts: Tormentil, Figwort, Senna leaf. Dose: Liquid extracts: 1-2 teaspoons. Tinctures: 2-3 teaspoons. Powders: 750mg (three 00 capsules or half a teaspoon) 2-3 times daily.

Practitioner. 5 drops Tincture Belladonna to 100ml water. 1 teaspoon hourly. For severe pain.

Formula. Liquid extract Figwort 15ml; Liquid extract Black root 30ml; Valerian 10ml; Tincture Goldenseal 2ml; Syr. Senna 60ml. Distilled water to 240ml. Dose: 2 teaspoons in water after meals.

Enema. Chamomile infusion. (*Arthur Barker FNIMH*).

Diet. Lacto-vegetarian. Salt-free. Slippery Elm gruel.

PRODUCT LICENCE. To safeguard the consumer, the Medicines Acts 1968 and 1971 require a product licence to be held by the manufacturer for every product sold or prescribed with a medical claim. The Product Licence, issued under the authority of the Medicines Control Agency, is the warrant for the legal manufacture, assembly, sale and supply of a medicine in the UK.

Medicines that meet the required criteria are granted a full Product Licence. The criteria is quality, safety and effectiveness. The condition of quality devolves upon the manufacture and assembly of a herbal medicine on suitable premises under the supervision of a fully qualified pharmacist or approved person, with a proper system of quality control.

As regards efficacy, the Licensing Authority bears in mind the traditional nature of herbal products and realise that it would be unrealistic to require special studies such as clinical trials. Instead, it will accept evidence found in established official and herbal pharmacopoeias to support an application for a licence. They feel "that an absence of scientific proof should not prevent continued use by the public of herbal treatments they have come to rely on".

The Licensing Authority will accept evidence of efficacy when based on appropriate bibliographies and traditional use. No advertisement or representation of the product shall state or imply that efficacy is based on evidence other than those bibliographies and traditional use.

The Department needs to be convinced that a remedy or combination of remedies is safe. Evidence of safety will be required.

Relevant references should accompany each licence application. Where licences are granted, the Licensing Authority requires the label to include such statements as: "A herbal remedy traditionally used for the symptomatic relief of . . ." (complaint). The Department regards this as a safety measure "in case the symptoms are in fact the beginning of something more serious than a self-limiting minor condition". Other statements include: "If symptoms persist consult your doctor"; the word "symptomatic" would be omitted if inappropriate.

Doctors can prescribe herbal products "for whatever purposes they think fit, including indications not covered by a licence. However, promotion of the product has to be restricted to indications given on the product licence".

Application forms are available from: The Medicines Control Agency, Market Towers, 1 Nine Elms Lane, London SW8 5NQ.

The Bach remedies do not fall under the testing requirements of the Act. See: MEDICINE'S ACT 1968.

Any preparation described as a herbal remedy or phytomedicine is regarded as an essentially medicinal product requiring a product licence. Exemption from licensing may apply if certain constraints are observed. If a product is in that category, the restriction of Section 12 (2) (f) of the Act applies that there should be no written recommendation for its use, and no instruction as regards dosage.

For exemption under Section 12 of the Act a supplier is only allowed to specify the name of the plant. No other name can be given nor must there be written recommendations as to its use.

Any preparation referred to as a herbal *tablet*, not a herbal *remedy*, is considered to be outside the Medicines Act.

The product shall not be recommended to be used for any purposes other than those specified in Part 1 of the Schedule of Clinical Indications of the relevant product licence.

Sold without a licence, a herb is classified as a food, and while it can be sold in the market-place, no claims can be made for healing action.

A licence continues in force for five years. All licences are subject to the requirements of EC Directive 65/65 as amended by EC Directive 83/570.

Applications for a product licence require the following information: Name of Product, Pharmaceutical form (tablets, etc), Legal Status (General Sales List or other rating), Method of retail sale and supply (health food stores, pharmacies, etc). Active constituents. Clinical indications and route of administration: i.e. a traditional herbal remedy for relief of restlessness . . . oral. Recommended dose and dosage schedules for adults, elderly patients and children. Contra-indications. Interactions (with other remedies or drugs). Effects on ability to drive and use machines. Known undesirable effects. Use in pregnancy and lactation (all medicines are usually avoided during pregnancy unless prescribed by a doctor). Special warnings and precautions. Overdosage. Incompatibilities. Other constituents (coating, excipients, etc). Precautions for storage. Nature of container. Pharmacological particulars. Pharmacokinetic particulars. Manufacture of dosage form.

Product licences are granted to herbal medicines only for "self-limiting" illnesses, such as colds, sore throats, haemorrhoids and headaches. No claims are allowed for potentially chronic illness such as arthritis, glaucoma, asthma or high blood pressure.

PROGESTERONE. PROGESTOGENS. Progesterone is a female sex hormone secreted in the ovary by the corpus luteum during the second half of the menstrual cycle. It prepares the lining of the womb to receive the fertilised egg. Some herbs, having a similar effect, are known as *progestogens* and which are given for progesterone-deficiency states. They are usually administered from days 15 to 28 of the menstrual cycle.

The synthetic form is known as progestin, of which is recorded: side-effects – rise in blood pressure, dizziness, depression, fatigue, cystitis and headache. It carries an increased risk of birth defects, stroke and blood clots.

Important phyto-alternatives: Agnus Castus, Helonias, Lady's Mantle, Sarsaparilla.

PROLAPSE, RECTAL. Downward displacement of the rectum or anus from loss of elasticity in connective tissue. Mucosal prolapse is sometimes seen in children during straining at stool, the condition normally clearing up within a few months. Often associated with constipation, chronic diarrhoea or cystic fibrosis. The lower end of the bowel may extrude after going to stool. In adults, especially with the elderly, may occur with coughing.

Treatment. Sponge carefully with cold water and hold in position by a small pad of cotton wool bandaged into position. In children, the mother should be able to reduce manually after each motion.

Tea. Strong infusion Raspberry leaves, Witch Hazel leaves, Pilewort leaves or Shepherd's Purse. 1 heaped teaspoon to each cup water; infuse 15 minutes. Strain. One cup 2-3 times daily.

Maria Treben's Tea. Lady's Mantle herb. 2 teaspoons to each cup boiling water; infuse 15 minutes. Half-1 cup thrice daily.

To strengthen muscles of pelvis: Liquid Extract Aletris (True Unicorn root), 15-30 drops (adults), 1-5 drops (infants), in water or honey, 2-3 times daily.

Formula. Aletris 2; Figwort 2; Senna 1. Dose: liquid extracts: 1 teaspoon. Tinctures: 2 teaspoons. Powders: 500mg (two 00 capsules or one-third teaspoon) 2-3 times daily.

Topical. Strong decoction: any one: Tormentil root, Oak bark, Sweet Sumach, Bayberry. Inject 1 cupful into rectum by enema or gravity douche.

PROLAPSE, WOMB. Downward displacement of the womb into the vagina from weakness of its supporting ligaments.

Symptoms. The neck of the womb may extrude through the vagina, "something falling out of the vagina". Incontinence of urine on exertion, coughing or excitement.

Treatment. Surgery is usually successful, though some are treated with a ring pessary. Where neither of these measures are possible, uterine astringents may afford some relief, a popular one being *Lady's Mantle*, taken as tea. Maria Treben combines this with equal parts of Shepherd's Purse. For use in a Sitz bath she advises strong Yarrow tea.

Alternatives as follows:– *Combination*. Herbs. Equal parts. Horsetail, Shepherd's Purse, Lady's Mantle. 1oz to each 1 pint boiling water; infuse 15 minutes. 1 cup before meals.

Powders (*Dr F.H. England*). Parts: Black Haw 4; Cramp bark 4; Wild Yam 3; Blue Cohosh 3; Skullcap 2; Ladies Slipper 2. Mix. Sift. Dose: quarter of a teaspoon thrice daily.

Aletris. See entry.

Liquid Extracts. (1) Equal parts Helonias and Aletris. 15-30 drops every 3 hours (*Dr F. Ellingwood*). (2) Hemlock Spruce (tsuga) BPC (1934). Liquid Extract: 1-4ml. (3) Beth root. (*A.W. & L.R. Priest*). Thrice daily.

Vaginal douche. Strong decoction of Yellow Dock, Oak bark, or Walnut bark. 1oz to 2 pints water gently simmered 20 minutes; strain and inject warm. OR:– 2-3oz fresh washed Lady's Mantle crushed with rolling pin and added to 2 pints boiling water; infuse 15 minutes. Strain and inject warm. Relaxation on a slant-board (feet above height of head) facilitates injection into vagina.

To strengthen pelvic floor: Lady's Mantle.

Yoga. Pelvic floor muscle exercises.

PROPHYLACTIC. An agent to strengthen the immune system and thereby assist the body's defences against infection. See: ANTIBIOTICS, ANTIVIRALS.

PROPOLIS. A resinous exudate collected by bees from leaf buds of certain trees, chief of which is the poplar (*populus nigra*). Such exudates are modified by enzymes from a bees glands as they process it for use as a cement to secure the structure of the hive and to seal-over fissures as a draught excluder. Propolis also protects the hive

from infection. Rich in fats, amino acids, alcohol ethers and trace elements: iron, copper, manganese, zinc. High vitamin content; particularly B group, C, E, P, and proto-Vitamin A, all of which tend to preserve good health in old age.
Action: antibiotic (non-toxic), fungicide, mild anodyne to assuage painful skin lesions, burns. Used as a mild anaesthetic in dentistry and oral surgery. Kills harmful bacteria. Assists athletic performance and promotes well-being. Effective in promoting regeneration of collagen, cartilage, bone and dental pulp.
Topical: antiseptic. Immune stimulant.
Uses. Acute inflammation of the throat, tonsillitis and other infections (gargle with tincture, lozenges). Tinnitus (emulsion). Gingivitis. Halitosis. Acne, slow-healing skin ulcers and wounds. For external conditions, usual to give treatment internally by tincture or capsule and externally by ointment or emulsion. Stomach ulcer (Tincture 1 part to 10 parts alcohol) 5-10 drops in water, or 1 capsule containing powder thrice daily, half an hour before meals. Urinary disorders, cystitis infection (2 capsules night and morning). Candida albicans.
Preparations. *Tincture. (USSR)*. 40 grams dry Propolis macerated for 3 days in 100ml 70 per cent alcohol; shake daily, filter. 4-5 drops in half a glass water, thrice daily, or more frequently for acute cases.
Alternative tincture. 1 part powdered propolis macerated in 10 parts 90 per cent alcohol for 3 days; shake daily, filter. Dose: 4-5 drops in water, as above.
Alternative tincture: "Salvaskin".
Capsules. 100mg finely ground powder. One capsule thrice daily.
Pastilles or Lozenges. Sore throat. With Aniseed and Liquorice. (*Power Health*)
Gargle or Mouth Wash. Tincture Propolis: 4-5 drops in half a glass water, as necessary.
Emulsion. Take 40 per cent alcoholic tincture: mix with 4 times its weight in Maize oil (or Olive oil). Soak plug of cotton wool; insert in ear and leave 36 hours, (tinnitus). (*Dr Len Mervyn*)
Ointment. Heat over a low gas: parts – Propolis powder (1); Lanolin (2) and Sunflower seed oil (10). Stir to a smooth consistency. For burns, shingles, ear infections, and as a cosmetic.
Propolis tooth paste. Regular use for healthy gums, bad breath, mouth ulcers.

Some people are allergic to Propolis which may manifest as an itchy rash, contact dermatitis (as with some beekeepers); this disappears as soon as the substance is discontinued. Excess tincture on the skin is removed by lemon juice.
Precaution. Exacerbates wet-eczema.

PROSECUTIONS. Prosecutions under the Medicines Act 1968 include:
1. Selling a medicinal product without a Product Licence, contrary to Section 7(2).
2. Selling a medicinal product by way of wholesale dealing without a wholesale dealer's licence, contrary to Sections 8(3) and 45(1).
3. Assembly of medicinal products without a manufacturer's licence.
4. Supplying Prescription Only medicines to an unauthorised person, contrary to Regulation 5(1) of the Medicines (Sale and Supply) (Miscellaneous Provisions) regulations 1980.
5. Breach of Advertising Regulations, and Regulation 2 of the Medicines (Advertising to the Medical and Dental Practitioners) Regulations 1978.
6. The sale or offering for sale of medicinal products which are not on the General Sales List on premises from which is operated a non-pharmacy business.
7. Unlawful importing of a medicinal substance without a Product Licence.
8. Selling a medicinal product not of the nature and quality demanded by the purchaser, contrary to Section 64(1).
9. Labelling offences.

PROSTAGLANDINS. Hormone-like messengers responsible for the control of important body functions. Unlike hormones that are secreted by the endocrine glands, they have a life of only a few seconds between the time when produced and their effect. Some constrict blood vessels of the brain and induce a migraine attack. They play a decisive role in the initiation of pain. Aspirin relieves pain as it prevents or antagonises the formation of certain prostaglandins. Herbalists believe that plant medicines are the natural normalisers for irregularities of prostaglandin function.

Inflammation and pain in rheumatic disorders are ameliorated when prostaglandin-blocking agents are given (Guaiacum, Feverfew, Yarrow). Blockers are useful to minimise the effect of strokes, thrombosis and heart failure.

Prostaglandins cause the womb to contract, thus inducing abortion or premature labour. They produce some inflammatory changes, raise and lower blood pressure, transmit nerve impulses and regulate metabolism.

Evening Primrose oil contains gamma linolenic acid (GLA) which converts to prostaglandin E1 (PGE1), a lack of which is related to multiple sclerosis, cystic fibrosis, eczema, asthma, breast disease, hyperactivity in the young and many allergies. This is but one example of how herbs may regulate or act as precursors of prostaglandins. Others include Slippery Elm and Goldenseal that appear to have a strong PG-effect inhibiting gastric acid secretion.

Vitamins B6, C and E, niacin and the mineral Zinc are essential among other factors for production of prostaglandins.

PROSTATE GLAND. Prostatitis – inflammation of. Benign prostatic hypertrophy BPH. Non-malignant enlargement of the prostate gland leading to obstruction of the urethra and interference with free flow of urine. May be a legacy from mumps in early life. Where inflamed, Gram negative organisms usually involved.
Symptoms. Urinary frequency; urgent desire to urinate at night. Pain in the crotch and low back. Rectal palpation reveals a not-so-tender gland. If obstruction is prolonged uraemia may follow. Acute or chronic retention of urine.
Alternatives:– *Tea*. Formula: equal parts – Horsetail, Pulsatilla, Goldenrod. 1-2 teaspoons to each cup boiling water; infuse 5-15 minutes; 1 cup thrice daily.
English traditional: Horsetail tea.
Tablets/capsules: Ginseng, Echinacea, Pulsatilla.
Formula. Black Willow 1; Saw Palmetto 2; Hydrangea half; Poke root half; Thuja quarter. Liquid extracts: 1 teaspoon. Tinctures: 2 teaspoons. Powders: 500mg (two 00 capsules or one-third teaspoon). Thrice daily.
Liquid extract Thuja: 5-10 drops in water thrice daily.
Dr Arthur Vogel. Saw Palmetto 93 per cent; Goldenrod 3 per cent; Echinacea 2 per cent; Poplar trem (aspen) 1.5 per cent; Larkspur 0.5 per cent. (*Prostasan*)
Gerard House. Pulsatilla tablet. Powdered Marshmallow 50mg; Barberry bark 50mg; Horsetail 50mg; Extract Avena sativa 3:1 33mg; Extract Pulsatilla 3:1 16mg.
Dr Finlay Ellingwood; physiomedicalist: Goldenrod tea from blossoms and roots.
Dr Rudolph Breuss; physiomedicalist: Willow herb tea (epilobium pariflorum).
T. Moule, MBNOA: Parsley tea.
Ginseng. Decreases prostate weight but increases testosterone.
Flower pollen. Used successfully in Sweden for over 25 years.
Saw Palmetto: inhibition of testosterone production favours relief.
Nettles. A German study has shown that a compound derived from Urtica diocia (stinging nettle) marketed as Prostatin positively influences prostatic adenoma and its clinical symptoms. Benefits from extracts of the roots are reported.
Saw Palmetto. Dihydro-testosterone (DHT), a product of the breakdown of testosterone stimulates cells of the prostate gland to multiply and is responsible for benign enlargement. It has been discovered that Saw Palmetto (S., serrulata; S., repens) prevents testosterone being converted to DHT, thus confirming its long traditional use.
Protat. Liquid extracts: Tansy 40 per cent; Oats 35 per cent; Uva Ursi 5.9 per cent; Buchu 5.9 per cent; Saw Palmetto 1.2 per cent; Pulsatilla 0.65 per cent.
Pumpkin seeds: quarter to half a cup daily for zinc content.
External. Sitz bath twice weekly. Cold water packs over low abdomen held in position by a pair of shorts. Being an anti-infective and anti-inflammatory, the insertion of 2 or more Garlic capsules into the rectum at night may be indicated. Suppositories for insertion into anus: Liquid extract Poke root, 1 part to 8 parts cocoa butter. Solidify in a refrigerator.
Diet. Problems linked to the prostate gland could be caused by a lack of soya in the Western diet. Soya has a prostate-protective effect. Essential fatty acids: oily fish or fish oil supplements. Limit alcohol and cholesterol-rich foods. Zinc has been shown to reduce size of the gland; see ZINC FOODS. Pesticides are detrimental to testosterone; therefore additives, pesticides and hormone-contaminated foods should be avoided. Accept: watercress, parsley, beet, sesame, pecan and cashew nuts.
Supplements. Flax seed oil: 1 tablespoon morning and evening. Glutamic acid: 200mg daily. Copper 2mg daily. Zinc: 15mg daily. Vitamin B6 50mg.
Note. Routine rectal examination of men aged over 55 to be carried out annually.

PROTEIN. The member of a group of substances which form the physical materials of tissues and fluids: muscles, blood cells, hair, nails, hormones, etc. They are made of amino acids linked together in long chains of atoms, and coagulate by heat. Proteins may be vegetable or animal; the major source being animal foods: fish, milk, eggs and meat. Vegetable proteins include the groups legumes, cereals, seeds and nuts. Those with the highest biological value are the legumes and pulses, the richest being soya bean which contains 40 per cent. A surplus of protein is converted into energy.

Protein is used to build and repair bones, teeth, organs, muscles, and to produce blood and other body fluids.

PROTEINURIA. Albuminaria. Presence of albumin in the urine.
Causes: kidney damage allowing proteins to pass from the blood into the urine as in Bright's disease and infective fevers. Neglect favours the onset of heart disease.
Treatment: same as for Bright's Disease, Chronic.

PRUNE. Plum. *Prunus domestica L. Part used*: fruit (prunes).
Constituents: malic acid, sugar, pulp, oil (kernel), amygdalin (kernel). Minerals: calcium, iron, potassium, magnesium, phosphorus. Vitamins: A, B1, B3, C. Higher in B2 than any other fruit for mental health and emotional balance.
Action: nutritive, laxative.
Uses. To raise haemoglobin levels and red cell

count in iron deficiency states. Being high in magnesium, excretion of excess calcium by the kidneys is promoted. This action is useful for hardening of the arteries. Deposition of calcium salts in joints, as in arthritis, is indirectly reduced.

Fruits too well known to require description.

PRURIGO. Chronic skin disease with pimples and intense itching. Chiefly of nervous origin. Pimples are deep-seated, beginning early and continuing until late in life. An acute form (summer prurigo) is caused by onset of warm weather. Lymph glands are swollen in incurable cases.
Alternatives. *Teas*. Burdock, Clivers, Figwort, Nettles, Red Clover.
Decoction (cold). Barberry root. One teaspoon to each cup cold water steeped overnight. Dose: 1 cup morning and evening next day.
Tablets/capsules. Blue Flag root, Devil's Claw, Echinacea, Poke root, Seaweed and Sarsaparilla.
Powders. Formula. Senna leaves 5; Echinacea 2; Blue Flag 1. Dose: 500mg (two 00 capsules or one-third teaspoon) thrice daily.
Liquid Extracts. Formula. Equal parts: Echinacea, Milk Thistle, Senna, Fennel. Dose: 1 teaspoon thrice daily.
Tinctures. Formula. Echinacea 2; Burdock 1; Turkey Rhubarb 1; Peppermint quarter. Dose: 1-2 teaspoons thrice daily.
Topical. Oils: Castor, Evening Primrose, Aniseed, St John's Wort, Garlic.
Creams/ointments: Chickweed, Comfrey, Marshmallow and Slippery Elm.
Lotion: 2-3 drops Tea Tree oil in teaspoon Almond oil. If too strong Tea Tree oil can be diluted many times.
Diet. Gluten-free.
Supplements. Vitamin A (7500iu). B-complex, B2, B3, B6, Biotin, Zinc.

PRURITUS. Pruritus is the most common symptom of skin diseases. An elegant word for itch. See: ITCHING.

PSITTACOSIS. Disease associated with birds, especially parakeets, parrots, pigeons, canaries and poultry. Toxic pneumatitis. The micro-organism may infect humans causing a rare kind of pneumonia. Spread by inhaled feathers and faeces dust, and from human to human by coughing.
Symptoms. Flu-like fever, productive cough with blood-stained foul-smelling yellow sputum. Malaise, depression, "always tired".
Treatment. Bedrest. Expectorants to increase and eliminate mucus. Sometimes in form of cough mixture: Pleurisy root, Balm of Gilead. Comfrey.
Herbal antibiotics lethal to chlamydia psittace: Echinacea, Goldenseal.
Diet. Fresh fruits and vegetables and added Vitamin C to support immune system.

PSOAS ABSCESS. Disease of the lumbar spinal column, usually tubercular which invades the sheath of the psoas muscle along which it passes to the upper thigh. Symptoms resemble hip disease. See: ABSCESS, with special reference to Echinacea internally, and Comfrey poultice externally.

PSORALEA CORYLIFOLIA. Seeds. Isolation of an anti-staphylococcal fraction for use in leucoderma and other skin diseases. (*Indian Journal of Pharmacy, 26: 141: 1964*)

PSORIASIS. An unsightly dry recurring non-contagious skin disorder with red scaly patches covered with silvery scales. Begins with blebs and progresses with a scale which flakes off leaving moist-looking but dry bright red surface.

Eruptions are symmetrical, preferably elbows, ears, knees, legs, scalp and low back. May be associated with a damaging form of polyarthritis similar to rheumatoid arthritis. Attacks fingernails, leaving them discoloured, pitted, cracked or split. Pitted nails can confirm diagnosis. Rare under age of ten. Usually first appears in early adult life. Cases are low in blood bromine. An old physio-medico specific is Blue Flag root and Poke root. Another combination that works well is Poke root and Dandelion root.

Though it is said there is no cure, herbs can keep it under control. Knowledge of herbal treatment has improved over recent years, adopting such agents as Evening Primrose, Aloe Vera and Dandelion.

Topical steroids may clear lesions but they have a high relapse rate and are subject to side-effects.

The addition of a nervine to a prescription helps support resistance – Skullcap, Valerian, Mistletoe, Passiflora.
Alternatives. Balm of Gilead, Bitter Lemon, Blue Flag root, Burdock root, Chickweed, Clivers, Dandelion, Echinacea, Figwort, Goldenseal, Linseed, Mountain Grape, Queen's Delight, Red Clover, Sarsaparilla, Thuja, Yellow Dock. Bitter Melon. Chaparral, Figwort, Liquorice root.
Tea. Formula. Equal parts: Burdock leaves, Clivers, Figwort, Liquorice root. 1 heaped teaspoon to each cup boiling water; infuse 10 minutes; half-1 cup thrice daily.
Tablets/capsules. Blue Flag root, Dandelion root, Devil's Claw, Echinacea, Poke root, Seaweed and Sarsaparilla.
Formula No 1. Echinacea 2; Blue Flag root 1; Valerian 1; Liquorice quarter. Dose – Powders: 500mg (two 00 capsules or one-third teaspoon). Liquid Extracts: one 5ml teaspoon. Tinctures: one to two 5ml teaspoons. Thrice daily.
Formula No 2. Yellow Dock root 2; Poke root 1; Valerian 1; Liquorice quarter. Dose – Powders: 250mg (one 00 capsule or one-sixth teaspoon).

Liquid Extracts: 15-30 drops. Tinctures: 30-60 drops. Thrice daily.
Formula No 3. Dec Jam Sarsae Co Conc BPC Fl oz 1 (30ml); Fl Ext Echinacea fl oz half (15ml); Fl Ext Stillingia sylvatica 30 min (2ml); Tincture Hydrastis BPC 1949 30 min; Syr Sennae fl oz 2; Aquam to 8 fl oz (240ml). Sig: one dessertspoon (8ml) after meals, tds. (*Arthur Barker*)
Decoction. Equal parts: Burdock, Valerian, Sarsaparilla, Dandelion. 1oz (30g) to 1 pint (500ml) water; bring to boil; simmer gently 20 minutes. Dose: half cup thrice daily.
Topical. Oils, creams, etc help lubricate the skin for flaking and dryness when free from perfume or colouring. In moist areas creams are preferred to ointments (Chickweed or Comfrey root).
Oils. Castor, Evening Primrose, Vitamin E.
Slippery Elm powder may be used as a dusting powder.
Slippery Elm paste is made by mixing a little powdered Slippery Elm in teaspoon Almond oil.
For cases of chronic plaque psoriasis: dilute Tea Tree oil with few grains powdered Myrrh.
Moisturising creams: Chamomile, Chickweed, Yarrow, Aloe Vera. There is considerable support for the use of herbal anti-fungals.
Baths. Baths should not be taken hot, but tepid. An old sock may be filled with bran, oatmeal, Chamomile, Yarrow or Elderflowers and infused in 1 pint boiling water before the bath is taken. Strain; pour the infusion into the bath and use the sock as a sponge.
Cleansing and De-scaling lotion. 5 drops Oil Juniper to 2 teaspoons Almond oil.
Epsom salts bath. To remove scales – but not where skin is cracked.
Dead Sea Salt baths. Salt from the Dead Sea is rich in magnesium, bromine and potassium but low in sodium ions. Has been responsible for many cures from biblical times, claim Israeli scientists.
Diet. See: DIET – SKIN DISEASES. Eskimos do not acquire psoriasis because their diet is chiefly fish.
Supplements. Daily. Vitamin A, 7500iu; Vitamin E, 400iu. Selenium 200mcg; Zinc 15mg.
Dr John Mansfield. Treat sufferers as if they had candida – with an anti-candida diet which is free from sugar, yeast foods and all refined carbohydrates (white flour, etc).
Note. Psoriasis is an embarrassing condition. Cure may not be possible but it can be well-controlled.

PSYCHIATRIC ILLNESS. See: NERVOUS SHOCK.

PSYCHOTROPICS. Psychosomatic herbs. Psychopharmacology includes herbal tranquillisers, narcotics, stimulants, antidepressants, sedatives and psychodelics. Some herbs appear to bring about a little-understood mental and emotional adjustment, as for timid tearful women reacting favourably to Pulsatilla. An infusion of St John's Wort is said to have been used to good effect for excitement and unnatural enhancement of the intellectual powers with erotic ideas, fixed and staring eyes, painful sensitiveness to hearing and sense of smell. Agoraphobia and claustrophobia have been known to yield to Aconite. Liver herbs have a reputation for relief of melancholia, and Calamint for the sorrowful spirit. John Gerard writes: "The seed of Calamint relieves infirmities of the heart, taking away melancholly, and making a man merry and glad." Psychotropics include Valerian, Lavender, Passion flower and Californian Poppy.

PSYLLIUM SEEDS (dark). Flea seeds. Plantago psyllium L. For Psyllium seeds (pale or light) see: ISPHAGHULA.
Action: demulcent, bulk-laxative.
Uses. Chronic constipation, irritable bowel, mucous colitis, dysentery, (*Indian traditional*) Cystitis BHP (1983).
Preparations. Dosage: same as for Psyllium seeds (pale).
Poultice: with Slippery Elm for boils, abscesses, etc.

PTYALISM. Excess salivation. See: SALIVA.

PULMONARY. Relating to the lungs.

PULSATILLA. Pasque flower. *Anemone pulsatilla L. German*: Kuhschelle. *French*: Pulsatille. *Spanish*: Anémona pulsatilla. *Italian*: Coronaria. *Chinese*: Pai-tou-wêng. Dried herb.
Constituents: anemone camphor, saponins, lactones.
Action: female nerve relaxant, mild *sedative*, alterative, antibacterial, mild analgesic, antispasmodic.
Uses. Inflammation of ovaries, testicles, epididymus, prostate gland, and genito-urinary infections generally. Absent or painful menstruation with headache, PMT, menopausal hot flushes, inflammation of the bladder, anxiety neurosis, tearful over-sensitive women, pains that flit from joint to joint. Hyperactivity, insomnia. Measles, chickenpox, mumps in children. Benzodiazepine or Valium addiction – to assist withdrawal. Frequent micturition by men at night. Styes (topical). Adrenal exhaustion. Schizophrenia. Senile dementia. Believed influence upon some obsessive mental illnesses. Hearing loss (Pulsatilla plus Hawthorn; equal parts).

Combines well with Passion flower and Jamaica Dogwood for hyperactivity and sleeplessness.
Preparations. From the dried plant only. Average dose: 0.1 to 0.3g thrice daily or as prescribed.
Liquid Extract BHC Vol 1. 1:1, 25 per cent ethanol. Dose: 0.1 to 0.3ml.
Tincture BHC Vol 1. 1:10, 25 per cent ethanol. Dose: 0.5 to 3ml.

Tablets/capsules. 250mg (one 00 capsule).
Precaution. Fresh plant should not be used. GSL

PUMPKIN SEEDS. *Cucurbita pepo. Cucurbita maxima*, Duch.
Constituents: B vitamins, Vitamin A, and minerals: calcium, iron, phosphorus, zinc; nutrient, linoleic acid, cucurbitacins.
Action: anthelmintic – important worm remedy, ground and mixed with honey. Diuretic – infusion of 2-3 teaspoons seeds in cup boiling water; infuse 10 minutes – half-1 cup freely. Male hormone-like effect on prostate gland.
Uses. Because of their antimitotic effect are used to arrest enlargement of prostate gland. Cystitis. Minor kidney dysfunction. Tapeworm (see entry). Schistosomiasis. (*Dr W.A.R. Thomson (1976) 138*)
Preparations. Seeds, or puree mixed with honey, eaten freely.
Tea: 2-3 teaspoons seeds to cup boiling water; infuse 10 minutes; drink freely as a male tonic. OR:– chew 2-3 teaspoons seeds daily.
Face mask: puree applied to skin for dryness and wrinkling.

PURGATIVE. An agent placed between a laxative and a hydragogue in degree of evacuation. More drastic than an aperient or laxative. Usually combined with a carminative to prevent griping.

Aloes, Butternut, Cascara sagrada, Castor oil, Jalap root, Poke root (large doses), Senna leaves (stronger than the pods), Turkey Rhubarb, Yellow Dock.

PURPURA. Discoloration of the skin or mucous membranes by surface bleeding. The result of blood vessel fragility. Causes are numerous, including scurvy (Vitamin C deficiency), haemophilia, anaemia, septicaemia, auto-immune diseases or deficiency of platelets in the blood to promote coagulation. Effective treatment depends upon correct diagnosis of the underlying condition which needs must receive priority.
Treatment. Depends on the cause.
Tea. Equal parts: Buckwheat and Alfalfa.
Tablets/capsules. Hawthorn, Rutin, Motherwort.
Formula. Equal parts: Hawthorn, Motherwort, Ginkgo. Dose: Liquid extracts: 1-2 teaspoons. Tinctures: 2-3 teaspoons. Powders: 750mg (three 00 capsules or half a teaspoon). Thrice daily.
Topical. Witch Hazel water or lotion. Vitamin E cream. Tincture Arnica: 20 drops in 100ml water.
Diet. Abundant Vitamin C (oranges and other citrus fruits). Low cholesterol. Low-salt.
Vitamins. A. B-complex, C (1-2g daily), E (1,000iu daily).
Minerals. Magnesium. Potassium.

PURSLANE, GARDEN. *Portulaca oleracea. Portulaca sativa. German*: Garten Portulak. *French*: Pourpier. *Spanish*: Verdolaga. *Iranian*: Turuk. *Arabian*: Baklat-al Humaka Kurfah. *Indian*: Lumak. *Malayan*: Karichira. *Italian:* Porcellana. Herb, seeds, juice. No longer used medicinally. A rich non-fish source of EPA suitable for the vegetarian approach.
Constituents: potassium oxalate, mucilage.
Action: refrigerant, to reduce body heat. Mild antispasmodic, diuretic.
Uses. Headache from nervous excitability, (2 teaspoons leaves to cup boiling water). Sore throat, sore gums (juice used as a mouth wash and gargle). For severe pain in the urethra with strong desire to pass water (2-3 teaspoons fresh juice). Dry coughs (teaspoon fresh juice with honey). Muscular rheumatism, gout (leaves used as a poultice). Ulcers and sores (juice used as an antiseptic and healer).
Note. This weed is the richest source of n-3 fatty acids yet examined. Purslane is eaten extensively as a vegetable in soups and salads in eastern Mediterranean countries. The entire plant is edible: can be eaten raw, cooked, or pickled; and has a mild acid taste and a fatty or mucilaginous quality. (*Journal American Oil Chemists Society 1991 68 198-9*)

PYELITIS. Inflammation of a part of the kidney known as the pelvis. Kidney substance is involved, together with the ureter, inflammation spreading upwards from the bladder. The common urinary pathogen is E. Coli, though streptococcus and pseudomonas are possible. May follow fevers, produce pus, painful urination, rigor and loin pain.
Symptoms. Loss of weight, frequency, sense of unwellness and vomiting.
Predisposing factors: prostate gland disorder, pregnancy, diabetes mellitus, suppressive effects of steroids, old age, renal stone or other obstruction, surgical instruments used on the genito-urinary tract. In the newly-married it can appear as 'honeymoon pyelitis' with shivering fit, pain, and scanty cloudy urine.

Diagnosis should take into account possible foci of infection elsewhere: decayed teeth, tonsils, blood disorders.
Treatment. Simple specifics may clear most conditions without incident. However, serious cases may develop requiring skilled attention.
Indicated: urinary antiseptics, i.e. Buchu; anti-inflammatories (Dandelion). Juniper should not be given for active inflammation.
Teas. Agrimony, Bearberry, Buchu, Celery, Cornsilk, Marshmallow, Plantain, Pellitory-of-the-wall. Drink freely.
Tablets/capsules. Boldu, Buchu, Celery, Juniper, Saw Palmetto.
Formula. Equal parts: Bearberry, Buchu, Echinacea. Mix. Dose: Powders: 750mg (three 00 capsules or half a teaspoon). Liquid extracts:

1-2 teaspoons. Tinctures: 1-3 teaspoons. In water or cup of Cornsilk tea, thrice daily.
Formula. A. Barker FNIMH. Liquid extract Hydrangea, 1 fl oz (30ml) . . . Liquid extract Damiana, half an ounce . . . Liquid extract Cornsilk half a fluid ounce . . . Tincture Goldenseal 30 minims (2ml). Syrup Marshmallow to 8oz (240ml). Dose: 1 dessert-spoon (8ml), thrice daily.
Formula. Dr Finlay Ellingwood. Tincture Wild Indigo 25 drops; Tincture Gelsemium 16 drops; Tincture Staphysagria 12 drops; Echinacea 180 drops (12ml); Aqua to 60ml. Dose: 60 drops (5ml) hourly.
R.J. King MD, Pontine, Illinois. Tincture Echinacea 30 drops; Tincture Chimiphilia 10 drops; in water 3-5 times daily.
Formula. A. Barker FNIMH. Pus in the urine. Liquid extract Hydrangea 30ml; Liquid extract Echinacea 15ml; Liquid extract Scolopendrium vulgare 15ml. Tincture Goldenseal 2ml. Ess Menth virid 2ml. Aqua to 240ml. Dose: 8ml every 4 hours.
Topical. Hot poultices to the small of the back, with infusions of Horsetail, Elderflowers, Goldenrod or Yarrow. Hip baths.
Frequent drinks of bottled or spring water; herbal teas.
Supportives: bedrest. Electric blanket or hot water bottle to loins.

To be treated by or in liaison with a qualified medical practitioner.

PYLORIC STENOSIS. Narrowing of passage from the stomach to the duodenum causing obstruction to outflow of gastric contents.
Causes: scarring of pylorus muscle, usually from peptic ulcer; congenital. Also caused by spasm.
Symptoms: congenital – projectile vomiting of baby after feed, constipated, dehydration if vomiting persists. In adults: vomiting, with loss of weight; almost the whole of meals brought up.
Treatment. Hospitalisation may be necessary.
Tea: German Chamomile.
Formula. Equal parts: Bayberry, Chamomile, Marshmallow. Dose: Liquid extracts: 1-2 teaspoons. Tinctures: 2-3 teaspoons. Powders: 750mg (three 00 capsules or half a teaspoon). Thrice daily before meals.
External. Castor oil packs twice weekly. Massage upper abdomen with hot Olive oil.
Diet. Lacto-vegetarian. Low salt. Slippery Elm gruel.

PYORRHOEA. A discharge of pus; usually referring to purulent inflammation of the gums and tooth sockets.
Treatment. Anti-infectives and lymphatics.
Tea: Equal parts, Red Clover, Clivers, Nettles. Mix. 1-2 teaspoons to each cup boiling water; infuse 15 minutes. 1 cup 3-4 times daily.
Tablets/capsules. Blue Flag, Echinacea, Goldenseal, Pulsatilla, Poke root, Red Clover, Sarsaparilla, Wild Indigo or Yellow Dock.
Formula. Echinacea 2; Goldenseal quarter; Poke root quarter; Myrrh quarter. Dose: Liquid extracts: 30-60 drops. Tinctures: 1-2 teaspoons. Powders: 250-500mg (one/two 00 capsules or one-sixth/one-third teaspoon) thrice daily.
Mouth wash alternatives. Aloe Vera gel or fresh juice. Slippery Elm. Natural Lemon juice, Tea Tree oil (5 drops to glass of water). Where non-available, use Eucalyptus oil, 1-2 drops in honey. Powdered Myrrh rubbed into gums.
Diet. Lacto-vegetarian.
Vitamins. A. B-complex, B6, C (2-3g daily).
Minerals. Calcium. Zinc. Iron.

PYRROLIZIDINE ALKALOIDS (PAs). Basic organic substances in some plants, notably Comfrey, Borage and Coltsfoot, and which have been found to be responsible for disease of veins of the liver, known as hepatic veno-occlusive disease (HVOD). While laboratory experiments have shown some to be toxic to animals, a serious debate commenced in the 1960s has not yet been satisfactorily concluded regarding their use on humans. In the meantime as a precautionary measure some restriction has been placed on plants containing PAs. A consensus of opinion settles for a small amount of risk following large doses which may cause intolerance reactions and liver damage in some individuals.

Plants containing PAs are contra-indicated in pregnancy and lactation, and their use limited to six weeks in any one year. There is a growing body of opinion to support the belief that a plant which has, without ill-effects been used for centuries and capable of producing results is to be recognised as safe and effective. In the clinical use of PAs potential benefits must be balanced against possible risks. Comfrey, one of the most popular plants containing PAs, is believed to possess a positive benefit-to-risk ratio.

Manufacturers have been advised that inclusion of PAs in herbal preparations is no longer acceptable.

Over 600 remedies contain PAs including: Borage, Buglass (*Echium vulgare L*), Butterbur, Dusty Miller (*Cineraria maritima L*), Coltsfoot, Comfrey (absent in Symphytum officinale), Groundseal, Jerusalem artichokes, Houndstongue, Life root, Rosebay Willowherb.

Q FEVER. An infection transmitted by *Coxiella burneti*, commonly found in cattle. First described in Australian abattoir workers in 1937. The organism may infect mammals and birds but cattle and sheep are chiefly responsible for human infections. A notifiable disease.
Symptoms: Incubation period – 9-28 days. Fever, muscle and chest pains, headache, dry cough.
Complications: pneumonia, endocarditis.
Treatment. Anti-microbials. Lymphatic cleansers.
Formula. Echinacea 2; Goldenseal 1; Myrrh half. Dose: Liquid extracts: 30-60 drops. Tinctures: 1-2 teaspoons. Powders: 250-500mg (one/two 00 capsules or one-sixth/one-third teaspoon) thrice daily.
Diet. 3-day fast, followed by raw green salads and fruits for further 3 days.
Vitamins: A. C (1-2g daily).
Minerals. Calcium. Iron.

Treatment by or in liaison with a general medical practitioner.

QUALITY CONTROL. The Ministry demands a high degree of production and quality control in processing. They prefer full automation in order that the end-product may be of exceptional quality and purity.

Products are expected to comply with the highest pharmaceutical standards and legislative criteria although a company should have its own exacting internal requirements.

Variations of active ingredients are unsuitable for a number of reasons. Plants grown during a season of excessive cold or heat, diminished rainfall, or on an impoverished mineral condition of the soil may result in imperfect material with possible reduced potency.

The Quality Control laboratory of an efficient manufacturing company will inspect all incoming raw material with a series of visual, physical and chemical tests, with chromatographic analysis of principal constituents. This checks herbs for the correct genus and species. Tests are also carried out for traces of heavy metal dust (lead, cadmium, zinc, etc), pesticides and other harmful pollutants. Samples that do not measure up to standards laid down by the Medicines Control Agency are rejected and returned to the supplier.

A Quality Control Unit will comprise a Receiving Area where crude herbs are sampled for cleanliness and potency. Their next stage may be a blending room where a tornado mill pulverises ingredients to ensure a high degree of product uniformity.

In the case of tablets, capsules, etc, the next stage is likely to be the Department where the tablets are formulated and pressed out. The tablet-press is usually computer-controlled. Further tests are necessary before a batch is released to pass further along the production line.

The next stage is entry of the finished tablet into an automated packaging machine that fills, seals, codes and overseals each product with documentation of batch. A final examination is made before a consignment is despatched.

A modern laboratory will include computerised instruments to test each batch for potency, purity and shelf life. All such tests enhance the role of traditional medicines and offer the public maximum protection. Nothing is left to chance.

QUASSIA. *Picrasma excelsa*, Lindt., *P. Amara L. German*: Simarubabaum. *French*: Simaroube officinale. *Italian*: Simaruba. *Indian*: Kashshing. Wood chips.
Constituents: alkaloids, quassinoids.
Action: anthelmintic, tonic *bitter*, orexigenic. To increase flow of gastric juice and saliva. Insect repellent.

Quassimarin is reported as having anti-leukaemic properties. (*S.M. Kupchan & D.R. Streelman, J. Org.Chem., 41, 3481, 1976*) Used for fevers by natives.
Uses. Lack of appetite, indigestion. Cirrhosis of the liver (temporary relief of symptoms). Worms – to eliminate nematode, internally or by enema.
Topical: infusion is used as a skin wash for scabies, fleas and other parasites.
Preparations. Thrice daily.
Tea: 1 heaped teaspoon chips in each cup cold water; steep overnight. Dose, half a cup. Tea may be used externally for body lice.
Powder. 500mg (two 00 capsules or one-third teaspoon).
Tincture Quassia BP (1948). Dose, 2-4ml in water.
Enema. 1oz to 2 pints warm water. Infuse 20 minutes. Strain, inject.
Quassia cups. Up to World War II cups were made from Quassia wood; water drunk from them had a tonic effect. GSL

QUEBRACHO. *Aspidosperma quebracho*, Schlecht. Bark. The 'digitalis' of the lungs.
Constituents: tannins, indole alkaloids, sterols.
Action: antispasmodic, anti-asthmatic, tonic bitter, hypotensive, diuretic, uterine sedative, peripheral vaso-constrictor, local anaesthetic (mild).
Uses. Breathing difficulties associated with heart and lung disease. Upper respiratory distress following climbing mountains and physical exhaustion. Rarely used in modern herbalism, but still an effective remedy.
Preparations. Thrice daily.
Concentrated infusion, BP; dose, 2 to 4ml.
Liquid Extract: dose, 0.5 to 1.5ml in water.
Tincture: 1 part bark to 10 parts 45 per cent alcohol; macerate 8 days, shake daily, filter. Dose, 2 to 4ml in water.

Note. Large doses nauseating. Practitioner use only.

QUEEN'S DELIGHT. Yaw Root. *Stillingia sylvatica L. German*: Chinesicher Talgbaum. *French*: Stillingie. *Italian*: Albero del sego. *Part used*: dried root.
Constituents: tannin, an acid resin, indole alkaloids including quebrachamine.
Action: alterative, traditional blood purifier, expectorant, diaphoretic, lymphatic, antispasmodic, circulatory stimulant.
Uses. Scrofula and chronic disorders of the lymph glands, elephantiasis, skin diseases with moist discharge (weeping eczema, etc). Bone pains, chronic periosteal rheumatism as in hip arthrodesis, etc. Popular plant medicine for syphilis and other STD in the Southern States of America before age of modern medicine. Piles, congested liver, hoarseness, bronchitis.
Combinations: (1) With Sarsaparilla as a lymphatic stimulant. (2) With Poke root for early stages of glandular fever.
Preparations. Half-2g thrice daily.
Decoction. Half-1 teaspoon to each cup water gently simmered 20 minutes. Dose, one-third to half a cup.
Liquid Extract. 10-30 drops in water.
Tincture BHP (1983). 1:5 in 45 per cent alcohol. Dose, 1-4ml.
Powder. 500mg (two 00 capsules or one-third teaspoon).
Practitioner use only. Large doses emetic and cathartic.

QUIET LIFE. Formula: each tablet contains – Motherwort 34mg; Wild Lettuce 4:1 7.25mg; Hops 75mg; Passion flower 58mg; Valerian 4:1 12.50mg; Thiamine hydrochloride (Vitamin B1) BP 0.71mg; Riboflavin (Vitamin B2) BP 0.57mg; Nicotinamide BP 4.49mg. Two tablets twice daily, plus two at bedtime. For everyday stresses, strains and to promote sleep. (*G.R. Lane's Health Products, Gloucester, U.K.*)

QUILLAIA BARK. Soap bark. *Quillaja saponaria*, Molina. Dried inner bark.
Constituents: saponins, tannins, calcium oxalate.
Action: stimulating expectorant, emulsifying agent, detergent.
Uses. Bronchitis. Aortic disease with heart enlargement. Skin disorders. Once used as a substitute for soap.
Preparations. A strong decoction is used to wash the skin in cases of vermin.
Liquid Extract BPC (1973). Dose 0.125 to 0.25ml.
Practitioner use. Large doses emetic.

QUINCE. *Cydonia oblonga*, Mill. Seeds and fruit pulp. Source of Vitamin C.
Constituents: amygdalin, tannins, oil, mucilage.
Action: demulcent, nutrient.
Uses. Irritable bowel, dysentery, sore throat and mouth, dry cough, constipation. Mild burns: stand seeds in water overnight; collect mucilage in the morning and apply. Eaten freely as a fruit.

QUINSY. Peritonsillar abscess. An acute 'strep' infection in the space round the tonsils with suppuration. Follows an attack of tonsillitis.
Symptoms. Pain on swallowing and on opening mouth. Soft palate inflamed; uvula swollen, foul breath, earache. Lymph nodes on affected side enlarged. Temperature.
Treatment. Bedrest.
Alternatives:– *Teas*: Cudweed, Hyssop, White Horehound, Raspberry leaves, Marshmallow leaves, Red Sage.
Natural lemon juice.
Diaphoretic teas to promote sweating, including Yarrow, Angelica, Elderflowers, etc.
Traditional. Combine equal parts, herbs: Hyssop, Centuary, White Horehound. 1 heaped teaspoon to each cup boiling water; infuse 5-15 minutes. Half-1 cup every 3 hours.
Formula. Echinacea 1; Sage 1; Poke root half; Myrrh quarter. Dose: Liquid extracts: 1 teaspoon. Tinctures: 2 teaspoons. Powders: 500mg (two 00 capsules or one-third teaspoon) every 3 hours.
Gargle. Any one of above teas. OR:– 5 drops Tincture Goldenseal in water, freely.
Cold compress wrapped round neck.
Fomentation, on linen wrapped round throat: any one – Lobelia, Ragwort, Slippery Elm. OR:– drops Oil of Peppermint.
Practitioner. May be necessary to puncture swelling to release pus, with immediate relief.
Diet. 3-day fast with plenty of fluids: herb teas, fruit juices.
Supplements. Daily. Vitamin A 7500iu. Vitamin C 1g. Zinc 15mg.

RABIES. Hydrophobia. Virus infection transmitted by the saliva of an infected animal to man through licking or biting. A notifiable disease. Treatment by or in liaison with a general medical practitioner. Within 10 days the virus travels up the axons of the nerves to the brain. Incubation period is anything from 1 week to 1 year.
Symptoms. Mild fever, sore throat, headache, nausea. Malaise gives way to convulsions (spasms may occur every 5 minutes) with frothing at the mouth. The crisis deepens into maniacal hysteria. "Cannot tolerate the sight of water", hence its early name: hydrophobia. James T. Kent MD describes it: "A vicious dog will take hold of your thumb, hand or wrist, and run his teeth through the radial nerve . . . causing a lacerated wound. That wound needs Hypericum which prevents tetanus."
Treatment. Speed is essential. Treatment is available from the nearest hospital intensive care unit but time and distance may be delaying factors. Plant medicines were used for centuries for this infection.

Before the doctor comes:
(1) Thoroughly cleanse the wound. Where water is not available, suck wound to remove poison.
(2) Wipe area of the bite with strong alcohol (Vodka, etc). Old school herbalists used one of the following tinctures: Hypericum (St John's Wort), Calendula (Marigold) or Myrrh. Follow with Slippery Elm poultice.
(3) If patient is able to drink, give strong infusion of Skullcap for spasmodic closure of the jaws and rigid face muscles. The other name for Skullcap is Mad-dog. 2 teaspoons to each cup boiling water: infuse 5-10 minutes. Drink freely. A sprinkle of Cayenne Pepper to each dose enhances efficacy.
Practitioner. Liquid Extract Skullcap BHP (1983) (1:1 in 25 per cent alcohol). Dose: 15-60 drops every 15 minutes.
Supplement: Vitamin C, 2g every 2 hours.
Chinese medicine – Rohdea japonica (Roth.)
Where professional treatment is not available, indigenous plants to relieve spasmodic muscular contractions include: Black Cohosh, Lobelia, Skunk Cabbage. Wild Yam.

RADIATION. Low level. Exposure to electromagnetic energy from electric and electronic equipment has become a factor in modern life. Radiation protection is offered by amino acids cysteine and glutathione; Vitamins A, C, and E; minerals Selenium and Zinc. See also: BIOSTRATH, FREE RADICALS and RADIATION SICKNESS.

Russian clinical study reveals some benefit from Ginseng (Eleutherococcus senticosus (ES)).

RADIATION SICKNESS. Caused by over-exposure to radiation such as X-rays, television screens and to an atmosphere polluted by such disasters as Chernobyl.
Treatment, and protectives. Anti-oxidants. 'Binders' – nutrients which bind with radioactive substances in the gut but do not enter the bloodstream and are excreted in the usual way. Radio-active strontium will bind with sodium alginate from seaweed.
Teas, tablets, nutrients, etc: Alfalfa, Buckwheat (rutin). Seaweed and Sarsaparilla. Kelp. Pollen (for its high content of pantothenic acid regarded as a protective). Apples (for their pectin) three or more daily. Evening Primrose, Siberian Ginseng, Pectin tablets. Sunflower seeds (handful). German Chamomile.
External tissue injuries, radiation burns on eyes, etc: Aloe Vera gel, or juice from fresh leaf.
Diet. Lacto-vegetarian.
Vitamins, Minerals. (*Leon Chaitow*) Daily: Vitamin C (with bioflavonoids) 1-3g. Vitamin E, 400-800iu. Pantothenic acid, 100-500mg. Selenium, 50-100mcg. Calcium and Magnesium (Dolomite or bonemeal).
Selenium alginate. (*Larkhall labaratory*)
Biostrath Elixir. Administration of Biostrath Elixir before radiation has proved itself to be a radioprotective agent. (*Professor Hedi Fritz-Niggli, Director, Institute of Radiobiology, University of Zurich; Radiation Protection Specialist for World Health Organisation*)
Tinctures, liquid extracts, powders. Combine parts: Oats (avena) 3; Skullcap 2; Cramp bark 1; Barberry 1; Ginger half. Tinctures: 1-2 teaspoons. Liquid extracts: 30-60 drops. Powders: quarter teaspoon. In water or honey every 2 hours acute cases; thrice daily, chronic.

RAGWORT. Stinking Nanny. St James' Wort. *Senecio jacobaea L. German*: Jacobi Grieskraut. *French*: Senecon. *Spanish*: Zuson. *Italian*: Giacobea. Fresh leaves.
Constituents: pyrrolizidine alkaloids, volatile oil.
Ointment or dried aerial parts (fine cut) used as a poultice for rheumatoid arthritis, gout, lumbago, sciatica (pain relief).
Lotion: 1 part flowers to 10 parts alcohol (gin, vodka, etc).

External use only.

RANSOM, WILLIAM & SON LTD. (Established 1846), Hitchin, Hertfordshire, England. Makers of medicinal extracts, distillers of essential oils. Specialise in plant extracts. "One of the most ambitious research and development programmes of its kind." Totally independent company with a remarkable reputation built on the traditions of quality and service. Its historical associations, its developments through a century of fundamental change and its present pre-eminence in the pharmaceutical industry for plant medicines is unique. World-wide suppliers, part of their crude material comes from their medicinal plant farm at Hitchin. For over a century, a successful business has provided both pharmacists and herbalists with reliable concentrated extracts, tinctures, mixtures, oleoresins, powders, elixirs, decoctions and volatile oils including English-grown and distilled Chamomile, Lavender and Peppermint. Also distillers of Buchu, Valerian, etc.

RASPBERRY LEAVES. *Rubus idaeus L.* Dried leaves, fine cut.
Constituents: tannins, polypetides, flavonoids.
Action: pre-natal aid, astringent tonic, antispasmodic, parturient with a reputation for painless and easy delivery in straightforward births.
Uses. Pain or profuse bleeding of menstruation. Helpful last 2 months of pregnancy to tone uterine muscles. Promotes milk production. Mouth ulcers, sore throat, tonsillitis (gargle and mouth wash). Vaginal discharge (douche). Sickness and nausea of pregnancy.

Combines well with Motherwort (equal parts) for threatened miscarriage. Combines with Marshmallow and Agrimony (equal parts) for diverticulitis and bowel disorders.
External. Tea used as an eye douche for conjunctivitis.
Preparations. Thrice daily.
Tea: 1oz (30g) leaves to 1 pint boiling water; infuse 15 minutes. Adults: 1 cup. Young children: wineglassful. Babies: teaspoon doses.
Liquid extract. 1-2 teaspoons in water.
Tablets/capsules. Popular formula. Raspberry leaf 300mg; Marshmallow 37.5mg; Motherwort 30mg. One, thrice daily, after meals.
Note. In preparation for birth drink one cup daily during the last two months of pregnancy and freely throughout labour.

RAT BITE FEVER. A relapsing fever with local inflammation and glandular swelling. Infection caused by gram negative bacteria.
Treatment: same as for RABIES.

RAUWOLFIA. *Rauwolfia serpentina*. Indian Snakeroot.

A powerful agent for reduction of high blood pressure. Cardiovascular, brain relaxant. Used in psychiatric medicine. For prescription by a qualified medical practitioner only. Prescribed in cases of arrhythmia for slowing down the heart muscle. Sometimes combined with Valerian (Rauvolfia 1; Valerian 2).
Extract: oral administration: 2mg once daily.

RAYNAUD'S DISEASE. Raynaud's phenomenon. An exaggerated constrictive response to cold. White, numb fingers, toes, ears and nose which later give way to swelling and blue colour. An immune disorder. 60-90 per cent sufferers are women. Winter is the worst time for spasmodic contraction of small arteries and veins. Concerned with *both* hands, or feet.

The condition is higher among migraine sufferers; and has been known to improve from migraine treatments. Patients are always chilly and have to wrap up well to keep attacks at bay. Unchecked, the condition may damage vessel walls and terminate in gangrene.
Treatment. An increase in Calcium intake as from summer months ensures vaso-dilation, causing tissues to relax, and improving blood flow. Adrenaline antagonists. Anti-spasmodics. Where it attacks the feet treat as for Buerger's disease.
BHP (1983). Severity and frequency reduced by Prickly Ash bark: internally.
Ellingwood. Cactus: internally.
Teas. Ginkgo, Green Buckwheat.
Tablets/capsules. Rutin, Ginkgo, Prickly Ash.
Formula. Valerian 1; Pulsatilla 1; Prickly Ash 2; Ginkgo 2; Cayenne Pepper quarter. Dose – Powders: 500mg (two 00 capsules or one-third teaspoon). Liquid Extracts: 30-60 drops. Tinctures: 1-2 teaspoons. Thrice daily. Where evidence of heart failure: add 15 drops Hawthorn.
Topical. Massage arms and shoulders with massage oil. Tincture Arnica as a lotion. Osteopathy to four upper dorsals. Avoid cold, wet and exposure.
Diet. Avoid milk, red meat, iced drinks. Reduce tea and coffee. 4 or 5 small hot meals daily. Oily fish. Two tablespoons virgin Olive oil daily – see: OLIVE OIL. Hay diet. Daily salad of green vegetables with Cider vinegar dressing. Ginger.
Supplements. Daily. Evening Primrose capsules to stimulate fibrinolysis and reduce severity of attacks. Vitamin E 200iu. Multivitamin. Calcium citrate tablet at meals.
Supportive. Avoid immersing hands in cold water. Wear gloves in cold weather. Electrically-heated gloves, free if supplied by a hospital consultant.

Treatment is the same for 'vibration-white finger' from industrial use of vibrating tools – a condition often confused with Raynaud's disease.
Information. The Raynaud's and Scleroderma Association, 112 Crewe Road, Alsager, Cheshire ST7 2JA.

RED BLOOD CELLS. Erythrocytes. Blood cells contain haemoglobin, a pigment; and which transports oxygen throughout the body. Differ from white blood cells that do not contain haemoglobin.

RED BUSH HERBAL TEA. See: ROOIBOSCHE TEA.

RED CLOVER. Trefoil. *Trifolium pratense L.* *German*: Wiesenklee. *French*: Triolet. *Spanish*: Trébol. *Italian*: Moscino. Flowerheads. Used by

Hippocrates and physicians of the Ancient World.
Constituents: flavonoids, isoflavones, resins, coumarins, minerals, vitamins.
Action: deobstruent, antispasmodic, alterative, sedative, expectorant. Mild stimulating and relaxing alterative with affinity for throat and salivary glands. (*Priest*) Anti-inflammatory. Reputed antineoplastic for reduction of tumours and hard swellings, especially of ovaries and breast. Has a long traditional reputation as a drink for cleansing the lymphatic vessels through which cancer is believed to spread.

"Clinicians have found it sometimes prevents ulceration, retards progress of tumours and improves general condition." (*Dr Fetter H.R. XIV, 431*)
Uses. Mouth ulcers and sore throat (strong tea gargle, swallowing a mouthful at each session). Skin diseases: scrofula, eczema, old sores that refuse to heal. Promotes healthy granulation tissue. Dr Margaret Wilkenlow used Red Clover to good effect for cough and night sweats of tuberculosis. Whooping cough, bronchitis in children (tea drunk freely).
Combination: (1) With Yellow Dock for chronic skin disease BHP (1983). (2) With Chaparral and Ginseng for cachexia, anaemia, wasting, and chronic blood disorders.
Preparations. Thrice daily.
Tea. 1oz to 1 pint boiling water; infuse 15 minutes; dose – 1 cup.
Liquid Extract BHC Vol 1. 1:1, 25 per cent ethanol. Dose: 2-4ml.
Home tincture. 1 part flowers to 5 parts vodka; macerate 8 days. Decant. Dose: 5-10ml (1-2 teaspoons).
Original Red Clover Compound. Parts: Red Clover 32, Queen's Delight 16, Burdock root 16, Poke root 16, Barberry 16, Cascara 16, Prickly Ash 4. Mix. Dosage: Liquid Extract: 4-8ml.
Powder. 750mg (three 00 capsules or half a teaspoon).
Tablets/capsules. Red Clover, Chaparral and Ginseng.
Jason Winter's tea. GSL

RED EYE. Congestion of conjunctiva or haemorrhages. Conjunctival injection. Red patches on the white of the eye. Cause may be superficial or serious (a symptom of glaucoma or iritis). Where not due to pink eye or glaucoma, treatment is same as for iritis.
Practice: Goldenseal drops.

RED ROOT. *Ceanothus americanus*. See: NEW JERSEY TEA.

RED VINE. *Vitis vinifera L. German*: Weinrebe. *French*: Vigne. *Spanish*: Enredadera. *Italian*: Vite. *Iranian*: Angura. *Chinese*: P'u-t'ao. *Malayan*: Munteri. *Part used*: leaves. Contains Vitamin C. Vitamin P effect.
Constituents: grape sugar, malic acid, gum.
Action: vein restorer. Alterative. Astringent (external). Antidiarrhoea.
Uses. Capillary fragility, varicose veins, piles, chilblains, hardening of the arteries. Excessive menstrual bleeding, irritable bowel. Menopause – to normalise the circulation.
Preparations. *Tea*: 1 heaped teaspoon to cup boiling water: infuse 15 minutes. Half-1 cup thrice daily.
Powder, capsules: 250mg. 2 capsules thrice daily.

REES EVANS CANCER CURERS. A Welsh family with a cancer clinic in Cardigan from 1900 to the 1950s. David, last of the line, practised in Hampstead and was at the centre of a fierce public controversy in 1950 when patients demanded recognition of his work. Since the days when uncles John and Daniel gathered sun spurge from hills of the surrounding country, David carried on the family tradition using, among other remedies, Blood root for breast conditions.

Hannon Swaffer, well-known journalist, toured Cardiganshire to interview those who had been cured of cancer – among them a Mrs Rose Chambers who showed him, preserved in a bottle of alcohol, a cancer the size of a grapefruit which David Rees Evans had removed from her breast ten years before. She was feeding a baby with the breast a surgeon wanted to remove. Evidence was produced to on-the-spot investigators of cases successfully treated. The Ministry of Health promised 'a full and fair' enquiry. Turning down a huge American dollar offer to buy his method and treatment he returned to England intending to offer his discoveries to a suitable authoritative body.

The Enquiry called for by Aneurin Bevan under the chairmanship of Sir Robert Robinson never materialised because the Committee refused to investigate cases under treatment. Queen's Counsel considered "unjustifiable" an attempt by physicians to eliminate from the scope of the enquiry rodent ulcer cases with which Rees Evans had been singularly successful.

REFLUX. A backward flow of food to the mouth from the gullet or stomach. Gastro-oesophageal reflux disease (GORD).
Causes: loss of oesophageal sphincter muscle tone brought about by antacids, aspirin or other non-steroidal anti-inflammatory drugs.
Symptoms: vomiting, difficult swallowing, respiratory symptoms, regurgitation. Other conditions that may be present: hiatus hernia, acid dyspepsia.
Treatment. Any underlying cause should be treated. Acid-neutralisers, gastric emptying improvers, peristalsis restorers. A number of alginate components are used for preparations,

chiefly Wrack Seaweed (*Ascophyllum nodosum*).
Pain: Cramp bark. Liquorice root. Wild Yam.
German Chamomile tea, freely. To increase gullet peristalsis, accelerate gastric emptying and to reduce acidity.
Slippery Elm bark powder. Long-lasting antacid barrier; protects gullet mucosa and allows progressive healing of lesions. Gruel freely during the day.
Alternatives: Comfrey, Marshmallow.
Papaya fruit. Temporary relief of symptoms.
Potato water. Temporary relief of symptoms.
French traditional. Half-1 teaspoon crushed Coriander seeds; infuse in cup of boiling water. 1 cup freely.
Diet. Bland. Low salt. Low fibre. Avoid spices and hot peppery foods and alcohol.

REFORMED PRACTICE OF MEDICINE. A school of natural medicine drawing its membership from the orthodox medical profession at the beginning of the 19th century, continuing until the advent of modern scientific medicine when their many useful discoveries were eclipsed. They were among the first to reject blood-letting arguing: "instead of drawing-off the vital fluid upon which the restorative principle depends, we prescribe means to equalise its circulation". At first they were known as botanic physicians.

Their *Vis Medicatrix Naturae* read: "We regret the indiscriminate use of minerals and such agents as tend to impair the integrity of the system, substituting safe botanical agents. Our fundamental principles are:
1. "We believe in the existence of an inherent curative power in the body's constitution, the constant tendency of which is to throw off disease.
2. "Every disease state or perverted action is initiated by Nature to bring about a healthy reaction.
3. "That all the physician can reasonably claim is to act in the capacity of a hand-maid or servant of Nature.
4. "That we will only prescribe remedies in harmony with this Vis Medicatrix Naturae."

These early eclectic physicians stringently tested information acquired by clinical experience at the bedside of the patient. Among those early pioneers were Dr Wooster Beach, Dr Finlay Ellingwood, Dr Samuel Thomson.

Contemporary writers highly praised this move towards natural medicine, welcoming the discovery of podophylin (*American Mandrake*) and leptandrin (*Black root*) as substitutes for mercury and antimony.

REFRIGERANT. A cooling tea for relief of fever and thirst. Also used topically as a lotion.

Balm, Borage, Greater Burnet, Liquorice root, Scarlet Pimpernel, Cinnamon, Houseleek, Blackcurrant fruit, Raspberry fruit.

REHMANNIA ROOT. Di-huang (Chinese). Jio (Japanese). Rehmannia glutinosa var. purpurea (Scrophulariaceae).
Action: anti-anaemic, antipyretic, tonic, immunosuppressant. (*Planta Medica, 1989, 55/5. pp 458-62*)

REISHI MUSHROOM. (Ganoderma lucidum).
Contains glucans of same structure as lentinan, as found in Shiitake. Contains germanium which helps oxygenate cells.
Action. Anti-tumour (animal studies). Hypotensive, antiviral, immunostimulant, antitussive, expectorant. Antihistamine. Antibacterial.
Uses. Contains adenosine which inhibits platelet aggregation and thrombocyte formation. High blood pressure. Chronic asthma. Popular Chinese remedy in syrup for bronchitis

Officially recognised in Japan as a cancer treatment. Candida, chronic fatigue syndrome, and side-effects of radiation and chemotherapy. Helpful for high blood pressure, allergies and to reduce blood fat.
Preparation. *Powder*. 1 teaspoon daily for immune enhancement. 2 teaspoons for cancer and AIDS to enhance immune response.

Works well with Shiitake Mushroom. Used for HIV, AIDS, and ME. (*Information: International Journal of Alternative and Complementary Medicine, July 1992, p15-16*)
Diet. Reishi is marketed as a food with no claims made.

No known side-effects.

REITER'S SYNDROME. A form of arthritis of knees, ankles and sacro-iliacs, first described by Hans Reiter, German bacteriologist.
Symptoms. Conjunctivitis, irritable skin rash simulating psoriasis, urethritis, inflammation of membranes of mouth and alimentary canal. Occurs in adolescent youths. Also seen in old cases of diarrhoea after cure. Believed to be a disease of suppression – a resurgence of disease in another form following suppression by drug therapy, etc. May follow urethritis or dysentery.
Alternatives. Bearberry, Bogbean, Burdock root, Celery, Dandelion root, Gotu Kola, Gravel root, Juniper (*Hyde*). Meadowsweet, Wintergreen.
Tea. Combine Meadowsweet 1; Gotu Kola 1; Juniper berries half. 1 heaped teaspoon to each cup boiling water; infuse 15 minutes; half-1 cup thrice daily.
Decoction. Combine Echinacea 2; Burdock root 1; Valerian root half; Liquorice half. 4 teaspoons to 1 pint (500ml) water gently simmered 20 minutes. Dose: half-1 cup thrice daily.
Formula 1. Powders. Equal parts: Kava Kava, Echinacea, Valerian. Liquorice (half). Dose: 500mg (two 00 capsules or one-third teaspoon) thrice daily.
Formula 2. Liquid extracts or tinctures.

Sarsaparilla 2; Kava Kava 1; Yellow Dock root 1; Liquorice half. Dose: Liquid extracts: 1 teaspoon. Tinctures: 2 teaspoons. Thrice daily.
Practitioner. Analgesic. Tincture Gelsemium: 10 drops in 100ml water. Dose: 1 teaspoon every 2 hours.
Topical. Evening Primrose oil, Jojoba oil, Castor oil packs to knees, Chamomile soaks for ankles.
Diet. Low salt. Low fat, Lacto-vegetarian. Oily fish.
Supplements. Vitamins A, C, D, E.
Natural lifestyle. No general treatment to meet every case is available.

REJUVENATION. While it is not possible to restore powers of youth, all people seek to function at their maximum capacity at whatever age. There are herbs which history claims to reinvigorate and breathe new life. Few agents stimulate the blood and glands more effectively or harmlessly that Gotu Kola, Ginseng, Kola, Saw Palmetto or Damiana, usually available as teas, tablets, powders or tinctures.

RELAPSING FEVER. Tick fever. Infection transmitted by a spirochete, *Borrelia duttoni*, from infected animals to humans. Patient has high fever which returns to normal. After a few days it again rises, followed by relapse, and the pattern is repeated.
Symptoms. Shivering, skin rash, high fever, vomiting and general pain. Incubation period: 7 days.
A notifiable disease under the Public Health (Control of Diseases) Act 1984.
Alternatives. Anti-infectives. Severity of the fever may be reduced by opening the bowels at the outset with a copious enema of Chamomile infusion or warm water. Follow with liver pill or tablet.
Formula. Echinacea 2; Yarrow 2; Pleurisy root 1. Mix.
Decoction: half an ounce to each 1 pint water gently simmered 20 minutes. Dose: 1 cup every 2 hours.
Liquid extracts: 1 teaspoon.
Tinctures: 2 teaspoons.
Powders: 500mg (two 00 capsules or one-third teaspoon) – every 2 hours.
Practitioner. Tincture Aconite: 5 drops to 100ml (half a glass) water: 1 teaspoon hourly until temperature falls.
The patient should drink all the cold water desired. If urine is scanty give 2-3 drops Oil Juniper in teaspoon honey every 4 hours. When collapse threatens: 10-20 drops Antispasmodic Drops; or 5-10 drops Tincture Capsicum (Cayenne); or 5-10 drops Tincture Myrrh; in water or hot drink, hourly.
Diet. Lacto-vegetarian. Slippery Elm gruel, Irish Moss products.

Treatment by or in liaison with a general medical practitioner.

RELAXANTS. See: SEDATIVES.

RELAXATION. Can help to prevent coronary heart disease and alleviate a number of nerve disorders by reducing blood pressure.
Teas: Lime flowers, Betony, Skullcap.
See also: STRESS.

RENAL. Refers to the kidney.

RENAL CALCULUS. Presence of mineral concretions in the pelvis of the kidney, and ureter. Stone. See: STONE IN THE KIDNEY.

RENAL COLIC. The attempted passage of a stone or gravel along the ureter from kidney to bladder. Excruciating agony with sweating and vomiting, causing patient to faint. When stone glides into the bladder the ordeal comes to an end. Urine, scanty and blood-coloured.
Alternatives. *Powders*. Formula: Lobelia 1; Cramp bark 1. Mix. Dose: three 00 capsules or half a teaspoon every half hour until relief.
Tinctures. Valerian 1; Gravel root 1; Hydrangea 1; Sea Holly 2. Mix. One 5ml teaspoon in water, every half hour.
Tincture Lobelia Simplex: 30 drops in water every half hour.
Practitioner. Tincture Belladonna: 5 drops to 100ml water; dose, 1 teaspoon every 15 minutes.

RENAL FAILURE. Progressive erosion of kidney substance associated with retention of fluids. The end-effect of many diseases including high blood pressure, drug reactions, polycystic kidney, acute or chronic kidney disease.
Symptoms: loss of weight, dry skin, falling hair, headache, digestive weakness, deficient urine secretion, possible heart failure, increasing blood pressure and other symptoms followed by coma. Specific modern hospital treatment (dialysis, etc) is necessary. See: BRIGHT'S DISEASE, CHRONIC.
Vigorous treatment for septic conditions. Treatment by or in liaison with a general medical practitioner.

REPETITIVE STRAIN INJURY (RSI). A general term for painful spasms in hands, arms, neck, shoulders, or back. In the USA it is believed to be the most common cause of lost working hours. First recorded among leather workers and copper beaters of Ancient Babylon and in recent years among production line workers. Also a white-collar injury, particularly in offices where data processing and keyboard work is carried out.
Symptoms. Agony in performing the simplest tasks – putting on and taking off clothes, turning

the key in a lock. Patient may awaken one morning to find himself/herself crippled; pain may be so bad that the sufferer dreads being touched.
Alternatives. White Willow, Hops, Astragalus root, Valerian, Shiitake Mushroom, Avena (oats), Siberian Ginseng, Pollen.
Tea: equal parts, Vervain, Valerian. 1 heaped teaspoon to each cup boiling water; infuse 15 minutes; 1 cup 2-3 times daily.
Tablets/capsules. Ginseng (Siberian), Valerian.
Practitioner. Tincture Arnica: 2-3 drops as prescribed.
Diet. Low salt, Oats (porridge etc), oily fish or fish oils.
Supplements. Kelp, Vitamin B-complex, B6, Magnesium, Zinc.
Aromatherapy. Oil Rosemary massage: 6 drops in 2 teaspoons Almond oil.
Supportives. Osteopathy where indicated. Appropriate seating while at work, regular screen breaks, foot rests, adequate lighting according to requirements of the Health and Safety at Work Act, 1974. Any ache or pain should be immediately reported to the management.
Information. RSI Association, Chapel House, 152 High Street, Yiewsley, West Drayton, Middlesex UB7 7BE.

RESEARCH. The purpose of good clinical research is to provide a bridge between orthodox and alternative medicine. Objective evidence is essential to support the efficacy of herbal medicine and to establish a link between the chemical interactions within each remedy and the evidence of its traditional use.

Much valuable work is being carried on by Messrs Madaus (Germany), Arkopharma (France), Gerard House (UK), other European and American pharmaceutical companies, and by the Scientific Committee of the British Herbal Medicine Association.

First of its kind in the Western world, is the Centre for Complementary Health Studies at the University of Exeter, Devon, UK, offering postgraduate degree courses (BPhil and MPhil) in studies including herbalism, homoeopathy and Naturopathy.

RESINS. Amorphous, inflammable substances from trees or plants, insoluble in water but soluble in alcohol.
Chief resins: Guaiacum, Scammony, Burgundy Pitch, Mastic, Copaiba.
Gum resins: resins mixed with gums: Myrrh, Olibanum, Galbanum, Gamboge, Asafoetida.
Oleo-resins: resins mixed with volatile oils.
Those occurring naturally: Canada balsam, Oregon balsam, gum Turpentine.
Those obtained by solvent extraction: Ginger, Capsicum.

RESORPTIVE. For exernal use for bruises or extravasation of blood into surrounding tissues; to promote re-absorption.

Arnica, Comfrey root, Herb Robert, Sanicle, St John's Wort.

REST HARROW, Prickly. *Ononis spinosa L. German*: Hauhechel. *French*: Bugrane. *Spanish*: Detienbuey. *Italian*: Bulimacola. *Parts used*: roots, leaves, flowers.
Constituents: flavonoids including rutin, triterpenes, volatile oil, phenolics, lectins.
Action: diuretic, anti-inflammatory, anti-lithic.
Uses. Rheumatism, gout, skin disorders. Kidney and bladder disorders, gravel and small stone. (*French traditional*)
External: leaves as a poultice for wounds and injuries.
Preparation. *Tea*: 1 heaped teaspoon to each cup boiling water; infuse 15 minutes. 1 cup 2/3 times daily.

RESTLESSNESS. Need for constant motion. "Jitteriness" in the legs (restless leg syndrome) or shoulders and arms. Twitching limbs when resting. Common in the elderly. Associated with varicose veins, neuritis, iron deficiency anaemia, etc. Where persistent an underlying cause should be sought and treated accordingly.
Nervous restlessness of pregnancy – see: PREGNANCY.
Alternatives. *Teas*: German Chamomile. Balm. Skullcap. Lime flowers. Passion flower.
Tablets/capsules. Skullcap, Mistletoe, Valerian, Chamomile.
Formula: equal parts, Hops, Passion flower, Valerian. Dose: powders, quarter of a teaspoon. Liquid extracts: 30-60 drops. Tinctures: 1-2 teaspoons. In water or honey, thrice daily.

Severe cases may require muscle relaxants: Cramp bark or Black Cohosh.
Practitioner. Tincture Gelsemium BPC (1963). 10 drops in 100ml (half cup) water: one teaspoon (acute) hourly; (chronic) thrice daily.
Aromatherapy. Massage with oils of Chamomile or Lavender: 6 drops to teaspoon Almond oil.
Diet. See: DIET – GENERAL. Avoid coffee, strong tea, caffeine. Iron-rich foods.
Supplements. Daily: Folic acid: 20mcg (adults), 10mcg (children). Floradix – a pre-digested iron preparation. Vitamin E 400iu for twitchy hands and feet. Zinc. Magnesium.
Supportives. Cool showers, swimming, yoga.
Note. Elderly people who complain of restless legs in bed at night can benefit from iron supplements but their condition needs to be investigated for any underlying cause of iron depletion.

RETENTION OF URINE. A condition in which the bladder is distended with urine but expulsion is obstructed. Differs from *suppression* in which the kidneys fail to produce urine. Inability to urinate. In *retention* urine is secreted by the kidneys but is held up in the bladder due to a number of causes.

In men, a common cause is enlargement of the prostate gland or stricture (narrowing of the urethra). Where acute, passage of a catheter must be carried out immediately. If this is not possible, 30 drops Liquid Extract Lobelia in water should be given half hourly. Damage to the lumbar vertebre, pressure from a tumour or prolapsed womb may cause spasm of the sphincter muscle and call for anti-spasmodics.

In the latter months of pregnancy retention is possible for which Raspberry leaf or Motherwort tea frequently resolves. Where due to fibroids of the womb, see FIBROIDS. Some relief has been found for temporary paralysis of the bladder from spinal injury, poliomyelitis or other infections, from Liquid Extracts, Lobelia, Skullcap, and Ephedra; equal parts. Dose: 15-60 drops, when necessary, according to the case.

Retention is sometimes due to hormonal problems in the woman; where this pertains, the following should be taken as supplements: Vitamin B6, 50mg, 3 times daily; and Evening Primrose (Efamol) two 250mg capsules, 3 times daily.

Alternative treatment. Teas and decoctions are used sparingly, because of increasing volume of urine to be voided.

Tablets/capsules. Lobelia, Black Cohosh.

Powders. Formula. equal parts: Black Cohosh, Cramp bark, Valerian. 500mg (two 00 capsules or one-third teaspoon). Hourly, until normal flow is continued.

Tincture Vervain. One teaspoon every 2 hours. Vervain relaxes sphincter spasm.

Practitioner. Tincture Gelsemium: 10 drops in 100ml water; dose, 1 teaspoon every half hour. For pain and to facilitate micturition.

The Inca writer, Garcilase de la Vega (1539-1616) recorded the use of maize (corn) for retention. Today, it is common for fine silky threads of the stigma from the female flowers, Cornsilk, not the grain itself, to be used as a tea, half-1oz to a teapot filled with boiling water to be drunk as desired.

Supportive. Sit in a hot bath.

RETINITIS. Inflammation of the retina of the eye by over-exposure to light or many varied conditions: kidney disease, tuberculosis, high blood pressure, hardening of the arteries, diabetes mellitis, etc. Perhaps the most common cause today is diabetes; having been demonstrated that patients receiving eight 500mg Evening Primrose oil capsules daily (360 GLA) respond well. (*JAM Dec. 1986, p.17*)

Refer to eye specialist.

Internal. Tincture Bryonia alba: 20 drops (adult), 5-10 drops (child), in water every 2 hours. Where traced to STD, treat as for syphilis. Eyebright is contra-indicated.

Tea: Pulsatilla herb: half a teaspoon to each cup boiling water. 1 cup morning and evening.

Liquid Extract: Pulsatilla BHP (1983): 2-5 drops, morning and evening.

Periwinkle (vinca minor) tea: congestion of blood in the retina.

Ginkgo biloba.

Diet. Bilberries. Avoid peppers and spicy foods. Low salt.

Supplements. Vitamin C, 1g thrice daily. Vitamin E, one 400iu capsule, morning and evening. Beta-carotene. Selenium, Zinc.

RETINITIS PIGMENTOSA. An inherited slowly degenerative disease of nerves of the retina.

Symptoms: night blindness leading to progressive blindness, sensitive to sunlight. No cure possible.

Alternatives. Limited efficacy. Build up general health and retinal efficiency with silica-rich herbs (Horsetail, Blessed Thistle, Oats), vitamins and minerals. Buckwheat (Rutin) maintains resilience of retinal vessels and stimulates blood supply to the eyes.

Evening Primrose oil capsules: two capsules morning and evening.

Tea: any of the above herbs: one heaped teaspoon to each cup boiling water; infuse 15 minutes; half-1 cup once daily.

Bilberries. A considerable amount of anecdotal evidence exists recording successful use of Bilberries for improvement.

Dr Grace Halloran, Eye Health Education Centre, Santa Rosa, California, was diagnosed having retinitis pigmentosa at the age of 24. Her eyesight was not restored to normality but was considerably improved by simple home treatments, including acupressure, biofeedback and nutrition.

Diet. Low salt, High fibre. Bilberries.

Supplements. Daily. Vitamin C, 100mg. Vitamin E, 200iu. Beta-carotene. Selenium, Zinc.

Supportives. Autogenic meditation and healing visualisations, aided by sessions of reflexology, spiritual healing and massage, especially to counter effects of muscular tension. Affirm to yourself: "I am not going to remain blind permanently." Mind over blindness. Photochromic sunglasses.

RETINOPATHY. Degenerative change in blood vessels of the retina due to high capillary pressures or atrophy.

Etiology. Diabetes mellitus, high blood pressure, kidney disorder, chronic infections such as tuberculosis or syphilis. Fragility of capillary walls leads to retinal haemorrhage (see entry).

Toxaemia of pregnancy.
Treatment. The underlying cause must receive treatment.
Periwinkle (vinca minor) tea: congested blood flow. Limited success.
Ginkgo biloba: for capillary circulation.
Bilberries. A farmer with diabetic retinopathy was nearly blind and had his sight successfully restored after taking Bilberry extract for three months, enabling him to resume normal life on the farm. Even blood sugar levels significantly stabilised. (*Paul Keogh ND*)
Diet. Low salt. High fibre. Bilberries.
Supplements. Daily. Vitamin C, 500mg. Vitamin E, 400iu. Beta-carotene. Evening Primrose 500mg. Selenium, Zinc.
Note. A preliminary therapeutic trial on patients with ageing macular degeneration or diabetic retinopathy showed that supplementation with beta-carotene, Vitamin C, Vitamin E and Selenium halted the progression of degenerative changes, and in some cases even brought some improvement. *(Age and Ageing, 1991, 20 (1) 60-9)*

REYE'S SYNDROME. Rare children's disease with damage to the nervous system. May strike healthy children recovering from a feverish illness such as chickenpox, influenza or other virus infections. Swelling of the brain, liver and kidneys. Aspirin poisoning suspected. Children taking aspirin are 25 times more likely to develop the disease.
Symptoms. Severe vomiting (Black Horehound), delirium (Skullcap) and convulsions in later stages (Cramp bark). Patient is listless, feverish, with running nose and possible earache, cough, sore throat. Survivors may suffer irreversible brain damage and fatty deposits in the liver.
Treatment. Parents are advised to avoid aspirin for feverish children. Though the disease follows a viral infection it is also a neurological disorder for which nervine herbs are indicated.
Acute. Tea. Combine equal parts: Chamomile flowers, Elderflowers, Lime flowers. 2 teaspoons to each cup boiling water; infuse 5-15 minutes. 1 cup freely.
Chronic. Formula. Ginkgo 2; Echinacea 1; Vervain 1; Goldenseal half. Dose: Liquid Extracts: 1 teaspoon. Tinctures: 2 teaspoons. Powders: 500mg (two 00 capsules or one-third teaspoon). Thrice daily.
Diet. 3-day fast on herb tea and fruit juices followed by lacto-vegetarian diet. Papaya fruit.
Supplements. Daily:– Vitamin A, 20,000iu. B-complex 50mg. Bromelain 300mg. Zinc 15mg.
Note. Aspirin is frequently given to prevent clotting of the blood. Garlic is a safer agent with the ability to block blood platelet aggregation.

Treatment by or in liaison with a general medical practitioner.

RHATANY ROOT. *Krameria triandra*. Dried root.
Constituents: tannins.
Action: tonic, astringent, haemostatic, anti-microbial.
Uses. Bleeding from mucous surfaces and from the lungs, as in tuberculosis. See: UMCKALOABO. Haemorrhoids. Excessive loss of menstrual blood. Incontinence of urine. Irritable bowel, colitis. Sore throat (gargle and mouth wash). To strengthen the gums.
Preparations. *Decoction*. 30g in 500ml water gently simmered 5 minutes; infuse 15 minutes. Dose, half-1 cup, thrice daily.
Tincture Krameria BPC (1949). Dose, 2-4ml, thrice daily, in water. GSL

RHEUMATIC DISEASES embrace a wide group of disorders. They include inflammatory disorders of muscles, joint stiffness, and various forms of arthritis. Treatment will differ according to type.

See: ANKYLOSING SPONDYLITIS. ARTHRITIS, Juvenile. ARTHRITIS, Bowel-related. ARTHRITIS, Gonococcal. ARTHRITIS, Infective. ARTHRITIS, from leprosy. ARTHRITIS of Infective hepatitis. ARTHRITIS of lupus. ARTHRITIS, Menopausal. ARTHRITIS from an attack of mumps. ARTHRITIS, Osteo. ARTHRITIS, Psoriatic. ARTHRITIS, Rheumatoid. ARTHRITIS, Tuberculous. CHARCOT'S DISEASE. COLLAGEN DISEASES. FIBROSITIS. GOUT. LUMBAGO. MARFAN'S SYNDROME. OSTEOMALACIA. PAGET'S DISEASE. POLYMYALGIA RHEUMATICA. RHEUMATIC FEVER. REITER'S SYNDROME. SCIATICA. SCLERODERMA. SJÖGREN'S DISEASE.

It is a consensus of practitioner opinion that a diet high in seafood is of value for most of the rheumatic diseases. See: FISH OILS. For pain, a substitute for aspirin may be found in White Willow bark which is more acceptable to the stomach. Consider low zinc levels.

A Norwegian study has shown that a change-over to vegetarian foods normalised dietary fatty acids and reduced inflammation in rheumatic disorders. Patients were allowed only Garlic, herb teas, vegetable soups and juices for first seven to ten days. Meat free and gluten-free food was eaten every second day. For the first three months citrus, salt, refined sugar, tea, coffee, strong spices, alcohol and dairy products (including milk) were avoided. After this period dairy products and gluten foods were gradually restored to the diet. Stronger hand-grips and improvement in painful and swollen joints reported. (*National Hospital, Oslo*)

Lemons and lemon juice should be avoided. At first, the juice may remove some calculi from the body, but after clearing the bloodstream it begins to remove calcium from muscles and bones which leads to degeneration.

RHEUMATIC FEVER. An acute feverish bacterial infection with inflammation of joints and the heart. Joints: hot, painful, enlarged. Mostly children 5-15 years. Moves from joint to joint. Sustained fever may affect the brain (chorea), skin (erythema) and heart (carditis). Night sweats.

Streptococcal infection first invades the throat 2 or 3 weeks before affecting the joints. Swollen joints and pericardial effusion subside but may be followed by a heart problem in later life. Differs from juvenile arthritis and osteomyelitis. "It hurts just to be touched."

First consideration is to arrest the spread of streptococcal infection (Echinacea). Other antibacterials: Wild Indigo (Baptisia), Holy Thistle (Cnicus), Myrrh (Commiphora).

Treatment. Complete bedrest during active synovitis. Treatment for heart failure as well as inflamed joints.

Alternatives. Agrimony, Balm of Gilead, Balmony, Bogbean, Heather flowers, Meadowsweet, Motherwort, Yarrow.

Tea. Equal parts: Holy Thistle, German Chamomile, Yarrow. Mix. 1 heaped teaspoon to each cup boiling water; infuse 15 minutes; 1 cup every 2 hours for acute condition.

Tablets/capsules. Devil's Claw, Echinacea, Hawthorn, Motherwort.

Alternative formulae:– *Powders*: Echinacea 2; White Poplar 1; Bogbean 1; Guaiacum quarter. Mix. Dose: 500mg every 2 hours for acute condition.

Liquid extracts: Echinacea 2 Prickly Ash 1; Hawthorn 1; Guaiacum quarter; Liquorice quarter. Mix. Dose: 1 teaspoon. Every 2 hours for acute condition.

Tinctures. Echinacea 2; Meadowsweet 2; Motherwort 1; Devil's Claw 1. Mix. Dose: 1-2 teaspoons every 2 hours for acute condition. Childrens' dose: quarter to half adult dose.

Topical. Bathe joints with strong infusion of Lobelia, Ragwort, Chickweed or Wintergreen. Plantain salve. Camphorated oil. Comfrey leaf poultice. Tea Tree oil: 2 drops to 2 teaspoons Almond oil.

Diet. 3-day fast on fruit juices and herb teas. Vitamin C drinks (orange, lemon juice). Followed by lacto-vegetarian diet and regular raw food days. Salt-free.

Supplements. Vitamins A, C, D, E, bioflavonoids, pangamic acid. Removal of bad teeth or tonsils.

RHINITIS. Inflammation of mucous membranes of the nose with attacks of sneezing, nasal discharge and blocked nose. Allergic rhinitis (hay fever) may include conjunctivitis, sore throat and deafness from obstruction in the Eustachian tubes. Cause may be a wide range of allergens from house dust to food additives. May be complicated by nasal polyps. Treat as for HAY FEVER.

RHUBARB, Garden. Rheum rhaponticum. A mild stimulant for the production of oestrogen. Of value for the menopause and oestrogen deficiency.

RHUBARB, TURKEY. *Rheum officinale* Baill, *Rheum palmatum L.* (Not the English or European rhubarb.) *German*: Pontischir. *French*: Rhapontic. *Spanish*: Rhubarbo. *Italian*: Rabarbaro. *Iranian*: Chukri. *Indian*: Râvandehindi. *Chinese*: Huangliang. Dried rhizome and bark.

Constituents: anthraquinone compounds, calcium oxalate, rutin, tannins, fatty acids.

Action: laxative, astringent-bitter, gastric stimulant, anti-inflammatory, stomachic, tonic, antiseptic.

Uses. Tincture of Rhubarb was once one of the most popular remedies for constipation. Today it is advised for non-persistent constipation only. Disorders of liver, gall bladder and stomach. Diarrhoea, dysentery, Crohn's disease. Uric acid diathesis (gout). Diverticulosis. Toxaemia from over-consumption of animal protein. Gastro-enteritis.

Combinations. (1) Turkey Rhubarb 1; Guaiacum quarter; Sarsaparilla 2; rheumatism and arthritis, temporary relief. (2) Turkey Rhubarb 1; Echinacea 2; Goldenseal quarter; amoebic dysentery. Doses: Liquid extract: 2-4ml.

Preparations. Once daily, usually at bedtime.

Powder. 500mg (two 00 capsules or one-third teaspoon).

Tincture Rhei Co BP: dose, 2-4ml.

Not taken in pregnancy, lactation or where intestinal obstruction if suspected. Said to be the ancient Sanskrit remedy; Soma, for courage, wisdom and longevity. GSL

RHUS TOXICODENDRON. Poison oak, Poison ivy. *Toxicodendron radicans L.* Leaves and stems.

Action: alterative, with special reference to non-irritative skin disorders. Discontinue if itching ensues.

Preparations. *Tincture* in 60 per cent alcohol 1:10. BHP (1983). Dose 0.06-0.12ml.

Rhus Tox Ointment. Anthroposophic. Constituents: 100g contains: Rhus toxicodendron tincture (1=2) 10ml in a base containing lanolin, beeswax and vegetable oils. Apply on a dry dressing (*Weleda*). Popular as a homoeopathic remedy.

RICKETS. Bone disease of children caused by a lack of Vitamin D. In adults, an insufficiency of this vitamin causes osteomalacia. See: OSTEOMALACIA.

Vitamin D is formed in the skin as the result of ultra-violet radiation, and upon the body's ability

to metabolise calcium and phosphorus. Basically rickets follows lack of exposure to sunlight (ultra-violet rays).
Symptoms. Rickets in infants means late crawling and walking, restlessness, insomnia and a delay in closure of the fontanelles of the skull. Epiphyseal cartilages of the long bones are enlarged, particularly those of the ribs (rachitic rosary).
Deformities: pigeon-chest, bow legs, etc.

Rickets is a problem among Asian communities because of a Vitamin D deficiency in their diet. In a tropical climate children receive adequate Vitamin D from direct sunlight, but this is not the case in Britain and other Northern climes. The Department of Health favours supplementation of the vitamin with their diet.
Alternatives. Nettles are a source of easily assimilated calcium (*A. Vogel*). Nettle tea may be drunk freely.
Other natural sources of calcium: taken as teas, etc: Comfrey leaves. Oats (Avena sativa), Lobelia, Plantain, Silverweed, Clivers, Rest Harrow, Shepherd's Purse, Scarlet Pimpernel, especially: Horsetail.
Tea. Formula. Equal parts: Plantain, Horsetail, Silverweed. Mix. 1-2 teaspoons to each cup boiling water simmered gently 5 minutes. Half-1 cup 3-4 times daily.
Decoction. Gentian. 1 teaspoon to each cup cold water left to steep overnight. Half-1 cup before meals.
Tablets/capsules. Iceland Moss. Kelp. Lobelia. Raspberry leaf. Red Clover.
Powders. Equal parts: Horsetail, Gentian, pinch Cayenne. Dose: 500mg (two 00 capsules or one-third teaspoon) thrice daily.
Liquid Extracts. (1) Mix: Oats (*Avena sativa*) 3; Gentian 1; Raspberry leaves. Few drops Capsicum. Dose: 15-60 drops thrice daily before meals.
(2) Mix. Oats 2; Chamomile 1; Comfrey 1; Vervain half. Mix. Dose: 1 teaspoon according to age in sweetened warm water or milk, before meals. Flavour with Liquorice, if necessary. (*Eric F. Powell*)
(3) Mix. Echinacea 1oz; Boneset half an ounce; Horsetail half an ounce; Oats 2. Flavour with Liquorice, or honey. 15-60 drops, according to age, in water before meals.
Diet and Supplementation: see: CALCIUM DISORDERS.
Comfrey. Potential benefit outweighs possible risk.

RICKETTSIA. Microorganisms that resemble viruses and bacteria and which are responsible for typhus, Rocky Mountain spotted fever and other fevers for which herbal antibiotics, antivirals or antibacterials are indicated.

RIGHT TO PRACTISE. Any British subject has the *freedom* to practise herbalism or any other kind of alternative medicine under Common Law, with or without qualifications, provided he does not commit an offense, such as purporting to be a qualified doctor, harming or causing the death of a person. He is not granted the *right* to practise.

RINGWORM (Tinea). A contagious skin disease caused by a fungus or vegetable parasite (Trichophyton).
Main forms: Tinea tonsurans (of the scalp); Tinea barbae (beard); Tinea cruris (groin); Tinea pedis (feet); Tinea circinata (of the body); Tinea favosa (nails); or Tinea versicola (honeycomb ringworm). Athlete's foot is a common form. Sweating aggravates.

Many sources of contagion, including microsporum from kittens and puppies. A ringworm of farmers may be picked up from gates or cattle-markets. When on the scalp, circular lesions with raised borders may confirm diagnosis. Hair should be cut short and washed with best quality castile soap, or soapwort (*saponaria officinalis, L*). Internally, Poke root has a reputation of efficacy.

Ringworm on the body is very easily overcome; it is more difficult on the face and scalp, especially children.
Alternatives. *Teas.* Angelica, Centuary, Chickweed, Clivers, Dandelion leaves, Gotu Kola, Ground Ivy, Liquorice root, Marigold, Red Clover.
Tablets/capsules. Blue Flag root, Echinacea, Poke root.
Formula. Echinacea 2; Poke root 1; Thuja half. Dose – Powders: 250mg (one 00 capsule or one-sixth teaspoon). Liquid Extracts: 15-30 drops. Tinctures: 30-60 drops. Thrice daily.
Practitioner. Tinctures 1:5. Echinacea 5ml; Baptisia tinctoria 5ml; Galium aparine 10ml; Phytolacca decandra 10ml; Rumex crispus 10ml; Stillingia sylvatica 10ml; Arctium lappa 10ml. Aqua to 100ml. Sig. 5ml (3i) tds aq.cal.pc.
Topical. Tincture Blood root as a lotion. (*Arthur Barker*)
Lotion: Tincture Blood root 5ml; Liquid Extract Thuja 10ml; Distilled Extract Witch Hazel to 240ml. (*North American Eclectic School, 1890*)

Scald half an ounce Lobelia herb in half pint boiling water in a covered vessel. Strain. Add 10 drops Tincture Myrrh. Use as a lotion morning and evening. Has a drying effect; follow with Comfrey cream. (*George Stevens*)
Tincture Calendula (Marigold). An antiseptic cell proliferant and anti-inflammatory. Good response usually follows within 48 hours for ringworm of the feet. (*I. Melrose MNIMH*)
Tea Tree oil. Dilute. May be diluted many times.
Aloe Vera. Edgar Cayce.
Ointments. Thuja, Plantain, Chickweed,

Marshmallow, Aloe Vera.
Oils. Castor, Evening Primrose, Eucalyptus, Garlic.
Cod Liver oil. Good responses observed.
Butternut. Green rind of *Juglans cinera* as a skin-rub.
Diet. See: DIET – SKIN DISEASES.

RNA. Ribonucleic acid – by which genetic intelligence is conveyed from the DNA to tissues in which new cells and replacement protein are synthesised.

ROBERTS, Captain Frank, MC. MNIMH. Distinguished West Country herbal practitioner. Papers on modern herbalism. Books: *Herbal Cures for Duodenal Ulcer and Gall Stones* (Thorsons). *Modern Herbalism for Digestive Disorders (1981)* (Thorsons); originally published in 1957 as *The Encyclopaedia of Digestive Disorders*. Guidance offered to causes, symptoms and herbal prescriptions based on clinical experience.

ROCKY MOUNTAIN SPOTTED FEVER. An infectious rickettsial disease caused by *Rickettsia rickettsii*, transmitted by ticks. Occurs in the USA and South America.
Symptoms. High fever, muscle pains, headache, dry unproductive cough. Four days after its sudden onset an irritative rash appears on arms and legs, spreading over the whole of the body. If untreated, delirium and pneumonia supervene.
Treatment. Hospitalisation. While vaccines are available, herbal agents of history are still used in primitive communities. Bowels constipated; relief with a Yarrow or Chamomile enema assists recovery.
Tea. Combine equal parts: Gotu Kola, Yarrow, Chaparral. 2 teaspoons to each cup boiling water; infuse 15 minutes. Half-1 cup freely.
Decoction. Combine half ounce each: Pleurisy root, Ladyslipper and Ginger in 1 pint (500ml) water; bring to boil, simmer 5 minutes. Strain. Dose: half-1 cup freely.
Tinctures. Combine, Chaparral 1; Echinacea 2; Goldenseal quarter. Dose: 1-2 teaspoons in water or honey every 2 hours.
Diet. 3-day fast on fruit juices and abundant herb teas.
Chaparral. Traditional Indian remedy for Rocky Mountain fever.

RODENT ULCER. Basal cell epithelioma. May occur anywhere on the body but mostly on exposed surfaces, commonly on the face. Slow-growing smooth pearly nodule which eats into soft tissues and bones. Tendency to spread and deform. Biopsy confirms.

Whatever treatment is adopted, large amounts of Vitamin C are essential (2-3 grams daily).

Alternatives. *Tea.* Gotu Kola, Red Clover, Yellow Toadflax, Plantain. Singly or in combination – 1-2 teaspoons to each cup boiling water; infuse 15 minutes. 1 cup thrice daily.
Decoction. Roots: Burdock, Yellow Dock, Queen's Delight. Mix. Half an ounce (15g) to 1 pint (500ml) water simmered gently 20 minutes. Half-1 cup once or twice daily.
Tablets/capsules. Ginseng, Chaparral, Red Clover, Echinacea, Poke root.
Powders. Mix: Echinacea 2; Yellow Dock 1; Queen's Delight 1; Ginger quarter. Dose: 500mg (two 00 capsules or one-third teaspoon), thrice daily.
Tinctures. Mix. Condurango 1; Yellow Dock 1; Thuja 1. 20-40 drops increasing to 30-60 drops in water 3 times daily.
Topical. (1) Fresh juice Yellow Toadflax. (2) Strong tincture of American Mandrake (*podophylum peltatum*). (3) Liquid extracts or fresh juices (to be preferred) Blood root, Great Celandine, Dandelion, or Houseleek. 3-5 drops of any one, to eggcup distilled extract Witch Hazel wiped over area as frequently as practical. Reported success with Castor oil.
Wm Salmon MD, physician, records success with the juice of Yellow Toadflax (fluellen) on a patient whose nose was almost consumed with cancer and which was entirely cured.
Diet. Avoid hot spicy foods.
Supplements. Vitamins A, C, D. Selenium. Zinc.

Treatment by or in liaison with a general medical practitioner.

ROOIBOSCH TEA. *Aspalathus linearis*. Contains cyclopine. Leaves. A tea drunk by bushmen and Hottentots in the Cape district of South Africa. Bush tea. Rich in Vitamin C and minerals: manganese, potash, magnesium, iron, and phosphate. An alternative to domestic tea. Its anti-histamine effect is useful in cases of allergy such as hay fever and milk allergy. Offers a caffeine-free, low-tannin beverage that promotes digestion and assists liver and kidney function. As a mild antispasmodic is of value for muscular cramps and rheumatic aches and pains. Contains sufficient natural fluoride to resist tooth decay. (*South African Division of the International Association of Dental research*). Teabags available.

ROSACEA. See: ACNE ROSACEA.

ROSE. *Rosa Gallica L. Rosa Damascena* Mill. *Rosa centifolia*. Family: Rosaceae. *French*: Eglantine, Rosa de Damas. *German*: Weisse Rose. *Italian*: Rosa bianca. *Spanish*: Rosa blanca, Rosa centifolia. *Turkish*: Kirmiz. Rose oil of the highest quality comes from Bulgaria where its distillation has been a major industry since the 17th century.

Constituents. Oil containing nerol, geraniol, geranic acid, eugenol, myrcene and other constituents. Source of Vitamin C.
Action. Mild sedative, mild local anaesthetic, anti-inflammatory, laxative, liver protector, antidepressant, aphrodisiac, cardioactive. Cooling skin astringent (topical). Increases bile-flow. Anti-viral, menstrual regulator.
Uses. To reduce high cholesterol levels. "To raise the spirits and cheer the heart" (*Traditional*). Rose water as a lotion for inflamed eyes. As a vehicle for other medicines. Vaginal irritation and dryness.
Preparation. Oil of Roses. Concentrated Rose Water BPC 1949. Rose oil BPC 1949.
Study. "Recent scientific research on Rose oil has yielded interesting results. Reportedly, Rose oil includes spasmolytic, sedative, local anaesthetic, antiseptic, antiparasitic, anti-inflammatory, laxative, digestive, hypolipidemic and cardiotonic properties. an ointment called "Rosalin" was tested against many micro-organisms with positive results, particularly the treatment of acute radio-dermatitis and late radion-necrosis. It also showed benefit to cancer patients receiving radiation therapy.

"Another preparation, "Girostal", containing Rose oil and Vitamin A, appears to have a blood lipid lowering (hypolipidemic) effect, especially in gall stones and fat degeneration. "Rosanol", capsules of 33mg pure Rose oil is reportedly effective for some disturbances of the bile-forming function of the liver. Psychological studies indicate that Rose oil can induce "sweeter dreams" and increase concentration and rate of work capacity. Safety studies indicate that Rose oil has a very low oral toxicity in humans." (*W.S. Brud and I. Szydlowska, "Bulgarian Rose Otto: Priceless Perfume, Precious Medicine". International Journal of Aromatherapy, Aut. 1991, Vol 3, No 3, pp.17-19*) GSL

ROSEBAY WILLOW-HERB. *Epilobium angustifolium L.* Rhizome and flowers. Leaves once used as a substitute for tea.
Action: astringent, antidiarrhoeic, demulcent, haemostatic, antimicrobial (mild). Leaves are diuretic. Externally: as an emollient, vulnerary.
Uses. Weak stomach, gastro-enteritis, dysentery, summer diarrhoea in children. Diarrhoea of typhoid fever. Colitis, diverticulosis. Mouth ulcers, pharyngitis (gargle and mouth wash). Infantile eczema (ointment made from the leaves). Cystitis, irritable bladder (leaf tea).
Preparations. *Tea*: 2 teaspoons dried leaves or flowers to cup boiling water; infuse 15 minutes. Half-1 cup freely.
Decoction (rhizome): 1 teaspoon to cup water gently simmered 15 minutes. Half cup, thrice daily.
Home tincture: dried rhizome 1 part, in 10 parts 45 per cent alcohol. Macerate 8 days. Decant. Dose: 1-2 teaspoons in water, thrice daily.
Ointment: 1 part dried leaves to 8 parts vaseline in gentle heat, half hour.

ROSE HIPS. Wild rose. Dog rose. *Rosa canina L.* Fruits (hips) are gathered in the autumn, halved and allowed to dry-out. Source of Vitamin C, in which plant it was first discovered. Contains also: Vitamins A, B1 and B2, in the pulp.
Action: anti-gall and kidney stone; diuretic, astringent, laxative (mild).

Because of a lack of a major enzyme in the human liver, the body in unable to manufacture its own Vitamin C (ascorbic acid) from glucose – as most members of the animal kingdom can do – it has to be taken into the body from outside sources, one of which is the Rose Hip.

As a fitness tea, Rose Hips help maintain a healthy collagen – the gelatinous substance that holds trillions of individual cells together and which offers a limited protection against viral infections.

Long before the discovery of Vitamin C, Rose Hip tea was used for the common cold and locally for inflamed or bleeding gums.
Preparations. *Tea*. 1-2 teaspoons Rose Hips, or half a teaspoon powder, to each cup boiling water: 1 cup freely. Teabags available. The combination Rose Hips and Hibiscus offer an alternative to caffeine drinks.
Tablets, capsules, etc. See: VITAMIN C. GSL

ROSEMARY. Sea dew. *Rosmarinus officinalis L. French*: Encensier. *German*: Rosmarin. *Spanish*: Romere. *Italian*: Rosmarine. *Chinese*: Mi-tieh-hsiang. *Parts used*: leaves and terminal twigs.
Constituents: flavonoids, diterpenes, volatile oil, rosmarinic acid.
Action: antibacterial, antidepressant, antispasmodic, antiseptic, circulatory tonic, diffusive stimulant, diuretic, sedative, mild substitute for Benzodiazepine drugs. Used in European pharmacy to strengthen the heart and allay arteriosclerosis.
Uses. Migraine headaches, or those from high blood pressure. Headache of gastric origin or emotional upset, psychogenic depression, cardiac debility, giddiness, hyperactivity, tremor of the limbs, flitting pains from joint to joint. Inflammation of the gall bladder, jaundice. Cirrhosis: to aid function of the liver. (*Jung & Fournier*) To strengthen blood vessels by decreasing capillary fragility and permeability. (*Kiangsu – 1738*) Chronic fatigue syndrome (ME). Syncope.
Combinations. With Lavender for depression: mix equal parts. With Valerian for headache of migraine or high blood pressure: mix equal parts. Half a teaspoon to each cup boiling water; doses half-1 cup.

Preparations. Thrice daily.
Tea: half-1 teaspoon to each cup boiling water: infuse 15 minutes; dose, half-1 cup. Cover cup with saucer to prevent escape of essential oil.
Liquid extract: 30-60 drops in water.
Rosemary wine: 30g fresh terminal shoots steeped 1 week in bottle white wine; half-1 wineglass.
Spirit of Rosemary, BPC 1934. Practitioner use. 3-5 drops in honey.
External:– Rosemary Liniment. Handful (approximately 50g) in 500ml (1 pint) alcohol; steep 1 week in a cool place; shake daily; filter. Massage into painful joints and stiff muscles.
Oil of Rosemary. Diluted, use as a lotion on areas where lice are suspected.
Rosemary chest-rub. 3-5 drops oil in 2 teaspoons Almond oil, for relief of respiratory distress.
Douche. Handful fresh or dried leaves in 2 pints boiling water; strain when cool. Use warm for vaginal discharge, parasite deterrent or to allay hair fall-out. Add to bath water for a Rosemary bath. GSL

ROSEMARY AND ALMOND OIL. Lotion or massage oil to relax muscles prior to manipulation. For rheumatism, arthritis, lumbago, backache.
Ingredients: 60 drops oil Rosemary to 8oz oil of Almond.
Shake briskly. Store in cool place.

ROUNDWORMS. Nematodes. Found in most parts of the world. May not be serious but difficult to totally eliminate. Usually a family ailment. Worms – white, threadlike.
Causes: eating food with unwashed hands, contact with pets and soil.
Symptoms: worms observed in stools, child sucks thumbs or fingers. Itching is worse at night. No passage of blood. Gritting teeth during sleep, bed-wetting, always hungry, dark circles under eyes. Getting on hands and knees in sleep.
Alternatives. Anthelmintics Carrots are anthelmintic.
Teas: Mugwort, Southernwood, German Chamomile, Wormwood. May also be given as an enema: 1oz to quart boiling water allowed to cool, strain; inject warm.
Tea: Combine equal parts; Sage, Balmony, Vervain. 2 teaspoons to each cup boiling water; infuse 15 minutes. Half-1 cup thrice daily. (*Melville Keith MD*)
Molasses. Half a teaspoon Wormwood powder in half a cup molasses. Dose: 1 teaspoon night and morning for 3 days, followed by a dose of Senna or Epsom's salts.
Traditional. Insert sliver of Garlic (or onion) into rectum at night. Repeat.
Pumpkin seeds. About 100 fresh inner seeds of Pumpkin. Take on rising. Follow in 2-3 hours with laxative.
Quassia Chips. 2 teaspoons steeped in teacup Cider vinegar. Dose: 3-4 teaspoons in water thrice daily, before meals.
Practitioner. Tinctures: Butternut half an ounce; Guaiacum quarter of an ounce; Lobelia half an ounce. Capsicum fort 3 drops. Dose: 5-10 drops, thrice daily. Children over five – 1 drop for each year of age, in honey.
Decoctions. White Poplar bark or Wild Yam root.
Powders. Formula. (*Dr F.H. England*) Poplar bark 2; Balmony 2; Bitter root 1; Cayenne quarter. Dose: 500mg (two 00 capsules or one-third teaspoon) thrice daily. Not given in pregnancy or to children under 10.
Diet. Paw Paw fruit. 2 or 3 grated raw carrots daily.
Enema. Any one of the above teas: 1oz to quart boiling water; allow to cool; strain, inject warm.

ROYAL JELLY. Queen Bee jelly. A secretion from the salivary glands of the worker bee. A special food for development of the queen bee. Contains 10 hydroxy-delta 2-decenoic acid known to have bactericidal properties. Rich in amino acids, vitamins and metabolites. Cannot be synthesised. A concentrated food which imparts extraordinary powers to the queen bee. Enables her to grow much larger, to become more fertile, to live 30 times longer than other bees and ensures immunity to most infections that invade the hive.
Action: antibiotic, endocrine gland stimulant, immune enhancer, anti-anorexic, digestive. Contains vitamins: B1, B2, B3, B5, B6, biotin, inositol, folic acid and Vitamin C.
Uses. Energy-source for the aged, to stimulate appetite, to increase metabolic processes, defence against infection, ability to handle stress; for healthy skin, hair and nails. For improved blood count and increase in weight. Antidote to stress, natural antibiotic and to restore diminished sexual function.
Preparations. Capsules. Combines well with honey, wheat germ oil, pollen, Ginseng and Vitamin C for an instant energy boost. Royal Jelly is combined with Jojoba oil and Vitamin E to make a cream for skin protection.
Note: of value for healthy pets.

RUBEFACIENT. External use. An agent to draw a rich blood supply to the skin, increasing heat in the tissues, thus aiding absorption of active constituents of lotions, creams, etc. Also given to relieve the aches of rheumatism.
Black Bryony, Cayenne, Garlic, Ginger, Horseradish, Kava Kava, Mustard. Oils of Peppermint, Rosemary, Thyme, Wintergreen, Lavender.

RUE. Herby grass. Herb of Grace. *Ruta graveolens L. German*: Garten raute. *French*: Rue des Jardins. *Italian*: Rue. *Chinese*: Yun-hsiang-ts'au.

Part used: herb. One of the sacred herbs of the ancient world. Once used by the Roman Catholic Church for exorcism.
Constituents: coumarins, lignans, flavonoids including rutin, alkaloids, volatile oil.
Action: antispasmodic, anti-tussive, emmenagogue, abortifacient, ophthalmic, anti-hysteric, anti-epileptic, carminative.
Uses. For suppression of menses from cold or shock. To promote menstrual flow after months of absence. Used as an eye-douche for over-use of eyes, eyes that tire easily, weak eyes with a tendency to inflammation. Headaches due to eye strain. Bruised bone, cartilage troubles, ganglion of wrist (tea internally, compress externally). Dry skin, to promote perspiration; Bell's palsy (tea). Mouth ulcers (mouth wash). Dimness due to eye-strain (douche). Sprains of wrists and ankles (compress). Rue tea is a traditional remedy for multiple sclerosis. Internal use today discouraged in modern practice.
Preparations. Average dose, half-1 gram. Thrice daily.
Tea: quarter of a teaspoon to each cup boiling water. Infuse 15 minutes. Dose: half-1 cup. May be used externally as a douche.
Powdered herb. Fill No 3 capsules. 1-2 capsules morning and evening.
Liquid Extract. 5-15 drops in water.
Poultice: for bone injuries (with or without Comfrey)
Ruta Ointment. Anthroposophic. Ruta graveolens tincture (1:3) 15 per cent. Apply on dry dressing. (*Weleda*)

Not used in pregnancy. Excessive handling of the fresh plant may cause 'contact dermatitis'. Practitioner use only.

Effective medicine for chickens. GSL

RUPTURE. See: HERNIA.

RUPTUREWORT. *Herniaria glabra, L.*
Constituents: herniarine and paronychine, saponins.
Action: diuretic. Action is the opposite of Bearberry. Renal antispasmodic.
Uses. Kidney and bladder. Dropsy: cardiac or renal.
Preparation. *Tea*. 1-2 teaspoons (dried), 3-4 (fresh) plant, to each cup boiling water; infuse 10-15 minutes. 1 cup thrice daily.

RUTA. See: RUE.

RUTIN. A flavone glycoside found in Buckwheat, Tobacco, Eucalyptus, etc. It is part of the Vitamin P complex (bioflavonoids) used as a protection against capillary fragility. Where this condition of the tiny blood vessels is associated with high blood pressure haemorrhages are possible, resulting in apoplexy, retinal haemorrhage or bleeding from the lungs. Capillary haemorrhage may appear as bruising or petechiae.

Prescribed for high blood pressure, varicose veins, hardening of the arteries, chilblains.
Popular source: Eucalyptus.
Tablets. Rutivite. 570mg dried green Buckwheat, providing 30mg natural source Rutin. Potter's: 60mg tablets.
Tea. Rutivite Green Buckwheat Herb Tea. May be mixed with ordinary tea or taken by itself. (*Rutin Products Pocklington, Yorks, UK*)
Powder. Available in 120mg capsules.

SACRO-ILIAC STRAIN. To support physiotherapy or osteopathy.
Combination: equal parts Buchu, Valerian, Cramp bark. Dose: Powders – two 00 capsules or one-third teaspoon. Liquid Extracts: 1 teaspoon. Tinctures: 2 teaspoons. Pinch of Cayenne Pepper enhances action.
Ligvites: *Gerard House*.

SADDLE-SORE. Dyspareunia. Strain of levator muscles by horse-riding. Massage with Peanut oil, Comfrey cream or Aloe Vera gel.

SAFFLOWER. *Carthamus tinctorius*.
Safflower seed oil, a polyunsaturated fat, contains 75 per cent linoleic acid and is a nourishing source of fats rich in essential fatty acids. Prevents hardening of cholesterol in the arteries and aids prevention of arteriosclerosis, coronary heart disease and kidney disorders. Cold-pressed. Beneficial in diabetes. Combines with cholesterol to form and repair connective tissue. Externally, eczema and roughness of the skin are soothed by its healing properties.

SAFFRON. *Crocus sativus L. German and French*: Safran. *Spanish*: Azafran. *Italian*: Zafferano. *Indian*: Kesara. *Arabian*: Zafran. *Chinese*: Fan-hung-kua. *Iranian*: Karkum. *Malayan*: Konger. *Part used*: flower pistils collected in the autumn.
Constituents: crocins, volatile oil, fixed oil, pigments, Vitamins B1 and B2.
Action. Aphrodisiac, sedative, antispasmodic, diaphoretic, expectorant. Has been used as an anti-tumour agent in primitive communities. Emmenagogue.
Uses. Dry cough, whooping cough, bronchitis, insomnia, hysteria, haemopysis, menstrual disorders, depression. Today's use chiefly confined to food flavouring and colouring. Not used in pregnancy.
Preparations. *Tincture*. 1 part to 5 parts 60 per cent alcohol; macerate 8 days; shake daily; filter, bottle. Dose: 5-15 drops in water thrice daily.
Powder: dose 0.5 to 2.5g, thrice daily. GSL

SAGE. Red sage. *Salvia officinalis L. German*: Salbei. *French*: Sauge. *Spanish*: Salvia. *Italian*: Salvia grande. *Chinese*: Tan shēn. *Indian*: Salbia. Dried leaves.
Constituents: diterpene bitters, volatile oil, flavonoids, rosmarinic acid.
Action. Astringent, antiseptic, carminative, circulatory stimulant, bactericidal, antibiotic, diaphoretic, digestive, anti-inflammatory, antispasmodic, oestrogenic. Folk medicine associates it with longevity.
Uses. Sore throat, laryngitis pharyngitis, to reduce blood sugar, tonsillitis. Inflammation or ulceration of mouth, gums and throat. Respiratory allergy. Excessive sweating, night sweats (cold Sage tea). Flatulence, loss of appetite, weak stomach. Chronic gastro-intestinal catarrh. Headache, anxiety and nervousness in the aged. To arrest breast milk production. Depression, vertigo. Hot flushes of the menopause. Poor memory. Mental confusion. To reduce high sugar levels in diabetics. Combines well with Tincture Myrrh: 5-10 drops Myrrh to cup of Sage tea.
Topical. Tea as a shampoo rinse to allay onset of greying hair.
Preparations. Average dose: 1-4 grams. Thrice daily.
Tea: half-1 teaspoon to each cup boiling water: infuse 15 minutes. Add pinch Cayenne Pepper for chronic conditions. Dose: half-1 cup; or used as a gargle and mouthwash.
Sage oil. External use only.
Liquid Extract: 15-30 drops, in water.
Tincture: 30-60 drops, in water.
Powder. Two 220mg capsules 4 times daily. (*Arkocaps*)
Not indicated in high blood pressure, presence of blood in the urine, pregnancy or epilepsy.

SAGEBRUSH, BIG. *Artemisia tridentata*, Nutt. Compositae. Leaves and flowering tops. American plant.
Constituents: alkaloids, flavonoids, coumarins, Camphor, Thujone, Borneol.
Action. Blood purifier, carminative, bitter tonic, stimulant, analgesic, antiseptic, laxative, anti-bacterial, anti-microbial, diaphoretic, antibiotic. Anti-neoplastic activity (*Navajo Indians*).
Uses. Pains of rheumatism and arthritis. Diarrhoea, gastro-intestinal irritation, head colds (inhalant), bronchitis (to increase expectoration).
Preparations. *Decoction*: 1 teaspoon to 2 cups water; bring to boil; simmer 10 minutes. Dose: half a cup thrice daily. Taken hot for first stages of fevers, influenza etc. Used also, topically, as a wash for open ulcers and wounds.
Powder. Taken in capsules to mask the bitter taste, usually combined with an aromatic (Peppermint) for patient compliance. Also used topically for healing of ulcers and wounds.
Sagebrush Brandy. Early American pioneer's 'cure-all' – leaves steeped in brandy.
Tincture. 1 part crude material to 5 parts 60 per cent alcohol.
Note. "No other plant is more closely associated with the American 'old West' than Sagebrush . . . Besides being a necessary source of winter nutrients for browsing wildlife and grazing livestock, it has provided knowledgeable humans with an abundant supply of medicinally active compounds." (*Dr Francis Brinker, British Journal of Phytotherapy, Vol 2 No.3 1991/92*)

SAINT VITUS DANCE. See: CHOREA.

SALAD DRESSING. *Ingredients*: Eggs 3, Olive oil 4oz, Cider Vinegar 7oz, Mustard flour 1oz, Salt half an ounce, Powdered Ginger 2g, Cayenne 0.5g. Mix.

SALICYLATES. Salts of salicylic acid (salix – willow) sometimes used in rheumatism, gout and acid conditions.
Food sources: almonds, apples, apricots, cherries, cucumber, grapes, peppermint, peaches, prunes, tomatoes, White Willow bark, Wintergreen, Poplar, Meadowsweet.

SALIVA. Watery, alkaline fluid secreted by the salivary glands of the mouth. An excess is known as ptyalism for which Sage tea is a known corrective.
Practitioner: To reduce. Tincture Stramonium BP (1973). 5-30 drops.
To increase saliva: Red Clover tea. Bitters. See: BITTERS.

SALMONELLA. The name of a large group of germs that cause bowel infection and gastroenteritis. The commonest cause of food poisoning by water or food borne infection by a rod-shaped bacteria of which family over 250 members have been identified. Pets, cattle, pigs and poultry can harbour the germ which is responsible for 95 per cent cases of food poisoning.

The organisms may be found in cooked meats and particularly chicken and eggs. A strain was once traced to chocolate bars. Such form of food poisoning is usually due to under-cooking. Some of the milder forms manifest as enteritis but the most virulent may cause typhoid and paratyphoid: see entries. A notifiable disease.

Vomiting may occur 1-12 hours after eating contaminated food. Colic in the abdomen is soon followed by diarrhoea. Onset may simulate gastric flu especially where there is raised temperature, headache and general weakness.
Alternatives. *Abundant herb teas*: Nettles, Gotu Kola or Buckwheat, with a few grains Cayenne, Ginger or Cinnamon.
Tablets/capsules. Echinacea, Goldenseal, Wild Yam.
Powders. Formula. Echinacea 2; Myrrh 1; Goldenseal 1. Liquorice half. Dose: 500mg (two 00 capsules or one-third teaspoon) 3-4 times daily.
Tinctures. Alternatives:– (1) Combine: Wild Yam 1; Echinacea 2; White Bryony 1. (2) Echinacea 2; Fringe Tree 1; Goldenseal quarter. Dosage: one 5ml teaspoon in water 3-4 times daily.
Tea Tree oil. 3-5 drops in honey or water. If too strong may be diluted many times. (*Dr Paul Belaiches, Faculty of Medicine, University of Paris*)
Diet. Slippery Elm gruel. Yoghurt. No coffee, tea or other stimulants as long as the acute condition lasts.
Precaution: careful handling of cooked meats, especially in hot weather. Eggs should be solid boiled or well-cooked. See: THE COCKROACH.

Treatment by or in liaison with a general medical practitioner.

SALPINGITIS. Infection of the Fallopian tubes. Acute or chronic. Ovaries may also become inflamed. Commonly associated with infection following sexual intercourse. May occur after abortion, use of IUDs and childbirth. In past years the chief cause was tuberculosis.
Symptoms. (*Acute*): fever, tenderness, low abdominal pain, purulent vaginal discharge, vomiting.
(*Chronic*): persistent dull pain in abdomen, painful sexual intercourse, weight loss, general malaise, backache. Lining of the tubes may become scarred and form a blockage. It is important to have the condition confirmed by expert medical opinion as soon as possible as the canal may become blocked by scars and sterility ensue.
Alternatives. *In general use*: Agnus Castus, Chamomile, Cramp bark, Echinacea, Goldenseal, Helonias, Pulsatilla, Wild Yam. All are available as powders, liquid extracts or tinctures.
Formula. Agnus Castus 2; Helonias 2; Myrrh quarter. Dose: Powders: 500mg (two 00 capsules or one-third teaspoon). Liquid extracts: 1 teaspoon. Tinctures: 2 teaspoons. In water or honey. Thrice daily.
A. Barker, FNIMH. Liquid Extract Cramp bark half a fluid ounce; Liquid Extract Chamomile half a fluid ounce; Liquid Extract Hops 60 drops; Tincture Goldenseal 30 drops. Liquid Extract Marshmallow 1 fluid ounce. Water (preferably, distilled) to 8 fl oz. Dosage: 2 teaspoons every 4 hours.
Practitioner: for excessive pain. Tincture Gelsemium BPC (1973) 10 drops in 100ml (half glass water): 1 teaspoon hourly.
Of tubercular origin: add 1 part Rhatany root.

Treatment by or in liaison with a general medical practitioner.

SALUS-HAUS Company. Founded in 1916 by Dr Otto Greither. Active, out-going enterprise for the harvesting and supply of medicinal herbs. Supports complex technologies behind the production of high-quality specialities which have gained world-wide reputation. Herbs grown in their natural surroundings. Strict quality control. Liquid food supplements prepared at low-temperature process of extraction. Extensive research programme. Plant situated at the foot of the Bavarian Alps. Products include Floradix, Borage oil capsules, Siberian Ginseng capsules, Garlic and Hawthorn and Mistletoe capsules, and a wide range of herb teas and preparations.
Addresses: PO Box 1180, 8206 Bruckmühl, West

Germany. Salus (UK) Ltd, Woolston Grange, Warrington, Cheshire, England.

SANDALWOOD. *Santalum album L.* Oil. Antiseptic and bacteriostatic against staphylococcus aureus (gram positive bacteria). Modern scientific research confirms a long traditional belief among the Australian aborigines of its effective use as a urinary antiseptic for chronic cystitis. Chinese medicine confirms. Contains a volatile oil.
Preparations. Thrice daily.
Oil Sandalwood: 3-5 drops in honey.
Liquid Extract: 1-4ml in water. GSL

SANDFLY FEVER. See LEISHMANIASIS.

SANICLE. Snake root. *Sanicula europaea L. German and Dutch*: Sanikel. *French*: Sanicle. *Italian*: Sanicola. Dried flowering plant.
Constituents: allantoin, saponins, essential oil, rosmarinic acid.
Action. Anti-inflammatory, astringent (mild), antitussive, expectorant, carminative.
Uses. Dry cough, sore throat, bronchitis, inflammation of mucous surfaces. Infected gums, ulcers (mouthwash). Varicose veins. Flatulence. Piles (ointment). Burns, minor injuries, cuts, etc (compress).
Preparations. Thrice daily.
Tea: 1 teaspoon to each cup boiling water; infuse 10 minutes. 1 cup.
Liquid extract: 1-2 teaspoons, in water. GSL

SAPONINS. Saponins are glycosides that have a detergent action on internal mucosa. They produce a soap-like frothing effect when agitated in water. There was a time when some were used externally, as Soapwort for body cleansing before the age of commercial soaps. They resemble steroid hormones.

Some are expectorants: Polypody root, Scarlet Pimpernel, Beth root. Some are anti-inflammatories: Butcher's Broom, Horse Chestnut, Sarsaparilla. Others relate to skin and kidneys.

They may be referred to as Adaptogens, appearing to have the ability to 'adapt' or 'normalise' abnormalities of the endocrine glandular system. Diogenin, a saponin of Wild Yam, is similar in structure to cortisone and used as a base for steroid synthesis. Other saponins include: Helonias, Ginseng, Fenugreek, Sanicle, Pilewort, Cornsilk, Cowslip, Chickweed, Golden Rod, Helonias, Soapwort and Sarsaparilla.

Saponin herbs and foods reduce high cholesterol levels and lower the risk of heart disease. Most effective are: Chickpeas, Alfalfa, Lentils and Fenugreek.

Other plants that contain significant levels of saponins: Lime flowers, Liquorice, Ginseng, Thyme, Nutmeg, Mung beans, Broad beans, Soya beans, Azuki beans, Egg plant, Sunflower, Oats, Garlic, Spinach, Asparagus, Sesame seed, Leeks, Indian tea, Kidney beans, Green peas, Asparagus, Aubergines, Quinoa, Blackberries, Sage, Thyme.

There is evidence that colon cancer risk may be reduced by saponins.

SARCOIDOSIS. Sarcoid. A chronic disorder believed to be due to an exuberant response of the body's immune cells to an unidentified invader. Cells cluster together in tiny nodules, or sarcoids (the name comes from the Greek for flesh). Organs affected may be the liver, spleen, skin, eyes, nervous and blood systems, salivary glands, and especially the lungs. It has features similar to tuberculosis. Has been known to follow use of The Pill.
Symptoms. Blurred vision, total fatigue, facial palsy, fever, lumps on the skin. May masquerade as multiple sclerosis, myalgic encephalomyelitis (ME) and glandular fever. Enlarged lymph vessels, joint pains, breathlessness during or after heavy exercise.
Treatment. Alteratives, lymphatics.
Teas. Red Clover, Gotu Kola, Horsetail.
Formula. Echinacea 2; Goldenseal 1; Poke root half. Liquid extracts: 30-60 drops. Tinctures: 1-2 teaspoons. Powders: 250-500mg (one or two 00 capsules, or one-sixth to one-third teaspoon). Thrice daily.
Tincture Thuja: 3-5 drops in water, night and morning.
Diet. Lacto-vegetarian.

See also: SCAR TISSUE.

This condition should be treated by or in liaison with a registered medical practitioner.

SARSAPARILLA. *Smilax officinalis*. Chiefly *Sarsaparilla aristolochiaefolia*, Mill. *German*: Sarsaparille. *French*: Salsepareille. *Spanish*: Zarzaparrilla. *Italian*: Salsapariglia. *Iranian*: Maghrabi. *Arabian*: Ashbah. *Indian*: Salasá. Dried root and rhizome.
Constituents: saponins, parillin, resin, oil.
Action. Antirheumatic, anti-itch, anti-inflammatory, diaphoretic, diuretic, antiseptic, powerful blood tonic, metabolic stimulant, immune enhancer. Pituitary stimulant and substitute for adrenal steroid. Contains the male hormone, testosterone, and cortin a hormone which regulates metabolism and produces a balanced haemostatic function. Has a progesterone-like effect which produces heavier muscle tone.
Uses. Used by sports-people to build up the body and to improve performance. Pre-menstrual tension, impotence and sexual debility, rheumatism, gout, vaginal and anal itching. Chronic skin eruptions: psoriasis, eczema. Leprosy – as an adjunct to primary treatment BHP (1983). Bacterial dysentery. Mercurial poisoning. These conditions are confirmed in Chinese medicine.

Reported use for cancer. (*J.L. Hartwell, 33, 97, 1970*).

A past generation of eclectic physicians combined it with Echinacea and Goldenseal for sexually transmitted diseases. Works well with Burdock and Yellow Dock (equal parts) for itchy skin disorders.

Preparations. Thrice daily.

Decoction. Half an ounce to 1 pint water, gently simmer 20 minutes; dose half-1 cup.

Liquid extract BHC Vol 1. 1:1, 50 per cent ethanol. Dose 2-4ml.

Powder. 500mg (two 00 capsules or one-third teaspoon).

Tablets. Sarsaparilla is chiefly used in combination with other agents. Popular combination: from powders – Guaiacum resin BHP (1983) 40mg; Black Cohosh BHP (1983) 35mg; White Willow bark BHP (1983) 100mg; Extract Sarsaparilla 4:1 25mg; Extract Poplar bark 7:1 17mg.

Jamaica Sarsaparilla Liquid. (*Potter's*) *Ingredients*: each 10ml dose contains the aqueous extractive from 0.5g Sarsaparilla root with Tincture Capsicum BPC 0.03ml; Glycerin BP 1ml: Liquorice Liquid Extract BP 0.78ml; Peppermint oil BP 0.003ml in a flavoured sweetened vehicle. GSL

SASSAFRAS. Ague tree. *Sassafras albidum* (Nutt.) *German*: Sassafrasbaum. *French and Spanish*: Sassafras. *Italian*: Sassafraso. Root bark. *Keynote*: rheumatism.

Constituents: alkaloids, tannin, volatile oil, resin, lignans.

Action. Anti-rheumatic, diuretic, stimulating diaphoretic, powerful blood tonic, carminative.

Uses. Aches and pains of rheumatism, gout, chronic skin disorders, kidney complaints, high blood pressure. Infestation, lice, fleas: (oil, external).

Preparations. Thrice daily.

Tea: quarter of a teaspoon to each cup boiling water; infuse 15 minutes. Dose: quarter to half a cup.

Powder: 0.5-2g.

Oil: external use only.

Liquid Extract: 5-30 drops.

Though highly regarded in history for rheumatic pain, evidence of toxicity has been reported. No longer advised for internal use.

SATURATED FATS. Fats derived from warm-blooded animals and which contain a high concentration of hydrogen. They are solid at room temperature and contain a white waxy substance called cholesterol. This occurs naturally in the blood but tends over the years to build up on the inner lining of arteries, raising blood pressure and causing blockages that lead to heart attacks and strokes.

Saturated fats are found in milk, cheese, cream, butter, margarine, dripping, lard, suet, fatty meats, chocolate.

SATYRIASIS. Insatiable sexual desire in men. Hops, Black Willow – as teas, tablets, powders or liquid extracts.

Extreme cases: 1-2 drops Tincture Camphor in teaspoon honey. Wearing of a Camphor locket. Chinese Barefoot medicine – Sage tea.

Dr A. Vogel: Wormwood or Hops tea, or lemon juice.

External. Cold water douche over genitals.

SAW PALMETTO. Sabal. *Serenoa serrulata*, Hook. *Part used*: berries. *Keynote*: endocrine system.

Constituents: fixed oil, essential oil, polysaccharides.

Action. Adaptogen, urinary antiseptic, tonic nutrient, endocrine stimulant, diuretic, sedative, anti-catarrhal. Mild antispasmodic.

Uses. Benign enlargement of the prostate gland, absence of sex drive. Inflammation or catarrh of the urinary tract, painful urination. Impotence. Cachexia and wasting diseases to increase weight and strength. Rapid loss of weight. Undeveloped pelvic organs. To assist bust development.

Combines well with Horsetail and Hydrangea for prostatitis.

Preparations. Thrice daily.

Decoction. Quarter to half a teaspoon crushed berries to each cup water gently simmered 15 minutes; dose, half-1 cup.

Liquid Extract, BPC (1934). Dose: 0.6-1.5ml (10-25 drops).

Tablets/capsules. Combination with Kola and Damiana.

Serenoa repens. Two 80mg tablets or capsules twice daily.

Note. Controlled trials have shown that the plant (extract) can reduce benign enlargement of the prostate gland thus allowing urine to flow more freely and obviating frequency at night. GSL

SCABIES. Used to be called "The Itch". Invasion of the skin by the mite acarus scabei (sarcoptes) like a cheese mite in burrows with intense irritation, worse by warmth (in bed). Contact may be venereal.

Symptoms. Sense of intense heat and intolerable itching preventing sleep. Usually spreads from the hands which become red and scabby.

Care of the nails (cutting and scrubbing) is necessary, as the mites can be found under fingernails because of scratching other parts of the body. Underclothes and other clothing should be boiled.

Diagnosis is not simple. As a scabious epidemic happens only once every 15 to 20 years it is hardly surprising that many practitioners may not be sure of the differential diagnosis. It may be confused with eczema, nettle rash, allergies or herpes. In adults it rarely occurs above the chin line. It may be some weeks before the itching settles.

Alternative treatment. Internal treatment is of little value except for anti-histamines.

Topical. Remove the mite from its burrow with a sterilised needle. Traditional orthodox pharmacy used sulphur ointment which rapidly destroys the parasite. Scrub skin vigorously with soap and infusion of *Quassia*. Apply essential oils: Quassia, Aniseed, Sassafras, Garlic or Tea Tree oil.

"If there is one thing those tiny insects hate, it is alcohol" records Hamdard; page 201. "In olden times wine was mixed with *natron* for external use."

Tansy – strong decoction of.

Quassia: used as a dusting powder.

Camphor: extract or tincture as a lotion.

"Over the affected area wrap a length of flannel or suitable material steeped in oil of turpentine." (*Dr Finlay Ellingwood*)

Tincture Calamus: good results reported.

SCALDS. See: BURNS.

SCAR TISSUE. Cicatrix. Fibrous tissue resulting from the healing of a wound, burn, or incision after surgical operation. Keloid scar. Internal scarring of stomach or intestines may lead to obstruction.

Aloe Vera (internally and externally). Vitamin E (500iu-1,000iu daily). Edward Cayce advises: Camphorated olive oil externally.

Aromatherapy, to reduce scar tissue: 3 drops Lavender oil to 2 teaspoons Almond or other vegetable oil; moisten gauze and apply. Renew twice daily, or more frequently to reduce pain.

SCARLET FEVER. Acute streptococcal infection with scarlet skin rash and tonsillitis. A notifiable disease.

Cause: group A beta haemolytic streptococci. Transmission is by droplet infection or contaminated food. Incubation: 2-4 days.

Onset: sore throat, vomiting, shivering, tonsils enlarged and throat red. Red rash appears first behind the ears before spreading over whole body. Pale ring around mouth in contrast with flushed face. "Strawberry tongue" – red spots on a white milky background. After attack skin flakes off; hair may fall out.

Complications: heart, kidney, throat, ear troubles and rheumatism. When any rash appears on a child with fever it is always safer to call the practitioner.

Alternatives. *Teas*: Boneset, Elderflowers and Peppermint, Yarrow, Thyme, Marigold.

Formula. Equal parts: Echinacea, German Chamomile, Marigold. Dose. Liquid extract: 1 teaspoon. Tinctures: 2 teaspoons. In water every 2 hours. Children: 1 drop for each year of age to 5, 2 drops to 10 years thereafter.

Jethro Kloss. "I have seen some of the worst cases cured even when there was no hope of recovery by 1 teaspoon Antispasmodic-Acid-Tincture of Lobelia in a little water every half hour. Keep in a warm room; wash body all over in vinegar and hot water. Wipe dry, followed by *clean* bed attire and bedding. Back to bed with warm herbal teas and half a teaspoon of the Antispasmodic tincture. I have never lost a single case by death."

Where the following are at risk add: kidneys (Buchu), heart (Hawthorn), middle ear (Poke root), with enlarged lymph nodes (Agnus Castus). With constitutional disturbance, add Echinacea to sustain powers of resistance. Unhealthy membranes (Goldenseal), nervousness (Skullcap).

Throat gargle. Few drops tincture Myrrh or Goldenseal in water.

Topical. Wipe with oil from Vitamin E capsules.

Treatment by or in liaison with a general medical practitioner.

SCHILCHER, Professor Heinz. Research and teaching, University of Berlin. Managing Director, The Institute of Pharmaceutical Biology. Teaching and research at Universities of Munich, Marburg and Tubingen. 110 publications on quality control, standardisation and effectiveness of plant-derived medicines. Chairman of Committee E (Committee of the German Health Authorities responsible for monographs of plant medicines).

SCHISANDRA. Schisandra sinensis. *Part used*: fruit.

Action. Stimulant. Anti-fatigue. Adaptogen. Anti-stress.

Uses. Sportsman's aid, to improve athletic performance and endurance. To enhance mental performance in students' examinations or in exacting professional work. Assists the immune system. Recovery after surgery.

Preparation. *Powders*. 250mg (or one 00 capsule) 3-4 times daily.

Chinese Medicine. Schisandra is widely used in China both in barefoot and orthodox medicine.

SCHISTOSOMIASIS. See: BILHARZIASIS.

SCHIZOPHRENIA. Dementia praecox. Acute or chronic.

A psychotic condition which may be genetic or the result of a disturbed body biochemistry changing the way a person thinks, feels, hears, sees, tastes, smells – even conversion of a responsible student to an emotionally disorientated teenager. Immature personality. Paranoid. The chemical messenger Dopamine over-stimulates sufferers.

The disorder may run in families, developing at puberty. Degenerative change in the frontal cortex of the brain, 30 per cent showing widened ventricles. Disturbed circulation of CSF (cerebro-spinal-fluid) which could be an indication for cranial osteopathy.

A critical event in the life, such as bereavement, divorce, can precipitate onset, causing withdrawal from the real world into a private personal world. Children may be vulnerable to a malignant environment at school or at home. While spastics are often happy in their own world, the schizophrenic is downright unhappy most of the time.

Symptoms. Peculiar behaviour. Deterioration of intellect. Apathy, delusions, hallucinations, poverty of speech, melancholia, lack of interest, extreme weakness, fatigue from least effort, cannot concentrate the mind, vague anxiety and fears, impaired learning ability, nervous breakdown, possible thyroid problems, subject to allergies and low blood sugar, drug addiction, suicidal tendencies. If left untreated, recovery rate is 35 per cent.

The Missing Link in the treatment of schizophrenia is zinc, according to Dr Carl Pfeiffer, internationally-known psychiatrist. "A common cause is excessive levels of copper, caused by copper water pipes, and deficiencies in the trace elements zinc and manganese, caused by a junk food diet."

People born five months after the 1957 influenza epidemic show an 88 per cent excess in schizophrenia say researchers based at King's College Hospital and Westminster Hospital, both of London. A flu epidemic thus offers one possible cause of the disturbance.

Pregnant mothers who catch flu during the middle months of pregnancy increase their risk of having a child who develops schizophrenia, the most common serious mental illness.

Treatment. Results from conventional neuroleptic drugs are poor. A competent psychiatrist should be seen. Practitioners using large doses of vitamins and minerals claim 80 per cent success, which suggests it may be a deficiency disease.

Alternatives. Black Cohosh, Blue Cohosh, Chamomile, Cramp bark, Evening Primrose, Hops, Jamaica Dogwood, Lobelia, Passion flower, Skullcap, Stramonium, Valerian, Wild Lettuce, Mistletoe, Skunk Cabbage, Rosemary, Lady's Slipper.

Tea. Formula. Equal parts: German Chamomile and Passion flower. 1 heaped teaspoon to cup boiling water; infuse 5-15 minutes. 1 cup thrice daily.

Formula. Passion flower 2; Valerian 1; Rosemary 1; Ginger half. Dose. Powders: 500mg (two 00 capsules or one-third teaspoon). Liquid extract: 1 teaspoon. Tinctures: 2 teaspoons. Thrice daily in water or honey.

Practitioner. Tr Rosemarinus 20ml
Tr Cypripedium pub . . . 20ml
Tr Berberis aquifol . . . 20ml
Tr Capsic fort BPC 0.05ml
Distilled water . . . . to 100ml
Sig: 5ml in medicine glass with water: tds after meals.

With chronic depression: Ginseng. A starting dose (800-1,000mg) daily, twice-daily doses. Predominantly positive symptoms: starting dose 1,000-1,200mg daily, twice-daily doses increasing if necessary to 1,800mg daily. Avoid during pregnancy, (particularly first 16 weeks) menstrual troubles and during the menopause when it may stimulate hormone production.

Pulsatilla. Recommended. (*N. Gosling FNIMH, in "The Herbal Practitioner", Apr 79, p.11*)

Vitamin and Mineral Supplementation. Acute cases can be due to a lifetime deprivation of Vitamins B1, B3, B6, B12, C, E, zinc, manganese and folic acid. Some cases have a personal genetic need for higher than average quantities of these vitamins, daily.

Diet. Foods with a specific reference to the thyroid gland and to general nutrition: Kelp, Parsley, Iceland Moss, Irish Moss, Romaine Lettuce, turnip tops. Avoid coffee, sugar and alcohol. Gluten-free diet: good results reported. Sugar intolerance is one of the main causative factors.

Supplements: Vitamins B3, B6, B12, Folic acid. Minerals: Magnesium, Manganese, Zinc.

SCHOENENBERGER PLANT JUICES. Whole plant juices are pressed from freshly harvested organically grown herbs without the use of preservatives and meet the German Medicines Act standards. Obtainable in the UK from: Phyto Products Ltd., 3 Kings Mill Way, Hermitage Lane, Mansfield, Notts NG18 5ER.

SCHULZ, Professor Dr Volker. Specialist in internal medicine, Faculty of Medicine, University of Cologne, West Germany. Managing Director, Department of Medicine, Lichtwer Pharma, which specialises in phytomedicines (herbal medicines). Developed the largest clinical research programme on Garlic in the world. Distinguished for his organisation of international symposia on Garlic.

SCIATICA. Neuralgia pain caused by irritation of, or pressure on the sciatic nerve which runs down the back and side of the leg. May arise from roots of the spinal cord, with loss of sensation, dull ache or lancinating pain anywhere in the buttocks to the big toe.

Causes. 'Slipped disc', osteoarthritis, spinal disc degeneration and effects of pressure. Where not due to any maladjustment of the lumbar vertebrae, inflammation of the nerve (neuritis) may be due to a number of causes including cold and inflammation from rheumatism, fibrositis, gout. Kidney or bowel function should be borne in

mind; any congestion may be responsible for pressure on the nerve. For this purpose a diuretic (Buchu) or evacuant (Senna) should be added to a mixture.
Alternatives. Barberry, Bearberry, Black Cohosh, Bogbean, Cayenne, Celery, Dandelion root, Dogwood (Jamaican), Lobelia, Prickly Ash bark, St John's Wort, Valerian, Wild Thyme, Wintergreen, Yarrow.
Dr John Christopher: Brigham tea, Burdock root, Chaparral, Sassafras root, Wintergreen.
David Hoffman, MNIMH: Black Cohosh, Jamaica Dogwood, St John's Wort, Yarrow.
Tea. Equal parts: Celery seeds, Buchu, Valerian. Mix. 1 heaped teaspoon to each cup boiling water; infuse 15 minutes; 1 cup thrice daily.
Barberry. Tea. 1 heaped teaspoon bark to cup cold water; steep 8 hours (or overnight); 1 cup morning and midday.
Decoction. Equal parts: Black Cohosh and Prickly Ash bark. 4 heaped teaspoons to 1 pint (500ml) water gently simmered 20 minutes. Half-1 cup thrice daily.
Oil of Juniper. 2-3 drops in teaspoon honey: morning and midday.
Tablets/capsules. Black Cohosh, Lobelia, Prickly Ash bark, Ligvites, Devil's Claw.
Alternative formulae:– *Powders*. Black Cohosh 1; Valerian 1; Juniper half. Mix. Dose: 500mg (two 00 capsules or one-third teaspoon) thrice daily.
Liquid extracts. Bogbean 2; Bearberry 1; Black Cohosh 1; Valerian 1. Dose 1-2 teaspoons in water or cup Dandelion coffee, thrice daily.
Tinctures. White Willow 2; Black Cohosh 1; Juniper half. Mix. Dose: 1-2 teaspoons in water or cup Dandelion coffee.
Practitioner. For pain. Tincture Gelsemium: 10 drops in 100ml (half cup) water. Dose: 1 teaspoon hourly.
Biostrath Willow Formula. For symptomatic relief.
Topical. Capsicum lotion, liniment or ointment. Camphorated oil. Hot bran poultice to low back. Warm water enema. Castor oil pack: Castor oil layered on cotton wool or other suitable material wrung out in hot water.
Aromatherapy. Horseradish, St John's Wort, Juniper. Two drops each essential oil to two teaspoons carrier oil. Mild analgesic to lumbar area prior to manipulation.
Diet. No tea, coffee or caffeine drinks. If feet and legs are cold use sprinkles of Cayenne pepper at table.
Supplements. Daily. Vitamin B-complex, B1 (25mg), D, E. Magnesium. Zinc.

If severe, few days bedrest. Hard board under mattress. Regulate bowels. Deal with overweight problems. Osteopathy or chiropractic for lumbar displacement.

SCLERITIS and EPISCLERITIS. Inflammation of the sclera – a tough membrane forming the outer covering of the eyeball. May be associated with rheumatoid arthritis or other collagen disorders. Sometimes accompanies polyarteritis nodosa. Eye has the appearance of raw meat.
Treatment. Internal: Formula: Echinacea 3; Goldenseal 1; Valerian half. Dosage. Powders: 500mg (two 00 capsules or one-third teaspoon). Liquid Extracts: 30-60 drops. Tinctures: 1-2 teaspoons. Thrice daily.
Topical. Goldenseal eyedrops. Witch Hazel packs kept in place by eye-goggles. Elderflowers eye douche.
Evening Primrose capsules: one 500mg, thrice daily.
Echinacea. Good responses observed.
Diet. Vitamin A foods, Cod Liver oil, Bilberries.
Supplements: daily: Vitamin A 7,500iu, Vitamin B2 10mg, Vitamin C 3g. Vitamin E 500iu, Beta-carotene. Zinc.

SCLERODERMA. A collagen disturbance. A 'hidebound' condition with rigidity and pigmented patches. Fibrosis. Begins in middle life. Female dominence. Sometimes involves gullet, lungs and heart. May not be curable. 75 per cent of patients have gullet dysfunction. Like other rheumatic conditions, scleroderma is believed to be a disorder of the immune system when that system appears to attack itself by producing damaging antibodies. A link has been suspected between silicone implants and scleroderma.
Symptoms. Shiny smooth skin, mask-like face; impaired circulation particularly of the hands.
Alternatives. Black Cohosh, Bladderwrack, Blue Cohosh, Boldo, Comfrey, Hart's Tongue Fern (Hyde), Liquorice, Prickly Ash, Blue Flag.
Decoction. Blue Cohosh 1; Prickly Ash bark 1; Liquorice half. Mix. 4 teaspoons to 1 pint (500ml) water gently simmered 20 minutes. Dose: half-1 cup thrice daily.
Powders. Mix: Black Cohosh 1; Liquorice 1; Cramp bark 1. Dose: 500mg (two 00 capsules or one-third teaspoon) thrice daily.
Tincture Colchicum BP. 5-20 drops in water morning and evening. (Practitioner use only)
Topical. Castor oil packs. Epsom salt soaks.
Diet. Low fat, low salt, high fibre, seafood, egg-yolk. Abundance of green salads: lettuces, radishes, watercress etc, oily fish.
Supplements. Daily. Vitamin B-complex, Vitamin B6, Vitamin C (200mg), Vitamin E (400iu) to increase iron absorption by the thyroid gland. Zinc 15mg.
Note. The majority of patients with scleroderma have Raynaud's disease – but the reverse is not true.

SCREENING. Before acceptance, a manufacturer will rigorously screen ingredients for herbicides, pesticides, bacteria, chemical fertilisers, heavy metals, pollutants and contaminants generally, including radiation. Animal testing and the use of parts of dead animals is discouraged.

SCROFULA. Tuberculosis of the lymphatic glands in the neck.
Causes: poor nutrition, lack of fresh air and exercise, unhealthy living conditions; in young people. The ancients blamed the spread of scrofula on pigs, it being observed in swine. It was called King's Evil because Edward the Confessor pretended to cure it by touch. Samuel Johnson was touched by Queen Anne in 1712.
Symptoms. Swollen glands of the neck.
Alternatives. *Decoction*. Irish Moss. Half a cup freely.
Tablets/capsules. Echinacea, Blue Flag, Iceland Moss.
Formula. Echinacea 2; Comfrey 2; Irish Moss 1; Blue Flag 1; Cloves half. Dose. Powders 500mg (two 00 capsules or one-third teaspoon). Liquid extract: 1 teaspoon. Tinctures: 2 teaspoons. Thrice daily in water or honey.
Devil's bit and Burdock leaf tea. Equal parts: 1oz to 1 pint boiling water; infuse 15 minutes. 1 cup freely. "I have known this to cure hundreds of cases." (*John Wesley, preacher*)
Dr Christopher. Fomentation of swollen glands with 1 part Lobelia and 3 parts Marshmallow root in 2 pints boiling water.
Dr A.L. Coffin. Bran and Slippery Elm poultice; apply cold, renew when dry.
Dr Madaus, Cologne, West Germany. Swollen lymph nodes – Agnus Castus. With chronic nasal discharge – Garlic.
Arthur Barker. Liquid Extracts: Black root 1 fl oz; Couchgrass half a fluid ounce; Lungwort half a fluid ounce; Marigold half a fluid ounce; Extract Liquorice 1 fl oz; water to 8oz. Dose: 2 teaspoons after meals.
Comfrey. Potential benefit outweighs possible risk.
Diet. Low salt and fats. Abundant green salads and fresh fruit.
Vitamins. A. B-complex. C.
Treatment by or in liaison with a general medical practitioner.

SCURVY. Deficiency disease from lack of Vitamin C. If untreated leads on to severe constitutional weakness with bone defects and capillary bleeding.
Symptoms. Irritability, fatigue, joint pains, weight loss, spontaneous bruising, bleeding of gums, cuts, wounds refuse to heal. In infancy, limbs are limp because of bone pain; there may be anaemia with fever, anorexia and irritability.
Alternatives. *Traditional teas (UK)*. Vervain, Nettles, Clivers. (*John Wesley*)
Decoction. Burdock root. Yellow Dock root.
Tincture Guaiacum. 2-3 drops in water or honey thrice daily.
Tincture Myrrh. 3-5 drops in water or honey, thrice daily.
Diet. High protein. Abundant citrus fruits.
Vitamins. A. Folic acid. Vitamin C (1-3g daily).
Minerals. Iron.

SCURVY GRASS. Spoonwort. *Cochlearia officinalis L. German*: Loffelkraut. *French*: Cranson officinal. *Spanish*: Coclearia. *Dutch*: Lepelkruid. *Italian*: Coclearia. *Part used*: herb.
Constituents: glucosinolates.
Action. Antiseptic, aperient, anti-scurvy, diuretic.
Uses. Once in demand by seamen for prevention of scurvy before discovery of Vitamin C. Acne, bleeding of the gums and other Vitamin C-deficient symptoms.
Preparation. *Tea*. 1 heaped teaspoon to each cup boiling water; infuse 10 minutes. Dose: half-1 cup thrice daily. Tea also used as a wash for mouth ulcers.

SEA HOLLY. Eryngo. *Eryngium maritimum L. German*: Mannstreu. *French*: Panicaut. *Spanish*: Eringe. *Italian*: Cardio stellario. Dried root.
Keynotes: kidneys and bladder.
Constituents: coumarins, saponins, flavonoids, plant acids.
Action. Stone-solvent, anti-inflammatory, expectorant, antispasmodic, galactagogue, diaphoretic, diuretic (herb).
Uses. Stone in the bladder, gravel, blood in the urine, renal colic. Enlarged prostate gland; to promote menses; whooping cough (expectorant).
Combines well with Horsetail (equal parts) for blood in the urine.
Preparations. Average dose, 2-4 grams or fluid equivalent. Thrice daily.
Decoction. Shredded root: 1 teaspoon to each cup water simmered half a minute; infuse 10 minutes. Dose, 1 cup.
Liquid Extract: half-1 teaspoon in water.
Diet. Boiled root is an article of diet. GSL

SEAWEED AND SARSAPARILLA. Well-known traditional combination. Blood purifier for toxaemia and debility. Iodine content offers support for the thyroid gland. Once taken at conclusion of winter as "spring medicine". Believed to protect the body from mild radiation.
Sports people: two tablets at meals as part of fitness routine.

SEBORRHOEA. Mild inflammation of the scalp, more unsightly than serious. When sebaceous glands become over-active or attacked by bacteria dry scales fall like frost. Soaked with serum, scales itch and irritate. Regarded as an effort by nature to eliminate cellulites (toxic

wastes) through the skin. Sometimes a constitutional problem. Cradle cap is a crusting of the scalp of infants. Hydrochloric acid deficiency frequently a factor.
Alternatives. Betony, Blue Flag root, Burdock, Chamomile, Echinacea, Gotu Kola, Nettles, Poke root, Quassia chips, Rosemary, Sarsaparilla, Southernwood, Yellow Dock.
Tea. Formula. Equal parts Alfalfa, Nettles, Rosemary. 1 heaped teaspoon to each cup boiling water; infuse 15 minutes. 1 cup 2-3 times daily.
Decoction. Equal parts: Burdock root, Dandelion, Yellow Dock root. Mix. 1oz (30g) to 1 pint (500ml) water gently simmered 20 minutes. Dose: half-1 cup thrice daily before meals.
Tablets/capsules. Blue Flag root, Echinacea, Poke root, Sarsaparilla.
Formula. Equal parts: Blue Flag root, Burdock root, Rosemary. Dose – Powders: 250mg (one 00 capsule or one-sixth teaspoon). Liquid Extract: 15-30 drops. Tincture: 30-60 drops. Thrice daily.
Burdock powder. Two 270mg capsules, thrice daily. (*Arkocaps*)
Topical. Wash with Periwinkle (Vinca major) tea or Quillaia bark decoction.
Scalp-rub: Lotion – 1 part Castor oil to 10 parts Vodka.
Dr D.C. Jarvis, Vermont, USA. Corn oil, internally and externally. Wash with Rosemary tea.
Diet. See: DIET – SKIN DISEASES.
Supplements. Betaine hydrochloride. B-complex 50mg; Biotin 3mg; morning and evening. Selenium 200mcg; Zinc 15mg; once daily.

SEDATIVES. 'Calmer-downers'. Herbs to relax the central nervous system: to reduce nerve tension, excitability, hyperactivity; to subdue restlessness and induce sleep. All diaphoretics, anxiolytics and antispasmodics are relaxants. Often of value in the treatment of mental illness. Teas, powders or tinctures of the following.
Balm, Betony, Black Cohosh, Blue Cohosh, Boldo, Catmint, Chamomile, Condurango, Cowslip, Dogwood (Jamaican), Evening Primrose, Ginseng (American), Hops, Kava Kava, Ladyslipper, Lavender, Lime flower, Lobelia, Mistletoe, Motherwort, Passion flower, Pulsatilla, Rosemary, Skullcap, St John's Wort, Skunk Cabbage, Valerian, Vervain, Wild Cherry bark, Wild Lettuce, Wild Yam.
Practitioner use: Gelsemium, Stramonium.
Brain: Passion flower, Skullcap, Valerian.
Bronchi, lungs and throat: Lobelia, Elecampane, Ephedra.
Liver: Boldo, Black root.
Heart: Motherwort, Poke root
Intestines: Senna, Wild Yam.
Kidneys: Clivers, Corn Silk.
Colon: Wild Yam.
Meningeal: Black Cohosh.
Muscles: Cramp bark.
Stomach: Chamomile, Hops.
Skin: Elderflowers, Catmint.
Nerves: see: ANTISPASMODICS.
Genito-urinary: Blue Cohosh.
Spine: Ladyslipper, St John's Wort.
Oats (*Avena sativa*) is a mild relaxing nervine but not for those who are gluten-intolerant.

SEIZURE. Convulsions or loss of consciousness caused by rupture of a blood vessel or spasm in the brain. See: STROKE.

SELENIUM. Essential nutrient. Occurs naturally in the soil but distributed unevenly throughout the world. RDA 0.05 to 0.2mg.
Deficiency. Anaemia, heart disease, liver disorders. The correlation between low serum levels and cancer is impressive. In communities where food and water are low in this element high rates of cancer and heart disease are observed. Smoker's lung.
Body effects. Promotes activity of blood cells, red and white. Arrests ageing process. Scavenges unwanted free-radicals. Enhances body's self-healing ability. Health of heart and thyroid gland.
Sources. Wholegrain flour and cereals, fish, egg-yolk, meats, liver, kidneys, nuts, mushrooms, asparagus, onions.
Herbs: Garlic, Horsetail, Horseradish, Kelp.
Note. Prescribed as an anti-oxidant to detoxify the body against poisonous metals of cadmium, lead and mercury.

SELF-HEAL. Prunella vulgaris. Leaves and young shoots. Much used in Chinese Barefoot Medicine as a cooling herb for fevers.
Constituents: Vitamins A, B, C, K, flavonoids, rutin.
Action. Leaves and stems: antibacterial, astringent, diuretic, hypotensive (reduces blood pressure). Flower spikes are liver-restorative. Hypotensive. Anti-tumour. Powerful antioxidant.
Uses. Injuries, wounds with bleeding. Haematuria (blood in the urine). High blood pressure.
Preparations. *Tea*: 1 teaspoon dried herb, or 2 teaspoons fresh herb to each cup boiling water; infuse 10 minutes. Dose: 1 cup 2-3 times daily. Professional opinion should be sought for blood in the urine and serious injury. The tea is used also as a gargle and mouth wash for laryngitis.
Eyewash: 5-10 drops fresh juice in eyebath half-filled with milk; used as a douche for conjunctivitis or eye injury.
Ointment: for bleeding piles.
Poultice: pulp of washed fresh leaves for healing of wounds. GSL

SENEGA. Snake root. *Polygala senega L.* *German*: Senega-Kreuzblume. *French*: Polygale.

Spanish: Serpentaria Senegalés. *Italian*: Poligala della Virginia. *Keynote*: respiratory organs. Practitioner use only.
Constituents: phenolic acids, triterpene saponins.
Action. Expectorant, diaphoretic, emetic, anti-inflammatory.
Uses. Bronchitis, bronchial asthma, croup. Dr Tennant, Scottish physician, witnessed recovery from the bite of a rattlesnake after use of this plant, and used it with success for pleurisy and pneumonia. Boiling water destroys its properties. It is usually given in Liquid Extract or Tincture form. Psoriasis, eczema.
Preparations. *Liquid Extract BPC (1968)*. 0.3 to 1ml (5-15 drops).
Tincture, BPC (1968). Dose, 2.5 to 5ml.
Powder. 260mg, capsules. 2 capsules thrice daily between meals. (*Arkocaps*)
Precaution. Overdosing causes vomiting. GSL

SENILITY. See: DEMENTIA.

SENNA LEAF. *Cassia senna L.* (*Cassia angustifolia*) (*Cassia acutifolia*). Action and uses, same as for Senna pods.
Preparations. One dose daily, usually at bedtime.
Dried leaves. Half to 1 teaspoon in each cup boiling water; infuse 15 minutes. Dose, half to 1 cup.
Liquid Extract BHP (1983). 1:1 in 25 per cent alcohol. Dose 0.5-2ml.
Powder. Three 220mg capsules morning and evening. (*Arkocaps*)
Store out of the light in airtight containers. GSL

SENNA PODS. Tinnivelly (*Cassia angustifolia*). Alexandrian (*Cassia acutifolia*). *German*: Sennacassie. *French*: Cassia séné. *Spanish*: Stat. *Italian*: Sena di Levante. *Iranian*: Sona-mukhi. *Indian*: Shon-pat. *Arabian*: Pero-sama-e-Hindi. *Chinese*: Chüeh-ming. *Keynote*: constipation.
Constituents: Senna is one of a group of remedies containing anthraquinones responsible for its action.
Action. Stimulant laxative, anti-tumour.
Uses. Constipation: a little Ginger prevents griping. Well-suited for confined bowels of fevers. Suitable in presence of gall bladder disorders. As chronic constipation is likely to be related to a disorder elsewhere in the body, the original cause must be found and given priority treatment. To reduce secretion of nursing mother's milk.
Preparations. *Tea*: dried pods (Alexandrian) 3-6 pods. (Tinnevelly) 4-12 pods. Steep in cup warm water overnight. Children 6-10 years: half adult dosage.
Liquid Extract BPC (1973): dose 0.5-2ml in water.
Senokot. Gentle family laxative. (*Reckitt & Colman*) Granules and tablets. Dose: 1 to 2 heaped 5ml spoonfuls of granules, or 2 to 4 tablets.
ESCOP European monograph. Indications: Constipation and all cases in which easy defecation with soft faeces is desirable, e.g. in cases of anal fissures, haemorrhoids and after rectal and abdominal surgery, as well as for bowel clearance before surgery and in diagnostic investigations.
Contra-indications: inflammatory colon diseases (e.g. ulcerative colitis, Crohn's disease), ileus, appendicitis, abdominal pain of unknown origin.
Side-effects: if used correctly, side effects will be minimal. GSL

SEPSIS. Sepsis is a condition of putrefaction caused by the growth and multiplication of harmful micro-organisms at the expense of the host. Therapy may demand antibacterials, antivirals or antiseptics.
Asepsis: a condition of being free from harmful micro-organisms.
See: SEPTICAEMIA.

SEPTICAEMIA. Blood poisoning. Bacterial invasion of the blood. Blood-borne infection to parts of the body. Compare, toxaemia; pyaemia.
Symptoms. Shivering followed by high fever, skin rash, red streaks, malaise. Symptoms vary according to part of the body affected.
Alternatives. *Decoction*. Formula. Blue Flag root 1; Burdock 2; Yellow Dock 2; Liquorice quarter. Prepare: 1oz to 2 pints water gently simmered 20 minutes. Strain. 1 wineglass every 2 hours (acute) thrice daily (chronic).
Powders. Formula. Echinacea 2; Blue Flag 1; Cloves half. Dose: 500mg (two 00 capsules or one-third teaspoon) every 2 hours (acute), thrice daily (chronic).
Liquid extracts. Formula. Wild Indigo 1; Goldenseal half; Myrrh half. 10-30 drops in water or honey every 2 hours (acute); thrice daily (chronic).
Tinctures. Formula. Echinacea 2; Myrrh half; Goldenseal half. Dose: 1 teaspoon in water or honey every 2 hours (acute); thrice daily (chronic).
Respiratory problems: add Iceland Moss, 1 part.
External lesions. Dusting powder or poultice: Slippery Elm, Comfrey, Aloe Vera, Plantain.
Septic sore throat. Dark red swelling, pain on swallowing, swollen glands at angle of the jaw. Equal parts: Poke root and Echinacea: 15-60 drops to glass water; gargle freely.
Diet. 3-day fast, followed by lacto-vegetarian diet.
Supplements. Vitamin A, B-complex, C (1-3g daily), Vitamin E (1,000iu daily), Magnesium, Iron, Potassium.
Treatment by or in liaison with a general medical practitioner.

SERENITY TEA. *Ingredients*: Betony 3; Mistletoe 1; Skullcap 1; Vervain 1; Valerian half.

Mix. 1 heaped teaspoon to each cup boiling water; infuse 15 minutes; 1 cup as desired. To unwind after prolonged stress or promote sleep.

SERUM SICKNESS. Anaphylactic shock. A reaction with fever, glandular swelling, skin rash and joint pains following injection of serum (as in vaccination) resulting in collapse.
Treatment: *Acute*: Ephedra. (*Malcolm Stuart, Herbs and Herbalism*)
Chronic – Thuja: Liquid Extract, 3-10 drops in water thrice daily.

SESAME SEEDS. *Sesamum indicum*. Valuable source of vitamins and minerals. Contain 45 per cent protein and 55 per cent edible oil.
Action. Laxative, nutritive, demulcent, emollient, powerful antioxidant. Promotes formation of blood platelets and combats anaemia (Vitamin T). Keeping properties of the oil are due to its resistance to oxidative rancidity. The oil is believed to have anti-tumour activity.
Uses. Dietary deficiencies. Maintenance of good health. Natives who daily eat the seeds and drink the oil are noted for their endurance, mental and physical, and for longevity. Genito-urinary inflammation and infection. Tahini is made from ground Sesame seeds. Seeds used as a poultice.

SEXUAL DEBILITY. Inadequacy due to lack of vitality. Sexual vigour reflects hormonal activity. To stimulate hormonal secretion of ovaries and testes: Damiana, Gotu Kola, Siberian Ginseng, Saw Palmetto. Specific for women: Pulsatilla, Motherwort, Helonias. Low pituitary (Sarsaparilla). Low thyroid (Kelp) may require attention.
Alternatives. *Tea*. Gotu Kola: quarter of a teaspoon to each cup boiling water; infuse 5 minutes; add honey for sweetening.
Tablets/capsules. Motherwort, Siberian Ginseng. Traditional combination USA: Damiana, Kola, Saw Palmetto.
Formula. Siberian Ginseng 2; Damiana 1; Saw Palmetto 2. Dose. Powders: 500mg (two 00 capsules or one-third teaspoon). Liquid extracts: 1-2 teaspoons. Tinctures: 2-3 teaspoons. Thrice daily in water or honey.
Evening Primrose oil capsules: two 500mg capsules morning and evening.
Diet. Wholefoods, wholewheat cereals, wheatgerm, honey, eggs.
Supplements. Vitamin A. B-complex, Brewer's yeast. Vitamin E (one 500iu capsule morning and evening). Magnesium. Zinc.

SEXUAL DRIVE EXCESSIVE. Increased libido. See: SATYRIASIS (men). NYMPHOMANIA (women).

SEXUAL INTERCOURSE, PAINFUL. Dyspareunia. In the female – apply Aloe Vera gel or Olive oil to vagina. In men – the underlying cause should be treated.

SEXUALLY TRANSMITTED DISEASES (STD). The term venereal disease has been superceded by STD. Most are extremely contagious. One in four Westerners between the ages of 15 to 55 will acquire an STD sometime in his or her lifetime. A GU specialist predicts that by the year 2000 one in every three women will become infertile because of an infection of the reproductive organs. More than 25 diseases are known, many growing resistant to modern drugs. They are a frequent cause of infertility by hyperplasia which blocks the Fallopian tubes. STDs include those arising from ulcerations of mouth and pharynx transmitted by oral sex.

The spread of HIV infection and the development of AIDS have given a new dimension to STD diseases, for AIDS is now a global problem introducing a new era in world history.
Treatment. Over the past 100 years medical literature contains abundant references to the efficacy of deep-acting plant medicines that inhibit growth of organisms responsible for gonorrhoea, syphilis, genital herpes and trichomoniasis.
Powerful alteratives: Goldenseal, Sarsaparilla, Wild Indigo, Poke root, Echinacea, that chemically alter vaginal and urethral mucus.
Notification. All STDs are notifiable and to be treated by an infectious diseases specialist.

See under specific diseases: GONORRHOEA, SYPHILIS, GENITAL HERPES, CHANCRE, CRABS, INFERTILITY (from STD). NON-SPECIFIC URETHRITIS, AIDS, HEPATITIS B, SCABIES, LICE.

SHAKERS, The. Their proprietary medicines.

In 1774 a small band of religious enthusiasts emigrated from England to America, eventually settling near Albany. Because of their inspired ritual dancing, they had first been called 'Shakers' in England while still associated with the dissident Quaker group called 'Shaking Quakers'. The handwritten volumes of medical recipes for everyday use in Shaker villages contain many Thomsonian remedies. From the beginning, the self-sufficient Shaker communes prepared all their own remedies. Then, in order to make maximum use of their land and labour, several villages began to sell herbs and their seeds in the first decade of the 19th century. They sold a wide variety of at least 200 botanical simples, sometimes packaged dry in tins, cardboard cylinders, or paper-wrapped 'bricks' of pressed plant material; sometimes as solutions in glass jars or as ointments in ceramic jars.

Brown's pure extract of English Valerian (also called Shaker Anodyne) was made by the commune at Enfield and was purported to be a "gentle stimulant . . . but without narcotic effect", and that in large doses it could control nervous symptoms, although it was "an uncertain remedy".

Several Shaker communities relied on "brand-name" remedies to stabilise their incomes. One such remedy was Dr J. Corbett's Compound Concentrated Syrup of Sarsaparilla, an aqueous mixture of Sarsaparilla root, Pipsissewa, Yellow Dock root, Dandelion, Thorough Wort, Black Cohosh, Elderflowers, Epsom salts, Juniper berries, Blue Gentian, Pokeweed root, sugar and alcohol, which was promoted as a blood purifier. Another was Mother Seigel's Curative Syrup which contained, on a weight/volume basis in simple syrup:

Aloes	1.25%
Black Cohosh root	1.39%
Butternut root	0.87%
Capsicum	0.14%
Colocynth extract	0.28%
Culver root	0.87%
Dandelion root	0.87%
Gentian root	0.28%
Pipsissewa	0.69%
Poke root	0.87%
Salt	1.67%
Sassafras	1.39%
Stillingia root	0.87%

Advertisement for the syrup said that it contained 5 alkaloids: a soporific, a diaphoretic, a diuretic, a laxative that acted on the liver, and an alterative that acted on "the glands" to minimise both the acidity and the alkalinity of the body's fluids. Lyman Brown's Seven Barks contained: Black Cohosh and Bloodroot (expectorant and muscle toner), Blue Flag Iris and Butternut (to clear the bowels), Goldenseal and May Apple (a kidney remedy), Lady's Slipper (nerve calmer) and Sassafras (for the skin and blood). (*Bulletin of the History of Medicine 1991 65 (2) 162-84*)

SHELL FISH POISONING. Stomach and bowel disorder due to microbial pollution of shellfish through direct discharge of raw sewerage into rivers or the sea. Saxotoxins, present in some planktons, may be taken into the body from cockles, mussels and scallops. Enteric fever.
Treatment: as for TYPHOID FEVER.

SHELLARD, E.J., BPharm, PhD(Lond), Hon DSC (Warsaw Medical Academy), FPS, CChem, FRSC, FLS. Emeritis Professor of Pharmacognosy, University of London. Important scientific papers on herbal medicine including: *Some Pharmacognostical Implications of Herbal Medicine and Other Forms of Medicine Involving Plants*. Scientific advisor to The British Herbal Pharmacopoeia.

SHEPHERD'S PURSE. *Capsella bursa-pastoris L. German*: Hirtenfaschel. *French:* Bourse de Pasteur. *Spanish*: Borsa de Pastor. *Italian*: Borsa di Pastore. Dried herb.
Constituents: histamine, tyramine, flavonoids, plant acids.
Action. Haemostatic, urinary antiseptic, diuretic, astringent, hypotensive, emmenagogue, anti-uric acid, circulatory stimulant.
Uses. Blood in the urine, from the urinary tract or from the womb. Excessive bleeding from the womb; fibroids to control bleeding. Red 'brick-dust' in the urine. Leucorrhoea. Catarrh of the bladder. Irritable bowel. Vomiting of blood as from the gullet, stomach or duodenum. Once used as a substitute for quinine for malaria and other protozoal fevers. Nosebleeds.

Combines well with Goldenseal for internal bleeding.
Preparations. Average dose, 1-4 grams or fluid equivalent. Thrice daily.
Tea. 1 heaped teaspoon to each cup boiling water; infuse 15 minutes. Dose, half-1 cup.
Liquid Extract BHP (1983) 1:1 in 25 per cent alcohol: dose, 15-30 drops.
Tincture. 1 part herb to 5 parts 45 per cent alcohol; steep 8 days, shaking daily. Dose, 1-2 teaspoons in water.
Rademacher's Continental Tincture: 20-30 drops. 3-4 times daily.

Not used during pregnancy. GSL

SHIGELLA. See: DYSENTERY, BACILLARY.

SHIITAKE MUSHROOM. *Lentinus edodes*. Eaten as food and medicine in the Far East and South America. Old Chinese medicine.
Constituents: triterpenes, polysaccharides. Contains lentinan, the most powerful natural immune stimulant and restorative known; also inteferon inducer. (*Paul Callinan MSc, ND, medical scientist*)
Action. Antiviral. Anticancer. Cholesterol-lowering.
Uses. Gastric and colorectal cancer. Said to help prevent AIDS infection. Inhibits metastasis with little toxic side-effect. Arthritis. Myalgic encephalomyelitis (ME). Lessens side-effects of radiation and chemotherapy.

SHINGLES. See: HERPES ZOSTER.

SHOCK. Two types. (1) Emotional, caused by sudden fear; (2) physical (road accident, electrocution, etc). Blood supply falls below a certain level. May follow trauma or surgery, leading to a fall in heart output. For emotional shock: see NERVOUS SHOCK.
Symptoms. Cold sweat, rapid pulse, breathlessness, anxiety, weakness, restlessness, extreme thirst, sweating, shivering, giddiness, confusion,

drowsiness.
Treatment. Bedrest with induced warmth. Elevate foot of bed. Avoid alcohol. To boost blood circulation: few grains Cayenne pepper or 3-5 drops tincture Capsicum or "Life Drops" in a cup of tea. Give abundant fluids: herb teas – Alfalfa, Sage, Ginger, etc.
To restore blood level in absence of saline drip: strong decoction (or powders), any one – Irish Moss, Iceland Moss, Comfrey tea, Slippery Elm.
Inhalation, of Camphorated oil or Oil of Rosemary.
Practitioner: Ephedra.
With nervous prostration: Skullcap tea.
Severe cases: strong coffee enema.
Diet. High protein.
Vitamins. B12. C. PABA.
Minerals. Calcium. Manganese, Iron.

SHOULDER, PAINFUL. See: BURSITIS.

SIALAGOGUE. A herb to increase production of saliva, and assist digestion of starches.
Blood root, Blue Flag root, Cardamom, Cayenne, Centuary, Gentian, Ginger, Lobelia, Mouse Ear, Prickly Ash, Quassia, Queen's Delight, Senega.

SICK BUILDING SYNDROME. A condition responsible for sickness absence among employees working in air-conditioned offices and inadequate ventilation. May include chemical hazards from solvents used in factories, photocopies, cleaning fluids, etc. (*Guy's Hospital, London Report*) The radiation factor surrounding computer display screens contribute to a polluted atmosphere. *BMJ. Vol 290, 321.20* refers to environmental respiratory and other related ailments.
Symptoms. Skin rash, headache, dizziness, fatigue, cough, irritability, itching, forgetfulness. Eye, nose and throat irritation, dry throat. Prone to colds and flu.
Alternatives. *Teas*. Alfalfa Ginseng, Sage, Chamomile, Thyme, Buckwheat.
Tablets, Powders, Liquid extracts, or Tinctures: Echinacea, Goldenseal, Myrrh.
Irish Moss: with loss of weight.
Iceland Moss: chesty cough.
Gargle and mouth wash. 3-5 drops, Tincture Myrrh or Tincture Goldenseal in glass of water, morning and evening.
Presence of simple pot plants: Chrysanthemums, English Ivy, Peace plant and especially the Spider plant: for removing fumes of chemicals and solvents from the atmosphere. A number of plants display curled and dying leaves or show abnormal growth when exposed to chemicals that give people headaches and dizziness.
Preventative. Suggested. 2-3 Garlic capsules at night.
Note. Cleaning air-conditioning plant brings no improvement in symptoms, but there is a marked reduction when chairs and carpets are steam-cleaned and furniture and papers dusted.

SICK ROOM SPRAY. Oil of Lavender 50 drops. Oil of Eucalyptus 20 drops. Vodka to 8oz. Dissolve. Use as spray, OR: place an electric light bulb in the fluid to produce slow evaporisation of 20/40 drops in a little water.

SIDE EFFECTS. Unwanted effect. Adverse effects seldom follow moderate use but may occur where used in excessive doses or for long periods. Examples include Liquorice; though helpful to raise a low blood pressure, may cause retention of fluid in the tissues. Ginseng is capable of producing high blood pressure if taken in excess. Irritation of the stomach may follow Juniper oil. Being abortifacients, Broom, Devil's Claw and Pennyroyal oil should not be taken in pregnancy. Fresh Feverfew may blister the tongue in sensitives.
The Committee of Safety of Medicines requires doctors to notify the Adverse Reactions Monitoring Unit of the Department of Health under a Yellow-Card scheme of any adverse reactions to over-the-counter alternative medicines. (*CSM., Current Problems 1986, No 16:477*)
A few herbs are regarded as having subtle toxicity such as Comfrey (taken internally) which contains minute amounts of pyrrolizidine alkaloids said to be toxic to the liver in animals. Evidence of toxicity of most herbs in general use is inconclusive. See: WHOLE PLANT.

SIDS. Sudden infant death syndrome. Also known as cot (or crib) death: a respiratory disorder affecting some infants under the age of six months.
At risk: boys of low birth weight.
During sleep, breathing of infants is irregular, sometimes completely arrested. Death may occur if breathing ceases for more than 20 seconds. Stress-induced deaths such as those of chickens occur in other species. Livers of such infants and chickens are found to be low in biotin. Almost all suffer a lack of oxygen. Cyanotic episodes.
Most of such deaths are believed to be in bottle-fed babies. Breast feeding appears to be a protective factor. Biotin is seldom added to baby foods. Biotin: low levels in stillborn children. Maternal smoking may double the risk of SIDS. (*Swedish study*)
Magnesium deficiency in the pregnant mother is another factor, causing histamine shock leading to SIDS. It is now known that such children also have low levels of an essential fatty acid DGLA in the liver. This substance is necessary for production of 1-prostaglandins that are biologically important. Baby foods are low in essential fatty acids and breast feeding offers a natural

alternative.

Fifty per cent of infants show symptoms before death. Where an infant presents with a 'cold' or evidence of excessive fluid loss, dehydration, usually from diarrhoea, a weak infusion of German Chamomile should be given in teaspoon doses, freely. Fracture an Evening Primrose capsule (for DGLA) and squeeze contents into the mouth. Biotin should be given to every mother and infant after birth.

Babies should be kept away from smoke. Mothers should not smoke from before conception until at least a year after birth. Parents should lay infants to sleep on their backs which has been shown to reduce the risk of cot death. Deaths are higher among those laid to rest on their fronts.

Supplementation. Magnesium to make good deficiency and sustain the heart.

Supportive. Gentle cranial osteopathy in first few weeks of life.

Note. Babies should be covered at night with blankets rather than a duvet. Babies put to bed heavily wrapped and in rooms where heating is on all night are more likely to be victims of the syndrome. Over-heating is a key risk factor.

SILICA. Quartz, pure flint, silicon dioxide. An outstanding example of how a mineral can be therapeutically useless in its natural form yet a powerful immune enhancer when a constituent of a plant. An element that not only imparts rigidity and skeletal stability to grasses, grains and bamboos of the plant world but to cellular tissue of the human body. Traces of silica are found in the blood, skin and nails, all of which are supplemented when plants containing the element are consumed. Silicic acid increases production of white cells; the acid is released and becomes soluble in decoction.

Silica-rich plants promote pus formation and assist the immune system to cleanse the body of self-poisoning toxins or infection. Professor Schultz, Griefswald University, discovered silica in the lens and other structures of the eye.

All tissues depend on silicea for elasticity. As a calcium fixer any deficiency spells an increase in body calcium with consequent loss of elasticity. It ensures rigidity of the spine. The bamboo contains 70 per cent silica and is an example of resilience under tension. It is essential for the healing of wounds and bones. Studies show that coronary thrombosis may follow silica deficiency due to loss of elasticity in arterial walls.

Source plants: Alfalfa, Oatstraw, Horsetail, Kelp.

Silica tea. 1 heaped teaspoon Horsetail to each cup water; gently simmered 15 minutes. Dose: 1 cup, cold, 1-3 times daily.

SILICOSIS. A pneumoconiosis from inhalation of quartz dust by miners. Fibrous nodules form on the surface of the lung, developing slowly over 5-25 years. Irritation is believed to be chemical in nature, with collagen formation. Acute infections such as influenza cause these nodules to coalesce and form massive fibrosis.

Symptoms. Breathlessness, chest pains, hoarseness, sleeplessness, poor appetite; cough (dry) is not common. Later stage: spitting of blood, bronchiectasis. Fever rare except from infection. TB should also be suspected.

Treatment. No cure is possible. Expectorants encourage, through expectoration, elimination of dust particles. Demulcent nutrients are usually cell-proliferants and promote tissue renewal: Irish Moss, Comfrey, Fenugreek seeds. Good responses have been observed from Elecampane leaves and root.

Comfrey. Potential benefit outweighs possible risk.

Irish Moss. 2 teaspoons to half a pint water. Simmer gently 20 minutes. Do not strain. Eat with honey, freely, with the aid of a spoon. Comfrey root and Fenugreek seeds prepared and eaten in the same way.

Tablets/capsules. Lobelia. Garlic. Slippery Elm. Fenugreek.

Formula. Powders. Pleurisy root 1; Lobelia 1; Irish Moss 2. Dose: 750mg (three 00 capsules or half a teaspoon) thrice daily.

Alternative formula. Liquid extracts, tinctures. Pleurisy root 1; Lobelia 1; Yarrow 2. Dose: Liquid extract: 1-4ml. Tincture: 2-5ml.

External. Chest rub with Olbas, Camphorated, Rosemary or Cedarwood oils.

Inhalant: see: FRIAR'S BALSAM.

Diet. Low fat, low salt, high fibre.

SILVER BIRCH. See: BIRCH, EUROPEAN.

SILVERWEED. *Potentilla anserina L. German*: Wilder Rainfarn. *French*: Potenille. *Italian*: Potentilla anserina. Leaves, flowers.

Constituents: bitters, tannins.

Action. Anti-inflammatory, astringent, antispasmodic (mild), odontalgic, diuretic, digestive, haemostatic. Used by old gardeners for cuts, wounds and as a local anaesthetic.

Uses. Pyrrhoea, gingivitis, sore throat (mouth wash). Kidney and bladder disorders, gravel, stone in the bladder. Painful menstruation. Inflamed irritable bowel, colic, diarrhoea that defies other agents. Stomach and intestines: inflammation of the rectum, bleeding piles, (tea used as a lotion). Leg ulcers, dusted with powder. Tetanus (*French traditional*). Strong tea used as a lotion.

Preparations. *Tea*: 1-2 teaspoons to each cup boiling water; infuse 10 minutes, strain. Dose, half-1 cup, thrice daily.

Liquid Extract: 30-60 drops, in water, thrice daily.

Compress: pulp of fresh leaves for wounds that refuse to heal.

SINUSITIS. Inflammation of mucous membrane of cavities within the skull bones that connect with the nose. Sinuses become blocked with excessive secretion from colds, fevers (influenza, etc), allergy, dental infections or nasal obstruction (polyp, deviated septum, etc). May result from chronic catarrh. Cause may be smoking or insufficient Vitamin A. Infection may be picked up in aircraft due to an unhealthy mixture of air of poor quality on board.
Symptoms. Swollen membrane or obstruction causes patient to breathe through the mouth. Muco-purulent discharge. Loss of sense of smell, headache, tenderness of sinuses.
Treatment. De-congestant nasal drops. Nasal vasoconstrictors to promote drainage.
Of Therapeutic Value. Chamomile, Elderflowers, Eucalyptus, Eyebright, Garlic, Goldenseal, Hyssop, Myrrh, Lobelia, Thyme, Plantain, Peppermint, Poke root, Thyme, Wild Indigo, Plantain, Lavender (anti-microbial).
Yarrow tea. 1-2 teaspoons to cup boiling water; infuse 5 minutes. Half-1 cup thrice daily.
Tablets/capsules. Garlic, Lobelia, Poke root, Goldenseal.
Powders. Combine equal parts: Goldenseal, Myrrh, Lobelia. 250mg (thrice daily).
Practitioner. Tinctures: equal parts: Poke root, Wild Indigo, Ephedra. 15-30 drops in water or honey thrice daily.
Fenugreek seeds. Tea: or pulverise seeds in a blender and sprinkle on cereals or salads.
Dr A. Vogel. Combination: Butterburr, Iceland Moss, Plantain.
Aromatherapy: dilute Chamomile oil gently massaged over bridge of the nose and cheekbones.
Nasal snuff. Powders of Myrrh, Bayberry or Blood root.
Decongestants. Olbas oil. Oils of Peppermint or Eucalyptus.
Inhalants. Friar's balsam. Neroli oil. Olbas oil.
Diet. High protein.
Vitamins: A. C. E.
Preventative: 2-3 tablets/capsules Garlic at night.
Hopi Indian Ear Candles. For mild suction and to impart a perceptible pressure regulation on sinus cavities.

SITZ BATH. To improve function of circulatory and nervous system. It is of especial benefit to the pelvic musculature, toning and soothing smooth muscle.

The patient sits navel-deep in a hip bath, but with legs outside. Modern practice at health farms is to prepare two baths: one cold, the other with hot water. Each bath is taken alternately – 3 minutes in the hot, and 1 minute in the cold bath. The routine may be carried out one, two or three times – finishing with the cold. If a hip bath is not available, the person may sit *across* his bath in cold water, after first had a hot bath or risen from a warm bed.

To the hot bath may be added 2 pints infusion of Chamomile or Rosemary: 1oz fresh or dried leaves and flowers to each quart of boiling water.
Pelvic disorders. 1oz (30g) Herb Bearberry, or Buchu. Simmer in 2 gallons water for 20 minutes. Dilute with warm water if necessary. Strain. To be sat in, knees and chest exposed for as long as tolerated. Top-up with warm water. Of value for shingles.

SJÖGREN'S DISEASE. Auto-immune disorder affecting lachrymal and salivary glands that may be associated with rheumatoid arthritis. Swedish ophthalmologist. Has certain special characteristics: lachrymal and salivary glands lacking secretion. Dry eye, in which the person is incapable of crying. Sore throat. Lupus sometimes present. Condition also linked with allergies and EFA deficiencies.
Alternatives. Blue Cohosh, Liquorice, Mountain Grape, Poke root, Wild Yam.
Powders. Mountain Grape 2; Blue Cohosh 1; Poke root half; Ginger root quarter. Mix. Dose: 500mg (two 00 capsules or one-third teaspoon) thrice daily. In water or Fenugreek tea.
Tinctures. Elecampane 2; Mullein 1; Blue Cohosh 1; Liquorice half. Mix. Dose: 1-2 teaspoons. In water or Fenugreek tea.
Evening Primrose oil. As artificial tear-drops.
Diet. Oily fish. Oatmeal. Agar Agar.
Supplements. Vitamin A, (7,500iu). B-complex, B6. C, (500mg). Beta-carotene. Zinc.
Preventative: Garlic.

SKELETON, John, MD. Physician, USA. Pupil of English Dr Albert Coffin (1798-1866). Medical reformer. Books: *Family Medical Adviser; Plea for the Botanic Practice of Medicine; Science and Practice of Botanic Medicine; Pathology and Cure of Cholera; Epitome of the Botanic Practice of Medicine*. Editor: *Botanic Record*.

SKIN CLEAR LOTION, (*Potter's*). Deep cleansing lotion prepared from Witch Hazel leaves and Benzoin gum for external use. Antiseptic.

SKIN DISORDERS. Surface texture of the skin may undergo many different forms of change as a result of invasive microbes or toxic elimination. Most skin disorders run according to specific patterns, usually classified as follows.
1. *Disturbances of the secreting system* (sweat and sebaceous glands). Acne, wens, cysts, seborrhoea, etc.
2. *Inflammatory conditions*. Pimples, vesicles, scaly lesions, erythema, dermatitis, erysipelas, nettle rash, lichen rubor planus, eczema, syphilis, lupus vulgaris, herpes (shingles), impetigo,

pemphigus.
3. *Swellings or degeneration*. Disorders relating to growth, atrophy and wasting, hypertrophy (excessive thickening by increase in tissues), pigmentation.
4. *Neuroses*. Those brought on by nervous conditions that may cause bed sores, varicose ulcers, pruritus; or from stress conditions (Nettles).
5. *Parasitic invasion*. Ringworm, candida from vegetable moulds, scabies from mites, disorders caused by lice.

See entry for individual disorder: ATHLETE'S FOOT, DANDRUFF, DERMAGRAPHIA, DERMATITIS, FOLLICULITIS, IMPETIGO, INTERTRIGO, LICE, NETTLE RASH, PITYRIASIS, PRURIGO, PSORIASIS, RINGWORM, SCABIES, SEBORRHOEA, ZERODERMA.
Diet: See – DIET, SKIN DISORDERS.
Note. For most forms of skin disease special consideration should be given to the role of the eliminatory organs in disposing of metabolic wastes and toxins from the system. Dandelion, Blue Flag or Sarsaparilla roots are only a few agents relative to the liver, pancreas, intestines and bowel. Stimulation of the endocrine system may be necessary: Agnus Castus (female); Sarsaparilla (male).

SKIN FOOD. Most skin foods contain wool fat or coconut oil which tends to produce acne when a person may sleep with them on at night. Satisfactory substitutes are preparations of Comfrey, Irish Moss, and Almond (oil).

SKIN: HERBS FOR. See: VULNERARY.

SKULLCAP. Quaker Bonnet. Mad dog. *Scutellaria lateriflora L. German*: Kappenhelmkraut. *French*: Scutellaire. *Spanish*: Craneo gorra. *Italian*: Scutellaria maggiore. *Chinese*: Huang-ch'in. *Part used*: dried herb. *Keynote*: nerves. One of the most widely used of herbal medicines.
Constituents: scutellarin, a flavonoid glycoside, oil, tannins, iridoids.
Action: antispasmodic, anticonvulsive, relaxing nervine, brain and CNS vasodilator, hydrophobic, sedative.
Uses. Benzodiazepine addiction, to assist withdrawal. Pressive headache, migraine, premenstrual tension, disturbed sleep, nervous stress following bereavement or shock.

"Its calming effects on the nervous system are widely known." (*Dr John Clarke*)

Supporting nervine for workaholics compelled to work long hours with resulting mental exhaustion.

"Depression of nervous and vital powers after long illness, over-exercise, over-study, long-continuing and exhausting labours." (*Dr C. Hale*)

Dr Compton-Burnett's chief remedy for nervous debility following influenza. Of value in myalgic encephalomyelitis, aftermath of stroke, epilepsy.
Mad-dog bites: old traditional remedy for rabies.
Preparations. Average dose, 1-2 grams, or equivalent in fluid form. Thrice daily.
Tea: half-1 teaspoon to cup boiling water; infuse 15 minutes. Dose, half-1 cup.
Liquid Extract BHP (1983), 1:1 in 25 per cent alcohol; dose 1-2ml (15-30 drops) in water.
Tincture BHP (1983), 1:5 in 45 per cent alcohol; dose 2-4ml (30-60 drops) in water.
Traditional combination: Skullcap, Valerian and Mistletoe (equal parts). Herb, root and leafy twigs: 1 heaped teaspoon to each cup boiling water. Dose: half-1 cup. Also combines well with Hops and Passion flower for hyperactivity; and with Valerian for hysteria, epilepsy and drug addiction.

Large doses said to cause giddiness. GSL

SKUNK CABBAGE. *Symplocarpus foetidus L. German*: Drackenqurz. *French*: Draconte. *Italian*: Dragonzio. Roots, rhizomes.
Constituents: resin, essential oil.
Action. Antispasmodic, antitussive, anti-fever, diaphoretic, mild sedative BHP (1983), expectorant.
Uses. Bronchial asthma, dry cough, whooping cough, early stage of fevers.
Preparations. Average dose, half to 1 gram, or equivalent. Thrice daily.
Powder. 250mg (one 00 capsule or one-sixth teaspoon).
Liquid Extract. 0.5 to 1ml.
Tincture BHP (1983) 1 part to 10 parts 45 per cent alcohol; dose, 2 to 4ml (15-60 drops).

SLEEP APNOEA. See: SNORING.

SLEEP – PROFOUND. See: NARCOLEPSY.

SLEEP, TALKING IN. *Wessex traditional* Rue leaves steeped in vinegar: 2-3 teaspoons at night.

SLEEP WALKING. Somnabolism. Mugwort tea: 2 teaspoons to each cup boiling water; infuse 15 minutes. Drink half-1 cup warm at bedtime. (*Dr Wm Boericke*)

SLEEPING SICKNESS. African trypanosomiasis. Caused by trypanosomes (protozoans) transmitted by the bite of a tsetse fly. Patient should be under the supervision of a specialist in tropical diseases. Deficiency of Selenium is a feature of the disease.
Formula. Prickly Ash 2; Mountain Grape 1; Wild Indigo 1. Dose. Powders: quarter to half a teaspoon. Liquid Extracts: 30-60 drops. Tinctures: 1-2 teaspoons. In water or honey every 3 hours.
Selenium: 200mcg daily.

SLEEPLESSNESS. See: INSOMNIA.

SLIPPED DISC. Intervertebral disc prolapse. Herniated nucleus pulposus. An acute lumbago and sciatica due to weakening of the annulus fibrosus and bursting through of nuclear material with severe nerve root pain. Usually one-sided.
Causes: heavy lifting, bending, unequal stresses, twisting.
Symptoms. Numbness of low back, severe muscle spasm, inability to stand erect, pain on sneezing and coughing. Nerve tension followed by exhaustion. Associated with pains in calf, sole or knee.
Diagnosis: poor ankle jerks. Straight leg raising is restricted. Loss of reflex.
Treatment. *Prickly Ash*. Thrice daily.
Liquid Extract BHP (1983): 1-3ml.
Tincture BHP (1983): 2-5ml.
Topical. Papaya poultice. No hot fomentations or application of heat. Three-tincture liniment: equal parts, Arnica, Calendula and Hypericum.
X-ray confirms. Chiropractic or osteopathy when acute stage subsides.

SLIPPERY ELM. Red elm. *Ulmus fulva*, Michaux. *German*: Ulme. *French*: Orme. *Italian*: Olmo. Contains a mucilage, chiefly galactose. Dried bark after peeling. One of the most widely used herbal agents.
Action. Soothing demulcent, nutrient, expectorant, antitussive. Topically as an emollient. The addition of a few grains of powder or drops of Tincture of Myrrh enhances its antiseptic and healing action. Long-lasting antacid barrier. Contains an abundance of mucilage.
Uses. Inflammation or ulceration anywhere along the digestive tract. Gastric or duodenal ulcer, acute or chronic dyspepsia and wind, diverticulosis, colitis, before a journey to allay travel sickness, summer diarrhoea in children (also enema), irritable bowel, before festivities to avoid 'hangover'.

Its blanketing action protects the gastric mucosa from the erosive effects of too much acid. Gastro-oesophageal reflux is one of the most common causes of dyspepsia; Slippery Elm powder protects the oesophageal mucosa and relieves pain of indigestion. Lasting protection against acid reflux. Suppresses acid production during the night when mucosal damage may occur. Together with carminatives such as Chamomile or Ginger it allays abdominal distension, reflux oesophagitis and hiatus hernia.

Of value during convalescence. Cachexia and wasting diseases to increase body weight. Boils, abscesses or discharging wounds, varicose ulcer (poultice or ointment). Vaginitis (powder on tampon).
Preparations. *Tablets/capsules*. Powdered Slippery Elm BHP (1983): 400mg. Freely.
Powder. Taken as a food (gruel) mixed into a paste before adding boiling water or milk: quarter to half a teaspoon to each cup. Sprinkle powder on porridge or muesli.
Poultice. 1-2 teaspoons powder mixed into a paste with a little water and spread over dressing.
English traditional 'drawing' ointment: Marshmallow and Slippery Elm.
No serious gastro-intestinal side-effects. GSL

SLOAN'S VAPOUR RUB. *Active ingredients*: Camphor 6.5 per cent; Menthol 3.2 per cent; Thymol 1.1 per cent; Oil Eucalyptus 3.0 per cent; Oil Turpentine 3.0 per cent; Oil Rosemary 2.0 per cent; Oil Pine needles 0.7 per cent. For massage into chest, throat and back. Body heat slowly releases medicated vapours that bring comfort and a measure of relief to inflamed membranes of nose, throat and to relieve tightness of the chest. Avoid contact with eyes and sensitive parts. By the makers of Sloan's Liniment.

SMALLPOX. An acute infectious disease caused by poxvirus variolae. Now abolished world-wide as a result of vaccination. A notifiable disease under the Public Health (Control of Diseases) Act 1984. Incubation period 12 days. Patient infective from third day of onset. Invasion is by virus released from erupted blisters that ride on dust particles and water droplets, via the respiratory tract. Spreads by contact with a patient or his clothing. Expert diagnosis essential as it may be mistaken for chickenpox. The virus may survive at room temperature for up to three years.
Symptoms. High fever, muscle pains, vomiting, chill, headache, pink skin rash invading the whole body; spots become blisters with pus, progressing to scabs that drop off to leave pitted areas.
Treatment. Isolation in hospital. Commence with an emetic.
Thuja. "Dr Busby, Iowa, USA, a few years ago obtained excellent results. Oil of Thuja was applied to the vesicles. Internally, 3-10 drops were given every 2 hours. This did away entirely with the vesicles and pustules, leaving a smooth skin and promoting healthy recovery." (*Finlay Ellingwood, MD*)

Dr Boenninghausen, German physician, found Thuja both preventative and curative in an epidemic of smallpox. It aborted the process and prevented pitting. (*John Clarke, MD*)
Indian Cup. (*Sarracenia purpurea*) Native plant of Nova Scotia. Specific used by Indians to prevent smallpox. "It will cure smallpox in its various forms within 12 hours after the patient has drunk the decoction. However alarming the eruptions, the peculiar action of the plant is such that very seldom is a scar left to tell the story. If the variolous matter is washed out with the decoction, the disease loses its contagious properties." (*Dr Frederick W. Morris*)
Diet. No solid food. Abundant Vitamin C fluids (orange and other juices) to maintain level of

body fluids. Intravenous fluids may be necessary. *Note.* Smallpox is one of man's deadliest viral enemies. In 1980 the World Health Organisation declared the world was now officially free from smallpox due to vaccination, which practice appears to be the only effective protective at the present stage of medical science.

Treatment by a general medical practitioner or hospital specialist.

SMARTWEED. See: WATER PEPPER.

SMELL and TASTE, LOSS OF.
Causes: aftermath of the common cold, influenza, etc. Catarrh, smoking, head injuries, blockage of the nose by polyp or other obstruction. Senses of smell and taste decline with age.
Alternatives. Iceland Moss, Kelp, Poke root, or Echinacea. Tablets, extracts, powders, or tinctures.
Diet. Lacto-vegetarian. Papaya fruit.
Vitamins. B-complex. C. E.
Minerals. Zinc.

SMOKER'S HEART. Irritable heart from excessive smoking. Ginseng is popular remedy. Where accompanied by erratic irritability – Kola; diminished urine output – Lily of the Valley; feeble pulse and palpitation – Hawthorn; with accelerated beat – Bugleweed. Chronic tobacco heart – Cactus.
Formula. Combine tinctures: equal parts: Kola, Hawthorn and Dandelion. Dose: 1 teaspoon in water thrice daily.
Diet. See: DIET – HEART AND CIRCULATION. Foods rich in the following vitamins and minerals:–
Supplements. Daily. Vitamins A, B-complex, B6, B12, C and E. Calcium, Selenium, Zinc.

SMOKING. Harmful in many ways. Clouds the sense of taste and smell, irritates air passages, promoting lung and heart disease. The action of nicotine constricts blood vessels, increases heart rate and raises blood pressure. Cigarette smoking predisposes to atherosclerosis. Increased vitality, alertness, increased energy and improved appetite follow elimination of nicotine. For cleansing the body of its ill-effects – Red Clover tea. To counter effects of nicotine some women find Chamomile tea helpful. The most popular remedy is *Lobelia*, (tablet: Potter's Herbal Supplies – 32.5mg with excipient to 200mg).
Traditional: chew a small nugget of Dandelion root when urge is strong.
Alternative: Tincture Goldenseal, 3 drops in water, thrice daily.

It is possible to stop smoking by use of substances which block taste enzymes, such as zinc. No treatment is successful without strong motivation. Smokers are about four times as likely to develop Crohn's disease as non-smokers. (*Professor Michael Langman*)

Smoking robs the body of the mineral Selenium which is helpful for prevention of smoking-related diseases. (*Danish Report*)
Protection from other people's smoke: anti-oxidant supplements: Vitamins A, C, E. Mineral: Zinc.
Lobelia. Main constituent lobeline is chemically similar to nicotine without being addictive. Nicotine withdrawal is assisted by Lobelia.
Oat grass (Avena sativa). One of the chief ingredients of a phytotherapist's prescription to discourage smoking.
Liquorice root – chewed to reduce the craving for nicotine.
Vitamin C. Each cigarette smoked uses up 25mg Vitamin C. Vitamin C mops up free radicals and guards the adrenal glands.
Diet. Lacto-vegetarian. Lecithin, for production of acetylcholine essential to efficient brain function. Tyrosine amino acid. Vitamins C, E, and foods rich in Zinc – Sunflower seeds, Pumpkin seeds. Restrict intake of starches. Those who give-up the habit of smoking crave carbohydrates and tend to put on weight by eating more sweet carbohydrate foods.
Note. Smokers have lower levels of beta-carotene in their blood and should eat liberally of beta-carotene foods, especially raw carrots. Smoking reduces chances of pregnancy.

SMOKING MIXTURE. Coltsfoot is the chief ingredient of many smoking mixtures or may be used alone for that purpose.
Formula: herbs fine-cut: parts – Coltsfoot 2; Chamomile flowers half; Thyme half; Eyebright 1; Wood Betony 1; Rosemary half. Mix.
To reduce desire for smoking: Lobelia tablets.

SNAKE BITE. Snake venom varies in virulence according to species. Some affects the nerves, triggering violent delirium, others acting as anti-coagulants in the blood. In primitive communities where modern hospital facilities are not at hand, plant medicines provide the only antidotes.

The only poisonous snake in Britain is the adder for which Skullcap tea was used before the age of serum therapy. Other European agents include decoctions of Yellow Dock or Burdock. Apothecaries prescribed Tincture Myrrh 3; Tincture Capsicum 1. Dose: 5-15 drops every half hour, or as frequently as tolerated. A popular remedy was to bind a cut onion on the wound.

History records the Seneco tribe of Indians (USA) using Senega (Seneco snake root). In the state of Virginia, Virginia snake root enjoyed a similar reputation. For rattlesnake bite, Dr A.C. Brook, Kansas, records: "15 drops Echinacea, Liquid extract, hourly for virulent fever".

Snakeroot (Rauwolfia), from which reserpine of modern pharmacy is extracted had a place in early Hindoo and Chinese medicine as an antidote to snake venom.

Treatment by a general medical practitioner or hospital specialist.

SNEEZING. To promote. To stimulate mucous membranes to increased secretion to clear the head, relieve congestion: powdered Bayberry as a snuff. See: SNUFF.

SNEEZING. Uncontrollable. Lobelia (tea, tablets, tincture, etc). German Chamomile tea. Sniff water up the nose to wash out pollens or other irritants. Vitamin C 1-2g daily believed to have an anti-histamine effect.

SNORING. Sleep apnoea. The basic problem of snorers is their soft palate which may be relaxed, with wide floppy uvulas that obstruct the pharynx. Sleep apnoea can be a serious condition resulting in unfreshing sleep, the sufferer falling asleep during the day at work, or when driving. It is a feature of hypothyroidism (myxoedema); search for stigmata. Alcohol and drugs may cause muscle relaxation in the pharynx area, narrowing the airway. A link between high blood pressure and snoring has been confirmed.

Snorers are more than twice as likely to have a stroke than non-snorers. (*Dr J. Palomaki, Helsinki University Central Hospital*)

Alternatives. Astringent gargle at bedtime: teas from any one: Raspberry leaves, Sage, Cranesbill. OR:– 5-10 drops tincture Myrrh in a glass of water.

Tea. Cup of Chamomile tea, late evening.

Tincture. Ephedra. (Practitioner use).

Avoid sleeping tablets.

If snoring occurs only when sufferer sleeps on back – a cork sewn into pyjamas sometimes effective.

Refer to Ear, Nose and Throat surgeon for underlying obstruction (polyp, etc).

Where the condition persists over months, consider treatments under ANGINA and HYPERTENSION.

SNOWFIRE HEALING TABLET. *Ingredients*: Oil Lemon 0.01 per cent, Oil Citronella 0.06 per cent, Oil Cloves 0.04 per cent, Oil Cade 0.04 per cent, Benzoin 0.02 per cent, Oil Thyme 0.01 per cent.

Uses. Chilblains, chapped surfaces, cracked lips, etc.

SNUFF. Temporary relief of nasal catarrh, runny eyes and nose. Equal parts of fine powdered barks: Witch Hazel, White Oak, Wild Cherry. Mix. Use as an inhalant as necessary.

Alternatives: use singly: powdered Ginger, Bayberry, Sneezewort.

SOAPWORT. Bouncing Bet. *Saponaria officinalis L. French*: Saponaire. *German*: Seifenkraut. *Spanish*: Saponella. *Italian*: Saponaria. Contains saponins. Leaves, root.

Action. Laxative, diuretic, expectorant, cholagogue, detergent, powerful blood tonic.

Uses. To increase bile flow, respiratory disorders, bronchitis, sore throat. Scale skin diseases (tea, internally and as a lotion). To increase milk in nursing mothers. Once used as a vegetable soap for personal hygiene and for cleansing and restoring old fragile fabrics (curtains, tapestries, etc). Used by early herbalists for dry coughs.

Preparations. Practitioner use only. Thrice daily.

Tea: 1oz to 1 pint boiling water; infuse 15 minutes. Dose, half-1 cup.

Decoction (root). Half an ounce to 1 pint water gently simmered 20 minutes. Dose: half-1 cup.

Liquid Extract: 15-30 drops, in water.

Lotion: tea used locally. Soapwort Skin Tonic to cleanse and refresh the skin.

S.O.D. See: DISMUTASE ENZYMES.

SODIUM. Important mineral constituent of the body. Its role is controlled by the kidneys and any excess may lead to fluid retention in the tissues, and hypertension. The reverse (hypotension) is caused by depletion of salt as in Addison's Disease. Regulates quantity of fluid entering into blood and tissue cells (osmosis). Maintains acid/alkali balance.

RDA 2000mg (common salt – 5 grams).

Sources. Common salt (sodium chloride). Most foods. Meats, fish, smoked foods.

Herbs: Black Willow, Chives, Calamus, Clivers, Devil's Bit, Fennel seeds, Irish Moss, Meadowsweet, Mistletoe, Nettles, Okra pods, Rest Harrow, Shepherd's Purse, Sorrel, Watercress.

SOFT EXTRACT. A soft extract is prepared by exhausting a herb by percolation or maceration in alcohol, the larger part of which is removed by evaporation. Differs from a liquid extract where the evaporation is carried further. Total evaporation of fluids results in a solid extract. A high proof spirit may be added to preserve against decomposition.

SOLDIER'S NERVE STRAIN. Nerve strain may be so great as to threaten the heart and lower blood pressure thus reducing ability to discharge his duties. Ginseng was used by the Chinese in the battles of antiquity because of its property of reviving nervous and physical exhaustion.

SOLID EXTRACTS. Prepared by totally exhausting the fresh juices or strong infusions by maceration or percolation with a suitable menstruum – usually alcohol – the greater part of which is removed by evaporation. Such extracts are widely used in the manufacture of pills, compressed tablets, ointments, or for 'running-up' into liquid extracts or tinctures.

SOLVENT SYNDROME. Ailment caused by ingestion of, or body contact with toxic chemicals used in the modern office or factory. Dry toners are likely to become airborne dust contaminants. Solvent mixtures include ethyl-alcohol, dethyl ether, actane and acetone, all of which are mildly irritating to mucous membranes.
Treatment. Same as for PHOTOCOPIER SYNDROME.

SORE. A tender injured or diseased spot that will not heal.
To encourage granulation and ease pain: Red Clover. Peach leaves, Marigold, Comfrey.
Topical. Fomentations of Comfrey or Marshmallow roots. Honey dressings.
Aromatherapy. Apply: Eucalyptus, Lavender, Lemon, Bergamot or Tea Tree oils diluted with a few drops of a carrier oil.

SORE THROAT. Simple 'acute' throat. A symptom of many disorders the underlying condition of which should receive priority.
Alternatives. *Teas*. Chamomile, Fenugreek seeds, Juniper, <u>Lemon juice</u>, Goldenrod, Marigold flowers, Marjoram, Marshmallow, Mullein, Raspberry leaves, <u>Sage</u>, Silverweed, Tormentil.
Tablets/capsules. Feverfew, Goldenseal, Echinacea, Lobelia, Myrrh, <u>Poke root</u>, Slippery Elm.
Gargle. Aloe Vera gel or fresh juice. Cider vinegar.
Cold packs: renew 2-hourly.
Diet. 3-day fruit juice fast. No solid foods.
Supplements. Vitamin A (7,500iu daily). Vitamin C (1 gram thrice daily). Beta-carotene 200,000iu. Zinc 25mg.

SORREL. *Rumex acetosa L. French*: Osielle. *German*: Ampfer. *Italian*: Acetosa. *Spanish*: Acedera. *Part used*: leaves.
Constituents: oxalic acid, potassium oxalate, anthraquinones, Vitamin C, flavonoids.
Action. Diuretic, refrigerant, alterative.
Uses. Offensive breath. Gingivits. In *Acetaria*, John Evelyn writes: "Sorrel sharpens the appetite, assuages heat, cools the liver, strengthens the heart. It is an anti-scorbutic, resisting putrefaction. In salads it imparts a grateful quickness (*piquant flavour*) to the rest . . ."

Leaves may be eaten raw in salads, boiled as spinach or made into a soup which the French regard as a stimulating tonic. Its properties are reduced on application of heat.

SOUR CHERRY. *Prunus cerasus L. German*: Kirsche. *French*: Cerisier. *Italian*: Ciliegio. *Part used*: fruit stalks.
Constituents: amygdalin (bark), a bitter principle.
Action. Diuretic. Genito-urinary anti-inflammatory.
Uses. Cystitis, oedema, water retention.
Preparation. *Decoction*: 1oz stalks to 1 pint water gently simmered 20 minutes. Dose: quarter to half a cup thrice daily. Practitioner use.

SOUTHERNWOOD. Lad's love. *Artemisia abrotanum L. German*: Ebberante. *French*: Aurone. *Spanish*: Abrotana. *Italian*: Abrotano. Well-known garden plant. Flowering tops.
Action. Mild antiseptic, anthelmintic, stomachic, emmenagogue, cholagogue, bitter.
Topical: insect repellent when rubbed into skin.
Uses. Weak stomach, feeble appetite, Raynaud's disease, worms in children, engorgement of veins and capillaries, to restore menstrual flow. Ailing children and thin people wanting to increase weight. Anxiety neurosis with nerve weakness.
Preparations. Average dose, 2-4 grams, or equivalent. Thrice daily.
Tea: half to 1 teaspoon to each cup boiling water; infuse 10 minutes. Dose, half-1 cup.
Liquid Extract BHP (1983). 1:1 in 25 per cent alcohol. Dose 2-4ml.

Not taken in pregnancy.

SOYA BEAN. "Meat without bones." Valuable source of protein (over 35 per cent) and fat (20 per cent). Nourishing body-builder. One of the few foods to contain all 22 health-giving amino acids. Rich source of lecithin (brain and nerve food and protector of heart and arteries). Contains linoleic acid, most important of the polyunsaturated fatty acids. By these contents, soya plays an important role in emulsifying and excreting deposits of cholesterol that may accumulate in the bloodstream.

Soya milk is a blend of water and dehulled soya beans; easily digested, its fat content being less than cow's milk and which is suitable for those with allergy to dairy products.

Soya bean sprouts contain Vitamins A, B, C, E, and minerals: calcium, copper, iron, magnesium, manganese, phosphorus, sulphur and zinc.

For tired business-man syndrome in need of a brain restorative. Precursor of female hormone for "The Pill", replacing Mexican Yam (Dioscorea villosa). (*Herbalgram, No 25*)

Soybeans appear to contain several potential anticarcinogens.

SPANISH TUMMY MIXTURE. (*Potter's*) For non-persistent diarrhoea.
Active ingredients: each 5ml contains 20 per cent alcoholic extractive (1:1) from 750mg Blackberry root bark; 45 per cent alcoholic extractive (1.5) from Catechu 0.25ml; 50 per cent

alcoholic solution (3:100) of Gingerin 0.187ml; Cinnamon oil BP and Clove oil BP of each 0.0015ml in a sweetened vehicle. Dose: 1 teaspoon (5ml) in a little water.

SPASMOLYTIC. Another name for anti-spasmodic.

SPEARMINT. *Mentha viridis*, Hort. *Mentha sativa, L. French*: Menthe verte. *German*: Grüne Rossiminze. *Spanish*: Menta verde. *Italian*: Menta verda. *Parts used*: leaves, essential oil. "The smell rejoices the heart." (*Turner*) Resembles Peppermint in its action.
Constituents: essential oil, flavonoids.
Action. Antispasmodic, carminative, diaphoretic, stimulant.
Uses. Feverish conditions in children. First stages of the common cold and influenza. Flatulence, dyspepsia, abdominal cramps (until the doctor comes), cholera, biliary colic, strengthens memory, sometimes allays headache. Feeble appetite (even the very smell may give one an appetite).
Preparations. *Tea*: 1 teaspoon dried herb to each cup boiling water; infuse 10 minutes. Half-1 cup. Fretful children: teaspoonful doses.
Oil of Spearmint: 1-3 drops in honey, or mashed banana. Children: dilute ten times.
Cultivated for culinary use.

SPEEDWELL. *Veronica officinalis L. German*: Ehrenpreis. *French*: Véronique. *Spanish*: Veronica. *Italian*: Veronic. *Part used*: herb.
Constituents: flavonoids, iridoid glycosides.
Action. Diuretic, alterative, tonic, vulnerary, expectorant.
Uses. Scrofulous disorders, catarrh, skin diseases.
Preparation. *Tea*: 1 heaped teaspoon dried herb to each cup boiling water: infuse 15 minutes. Half-1 cup thrice daily. Drunk as a country tea before the days of Indian tea.

SPERMACETI. A wax extracted from the sperm whale, once used as a base for ointments and creams.
Alternatives: Almond oil, Peanut oil, Irish Moss, Comfrey mucilage.

SPERMATORRHOEA. Involuntary discharge of semen without orgasm.
Causes: neurasthenia, anaemia or sexual debility.
Alternatives. *Of therapeutic value*. Black Willow, Sarsaparilla, Skullcap, Thuja. Yellow Parilla. (*South American traditional*) Hops.
Skullcap tea (*French traditional*).
Sage tea *(Malaysia)*.
Tablets/capsules. Seaweed and Sarsaparilla. Thuja.
Formula. Black Willow 2; Sarsaparilla 1; Thuja half. Dose. Powders: 500mg (two 00 capsules or one-third teaspoon). Liquid extracts: 1 teaspoon. Tinctures: 2 teaspoons. 2-3 times daily.
Diet. To build up general health.
Supplements. B-complex, B6, B12. Calcium, Magnesium, Zinc, Bee pollen.

SPERMICIDAL CONTRACEPTION. The use of spermicides for the purpose of contraception may cause a number of grave disorders ranging from genital herpes to toxic shock syndrome. They are a suspected cause of Down's syndrome. Where contraception by spermicide fails some women have an increased risk of birth defects.

Spermicides may also be responsible for vaginal irritation and inflammation for which powerful alteratives are indicated: Goldenseal, Echinacea, Wild Indigo, Myrrh, Blood root.
Teas: Red Clover, Gotu Kola, Plantain. (Also used as a douche.)
Tablets/capsules. Goldenseal, Echinacea, Poke root.
Combination. Equal parts tinctures Goldenseal and Myrrh. 5-20 drops in water or honey, thrice daily.

SPIKENARD. *Aralia racemosa, L.* A perennial plant of the Ginseng family. *Part used*: rhizome and root.
Constituents: essential oil, glycoside.
Action. Alterative, warming stimulant, soothing expectorant, diaphoretic. Similar to Ginseng in its action towards rapid recovery from physical and mental exhaustion.
Uses. Allays irritation of the respiratory mucous membranes. Whooping cough, pleurisy, bronchitis. Used by early American frontiersmen for tuberculosis. Rheumatism. Skin diseases.
Preparations. Thrice daily.
Decoction. 15g to 250ml (half an ounce to 1 pint) water gently simmered 5 minutes; strain when warm. Dose, half cup.
Liquid Extract: 30-60 drops, in water.
Cough medicines: traditional ingredient of.

SPINA BIFIDA. Failure of the spinal bones to close over nerves arising from the lower end of the spinal cord. May cause paralysis of the legs and incontinence. Associated with poverty, bad housing and is more common in Celtic races and among the sikhs. Most common cause is folic acid deficiency. Prevention only.

A woman of childbearing age should increase her consumption of food rich in Folic acid, such as Brussels sprouts, spinach, green beans, oranges, potatoes, wholemeal bread, yeast extract. New evidence suggests health is determined before birth by a mother's condition during pregnancy. The UK Department of Health advises 400 micrograms (0.4mg) Folic acid until the twelfth week of pregnancy. If a woman has had a spina bifida baby, about 5 milligrams is recommended. "A 75 per cent protection against neural tube defects is possible in women taking a Folic acid-containing vitamin in early pregnancy." (*Oregonian, 11-25-89, p11*) To be taken before conception also.

"Consideration should be given to including Vitamin B12 as well as Folic acid in any programme of supplementation or food fortification to prevent neural tube defects." (*Quarterly Journal of Medicine, Nov 1993*)

Supplements. Calcium, Iron, Magnesium, Zinc. Multivitamin. See: FOLIC ACID. Vitamin B12.

Treatment by or in liaison with a general medical practitioner.

SPINAL CORD INJURY. As caused by injury, trauma, disc protrusion or pressure on the cord by tumour.

Symptoms. Sensory or motor loss, pain, loss of control of bladder or bowel, backache, muscle weakness.

Treatment. Treat underlying cause. Even where a situation may appear hopeless, some small amelioration of symptoms may be possible by spinal restoratives: Hops, Ladyslipper, Galangal, True Unicorn root, False Unicorn root.

For injury, Comfrey and Horsetail help mend and strengthen bones.

Treatment by or in liaison with an orthopaedic surgeon or general medical practitioner.

St John's Wort has a long traditional reputation for spinal injury.

Decoction. Equal parts: Skullcap, Mistletoe and Valerian. Mix. 1oz to 1 pint water gently simmer 5 minutes, half-1 cup thrice daily.

Tenderness on pressure of spinal vertebre – Tincture Bryonia, 5-20 drops in water, thrice daily.

Formula. St John's Wort 2; Comfrey 1; Black Cohosh half; Liquorice quarter. Dose. Powders: 500mg.

Liquid extracts: 1 teaspoon. Tinctures: 2 teaspoons. Thrice daily.

Vitamin E. Tissue bleeding and oedema due to suppressed blood flow may arise from free radical activity in cell membranes which condition may be successfully met with Vitamin E: 500mg thrice daily.

Propolis. To promote regeneration of collagen, cartilage and bone.

See entries for specific conditions: SLIPPED DISC, SPONDYLOSIS, OSTEOPOROSIS, LUMBAGO, BACKACHE.

SPIRULINA. A nutritious food supplement prepared from plant plankton; a blue-green micro-algae. It contains no less than 18 amino acids; including 8 essential amino acids which the body cannot produce from its own resources and have to be daily replaced by food. Rich in beta-carotene, Vitamin E and iron.

It grows naturally on alkaline lakes for its high level protein, vitamins and minerals. 100 grams of spirulina yields 50-70 per cent of protein. Its exceptional level of Vitamin B12 (160 mcg) is of special interest to vegetarians, vegans and non-meat eaters who, unless they study their diet carefully, may be deficient of this important vitamin. Active against the AIDS virus.

Eaten by sportsmen, body builders and slimmers who desire maximum nutrition from a minimum of food bulk. Past civilisations harvested algae for food, including the Aztecs. Its blood purifying and hypotensive properties are made possible by its high chlorophyl content. The product comes from Japan where the algae is cultivated in large water reservoirs.

Spirulina contains a Vitamin F factor (GLA). It also contains iodine necessary for efficiency of the thyroid gland. As the thyroid regulates metabolic rate, spirulina may effect weight reduction and contribute to the body's sense of well-being.

A useful supplement taken during purifying diets, fasts and cleansing regimes.

SPLEEN. An abdominal organ which stores blood. Produces white blood cells and stores any excess of red cells. Important part of the immune system. Enlargement (splenomegaly) occurs in many diseases, benign and malignant: anaemia, malaria, leukaemia. Bacterial infections would be treated according to the basic disorder. One cause of enlargement is latent vaccinosis and little progress may be made until this condition is resolved by Thuja.

Symptoms. Deep-seated pain in left hypochondrium, impaired appetite, sallow or yellow skin, scanty urine, physical weakness. Enlargement may simulate heart disease. Electrocardiogram confirms. In the past the spleen was believed to be inessential to health (like the appendix), but it is now known that people without a spleen have a greater risk of severe infection than those with a spleen. Travellers without a spleen should take special precautions against the risk of malaria.

Historical. "During the late Civil War I used New Jersey tea for inflammation of the spleen and was well-satisfied with the results that for six years I do not remember using anything else for an enlarged spleen. I have used it in the worst cases I ever saw, from infancy to old age; I have yet to hear of its failure in any case." (*E. Hale MD*)

Of therapeutic value. Fringe Tree bark, Black root, Goldenseal, Bayberry, Echinacea, Hart's Tongue fern, Grindelia, New Jersey tea. Barberry is an old spleen remedy which combines well with Bayberry. BHP (1983) recommends Fringe Tree, Peruvian bark and Hart's Tongue fern. Mountain Grape appears in USA pharmacopoeias. For a malarial spleen – Dandelion, Peruvian bark. American Bearsfoot. (*Priest*)

Formula. Echinacea 2; Fringe Tree bark 1; Barberry 1; Thuja quarter. Dose. Powders: 500mg (two 00 capsules or one-third teaspoon). Liquid extracts: 1 teaspoon. Tinctures: 2 teaspoons. Thrice daily.
New Jersey tea. Now little used in American herbal practice.
Agrimony tea. For mild recurrent splenic disorders.
Astragalus. Very popular "spleen tonic" in Chinese medicine. Liver and spleen protective in chemotherapy.
Successes recorded: Periwinkle (Vinca rosea), Poke root (hardened spleen), Wild Strawberry leaves and root. Nettle tea.
Tamarinds. "Tamarinds (nutritive) are accounted specific for spleen disorders to lessen its size. In the East they used to drink out of cups made of this wood to cure those illnesses." (*Joseph Miller*)

In herbal treatment of the spleen it is often observed that for some unaccountable reason output of urine is increased and an eliminative diarrhoea initiated.
Thuja, tincture BHP (1983): 5-15 drops, thrice daily.
Splenectomy. The risk of infection after this operation is high enough to justify the precaution of taking a pinch of Echinacea powder, or one tablet daily. In children under 12, half a tablet/capsule (30-40mg) suffices. In the absence of Echinacea other herbal antibiotics are available, including Garlic.
Diagnosis. A craving for sweet foods, as part of the symptom picture, could suggest disorder of the spleen.
Vitamins. A. B12. C. D.
Minerals. Iron, Zinc.
Caution. People without a spleen should consult their doctor or practitioner if infection occurs. The main sign is fever. Others may be cough, headache, sore throat or severe abdominal pain.

SPONDYLOSIS. Osteo-arthrosis of the spine (cervical or lumbar) with pain and restriction of movement. May follow 'slipped disc', congenital deformities, injury, stress. Where present in the neck area (cervical spine) pain radiates to shoulder and arm; when in the sacroiliac area, to the legs.
Treatment: as for ANKYLOSING SPONDYLITIS.

SPORTS' INJURIES. See: ABRASIONS, BRUISES, CUTS, SPRAINS, etc.

SPORT'S TRAINING. By their high mineral content some herbs promote well-being and upbuilding of the body. Comfrey herb increases the condition and performance of race horses, Irish Moss keeps respiratory membranes in a healthy condition, and Buckwheat maintains resilience of arteries and veins.
During sports training: Alfalfa tea. Eggs, Safflower oil, brewer's yeast, Vitamin C, Dolomite, Vitamin E, Thiamine, Zinc.
Tablets/capsules. Alfalfa tablets 500mg. (*Meadowcroft*) Alfalfa capsules 240mg powder (*Arkopharma*).
Sports injuries. Comfrey cream. Aloe Vera gel. Marigold ointment.
Aromatherapy. Lavender oil (mild analgesic).
Formula. Powders. Mix equal parts: Ginger, Alfalfa, Gotu Kola, Siberian Ginseng. Dose: 500mg (two 00 capsules or one-third teaspoon), before meals thrice daily. For intensive exercise.

SPOTTY FACE. Treatment as for ACNE.

SPRAIN. Injury to ligaments surrounding a joint, stretched or torn. Differs from a 'strain' which is injury to a muscle where fibres are torn or stretched.
Treatment. Elevate and support limb. Apply ice-pack or packet frozen peas to ease pain or immerse in cold water.
Internal. Antispasmodic, Life Drops or pinch of Cayenne in cup of tea.
Topical. Witch Hazel water. Wipe with Cider vinegar or infusion of daisy flowers. Tincture Arnica.
Poultice: Comfrey, St John's Wort, Marigold or Arnica. Follow with Comfrey cream or Aloe Gel, with compression bandaging.
Traditional (Norfolk, England). Egg-white mixed with raw cabbage juice.
Aromatherapy. Oils of Chamomile or Lavender: 6 drops in two teaspoons Almond or Olive oil; massage.

SPRING MEDICINE. Half an ounce each: Yellow Dock, Sarsaparilla, Agrimony, Burdock. Mix.
Method: place quarter of mixture in 1 pint cold water and bring to boil; simmer gently 20 minutes. Drink cold, half to 1 cup thrice daily, after meals.
Alternative. Equal parts: Nettles, Dandelion root, Balm. Mix. 2 teaspoons to each cup boiling water; infuse 15 minutes: 1 cup 2-3 times daily.
Other blood tonics, for annual cleansing of the blood: Parsley, Watercress.

SPROUTS. Home seed germination. Source of vitamins grown in the kitchen. Health-giving values of sprouted seeds, beans, peas, etc, first discovered and recorded by the Chinese Emperor, 2939BC. One of the purest forms of crisp, fresh, flavoursome vitamin-packed nutrition. Inexpensive means of obtaining vital vitamins and minerals. They increase mineral, enzyme and chlorophyll levels and contain cell-building

amino acids such as lysine and tryptophane.
Popular sources: Wheat, Rye, Corn, Barley, Oats, Millet, Beans, Chick-peas, Alfalfa, Fenugreek, Lentils, Clover, Cress, Kale, Radish, Dill, Parsley, Sesame, Caraway, Purslane, Lettuce, Celery, Mung beans, and especially Soybean. On sprouting, Soybeans acquire an increase of 550 per cent Vitamin C; wheatgrains yield 300-400 per cent increase in the B-vitamins. Being rich in chlorophyll they sweeten bad breath.

Sprouted seeds spring to life initiating synthesis of Vitamins C, E and carotene (Vitamin A precursor). They produce trace elements, particularly iron and zinc in Alfalfa; protein, enzymes, and break down starch into easily-digested sugars. Bean sprouts are an everyday dish in China.
Method: grains, beans, seeds, etc, should be soaked in twice their volume of water for 24 hours. Spread on a damp cloth and place in the light, as near a window. Wash seedlings two or three times a day in running water, drain. Must not be allowed to dry. Sprouts may be eaten with salads, cereals or as garnishes to other vegetables. Will refrigerate up to 8 days.

SPRUE. Two types; that of the tropics and of the temperate zone. Intestinal disorder with malabsorption of food, especially fats. May simulate pancreatitis, coeliac disease or amyloidosis. Allergy to gluten (temperate zones).
Symptoms. Cracks at corner of mouth (Vitamin C deficiency). Scarlet tongue (Vitamin B deficiency). Loss of hair on head. Malaise, dry skin, weight loss, swelling of ankles, muscle weakness, diarrhoea with large fatty stools.
Positive diagnosis: stools float.
Treatment. (*Indian*) Fenugreek seeds decoction. Freely.
Tincture Myrrh: 5-20 drops in water thrice daily.
(*European*) *Tea*. Equal parts, Agrimony, Meadowsweet. 1-2 teaspoons to each cup boiling water; infuse 15 minutes. 1 cup thrice daily.
Alternatives: Equal parts, tinctures Goldenseal and Wild Yam: 5-15 drops in water or honey thrice daily. Aloe Vera juice, or gel.

Warm hip baths.
Diet. Gluten-free. Unpasteurised yoghurt. Raw carrot juice.
Vitamins. A. B-complex, B6, B12, Folic acid, C. D. E. K.
Minerals. Iron. Magnesium.

SQUAW VINE. Partridge berry. *Mitchella repens L.* Whole plant. *Keynote*: Genito-urinary system.
Constituents: mucilage, glycosides, alkaloids.
Action. Parturient, diuretic, uterine tonic, emmenagogue, astringent.
Uses. Even today, an infusion is drunk by West Indian women during pregnancy for easy and safe delivery. For weak, anaemic teenagers who find themselves pregnant – to strengthen nerves, circulation and to promote development of a healthy foetus. Also used for sore nipples, painful menstruation, bladder irritation, dropsy, suppression of urine, and to assist the womb back to normal after childbirth. Candida.

Combines well with Raspberry leaves for pregnancy and threatened miscarriage. With Oatstraw for neurasthenia; with Cramp bark for severe uterine cramps.
Preparations. Average dose, 2-4g or fluid equivalent. Thrice daily.
Tea: 1 teaspoon to each cup boiling water; infuse 15 minutes; dose, half-1 cup.
Tincture: 1 part to 5 parts 45 per cent alcohol; steep 8 days, shake daily. Filter. Dose, 15-60 drops.
Liquid Extract: 2-4ml in water.

Once known as Motherhood tea. GSL

SQUILL. Scilla. White Squill. *Urginea maritima L.* Baker. *German*: Meerzwiebel. *French*: Ognon marin. *Spanish*: Escila. *Arabian*: Basal-el-unasala. *Italian*: Scilla marina. Dried bulb. One of the oldest plants known to medicine. Earliest mention is in the Ebers Papyrus. So effective it proved for cardiac dropsy that it became an object of temple worship.
Constituents: cardiac glycosides, flavonoids.
Action. Expectorant, antispasmodic, emetic, diuretic, cathartic. Antitussive. Cardiotonic: has a digitalis-like effect.
Uses. 'Dry' respiratory conditions in need of a positive expectorant; whooping cough, bronchial asthma. Promotes fluid elimination in heart disease.
Topical: hair tonic of Red Squills and Methanol for dandruff and seborrhoea.
Preparations. As prescribed. Practitioner use only.
Liquid Extract. 1-3 drops in water.
Tincture BPC (1973). Dose 0.3 to 2ml.
Ingredient: Balm of Gilead Cough Mixture.
Powder: 60-200mg.

Small doses advised; a gastric irritant. Not given with digitalis or in dehydration of body fluids. GSL

STAPHYLOCOCCUS. One of the commonest infectious micro-organisms or bacteria made up of cocci aggregated like a bunch of grapes. May produce infection of the skin with pus formation; boils, styes. The superbug. Kidney patients are particularly vulnerable to the infection.
German Chamomile (matricaria) contains compounds including chamazulene which is active against Staphylococcus aureus.
Other herbs include: Echinacea, Goldenseal, Myrrh, Wild Indigo.

STAR OF BETHLEHEM. *Ornithogalum umbellatum L.* Member of onion family. *French*:

Dame d'onze heures. *German*: Doldiger Milchstern. *Italian*: Bella di undici ore. *Part used*: bulb.

Action. Anti-tumour, unproven.

Uses. Gastric and duodenal ulceration. Of value for cancer of the stomach recorded by Dr Robert Cooper.

Practitioner use only.

STATUTORY INSTRUMENTS.

The Medicines Act 1968, Order 1977, No 2128 (c71).

The Medicines (Supply of Herbal Remedies) Order 1977, No 2130.

The Medicines (General Sales List) Order 1977, No 2129 which includes remedies that may be supplied otherwise than to a pharmacy.

The Medicines (Prescription only) Order 1977, No 2127 listing drugs, a few of vegetable origin which may be supplied only by a pharmacist on the prescription of a registered physician.

The Medicines (Miscellaneous Provision) Regulations 1977, No 2132. including definition of terms, enforcement authorities and the wholesale supply of permitted medicinal substances 5 (4) (p).

STD. Sexually Transmitted Disease.

STEINER, RUDOLPH, Dr. 1861-1925. Austrian scientist and founder of the Anthroposophical Society. Gifted with extraordinary powers of perception, he was known by his comperes as the 'spiritual scientist'. Gained a PhD degree at Rostock University and edited Goethe's scientific works. Was one of the first to adopt the Holistic approach. An advocate of herbal medicine, he sought to reveal the presence of unseen energies as the 'soul' of plants. Intuition led him to believe that such forces were attracted from the steller sphere within the cosmos and, through the plant kingdom were converted into healing alkaloids, glycosides, etc.

Steiner taught the doctrine of re-incarnation and vegetarianism. For children he initiated a system of 'curative education' and introduced dancing, painting and music as therapies. He revived the art of eurythmics which ' expresses the gestures inherent in speech and music".

See: ANTHROPOSOPHICAL MEDICINES.

STERILITY. See: INFERTILITY.

STERNUTATOR. A herb to provoke sneezing.

Soapwort, Black Pepper, Snuff, Mustard.

STEROIDS. Chemicals produced naturally in the body from a group of organic compounds. A number of diseases respond to synthetic steroids which are used to replace the body's natural production of hormones in adrenal deficiency states – such as adrenal exhaustion, Addison's disease, or surgical removal of the gland.

By suppressing activity of the adrenal cortex the body loses its ability to produce its own natural hormones. Consequently the patient on a maintenance dose should not stop this abruptly, but gradually, over a period.

Synthetic steroids effectively combat rheumatoid arthritis, rheumatic fever, skin diseases and asthma. But their administration is not without side-effects, chief of which is a reduction of the inflammatory response by the immune system. Their effect upon the white blood cells is to reduce their power against infection.

Other problems: heart failure from fluid retention and increased blood pressure, brittle bones, muscle weakness, bruising and thinning of the skin, disrupted menstrual periods, blood clots and unexplained headaches.

Cortico-steroids are synthetic preparations possessing the same anti-allergy, anti-inflammatory effects of the natural steroid. See: CORTICO-STEROIDS.

If exposed to the virus, patients on steroids who have not had chicken pox should seek medical attention.

STIFF NECK. See: TORTICOLLIS.

STIFF NECK SALVE. *Ingredients*: Essential oils, Cajeput, Eucalyptus, Thyme, 20 drops each. Camphorated oil 10 drops. Tincture Capsicum (cayenne) 30 drops. Beeswax 2oz. Gently heat 16oz Sunflower seed oil. Add beeswax and dissolve. Add other ingredients. Stir well. Pour into jars.

Useful to prepare muscles and joints for osteopathic manipulation.

STILL'S DISEASE. After the name of England's Dr Still. A form of polyarthritis in children presenting as a systemic illness with fever and rash. Cod Liver oil proves helpful.

See: JUVENILE RHEUMATOID ARTHRITIS.

STIMULANTS. Herbs that spur the circulation, increase energy, and inspirit physical function. A herb which stimulates the spinal cord, therefore, increases the reflex movements. They are also prostaglandin stimulants.

Brain. Ephedra (Ma-huang). Kola nuts.

Circulatory system (blood vessels and lymphatics). Bayberry, Prickly Ash, Nettles, Ginger, Cayenne, Wahoo bark, Horseradish, Cinnamon, Siberian Ginseng.

Endocrine glands. Gotu Kola. Sarsaparilla.

General. To stimulate the whole body. Cayenne, Prickly Ash, Cloves, Ginger, Horseradish, Turkey Corn.

Heart. Figwort, Hawthorn, Thuja, Wahoo.

Liver. Boldo, Dandelion, Fringe Tree bark.

Intestines and bowel. Balmony, Goldenseal,

Peppermint.
Involuntary muscle. Goldenseal.
Kidney. Buchu, Juniper berries.
Muscle. White Ash (Fraxinus americanus), Bayberry.
Nerves. Thuja.
Respiratory. Lungs, bronchi, nose and throat. Lobelia, Bittersweet, Poplar bark, Senega, Squills, Cowslip, Soapwort, Cubebs, Thuja.
Spinal. Central nervous system. Cramp bark, Kola nuts, Yerbe mate.
Stomach. Balmony, Gentian, Germander, Nutmeg, Peppermint, Quassia.

STOMACH DISORDERS. Most common disorders confined to the stomach are gastritis, gastro-enteritis and peptic ulcer. However, abnormal conditions elsewhere may be closely related to stomach dysfunction.

See: ABDOMINAL PAIN, ACIDITY, APPETITE – LOSS OF, DIARRHOEA, DYSPEPSIA, FLATULENCE, FOOD POISONING, GASTRITIS, GASTRO-ENTERITIS, HAEMORRHAGE, HYPERCHLORHYDRIA, NAUSEA, PEPTIC ULCER, PYLORIC STENOSIS, SPANISH TUMMY.

STOMACH FLU. See: GASTRO-ENTERITIS.

STOMATITIS. Sore or inflamed mouth with or without ulcers. Aphthous ulcer. May occur in fungal infections (thrush) – candidiasis.
Etiology: run-down condition. May be associated with infections from elsewhere: acute leukaemia, scurvy, stress, Vitamin C deficiency. Sometimes related to menstrual problems (Evening Primrose) or digestive disorders (Slippery Elm) which require specific treatment.
Symptoms. Profuse salivation, bad breath, slight fever, "out of sorts". Red and swollen mucous membrane.
Treatment. Any underlying condition must receive attention. Consult a dentist for dental problems.
Principle agents: Echinacea, Myrrh, Goldenseal, Poke root, Thuja.
Alternatives. *Teas*. Avens, Bistort, Chamomile (German), Ground Ivy, Ladies Bedstraw, Lime flowers, Lovage, Marigold flowers, Marshmallow leaves, Raspberry leaves, Red Sage BHP (1983), Sanicle, Slippery Elm (decoction), Violet leaves.
Salmon's Herbal. Wild Strawberry leaves, fruits or roots.
Tablets/capsules. Liquorice, Echinacea, Goldenseal, Poke root, Slippery Elm (chewed), Thuja, Blue Flag root, Devil's Claw, Garlic, Red Clover.
Formula. Echinacea 2; Myrrh 1; Goldenseal 1. Dose: Powders: 250mg (one 00 capsule or one-sixth teaspoon). Liquid extracts: 15-30 drops. Tinctures: 1-2 teaspoons. Thrice daily.
Evening Primrose oil capsules. 1,500mg daily.
Mouth Wash. Equal parts tinctures Myrrh and Goldenseal: 10-20 drops in a glass of water, freely.
Alternatives: Ladies Bedstraw or Wild Strawberry tea. Essential oils: Bilberry, Geranium or Lemon, 3 drops, any one, in a glass of water.
Diet. Slippery Elm gruel, yoghurt, Lactobacillus acidophilus. Avoid highly spiced food.
Supplements. Daily. Thiamine 300mg, Vitamin B-complex, B6 150mg, Vitamin B12, Folic acid, Vitamin C (1g), Riboflavin 20mg. Vitamin E (400iu), Iron, Zinc.
Prevention. Strengthen immune system with 2-3 Garlic capsules at night.

STONE – IN THE BLADDER. Due to imperfect body chemistry following poor nutrition. Stones commence with a nucleus which may be a plug of dry mucus or dead bacteria encrusted with lime salts, uric acid or other urinary deposits.
Symptoms. May follow a recent history of 'gravel' in the urine, with pricking or tingling in the penis or vagina. Pain is felt in the perineum and down the thighs. At times a flow of urine may be immediately arrested before the bladder is empty. Few drops of blood after urination.

Diagnosis is confirmed by X-ray. Phytotherapy may reduce size of stone and eliminate sandy gravel. Surgical operation mostly successful.
B. Morris, MD, Canada, writes: "An injection of Castor oil had the great effect of relieving stone in the bladder. I first rid myself of the contents of the bladder, then with a syringe inject two ounces Castor oil. I cannot express my feelings at the change brought about at its introduction direct into the bladder. It seems that a new lower half has been given me. Thereafter, the bladder was supplied with 2-3 ounces Castor oil and soon every symptom vanished."
General treatment – same as for GRAVEL.

STONE, IN THE KIDNEY. Presence of solid constituents in pelvis or drainage system of the kidneys, or in the ureter. Mainly calcium, such deposits may range from 'sand' or 'gravel' to concretions as large as a golf ball. Layers of lime salts form round a nucleus which may be a speck of mucin or small mass of tube casts. Calcium precipitated in the wrong place.

Renal colic is an attempted passage of the stone down the ureter with loin pain on the affected side radiating down into the vagina or scrotum. Such excruciating agony may cause the patient to double-up with pain under the ribs, worse on movement, with possible fainting.

The abdominal surface is very sensitive. Jolting movements may precipitate blood in the urine. Pressure, caused by apposition of the stone's surface or by pressure on the pelvis of the kidney can cause suppuration.

Predisposing factors: increased acidity of the urine, frequent doses of stomach powders, tablets, etc for gastric ulcer and dyspepsia. Formation of kidney stones may be linked to tap water with high level calcium, but if such water is first boiled much of its mineral content is deposited on the sides of the kettle. A growing practice is to drink bottled spring water with a low calcium content.

While many stones are removed surgically, and some broken-up in situ by ultrasonic beam, there are convincing cases of dissolution of kidney stones by traditional plant medicines as listed in the BHP (1983): Marshmallow leaf, Couchgrass, Parsley Piert, Bearberry, Stone root, Wild Carrot, Sea Holly, Gravel root, Hydrangea, Corn Silk and Pellitory of the Wall. (Anti-lithics)

Horsetail is widely used for bleeding from the kidney caused by stone, being a natural healer for urinary mucous membranes.

Oxalate stones may take months (even years) to resolve.

Urinary demulcents protect delicate mucous surfaces: Couchgrass, Cornsilk, Marshmallow. Where there is pus formation urinary antiseptics are indicated: Echinacea, Bearberry, Buchu, Juniper.

If bleeding is present consult a qualified medical practitioner. Obstruction to flow of urine is a matter for urgent relief.

It is known that excess activity of the parathyroid gland promotes formation. Other causes may be Paget's disease, bone cancers and metabolic disturbance through increased activity of the thyroid gland.

The fresh dried stigmas and styles of maize, known as 'Cornsilk' are widely used as an anti-lithic. However, the whole of the grain is soothing and healing to kidney structure The Inca writer, Garcilaso de la Vega (1539-1616) left these observations:

"I am impressed with the remarkable curative properties of corn (maize), which is not only the principle article of food in America, but is also of great benefit in the treatment of affections of the kidney and bladder, among which are calculus and retention of urine. The best proof I can give is that the Indians, whose usual drink is made of corn, are afflicted with none of these diseases."

The Cherokee Indians used Hydrangea root for stone or gravel.

Alternatives. *Teas*: Corn Silk, Couchgrass, Bearberry, Pellitory of the Wall, Marshmallow leaves, Wild Carrot, Dandelion leaves.

Decoction. Combine: Sea Holly 2; Gravel root 1; Hydrangea 1. Singly or in combination. 1-2 teaspoons to each cup water gently simmered 20 minutes. Half-1 cup thrice daily.

Powders. Formula: equal parts, Dandelion root, Marshmallow root, Stone root. Dose: quarter to half a teaspoon (375-750mg or 2-3 00 capsules) thrice daily.

Liquid Extracts. Stone root 1; Gravel root 1; Lobelia half; Ginger root half. Mix. Dose: 1 teaspoon thrice daily.

English traditional. Horsetail tea.

Tinctures. Formula. Gravel root 10ml; Parsley Piert 10ml; Marshmallow root 20ml; Lobelia simplex, BPC (1949) 5ml. Ginger (fort) BP 2ml. Aqua to 100ml. Dose: one 5ml teaspoon in water thrice daily.

Topical. Every two days: hot fomentations of Ginger. Teaspoon powdered Ginger to half cup boiling water; stir well, spread on linen or other suitable material for application over painful area. OR: Castor oil pack.

Diet. No dairy products, calcium of which disposes to stone formation. Dandelion coffee. No tap water; only bottled low-calcium waters. Vitamins A, B6, C and E. Broccoli, oranges.

Supportives. Magnesium has been credited with resolving stone. A coffeespoonful Epsom salts in tea at breakfast is a well-known preventative for those prone to formation of renal calculi. See: HAEMATURIA (Note).

Renal colic. Refer to entry for passage of stone.

STONE ROOT. Knob-root. *Collinsonia canadensis L. German*: Kanaddische collinsonie. *French*: Baume de Cheval. *Italian*: Collinsonia.

Part used: rhizome.

Constituents: essential oil, magnesium salts, saponins, resin.

Action. Anti-lithic, diaphoretic, diuretic.

Uses. Kidney stone. Gravel. Gall stone. Dr F.G. Hoener claimed success in its use for cholera, dysentery and gastro-enteritis. Dropsy from heart disease. Itching anus or piles.

Combines well with Corn Silk for stone; with Wild Yam for diverticulitis and Crohn's disease.

Preparations. Average dose, 1-4 grams or fluid equivalent. Thrice daily.

Liquid Extract BHP (1983) 1:1 in 25 per cent alcohol; dose, 1-4ml.

Powder. Add a pinch Cayenne and fill No 00 capsules; dose, 2 capsules, or one-third teaspoon in honey.

Tincture BPC (1934). 1:5 in 40 per cent alcohol; dose 2-8ml in water. GSL

STORAX. Sweet gum. Styrax. *Liquidambar orientalis*, Mill. *Part used*: balsam.

Constituents: triterpene acids.

Action. Stimulating expectorant, antiparasitic, antiseptic, antimicrobial, anti-inflammatory.

Uses. To aid excretion of phlegm in bronchitis, and pulmonary affections as an inhalant. See: FRIAR'S BALSAM. Parasitic skin diseases such as scabies (ointment).

An ingredient of Friar's balsam. GSL

STORING OF HERBS. Containers should be airtight to prevent escape of volatile oils. Herbs should be stored out of the light and air and in a cool dry place. The least trace of moisture introduces mildew which may spoil a whole consignment. Herbs are stored in paper bags, tins or stoppered jars; never in plastic bags or containers. Store medicines in a dry, cool place, safely locked away from children.

STRAMONIUM. Thorn apple. *Datura stramonium L. German*: Stechapfel. *French*: Endormie. *Spanish*: Erba del diavolo. *Italian*: Pomo spina. *Indian*: Dhatura. *Arabian*: Jous-ul-mathel. *Iranian*: Korz masali. *Malayan*: Rotiku bung. Seeds, leaves, tops.
Constituents: alkaloids – hyosine, hyosyamine, atropine.
Action. Anti-asthmatic, antispasmodic, nerve-sedative, senility.
Uses. Asthma; leaves also smoked for relief. Whooping cough. In common use for rabies in China. Temporary relief from Parkinsonian tremor recorded.
Combinations. With Ephedra for asthma; Mouse-Ear for whooping cough; Lobelia for asthma.
Traditional inhalant: herb or powder burnt and allowed to smoulder. An ingredient of smoking mixture and asthma cigarettes.
Preparations. Use confined to practitioners only.
Liquid Extract BP (1968): dose, 0.06 to 0.2ml.
Tincture BP (1973): dose 0.5 to 2ml.
Powder: 0.06 to 0.2 grams.
Contra-indications: heart failure, abnormal irritability, prostatitis, pregnancy or depressant drugs.
Pharmacy only, herbal practitioners being exempt up to 150mg daily (50mg per dose).

STRAWBERRY, WILD. *Fragaria vesca L. German*: Erdbeere. *French*: Fraisier. *Spanish*: Fresca. *Italian*: Fragola. *Parts used*: leaves, rootstock.
Constituents: essential oil, tannins, flavonoids, glycosides.
Action. Haemostatic, astringent, laxative, diuretic, anti-scurvy.
Uses. Excessive menstruation, bleeding piles, irritable bowel, colitis, kidney or bladder gravel, gall-stone, to reduce bust measurement and arrest flow of milk in nursing mothers. To reduce uric acid levels in the blood. Reduction of enlarged spleen reported.
Preparations. Dried leaves were once used as a substitute for Indian tea.
Tea: 1-2 teaspoons to each cup boiling water; infuse 10 minutes, half-1 cup freely.

Cultivated Strawberry leaves do not possess the same properties.

STREPTOCOCCUS. Bacterial organism: streptococcus pyogenes. Most common of all bacteria, made up of cocci arranged like a string of beads, wreath-like as seen under the microscope. Most are harmless; others however may attack wounds as septicaemia, or cause such infections as erysipelas, scarlet and rheumatic fevers. Sometimes the bacteria takes on a life-threatening character, as in Flesh-Eating disease. There is a correlation between 'strep' throat infections and subsequent rheumatic heart disease.

Most streptococcus respond to herbal antibacterials and antivirals, chief of which are Echinacea, Myrrh and Goldenseal. Routine gargling with Tincture Myrrh (10-20 drops to each glass of water) can save the waiting period of a day or more required to grow laboratory cultures.

STREPTOMYCIN. Antibiotic used to combat a number of bacteria, especially one responsible for tuberculosis. Used also for a number of other infections. Careful control is necessary because of disturbing side-effects, one being damage to the auditory nerve concerning balance; another for tinnitus.
Alternatives sometimes used with success: Myrrh, Camphor, Echinacea, Wild Indigo.

STRESS. The 20th century disease. To be alive is to be under a certain amount of stress. It is needed by all who wish to perform at their best. Yet it is a major factor in high blood pressure, heart attacks, strokes and coronary artery disease. No other single cause is responsible for the world-wide escalation of alcohol and drug abuse.

Common sources of stress are marriage difficulties, separation or divorce, personal illness, unemployment, bereavement, suppressed anger. Physically-fit people can take vast pressures. Maintenance of a good general health is called for, with change of pace, maybe change of lifestyle, exercise in the open air, yoga or other relaxation techniques.
Alternatives. To help raise tolerance to stress: Balm, Betony, Black Cohosh, Borage, Cayenne, German Chamomile, Roman Chamomile, Damiana, Gentian, Ginseng, Ginkgo, Motherwort, Hops, Eleutherococcus, Lobelia, Kola, Lime flowers, Mistletoe, Oats, Pulsatilla, Passion flower, St John's Wort, Skullcap, Valerian, Vervain, Wild Lettuce. Any of these taken as a tea, tablet, powder, liquid extract or tincture.
Calmer-Downer tea: equal parts, German Chamomile, Balm, Betony. 1 heaped teaspoon to each cup boiling water; infuse 15 minutes. Half-1 cup freely.
Powders. Mix, equal parts: Passion flower, Wood Betony, Valerian, Kola, Siberian Ginseng. Fill size 00 capsules. Dose: 2 capsules or one-third teaspoon morning and evening (500mg).

Practitioner. Alternatives: (1) Tincture Gelsemium BPC (1973). Dose: 10 drops in 100ml (half a cup) water; 1 teaspoon 3-4 times daily. (2) Combine equal parts: Tinctures, Wild Lettuce, Jamaica Dogwood, Skullcap. Dose: 30-60 drops in water or honey. Thrice daily.
Aromatherapy. Massage. 6 drops oil of Lavender in 2 teaspoons Almond oil.
Diet. High protein. Maintain potassium levels by eating potassium-rich foods, bananas.
Vitamins. A. B-complex, B6, B12, Folic acid, Pantothenic acid, C. D. E. Evening Primrose.
Minerals: Magnesium, Zinc.

STRETCH MARKS. Stretch marks are thin purple lines that fade into silvery streaks appearing usually on hips, breasts, buttocks or stomach when skin is over-stretched as in pregnancy. Women who in pregnancy put on most weight acquire most stretch marks. Their presence is associated with lack of protein Vitamin B6 and Zinc, elements essential for production of sound collagen tissue.
Alternatives. *To give high level elasticity*. Comfrey tea, Irish Moss, Iceland Moss, Fenugreek seeds.
Topical. Massage with Almond oil or Cocoa Butter to tone connective tissue and stimulate circulation. Follow with Vitamin E cream. After pregnancy: Aloe Vera gel or cream.
Diet. See: DIET – GENERAL.
Supplements. Daily. Vitamin B6 50mg. Vitamin E 400iu. Zinc 15mg.
Check for diabetes.

STRICTURE. Narrowing of a tube or passage such as the urethra, gullet or rectum. Caused by the formation of scar tissue after repeated inflammation.
See: URETHRAL STRICTURE. OESOPHAGEAL STRICTURE.

STROKE (Apoplexy). A sudden and severe attack in the cardiovascular system caused by the bursting of a blood vessel or by a clot in the brain. Brain damage follows escape of blood into the delicate nerve cells. High blood pressure may cause rupture of a vessel, usually in the aged with hardening of the arteries. Where there is no high blood pressure it is likely to be due to thrombosis.
A stroke may be immediate, with collapse and unconsciousness; or a slowly-developing paralysis while the person is still conscious. Can also result from narrowing of the carotid artery in the neck due to atheroma. Paralysis on one side of the body, with lack of sensation is usual. The face is distorted downwards towards the side affected. Breathing may be a violent snoring. In bed, or on the floor, diagnosis is assisted by passive movement of an arm or leg on one side while the other is without movement.
Symptoms include: numbness, 'pins and needles' or heaviness of affected limbs, temporary blindness, tinnitus (roaring in the ears), dizziness, impaired speech and mental confusion. A 'little stroke' may occur without evidence of clotting or bleeding due to cerebral spasm. Partial or temporary paralysis may pass off within a few days.
Recognition. Haemorrhage: from emotional or physical exertion. Vomiting. Headache. Distressed breathing. Loss of consciousness. Rapid onset. Face flushed.
Thrombosis. Commonest cause. Slower onset. Gradual deterioration over hours. Cause: high blood pressure or diabetes. Face pale.
Embolism. Usual signs, but with no loss of consciousness. Headache. Confusion.
Call for doctor immediately. Lay patient on a bed or the floor. Apply hot water bottles to feet, cold packs to head. Keep airway clear and disturb as little as possible. Official medicine regards Aspirin as effective in preventing death from heart attack.
Treatment. On discharge from hospital to promote recovery: peripheral vasodilators with heart and nerve agents. Where the cause has been related to high blood pressure: see – BLOOD PRESSURE, HIGH. Attention to bowels: constipation may increase arterial pressure.
Alternatives:– *Teas*: of value – Buckwheat, Gotu Kola, Hawthorn, Hyssop, Lime flowers, Mistletoe, Yarrow.
Tea combination: Equal parts, Hawthorn, Mistletoe, Lime flowers, Yarrow. One heaped teaspoon to each cup boiling water; infuse 10-15 minutes; dose – 1 cup thrice daily.
Powders. Formula. Ginkgo 2; Hawthorn 1; Mistletoe 1; Yarrow 2. Dose: 750mg (three 00 capsules or half a teaspoon) thrice daily.
Tinctures. Hawthorn 1; Lime flowers 2; Mistletoe 1; Rosemary half; Yarrow 1. Dose: 1-2 teaspoons thrice daily.
Ginkgo: rich in bioflavonoids that strengthen capillaries.
Practitioner. Formula. Liquid extract Lady's Slipper 5ml; Liquid extract Hawthorn 5ml; Liquid extract Yarrow 30ml; Liquid extract Lily of the Valley 5ml; Liquid extract Oats (avena sativa) 30ml; Tincture Capsicum 0.3ml. Sig: 5ml (3i) tds pc sine aq.
Gelsemium, or Dr Thomson's 3rd Preparation of Lobelia at the discretion of the practitioner.
Diet. Vegetarian. Avoid coffee, alcoholic stimulants, eggs. Accept: soya and other products rich in lecithin. Fish oils. Low salt. Foods rich in cholesterol should be kept to a minimum: fat meat, butter, cheese, milky drinks, caramel cakes, chocolate and cream.
A British study demonstrates how onions reduce the chances of having a stroke, favouring clotting power of the blood. Researchers in the Netherlands found that men who ate more than 20 grams of fish

a day had a 51 per cent reduction in risk of stroke compared with men eating less fish. They suggested the effect might be due to polyunsaturated fatty acids in fish reducing clotting.
Supplements. Vitamin A, B-complex, inositol, C (time-release), chromium, selenium. Heavy doses of Vitamin E are shown to assist breathing, allay anginal pains and sustain the heart – up to 1,500iu daily.
Garlic. Anticoagulant: 2-3 capsules or tablets at night.
Note. Care should be taken to avoid powerful diuretics with frequent voiding of urine. Muscles should be kept active by gentle movement.

Treatment by or in liaison with a general medical practitioner.
The Stroke Association. The only charity in England and Wales with the single purpose of preventing stroke and helping those sufferers and their families. Home-visiting services, welfare grants, leaflets and videos. CHSA House, Whitecross Street, London EC1Y 8JJ. Tel: 071 490 7999.

STROPHANTHUS. *Strophanthus kombé*, Oliver. Dry ripe seeds. Well-documented in medical literature. Seeds yield G-strophanthin an arrow-tip poison among African forest people.
Constituents: cardiac glycosides.
Action. Heart sedative: effect is not as cumulative as Digitalis.
Uses. Asthma from cardiac failure, fatty degeneration of the heart. Goitre with heart weakness. (*Dr Finlay Ellingwood*) Where rapid heart response is required, sometimes used instead of Digitalis. Does not slow the heart as much as Digitalis. Of value in failure of compensation as in mitral disease and in extremely critical heart conditions. Raises blood pressure; increases force of the heart beat.
Preparation. *Tincture Strophanthus BP (1948)*. 0.12 to 0.3ml (2 to 5 minims).
Note. Used by injection given by a medically qualified practitioner. German physician Dr Berthold Kern treats with oral G-strophanthin and has shown how the African plant extract can prevent death from heart attack and who has experienced no fatal infarcts. The agent is used by 5,000 West German doctors. In the UK, is available as oil and capsules. Prescription only medicine (POM).

STUPOR. A state of complete psychomotor inhibition but with retained consciousness. Patient motionless, does not speak, is oblivious to surrounding activity, depressed, numbed by grief (bereavement), dopiness from drugs, alcohol, fatigue. May follow excited noisy behaviour or epileptic fit.
Treatment. Antidepressants. In compounding prescription due regard should be given to the thyroid and parathyroid glands, liver and kidneys.
Alternatives. Yerbe mate tea. Rosemary tea. Damiana, Kola and Saw Palmetto (standard combination). Ginseng, Ginkgo.
Formula. Equal parts: Balmony and Ginkgo. Dose. Powders: 500mg (two 00 capsules or one-third teaspoon). Liquid extracts: 1 teaspoon. Tinctures: 2 teaspoons. Every 2 hours (acute). Thrice daily (chronic).
Cayenne pepper: few grains (or few drops Tincture Capsicum) in cup of tea or other beverage.
Diet. Oatmeal.

STYE. Hordeolum. Bacterial infection of an eyelash follicle. Associated with BLEPHARITIS. See: EYE – INFECTION OF.

STYPTICS. See: HAEMOSTATICS.

SUB-LINGUAL DELIVERY. Under-the-tongue administration of herbal powders, tinctures and nutritional substances becomes increasingly popular among practitioners. When swallowed, capsules, tablets and other preparations enter the stomach where their efficacy may be eroded by the presence of stomach acid.

When placed under the tongue substances come into closer contact with blood vessels than by any other route. Absorption is rapid and the remedy readily available for use. Under this technique a medicinal substance can by-pass the liver and therefore avoids chemical change. The under-the-tongue route for a specific powder, say, Cinnamon, Sage or Thyme, may require a small pinch or a few grains; it is claimed that this would be as potent as four to six times the quantity in capsule or tablet. Moreover, speed of action is greater. A substance can be absorbed into the bloodstream as fast as when injected by a doctor with a hypodermic syringe. One advantage of this method is the absence of binders, fillers and additives and the allergies they may encourage.

SUCCUSION. The simple act of vigorously shaking an electuary or herbal medicine in its container is believed to enhance the potency of its contents, releasing latent powers. Magnetism is imparted to a substance like amber by prolonged rubbing. Friction produces an increase in kinetic energy. A physiotherapist makes use of this elementary physical law when he massages the bodies of his patients. Energy generated by bottle-shaking is stored in the molecules as a charge of static electricity which activates the ingredients. The success of homoeopathy is believed to be partly due to this law.

SUDORIFICS. See: DIAPHORETICS.

SUICIDAL TENDENCY. Suicide is often contemplated when in depression and may be aggravated by poor nutrition. Diet should be high in protein, low-salt, low-cholesterol, and high in fibre. Skullcap is a brain-tonic and Ginseng (Eleutherococcus) an antidepressant used by Soviet scientists for mental anxiety.

Low concentration of serotonin in the cerebrospinal fluid can cause depression and suicidal anguish. Any emotional 'low' reacts favourably to the supplement tryptophan which is a precursor of serotonin and prescribed by a general medical practitioner only.

Ginkgo. Encouraging results reported.

SULPHUR. Non-metallic trace element essential to health. RDA not known.
Deficiency. Skin disorders.
Body effects. Healthy skin, hair and nails.
Sources. Prime source – Garlic. Others – Broom, Coltsfoot, Eyebright, Fennel seed, Meadowsweet, Mullein, Nettles, Pimpernel, Plantain, Rest Harrow, Horsetail, Shepherd's Purse, Silverweed, Watercress.

SUMA. Wild Brazilian shrub. "Para Toda".
Constituents: pfaffosides.
Action. Adaptogen, immune stimulant, nervine. Hormone stimulant believed to be the female equivalent of Ginseng.
Uses. Excessive stress. Physical and mental fatigue. Low blood pressure. Lack of appetite. Sexual debility.
Preparation. *Average dose*: powder: 750mg (three 00 capsules or half a teaspoon) thrice daily.

SUMACH, SWEET. *Rhus aromatica* Ait. *German*: Echter perückenstrauch. *French*: Fustet. *Italian*: Scuatano. Root bark. *Keynote*: genito-urinary system.
Constituents: free malic acid, tannic and gallic acid, oil, resin.
Action. Astringent, diuretic, anti-hyperglycaemic, adaptogen.
Uses. Urinary incontinence and frequency, blood in the urine. Inflammation of bladder, rectum or colon. Colitis, diverticulosis, irritable bowel, dysentery, bed-wetting, menopausal flooding. Lowers blood sugar, which may be the reason for its long traditional reputation in America for diabetes.
Preparations. Average dose 1-2 grams, or fluid equivalent. Thrice daily.
Decoction: half-1 teaspoon to each cup water gently simmered 20 minutes. Dose, half a cup.
Liquid extract: dose, 15-30 drops. GSL

SUMBUL. Musk root. *Ferula sumbul*, Hook.
Constituents: volatile oil, two balsamic resins, bitter principle.
Action. Antispasmodic, nerve tonic.
Uses. Nervous excitability, brain storm, convulsions, hysteria. Ovarian neuralgia, absence of menses, menopausal hot flushes, bronchitis.
Preparations. *Liquid Extract*: 1-2ml. Thrice daily.
Tincture: 2-4ml thrice daily. GSL

SUMMER SAVOURY. *Satureja hortensis, L.*
Constituents: tannins, mucilage, phenols, essential oil.
Action. Carminative, stomachic, antiseptic, diuretic, expectorant, anthelmintic, aphrodisiac.
Uses. To aid digestion and promote appetite. Irritable bowel, colitis.
Preparation. *Tea*: 2 teaspoons to each cup boiling water: infuse 10-15 minutes. Dose 1 cup thrice daily.

Salad ingredient at table.

SUN-BURN. Due to over-exposure of the skin to intensive bursts of strong sun. Public awareness of the potential dangers of sunbathing demand creams or oils to absorb and block an excess of ultra-violet rays penetrating the skin. Destruction of the ozone layer (which normally blocks some U.V. light) increases the risk of malignant melanoma through production of excess free-radicals in the body, which encourages abnormal reproduction of cells possibly leading to cancer of the skin.
Alternatives. *Teas*. Singly, or in combination: Elderflowers, Boneset, Yarrow, or other diaphoretics to induce sweating and epidermal recovery.
Topical. Aloe Vera, fresh juice from leaf, or gel. Jojoba. Marigold infusion – cold compress.

Creams to absorb UV radiation are: Houseleek, Evening Primrose. Contents of Vitamin E capsule wiped over affected area. Wipe with slice of cucumber. Yoghurt with lemon juice.

Aromatherapy. Re-moisturise with 2 drops each Marigold (calendula) and Hyssop essential oils in 2 teaspoons Almond oil.
Cider vinegar. Add teacupful to bath water.
Suntan Lotion. Old Vermont Remedy. Combine equal parts Olive oil and Cider vinegar. Vinegar protects the skin from burning. Shake well before use.
Diet. See: DIET – SKIN DISEASES.
Supplements. Beta carotene (to quench free-radicals), Vitamin A. Vitamin C (1g morning and evening). Vitamin E (one 500iu capsule morning and evening). Selenium, Zinc. To prepare skin for excessive sunshine: Vitamin B6 (50mg); PABA (every day for one week before exposure).
Note. Even dull skies carry ultra-violet light, and sunburn in childhood is a risk factor.

SUNDEW. *Drosera rotundifolia L. French*: Rosée du soleil. *German*: Runder Sonnentau. *Italian*: Erba da fottosi. Lichen.
Constituents: flavonoids, naphthaquinones.
Action. Expectorant, soothing demulcent, anti-

spasmodic, antitussive. Vitamin K-like effect which assists antispasmodic action in whooping cough.

Bacteriostatic and bacteriocidal action against staphylococcus aureus. (*Complementary Medical Research Vol 2, No 2, p.139*)

Uses. Asthma, bronchitis, constant dry tickling cough, loss of voice. Chronic indigestion with bronchial spasm: violent coughing attacks ending in vomiting. Whooping cough. Arteriosclerosis.

Preparations. Average dose, 1-2 grams or fluid equivalent. Thrice daily, or 2-hourly for acute cases.

Tea. Half-1 teaspoon to each cup boiling water; infuse 15 minutes; dose, half-1 cup.

Liquid Extract BHP (1983). 1:1 in 25 per cent alcohol. Dose: 0.5 to 2ml.

Tincture BHP (1983). 1:5 in 60 per cent alcohol. Dose: 0.5 to 1ml.

Contra-indications: tuberculosis of the lungs. Terminal stage of any severe lung disease. A harmless side-effect is a dark-brown discoloration of urine. GSL

SUNFLOWER SEEDS. *Helianthus annuus L.*

Action. Expectorant, diuretic, anti-cholesterol, nutritive.

Uses. Seeds are high in B vitamins and Vitamin E, and therefore good for muscles, nerves and blood vessels. Rich in a wide spectrum of minerals, including zinc. In Russia the seeds are a staple item of diet. Habitual eating of the seeds is said to build-up physical endurance and resistance against disease, as well as preserve natural sight for a long time without glasses. Up to half a cup of seeds may be eaten daily by sportspeople to strengthen muscles and improve performance.

Seed and oil reduce cholesterol deposits, help reduce high blood pressure, and prevent heart failure.

Rich in linoleic acid. See: LINOLEIC ACID. GSL

SUNSTROKE. See: HEATSTROKE.

SUPPOSITORY. Bolus. A vehicle, usually cartridge-shaped, to be inserted into a body cavity such as the rectum, vagina or urethra. Powdered herbs are worked into cocoa butter until the consistency of dough and rolled out with the hands or rolling-pin until finger-thickness. Cut into one-inch pieces and harden off in a refrigerator.

This should be a most important item of modern herbal pharmacy as it can bring into direct contact with abnormal tissues in the rectum or vagina certain antibiotic, antiviral and anti-neoplastic herbs.

Witch Hazel, Figwort, Pilewort, are used per rectum for haemorrhoids; Goldenseal, Echinacea, Squaw Vine, for vaginal inflammation, tumour, thrush. Usually applied at night with adequate precaution to protect clothing.

For application to cysts and tumours John Christopher and Michael Tierra advise: Equal parts: Squaw Vine, Slippery Elm, Yellow Dock, Comfrey, Marshmallow root, Chickweed, Goldenseal root, Mullein leaves. Mix powders and add tablespoon to small amount of cocoa-butter; prepare as above.

SUPPRESSION OF URINE. Failure of the kidneys to secrete urine.

Causes: stone, injury, pyelitis, renal failure. Suppression as well as retention may occur in drug poisoning.

Treatment. *Teas*: any one: Corn Silk, Wild Carrot, Couchgrass, Buchu, Spearmint, Parsley root.

Simple suppression from cold or 'nerves': 3-10 drops Oil Juniper in teaspoon honey hourly.

Slippery Elm gruel. (*Dr Samuel Stearn*)

Hop Poultice for pain.

This condition should be treated by or in liaison with a qualified medical practitioner.

SUPPURATION. Pus-formation as in an infected wound caused by pyogenic microbes. See: ABSCESS, and specific infections.

SURGERY. Occasions arise when a surgical operation is required. Of European reputation is the Royal College of Surgeons which sets standards of surgical excellence and is dedicated to professional performance, education, training and research. The qualifications FRCS inspire confidence and are a natural choice of the discerning patient.

SURGICAL OPERATION. Herbal medicine has its limitations. Surgery may be necessary. Much can be done to build up powers of resistance before the day of admission to hospital. Honey, bee pollen and Slippery Elm are great strengtheners and may be taken at meals. With possible loss of blood, surgery (dental or general) makes a heavy demand on the body's mineral reserves. These may be provided by teas: Alfalfa (richest source of trace elements), Irish Moss (iodine), Chiretta and Fenugreek seeds.

After operation. Combine: 5 drops each: Tincture Arnica, Tincture Calendula (Marigold), Tincture Hypericum (St John's Wort), to half a glass water (100ml). Dose: one teaspoon hourly to help dissipate shock and mobilise the body's recuperative powers.

Skullcap tea. For nerve weakness.

Local. To restore flesh which has been abnormally stretched and bruised. Bathe with weak tincture Arnica, St John's Wort or decoction Comfrey root.

Vitamins. A. B-complex. B12. C (500mg). E (1,000iu) daily. Mineral: Zinc.

Note. Do not take a surgeon's qualifications for granted. Your operation should be performed by an accredited member of the Royal College of Surgeons (FRCS) in Britain, The American College of Surgeons (FACS) in America, or senior body in other countries.

SWEAT RASH. Miliaria. See: PRICKLY HEAT.

SWEATING. Absence of.
To induce: Teas: Elderflowers, Catmint, Yarrow. All diaphoretics promote sweating.
Life Drops. Composition Essence.
Composition powder. 1 teaspoon in cup of tea, freely.
Diet. Cayenne pepper at table. Spicy foods. Curry.

SWEATING. Excessive. Most cases are due to natural causes. However, it may be due to constitutional disturbance when it is necessary to treat the underlying condition. Night sweats are usually due to temperature rise and are frequent in malaria and tuberculosis. Where lung or kidney disease is suspected, treatment should relate. Menopausal sweating is a natural phenomenon.
Alternatives. Agnus Castus (hormone disorders); Burdock (under arm); Thuja (cadaver-like smell). Sage, Boneset.
Teas. Made with boiling water and best taken cold. Boneset, Lady's Mantle, Horsetail, Yerbe Santa, Nettles, Hops, Rosemary. Most popular: Garden Sage.
Traditional tea. Combine equal parts: Horsetail, Lady's Mantle, Garden Sage. 1 heaped teaspoon to each cup boiling water; infuse until cold. Dose: 1 cup morning and evening.
Dr Finlay Ellingwood. Liquid Extract or tincture Passion flower. 5-10 drops in water every half hour until asleep.
Practitioner. Tincture Belladonna, BP (1980). Dose: 0.5-2ml, in water. Jaborandi.
Formula. Sage 2; Buchu 1; Dandelion half. Mix. Dose. Powders: 500mg (two 00 capsules or one-third teaspoon). Liquid extracts: 1 teaspoon. Tinctures: 2 teaspoons.
Aromatherapy. External use; hands, underarm, etc. 6 drops Sage oil to 15ml Almond oil.
Footbath. Hot sweaty feet. 1 kilo pine needles boiled in 2 litres water 10 minutes. Alternatives: Tansy, Witch Hazel.
Cold sponge-down followed by brisk friction-rub with hands or a coarse towel.
Diet. Avoid hot spicy foods, Cayenne, Ginger, Horseradish and alcohol. Increase protein.
Supplements. Vitamin C. Dolomite. Potassium, Zinc.

SWEDISH BITTERS. A combination of traditional herbs popularised by the famous Swedish physician, Dr Clause Samst and afterwards rediscovered by the Austrian Herbalist, Maria Treben, consisting of 11 herbs macerated in alcohol to form a tincture.
Constituents: 10gm Aloe (for which Gentian root or Wormwood herb may be substituted); 5gm Myrrh; 0.2gm Saffron; 10gm Senna leaves; 10gm Camphor (natural); 10gm Rhubarb root; 10gm Zedoary; 10gm Manna; 10gm Venetian Theriac, 5gm Blessed Thistle root, 10gm Angelica root.
May be taken internally or used externally as a compress. Taste is strong and bitter. A persuasive liver stimulant. An important combination for purifying and detoxifying the system.

SWEDISH BITTERS ELIXIR. (*Pronatura, West Germany*) *Ingredients*: alcohol (17.5 per cent volume) containing alcoholic extracts from Manna, Aloe, Senna leaves, Rhubarb root, Zedoary root, Angelica root, Black Snake root, Valerian root, Ceylon-Cinnamon bark, Malabar cardamoms (Myrrh), Carline Thistle root, Myrrh, Camphor and Saffron. Liquid herbal extract. Based on a 16th century recipe of Paracelsus.

SWEET CICELY. Sweet bracken. See: CHERVIL.

SWOLLEN ANKLES. See: FLUID RETENTION SYNDROME.

SYCOSIS. Barber's itch. See: FOLLICULITIS.

SYDENHAM'S CHOREA. St Vitus dance. Dancing mania. A nervous disorder with contortion of the facial muscles and limbs. A disease of childhood, girls more than boys: ages 5 to 15 years. Associated with valvular heart disease just as is rheumatic fever.
Causes: irritation of the cerebro-spinal system by rheumatic fever, streptococcal or other infection.
Symptoms. Jerky movements, weak muscles, debility, cold hands and feet, low blood pressure, irritability, irregular or absent menses, grunting, child drops articles.
May be brought on by over-study, 'outgrowing one's strength', insufficient rest. The condition differs from Huntington's chorea which appears in middle life, with mental defection.
Treatment. Bedrest. Nerve relaxants to help control the nervous contortions (Lobelia, Skullcap, Ladyslipper, Passion flower etc). To combat rheumatic fever (Echinacea, Wild Indigo, Myrrh, Garlic, Yarrow, etc). Popular conventional treatment is aspirin, for which White Willow is a mild substitute.
Alternatives:– *Tea*: Combine Passion flower, Motherwort, Skullcap. Equal parts. 2 teaspoons to each cup boiling water; infuse 15 minutes. Half-1 cup thrice daily.
Decoction: (1) Combine equal parts: Fringe Tree bark, Black Cohosh, White Willow. OR:–

(2) Combine equal parts: Motherwort, Skullcap, Mistletoe. Prepare: 2 teaspoons to each large cup water gently simmered 20 minutes; dose; half a cup thrice daily.
Tablets/capsules: Kelp, Valerian, Mistletoe, Skullcap, Passion flower, Lobelia, Helonias (especially girls).
Powders: Black Cohosh, with few grains Cayenne pepper. Dose: 500mg (two 00 capsules or one-third teaspoon) thrice daily.
Tinctures: combine: Echinacea 2; Black Cohosh 1; Oats 1. 1 teaspoon in water thrice daily.
Eclectic School, (*Ellingwood*) regarded Black Cohosh almost specific, 10-20 drops in water thrice daily. (*T. Jensen MD*)
Practitioner: When inco-ordinated movements are uncontrollable: Tincture Gelsemium 5 drops (0.3ml) as indicated.
BHP (1983) combination: Jamaica Dogwood, Hops, Valerian.
John Wild MD, claims to have successfully treated cases with tincture Mistletoe made from the bruised leaves – 5-10 drop doses, in water.
Dr Melville Keith commenced all treatments with an emetic.

Irritation of the brain and nerves is often due to a disordered stomach and intestines for which Hops, Meadowsweet or Betony may be added.
Formula. Tinctures. Feverfew 10-30 drops; Echinacea 10-20 drops; Cayenne (capsicum) 10-20 drops. Dose every 2-3 hours according to symptoms. (*Dr S. Clymer, Nature's Healing Agents*)
Diet. Build sound nutrition with wholefoods. Oatmeal porridge or muesli.
Supplementation. Calcium and Magnesium. Zinc. Vitamins B6, B12, C, D, E.
General: removal of bad teeth or infected tonsils. Look to eyes for astigmatism requiring correction by glasses.

Treatment by or in liaison with a general medical practitioner only.

SYNCOPE. See: FAINTING.

SYNDROME. A group of symptoms that define the character of a disease.

SYNERGIST. A medicine which aids or works well with another. An adjuvant correlating and co-operating well with another, i.e. the old traditional nerve combination: Skullcap, Valerian and Mistletoe, each known to enhance the action of the other. "The total is greater than the sum of its parts."

SYNOVITIS. Inflammation of the synovial membrane of a joint, tendon or bursa. See: BURSITIS, ARTHRITIS, TENOSYNOVITIS.

SYPHILIS. Highly contagious sexually transmitted disease (STD) caused by the spirochete *Treponema pallidum*. Corkscrew in shape, it can worm its way into almost every kind of tissue. May be acquired or congenital. Infants may never develop its symptoms. A notifiable disease.

Treatment by a hospital infectious diseases specialist.
Symptoms. Usually become apparent about 3 weeks after contact. Disease marked by three stages: (1) primary and secondary (2) latent when the disease seems to disappear and (3) tertiary (late) stage. A blood test (Wasserman) is necessary to confirm diagnosis.
Primary. With a sore (chancre), a painless red swelling about the size of a small marble which ulcerates and forms a scab with a depression in the middle. Swollen lymph glands.
Secondary. General non-itch skin rash. Discoloured patches of mucous membrane. Flat warts (condylomata). Enlargement of spleen, liver and lymph glands. Followed by the latent stage.
Latency period. Disappearance of obvious symptoms.
Tertiary. The disease may last as long as 10-15 years before it again manifests; within this time heart, brain and spinal cord may be affected. Swellings of skin and bones. Paralysis may supervene with mental deterioration. General paralysis of the insane (GPI).

Today multiple infection is common; syphilis may co-exist with other STDs.
Treatment. Penicillin. Historical literature abounds with cases of the disease being controlled by herbal anti-bacterials. "The results I have had curing syphilis would convince the most sceptical," wrote Dr Finlay Ellingwood. (*Ellingwood Therapeutist vol 12. No 3*) He treated hundreds of cases at the turn of the century with Liquid Extract Echinacea, 30 drops; and Liquid Extract Thuja, 10 drops, in water, thrice daily. Tissue damage can never be repaired.
Skin eruptions: Barberry.
Lymph glands: Poke root.
Dry scaly eczema: Blue Flag root.
Purplish ulceration of mouth and throat: Wild Indigo and Thuja.
Sore throat: local swabs with Goldenseal, Myrrh and Blood root.
Venereal warts: paint with liquid extract Thuja.
W.H. Black MD. (*Ellingwood*) Liquid Extract Poke root 2 drams; Liquid Extract Echinacea half an ounce. 1-2 teaspoons, thrice daily. Most practitioners are inclined to be sceptical of such simple combination but the doctor claimed good results over 40 years.
Dr Rush, Bennett Medical College, (*Ellingwood*). Red Clover Compound, original formula. 32gr Red Clover; 16gr Queen's Delight; 16gr Burdock; 16gr Poke root; 16gr Water Barberry; 16gr Cascara; 4gr Prickly Ash. Dr Rush writes:

"Thousands of cases have been successfully treated by such vegetable alternatives and the relief when achieved leaves the patient in excellent condition. The thing that is necessary is confidence and persistence."

Sore throat. Formula. Equal parts: Tinctures Thuja, Echinacea, Blue Flag root. Dose: 15-30 drops thrice daily, internal. 20 drops to glass water as a gargle, freely. (*American Eclectic School*)

Historical. Oviedo (1526) advises Guaiacum; Monardes (1570) – Sarsaparilla; Samuel Thomson (1800) – Lobelia. The use of Blue Lobelia, a variety of Indian Tobacco, by the Iroquois Indians as a venereal remedy was the subject of a paper by John Bartram in 1751. (*Virgil Vogel*)

SYRINGOMYELIA. Congenital disease of the lower brain and spinal cord in which cavities form within the cord, in the neck.

Symptoms. Loss of sensation over the shoulders and arms. Weakness of legs. Difficulties in swallowing, speech and sense of balance, terminating in paralysis.

No treatment can cure or arrest, yet general nerve and constitutional tonics may strengthen and sustain.

Alternatives. *Tea*: combine equal parts: Skullcap, Alfalfa, Oats. 1-2 teaspoons to each cup boiling water; infuse 15 minutes. Half-1 cup as desired.

Tablets: Prickly Ash, Ginseng, Gentian.

Tinctures: combine, Kola 1; Prickly Ash 1; Oats (Avena sativa) 2. Dose: 15-60 drops in water or honey thrice daily.

Diet. Gluten-free.

Treatment by or in liaison with a general medical practitioner.

SYRUP. A fluid preparation of herbs containing a sufficient quantity of sugar, either to make it more palatable or to preserve.

Examples: syrup of Orange, Lemon, Virginian Prune, Rhubarb root, Red Poppy petals, Squills, Senna, Tolu, Ginger.

Modern pharmacy views with disfavour administration of sugar-sweetened medicines to children. An alternative is honey, used as sweetening for teas, decoctions, tinctures, etc.

SYSTEMIC. Referring to the whole of the body.

TABEBUIA TREE. See: LAPACHO TREE.

TABES DORSALIS. Locomotor ataxia. Degeneration of nerve fibres of the spinal cord due to advanced syphilis. May not manifest until lapse of 10-20 years after infection. Unsteady and high-stepping gait. Loss of control of bladder with incontinence. Most distressing symptoms include 'lightning' stabbing pains in the legs and abdomen, with vomiting. Weakness, nervous prostration.

Treatment. Condition incurable, but increase in muscle and nerve tone makes the lot easier for the sufferer. Supportives for the central nervous system: Yerba mate tea, Kola nuts, Ginseng, Cramp bark, St John's Wort, Bayberry bark, Thuja, Damiana (Curzon), Lady's Slipper, Gotu Kola, Rosemary.

By the time tabes has developed, treatment for syphilis will be too late, yet the addition of a traditional chronic syphilis remedy may benefit: Sarsaparilla, Queen's Delight or Prickly Ash.

Formula. Cramp bark 2; Thuja 1; Damiana (Curzon) 1. Mix. Dose. Powders: 250-500mg (1-2 capsules 00 or quarter to one-third of a teaspoon). Liquid Extracts: 30-60 drops. Tinctures: 1-2 teaspoons. Thrice daily. See: SYPHILIS.

Treatment by a general medical practitioner or hospital specialist.

TABISHIR. See: BAMBOO.

TABLETS. Compressed powders or extracts are the most popular form of taking herbs. Most tablets on the herbal market contain simple dried, powdered herbs with no destructive refining and processing.

The modern trend is against the use of sugar, solvents, starches, preservatives, artificial flavouring and chemical dyes. It is in favour of natural excipients, fillers, and binders which hold the tablet together. These include vegetable oils, Acacia or Guar gums, propolis, alginic acid from seaweed, calcium phosphate and rice bran. Gum tragacanth is sometimes used for its thickening, emulsifying and suspending ability. Irish Moss makes a good binder, emulsifier and stabiliser.

Coating is important for storage life; for which maize protein (zein) is popular. An aqueous cellulose process uses water and vegetable cellulose to ensure stability of ingredients. Some tablets need to be of 'sustained release' in order that their contents be released slowly over 8-12 hours to prolong absorption period and ensure an efficient bioavailability. An enteric-sealed tablet is one devised to dissolve in the duodenum and intestine rather than the stomach.

Anti-allergens and hypo-allergenics today replace some allergenic substances once used, such as iodine, yeast, preserves, artificial colouring, flavouring, gluten or salt. As far as is known, no animals are involved in research and experiment in the manufacture of herbal products.

Labels on tablet containers must conform with requirements of The Medicines (Labelling and Advertising to the Public Regulations 1978). See: LABELLING OF HERBAL PRODUCTS.

Dosage of tablets varies according to each product. As a general average: Adults (over 12), 2 tablets thrice daily. Children (5-12 years) 1 tablet 2-4 times daily according to age. Carton-cap seals should not be broken.

Keep tablets out of sight and reach of children. All tablets should be packed in containers with safety closures against the attention of children.

Tablets should be stored in a cool dry place out of the light.

Patients should remain standing for at least 90 seconds after taking tablets, followed by sips of water. Swallowing failure is possible when taken in the recumbent position when the tablet may adhere to the oesophageal membrane, delaying disintegration time.

TACHYCARDIA. Rapid heart beat. Sinus tachycardia. One hundred or more beats per minute. Paroxysmal tachycardia has a steady rate of 180 or more of sudden onset and offset due to an abnormal (ectopic) pace-maker cell in the atrium or ventricle wall. It is sometimes arrested by firm pressure on the eyeballs or on the carotid sinus in the neck.

Causes: abnormality of the heart's pacemaker, emotional shock, anxiety, excitement, blood disorder, over-active thyroid gland, anaemia, feverish conditions, infections, kidney disorders, common drugs, coffee, strong tea, alcohol. A rise in heart rate always keeps pace with a rise in temperature.

Symptoms. Breathlessness, rapid beat, fainting, excessive urination.

Alternatives. Treat underlying cause. BHP (1983) recommends Bugleweed, Passion flower, Broom, Mistletoe.

Simple tachycardia: Motherwort.

Paroxysmal tachycardia: Hawthorn.

Of thyroid origin: Bugleweed. (Madaus)

With feeble pulse: Lily of the Valley.

Associated with high blood pressure: Lime flowers.

Tea. Single, or in combination of equal parts: Passion flower, Lime flowers. 1-2 teaspoons to each cup boiling water; infuse 15 minutes; 1 cup once or twice daily, or every 3 hours acute cases.

Tablets/capsules. Passion flower. Valerian. Mistletoe. Motherwort.

Formula. Equal parts: Motherwort, Lily of the Valley, Valerian. Mix. Dose: Powders: 500mg (two 00 capsules or one-third teaspoon). Liquid extracts: 1 teaspoon. Tinctures: 2 teaspoons. Thrice daily.

Practitioner. Valerian 2; Strophanthus 1. Mix.

Dose: Liquid extracts: 8-15 drops. Tinctures: 15-30 drops. Thrice daily.
Dr Finlay Ellingwood. "Give Poke root, Blue Flag root, Bugleweed and Cactus."
Spartiol Drops (Broom). 20 drops thrice daily for periods of 4 weeks. (*Klein*)
Diet. See: DIET – HEART AND CIRCULATION.
Note. Tachycardia may often be relieved by pressure of the eyeballs.

TAENIFUGE. An agent, such as Male Fern, to induce expulsion of tapeworms from the body of the host. See: ANTHELMINTICS.

TALBOR, SIR ROBERT. English herbalist who settled near the Essex Marshes to study the ague which was endemic. A scholarly man, he proceeded by observation and experiment to employ herbs in the treatment of fevers. Though unqualified, he attracted rich and poor and was so successful that visits from high European society compelled him to open in London where he developed the most famous and fashionable practice of his day.

After curing King Charles II of a malignant fever he was granted a knighthood and made Physician to the King much to the chagrin of the College of Physicians. Stung by this affront and by his refusal to purge or bleed his patients his life was a running battle with the Medical Establishment. However, neither the College nor the illustrious Thomas Sydenham could any longer hold back the flood-tide demand for the remedy responsible for Talbor's success, known in those days as Jesuit's powder. Thus, an unknown herbalist rose to be the first to introduce Peruvian bark (Quinine) into Europe for the cure of malaria.

TALCUM POWDER. Take cornflour. Sieve to rub out lumps. Add a few drops of essential oil (say Patchouli, Bergamot, Rose). Shake daily for 7 days. Pack into sprinkler and use.

The talcum of conventional pharmacy is finely-ground magnesium silicate. When changing nappies, Aloe Vera or Evening Primrose lotion or cream – or even warm towels – should be used in its place.

TAMARINDS. Tamarind fruit. *Tamarindus indica, L. German*: Tamarinde. *French*: Tamarin. *Spanish*: Tamarindo. *Italian*: Tamarindizio. *Iranian*: Ambala. *Indian*: Tentula. *Chinese*: An-me-lo. *Part used*: fruit pulp.
Constituents: volatile oil, vitamins, sugars, plant acids.
Action. Laxative, nutritive.
Uses. Has a long traditional history in the East for splenic disorders. Excessive acidity. Abnormal thirst. Constipation. As a cooling drink for fevers.
Preparations. An ingredient of Confection of Senna once widely used for constipation and malnutrition.
Cups were made out of the wood from which was drunk water and fluids, for splenic enlargement. Known as Indian dates the fruit may be eaten for above purposes.
Confection of Senna, BPC 1949: dose, 4-8 grams.

TAMPONS. A tampon or polyurethane sponge offers a useful vehicle for conveying a medicament to a cavity of the body. Moistened with a little dilute Liquid Extract Goldenseal, or with Slippery Elm paste before insertion into the vagina. Will stay in place by contact with the wall of the vagina for a considerable period of time.

TANNINS. Related to tannic acid. Acid astringents that coagulate protein and inhibit the laying-down of fatty deposits as in cellulitis and obesity. By contracting living fibre they reduce secretion and excretion and are useful to arrest external bleeding, catarrhal discharges, diarrhoea, etc (Oak Bark, Cranesbill). Useful for affections of mouth, throat, vagina, rectum and other internal surfaces. They inhibit digestion of proteins. Lime flower tea is one of the few herbs low in tannin that promotes digestion. Water soluble. Tannins are used to turn animal hides into leather. They are present in tea and coffee and to a lesser extent in other herbs including Agrimony, Archangel (*Lamium album L.*), Greater Burnett, Catechu, American Cranesbill, Witch Hazel.

TANSY. *Tanacetum vulgare L. German*: Rainfarn. *French*: Tanaisie. *Italian*: Tanasia. Leaves, flowers and terminal stems.
Constituents: sesquiterpene lactones, volatile oil, flavonoids.
Action. Emmenagogue, anthelmintic, antispasmodic, vermifuge, bitter, carminative.
Uses. Absence of menstruation. Expulsion of round worms (enema). Body lice, scabies, fleas, etc: wash with strong tea.
Preparations. Average dose, 1-2 grams or fluid equivalent. Thrice daily.
Tea: quarter to half a teaspoon in each cup water brought to boil; vessel removed at boiling point. Dose, one-third to half a cup.
Liquid Extract: 15-30 drops in water.
Enema (for worms): 1oz to 2 pints boiling water; infuse until cool, strain, inject warm.

Convulsions with toxicosis may follow large doses. Not used in pregnancy. External use only. Of historic interest.

TAPEWORMS. Cestodes. Parasitic worms of considerable length shaped like pieces of tape. Such worms living in the human intestines are *Taenia solium* (from pigs), *Taenia saginata* (cattle), *Diphyllobothrium latum* (fish). Human infestation is possible after eating undercooked meat, especially fresh uncooked cod fish and that which is sold in the cured and dried form, known as 'bakalar'.

Symptoms. Segments of tapeworm seen in the faeces, loss of weight, rarely pain. Children become irritable, twist and turn in their chair, have an itchy nose, are all 'skin and bone' and with possible anaemia due to worms pillaging vital nourishment.

Treatment. Not generally known that worms cannot well tolerate Cayenne pepper (Capsicum). Simple regime:–

Powders. Combine Slippery Elm 15; Cayenne 1. Dose: 250-750mg, or one-sixth to half a teaspoon. Abstain from food after evening meal of the previous day. On rising take dose according to age. Children 5 to 12 years: 250mg. No breakfast. Four hours later take dose of laxative: Senna, cleansing herbs or Castor oil. Repeat the process the next day or two, if necessary.

Alternatives. Poplar bark decoction or powder. Balmony tea. Wild Strawberry leaves and root; decoction. Pumpkin seed. (*Dr Wm Boericke*) Pomegranate bark decoction.

Chenopodium oil (American Wormseed) has now been superceded by the drug Niclosamide but is still effective for stubborn cases in doses of 15 to 20 drops in honey on rising. Repeat after 2 hours. Within 2-3 hours of the last dose follow with a laxative. Not for children under 12 years.

See also: HYDATID DISEASE.

Pumpkin seeds. Procedure: patient fasts 24 hours. Take a strong laxative: Senna, Castor oil, etc. Follow with 2oz seeds beaten into a pulp and mixed with a little honey. Add water to 1 pint. The whole is drunk at intervals throughout the day and followed after 3-4 hours of last dose with another draft of laxative.

Note. Three things can prevent and cure: Quinine, as used against malaria; Castor oil, as for constipation; and Garlic, well-known in any kitchen. Caffeine revives the tapeworm. Thus it is advised to drink less coffee and more 'schweppes'; more fruit and less starchy food. (*Z. Reut PhD, DSc, Journal, Royal Society of Health, Dec 91 p.251*)

TARTRAZINE POISONING. Allergy arising from tartrazine (E102) additive as found in foods, colour confectionery, etc. It is a synthetic yellow azo dye appearing in chewing gum, smoked fish, soft drinks, tinned peas, salad cream and some convenience foods. May cause behaviour disturbance, hyperactivity in children.

Symptoms. Drying of mucous secretions with exacerbation of asthma and chest conditions. Reactions include hay fever, eczema and irritable skin rash.

Treatment. Expectorants to promote secretion of mucus: Irish Moss, Slippery Elm, Garlic.

For skin reactions: Nettle tea (internal); Witch Hazel water (external).

Weakness of sight: Eyebright tea (external).

TASTE OF HERBS. Evidence from many cultures throughout history demonstrates that each flavour has a specific pharmacological trait. The following are the six classifications (the Chinese have five, combining astringent with sour).

SOUR – acting on the liver and gall bladder, e.g. Myrica, Rubus, Lemon.

BITTER – heart and small intestine, e.g. Gentiana, Rumex, Chicory.

SWEET – stomach, spleen and pancreas, e.g. Glycyrrhiza, Panax spp., honey.

PUNGENT – lungs and colon, e.g. Zingiber, Mentha, Garlic.

SALTY – kidneys, adrenals, bladder, e.g. Apium, Fucus, Tamari.

ASTRINGENT – skin, in Ayurvedic medicine, e.g. Commiphora, Hamamelis, apples.

(*Walter Kacera, in Canadian Journal of Herbalism, Jan 1994*)

TEA. Thea chinensis. *Camelia sinensis L.* Habitat: China, Pakistan, Sri Lanka, Kenya, etc. Leaves. Popular national beverage. Tonic properties due to tannin and caffeine.

Action. Nerve and circulatory stimulant. Antitoxic. Diuretic.

Tea is anti-Vitamin B1 (thiamin) essential for the nervous system. Too much tea may cause polyneuritis (muscle weakness). B1 deficiency symptoms disappear when domestic tea is reduced or discontinued. British politician, Tony Benn, suffered severe polyneuritis when drinking more than 50 cups daily. People prone to peptic ulcer should avoid strong tea which increases acidity. Tea is shown to reduce iron and protein absorption.

Before introduction of Indian and Chinese teas into the U.K., native teas were made from local herbs: Agrimony, Raspberry leaves, Lemon balm, Dandelion leaves, and Wood Betony. Combined, equal parts may still be acceptable to the palate. For sunburn, tired eyes or headache – saturated teabag used as a wash.

Antidotes to excessive tea-drinking: Peruvian bark, Wild Yam, Gotu Kola, Thuja.

TEAS. Herbal infusions or tisanes. Should be prepared in enamel, non-plastic, non-aluminium, china or other suitable vessel. Unless otherwise stated, preparation is with 1 heaped (5ml) teaspoon dried herb to cup (250ml or 8 fl oz) boiling water. Add one cup of water for each additional teaspoon.

To make a larger quantity: infuse 30g (1oz) dried herb or 75g fresh herb in 1 pint (500ml) boiling water for which purpose a vacuum flask is perfect. Infusions made in closed or covered vessels are proof against escape of valuable volatile oils in such herbs as Elderflowers, Peppermint, Juniper berries, Spearmint and Yarrow. Where a teapot is used, it should contain no old tannin deposits left from conventional teas. Standard dose: half-1 teacup thrice daily.

Most infusions work better when taken hot: as for feverish conditions, colds, influenza and other acute crises. Diaphoretics are taken hot to induce perspiration, as also are expectorants to loosen phlegm, febrifuges to reduce high body temperature, hypnotics to induce sleep.

After preparation in boiling water some infusions work better when allowed to stand until they are cold. Such infusions include some alteratives for purification of the blood, bitters to sharpen appetite, diuretics to promote the flow of urine, haemostatics to staunch bleeding, vermifuges to expel worms and tonics to stimulate metabolism. *Cold water infusions.* Some plants yield their constituents to cold water without application of heat. Extraction at room temperature may avoid possible loss of potency in some plants that suffer on application of heat. Materials are steeped for a period of 8 hours, or overnight. Such include Gentian root, Wormwood, Calumba root, Barberry bark, Quassia Chips, Mistletoe leaves, Valerian. Cold milk may serve as an alternative to water.

Simple domestic herbal teas make good alternatives to caffeine/tannin beverages that hinder digestion of proteins. Teas, unlike decoctions, are never boiled. If sweetening is required, as for children, honey should be used in preference to artificial sweeteners. For chronic conditions teas may be taken for weeks but with a break of a week after each period of 6 weeks.

Teas may be made from one remedy only. However, experience of centuries has shown that plants have their own affinities and one may work better in the presence of another, interacting with it to produce increased activity (synergism). A second agent may be added to enhance action of the basic remedy. To these, a third may be added as a stimulant, relaxant or other regulator. For instance, a combination for dyspepsia might include Meadowsweet 3 (basic), Dandelion 1 (enhancer), Peppermint 1 (gastric stimulant). There is a movement away from omnibus prescriptions of many different remedies of varying action towards combinations of few ingredients, each for a specific purpose.

Teabags are available for a number of herb teas.

TEA TREE OIL. Essential oil of *Melaleuca alternifolia*, an aromatic shrub of the myrtle family. The non-irritating, non-poisonous oil from the leaves and terminal branches used chiefly externally.

Action. Germicidal, antifungal, pus solvent and tissue cleanser. Safe antiseptic to use with children and which compares favourably with most broad spectrum antibiotics. Being a specific for *staphylococcus aureus* it is indicated in surgery and dentistry. "Finest antiseptic known to man." (*Australian Medical Journal, Aug 1930, p.284*) Said to be five times more bactericidal than carbolic acid. Antiviral.

Uses. Vaginitis, urethritis, cystitis, herpes, leg ulcers; ulcers of throat, mouth and gums. Aboriginals used it for skin diseases and infected wounds. Claimed to be effective against septicaemia, dispersing festering matter. Fungal infections: monilia, thrush, candida albicans, athlete's foot, infected nails. Impetigo, warts, pimples, boils, lice infestation, ringworm. Cold sores, acne (lotion). Stings and bites: mosquitoes, fleas, etc. Scalp disorders (lotion). Animals – mange in dogs, cats and horses (lotion). Appendicitis (lotion to massage McBurney's point).

Australian studies show that the watery solution dissolves pus, leaving surfaces of infected wounds and ulcers deodorised and clean. When dirty wounds are washed or syringed with a 10 per cent watery solution, embedded dirt and debris are loosened and carried away. (*Eduardo F. Pena, MD*)

Preparations. Oil should not be used internally except on the advice of a practitioner, neither be applied neat to the skin. It can be diluted many times. Available in creams, shampoos, lotions, cosmetics and burn preparations.

Lotion. Emulsify 40 per cent solution of Tea Tree oil in castile soap and containing 13 per cent isoprophyl alcohol. This emulsion easily mixes with water. For vaginal infection, surgical and dental work. Marketed in the United States under name: "Melassol".

Inhalant. Sprinkle few drops on handkerchief, or add to boiling water, cover head, and inhale.

Aerosol. For sinus congestion and external ulceration: 1 per cent oil added to a suitable base.

Tea. Bushmen would add a few leaves to a tea pot and brew.

TEETH. Decay. Dental caries. Commences with a jelly-like plaque on the surface enamel. Plaque harbours bacteria which produces acid, dissolving the enamel and exposing the underlying dentine. Decay proceeds towards the central pulp causing pain when it reaches the root canals. Untreated, dental abscess may follow.

Dental decay requires expert treatment with possible extraction. Where an eroded area is drilled the cavity should be filled with a non-mercurial amalgam. Owing to the effect of mercury on the central nervous system and circulatory vessels, it is being replaced by a ceramic material without ill-effects such as may follow the use of mercury fillings: depression, memory failure, and inflammation of the upper respiratory tract.

Dental enamel is a unique tissue, being the most highly calcified component of the body, containing 90 per cent calcium phosphate. Thus calcium supplements are indicated. Any underlying cause should be treated. Chronic infection of the teeth may track a long way from its source and present as a sinus on the face, or neck. Research has shown that Liquorice arrests the growth of bacteria and deposition of plaque. Care should be taken to see that Lemon juice does not come into direct contact with the teeth, the enamel of which it erodes.

Treatment. *Antimicrobials*: Goldenseal, Myrrh, Echinacea, Liquorice.

Decaying teeth should be extracted. Where not possible, chew Comfrey (tablets, powder or root) and compress a moistened mass into the cavity; allow to remain as long as possible. For toothache, plug tooth with cotton wool moistened with 5-6 drops Oil of Cloves or Oil of Peppermint (mild analgesics).

Traditional. Chew leaves of Plantain, Houseleek, Marshmallow or Chamomile. Tincture Myrrh mouth rinse. Liquorice.

Prickly Ash bark. Decoction, tincture or Liquid Extract. (*Wm Cayce*)

Internal. Echinacea, Kelp, Garlic, Sunflower seeds.

Supplementation. Vitamins A, C and D; in the absence of these teeth break down and loosen. Minerals: Potassium, Dolomite for magnesium and calcium. Iron. Zinc.

Supportives. Cranial osteopathy to correct any unbalanced temporo-mandibular joints. Change toothbrush every three months.

Diet. See: DIET – HIGH FIBRE.

TEETH EXTRACTION. Do not disturb socket or blood clot with fingers, tongue or rinsing. If excessive bleeding occurs, place small handkerchief folded into a pad saturated with distilled extract of Witch Hazel over the socket and bite hard until bleeding stops.

Alternatives. Comfrey, Echinacea or Marigold. To promote healing.

Mouth wash. 5-10 drops Tincture Myrrh in water.

St John's Wort. Pains radiating along the course of a nerve. Two tablets every half hour. Facial neuralgia.

Practitioner. For violent trembling and nervous agitation: Tincture Gelsemium BPC (1963), 2-5 drops in water.

Chamomile flowers. 1 cup tea for exquisitely painful teeth before and after extraction.

Marigold tea. To arrest excessive bleeding.

Tea Tree oil. 2 drops in glass of water: anti-infective mouthwash.

Supplementation. Vitamin C (1g daily). Dolomite. Calcium.

TEETH GRINDING. Bruxism. May be due to worms, stress or low mineral levels.

Sage, Fennel, Papaya or Peppermint.

Nutrients: Dolomite, Kelp, Calcium, Iron. Magnesium, Zinc.

TEMPERAMENTS. The temperament is the peculiar physical character and mental disposition of an individual. An occasional dose of one's constitutional remedy may prove preventative of diseases peculiar to the temperament.

Lymphatic. Large, well-formed body with tendency to be fat. "Lazy", phlegmatic, fair complexion, light hair, flesh soft – Agnus Castus. German Chamomile. Kelp.

Scrofulous. Lobelia. Elecampane. Poke root.

Hydrogenoid (cannot tolerate much moisture). Yarrow.

Psoric (sycotic). Thuja.

Nervous (or mental temperament). Large brain, large frontal lobes. Great activity of brain and nervous system. Ginkgo.

Bilious (choleric). Well developed bony system. "Wiry." Hair dark, skin sallow. Subject to liver trouble. Dandelion root.

Sanguine. Full-blooded, robust. Light auburn or red hair; large veins and arteries. Chest and muscles well developed. Hawthorn.

May be taken as herb teas, powders, extracts or tinctures.

TENNIS ELBOW. Radiohumeral bursitis. Pain and tenderness of the epicondyle of the humerus. Miner's, golfer's, tailor's, jogger's or pudding-mixer's elbow – in fact, anything arising from an excessive backward stretching of tendons. Aggravated by twisting and gripping.

Alternatives. Anti-inflammatory agents with specific reference to bones: Guaiacum, Devil's Claw, Black Cohosh, Prickly Ash, Bamboo gum. Celery seed tea.

Topical. Arnica tincture or lotion. Cold pack. Poultices of Chamomile, Mullein or Comfrey.

Supplements. Magnesium, Zinc.

Supportives. Osteopathy or Chiropractic. Acupuncture to block pain impulses. A simple arm-sling helps rest the joint.

TENOSYNOVITIS (TSV). Inflammation and swelling of tendon sheaths. Common repetitive strain injury associated with work requiring rapid repetitive gripping and twisting movements as in industry. Tennis or golfer's elbow.

Symptoms. Numbness, aching wrists, tingling in fingers, pain on movement. Commonest site: wrist, fingers and thumb.

Alternatives. *Internal*. Cramp bark, Black Cohosh, Devil's Claw, Jamaica Dogwood, Wild Lettuce, Valerian, Ladyslipper, Cowslip root (Biostrath). Any one, taken in decoction, liquid extract, tincture, powder, etc.

Topical. Arnica cream or lotion.

Supplements. Vitamins B6. Calcium, Magnesium.

TENSION, Nervous. See: STRESS.

TESTICLES – SWELLING OF. May be due to:–
Trauma. For physical injury paint scrotum with tincture Arnica or St John's Wort. Ruptured testicle requires hospital treatment.
Torsion. Sudden testicular swelling and pain. Comfrey poultice.
Epididymo-orchitis. Sudden pain and swelling – refer to hospital for acute condition. If unresolved, suspect tumour. Comfrey poultice. Internal treatment – see below.

Non-painful swellings include scrotal nodules, cystic swellings, epididymal carcinoma and infective conditions which should be referred urgently to hospital.
Alternatives. *Tea*. Cornsilk. Add 5 drops Tincture or Liquid Extract Goldenseal. Drink freely.
Decoction. Formula: equal parts. Kava Kava root, Couchgrass, Marshmallow root. Half an ounce (15g) to 1 pint (500ml) water, simmered gently 20 minutes. Dose: 1 cup freely.
Powders. Echinacea 2; Kava Kava root 1; Sarsaparilla 1; Pinch Cayenne. Dose: 500mg (two 00 capsules or one-third teaspoon) thrice daily and at bedtime.
Tinctures. Kava Kava root 1; Goldenseal quarter; Thuja quarter; Marshmallow root half; Pulsatilla 1. Dose: 1-2 teaspoons thrice daily.
Dr Arthur Vogel. Saw Palmetto berries.
Note. Testicular tumours are usually painless. Surgical treatment may be required if the testicle is to be saved.

TESTOSTERONE. Male hormone produced in the testes, or synthetically. Essential for development of the male sexual organs. Precursors for maintenance of a balanced male endocrine function: Ginseng, Sarsaparilla, Liquorice.
To promote testosterone: zinc.

Preparations of the hormone have surged in popularity among athletes, enhancing performance.

TETANUS. Lockjaw. Caused by a toxin, *Clostridium tetani* spores that may remain many years in the soil from which infection spreads. Occurs when a wound, scratch or cut, is contaminated. Over half reported cases are from gardening injuries. See: NOTIFIABLE DISEASES.
Symptoms. Stiffness of arms, neck and jaw. As fever heightens the mouth can be opened only with difficulty; facial muscles rigid, convulsions develop and in the absence of effective treatment death may supervene.
Treatment. Hospitalisation. Key agents are Lobelia or Gelsemium for their powerful antispasmodic action. Echinacea for its antitoxic effect. Should sedation be needed: Valerian.
Eclectic School. Tincture Lobelia 3 drops, Tincture Echinacea 10 drops, in water, hourly. Add Tincture or Liquid Extract Skullcap or Valerian, 5 drops, if necessary, for delirium.
Practitioner. Tincture Gelsemium, five drops (0.3ml) in water, to relax muscles, open the mouth, unclench teeth and promote perspiration which in itself helps reduce tension.
In absence of above. St John's Wort, Cramp bark, Thomson's 3rd preparation of Lobelia.
Topical. Wash wound with half a pint water to which has been added 1 teaspoon Tincture St John's Wort (Hypericum), or 1 teaspoon Tincture Marigold (Calendula). Steep clean dressing in the solution; apply.
Hypericum. St John's Wort. Homoeopathic version used with success by James T. Kent MD.

Treatment by or in liaison with a general medical practitioner.

THALASSAEMIA. One of a group of haemolytic anaemias. Disorder that affects red blood cells. When due to inheritance of an abnormal gene from both parents it is known as Thalassaemia major; when from one parent, Thalassaemia minor. Liver, spleen and bone tissue enlarge as more red cells are demanded.
Symptoms. Pallor, easily tired, enlarged spleen, leg ulcer, breathlessness. Bones easily fracture. Iron is deposited in the tissues and heart failure possible. Those at risk should submit themselves for screening.
Treatment. The mainstay of treatment involves lifelong blood transfusions to replenish red cell numbers.

Treatment by hospital specialist or general medical practitioner.
Tinctures. Equal parts – Echinacea, Dandelion, Red Clover, Gentian. Dose: 1 teaspoon thrice daily in water or honey.
Hawthorn tablets for heart involvement.

THEOPHRASTUS. 372-287 BC. Father of Botany. Greek philosopher and friend of Aristotle who bequeathed to him his library and garden. Under him the classification of plants blossomed into an ordered science. Author of 277 books including *Causes of Plants*. His *History of Plants* was translated into English by Sir Arthur Hort in 1916 (2 volumes).

THIN PERSON, The. To increase weight: tea, tablets, decoctions of Fenugreek seeds, Alfalfa, Irish Moss, Slippery Elm, Agnus Castus, Wild Yam, Kelp.
Gentian. 1 teaspoon grated root in cup cold water steeped overnight. Half a cup, morning and evening.
Combination, tea. Equal parts: Alfalfa, Balm, Oats. 2 teaspoons to each cup boiling water; infuse 15 minutes. 1 cup freely.
Diet. See: DIET – THIN PEOPLE.
Vitamins. B-complex. F.
Note. Thinness is a result of all serious disorders. Growth retardation is common in chronic asthma,

chronic infections and thyroid disorders. The thyrotoxic child is thin, tall and usually has a goitre. See relevant entries.

THIRST. Desire for fluids. A symptom of conditions – vomiting, excessive passage of urine, diarrhoea, haemorrhage, diabetes mellitis (or insipidis), sweating. See entries of specific disorders. In excessive thirst there is potassium loss but salt gain.

THOMSON, SAMUEL. 1769-1843. American medical reformer. Said to have revolutionised American medicine. Of humble origin, Thomson spent his early life on his father's farm where he befriended a local herb collector and dealer from whom he learnt identification of plants and the elements of natural healing.

By experimenting on himself he made important discoveries of the properties of a number of plants which have since passed into orthodox pharmacy. These include Lobelia (Indian tobacco) and Capsicum (red pepper) which he used in his practice. Fame quickly sprang to nationwide success, generating a huge demand for the new medicines. Having chewed Lobelia (which acts upon the vomiting centre of the brain) he was able to offer to the orthodox profession a harmless alternative to the deadly mercury used as an emetic for cleansing the stomach and inducing perspiration.

Once, in an epidemic, he cured 28 people suffering from dysentery with Capsicum steeped in a tea of Sumach leaves.

Ready for an alternative to blood-letting, many young doctors eagerly adopted his system, while the public devoured his books much to the embarrassment of established professionals. So successful were the "Eclectics" led by Thomson that they threatened to supplant the "Regulars" in the confidence of the public.

Dr Thomson's favourite stock prescriptions are still found in today's herbal dispensary: No 6 of which is: *Antiseptic for malignant and serious throat conditions* – 2oz powdered gum Myrrh and half an ounce Powdered Capsicum steeped in 40oz alcohol. Stand 7 days, shaking daily. Filter. Bottle. Dose: 5 drops in water as a gargle and mouth wash.

THREE OILS. A popular mixture of oils of Eucalyptus, Camphor and Amber oils (equal parts), the latter derived from the resins of various trees. A rub for rheumatism of the joints or applied to the chest for bronchitis or whooping cough. An alternative to camphorated oil which has gone out of fashion and is superceded by Olbas oil.

THROAT, ULCERATED.
Treatment: as for QUINSY.

THROMBOCYTOPAENIA. A decrease in the number of platelets which are responsible for blood-clotting. Failure of platelet production occurs in aplastic anaemia, leukaemia, alcoholism and irradiation. The main causes of increased platelet destruction are drugs, viral infections and autoimmune disorders. Referral to a haematology clinic is essential.
Symptoms. Bleeding. This may occur as bruises under the skin (petechiae) or excessive haemorrhage.
Treatment. Attention to the underlying cause.
Of value: teas – Rutin, Alfalfa, Irish Moss, Red Clover, Gotu Kola, Yarrow, Nettles.
Formula. Bladderwrack 2; Fringe Tree bark 1; Yellow Dock 1; trace of Cayenne powder or few drops Tincture Capsicum. Dose. Powders: 500-750mg (2-3 capsules 00 or quarter to half a teaspoon). Liquid Extracts: 1-2 teaspoons. Tinctures: 1-3 teaspoons. Thrice daily, as tolerated in the presence of corticosteroid drugs.
Diet. High protein.
Supplements. B-complex, B1, B6, B12, C, E, Calcium, Zinc.

THROMBOLYTIC. A thrombolytic works by dissolving clots that block the coronary arteries.
Hawthorn, Prickly Ash bark, Marigold.

THROMBOSIS. A blood clot in an artery or vein. When it breaks free from its original site, it becomes an embolism.
Diet. Greenland eskimos hardly ever suffer from coronary disease. This is due to their fish-rich diet. Polyunsaturated fish oils have a cholesterol-lowering effect and reduce development of atheroma, offering protection against thrombus formation.

See: ATHEROSCLEROSIS, CEREBRAL THROMBOSIS, VENOUS THROMBOSIS, STROKE, GANGRENE. Where condition does not fall within these categories, consult CORONARY HEART DISEASE (CHD).

THRUSH. Oral thrush in children. A fungus disease. Sickly, poorly-fed children may have a dry sore mouth and lips with pale patches on tongue and gums. May occur on change from breast to cow's milk in babies. Dummy-sucking is associated with a greater prevalence of thrush.
Alternatives. Swab or spray mouth with:–
1. 1 teaspoon Witch Hazel in half cup of water.
2. 2-5 drops Tincture Myrrh in glass of water.
3. Aloe Vera juice or gel.
4. Comfrey leaf tea.
5. 50ml Tincture Calendula (Marigold) with one drop essential oil of Tea Tree, Thyme or Oregano. Add 2-3 drops of the mixture to a little water and spray into the baby's or child's mouth. (*Anne McIntyre MNIMH*)
6. Pulsatilla.

Diet. Yoghurt has been shown to inhibit infection.
Supplements. Vitamin A, C. Zinc.
Garlic. 1-2 tablets or capsules at night.

THUJA. Arbor-vitae. Tree of Life. *Thuja occidentalis L. German*: Lebensbaum. *French*: Arbre de vie. *Spanish*: Tuya. *Italian* Tuja. *Chinese*: To. New growth terminal twigs One of the most important agents of the herbal pharmacopoeia.
Constituents: flavonoids, thujone.
Action. Vaccinial antidote, antisycotic, antibacterial, anti-viral, diuretic, emmenagogue, expectorant, nerve tonic, febrifuge.
Uses. A substitute for children to whom vaccination is inadvisable.

"Thuja exercises a peculiar influence over abdominal growths and tissue degeneration, especially that of an epithelial character. It is a positive remedy for cancers of different varieties, tumours, warts, fungoid growths of the skin or mucous membrane." (*Dr Finlay Ellingwood*)

"I found Thuja preventative and curative in an epidemic of smallpox, and prevents pitting," writes (*Dr C.M.F. von Boenninghausen (1785-1864)*). He used it for "the vaccinal taint – that profound, often long-lasting morbid constitutional state engendered by the vaccine virus . . ."

Used for cancer of the womb by the Eclectic School of Physicians, late 19th century. Warts (soft or figwarts) surrounding the anus, genitals; anal fissure; topical and oral. Absent menses, ovarian pains. Would appear to be of value for AIDS.

Itchy skin disorders, urinary infections with pus, bed-wetting of children at night, frequency in adults, auto-toxaemia, ill-effects from excessive drinking of coffee and tea.
Preparations. Average dose, 1-2 grams, or fluid equivalent. Thrice daily.
Decoction. Half an ounce to 1 pint water gently simmered 10 minutes. Dose, quarter cup. Also used externally as a lotion.
Liquid Extract. 5-15 drops in water.
Tincture BHP (1983). 1 part to 10 parts 60 per cent alcohol. Dose, 1-2ml.
Oil: Cedar leaf. As an ointment in a suitable base.
Contra-indications: pregnancy, lactation.

THYME, GARDEN. Common Thyme. *Thymus vulgaris L.* Dried leaves and flowering tops. Contains a valuable essential oil (thymol).
Other names and constituents: see – WILD THYME.
Action. Antibacterial, antiviral, anti-parasitic, antispasmodic, antifungal, tonic, carminative, anti-oxidant, expectorant, anti-cough, antiseptic.
Uses. Infections of the respiratory organs, throat, bronchi, urinary tract. Spasmodic dry cough, whooping cough. Irritable bowel and bed-wetting in children, worms, waterbrash. Overwork. Mouth ulcers (mouthwash), sore throat (gargle). Chronic grumbling appendix. To break the alcohol habit – tea or tincture. Streptococcal infection. Salpingitis.
External. Fresh plant pulped by old-time gardeners to use as a compress for minor wounds, cuts, abrasions, scabies, warts.
Preparations. Average dose, half-4 grams, or fluid equivalent. Thrice daily, or 2-hourly for acute cases.
Tea: half-1 teaspoon to each cup boiling water; infuse 10 minutes in covered vessel. Half-1 cup freely. Also as a gargle and mouth rinse.
Tincture BHP (1983). 1:5 in 45 per cent alcohol. Dose 2-6ml in water.
Powder. Two 250mg capsules thrice daily. (*Arkocaps*)
Antiseptic lotions, creams. Oil of Thyme: inhalant for respiratory disorders.
Thyme bath. For respiratory disorders, chronic cough, difficult breathing and as a refreshing tonic. Handful of fresh or dried herb to 1 pint (500ml) boiling water: infuse 20 minutes in covered vessel, strain; add to bath water.
Note. Large doses sometimes necessary for adequate response. Avoid in pregnancy. GSL

THYME, WILD. Mother of Thyme. *Thymus serpyllum L. German*: Wilder thymian. *French*: Serpolet. *Spanish*: Tomillo. *Italian*: Timo serpillo. *Iranian*: Hasha. *Indian*: Ipar. Herb.
Constituents: tannins, gum, flavonoids, volatile oil, caffeic acid.
Action. Antiseptic, antibacterial, anti-oxidant, antifungal, antitussive, antispasmodic, expectorant, diaphoretic, anthelmintic, carminative, diuretic, mild sedative, anti-candida, antiviral.
Uses. Infections of the respiratory organs, throat, bronchi, whooping cough. Common cold – to induce perspiration that may shorten its duration. Otitis media (internally and eardrops). Sinusitis. Streptococcal infection. Sore throat – as a gargle. Gingivitis – as a mouthwash. Painful or delayed menstruation. Round worms in children. Leucorrhoea and other mild vaginal discharges. Mastitis – washed and pulped herbs used as a poultice. Nightmare. To break the alcohol habit: tea or tincture.

Combines well with Tincture Myrrh for infective sore throat.
External. Healing of wounds and ulcers (tea used as a lotion). In liniments for aching muscles.

Not used in pregnancy.
Preparations. Average dose, 0.6 to 4g or fluid equivalent. Thrice daily; or every 2 hours in acute cases.
Tea. Quarter to 1 heaped teaspoon to each cupful boiling water; infuse 15 minutes. Dose, one-third to 1 cup.
Liquid Extract. 10-60 drops, in water.
Tincture. 1 part to 5 parts alcohol: macerate 8 days, strain, bottle. Dose, 30-60 drops, in water.

Also as a gargle and mouth rinse.
Oil of Thyme. 2-3 drops in honey. Ear drops: 3 drops to teaspoon Almond oil. Mix. Inject 2-3 drops, morning and evening.
Bio-Strath Thyme formula.
Thyme bath. Same as for GARDEN THYME.
Wild Thyme Cleansing Cream.

THYMOL. A volatile oil extracted from a number of species of Thyme, possessing the properties of those plants. Mostly used as an antiseptic mouth wash or gargle. Also a deodorant and fungicide. Bactericidal action is greatly reduced in the presence of protein and should not be used near meals.
Preparation: Thymol BP.
See: THYME, WILD. THYME, GARDEN.

THYMOLEPTIC. Another term for an antidepressant.

THYMUS GLAND. The key centre in the body's immune (defence) system. Controls the behaviour and storage of white blood cells which combat invading viruses and bacteria. A synergist. The gland shrinks rapidly in severe stress and suffers when nutrition is poor. (*Dr Hans Selye*) What supports the thymus gland also aids the immune system.

The gland receives white cells (lymphocytes) via the blood stream after they have been produced in the bone marrow. These cells are immediately conscious of the presence of invading enemy bacteria and alert the thymus to organise the body's defence in the production of antibodies.
To stimulate thymus activity: Echinacea angustifolia, Goldenseal, Liquorice, Mistletoe. Vitamin B6. Zinc.
Supplements known to have a reference to the thymus:–
Vitamins. A. B-complex. Vitamin B6. Vitamin C. Vitamin E. Beta-carotene.
Minerals. Copper, Iron, Manganese, Zinc.
See: FREE RADICALS.

The thymus is especially involved in the menace of HIV, being protector of the T cells. HIV positive people could become a victim of AIDS.

THYROID GLAND – GOITRE. Enlargement of the thyroid gland. Usually due to deficiency of iodine. Less common causes: cyst or benign tumour of glandular tissue, inherited disorders or inflammation of the gland by bacteria or virus. Non-toxic (simple) goitre is where the gland is enlarged but no hyperthyroidism exists. Lack of iodine in the diet causes diffuse enlargement of the gland to achieve normal secretion. Overactivity of the gland in Graves' disease (hyperthyroidism) produces excess thyroxin and causes the body to burn up its food and oxygen at a rapid rate, increasing metabolism abnormally. See: THYROTOXICOSIS. Enlargement may be present in both hyper- and hypothyroidism. The neck is swollen just beneath the Adam's Apple, with or without pain.
Alternatives. Iodine-deficient goitre requires iodine-rich foods – see: IODINE. Bladderwrack is a key remedy. Hard goitre – Poke root. Soft goitre – Blue Flag root. Persevere for months. Inflammation of the gland – Agnus Castus. Kelp.
Hard Goitre. Combine liquid extracts: Bladderwrack 2; Fringe Tree 1; Poke root half. One 5ml teaspoon in water thrice daily.
Soft Goitre. Combine liquid extracts: Bladderwrack 2; Blue Flag root half; Horsetail 1. One 5ml teaspoon in water thrice daily.
Goitre with severe nervous agitation. Combine liquid extracts: Bladderwrack 2; Valerian 1; Passion flower 1. 30-60 drops in water thrice daily.
Cyst on the gland. Bladderwrack 2; Clivers 2; Fringe Tree 1. One 5ml teaspoon in water thrice daily.

Dr F.J. Norton (*Ellingwood*) relates: "In the treatment of goitre no one single remedy has as wide a range as Blue Flag root. It is claimed that in the treatment of exophthalmic goitre Poke root and Cactus are superior to some methods; Blue Flag combines with these."
Farida Davidson. Nettles, Bladderwrack, Bugleweed, Parsley leaves, Kelp, Irish Moss, Iceland Moss.
Diet: Low protein. Cabbage, cauliflower, kale, spinach, Brussel sprouts, turnips and beans all adversely affect the thyroid gland and should be taken in small amounts.
Supplements. B-complex vitamins. Magnesium, Potassium, Selenium.

THYROID, UNDERACTIVE.
Treatment: as for MYXOEDEMA.

THYROTOXICOSIS. Overactivity of the Thyroid gland. Excessive production of thyroid hormones (thyroxine, etc) which increase the metabolic rate. Also known as Grave's Disease or hyperthyroidism. More common in women. Causes include anxiety and emotional shock.
Symptoms. Sweating, hunger which is never sated, fatigue, weight loss, intolerance of heat, nervousness, diarrhoea, staring eyeballs, brittle nails, thin hair, menstrual disorders, trembling hands, swelling of the neck just below the Adam's Apple, rapid heartbeat.
Treatment. Bugleweed is a thyroxine antagonist BHP (1983); it also regulates pituitary thyrotropic activity. Cactus is added to strengthen the heart (*Priest*). Eric Powell favours Horsetail; tincture made from fresh (not dried) plant.
Tinctures. Alternatives. (1) Combine equal parts, Bugleweed and Motherwort. (2) Com-

bine Bugleweed 2; Cactus 1; Valerian half. (3) Combine Bugleweed 2; Pulsatilla 1; Blue Flag root half. Dose: 1-2 teaspoons in water thrice daily.
John Christopher USA. Parsley.
Mutellon. Bugleweed, Motherwort, Valerian. (*Klein*)
Diet. Low protein, high fat (cheese, cream, milk). Iodine-rich foods – see: IODINE. Avoid cabbage.
Nutrients. Vitamins A. C. Calcium.
Supportives. Relaxation techniques. Avoid stress situations.
Palpitation of thyroid origin: Tea – equal parts Motherwort and Balm. 1-2 teaspoons to each cup boiling water: infuse 5-15 minutes: 1 cup 2-3 times daily.

THYROXINE. Thyroid hormone. Crystalline substance containing iodine found in the thyroid gland. A synthetic form is administered to cases of diminished function of the gland (myxoedema, cretinism). Lowers bone density.
Adverse effects: nervous excitability, rapid heart beat, sweating. In the treatment of a defective thyroid gland, it may sometimes be necessary for this hormone to be used.
Supportive treatment may include: Kelp, Bugleweed, Hawthorn.

TIC DOULOUREUX. Trigeminal neuralgia. See: FACIAL NEURALGIA.

TIGER BALM. *Ingredients*: Menthol BP 8 per cent. Clove oil BP 15 per cent. Cajeput oil BPC 12.9 per cent. Camphor BP 24.9 per cent. Peppermint oil 15.9 per cent. Paraffin 36.8 per cent. Muscular aches and pains. Massage cream used by sportsmen and aromatherapists. External use only. Made in Singapore.

TIGER NUTS. Earth almonds, chufa nuts. Strengthening nutrient. Has a mild bactericidal effect.
Uses. To increase flow of milk in nursing mothers. Roasted nuts offer a palatable substitute for coffee. A sprinkle of the ground nuts on muesli or various dishes offers a mineral-rich supplement. May also be eaten whole by children in place of sweets for enhancing resilience of the immune system.

TILKE, Samuel, Westcott. English medical reformer. Self-taught herbalist whose efforts attracted the attention of some members of the House of Lords who prevailed on him to settle in London where he built a highly successful practice in Manchester Square. His spectacular cures became the talk of the town. He wrote books and numerous publications of which few survive. He often featured favourably in the "Times"; one reference being: "Any man who makes such unceasing efforts to alleviate the sufferings of humanity in diseases that defy medical skill is entitled to honorable mention."

Tilke relied on Holy Thistle to build up old broken-down constitutions; Tormentil as a powerful astringent for bowel disorders, piles etc; and Marshmallow as a diuretic. His favourite poultice was Wormwood.

TINCTURE. Tinctures are concentrated liquid extracts of the soluble constituents of roots, barks, seeds or aerial parts of plants to preserve their vital properties. Being aqueous (watery) in character, infusions and decoctions have a very limited life – not more than a day or two. Tinctures made from alcohol (usually ethyl alcohol) or glycerine and water, ensure preservation for a number of years. For leaves, flowers and aerial parts generally, 25 per cent alcohol is usually sufficient strength, but many require 60-90 per cent.

If fresh leaves, flowers etc are used, they should be gathered dry when their properties are at their height. This may vary with each plant but a good rule is when the sun is on them or in fine weather. Chop, pound to pulp and weigh: twice the amount of fresh plant is necessary.

Average strength is 1 part herb material to 5 parts alcohol/water mixture. Some plant materials may be 1 part to 10 parts of the menstruum.

Place 4oz (120g) dried material or powder in a closed vessel (wide-mouthed bottle or vacuum flask with a tight closure). Pour on 1 pint (20 fl oz or half a litre) alcohol/water mixture (25 parts alcohol with 75 parts water). Set aside in a cool dark place. Shake well morning and evening. Length of maceration time is usually 14 days for leaves etc but fibrous roots, barks and resins may take as long as 3 weeks. Separate tincture by decanting, straining and filtering. Store, preferably in well-stoppered amber-coloured bottle. Vodka is frequently used as a form of alcohol.

Wines (sherries, Madeira, orange, etc), may be used to make a mild unstable tincture of leaves and flowers but because of their low alcohol content are unsuitable for denser material. Agrimony, Chamomile, Elderflowers, Peppermint, Thyme and Yarrow respond well to most wines.
Example: open bottle of sherry; pour off two glassfuls. Insert sprig of Rosemary, Lavender, etc, and leave in a cool place, out of the sun, for 8 days.

Some tinctures are made from vinegar, (Lobelia, Squills). The degree of extraction with vinegar is lower than with alcohol.

Some tinctures demand a high percentage of alcohol: gum Myrrh, Aloes, Guaiacum (90 per cent). Percentage varies according to the ability of the menstruum to extract the vital constituents from the plant. For external treatments, a cheaper alcohol is sometimes used.

While manufacturers use Ethanol, most tinctures require only 25-30 per cent alcohol; this is an area in which wines and vodka can serve well. Vodka is excellent for home-made tinctures.

An example of how a tincture is usually expressed:– 1:5 in alcohol = 1 part powder or crude material to 5 parts alcohol. Tinctures should not be made from methylated, industrial or iso-propyl alcohol.

Glycerine tincture. Take 2 parts glycerine to 4 parts distilled water to make 1 pint. Add 4 ounces (120 grams) powdered herb and macerate 14 days in a well-capped bottle; shake daily; strain and bottle. Glycerine tinctures were once popular but alcohol is now considered a more efficient preservative.

Dosage. The amount of tincture prescribed as a single dose may vary from a few drops to 1-2 teaspoonfuls. The small volume of alcohol is usually well-tolerated. Where there is aversion or allergy the dose may be taken in hot water from which alcohol soon vaporises into the atmosphere leaving only medicament and water. The bottle should be shaken before use to remix any natural sediment.

"Shake the bottle" means more than a cursory agitation of sediment. An older generation of herbalists believed that a vigorous shaking (succussion) enhanced efficacy. See: SUCCUSSION.

Where digestion is imperfect a morsel of cheese assists absorption. Raw apples are natural antidotes to over-dosing or allergy. Like good wines, a tincture takes time to mature – it is a living thing.

TINNITUS. A sensation of noises in the ear: buzzing, ringing, singing, "escaping steam". Intermittent or continuous. May drive its victims to the point of suicide. Not always accompanied by loss of hearing. In the West one-third people have it. Common among the elderly. Sensation is different from the hallucinations of voices in the head which are psychogenic in origin.

Causes are legion: foreign bodies, wax, catarrh, earache or discharge, deafness, anaemia, high or low blood pressure, dental caries, impacted molars, vertigo, bleeding from the ear, Meniere's disease, toxicity from quinine, diuretics or other drugs such as aspirin (rheumatic patients on heavy doses), minute intracranial aneurysm of veins or arteries, arterio-sclerosis of the carotid artery, chronic incurable ear disease, cervical disc lesions (resolved by osteopathy).

After ruling out these conditions, the major cause is noise-induced: exposure in industry, explosives as in firing guns. The wearing of personal stereos may raise noise-levels of up to 124 decibels which is capable of ear damage. Listening to highly-amplified music or speech as in discos.

For sensory hearing impairment and degenerative changes of the cochlea – Skullcap, Ladyslipper, Hops, Passion flower. Hawthorn can be successful when the condition is associated with heart and circulatory disorders. Garlic, either the corm at table or 2-3 capsules at night enjoys an impressive record.

Treatment. Discover cause where possible.

Principle remedies: Hawthorn, Mistletoe, Black Cohosh. Ginkgo.

When associated with arterio-sclerosis: Black Cohosh.

Sluggish circulation: Cayenne.

Suspected infection: 2-3 drops Onion juice injected into the ear.

Migraine: Feverfew.

Nervous origin: Skullcap.

Catarrh: Ground Ivy.

From past infections: Echinacea.

Kidney weakness: Horsetail.

High blood pressure: Lime flowers.

Low blood pressure: Cayenne.

Rheumatic conditions: White Willow.

With long history of earache in childhood: Goldenseal.

Ginkgo. Favourable results reported. Tablets, capsules, liquid extracts or tinctures. Leaf tea: 1-2 teaspoons to cup water, bring to boil; simmer 5 minutes. 1 cup morning and evening.

Cowslip tea. (*William Boericke MD*)

Aconite. Homoeopathic preparation. Commence 2 tablets hourly.

Romany Chal tea. Equal parts: Horsetail, Ground Ivy, Vervain, Yarrow. 1-2 teaspoons to each cup boiling water; infuse 5-15 minutes. Wineglassful thrice daily.

Formula. Hawthorn 2; Black Cohosh 1; Ground Ivy 1; Mistletoe 1. Mix. Dose. Powders: 500mg (two 00 capsules or one-third teaspoon). Liquid extracts: 1 teaspoon. Tinctures: 2 teaspoons. Thrice daily.

Topical. 'Onion juice dropped into the ears eases the pains and noises in them.' (*Nicholas Culpeper (1616-54)*) Dilute Garlic juice.

Diet. Avoid refined foods, dairy products, caffeine, alcohol, cola drinks, smoking, salt. By reducing cholesterol levels a low-fat diet improves the condition. Copious drinks spring water, fruit juices.

Supplementation: Calcium, Magnesium, Zinc. Vitamins A and D.

Supportives: yoga, biofeedback, meditative and relaxation techniques. Removal of wax obstruction. Hopi Indian Ear Candle, for mild suction and to impart a perceptible pressure regulation on aural fluids.

Information. British Tinnitus Association, 14-18 West Bar Green, Sheffield S1 2DA.

TIREDNESS. To be distinguished from *fatigue* and exhaustion which occur when the body is physically pushed beyond its normal limits.

Tiredness is often overlooked as a symptom of ill-health – as in heart disease. Rather than excess fats in the blood, tiredness is at the root of many strokes and heart attacks. It follows anger, lack of sleep, 'job dissatisfaction'. Destructive emotions such as a virulent hatred, anger, and malignant envy result in self-inflicted tiredness, later manifesting as cardiac arrest.

Patients demanding too much of their body may need a change of lifestyle and at most, simple cardiac supports: Hawthorn, Motherwort. Juniper berries, oil or tea, offer a refreshing general invigorator.

Aromatherapy. Inhalant: 10 drops any of the oils of Lemon, Lavender or Clary-Sage on a tissue.

Diet, vitamins and minerals. See: EXHAUSTION.

TOADFLAX. Butter and eggs. *Linaria vulgaris*, Mill. *German*: Leinkraut. *French*: Linaire. *Spanish*: Linaria. *Italian*: Urinaria. *Part used*: herb.

Constituents: two glycosides – linarin and pectolinarin, flavonoids, peganine (alkaloid).

Action: astringent, antiscrofula, hepatic, detergent, diuretic, blood tonic.

Uses. Mild liver tonic for jaundice and chronic skin disorders; dropsy, piles, constipation. For tubercula tendency. To improve nutrition of children with calcium deficiency and wasting diseases, increasing weight and strength. Has proved effective for some obscure blood disorders in children.

Preparations. *Tea*: 1 teaspoon to each cup boiling water; infuse 10 minutes. Half-1 cup thrice daily.

Compress: pulped leaves and flowers for minor injuries, cuts, abrasions, etc.

TOBACCO SMOKE ABSORBER. Mix: Oil Eucalyptus 1 part; Oil of Lemon 1 part; Vodka 20 parts. Use as a spray. OR:– place an electric light bulb in the fluid to promote slow evaporation of 20-40 drops in a little water.

TOFU. Popular soya bean product. Traditional, natural food discovered by a Chinese prince in 164 BC but now prepared fresh each morning throughout Japan. The most important soy bean low-cost protein throughout East Asia. Said to be the protein backbone of the diet for more than one billion people. Unlike animal protein sources, it is entirely free of cholesterol and high in polyunsaturated fats. Enjoys a renaissance among health-minded people the world over.

A perfect substitute for meat in disorders such as kidney troubles, high blood pressure, gout, where minimum residue of by-products of protein digestion relieves strain on kidneys and minimises body wastes. Only 52.6 calories per 100 grams. Sought by dieters and weight-watchers.

This soybean curd rapidly establishes itself in Western diet, used for salads, sandwiches, spreads, hors d'oeuvres, soups, sauces; egg, vegetable and grain preparations. A perfect protein from babies to grandparents, containing iron, B-vitamins and calcium. A 100 per cent vegan product.

TOILET POWDER. Soothing and healing. Rice starch or rice powder is the chief ingredient. Add 1 part Orris root to 10 parts rice powder. Add, a sufficiency of perfume or essential oils of personal choice: Lavender, Rose, Geranium, Bergamot, etc.

TOILET VINEGAR. Has a prophylactic effect preventing the spread of mild infectious diseases. Vinegars are aromatic, cooling and refreshing. Singly or combined, take a few drops oil of Bergamot, Cinnamon, Sweet Orange flower, Lemon, Lavender or other perfume of personal choice; add to 4oz Cider vinegar. Shake well. Good for greasy skins.

TOLU BALSAM. *Myroxylon balsamum*, Harms. *Part used*: balsam.

Constituents: triterpenoids, benzoic acid, Cinnamic acid.

Action: stimulating antiseptic expectorant.

Uses. For dispersing congealed mucus that coughing and hawking fail to remove. Chronic catarrh.

External: sore nipples, bedsores, lips, minor injuries.

Inhalant: laryngitis, whooping cough, croup.

Reportedly used in treating cancer. (*J.L. Hartwell, Lloydia, 33, 97, (1970)*)

Preparation. Tincture Tolutana BP. Dose, 2-4ml. GSL

TOMATO. Contains rutin (anti-haemorrhage factor). Vitamins A and C.

Uses. Capillary haemorrhage.

TONG KWAI. An adaptogen. As Ginseng is taken by men as an aphrodisiac, Tong Kwai is taken by women for the same purpose. Women's Ginseng.

TONGUE. See: GLOSSITIS.

TONGUE, BLACK, HAIRY. Hyperplasia of the filiform papillae which may become very long. A pigment-producing bacteria is responsible for the blackness, together with an overgrowth of fungi.

Causes: antibiotic therapy, smoking, poor dental hygiene.

Treatment. Mouth wash and gargle: 5 drops Tincture Myrrh or Goldenseal in half glass water, thrice daily. Few sips swallowed.

Alternative: Cider vinegar.

TONICS. Herbs that increase the tone of body tissues. To assist oxygen-bearing elements in the blood, augmenting metabolic processes and promoting nutrition. They impart added strength and vitality. Tonics should be taken cold, of moderate strength, and not too frequently repeated. While dosage will vary according to the herb, the average dose is a cup of infusion or wineglass of decoction before meals, thrice daily. Children: quarter to half dose according to age.

Agrimony, Bayberry, Betony, Bogbean, Boldo, Chamomile, Dandelion, Fringe Tree bark, Gentian, Goldenseal, Hops, Ginseng, Quassia Chips, White Poplar bark, Wild Cherry bark, Yellow Dock root, Dang gui, Fenugreek, Asparagus root, Rehmannia.

Of the above, some have an effect upon a specific organ or system:– Coltsfoot (lungs), Bayberry (intestines), Dandelion (liver), Fringe Tree bark (pancreas), Goldenseal (mucous membranes), Oatstraw, Oats (nervous system), False Unicorn root (uterus).

TONSILLITIS. Inflammation of the tonsils. Infection may be viral or streptococcal. Acute or chronic. The chronic condition may be due to auto-toxaemia. When the eliminatory organs (bowels, kidneys, lungs) fail to expel accumulations of impurities an extra burden is placed on the lymphatic (de-toxifying) system, which includes the tonsils. They become chronically swollen but surgical removal is not advised unless absolutely necessary.

Symptoms. Fever, difficulty in swallowing, sore throat, inflamed tonsils, pus or exudate.

Alternatives. Agnus Castus (enlarged inflamed tonsils), Black Catechu, Cudweed (marsh), Echinacea, <u>Lemon juice (fresh)</u>, <u>Pineapple juice</u>, Myrrh, <u>Poke root</u>, Raspberry leaves, Red Sage, Rose hip tea, Slippery Elm, <u>Thuja</u> (enlarged lymph nodes), Wild Indigo.

Teas. Chamomile tea plus 5 drops Liquid Extract Poke root thrice daily. Combination: equal parts, Red Sage, Raspberry leaves. 1-2 teaspoons to each cup boiling water; infuse 15 minutes. 1 cup freely.

Tablets/capsules. Thuja, Echinacea, Myrrh, Agnus Castus.

Formula. Echinacea 2; Poke root quarter; Myrrh quarter; Thuja quarter. Dose: Powders: 500mg (two 00 capsules or one-third teaspoons). Liquid extracts: 1 teaspoon. Tinctures: 2 teaspoons. In water or honey every 2 hours (acute); thrice daily (chronic).

Dr Thakhur Qam Dhari Sinha, India. "I have treated many cases of severe chronic tonsillitis with various remedies, internal and external, but nothing has given such satisfaction as *Thuja* painted over the affected area. Mix equal parts Liquid Extract (or tincture) Thuja and glycerine. I also give blood purifying tablets, one every 3 hours."

Abscess on tonsils: Chamomile tea with 5 drops Tincture Goldenseal, thrice daily.

Preventative. Tincture Thuja, 3 drops at night. Vitamin C 400mg daily.

Gargle. Any of the above. OR:– 5 drops Tincture Goldenseal, Myrrh, Echinacea, Thuja OR Tea Tree oil in half a tumbler water. Gargle freely, or use any one in an atomiser spray. Lemon juice. Pineapple juice.

Cold compress around neck; linen or suitable material saturated with Witch Hazel.

Diet. 3-day fast on fruit juices. Abundant Vitamin C (oranges and citrus fruits). Follow with protein diet.

Vitamins. A. B-complex. C (1g daily). Folic acid.

Minerals. Iodine. Selenium (50mg), Zinc (15mg) daily.

TOOTH PASTE. Ayurvedic healing science advises the use of Neem from the East Indian Neem tree (*Azadirachta indica*) which has a long history for cleaning teeth in Southern Asia. Fennel tooth paste.

TOOTH POWDER. For cleansing, anti-tartar formation, to firm-up gums, keep teeth free from infection and to sweeten the breath.

Equal parts: Bayberry, Gum Myrrh, Cuttlefish bone and Orris root powders. Mix. Store in air-tight tin or jar. Use freely.

Alternatives: (1) Equal parts, powders, Oak bark, Comfrey root, Horsetail, Lobelia, Cloves, Peppermint. Mix. (2) Equal parts, powders Bistort root, Bayberry bark, Orris root (*Dr John Christopher*).

TOOTHBRUSH TREE. *Salvadora persica*. Native of India and the Middle East where it is used as a chewing stick for protection and cleaning of teeth. Of value for removal of tartar, healing of mouth ulcers and bleeding gums.

TOPICAL. A term used for the route of administration of a herb or herbal product, applied directly to the part treated, i.e. an ointment applied to a skin eruption.

TORMENTIL. Septfoil. *Potentilla tormentilla*, Neek. *Potentilla Erecta*, Rausch. *German*: Blutwurz. *French*: Tormentille. *Spanish*: Sictun kama. *Italian*: Tormentilla. *Keynote*: irritable bowel.

Constituents: 10-30 p.c. tannin, resin, 'tormentil red' colouring matter.

Action. A welcome gentle-acting tonic astringent for distressing irritable bowel disorders. Haemostatic and styptic (external).

Uses. Irritable bowel including colitis, cholera, piles, diverticulitis (with ulceration), gastro-intestinal irritation, bleeding or ulceration. Mouth

ulcers, sore gums, sore lips (mouthwash or chew root or leaves). Leucorrhoea, as a vaginal douche. Tea is used as a lotion for ulcers, minor injuries and sores that refuse to heal.
Preparations. Average dose, 2-4 grams or fluid equivalent, thrice daily.
Tea: 1 heaped teaspoon to each cup water gently simmered 5 minutes; dose – half-1 cup.
Liquid extract: half-1 teaspoon in water.
Tincture BHP (1983): 1:5 in 45 per cent alcohol. Dose, 2-4ml.

TORTICOLLIS. Wry neck. Spasm of the neck muscles. Contraction of one of the strong sterno-mastoid muscles, twisting the head to one side. Stiff neck through sitting in a draught or from general toxic condition. Head cannot be turned away from the affected side. Movements of head and neck painful. Search for septic foci such as bad teeth.
Causes: may include rheumatism, hysteria, injury.
Alternatives. Black Cohosh, Celery, Cramp bark, Devil's Claw, Guaiacum (anti-inflammatory), Poke root (mild analgesic), Prickly Ash (anti-rheumatic), Sarsaparilla (powerful blood tonic to correct toxaemia), Wild Yam (to relax muscles).
Teas. Yerba mate tea. Celery seed tea.
Decoction. White Willow 2; Sarsaparilla 2; Wild Yam 1; Valerian 1; Ginger root half. Mix. 4 teaspoons to 1 pint (500ml) water gently simmered 20 minutes. Dose: wineglass thrice daily.
Tablets/capsules. Black Cohosh, Celery, Devil's Claw, Wild Yam, Ligvites.
Powders. Formula. White Willow 3; Guaiacum 1; Celery 1; Black Cohosh 1; Ginger half. Dose: 750mg (three 00 capsules or half a teaspoon). Thrice daily.
Formula, liquids. Jamaica Dogwood 1; Black Cohosh 1; Devil's Claw 1; Guaiacum quarter; Liquorice quarter. Mix. Dose: Liquid extracts: 1 teaspoon. Tinctures: 2 teaspoons. Thrice daily.
Tincture Cramp bark: 1-2 teaspoons, thrice daily.
Topical. Capsicum salve. Stiff-neck salve. Jojoba oil, Evening Primrose oil. Hot pack: towel wrung out in hot water and applied at night.

Gentle massage of neck from base of the skull downwards, including shoulders and upper spine with warm Olive oil. Radiant heat. Osteopathy or Chiropractic.
Diet. Abundant Vitamin C drinks (orange, lemon). Low salt. Lacto-vegetarian. Oily fish.
Supplements. Vitamin B6, C, Zinc.

TOXAEMIA. See: AUTO TOXAEMIA.

TOXIC SHOCK SYNDROME (TSS). A magnesium deficiency disease due to vaginal contraceptive devices and highly absorbant brands of sanitary towels, sponges and tampons used by menstruating women. Polyester and polycrylate rayon fibres leech magnesium from the body, thus hindering its natural defences against shock and favouring production of staphylococcus aureus toxins.
Symptoms. High fever to 102°F, or higher; dizziness, diarrhoea, vomiting, dusky 'sunburn' rash, sudden drop in blood pressure leading to shock. Liver failure, ulceration of the cervix, or coma may follow.
Treatment. Discontinue use of tampons, etc. Goldenseal alters the cervical mucus towards normality. Cornsilk tea, freely.
Formula. Pleurisy root 2; Goldenseal 1; Agnus Castus 1; few grains Cayenne pepper or drops Tincture Capsicum. Dose: Powders: 750mg (three 00 capsules or half a teaspoon). Liquid extracts: 1-2 teaspoons. Tinctures: 1-3 teaspoons. In water or honey every 2 hours (acute), thrice daily (chronic).
Douche. 1 part Cider vinegar to 5 parts boiled water allowed to cool. OR:– apply Aloe Vera juice or gel with applicator, per vagina.
Enema. Strong coffee.
Diet. 3-day fast. Fruit juices only. High protein to follow.
Vitamins. A. B12. C (1-3g daily). E (1,000iu daily).
Minerals. Magnesium, Iron, Manganese, Zinc.
Note: Tampons not to be worn at night. Use of dioxin-free tampons, changed regularly. Tampons should not be used in the presence of genital infection. Present-day medical practice discourages the use of tampons.

TOXOCARIASIS. Occurs mostly in children following infection by the larvae of the round-worm *Toxocara canis* found in dogs, or *Toxocara cati* in cats. Eggs are excreted in an animal's faeces and spread by contaminated soil. Microscopic eggs of the parasite enter homes on soles of shoes or on paws of household pets.
Symptoms: fever, enlargement of liver and spleen, breathing difficulties with cough, skin rash. Inflammation of the retina of the eye with damage to vision. Fatigue, allergies, abdominal pain, heart and arterial problems.
Treatment. Anthelmintics, anti-inflammatories.
Teas. Betony, Thyme, Wormwood. German Chamomile.
Traditional. Pumpkin seeds (5-6 seeds thrice daily). Papaya fruit, as desired. Onions (diet). Burdock and Sarsaparilla beer. Senna pods (see entry). Pomegranate seeds, as desired.
Garlic. 2 capsules at night. 2-3 inserted into rectum at night.
Quassia chips. 2 teaspoons in each cup cold water steeped overnight, or 8 hours. Internal: one-third cup thrice daily. Enema: half an ounce to 1 pint used warm, twice weekly.
Chamomile enema. 2 teaspoons flowers to 2 pints boiling water. Strain; inject warm at bedtime.

Pregnancy. It is wise to avoid uncooked meats and the presence of cats and dogs.

TOXOPLASMOSIS. A cat-borne disease. Causative organism: *Toxoplasma gondii* contracted from raw incompletely cooked meats or from dried faeces from a cat's litter box or garden soil. A mild flu-like complaint capable of blindness and brain damage.
Symptoms: painful lymph nodes, infections of the eyes, fever. Effect upon a foetus may be blindness, cleft palate, retarded mentality or abortion. Pregnant women should not be exposed to a kitten's faeces. Scarring of the retina may occur sometime after birth.
Alternatives. Echinacea, Poke root, Goldenseal.
Formula. Echinacea 2; Thyme 1; Poke root quarter; Goldenseal quarter. Mix. Dose: Powders: 500mg (two 00 capsules or one-third teaspoon). Liquid extracts: 1 teaspoon. Tinctures: 2 teaspoons. In water or honey every 2 hours (acute); thrice daily (chronic).
Note. Cats may excrete a parasite that can infect a pregnant woman with toxoplasmosis which can cause severe abnormalities in her unborn baby.
Precautions. Avoid eating raw or under-cooked meat; wash hands carefully after handling raw meat; wear gloves and wash hands thoroughly after gardening; change cat litter daily, and wear gloves in doing so. Avoid unpasteurised goat milk products.
Information. Toxoplasmosis Trust, 61-71 Collier Street, London N1 9BE.

TRACE ELEMENTS. Minerals essential for life include: iron, cobalt, copper, molybdenum, selenium, chromium, manganese, vanadian, nickel, tin, iodine, silica, zinc, etc.

These may be found in varying concentrations in all herbs, but some plants may have an affinity with a certain mineral, such as Horsetail (silica), Kelp (iodine), the Dock family (iron), Nettles (calcium and iron), Sunflower seeds (zinc).

TRACHEITIS. Inflammation of the trachea (windpipe). The trachea extends from the larynx to the bronchi. Due to viral or bacterial infection spreads downwards from the throat.
Treatment: same as for LARYNGITIS.

TRACHOMA. A contagious disease infecting the membrane investing the front of the eye (conjunctiva). Causative organism: *Chlamydia trachomatis.* A cause of blindness in tropical countries.
Symptoms. Severe reddened conjunctivitis. Watery eyes, swollen lids, dread of light (patient shields his eyes with his hands when looking at you). Small masses on the membrane harden, blurring vision, ending with loss of sight.
Treatment. Hospitalisation. First clean the lids with common salt wash. Early treatment with anti-infectives to prevent scarring. Scarring may have to be removed by corneal graft which is usually successful. Traditional treatment in India is to bathe eyes with Gotu Kola tea.
Teas or tablets: Wild Thyme, Nasturtium, Agnus Castus.
Formula. Echinacea 2; Myrrh half; Goldenseal half. Mix. Dose: Powders: 500mg (two 00 capsules or one-third teaspoon). Liquid extracts: 1 teaspoon. Tinctures: 2 teaspoons. In honey or water every 2 hours (acute); thrice daily (chronic).
Topical. Goldenseal Eye Drops.

Vitamin C is a powerful antibacterial (1-2g daily).
Garlic capsules: 2-3 at night.

Treatment by or in liaison with a general medical practitioner.

TRAGACANTH, GUM. *Astragalus gummifer.*, Labill. *Part used*: gum exudation.
Constituents: tragacanthin, polysaccharides.
Action. Demulcent, mucilage, emollient, vehicle for heavy powders. Laxative. Inhibits growth of cancer cells. (*J.F. Morton, 1977, Major Medicinal Plants: Botany Culture and Uses: Thomas, Springfield, Illinois, USA*)
Uses. Irritations of the internal mucosa. Foreign bodies in the alimentary canal, colitis, dry coughs, bronchitis.
Preparations. *Powder*: average dose, 1-2 grams, thrice daily. Used in the manufacture of tablets, lozenges and suppositories as a base. GSL

TRAINING OF THE MEDICAL HERBALIST. The National Institute of Medical Herbalists is the senior professional body of qualified practitioners. Candidates for membership are required to pass examinations of the School of Phytotherapy or have taken the postgraduate degree in Complementary Health Studies, Exeter University. A stipulated period of clinical practice must be completed before the final examination is taken.

See: POST GRADUATE DEGREE IN COMPLEMENTARY HEALTH STUDIES. PHYTOTHERAPY – SCHOOL OF. NATIONAL INSTITUTE OF MEDICAL HERBALISTS.

TRANQUILLISER. A nerve relaxant. See: SEDATIVE.

TRANSDERMAL PATCHES. Oestrogen patches to control menopausal symptoms have been in use a number of years. The technique of applying an agent to the skin and expecting it to act elsewhere through absorption, proves to be an important development in modern medicine.

A circular adhesive skin patch, the size of a £1

coin, is seen as the potential to give a remedy a controlled release.

Transdermal preparations include the sticking of a patch containing the drug Hyoscine behind the ear of orchestrial wind instrumentalists to arrest salivation during a performance. It will also cure or prevent motion sickness. Return to normal is immediate upon removal of the patch.

This new mode of administration is popular among some doctors who find patient-compliance high. Over-dosage is rare. The action of the remedy may be switched on and off at will. In children, it offers an alternative to injections. It is seen as a way of avoiding the systemic side-effects of deep-acting remedies such as Nux Vomica, Gelsemium, Stramonium and Colchicum.

Pain-relief with the aid of analgesics attached to the head for headache or to the joints for rheumatoid conditions offers a fascinating field of study. It is claimed that such a patch when plugged with cotton wool saturated with Tincture of Arnica can exert a beneficial influence upon the heart.

TRAVEL DIARRHOEA. See: DIARRHOEA.

TRAVEL SICKNESS. See: MOTION SICKNESS.

TREBEN, MARIA. (1907-1991) Austrian Herbalist with nationwide practice. Author: *"Health Through God's Pharmacy"*. Experiences of herbal healing with prescriptions for specific diseases. European best-seller of over three million copies in one year. In Maria's own words: "At a time when the majority of mankind has moved away from life's natural ways, when illness, caused by a changed attitude to life threatens, we should turn again to medicinal herbs which God in His goodness has provided for us since time immemorial. As Abbe Kneipp (famous European herbalist) says: 'There is a plant for every illness'."

TREMOR. Practitioner: Datura stramonium. 5 drops tincture twice daily as initial dose, increasing dose by 2 drops per day every 3 days until effective. Stabilise at 10 drops twice daily. Background treatment of Skullcap and Oats. (*Ann Dunning, MNIMH*)

Combination of Vitamins C and E may delay appearance of tremor, loss of balance and rigidity in Parkinson's disease.

TRENCH FOOT. Frostbite of the foot, with severe neuritis. Toes without sensation and swollen from fluid retention. Blister formation. Skin should be kept dry by dusting with Slippery Elm powder. Where skin is broken, apply Marigold (Calendula) cream or lotion. Where unbroken, Arnica, Comfrey or Chickweed cream or ointment.

See also: FROSTBITE.

TRENCH MOUTH. Painful ulceration of mucous membranes of the mouth and throat. See: VINCENT'S ANGINA.

TRICHINOSIS. Caused by eating undercooked pork, bacon or ham that may contain cysts of the parasite: *Trichinella spiralis* which discharges its larvae into the stomach and intestines.
Symptoms: fever, loss of appetite, abdominal pain and swelling, nausea, diarrhoea, nervous irritability, swelling of eyelids, abnormal sensitivity to light (photophobia), conjunctivitis, marked prostration. Muscles become painful, stiff and weak. Liver and lungs may be affected and myocarditis develop into heart failure.
Treatment. Until hospitalisation is possible. When ingestion of infected pork, etc has been confirmed, an emetic should be given with all possible speed: 1 heaped teaspoon Lobelia herb to cup boiling water; infuse 5-10 minutes. Repeat until stomach has been cleared. If not available, see EMETICS. The bowels, also, should be emptied by use of Senna tea or other strong laxative to completely clear the bowel and intestines. Emesis is half the battle. Once the parasite has invaded the muscles medication is of little value, except to build up strength. The disorder will impose a severe strain on the body's recuperative powers and there is no substitute for nourishing wholefoods, multivitamins and minerals.
European traditional: High Garlic.
Chinese Barefoot: Gotu Kola tea, freely.
Australia. Tea Tree oil – powerful anti-parasitic. 2-3 drops in water or honey every 3 hours. If too strong may be diluted many times.
Tinctures Myrrh and Goldenseal, equal parts. 5-20 drops in water every 2 hours.
Diet. 3-day fast followed by high protein.
Vitamins. A. B-complex, B1, B2, B6, B12, C, D, K.
Minerals. Calcium, Iron.

Treatment by a general medical practitioner or hospital specialist.

TRICHOMONIASIS. Infection of the genito urinary tract with protozoan – *Trichomonas vaginalis*. Sexually transmitted vaginitis, cystitis and urethritis in females. In males: prostatitis, urethritis, cystitis. May be present in the vagina for months until triggered off by nylon pants, trousers, tights.
Symptoms. Greenish yellow offensive vaginal discharge. Itching and irritation of vulva, strawberry-spotted vagina. Inflammation of Bartholin's gland, bladder and vagina. Frequency of urine. Discharge not as frothy as candida. Painful intercourse.
Alternatives. Both partners should be treated.
Tablets/capsules. Thuja. Agnus Castus. Goldenseal. Garlic.
Formula 1. Kava Kava 2; Goldenseal 1; Thuja

quarter. Mix. Dose: Powders: 250mg (one 00 capsule or one-sixth teaspoon). Liquid extracts: 15-30 drops. Tinctures: 30-60 drops. In water or honey thrice daily.
Formula 2. Squaw vine 1; Kava Kava 1; Agnus Castus 2. Mix. Dose: Powders: 500mg (two 00 capsules or one-third teaspoon). Liquid extracts: 1 teaspoon. Tinctures: 2 teaspoons. In water or honey thrice daily.
Camphor, oil of: 1-2 drops in honey or water, 3-4 times daily for intense irritation of sexual organs.
Topical, and per os. (1) After thoroughly washing vulva and vagina follow with insertion of tampon impregnated with solution of 2 drops Tea Tree oil to 4oz (120ml) boiled water. If too strong drops may be diluted many times. Patient removes tampon after 24 hours, and replenish. (2) Douche. 5 drops Tea Tree oil to 2 pints boiled water, as an injection. (3) Zinc and Castor oil cream. (3) Thuja ointment. (4) Garlic ointment.
Diet. Low fat. Garlic, onion, yoghurt.
Mineral. Zinc.
Note. Garlic commended.
Treatment by a general medical practitioner or hospital specialist.

TRIGLYCERIDE. The chief constituent of a fat or oil. A compound with one molecule of glycerol and three molecules of fatty acids. Produced by the liver from starches and which in excess may cause atherosclerosis. Too many triglycerides thicken the blood and block capillaries or sometimes arteries. Ingestion of too much sugar may predispose. Treatment should include a liver remedy (Dandelion, Boldo, etc).
Triglycerides are linked to heart disease mortality in women. (*Norwegian Study: Stensvold I et al, BMJ 1993, 307: 1318-22*)

TRYPANOSOMIASIS, African. See: SLEEPING SICKNESS.

TRYPTOPHAN. L-Tryptophan. One of the 8 essential amino acids. Necessary to maintain a balance in the body's protein and required to produce niacin (B3). A niacin deficiency may cause skin disorders. A neurotransmitter chemical in the brain, called serotonin, helps control moods and mental behaviour. To produce serotonin, tryptophan is essential.
Action: anti-stress, relaxant, anti-depressant.
Uses: sleep problems, anxiety symptoms, examination stress.
Tryptophan occurs naturally in peanuts, peas and beans. Also present in meat, fish, yoghurt and chicken. Highest in turkey (turkey sandwich at night).
Alternatives: Passion flower, Skullcap, Valerian, Oats, Lime flowers, Jamaica Dogwood. See: EOSINOPHILIA.
Pumpkin seeds. A natural source of tryptophan. 200 grams of Pumpkin seeds will produce a gram of tryptophan. Since lack of availability of this essential amino acid due to UK Government action, Pumpkin seeds become popular for depression.

TUBERCULOSIS. Infectious notifiable disease caused by the *bacillus tuberculosis*, discovered by Koch. Onset is generally in the lung, but any organ may be invaded. Common sites are lungs, bone, lymph nodes, kidneys, genital organs, each of which produces its own set of symptoms.
Symptoms. Night sweats, loss of weight, feeble strength and a rise in temperature every evening. Pulmonary tuberculosis (of the lungs) produces sputum streaked with blood, cough, and sometimes haemoptysis (bleeding). When occurring elsewhere, may cause bone swelling, cold abscesses, blood in the urine.
With the introduction of BCG vaccination the morbidity and mortality from tuberculosis has decreased enormously in this century. However, despite its initial success, the disease is still very much with us today. The current increase is associated with AIDS infection. Echinacea antidotes ill-effects of BCG vaccine. For tuberculosis of the lymphatic glands, see SCROFULA.
Treatment. *Tuberculostatics*: Elecampane, Comfrey, Iceland Moss.
Treatment varies according to organ involved and to the constitution of the patient. To meet individual needs, treatment will be varied many times during the course of the disease. Key remedies are Elecampane and Echinacea. In a series of tests, showing the action of these remedies upon tubercle bacilli, Dr von Unrich, one-time Medical Officer in the U.S. Army came to the conclusion that these two "antagonise Koch's bacillus and quickly antidote virulent toxins in a number of the worst forms of infection".
Inflamed joints: Echinacea, with Elecampane root.
Night sweats: Sage tea.
Tea: Combine, Hyssop 1; White Horehound 1; Comfrey leaves 2; Liquorice root quarter. 1oz of the mixture to 1 pint boiling water. Infuse 15 minutes. Half-1 cup 3-4 times daily. May be stored in a thermos flask.
Decoction: Irish Moss: see entry.
Potter's formula has been used for over 150 years. Parts: Marshmallow root 1; Liquorice root 2; English Linseed 2; Iceland Moss 2; Goldenseal 1; Life root 1; Pleurisy root 1. Prepare as a decoction.
Powders. Mix: 1oz Marshmallow root; 1oz Liquorice; half an ounce Lobelia herb; half an ounce Valerian; Coffeespoon Cayenne. Half-1 level teaspoon in honey or hot beverage. (*Arthur Barker*)
Tinctures. Combine equal parts Echinacea and Elecampane. Add 1 teaspoon of the mixture to

1 cup Comfrey root decoction. Dose: half-1 cup with honey, thrice daily. If Elecampane not available substitute Pleurisy root.

Spanish traditional. As recorded by explorer-botanist Alec de Montmorency: "The Koch bacillus may be destroyed in the body by the sap of the cooking banana (Plantain)".

Tuberculosis of kidneys. Cup Yarrow tea to which 10 drops Liquid Extract Echinacea added. Thrice daily.

White Birch. (Betula alba) The Creeks, North American Indians, used White Birch for the disease. (*Swanton: Social and Religious Beliefs and Practices of the Chickasaw Indians" 1924-1925, 659*)

Comfrey root. Has been an important ingredient in formulae for tuberculosis in the past: its potential benefit outweighs possible risk.

Lobelia (or other emetic) once weekly to cleanse the stomach was favoured by the Eclectic School. It has a cleansing effect upon the lungs also, assisting removal of accumulated mucus and bringing a sense of relief for many hours. Lobelia emetics do not weaken but increase strength.

Fish oils. Tuberculosis demands a high level of Vitamins A and D. Cod Liver oil was widely used for the disease in the 1920s for strength and building up tissue.

Diet. The Catawbas Indians used Slippery Elm gruel and Alfalfa tea. Pasteurisation of milk considerably reduces risk of infection.

Vitamins. A. B6, B12, Niacin, C, D.

Minerals. Calcium, Iron, Phosphorus, Zinc.

Historical. See entry: UMCKALOABO. (*Steven's Cure*)

Note. The phenomenal rise of the disease in recent years is directly related to the increase in HIV infections (*World Health Organisation*). An increasing number of victims of AIDS show signs of tuberculosis; a skin test may prove positive while the person shows no signs of clinical disease. The AIDS virus activates previously dormant tuberculosis by weakening patients' defences.

Treatment by general medical practitioner or tuberculosis specialist.

TULIP TREE. *Liriodendron tulipifera L.* *French*: Tulipier. *German*: Tulpenbaum. *Italian*: Tulipifero.

Action: astringent, antiseptic, febrifuge, aromatic, stimulant, antiperiodic. Bitter tonic.

Uses, internal. Intermittent fevers.

Topical: sore throat, mouth ulcers, spongy gums, infected teeth (decoction used as a mouth wash and gargle).

Preparations. Thrice daily.

Decoction, inner bark. 15g (half an ounce) to 500ml (1 pint) water gently simmered 10 minutes; half-1 cup.

Liquid extract: 15-45 drops in water.

TUMOUR. Neoplasm. A spontaneous new growth – malignant (cancerous) or benign (non-cancerous).

Differential diagnosis: a malignant tumour infiltrates other body tissues, whereas a benign one does not spread or infiltrate.

Medical literature has an abundance of cases of successful use of plant medicines which warrant investigation in depth. The following have a long traditional reputation for resolution of tumours but which cannot always be confirmed in the laboratory.

Burdock root, Clivers, Chickweed, Comfrey, Chaparral, Fenugreek seeds, Greater Celandine, Red Clover, Wild (not cultivated) Violet, Thuja, Yellow Dock.

A Slippery Elm poultice may soften hard (non-malignant) tumours.

Diet. Gerson diet.

Vitamins. A. B12, C. P (bioflavonoids).

Minerals. Chromium, Manganese, Nickel, Selenium, Molybdenum, Sulphur, Zinc. These form part of a multi-vitamin capsule or tablet.

Treatment by a general medical practitioner or hospital specialist.

TUMOUR – OF THE ABDOMEN. Dr Compton Burnett records the case of male of 60 years with an abdominal tumour arising from a fall on the left side. Six surgeons declared it inoperable. He prescribed Common Daisy (*Bellis perennis*) and the splenic remedy, New Jersey tea (*Ceanothus*) in alternation. Seventeen days later the man was able to visit Burnett. The tumour had rapidly diminished. Ten weeks after the first visit the tumour had disappeared. Cure was permanent. Daisy has removed tumours after a blow – especially a blow on the breast. It is useful where a tumour follows a bruise. Daisy is also known as the English Arnica.

For a similar condition Dr Wm Boericke advises Star of Bethlehem.

Treatment by a general medical practitioner or hospital specialist.

TUMOUR – ADRENAL GLAND. May be medullary or cortical. At first they promote excessive hormonal secretion, but later have the opposite effect.

Medullary tumour symptoms: high blood pressure, fainting, sweating, violent palpitation, the feeling that one's last hour has arrived.

Cortical tumour symptoms: rapid production of steroid hormones, deepening voice, masculine characters, clitoris enlarges, excess pubic and facial hair. Cushing's syndrome.

Mistletoe tea.

Formula. Sarsaparilla 3; Liquorice 1; Ginseng 1; Thuja quarter. Mix. Dose: Powders: 500mg (two 00 capsules or one-third teaspoon). Liquid extracts: 1 teaspoon. Tinctures: 1-2 teaspoons in

water (or cup of Mistletoe tea) thrice daily. Supportive to conventional medical treatment.
Diet. As for ADDISON'S DISEASE.

Treatment by a general medical practitioner or hospital specialist.

TUMOUR – BRAIN. For the purposes of herbal treatment all expanding lesions of the skull are regarded as tumours. They may comprise neoplasm, haemorrhage, abscess, osteoma of the bone; tumours of the meninges, cranial nerves, supportive tissue, etc. All these increase intra-cranial pressure and require cerebral relaxants to relieve tension. Anti-tumour agents with specific reference to this condition include: Mistletoe, Thuja, Echinacea and Sweet Violet (the wild, not cultivated variety). Nerve restoratives such as Skullcap and Ladyslipper would find a place in a prescription to sustain the nervous system.
Symptoms. Headache, nausea and vomiting. Convulsions, drowsiness, mental deterioration.
Treatment. Supportive to conventional medical treatment.
Relaxing teas. Singly, or in combination: Lime flowers, Lemon Balm, Wood Betony, Red Clover, Valerian.
Powders. Mistletoe 1; Valerian 1; Passion flower 2; Thuja quarter. Mix. Dose: 750mg (three 00 capsules or half a teaspoon) in honey or banana mash 3 or more times daily. May be followed by a cup of relaxing tea.

Treatment by a general medical practitioner or hospital specialist.

TUMOUR – OF THE GULLET. Oesophageal swelling.
Symptoms. Sense of food being obstructed on its way down to the stomach (dysphagia). Pain.
Treatment. *Supportive to conventional medical treatment.*
Tea. Periwinkle, Red Clover, Hydrocotyle, Violet leaves: equal parts. 1 heaped teaspoon in each cup boiling water; infuse 5-10 minutes. One cup freely. Add honey if necessary.

Treatment by a general medical practitioner or hospital specialist.

TUMOUR – OF THE KIDNEY. Renal tumour or neoplasm may arise from the pelvis, capsule or parenchyma of the kidney. Not common.
Symptoms. Blood in the urine. Cachexia. Anaemia. Colic from trapped blood clots in the ureter. Abdominal mass may be readily palpable. Persistent loin pains. Loss of weight.
Treatment. *Supportive to conventional medical treatment.*
Fenugreek tea.
Supplementation. Vitamin C shown to help renal carcinoma. (*Cancer Research Vol 43, 10, 4638-42 (1983)*) RDA – 2-3 grams daily.

Treatment by a general medical practitioner of hospital specialist.

TUMOUR – PINEAL GLAND. Not common among adults. Speeds up puberty; a cause of water on the brain. Light reflexes impaired. Some loss of sight and hearing. Intra-cranial pressure increases requiring brain relaxants.
Treatment. *Supportive to conventional medical treatment.*
Teas. Red Clover, Gotu Kola, Vervain, Ladyslipper, Mistletoe.
Tablets/capsules. Jamaica Dogwood, Valerian.
Formula. Passion flower 2; Mistletoe 1; Gotu Kola 1. Mix. Powders: 750mg (three 00 capsules or half a teaspoon). Liquid extracts: 1-2 teaspoons. Tinctures: 1-3 teaspoons. Once or more daily.

Treatment by a general medical practitioner or hospital specialist.

TUMOUR – PITUITARY GLAND. May be adenoma or carcinoma, resulting in increased output of the growth hormone in gigantism or acromegaly. In gigantism parts of the body may enlarge before puberty. In acromegaly parts of the body – usually face, hands and feet – may enlarge after puberty.
Supportive to conventional medical treatment.
Wild Yam. Tablets, tinctures, liquid extracts or powder.

Treatment by a general medical practitioner or hospital specialist.

TURKEY CORN. Turkey pea. *Dicentra cucullaria, L. Part used*: root.
Constituents: alkaloids.
Action: general stimulant, diffusive tonic, diuretic, alterative, anti-syphilitic, anti-scrofula.
Uses. Once widely used in America for blood disorders, including syphilis and the chronic sequelae following infection – rheumatism, etc. Stirs the body into activity from torpid and sluggish conditions affecting the blood stream, mucous membranes and lymphatic glands. Menstrual disorders.
Traditional combination: equal parts – Turkey Corn, Prickly Ash, Burdock and Queen's Delight.
Preparations. Average dose, half-1 gram or fluid equivalent, thrice daily.
Decoction. 15g (half an ounce) to 500ml (1 pint) water gently simmered 20 minutes. Dose: half-1 cup.
Liquid extract: 30-60 drops.

TURMERIC. Curcuma. *Curcuma longa, Curcuma domestica, L.* Spice. *Part used*: rhizome.
Constituents: volatile oil, vitamins, minerals, yellow pigment curcumin.
Action. Aromatic, blood purifier, stomachic,

anti-oxidant, carminative, cholagogue, choleretic, bile stimulant. Detoxifier and regenerator of liver tissue. Anti-inflammatory for arthritis, skin disorders and asthma. Anti-tumour activity. Anti-cancer.

Harvard Medical School. Curcumin inhibits HIV-1 replication and p24 antigen expression in cells chronically and acutely affected.

Uses. Dyspepsia. To lower cholesterol levels. Liver and gall bladder diseases. Rheumatoid arthritis. Salmonella.

Diabetes: to boost insulin activity. (*American Health, 1989, Nov 8, p96*)

Vomiting of pregnancy. Anti-platelet activity offers protection to heart and vessels. To reduce high plasma cholesterol.

Spice, for use at table: 250-500mg once or twice daily. An ingredient of curry powders.

Medicine for specific disease: 1-2 grams daily.

Turmeric controls cholesterol.

An article by Kerry Bone discusses the astonishing pharmacological properties of Curcuma longa. Studies have revealed it to be antioxidant, anti-inflammatory, anti-platelet, cholesterol lowering and potentially anti-tumour. Curcumin, its yellow colouring, was the strongest free-radical scavenger, as effective as the antioxidant BHA. The cholesterol-lowering effect is equal to clofibrate. It inhibits gram positive bacteria, is highly toxic to Salmonella, and has a protective action against hepatotoxicity. It also protects against DNA damage in lymphocytes. (*British Journal of Phytotherapy, Vol 2, No 2*)

TURNER, WILLIAM. 1510-1568. Father of English botany. Son of a tanner. A Northumbrian with strong Protestant convictions which led him to flee England. He wandered around Europe, finally studying under Conrad Gerner in Switzerland where he was introduced to European herbals of the day. Book: *A New Herball* (1511), with beautiful wood-cuts is now a collector's piece of value. "This notable work," wrote Eleanor Sinclair Rohde, "is the only original work on botany written by an Englishman in the 16th century." It was published in three separate parts and dedicated to Queen Elizabeth I.

TWITCHING. See: RESTLESSNESS.

TYMPANITES. Abdominal distention with gas or air.

Causes: irritable bowel syndrome, obstruction of the intestines or air-swallowing.

See: FLATULENCE.

TYPHOID FEVER. Serious infective notifiable fever caused by *Salmonella typhi* spread by infected food, water, dairy produce, seafood (raw oysters, etc). Occurs mostly in the Indian sub continent and Mediterranean countries. The organism is present in the faeces of some people known as carriers for years, yet remain healthy. Partiality for the gall bladder. High standards of hygiene have almost eliminated it in the West. Incubation period: 5-10 days.

Symptoms. *First week*: may go undetected but later the patient becomes dull with sensation of influenza. Abdominal discomfort, muscle pains. Step-ladder temperature to 104°F.

Second week: patient apathetic, with enlarged spleen, rose-coloured patches on skin, invasion of lymph glands, bleeding from the bowel.

Third week: crisis, with swollen abdomen and coma. Severe diarrhoea and relapse, ulceration, with possibility of perforation. Cough, nose-bleeds. The tongue is long, narrow-pointed and coated dark brown or black. Symptoms of the milder form: (paratyphoid fever) are the same but run a shorter course.

Treatment. Hospitalisation. Bed isolation. Patient should make-good fluid losses with abundant herb teas which also act as diaphoretics to lower temperature.

Chamomile, Yarrow, Raspberry leaves, Sage, Wild Cherry bark (decoction), Skullcap (mental confusion), Pleurisy root (decoction), Rosemary and Raspberry leaves.

At the close of the 19th century, medical practitioners of the Eclectic School of America had plenty of experience in dealing with this killer disease. Dr Finlay Ellingwood records that Witch Hazel, Thuja, Stone root and Shepherd's Purse were most serviceable (Liquid Extract 5-10 drops in water, hourly). He writes: "Baptisia (Wild Indigo) is indicated when the tongue is dry and with a brown or black coat; when mucous membranes are dark red or purple; when the breath and discharges are fetid. He writes:–

"Where there is excessive abdominal tenderness on pressure, with sharp cutting pains tending to peritonitis, Tincture Bryonia, (Liquid Extract 5-10 drops, hourly) usually controls temperature and reduces inflammation. May be indicated in the third week when there is marked prostration and physical exhaustion. Haemorrhage is almost an unknown complication with those who have used Echinacea in typhoid."

Dr A.W. Fisher, writes in the Medical World: "Small doses of Echinacea seem to help the blood free itself of its burden and render it abler to fight its battle."

Alternatives. *Tinctures*. Bayberry 1; Pleurisy root 2; Motherwort 1; Echinacea 2; Ginger half. Dose: 1 teaspoon every 2 hours.

Dr Margaretha Wilkenloh's treatment. One or two drops Wood Turpentine in honey or sweetening, every 2 hours. Turpentine is soothing to irritable membranes, destroys bacteria and stimulates mucous secretion. Another authority advises 5 drop doses every 2 hours enclosed in a gelatin capsule.

Tea. Equal parts: Wood Betony. Meadowsweet. Great Burnet. Agrimony, Vervain, Raspberry. Mix. Infuse in 1 and a half pints (750ml) for 10 minutes. Strain. Half a teacupful doses are taken hot every 15 minutes until all consumed. This usually relieves sickness, vomiting and delirium. A pinch of Cayenne should be added to each dose. Follow with teaspoon Antispasmodic drops or third preparation of Lobelia, every 3 hours in small teacup of warm water. Sponge down body with vinegar and warm water. (*Richard L. Hool MNAMH. From: Herb Doctor 1916*)
Practitioner. Treatment will vary according to individual case. Combine tinctures of Aconite and Belladonna. 5-10 drops hourly in wineglassful water prevents local congestion, equalises the circulation and is appropriate in the early stages where the skin and extremities are icy cold and circulation feeble.
Tincture Baptisia (Wild Indigo) BPC (1934). Dose 2-5ml in water 3 or more times daily.
External. Where fever is on the increase sponge down with hot water and Epsom's salts or vinegar, permitting the mixture to evaporate on the surface. Follow with wet pack at body temperature which imparts a sense of comfort and rest. Replace pack as necessary.
Enema. As tolerated. 10-20 drops of tinctures or liquid extracts: Wild Indigo, Goldenseal, Myrrh, Echinacea, Witch Hazel; or 2 tablespoons vinegar . . . to 2 pints boiled water allowed to cool. Inject tepid. Sleep with eyes half open means the intestinal tract is under severe irritation requiring a strong Catnep enema; 1oz herb to 2 pints boiling water.
Diet. Fasting necessary; fruit juices and herb teas only, with plenty of water, as tolerated. Boil all drinking water. Regulate bowels. No alcohol or caffeine beverages.
Supplementation. To build up after attack: multivitamins, calcium, magnesium, potassium, iron, Vitamin B-complex. Minerals are needed to replace those drained away during the illness.
Treatment by a general medical practitioner or hospital specialist.

TYPHUS. A severe feverish condition caused by the organism: *Rickettsia.* Infection may follow a bite from the human body louse or from inhaling airborne louse faeces. The parasite sucks blood from an infected person and passes on the infection to another, as in concentration camps and closed communities. Also transmitted by rats and mice. A notifiable disease under Public Health (Control of Diseases) Act 1984.
Symptoms: general malaise, headache, drowsiness, pain in muscles with rigors, vomiting, facial features sometimes obliterated. Rash: small red spots which change colour and resemble black bruises. Low muttering delirium.
Treatment. Herbal antibiotics. Diaphoretic drinks favourably influence action of the skin to eliminate morbific material thus relieving pressure on the internal organs. Such include: one or more of the following teas: Yarrow, Elderflowers and Peppermint, Catnep, Boneset.
Formula. Echinacea 2; Poke root half; Wild Indigo quarter; Fringe Tree bark quarter. Dose: Powders: 750mg (three 00 capsules or half a teaspoon). Liquid extracts: 1-2 teaspoons. Tinctures: 1-3 teaspoons. In water or honey every 2 hours (acute), thrice daily (chronic).
External. Sponge surface of the body with cold water and vinegar. Apply cold to head. De-louse.
Treatment by a general medical practitioner or hospital specialist.

ULCERATION. Breakdown through infection or injury of an area of skin or mucous membrane which may lead to infection or haemorrhage. Common in lower leg in association with varicose veins.

Trapped white cells in capillaries. Because of inadequate venous pressure they become activated, triggering venous disease that develops into ulcers. (*John Scurr & Colleagues, Middlesex Hospital Venous Research Unit*)

Formula. Echinacea 2; Goldenseal half; Myrrh half; Liquorice quarter. Mix. Dose: Powders: 500mg (two 00 capsules or one-third teaspoon). Liquid extracts: 30-60 drops. Tinctures: 1-2 teaspoons. In water or honey thrice daily.

Throat. Any of the following *teas*: Raspberry leaves, Yarrow, Red Sage, Agrimony, Clivers, White Horehound, Marshmallow leaves, Mullein, Plantain, Coltsfoot.

Alternatives. *Gargle*. (1) 5-10 drops tincture Myrrh to glass of water.

(2) Strong teas from any of the above teas.

(3) Cider vinegar: 2 teaspoons to glass water.

Poultice. Comfrey root, Aloe Vera, Slippery Elm or Lobelia.

Honey dressings.

Mouth and lips. Aphthous ulcer with painful blisters. May be related to weakness and debility or may follow colds and influenza due to shortage of Vitamin C or new infection. Houseleek is almost specific for ulcerated lips. Aloe Vera gel.

A. Barker. Liquid Extract Black root half an ounce; Liquid Extract Bayberry 60 drops; Liquid Extract Burdock 60 drops; Tincture Goldenseal 30 drops. Essence of Peppermint 20 drops. Distilled water to 8oz. Dose: 2 teaspoons, in water, every 3 hours.

Tongue. Treat internally for auto-toxaemia. Fresh juices of Clivers and Houseleek (singly or in combination). Half-1 wineglassful, 3-4 times daily. Propolis.

Skin and genital organs. Raw potato juice. Fenugreek tea. Raw Linseed. Garlic. Ointments of St John's Wort, Chickweed, Slippery Elm, Goldenseal, Marshmallow, Bayberry, etc.

Role of honey. "Necrotic and gangrenous tissue gradually separated from the floor and wall of the ulcer allowing it to be removed without pain. The swelling subsided and weeping ulcers were dehydrated." (*A surgeon from the University Teaching Hospital, Northern Nigeria, describes the use of honey on 59 patients, in British Journal of Surgery*)

Honey may control the pain and encourage healing of mouth ulcers and all external ulceration.

ULCERATIVE COLITIS. Ulceration of the colon with stool frequency, abdominal pain and bloody diarrhoea. Mucous lining undergoes steady erosion with abscess formation. Colon becomes narrower and shorter Ineffectual straining at stool leading to nervous exhaustion. Worse in winter. Complications include perforation, fistula, rectal bleeding. Condition is now known as ischaemic colitis.

Differential diagnosis. From irritable bowel syndrome, dysentery, nervous bowel. Cracks or ulcers at corners of the mouth are often a good marker of UC.

Alternative treatment. Comfrey (membrane regeneration), Goldenseal (antibacterial), Cranesbill (to control bleeding), Poke root (intestinal ulceration), Wild Indigo (antipyretic).

Tea. Combine, equal parts: Agrimony, Comfrey, Meadowsweet. 1-2 teaspoons to each cup boiling water; infuse 5 minutes. 1 cup 3-4 times daily.

Fenugreek tea contains healing mucilage that soothes irritated membranes and assists peristalsis by eliminating excess mucous.

Powders. Formula. Marshmallow root 2; Cranesbill 1; Goldenseal half. Mix. Dose: 750mg (three 00 capsules or half a teaspoon) thrice daily. Acute condition: 2 hourly.

Liquid extracts: Formula. Wild Yam 1; Marshmallow root 1; Goldenseal quarter; Hops quarter; Stone root quarter. One teaspoon in water thrice daily.

Tincture. Greater Burnet BHP (1983). 1:5 in 45 per cent alcohol. Dose: 2-8ml, thrice daily in water.

Peppermint oil. 2 drops with meals.

Aloe Vera juice. 2-3oz juice thrice daily.

Comfrey tea. English traditional.

Slippery Elm. Quarter to half a teaspoon in water thrice daily.

Diet. Fast 3 to 10 days during which no solid food is eaten. Abundant fluids, apple juice, carrot juice, herb teas, spring water. The fast is broken slowly by a bland diet of ripe banana and Slippery Elm or dried milk powder. Baked apple, steamed vegetables, cooked potatoes, well-cooked well-chewed brown rice, steamed fish, low-fat cheese, unpasteurised yoghurt, carob bean powder, soya milk. Avoid dairy and wheat products and high-fibre foods. Gluten-free diet: success reported.

Supplements. Daily. Vitamin A 15,000iu, Vitamin B-complex with high Vitamin B12. Vitamin C 500mg. Kelp 800mg. Vitamin P (Buckwheat leaf).

Cold compress over abdomen to reduce inflammation.

Colonic hydrotherapy – cleans the colon of accumulated wastes.

UMCKALOABO. The tribal name of a South African root used in the treatment of tuberculosis. In 1897 a young mechanic fell ill with tuberculosis. His doctor advised him to settle on the plateau of South Africa for survival. He met a witch doctor who cured him by boiling a native remedy – Rhatany root (*krameria triandra*), a powerful germicide.

After assuring a permanent future supply of the root, Charles Stevens returned to England where he settled in Wimbledon treating successfully without charge sufferers of the disease. His action excited hostility of the orthodox profession of the day and there followed two disastrous law-suits with the British Medical Association. In spite of the public disgrace he sustained at the instigation of the highest medical authority in the land, subsequent medical opinion formed the belief that the plant proved beneficial to all surgical and pulmonary forms of tuberculosis with the exception of certain specially virulent and complicated forms. There is evidence of its endowment with anti-tuberculosis properties offering a specific effect upon Koch's bacillus with a complete absence of toxicity. It was sold as "Steven's Cure" until the advent of the Pharmacy Act of 1933.

UNDERWEIGHT. See: THIN PERSON, The.

UNICORN ROOT, FALSE. See: HELONIAS.

UNSATURATED FATS. Those that contain a low concentration of hydrogen. They are liquid at room temperature and come largely from the vegetable kingdom. Vegetable fats are made up of unsaturated fatty acids and are found in Soy-bean, Safflower, Corn, Cottonseed, Olive oil and other so-called 'golden oils'. This means they are able to take-on extra atoms of hydrogen. The oils tend to lower cholesterol levels and are a safeguard against high blood pressure and heart disorders.

Polyunsaturated fats are also found in wholegrains, wheatgerm and green leafy vegetables.

URAEMIA. A condition in which waste products (urea etc) normally excreted by the kidneys are held-up in the blood and which poison the central nervous system.
Symptoms. Nausea, vomiting, extreme weakness, headache, dry mouth, thirst, stupor, twitching of muscles, alternating lethargy and restlessness, laboured breathing, and the passage of small quantities of dark and concentrated urine. Patient complains of feeling cold. Coma possible.

When kidneys fail alternative avenues of waste fluid elimination must be found. One of these would be use of diaphoretics to encourage free perspiration to sweat out impurities via the skin. Another may be attention of bowels; a timely laxative assisting elimination by the bowel. A heavy intake of fluids, 3-5 pints daily is necessary: bottled or spring water or Cornsilk tea.
Treatment. While specific hospital treatment is essential, phytotherapy offers positive primary or secondary treatment. Powerful alteratives and diuretics are available to de-toxify the blood and promote the flow of urine. To stimulate renal function:–
Teas: Parsley root, Yarrow, Parsley Piert, Lime flowers, Corn Silk.
Formula. Equal parts: Barberry bark; Hydrangea; Echinacea. Dose: Powders: 750mg (three 00 capsules or half a teaspoon). Liquid extracts: 1-2 teaspoons. Tinctures: 1-3 teaspoons. Three or more times daily.
Practitioner. Tincture Wild Indigo (BPC 1934) 30ml; Tincture Echinacea 20ml; Tincture Buchu 20ml. Aqua to 100ml. Dose: one 5ml teaspoon in water or cup Cornsilk tea, 3 or more times daily.
Arthur Barker FNIMH. Liquid Extract Corn Silk 30ml. Liquid Extract Marigold 15ml. Liquid Extract Echinacea 15ml. Liquid Extract Hydrangea 4ml. Ess Menth Virid 1ml. Aqua to 250ml. Dose: 2 teaspoons 3-4 times daily.
Topical. Alternate hot and cold body sponge-down frequently. Sweat baths. High enemas.
Diet. Restricted protein. No meat, fish, poultry, eggs or dairy products. Lacto-vegetarian diet.

Condition should be treated by hospital urologist.

URETHRA. The tube from the bladder or penis through which urine is excreted from the body.

URETHRAL STRICTURE. Narrowing of the urethra resulting in a diminished flow of urine to a thin stream. Untreated may lead to stoppage and pain from distension of the bladder.
Alternatives. While cure may not be possible, the following are found to be helpful: Sea Holly (Eringo), Horsetail, Thuja, Echinacea.
Tea: Mullein herb. (*Jethro Kloss*) 2 teaspoons to each cup boiling water; infuse 15 minutes; one cup freely.
Formula. Olive oil 4oz; Oil Thuja 15 drops; Liquid Extract Echinacea 15ml. Mix. Dose: 5-10 drops in water, 3-4 times daily. (*Finlay Ellingwood MD*)
Horsetail, Liquid Extract, BHP (1983). Dose: 1-4ml (15-60 drops) in water, thrice daily.
Practitioner. Tincture Belladonna BPC 1963. Dose: 10 drops in 100ml water (half glass); 1 teaspoon every 2 hours for pain.

URETHRITIS. Inflammation of the urethra due to non-specific infection or sexually transmitted disease. May be with strangury (constant desire to pass water) but only a few drops passed.
Symptoms. Scalding pain on passing water, irritation, urinary outlet red and sticky.

A tissue-change known as urethral fibrosis (indurata penis plastica) or thickening may follow infection for which condition the following have been found helpful: Kava Kava, Saw Palmetto, Horsetail. For presence of pus: Echinacea, Yarrow, Bearberry.
Alternatives. A favourite combination is Sea Holly, Gravel root and Hydrangea. The causative organism should be identified where possible,

though there may be cases of simple inflammation due to no specific infection.
BHP (1983) recommends: Buchu, Couchgrass, Marshmallow leaf, Celery seed, Bearberry, Horsetail, Sea Holly, Gravel root, Hydrangea, Matico leaves, Kava Kava, Saw Palmetto berries, Corn Silk.
Teas. Buchu, Celery seed, Bearberry, Corn Silk, Marshmallow leaves.
Decoctions. Couchgrass, Gravel root, Horsetail, Hydrangea, Kava Kava, Saw Palmetto berries, Sea Holly.
Formula. Echinacea 2; Kava Kava 1; Saw Palmetto half. Dose: Powders: 500mg (two 00 capsules or one-third teaspoon). Liquid extract: 1 teaspoon. Tinctures: 2 teaspoons. Three or more times daily in water or cup of Cornsilk tea.
Practitioner. Sandalwood oil: 10 drops in honey 3-4 times daily.
Topical. Irrigation of the bladder by catheter and gravity douche: two pints boiled water with 2ml Liquid Extract Thuja warm.

To be treated by or in liaison with a qualified medical practitioner.
For STD infection: see GONORRHOEA.

URIC ACID DIATHESIS. Uric acid is a waste product of metabolism and is formed in the body from the breakdown of tissue proteins. When in excess, uric acid crystals inflame tissues resulting in gout. Some people have a natural or genetic predisposition to produce an excess of uric acid. Excess in the urine may cause kidney stone.
Alternatives. *Uricosuric agents*: Nettles, Yarrow, Celery seed. Wild carrot. Nettle tea said to be specific.
Diet. Dandelion coffee.

URINARY ANTISEPTIC. A germicidal action of a herb (chiefly by its essential oils) destructive to harmful bacteria in the urine when excreted from the body via the kidneys, bladder and ureters.

Angelica root, Bearberry (*Biostrath*), Boldo, Buchu, Celery seed, Couchgrass, Goldenrod, Heather (Calluna vul.), Juniper, Matico leaves, Meadowsweet, Saw Palmetto, Shepherd's Purse, Silver Birch, Yarrow.

URINARY DEMULCENT. A soothing, anti-irritant used for the protection of sensitive surfaces of kidney tubules and ureters against friction, i.e., combined with anti-lithics, Corn Silk minimises damage by the presence of stone.

Boldo, Couchgrass, Marshmallow leaf.

URINARY HAEMOSTATICS. Urinary astringents. Agents that arrest bleeding from the kidneys. All cases of such bleeding should be under the supervision of a general medical practitioner.

Beth root, Burr-Marigold, Horsetail, Lady's Mantle, Plantain, Shepherd's Purse, Tormentil.

URINE, BLOOD IN. See: HAEMATURIA.

URINE – FREQUENCY OF. See: FREQUENCY OF URINE.

URINE, PAIN ON PASSING. Dysuria. Painful micturition.
Causes: gravel, cystitis, urethritis, stricture. Spastic dysuria (difficult urination) is due to spasm of the bladder and requires urinary antispasmodics.
Alternatives. Used in professional practice: BHP (1983) – Buchu, Bearberry, Gravel root, Clivers, Parsley root, Heartsease. Eclectic Physicians (North American school) of the late 19th century regarded a strong infusion of Agrimony as specific.
Teas. (Infusions) Agrimony, Alfalfa, Corn Silk, Barley, Elderflowers, Plantain, Vervain.
Decoctions. Broom, Cramp bark, Black Cohosh, Golden Rod, Sea Holly.
Tablets/capsules. Buchu. Antispasmodic. Black Cohosh.
Powders. Formula. Equal parts: Black Cohosh, Buchu, Cramp bark. Dose: 750mg (three 00 capsules or half a teaspoon). Thrice daily.
Practitioner. Liquid Extract Agrimony 10.5ml; Liquid Extract Black Cohosh 1.75ml; Liquid Extract Pulsatilla 1.2ml; Tincture Belladonna 1ml. Aqua to 4oz (120ml). Sig: one teaspoon every two hours until relief is felt, then every 4 hours. (*G.A. West MD., Dulmuth, Minn, USA*)
Note. "I learned that my old-time remedy was more decidedly remedial for painful urination than our newer prescriptions. Thirty-five years ago, with confidence of cure, I prescribed a tea of Buchu leaves (or its equivalent in tincture) and Linseed. Six to eight teaspoonfuls of each was steeped in one pint boiling water; stirred, and allowed to stand all night. All had to be drunk the following day. The two had only to be continued until the patient was relieved." (*George Hare MD, Kirkland, Texas*)
Formula. Tinctures. Horsetail 5-20 drops; Couch grass 20-40 drops; Corn Silk 10-20 drops. Dose: three or more times daily. (*Alma Hutchens, in Indian Herbology of North America*)

URTICARIA. See: NETTLERASH.

UTERINE. Pertaining to the womb (uterus).
Uterine analgesic: Blue Cohosh (Priest).
Uterine relaxant: Black Haw bark.
Uterine stimulants: Blue Cohosh, Cotton root/bark, Thuja.
Uterine tonics: Agnus Castus, Black Cohosh, Blue Cohosh, Helonias root, Motherwort,

Mugwort, Parsley, Raspberry leaves, Southernwood, Squaw Vine, White Pond Lily (American).

UVA-URSI. *Arctostaphylos uva-ursi*, Spreng. See: BEARBERRY.

UVEITIS. Inflammation of all or part of the uveal tract (iris, choroid, ciliary body). Symptoms differ according to which part of the eye is affected. It is a feature of some fevers. Where it affects the back of the eye it is called choroiditis; the front of the eye, iritis.

Causes: spread of fungi, organisms, protozoa; diabetes, arthritis.

Treatment. Febrifuges, alteratives, anti-inflammatories.

Tea: equal parts, Red Clover, Elderflowers, Yarrow. Mix. 1-2 teaspoons to each cup boiling water; infuse 5-15 minutes. Half-1 cup every two hours, acute cases; thrice daily (chronic).

Douche: with aid of an eyebath: Aloe Vera gel.

VACCINATION. Vaccination is inoculation with a vaccine to induce immunity against a specific disease. It always involves an element of risk. Vaccinosis refers to a feverish state and local reaction at the point where the vaccine is injected. The term refers also to the profound often long-lasting period of chronic indefinite ill-health which so often follows. Many people date their ill-health from a so-called "unsuccessful vaccination".
Treatment. *Key agent*: Thuja. *Runner-up*: Echinacea.
Thuja. "A most reliable property of Thuja is its use in small doses to prevent ill-effects from vaccination for smallpox. It has been given in so many cases and entirely controls the fever and other symptoms induced by severe effects of vaccination." (*Dr Finlay Ellingwood*)
Case history: "Small boy, purulent onychia, intractible. Nail removed and thumb healed. Then appeared abscesses in different parts of the body till it was discovered that he had been eight times vaccinated by a persistent and conscientious G.P. *Thuja* promptly ended the trouble." (*Professor Maitland, Manchester Pathological Society, 1933*)
Tincture Thuja BHP (1983), 1:10 in 60 per cent alcohol. Dose: 15-30 drops, thrice daily. Externally: paint over lesion.
Echinacea. For swollen arm with discharging sore. Cover with cotton wool soaked in Tincture Echinacea BHP (1983), 1:5 in 45 per cent alcohol. Cover with a protective. Replenish when dry a number of times. Internally: 15-30 drops in water, thrice daily.

VAGINAL CANDIDIASIS. Vaginal thrush. See: CANDIDA, VAGINAL.

VAGINAL WARTS. Thuja. See: WARTS.

VAGINISMUS. Spasmodic contractions of muscles enveloping the vaginal canal that make sexual intercourse painful.
Alternatives. Beth root, Black Cohosh, Black Haw, Chamomile, Cramp bark, Ladyslipper, Lobelia, Motherwort, Mugwort, Peony root.
Teas. Chamomile, Ephedra, Lobelia, Motherwort, Mugwort.
Decoctions. Beth root, Black Cohosh, Black Haw, Cramp bark, Ladyslipper, Peony root.
Formula. Equal parts: Black Cohosh, Cramp bark, Valerian. Mix. Dose: Powders: 375mg (quarter of a teaspoon). Liquid extracts: 30-60 drops. Tinctures: 1-2 teaspoons. Morning and evening, and when necessary. In water, honey or banana mash.
Practitioner. Ephedra.
Topical. To improve quality of the vaginal mucosa: Evening Primrose oil, Aloe Vera or Comfrey cream.

VAGINITIS. NON-SPECIFIC. Term used for inflammation of the vagina with no evidence of candida albicans, trichomoniasis or gonorrhoea but associated with a vaginal discharge. Not leucorrhoea.
Causes: cold, anaemia, polyps, allergy, shingles, stress, inflammation of the womb, overactive sexuality, tight jeans, trousers, man-made fibre pants instead of cotton. A common cause is the use of super-absorbant tampons of the regular brand varieties, especially those with plastic inserters. Spontaneous healing may occur when tampons discontinued.
Symptoms. Discharge, itching, spotting of blood, urination frequent and painful, ulceration possible.
Treatment. Where due to the menopause (Black Cohosh); ovarian insufficiency (Rosemary); ovarian overactivity (Agnus Castus); offensive discharge (Camphor); persistent pain (White Pond Lily).
Internal: Tea, mix parts: Raspberry leaves 1; Nettles 1; Rosemary half; Valerian 1. One heaped teaspoon to each cup boiling water; infuse 5-15 minutes. Drink freely.
Tablets/capsules. Pulsatilla, Agnus Castus, Echinacea.
Formula. Echinacea 2; Goldenseal 1; Agnus Castus 2. Mix. Dose: Powders: 500mg (two 00 capsules or one-third teaspoon). Liquid extracts: 1 teaspoon. Tinctures: 2 teaspoons. In water or honey.
Topical. Evening Primrose oil capsules. Smooth over vagina with contents.
Calendula and Hydrastis pessaries. The Nutri Centre, 7 Park Crescent, London W1N 3HE.
Goldenseal Drops. 2-3 drops in teaspoon water. Insert with dropper.
Douche. German Chamomile tea. Yoghurt as a lotion. Cold pack.
Slippery Elm stick. Insertion to relieve irritation.
Tea Tree oil. Vaginal pessaries containing 200mg of oil distilled from the Tea Tree in a vegetable base. (*The Herbal Apothecary, Syston, Leicester*)
Diet. See: DIET – GENERAL.
Supplements. Daily. Vitamin A (7,500iu), Vitamin C (1g); Vitamin E (200iu), Vitamin B6 (100mg), Zinc (15mg).
Garlic tablets or capsules: 3 at night. Good responses reported.

VALERIAN. All Heal. *Valeriana officinalis L.s.l. German*: Baldrian. *French*: Herbe aux chats. *Spanish*: Valeriana. *Italian*: Amantilla. *Arabian*: Sumbul-ul-asfar. *Indian*: Sugandha. *Iranian*: Sumbul-ul-tib. *Parts used*: rhizome, root.
Constituents: alkaloids, essential oil, valepotriates, organic acids.

The Spikenard of the New Testament. One of Nature's gentlest, non-toxic, non-addictive tranquillisers.

Action. Favourably influences the CNS, acting as a natural relaxant to the higher nerve centres. Antibiotic against gram-positive bacteria. (*Rashid, M.H. et. al. Pak.J. Forest 22 (4), 439-45, 1973*)

Sedative, hypotensive, hypnotic, carminative, mild anodyne for temporary relief of pain, expectorant, aromatic, antidiuretic, relaxant, spasmolytic.

Uses. Has been used for its calming effect since Hippocratic times. Nervous tension, excitability, convulsions in infants, sleeplessness, restlessness, palpitation, high blood pressure, hypochondria, irritability, excessive nerve stress, mental confusion, tensive headache, migraine, epilepsy, menstrual pain, muscle and intestinal cramps, bronchial spasm, smoker's cough, insomnia.

As effective as benzodiazepines in relieving anxiety states. Valium, Librium and benzodiazepine addiction – to assist withdrawal without evidence of dependence or abuse potential. Menopausal restlessness. Used with some success in shell- and air-raid-shock in World War 2 without depressing vital functions and mental activity. Tension headaches.

External. Decoction used as an antiseptic lotion for discharging wounds that refuse to heal.

Tablets/capsules. One to two 200mg, 2-3 times daily.

Combinations. Often formulated with Wild Lettuce, Jamaica Dogwood, Hops, Skullcap, Passion flower, according to the case. With Motherwort for heart conditions. With Oatstraw and Skullcap for myalgic encephalomyelitis. With Mistletoe and Lime flowers for high blood pressure and epilepsy.

Pregnancy. May be used during pregnancy and lactation.

Preparations. Average dose, 1-3g (tea) or fluid equivalent, thrice daily.

Infusion. 1 teaspoon to cup boiling water; infuse 10-15 minutes. Dose: half-1 cup.

Decoction. Half-1 teaspoon to cup cold water; cover, stand overnight. Dose, half-1 cup.

Powder. 270mg capsules: 3 capsules morning and evening. (*Arkopharma*)

Liquid Extract. BPC (1963) 1:1 in 60 per cent alcohol; dose, 0.3-1ml.

Tincture (simple) BPC (1949). 1:8 in 60 per cent alcohol; dose, 4-8ml.

Tincture, (EM). 1:5, 1-3ml up to 3 times daily.

"The tincture is the most widely used preparation and is always useful, provided that the single dose is not counted in drops, but that half-1 teaspoonful is given, and indeed sometimes two teaspoonfuls at one time. Valerian tea can be effectively enhanced by adding a teaspoonful of the tincture to a cup of the tea." (*Herbal Medicine, by Rudolf F. Weiss MD., Beaconsfield Publishers, UK*)

Essential oil of Valerian (anti-inflammatory, anti-spasmodic). 1-3 drops in honey or mashed banana.

Valerian bath. To promote sleep after nervous exhaustion. 2 handfuls bruised or crushed root in muslin bag or length of nylon stocking. Infuse 30 minutes in 2 pints boiling water. Strain, add to bath water or use bag as sponge.

Side effects. None known, no change in brain-wave activity or hangover recorded although it should not be prescribed for severe depressive states. Large doses cause giddiness and mental confusion. Lacks the side-effects of some sedative drugs including the barbiturates and benzodiazepines. No dependence or withdrawal symptoms reported.

Store in a well-closed container out of the light.

Similar uses are reported in the literature of Europe, China, India and Egypt.

Note. After Chamomile, Valerian is Europe's most popular herb.

No evidence of dependence in clinical use.

VALERIAN, AMERICAN. See: LADY'S SLIPPER.

VALIUM ADDICTION. St John's Wort, tablets, tea or tincture. See: DRUG DEPENDENCE.

VAPOUR BATH. Sweat bath. To induce profuse perspiration to eliminate impurities and equalise the circulation. Sometimes advised for chronic arthritis, auto-toxaemia. Patient sits naked on a chair with legs on a stool. A bowl is placed beneath the chair. A large sheet or blanket is flung round the patient, enclosing the chair. The bowl is filled with boiling water or an infusion of Elderflowers, Yarrow or other diaphoretic. Sheet should fit snugly about neck. To assist, patient may drink freely a tea of Balm, Yarrow, Elderflowers or other diaphoretic. Add more boiling water to keep up temperature. After sweating, dry well; rub vigorously with a rough towel before bedrest.

VARICOCELE. Swelling of veins of the spermatic cord around a testicle. More common in left than in right testicle. Seldom causes serious symptoms. Treatment invariably relieves.

Alternatives. Agnus Castus decoction, freely (*Doeden's Herbal*). Sarsaparilla. Saw Palmetto. Prickly Ash, Horsechestnut, Yarrow.

Tablets/capsules. Agnus Castus, Horsechestnut.

Formula. Prickly Ash 1; Agnus Castus 2; Horsechestnut half. Mix. Dose: Powders: 500mg (two 00 capsules or one-third teaspoon). Liquid extracts: 1 teaspoon. Tinctures: 2 teaspoons. Thrice daily in water or honey.

Horsechestnut (Aesculus) Capsules 200mg. 2 capsules thrice daily.

Topical. Frequent douching with cold water finishing-off with Witch Hazel wipes. Scrotal support.
Diet. See: DIET – GENERAL.
Vitamin. E (400iu daily).
Mineral. Zinc.

VARICOSE ULCER (or mixed ulcer). Often started by injury to the veins. Appears mainly on lower third of leg. Not usually painful. May arise from varicose veins following months of bad circulation. Usually the end of a series of changes in the skin and underlying tissues accompanied by pigmentation, eczema and induration. See definition of 'ulceration'.
Treatment. Encourage venous return. Attend to general health problems, i.e. iron-deficiency anaemia. Bedrest for few days favours granulation of tissue. Regulate bowels. Leg ulcers take longer to heal in the presence of oedema (fluid retention): diuretics assist recovery.
Alternatives. Bayberry, Chamomile (German), Beth root, Chickweed, Cranesbill (American), Fenugreek seed, Holy Thistle, Hops, Marigold, Marshmallow root or leaf, Slippery Elm, Wood Sage, Wild Indigo.
Teas. Chamomile (German), Chickweed, Comfrey leaves, Holy Thistle, Hops.
Tea. Combine: equal parts: Comfrey leaves; Aloe leaves; Marigold petals. 1-2 teaspoons to each cup boiling water; infuse 5-15 minutes. 1 cup thrice daily.
Decoction. Combine: Comfrey root 1; Slippery Elm bark 1; Aloe leaves half; Goldenseal root quarter; Liquorice quarter. 1-2 heaped teaspoons to half a pint (250ml) water gently simmered 20 minutes. Strain. Dose: half a cup thrice daily.
Formula. Comfrey root 2; Holy Thistle 1; Hops quarter; Cayenne quarter. Mix. Dose: Powders: 500mg (two 00 capsules or one-third teaspoon). Liquid extracts: 1 teaspoon. Tinctures: 2 teaspoons. Thrice daily in water or honey.
Comfrey. Potential benefit outweighs possible risk.
Topical. The following alternatives all promote healthy granulation. (1) Few drops Tincture Echinacea or Tincture Myrrh to a cup of boiled water as a lotion for cleansing. (2) Castor oil. (3) Aloe Vera on sterile dressing.
Compress: 1 part Tea Tree oil to 4 parts Olive oil. Spread lotion on suitable material. Replenish when dry. If treatment cleans off old scab, regard as favourable, prior to healing.

Zinc and Castor oil ointment has been responsible for many cures. Alginate dressings, from the calcium salt of alginic acid, may be used as a base for ointments, etc.

New Zealand Manuka honey.

Comfrey or Chickweed cream or ointment. Pulp of fresh plants: Plantain, Comfrey, Chickweed, Aloe Vera.
Cornish traditional: Equal parts dried Comfrey root and refined china clay.
Norfolk traditional: Cabbage leaf poultice.

Powdered Comfrey root mixed into a paste with a little milk.
To inhibit profuse discharge: dusting powder – Bayberry.

Dressings supported by bandage below the knee to the base of the toes, with overlaying support bandage.
Diet. Lacto-vegetarian.
Supplementation. Vitamins A, B6, B12, E, K, C. Minerals – Magnesium, Zinc. 2-3 Garlic capsules at night.

VARICOSE VEINS. Veins that become abnormally twisted and enlarged.
Causes: damage to the valves or by increased blood pressure. Damage to the valves is mostly due to venous thrombosis. High blood pressure causes deposition of fibrin, thereby blocking diffusion of nutrients and oxygen to the skin leading to weakness of the veins. May be the result of tight jeans, obesity, sedentary occupation, crossing of legs, pregnancy, abdominal tumour as from ovarian cyst or fibroid of the womb.
Symptoms. Aching legs, veins visibly distorted, night tingling, firey or sensation of crawling ants. Where they appear in the rectum they are known as piles, or around a testicle (varicocele).
Treatment. Vaso-constrictors and agents to prevent further deposition of fibrin. Hawthorn to sustain the heart; Buckwheat to strengthen the veins; Stone root to stimulate the abdominal circulation.
Alternatives. Cayenne, Echinacea, Ginseng, Ginger, Red Vine, Goldenseal, Horsechestnut, Kelp, Motherwort, Parsley, Bilberry, Prickly Ash, Pulsatilla, Witch Hazel, Yarrow, Butcher's Broom.
Tea. Formula. Combine equal parts: Motherwort, Parsley leaves and Yarrow. 1 teaspoon to cup boiling water; infuse 15 minutes. 1 cup 2-3 times daily. Drink cold.
Tablets/capsules. One of each before meals – Prickly Ash, Ginseng, Goldenseal.
Varicose veins of pregnancy – see PREGNANCY.
Formula. Motherwort 2; Prickly Ash 1; Stone root half. Mix. Dose: Powders: 500mg (two 00 capsules or one-third teaspoon). Liquid extracts: 1 teaspoon. Tinctures: 2 teaspoons. In water or honey.
Horsechestnut drops. (*Dr A. Vogel*) 15-20 drops thrice daily. Horsechestnut is a key agent for veins, as Garlic and Ginkgo for the arteries.
Topical. To improve circulation: Witch Hazel water.
Dr A. Vogel Salve: Witch Hazel 9 per cent; St John's Wort oil 5 per cent; Echinacea 3 per cent; Wheat Germ oil 2 per cent.
Comfrey, cream or ointment: good responses

reported.
Aesculus gel or ointment, gently applied.
Rosemary bath. Muslin bag containing handful fresh Rosemary leaves in bath.
Diet. High protein. Lecithin. Buckwheat tea.
Supplements. Daily. B-complex, C (500mg), E (400iu), Bromelain. Calcium, Copper, Iodine, Magnesium.
Supportives. Rest. Elevation. Slant board. Raise foot of bed on blocks. Allow cold tap to run water over affected parts. Graduated elastic stocking compression. Varicose veins should not be massaged.

VASCULAR. Referring to blood vessels.

VASCULITIS. Inflammation of a vessel. Inflammation and blockage of a small artery will result in an area of infarction but blockage of a small capillary rarely causes serious problems and usually appears as small purple marks on the skin. The condition may manifest as polyarteritis nodosa, hypersensitivity vasculitis or arteritis.

VASECTOMY. Voluntary sterility. A surgical operation in which the two tubes, vasa deferentia, that carry male sperm from the testicles to the ejaculatory ducts are severed for the purpose of birth control. Long term health risks may include atheroma and congestive epididymitis.

Long-term safety of the procedure has been questioned, and in particular the possibility of risk of prostatic adenocarcinoma.
Important tonics for the male include: Ginseng, Gotu Kola, Sarsaparilla and zinc supplements.

VASO-CONSTRICTORS. Agents that constrict blood vessels for the purpose of increasing blood pressure, reducing secretions (as in catarrh), stasis and congestion. Most astringents are vaso-constrictors.

VASO-DILATORS. Herbs that promote production of prostaglandins to relax the muscular coating of blood vessels, opening them up to permit an increased circulation of blood. Vaso-dilators may open-up circulation of the whole body – general vaso-dilators, or expend their influence on a single organ or system – broncho vaso-dilators, coronary vaso-dilators, peripheral vaso-dilators (also known as circulatory stimulants).

Vaso-dilators can be used for hypertension to reduce blood pressure. A peripheral vaso-dilator such as Lime flowers affects blood vessels of the limbs and improves the circulation. A coronary vaso-dilator (Hawthorn) increases blood flow through the heart and is useful for angina. Other important vaso-dilators are: Yarrow, Ephedra, Garlic and Feverfew.

VEGETABLE COUGH REMOVER. Each 10ml contains: Black Cohosh 10mg; Ipecac BP 13mg; Lobelia BPC 24mg; Pleurisy root 24mg; Skullcap 25mg; Liquid Extract Elecampane (1:1 21 per cent alcohol) 0.15ml; Liquid Extract Horehound (1:1 21 per cent alcohol) 0.2ml; Liquid Extract Hyssop (1:1 21 per cent alcohol) 0.15ml. Also contains Capsicum, Skunk Cabbage, Valerian, Aniseed oil, Myrrh Tincture, Liquorice extract; in a sweetened vehicle. (*Potter's, UK*)

VENOUS THROMBOSIS. Milk leg, white leg. The formation of a blood clot in a vein. Phlebothrombosis is the presence of a clot without inflammation of the vein. Thrombophlebitis is clotting associated with inflammation of a vein.
Causes: damage to a vein by infection, injury, or by auto-immune disorder which occurs when the body reacts against itself. See: AUTO-IMMUNE DISEASE and FREE-RADICALS. The use of oestrogen and other hormones predispose. Symptoms vary according to the types: (1) superficial vein or (2) deep vein, with danger of pulmonary embolus.

Superficial vein thrombosis, is concerned with minor vessels, but when a deep vein is involved there may be clotting in vessels of the leg, calf and pelvis. Causes may be the 'long-sit' stasis, when immobility arrests the flow of blood and enhances clot formation. Common causes of 'deep vein' are sitting in a deck-chair, being bedfast, "The Pill", pregnancy and low heart output. Recurrent attacks of influenza may bring about adverse changes in blood vessels. Pain (intermittent claudication) is always present. Leg heavy and sensitive to touch. Pulse rapid.

Witch Hazel (externally) promotes venous circulation and Buckwheat (Rutin) (internally) strengthens walls of the veins.
Treatment. Anticoagulation measures to prevent spread.
Teas. Nettles, Motherwort, Lime flowers, Buckwheat, Yarrow.
Formula. Powders. Horsetail 2; Hawthorn 2; Echinacea 1. Pinch Cayenne. Dose: 750mg (three 00 capsules or half a teaspoon. Thrice daily.
Liquid extracts. Equal parts: Yarrow, Hawthorn, Echinacea. Few drops Tincture Capsicum. Mix. Dose: 1 teaspoon thrice daily.
Tinctures. Hawthorn 2; Echinacea 1; Black Cohosh half. Mix. 2 teaspoons thrice daily.
Evening Primrose oil. 4 x 500mg capsules daily.
Garlic (capsule, tablet or bulb). "Garlic contains an anti-clotting component (adenosine) which blocks blood platelet aggregation and helps combat disease of the heart and blood vessels." (*Dr Martin Bailey, Georgetown University, USA*)
Old Grecian: Agrimony and Comfrey leaf tea (equal parts).
Tablets/capsules: Echinacea, Kelp, Rutin.

Dr Finlay Ellingwood: Mix. Tincture Stone root 2; Tincture Black Cohosh 1. Dose: 10 drops every 2 hours (acute), thrice daily (chronic).
Topical. Cold packs sprinkled with one of the following liquid extracts or tinctures: Calendula (Marigold), Arnica (where skin is unbroken), St John's Wort, Yarrow.
Alternative. Distilled extract of Witch Hazel. Substitute for surgical spirit – Vodka compress.
Diet. See: DIET – HEART AND CIRCULATION.
Supplements. Daily. B-complex, Niacin, Pantothenic acid, Vitamin C (5-10g), Vitamin E (1,000iu). Copper, Iodine, Magnesium.

VERMIFUGE. See: ANTHELMINTIC.

VERRUCA. A wart, as appearing on soles of the feet. See: WART.

VERTIGO. A disturbance of balance. Sensation of spinning in space or the world rotating round the individual.
Causes: middle ear disease or any disorder of the auditory nerve, brain, eyes; alcohol, drugs, toxaemia, food poisoning, high or low blood pressure, migraine, epilepsy, temporary emotional stress, Meniere's disease.
Symptoms. Nausea, vomiting, buzzing in the ears, flickering of the eyes, tendency to fall sideways.
Treatment. According to the cause, which may be one of the above conditions. To restore circulation in simple conditions – Life Drops. Teas of Wood Betony, Hawthorn blossoms, Buckwheat (rutin), Periwinkle (Vinca minor), Cayenne, Hops.
Persistent cases. Prickly Ash, Ginkgo, White Willow, Hawthorn (cardiac), Buchu (kidney), Ladyslipper, Valerian, Pulsatilla (menstrual).
Tinctures. Ginkgo 2; Hops (lupulin) 1; Rutin 1; Valerian 1. Few drops Tincture Capsicum (Cayenne). 1-2 teaspoons in water thrice daily.
Cider Vinegar. 2-3 teaspoons to glass water, thrice daily.
Practitioner. Tincture Gelsemium BPC 1963. 10 drops in 100ml water. Dose: 1 teaspoon hourly.
Diet. Fat-free, salt-free, sugar-free, avoid eggs. Regular raw foods, salads, fruits, etc.
Supplementation. Vitamins: B-complex, B6, B12, C, E. Minerals: Calcium orotate, zinc.

VERVAIN. Pigeon's grass. *Verbena officinalis L. German*: Eisenkraut. *French*: Verveine. *Spanish and Italian*: Verbena. Herb. Sacred to Greeks and Druids. *Keynote*: nervous system.
Constituents: alkaloids, choline, volatile oil, flavonoids.
Action. Antispasmodic for relief of tension and stress. Stimulating relaxing nervine with affinity for liver and kidneys. Sedative, diaphoretic, hypnotic, thymoleptic, galactagogue, alterative, emmenagogue, aphrodisiac, anti-diarrhoeic.
Uses. Post viral fatigue syndrome, ME. Nervous exhaustion from prolonged physical exertion. Epilepsy and convulsions (traditional). Congested liver, jaundice. Promote production of milk in nursing mothers. Amenorrhoea.
Psychiatry. Has proved of moderate value for post-operative depression, paranoidal tendency, 'nervous breakdown', agarophobia.
Combines well with Oats (equal parts) for liver depression: with Chamomile for post-natal depression.
Preparations. Average dose 2-4 grams or fluid equivalent, thrice daily.
Tea: 1-2 teaspoons to each cup boiling water; infuse 15 minutes; half-1 cup.
Liquid Extract: half-1 teaspoon in water.
Tincture BHP (1983): 1:1 on 40 per cent alcohol. Dose, 5-10ml in water.
Not used in pregnancy. GSL

VESICANT. An agent applied externally to induce blistering as in past use of White Bryony to cause blisters to appear on joints to absorb effusions of fluid (house-maid's knee, gout, etc). Blistering was claimed to ameliorate deep-seated pain of pleurisy or severe backache.

VICK VAPOUR RUB. Contains, Menthol 2.82 per cent, Camphor 5.25 per cent, Turpentine oil 4.77 per cent, Eucalyptus oil 1.35 per cent, Nutmeg oil 0.48 per cent, Cedar wood oil 0.45 per cent, and Thymol 0.1 per cent. To ease difficult breathing. Mild analgesic for rheumatic aches and pains. (*Richardson-Merrell*)

VINCENT'S ANGINA. Trench mouth. An acute membranous inflammation of the gums, tonsils and pharynx with yellowish green exudate which when removed leaves a bleeding ulcer. Cause due to one of two forms of bacteria: fusiform bacillus; the other – spirillum. May be mistaken for diphtheria.
Symptoms. Bleeding gums, bad breath, slight fever, ulceration of tongue and inner cheeks.
Alternatives. Echinacea, Poke root, Goldenseal, Myrrh.
Tea: German Chamomile.
Formula. Echinacea 2; Goldenseal half; Myrrh quarter. Mix. Dose: Powders: 500mg (two 00 capsules or one-third teaspoon). Liquid extracts: 1 teaspoon. Tinctures: 2 teaspoons. Thrice daily in water or honey.
Mouth Wash and Gargle. Equal parts, tinctures Myrrh and Goldenseal. 10-20 drops in glass water, freely.
Evening Primrose capsules: 1,500mg daily.
Garlic capsules: 2-3 at night.
Treatment by or in liaison with a general medical practitioner.

VINCHRISTINE. From an alkaloid of the periwinkle, Vinca rosea (*Catharanthus roseus*). An anti-tumour agent used as an anti-mitotic to inhibit cell-division in acute leukaemia, Hodgkin's disease and other chronic malignant lymphatic swellings. Administered by a physician by injection. Vinblastine is from the same source and has a similar action. Given only in combination with other medicines.

VINEGAR. Vinegar is sometimes used as a menstruum for herbal medicines. One of the most popular is Sage vinegar. Take 1 pint pure malt or cider vinegar, or white wine vinegar, and add pulped Sage leaves to saturation point. Macerate 14 days; shake daily, strain. Dose: 20-40 drops in water thrice daily. To stimulate metabolism in old age or in feeble constitutions.

By the same method may be prepared Lobelia, Horseradish, Gentian, Wormwood, Burnet. Basil and Fennel make good salad dressings. Burdock root steeped in cider vinegar is used as a lotion for removal of scabs in chickenpox. Chamomile vinegar (2/3 teaspoons to glass of water) is taken as a daily health drink.

VIOLET, SWEET. Blue violet. *Viola odorata L.* Leaves and flowers. *German*: Veilchen. *French*: Violette. *Spanish*: Violetta. *Italian*: Viola odorosa. *Chinese*: Hu-chin-ts'ao. Mentioned in the Koran.
Constituents: saponins, mucilage, alkaloid, phenolic glycosides.
Action. Anti-neoplastic – orally, or externally (poultice), antiseptic (mild), soothing expectorant.
Uses. Has a long traditional reputation as a mild analgesic for cancer of the lungs, alimentary canal, and breast (poultice). When the wife of General Booth, Salvation Army Chief, was dying of cancer the one drink that gave her relief from the pain was Violet leaf tea made from leaves foraged from railway embankments by devoted members of the Army.

Lady Margaret Marsham, 67, was cured of a malignant tumour in the throat (epithelioma of tonsil) with Violet leaf tea (1oz to 1 pint boiling water) teacupful taken freely. Compresses of the leaves were also applied, with immediate relief from pain and breathing difficulties. Within 7 days the swelling disappeared; within 14 days the tonsil growth also.
Other uses: bronchitis and children's chest troubles, mouth ulcers (tea used as a mouthwash), congested lymph glands, cystitis – with hot acid urine, urethritis, vaginal trichomonas, fibroids – as a douche to alleviate pain. Persistent cough.
Preparations. The traditional method is by simple infusion (tea) from which best results are achieved – in preference to use of alcohol. Past successes have shown that use of the wild plant, and not the cultivated, is the more successful. Average dose, 2-4 grams or fluid equivalent, thrice daily.
Tea: 1-2 teaspoons to each cup boiling water; infuse 15 minutes. Dose, half-1 cup freely.
Liquid Extract: (From the fresh leaves) half-1 teaspoon in water.
Home tincture: fresh leaves in white wine to saturation point. Macerate 8 days. Decant. 2-5 teaspoons as above. GSL

VIRGINIA SNAKE ROOT. *Aristolochia serpentaria*. Rhizome.
Action. Antispasmodic, tonic nervine, anti-inflammatory, hepatic (mild).
Uses. Indigestion, mild liver upsets, nausea, vomiting. Being a ready diaphoretic and well-tolerated by the stomach, was once used for febrile conditions.
Preparations. Average dose: 50-100mg, or fluid equivalent, thrice daily.
Powder: above quantity to cup of boiling water; infuse 15 minutes; dose half-1 cup.
Tincture: 5-15 drops in water. Use in phytotherapy declining. GSL

VIRUS. A living agent so small that it avoids detection by the average microscope. Appears as a living point of protein and causes such diseases as measles, poliomyelitis, chickenpox, mumps and the common cold. Viruses destroy epithelium and can be an important factor in chronic obstructive lung disease. They can only live and multiply within a living cell.
Herbal anti-virals include: Balm, Hypericum, Echinacea and Garlic.

VISCEROPTOSIS. Prolapse of the visceral organs, usually of the abdomen, due to lack of tone, overstrain or sedentary habit. Only partial success possible.
Tea. Combine, equal parts: Shepherd's Purse, Ladysmantle, Horsetail. 1 heaped teaspoon to each cup boiling water; infuse 5-10 minutes. 1 cup thrice daily.
Tablets/capsules. Bladderwrack. Motherwort. Poke root.
Formula. Equal parts: Bladderwrack, Clivers, Motherwort. Mix. Dose: Powders: 750mg (three 00 capsules or half a teaspoon). Liquid extracts: 1-2 teaspoons. Tinctures: 1-3 teaspoons. Thrice daily in water or honey.
Cider vinegar.

VITAMIN A. Anti-bacterial, anti-viral to increase resistance against infection. Retinol. Fat soluble. RDA 0.75mg: nursing mothers 1.2mg.
Deficiency. Unable to see in dim light (night blindness). Corneal injury, hair loss, dry skin, weight loss, crumbling fingernails, acne. Hearing loss.
Body effects. Healthy mucous membranes, eyes, skin. Vision improvement. Bone development.

Normal growth. Protein synthesis, immune stimulant, lung protective. Reproduction and sexual virility. Anti-inflammatory for respiratory organs.
Sources. Red and yellow-coloured vegetables (carrots etc). Dairy produce, fish liver oils, wholegrain cereals, wheatgerm, beet greens, turnip greens, spinach, apricots, peaches, asparagus, endive, kale, alfalfa, dandelion leaves, parsley, watercress.

Butter is a good source of Vitamin A because of the Beta-carotene (the strong pigment that gives it a yellow colour) is converted into Vitamin A in the body.
Notes. Not advised in pregnancy. Even pre-cancerous cells have been known to revert after a deficiency has been made up. Large doses toxic.

See entry: BETA-CAROTENE.

VITAMIN B1. Aneurin, thiamin. Water soluble. RDA 1-3mg. Digestant, nervine, nutrient.
Deficiency. Digestive disorders – nausea and vomiting. Slow heart beat. Depression, irritability.
Body effects. Healthy nervous and muscular systems. Mild pain-killer. Carbohydrate metabolism, cell oxidation, appetite, nerve impulses, function of heart and muscles.
Sources. Wholegrain cereals, wheatgerm, brewer's yeast, yeast extract, meal, poultry, seafood, potatoes, pulses, nuts, brown rice, beans, green vegetables. Dessicated liver. Fenugreek seeds. Kelp.

VITAMIN B2. Lactoflavin, riboflavin. Water soluble. RDA 1.3-1.6mg.
Deficiency. Insomnia, dizziness, hair loss, inflammation of lips and tongue. Cataracts. Watering eyes; sensation of sand under eyelids. Difficulty in seeing how to drive in twilight. Dim vision. Itching eyes.
Body effects. Healthy mucous membranes, skin, eyes. Growth factor, metabolism of fats, carbohydrates and proteins.
Sources. Meat, poultry, kidney, liver, cheese, yoghurt, eggs, milk, seafood, lima beans, peas, pulses, wholegrain cereals, wheatgerm, brewer's yeast, yeast extract, soya beans and flour. Kelp, Fenugreek seeds, saffron, dulse seaweed, Gotu Kola.

VITAMIN B3. Niacin, nicotinic acid. Water soluble. RDA 18mg.
Deficiency. Digestive disorders, nausea and vomiting, loss of appetite. Irritability, insomnia, headaches, depression. Fatigue, diarrhoea, pellagra.
Body effects. Healthy nervous system, skin, hair, circulatory system and adrenal glands. Carbohydrate metabolism. Blood cholesterol.
Sources. Meat, poultry, liver, kidney, fish, brown rice, brewer's yeast, yeast extract, eggs, cheese, nuts (especially peanuts), dried fruit, soya beans and flour, wheatgerm, peas and beans, globe artichokes. Herbs: Alfalfa, Burdock seed, Fenugreek seeds, Parsley, Watercress.
Note. No more than 500mg to be taken daily except under supervision.

VITAMIN B5. Pantothenic acid. Water soluble. RDA 4-7mg.
Deficiency. Allergy, fatigue, cramp, muscle tremors, physical exhaustion, insomnia, respiratory distress, burning feet and tender heels.
Body effects. Healthy skin, hair and nervous system. Produces antibodies to support the immune system. Adrenal glands and gastro-intestinal tract. Co-ordination of limbs and muscles on walking.
Sources. Produced in the human intestinal tract. Liver, heart of beef and chicken, egg yolk, beans, peanuts, tomato, sweet potato, broccoli, wheatgerm, brewer's yeast, buckwheat flour, sunflower seeds, oranges.

VITAMIN B6. Pyridoxine. Water soluble. RDA 25mg (Boots).
Deficiency. Pre-menstrual tension.
Body effects. Production of adrenalin, insulin and antibodies; formation of red blood cells; enzyme activator, RNA and DNA synthesis. Metabolism of fats, carbohydrates and proteins. Health of nerves and muscles. Hair loss.
Sources. In most foods. Lean meats, liver, fish, milk, egg yolk, brewer's yeast and yeast extracts, soya beans and flour, wholegrain cereals, buckwheat flour, sunflower seeds, pulses, peanuts, walnuts, green vegetables – especially cabbage, raisins, bananas, prunes.

VITAMIN B12. Cyanocobalamin. Water soluble. RDA 2mcg (nursing mothers and pregnant women 4mcg). Cannot be produced in the body and has to be taken up in food.
Deficiency. Anaemia, loss of appetite, weakness of nervous system. Hearing loss. Important for mental health. Spina bifida. Pernicious anaemia. Subacute combined degeneration of the spinal cord.

"Insomnia, paranoia, depression mania – even psychosis." (*Dr H.L. Newbold, Journal Medical Hypotheses*)
Body effects. Healthy nerve tissue. Metabolism of fats, carbohydrates and proteins. Formation of red blood cells. RNA and DNA synthesis. Growth factor.
Sources. All foods of animal origin: meat, liver, kidney, dairy products, cheese, egg yolk, fish, wheatgerm, yeast, spinach, lettuce. Herbs – Alfalfa, Kelp, Dulse.

VITAMINS – BIOFLAVONOIDS. Rutin. Vitamin P.

Deficiency. Varicose veins. Infection. Inflammation.
Body effects. Anti-bacterial. Anti-inflammatory. Blood vessel protector.
Sources. Always associated with Vitamin C in fruits and foods. Citrus fruits – pulp and skin. Green peppers, grapes, apricots, paprika, broccoli, tomatoes, buckwheat flour.

VITAMIN – BIOTIN. Member of B-complex. Water soluble. RDA: 0.1-0.2mg.
Deficiency. Rare. Metabolism of fats, carbohydrates and proteins. When diet is low in carbohydrates it has the property to synthesise glucose. Health of bone marrow, skin, hair, nerves, sex and sweat glands. Anaemia – pale smooth tongue. Hair loss, eczema, high cholesterol levels. Loss of reflexes. Impaired mental health, depression, sleepiness, fatigue.
Sources. Meat, liver, kidney, fish, egg yolk, yeast, wheatgerm, oats, wholegrain cereals, unpolished rice, nuts, fruits.

VITAMIN C. Ascorbic acid. Water soluble. RDA 30mg (pregnant women 60mg). Anti-oxidant.
Deficiency. Poor resistance to infection, physical weakness, anaemia, muscle degeneration, fatigue, irritability, scurvy.
Body effects. Increased resistance to infection. Absorption of iron, control of blood cholesterol. Anti-stress. Anti-histamine effect. Healthy tissues of blood vessels, bones, skin, teeth, gums, cartilages and collagen. Growth factor in children. Health of spleen and reproductive organs.
Sources. Citrus fruits (fresh). Acerola cherry, black currants, guava fruit, grapefruit, lemons, oranges and all other fruits. Vegetables (fresh) – parsley, kale, green peppers, potatoes. Herbs – Burdock seed, Chillies (capsicum), Elderberries, Horseradish, Marigold, Oregano, Rosehips, Paprika, Watercress. An orange contains 75mg Vitamin C.

VITAMIN – CHOLINE. B-complex vitamin. Constituent of lecithin. Fat emulsifier: essential for breakdown of fats and to prevent build-up of cholesterol on arterial walls. RDA 500-1,000mg.
Deficiency. High cholesterol, high blood pressure, memory lapse, dizziness, Alzheimer's disease, angina, atherosclerosis.
Body effects. Protective for myelin sheaths that cover nervous tissue. Strengthens weak capillary walls. Nervous system: makes acetylcholine to bridge synapse between nerves and muscle. Function of brain, liver, circulatory system, nervous system and to regulate blood pressure.
Sources. Beef liver, fish, eggs, lecithin, brewer's yeast, peanuts, soybeans or flour.
Note. Its action is enhanced in combination with Vitamin A.

VITAMIN D. Cholecalciferol. Fat soluble. RDA 10mcg.
Deficiency. Bone disorders, cramp, dental caries, muscle weakness, osteomalacia, rickets.
Body effects. Absorption of calcium and phosphorus for teeth and bones. Regulates heart beat. Assists absorption of calcium and phosphorus from the intestines.
Sources. Action of sunlight on the skin, dairy products, fish liver oils (Cod Liver oil etc). Oily fish: mackerel, salmon, tuna, sardines, halibut, egg yolk, margarine, sprouted seeds.

VITAMIN E. D-Alpha Tocopherol. Fat soluble.
Deficiency. Heart disorders. Infertility.
Body effects. Protection against harmful environmental effects. Anti-oxidant which reduces oxygen requirements of muscles. Healthy blood cells; their membranes especially. Anticoagulant, dissolves blood clots, protects walls of veins and arteries. Healing skin without a scar.

"The oil reduces the risk of skin cancer from the sun." (*University of Arizona College of Medicine and Cancer Center*)

Protects against loss of Vitamin C. Delays onset of cataracts. Protects the eye from damage.
Sources. Richest sources are seed oils, cold-pressed. Wholegrain cereals, nuts, seeds, pulses, brown rice, egg yolk, margarine, green vegetables, turnip greens. Oils of Wheatgerm, Soya bean, Safflower, Corn, Tung, Cottonseed, Olive, Sunflower. Herbs: Alfalfa, Avena Sativa, Kelp, Dandelion leaves, Dulse, Linseed, Sesame seed.
Notes. (a) Cream, preferably lanolin-free, helps prevent premature ageing of dry skin.
(b) Dosage of over 1,000iu daily should be under supervision.
(c) Not given in presence of mitral disease or rheumatic heart.
Note. Use with caution in cases of over-active thyroid gland, diabetes, rheumatic heart disease and high blood pressure.

VITAMIN – FOLIC ACID. Folate, pteroylglutamic acid, Vitamin B9. RDA 0.3mg (pregnancy 0.4mg).
Deficiency. Anaemia, extreme weakness. Lack of concentration. Irritability, insomnia. Low levels of Vitamin B12. Spina bifida. Research shows that those with low blood levels of folic acid are five times more likely to develop cancer than those with high levels. In women, it may strike as cervical malignancy.
Body effects. Formation of red blood cells. Metabolism of fats, carbohydrates and proteins. RNA and DNA synthesis. Healthy hair and skin, fetus growth, healing of wounds, mental illness.
Sources. Meat, liver, kidney, brewer's yeast, yeast extract, egg yolk, wheatgerm, green vegetables (especially beet greens), endive, kale, spinach, turnips, asparagus, fresh fruit.

Notes. (a) Pregnant mothers are advised by the Medical Research Council to take Folic acid – part of the B-group – to help protect against neural tube defects; severe birth defects of spina bifida, and hydrocephalus.
(b) The risk of cleft lip or palate was cut 42 per cent after mothers had taken Folic acid supplements one month prior to conception and two months post-conception. (*California Births Control Monitoring Program*)
(c) Where daily dose exceeds 500mcg, Folic acid becomes a Prescription Only Medicine (POM). No known side-effects.

VITAMIN – INOSITOL. Member of the B-complex. Occurs in high concentration in the human brain.
Deficiency. Psoriasis in patients whose cholesterol levels are above normal.
Body effects. Prevents accumulation of fatty acids. Function of liver, kidney, stomach, spleen and brain. Lowers serum cholesterol in diabetics.
Sources. Brown rice, brewer's yeast, beef heart, eggs, liver, meat, kidney, wholegrain cereals, molasses.

The human body has the ability to synthesise this vitamin through the action of intestinal flora.
Notes. Taking inositol as an isolated vitamin is not recommended. It may be combined with Vitamin E, in which form it has acquired some success in treating nerve damage in certain forms of muscular dystrophy.

VITAMIN K. Menadione. Fat soluble. RDA 70-140mcg. Vital for blood coagulation.
Deficiency. Spontaneous bleeding, nosebleeds, bruising of the skin, diarrhoea.
Body effects. To hasten blood clotting. Anti-haemorrhage. Protection against side-effects of aspirin and sulpha drugs. Has been identified with radiation treatment and X-rays as Vitamin K destroyers. Bacterial replacement with lacto-bacillus, yoghurt and acidophilos re-establishes intestinal flora necessary for the assimilation of Vitamin K following the use of antibiotics.
Sources. Synthesised in the intestinal tract. Beef liver, eggs, potatoes, tomatoes, cabbage, Brussel's sprouts, lettuce, broccoli, spinach. Herbs: Alfalfa, Kelp, Shepherd's Purse.
Note. Vitamin K injections given to the newborn to prevent potentially fatal bleeds into the brain are found to double children's risk of developing leukaemia. No such risk is found linked with oral use.

VITAMIN – PABA. Para-aminobenzoic acid. Constituent of folic acid. Stimulates intestinal flora to produce folic acid. Utilises pantothenic acid.
Deficiency. Anaemia. Skin disorders.
Body effects. Metabolism of proteins. Formation of red blood cells. Antagonist to sulpha drugs. Of value as a sun-screen; a possible preventative of skin cancer. Carrier of oxygen from blood to lungs, muscles and vital organs. Antistress factor. Vitiligo – success reported.
Sources. Liver, yeast, wheatgerm, eggs, molasses, rice bran, porridge oats, maize, barley, apricot kernels.

VITAMIN Q10. Coenzyme. Prophylactic. Heart medicine. Success reported in various seemingly unrelated diseases: atherosclerosis, chronic fatigue syndrome, gingivitis (gum disease). Cancer protective. Best known European brand: BioQuinone Q10.

VITILIGO. Cause unknown. Often associated with auto-immune based disorders affecting the thyroid, adrenal and pancreas glands. Fifty per cent of known cases appear before the age of 20. De-pigmentation. Also results from self-destruction of melanocites, with disappearance of melanin – the chemical that produces pigment of the skin. Pale patches appear mostly on face and neck. There is no cure, although certain agents appear to be indicated.
Treatment. Immune-positive agents.

Prolonged use of topical steroids (standard treatment) on the face may cause skin damage. Frequent application of Comfrey ointment or Aloe Vera gel are both well-tolerated, having no adverse systemic effects. Some authorities observe a segmental distribution of areas of pale skin, suggesting it often follows the path of a nerve. Inclusion of a nerve agent (Valerian) in a prescription may be indicated.
Internal. To strengthen immune system. Formula. Yellow Dock 2; Poke root half; Horsetail half; Valerian half; Liquorice quarter. Dose: Powders: 500mg (two 00 capsules or one-third teaspoon). Liquid extracts: 1 teaspoon. Tinctures: 2 teaspoons. Thrice daily in water or honey.
Topical. 4oz Witch Hazel water to which 1 teaspoon extract Butternut added. Frequent use as lotion.
Oil of Bergamot. Discoloured areas painted and exposed to the sun or ultra-violet light. Practice now discontinued.

VODKA. A colourless spirit distilled from malt, rye and potato. Sometimes used as a menstruum for extraction of herbal constituents as an alternative to pure alcohol. Similar spirits: pastis, schnapps, aquavit, arrack, ouzo, mescal and tequila. A typical Russian spirit.

VOGEL, Dr. Alfred C.A. Swiss naturopath, herbalist, author and lecturer. Revived interest in herbal medicine in Switzerland. Book: *Nature Doctor*, (1977). Learnt the fundamental principles of herbal medicine from his parents and from primitive peoples during his travels to parts of the world. Founder of Bioforce Ltd, one of the important companies in the field of herbal research. From the bedside of the patient he learnt "Nature is the first and best teacher for the conscientious observer". Well-respected in his field. Dr Vogel calls the medicinal plant a prescription given to us by the Creator. "True, we are able to define the individual major substances of this prescription, yet the whole of it remains hidden from us."

VOGEL, Dr. Virgil J. University of Chicago. Book: *American Indian Medicine*, (1982), USA. Comprehensive history. Its purpose is to show the effect of Indian medicinal practices on the white civilisation. Lists Indian herbs which have won a place in the *Pharmacopoeia of the United States*.

VOICE, LOSS OF. Aphonia.
Treatment: as for LARYNGITIS.

VOLATILE OILS. See: ESSENTIAL OILS.

VOMITING. Emesis. Forceful expulsion of contents of the stomach. Reverse of peristalsis.
Causes: peptic ulcer, gastritis (inflammation of lining of the stomach), shock, intestinal obstruction, pressure on the brain by tumour or encephalitis, or by loss of sense of balance as in ear infection. Babies may vomit frequently, but not always serious. Prolonged vomiting may produce dehydration that demands practitioner treatment.
Treatment. For simple uncomplicated conditions: see NAUSEA.
Antemetics: *Teas*: Avens, Balm, Black Horehound, Bogbean, Cayenne, German Chamomile, Cinnamon, Cloves, Fennel, Meadowsweet, Artichoke leaves, Parsley leaves. Chew small segment crystalised Ginger, or Liquorice. Few drops simple Oil of Peppermint may be convenient and effective.
Vomiting of infants – Spearmint tea, teaspoon doses.
Useful combination: Meadowsweet and Black Horehound tea.
Formula. Persistent vomiting. Equal parts: Galangal, Turkey Rhubarb and Ginger. Mix. Dose: Powders: 750mg (three 00 capsules or half a teaspoon). Liquid extracts: 1 teaspoon. Tinctures: 1-2 teaspoons. Every 2 hours acute cases. Not used in presence of peptic ulceration.
Tincture Cardamoms Co BP (1973). Dose: 30-60 drops.
Prolonged, uncontrollable: 1 drop Oil of Camphor in honey, half-hourly.
Diet. Lacto-vegetarian. Table-salt. Pinch of Nutmeg in food.
Vitamins. B-complex. B6, C (1g tablet daily).
Minerals. Dolomite.

VULNERARY. A plant whose external application has a cleansing and healing effect on open wounds, cuts and ulcers by promoting cell repair. An older generation of herbalists believed the fresh plant was more effective but extracts, creams, lotions, and similar preparations are more widely used today because of their utility. Many of such plants are haemostatics or astringents with power to arrest bleeding.

All Heal (Prunella vulgaris), Aloe Vera, Cranesbill (American), Comfrey, Elderflowers, Goldenseal, Gotu Kola, Ground Ivy, Heather flowers (Calluna), Horsetail, Marigold flowers, Marshmallow root, Myrrh gum powder, Nutmeg powder, Plantain, Purple Loosestrife, St John's Wort, Self-heal, Slippery Elm powder, Tormentil, Witch Hazel, Wood Sage.

VULVITIS. Inflammation of the vulva with pale white patches.
Treatment: same as for VAGINITIS, NON-SPECIFIC.

VULVOVAGINITIS. Inflammation of both the vulva (vulvitis) and the vagina (vaginitis).
Treatment: same as for VAGINITIS, NON-SPECIFIC.

WAHOO BARK. Spindle tree. *Euonymous atropurpureus* Jacq. *French*: Fusain. *German*: Spindelbaume. *Italian*: Fusano. *Spanish*: Bonetero. *Indian*: Barphali. *Part used*: root bark, stem.
Constituents: alkaloids, sterols, tannins, cardenolides.
Action. Liver agent, cholagogue, diuretic, alterative, laxative, antiperiodic, antiparasitic, stimulant. Frontiersmen regarded it as an anti-syphilitic. Winnebago.
Uses. Indian women used a decoction for womb troubles. Torpidity of the liver, gall bladder disorder, jaundice. Constipation of liver origin. Proteinuria.

Not given in pregnancy and lactation.
Preparations. Average dose. 0.3-1g, or fluid equivalent, thrice daily.
Decoction. Quarter to half a teaspoon powder, or half-1 teaspoon bark shavings, to each cup water gently simmered 10 minutes. Dose, half a cup.
Liquid Extract. 5-15 drops in water.
Tincture. 10-40 drops in water. GSL

WALNUT. *Juglans regia L. German*: Walnuss. *French*: Noyer. *Italian*: Noce comune. *Parts used*: leaves, bark. Walnuts are rich in omega 3 fatty acids.
Constituents: volatile oil, naphthaquinones, flavonoids, tannins.
Action. Alterative, astringent, laxative, hypoglycaemic (mild), detergent, anti-inflammatory, anti-scrofula.
Uses. Tubercula tendency; thin people desiring to put on weight; irritable bowel; said to delay hardening of the arteries. Indigestion. Eczema. Tea drunk orally or used as a wash for skin disorders and shingles. Inflamed eyelids (wash).
Preparations. Thrice daily.
Tea: 1-2 teaspoons dried herb to each cup boiling water; infuse 15 minutes. Dose, half-1 cup, or use as a wash.
Liquid Extract: dose, 4-8ml in water.
Tincture: leaves or green fruit. 1 part to 5 parts 40 per cent alcohol; macerate 8 days, decant. Dose, 1-3 teaspoons in water.
Compress: 30g fresh or dried leaves to 500ml water gently simmered 1 minute. Allow to cool. Soak suitable material and apply.
Note. Eating walnuts led to a lower risk of a coronary and with cholesterol levels falling by 20 per cent.

WARFARIN. An anticoagulant drug to prevent blood clotting in thrombosis and atherosclerosis. *Adverse effects*: loss of hair, irritable skin rash, blood in the urine and bleeding of the gums.

For moderate alternatives see under HEART, ATHEROMA, THROMBOSIS.

WARTS. A *papova* virus infection of the skin. The common wart varies in colour from pink to dark brown. Plantar warts are flat and painful on weight-bearing parts of the foot. Molluscum contagiosum are flesh-coloured. Many warts disappear as mysteriously as they come except those on genitals and finger-tips. Genital (venereal warts, condylomata) are usually sexually transmitted, the primary underlying cause of which should be treated. Warts on finger-tips are common among nail-biters, are long-lived and difficult to treat. Seborrhoeic warts are benign tumours common in the over-50 age group; bits may separate when rubbed.
Treatment. Keratolytics. Alteratives.

A cause may be vaccination for which *Thuja* is specific. Where possible, chemical solvents should be avoided. There are hundreds of wart cures, including rubbing with radishes, fig leaves, Marigold flowers, Sloe, Houseleek or Aloe Vera juice; also fresh juice of onions, Garlic, Dandelion, or Greater Celandine. Castor and Jojoba oils have their successes. Vulval warts have responded favourably to Aloe Vera.
Thuja. Tincture. (Internal): 5 drops in water, morning and evening.
Topical. Use of tincture Thuja as a lotion.
Slippery Elm powder. Moisten and apply.
American Mandrake. Low-dose podophyllin solutions. 0.5 per cent podophyllotoxin for penile warts; applied twice daily for 3 days.
Other effective agents. Internally and externally: Echinacea, Horsetail.
Note. All cases of genital warts should be referred to genito-urinary clinics for screening of co-infections. Such warts may follow candida or chlamydia.

WASTING. See: CACHEXIA.

WATER BRASH. See: INDIGESTION.

WATERCRESS. *Nasturtium officinalis L. French*: Cresson de fontaine. *German*: Brunnenkresse. *Italian*: Crescione di fonte. *Spanish*: Berro. *Chinese*: Ting-li. *Part used*: leaves.
Constituents: iron-compound mineral salts, phosphates, potash, iodine, sulphur, folic acid that build up impoverished blood. Its manganese relates to the pituitary gland.
Action. Hypoglycaemic, diuretic, expectorant, odontalgic, nicotene solvent, antiscorbutic, blood enricher.
Uses. The ancient Persians gave it to their children for sound physical development doubtless due to its complex of trace minerals. Catarrh of the respiratory organs, kidney and bladder disorders; renal stone (*Dodoens*). Chronic rheumatism, metabolic disorders, skin eruptions, anaemia – to restore colour to ashen cheeks.
Preparation. *Fresh juice*: 1-2 teaspoons, thrice daily.

Diet. Ingredient of salads.
Note: Watercress contains four times as much Vitamin C, weight for weight as lettuce, and more calcium than whole milk. One of the richest sources of Vitamin A and dietary fibre. Offers 14 calories per 100g.

WATER PEPPER. Smartweed. Arsesmart. *Polygonum hydropiper L. German*: Pfeffer-Knotĕrich. *French*: Curage. *Italian*: Poligono. Herb; dried or fresh.
Constituents: polygonolide, sesquiterpenes, flavonoids.
Action. haemostatic, astringent, anti-inflammatory, antifungal, diuretic, emmenagogue, stimulant, styptic.
Uses. Delayed menstruation. Amenorrhoea in teenage girls to promote healthy monthly flow; periods absent for months – to re-establish. Minor injuries, cuts, etc, to arrest bleeding. Bleeding piles. Athlete's foot (powdered leaves or diluted tincture).
Preparations. 1 to 3 times daily.
Tea: 1 teaspoon to each cup boiling water; infuse 10 minutes; dose, half-1 cup.
Tincture. 1 part dried or fresh herb to 5 parts 45 per cent alcohol. Macerate 8 days, shake daily; strain and store in an amber-coloured bottle. Dose, 30-60 drops in water.
Not used in pregnancy.

WATER PLANTAIN. Mad-dog weed. *Alisma plantago, L. French*: Plantain d'eau. *German*: Froschlöffel. *Italian*: Piantaggine aquatica. *Spanish*: Plátano agua. *Chinese*: Tsê-hsieh.
Action. Diuretic, diaphoretic.
Uses. Irritability of the bladder, gravel, painful urination. Snakebite (*South American traditional*). Rabies (hydrophobia) (*German traditional*). Antidote to mad-dog bite (*Russia*).
Preparation. *Tea*: 1-2 teaspoons to each cup boiling water; infuse 10 minutes. Half a cup thrice daily. Taken freely in emergency.

WATER RETENTION. See: FLUID RETENTION SYNDROME.

WATER TROUBLES.
See: KIDNEY DISORDERS.

WEAKNESS. Debility. Lassitude. Asthenia. Symptomatic of a number of disorders. Lack of vitality and physical strength from nervous fatigue, under-nourishment, over-work, poor food, surgery, etc. In every case of weakness low blood pressure is associated.
Alternatives. Alfalfa is rich in minerals and a daily tea readily imparts strength provided that newly found well-being is not dissipated by a continuation of debilitating living habits, smoking, alcohol or lack of exercise. For poor resistance to infection – Echinacea.
Teas. Irish Moss, Iceland Moss, Agrimony, Wood Betony, Wormwood, Chamomile, Oats, Rosemary, Siberian Ginseng, Red Clover, Fenugreek seed, Gotu Kola.
Tea. Combination. Equal parts: Agrimony, Alfalfa, Oats. 1-2 teaspoons to each cup boiling water; infuse 5-10 minutes. 1 cup thrice daily.
Decoction. Gentian root. 1-2 teaspoons to each cup cold water left to steep overnight. Half-1 cup before meals thrice daily.
Tablets/capsules. Damiana. Chamomile flowers. Goldenseal. Ginseng. Hawthorn, Pulsatilla, Kelp, Agnus Castus.
Traditional combination: Saw Palmetto, Damiana, Kola.
Formula. Equal parts: Ginseng, Alfalfa, Oats, Ginger. Mix. Dose: Powders: 750mg (three 00 capsules or half a teaspoon). Liquid extracts: 1-2 teaspoons. Tinctures: 1-3 teaspoons. Thrice daily in water or honey.
Chinese medicine. Liquid Extracts: Combine, Ginseng 2; Don quai 2; Liquorice 1; Ginger 1. Half-1 teaspoon in water before meals thrice daily.
Practitioner. Tincture Peruvian bark (BPC 1949). Dose: 2-4ml thrice daily before meals.
Diet. Kelp, Slippery Elm, Irish Moss, Horse Radish.
Nutrients. Superoxide dismutase. Brewer's Yeast. Multivitamin. Remove risk factors – holiday, adequate rest.

WEAVER FISH STING. The sting of the weaver fish's dorsal fin is so intensive that trawlermen have been known to cut off their toes to obtain relief.
Internal: Echinacea. *External*: plunge the foot in very hot water – the toxin is destroyed by heat. (*Dr David Wynne Evans, Welsh general practitioner*)
When someone treads on a weaver fish an ice-pack should not be applied. The burning end of a lighted cigarette should be held close to the skin of the victim where the sting has penetrated for dramatic relief.

WEIL'S DISEASE. See: LEPTOSPIROSIS.

WEISS, Rudolf Fritz MD. Distinguished German physician. Professor of phytotherapy and herbal medicine. Modern textbook – a systematic study of herbs within the framework of clinical diagnoses. (*"Herbal Medicine" – Beaconsfield Publishers, Beaconsfield, England*)

WELEDA. Specialists in anthroposophic medicine. Preparation of a healing remedy is regarded as a spiritual activity; "a plant is more than its chemical components". Treatment is related to a patient's personality as well as to illness, and it is to a person's spirit as well as his body that treatment is directed. Weleda's comprehensive range of mother tinctures and potencies are produced for this purpose and for use by the doctor who has cultivated his powers of spiritual awareness.

Plants are gathered from Weleda's own gardens, organic cultivation ensuring the vitality of growth essential for medicinal plants. Some are collected from their natural habitat. All are prepared according to instructions left by Dr Rudolph Steiner for proper drying, preservation of aroma and essential oil content.

Weleda is based on the work of Dr Rudolph Steiner, founder of the Anthroposophical movement which regards the human being as an entity comprised of body, soul and spirit, and through these connected with the plant kingdom.

The first Weleda company was started in Switzerland in 1921. Twenty-five companies throughout the world now bear its name, each dedicated to Steiner principles. A quarter of their output is accounted for by servicing individual prescriptions from doctors and hospitals. Stocks are carried by over 2,000 chemists and health food shops.
Address: Weleda (UK) Ltd., Heanor Road, Ilkeston, Derbyshire DE7 8DR. Tel: (0602) 309319.

WENS. Wens are cysts caused by blockage of a sebaceous gland and are filled with a fatty material. Usually removed by a surgeon who opens-up and removes the contents. A Castor oil compress a few nights, softens before excision. John Clarke MD reports use of injection of a few drops fresh Poke root juice to reduce.

WESLEY, John. The great Methodist Reformer. Book: *Primitive Physic*: or an easy natural method of curing most diseases. Edited by William Paynter, (1958), Plymouth. Reprint of remedies in author's 1755 edition, with some additional prescriptions. Of historic interest.

WHEATGRASS. Juice from 3-4 day sprouted wheat grains is rich in chlorophyll and enzymes. Wheatgrass is the crop from germinated seed of wheat grains as sown on flat trays or in flowerpots, chiefly in the kitchen. When 2-3 inches high the green spears are "reaped" with scissors or shears, chopped, and added to salads for a rich source of trace minerals. It is a natural source of superoxide dismutase (SOD) an important enzyme in detoxifying the body.

WHEEZING. A rasping sound heard in some breathing troubles from inflammation of the bronchial tubes. Lobelia or Iceland Moss. 2 teaspoons Cider vinegar and 1 teaspoon honey in a little water, freely. Underlying cause should be treated.

See: BRONCHITIS, TRACHEITIS, ASTHMA.

WHITE DEAD NETTLE. Blind nettle. *Lamium album L. German*: Weisse taubnessel. *French*: Ortie blanche. *Italian*: Lamio bianco. *Part used*: flowering tops.
Constituents: saponins, tannins, amines, Lamiine (alkaloid), flavonoids.
Action. Haemostatic, astringent, diuretic, expectorant, anti-inflammatory, vulnerary, antispasmodic, menstrual regulator.
Uses. Profuse or painful menstrual bleeding, cystitis, diarrhoea, irritable bowel, prostatitis, catarrh, bleeding piles. Offensive vaginal discharge (douche). Respiratory catarrh.
Preparations. *Tea*: 1-2 teaspoons to each cup boiling water; infuse 10 minutes; dose 1 cup thrice daily. Used also as an eye douche.
Vaginal douche: 2oz to 2 pints boiling water; infuse till cool; strain, inject.
Diet. Leaves in spring may be cooked as spinach.

WHITE POND LILY. American waterlily. Water nymph. *Nymphaea odorata*, soland. *French*: Nénuphar blanc. *German*: Seeblume. *Italian*: Ninfea bianca. *Spanish*: Ninfea blanca. *Parts used*: roots, leaves, flowers.
Constituents: alkaloids, flavonoids, gallic acid.
Action. Anaphrodisiac, demulcent, astringent, antimicrobial. (*Fletcher Hyde*)
Uses. Chronic vaginal discharge, ulceration of the cervix. Once in general use for fibroids of the womb (douche). Prostatitis, diarrhoea, irritable bowel. Sore throat (gargle). To reduce sexual drive.
Preparations. Average dose, 1-2g or fluid equivalent, thrice daily.
Tea: half-1 teaspoon to each cup water gently simmered 2 minutes; allow to cool; dose, half-1 cup.
Liquid Extract BHP (1983): 1:1 in 25 per cent alcohol; dose 1-4ml.
Douche: 2oz leaves or 1oz root to 2 pints water gently simmered 2 minutes. Strain; inject warm.
GSL

WHITE POPLAR BARK. Quaking aspen. *Populus tremuloides*, Michx. *French*: Peuplier blanc. *German*: Weisse Pappel. *Italian*: Popolo bianco. *Spanish*: Alamo. *Chinese*: Pai-yang. *Parts used*: leaves, bark. Contains salicin, populin, lignan, tannins.
Action. Tonic-stimulant, anti-rheumatic, antiseptic, anti-inflammatory, analgesic (mild), stimulant. Febrifuge, with an action similar to Peruvian bark but without cumulative effects of the latter.
Uses. Rheumatoid arthritis. Weak digestion, dyspepsia, general debility, irritable bowel, low metabolic tone.
Preparations. Average dose, 1-4 grams or fluid equivalent, thrice daily.
Decoction. 1-2 teaspoons to each cup water gently simmered 10 minutes; dose, half-1 cup.

Liquid Extract BHP (1983). 1:1 in 25 per cent alcohol; dose, 1-4ml in water. GSL

WHITLOW. Felon. Inflammation with redness, throbbing and swelling of finger-tip from prick of a needle or other minor injury which has exposed the root of the nail or tendon sheaths to infection. Worse hanging hand downwards. Tenderness. Enlargement of hands or glands under arms. Infection chiefly staphylococcal (Myrrh). Often seen on the hands of nurses and technicians handling septic material. Sometimes due to fungus.
Treatment. As for blood-poisoning, with alteratives. Internal.
Teas: Nettles, Red Clover, Plantain, Clivers.
Tablets/capsules: Blue Flag root, Echinacea, Sarsaparilla, Devil's Claw, Goldenseal. Wild Yam.
Formula. Equal parts: Echinacea, Devil's Claw. Mix. Dose: Powders: 500mg (two 00 capsules or one-third teaspoon). Liquid extracts: 1 teaspoon. Tinctures: 2 teaspoons. Thrice daily in water or honey.
Tincture Thuja BHP (1983): 5 drops in water morning and evening.
Topical. Keep hands out of water. Wear finger stall. Paint with: neat Tea Tree oil, Tincture Myrrh, Marigold, St John's Wort, Blood root, or Evening Primrose oil.
Potato poultice: raw, cold. Renew morning and evening.
Hot compress: Slippery Elm, Lobelia, Chamomile, Comfrey. Finish off with ointment of Comfrey or of Marshmallow and Slippery Elm.

Cut hole in lemon and encase whole finger, wearing like a thimble.
Fungus infection. See: ANTI-FUNGALS.
Dr M.E. Moore, Winchester, advises toothpick dipped in Friar's Balsam and applied to cracks twice daily.

Minor surgery may be necessary.

WHOLE PLANT, The. Orthodox medicine believes that by isolating the active parts of a plant, side-effects are less likely to occur because of its 'purity'; moreover, the preparation would become more potent. It is the practise of the *herbalist* to base his treatments upon the whole plant in the belief that the whole plant has natural in-built safeguards. Plant pharmacology has been shown to differ from the pharmacology of isolated substances.

The number of agents used for rheumatism runs into hundreds, but part of the training of the qualified herbalist equips him to understand plant pharmacology and to assess which remedy matches the patient's totality of symptoms.

By use of the Whole Plant the active principle is assisted by other components all working within the one context. The synergistic effect is important.

When alkaloids etc are isolated and concentrated in their chemically pure state, a hazard to health may arise. It is assumed that Nature does not intend one of its constituents to be isolated from others with which it works in harmony. A more 'balanced' action is desirable.

It is noted that the pure crystalline alkaloid of quinine may throw-up side-effects entirely absent from use of the crude bark of the Cinchona tree. Clinical experience has shown that a simple decoction of its bark possesses properties absent in the isolated preparation.

"A herbal remedy such as Lily of the Valley leaves contains several cardio-active glycosides that are released sequentially in the body; the result is a lengthening of the cardiac response and the avoidance of an abrupt and undesirable peak in plasma concentration. Certain non-cardioactive glycosides also present increase almost 500 times the water solubility of *convallatoxin* and *convallatoxol*. Other glycosides act synergistically by occupying protein binding sites and thereby effecting a high plasma concentration of active glycosides with correspondingly increased bioavailability. The combination occurring in the leaf has many therapeutic advantages over the isolated glycosides – a fact of general application that seems to be appreciated by those practitioners who prescribe Digitalis (foxglove) leaf in preference to Digoxin in certain cases." (*F. Fletcher Hyde*)

The whole is greater than the sum of its parts.

WHOOPING COUGH. A children's infectious notifiable disease with paroxysmal coughing. Pertussis. Convulsive coughing is followed by the characteristic 'whoop' on breath intake. Transmitted by droplet infection. One attack usually confers immunity. Incubation: 5-6 days. Isolation 21 days from first whoop. Three stages of the disease: (1) catarrhal (2) spasmodic (3) decline.

Early symptoms are a cold with inflammation of mucous membranes lining the air passages, sneezing, watery eyes and harsh cough. Cough develops in severity until after 7 days it becomes convulsive. After 14 days comes the 'whoop' followed by vomiting. Children under 7 years most affected.

After-care is important, the immune system depleted. Echinacea should be taken daily for one month to build up resistance to other infectious diseases generally.
Treatment. Bedrest. Plenty of fluids. Abundant herb teas. Expectorants. The Eclectic School asserts: "The secret of successfully treating whooping cough by herbs, is the use of emetics to make the patient sick. Once a good evacuation of the stomach is achieved, the battle is half over."

Labrador tea is still given in country areas of Sweden. Barefoot doctors of China use Ephedra,

but in European medicine its use is restricted to general medical practitioners and qualified phytotherapists.
Alternatives. *Tea*. (*E.G. Jones MNIMH*) Equal parts: White Horehound, Coltsfoot, Mouse Ear, Wild Thyme. Mix. 1-2 teaspoons to each cup boiling water. Infuse 5-15 minutes. Half-1 cup every 2 hours acute cases. Children under 5 – teaspoonful freely.
Tea. (*John Lust*) Equal parts: Thyme, Mouse Ear, Liquorice, Coltsfoot. Steep 2 tablespoons mixture in 3 cups boiling water 30 minutes, covered. Strain and sweeten with honey. Dose: 1-4 tablespoons 4 times daily between meals, dose depending on age.
Tea. (*Yorkshire traditional*) Equal parts: Mullein and Wild Thyme. Mix 2 teaspoons to each cup boiling water; infuse. 1 cup freely. Children under 5 – teaspoonful sips freely.
Decoction. Any one: Black Cohosh, Wild Cherry bark, Spanish Chestnut leaves Elecampane root. Prepare: 1oz (30g) to 1 pint (500ml) water; simmer gently 20 minutes. Dose: half-1 cup every 2 hours.
Tablets/capsules. Lobelia, Garlic, Iceland Moss.
Practitioner. Formula. Equal parts: Wild Cherry bark, Ephedra, Wild Thyme. Mix. Dose: Powders: 750mg (three 00 capsules or half a teaspoon). Liquid extracts: 1-2 teaspoons. Tinctures: 1-3 teaspoons. Children 5-12 years – one-third dose. After 12 years regard as an adult. Not given to children under 5. Thrice daily; every 2 hours acute cases.
Practitioner. As indicated: Stramonium, Blood root, White Squills, Belladonna.
External. Olbas oil massage on chest and back.
Aromatherapy. Inhalation of essential oils: Caraway, Eucalyptus, Thyme. Pine, Anise. Also use as chest-rub diluted in carrier oil: 2 teaspoons Almond oil.
Diet. No dairy products or gluten grains. Low salt. Low starch. Abundant Vitamin C drinks – orange juice and citrus fruits.
General. Regulate bowels. Hot bath 10-15 minutes at bedtime. Many children have cold feet and chilly pale skin.
Preventative during epidemic: Garlic oil capsules: 2 capsules night and morning for 7 days.
Treatment by or in liaison with a general medical practitioner.

WILD CARROT. *Daucus carota L. German*: Karrotten. *French*: Carotte. *Italian*: Carota. Dried herb. *Keynote*: stone.
Constituents: volatile oil, flavonoids, daucine (alkaloid).
Action. Anti-lithic (stone-resolvent), diuretic, carminative. Pro-Vitamin A.
Uses. Kidney or bladder stone, gravel, dropsy, retention of urine. Dysentery and worms (*Chinese Medicine*). Hot flushes of the menopause, night blindness, ultra-violet radiation.
Preparations. Thrice daily. Believed to produce best results by simple infusion.
Tea. 1-2 teaspoons to each cup boiling water; infuse 15 minutes; dose – 1 cup.
Wild Carrot is an ingredient of many herbal diuretics, i.e. Tea: Wild Carrot 15 per cent; Bearberry 15 per cent; Couchgrass 15 per cent; Buchu 10 per cent; Alfalfa 45 per cent. Preparation as above.
Tincture. 1 part to 5 parts vodka; macerate 8 days; decant. Dose: 1-2 teaspoons.

WILD CHERRY BARK. Virginia prune. *Prunus serotina*, Ehrh. *German*: Sauerkirsch. *French*: Griottier. *Spanish*: Cerezo. *Italian*: Ciliegio. *Chinese*: Ying-t'ao.
Constituents: tannins, scopoletin, prunasin.
Action. Astringent, sedative (mild), digestant, antitussive, antispasmodic, pectoral.
Uses. Hacking cough, whooping cough, asthma, bronchitis, croup, catarrh. No longer used to control the cough of pulmonary tuberculosis. Irritable bowel: the Penobscot Indians steeped the bark in boiling water for diarrhoea. A tonic in convalescence. The common cold (tea).
Preparations. Thrice daily.
Tea. Half a teaspoon to each cup boiling water; infuse 15 minutes; dose – half-1 cup.
Powder. 500mg (two 00 capsules or one-third teaspoon).
Liquid extract. 1-2ml, in water.
Tincture, BPC 1949. 2-4ml.
Wild Cherry syrup. 3-10ml.
Store dry and in the dark. GSL

WILD INDIGO. Yellow indigo. *Baptisia tinctoria* R.Br. *German*: Baptisie. *French*: Baptisie sauvage. Dried root, shredded. *Keynote*: infection.
Constituents: flavonoids, coumarins, isoflavones, baptisin (a bitter principle).
Action. Powerful antiseptic alterative. Febrifuge for non-specific continued fevers arising from blood infection. "Resembles Echinacea but has a more specific reference to enteric and typhoid conditions." (*E.H. Ruddock MD*)
Immune stimulant. "Roots contain a strong lymphocyte DNA synthesis-stimulating activity." (*Planta Medica 1989, 55(4), pp 358-63 (Ger).*)
Uses. One of the first agents that sprang to the minds of old-time American physicians for typhoid. Fevers and septic conditions. Said to produce antibodies to counter typhus organisms. "The specific indication for Baptisia is a dusky purplish colour of the face and tongue, like one exposed to cold; the face expressionless" (*Dr Finlay Ellingwood*).
Exhausting feverish conditions that go on a long time. Epidemic influenza with violent gastro-intestinal symptoms. Lymphatic infections with enlarged nodes. Bacillus Coli infection.

Infective sore throat, mouth ulcers, ulcered gums, tonsillitis, pharyngitis (mouthwash and gargle). Amoebic dysentery, ulcerative colitis, foul evil-smelling discharges. Boils. Stricture of the oesophagus. Leucorrhoea (douche).
Popular combination: Myrrh and Echinacea (equal parts).
Preparations. Average dose, 0.5-1 gram or fluid equivalent, thrice daily.
Decoction. Quarter to half a teaspoon to each cup water gently simmered 20 minutes; dose, half-1 cup.
Liquid Extract BHP (1983). 1:1 in 60 per cent alcohol; dose, 0.3-1.3ml in water.
Tincture. Dose: 1-2.5ml in water. GSL

WILD LETTUCE. *Lactuca virosa L. German*: Wilder lattich. *French*: Laitue vireuse. *Spanish*: Lechuga. *Italian*: Lattuga velenosa. *Arabian*: Bazrul-khasa. *Iranian*: Tukhme-kahu. *Indian*: Kahu-khaskabija. *Chinese*: Ku-chin-kan. Leaves; dried juice (latex).
Constituents: flavonoids, lactucin, hyoscyamine.
Action. Nerve relaxant, mild analgesic, mild hypnotic, sedative, antispasmodic, anaphrodisiac. Once used as a substitute for opium.
Uses. Hyperactivity in children, nervous excitability, anxiety, restlessness: to resolve physical stress and promote healthful sleep. Irritable cough, smoker's cough. Nymphomania. Muscle pains. Insomnia.
Combines well with Passion flower and Valerian for chronic insomnia.
Preparations. Thrice daily. Often formulated with Valerian, Hops, Chamomile or Passion flower.
Popular combination: with Passion flower and Hops (equal parts) for insomnia.
Tea. Half-1 teaspoon to each cup boiling water; infuse 15 minutes; dose, half a cup.
Liquid extract BHC Vol 1. 1:1, 25 per cent ethanol. Dose: 0.5-4ml.
Large doses may produce stupor and confusion.
GSL

WILD YAM. Colic root. Rheumatism root. *Dioscorea villosa L. German*: Wilde-yam. *French*: Igname indigène. *Italian*: Dioscoria salvatica. Dried rhizome. *Keynote*: colicky cramps.
Constituents: saponins for manufacture of steroids.
Action. Antirheumatic, visceral, anti-inflammatory, muscle relaxant, cholagogue, diaphoretic, cardiac sedative (mild angina), antibilious. Believed that its anti-inflammatory action is due to a steroidal effect. Wild Yam is the starting material in the manufacture of steroidal preparations: cortisone, sex hormones, "The Pill", and anabolic hormones.
Uses. Adrenal exhaustion, inflammatory rheumatism, rheumatoid arthritis, stomach and muscle cramps. Biliary, gall stone, renal and intestinal colic; dysentery; persistent nausea and vomiting to promote bile flow. Diverticulosis, appendicitis, together with few grains powder or drops of tincture Ginger. To aid liver function in degenerative disease. Pain in the womb and ovaries; hormone imbalance associated with the menopause. Intermittent claudication. Spasmodic asthma. Threatened miscarriage (add quarter of a teaspoon powdered Ginger to 1 teaspoon powdered Wild Yam). Sharp pains of whitlow (locally).
Preparations. Average dose, 2-4 grams or fluid equivalent, thrice daily
Decoction. 1 teaspoon to each cup water gently simmered 20 minutes. Dose, half-1 cup.
Liquid Extract BHP (1983). 2-4ml in water.
Tincture BHP (1983). 1 in 5 in 45 per cent alcohol; dose, 2-10ml in water.
Popular combination for rheumatoid arthritis: equal parts powders: Wild Yam, Cramp bark, Black Cohosh. Dose: 500mg thrice daily.
Caution. Avoid in pregnancy.

WILLOW, BLACK. *Salix nigra*, March. *German*: Trauerweide. *French*: Saule pleureur. *Spanish*: Sauce negro. *Italian*: Salice Plangente. *Indian*: Bani jurni. *Part used*: dried bark.
Constituents: salicin, gum, wax.
Action. Anaphrodisiac, tonic nervine, astringent, febrifuge.
Uses. To reduce sexual activity, nymphomania, satyriasis, nocturnal emissions, masturbation, spermatorrhoea, prostatitis, ovarian neuralgia.
Once a substitute for potassium bromide, but without a depressant effect.
Combination: with Tincture Myrrh and Goldenseal for purulent discharge.
Preparations. Thrice daily.
Decoction. 1 heaped teaspoon to each cup water gently simmered 1 minute; infuse 15 minutes; dose, half-1 cup.
Liquid Extract. Half-1 teaspoon in water.

WILLOW, WHITE. *Salix alba L. French*: Saule blanc. *German*: Silberweide. *Italian*: Salcio bianco. *Chinese*: Liu. Dried bark.
Constituents: flavonoids, tannins, phenolic glycosides.
In 1838 chemists identified salicylic acid in the bark of White Willow. After many years, it was synthesised as acetylsalicylic acid, now known as aspirin.
Action: antirheumatic, antiseptic, mild pain-killer; antipyretic with power to arrest inflammatory processes and reduce fever.
Uses. Inflammatory rheumatic states, painful muscles and joints; gout, fevers associated with rheumatism and gout, collagen disorders, rheumatoid arthritis, rheumatic fever, lumbago, sciatica, neuralgia. Ankylosing spondylitis BHP (1983). Skeletal backache.

Diarrhoea, dysentery. Deaths from heart attack may be reduced by treating patients with White Willow together with a clot-dissolving remedy (Lime flower tea).

Combines well with Guaiacum, Black Cohosh and Celery seeds for rheumatoid arthritis BHP (1983). Charcoal from the wood is still used for water brash. Combines well with Rosemary for headache, equal parts.

Preparations. Average dose: 1-3 grams or fluid equivalent, thrice daily, or as prescribed by a practitioner.

Decoction. Half a teaspoon dried bark to each cup of water gently simmered 1 minute; infuse 15 minutes; dose, half-1 cup.

Liquid Extract. 1:1 in 25 per cent alcohol. Dose, 1-2ml.

Tablets/capsules. Chiefly in combination with other agents.

Biostrath Willow Formula. Herbal product containing Candida yeast cultures and plant extracts: White Willow bark and Primula root for symptomatic relief of muscular pain. GSL

WILSON'S DISEASE. A rare congenital disease with abnormal accumulation of copper in the body, especially in brain, nerves and liver. May manifest as jaundice or cirrhosis. When high levels appear in the brain dementia ensues.

Treatment. Symptomatic only.

Tea. Combine, Alfalfa, Agrimony, Skullcap. Infuse 15 minutes. 1 cup thrice daily.

Supplements. B6 (25-50mg daily). ". . . the remedy Zinc (150mg daily) proves effective." (*Dr George E. Shambaugh, Northwestern University Medical School, Chicago*)

WIND. See: FLATULENCE.

WINDPIPE. Infection of. See: TRACHEITIS.

WINE. Hippocrates was one of the first to advocate the use of wine in the healing of the sick. Prescription of wine has arrested the progress of much acute and chronic disease, and has played no small part in prevention. Dry wines have been advised for diabetes. Most kinds offer a ready tranquilliser, an energy-generator and a digestive aid taken with food. To the elderly it is a mild sedative, relieving tension and improving nutrition. It has been known to help anorexia nervosa and reduce the risk of heart disease.

Medical authority agrees that a little wine can be good, but with exceptions: pregnancy, gastric ulcer, intestinal lesions, liver and kidney disorders, epilepsy and those taking drugs.

It was St Paul who told Timothy to drink no water, but a little wine for his stomach's sake and other infirmities. Some hospitals recognise the value of wine with food. A little wine and a piece of cheese are believed to relax and promote sleep.

WINTER CABBAGE. *Brassica oleracea*. Contains sulphur, iodine and other minerals. Physicians of the Ancient World employed the vegetable cabbage as medicine as well as food. Peptic ulcer, wounds that refuse to heal, rheumatism and collagen diseases. 1-2 teaspoons fresh juice morning and evening. Avoid in hyperactive thyroid gland.

WINTERGREEN. Checkerberry. Teaberry. *Gaultheria procumbens L. French*: Thé du Canada. *German*: Wintergrün. *Italian*: Tè di montagna. *Keynote*: rheumatism.

Constituents. Leaves contain methyl salicylate – a source of salicin – and other phenolic compounds.

Action. Antirheumatic, anti-inflammatory, aromatic, tonic, astringent, diuretic, analgesic (mild), galactagogue, stimulant.

Uses. Rheumatoid arthritis, inflammation of the joints, painful muscles, gout, backache, lumbago, sciatica, neuralgia, sprains. Intercostal neuralgia.

Preparations. Average dose, 0.5-1 gram, or fluid equivalent, thrice daily.

Tea: 1 teaspoon dried leaves to each cup boiling water; infuse 15 minutes; dose, quarter to half a cup.

Liquid Extract BHP (1983): 1:1 in 25 per cent alcohol. Dose, 0.5-1ml, in water.

Tincture, fresh leaves: 1 part to 5 parts 60 per cent alcohol. Macerate 8 days, shake daily; strain, bottle. Dose, 1-2ml.

Oil of Wintergreen: an ingredient of lotions, creams.

Wintergreen Liniment: Oil Wintergreen 20 drops; Oil Peppermint 10 drops; Oil Camphor 5 drops; 1oz soft soap; 4oz alcohol. Mix. Shake well.

Compress: 1oz to 1 pint boiling water; infuse 30 minutes. Steep linen or suitable material and apply for muscle pains. GSL

WINTERS, Jason. Terminal cancer patient, given 3 months to live, set out on a world search for healing herbs. Was successful in self-treatment for infiltrating squamous cell carcinoma wrapped round the carotid artery and attached to the wall of the jugular vein.

Treatment: Red Clover blossoms, Chaparral herb and a known spice, drunk as a simple tea.

Book: *Killing Cancer*.

WITCH HAZEL. Hamamelidis. Winter Bloom. *Hamamelis virginiana L. French*: Hamamélide. *German*: Zaubernuss. *Italian*: Amamelide. *Spanish*: Hamamelis, carpe. *Chinese*: Chin-lü-mei. Bark, leaves.

Constituents: Vitamin P to protect capillaries and small blood vessels: tannins, flavonoids, saponins.

Action. Haemostatic, anti-inflammatory, cooling, cleansing astringent. Entry to be found in all European Pharmacopoeias.

Uses. Spontaneous bruising and capillary

fragility induced by steroid therapy, tendency of skin to bleed, phlebitis, itchy varicose veins, chilblains, to refresh a tired skin, piles – blind or bleeding, to wash wounds. Nose-bleeds – plug with saturated cotton wool swab. All respond favourably to external use of distilled extract of Witch Hazel.
Conjunctivitis: 10 drops distilled extract to an eyebath half-filled with water (douche).
Tired eyes: cotton wool swabs saturated with the extract and placed over each eye for eye-fatigue or soreness, for freshness.
Preparations. No longer used internally.
Distilled extract of Witch Hazel, neat or dilute.
Hametum ointment (*Schwabe*).
Dr A. Vogel's Witch Hazel Salve. Witch Hazel 9; St John's Wort oil 5; Echinacea 3; Wheat Germ oil 2.
Pond's Extract: A proprietary cosmetic water distilled from the leaves.
Compress: 1oz leaves to 1 pint boiling water: soak pad of suitable material in the liquor and apply.
Injection: 1 part Tincture to 10 parts boiled water, for itching piles or vaginal irritation.
Shoots of the tree are used as divining rods for water and metals. GSL

WITHERING, Dr William. Pioneer of the medicinal use of the Foxglove (digitalis). Son of an apothecary. Born in Wellington, Shropshire 1741. Practised in Stafford and Birmingham. Published "An Account of the Foxglove and some of its Medicinal Uses" in 1785 after being converted to use of the plant by an old woman herbalist he found using it successfully for heart failure.

WOMB. Uterus. A pear-shaped organ, about 7.5cm long, located between the female rectum and bladder, in which the developing foetus is nourished. The endometrium (inner lining of cells) responds to various hormones secreted by endocrine glands which govern the menstrual cycle. Two oviducts (fallopian tubes) rise from its upper surface and communicate with the ovaries. The neck of the womb (cervix) connects with the vagina. A number of gynaecological disorders may arise, for which the appropriate entry should be consulted.
See: AMENORRHOEA, DYSMENORRHOEA, ENDOMETRITIS, ENDOMETRIOSIS, FIBROIDS, HYSTERECTOMY, LEUCORRHOEA, MENORRHAGIA, METRORRHAGIA, OVARIES, PROLAPSE, MENSTRUATION.

WOOD SAGE. Garlic sage. *Teucrium scorodonia L. German*: Wald Gamander. *French*: Ambroise. *Italian*: Camendrio salvatico. Dried herb.
Constituents: flavonoids, diterpenes, iridoids.
Action. Antirheumatic, astringent tonic, diaphoretic, febrifuge, emmenagogue, antiseptic.
Uses. Early stages of fever, influenza, rheumatic fever, chest infections. Delayed menstruation.
External: a cleansing wash for open discharging sores, boils, ulcers and suppurating wounds.
Preparations. Average dose, 2-4 grams or fluid equivalent, thrice daily.
Tea: half-1 teaspoon to each cup boiling water; infuse 15 minutes; dose, half-1 cup.
Liquid Extract BHP (1983): 1:1 in 25 per cent alcohol; dose, 2-4ml (30-60 drops) in water. GSL

WOODRUFF. Sweet Woodruff. *Asperula odorata L.* Herb.
Constituents: anthraquinones, flavonoids, iridoids, nicotinic acid, tannins.
Action. Diuretic, carminative, digestive tonic, anti-inflammatory, anti-migraine.
Uses. Migraine. Congested liver and to support a weak stomach. One of the national domestic teas drunk before the importation of colonial teas into Britain. Contains coumarin, an anticoagulant, large doses of which may cause giddiness and confusion. To promote sleep. Varicose veins. Phlebitis.
Preparation. *Tea*: 1 teaspoon herb to each cup boiling water; infuse 5-10 minutes; cup morning and evening.

WORMS. Several types of worms live in the human intestines and other body tissues. They are of three types: roundworms (nematoda), tapeworms (cestoda), and flukes (trematoda). In the intestine worms are the cause of feeble absorption of nutrients and dispose to anaemia.
See: ROUNDWORMS, TAPEWORMS, FLUKES.
Nearest known preventative – Garlic.

WORMWOOD. *Artemisia absinthum L. French*: Absinthe alvine. *German*: Wermut. *Italian*: Assenzio. *Indian*: Mastaru. *Sanskrit*: Indhana. *Russian*: Polin. Dried leaves and tops.
Constituents: phenolic acids, volatile oil, sesquiterpene lactones.
Action. Digestive, mental, stomach, bile and gastric juice stimulant. Antiparasitic, anthelmintic, anti-inflammatory, aromatic tonic bitter, carminative, choleretic. Immune enhancer.
Uses. Feeble digestion, liver and gall bladder congestion with yellow tinge of skin and sclera of eyes (jaundice). Depression of liver origin, foul breath, lack of appetite, nausea, vomiting. To promote stomach acid production in the elderly. Abnormal absence of periods. Benzodiazepine addiction – to assist withdrawal. Travel sickness, before a journey. Paracelsus advised drops of Oil of Wormwood in honey as a diuretic and to expel wind. Used to make "absinthe" historical drink.
Worms: to expel – strong tea injected into rectum by enema.
Preparations. Properties deteriorate on application of heat. Average dose, 1-2 grams or fluid

equivalent. Thrice daily.
Tea: 1 teaspoon to each cup cold water steeped overnight and drunk in the morning.
Liquid Extract BHP (1983): 1:1 in 25 per cent alcohol. Dose 1-2ml, in water.
Tincture: 1:10 in 45 per cent alcohol. Dose: 1 teaspoon (5ml) thrice daily.
For worms: single dose (5-10ml) much diluted, taken on empty stomach. Repeat fortnightly. (*Hein H. Zeylstra, FNIMH*)
Powder: 250mg. (One 00 capsule or one-sixth teaspoon).
Medicinal wine (*Russia*): 1 pint Vodka to which is added 5 to 10 Wormwood sprigs and left to steep for 3 days, shake daily, strain; dose – half-1 wineglass once or twice daily for rheumatism, travel sickness or as a tonic.
Vermouth: pleasant way of taking Wormwood. Sweet or dry, the base of all true Vermouth is the grape with the addition of Wormwood according to ancient formulae.
Compress: suitable material immersed in hot infusion (1oz to 1 pint boiling water) wrung-out, and applied to muscles for rheumatic pain.
Contra-indications: large doses, high blood pressure, pregnancy, heart failure. Alcohol preparations should not be taken over a long period of time. GSL

WORMWOOD, SWEET. Sweet Annie. *Artemisia annua*. Traditional Chinese medicine, Qinghaosu, for malaria.

WOUNDS. A wound is a disruption of tissues in any part of the body due to injury. A contusion is bruising of soft tissues beneath the skin, with pain and swelling. A haematoma is where a local extravasation of blood occurs. A laceration is a ragged torn wound. From severe wounds there is always the possibility of collapse from shock. Internal treatment assists recovery.
Alternatives. Internal. Comfrey is a demulcent-astringent-vulnerary which promotes cell proliferation and granulation of tissue, especially wounds with broken bones. Equal parts Comfrey root and Horsetail form a powerful healing combination. Also used as a compress.
Marigold (Calendula) for cuts, lacerations and to arrest bleeding. Also as a compress.
St John's Wort (Hypericum). Injuries to areas rich in nerves, i.e. finger tips, toes Shock. Protection against tetanus.
Chamomile tea. Shock. Also to cleanse. 10-20 flowers to each cup boiling water.
Infected purulent wounds: Echinacea, Goldenseal or Myrrh.
First aid antiseptics and cleansers. Mashed Garlic, Witch Hazel water, Irish Moss, Plantain juice, Houseleek juice, Tincture Myrrh, Tincture Goldenseal.
Topical. Dehydration delays wound healing.
Slippery Elm poultice: moisten and apply for cuts and wounds.
To staunch flow of blood. See: BLEEDING.
Wounds that refuse to heal. Combine tinctures: Echinacea 2; Fringe Tree 1; Horsetail 1. Two teaspoons in water thrice daily. Edgar Cayce: "apply soft pad of cloth saturated with Castor oil overnight; for a few nights, and keep in place with an elastic bandage".
Pain or discomfort from scar formation. Apply Castor oil.
Gunshot wounds. Equal parts, tinctures, Echinacea and Myrrh. 30-60 drops every 3 hours. (*World War 1*)
Wine. The healing effect of wine should not be overlooked. All wines are antiseptic.
Vitamins. A. B6, B12, PABA, E. K.
Minerals. Magnesium, Zinc.

WRINKLES. Furrows between folds of skin due to loss of subcutaneous fat. May be caused by emaciating illness or age. They first appear on the face around the eyes (crow's feet) and on the forehead. A recently discovered cause is smoking which wrinkles the skin ten years sooner than that of non-smokers because nicotine constricts blood vessels near the skin-surface. This makes it difficult for blood to convey nourishment to the skin cells and carry away wastes.
Alternatives. *Massage lotion*. 3 teaspoons each: oils of Almond, Soya and Wheatgerm. Add 3 drops oil Galbanum. Light massage followed by a warm compress. Calendula moisturiser. St John's Wort. Borage oil.
Seaweed baths, to retard ageing of the skin.
Evening Primrose oil. Claims made for its internal use for softening and firming dry skin of scraggy necks.
Diet. Buckwheat flour added to stews, casseroles and soups. Buckwheat contains rutin, helpful for reduction of varicose veins, arteriosclerosis and bad circulation – discourages wrinkles. Fish, such as herrings where the hair-like bones can be eaten as a source of calcium.
Supplements. Vitamins A and E. Cod Liver oil may restore loss of subcutaneous fat. Calcium. Zinc.

Do not expose unprotected skin to the sun for long periods. Protect the skin from the drying effect of central heating with moisturiser.

WRITER'S CRAMP. See: CRAMP.

XIA KU CAO. See: SELF-HEAL.

X-RAY BURNS. Castor oil. Aloe Vera juice or gel. Honey. See also: RADIATION SICKNESS.

XANTHELASMA. Formation of small yellow plaques containing "foam cells" in corners of the upper and lower eyelids.
Cause: presence of too much fat in the blood. Associated with diabetes and atheroma.
Treatment. Of limited success.
Internal. Poke root. Tablets, powders or tinctures.
Topical. Fresh Poke root juice. Aloe Vera gel.
Diet. "Continued over a number of years, a diet low in fats promotes the withdrawal of cholesterol from tissue deposits." (*The Lancet, 7741 Vol 1 (1972)*)

XERODERMA. An ichthyosis-like dry, rough skin which scales off.
Treatment. Alteratives (Burdock, Yellow Dock, Poke root etc) with attention to the thyroid gland.
Formula. Equal parts: Echinacea, Clivers, Kelp. Dose – Powders: 500mg (two 00 capsules or one-third teaspoon). Liquid Extracts: one 5ml teaspoon. Tinctures: two 5ml teaspoons. Thrice daily.
Practitioner. Tinctures. Formula. Stillingia sylvatica 2ml; Sambucus nigra 25ml; Echinacea angustifolia 20ml; Smilax 20ml; Lycopus europaeus 5ml; aqua to 100ml. Sig: 5ml (3i) aq cal pc.
Topical. Creams or lotions: Chickweed, Comfrey.
Diet. Gluten-free.
Supplements. Vitamin A, B-complex, B6, Kelp, Zinc.

XEROPHTHALMIA. Dryness of eyes. Reduced tear secretion caused by Vitamin A deficiency. May also be associated with hypothyroidism, lid paralysis, tumour or auto-immune disturbance. A component of Sjögren's syndrome. Common in Asian-developing countries. Mucous membranes lose their smooth surface and become keratinised. They then develop into a ready culture media for bacteria. Vitamin A deficiency weakens the body's defence system leading to respiratory disorders, etc. Also due to tear-duct obstruction by fistula of the lachrymal duct.

A common present-day cause is a deficiency of essential fatty acids (EFAs).
Alternatives. To promote tears: Angelica, Devil's Claw, Ginkgo, Yarrow, taken as teas, tablets or tinctures. Garlic – corm in salad, or 2 capsules at night. The act of peeling onions. Pumpkin seeds. Use of Cayenne pepper at table.
Evening Primrose capsules: one 500mg, morning and evening.
Topical. Castor oil eye drops.
Snuff. Use of powders of Lobelia or Blood root in nostril nearest affected eye.
Diet. Bilberries (fresh) as desired. High protein, low salt, oily fish, carrots and carrot juice, brewer's yeast. Polyunsaturated fats for EFAs: oils of Corn, Safflower and Sunflower.
Supplements. Daily. Vitamin A 7,500iu for immediate improvement; avoid large doses, especially in pregnancy. Vitamin B-complex, Vitamin B2 10mg, Vitamin B6 10mg, Vitamin C 400mg, Vitamin E 400iu. Beta carotene. Zinc 15mg.
At bedtime: 2 Garlic tablets/capsules.

YARROW. Milfoil. Nosebleed. *Achillea millefolium L. French*: Mille feuille. *German*: Schafgarbe. *Italian*: Achillea. *Russian*: Nastoika. *Part used*: whole herb. Once referrred to as the Englishman's quinine.
Constituents: flavonoids, volatile oil, sesquiterpene lactones, plant acids, alkaloids.
Action. Anti-inflammatory antispasmodic, *diaphoretic*, haemostatic, antiscorbutic, antipyretic, anti-rheumatic, choleretic, bitter, diuretic (cold tea), urinary antiseptic, hypotensive, carminative, peripheral vasodilator to open-up surface vessels enabling more blood to be circulated. Digestive tonic. A gentle relaxant like Chamomile. Emmenagogue.
Uses. Used internally and externally for a wide range of conditions. For temperature reduction in the early stages of fevers, influenza, the common cold. Dry skin and absent perspiration. Measles, chicken pox and feverish children's complaints. Haemorrhage of mucous surfaces, nosebleed. High blood pressure with thrombosis – cerebral, coronary or other BHP (1983). Biliary colic, diarrhoea, dysentery, stomach cramps (tea, with cold wet packs externally), obstructed menstruation, non-specific vaginal discharge (injection), to cleanse wounds (tea). An ingredient of Maria Treben's tea. Internal and external bleeding. For toning veins (varicose veins). To prevent blood clots.
Combinations. Nettles and Lime flowers for high blood pressure BHP (1983). With Elderflowers and Peppermint for colds and feverish conditions.
Preparations. *Tea*. One heaped teaspoon to each cup boiling water; infuse 10 minutes. 1 cup thrice daily (chronic); every 2 hours (acute).
Liquid extract BHC Vol 1. 1:1, 25 per cent ethanol. Dose: 1-2ml.
Tincture BHC Vol 1. 1:5, 25 per cent ethanol. Dose: 2-4ml.
Fresh juice from leaves and flowers. Half-1 teaspoon.
Poultice, fresh leaf, for cleansing wounds.
Reference: Martindale Extra Pharmacopoeia, 27th edition.
Contra-indication: large doses may cause headache.
Yarrow Bath: to lessen pain and inflammation. Handful dried or fresh flowers or leaves in 1 pint (500ml) boiling water; infuse 15 minutes: strain and add to bath water. GSL schedule 1

YAWNING. Cause is usually due to oxygen exhaustion or poor ventilation – Vitamin E, Honey, Cayenne Pepper, Cinnamon.
Due to over-eating: Calamus, Oil of Peppermint, Ginger.
Fatigue: Gentian root, Ginseng.
Where due to anxiety and fear Skullcap tea, Balm tea.
Due to chronic insomnia: Ladyslipper.
Supplement: Zinc.

YAWS. An infectious tropical disease caused by *Treponema pertenue*, a close relative of the bacteria that causes syphilis.
Treatment by herbal antibiotics.
See: SYPHILIS.

YELLOW DOCK. *Rumex crispus L. French*: Oseille d'Amérique. *German*: Amerikanischer sauerampfer. *Italian*: Acetosa d'America. *Spanish*: Bardana. *Chinese*: Chin-ch'iao-mai. *Part used*: root. Mineral rich.
Constituents: anthraquinone glycosides, oxalates, tannins.

Roots possess the property to attract iron from the soil which is transmuted into organic iron in the plant tissues. An older generation of herbalists sprinkled iron-filings on soil on which they grew Yellow Dock. The plant thus became "enriched" with the metal; extracts and tinctures made from its roots made invaluable blood-enrichers for the treatment of simple iron-deficiency anaemia. Also contains sulphur, of value in chronic skin disorders.
Action. General alterative tonic, bitter, laxative, lymphatic, cholagogue.
Uses. Disorders of the spleen, lymphatic glands, to promote the flow of bile in liver congestion and jaundice. Chronic dry itchy skin eruptions, boils, shingles, pruritus, rheumatism, ulceration of the mouth (mouthwash).
Popular combination. Equal parts Blue Flag root, Yellow Dock root and Dandelion. Tinctures, 10 drops each in 4oz water; dose, 1 teaspoon thrice daily for enlarged glands in children.
Preparations. Average dose, 2-4 grams or fluid equivalent, thrice daily.
Decoction. Half an ounce to 1 pint water simmered gently 20 minutes. Dose, half-1 cup.
Liquid Extract. One teaspoon in water.
Tincture BHP (1983). 1:5 in 45 per cent alcohol; dose, 1-2ml in water. GSL

YELLOW FEVER. An acute tropical virus infection transmitted by the mosquito: *aedes aegypti*. Common in South America and Africa. Incubation: 3-5 days. A notifiable disease.
Symptoms. Sudden attack of shivering with high fever but patient feels cold and chilly. Painful bones and head, vomiting, sensitivity to bright lights, confusion. After 4 days, temperature returns to normal with appearance of recovery. However, fever returns with jaundice and blood appears in urine, from the mouth and under the skin.
Prognosis: liver and kidney failure; heart and brain to lesser extent. Coma.
Treatment. Intravenous fluids to combat dehydration. Abundant diaphoretic herb teas open pores of the skin inducing a copious perspiration which serves to eliminate toxins and reduce temperature: Yarrow, Boneset, Catnep or others as available.

Appropriate: Anti-nauseants, Febrifuges, Hepatics, Diuretics. Skilled medical and nursing attention necessary.
Traditional: Orange leaf tea (improved by addition of few grains Cayenne pepper or drops of Tincture Capsicum).
Formula: supportive to physician's primary treatment. Equal parts: Lobelia, Wahoo and Ginger. Dose: Powders: 750mg. Liquid extracts: 1-2 teaspoons. Tinctures: 1-3 teaspoons. Every 2 hours in water or honey.
Enema: to remove toxic material and relieve delirium. 2 handfuls Bay leaves to 1 quart (3 and a half litres) boiling water; infuse until warm; inject every 2-3 days.
Diet. No food except Slippery Elm gruel until appetite returns. Abundant Vitamin C drinks – orange and citrus fruits.

Treatment by a general medical practitioner or infectious diseases specialist.

YELLOW PARILLA. Moonseed. Yellow Sarsaparilla. *Menispermum canadense L. Part used*: root.
Constituents: menispine, berberine, tannin, resin.
Action. Powerful alterative and outstanding lymphatic. Stomachic, diuretic, bitter tonic, laxative, diaphoretic. Action similar to Sarsaparilla. When the latter proves ineffective, invariably Yellow Parilla will take over and relieve – possibly cure.
Preparations. Thrice daily.
Powdered root: quarter of a teaspoon in water or honey.
Liquid Extract: 30-60 drops in water.

YERBA SANTA. Gum bush. *Eriodictyon glutinosum*, Benth. *Part used*: leaves.
Constituents: flavonoids, resin.
Action. Expectorant, febrifuge, respiratory stimulant, tonic, aromatic, antispasmodic.
Uses. Coughs producing much sputum. Bronchial catarrh, bronchitis, asthma.
Preparations. *Liquid Extract*: dose, 2-4ml in water thrice daily.
Powdered leaves: quarter of a teaspoon in honey or mashed banana, thrice daily, or as prescribed for acute cases.
Poultice: for wounds, insect or animal bites; bruises.

YOGHURT. In milk which has been predigested by the yogurt culture milk sugar is broken down into lactic acid, thus it is more easily tolerated by those allergic to ordinary milk. Yogurt produces valuable B group vitamins in the intestines.

Professor Metchnikov, Russian biologist found a colony of Bulgarian people living to 100 years and who had eaten yogurt all their lives. He discovered the acid-making bacteria which he named *Lactobacillus bulgaricus*. A carton of natural yoghurt contains fewer calories and more protein than a glass of milk, which accounts for its popularity with weight-watchers.

Yoghurt has proved effective in controlling bacteria that causes dysentery, cholera and diarrhoea, and has helped fight staphylococci and streptococci by its antibiotic effects. It has proved effective for high blood pressure, lowering cholesterol levels, healing chronic internal and surface ulceration. Ethnic groups that eat yoghurt daily are said to be free of gastro-intestinal cancer. Yoghurt douches are used to treat women with vaginal and uterine conditions, it being given for anti-cancer effect. Healthy people take it for added vigour and vitality. For many people it is an important item of diet. Variations of flavour and content are made by mixing with orange, tomato, lemon and other fruit or vegetable juices.

YOHIMBE BARK. *Pausinystalia yohimbe* (K. Schum) Pierre. *Part used*: bark.
Constituents: yohimbine (indole alkaloid).
Action. Aphrodisiac.
Use. Sexual debility.
Preparation. *Liquid Extract*: dose, 2-4ml in water thrice daily.

Prescription by registered medical practitioner only.

YUCCA. *Yucca bacata; Yucca glauca; Yucca brevifolica*. Joshua tree. Soap tree. A source of natural soap used by the Navajo Indians for washing their hair and bodies.
Constituents: saponins, sarsasapogenin, similagenin and sapogenin which is similar to the Mexican Yam used to produce the progesterone hormone. Natural source of progesterone used in gynaecology for bleeding of the womb and menstrual disorders. Its steroidal saponins act as an anticoagulant to resolve clumping of blood cells.
Action. Cardiac stimulant, anti-inflammatory (rheumatism and arthritis), diuretic, cholagogue (saponins), blood purifier. Ability to shrink tumours.
Uses. Hormonal imbalance, varicose veins, acne (a hormone disturbance), ulcers of mouth and skin, to cleanse gall bladder.
Cataract: Navajo Indians used it with iodine to restore sight to blind animals.
Preparations. Tea. Liquid extract.

ZAM-BUK. *Active ingredients*: Eucalyptus oil 5 per cent, Camphor 1.8 per cent, Thyme oil 0.5 per cent, Colophony 2.5 per cent and Sassafras oil 0.65 per cent Healing antiseptic ointment.

ZERODERMA. See XERODERMA.

ZINC. Trace element essential at every stage of life from the cradle to the grave. Involved in the production of over 80 hormones. A necessary component in a number of enzyme systems that regulate metabolic activities in animals and plants. Specialisation of T-cells and metabolism of essential fatty acids. Linked with production of insulin.

Helps form enzymes that enable proteins to become 'building blocks' for new cells. Its effects include the healing of wounds, fertility, and stimulation of the immune system.

Deficiency. Delayed sexual maturity, infertility, foetal growth arrest, hyperactivity in children, loss of appetite, loss of sense of taste and smell, anorexia nervosa, loss of hair, inability of wounds to heal, frequent colds and infections, osteoporosis, acne, epileptic attack, white marks on finger nails, eczema, greasy skin, stretch marks, body odour, dwarfism. Mental ill-health. Zinc-deficient mothers suffer post-natal depression and have lactation difficulties. Child deformities have occurred with hypertrophy of mucous membranes of the gullet and with under-developed gonads.

Sources. Red meat, liver, dairy produce, egg yolk, herrings, shellfish (especially oysters), wholegrain flour, brewer's yeast, brown rice, beans, dried fruits, molasses, wheatgerm, onions, garlic, pumpkin seeds, sunflower seeds. Fenugreek seeds. A high protein diet is necessary to enhance the body's ability to utilise zinc. Citrus fruits increase, while wheaten products decrease absorption of zinc.

Notes. A diet low in essential fatty acids requires more zinc, as also would one high in processed fats: chips, pastry. A diet rich in Vitamins B6 and C requires less zinc. Coffee and alcohol inhibit absorption. The zinc content of diet depends chiefly upon the dietary protein content. Only 20 per cent of the mineral is absorbed by the average person.

Alcohol. Alcohol flushes zinc out of the liver into the urine.

RDA 15mg. 20mg (pregnant women). 25mg (nursing mothers).

ZOSTER, Herpes. See: HERPES.

LATIN/ENGLISH PLANT INDEX

. . . showing the standard botanical names of medicinal plants.

Latin	English
A	
Abies balsamea	Canada balsam
Acacia catechu (Willd)	Catechu, Black
Acacia senegal	Acacia gum
Achillea millefolium, L.	Yarrow, Milfoil
Aconitum napellus, L.	Aconite
Acorus calamus, L.	Sweet flag. Calamus
Adiantum capillus-veneris	Maidenhair Fern
Adonis vernalis, L.	Spring Adonis, Pheasant's eye
Aegle marmelos	Bael
Aesculus hippocastanum, L.	Horse Chestnut
Agrimonia eupatoria, L.	Agrimony, Cocklebur
Agropyron repens	Couchgrass
Ajuga reptans	Bugle
Alchemilla vulgaris, L.	Lady's Mantle
Aletris farinosa	Aletris
Alisma plantago	Water Plantain
Alkanna tinctoria	Alkanet
Allium cepa	Onion
Allium sativum, L.	Garlic
Allium ursinum, L.	Bear's Garlic
Aloe arborescens	Aloe
Aloe barbadensis	Aloe Vera
Aloe ferox. Aloe perryi	Cape Aloe
Aloysia eriphylla	Lemon Verbena
Alpinia officinarum (Hance)	Galangal
Alstonia constricta	Alstonia bark
Althaea rosea	Hollyhock
Althaea officinalis, L.	Marshmallow
Amaranthus hypochondriacus	Amaranth
Ammi visnaga, (L) Lam.	Khella, Visnag
Amygdala dulcis	Almond oil
Anacardium occidentale	Cashew tree fruit
Ananassa sativa	Pineapple juice
Anagallis arvensis	Pimpernel, Scarlet
Ananassa sativa	Bromelain
Anemone pulsatilla	Pulsatilla
Anethum graveolens, L.	Dill
Angelica archangelica, L.	Angelica (or Garden Angelica)
Angelica shkiokiana	Angelica, Japanese
Angelica sinensis	Dong Quai, Angelica, Chinese
Anthemis nobilis	Chamomile flowers, Roman, Garden or English Chamomile
Aphanes arvensis	Parsley Piert
Apium graveolens	Celery seed
Apocynum androsaemifolium	Bitter root
Apocynum cannabinum, L.	Indian Hemp, Canadian Hemp
Arachis hypogaea	Arachis
Aralia racemosa, L.	Spikenard
Arctium lappa	Burdock, Great Burdock
Arctostaphylos uva-ursi	(Common) Bearberry
Areca catechu, L.	Betelnut palm, Areca nut
Aristolochia clematitis	Birthwort
Aristolochia longa	Birthwort
Armoracia rusticana	Horseradish
Aristolochia serpentaria	Virginia Snake Root
Arnica montana, L.	Arnica, European Arnica
Artemisia abrotanum	Southernwood
Atemisia absinthium, L.	Wormwood
Artemisia annua	Wormwood, Sweet
Artemisia tridentata	Sagebrush
Artemisia vulgaris, L.	Mugwort
Asarum europaeum, L.	(European) Wild Ginger
Asclepias tuberosa	Pleurisy Root
Asclepias, L.	Milkweed genus
Asclepias tuberosa, L.	Butterfly weed
Aspalathus linearis	Rooibosch Tea
Asparagus officinalis	Asparagus
Asperula odorata, L.	Sweet Woodruff
Asplidosperma quebracho	Quebracho
Astragalus gummifer	Tragacanth
Astragalus membranaceus	Huang Qi
Atropa belladonna, L.	Belladonna, Deadly Nightshade
Avena sativa	Groats, Oats
Azadirachta indica	Neem
B	
Bamboo	See: Tabishin
Ballota nigra	Horehound, Black
Bambousa arundinacea	Bamboo
Baptisia tinctoria	Wild Indigo
Barosma betulina	Buchu
Bearberry	See: Arctostaphylos, Uva Ursi
Bellis perennis	Daisy
Berberis aquifolium	Mountain Grape
Berberis vulgaris, L.	(European or Common) Bearberry
Beta vulgaris	Beetroot
Betonica officinalis	Betony
Betula pendula, Roth	Birch
Bidens tripartita	Burr Marigold
Birch, European	See: Silver Birch
Bisr Khil	Khil plant
Borago officinalis, L.	Borage
Boswellia carteri	Olibanum
Boswellia serrata	Boswellia

Latin	English
Boswellia thurifera	Frankincense
Brassica alba, Brassica nigra	Mustard, Common
Brassica oleracea	Winter Cabbage
Bryonia alba	Bryony, White
Bryonia dioica, Jacq.	Red Bryony, Wild Hop
C	
Calaminta ascendens	Calamint
Calendula officinalis, L.	Marigold, Pot Marigold
Calluna vulgaris	Heather flowers
Camelia sinensis	Tea
Camellia thea	Green Tea
Capsella bursa-pastoris	Shepherd's Purse
Capsicum	Chillies
Capsicum annuum, L.	Green Pepper, Chili Pepper
Capsicum minimum (Roxb)	Cayenne
Carica papays, L.	Papaya
Carthamus tinctorius	Safflower
Carum carvi, L.	Caraway
Cassia angustifolia	Senna Pods
Cassia augustifolia, Vahl	(Alexandrian) Senna
Cassia senna	Senna Leaf
Castanea sativa, Mill.	Spanish or European Chestnut
Castor oil	See: Palma Christi
Catharanthus roseus	Periwinkle
Caulophyllum thalictroides	Blue Cohosh
Cayenne	See: Capsicum
Ceanothus americanus, L.	New Jersey tea, Redroot
Centaurium Erythraea	Centuary
Centaurium umbellatum	Centuary
Centella asiatica	Gotu Kola
Cephaelis ipecacuanha	Ipecac, Ipecacuanha
Ceratonia siliqua	Carob bean
Cetraria islandica	Iceland Moss
Chamaelirium luteum	(Gray) Helonias
Chelidonium majus, L.	Celandine, Celandine Poppy
Chelone glabra	Balmony
Chenopodium album	Fat Hen
Chenopodium elidum	Arrach
Chervil	See: Sweet Cicely
Chimaphila umbellata	Pipsissewa
Chionanthus virginicus, L.	Fringe Tree
Chondrus crispus	Irish Moss
Chrysanthemum vulgare	(Common) Tansy
Chyamopsis tetragonobulus	Guar Gum
Cichorium intybus, L.	Chicory, Succory
Cimicifuga racemosa	Black Cohosh, Black Snakeroot
Cinchona	See: Peruvian bark
Cinchona succirubra, Pav.	Yellowbark Cinchona
Cinnamomum camphora	Camphor
Cinnamomum cassia	Cinnamon, Chinese
Cinnamomum zeylanicum	Cinnamon
Citrus aurantium, L.	Bitter Orange, Sour Orange
Citrus limonum	Lemon
Claviceps purpurea	Ergot
Cnicus benedictus, L.	Blessed Thistle
Cocillana	See: Guarea
Cochlearia officinalis, L.	Scurvy grass, Spoonwort
Cocos nucifera	Coconut oil
Coffee arabica, L.	Coffee
Cola	See: Kola nuts
Cola acuminata	Cola
Colchicum autumnale, L.	Autumn Crocus, Meadow Saffron
Collinsonia canadensis	Stone Root
Commiphora molmol	Myrrh
Commiphora mukul	Gugulon
Conium maculatum	Hemlock
Convallaria majalis, L.	Lily-of-the-Valley
Copaifera langsdorffi	Copaiba
Corydalis cava	Corydalis
Corallorhiza odontorhiza	Crawley Root
Coriandrum sativum	Coriander
Crataegus oxyacantha, L.	(English) Hawthorn
Crataegus monogyna, Jacq.	(English) Hawthorn
Crocus sativus	Saffron
Cucumis sativus	Cucumber
Cucurbita peop. L.	Pumpkin, Squash
Cuminum cyminum	Cummin
Cupressus sempervirens	Cypress
Curcuma longa, L.	Turmeric
Cydonia oblonga, Mill	Quince
Cymbopogon winterianus	Citronella
Cynara scolymus, L.	(Globe) Artichoke
Cynoglossum officinale, L.	Hound's Tongue
Cypripedium pubescens	Lady's Slipper
Cytisus scoparius, (L), Link	(Scotch) Broom
D	
Datura stramonium	Stramonium, Thornapple, Jimsonweed
Daucus carota	Wild Carrot
Devil's Claw	See: Harpagophytum
Dicentra cucullaria	Turkey Corn
Digitalis purpurea, L.	Foxglove
Digitalis lanata J.F. Ehrh	Grecian Foxglove
Di-huang (Chinese)	Rehmannia Root
Dioscorea villosa, L.	(Wild) Yam
Dorema ammoniacum	Ammoniacum
Drosera rotundifolia, L.	Sundew
Dryopteris fillix-mas	Male Fern

Latin	English
E	
Echinacea angustifolia, DC.	Purple Coneflower
Eleutherococcus senticosis	Ginseng, Siberian
Elettaria cardamomum	Cardamom seeds
Ephedra sinica, Stapf	Ephedra, Joint Pine. Ma-huang
Epilobium angustifolium	Rosebay Willow-Herb
Equisetum arvense	Horsetail
Erigeron canadensis, L.	Fleabane, Horseweed
Eriodictyon glutinosum	Yerba Santa
Eryngium maritimum	Sea Holly
Erythroxylum coca, Lam.	Coca
Eschscholzia californica	California Poppy
Eucalyptus globulus, Labill	Eucalyptus, Blue Gum (tree)
Eugenia caryophyllus	Cloves
Eugenia jambolana	Jambul
Euonymous atropurpureus	Wahoo Bark
Eupatorium cannabinum, L.	Hemp Agrimony
Eupatorium perfoliatum	Boneset
Euphorbia hirta	Euphorbia
Eupatorium purpureum	Gravel Root
Euphrasia officinalis	Eyebright
F	
Fagopyrum esculentum	Buckwheat
Ferula asa-foetida	Asafoetida
Ferula gummosa	Galbanum
Ferula sumful	Sumbul
Filipendula ulmaria	Meadowsweet
Foeniculum vulgare, Mill.	Fennel
Foxglove	See: Digitalis
Frangaria vesca, L.	(Woodland) Strawberry
Frangula alnus	Frangula Bark
Frangula alnus, Mill.	Alder Buckthorn
Frangula bark	See: Buckthorn
Fraxinus excelsior	Ash
French bean	See: Dwarf Bean
Fucus vesiculosis, L.	Bladderwrack
Fumaria officinalis, L.	Fumitory, Earth Smoke
G	
Galega officinalis, L.	(European) Goat's Rue
Galipea officinalis Han.	Angostura Bark
Galium aparine	Clivers
Galium verum, L.	Bedstraw, Our Lady's Bedstraw
Ganoderma lucidum	Reishi Mushroom
Gaultheria procumbens, L.	Wintergreen, Teaberry, Checkerberry
Gelidium amansii	Agar Agar
Gelsemium sempervirens	Yellow Jessamine

Latin	English
Gentiana lutea, L.	Yellow Gentian, Drug Gentian
Geranium maculatum	Cranesbill, American
Geranium robertianum, L.	Herb Robert
Geum urbanum, L.	Avens, Herb Bennet
Ginkgo biloba, L.	Ginkgo, Maidenhair
Glycyrrhiza Glabra. L.	Liquorice
Gossypium herbaceum	Cotton root
Gotu Kola	Indian Pennywort
Gnaphalium uliginosum	Cudweed, Marsh
Gratiola officinalis, L.	Hedge Hyssop
Grindelia camporum	Grindelia
Guaiacum officinale, L.	Lignum Vitae
Guarea rusbyi	Cocilla
H	
Haematoxylon campechianum	Logwood
Hamamelis virginiana, L.	Witch Hazel
Harpagophytum procumbens, DC	Devil's Claw
Hedera helix, L.	Ivy
Helianthus annuus	Sunflower Seeds
Helleborus niger	Christmas Rose
Helonias	Unicorn Root, False
Heracleum brunonis	Cow Parsley, Himalayan
Herniaria glabra, L.	Rupturewort
Hieracium pilosella	Mouse Ear
Hordeum distichon	Barley
Huang Qi	Astragalus
Humulus lupulis, L.	(Common) Hop
Hydnocarpus kurzii	Chaulmoogra
Hydrangea arborescens	Hydrangea
Hydrastis canadensis, L.	Goldenseal
Hyoscyamus niger, L.	Henbane, Hyoscyamus
Hypericum perforatum	Hypericum, St John's Wort
Hyssopus officinalis	Hyssop
I	
Ilex aquifolium	Holly
Ilex paraguariensis, St. Hil	Paraguay Tea, Mate
Inula helenium, L.	Elecampane, Scabwort
Iris florentina	Orris Root
Iris versicolor	Blue Flag Root
J	
Jasminum officinale	Jasmine
Jateorhiza palmata	Calumba
Juglans cinera	Butternut
Juglans regia, L.	Walnut (English)
Juniperus brasiliens	Catuaba
Juniperus communis, L.	(Common) Juniper
K	
Krameria triandra	Krameria, Rhatany

Latin	English
L	
Lactuca virosa	Wild Lettuce
Lady's Slipper	See: Cypripedium. Valerian, American
Lamium album, L.	White Deadnettle
Lapacho tree	Ipe Roxo Tree, Pacho Tea, Tabebuia Tree
Larrea divaricata	Chaparral
Laurus nobilis, L.	Bay
Lavandula angustifolia, Mill.	Lavender
Lawsonia alba	Henna
Ledum latifolium	Labrador Tea
Lentinus edodes	Shittake Mushroom
Leonurus cardiaca, L.	Motherwort (Common)
Levisticum officinale	Lovage
Ligustrum lucidum	Nu Zhen Zi
Linaria vulgaris	Toadflax
Linum usitatissimum, L.	Flax, Linseed
Liquidambar orientalis	Storax
Liriodendron tulipifera	Tulip Tree
Liriosma ovata	Muira-Puama
Lithospermum officinale	Gromwell
Lobelia inflata, L.	Indian Tobacco, Lobelia
Lycopodium clavatum	Club Moss
Lycopus Europaeus	Gipsywort
Lycopus virginicus, L.	Bugleweed
M	
Maeso lanceolata	Orange berries
Malpighia punicifolia	Acerola
Malva sylvestris, L.	High Mallow, Common Mallow
Mandragora officinalis, L.	Mandrake
Maranta arundinacea	Arrowroot
Marigold	Calendula
Marrubium vulgare, L.	Horehound
Marsdenia condurango	Condurango
Matricaria chamomilla, L.	German or Wild Chamomile
Medicago sativa	Alfalfa
Melaleuca alternifolia	Tea Tree Oil
Melaleuca leucadendron	Cajuput
Melilotus officinalis	Melilot
Melissa officinalis, L.	Balm
Menispermum canadensis	Yellow Parilla
Mentha piperita, L.	Peppermint
Mentha pulegium	Pennyroyal
Mentha viridis	Spearmint
Menyanthes trifoliata, L.	Buckbean, Marsh Trefoil, Bogbean
Mitchella repens	Squaw Vine
Momordica charantia	Karela, Bitter Melon
Monarda didyma, L.	Oswego tea, Bergamot
Morus	Mulberry genus
Myrica cerifera	Bayberry
Myristica fragrans (Houtt)	Mace
Myristica fragrans (Houtt)	Nutmeg
Myroxylon balsamum	Tolu Balsam
N	
Nasturtium officinale	Watercress
Nelumbo nucifera	Lotus
Nepeta cataria	Catmint
Nepeta hederacea	Ground Ivy
Nerium oleander, L.	Oleander
New Jersey tea	Red Root
Nymphaea odorata	White Pond Lily
O	
Oats	Avena sativa
Ocimum basilicum	Basil
Oenothera biennis	Evening Primrose
Olea europaea, L.	Olive
Ononis spinosa, L.	Restharrow, Prickly
Ophioglossom vulgatum	Adder's Tongue
Opuntia	Cactus
Origanum vulgare, L.	(Wild) Marjoram, Oregano
Ornithogalum umbellatum	Star of Bethlehem
Orthosiphon stamineus	Java Tea
P	
Paeonia mascula, L.	Peony
Panax quinquafolius, L.	Ginseng, American
Panax ginseng, C.A. Mey	Ginseng, Asiatic
Papaver somniferum, L.	Opium Poppy
Papaya	Paw Paw
Para toda	Suma
Parietaria diffusa	Pellitory of the Wall
Passiflora incarnata, L.	Wild Passionflower, Maypop
Paullinia cupana	Guarana
Pausinystalia yohimbe	Yohimbe Bark
Petasites hybridus	Butterbur, Sweet Coltsfoot
Petroselinum crispum	Parsley
Peucedanum ostruthium	Masterwort, Hogfennel
Peumus boldus, Mol	Boldo
Pfaffia paniculata	Pfaffa
Phaseolus vulgaris, L.	Bean (Common), Haricot, Kidney
Phyllitis scolopendrium	Hart's Tongue
Physostigma venenosum	Calabar Bean
Phytolacca americana, L.	Poke Root
Picrasma excelsa	Quassia
Pilocarpus pennatifolius	Jaborandi
Pimento officinalis	Allspice
Pimpinella anisum, L.	Aniseed, Anise
Pimpinella saxifraga, L.	Burnet saxifrage
Pinus sylvestris, L.	Scot's Pine
Piper angustifolium	Matico
Piper cubeba	Cubebs

Latin	English
Piper methysticum, G. Forst	Kava, Kava-Kava
Piscidia erythrina	Jamaica Dogwood
Plantago major	Plantain
Plantago ovata	Ispaghula Seeds (Pale)
Plantago psyllium, L.	Psyllium
Podophyllum peltatum, L.	Mayapple. Mandrake, American
Polemonium reptans	Abscess root
Polygala senega, L.	Senega
Polygonum aviculare	Knotgrass
Polygonum bistorta	Bistort
Polygonum hydropiper, L.	Water Pepper
Polygonum multiflorum	He Shou Wu
Polypodium vulgare, L.	Polypody, Sweet Fern
Polymnia uvedalia	Bearsfoot, American
Populus gileadensis	Balm of Gilead
Populus tremuloides	White Poplar Bark
Portulaca oleracea	Purslane, Garden
Potentilla anserina	Silverweed
Potentilla erecta	Tormentil
Primula veris, L.	Cowslip, Oxlip
Primula vulgaris	Primrose
Prunella vulgaris	Self-Heal
Prunus armeniaca	Apricot
Prunus cerasus	Sour Cherry
Prunus domestica	Prune
Prunus dulcis var.amara	Bitter Almond
Prunus persica	Peach Tree
Prunus serotina	Wild Cherry Bark
Pulmonaria officinalis, L.	Lungwort
Pulsatilla vulgaris, Mill	Pulsatilla
Punica granatum	Pomegranate
Q	
Quaiacum officinale	Lignum vitae
Quercus robur, L.	Oak
Quillaja saponaria	Quillaia Bark
R	
Ranunculus ficaria	Pilewort
Raphanus sativus	Black Radish
Rauvolfia serpentina	Indian Snakeroot
Rhamnus frangula, L.	Frangula Bark
Rhamnus purshiana, DC	Cascara Sagrada
Rheum palmatum, L.	Rhubarb, Turkey
Rheum rhaponticum	Rhubarb, Garden
Rhus aromatica	Sumach, Sweet
Ribes nigrum, L.	Black Currant
Ricinus communis, L.	Castor Oil Plant
Rooibosch tea	Red Bush Tea
Rosa canina L.	Dog Rose, Rose Hips
Rosa gallica, Rosa Damascena, Rosa centifolia	Rose
Rosmarinus officinalis, L.	Rosemary
Rubia tinctorum L.	Madder
Rubus fruticosus, L.	Blackberry, Bramble
Rubus idaeus	Raspberry

Latin	English
Rumex crispus, L.	Yellow Dock
Ruscus aculeatus	Butcher's Broom
Ruta graveolens, L.	Rue
S	
Salix alba, L.	White Willow
Salix nigra	Willow, Black
Salvia officinalis	Sage
Salvia sclarea	Clary
Sambucus ebulus, L.	Dwarf Elder
Sambucus nigra, L.	Elder
Sanguinaria canadensis, L.	Bloodroot
Sanguisorba officinalis	Burnet, Greater
Sanicula europaea, L.	Sanicle
Santalum album	Sandalwood
Saponaria officinalis, L.	Soapwort, Bouncing Bet
Sarothamnus scoparius	Broom
Sassafras albidum	Sassafras
Satureja hortensis	Summer Savoury
Schisandra sinensis	Schisandra
Scrophularia nodosa	Figwort
Scutellaria lateriflora	Skullcap
Selenicereus grandiflorus	Cactus, Night-blooming Cereus
Sempervivum tectorum	Houseleek
Senecio aureus	Life Root
Senecio jacobaea	Ragwort
Senecio maritimus	Cineraria maritima
Serenoa serrulata	Saw Palmetto
Sesamum indicum	Sesame Seeds
Silybum marianum	Milk Thistle
Simmondsia chinensis	Jojoba
Smilax officinalis	Sarsaparilla
Solanum dulcamara	Bittersweet
Solanum tuberosum	Potato
Solidago virgaurea	Goldenrod
Spigelia marilandica	Pinkroot
Spiranthes autumnalis	Lady's Tresses
Stillingia sylvatica	Queen's Delight
Strophanthus kombe	Strophanthus
Strychnos nux-vomica	Nux-vomica
Styrax benzoin	Benzoin, Friar's Balsam
Swertia chirata	Chirata
Symphytum officinale	Comfrey
Symplocarpus foetidus	Skunk Cabbage
T	
Tamarindus indica	Tamarinds
Tamarix mannifera	Manna
Tamus communis	Bryony, Black
Tanacetum parthenium	Feverfew
Taraxacum officinale	Dandelion
Teucrium chamaedrys, L.	Germander
Teucrium scorodonia	Wood Sage
Theobroma cacae	Cocoa
Thuja occidentalis	Arbor-vitae
Thymus serpyllum	Thyme, Wild
Thymus vulgaris, L.	Thyme, Garden

Latin	English
Tilia cordata, Mil	Lime flowers
Toxicodendron radicans	Rhus Toxicodendron
Trifolium pratense	Red Clover
Trigonella foenum-graecum, L.	Fenugreek
Trillium erectum	Beth Root
Tropaeolum majus, L.	Common or Garden Nasturtium
Tsuga canadensis	Pinus Bark
Turnera diffusa, Wild	Damiana, Curzon
Tussilago farfara, L.	Coltsfoot
U	
Ulmus fulva	Slippery Elm
Umbilicus rupestris	Pennywort
Uncaria gambier (Robx)	Catechu, Pale
Urginea maritima	Squill
Urtica dioica/Urtica urens, L.	Nettles
V	
Vaccinium myrtillus, L.	Bilberry, Whortleberry
Vaccinium oxycoccos	Cranberries
Valeriana officinalis, L.	Valerian
Verbascum thapsus	Mullein
Verbene officinalis	Vervain
Veronica officinalis	Speedwell
Veronicastrum virginicum	Black Root
Viburnum opulus	Cramp Bark
Viburnum prunifolium, L.	Black Haw, Stagbush
Vinca, L.	Periwinkle genus
Viola odorata, L.	English or Sweet Violet
Viola tricolor	Heartsease
Viscum album, L.	Mistletoe
Vitex agnus-castus, L.	Agnus Castus
Vitis vinifera, L.	Grape, Vine, Red Vine
Vivia faba	Broad Beans
W	
Wahoo	Euonymus
Y	
Yucca bacata, Yucca glauca, Yucca brevifolica	Yucca
Z	
Zanthoxylum clavaherculis	Prickly Ash
Zea mays	Corn Silk
Zingiber officinale, Roscoe	Ginger

BIBLIOGRAPHY

BEACH, Wooster. *The British and American Reformed Practice of Medicine,* (London and Birmingham, 1859).

BIGELOW, Jacob. *American Medical Botany.* 3 volumes, (Boston, 1817-1820).

BRITISH JOURNAL OF PHYTOTHERAPY. See entry.

BUCHAN, William. *Domestic Medicine*, or, a treatise on the prevention and cure of disease by regimen and simple medicine, (1797).

BUCKMAN, D.D. *Herbal Medicine: The Natural way to Get Well and Stay Well*, (1983). Rider, London, in association with The Herb Society. How to make herbal medicine, collection and storage of herbs, suppliers, etc.

BUDGE, Earnest Wallis. *The Divine Origin of the Craft of the Herbalist*, (London, 1928). The Society of Herbalists. Origins of herbal medicine.

COFFIN, Albert. *A Botanic Guide to Health*, (London, 1866). *Botanical Journal and Medical Reformer*, (London, 1849-1859).

COOK, William H. Physician. *Woman's Herbal Book of Health*. One-time textbook for the practitioner and guide for wife, mother and nurse, (Southport, UK, 1866). *Science and Practice of Medicine*, (London, 1916).

CULPEPER, Nicholas. *The Complete Herbal*. Of historical interest.

FOX, William. *The Working Man's Model Family Botanic Guide*, (Sheffield, 1904). Still popular among the British public.

GERARD, John. *The Herbal, or General History of Plants*. The complete 1633 edition as revised and enlarged by Thomas Johnson, (Dover Publications Inc., New York). Herbal classic.

GRACE MAGAZINE. Quarterly. Healing by natural methods. Research abstracts on herbal and holistic subjects. New developments in research and alternative/complementary medicine. Positive lifestyle, spiritual refreshment. Grace Publishers, Mulberry Court, Stour Road, Christchurch, Dorset BH23 1PS.

GREENFILES. Quarterly newsletter of research abstracts for the herbal practitioner. Recent developments in alternative medicine. Materia medica, nutrition, pathology, therapeutics, news items. Brenda Cooke and Pat Jones, 138 Oak Tree Lane, Mansfield, Notts NG18 3HR.

GRIEVE, Mrs M, FRHS. *A Modern Herbal* – edited by Hilda Leyel – (London, 1931). First complete encyclopedia to appear since the days of Culpeper. Over 1,000 English and American plants, description and medical uses.

GRIGGS, Barbara. *Green Pharmacy:* a history of herbal medicine, (1981). Story of herbalism down the ages. *The Home Herbal:* a handbook of simple remedies, (London, 1983).

HERBALGRAM. Educational Publication of the American Botanical Council and the Herb Research Foundation. PO Box 201660, Austin Texas 78720-1660, USA. Tel: 512/331-8868. A non-profit research organisation directed by leading medicinal plant experts. Latest research, legal information, market updates, literature reviews. Invaluable resource for the professional and layperson.

HOFFMANN, David. Exponent of Holistic Herbalism. *The Holistic Herbal*, Findhorn Press (1983). *The Herb User's Guide:* basic skills of Medical Herbalism, (Thorsons, 1987).

HOOL, Richard, Lawrence. Member, National Institute of Medical Herbalists, and of the American Physio-Medical Association; co-editor, *The Herb Doctor. British Wild Herbs and Common Plants, Their Uses in Medicine*, (1924); abridged from *The Standard Guide to Non-Poisonous Herbal Medicine* (edited by W.H. Webb).

Hool prescribed herbal treatment for typhoid fever which enjoyed wide acceptance at the beginning of the 20th century.

HUTCHENS, Alma R. *Indian Herbology of North America*, (Ontario, 1974). Canadian herbalism. Commended for the serious student.

HYATT, Richard. *Chinese Herbal Medicine:* ancient art and modern science, (1978). Practice of Chinese herbal Medicine, with description of plants from the Chinese Pharmacopoeia.

JOURNAL OF ALTERNATIVE AND COMPLEMENTARY MEDICINE (JACM). An independent monthly magazine for alternative practitioners. Contributions cover a wide range of unorthodox therapies and promote the holistic concept of disease. Green Library, Homewood House, Guildford Road, Chertsey, Surrey KT16 0QA.

KEITH, Melville C. MD (USA). Powerful protagonist of the Thomsonian system of herbal medicine. *Domestic Practice and Botanic Handbook*, (USA, 1901).

KLOSS, Jethro (1863-1946). Consulting Medical Herbalist of 40 years experience.

Converted to herbal medicine after being given up by his physicians of a serious nervous disorder, healing himself with herbs and natural diet. *Back to Eden*: (USA, 1939). Popular with the American public.

KOURENNOFF, Paul, M. *Russian Folk Medicine*; translated by George St George, 1970. 350 Russian remedies.

KREIG, Margaret. *Green Medicine*, (London, 1965).

LEYEL, Hilda. *Consulting Herbalist*, (1880-1957). Fellow of the Royal Institution. Founder of the Society of Herbalists (now incorporated with the Herb Society) and the Culpeper shops. Her pioneering spirit of the 1920s and 1950s fought for the survival of herbal medicine endangered by the Pharmacy and Medicines Bill 1941. Friends rallied to her support and were able to modify some of the extreme aspects of the Bill. Opened the first Culpeper shops in 1927, selling herbal medicines, foods and cosmetics.

Prolific writer: *Herbal Delights, Heartsease, Magic of Herbs, Compassionate Herbs, Elixirs of Life, The Truth About Herbs, Cinquefoil:* herbs to quicken the five senses, (1957), *Green Medicine*, (1930). Editor of Mrs Grieve's *Modern Herbal*.

LUST, John. *The Herb Book*, (New York, 1974).

LYLE, T.J. Professor Therapeutics and Materia Medica, Chicago Physio-Medical College. Skilled practitioner. Book: *Physio-Medical Therapeutics, Materia Medica and Pharmacy* was until recent years a standard textbook of the National Institute of Medical Herbalists. Classic; first published 1897. Practitioner's constant companion.

MESSEGUE, Maurice. Provencal herbalist. Son of a farm-worker who handed down to him the traditional knowledge of generations, he used cabbage leaves for bandaging wounds, watercress for clearing lungs, and fennel for menstrual difficulties. Books: *Of Men and Plants; Way to Natural Health and Beauty; Health Secrets of Plants and Herbs*.

MEYER, Joseph E. Herbal practitioner. Author: *The Herbalist*, (1960). First published 1918. Popular with the American public.

PARACELSUS (edited by J. Jacobi), *Selected Writings*, (London, 1951).

POTTER'S NEW CYCLOPAEDIA OF BOTANICAL DRUGS AND PREPARATIONS, by R.C. Wren, FLS. Revised by Elizabeth M. Williamson, B.Sc., MPS., and Fred J. Evans, B.Pharm., PhD., MPS. Uses, preparations, doses, synonyms and characters of botanical drugs used in medicine, (*C.W. Daniel Company Ltd*).

PRIEST, Albert W. and L.R. Distinguished herbal practitioners. Book: *Herbal Medication: a Clinical and dispensary handbook*, (1882). Commended to students and qualified practitioners.

RODALE, J.I. *Hawthorn Berry for the Heart*, (1971).

SALMON, William. Physician. Seplasium: *The Compleat English Physician*, (London, 1692).

SKELTON, John. *The Family Herbal and Botanic Record*, (Leeds, 1855). *The Epitome of the Botanic Practice of Medicine*, (Leeds, 1855). *The Family Medical Advisor*, (Leeds, 1852). *A Plea for the Botanic Practice of Medicine*, (London, 1853). *The Science and Practice of Medicine*, (1870); re-published by the National Association of Medical Herbalists, 1904.

STUART, Malcolm. Book: *Encyclopedia of herbs and herbalism*, (1979). London. Information on 420 important herbs.

THOMSON, Samuel. *A narrative of the life and Medical Discoveries of Samuel Thomson*, (Boston, 1825).

THOMSON, W.A.R. Physician. *Herbs That Heal*, (London, 1976).

TIERRA, Michael. *The Way of Herbs*, (Santa Cruz, 1980).

TURNER, William. *A New Herball*, (London, 1551). Herbal classic.

UNITED STATES DISPENSARY, 1880-1960, 5th-25th editions. J.B. Lippincott USA. Includes herbs of sufficient efficacy to appear in the most important Pharmacopoeia.

VOGEL, Virgil J. *American Indian Medicine*, Norman, University of Oklahoma Press, 1970. Indian theories of disease and methods of combatting it. Lists Indian herbs that have gained acceptance into the Pharmacopoeia of the United States and the National Formulary.

WEISS, Rudolf Fritz MD. *Herbal Medicine*. English edition from the original German. Takes account of research findings to 1988. For the practitioner and advanced student. Beaconsfield Publishers Ltd, Beaconsfield, UK.

WITHERING, William. *An Account of the Foxglove*, (Birmingham, 1785).

PROFESSIONAL AND TRADE ASSOCIATIONS

American Botanical Council & Herb Research Foundation
PO Box 144345, Austin, TX, USA. 78714–4345.
Phone: 512/926/4900.
Fax: 512926–2345.
Magazine: Herbalgram; an educational project

Ayurvedic Living
PO Box 188,
Exeter,
Devon EX4 5AB.

British Herbal Medicine Association
25 Church Street,
Stroud,
Glos. GL5 1JL.

The British Herb Growers Association
c/o NFU,
Agriculture House,
London SW1X 7NJ

The Herb Society
134 Buckingham Palace Road,
London SW1W 9SA

National Institute of Medical Herbalists
56 Longbrook Street,
Exeter EX4 6AH

The National Medicines Group Secretariat
PO Box 5,
Ilkeston,
Derbyshire DE7 8LX

The Register of Chinese Herbal Medicine
98b Hazelville Road,
London N19 3NA

National Herbalists Association of Australia
(Queensland Chapter)
Montville Road,
Mapleton,
Queensland,
Australia 4560

Verband der Reformwaren-Hersteller
(VRH) e.V.
D-6380 Bad Homburg v.d. H.
Hessenring 73,
Postfach 2320,
Germany

The Auckland Herb Society
PO Box 20022,
Glen Eden,
Auckland 7,
New Zealand

The Tasmanian Herb Society
12 Delta Avenue,
Taroona,
Tasmania 7006

The Chinese Medical Practitioners Association
170 Johnston Road,
Hong Kong

The Chinese Medicine and Acupuncture Research Centre
22nd floor,
322-324 Nathan Road,
Kowloon,
Hong Kong

The Botanical Society of Japan
c/o University of Tokyo,
3 Hongo,
Bunkyo-ku,
Tokyo,
Japan

Associazione Nazionale Erboristi e Piante Officinali (ANEPO)*
Via E.S. Piccolomini 159,
53100 Siena,
Italy

The Icelandic Nature Health Society
Laufasvegi 2,
Reykjavik,
Iceland

Swedish Herbal Institute (Svenska Örtmedicinska Institutet KB)
Bellmansgatan 11,
411 28 Göteborg,
Sweden

Société de Recherches et de Diffusion de Plantes Medicinales
8 rue St Marc,
Paris 2e,
France

HERBAL SUPPLIERS

BALDWIN G. & Co
171-173 Walworth Road,
London SE17 1RW.
Tel: 0171 703550.

Herbs, roots, barks, dried flowers, fluid extracts, tinctures, Essential, vegetable and aromatherapy oils. Potter's, Blackmore's and Gerard House preparations. Mail order service.

CULPEPER Ltd (Head office)
Hadstock Road,
Linton,
Cambridge CB1 6NJ.
Tel: 01223 894054.

EAST-WEST HERBS Ltd
Langston Priory Mews,
Kingham,
Oxon OX7 6UP.
Tel: 01608 658862.

GALEN HERBAL SUPPLIES Ltd
Unit 17,
St David's Industrial Estate,
Pengham,
Blackwood,
Gwent NP2 1SW.
Tel: 01443 820024.

Fluid extracts, tinctures, etc.

THE HERBAL APOTHECARY
103 High Street,
Syston,
Leicester LE7 1GQ.
Tel: 0116 2602690.

Tinctures, fluid extracts and B.P. special extracts, fresh extracts, essential oils, creams, ointments, pessaries, powders, capsuling service.

1/5/98:
MAYWAY HERBAL EMPORIUM
43 Waterside Trading Estate
Trumpers Way, Hanwell,
London W7 2QD.
Tel: 0181 8936873.

NAPIER'S
Herbalist,
18 Bristo Place,
Edinburgh EH1 1EZ.
Tel: 01465 861625.

NEAL'S YARD REMEDIES
15 Neal's Yard, Covent Garden,
London WC2H 9DP.
Tel: 0161 8317875

PHYTOPRODUCTS
Park Works,
Park Road,
Mansfield Woodown,
Mansfield,
Notts. NG19 8EF.
Tel: 01623 644334.

POTTERS HERBAL SUPPLIES
Leyland Mill Lane,
Wigan,
Lancs WN1 2SB.
Tel: 01942 405100

See entry: Potter's.

AROMATHERAPY OILS SUPPLIERS

BUTTERBUR & SAGE
101 Highgrove Street
Reading RG1 5EJ

HARTWOOD AROMATICS
Hartwood House,
12 Station Road,
Hatton,
Warwicks CV35 7LG

NORMAN & GERMAINE RICH
2 Coval Gardens,
London SW14 7DG

SHIRLEY PRICE AROMATHERAPY
Wesley House,
Stockwell Road,
Hinckley,
Leics LE10 1RD

CAPSULE-MAKING MACHINES & CAPSULES

DAV-CAPS
PO Box 11,
Monmouth,
Gwent NP5 3NX

THE HERBAL APOTHECARY
103 High Street,
Syston,
Leicester LE7 8BC

OINTMENT BASES & PHARMACY SUPPLIES

BUTTERBUR & SAGE
See: Essential Oil Suppliers

POTTERS HERBAL SUPPLIES
Leyland Mill Lane,
Wigan,
Lancs WN1 2SB.
Tel: 01942 405100

THE HERBAL APOTHECARY
103 High Street,
Syston,
Leicester LE7 8BC